Global Crises, Global Solutions

A unique publication exploring the opportunities for addressing ten of the most serious challenges facing the world today: climate change, communicable diseases, conflicts, access to education, financial instability, governance and corruption, malnutrition and hunger, migration, sanitation and access to clean water, and subsidies and trade barriers. In a world fraught with problems and challenges, we need to gauge how to achieve the greatest good with our money. *Global Crises, Global Solutions* provides a rich set of arguments and data for prioritising our response most effectively. Each problem is introduced by a world-renowned expert who defines the scale of the problem and describes the costs and benefits of a range of policy options to improve the situation. Debate is encouraged through the addition of two sets of 'alternative perspectives' for each proposal, each also written by an internationally recognised expert. The complete set of policy proposals is evaluated by eight of the world's top economists – including three Nobel Laureates – from North America, Europe and China, who attempt a ranking of the most promising options. Whether you agree or disagree with the analysis or conclusions, *Global Crises, Global Solutions* provides a serious, yet accessible, springboard for debate and discussion.

Contributors: Bjørn Lomborg (editor). The proposal authors: Kym Anderson, Jere R. Behrman, William R. Cline, Paul Collier, Barry Eichengreen, Philip Martin, Anne Mills, Lant Pritchett, Frank Rijsberman and Susan Rose-Ackerman. The perspective paper authors: Tony Addison, Jens Christopher Andvig, Simon Appleton, Roger Böhning, John J. Boland, Jean Cartier-Bresson, David B. Evans, Peter Blair Henry, Michael D. Intriligator, Alan S. Manne, Robert Mendelsohn, Arvind Panagaryia, Jan Pronk, Mark Rosenzweig, T. Paul Schultz, Peter Svedberg, Jacques van der Gaag, Ludger Wößmann, Charles Wyplosz. The expert panel: Jagdish N. Bhagwati, Robert W. Fogel, Bruno S. Frey, Justin Yifu Lin, Douglass C. North, Thomas C. Schelling, Vernon L. Smith, Nancy L. Stokey

Global Crises, Global Solutions

Edited by

BJØRN LOMBORG

PUBLISHED BY THE PRESS SYNDICATE OF THE UNIVERSITY OF CAMBRIDGE
The Pitt Building, Trumpington Street, Cambridge, United Kingdom

CAMBRIDGE UNIVERSITY PRESS
The Edinburgh Building, Cambridge CB2 2RU, UK
40 West 20th Street, New York, NY 10011–4211, USA
477 Williamstown Road, Port Melbourne, VIC 3207, Australia
Ruiz de Alarcón 13, 28014 Madrid, Spain
Dock House, The Waterfront, Cape Town 8001, South Africa

http://www.cambridge.org

First published 2004

Printed in the United States of America

Typeface Times 9.5/12 pt. and Formata   *System* LaTeX 2_ε [TB]

A catalogue record for this book is available from the British Library

ISBN 0 521 84446 0 hardback
ISBN 0 521 60614 4 paperback

This book was made possible by generous donations from
    The Tuborg Foundation, and
    The Carlsberg Bequest to the Memory of Brewer I.C. Jacobsen

---

Because of the unusual speed of publication of this book after the Copenhagen Consensus sessions, it has not
proved possible to provide complete details for approximately twenty of the author-date references cited in the
text. The publisher will continue to attempt to provide this information, and it will be displayed on the
Cambridge University Press website at http://www.cambridge.org/globalcrises

---

Contents

Figures

Tables

Boxes

Contributors

Chapter Authors

Kym Anderson is Professor, Centre for International Economic Studies, University of Adelaide. His research areas are in microeconomics, international trade, agricultural economics and development economics. His most recent publications include *The WTO and Agriculture* (with T. Josling, a two-volume set, for the series of readings on Critical Perspectives on the World Trading System, London: Edward Elgar, 2004) and (editor) *The World's Wine Markets: Globalization at Work* (London: Edward Elgar, 2004).

Jere R. Behrman is William R. Kenan, Jr., Professor in Economics and Director, Population Studies Center, University of Pennsylvania. His research areas are in health, nutrition and education; family and household processes and distribution of resources within and across generations; labour markets; and policy and project evaluation in the social sector. His most recent publications include 'Returns to Birthweight' (with M. Rosenzweig, *Review of Economics and Statistics*, 2004) and 'Does Increasing Women's Schooling Raise the Schooling of the Next Generation?' (with M. Rosenzweig, *American Economic Review* 92(1), 2002).

William R. Cline is Senior Fellow, Institute for International Economics and the Center for Global Development in Washington, DC. His research areas are in capital flows, debt and debt relief, economic growth, financial crises, foreign direct investment, global warming, international finance, macroeconomic policy, poverty, trade policy and agreements. His most recent publications include *Trade and Income Distribution* (1997) and *An Index of Industrial Country Trade Policy toward Developing Countries* (CGD Working Paper, 14, 2002).

Paul Collier is Professor and Director of the Centre for the Study of African Economies, Oxford University. His research areas are within macroeconomics: external shocks, exchange rate and trade policies; within microeconomics labour and financial markets, and rural development; within political economy: the process of policy reform and 'restraining the state'; African economies, especially in the area of open economy macroeconomics. His is currently researching the transition from civil war. His most recent publications include *Breaking the Conflict Trap: Civil War and Development Policy* (Oxford University Press, 2003).

Barry Eichengreen is The George C. Pardee and Helen N. Pardee Professor of Economics and Political Science, University of California, Berkeley. His research areas are the history and current operation of the international monetary and financial system. His most recent publications include *Capital Flows and Crises* (MIT Press, 2003); *Financial Crises and What to Do About Them* (Oxford University Press, 2002).

Philip Martin is Professor, Chair, UC Comparative Immigration and Integration Program, University of California, Davis. His research areas are immigration, farm labour and economic development. His recent publications include 'International Migration: Facing the Challenge' (with J. Widgren, Population Reference Bureau, *Population Bulletin*, 57(1), 2002) and 'The Mirage of Mexican Guest Workers' (with M.S. Teitelbaum, *Foreign Affairs*, 80(6), 2001).

Anne Mills is Professor of Health Economics and Policy, London School of Hygiene & Tropical Medicine. Her research areas are health services research, health systems, malaria, health care financing and health policy. Her recent publications include *International Public Health* (with M. Merson and R. Black, Gaithersburg: Aspen Publishers, 2001) and *Reforming Health Sectors* (London: Kegan Paul, 2000).

Lant Pritchett is Lecturer in Public Policy and Faculty co-chair MPA/ID program, Kennedy School of Government. His research areas are poverty and vulnerability, social capital, health, safety net programmes, economic growth, education, participatory project approaches and trade. His most recent publications include 'Does Learning to Add up Add Up' (forthcoming in *Handbook of Education Economics*, North-Holland, 2005) and *World Development Report 2004: Making Services Work for the Poor* (with the WDR2004 team, Oxford: Oxford University Press for the World Bank, 2004).

Frank Rijsberman is Director General, International Water Management Institute, Colombo, Sri Lanka, Professor at UNESCO-IHE, International Institute for Water Education, Delft and Wageningen University and Research, Wageningen. His research areas are natural resources management research and consulting, specifically for fresh water resources, coastal zones, soil erosion, environmental management and climate change/ sea level rise. His recent publications include 'Can Development of Water Resources Reduce Poverty?' (*Water Policy*, 5(5–6), 2004) and 'Water, Food and Environment: Conflict or Dialogue?' (with A. Mohammed, *Water Science and Technology*, 47(6), 2004).

Susan Rose-Ackerman is Henry R. Luce Professor of Jurisprudence, Yale University, Law School and Department of Political Science. Her research areas are administrative law, law and economics, corruption, regulation and political economy, social choice, comparative administrative law, and law and economic development. Her most recent publications include *Corruption and Government: Causes, Consequences and Reform* (1999) and *Controlling Environmental Policy: The Limits of Public Law in Germany and the United States* (1995).

Perspective Paper Authors

Tony Addison is Professor, Deputy Director, Project Director, Senior Research Fellow, World Institute for Development Economics Research (WIDER) of the United Nations University (UNU). His research areas are the relationship between conflict, reconstruction and economic reform in Africa, fiscal policy (public spending, taxation, and macro-fiscal policy) in low-income countries and development economics and advanced development economics.

Jens Christopher Andvig is Senior Researcher, University of Oslo. His research areas are the economics of corruption with an emphasis on the auction systems of public contracting, fluctuations in public activity levels, international spillover mechanisms of economic crimes and child labour in developing countries.

Simon Appleton is Senior Lecturer in Economics, School of Economics, University of Nottingham. His research areas are poverty and human resources with application to sub-Saharan Africa.

Roger Böhning is Director, Programme on Promoting the Declaration on Fundamental Principles and Rights at Work, International Labour Office, Geneva. His research areas are the effectiveness of immigration and integration policies in western Europe; indicators of the achievement of human rights in the labour field.

John Boland is Professor Emeritus, Environmental Economics and Policy, Department of Geography and Environmental Engineering, The John Hopkins University, Baltimore, MD. His research areas are urban water supply and sanitation; water use forecasting; public utility tariff design; water resource planning and management; and environmental policy.

Jean Cartier-Bresson is Professor of Economics, Université de Versailles, Saint-Quentin en Yvelines, France. His research areas are development, public economy, the global governance agenda and the uses and abuses of estimates of different forms of illegal transactions.

David Evans is Director, Department of Health System Financing, Expenditure and Resource Allocation (FER), World Health Organisation. His research areas are the burden of disease, the costs and effects of interventions to reduce that burden and their impact on population health, and the responsiveness and fairness of financial contributions of health systems.

Peter Blair Henry is Associate Professor of Economics in the Graduate School of Business, Stanford University. His research areas are international finance and macroeconomics, particularly the real effects of asset price responses to stabilisation, liberalisation and reform in emerging economies; and economic growth and development.

Michael Intriligator is Professor of Economics, Political Science and Policy Studies, University of California, Los Angeles, and Senior Fellow, Milken Institute. His research areas are economic theory and mathematical economics, econometrics, health economics, strategy and arms control.

Alan Manne is Professor Emeritus of Operations Research at Stanford University. His research area is climate change.

Robert Mendelsohn is Edwin Weyerhaeuser Davis Professor, Professor of Economics, and Professor in the School of Management. His research areas are resource economics with special emphasis on valuing the environment, impact from climate change, impacts of air pollution and conservation of tropical forests.

Arvind Panagaryia is Professor of Economics at Columbia University. His research area is trade reforms in developing countries and free trade areas.

Jan Pronk is Professor of Theory and Practice of International Development, Institute of Social Studies; he was the former Minister for Development Cooperation, the Netherlands, and Special Envoy,

Secretary General, United Nations, for the World Summit on Sustainable Development. His research areas are international development, international cooperation, development aid, national development policy making, trade and development, environment and development, poverty and sustainable development and EU policy-making.

Mark Rosenzweig is Mohamed Kamal Professor of Public Policy, at Kennedy School, Harvard University. His research areas are the consequences of the Indian green revolution for schooling attainment, household structure, and deforestation; the impact of local democratisation on the distribution of public services in India; the effects of maternal schooling on children's human capital; and the consequences of low birthweight.

Paul Schultz is Malcolm K. Brachman Professor of Economics, Department of Economics, Yale University. His research areas are schooling, health and mobility in development, income distribution and endogenous household composition and gender inequalities.

Peter Svedberg is Professor of Development Economics, The Institute for International Economic Studies. His research areas are the causes and effects of undernutrition and measurement problems.

Jacques van der Gaag is Professor of Development Economics, University of Amsterdam, Dean of the Department of Economics and Econometrics. His research areas are the economics of poverty, structural adjustment, labour markets, health and education economics and social policy.

Ludger Wößmann is Head of Department, Research Department 'Human Capital and Structural Change', ifo Institute of Economic Research at the Ludwig-Maximilians-Universität. His research areas are education economics, growth economics and structural change.

Charles Wyplosz is Professor of Economics, and Director of the International Centre for Money and Banking Studies, Graduate Institute of International Economics, Geneva. His research areas are monetary affairs, currency crises and the international monetary system.

The Experts

Jagdish N. Bhagwati is Professor, Economics Department, Columbia University. One of the foremost international trade theorists of his generation, he has also made contributions to development theory and policy, public finance, immigration and to the new theory of political economy. He is a Director of the National Bureau of Economic Research and was advisor to India's Finance Minister on economic reforms. In 1971 Bhagwati founded the *Journal of International Economics*, the premier journal in the field today, and in 1989 *Economics & Politics*.

Robert W. Fogel is Charles R. Walgreen Distinguished Service Professor, University of Chicago. His foremost work concerns the role of the railways in the economic development of the United States, the importance of slavery as an institution and its economic role in the United States and studies in historical demography. In 1993, he shared the Nobel Memorial Price in Economics with Douglass North. His use of counterfactual analysis of the course of events and his masterful treatment of quantitative techniques in combination with economic theory, have had a substantial influence on the understanding of economic change.

Bruno S. Frey is Professor of Economics and Research Director, CREMA, University of Zurich, and Head of the Institute of Empirical Economics at the University. He has written extensively on public choice and non-market economics including happiness and economics, motivation and knowledge transfer and arts and economics.

Justin Yifu Lin is Professor and founding Director of the China Center for Economic Research (CCER) at Peking University and Professor at the Hong Kong University of Science and Technology. He is Vice President, Chinese Agricultural Economics Association, 1999–, Member of Advisory Council, Development Institute, Asian Development Bank, 1998–, Member, International

Advisory Committee for 2020 Vision for Food, Agriculture, and the Environmental Initiative, International Food Policy Research Institute (IFPRI), 1998–, Member, Academic Committee, XXIV International Agricultural Economists Association Congress and Member, Working Group on the Future of the OECD, the Reinventing Bretton Woods Committee, 1996–.

Douglass C. North is Spencer T. Olin Professor in Arts and Sciences, Washington University in St. Louis. In 1992 he became the first economic historian ever to win one of the economics profession's most prestigious honours, the John R. Commons Award. He is a founder of Washington University's Center for New Institutional Social Sciences and in 1993 shared the Nobel Memorial Prize in Economics with Robert Fogel. His research has focused on the formation of political and economic institutions and the consequences of these institutions on the performance of economies through time, including such areas as property rights, transaction costs, and the free rider problem. He is recognised as one of the founders of the 'new institutional economics', and has done important work on the connection of the cognitive sciences to economic theory.

Thomas C. Schelling is Distinguished University Professor, University of Maryland. He was the recipient of the Frank E. Seidman Distinguished Award in Political Economy and the National Academy of Sciences award for Behavioral Research Relevant to the Prevention of Nuclear War. He served in the Economic Cooperation Administration in Europe, and has held positions in the White House and Executive Office of the President, Yale University, the RAND Corporation and the Department of Economics and Center for International Affairs at Harvard University. He has published on military strategy and arms control, energy and environmental policy, climate change, nuclear proliferation, terrorism, organised crime, foreign aid and international trade, conflict and bargaining theory, racial segregation and integration, the military draft, health policy, tobacco and drugs policy and ethical issues in public policy and in business.

Vernon L. Smith is Professor of Economics and Law, George Mason University. He is a research scholar in the Interdisciplinary Center for Economic Science, and a Fellow of the Mercatus Center, all in Arlington, VA. In 2002 he shared the Nobel Memorial Prize in Economics with Daniel Kahneman. He has laid the foundation for the field of experimental economics, developing an array of experimental methods, setting standards for what constitutes a reliable laboratory experiment in economics. His work has been instrumental in establishing experiments as an essential tool in empirical economic analysis.

Nancy L. Stokey is Frederick Henry Prince Professor, University of Chicago. She is the current vice-president of the American Economic Association, co-editor of *Econometrica*, associate editor of the *Journal of Economic Growth* and has served as associate editor of *Games and Economic Behavior* and of the *Journal of Economic Theory*. An expert on economic theory and economic development, she examines the impact education and job training have on the development of national economies. She has shown that economies continue to expand when workforces adopt more complex skills, moving, for instance, from manufacturing into high technology.

Acknowledgements

The Copenhagen Consensus started as a simple but untested idea of prioritising global opportunities, and ended with a successful list, compiled by some of the world's top economists, attracting attention from all over the world. Making this project happen, both the Copenhagen Consensus and this book, has been possible only through a very dedicated effort by a large number of people. Now it is time to say 'thank you'.

Special thanks are due to the Prime Minister of Denmark, Anders Fogh Rasmussen, and to the Minister for Food, Agriculture and Fisheries, Hans Christian Schmidt (then Minister for the Environment), for their early recognition of the importance of the Copenhagen Consensus, and for their support of the project. The generous financial support of the Ministry of the Environment early on in the process was highly appreciated.

The Copenhagen Consensus also greatly benefited from the generous financial support of The Tuborg Foundation and The Carlsberg Bequest to the Memory of Brewer I.C. Jakobsen, who financed the individual chapters in this book. A generous grant from The Sasakawa Peace Foundation is also deeply appreciated.

Thanks also go to the Board of Directors of The Environmental Assessment Institute, especially the former Chairman, Director General, the Danish Plant Directorate, Dr Ole P. Kristensen, for his explicit support for the project in times of difficulty, and his successor, the present Chairman, Dr Knud Larsen.

The Copenhagen Consensus project would not have achieved the same impact without the invaluable support of *The Economist*. Particular thanks are due to deputy editor, Clive Crook, for his belief in the project and his strong support during the week's meeting in Copenhagen.

Many thanks should definitely be given to the participants and contributors for taking part in this innovative exercise and for the results they brought about. The Copenhagen Consensus would not have been possible without the invaluable contribution of the experts, the authors and the opponents, who provided an alternative perspective in their Perspective papers. They were all asked to perform an ambitious task under severe deadlines, yet they all produced sterling work that facilitated this groundbreaking achievement.

From planning the Copenhagen Consensus to making sure the participants reached the venue, the Copenhagen Consensus team deserves special acknowledgement for their enthusiastic commitment. With a surprisingly small staff, the Copenhagen Consensus Secretariat managed to meet virtually impossible deadlines and make the entire event run surprisingly smooth, an astounding achievement that was amply confirmed by the praise that they received from everyone during the week. The Copenhagen Consensus Secretariat consisted of: Project Manager, Henrik Meyer; Project Officer, Anders Kristoffersen; Administrative Officers, Tommy Petersen and Maria Jakobsen; Communications Manager, Anita Furu; Communications Officer, David Young.

The eight personal assistants who supported the eight experts during the week proved to have an indispensable role. Thanks go to Rico Jensen Busk, Jonas West Eilersen, Linda Harrison, Bjørn Juncker, Maria Skotte, Sonja Thomsen, Dorte Vigsø and Kasper Wrang.

Two other events during the Copenhagen Consensus week were indispensable in achieving the impact of the total project. The Copenhagen Consensus Youth Forum (see the section at the end of the volume), brought together young university students from all over the world to make essentially the same prioritisations as the economic experts. That this project also worked so well was due to the committed work of many people. The Copenhagen Consensus Youth Forum Secretariat consisted of: Project Manager, Clemen Rasmussen, Dorte Vigsø, Rasmus Brandt Lassen, Morten Kohl, Susanne Thomsen, Anni Bach, Annette Ludvigsen and Monica Hansen as well as Martin Livermore and Martin Ågerup. Finally, in getting the public involved, a presentation on the main street in Copenhagen was aptly overseen by Anja Skjoldborg Hansen and six student helpers.

Thanks also go to our external partners. 3. Dimension with Director Claus Sneppen and Project Managers Vita Clausen and Helle Rimmer made the Copenhagen Consensus run both smoothly and efficiently. Our web page looked eye-catching due to the work of No Zebra Director Jesper Holm Joensen and his team. The designers from Co & Co made the CC-logo and many of the other necessary materials – many thanks to Lars Toft and Anne-Marie Mortensen for their unwavering work when we made unreasonable changes even after deadlines had passed.

Finally, we are indebted to the team at Cambridge University Press for wanting to publish the hard work of the many contributors and participants in the Copenhagen Consensus, and for helping put it all together under severe time constraints.

A lot of people put their lifeblood into this project – and that is the reason the Copenhagen Consensus did so well. This book is dedicated to all of them. Thank you.

Bjørn Lomborg
Copenhagen, 9 August 2004

Abbreviations and Acronyms

ACP	Africa, the Caribbean and the Pacific
ACT	artemisinin-based combination therapy
ADB	Asian Development Bank
ADR	American Depository Receipts
ANB	annualised net benefits
APEC	Asia–Pacific Economic Cooperation
ARV	anti-retroviral therapy
ATC	Agreement on Textiles and Clothing (WTO)
BCR	benefit-cost ratio
CAP	Common Agricultural Policy (EU)
CBA	cost-benefit analysis
CEA	cost-effectiveness analysis
COI	cost of illness
CPI	consumer price index
CPI	Corruption Perceptions Index
CPIA	Country Policy and Institutional Assessment (World Bank)
DALY	disability adjusted life year
DPT	diphtheria, pertussis, tetanus (vaccine)
DSP	Dispute Settlement Procedure (WTO)
EBA	'everything but arms'
EBRD	European Bank for Reconstruction and Development
ECB	European Central Bank
EIA	Energy Information Administration
EITI	Extractive Industries Transparency Initiative
FAO	Food and Agriculture Organisation (United Nations)
FDI	foreign direct investment
FFE	Food for Education
FTA	free trade agreement
FTAA	Free Trade Area of the Americas
GATS	General Agreement on Trade in Services
GATT	General Agreement on Tariffs and Trade
ghgs	greenhouse gas emissions
GDP	gross domestic product
GM	genetically modified
GMO	genetically modified organism
GNI	Gross National Income
GSP	Generalised System of (tariff) Preferences
GTAP	Global Trade Analysis Project
GWP	gross world product
HDI	Human Development Index (United Nations)
HEFP	Health Economics and Financing Programme (UK)
HIPC	Heavily Indebted Poorer Countries

HMO	health maintenance organisation
IAG	International Advisory Group (World Bank)
IBRD	International Bank of Reconstruction and Development (World Bank)
IDA	International Development Agency (World Bank)
IFC	International Finance Corporation
IFIs	international financial institutions
IICR	Institutional Investor Credit Rating
ILO	International Labour Organisation
IMF	International Monetary Fund
IOM	International Organisation for Migration
IPCC	Intergovernmental Panel on Climate Change
IPR	intellectual property rights
IPTp	intermittent presumptive treatment of pregnant women
IRR	internal rate of return
IT	information technology
ITNs	insecticide treated (bed)nets
ITO	International Trade Organisation
IUGR	inter-uterine growth retardation
IWMI	International Water Management Institute
KP	Kyoto Protocol
LBW	low birth weight
LDCs	least-developed countries
MDG	Millennium Development Goals (UN)
MENA	Middle East and North Africa
MERGE	Model for Evaluating Regional and Global Effects (of ghgs reduction)
MFN	most favoured nation
MIGA	Multilateral Investment Guarantee Agency
NAEP	National Assessment of Economic Progress
NAFTA	North American Free Trade Agreement
NBFIs	non-bank financial intermediaries/ institutions
NGO	non-governmental organisation
NIEO	New International Economic Order
NTB	non-tariff barrier
OAS	Organisation of American States
ODA	Official Development Assistance
OECD	Organisation for Economic Cooperation and Development
PHC	primary health care
PPP	purchasing power parity
PRGF	Poverty Reduction and Growth Facility (IMF)
PSE	producer support equivalent
PTA	preferential trade areas
R&D	research and development
RDB	regional development bank
RBM	Roll Back Malaria (WHO, UNICEF)
SDRs	special drawing rights
SFE-IV	school fixed effects with instrumental variables
SGA	small for gestational age
SME	small and medium-sized enterprise
STD	sexually transmitted disease
STI	sexually transmitted infection
SSA	sub-Saharan Africa
TRIPS	Trade-Related Aspects of Intellectual Property Rights (WTO)

TRS	Temporary Resident Status (USA)
UNCTAD	United Nations Conference on Trade and Development
UNDP	United Nations Development Program
UNESCO	United Nations Educational, Scientific and Cultural Organisation
UNFCCC	United Nations Framework Convention on Climate Change
UNGASS	United Nations General Assembly Special Session
UNHCR	United Nations High Commission on Refugees
UNICEF	United Nations Children's Fund
UNWWDR	United Nations World Water Development Report
VLBW	very low birth weight
VSL	value of a statistical life
WBES	World Business Environment Survey
WHO	World Health Organisation
WHOPES	WHO Pesticides Evaluation Scheme
WMO	World Migration Organisation
WTO	World Trade Organisation
WTP	willingness to pay
YLL	year of life lost

Introduction

BJØRN LOMBORG

The Focus for the Consensus

At its heart, the focus for the Copenhagen Consensus was very simple – it was to address the current global crises and come up with a list of the best solutions. The core idea is simple: with scarce resources to tackle the problems of the world, prioritization is necessary. Not being willing to prioritize does not make the problem go away: it simply becomes less clear – and, most likely, more expensive to solve in the end. The result is that our ability to do good is less than it could have been. Thus, very simply we need to know *what we should do first*. The practical aim of the Copenhagen Consensus was an attempt to present the best information available from economic studies as a ranked list of the very best projects to do in the world.

Why was This the First Explicit Economic Prioritisation?

Surprisingly such an explicit economic prioritization has not been done earlier. There are several reasons for this.

Hard-to-Compare Alternatives

First, it involves comparing very different and hard-to-compare alternatives, such as tackling malaria by distributing insecticide-treated mosquito nets (ITNs) and dealing with civil wars by deploying peace-keeping forces. Yet, such trade-offs happen implicitly all the time through (lack of) actual investments by countries and international agencies. In reality, prioritizing between such disparate issues on the international level is little different from the decision to spend money on hospitals rather than opera houses in a national prioritization debate. The difference is mainly that on the national level we have well-established institutions and procedures (governments and appropriation laws) that force us to confront these choices more clearly.

Institutional Rigidities

Second, there may be strong institutional rigidity to prioritization between different agencies – for example, between different UN agencies. Part of this may simply be due to institutional risk aversion. While most organizations would like to have their issues end up at the top of a prioritized list, they would be terrified of ending up at the bottom. A rational institution would thus be disinclined to inter-agency prioritization. Partly, this may be due to bounded thinking within the single institution. While someone working with preserving cultural heritage may acknowledge that preventing HIV/AIDS is more important on a global level, the day-to-day prioritization and focus of attention is likely to be centred around cultural preservation issues.

Why Prioritise?

Third, and surprisingly, there seems to be a good deal of resentment about the whole idea. An important common denominator of this seems to be that we shouldn't have to prioritize. Prioritization is seen as bad, because whenever we prioritize we not only say where we should do more (which is good) but also where we should not at first increase our efforts (which is seen to be cynical). Of course, in an ideal world the critics would be right: prioritization would not be necessary. Governments *should* be able simultaneously to eradicate corruption, improve sanitation, end conflicts, global warming and malnutrition and win the war against communicable diseases. But in a world where resources are limited, it is important to make sure every dollar is spent in the best achievable way.

Thinking Outside the Box

Of course, within a single agency, prioritization is common. In essence, we can picture the individual agencies and areas of interest in the world as boxes. Within each box, prioritization is, if not embedded, then at least conceivable and is in fact regularly performed based on diverse criteria. What the Copenhagen Consensus tries to do is to spread this thinking outside the individual boxes, and to prioritize between all the different worthwhile projects.

While this may sound obvious, it is clearly not happening. Take the UN Millennium Development Goals (MDGs) which consist of a long list of desirable goals for 2015 (reduce by half the proportion of people living on less than a dollar a day, reduce by half the proportion of people who suffer from hunger, ensure that all boys and girls complete a full course of primary schooling, reduce by two-thirds the mortality rate among children under five, reduce by three-quarters the maternal mortality ratio, etc.). These goals are eminently laudable. They are estimated to cost around US$40–70 bn extra per year,[1] yet funding in such quantity does not seem to be forthcoming. So it is important to prioritize – what do we want first? The UN MDGs are also not the only commitments. The United Nations has committed to treaties regarding a wide range of subjects including sustainable development (in Rio), climate change (in the Climate Convention Framework), Convention against Transnational Organized Crime (Palermo), International Convention for the Suppression of the Financing of Terrorism (New York) and biological diversity (Cartagena Protocol on Biosafety). Moreover, we might also want to do other things such as preventing old conflicts from flaring up, increasing research in tropical diseases or improving financial sector lending.

What this basically tells us is *why* we should prioritize. If we don't we end up doing less well than we could otherwise have done. But we also need to ask *where*, *how* and *what* we should prioritize.

Where Does the Copenhagen Consensus Prioritise?

'Doing-Good' Areas

Ultimately, national political decisions end up – directly or indirectly – prioritizing all resources available to the nation. One of the major guidelines for such prioritization is: 'who benefits?' This is immediately obvious when looking at how priorities are set in first world countries, where a new medical treatment may cost millions of dollars to postpone death by a year, while the average cost of saving a human life for one year in the third world is just $62.[2] Thus, in making a ranked list for good initiatives it is imperative to separate projects meant to increase welfare *within* as opposed to *outside* the country, the ones made for, some might say, selfish reasons as opposed to the ones made for unselfish reasons. (Making a list of all projects together, and treating all lives as equally worthy, would simply show that we should be investing much more in the developing world – on the order of 50–80 per cent of our GDP, which may be interesting but not very politically realistic or informative.) Since the actual prioritization within individual countries is well known and has a long historical legacy, the current Copenhagen Consensus is aimed at looking at the prioritizing of first world money outside the first world nations.

The Copenhagen Consensus can thus be said to be looking at the 'doing-good' areas. This does not just include the obvious Official Development Assistance (ODA), estimated at $58 bn annually.[3] It also includes all other efforts taken mainly to achieve benefits outside the first world national areas. Under this heading come peace-keeping forces, research into (say) tropical diseases, (parts of the) attempts to alleviate cross-boundary environmental pollution etc. Naturally, distinguishing between 'selfish' and 'unselfish' projects is necessarily somewhat vague. Yet the bottom line is that

---

[1] Devarajan, Miller and Swanson (2002).
[2] Hahn (1996, 236).
[3] OECD (2003).

the Copenhagen Consensus looks mainly at the c. 1 per cent of GDP that rich nations set apart to do good outside their countries, and not at the 99 per cent they spend doing good within their national boundaries.

Military Spending and Free Trade

These considerations are also relevant for two of the most hotly debated issues for inclusion in the Copenhagen Consensus: military spending and free trade.

Every year the world spends almost $1,000 bn on military expenditure.[4] Could this money not be better spent elsewhere? Why was this not considered within the Copenhagen Consensus? It was not, for two reasons. First, military spending is not primarily motivated by doing good – by increasing welfare outside the donating country. If anything, military spending can typically be seen as the utmost in 'selfish spending'. Bringing in military spending would be no more sensible than bringing in national hospital spending, to be compared with third world hospital spending. Second, even if some military spending could be argued to be unselfish, we have no academic agreement on its benefits. Take the Iraq War, where we might find some agreement as to its immediate costs. Yet, some scholars would find that its benefits far outweigh its costs (bringing democracy to the region, sending a powerful signal to other, potentially rogue nations) whereas others could equally well argue that the benefits would be small or even strongly negative (incurring further costs on the region, jeopardizing its stability, leaving other rogue states unchecked). Thus, with the current lack of consensus of a cost-benefit analysis (CBA) in International Relations, it would be unlikely that the inclusion of such initiatives as military expenditure would give more information on the prioritization between different projects.

The second inclusion issue in the Copenhagen Consensus was the question of free trade. This issue was included although national trade policies are typically seen as protecting domestic interests. Yet the standard economic point is that such a view is incorrect, as free trade benefits both developed and developing nations and that trade protection pro-

tects only certain, smaller domestic interests. Thus, promoting free trade is a classic win–win situation where first world nations can easily see trade as an almost free (or indeed a negative-cost) instrument to do good in the world.

How Does the Copenhagen Consensus Prioritise?

The ranking in the Copenhagen Consensus is based on a CBA, measuring the costs and benefits to a global community at the relevant prices. In making a CBA, one of the primary preconditions is that the change is *marginal* (so that the models may still be able to handle the changes proposed). This was achieved by making the focal question for the Copenhagen Consensus: 'where should the world invest, say, $50 bn *extra* over the next four years to do the most good?' Such an amount ($12.5 bn/year) represents a 20 per cent increase of the present-day ODA. Notice that this does not mean that the Copenhagen Consensus makes any decision on what would be an appropriate level of *extra investment*. If one only invests another $5 bn/year, the list will still make sense, only we cannot do as much. Likewise, if we were to invest another $25 bn/year, we could go even further down the list.

Finally, notice that the Copenhagen Consensus prioritizes only *extra* resources spent, since it is looking only at where the best opportunities are to be found. Opportunities ending up far down the list are not necessarily bad, only less attractive than those higher-up.

What Does the Copenhagen Consensus Prioritise?

Problems and Solutions

When we talk about doing something about the world's woes, we typically talk about *problems*: this is the current organizing principle in thinking about the state of the world. However, when we have to

---

[4] $956 bn in 2003, from Stockholm International Peace Research Institute, http://web.sipri.org/contents/milap/milex/mex_trends.html.

make a ranked list of actions, we really have to focus on *solutions*. In essence, it does not make sense to talk about ranking the world's problems, for two reasons. First, many 'big' problems do not have any well-defined, technical solution. War is surely a 'big' problem, but we have no general solution to it. This is also why in the Copenhagen Consensus, the focus lay on conflicts and arms proliferation, which actually does have some fairly identifiable solutions, such as deploying peace-keeping forces.

Second most problems get progressively harder to solve as we move closer to completion. Take supplying clean drinking water. Giving access to the first 50 per cent of the population who currently do not enjoy access to clean drinking water can be done fairly cheaply. However, as we contemplate giving another 45 per cent access, the price will increase, as we have to supply people more isolated and further away from an appropriate water source. The last 5 per cent might turn out to be very expensive and the last person (perhaps on an isolated mountaintop) will be utterly impossible. Thus, measuring the cost of the world's problem with supplying clean drinking water is undefined. What the Copenhagen Consensus points out is that in moving forward we should not focus on problems (or challenges), but rather on realistic solutions (or *opportunities*). Opportunities mean that we have both a technical solution to the problem and that its cost is well defined. The opportunity concerning clean drinking water could be providing clean water to, say, 50 per cent of the population who do not have access.

The Copenhagen Consensus Process

Compilation of Challenges

The first task of the Copenhagen Consensus was to compile a list of all *major challenges facing humanity* (see table on p. 5). This was in line with the view that challenges and not opportunities are the organizing principle of thinking about the state of the world. Two main approaches to collecting a gross list of challenges were considered. The one we settled on was to scan all major UN publications over the years 2000–3: if an issue was suf-

ficiently important and global to merit consideration at the Copenhagen Consensus, it was unlikely that it would have gone unmentioned in any UN publication, given the UN commitment to follow and tackle global problems. This scan resulted in a multitude of challenges, which we managed to narrow down to a list of thirty-one. Of course, in narrowing down some of the challenges, some level of discretion had to be applied. Moreover, the thirty-one challenges were not exactly at the same level, and to some extent were cross-cutting. This was considered unavoidable and unharmful, since the goal of the list was didactic and meant only to organize the eventual list of opportunities.

As a further check on the gross list, it was discussed by two Danish focus groups, consisting, respectively, of economists and non-economists. The groups came up with only one extra issue, the digital divide. This reassured us that the process indeed had captured the most important challenges facing humanity.

The other main approach considered was to survey UN organizations and NGOs for their views on the main challenges. The advantage would have been to have immediate credibility since no challenges could later be claimed to have been left out. However, we decided against this method, partly because the first option gave a list of challenges that was generally seen as reasonable, partly because a survey could potentially have taken a very long time, with no guarantee that all organizations would participate.

Making a Manageable List of Challenges

Since the challenges would later have to be independently analysed by specialists and also deliberated by experts present in Copenhagen, it was imperative to limit the total number of considered challenges, and for a variety of practical reasons the number was set at ten. Here, we asked the experts to come up with their best initial estimates as to which of the thirty-two challenges would have the most promising opportunities in terms of CBA. From the feedback, the Copenhagen Consensus secretariat formulated the ten challenges presented on p. 5. This whittling down of the challenges was

The 32 Original General Challenges Facing Humanity	The Final 10 Challenges Found to Hold the Most Promising Opportunities
Economy Digital divide Financial instability Lack of intellectual property rights Money laundering Subsidies and trade barriers Transport and infrastructure	Climate change Communicable diseases Conflicts and arms proliferation Access to education Financial instability Governance and corruption Malnutrition and hunger Migration Sanitation and access to clean water Subsidies and trade barriers
Environment Air pollution Chemical pollution and hazardous waste Climate change Deforestation Depletion of the ozone layer Depletion of water resources Lack of energy Land degradation Loss of biodiversity Vulnerability to natural disasters	
Governance Arms proliferation Conflicts Corruption Lack of education Terrorism	
Health and population Drugs HIV/AIDS Human settlements Lack of people of working age Malaria Living conditions of children Living conditions of women Non-communicable diseases Undernutrition/hunger Unsafe water and lack of sanitation Vaccine-preventable diseases	

not as restrictive as it might seem, since the goal was only to find the *best* opportunities. Thus, if opportunities belonging to a challenge that was dropped would have come in higher in an absolute (theoretical) ranking than other opportunities included, this would be important only if they were at the very top of the list. If we momentarily think of each challenge being solved by just one opportunity, this can be formulated easily: what matters in the Copenhagen Consensus is just that the top challenges are included (the true 1–5), whereas the accuracy matters little towards the lower end (whether the true 10 made it, or whether it was replaced by the true 11) because it makes no difference to the policy relevant conclusions.

Identifying the Best Opportunities and Cost-Benefit Estimates

The Ten Challenge Papers

With the ten challenges identified, a renowned economics specialist within each field was approached to write what we called a 'challenge paper' (chapters 1–10 in this volume). Challenge paper authors (CPA) were asked to cover three issues:

- First, give a brief overview of the *dimensions* of the challenge.
- Second, identify between one and five *practicable opportunities to address the challenge*. These opportunities should try to fulfil two, only partly

overlapping criteria. Partly, they should represent what the CPA believed to be the best or politically most relevant opportunities on the basis of CBA; partly, they should be formulated such that the CBAs already present in the literature fairly easily could be applied to the opportunities.

- Third, the paper should make an *extensive overview of the CBAs in the literature* and apply it to the different opportunities.

VSLs and Discount Rates

Two of the most critical factors in making a CBA are the so-called *value of statistical life* (VSL) and the *discount rate*. In making decisions that will save lives, we need to know the worth of the lives saved; this is what VSL gives us. It is often seen as immoral to put a price tag on lives – and, of course, in a perfect world, all lives would be priceless. But real policy decisions mean that some lives get saved while others don't. Say that politicians could build a roundabout for $9 m and save one life. If the roundabout does not get built, it means that the politicians valued that life at less than $9 m – that their VSL was less than $9 m. In general, most public and private decisions implicitly give us an indication of the worth of saving a statistical life, and this general value goes into the CBA.

Likewise, CBAs have to allow for the fact that not all costs and benefits occur at the same time. If we pay $10 today and get $16 in ten years, a thoughtless calculation seems to indicate a $6 benefit. But of course we could also have invested the $10. Had we got 5 per cent yearly interest, it would actually have become $16.29 in ten years. Getting just $16 would thus have been a disappointment. To make the cost and benefit comparable, all amounts are typically discounted to *today's* value. Yet, making this discounting heavily depends on assumptions about future interest rates and moral arguments – essentially a question of how important one evaluates the *future relative to the present*.

Since we were asking CPAs to base themselves mainly on the existing literature, we found that it would be too restrictive to make prescribed values for VSL and the discount rate, since these vary greatly with individual disciplines. Instead we decided that in the review of the literature each area should use its own typical estimates, and the

experts later find a common ground. In retrospect, we should perhaps have made a set of different values against which the CPAs could have tabulated their findings. As the Copenhagen Consensus 2004 stands, the experts were left to make this adjustment themselves which perhaps contributed towards their rejection of making cost and benefit estimates.

The Perspective Papers

After identifying the CPA, we commissioned two more scholars to provide a commentary and an alternative perspective on the challenge paper. These experts were called 'opponents' to emphasise their obligation to stress the differences and uncertainties, but since most of the 'opponent papers' showed more agreement than disagreement, we have called them 'Perspective papers' and they follow each chapter in the volume. The use of opponents ensured that important CBAs or other strands of the literature were not accidentally left out of the discussion. If necessary, the opponents could also suggest a new opportunity, requiring them to identify the relevant literature to make it possible for the experts to assess the costs and benefits of this new choice. While several Perspective paper authors briefly mentioned other opportunities in closing, none unfortunately gave enough documentation to make a ranking possible.

Finding the Experts

Economists and Prioritisation

The job of the experts was to make rankings of the opportunities, based on the evidence given by the specialists. Two main considerations went into their selection. First, they had to be economists. Some considered this controversial, arguing that other scholars, such as natural scientists and philosophers, should have been included. However, the argument for restricting the selection of experts (and indeed specialists) to economists was that the focus of the Copenhagen Consensus was economic prioritization. Just as you ask a climatologist about the climate, and a malaria expert about malaria, you ask an economist about prioritization. If, instead, one places a climatologist and a malaria expert together, they will probably agree that opportunities within both fields are very good but will be unlikely to be able to agree as to which opportunity is the better investment.

Perspective on Social Issues

Second, the experts had to be highly respected economists with a broad perspective on social issues. A list of some fifty economists was seen to fulfil these requirements, including many Nobel Laureates, who are typically awarded the prize as a testimony both to their outstanding contributions and also to their general abilities in economics. Most of the economists whom we approached were interested, but the main challenge was to find a team of people who would have time to both meet up five days in Copenhagen and take the time to read some 600 pages of material beforehand. Some critics of the enterprise expressed a concern that selecting top economists would mean that they would be heavily skewed towards older, male Americans. This is a characteristic of the profession, not of our selection criteria, as is most evident in the Nobel Prize distribution. American universities host many of the world's best economists; since 1994, of the twenty economists who have received the Nobel Prize, fifteen have been economists with US citizenship. No women have ever received the prize. Only one developing country citizen (Amartya Sen, 1998) has received it.

Anticipated Bias

Our final list did include one Chinese, one ethnic Indian as well as one female economist. However, in our view these numbers were not important. The defining criterion was that our expert panel comprised outstanding economists, because they were not to represent their own viewpoints or their own considerations, but to tell us what, in the view of the data, what was their best, professional evaluation of the rankings of opportunities. It is perhaps worth mentioning that any anticipated biases of the expert panel were tested against the simultaneous exercise of the Copenhagen Consensus Youth Forum which came to conclusions that were broadly consistent with the Copenhagen Consensus conclusions.[5]

The Copenhagen Setup

The schedule in Copenhagen consisted of five days with two sessions per day, dealing with one challenge in the morning and one in the afternoon. Each three-hour session was started by a short presentation by the CPA and with comments by the opponents (about forty minutes). After this, CPAs and opponents were questioned by the experts for about one hour. Then, in the final hour, the specialists left and the experts discussed their various reasons and considerations for their proposed ranking, which they would then perform before ending the session.

The Final Ranking

The job of the experts was to rank all the suggested opportunities in a single list. It was originally anticipated that they would be able to make numerical estimates of the costs and benefits of the individual opportunities, but early in the process the experts declined to do this given the evidence and time constraints brought before them. One of the challenges for Copenhagen Consensus 2008 will be to provide more information and innovative ways of providing more time to allow the experts to make the numerical estimates. For the Copenhagen Consensus 2004 the experts gave only relative rankings though still categorizing the opportunities from 'very good' to 'bad' projects.

It was also originally envisioned that the experts would be ranking the issues entirely by benefit-cost ratios (BCRs) (i.e. how much good each opportunity would provide for its cost). However, as the experts did not give numerical estimates, they decided at the end only to let the ranking be 'guided predominantly by considerations of economic costs and benefits'.

The innovative methodology of the Copenhagen Consensus remained intact, however. The main

---

[5] In his discussion of the Youth Forum, Christian Friis Bach makes much of the fact that the participants picked different opportunities, but of course, the main issue is that the lists of challenges were very similar. Moreover, he points out that you correctly have to make choices between condoms and clinics, but the hard question remains: Should you save, say, 1 m lives through condoms or 100,000 through an equivalent spending on clinics?

issue was to make it possible for each expert to make his or her own judgement on the basis of the evidence on the ranking, while making it possible for the entire expert panel to automatically issue a single, joint list. This was achieved by taking the median of the expert rankings as the ranking in the common list. This procedure was accepted before-hand by all experts and provided a common rank-ing while being strategy-proof (one expert changing his or her ranking at the extreme would not make the general ranking change greatly). Moreover, had the experts given numerical estimates of costs and benefits, the median methodology would still have worked.

Using the Copenhagen Consensus

The Copenhagen Consensus is based on the idea that academic information should be brought to the general public to make a better contribution to democratic decision-making. This entailed getting information into the media, about the Copenhagen Consensus project, the information on the individ-ual challenges and the final ranking. The Copen-hagen Consensus teamed up with *The Economist* to disseminate information about all three stages. *The Economist* printed a page about the process, five pages about five of the challenges, publishing the other five on their web site, and a three-page story on the outcome. The Copenhagen Consensus process was brought to much wider public attention through numerous op-eds (printed in many news-papers around the world, from *The Times* and *Wall Street Journal*, through the *Hindustan Times* in India to *Revista Cambio* in Colombia). Moreover, we had press conferences in Denmark, London and Washington, DC. We also sought to team up with national newspapers to publish information on the individual challenges. We had a lot of news stories and op-eds on the result of the Copenhagen Consen-sus and we expect that the publication of this book (and of a simplified version for high-school stu-dents) will further encourage the discussion about global priorities.

The Copenhagen Consensus results should be disseminated through media, public discourse and publications of the background material and results. However, the process does not stop here, and it is envisioned that the Copenhagen Consensus will be repeated in 2008, taking into account the shortcom-ings of the present Copenhagen Consensus, how the world has changed and how some priorities have al-ready been dealt with.

Finally, it is our hope that the Copenhagen Consensus methodology will be used for other prioritization issues, such as Brazilian education or American environmental policies. This will re-quire very little change in the original setup and deliver easily accessible and succinct information to the public and policy-makers alike. If Brazil looked at its education policies, it could make a list of educational challenges, identify economists to write papers with opportunities within each, con-vene a group of eminent economists to evaluate the evidence and produce a prioritized list to show where Brazil would get the most for its educational investments.

Conclusion

Part I of this book takes the reader through a broad field, from climate change (chapter 1) to subsidies and trade barriers (chapter 10), and gives the best estimates of costs and benefits to the suggested op-portunities. Part II reports on the conclusions of the expert panel as well as their individual esti-mates and comments. The bottom line is that the Copenhagen Consensus suggests a way in which it might be possible to address head-on the issues of prioritisation. Many people have criticised this project – that prioritisation should be necessary at all. Yet, imagine if doctors at an overstretched hospital refused to perform triage on outpatients, but instead coped with patients as they arrived, focusing more attention on those whose families made the most fuss. We would never accept such an approach in the hospital – the approach would be unjust, waste precious resources and cost lives. We should not accept it for the rest of the world, either.

In public discussion so far, the goodwill of dreamers rejecting prioritisation, seems to have captured the moral high ground. Are the realists really the ones making the evil prioritisations? Mea-sured by the effect on the world's most vulnerable,

I would tend to say exactly the opposite. It is not unethical to include knowledge about where we can do the most good. The Copenhagen Consensus is a deeply ethical project; but rather than playing to our bad conscience, it encourages positive and concrete action.

I am proud that the Copenhagen Consensus has achieved its goal of making a prioritised list of opportunities for the world. The experts have used their knowledge and insight; they have put in a great deal of effort to make estimates of concrete opportunities. The Copenhagen Consensus has already started an important world wide discussion on the prioritisation of the world's resources. I hope that this book will encourage and provide information for researchers, politicians and citizens to engage even further in this crucial debate.

References

Devarajan, S., M. J. Miller and E. V. Swanson, 2002: Development goals: history, prospects and costs, World Bank Policy Research Working Paper, http://econ.worldbank.org/files/13269_wps2819.pdf; summarized (slightly incorrectly) on the MDG's web-page, http://mdgr.undp.sk/PAPERS/WB%20MDG%20Costing.pdf

Hahn, R., 1996: *Risks, costs, and lives saved: getting better results from regulation*, Oxford University Press, Oxford

OECD, 2003: *Statistical annex of the 2003 development co-operation report*. http://www.oecd.org/document/9/0,2340, en_2649_37413_1893129_119687_1_1_37413,00.html

PART I

The challenges

Climate Change

WILLIAM R. CLINE

Introduction

This chapter is part of the Copenhagen Consensus initiative of Denmark's National Environmental Assessment Institute. This initiative seeks to evaluate the costs and benefits of alternative public policy actions in a wide range of key policy areas. For comparability, each of the studies in this programme identifies a limited number of policy actions and examines their respective costs and benefits. This chapter examines the issue area of abatement of greenhouse gas emissions to limit future damage from global warming. Three policy strategies are evaluated: (a) an optimal, globally coordinated carbon tax; (b) the Kyoto Protocol; and (c) a value-at-risk strategy setting carbon taxes to limit exposure to high damage. First, however, a considerable portion of this chapter must be devoted to the conceptual framework and key assumptions used in modelling costs and benefits from abatement of global warming.

The next section of this study briefly reviews the state of play in the scientific and international policy deliberations on global warming. It summarises the key findings of the 2001 review of the Intergovernmental Panel on Climate Change (IPCC) and reviews the status of the Kyoto Protocol. The next section discusses crucial methodological components that can drive sharply contrasting results in cost-benefit analyses (CBAs) of global warming abatement, including especially the question of appropriate time discounting for issues with century-scale time horizons. The next section briefly reviews the findings of my own previous studies on this issue as well as those of a leading climate–economic modeller. The next section sets out the model used in this study for analysis of the policy strategies: an adapted version of the Nordhaus and Boyer (2000) DICE99 model. Further details of this

adaptation are presented in the appendix (p. 39). The next three sections present this study's CBAs of each of the three policy strategies considered, and the final section draws an overview on policy implications.

The State of Global Warming Science and Policy

The 2001 IPCC Scientific Review

For some two decades the central stylised fact of global warming science has been that the 'climate sensitivity parameter' (hereafter referred to as CS) is in a range of 1.5°C–4.5°C equilibrium warming for a doubling of atmospheric concentration of carbon dioxide from pre-industrial levels.[1] The 2001 international review (Third Assessment Report, TAR) did not change this benchmark (IPCC 2001a). However, it did increase the amount of expected realised warming by 2100.[2] Whereas the 1995 Second Assessment Report (SAR) had projected that by that date there would be realised warming above 1990 levels of 1.0°C–3.5°C, the TAR raised the range to 1.4–5.8°C. This increase was primarily the consequence of lower projections than before for future increases in sulphate aerosols (which reflect sunlight and thus have a cooling influence) in light of increased expectation that

---

[1] 'Equilibrium' refers to the level attained after allowance for the time lag associated with initial warming of the ocean (ocean thermal lag), typically placed at some thirty years. Note that atmospheric carbon dioxide has already risen from 280 to 365 parts per m (ppm), corresponding to a rise in the atmospheric stock of carbon from 596 to 766 bn tons.

[2] 'Realised warming' is less than committed warming at any point in time because of ocean thermal lag.

developing countries will follow industrial countries in curbing sulphur dioxide pollution (Hebert,
2000; Barrett, 2003, 364).

Other main findings of the 2001 review include
the following. Global average surface temperature
rose by a central estimate of 0.6°C from 1861 to
2000, up by 0.15°C from the corresponding SAR
estimate through 1994.[3] '[M]ost of the observed
warming over the last 50 years is likely to have
been due to the increase in greenhouse gas concentrations' (IPCC 2001a, 10).[4] Snow cover has 'very
likely' declined by about 10 per cent since the late
1960s. There was 'widespread retreat of mountain
glaciers' in the twentieth century and the global average sea level rose 0.1–0.2 m. Since the 1950s, the
thickness of Arctic sea ice in late summer – early
autumn has likely decreased by 40 per cent. It is very
likely that precipitation increased 0.5–1.0 per cent
per decade over the twentieth century in the mid-
and high latitudes (>30°) of the Northern Hemisphere and by 0.2–0.3 per cent per decade in tropical areas (10°N–10°S), but that rainfall decreased
by about 0.3 per cent per decade over sub-tropical
areas in the Northern Hemisphere (10°N–30°N).
The report judged that it was 'likely' that during the twenty-first century there would be 'increased summer continental drying and associated
risk of drought', an 'increase in tropical cyclone
peak wind intensities', and an 'increase in tropical cyclone mean and peak precipitation intensities'
(IPCC 2001a, 15).

The 2001 report based the range of projected
warming on six benchmark scenarios (table 1.1). In

Table 1.1. IPCC Emissions Scenarios (GtC), 2050 and 2100

Case	Description	Emissions in: 2050	Emissions in: 2100
A1B	Rapid growth, population peaking mid-century, convergence, balanced fossil–non-fossil energy	16.0	13.1
A1T	Same as A1B but non-fossil technology emphasis	12.3	4.3
A1F1	Same as A1B but fossil-intensive technology	23.1	30.3
A2	Continuously rising population, slower growth, less technological change	16.5	28.9
B1	A1 growth and population; sharper decline in materials intensity; cleaner, more resource-efficient technologies	11.7	5.2
B2	Continuously increasing population, slower growth	11.2	13.8

Source: IPCC (2001a, 14–18).

the scenario with high economic growth and fossil-
fuel intensive technology (A1F1), global emissions
from fossil fuels and industrial processes multiply
from 6.9 GtC (bn tons of carbon) annually in 2000
to 30.3 GtC by 2100. In contrast, two of the scenarios based on optimistic assumptions about the
shift toward non-fossil technology (A1T and B1)
show emissions peaking at about 12 GtC by mid-
century and then falling back to 5 GtC or less by
2100. The wide range of projected emissions and
hence atmospheric concentrations, combined with
the range of CSs in the various climate (general
circulation) models, generates the relatively wide
range of projected possible warming by 2100. Although the report suggests that each of the scenarios
is equally likely, the analysis of this study will apply
a path that is close to the average of scenarios A1B,
A1F1, and A2).[5] The scenarios with a sharp drop
in carbon intensity (A1T and B1) are inconsistent
with a business as usual baseline in which there is
no carbon tax (or emissions ceiling) to provide an
economic incentive for carbon-saving technological change.[6]

The central message of the 2001 IPPC scientific
review is that the grounds for concern about global

---

[3] The earth's surface temperature changed little from 1860
through 1910, then rose relatively rapidly and steadily
through 1940. Thereafter there was a period of about four
decades of small but relatively steady temperature *decline*,
followed by a return to a renewed and more rapid warming
trend since 1980 (IPCC 2001a, 3).

[4] The report used 'likely' for 66–90 per cent chance, and
'very likely' for 90–99 per cent chance.

[5] The baseline used here is the same as in Cline (1992). This
shows emissions at 22 GtC in 2100, close to the 24.1 GtC
average for the IPCC's A1B, A1F1 and A2.

[6] Moreover, with the more rapid exhaustion of oil and gas
reserves than of coal, the carbon intensity of fuel could easily
rise toward the later part of the twenty-first century, as coal
generates almost twice as much in carbon emissions per unit
of energy (26 kg per mn British thermal units (BTU)) as natural gas and about one-quarter more than oil (Cline 1992, 142).

warming have strengthened rather than weakened. There is a greater degree of certainty than in earlier reviews that the warming observed in the past century is largely anthropogenic, and the range for projected warming over the twenty-first century has been ratcheted upward rather than diminished, and by an especially large increment (by 2.3°C) at the high-warming end.

Kyoto Protocol Impasse

The state of play in international policy action on global warming is one of impasse. At the Rio Earth Summit in June of 1992, some 150 countries agreed to the Framework Convention on Climate Change (UNFCCC). The agreement did not set hard targets for emissions, however. Two implementing Conferences of Parties followed, at Berlin in 1995 and Kyoto in 1997. The Kyoto Protocol set quantitative emissions ceilings for industrial countries (including Russia), but set no limits for developing countries (most importantly, China and India). Although US President Clinton signed the treaty in November 1998, he did not submit it to the Senate for confirmation, recognising that he could not obtain the required two-thirds majority. In March 2001, President Bush rejected the Kyoto Protocol, on the grounds that the science was uncertain and that the targets could be costly to the US economy. In addition, there was a strong sense in the US Congress that any international treaty would have to include developing countries in commitments on emissions ceilings; and the US Senate had voted 95–0 in the summer of 1997 that the USA should not sign any agreement that failed to impose emissions limits on developing as well as industrial countries and that would harm US interests (Barrett 2003, 369–71).

Despite the US refusal to ratify the Kyoto Protocol, by March 2001 there were eighty-four countries that had signed the agreement, and by November 2003 there were eighty-four signatories and 120 countries that had ratified it (UNFCCC 2004). However, to take effect the Protocol required not only that at least fifty-five countries sign, but also that countries accounting for 55 per cent of the 1990 total carbon emissions from Annex I parties (industrial and transition economies) did so. Russia

has been the key to implementation, because in the absence of US adherence, without Russia's participation the emissions threshold cannot be reached. In early December 2003, Russia's President Putin reaffirmed earlier reports that he did not intend to sign the Protocol (*The Guardian*, 5 December).

Rejection of the Protocol by both the USA and, apparently, Russia leaves little in place for international abatement other than plans adopted by some countries unilaterally. However, these self-imposed limits have largely not been met. The EU announced in October 1990 that by the year 2000 it would constrain emissions to their 1990 level; however, by 1992 it clarified that it would impose its carbon tax policy toward this end only if other OECD countries also did so, including the USA and Japan (Barrett 2003, 368).

The costs and benefits of the Kyoto Protocol are considered below. However, at present it is questionable whether the protocol remains of relevance. It would seem more likely that the international community will need to return to the negotiating table to arrive at a different type of agreement that will be adopted by all of the key players, including the USA and Russia. It is possible that an arrangement for nationally collected and internationally coordinated carbon taxes, including at least the major developing countries (and albeit perhaps with some later phase-in), could form the basis for such a regime. This is the underlying approach considered in the first and third policy strategies examined below.

Core Analytical Issues

Time Discounting

Before proceeding to the specific CBAs, it is first necessary to consider the issues and debates involved in the most important dimensions of the analysis. Perhaps the single most important and controversial conceptual issue in analysing global warming policy is *how to discount future costs and benefits* to obtain comparable *present values for policy judgements*. Most issues of public policy involve actions with costs and benefits spanning a few years or, at most, a few decades. Although the scientific analysis on global warming at first focused on the benchmark of a doubling of carbon dioxide concentrations, which was expected to occur within a few decades, by now the standard time horizon for primary focus has become at least one century. The principal scenarios and projections in the 2001 IPCC review were thus for the full period through 2100, and some additional analyses referred to effects several centuries beyond that date. Cline (1991) was the first economic analysis to propose that the proper time horizon for consideration was three centuries, on the basis that it is only on this time scale that mixing of carbon dioxide back into the deep ocean begins to reverse atmospheric buildup (Sundquist 1990). Cline (1992) estimated that on a time scale of 300 years, plausible emissions and build-up in atmospheric concentrations of carbon dioxide and other greenhouse gases could cause warming of 10°C even using the central (rather than upper-bound) value for the CS.

Typical economic analyses of costs and benefits tend to apply discount rates that simply make effects on these time scales vanish, for all practical purposes. For example, discounting at even 3 per cent annually causes $100 two centuries in the future to be worth only 27 cents today. Yet the essence of the global warming policy is taking potentially costly actions at an early date in exchange for a reduction of potential climate damages at a later date. The damage effects stretch far into the future, in part because they begin to occur with a lag of some three decades after the emissions (because of ocean thermal lag), but more importantly because they are recurrent annually over a span of some two centuries or more because of the time of residence of carbon dioxide in the atmosphere. The asymmetry in the timing of costs and benefits of action, when combined with the vanishing-point compression of present values of century-distant effects, means that casual application of typical discount rates can introduce a strong bias against any preventive action.

Cline (1992) sets out an approach to time discounting that addresses this issue while remaining fully within the tradition of the literature on social CBAs.[7] The key to this approach is to adopt zero as

the rate of time discounting for 'pure time preference,' or 'myopic' preference for consumption today over consumption tomorrow even when there is no expectation of a higher consumption level tomorrow. Ramsey (1928) called discounting for pure time preference 'a practice which is ethically indefensible and arises merely from the weakness of the imagination' (1928, 543). A second component of time discounting still remains valid in this approach, however: the discounting of future consumption on the basis of an expectation that per capita consumption will be rising so the marginal utility of consumption will be falling, or 'utility-based discounting'.

The proper rate at which to discount future consumption is thus the Social Rate of Time Preference, or SRTP, where:

(1) $\text{SRTP} = \rho + \theta g$,

where ρ is the rate of 'pure' time preference, θ is the 'elasticity of marginal utility' (absolute value) and g is the annual rate of growth of per capita consumption (Cline 1992, 1999). Most empirical research places θ in the range of 1–1.5, meaning that when per capita consumption rises by 10 per cent (for example), the marginal utility of an additional unity of consumption falls by 10–15 per cent. It is evident from 1) that if the future is considered to be a bleak outlook of perpetual stagnation at today's levels of global per capita income (i.e. $g = 0$), and if there is no 'pure' time preference ($\rho = 0$), then there would be no discounting whatsoever (SRTP = 0). If instead per capita consumption is expected to grow consistently at, say, 1 per cent annually, then even with zero pure time preference, the annual discount rate applied to future consumption would be 1.5 per cent (using $\theta = 1.5$).

The tradition of social CBA discounts future consumption effects by the SRTP. However, it also allows for a divergence between the rate of return on capital and the SRTP. This tradition thus requires that all capital (e.g. investment) effects be converted (i.e. expanded) into consumption-equivalents by applying a 'shadow price of capital', before discounting all consumption-equivalent values. On a basis of the literature, Cline (1992, 270–4) suggests a typical shadow price of capital of 1.6, so

---

[7] See Arrow (1966); Feldstein (1970); Arrow and Kurz (1970); Bradford (1975).

that a unit of investment translates into 1.6 units of consumption.

In the 1995 report of Working Group III of the IPCC (Bruce, Lee and Haites 1996), a panel of experts referred to the discounting method just reviewed as the 'prescriptive' approach (Arrow *et al.* 1996). It contrasted this method with the 'descriptive approach' based on observed market rates of return. The discounting method used by Nordhaus and Boyer (2000) is a good example of the latter. They apply a Ramsey-type optimal-growth model in which they employ a rate of pure time preference set at 3 per cent, based on observed capital market rates.[8] They take account of falling marginal utility by applying this discount rate to 'utility' rather than directly to consumption. Their utility function is logarithmic ($U = \ln c$, where U is *per capita* utility and c is *per capita* consumption). In this utility function, the absolute value of the elasticity of marginal utility is unity ($\theta = 1$). If *per capita* consumption grows systematically at 1 per cent, their overall discount rate is thus equivalent to about 4 per cent annually (3 per cent pure time preference plus 1 per cent from logarithmic utility). At this rate, $100 in damages 200 years from today shrinks to 0.04 cents in today's values. It would take savings of about $2,500 in avoided damages 200 years from today to warrant giving up just $1 in consumption today, at this rate. I continue to believe that this type of discounting, whether descriptive or not, trivialises the problem of global warming by introducing a severe bias against counting the damage experienced by future generations.[9]

A final conceptual issue in discounting using zero pure time preference involves implications for optimal saving and investment. Critics of the social cost-benefit approach sometimes argue that it must be wrong, because it would imply the need for a massive increase in saving and investment in order to drive the rate of return to capital down to the SRTP. Otherwise the economy would be suboptimal. A variant on this argument is simply that instead of investing in greenhouse abatement, society should invest more in other goods and services generally and thereby more effectively keep the future generations no worse off by compensating their environmental damages with additional goods and services.

The answer to the first variant of this argument is that public policy should be second-best when it cannot be first-best. It has proven extremely difficult to boost private saving and investment rates. So even though it might be socially optimal to do so, if in fact that is impossible, that reality should not be allowed to prevent action on global warming. It might be first-best to raise saving and investment simultaneously with adopting greenhouse abatement, but even in the absence of a boost to saving and investment it could be second-best to proceed with the greenhouse abatement.

The answer to the second variant of the capital argument, which I have called the 'Fund for Greenhouse Victims' approach, is that it is implausible (Cline, 1992, 265). Suppose that society could devote 1 per cent of GDP to reducing global warming, but instead chooses to invest this amount to compensate future generations for unabated warming. Even if the corresponding tax revenues and investments could be mobilised, this approach would not be credible. The extra capital assets thereby obtained would have life spans of 10–15 years, whereas the life span of the carbon abatement benefit is on the scale of two centuries. The beneficiaries of additional investments in schooling today would be today's youth, not the youth of two centuries from now. Moreover, if somehow additional goods and services for the future generations could be assured, those generations could easily place a much lower valuation on them than would be required to compensate them for the environmental damages.

Measuring Benefits

From the outset of economic analysis of global warming more than two decades ago, there has

[8] As discussed below, they allow for a slight decline in the rate of pure time preference over time.

[9] The dichotomy of 'descriptive' and 'prescriptive' is misleading, as it could be interpreted as implying that the former matches reality while the latter is based solely on theory. Yet it is quite 'descriptive', in terms of according with observed data, to argue that the rate of pure time preference is zero. It turns out that the real rate of return on US treasury bills – the only risk-free instrument (including freedom from risk of change in the interest rate) at which households can transfer consumption over time – has historically been about zero.

been far more empirical work on the side of calculating the cost of abatement than on the side of measuring the potential 'benefits' from *climate damage avoided*. Quantifying the potential damages is simply a far more elusive task. On the basis of then-available estimates by the US Environmental Protection Agency and other sources, Cline (1992) compiled benchmark estimates for damage that could be expected from warming associated with a doubling of CO_2. This damage turned out to be an aggregate of about 1 per cent of GDP (1992, 131). The largest damage was in agriculture (about one-quarter of the total damage); increases of electricity requirements for cooling in excess of reductions for heating (about one-sixth of the total); sea-level rise, adverse impact of warming on water supply and loss of human life from heat waves (each about one-tenth of the total); and forest loss and increased tropospheric ozone pollution (each about one-twentieth of the total). The estimate included a speculative and probably lower-bound number for species loss. Other potential losses (human amenity, human morbidity, other pollution effects of warming) were recognized but omitted from quantification.

The 1 per cent of GDP benchmark was about the same as suggested by Nordhaus (1991) who, however, specifically calculated only agricultural losses (far smaller) and sea level damages (somewhat larger) and arbitrarily assumed 0.75 per cent of GDP as a comfortable allowance for all other losses not specifically examined. Two other analyses quantifying broadly the same categories as in Cline (1992) reached similar magnitudes for the USA (Fankhauser 1995, at 1.3 per cent of GDP, and Tol 1995, at 1.5 per cent of GDP) and in addition extended the estimates to other parts of the world. A higher estimate of 2.5 per cent of GDP damage was obtained by Titus (1992), who however applied a higher $2 \times CO_2$ warming assumption (4°C) than in the other studies (2.5°). The Fankhauser and Tol studies obtained modestly higher damage estimates for non-OECD countries (1.6 per cent and 2.7 per cent of GDP, respectively).[10]

Cline (1992) also suggested benchmark damage for very-long-term warming with a central value of

6 per cent of GDP for warming of 10°C, on the basis of plausible non-linear relationships of damage to warming in each of the damage categories. This implied an average exponent of 1.3 for relating the ratio of damage to the ratio of warming (i.e. $6/1 = [10/2.5]^{1.3}$).

Subsequent damage estimates have tended to suggest somewhat lower magnitudes for $2 \times CO_2$ damage for the USA, but there has tended to be greater emphasis on the potential for larger damages in developing countries, in part because of lesser scope for adaptation. A 'Ricardian' model relating US land values to temperatures estimated by Mendelsohn, Nordhaus and Shaw (1994) suggested that a modest amount of warming might have positive rather than negative effects for US agriculture, but Cline (1996) suggested that this result was vulnerable to an overly optimistic implicit assumption about the availability of irrigation water.

Incorporating Risk of Catastrophe

A third issue that warrants emphasis is the question of catastrophic impacts. The most well known is that of the shut-down of thermohaline circulation in the Atlantic ocean. There is a 'conveyor belt' that involves the sinking of cold water near the Arctic and upwelling of warm water in the Southern Atlantic, giving rise to the Gulf Stream which keeps northern Europe warm. Increased melting of polar ice could reduce the salinity and specific gravity of the cold water entering the ocean there, possibly shutting down the ocean conveyor belt. The approach to this and other catastrophic risks in Cline (1992) is merely to treat them as additional reasons to act above and beyond the basic economic attractiveness of greenhouse abatement as evaluated in a CBA. The analysis of that study does incorporate risk in a milder form, however, by placing greater weight on upper-bound scenarios and (non-catastrophic) damage coefficients than on lower-bound combinations in arriving at an overall weighted BCR for action.

Nordhaus and Boyer (2000) make an important contribution in attempting instead to incorporate catastrophic risk directly into the CBA. On the basis of a survey of scientists and economists working in the area of global warming, they first identify a range of potential damage and associated

---

[10] For a survey of damage estimates, see Pearce *et al.* (1996).

probabilities of catastrophic outcomes. After some upward adjustment for 'growing concerns' in scientific circles about such effects (2000, 88), they arrive at estimates such as the following. The expected loss in the event of a catastrophe ranges from 22 per cent of GDP in the USA to 44 per cent for OECD Europe and India (2000, 90). The probability of a catastrophic outcome is placed at 1.2 per cent for 2.5°C warming and at 6.8 per cent for 6°C warming (the highest they consider). Using a 'rate of relative risk aversion' of 4, they then calculate that these probabilities and damages translate into a willingness-to-pay to avoid catastrophe of 0.45 per cent of GDP in the USA at 2.5°C and 2.53 per cent of GDP at 6°C, while the corresponding magnitudes are 1.9 per cent and 10.8 per cent of GDP, respectively, for both OECD Europe and India. The higher estimates for Europe reflect greater vulnerability (in particular because of the risk to thermohaline circulation). Other regions are intermediate.

Nordhaus and Boyer (2000) then directly incorporate this 'willingness-to-pay' directly into their damage function relating expected damage to warming. The result is a highly non-linear function, in which damage as per cent of GDP is initially negative (i.e. beneficial effects) up to 1.25°C warming, but then rises to 1.1 per cent of GDP for 2.5°C warming, 1.6 per cent of GDP for 2.9°C, 5.1 per cent of GDP for 4.5°C and 10 per cent of GDP for 6°C warming.[11] Although their direct incorporation of catastrophic risk is heroic, it surely captures the public's true concern about the possible scope of global warming damage more effectively than do the usual central estimates of benchmark $2 \times CO_2$ damage at 1 per cent of GDP or so.

Adaptation

This chapter examines the policy option of abatement of emissions contributing to global warming. A natural question is whether instead there could be an alternative policy of adaptation to climate change. In practice, adaptation turns into more of an inevitable concomitant of global warming rather than a viable stand-alone policy. The amelioration of climate damages feasible through adaptation tends to be already incorporated in the estimates of baseline damage, which in effect are 'damage net of costs and benefits of feasible adaptation'. Specifically, in the Nordhaus–Boyer damage estimates to be used in the present study, key components already take account of adaptation. Their relatively low damage estimates for agriculture and some other sectors are premised on incorporating net effects of adaptation.[12]

Carbon Taxes versus Quotas with Trading

The analysis of this chapter examines optimal carbon taxes in the light of potential reductions in climate damage through abatement. In principle, any optimal path for emissions and carbon taxes can also be translated into an equivalent path for global carbon quotas coupled with free market trading of these quotas. The market price of the quotas should wind up being the same as the carbon tax that generates the emissions path targeted. Countries receiving an abundant quota would tend to find their value in international trading would exceed the value in their domestic use and would tend to 'export' (sell) the quotas, while countries receiving relatively scant quotas in view of their energy–economic base would tend to 'import' (buy) them. There are several key practical differences, however. Perhaps the most important is that a regime of quotas would presume some form of allocation that would be unlikely to have the same distributional effects as a carbon-tax approach. In particular, quota allocations based substantially on population rather than existing total energy use would tend to redistribute quota 'rents' to large countries with low *per capita* income (India, China), whereas the carbon-tax approach would essentially distribute the quota-equivalents on a basis of existing economic strength and hence capability to pay the tax.

A second important difference has to do with the degree of certainty about the response of

[11] In the DICE99XL version of their model, the damage function (per cent of GDP) is: $d = 100 \times (-0.0045T + 0.0035T^2)$, where T is the amount of warming (°C) above 1990.

[12] Thus, Nordhaus and Boyer (2000, 70) state: 'many of the earliest estimates (particularly those for agriculture, sea-level rise, and energy) were extremely pessimistic about the economic impacts, whereas more recent studies, *which include adaptation*, do not paint such a gloomy picture'.

carbon-based energy supply and demand to prices. When pollution has sharply rising marginal damages, and supply–demand price elasticities are highly uncertain, set quotas (which are then traded) can be a better approach than taxes. When the marginal pollution damages are relatively constant but marginal abatement costs are steep, taxes can be a preferable approach in order to avoid excessive cost of overly ambitious emissions targets (Weitzman 1974). In practice, however, global warming policy has such a long time horizon that either a tax-based or a quota-based approach would seem capable of periodic review and adjustment.

Previous Cost-Benefit Analyses

In part because of the difficulty of measuring potential global warming damage, and hence the economic benefits of abatement, there are relatively few cost-benefit studies, whereas there are numerous estimates of costs of specified abatement programme. This section will highlight two principal previous studies: Cline (1992) and Nordhaus and Boyer (2000).[13]

Cline 1992

My study in 1992 examined a three-century horizon involving much higher future atmospheric concentration of greenhouse gases than had previously been considered. This was based in part on the analysis by Sundquist (1990), indicating that over this time span the atmospheric concentration of CO_2 alone could rise to 1,600 ppm, far above the usual benchmark of doubling to 560 ppm. Based on then existing projections of emissions through 2100 (Nordhaus and Yohe 1983; Reilly *et al.* 1987; Manne and Richels 1990), I calculated a baseline of global carbon emissions rising from 5.6 GtC in 1990 to a range of 15–27 GtC in 2100. Thereafter the baseline decelerated to about 0.5 per cent annual growth, but even at the slower rate reached

an average of about 50 GtC annually in the second half of the twenty-third century (Cline 1992, 52, 290). These projections were based on the view that there was abundant carbon available at relatively low cost, primarily from coal resources, to generate from 7,000–14,000 GtC cumulative emissions (Cline 1992, 45, based on Edmonds and Reilly 1985, 160), so that rising resource costs could not be counted upon to provide a natural choking-off of emissions by the market. Assuming atmospheric retention of one-half of emissions, and taking into account other greenhouse gases, I calculated realized warming of 4.2°C by 2100 and 'committed' warming of 5.2°C by that date under business-as-usual (non-abatement). For the very long term, I estimated 10°C as the central value for warming by 2300, using a CS of 2.5°C. I placed upper-bound warming (for CS = 4.5°C) at 18°C. As discussed above, the corresponding damage amounted to about 1 per cent of GDP for the central value by about 2050 (the estimated time of realized warming from CO_2 doubling above pre-industrial levels already by 2025), rising to a central estimate of 6 per cent of GDP by 2300 and, in the high-CS case, 16 per cent of GDP by 2275 (1992, 280).

On the side of abatement costs, several 'top-down' modelling studies then available provided estimates, which tended to cluster in the range of about 1–2 per cent of GDP as the cost of cutting carbon emissions from baseline by 50 per cent in the period 2025–50, and about 2.5 to 3.5 per cent of GDP as the cost of reducing emissions from baseline by about 70 per cent by 2075–2100 (Cline 1992, 184). One study in particular (Manne and Richels, 1990) suggested that by the latter period there would be non-carbon 'backstop' technologies that could provide a horizontal cost-curve of abundantly available alternative energy at a constant cost of $250 per ton of carbon avoided. For comparison, $100 per ton of carbon would equate to $60 per ton of coal (about 75 per cent of current market prices), $13 per barrel of oil, and 30 cents per gallon of gasoline.

Another family of studies in the 'bottom-up' engineering tradition suggested that there was at least an initial tranche of low-cost options for curbing emissions by moving to the frontier of already available technology in such areas as building standards

[13] The Working Group III review for the IPCC in 1995 identified only two other CBAs then available, and only one of them (Peck and Teisberg 1992) was published (Pearce *et al.* 1996, 215).

and higher fuel efficiency standards for vehicles. In addition, numerous studies suggested low-cost carbon sequestration opportunities from afforestation, which could, however, provide only a one-time absorption of carbon in the phase of forest expansion. Taking these initial lower-cost options into account, I estimated that world emissions could be cut by about one-third for as little as 0.1 per cent of world product in the first two decades; but that by about 2050 it would cost about 2 per cent of world product to cut emissions 50 per cent from the baseline. By late in the twenty-first century emissions could be reduced by up to 80 per cent from the baseline for still about 2 per cent of GDP in abatement costs, because of the widening of technological alternatives (Cline 1992, 231–2).

As discussed above, because of the later arrival of climate damage and the earlier dating of abatement measures, the discount rate is central to arriving at a CBA. Cline (1992) applies the SRTP method with zero pure time preference and conversion of capital effects to consumption equivalents, as summarized above. The study analysed a global policy of reducing emissions to 4 GtC and freezing them at that level. In the base case, the present value of benefits of damage avoided were only three-quarters as large as the present value of abatement costs. However, an examination of a total of thirty-six alternative cases showed that in several combinations of high damage (CS = 4.5°C, and/or damage exponent = 2 rather than 1.3, and/or base damage = 2 per cent of GDP rather than 1 per cent in light of unquantified effects) the BCR could reach well above unity. To arrive at an overall evaluation, and to give some weight to risk aversion, the analysis placed 1/2 weight on the base case, 3/8 weight on the upper-bound damage outcome and 1/8 weight on the lower-bound damage outcome. The result was a weighted BCR of 1.26 for reducing global emissions to 4 GtC annually and holding them to this ceiling permanently in the future (1992, 300).

Nordhaus' DICE Model

In a body of work spanning more than two decades, William Nordhaus has provided successive estimates of optimal carbon abatement (Nordhaus 1991, 1994; Nordhaus and Boyer 2000). His results have systematically found that while optimal abatement is not zero, neither is it very large. The most recent analysis (Nordhaus and Boyer 2000) finds that the optimal reduction in global carbon emissions is only 5 per cent at present, rising to only 11 per cent from the baseline by 2100. Correspondingly, the optimal carbon tax is only $9 per ton by 2005, rising to $67 by 2100 (2000, 133–5). Optimal policy reduces warming by 2100 by a razor-thin 0.09°C, or from the baseline 2.53°C to 2.44°C (2000, 141). Although this change is for all practical purposes negligible, the authors apparently judge that it will be sufficient to successfully 'thread the needle between a ruinously expensive climate-change policy that today's citizens will find intolerable and a myopic do-nothing policy that the future will curse us for' (2000, 7).

I have previously shown that the earlier version of the DICE model could generate far higher optimal cutbacks and optimal carbon taxes if pure time preference is set at zero in my preferred SRTP method (Cline 1997). However, the DICE model is an attractive vehicle for integrated climate–economic analysis. In particular, it provides a basis for identifying an optimal time path for emissions and abatement, whereas the 4 GtC ceiling experiment in Cline (1992) constitutes a single imposed policy target. Nordhaus has also made the model available for use by other researchers. The approach of this chapter is to use the model as a basis for evaluating alternative policy strategies, but only after making adjustments in certain key assumptions and, in some cases, calibrations. The change in the discounting methodology is the most important.

Before discussing the changes made to the model, however, it is useful to obtain a feel for the structure of DICE. The model begins with baseline projections of population, *per capita* consumption, carbon emissions and emissions of non-carbon greenhouse gases. Global output is a function of labour (population) and capital, which rises from cumulative saving. A climate damage function reduces actual output from potential as a function of warming. In the climate module, emissions translate into atmospheric concentrations and hence radiative forcing. Concentrations are increased by emissions but reduced by transit of CO_2 from the atmosphere to the upper and, ultimately, lower oceans, in a 'three-box' model. Warming is a function of radiative forcing, but also a (negative) function of the difference between surface and low-ocean temperature. This means that the ocean thermal lag between the date of committed and realized warming stretches out substantially as the CS parameter is increased, as discussed below.

There is a cost function for reduction of emissions from the baseline. This function is relatively low-cost at moderate cutbacks. Thus, in the Excel version of the most recent version of the model (hereafter referred to as DICE99NB), as of 2045 it would cost only 0.03 per cent of gross world product (GWP) to cut emissions from the baseline by 10 per cent; only 0.32 per cent of GWP to cut emissions by 30 per cent; and only 0.97 per cent to cut them by 50 per cent. Costs then begin to escalate, however, and it would cost 2.3 per cent of GWP to cut emissions by 75 per cent at that date.[14]

The model is optimized by a search method applying iterative alternative values of the 'control rate' (percentage cut of emissions from the baseline) and evaluating a social welfare function each time. Welfare is the discounted present value of future utility, and the utility function is logarithmic (as discussed above). The optimal carbon abatement path is that which maximizes welfare after taking account of both abatement costs and the opportunity for higher actual output as a consequence of lesser climate damage.[15] The nearly *de minimis*

cost of reducing emissions by 10 per cent, combined with the Nordhaus–Boyer conclusion that optimal cuts are below 10 per cent for most of this century, shows immediately that the driving force behind the minimal-action conclusion is not an assumption that it is costly to abate, but instead a calculation that there is very little value obtained in doing so. The minimal value of abatement benefits is in turn driven mainly by the discounting method.

Adapting the DICE99 Model

This study uses the Nordhaus–Boyer DICE99 model,[16] designated as DICE99NB. The preferred version in this study applies several modifications to obtain what will be called the DICE99CL model. The appendix sets out details on these modifications. This section sets out the reasons for the most important changes.

Rate of Pure Time Preference

For the reasons set out above, the preferred value for pure time preference (ρ above) is zero. The most direct way to show the importance of this parameter is to consider the results of DICE99NB when there are no other changes except for setting pure time preference at zero. In the Nordhaus–Boyer (NB) version, this rate begins at 3 per cent, and slowly falls over time (to 2.57 per cent by 2055, 2.26 per cent by 2105 and 1.54 per cent by 2155). Figures 1.1 and 1.2 show the optimal abatement profiles (carbon tax and percentage cut from the baseline) using DICE99NB with the original pure time preference and zero pure time preference, respectively. As shown, far more aggressive action is found optimal when pure time preference is set to zero. Thus, whereas by 2055 in the original version the optimal carbon tax is $33, when pure time preference is zero the optimal tax is $240 at that date. Optimal per cent cuts in emissions from baseline are in the range of 50 per cent through most of the twentieth century when pure time preference is zero, instead of 5 to 10 per cent as in the original case with 3 per cent pure time preference.[17]

Figures 1.1 and 1.2 refer to optimization of the DICE model with respect to the carbon tax

---

[14] This and other specific calculations using the model are obtained using the Excel spreadsheet version of DICE99 available at http://www.econ.yale.edu/~nordhaus/homepage/dicemodels.htm.

[15] Full optimisation of the model allows the savings rate to vary, as well as the carbon abatement rate.

[16] A more thorough analysis could be carried out by adapting the regional NB model, RICE, along the lines done here for the globally aggregate DICE99 model. This more extensive task was beyond the scope of the present chapter.

[17] The downward slope in the optimal cut curve in the case of zero time preference is probably exaggerated by the anomaly of a rising linear component of the abatement cost function, as discussed below. The Excel version of the cost curve to approximate the RICE results is meant to provide a close approximation only through 2100 and close to the optimal cut ranges identified in Nordhaus and Boyer (2000).

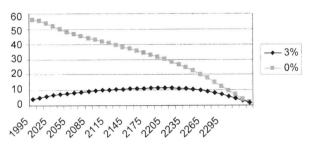

Figure 1.1. *DICE99NB optimal % cut from baseline at alternative pure time preference rates*

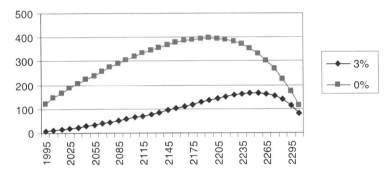

Figure 1.2. *DICE99NB optimal carbon taxes at alternative pure time preference rates*

only. If in addition the savings rate is allowed to be optimized, then in the variant with zero pure time preference the optimal control rates and carbon taxes are slightly higher, and the savings rate is far higher (averaging 33 per cent over the twenty-first century rather than 23 per cent as in the baseline).[18] However, as discussed above, 'full optimization' including a major boost to the savings rate, is not realistic. The analyses that follow optimize only the carbon tax and treat the savings rate as exogenous.

Discounting Future Consumption

As discussed above, the social cost-benefit approach uses the SRTP to discount future consumption. The adapted model does this directly, using an elasticity of marginal utility (θ) of 1.5 (absolute value) and identifying a cumulative *per capita* consumption growth rate (g) that is specific to each of the periods (decades) in the model. In this approach, there is no need further to shrink rising consumption by translating it into 'utility' through a logarithmic function (see the appendix).

Shadow-Pricing Capital

The SRTP method also requires conversion of all capital effects into consumption-equivalents. In practice, this principally involves an expansion of the abatement cost function to take account of the fact that a portion of the resources withdrawn to carry out abatement would come out of investment rather than consumption.

Baseline Carbon Emissions

Even though the more recent Nordhaus and Boyer (2000) study incorporates a higher climate damage function than in Nordhaus (1994), it arrives at about

---

[18] For example, in 2195 the optimal carbon tax is 44 per cent instead of 41 per cent with full optimization, and the carbon tax is $353 per ton insted of $320, for the zero pure time preference variant.

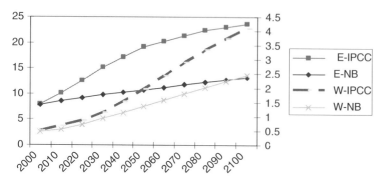

Figure 1.3. *Carbon emissions (left, GtC) and warming (right, °C)*

the same amount of optimal abatement. The main reason is that baseline emissions are scaled back in the later study, so there is less to cut back. Whereas global output by 2100 is set 13 per cent lower than before, with population 8.5 per cent higher (at 10.7 billion) but output per person 20 per cent lower (at $9,100 in 1990 prices), carbon emissions are 48 per cent lower than before (at only 12.9 GtC, down from 24.9 GtC; 2000, 5). The drop in carbon intensity (from 0.22 tons per $1,000 of GDP in the earlier study to only 0.13 tons) stems mainly from the authors' new view on a steeply rising cost curve for fossil fuel extraction after a cumulative 6,000 GtC carbon-equivalent has been used.

The basis for the sharp reduction in projected carbon intensity of output is not clear, however. In particular, with annual emissions averaging about 10 GtC in the twenty-first century, the new Nordhaus–Boyer baseline would exhaust only about one-sixth of the 6,000 GtC cumulative amount available before the sharp increase in extraction costs. As suggested above, my preferred baseline for emissions is still the path used in Cline (1992), which is also relatively close to the average of three of the four 'A' series in the IPCC 2001 report: A1B, A1F1 and A2 (table 1.1).[19] The other

scenarios tend to be inconsistent as 'business-as-usual' baselines, because they presume sharp drops in carbon intensity without any special economic incentive to prompt the corresponding technological change, in the absence of any carbon tax.

Figure 1.3 shows the contrast between the 3As emissions baseline from the IPPC and the much lower Nordhaus–Boyer baseline. In the IPCC average, emissions reach about 24 GtC in 2100 (the same as in Nordhaus 1994) whereas in the new Nordhaus–Boyer baseline they reach only 13 GtC. Figure 5.3 also shows the average projected baseline warming above 1990 for the 3As scenarios from the IPCC. By 2100, realized warming in the three IPCC scenarios averages 4.1°C. This is virtually the same as in Cline (1992), as discussed above, but is far above the 2.45°C in Nordhaus–Boyer. A major adaptation to the model, then, is to replace the emissions baseline, restoring it to a path much more like Nordhaus' previous projections. Further details on changes in the emissions and world output baselines are discussed in the appendix.

Other Adaptations

As discussed in the appendix, the climate module of DICE99NB generates a surprisingly low rate of atmospheric retention of emissions over the period of the first century, so in addition to a low emissions baseline there is an even lower build-up in atmospheric stock. The projections in IPCC (2001) provide a basis for relating atmospheric retention to emissions over this period, and this

[19] Note that other leading analysts of carbon emissions scenarios do not appear to have adopted drastic reductions like those of Nordhaus and Boyer. For example, Manne and Richels (2001) still apply a baseline that places global emissions at 21 GtC in 2100, down only moderately from their earlier projection of 26.9 GtC by 2100 (Manne and Richels 1991) and far above the new Nordhaus–Boyer level.

relationship is used as the basis for the adaptation of the model. This involves relatively modest alterations in the rates of transfer of CO_2 between the various 'boxes' of the three-box model, as discussed in the appendix.

Abatement Cost Function

Finally, a modification is made to the abatement cost function for the period after 2100. The Excel version of DICE99 has the seeming anomaly of a rising trend over time for the linear term in the abatement cost function, whereas it is usually judged that for any target percentage cut from the baseline, the economic cost (as a percentage of GDP) should fall over time thanks to the widening array of technological alternatives. Indeed, in the GAMS version of the DICE model, this term does fall over time. The use instead of a rising linear term in the Excel version reflects the need to make its optimization results track those of the more regionally detailed RICE model. Because the latter can take advantage of initial low-cost carbon abatement in developing and transition economy regions (for example), at the global level the gradual exhaustion of this opportunity is mimicked by having a rising rather than falling linear term for the abatement cost function. Although the result is successfully to track the optimal results of RICE for the first 100 years, Nordhaus has indicated that this cost function may not track well for the more distant future.[20]

The modification made here is to place a ceiling on the linear term in the abatement cost function, freezing it at its 2100 level for all later periods. This means that it does not reflect the falling-cost opportunities of a widening technological menu, but neither does it project rising cost of abatement. This approach implicitly makes the reasonable assumption that the process of exhausting the regional 'easy pickings' is complete by 2100.

Warming Baseline

The result of these changes to arrive at the adapted model, DICE99CL, is a substantially higher baseline for warming. In the NB baseline, warming reaches 2.5°C by 2100, 3.8°C by 2200 and 4.5°C by 2300. In the adapted (CL) baseline, warming

reaches 3.3°C by 2100, 5.5°C by 2200 and 7.3°C by 2300. While this is a more pessimistic projection than in the NB outlook, it is somewhat more optimistic than that of the three A-series scenarios of the IPCC (2001a) discussed above, which on average place warming by 2100 (above 1990) at 3.7°C (figure 1.3).

The DICE99CL baseline warming for the very long term (2300) is lower, at 7.3°C, than that in Cline (1992), at 10°C. The difference is attributable to the lower assumption in the model used here about the impact of non-carbon greenhouse gases. DICE99CL adopts the NB assumption that radiative forcing from non-carbon gases hits a ceiling of 1.15 wm^{-2} in 2100 and stays fixed at that rate thereafter. In contrast, Cline (1992, 53) assumed that the *ratio* of non-carbon to carbon radiative force remained constant after 2100 at its level projected by the earlier IPCC studies for that time (with a ratio of 1.4 for total to carbon radiative forcing). IPCC (2001a) did not project radiative forcing beyond 2100, but it did state that carbon dioxide would comprise a rising fraction of total radiative forcing during the course of the twenty-first century, a view potentially consistent with little increase in non-carbon radiative forcing after 2100. The overall effect is to place total radiative forcing by 2300 at 13.6 wm^{-2}, in contrast to the level of 17.5 wm^{-2} which it would reach if non-carbon radiative forcing remained proportional to carbon forcing at its 2100 ratio. In this important dimension, the adapted model here (DICE99CL) is considerably less pessimistic about the extent of very-long-term warming than was my original study (Cline 1992). From this standpoint, optimal abatement estimates may be on the low side, as the assumption that non-carbon radiative forcing does not rise after 2100 may be too optimistic.

[20] Personal communication, 8 January 2003. Note also that for the first century the Excel version of the DICE99 cost function generates abatement cost estimates that are comparable to those of other leading energy–economic models. Thus, in an OECD exercise implemented with three such models, the average cost of cutting emissions from baseline by 45 per cent in 2020 was 2.1 per cent of GWP; by 70 per cent in 2050, 2.9 per cent; and by 88 per cent in 2095, 4.7 per cent (Hourcade *et al.* 1996, 336; Edmunds and Barns 1992; Manne 1992; Rutherford 1992). The corresponding cost estimates using the DICE99 Excel function are 0.7, 2.1 and 4.3 per cent, respectively.

Policy Strategy 1: Optimal Carbon Tax

With the adapted model (DICE99CL) in hand, it is possible to apply it to examine key policy strategies for dealing with global warming. The first general policy would be for the international community to agree that all countries would levy carbon taxes. The rate for the taxes would be coordinated internationally, but each country would collect the tax on its own emissions and use the revenue for its own purposes. An attractive feature of this approach is that it could provide substantial tax revenue to national governments. In many countries, weak fiscal revenue performance has been at the root of serious macroeconomic breakdowns. A substantial source of new revenue could thus have favourable macroeconomic effects in many countries.

Figure 1.4 shows the path of the optimal carbon tax and optimal percentage cutback in carbon emissions from the business-as-usual baseline, using the adapted DICE99CL model. The optimal abatement strategy turns out to be relatively aggressive. Emissions would be cut from baseline by about 35–40 per cent early on, by nearly 50 per cent by 2100 and by a peak of 63 per cent by 2200. The corresponding carbon taxes would start out at $128 per ton, and then rise to $170 by 2005, $246 by 2025 and $367 by 2055, eventually reaching $1,300 in 2200 before tapering off. The higher baseline for emissions and warming mean that potential climate damage is greater than projected by NB, so the optimal cutbacks and carbon taxes are much higher than would be obtained in DICE99NB if the only change to their model were the enforcement of zero pure time preference (figures 1.1 and 1.2).

Table 1.2 reports the absolute levels of carbon emissions in the baselines and in the optimal cutbacks for three sets of studies: my 1992 study; the results of applying the DICE99NB model; and the adapted DICE99CL model. The baseline emissions are set in the DICE99CL model to be very close to those in Cline (1992), and are far above those in the DICE99NB baseline. In the first half of this century the optimal emissions in the DICE99CL model are intermediate between those in the NB optimal path and those of the Cline (1992) aggressive abatement path. Later in the horizon the absolute levels of emissions in the CL model begin to equal, and eventually exceed, those in the NB optimal path, but only because the CL baseline is so much higher than the NB baseline (so that the CL optimal path ends up being higher despite larger per cent cuts from baseline).

Figure 1.5 shows the amount of warming above 1990 for the CL baseline and for the optimal abatement. Whereas warming reaches 7.3°C by 2300 without action, under optimal abatement it is limited to 5.4°C – a level that is uncomfortably on the high rather than low side.

Figure 1.6 shows climate damage as a percentage of GWP in the base and optimal cases. The difference between the two curves represents the economic benefits of abatement. When these benefits are plotted in figure 1.7 against the abatement costs, both as a percentage of GWP, the characteristic timing asymmetry is strongly evident: abatement costs come earlier in the horizon, and benefits of damage avoided begin to exceed abatement costs only after several decades have passed. Even taking account of rising gross world product,

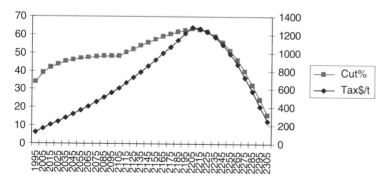

Figure 1.4. *DICE99CL optimal cut (% left) and carbon tax ($ right)*

Table 1.2. Baseline and Optimal Carbon Emissions (GtC), 1995–2295

	1995	2005	2015	2025	2055	2095	2145	2195	2245	2295
Baseline										
Cline (1992)	6.7	6.9	9.4	10.9	13.8	21.6	28.9	39.2	49.4	63.3
DICE99NB	7.3	8.2	8.9	9.5	11	13	15.3	17.2	16.8	9.7
DICE99CL	7	8.6	10.1	11.6	15.8	21.4	29	38	49.8	62.8
Optimal										
Cline (1992)a	4	4	4	4	4	4	4	4	4	4
DICE99NB	7.3	7.8	8.4	8.9	10.1	11.3	13.7	15.3	15.2	9.5
DICE99CL	7.3	5.7	6.3	6.9	8.6	11.2	13.0	14.3	22.4	48.6

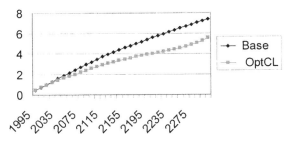

Figure 1.5. *Baseline and optimal warming (°C)*

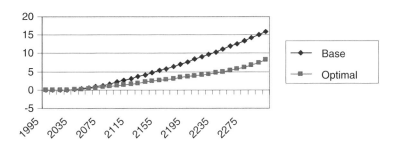

Figure 1.6. *Climate damage as % of GWP*

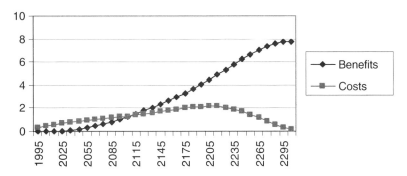

Figure 1.7. *Benefits and costs of optimal abatement (% GWP)*

it is easy to see from figure 1.7 that if effects after 2100 or so are essentially ignored by using a relatively high time discount rate, the level of abatement judged optimal when setting pure time preference at zero will be considered far too costly, demonstrating once again the centrality of the discounting methodology for policy analysis given the long time scales of this problem.

To recapitulate, the first policy strategy, economically optimal abatement, involves an aggressive programme that cuts global carbon emissions by an average of about 45 per cent from the baseline during this century and 55 per cent from baseline in the next century. This would require carbon taxes rising from about \$130–170 per ton through 2015 to about \$600 by 2100 and eventually \$1,300, before declining again. Using the discounting methodology set out above, and applying the percentage of GWP abatement costs and benefits of figure 5.7 to the projection of baseline GWP, this policy strategy would have abatement costs with a discounted present value of \$128 trillion (1990 prices) and benefits from avoided damage amounting to \$271 trillion. The BCR would thus be 2.1.

An implication of the result that the present value of benefits would be twice the present value of abatement costs is that there would be scope for more aggressive abatement that would still have positive net benefits, even though the ratio of benefits to costs would begin falling. That is, beyond the optimal amount of abatement, incremental benefits from damage avoided would begin to fall short of incremental costs.

An important specific instance of this point concerns the aggressive plan in Cline (1992): stabilization at 4 GtC. In a run of the DICE99CL model applying this ceiling, the climate effect of this stabilization is the limitation of warming to 3.2°C by 2300, compared to 7.3°C in the baseline and 5.4°C in the optimal abatement case. Abatement costs are considerably higher than in the optimal run here, reaching about 4 per cent of GWP by 2085 and reaching a plateau of about 5 per cent of GWP by 2205. (The cost estimate in Cline 1992, is instead a plateau of about 2.5 per cent of GWP by 2150 and

after: 1992, 280.) However, the DICE99CL estimates of benefits of the aggressive action plan (stabilization at 4 GtC) are also higher, as economic damage from warming is limited late in the horizon to a lower level (averaging about 1.5 per cent of GWP for the twenty-third century) than in the optimal path (averaging about 4.5 per cent of GWP through the twenty-third century but reaching 8 per cent by its end: figure 1.6). The discounted present value of benefits in the aggressive stabilization case amounts to \$435 trillion, and the present value of abatement costs, \$420 trillion, giving a BCR of 1.04. This is far lower than in the optimal case (figure 1.7, with a BCR of 2.1), but nonetheless shows net positive benefits. The more severe damage function in NB (2000) than in Cline (1992) is the reason why DICE99CL finds a (just barely) favourable BCR for the aggressive stabilization programme even though baseline warming in the very long term is lower at 7.3°C rather than the 10°C identified in Cline (1992).[21]

Policy Strategy 2: the Kyoto Protocol

The essence of the Kyoto Protocol (KP) is to have the industrial and transition economies cut emissions back to 5 per cent below 1990 levels and freeze them at that level, while allowing developing countries unlimited emissions. This strategy is inherently no more than second-best in at least two dimensions. First, it would seriously weaken prospective global abatement, given the probable large increase in developing country emissions. Second, despite the various vague provisions for 'trading' emissions (more fully among the 'Annex I' industrial countries but arguably between them and developing countries as well), the Kyoto structure inherently violates the least-cost solution of cutting emissions globally in a manner that equates the marginal cost of cutbacks across all countries.

Even so, it is possible that Kyoto is better than nothing, as it would contribute to at least some moderation of warming. The question is whether the benefits of this abatement would exceed the costs, taking account of the likely inefficiency of this strategy.

Nordhaus and Boyer (2000) find that the Kyoto targets have costs that exceed their benefits.

---

[21] In the central case, the Cline (1992) damage function is less than quadratic with respect to warming, while the NB function is more than quadratic.

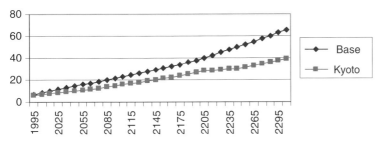

Figure 1.8. *Global carbon emissions (GtC), baseline and Kyoto*

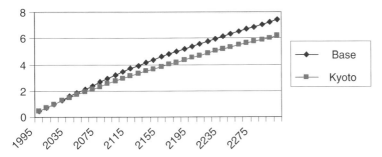

Figure 1.9. *Baseline and Kyoto warming (°C)*

However, this finding is driven by two assumptions that are questioned in the present study. First, they assume a minimal increase in industrial country emissions in the baseline from present-day levels. As a result, in their projections Kyoto makes almost no difference to future global emissions. By 2105, baseline emissions are at only 13.25 GtC; with Kyoto, they are 12.8 GtC. Not surprisingly, Kyoto makes almost no difference to warming, and has minimal damage avoidance benefits. Second, they use a rate of pure time preference of 3 per cent.

Cline (1992, 337) provides a sharply different picture of future industrial country emissions. For industrial OECD plus Eastern Europe and the former Soviet Union, emissions (excluding from deforestation) rise from 4.0 GtC in 1990 to 10.6 GtC in 2100 and 24.4 GtC by 2250. So there is plenty to cut under Kyoto.[22] Developing country emissions rise by even more, from 1.66 GtC in 1990 to 10 GtC in 2100 and 25.4 GtC in 2250, posing the main problem with Kyoto: it will fail to curb a massive build-up in emissions from developing countries.

It is possible to use the DICE99CL model as a point of departure for analysing costs and benefits of the KP. The first step is to obtain the KP baseline for global emissions. This is done by cutting the

controlled (Annex I) country emissions by 5 per cent below 1990 levels to 3.8 GtC and freezing them at this level, while projecting the baseline emissions just discussed for developing countries. The result is a significant cut in global emissions as the time horizon lengthens (figure 1.8), although far less of a cut than in the optimal strategy of the previous section. The emissions path and all of the rest of the KP analysis assume that all Annex I countries, including the USA, participate.

With the emissions path in hand, it is possible to apply the climate module of DICE99CL to obtain the corresponding warming. Similarly, the climate damage function of the model can be applied to obtain the corresponding damage as a per cent of world product. Figures 1.9 and 1.10 display the baseline and Kyoto paths for warming and climate damage. It is evident in figure 1.9 that Kyoto is disappointing as a strategy for limiting global warming, as it reduces warming by 2300 only from 7.3°C to 6.1°C. Even so, because of the high degree of nonlinearity in the NB damage function, the result is to cut global

[22] Note, however, that Manne and Richels (2001) project much lower baseline emissions by 2100 for the Annex I countries (6 GtC), combined with much larger emissions for developing countries (15 GtC), especially China.

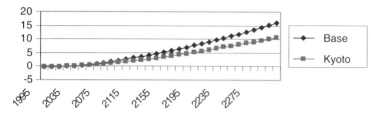

Figure 1.10. *Climate damage as per cent of GWP, baseline and Kyoto*

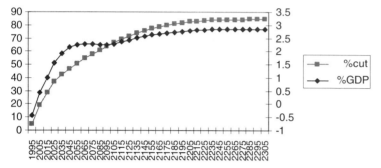

Figure 1.11. *Kyoto: industrial country emission cuts (left) and cost (right)*

climate damage by 2300 from 15.4 per cent of world product to 10.3 per cent.

What remains is to identify the abatement cost of the KP. This time, it is not appropriate to use the DICE99CL cost function, which is for global cuts. The core of the efficiency problem with Kyoto is that it does not take the lowest marginal cost cuts but instead imposes the cuts on a sub-set of the global economy: the industrial countries. Note that the issue here is in principle not one of *distribution* but *efficiency*. The same amount of total emissions could be obtained by lesser cuts in industrial countries, greater cuts in developing countries and transfers from industrial countries to compensate developing countries for the cuts made there.

The cost function, then, needs to be specified relative to the industrial countries. The mitigation cost survey in Hourcade *et al.* (1996) provides a basis for doing so. That study provides a summary

of twenty-nine studies with seventy-two emissions cut scenarios for the USA (1996, 304). Four studies show negative costs of emissions cuts. If these 'bottom-up' studies are omitted, the resulting point estimates provide a basis for regression estimates relating abatement cost as a percentage of GDP to the percentage cut in emissions from the baseline.[23] (This means that the summary regressions may tend to overstate rather than understate abatement costs, as they exclude the more optimistic bottom-up analyses.) These estimates confirm a falling cost over time for a given percentage cut from the baseline. Abatement cost estimates for Kyoto apply the 2020 regression for 2000–20 and the 2100 regression for all periods after 2100, and interpolate between the three benchmark regression years for all other periods. The resulting abatement costs as a percentage of industrial countries' GDP, and percentage cutbacks in emissions from baseline for these countries, are shown in figure 1.11.

Because industrial countries' GDP falls from 56 per cent of the world total (PPP basis) in 1995 to 36 per cent by 2100 and 28 per cent by 2300, the corresponding abatement costs as a percentage of world product are progressively smaller over time. Figure 1.12 shows the Kyoto abatement costs as a

[23] There are three regressions, one for each of three benchmark dates. For 2020, the result is: $z = -0.75 \ (-2.1) + 0.061 \ (6.8) \ C$; adj. $R^2 = 0.74$, where z is abatement cost as a percentage of GDP and C is the percentage cut in emissions from the baseline (t-statistics in parentheses). For 2050: $z = 0.63 \ (0.7) + 0.0332 \ (2.0) \ C$; adj. $R^2 = 0.16$. For 2100: $z = 0.11 \ (0.33) + 0.0325 \ (6.7) \ C$; adj. $R^2 = 0.73$.

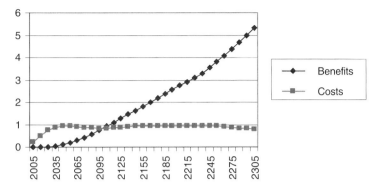

Figure 1.12. *Benefits and costs of Kyoto Protocol abatement (% world product)*

percentage of GWP, along with the benefits of Kyoto abatement as a percentage of world product. These benefits are simply the difference between baseline-warming climate damage and Kyoto-warming climate damage (from figure 1.10).

For the world as a whole, Kyoto abatement benefits overtake costs by 2100 and increasingly exceed them thereafter. It is the industrial countries who pay, however. Considering that their benefits as a percentage of GDP are the same curve as shown globally in figure 1.12, for the industrial countries Kyoto benefits overtake costs only by about 2200. On this basis, the resistance of some industrial countries to the Kyoto approach is understandable.

When the cost and benefit paths are applied to that for world product, and after augmenting the costs by a factor to adjust for shadow pricing of capital, and discounting using the SRTP method discussed above, the discounted present value of abatement benefits equals $166 trillion (1990 prices) and the costs equal $94 trillion, for a BCR of 1.77.[24] Somewhat contrary to the predominant view, then, the KP seems to pass a benefit-cost test globally, although it shows negative net benefits for the industrial countries. They enjoy a discounted present value of $55 trillion, but pay the discounted present costs of $94 trillion, so for their part alone they face a BCR of 0.58.

An important qualification to this estimate is that the benefit-cost calculus might be favourable for Europe as a sub-region within the industrial country group. Because the risk of thermohaline circulation shutdown poses the greatest potential damage to Europe, in their regional RICE model NB (2000,

160) find that Kyoto emissions ceilings would have a net positive benefit for Europe even in an arrangement in which emissions trading is allowed only within the OECD. This version has significant losses for the USA and for the world as a whole, however.

Quite apart from the unattractive cost-benefit calculation from the standpoint of industrial countries as a group, as noted the KP accomplishes relatively little in curbing warming. For the world as a whole, then, it is better than nothing, but not a persuasive answer to the problem of global warming. For industrial countries, its economic costs outweigh its economic benefits.

Policy Strategy 3: a Value-at-Risk Approach

In the 1990s, private financial firms have increasingly applied the approach of value-at-risk (VaR) in managing portfolio risk. Although the origins of this approach go back to Markowitz (1952), it was popularized by an influential study by a policy research group in the early 1990s (Group of Thirty 1993), and gained increasing attention because of the expansion of the derivatives market and the evolution of international bank regulation toward more sophisticated risk-related capital requirements for banks under rules developed by the Basel Committee.

---

[24] Abatement costs are multiplied by 1.13 to adjust for a shadow price applied to that portion of abatement resources that come out of saving rather than consumption.

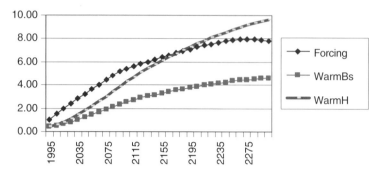

Figure 1.13. *Radiative forcing (w/msq) and warming (°C, NB baseline and 95% high)*

The VaR approach identifies the maximum value that a firm can be expected to lose during a specified horizon and up to a specified probability. In the financial sector, horizons tend to be a day or a month. Target probability levels tend to be in the high ninety percentiles. The historical volatilities and covariances of individual assets in a portfolio are estimated to arrive at such probabilities. As applied to global warming, a VaR approach would focus on the prospective damage that could occur up to a fairly high level of probability that actual damage would be no greater than the estimated amount. Cost-benefit models in this area do not yet appear to have emphasized stochastic approaches with confidence intervals, but it could be that both the scientific and economic literature will evolve in this direction.

A potentially crucial recent study on the scientific side estimates the probability distribution of the CS parameter (Andronova and Schlesinger 2001). Using sixteen radiative forcing models capturing greenhouse gases, tropospheric ozone, anthropogenic sulphate aerosol, solar forcing and volcanos, the study uses Monte Carlo simulations to generate alternative temperature histories over the past 140 years. On this basis, it identifies probability distributions for CS. The study finds that the 90 per cent confidence interval for CS is between 1.0°C at the lower end and 9.3°C at the upper end. This means that to arrive at a 95 per cent probability threshold for the climate analogue of VaR, it is necessary to evaluate damage with CS = 9.3°C. This

is more than twice the conventional 'upper-bound' benchmark of 4.5°C.

It is therefore useful to consider costs and benefits of greenhouse abatement using a CS of 9.3°C, rather than the base CS value of 2.9°C value in the DICE99 model in the analyses of the previous two sections. Abatement policy based on this parameter might be thought of as at least an approximation of identifying society's 'value-at-risk' up to a probability of 95 per cent. Alternative terminology for the same thing would be a 'minimax' strategy, which minimizes the maximum risk (up to a 'maximum' of 95 per cent probability).

Figure 1.13 returns to the DICE99NB baseline for emissions and radiative forcing to examine the influence of increasing the CS parameter. Figure 1.13 shows radiative forcing (wm^{-2}) and warming (°C) for the base and high-warming cases (CS = 2.9°C and 9.3°C). An important feature of the high-warming case shown in figure 1.13 is that equilibrium warming at the CS occurs with a much longer lag from the date of realized $2 \times CO_2$ radiative forcing when the CS is higher. Thus, the radiative forcing corresponding to a doubling of carbon dioxide is 4.4 wm^{-2}. If a grid is drawn to the horizontal axis, the NB baseline shows this amount of radiative forcing by 2075. For baseline warming, the corresponding warming of 2.9°C occurs in 2125, giving a thermal lag between committed and realized warming of fifty years. In contrast, for the high-warming case, the CS warming of 9.3°C does not occur until 2285, meaning that the thermal lag has lengthened to 210 years.[25] This effect tends to soften the potential damage, but also raises the question of whether the 300-year horizon is sufficient for analysing the effects of the 95 per cent probability CS.

[25] Wigley and Schlesinger (1985) first analysed the lengthening of the thermal lag for higher climate sensitivity parameters.

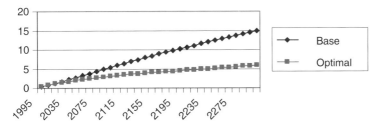

Figure 1.14. *Baseline and optimal warming for 95% high case (°C)*

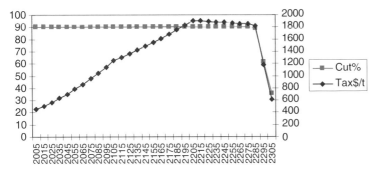

Figure 1.15. *DICE99CL 95% high optimal cut (left) and carbon tax (right)*

In the spirit of a VaR strategy, it is possible to repeat the optimal abatement analysis of strategy 1 above, once again applying the DICE99CL model but this time implementing it with a CS of 9.3°C. Figure 1.14 shows baseline warming in that model, along with high-CS warming for the same baseline of emissions and radiative forcing. By 2300, warming reaches 15°C, considerably higher than the 10°C reached in figure 1.13 because of the higher baseline emissions and radiative forcing in the CL than in the NB version. Optimal abatement policy curbs this warming to 5.9°C by 2300.

Figure 1.15 shows the corresponding optimal emissions cut from baseline and optimal carbon tax in the DICE99CL model for the case with CS = 9.3°C. This time, the adapted model's maximum allowed cut of 90 per cent from baseline becomes binding.[26] The time path for the optimal carbon tax begins at $450 per ton in 2005 and rises to a peak of $1,900 per ton in 2205.

In contrast, it turns out that if the only change to the NB model is to apply the high CS parameter, their optimal cuts and carbon taxes remain moderate. Thus, figure 1.16 shows that, in this test, optimal cutbacks begin at about 15 per cent and peak at

30 per cent, and the corresponding carbon taxes begin in the range of $32 per ton and peak at $425 per ton. These abatement intensities are far less than in the CL optimal results for high CS, and demonstrate that the effect of higher discounting and a lower emissions baseline in the NB analysis tend to place a relatively moderate ceiling on optimal action even if the 95 per cent high threshold is used for the CS warming parameter.

Returning to the CL version, when the climate sensitivity parameter is high the warming is sufficiently high (figure 1.14) to impose massive climate damage on the global economy. Baseline damage reaches 8.6 per cent of GWP by 2100 and a remarkable 68 per cent of GWP by 2300, given the strongly non-linear damage function. Optimal cutbacks reduce this damage to 2.1 per cent and 9.4 per cent of GWP at these two dates, respectively (figure 1.17).

[26] Correspondingly, through most of the period the carbon tax needed to arrive at this ceiling cut (at 90 per cent reduction) is considerably below the environmental shadow price associated with climate damage. Thus, as of 2025 (for example), the environmental shadow price is $1,820 per ton of carbon, whereas a carbon tax of $570 is sufficient to cut emissions by the maximum 90 per cent.

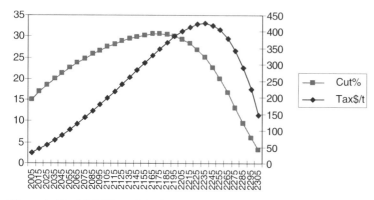

Figure 1.16. *DICE99NB 95% high optimal cut (left) and carbon tax (right)*

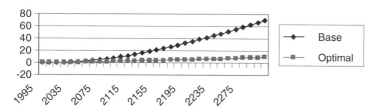

Figure 1.17. *Climate damage %GWP, 95% high case*

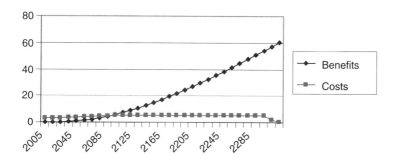

Figure 1.18. *Benefits and costs of optimal abatement with 95% high warming (%GWP)*

Figure 1.18 shows the abatement costs of optimal policy under the high-warming case. These average about 3.5 per cent of GWP in the twenty-first century and plateau at about 5 per cent of GWP thereafter. However, these abatement costs secure a much larger benefit in avoided damages. These benefits,

the difference between baseline and optimal damage in figure 1.17, are shown in figure 1.18 to reach about 7 per cent of world product by 2100, 17 per cent by the middle of the twenty-second century, 30 per cent by 2200 and, ultimately, about 60 per cent of GWP by 2300.

The discounted present value of benefits of damage avoided amounts to $1,749 trillion in the 95 per cent high-warming case. The discounted present value of abatement costs is $458 trillion, yielding a BCR of 3.8 to 1.[27]

In summary, in a cautious 'value-at-risk' approach in which abatement is based on high

[27] In the absence of abatement the damage to future consumption would be sufficient to require recalculation of the discount rate, as future period cumulative *per capita* income growth rates (*g*) would be much lower. The discounted present value of future damages would be considerably higher than using the unadjusted discount rate. However, optimal abatement would constrain damage to a small enough level that the adjustment in the discount rate would be minor.

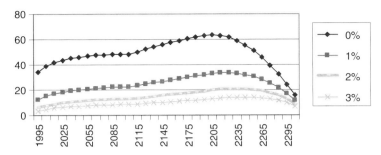

Figure 1.19. *Optimal % cut with alternative pure time preference rates*

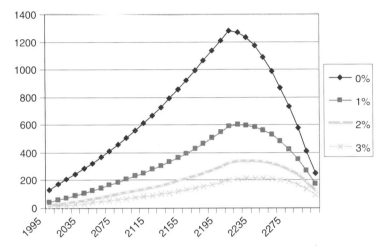

Figure 1.20. *Optimal carbon tax ($/t) with alternative pure time preference rates*

warming, with 95 per cent probability that the CS would be equal to or below the threshold used (CS = 9.3°C), optimal cutbacks would be the maximum considered feasible (90 per cent from the baseline) over practically the whole of the next three centuries, and carbon taxes would start at about $450 per ton, reach $740 by 2050, $1,200 by 2100 and rise to a peak of about $1,900 in 2200. This seemingly punitive abatement scenario would nonetheless be highly beneficial in net terms, with the present value of benefits of damage avoided almost four times that of abatement costs.

Impact of Alternative Discounting

All of the analyses so far apply a zero rate of pure time preference. Figures 1.19 and 1.20 show the impact of applying alternative rates of pure time preference in arriving at the optimal abatement path un-

der the central value of the CS (2.9°C for $2 \times CO_2$ warming). The strong influence of this change in the discount rate is evident in figures 1.19 and 1.20. For example, if the rate of pure time preference is set at 3 per cent, implying a total discount rate of about 4.5 per cent annually once the influence of rising *per capita* income and the elasticity of marginal utility are taken into account, the optimal cutback from baseline emissions remains below 10 per cent until the middle of the next century, whereas in this study's central case (zero pure time preference) the optimal cutback is in the range of 40–50 per cent in this century and is about 55 per cent by the middle of the next century (figure 1.19). Correspondingly, whereas by 2025 the optimal carbon tax is $245 per ton at zero pure time preference, the optimal tax at this date is $90 at pure time preference of 1 per cent, $45 at 2 per cent and only $26 at 3 per cent.

The major reduction of abatement found to be optimal in the base case as the pure time preference

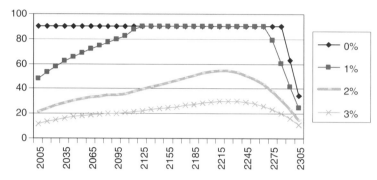

Figure 1.21. *95% high optimal cut (%) under alternative pure time preference rates*

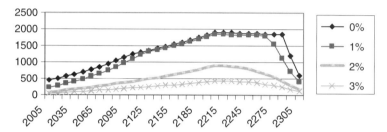

Figure 1.22. *95% high optimal carbon tax ($/t) under alternative pure time preference rates*

rate reaches 2–3 per cent is no surprise. The optimal cutbacks and carbon taxes over the present
century are broadly similar to those estimated by
NB, who start with a pure time preference rate of
3 per cent and allow only a gradual decline in this
rate over time. It is perhaps a greater surprise that
even in the high-damage case the degree of abatement is modest when a pure time preference rate of
2–3 per cent is used (figures 1.21 and 1.22). Thus,
whereas the optimal emissions cutback from baseline in the 95 per cent high-climate sensitivity case
is 90 per cent in 2025 with zero pure time preference, the cut drops to 58 per cent with 1 per cent
pure time preference, 27 per cent with 2 per cent
and 15 per cent with 3 per cent pure time preference. The corresponding optimal carbon taxes also
drop off rapidly, from $565 per ton to $339, $139
and $72 per ton, respectively.

[28] Another factor may be that the 'fix' in the model adaptation
here placing a ceiling after 2100 to an otherwise rising cost
abatement function present in the Excel version of DICE99
(contrary to a declining function in the GAMS version) may
insufficiently avoid overstatement of abatement cost by that
period.

The modest abatement at pure time preference of
3 per cent even with high climate sensitivity seems
to contradict the finding in Cline (1992, 302) that an
aggressive plan of abatement limiting global emissions permanently to 4 GtC has a favourable BCR at
3 per cent pure time preference if the CS is 4.5°C,
the damage function is quadratic and damage at
2.5°C warming is 1 per cent of GDP. Considering
that the latter two parameters are about the same
as in the DICE99 model and the 'value-at-risk' CS
is a much more severe 9.3°C here, it is apparently
a higher abatement cost function that discourages
much abatement in DICE99 even in the face of dramatic warming. Thus, abatement of 90 per cent
costs about 5 per cent of GWP annually by 2100
in the adapted DICE99CL model, whereas in Cline
(1992, 280) cutbacks this deep at this time horizon
cost only 2.5 per cent of GWP. The lower cost in
the Cline (1992) calculation reflects the assumption
there that a 'backstop technology' becomes available for non-carbon energy by that period, as argued
by Manne and Richels (1991).[28]

An alternative way to examine the influence of
the discount rate is to consider the impact on the
discounted present value of benefits and costs of

Table 1.3. Discounted Present Values at Alternative Rates of Pure Time Preference ($ trillion and ratios)

Abatement path:	Pure time preference (%)	Benefits	Costs	BCR
1 Optimal, base climate	0	270.96	128.47	2.11
sensitivity (figure 1.4)	1	36.04	35.83	1.01
	2	7.76	15.88	0.49
	3	2.45	9.38	0.26
2 Kyoto Protocol	0	165.68	94.12	1.76
(see text)	1	23.30	28.54	0.82
	2	5.24	13.06	0.40
	3	1.67	7.24	0.23
3 Optimal under 95% high-climate	0	1,748.52	458.38	3.81
sensitivity (figure 1.15)	1	229.60	144.07	1.59
	2	47.45	69.21	0.69
	3	14.26	41.76	0.34

the specific abatement paths identified to the policy options above. Table 1.3 reports the present values of the base-case 'optimal' abatement path, the Kyoto Protocol and the 'high-damage' optimal abatement path identified in policy options 1, 2 and 3 above, at alternative values of rate of pure time preference. As shown in table 1.3, in both 'optimal' cases 1 and 3, the discounted present value of benefits from limitation of climate damage exceeds the present value of abatement costs when the rate of pure time preference is 0 or 1 per cent, but benefits fall short of costs when this rate rises to 2 or 3 per cent. In the case of the Kyoto Protocol (2), the present value of benefits falls somewhat below the present value of costs even when the rate of pure time preference is 1 per cent.

Conclusion

This study has applied an adapted version of the DICE99 climate–economic model developed by Nordhaus and Boyer (2000) to examine the costs and benefits of alternative abatement strategies for dealing with global warming. The crucial model adjustments involve adopting zero pure time preference (but allowing for above-unity elasticity of marginal utility) in arriving at the proper time discounting for century-scale time horizons; and reverting to a much less optimistic baseline projection of carbon emissions than in the new NB estimates, which are far lower than in Nordhaus

(1994). Table 1.4 summarizes the benefit-cost results for the three strategies examined.

The first strategy is to identify and adopt an optimal path for abatement of carbon emissions, based on a carbon tax. Implicitly this tax is globally uniform, but it would be nationally collected and used. Using the adapted model (DICE99CL), the optimal reduction in carbon emissions from baseline averages about 45 per cent in this century and 55 per cent in the next. A carbon tax in the vicinity of $150 per ton would be applied over the next decade, rising to $600 by 2100. Global warming would reach 3.4°C by 2100 and 7.3°C by 2300 in the baseline. Warming would be reduced under optimal abatement to 2.6°C by 2100 and 5.4°C by 2300. The discounted present value of benefits of damages thereby avoided would amount to twice the present value of abatement costs.

It should be noted that this strategy involves much more aggressive abatement than that identified in Nordhaus and Boyer (2000), who place the optimal carbon tax at less than $10 per ton in the near future and only about $60 by 2100, and who correspondingly estimate optimal cutbacks from baseline at only about 5 per cent in the near term, rising to only about 11 per cent by 2100. It is also important to note that the policy of aggressive abatement suggested in Cline (1992), stabilizing global emissions at 4GtC annually, would just barely have present value benefits in excess of present value of costs. Although it would be less optimal than the path identified under policy 1, it

Table 1.4. Benefit-Cost Summary, Discounted Present Values[a] (trillion dollars at 1990 prices and ratios)

	Optimal carbon tax (A)	Kyoto Protocol (B)	Value-at-Risk carbon tax (C)
Benefits	271	166	1,749
Costs	128	94	458
Benefits/Costs	2.12	1.77	3.82
Annualized benefits	0.90	0.55	5.83
Annualized costs	0.43	0.31	1.53

Notes: [a] All cases use social rate of time preference for discounting. This equals the rate of pure time preference, set to zero, plus the amount of discounting to take account of improving living standards. The latter equals the elasticity of marginal utility (set at 1.5) multiplied by annual growth rate for *per capita* income (approximately 1%). All cases examine a 300-year horizon.
A   Base-case optimization yields a carbon tax beginning at $128 per ton of carbon equivalent, rising to $600 by 2100 and $1,300 by 2200. Global warming is limited to 5.4°C by 2300 instead of the baseline 7.3°C. Carbon cutbacks are 30–50% from the baseline in the twenty-first century and 50–60% in the twenty-second century.
B   Industrial and transition economies adhere to KP emissions targets; developing countries unrestrained from baseline emissions growth. By 2200 global emissions are 30 GtC instead of 40 GtC in baseline. Global warming is limited to 6.1°C by 2300 instead of the baseline 7.3°C. Costs of abatement are fully borne by industrial countries. Benefits of abatement are only 0.58 of costs, for these countries.
C   95% high CS of 9.3°C warming for 2 × CO₂ used to calibrate costs and benefits. Baseline warming reaches 15°C by 2300. Optimal emissions cutbacks are identified as the maximum allowed in model (90%), limiting warming by 2300 to 5.9°C. Optimal carbon tax begins at $450 per ton and reaches $1,900 per ton by 2200.

would limit warming substantially more (to 2.1°C by 2100 and 3.1°C by 2300). It could thus be more appealing than the optimal strategy identified as policy 1 to those who consider that even the substantially non-linear damage function in the NB model (adopted also in the DICE99CL version here) may understate potential damage.

The second policy strategy specifically examined is the KP. The model results indicate that this policy has a BCR above unity, but has several limitations. Because only the industrial and transition economies curb emissions, and given the large increase expected in emissions of developing countries not subject to limits, the KP attains considerably less limitation of future global warming and damages than under the optimal pol-icy. Warming would reach 6.1°C by 2300, rather than 5.4°C in the optimal policy. Moreover, for the industrial and transition economies subject to the Kyoto controls, the discounted present value of benefits would be less than the present value of abatement costs, as much of the benefits would accrue to the developing countries not restraining their emissions. The only question about this strategy is whether it warrants implementation as 'better than nothing.' In part, the answer depends on whether the climate policy area should be viewed as an additional area in which industrial countries should make income transfers to developing countries. Moreover, answering this question requires thinking about whether such transfers should be made over a centuries-scale horizon.

The third policy strategy is a risk-averse 'value-at-risk' approach. By analogy with common practice in financial firms, the global authorities might wish to base climate policy on projections that consider the damages that could occur up to a probability of 95 per cent that they would be no larger. For this purpose, it is possible to apply a recent estimate of the probability distribution for the CS. Andronova and Schlesinger (2001) estimate that this parameter would have to be as high as 9.3°C for a doubling of carbon dioxide to provide 95 per cent confidence that warming would be no higher. When the (adapted) model is applied using this parameter, global warming reaches 15°C by 2300. The optimal amount of abatement is the ceiling considered feasible in the model (a limit of 90 per cent cutback in emissions from baseline). Optimal carbon taxes begin in the range of $450 per ton and rise as high as $1,900 by 2205. The BCR for this approach is about 4:1, reflecting the extraordinary levels of climate damage eventually reached in the baseline (about 50 per cent of GWP by the second half of the twenty-third century). Although many would judge this strategy to be prohibitively costly and unduly risk-averse, it should not be dismissed out of hand. Its abatement costs average about 3.5 per cent of GWP in the twenty-first century and plateau at about 5 per cent thereafter. Many might consider this a price worth paying to assure with a high degree of probability that warming would not reach the extremely high levels that could otherwise be attained.

Appendix: Changes to the DICE99 Model

The DICE99 climate model of Nordhaus and Boyer (2000) is an elegant integrated climate–economic model that provides a basis for analysing optimal policy on global warming. A key feature of the model is that it examines a three-century horizon. As emphasized in Cline (1992), this is the proper time-scale for analysing the impact of CO_2 emissions, because it will take this long before the reduction of atmospheric CO_2 through mixing into the deep ocean will begin to reverse atmospheric buildup (Sundquist 1990).

The model (hereafter referred to as DICE99NB) has been made available to the public on the website of William Nordhaus.[29] Some of the text analysis directly applies this model. Most of the analysis, however, applies a revised version prepared by the present author for this study. These revisions have been adopted either because of an alternative conceptual framework (in particular, for time discounting) or because of an alternative long-term outlook for underlying economic variables (e.g. gross world product (GWP) and carbon emissions). This appendix discusses the changes made in the model.

A Gross World Product (GWP)

Real GWP is changed to track the projections in Cline (1992, 290). Purchasing power parity (PPP) values are used for developing countries. This boosts initial world product from $22.6 trillion (NB) to $35.7 trillion (CL).[30] It should be noted that by using market exchange rates rather than PPP values, the NB version tends to understate growth of world product because it gives a low weight to the more rapidly growing area. This scalar adjustment also requires a corresponding adjustment to initial world capital stock (from $47 trillion to $74 trillion). GWP in the model is obtained from

a production function involving capital (to the exponent 0.3, reflecting the share of capital), labour (to the exponent 0.7, for the share of labour) and a multiplicative term for total factor productivity (TFP). To obtain the same growth path for GWP as in Cline (1992), the growth of TFP is raised from 3.8 per cent per decade in NB to 6.5 per cent per decade in CL through 2205, then is cut to 3.2 per cent. Finally, as expansion of base-period capital stock only increases base-period GWP from $22.6 trillion to $25.8 trillion, the remainder of the expansion to the PPP base world product of $35.7 trillion is obtained by adding an initial multiplicative scalar (= 1.38) to the production function.[31]

B Emissions Coefficient

As discussed in the main text, the NB DICE99 carbon emissions baseline sharply reduces projected emissions from the earlier Nordhaus and Yohe (1983) projections used in part in determining the baseline for Cline (1992). To return to an emissions baseline that tracks that in Cline (1992), the growth rate of the coefficient of carbon emissions relative to GWP (σ) is moderated from an initial pace of -15.9 per cent per decade in NB to -4.6 per cent per decade in CL. This pace is held constant through 2205 and thereafter forced to zero to adhere to the Cline (1992) baseline.[32]

---

[29] http://www.econ.yale.edu/~nordhaus/homepage/homepage.htm.

[30] In 1990 prices. For clarity, NB is used to identify the NB version, and CL to identify the adapted version of this study.

[31] The changes reported in this paragraph are made in rows 15, 37 and 71 of the Excel spreadsheet version of DICE99, hereafter referred to as NBDxl.

[32] Row 22 in NBDxl. The 'rate of decrease in the growth rate of sigma' (row 23 in NBDxl) and the 'Acceleration

C Non-Carbon Radiative Forcing

'Exogenous forcing' from non-carbon greenhouse gases (O_t) is set in the NB model to start at -0.2 wm^{-2} (watts per m^2) in 1995, rise to $+0.2$ wm^{-2} by 2025 and continue rising until it reaches a plateau at 1.15 wm^{-2} by 2095. The initial negative figure appears to reflect the NB treatment of net cooling from sulphate aerosols. In the 2001 international scientific review, however, (IPCC 2001a, 7–8), radiative forcing as of 2000 above 1750 is estimated (all in wm^{-2}) at 1.46 for CO_2, 0.48 for methane, 0.34 for halocarbons and 0.15 for nitrous oxide, for the 'well-mixed' greenhouse gases (WMghgs), meaning 0.97 for the non-carbon WMghgs. Radiative forcing is set at -0.15 for stratospheric ozone depletion, $+0.35$ for tropospheric ozone, -0.4 for sulphate aerosols, -0.2 for biomass aerosols, -0.1 for organic carbon from fossil fuel burning and $+0.2$ for black carbon from fossil fuel burning, with a sum of -0.3 for these non-well-mixed greenhouse gas (NWMghgs) effects. The report also states that of the WMghgs, by 2100 only one-third of the radiative forcing will come from the three non-carbon gases.

Radiative forcing from non-carbon greenhouse gas sources in the base period (1995) can thus be set at 0.97 for WMghgs and -0.3 for NWMghgs, or a net of 0.67. In the CL baseline, which as discussed in the main text is close to the IPCC A series scenarios (excluding AT), by 2105 the atmospheric stock of carbon dioxide stands at 1,478 GtC (in comparison to 1,220 in NB), providing radiative forcing of 5.35 wm^{-2}. So one-third of this amount for the non-carbon WMghgs would amount to 1.76 wm^{-2}. If

we freeze the contribution of NWMghgs at their initial net level of -0.3, then by 2105 'exogenous forcing' would rise to 1.46 wm^{-2}. On this basis, the CL version of DICE99 sets O_t at 0.67 wm^{-2} in 1995, rising linearly to 1.46 wm^{-2} by 2105 and remaining constant thereafter.[33]

D Pure Time Preference

Pure time preference in CL is set to zero, as discussed in the main text.[34]

E Shadow-Pricing Capital

The social cost-benefit approach set out in Cline (1992) uses zero pure time preference, but also places additional weight on capital effects to take into account the gap between the social rate of time preference (solely based on utility discounting once pure time preference is zero) and return on capital. This is done by applying a 'shadow price of capital' to convert capital effects into consumption-equivalents. This effect is incorporated into CL by expanding abatement costs to take into account the extra consumption-equivalent costs associated with that portion of abatement costs likely to be at the expense of capital formation. For this purpose, it is assumed that 22 per cent of all abatement costs come at the expense of capital formation (rather than consumption), and that the shadow price of capital is 1.6 (based on Cline, 1992, 291).[35] This procedure leans against abatement, because it does not incorporate a similar shadow pricing of that portion of abatement 'benefits' – defined as the reduction in climate damage – that would accrue to increased capital formation as opposed to increased consumption.[36]

F Discounted Utility and Welfare

In NB, the discounted present value of utility in a future period equals the shrinking pure social time preference factor, multiplied by period population, multiplied by the logarithm of *per capita* consumption. As discussed in Cline (1992, 253), the

---

parameter' (row 24) are correspondingly both set at zero. In addition, the initial coefficient is rescaled from 0.274 to 0.165 GtC per trillion dollars of GWP to account for the larger value of PPP GWP (row 20).

[33] Row 54 in NBxl.

[34] Accordingly, in NBDxl both rows 63 (initial social rate of time preference) and 64 (rate of decline) are set to zero.

[35] The result is to multiply the abatement cost function, in row 7, by the scalar: $[1 + 0.22 * (v - 1)]$, where v is the shadow price of capital.

[36] However, as discussed in Cline (1992, 295), perhaps about half of the damages avoided would be in consumption-specific form.

logarithmic utility function is equivalent to a utility function with the elasticity of marginal utility set at unity. That study suggests that utility-based discounting can more appropriately use a central value of 1.5 for θ. In CL, therefore, the future period-specific utility becomes simply: $U_t = [R_t L_t c_t]/(1 + \theta g_t)^T$ where R_t is the period discount factor based on pure time preference (such that R always equals unity in the principal CL assumption), L is population, c is *per capita* consumption, θ is the absolute value of the elasticity of marginal utility, g_t is the cumulative average annual growth rate of *per capita* consumption from the initial year up through the end-year of the period in question and $T = 10t$ as each period is one decade. Total welfare is then simply the sum of discounted utility over all periods considered.[37]

In the optimal carbon-tax solution, the discount factor for each period $[1/(1 + \theta g_t)^T]$ is held constant at its baseline level. Otherwise the endogenous change in the cumulative *per capita* growth rate g alters the discount factor, posing an index number problem. Applying the *ex ante* discount factor path is analogous to applying a Lespeyres (base-period-weighted) price index.

G Atmospheric Retention

In the NB baseline for emissions and atmospheric concentration of carbon dioxide, from 1995 to 2095 the rate of atmospheric retention of emissions falls from 70 per cent in the first decade to 36 per cent in the last decade.[38] In contrast, from the detailed IPCC tables on emissions and atmospheric concentration (IPCC, 2001a, tables II.1 and II.2), it can be calculated that the atmospheric retention rate *rises* from 49 per cent in 2000–10 to 59 per cent in 2090–2100.[39] So it is necessary to alter the DICE99 equations determining the transit of carbon dioxide out of the atmosphere ('box 1' in the three-box model) into the biosphere and shallow ocean (box 2).[40] (Box 3 is the deep ocean, which can receive carbon dioxide only from box 2.) For this purpose, the CL version changes the coefficients ϕ_{11}, the share of atmospheric carbon from the previous period retained in the atmosphere in the current period, from

0.67 to 0.69; and changes the coefficient ϕ_{21}, for the share of previous-period atmospheric carbon lost to the biosphere-shallow ocean 'box,' from 0.33 to 0.31. It also changes ϕ_{12}, the share of box 2 carbon absorbed into the atmosphere, from 0.276 to 0.3, and ϕ_{22} (retained in box 2) from 0.609 to 0.585. These changes have the effect of maintaining the average atmospheric retention rate at about 50 per cent during the twenty-first century, which is more consistent with the IPCC projections.[41]

H Abatement Limit

In NB, the cut from baseline emissions can be as high as 100 per cent. The cut is driven by a formula that shows the percentage cut from the baseline as a function of the carbon tax. In CL, this formula is altered so as to limit the cut from baseline to no more than 90 per cent, on grounds of plausible feasibility.[42]

I Abatement Cost Function

For the reasons set out in the main text, the linear abatement cost term (b_1, row 7) is constrained in CL to a ceiling reached by 2105, rather than allowed to continue rising.

[37] In the Excel spreadsheet, these changes affect rows 94 (U_t) and 95 (welfare), and require insertion of a reference row reporting g_t. Note that the single summary value of welfare is merely ten times the sum over all periods of U_t.

[38] The rate of atmospheric retention is simply the change in the atmospheric stock of carbon from the beginning to the end of the period, divided by cumulative emissions over the period (which in turn is ten times the average between the annual rates of emissions at the beginning and end of the period).

[39] Note that the IPCC data are in parts per million (ppm). The stock of atmospheric carbon in GtC is approximately 2.12 times the atmospheric concentration in ppm.

[40] Rows 45-48 in NBxl.

[41] The DICE structure imposes a falling retention rate, whereas the IPCC models do not show this over the period through 2100. The changes adopted in CL yield an average retention rate of 52 per cent for this century, beginning at an overstated 97 per cent, and falling to 59 per cent by 2015–25 and to 44 per cent by 2095–2105.

[42] For this purpose, the initial scalar '1000' in row 99 is changed to '888'.

References

Andronova, N.G. and M.E. Schlesinger, 2001: Objective estimation of the probability density function for climate sensitivity, *Journal of Geophysical Research*, **106**(D19), 22605–12

Arrow, K.J., 1966: Discounting and public investment criteria, in A.V. Kneese and S.C. Smith (eds.), *Water research*, Johns Hopkins University Press, Baltimore, MD, 13–32

Arrow, K.J., W.R. Cline, K-G. Maler, M. Munasinghe, R. Squitieri and J.E. Stiglitz, 1996: Intertemporal equity, discounting, and economic efficiency, in J.P. Bruce, H. Lee and E.F. Haites (eds.), *Climate change 1995: economic and social dimensions of climate change*, Cambridge, University Press, Cambridge, for the Intergovernmental Panel on Climate Change, 125–44

Arrow, K.J. and M. Kurz, 1970: *Public investment, the rate of return and optimal fiscal policy*, Johns Hopkins University Press, Baltimore, MD

Barrett, S., 2003: *Environment and statecraft: the strategy of environmental treaty-making*, Oxford University Press, Oxford

Bradford, D.F., 1975: Constraints on government investment opportunities and the choice of the discount rate, *American Economic Review*, **65**(5), 887–99

Bruce, J.P., H. Lee and E.F. Haites (eds.), 1996: *Climate change 1995: economic and social dimensions of climate change*, Cambridge University Press, Cambridge, for the Intergovernmental Panel on Climate Change

Cline, W.R., 1991: Scientific basis for the greenhouse effect, *Economic Journal*, **100**, 904–19

1992: *The economics of global warming*, Institute for International Economics, Washington, DC

1996: The impact of global warming on agriculture: comment (on Mendelsohn, Nordhaus and Shaw, 1994), *American Economic Review*, **86**(5), 1309–11

1997: Modelling economically efficient abatement of greenhouse gases, chapter 7 in Y. Kaya and K. Yokobori (eds.), *Environment, energy, and economy: strategies for sustainability*, United Nations University Press, Tokyo

1999: Discounting for the very long term, in P.R. Portney and J.P. Weyant (eds.), *Discounting and intergenerational equity*, Resources for the Future, Washington, DC, 131–40

Edmunds, J. and D.W. Barns, 1992: Factors affecting the long-term cost of global fossil fuel CO_2 emissions reductions, *International Journal of Global Energy Issues*, **4**(3), 140–66

Edmunds, J. and Reilly, 1985: *Global energy: assessing the future*, Oxford University Press, Oxford

Fankhauser, S., 1995: *Valuing climate change. The economics of the greenhouse*, Earthscan, London

Feldstein, M.S., 1970: Financing in the evaluation of public expenditure, *Discussion Papers*, **132** Harvard Institute of Economic Research, Cambridge, MA

Group of Thirty, 1993: *Derivatives: practices and principles*, Global Derivatives Study Group, Group of Thirty, Washington, DC, July

Hebert, H.J., 2000: Future looks hot: UN panel says warming is worse than previously believed, Associated Press, 26 October

Hourcade, J.C., K. Halsnaes, M. Jaccard, W.D. Montgomery, R. Richels, J. Robinson, P.R. Shukla, P. Sturm, W. Chandler, O. Davidson, J. Edmonds, D. Finon, K. Hogan, F. Krause, A. Kolesov, E. La Rovere, P. Nastari, A. Pegov, K. Richards, L. Schrattenholzer, R. Shackleton, Y. Sokona, A. Tudini and J. Weyant, 1996: A review of mitigation cost studies, in J.P. Bruce, H. Lee and E.F Haites (eds.), *Climate change 1995: economic and social dimensions of climate change*, Cambridge University Press, Cambridge, for the Intergovernmental Panel on Climate Change, 296–366

IPCC, 2001a: J.T. Houghton *et al.*, *Climate change 2001: the scientific basis*, Cambridge University Press, Cambridge for the Intergovernmental Panel on Climate Change

2001b: Q.K. Ahmad *et al.*, *Climate change 2001: impacts, adaptation, and vulnerability*, Cambridge University Press, Cambridge for the Intergovernmental Panel on Climate Change

Manne, A.S. 1992: Global 2100: alternative scenarios for reducing emissions, OECD Working Paper, **111** OECD, Paris

Manne, A.S. and R.G. Richels, 1991: Global CO_2 emission reductions: the impacts of rising energy costs, *The Energy Journal*, **12**(1), 88–107

2001: US rejection of the Kyoto Protocol: the impact on compliance costs and CO_2 emissions, Stanford University, mimeo

Markowitz, H.G., 1952: Portfolio selection, *Journal of Finance*, **7**, 77–91

Mendelsohn, R., W.D. Nordhaus and D. Shaw, 1994: The impact of global warming on agriculture: a Ricardian approach, *American Economic Review*, **84**(4), 753–71

Nordhaus, W.D., 1991: To slow or not to slow: the economics of the greenhouse effect, *Economic Journal*, **101**(6), 920–37

1994: *Managing the global commons: the economics of climate change*, MIT Press, Cambridge, MA

Nordhaus, W.D. and J. Boyer, 2000: *Warming the world: economic models of global warming*, MIT Press, Cambridge, MA

Nordhaus, W.D. and G.W. Yohe, 1983: Future carbon dioxide emissions from fossil fuels, in National Research Council, *Changing Climate*, National Academy Press, Washington, DC, 87–153

Pearce, D.W., W.R. Cline, A.N. Achanta, S. Fankhauser, R.K. Pachauri, R.S.J. Tol and P. Vellinga, 1996: The social costs of climate change: greenhouse damage and the benefits of control, in J.P. Bruce, H. Lee, and E.F. Haites (eds.), *Climate change 1995: economic and social dimensions of climate change*, Cambridge University Press, Cambridge, for the Intergovernmental Panel on Climate Change, 179–224

Peck, S.C. and T. J. Teisberg, 1992: CETA: a model for carbon emissions trajectory assessment, *Energy Journal*, **13**(1), 55–77

Ramsey, F.P., 1928: A mathematical theory of saving, *Economic Journal*, **138**(152), 543–59

Reilly, J.M., J.A.E. Edmunds, R.H. Gardner and A.L. Brenkert, 1987: Uncertainty analyses of the IEA/ORAU CO_2 emission model, *The Energy Journal*, **8**(3), 1–29

Rutherford, T., 1992: The welfare effects of fossil carbon reductions: Results from a recursively dynamic trade model, Working Papers, 112, OECD/GD (92)89, OECD, Paris

Sundquist, E.T., 1990: Long-term aspects of future atmospheric CO_2 and sea-level changes, in R.R. Revelle *et al.*, *Sea-level change*, National Research Council, National Academy Press, Washington, DC, 193–257

Titus, J.G., 1992: The cost of climate change to the United States, in S.K. Majumdar, L.S. Kalkstein, B. Yarnal, E.W. Miller and L.M. Rosenfeld (eds.), *Global climate change: implications, challenges, and mitigation measures*, Pennsylvania Academy of Science, Easton, PA

Tol, R.S.J., 1995: The damage costs of climate change: towards more comprehensive calculations, *Environmental and Resource Economics*, **5**, 353–74

UNFCCC, 2004: United Nations Framework Convention on Climate Change, The convention and Kyoto Protocol, United Nations, New York; available at http://unfccc.int/resource/convkp.html

Weitzman, M.L., 1994: Prices and quantities, *Review of Economic Studies*, **41**, 477–91

Weyant, J.P. and J. Hill, 1999: The costs of the Kyoto Protocol: a multi-model evaluation, introduction and overview, *Energy Journal*, Special Issue

Wigley, T.M.L. and M.E. Schlesinger, 1985: Analytical solution for the effect of increasing CO_2 on global mean temperature, *Nature*, **315**, 649–52

Alternative Perspectives

Perspective Paper 1.1

ROBERT MENDELSOHN

It is no surprise that climate change is listed as one of the top ten pressing public policy issues in the Copenhagen Consensus. The global scale and potential seriousness of the impacts of cumulative greenhouse gas emissions (ghgs) make it indeed a challenge for world policy makers. William Cline's chapter 1 in this volume provides an important introduction to this complex dynamic question. The world must weigh the consequences of tampering with future climates against the cost of forgoing inexpensive energy from fossil fuels. It is by no means an easy choice and it requires all the skills that economists and natural scientists can muster just to comprehend what is at stake.

This Perspective paper examines Cline's chapter and seeks out issues or concerns with Cline's work. Cline's chapter does a good job of identifying why the world must be concerned with climate change. However, there are some problems with the presentation that need to be addressed. First, there are flaws in the economic logic of the chapter. Second, many recent empirical studies of climate change impacts have been omitted. Third, the cost-benefit analysis (CBA) is skewed. A corrected analysis suggests that Cline's chapter examines only strong to extremely aggressive abatement policies. We recommend a moderate abatement policy be added as a final policy alternative.

Ghgs accumulate in the atmosphere because they are assimilated back to earth very slowly. When judging whether or not to abate, the social decision maker must equate the marginal cost of abatement with the present value of the resulting stream of marginal damages (Nordhaus 1991; Falk and Mendelsohn 1993). As Cline notes, with greenhouse gases these impacts begin in thirty years and last for centuries. Because the stream of damage caused by current emissions lasts far into the future, we must take a long-range view of our current actions.

Although it is important to examine the consequences of today's actions far into the future, it is important not to confuse far future actions with what is done today. The impact of emissions that are made after 2100 has no bearing on what the world should do for the next thirty or even 100 years. By examining climate impacts 200–300 years from now, Cline mixes today's emissions with the emissions of far future generations. Instead of comparing the marginal cost of abatement in the near term (next thirty years) against the resulting stream of marginal damages, Cline compares the total cost of abatement for centuries against the total impacts for centuries. This mistake confuses our relatively benign emissions with much more dangerous emissions that could be made in the far future. Although Cline's projections are something to be afraid of, this aggregation over time makes us mistakenly attack the present generation for a problem that future generations might cause. Our first priority is to be responsible for what we ourselves do. We must stop current emissions because of what our emissions will do in the future. If every generation does the same, the problem will be taken care of over time.

Cline has made a very strong assumption by choosing to discount climate change impacts using a 1.5 per cent discount rate. He argues that we must use a 1.5 per cent rate to discount climate change impacts because they occur so far into the future. If we use a large discount rate, they will be judged to be small effects. However, this is circular reasoning, not a justification. Cline does not make a convincing case why only ghgs damage should be discounted at 1.5 per cent, not any other source of consumption. A dollar invested in the private sector can provide a stream of consumption at 4 per cent. Social funds are clearly limited. If we cannot invest in every desirable social activity, clearly we should begin by investing in our best social opportunities first. If climate change can earn only a 1.5 per cent return each year, there are many more deserving social activities that we must fund before we get to climate. Although climate impacts are long term, that does not justify using a different price for time.

Although Cline has done a good job of summarizing the literature through the early 1990s, there is an extensive literature that has been developed since then. The empirical estimates in Cline's analysis rely on studies that are over ten years old. Of course, if new work essentially supports the older figures, this would be a minor oversight. However, this is not the case. A series of studies on the impacts of climate change have systematically shown that the older literature overestimated climate damage by failing to allow for adaptation and for climate benefits (see Fankhauser, Tol and Pearce 1997; Mendelsohn and Neumann 1999; Tol 1999, 2002; Mendelsohn *et al.* 2000; Maddison 2001; Mendelsohn 2001; Sohngen, Mendelsohn and Sedjo 2002; Pearce 2003; Mendelsohn and Williams 2004). These new studies imply that impacts depend heavily upon *initial temperatures* (latitude). Countries in the polar region are likely to receive large benefits from warming, countries in the mid-latitudes will at first benefit and begin to be harmed only if temperatures rise above 2.5C (Mendelsohn *et al.* 2000). Only countries in the tropical and subtropical regions are likely to be harmed immediately by warming and be subject to the magnitudes of impacts first thought likely (Mendelsohn *et al.* 2000). Summing these regional impacts across the globe implies that warming benefits and damages will likely offset each other until warming passes 2.5C,

and even then it will be far smaller on net than originally thought (Mendelsohn and Williams 2004). Compared to the estimates presented in Nordhaus and Boyer (2000), the new benefit estimates are substantially smaller.

The smaller net global impacts imply lower optimal taxes. Nordhaus and Boyer (2000) predict marginal benefits that should start at about $10/ton and gradually rise to $60/ton of carbon by 2100. The new estimates suggest marginal benefits that start closer to $1–2/ton and rise to $10–20/ton by 2100. Lower marginal benefits, of course, imply more modest programmes. Cline is correct when he observes that even with the Nordhaus–Boyer estimates, the modest marginal damages imply meagre abatement programmes. The new empirical estimates suggest even more modest programmes.

Cline complains that impact research has not included low-probability high-consequence events such as shutting down the thermohaline circulation or suddenly losing the West Antarctic ice sheet. Without warm currents from the Atlantic, northern Europe would cool substantially. A sudden melting of huge ice sheets would cause sea level to rise dramatically. These changes would have large effects. The question, however, is whether one can realistically link current actions to these consequences. Although far future emissions could cause large enough changes in the earth's temperature to trigger such events, it is not probable that near-term emissions would do this. It is again a flaw of comparing total costs and total damage that leads Cline into this trap. Showing that far future emissions might cause catastrophic events does not in itself prove that current emissions will cause these events.

If one focuses on comparing the marginal impacts of current actions against the marginal cost, recent economic research suggests that the optimal ghgs policy is to start modestly. If damages rise more quickly in the future than we expect, the estimates can be adjusted and stricter policies can be imposed. For now, based on what we understand today, the optimal policy for controlling ghgs is actually a relatively modest programme.

What policies, then, are available to control ghgs? Clearly there are a host of tools available, from command and control, tradable permits and carbon taxes. There is no question that command and control has proven to be very expensive and undesirable. This is especially clear with a pollutant where the location of emissions makes no difference. We are interested in controlling the aggregate emissions in the entire world and only tradable permits and taxes will do that efficiently. Cline and many other economists advocate using taxes because the taxes would provide a new source of revenue for governments. However, tradable permits would do the job just as effectively. Permits could be granted to existing polluters in every country in the world. This gives firms the right to pollute up to the socially desirable amount of pollution, a policy that has been followed consistently for every regulated pollutant to date. It is not clear that ghgs should be treated differently. That implies that the tool of choice is a tradable permit. The government should allocate permits across existing users. Users should then be free to trade among each other to seek efficiency gains.

Another important question is how to abate carbon. Although the bulk of carbon emissions in the future come from burning fossil fuels, policy makers should consider more than just energy policies to reduce carbon emissions. Another important policy option is to include carbon sequestration in forests. By growing timber trees longer and by setting aside vast tracts of marginal forestland for conservation, land use policies can sequester a large stock of carbon in living forests. Following dynamic tax paths such as the Nordhaus and Boyer (2000) programme, it is optimal to construct a forest sequestration programme that sets aside carbon equal to one-half of the abatement in energy (Sohngen and Mendelsohn 2003). That is, forest sequestration should account for one-third of total abatement. This must be a world-wide effort because some of the most attractive lands to use for forest sequestration are in the low latitudes (Sohngen and Mendelsohn 2003).

One of the most important questions that the Copenhagen Consensus must address is how severe a programme of abatement makes sense for ghgs. Cline presents three basic options. The least expensive programme presented by Cline is the preferred policy from Nordhaus and Boyer (2000), which starts with taxes at $10/ton and lets them rise slowly to $60/ton by 2100. The next programme is Cline's own preferred policy, which starts at $150/ton and rises to $600/ton by 2100. He then introduces a more aggressive policy based loosely on risk that starts at $450/ton and rises to $1,200/ton by 2100.

Because economic research on impacts suggests that global net impacts are quite low for near-term emissions, Cline's policies appear to be overly aggressive. That is, Cline calls for abatement that is more expensive than the damage avoided. I consequently introduce a fourth policy that is more modest than even Nordhaus and Boyer (2000). Global market damages are closer to $1/ton for the near future. Doubling this value to take into account non-market damage and the expected value of catastrophes, the marginal damage per ton should begin at $2/ton. As carbon accumulates, this will increase speculatively to $20/ton by 2100.

Table 1.1.1 describes what these policies look like over the century and what the costs and benefits are likely to be. The benefits, in this case, are the discounted stream of benefits caused by another ton of emissions. Because the marginal damage of an emission is constant within a year, average and

Table 1.1.1. Benefits and costs of alternative options, 2010–2100

Options	2010	2050	2100
Mendelsohn 'optimal'			
Tax (marginal cost) ($)	2	10	20
Average cost ($)	1	5	10
PV damage ($)	2	10	20
Benefit/cost	2.0	2.0	2.0
Nordhaus and Boyer 'optimal'			
Tax (marginal cost) ($)	6	30	60
Average cost ($)	3	15	30
PV damages ($)	2	10	20
Benefit/cost	0.67	0.67	0.67
Cline 'optimal'			
Tax (marginal cost) $	150	375	600
Average cost ($)	75	187	300
PV damage ($)	2	10	20
Benefit/cost	0.027	0.053	0.066
Cline 'value-at-risk'			
Tax (marginal cost) ($)	450	825	1200
Average cost ($)	225	412	600
PV damages ($)	2	10	20
Benefit/cost	0.009	0.024	0.033

marginal damages are the same. I assume that average cost is about half of marginal cost. Only the modest programme has a benefit-cost ratio greater than 1. Cline teases the Nordhaus and Boyer (2000) programme for having such a little effect on abatement. However, the Nordhaus and Boyer (2000) programme is too costly with a benefit-cost ratio (BCR) of about 0.67. Cline's more aggressive policies earn only 1–7 cents per dollar spent on abatement.

How does the Kyoto Agreement look? This is a difficult question to answer because Kyoto is a short-term commitment made by a limited number of polluting countries. Developing countries, which will soon be responsible for half of ghgs emissions, made no commitments at all. Because of reductions in emissions in Eastern Europe and the introduction of North Sea oil and natural gas, European emissions are actually close to their 1990 levels. The commitments the Europeans made in Kyoto are quite modest and in line with the optimal policy. The commitments made by Japan and Canada are greater and look more like the Nordhaus and Boyer (2000) estimates. Because of growth since 1990, the USA is well above their 1990 level of emissions. To cut back to below 1990 levels requires the USA to effectively make a 30 per cent reduction in emissions. The US restrictions look much more like Cline's preferred policy. Kyoto is consequently a complex country-by-country agreement that includes everything from nothing to extreme measures. It is no surprise that the USA did not finally agree to Kyoto as it was negotiated.

In this Perspective paper, we present century-long emission trajectories to give decision makers a sense of what they are beginning to commit themselves to. However, we are by no means suggesting that governments lock themselves into an emission path for a century. There is no question but that we will learn a great deal about controlling ghgs and about climate change over even the next few decades. The optimal policy is to commit only to what one will do in the near term. Every decade, this policy should be re-examined in light of new evidence. Once the international community has a viable programme in place, it is easy to imagine the community being able to adjust its policies based on what new information is forthcoming. The trick is not to commit to a draconian programme that will solve this long-term problem immediately. Draconian programmes such as the ones offered by Cline are extremely poor investments. The world community simply should not support such extreme measures when there are so many other pressing issues at hand. The optimal response to ghgs is to start modestly. Build an international consensus to bring ghgs under regulation. Focus at first on putting together an efficient control programme. Armed with this solid foundation, the world will be able to tackle future emissions as they come.

References

Falk, I. and R. Mendelsohn, 1993: The economics of controlling stock pollution: an efficient strategy for greenhouse gases, *Journal of Environmental Economics and Management*, **25**, 76–88

Fankhauser, S., R. Tol and D.W. Pearce, 1997: The aggregation of climate change damages: a welfare theoretic approach, *Environment and Resource Economics*, **10**(3), 249–66

Maddison, D. (ed.), 2001: *The amenity value of the global climate*, Earthscan, London

Mendelsohn, R. (ed.), 2001: *Global warming and the American economy: a regional analysis*, Edward Elgar Publishing, Cheltenham

Mendelsohn, R. and J. Neumann (eds.), 1999: *The impact of climate change on the US economy*, Cambridge University Press, Cambridge

Mendelsohn, R., W. Morrison, M. Schlesinger and N. Adronova, 2000: Country-specific market impacts from climate change, *Climatic Change*, **45**, 553–69

Mendelsohn, R. and L. Williams, 2004: Dynamic forecasts of market impacts of global warming, *Integrated Assessment*, forthcoming

Nordhaus, W., 1991: To slow or not to slow: the economics of the greenhouse effect, *Economic Journal*, **101**(407), 920–37

Nordhaus, W. and J. Boyer 2000: *Warming the world: economic models of global warming*, MIT Press, Cambridge, MA

Pearce, D., 2003: The social cost of carbon and its policy implications, *Oxford Review of Economic Policy*, **19**

Sohngen, B. and R. Mendelsohn, 2003: An optimal control model of forest carbon sequestration,

Journal of American Agricultural Economics, **85**, 448–57

Sohngen, B., R. Mendelsohn and R. Sedjo, 2002: A global model of climate change impacts on timber markets, *Journal of Agricultural and Resource Economics*, **26**, 326–43

Tol, R., 1999: The marginal costs of greenhouse gas emissions, *The Energy Journal*, **20**(1), 61–81

2002a: Estimates of the damage costs of climate change, part 1: benchmark estimates, *Environmental and Resource Economics*, **21**, 47–73

2002b: Estimates of the damage costs of climate change, part 2: dynamic estimates, *Environmental and Resource Economics*, **21**, 135–60

Perspective Paper 1.2

ALAN S. MANNE

Introduction

This is intended as a response to William Cline's chapter 1 in this volume (Cline 2004). Climate change is a problem that requires an unprecedented degree of international consensus, and its consequences must be considered over a time horizon of unprecedented length. It would be a serious mistake to underestimate the difficulty of achieving a consensus. There are serious uncertainties on both the science and the economics. Cline has offered a useful challenge, but – in my judgment – it overstates the immediacy of the problem. In the allocation of limited global resources it does not warrant as much effort as dealing with poverty and disease in the developing nations.

Cline's chapter deals with three policy strategies: (1) an optimal carbon tax (or regional quotas); (2) the Kyoto Protocol; and (3) a value-at-risk approach. Because of space limitations, I will deal with only the first of these. There is widespread disagreement over the Kyoto Agreement. Despite the European consensus, neither the USA nor Russia has agreed to ratify it. For emissions control to be effective, the developing nations will also eventually have to join in. This is why an optimal carbon tax (or regional quotas) provides a more meaningful frame of reference than Kyoto.

Why not consider the value-at-risk approach? This is an exceedingly risk-averse criterion. If it is good to adopt a 95 per cent threshold for the climate sensitivity parameter, why not 99 per cent? Or an even higher value? Moreover, this criterion discards one of the principal parameters of dynamic decision analysis. It neglects the 'act, then learn' features of the problem. Yes, there is uncertainty, but eventually there is some resolution of this uncertainty. We may all be willing to agree that the climate sensitivity parameter could be as high as 9.5°C. But if the effects turn out to be this dramatic, it should not take very many years for us to reach a consensus on this aspect of the debate. Value-at-risk may be appropriate in considering financial risks, but it seems to be the wrong criterion for evaluating measures that might be employed to combat global climate change. It distracts us from taking more meaningful steps for dealing with the problem.

Benefit-Cost Analysis

Cline provides a useful introduction to benefit-cost analysis (CBA) in the area of global climate change. I have no real disagreement with his description of the components of costs and benefits. And I agree that there is very little difference between a policy in which nations are persuaded to adopt a uniform global tax and a policy in which regional emission quotas are assigned to individual nations, and there is 'banking'', 'borrowing' and international trade in these quota rights. In both cases, there is full 'when' and 'where' flexibility. That is, there is a market test for when and where emissions are to be reduced. Neither Cline nor I would disagree with the importance of arriving at an efficient allocation of resources. There is the further issue of equity, but this is where we need the participation of some imaginative political scientists.

My principal concern is that Cline has advocated a discounting strategy that is unduly alarmist. Moreover, by presenting a global approach through the DICE model, he has ignored

The author is indebted to Richard Richels for helpful comments. Thanks go to Charles Ng for research assistance.

the priorities of individual developing countries. For this reason, I will quantify my critique in terms of MERGE, a Model for Evaluating Regional and Global Effects of greenhouse gas emission reductions. This model represents joint work with Richard Richels and others. For details, see *www.stanford.edu/group/MERGE*. A computer listing is available at that website. MERGE contains sub-models governing:

- The domestic and international economy
- Energy-related emissions of greenhouse gases (ghgs)
- Non-energy emissions of ghgs
- Global climate change.

Each region's domestic economy is viewed as though it were a Ramsey–Solow model of long-term economic growth. The time paths of investment and consumption are strongly influenced by the choice of a 'utility' discount rate. This in turn may be governed by a prescriptive or a descriptive viewpoint.

Energy-related emissions in MERGE are projected through a 'bottom-up' perspective. Fuel demands are estimated through 'process analysis' and a 'top-down' production function of the inputs of capital, labour, electric and non-electric energy.

Each period's emissions are translated into global concentrations and in turn to the impacts on mean global indicators such as temperature change. The MERGE model may be operated in a 'cost-effective' mode – that is, supposing that international negotiations lead to a time path of emissions that satisfies a constraint on concentrations or on temperature change. The model may also be operated in a 'benefit-cost' mode – choosing a time path of emissions that maximizes the discounted utility of consumption, after making allowance for the disutility of abrupt climate change.

Individual geopolitical regions are distinguished in the MERGE model. Abatement choices are distinguished by 'where' (in which region?), 'when' (in which time period?) and 'what' (which greenhouse gas to abate?). There may be tradeoffs between equity and efficiency in these choices.

Population and Regional GDP Projections

Greenhouse emissions are *not* proportional to population and GDP, but they can be quite sensitive to these projections. For this purpose, we have used what we believe to be a middle-of-the-road projection of the global population – assuming that it will rise from 6 bn people in 2000 to 10 bn in 2100, and that it will stabilize thereafter. Virtually all of this growth will take place in the developing countries.

Separate projections are provided for each of nine regions. It is useful to draw a distinction between the four high-income regions: the USA, Western Europe, Japan, and Canada/Australia–New Zealand; and the five low-income regions: Eastern Europe and Former Soviet Union (FSU), China, India, Mexico and the OPEC nations and ROW (rest of world). The model employs ten-year time steps extending from 2000 through 2200. To reduce 'horizon effects', we shall report only the years through 2150 (see figure 1.2.1).

Population projections may be debatable, but there are even more controversies with respect to productivity and *per capita* GDP growth. Through

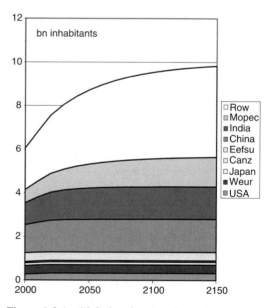

Figure 1.2.1. *Global and regional population, 2000–2150*

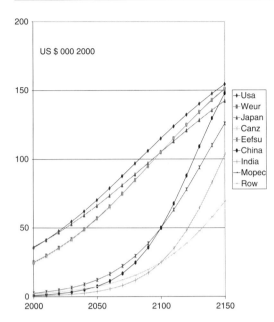

Figure 1.2.2. *Projections of GDP per capita, market exchange rates, 2000–2150*

All dollar values here are expressed in dollars of 2000 purchasing power, and are shown at market exchange rates. If instead we had employed 'purchasing power parity'(PPP), there would have been much higher initial GDP values for the low-income nations, but lower growth rates of GDP and of emissions. With PPP, we have found only minor changes for the high-income nations.

Market and Non-Market Damage

Typically, the benefits of slow climate change are expressed in terms of the damage avoided. When Nordhaus (1991) made his first efforts at quantification, the benefits were expressed in terms of avoiding crop losses, forestry damage, shoreline erosion, etc. For each of these sectors, it was possible to assign market values to the losses. There are prices for crops, timber and real estate. Later, it was discovered that some changes (e.g. CO_2 fertilization) could even lead to modest gains in some of these areas. There is an emerging consensus that market damage is not the principal reason to be concerned over climate change.

The more worrisome issue is the type of damage for which there are no market values. The 'non-market damage' includes human health, species losses and catastrophic risks such as the shutdown of the thermohaline circulation in the Atlantic ocean. Here we must rely on imagination and introspection. We can be sure of only one thing. This type of loss is of far greater concern to high-income regions than to those with low incomes; Bangladesh has more reason to be concerned about typhoons than about Arctic ice flows.

In MERGE, we have tried to allow for both market and non-market damage, but have focused our attention on the latter. Many calculations have been based upon CS, the climate sensitivity parameter. This is the equilibrium warming associated with a doubling of carbon concentrations over the pre-industrial level. A typical value for this parameter is an equilibrium warming of 2.5°C. For market damage, we have supposed that this amount of temperature rise would lead to GDP losses of only 0.25 per cent in the high-income nations, and to losses of

2020, we have taken over these projections from the 'reference case' defined by the Energy Information Administration (EIA 2003). Thereafter, we have extrapolated by using logistic functions. The initial point is the EIA projection for 2020. Each of these logistic functions converges to the identical asymptote. The 'limit to growth' is $200,000 *per capita*, but this limit is not reached for several centuries. This value is astronomical in comparison with today's incomes in India, China and other low-income nations; it was chosen so that there would not be an immediate decline in the growth rate of the high-income countries during the next two centuries.

For each of the nine regions, the third point along the logistic curve is an arbitrary individual estimate of the *per capita* GDP in the year 2100 (figure 1.2.2). These values were chosen so as to allow for a smooth transition post-2020 – and a *partial* convergence of the low-income countries to those with high incomes by 2100. For example, the USA grows from $36,000 in 2000 to $115,000 by 2100. India grows rapidly (from $500 to $25,000), but is still far behind the USA by the end of the century.

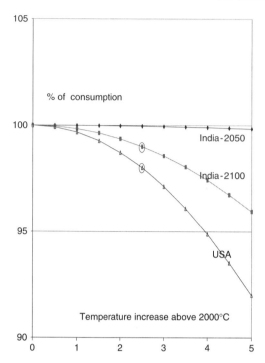

Figure 1.2.3. *Economic loss factor, non-market damage*

0.50 per cent in the low-income nations. From 2050 onward, recall that only a small amount of global GDP will originate in agriculture, forestry and fishing. At higher or lower temperature levels than the CS of 2.5°, we have made the convenient assumption that market losses would be proportional to the temperature change.

For non-market damage, MERGE is based on the conservative proposition that expected losses would increase quadratically with the temperature rise. That is, there are only small discernible losses at the temperature level of 2000, but the losses from possible catastrophes could increase radically if we go to higher temperatures. Figure 1.2.3 shows the admittedly speculative estimates that are currently used in MERGE. Different numerical values are employed, depending upon the *per capita* income of the region at each point in time. These loss functions are based on two parameters that define willingness-to-pay (WTP) to avoid a temperature rise: *catt* and *hsx*.

To avoid a 2.5° temperature rise, high-income countries might be willing to give up 2 per cent of their GDP. (Why 2 per cent? This is the total GDP

component that is currently devoted by the USA to all forms of environmental controls – on solids, liquids and gases.) In figure 1.2.3, this is expressed as an 'economic loss factor' of 98 per cent associated with a temperature rise of 2.5°. (The loss factor at 2.5° is circled on the two lower curves.) This factor represents the fraction of consumption that remains available for conventional uses by households and by government. For high-income countries, the loss is quadratic in terms of the temperature rise. That is, in those countries, the hockey-stick parameter $hsx = 1$, and the loss factor is:

$$ELF(x) = [1 - (x/catt)^2]^{hsx}$$

where x is a variable that measures the temperature rise above its level in 2000, and *catt* is a catastrophic temperature parameter chosen so that the entire regional product is wiped out at this level. In order for $ELF(2.5) = 0.98$ in high-income nations, the *catt* parameter must be 17.7°C. This is a direct implication of the quadratic function.

What about low-income countries such as India? In those countries, the *hsx* exponent lies considerably below unity. It is chosen so that at a *per capita* income of $25,000, a region would be willing to spend 1 per cent of its GDP so as to avoid a global temperature rise of 2.5° (see the loss factor circled on the middle curve). At $50,000 or above, India might be willing to pay 2 per cent. And at $5,000 or below, it would be willing to pay virtually nothing. To see how these parameters work out, consider the three functions shown in figure 1.2.3. At all points of time, the US *per capita* GDP is so high that *ELF* is virtually the identical quadratic function of the temperature rise. Now look at India. By 2100, India's *per capita* GDP has climbed to $25,000, and *ELF* is 99 per cent at a temperature rise of 2.5°. In 2050, India's *per capita* GDP is still less than $4,000, and that is why its *ELF* remains virtually unity at that point – regardless of the temperature change.

Caveat: admittedly, both *catt* and *hsx* are highly speculative parameters. With different numerical values, one can obtain alternative estimates of the WTP to avoid non-market damage. One example will be given below. Although the numerical values are questionable, the general principle seems plausible. All nations might be willing to pay something to avoid climate change, but poor nations cannot afford to pay a great deal in the near future. Their more immediate priorities will be overcoming domestic poverty and disease.

We are now ready to incorporate the *ELF* functions into the maximand of MERGE. The maximand is the Negishi-weighted discounted utility (the logarithm) of consumption – adjusted for non-market damages:

Maximand

$$= \sum_{rg} nwt_{rg} \sum_{pp} udf_{pp,rg} \cdot \log \left(ELF_{rg,pp} C_{rg,pp} \right)$$

where:

nwt_{rg} = Negishi weight assigned to region rg – determined iteratively so that each region will satisfy an intertemporal foreign trade constraint

$udf_{pp,rg}$ = utility discount factor assigned to region rg in projection period pp

$ELF_{rg,pp}$ = economic loss factor assigned to region rg in projection period pp

$C_{rg,pp}$ = conventional measure of consumption (excluding non-market damages) assigned to region rg in projection period pp.

Prescriptive and Descriptive Views on the Rate of Return

Consider a single region with a single good that may be used interchangeably for consumption and investment. For analytic purposes, it will be convenient to assume a 'first-best' world. In this case, it is straightforward to conclude that the rate of return on consumption must be identical to that on capital. For a model in which the maximand is the discounted utility of consumption, the rate of return (ROR) is:

$$\text{ROR} = \rho + \theta g,$$

where ρ = utility discount rate

θ = elasticity of marginal utility

g = growth rate of consumption.

The right-hand side is identical to the value that Cline calls SRTP (the social rate of time preference). We both agree that this represents the optimal

rate of return on consumption, but we part company when it comes to investment goods. In a 'first-best' world, I see no reason to distinguish between the rate of return on consumption and on investment. Cline refers to a 'shadow price' on capital, and states that this price is greater than unity, but does not define the constraints that lead to this price. This is not just an academic nicety; it is at the heart of the debate over prescriptive and descriptive views on the ROR.

There is another point of difference between us. The original DICE model refers to a single-region view of the world. In Nordhaus' later work on RICE, he describes a multi-region model, and he employs Negishi weights to ensure that each region satisfies an intertemporal balance of trade constraint. In Nordhaus and Boyer (2000, 112), the authors state that: 'The welfare weights were chosen so that the shadow prices on the period-specific budget constraints – the social marginal utilities of income – are the same across regions in each period at the social optimum'.

In MERGE, we have taken a simpler approach. We specify a uniform ROR among all regions, and do not impose constraints on capital flows – either between regions or between time periods. Because of the different growth rates in individual regions, we compensate by adopting region-specific and time-specific values of ρ, the utility discount parameter. MERGE allows for non-zero interregional capital flows, but it turns out that they are small. Like Nordhaus and Boyer, we employ a logarithmic utility function, and therefore set the elasticity of marginal utility, $\theta = 1$.

What are the values that we take for the ROR? To parallel Cline's case (a prescriptive approach), we follow the assumption that this is a constant 1 per cent per year throughout our planning horizon. Alternatively, as a descriptive (market oriented) approach, we shall assume that the ROR begins at 5 per cent per year in 2000, and that it declines linearly to 3 per cent by the horizon date of 2200. (A decline in the ROR would be consistent with a world in which there is an eventual slowdown of growth.) Now, what are the consequences of these two very different assumptions?

Perhaps the most important difference is the sensitivity to assumptions about the distant future. The

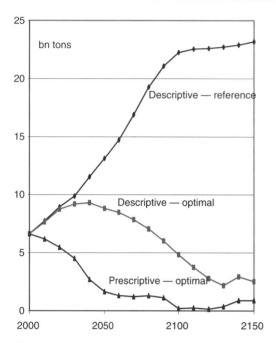

Figure 1.2.4. *Total carbon emissions, under alternative rates of return, 2000–2150*

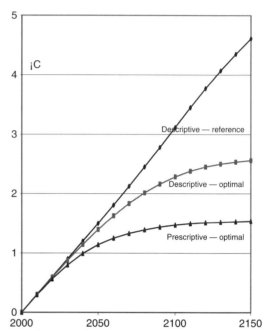

Figure 1.2.5. *Temperature increase, under alternative rates of return, 2000–2150*

prescriptive approach makes present decisions quite sensitive to distant-future uncertainties such as non-market damage costs. In the absence of near-term constraints on capital formation, the prescriptive approach also leads to an unrealistically rapid immediate build-up of capital. Most important for the climate debate, the prescriptive approach implies an immediate stabilization of global carbon emissions and a reduction of these emissions in the very near future (see the bottom line labelled 'prescriptive–optimal' in figure 1.2.4.) By contrast, the descriptive assumption implies that optimal behaviour will lead to only a gradual departure from the baseline (reference case) emissions path.

What are the consequence for mean global temperature? (See figure 1.2.5.) With the reference case (topmost line), emissions keep rising. It should come as no surprise that mean global temperatures then keep rising over the next two centuries. With the bottom line (prescriptive rates of return – optimal balancing of costs and benefits), the temperature increase is limited to about 1.5°C. With the middle line (descriptive rates of return – optimal balancing of costs and benefits), the tempera-

ture increase is higher, but eventually it stabilizes at about 2.5°C. Using market oriented criteria does *not* lead to indefinite postponement of abatement. But it does delay taking costly immediate measures. Most of the abatement occurs during the period when technology has improved, and abatement becomes less costly. At that time, more countries will have a higher GDP, and will be more willing to help pay for abatement. This is the consequence of using market oriented rates of return rather than those that might be suggested by social planners. We should probably move toward greenhouse gas abatement in the long run, but at a more gradual pace than advocated by Cline.

What are the cost differences between the prescriptive and the descriptive approach? Perhaps the most vivid difference appears in the efficiency price (in a 'first-best' world, a carbon tax) assigned to CO_2 (figure 1.2.6). With the discount rates suggested by the prescriptive approach, a high price is assigned to carbon abatement in the immediate future – about $300 per ton. With the lower discount rates suggested by the descriptive approach, we move toward a near-term efficiency price of only

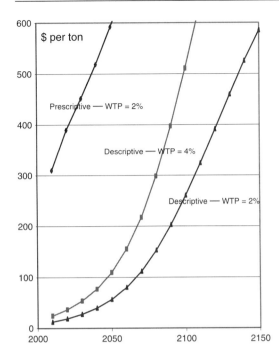

Figure 1.2.6. *Efficiency price of carbon,*
2000–2150

based on a WTP of 4 per cent for avoiding a temperature rise of 2.5°. This has a discernible effect upon the solution. With a doubling of the WTP, the efficiency price of carbon rises, but it does not skyrocket. The tax moves to $24 per ton during the immediate future. And for the balance of our planning horizon, the tax continues to be about twice that when the WTP = 2 per cent. Again, the tax rises at a rate that is consistent with a gradual departure from the reference case (status quo) emissions path. It is costly to do otherwise.

To summarize what has been said in this Perspective paper: if we are to avoid an indefinite rise in the world's temperature, ghgs must eventually be driven down to low levels. It would be wise to undertake this move over the next few centuries, but not over the next few decades. Meanwhile, it is important to undertake the research and development (R&D) that will facilitate the long-term move toward a low-carbon world.

$12. The market oriented ROR does not ignore the distant future, but it places less weight upon that future than does the prescriptive approach.

MERGE is designed to produce an 'optimal' trajectory, but we cannot be sure that it incorporates the most reasonable estimate of either the costs or the benefits of abatement. Suppose that we were to adopt a higher estimate of the WTP for non-market damage. Instead of a WTP of 2 per cent for high-income countries, imagine that these functions were

References

Cline, W.R., 2004: Climate change, chapter 1 in this volume

Energy Information Administration (EIA), 2003: *International energy outlook 2003*, US Department of Energy, Washington, DC

Nordhaus, W.D., 1991: To slow or not to slow: the economics of the greenhouse effect, *Economic Journal*, **101**(6), 920–37

Nordhaus, W.D. and J. Boyer, 2000: *Warming the world: economic models of global warming*, MIT Press, Cambridge, MA

Rejoinder to Perspective Papers 1.1 and 1.2

WILLIAM R. CLINE

Alan Manne (2004) and Robert Mendelsohn (2004) have vigorously pursued their mandate as 'opponents' to my chapter 1 on global warming (Cline, 2004). I welcome their critiques as an opportunity for sharpening the debate.

Let me begin with Mendelsohn, whose views in Perspective paper 1.1 are the more diametrically opposed to mine. He raises the following key concept: the world's present carbon emissions are 'benign' because currently the world is below optimal temperature, so why not let the future take care of itself and adopt its own abatement when the proper time comes? It should be emphasised that this is a radical position. Virtually all of the other optimal abatement analyses arrive at some degree of abatement even early in the horizon. They typically have a lesser cutback of emissions early and greater cutback later (including in my optimal path), but that results from the effect of discounting for rising utility and (in some cases) falling abatement cost as technological alternatives widen. None is premised on the notion that current emissions do not contribute at all to future damage because they are benign.

Set aside for the moment whether the optimal amount of global warming would be 2.5°C, which Mendelsohn appears to believe. Consider simply the following problem. Even if we wished to set the world's thermostat at 2.5°C above the pre-industrial level, it would be inadvisable to do nothing now and leave action to the future. The reason is that warming cannot be stopped on a dime. There is a thirty-year or longer ocean thermal lag from emissions to warming. There are also decades-long lags from construction of power plants and other carbon-

Table R.1.1. Implied Policy under Mendelsohn's LFTCI Strategy, 2005–2205[a]

	Emissions (GtC)	Cut from baseline (%)	Abatement cost (% GWP)	Warming (°C)
2005	8.59	0.45	0.01	0.69
2015	10.03	1.05	0.03	0.99
2025	11.41	1.48	0.04	1.28
2035	12.76	1.80	0.06	1.57
2045	14.11	2.04	0.07	1.84
2055	2.51	87.40	3.74	2.12
2065	2.60	87.50	4.04	2.38
2075	2.66	87.83	4.34	2.51
2085	2.68	88.35	4.65	2.58
2095	2.67	88.99	4.95	2.64
2105	2.77	89.09	5.26	2.69
2155	4.11	87.04	4.98	2.74
2205	7.34	81.96	4.38	2.91

Note: [a]LFTCI: Let the future take care of itself.

using capital stock today to the date when it is time to replace them.

Table R1.1 shows what Mendelsohn's 'Let the future take care of itself' (LFTCI) strategy would imply. Using the DICE99CL model (see Cline 2004), and even allowing for the tiny carbon tax proposed as optimal by Mendelsohn, baseline emissions would rise to 14 billion tons of carbon (GtC) by 2045.[1] By then, the future would have arrived: the world would have to stop emissions in their tracks by cutting them back to less than 3 GtC annually in order to hold global warming by thirty years later at close to 2.5°C. While we could enjoy *de minimus* abatement costs for the next four decades, suddenly in the fifth decade and after abatement costs would surge to about 5 per cent of world product in

[1] The DICE99CL model adapts the DICE99 model of Nordhaus and Boyer (2000).

Table R.1.2. Mendelsohn's Implied Optimal Warming, 2005–2305 (°C)

	Baseline Warming (°C)[a]	Carbon tax ($/tce)[b]	Emissions cut from baseline (%)	Optimal warming (°C)[a]	Abatement impact (°C)[a]
2005	0.687	1	0.45	0.687	0.000
2015	0.988	3	1.05	0.987	0.000
2055	2.124	11	2.22	2.116	−0.008
2105	3.464	21	2.60	3.436	−0.028
2155	4.576	31	3.06	4.530	−0.046
2205	5.563	41	3.29	5.500	−0.063
2255	6.504	51	4.09	6.426	−0.078
2305	7.413	61	4.92	7.316	−0.098

Notes: [a] Baseline, % cut and abatement impact calculated using DICE99CL (Cline 2004).
[b] Carbon tax: Mendelsohn (2004).

order to keep warming from going beyond Mendelsohn's benign limit.

We know from costly experience that political processes make it difficult to implement such sudden and wrenching policy changes. The fundamental problem with Mendelsohn's approach is that it fails to set the world on a path toward feasible limitation of warming to within the limit he considers benign (which itself involves a debatable tolerance of much more warming than in the past most in the scientific community would have considered safe). Even if somehow the path of emissions could be halted abruptly, there would be intergenerational inequity involved. The path in table R1.1 implies allowing global industrial emissions to rise from 1.2 tons of carbon *per capita* (tcpc) today to 1.5 tcpc by 2045, only to be followed by an abrupt reduction to 0.2 tcpc by 2055.

Mendelsohn calculates his own optimal abatement path. It involves setting an initial carbon tax of $1 per ton, raising it to $10 per ton by 2050, and to $20 by 2100. When this path of carbon taxes is applied to the DICE99CL model, it generates truly negligible reduction in warming. As shown in table R1.2, the resulting reduction from baseline warming amounts to less than three-hundredths of a °C by 2100, and less than one-tenth of a degree by 2300 (extrapolating Mendelsohn's straight-line tax path). It is highly misleading to use the phrase 'optimal abatement' in describing such a path. 'Optimal inaction' would be far more transparent – and,

indeed, much more in keeping with Mendelsohn's diagnosis of the problem.

Mendelsohn makes much of the argument that recent literature has downscaled the likely damage from global warming. He states incorrectly that my empirical estimates 'rely on studies that are over ten years old'. Instead, the climate damage function I use for the empirical estimates is from the DICE99 model of Nordhaus and Boyer (2000). They explicitly cite Mendelsohn and Neumann (1999), calling it 'the most optimistic outlook of the recent research' (Nordhaus and Boyer 2000: 70), so their chosen damage function should already have incorporated the benefit of Mendelsohn's advice about relatively recent findings. The Nordhaus–Boyer estimates already take account of a substantial reduction in damage estimates from the early levels for traditional effects in agriculture and elsewhere, because of adaptation opportunities. Nordhaus and Boyer introduce a component for willingness-to-pay to avert the risk of thermohaline circulation or other disaster, however. Mendelsohn is prepared for some reason simply to dismiss this component of damage. Surely this is assuming away what is potentially the most important part of climate damage.

Nordhaus and Boyer do allow for an initial zone of favourable rather than unfavourable effects of warming. Using the DICE99CL model, effects are favourable until cumulative warming (above 1900) reaches 1.28°C, which occurs by 2025. Further warming then begins to cause net damage. The

Nordhaus–Boyer limit for benign warming, then, is only half the amount proposed by Mendelsohn. In the DICE99CL baseline, warming reaches 2.5°C by 2070, and the Nordhaus–Boyer damage function places the adverse impact for this amount of warming at 1.1 per cent of world product, compared with Mendelsohn's zero net effect.

With respect to changes in the more recent literature, in my view the most important recent scientific information in this debate is the finding by Andronova and Schlesinger (2001) that the upper bound for benchmark $2 \times CO_2$ is not 4.5°C but 9.3°C at the 95 per cent confidence level. Mendelsohn is aware of this new evidence (we were both at a recent conference where it featured prominently, see Cato 2003) but for some reason chooses to ignore it when making his case that recent research should make us less rather than more concerned about global warming than we were in the 1990s.

Mendelsohn also attacks my discounting methodology as 'circular reasoning, not a justification.' This caricature may be what underlay the critique in the summary article in the *Economist* (2004).[2] Neither Mendelsohn nor the *Economist* recognises that I based the discounting method on a major body of economic literature concerned with social cost-benefit analysis (CBA).[3] Alan S. Manne, in contrast, in Perspective paper 1.2, not only recognises this approach but includes it as one variant in his calculations as the 'prescriptive' method, even though he prefers the alternative 'descriptive' approach. I do believe that the following logical syllogism is valid: (a) the distant future is important; (b) discount rates frequently used tend to make the distant future completely unimportant; so (c) the discount rates frequently used can be highly misleading for analysing the distant future. My chapter appeals to this logic only as introductory and motivational, however, and then turns formally to the existing theoretical literature as the basis for applying the Social Rate of Time Preference approach. I return to the discounting issue below.

Mendelsohn strongly prefers tradable permits to carbon taxes. It is not clear why, because he cites only past practice. It would not make much difference which instrument is used in his optimal policy, because his carbon fee is so small it would have little impact. Even by 2100 his $20 tax-equivalent would amount to only 6 cents on a gallon of gasoline (but a 25 per cent tax on coal). A key problem with tradable permits owned by historic producers, however, is that if the optimal carbon tax eventually reaches the range of several hundred dollars per ton of carbon, as in my optimal path, there would be an extreme transfer of wealth to the historic owners of the licences to emit. It would be far better to use this large incremental rent arising from incremental environmental scarcity for expenditure on other objectives, such as improvements in education and health.

Finally, Mendelsohn himself acknowledges that global warming would impose substantial damage immediately on tropical and sub-tropical regions. While he is comfortable at 'Summing . . . regional impacts across the globe,' it is implausible that the richer countries will make transfers to compensate the poorer tropical countries for their immediate damage, so Mendelsohn's diagnosis of benign warming up to 2.5°C not only excludes catastrophic risk but is also indifferent to the differentially adverse impact on poor countries. Fundamentally, however, he and I disagree on which is the greater 'trap': doing virtually nothing until it is too late (my concern), or taking 'draconian' action too soon (his).

Manne's framework for analysis is much closer to my own, and his differences are more nuanced. Indeed, over a time horizon of several decades his bottom line is not far from my own. His preferred 'descriptive optimal' path from his MERGE model cuts global carbon emissions from a baseline of 22.5 GtC in 2100 to 5 GtC. My optimal abatement path cuts global emissions from 21.4 GtC in approximately the same year (2095) to 11.2 million, a less dramatic cut than Manne's.

Manne's climate damage function is similar to, and potentially more severe than, that of Nordhaus and Boyer (and hence mine). He places 'market'

---

[2] 'To say that without using such a rate, abatement would be minimal is not a very persuasive reason', *Economist* (30 April 2004: 80).
[3] See Arrow (1966), Feldstein (1970), Arrow and Kurz (1970) and Bradford (1975).

economic damage for 2.5°C warming at 0.25 per cent of GDP for rich countries and 0.5 per cent of GDP for poor countries. He adds a 'willingness-to-pay' for avoiding 'non-market' damage associated with 2.5°C, set in his main case at 2 per cent of GDP for rich countries and 1 per cent for poor countries. This means his global damage is in the vicinity of 2 per cent of world product for 2.5°C warming, higher than the Nordhaus–Boyer 1 per cent of world product at this benchmark and of course far higher than Mendelsohn's zero net global damage for this warming.

Manne also incorporates cheaper opportunities over time for switching to non-carbon energy, the consequence of a widening technological menu for non-carbon energy than is available in the Nordhaus–Boyer abatement cost function. His optimal path cuts warming from 4.5°C by 2150 in the baseline to 2.5°C ('descriptive') or 1.5°C ('prescriptive'). My optimal results, even with what Manne would call 'prescriptive' discounting, are more pessimistic, cutting warming by 2150 from a baseline 4.5°C to 3.6°C. Manne's optimal carbon tax path (descriptive case) is also in the same order of magnitude as mine. His optimal tax in 2100 is $250 per ton using his lower (2 per cent of rich country GDP) valuation of willingness-to-pay for insurance against non-market damage, and $550 per ton using his higher variant (4 per cent for willingness-to-pay). My optimal carbon tax in 2100 is $560. All of these estimates are radically higher than Mendelsohn's $20 estimate.

So the first point to emphasise is that at least by 2100 or so Manne's results broadly support mine, especially when judged in comparison to Mendelsohn's analysis. In particular, unlike Nordhaus and Boyer, Manne does not accept the idea that previous projections of baseline carbon emissions should be vastly reduced because of new analyses of greater resource limitations and more rapidly rising extraction costs. (Nordhaus and Boyer cut their baseline emissions by almost half from Nordhaus' earlier work, or from 25 GtC in 2100 to 13 GtC.)

Manne's bottom line does differ substantially from mine, however, on the question of how early abatement should occur. His optimal carbon tax in 2020 even with the high willingness-to-pay is only $40 per ton of carbon, whereas my optimal tax

is by then $220. This result appears to be driven in part by cheaper carbon reduction costs later in the horizon thanks to technological change, and in part by his use of a higher discount rate.[4] Thus, Manne's 'descriptive' optimal cuts from the baseline are small until about 2040, then become increasingly deep. The availability of a falling unit cost abatement function from future technology change is absent in the Excel version of the DICE model (even as adapted to DICE99CL), suggesting that comparable depth of optimal cutbacks might be achievable at considerably lower carbon taxes than in my estimates. When Manne uses 'prescriptive' discounting, his optimal cutback timing is much more like mine and in fact the cuts are considerably deeper.[5]

This brings us to the key question of what is somewhat unfairly called 'prescriptive' versus 'descriptive' discounting. The core issue here is whether there is a zero or non-zero rate of 'pure' time preference for impatience. Ironically, whereas Ramsey (1928) called non-zero pure time preference 'ethically indefensible', modern users of his optimisation framework for saving and consumption regularly apply an impatience rate of 3 per cent per year or so, which of course squeezes values over a timescale of centuries down to virtually nothing. The descriptionists invoke observed rates of return on capital as the basis for allowing pure time preference this high. However, the closest empirical measure of pure time preference for the consumer, or the risk-free rate for transferring consumption over time, should be the real Treasury bill rate. Treasury bills have no credit risk and no interest rate risk (because of their short maturity). I have re-estimated this rate for the USA, and for the period 1949 through 2003 it turns out to be 1.1 per cent

---

[4] 'Most of the abatement occurs during the period when technology has improved, and abatement becomes less costly' (Manne 2004: 54).

[5] In this case Manne's optimal cutback by 2030 is from 10 GtC to 4.5 GtC, whereas my optimal cut is from 12.3 GtC to 7.1 GtC. Manne's prescriptive optimal carbon tax in the 'immediate future' is $300 per ton, or twice mine. In part, this may reflect the fact that his prescriptive specification is that the rate of return (and the Social rate of time preference, SRTP) is only 1 per cent, whereas mine is higher (see n. *a*, in Cline (2004, table 1.4)). Manne's prescriptive run also does not shadow price capital.

(calculated from IMF 2004). If the consumer truly insisted on 3 per cent annually just to compensate her for impatience (i.e. with no expected rise in consumption level and hence utility), then the US government could not issue Treasury bills as cheaply as it historically has done. Importantly, my sensitivity analysis in table 1.3 shows that when the rate of pure time preference is raised to 1 per cent, the paths of abatement estimated as optimal at zero pure time preference (1 for the central case and 3 for the value-at-risk case) still have a benefit-cost ratio (BCR) above unity (although the Kyoto Protocol no longer does).

The real motivation of the descriptionists in using a higher rate of pure time preference is that if zero (or 1 per cent) pure time preference is used, a gap arises between the rate of return on capital and the consumer discount rate. But that is the whole point of the social CBA approach: this gap should be taken account of by shadow pricing a unit of capital as being worth more than a unit of consumption. That is what I do in my method.[6] I would argue that the descriptionists assume away the gap between the consumer's time preference and return on capital by mistakenly imputing a high pure time preference rate, whereas taxes and capital market imperfections are a more plausible explanation for the gap. The descriptionists are actually prescriptionists when it comes to assuming the perfect capital markets and zero tax distortions needed for their formulation of the optimal growth and saving models.

That still leaves the question of what is special about global warming discounting. First, it is *intergenerational*. There is a long tradition holding that intergenerational discounting may require a framework different from that used for within-generational discounting. Second, I would argue that any problem, which has a horizon of three centuries, should use the same discounting method I apply. So global warming is special only insofar as it is one of the few areas with this long a time horizon. This method would be even more important to apply in, for example, issues of disposal of atomic waste. Third, however, I have no real problem with applying the SRTP approach to public policy decisions on timeframes of one or two decades, either. If doing so finds that greater amounts of public investment should be taking place than currently occur, the proper response should be to seek greater investment in the other areas as well, rather than to block climate change abatement on grounds that other social expenditures should be undertaken instead. Consideration of the BCRs estimated using the SRTP, after properly shadow pricing capital effects, should then make choices among the various areas on an equal footing. Note once again that this does not mean simply 'applying a discount rate of 1.5 per cent' to judge other areas comparably with the analysis in my chapter, because the SRTP will depend on how rapidly *per capita* income is growing in the relevant (nearer-term) period, and capital effects must be shadow priced.

When it comes to dilemmas for choosing between the environment and today's poor, moreover, it seems to me the debate has missed a key consideration. A carbon tax would raise revenue, and the lack of revenue is a key obstacle to achieving many social goals. Global revenue from my optimal carbon tax of about $200 per ton in 2015, when industrial emissions would be curbed from a baseline amount of 9.2 GtC to 5.4 GtC by the tax, would raise $1.1 trillion.[7] That can buy a lot of schooling and medicine.[8] So rather than coming at the expense of social spending, it is quite possible in practice that carbon abatement could facilitate social spending. Because of revenue realities, action in the climate change part of the Copenhagen Consensus agenda can perhaps more realistically be seen as complementary to, and enabling of, action in the other issue areas, rather than competitive with them.

---

[6] It should be pointed out, moreover, that in the initial decades of my baseline, the SRTP is not as low as the 1.5 per cent average over three centuries. Real *per capita* income rises at an average of 1.4 per cent from 1995 to 2015, so with an elasticity of marginal utility of 1.5, and with pure time preference at zero, the SRTP is 2.1 per cent.

[7] It is often pointed out that environmental taxes are a fragile basis for revenue because if they are successful they suppress the source of their own revenue. The point here is that a large revenue would be generated even after taking account of the reduction in emissions from baseline amounts.

[8] Although the more the revenue is diverted to social spending rather than used to reduce output-distorting taxes, the higher the abatement cost.

Returning more specifically to Manne's Perspective paper 1.2, he suggests that my 'value-at-risk' case is an inappropriate basis for policy. I acknowledge that it is included primarily as a warning rather than an immediate call for action as severe as it indicates. Nonetheless, there is something fundamentally disturbing in the fact that society values its money highly enough to take out insurance against the 95-percentile bad outcome in the financial sphere, but is unprepared to do the same when it comes to policies affecting the environment and future generations. At the very least the results for the value-at-risk case should be seen as supporting the extent of action called for in the central optimal abatement case (1) by illuminating how much greater warming damage, and hence warranted abatement, could be in the high-damage tail of the probability distribution.

References

Andronova, N.G. and M.E. Schlesinger, 2001: Objective estimation of the probability density function for climate sensitivity, *Journal of Geophysical Research*, **106**(D19), 22605–12

Arrow, K.J., 1966: Discounting and public investment criteria, in A.V. Kneese and S.C. Smith (eds.), *Water Research*, Johns Hopkins University Press, Baltimore, MD, 13–32

Arrow, K.J. and M. Kurz, 1970: *Public investment, the rate of return and optimal fiscal policy*, Johns Hopkins University Press, Baltimore, MD

Bradford, D.F., 1975: Constraints on government investment opportunities and the choice of the discount rate, *American Economic Review*, **65**(5), 887–99

Cato, 2003: Global warming: the state of the debate, Conference held at the Cato Institute, Washington, DC, 3 December 2003; proceedings available at www.cato.org/events/gw031212.html

Cline, W.R., 2004: Climate change, chapter 1 in this volume, available at www.copenhagenconsensus.com

Feldstein, M.S., 1970: Financing in the evaluation of public expenditure, *Discussion Papers*, **132** Harvard Institute of Economic Research, Cambridge, MA, August

IMF, 2004: *International financial statistics*, April, CD-Rom

Manne, A.S., 2004: Perspective paper 1.2 in this volume, available at www.copenhagenconsensus.com

Mendelsohn, R., 2004: Perspective paper 1.1 in this volume, available at www.copenhagenconsensus.com

Mendelsohn, R. and Neumann, 1999: *The impact of climate change on the United States economy*, Cambridge University Press, Cambridge

Nordhaus, W.D. and J. Boyer, 2000: *Warming the world: economic models of global warming*, MIT Press, Cambridge, MA

Ramsey, F. P., 1928: A mathematical theory of saving, *Economic Journal*, **138**(152), 543–59

Communicable Diseases

ANNE MILLS AND SAM SHILLCUTT

Summary

The Challenge of Communicable Disease

Between the 1950s and the 1990s, the world saw enormous health improvements. However, developing countries have benefited unequally from health gains, with many, especially in sub-Saharan Africa (SSA), continuing to experience high mortality. Children bear a major burden of ill health, with infectious and parasitic diseases the main killers. Adults experience substantial premature mortality. Within countries, poorer groups have considerably worse health than the better off. Analysis of avoidable mortality highlights the importance of communicable disease, which represents around 90 per cent of all avoidable mortality in almost all age–sex groups. The benefits of research mean that tools and approaches now exist to address the great majority of communicable disease, most notably malaria, TB and HIV/AIDS, as well as vaccine preventable diseases. However, large numbers of people do not have effective access to prevention and treatment, and die as a result.

The chapter focuses on three opportunities:

- Malaria control
- HIV/AIDS control
- Strengthening basic health services.

This categorisation has been chosen largely because malaria and HIV/AIDS are major causes of disease

Anne Mills and Sam Shillcutt are members of the Health Economics and Financing Programme (HEFP) which is funded by the Department for International Development of the United Kingdom. However the Department for International Development can accept no responsibility for any information provided or views expressed. We are very grateful to Catherine Goodman and Fern Terris-Prestholt for comments on the final draft, and more generally to our HEFP colleagues for support in tracing literature and discussion of drafts.

burden and economic losses; cost-effective interventions are known to exist for their control; there is recent literature which can be drawn on to estimate costs and benefits; and these diseases are currently the focus of world attention. Basic health services have been chosen as the third opportunity since they address a major part of the disease burden, and explicitly represent the infrastructure that needs to be in place for people's main health needs to be met.

The Economic Benefits of Improved Health

The relationship between *illness* and *income* is complex. Effects are felt both directly (through the immediate impact of ill health on productive activities) and indirectly, via the effects of illness on fertility, morbidity, mortality and intellectual capacity, and hence on the labour force size, composition and quality, and on the capacity of countries to engage in the global economy. Empirical studies of the relationship between disease and income fall into two categories: microeconomic and macroeconomic. The former study the link between disease and ill health at the household or individual level, usually documenting the costs imposed by disease on households but not explicitly the benefits of disease control, and categorising costs as direct and indirect. Such estimates are likely to underestimate the true economic impact of a disease on income, since they neglect the impact of *coping strategies* and the broader, dynamic consequences of disease for the economy as a whole. In contrast, macroeconomic studies assess the influence of a disease on income in cross-country comparisons. In principle, they are better able than microeconomic studies to reflect the wide-ranging and dynamic implications of ill health, but raise concerns as to the extent to which other influences on economic growth are adequately allowed for. Again, such studies usually document the cost of disease, but only by implication the benefits of *disease reduction*.

The most abundant literature is that on the cost-effectiveness of interventions, comparing intervention cost with benefits expressed in terms of health outcomes. Systematic approaches have recently been applied to the synthesis of both epidemiological studies and economic studies, making judgements on the quality of evidence, and facilitating conclusions on both the health outcomes of interventions and cost-effectiveness. However, using these studies to evaluate the efficiency of health interventions in units that are comparable across economic sectors requires placing a monetary value on human life.

Given the limitations of the literature in terms of both quantity and quality, and the need to be comprehensive and consistent, estimates of costs and benefits were where possible calculated by the authors based on the literature rather than limiting the chapter only to costs and benefits actually provided in the literature. Several different approaches were adopted. For the two diseases (malaria and HIV), evidence was drawn from three different sources:

- Studies of the macroeconomic impact of the disease
- Studies of the cost-effectiveness of interventions
- Evidence of the costs and health benefits of large-scale country programmes.

For basic health services, evidence was drawn from two different sources:

- Regression analyses that measured the efficiency of health expenditure in generating health outcomes
- The costs and health benefits of a package of interventions recommended in the 1993 *World Development Report*.

Where possible, costs and benefits were summarised as both annualised net benefits (ANB) adjusted for purchasing power parity (PPP) and benefit-cost ratios (BCR). A year of life lost was valued at 2003 *per capita* Gross National Income (GNI) (the ceiling ratio), and a discount rate (DCR) of 3 per cent applied. The sensitivity analyses tested a DCR of 6 per cent and a common ceiling ratio

of Int\$3,830 (the mean GNI for low- and middle-income countries). To assist comparison with other chapters in the volume, further sensitivity analysis tested values of US\$1,250 and \$100,000 per life.

Control of Malaria

Major reductions in the malaria burden and its eradication from temperate parts of the world gave reason for optimism in the mid-twentieth century. However, in the 1980s, commitment to programmes waned and resistance to medicines and insecticides increased. With the increased use of new combination drugs and a greater international commitment to financing malaria control, there is again reason to believe that the burden of malaria can be substantially reduced. SSA experiences over 90 per cent of the global burden of malaria; malaria causes around 20 per cent of the mortality of children under 5; and it is the most important single infectious agent causing death in young children. Cost-benefit estimates were therefore made for SSA, drawing on macroeconomic studies; on cost-effectiveness studies of insecticide-treated mosquito nets, intermittent presumptive treatment of pregnant women (IPTp), and combination therapy (ACT); and evidence from recent successful malaria control efforts in the KwaZulu Natal province of South Africa. Based on estimates from macroeconomic models, we predicted that the ANB of eliminating 50 per cent of malaria between 2002 and 2015 would be Int\$10–37 bn, with BCRs of 1.9–4.7. For the package of malaria control measures these were Int\$47.54 bn and 17, respectively. The ANB of the successful South African malaria control programme was Int\$19 m, and it was cost-saving.

Control of HIV/AIDS

The HIV/AIDS pandemic is devastating the economies of many low- and middle-income countries. Current estimates are that more than 22 m people have already died, 34–46 m are currently living with HIV/AIDS and 5.3 m new infections occur each year. The scale of the problem is such that it is considered a development issue and global security threat. The costs and benefits of approaches to addressing the epidemic were estimated, drawing on four different sources of information: a macroeconomic model of the gains to prevention in several north African and Middle Eastern countries at the 'nascent' stage of the epidemic; the costs and benefits of successful control in Thailand, at the 'concentrated' stage of the epidemic; evidence on the cost-effectiveness of a number of specific interventions in Africa; and estimates of the cost and health impact of the UN General Assembly Special Session (UNGASS) global programme (June 2001). For the group of North African–Middle Eastern countries, intervening now was estimated to save 15–30 per cent of 2000 GNP by 2025. In Thailand, the ANB of the AIDS control was Int$3.4 bn and BCR 14.2. BCRs of individual interventions were highly variable, but generally exceeded 2, with condom distribution and blood safety having BCRs of 466. The UNGASS package had ANB of Int$359.4 bn and BCR of 50.

Basic Health Services

The great majority of health interventions depend for successful and sustained implementation on an infrastructure of basic health services, consisting of community-based services, health centres and local hospitals. These can address much of the burden of ill health, including that from maternal and neonatal conditions, childhood illnesses such as diarrhoea, ARI and vaccine preventable diseases, and malaria, TB and HIV/AIDS. During the 1990s recommendations were made on a package of priority interventions to be delivered at this level. We estimated the costs and benefits of scaling up basic health services drawing first on evidence for Heavily Indebted Poor Countries (HIPC) countries of the relationship between health expenditure and health gains and the necessary increase in public spending to reach the Millennium Development Goal (MDG) child mortality target; and secondly estimates of the costs and health benefits of the package of interventions recommended in the 1993 *World Development Report*. The first approach gives ANB of Int$18.2 bn and BCR 2.1 (though benefits only for children are included). The 1993 *World Development Report* package gives ANB of Int$534.1 bn and BCR of 2.6.

Conclusions

All the sources of data used have severe shortcomings, which must inform the interpretation of the costs and benefits. In particular:

- The macroeconomic literature is quite inadequate as there are only two recent studies on malaria, and models for HIV require further development.
- Evidence on intervention costs and effects comes mainly from epidemiological trials; evidence of costs and health effects of large-scale programme implementation is very limited. Health effects were translated into a monetary value using a somewhat arbitrary ceiling ratio.
- For the basic health services opportunity, benefits only for children are valued in one approach although other population groups will benefit.
- Evidence from successful programmes is hard to interpret, since external factors may also have affected changes in health effects.

In addition, our estimates suffer from three further shortcomings:

- Available costs were usually costs to the provider, excluding costs to users
- We were unable to be explicit on which groups would benefit most under each of the challenges, and in particular on the extent to which the poorest would benefit.
- Macroeconomic estimates of benefits and calculations made from cost-effectiveness evidence do not reflect the same dimensions of benefits: the former reflects impact on income, while the second seeks to reflect impact on human welfare more broadly.

Given the weakness of the evidential base, it would be unwise to read too much into detailed differences between or within opportunities. However, a clear message from the calculations is that, in general, the benefits from investing in communicable disease control greatly exceed the costs. It remains unclear whether greater priority should be given to controlling one specific disease, such as malaria or HIV/AIDS, or to a package of priority health services, and the decision will depend to a considerable degree on total funding available. However it cannot be emphasised enough that these three opportunities are not completely independent – both malaria and HIV/AIDS control must include a substantial component of strengthening health services if they are to be successful.

Finally, it should be noted that the productivity of health expenditure is likely to be greater both in a supportive policy environment, and where complementary investments take place, for example in female education.

The Challenge of Communicable Disease

Between the 1950s and the 1990s, the world saw enormous improvements in health. Between 1960 and 1995, life expectancy in low-income countries improved by twenty-two years, in contrast to nine years in developed countries (Jha and Mills 2002). However, developing countries have benefited unequally from health gains (WHO 2003a): the large life expectancy gap between developed and developing countries in the 1950s has changed to a large gap between developing countries with persisting high mortality (mainly in SSA), and those who have experienced rapidly falling mortality (figure 2.1). For example, average adult life expectancy is below forty years in several countries in the developing world, particularly in those severely affected by HIV such as Botswana. Sierra Leone has the highest mortality rates for infants and children under five years old in the World (World Bank 2003a).

Of the 57 m deaths in the world in 2002, nearly 20 per cent were children under five, and 98 per cent of these were in developing countries (http://www.fic.nih.gov/dcpp/gbd.html). Communicable disea-

Table 2.1. Leading Causes of Death in Children in Developing Countries, 2002

Rank	Cause	No. (000)	% of all deaths
1	Perinatal conditions	2,375	23.1
2	Lower respiratory infections	1,856	18.1
3	Diarrhoeal diseases	1,566	15.2
4	Malaria	1,098	10.7
5	Measles	551	5.4
6	Congenital anomalies	386	3.8
7	HIV/AIDS	370	3.6
8	Pertussis	301	2.9
9	Tetanus	185	1.8
10	Protein-energy malnutrition	138	1.3
	Other causes	1,437	14.0
	Total	**10,263**	**100**

Source: WHO (2003a, p. 182).

ses represent seven out of the top ten causes of child deaths in developing countries, and account for around 60 per cent of all such deaths (table 2.1). Just over 30 per cent of all deaths in developing countries are of adults aged 15–59, in contrast to 20 per cent in developed countries, representing a substantial problem of premature adult mortality with strong economic implications. Within countries, the poorer groups have substantially poorer health than the better off: for example in Cambodia under-five mortality in the poorest quintile, 147 per 1,000, was three times that of the richest quintile, and in the Central African Republic, under-five mortality of 189/1,000 in the poorest quintile was double that of the richest quintile (World Bank 2004a).

The analysis of avoidable mortality undertaken by Working Group 5 of the Commission on Macroeconomics and Health (CMH) highlights the importance of focusing on communicable disease (Jha and Mills 2002). Avoidable mortality is a population's excess risk of dying before age 70, as calculated by comparison with the death rates in another population: in this case, non-smokers in the richest countries. Table 2.2 shows that almost 90 per cent of deaths in children under five are avoidable, and 84 per cent of deaths in women aged 5–29. Avoidable mortality due largely to communicable disease

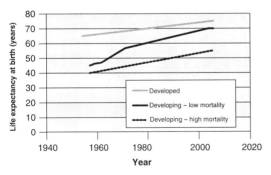

Figure 2.1. *Life expectancy at birth, 1955–2002*
Source: WHO (2003).

Table 2.2. Risk of Dying and Avoidable Mortality (%), Low- and Middle-Income Countries, 1998

Risk of dying	Males at ages			Females at ages		
	0–4	5–29	30–69	0–4	5–29	30–69
Low- and middle-income countries (a)	8.6	6.1	35.0	8.2	5.6	26.7
Non-smoking, high-income population (b)	1.2	2.2	19.2	1.0	0.9	12.6
Excess risk of dying (avoidable mortality) in low- and middle-income countries (c = (a) − (b))	7.3	3.9	15.7	7.2	4.7	14.2
Relative contribution of avoidable mortality to risk of dying in low- and middle-income countries (d = (c)/(a))	86	63	45	88	84	53
Relative contribution of Group 1^a causes to avoidable mortality	91	94	80	93	97	91

Note: ^{a}Communicable diseases, maternal conditions, perinatal conditions and nutritional deficiencies.
Source: Jha and Mills (2002).

represents around 90 per cent of all avoidable mortality in all age–sex classes other than middle-aged men, for whom it is 80 per cent.

Historically, rapid declines in mortality have been the result of access to better housing, sanitation and education, growing incomes, and public health measures such as vaccination. The benefits of research mean that tools and approaches now exist to address the great majority of the burden of communicable disease, most notably malaria, TB and HIV/AIDS, as well as vaccine preventable diseases. This helps to explain the current international focus on tackling these diseases. However, as table 2.1 demonstrates, large numbers of people do not have effective access to prevention and treatment, and die as a result. For example, coverage of DPT3[1] is under 50 per cent for children in households living below the poverty line of $1 per day (World Bank 2004a); and only 2 per cent of children are protected from malaria by sleeping under insecticide-treated mosquito nets in SSA (WHO 2003b).

The control of communicable disease – depending on the disease – is achieved by some combination of action through a health service infrastructure and through specific targeted efforts which in some instances depend on the infrastructure and in others are independent of it. Hence the evaluation of the case for controlling specific communicable

diseases cannot ignore its *relationship with the health system*. However, issues of whether successful health improvement can be achieved by general health system strengthening, or by targeted efforts focused on specific diseases, have been the subject of considerable controversy (Oliveira-Cruz, Kurowski and Mills 2003). The reality is that with the very unusual exception of diseases that can be eradicated (notably smallpox in the past and polio in the future), sustainable health improvement requires some combination of a strengthened and accessible health service plus focused efforts to strengthen the control of priority diseases. Nonetheless, given limited resources, there are choices to make, which this chapter seeks to evaluate.

The chapter has chosen to focus on three opportunities:

• Malaria control
• HIV/AIDS control
• Strengthened basic health services.

As emphasised above, this definition of the opportunities should not be taken to imply that these are completely distinct efforts. Expanded and improved basic health services are a precondition for malaria and HIV/AIDS control, though they also address a much broader range of conditions including other communicable diseases such as acute respiratory infections, diarrhoeal diseases,

[1] The third dose of the diptheria, pertussis, tetanus (DPT) vaccine, commonly used as a proxy for vaccination coverage.

TB, vaccine preventable diseases and maternal–perinatal conditions. This categorisation of opportunities has been chosen largely because malaria and HIV/AIDS are major causes of the disease burden and economic losses; cost-effective interventions are known to exist for their control; there is recent literature which can be drawn on to estimate costs and benefits; and these diseases are currently the focus of world attention. Strengthened basic health services have been chosen as the third opportunity since they address a major part of the disease burden affecting poor countries, and explicitly represent the infrastructure that needs to be in place for people's main health needs to be met.

The following section provides an overview of the economic benefits of improved health, discusses the availability of evidence and outlines the overall approach taken in the chapter to estimating costs and benefits. Subsequent sections address each opportunity. A final section discusses methodological weaknesses and limitations, and draws conclusions.

Assessing the Opportunities

The Economic Benefits of Improved Health and the Availability of Evidence

Health has both *consumption* and *investment* benefits. In other words, it is valued for its own sake, as well as a means to achieve other goals (such as a good income). The relationship between illness and income is complex, as illustrated in figure 2.2 (Ruger, Jamison and Bloom 2001). Effects are felt both directly (through the immediate impact of ill health on productive activities) and indirectly, via the effects of illness on fertility, morbidity, mortality and intellectual capacity, and hence on the labour force size, composition and quality, and on the capacity of countries to engage in the global economy.

Disease has been shown to have a major impact on the economy through such effects on productivity, education and investment. As people fall ill, they are less likely to be able to work, and less likely

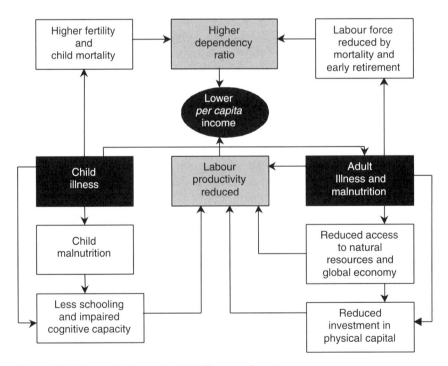

Figure 2.2. *Channels through which illness reduces income*
Source: *Ruger, Jamison and Bloom (2001).*

to be productive if they can. People have weaker incentives to invest in their education if it is uncertain that they will be alive to reap the benefits. There is also less incentive for people to save for their retirement, as shorter life spans reduce the value of saving and investment in productive assets. As foreign investors withdraw their money from disease-affected areas, the economic costs of disease are exacerbated (Bloom and Canning 2000). However, it has been argued that effective intervention can thrust the economy just as powerfully in a positive direction. Better health can lead to a demographic transition and economic growth in the long term. Initial reductions in child mortality are followed by a decline in fertility. As the flood of new children matures and reaches working age, and a larger proportion of people are able to contribute to the economy, the wealth of the society rises substantially, as is argued to have happened in East Asia between 1965 and 1992 (Bloom and Canning 2000). The massive improvements in public health that occurred in East Asia between 1965 and 1990 most powerfully show these effects, and may have accounted for as much as 1.68 percentage points of its annual economic growth rate during this period (Wagstaff 2002).

The CMH has argued that the impact of health on economic development has been underestimated (Ruger, Jamison and Bloom 2001; Alleyne and Cohen 2002), and that health improvements globally during the twentieth century contributed as much, or more, to improvements in economic welfare as the innovations and expansion in material goods and services. Such conclusions have been drawn from studies which seek to explore the determinants of economic growth – and, in particular, the influence of improved health status. From the perspective of this chapter, this literature presents two problems: it is not disease-specific; and it does not address well what type of action might best improve health.

Empirical studies of the relationship between disease and income fall into two categories: microeconomic and macroeconomic. The former study the link between income and disease/ill health at household or individual level. Usually they document the costs that disease imposes on the household, but not explicitly the benefits of *disease control*. Costs are commonly categorised as direct (household and government expenditure on prevention and treatment), and indirect (loss of productivity due to illness and death). There are strong reasons to believe that this simple methodology does not measure the true economic impact of a disease, not least because in response, households and firms adapt their productive activities, or 'cope'. *Coping mechanisms* are defined as strategies adopted by family members, friends and colleagues to minimise the effects of an illness on the welfare of all concerned (Over et al. 1992). Sauerborn, Adams and Hien (1996) identified eleven different kinds of household coping behaviours in response to illness episodes of all kinds in rural Burkina Faso. The most commonly used strategy was intra-household labour substitution in response to lost work time of household members. Direct costs were usually met by mobilising cash reserves and savings, selling livestock, or receiving gifts from other households.

Such strategies may have knock-on effects through depleted capital stock, lost savings and indebtedness. The sale of assets such as livestock potentially jeopardises the household asset base, with households emerging more vulnerable and less able to cope with further crises (Sauerborn, Adams and Hien 1996). A household without livestock, and unable to rely on gifts, may be forced to take out loans which could lead to serious debt and future impoverishment (Over et al. 1996). These knock-on effects ultimately affect supply or production through low saving and investment. This also means that the causal relationship by which disease affects the economy may not necessarily be through sick labour only, but also through lost capital and purchasing power.

The potential for labour substitution crucially affects the degree to which any loss of time is translated into a *loss of output*. Unemployment and underemployment are common features of underdeveloped economies, and farming is often undertaken communally, in households or extended families. In the event of temporary disability of a household member, the family workforce may provide a cushion, limiting the consequent loss of output. During some seasons, agricultural underemployment may be so prevalent that time lost by sick individuals can be fully compensated for. In the industrial and service sectors, other members of the workforce may similarly cover to some extent for sick colleagues.

However, even if market output is maintained, there may be costs associated with labour substitution, depending on the value of the activities from which the substituting labour is withdrawn (Over *et al.* 1996). Moreover, assessment of a single measure of household output, such as agricultural production, will not capture the total impact on household welfare, as it ignores the quantity and quality of home production such as food preparation or child care, and participation in other activities, such as education or social organisations.

Coping strategies are likely to respond not only to actual illness, but also to the *risk* of disease. The risk of poor health status may have a pervasive effect on economic incentives, behaviour and strategies (Stevens 1977). Households and firms respond with anticipatory coping strategies, ranging from insurance mechanisms to changes in the organisation of productive activities (Over *et al.* 1996). Although formal insurance is rare in developing countries, informal mechanisms are common, including social networks and community organisations, and incur administrative costs which produce efficiency losses in comparison with a risk-free setting. Precautionary measures affecting the organisation of economic activity are likely to have wide-reaching economic effects. High rates of absenteeism may engender labour supply responses such as limiting staff specialisation and maintaining labour reserves to reduce the risk of labour shortages at key times of the year, reducing the average labour productivity of all staff. Households may respond to the risk of high financial expenditure for serious illness by reducing their level of investment, or investing in assets which have higher liquidity but lower returns. Finally, the risk of disease may affect reproductive as well as productive strategies – for example, increasing desired family size to insure against high rates of child mortality and increase the family's ability to cope when illness occurs (Over *et al.* 1996).

The impact of these anticipatory coping strategies cannot be captured by comparing households or firms exposed to the same degree of risk because they reduce the average productivity of all households and firms, not just those experiencing illness during the study period. Microeconomic estimates

are thus likely to be an underestimate of the impact of disease on income.

In contrast, macroeconomic studies assess the influence of a disease on national income in cross-country comparisons, and methods and, data permitting, are better able than microeconomic studies to reflect the wide-ranging and dynamic implications of ill health. Again such studies usually document the cost of disease, but only by implication the benefits of *reduced disease*. Compared to microeconomic studies, the volume of the macroeconomic literature is far more limited. Apart from the many econometric difficulties encountered, such as omitted variable bias, there are problems in measures and data on disease prevalence, leading to some uncertainty on whether such studies really are picking up the impact of the disease in question.

There is some considerable overlap in the literature on the economic impact of malaria and that of HIV in terms of the mechanisms of influence. To a considerable extent, ill health has common effects on households and the broader economy, though these can also differ depending on the nature of the disease. In particular, HIV/AIDS affects primarily adults, and malaria affects mainly children (in high-burden settings), leading to some distinctly different effects (for example, malaria in children is unlikely to lead to the dissolution of a household, whereas HIV might well do so; severe malaria in children can have long-term effects on intellectual development). For convenience in reflecting the body of evidence on each of the diseases, the detailed evidence on economic impact is included in the disease-specific sections, although this inevitably leads to some repetition of mechanisms between sections.

Studies – of which there are many – which evaluate actual interventions have almost always employed the analytical approach of cost-effectiveness analysis (CEA) rather than cost-benefit analysis (CBA), thus calculating cost per unit of health effect (such as a life saved, or a Disability-Adjusted Life Year (DALY)[2] averted). Using these studies

---

[2] DALYs are probably now the most commonly used unit of health outcome. They sum years of life gained and years lived with disability, weighted by the severity of the disability.

to evaluate the efficiency of health interventions in units that are comparable across economic sectors requires a *monetary value* to be placed on a human life. This value, the value of a statistical life (VSL), is intended to represent the marginal cost or benefit of saving a life to society (Folland, Goodman and Stano 1997). Two approaches may be taken to determine the VSL. The *human capital* approach assumes that productivity is a proxy for utility and estimates the VSL in terms of the present value of an individual's future earnings. It can be assumed to provide a lower bound on the value of life. Alternatively, a *willingness-to-pay* (WTP) approach may be used, which assumes that an individual's preferences are reflected in his actual or hypothetical choices according to market prices. To translate cost-per-health effect into a monetary metric, either of these approaches may be used. While research on the willingness-to-pay for a human life has been carried out in high-income countries (Klose 1999), estimates for low-income countries rely largely on expert opinion. For example the CMH argued that, conventionally, each DALY can be valued at 'a multiple of annual income' (CMH 2001). Lower cut-off points are more normally applied in low- and middle-income country settings: for example $25 per DALY as a criterion for a 'highly attractive' intervention, and $150 for an 'attractive' intervention (c. 1996 values) (WHO 1996a). In contrast, it has been argued that the UK cut-off is around £30,000 (c. $54,000), and possibly as high as £45,000 (c. $80,000) (Devlin and Parkin 2004), reflecting approximately two times *per capita* income.

Two other issues arise in drawing on this cost-effectiveness literature, which stem from its origin in clinical trials. First, the evidence of efficacy produced by trials may provide a poor guide to the impact expected from routine service provision.[3] Secondly, such trials usually evaluate an intervention delivered on its own (e.g. insecticide treated

nets (ITNs) for malaria control) whereas in reality packages of interventions are provided (e.g. ITNs plus treatment of child fevers). Interventions may be synergistic or competing, making it difficult to extrapolate the benefits of packages. Finally, the quantity of literature is very limited with respect to both geographical coverage and the range of interventions that require evaluation.

Nonetheless, these cost-effectiveness studies represent an important source of evidence. Moreover, systematic approaches have recently been applied to the synthesis of both epidemiological studies and economic studies,[4] making judgements on the quality of the evidence, and drawing conclusions on both the health outcomes of interventions and cost-effectiveness. Given the existence of these syntheses for both malaria and HIV/AIDS interventions, this chapter relies on these reviews rather than the original studies.

Benefits of disease control include not only health benefits, but also resource savings, as when preventive interventions reduce the need for treatment. While some cost-effectiveness studies take these into account, in general they are often neglected, in part because of equity concerns: resources are saved only if used in the first place, and those population groups which have worst access to care will spend less (and have less spent on them).

Methodological Approach Adopted

Given the limitations of the literature, the following approach was adopted. In general, conservative assumptions were made. For each opportunity, several different approaches were adopted to estimate costs and benefits. For the two diseases (malaria and HIV), evidence was drawn from three different sources:

- Studies of the macroeconomic impact of the disease
- Studies of the cost-effectiveness of interventions
- Evidence of the costs and health benefits of large-scale programmes.

For basic health services, evidence was drawn from three different sources:

---

[3] Epidemiologists distinguish efficacy, that obtained under ideal conditions (usually a research study), with effectiveness, that obtained under more normal service conditions.

[4] The Cochrane library is one of the most up-to-date catalogues of reviews on the appropriateness and effectiveness of medical interventions, and can be accessed at http://www.cochrane.org/reviews/clibintro.htm

Table 2.3. Value of a DALY/YLL, 2001

Region	2001 PPP-adjusted *per capita* GNI (2003 Int$)	2001 *per capita* GNI (2003 US$)
Low- and middle-income	3,830	1,160
East Asia and Pacific	3,790	900
Europe and Central Asia	6,320	1,970
Latin America and Caribbean	6,900	3,580
Middle East and North Africa	5,430	2,220
South Asia	2,570	450
SSA	1,750	460
Thailand	6,230	1,940
South Africa	10,910	2,820

Source: Figures taken from World Bank (2003a).

- Regression analyses that measured the effectiveness of health expenditure in generating health outcomes
- A major report to determine the cost of interventions that should take priority
- An analysis that determined the costs and benefits of a package of interventions that was recommended in the 1993 *World Development Report*.

Given the limitations of the literature in terms of both quantity and quality, and the need to try and be comprehensive in estimates of costs and benefits, these were where possible calculated by the authors based on the literature rather than limiting the chapter only to the costs and benefits actually provided in the literature. This also enables the chapter to seek some degree of consistency in terms of years and scope of costs and benefits. Since the literature has very limited and patchy geographical coverage, rather than make heroic assumptions extrapolating country-specific analyses to the whole developing world, costs and benefits were calculated for the geographical entity from where the evidence came. While this means that estimates cover very different areas, taken together the evidence gives a sense of the *overall balance of costs and benefits*.

Given the geographical focus of this chapter, benefits accrue to the populations of low- and middle-income countries and, if valued according to exchange rate conversions, would understate benefits when compared to another challenge where benefits to high-income populations are included. Costs and benefits were therefore adjusted for purchasing power parity (PPP), and expressed in 2003 international dollars (Int$).[5] Each year of life lost (YLL), or DALY,[6] was valued at *per capita* Gross National Income (GNI). Depending on the population served, the corresponding GNI was used to represent this value, or ceiling ratio (table 2.3). While this choice of value is arbitrary, it is a conservative reflection of the level of its income the developed world is willing to spend on saving a year of life. To avoid disadvantaging low-income countries (since the lower their income, the lower the value of benefits), results were recalculated in the sensitivity analysis using a standard value of Int$3,830/YLL or DALY averted, the mean GNI for low-and middle-income countries. To assist comparison across other chapters in this volume, further sensitivity analysis valued benefits at values of US$1,250 and $100,000 per life (appendix 2, p. 108).

[5] Monetary values were converted from US$ to International dollars (Int$) by dividing the ratio of the PPP conversion factor to the local currency unit/US$ exchange rate (World Bank 2003a). To represent global regions, an average of the ratios of all countries with available data was taken.

[6] Both were used, depending on the original source. In general, for the conditions considered here which cause death, YLLs dominate in the DALY and so the values are very similar.

Costs were calculated from a *social perspective* (i.e. including costs to both providers and users) where data permitted, though they often reflected provider costs only. Reductions in treatment expenditures arising from disease prevention were included where possible.

To make results comparable to those in other chapters in the volume, estimates were presented in terms of annualised net benefit (ANB) and benefit cost ratios (BCR). Where absolute levels of benefits and costs could not be estimated from information given in the literature, benefits were estimated from cost-effectiveness ratios by dividing them by the ceiling ratio appropriate to the study. Where it was possible to estimate total costs and benefits, net benefit was calculated (1):

$$(1) \quad NB_{Individual} = (R_C * Benefits) - Costs$$

where R_c represents the ceiling ratio. Evidence of absolute costs and health benefits was given in two estimates from successful programmes (Brown 2003; Muheki, Barnes and McIntyre 2004). Costs and benefits for individuals were calculated for other estimates, and scaled up to incremental target coverage levels for the population in need (PIN) (2):

$$(2) \quad NB_{Total} = NB_{Individual} * Coverage * PIN$$

Where possible, costs and benefits were estimated for the period 2002–15 (to coincide with the MDGs) and MDG targets were used, where relevant, to establish the desirable scale of interventions. Costs and benefits were adjusted by a DCR of 3 per cent. Sensitivity analyses were used to explore the sensitivity of costs and benefits to changed assumptions, including a higher DCR (6 per cent) and the common valuations for life and life years.

For all models, it was assumed that scaled-up coverage targets were achieved instantaneously. Where specific evidence was unavailable, parameter values were extrapolated assuming linear growth rates and relationships between data points calculated as incremental values: additional amounts relative to the costs and benefits of existing programmes.

Control of Malaria

Identification and Description

Introductory Statistics

Malaria is the most important of the parasitic diseases of humans. Transmission occurs in 103 countries; more than 1bn people live in malarious areas; and between 1m and 3m people die from malaria each year. Malaria was eradicated from North America, Europe and Russia over the twentieth century, and for a period was substantially controlled in much of South Asia, but has resurged in recent decades. The increased threat from malaria is particularly a result of international neglect of the disease in the 1980s onwards, following the realisation that malaria eradication was not feasible and major and increasing problems of resistance to the most commonly used drugs and insecticides.

Malaria is caused by four different species of the genus *Plasmodium*, of which the most dangerous is *P. falciparum*. Human infection occurs when the malaria vector, a female mosquito of the *Anopheles* genus, inoculates sporozoites from its salivary glands when it bites humans. The parasite reproduces within the human host, and the disease is transmitted by gametocytes in the blood meal when further female anophelene mosquitoes feed on the infected individual.

Epidemiological Description

Malaria is primarily a tropical disease. *P. falciparum* predominates in SSA, which as a result bears over 85 per cent of the disease burden and 90 per cent of malarial deaths. *P. vivax* is more common in Central America and the Indian subcontinent. The epidemiology of malaria is complex, varying considerably from place to place. Transmission is termed 'stable' when infection occurs all year round. In these settings, small children are infected repeatedly early in life, and morbidity and mortality are considerable (WHO 2002a; UNICEF 2003). Through repeated infection children develop immunity, meaning that as adults they may suffer febrile episodes but are very unlikely to die from malaria. Pregnant women are the other population group at high risk, since their immunity is impaired, especially in the first pregnancy. In contrast, where transmission is low, unstable or very focal (termed 'unstable transmission'), immunity is not acquired and symptomatic disease may occur at all ages. Areas with unstable malaria are prone to epidemics – for example, northern India, Sri Lanka, Southeast Asia, southern Africa – which can cause many deaths.

The number of children dying of malaria rose substantially in eastern and southern Africa during the first half of the 1990s as compared to the 1980s, while in West Africa there was little change in the overall malaria mortality rate in children (WHO 2003b). The most likely explanation is the rapidly increasing levels of resistance to chloroquine (the most widely used treatment drug) in eastern and southern Africa.

Defining and Measuring the Malaria Disease Burden

Defining and measuring the health burden of malaria presents some major difficulties.

Mortality   Estimating the number of deaths due to malaria is notoriously problematic (Snow *et al.* 1999). *Post-mortem* questionnaires are relatively insensitive for detecting malaria deaths, because of the similarities between the symptoms of malaria and other severe diseases, such as pneumonia (Snow *et al.* 1992). Official reporting systems are often unreliable, as in many areas of Africa the majority of deaths occur at home and are not formally registered.

Malaria can contribute to death in young children in three main ways:

- an overwhelming acute infection can kill a child quickly
- repeated infections contribute to the development of severe anaemia, which substantially increases the risk of death
- low birthweight, a frequent consequence of malaria infection in pregnancy, is the major risk factor for death in the first month of life.

In addition, repeated infections make young children more susceptible to other common childhood diseases.

In SSA it is estimated that around 20 per cent of mortality of children under five is due to malaria, and malaria is the most important single infectious agent causing death in young children. Around 1m deaths (range 0.744–1.3m) are estimated to occur in Africa, more than 75 per cent of them in children (Breman 2001).

Episodes of Uncomplicated Malaria   Uncomplicated malaria is typically treated on the basis of clinical symptoms alone. 400–900m acute febrile episodes are thought to occur yearly in African children under five living in endemic areas (Breman 2001). If 30–60 per cent of these children were parasitaemic, as reported in some studies, malaria cases in children would be 200–450m annually. Older age groups in Africa have around 0.4–1 episodes of malaria a year, and probably 2 or more febrile episodes. World-wide, there may be well over 2bn febrile episodes annually resembling malaria.

Severe Disease   Severe malaria has two major clinical syndromes: malaria with respiratory distress; and malaria with neurological disturbance, or cerebral malaria (Marsh *et al.* 1996). These occur primarily among children, but also affect adults in areas of low or unstable transmission. An estimated 3 per cent of all attacks are severe, and in the absence of inpatient treatment around half of cases are likely to die (Goodman, Coleman and Mills 2000). Even with optimal management of treatment, case fatality rates for cerebral malaria are around 19 per cent, and would be much higher in many hospital settings in Africa given lack of resources and skilled staff.

Anaemia   Malaria is an important cause of anaemia in SSA (Snow *et al.* 1999). The severe form is a life-threatening condition in young children and often warrants blood transfusion, which increases the risk of HIV infection. In malaria-endemic areas, the incidence and age pattern of severe anaemia are strongly dependent on the intensity of *P. falciparum* transmission (Snow *et al.* 1994), and malaria control trials have been associated with significant reductions in the prevalence of anaemia in children and pregnant women (Alonso *et al.* 1991).

Malaria in Pregnancy   Anaemia is also a harmful manifestation of malaria in pregnancy. Pregnant women, as a result of malaria infection and especially in their first pregnancy, experience an increased risk of maternal anaemia, abortion, still birth and low birth weight, due to both prematurity and intra-uterine growth retardation (Shulman *et al.* 1996). This is of particular concern because low birth weight is associated with increased neonatal mortality (McCormick 1985).

Interaction with Other Diseases   In addition to its direct role in morbidity and mortality, malaria is also thought to have a significant indirect effect in conjunction with other common diseases such as measles, respiratory infections, diarrhoeal disease and malnutrition, although the extent of the indirect impact is difficult to measure and not well understood. Evidence for a significant indirect effect is bolstered by malaria control trials which have found much larger reductions in all-cause mortality than would have been expected from data on malaria-specific mortality alone (Alonso *et al.* 1991). Moreover, the use of ITNs has led to reductions in deaths attributed to acute respiratory infections, acute gastro-enteritis and malnutrition as well as malaria (Alonso *et al.* 1993). However, during the Garki project of residual spraying and mass drug administration, malaria control led to less than the expected impact on all-cause child mortality, which may be because children face 'competing risks' from other potentially fatal diseases, so that a reduction in malaria risk increases their likelihood of falling victim to another cause (Molineaux 1985).

Intellectual Development   Although evidence is limited, it is likely that malaria significantly affects intellectual development and since variations in reasoning ability, cognitive skill and years of schooling are considered to be important determinants of future variations in productivity and earnings of individuals (Boissier, Knight and Sabot 1985), the economic impact is likely to be significant. Survivors of cerebral malaria may be left with neurological sequelae including weakness in the limbs, speech disorders, behavioural disorders, blindness, hearing impairment, cerebral palsy and epilepsy. A review of comparable studies of African children found that 16 per cent of cerebral malaria survivors had

some kind of neurological sequelae at discharge, and for 6 per cent of children these defects persisted for at least six months (Snow *et al.* 1999). No data were available on residual sequelae among adults.

There is good evidence on the association between iron deficiency anaemia (IDA) and poor performance in infant development scales, IQ and learning tasks in pre-school children and educational achievement among school-age children (Pollitt 1997). Iron supplementation has been associated with improvement in mental development scale scores in infants (Pollitt *et al.* 1986) and significant increases in school achievement scores (Soemantri, Pollitt and Kim 1985). However, it is not clear whether these findings for IDA apply equally to children with the type of anaemia associated with malaria.

Malaria may also affect intellectual development through the impact on school attendance. A study in the Gambia of the effects of ITNs found that absenteeism because of fever was significantly higher in the control group (Aikins 1995).

Microeconomic Impact of Malaria

Microeconomic studies are concerned with impact at the level of a productive unit such as the household or firm. There is quite a voluminous literature, which we lack space to cover here but which is reviewed in Chima, Goodman and Mills (2003).

Evidence on direct costs suggests that households can spend quite substantial sums on prevention and especially treatment, and also that direct costs to governments are substantial (for example, an estimated 19 per cent of the Rwandan Ministry of Health recurrent budget, Ettling and Shepard 1991). In terms of indirect costs, the average time lost per episode for a sick adult ranges from one to five days, though these averages conceal considerable variation across individuals (Chima, Goodman and Mills 2003). In order to estimate total costs, Ettling *et al.* (1994), using data from Malawi, multiplied the cost per episode by the predicted number of episodes per year and average household size to obtain a total annual cost per household of $40.02, or 7.2 per cent of household income. For very low-income households the total cost was $24.89, equivalent to 32 per cent of income. Leighton and Foster

(1993) found that total household costs amounted to 9–18 per cent of annual income for small farmers in Kenya, and 7–13 per cent in Nigeria. Only one study, by Shepard *et al.* (1991), has attempted to use such data to estimate the overall economic cost of malaria morbidity and mortality in Africa. Based on extrapolations from four country case studies in Burkina Faso (one district), Chad (one district), Congo (Brazzaville) and Rwanda, the total direct and indirect cost in 1987 was estimated to be $1,064 m, $3.15 *per capita* and 0.6 per cent of the SSA GDP (1999 prices). The authors predicted that the total cost would increase substantially over time, based on projected increases in population, malaria incidence, the value of output and the cost of antimalarials.

However, this evidence on the microeconomic impact of malaria is in general partial and of questionable accuracy (Sachs and Malaney 2002; Chima, Goodman and Mills 2003), and there are many problems in using such data to reflect the burden to society or the potential benefits from control. Studies have generally focused on febrile illness, overestimating the burden of uncomplicated malaria but underestimating the costs of severe illness, other debilitating manifestations (especially neurological sequelae, anaemia and cognitive development) and mortality. Many studies use inadequate data to calculate indirect costs, failing to account for seasonal variations, the difference between the average and marginal product of labour and the ways households and firms 'cope' in response to illness episodes. An alternative approach has been to estimate the net impact on output by looking directly at the statistical association between malaria and agricultural output through a production function (Audibert, Mathonnat and Henry 2003). Findings have been contradictory, at least in part because of data and methodological weaknesses.

The evidence on the extent to which the burden falls more heavily on lower socio-economic groups is reasonably consistent (Worrall, Basu and Hanson 2003). Studies examining socio-economic status using assets, education and occupation all yield data that suggest an inverse relationship between the impact of malaria and socio-economic status.

Evidence on the impact of coping strategies in response to the *risk* of disease is fragmentary. Such strategies probably affect fertility decisions and crop choices, for example, but are difficult to identify since they reduce the *average productivity* of all households and firms, not just those experiencing illness during the study period. It is ironic that precautionary measures against the risk of malaria may lead analysts to conclude that the economic impact of malaria episodes is low, when the reverse is the case. For example, maintaining a labour surplus, which is very costly to firms or households, would permit a high degree of labour substitution in response to a single episode.

Macroeconomic Impact of Malaria

Studies of the macroeconomic impact of malaria have produced conflicting results. Barlow (1967) analysed the impact of near-eradication of malaria in Sri Lanka using a macro model which encompassed both demographic and economic variables, such as the labour force, savings and investment and public expenditure. He argued that, although there may have been a positive impact during the first decade, in the long run the growth of output would have been outstripped by population growth, reducing real income *per capita*. These conclusions should be treated with caution, for several reasons. The impact of malaria eradication on population growth in Sri Lanka has been a subject of great controversy, with some analysts arguing that its contribution was much lower than that assumed by Barlow. Borts (1967) argued that malaria control may change household savings behaviour if the productivity of capital is increased through, for example, the opening up of more productive land. More generally, models such as Barlow's have been criticised for overemphasising the role of capital formation in economic growth. Finally, the relevance of Sri Lanka's experience to contemporary Africa is questionable, given that population density and demographic trends are very different, and malaria interventions focus on control rather than eradication.

An alternative approach has been to use malaria as an explanatory variable in economic growth models in the style of Barro (1991). Gallup and Sachs (2001) used cross-country regression analysis to relate the growth in GDP *per capita* between 1965 and 1990 to initial income levels, initial human capital stock, policy variables, geographical variables and a 'malaria index', calculated as the product of the fraction of land area with endemic malaria in 1965 and the fraction of malaria cases that were *P. falciparum* in 1990. Their results suggested that countries with a substantial amount of malaria grew 1.3 per cent per year less between 1965 and 1990 (controlling for other influences on growth), and that a 10 per cent reduction in malaria was associated with 0.3 per cent higher growth per year. McCarthy, Wolf and Wu (2000) employed a similar cross-sectional regression approach to explore the impact of malaria on average *per capita* growth rate in three five-year periods. They proxied the malaria burden with data on the incidence of malaria episodes, to account for the impact of differing use of protective measures on actual morbidity with given exposure. They also found a significant negative association between malaria and economic growth, although the estimated impact differed sharply across countries. The impact was smaller than that found by Gallup and Sachs, exceeding 0.25 per cent per year in a quarter of the sample countries, and averaging 0.55 per cent for those located in SSA.[7]

These differences in growth rates translate into substantial differences in levels of income: for example, countries with intensive malaria had income levels in 1995 only 33 per cent that of countries without malaria, whether or not the countries were in Africa (Gallup and Sachs 2001).

The contrasts between these results and those based on direct and indirect costs and production functions highlight the need to develop a much deeper understanding of the mechanisms by which malaria affects households and economies. Without this, it is difficult to evaluate existing estimates, both micro and macro.

Alleviation of the Challenge: Interventions against Malaria

Compared to some tropical diseases, the epidemiological and cost-effectiveness literature on malaria is relatively strong for some key interventions (Goodman, Coleman and Mills 2000), though evidence of effectiveness is available almost only for individual interventions. In order to approximate a more realistic scenario, we identified a limited package of interventions whose total costs and benefits could be estimated.[8] Interventions were included that minimised the overlap of target groups while maximising the population coverage. Synergies in the costs and effects of different interventions were not considered due to lack of evidence. SSA was chosen as the geographical context, as 90 per cent of the global burden of malaria falls on this region.

The package evaluated included two preventive interventions targeted to different population groups and one treatment intervention. An ITN programme was included to reduce infections in children under five years in SSA, as trials have shown they reduce overall child mortality by 19 per cent (Lengeler 1998).[9] However, only a small proportion of African children under five years old actually receive this protection (WHO 2003b). Residual spraying of homes with insecticide and chemoprophylaxis of children were excluded from the package as they target the same individuals.

Intermittent presumptive treatment of pregnant women (IPTp) in their first pregnancy (primigravidae) was included to protect children from dying from complications associated with low birth weight (Gülmezoglu and Garner 1998). In 1986, the WHO advocated that all pregnant women living in

[7] Reasons for the differences between the two models remain to be fully explored. A potential explanation lies in the time frame used in each evaluation; Gallup and Sachs (2001) use a dataset that spans 1965–90 based on historical maps, while McCarthy, Wolf and Wu (2000) use WHO data between 1983 and 1997. A sizeable proportion of the advances in malaria control were lost during the 1980s, so the model by McCarthy, Wolf and Wu does not reflect many of the advances made previous to those years. Also, Gallup and Sachs use a malaria index, which ties the burden strongly to prevalence and geography. McCarthy, Wolf and Wu consider that the distribution and amount of national income, along with access to health facilities, reduces the detrimental effects to the economy. The measure that McCarthy, Wolf and Wu use ties malaria prevalence less strongly to the detrimental effects of the disease.

[8] This package should not be interpreted as a policy recommendation, but is selected purely for use here.

[9] Other age groups are likely to benefit from these nets, but to an unknown extent.

endemic areas be protected against malaria. Since concerns exist about the safety of prescribing new artemisinin-based combination therapies (ACTs) to pregnant women (WHO 2003c), and chloroquine (CQ) is associated with problems of resistance and compliance (Slutsker *et al.* 1994; Attaran, Barnes and Curtis 2004), sulfadoxine pyramethamine (SP) is the recommended prophylactic therapy. IPTp consists of two curative doses given during the first and second trimesters of pregnancy during antenatal care visits. Antenatal care is common (around 65 per cent coverage) in SSA; however, a considerable amount of scaling up of IPTp is needed, as few of these women currently receive antimalarials.

A switch to ACT in SSA plus dipstick diagnosis was included as the treatment intervention as existing therapies, such as CQ and SP, are declining in efficacy. The WHO has argued that appropriate and timely case management should be seen as a key component of any malaria control programme (WHO 1993). In reality, case management is often inadequate. The 2003 *African Malaria Report* reported that more than 80 per cent of children treated for malaria received CQ (WHO 2003b). A few countries have switched to SP, but resistance is expected to increase rapidly to this drug: for example in Burundi, resistance to SP is already 50 per cent (EANMAT 2004).

Artemisinin derivatives provide an efficacious alternative to SP, and using them in combination with longer-acting drugs is likely to slow the growth of resistance (Attaran, Barnes and Curtis 2004). Artemisinins are eliminated from the body relatively quickly, reducing the time that they spend at sub-therapeutic concentrations where drug resistance can develop.[10] These parasites can be residual parasites not yet cleared from the initial infection, or those inoculated by a new infectious bite. In theory, the longer-acting drug in the combination will protect the artemisinin derivative by maintaining therapeutic-levels as the artemisinin is eliminated (Bloland 2001). The shift to ACTs as first line treatment for malaria is already happening, and is likely to be implemented in all endemic countries. South Africa has fully switched its first-line drug policy to ACTs, and Tanzania, Zanzibar and Burundi are all in the process of making the change (WHO 2003b). Although the technology has still to be fully

developed for use in SSA, it is likely that dipstick diagnosis should accompany prescription of ACTs in some areas to avoid over-use of expensive drugs.

In addition to changing first-line therapy, scaling up programmes to expand malaria treatment coverage is needed urgently. Approximately 42 per cent of children with malaria receive antimalarials (WHO 2003b), and the majority of deaths in hospital occur within twenty-four hours of treatment, indicating that treatment was received too late (D'Alessandro 2004). Prime reasons for low coverage include poor physical accessibility of health facilities and low levels of affordability of treatment (Hanson *et al.* 2000).

Side Effects

Positive Side Effects

Positive side effects in terms of economic development and improved individual welfare are taken into account as far as possible in the calculations below, so are not further discussed here.

Negative Side Effects

Medical interventions have both benefits and risks. In general, the licensing process for drugs, vaccines and chemicals used to improve human health requires good evidence on adverse effects. Beyond this, WHO, as the global normative authority, may choose not to recommend that countries use a particular product if it judges the evidence of benefit or adverse effects to be not sufficiently strong, and the balance of risks and benefits not sufficiently positive. That said, trials of new products can never be done in all relevant settings, and some adverse effects are rare given the sample size of studies, but nonetheless may be sufficiently serious to warrant withdrawal of a product. Monitoring systems exist in the more developed world to check for adverse reactions, though are rarely 100 per cent effective given the difficulties of associating adverse effects

---

[10] When drugs are at sub-theraputic levels in the body, parasites with mutations that confer small selective advantages proliferate relative to the rest of the parasite population. If this type of drug pressure persists over time, resistance will spread, and treatment will fail for increasing proportions of people with malaria.

Table 2.4. BCRs in Malaria Control

Source	Country	Method	BCR
Barlow (1968)	Sri Lanka	Insecticide	146
Griffit, Rampana and Mashaal (1971)	Thailand	Chemoprophylaxis	6.5
Khan (1966)	Pakistan	Eradication programme	4.9
Livandas and Athanassatos (1963)	Greece	Eradication programme	17.3
Niazi (1969)	Iraq	Eradication programme	6.0
Ortiz (1968)	Paraguay	Insecticides	3.6
San Pedro (1967)	Philippines	Eradication programme	2.4
Democratic Republic of Sudan (1975)	Sudan	Control programme	4.6

Source: Barlow and Grobar (1986).

with the product. For products used exclusively in the developing world, it is unlikely that adverse effects will be quickly detected unless they are very obvious.

With respect to the malaria interventions considered here, side effects are not of major concern. Insecticides recommended for use on nets are evaluated by WHOPES.[11] SP has been chosen as the WHO recommended drug for use in IPTp; adverse effects do occur with SP, but are very rare. Artemisinin and ACTs have been used very widely in China and South East Asia, and appear to have few adverse effects (International Artemisinin Study Group 2004). One specific concern is that given limited government controls on the use of drugs in low- and middle-income countries, it is very difficult to regulate the use of new drugs once available on the local market. This has implications for the development of resistance. Drugs taken in doses inadequate to cure the infection, or drugs taken by an uninfected person who subsequently becomes infected, can expose the malaria parasite to sub-optimal drug levels, increasing the risk of resistance developing or being transmitted. Approaches to tackling this problem include international agreements with the pharmaceutical industry on marketing drugs; information campaigns to educate consumers on taking full courses of drugs; and drug retailer training programmes. However, since it is unlikely that such efforts will be fully

effective, continued investment in the discovery of new drugs is also needed. This comes at a cost, which currently falls mainly on public and charitable funds (channelled though public private partnerships such as MMV[12]), given the limited incentives for the industry to invest in drugs whose market is severely limited by low purchasing power.

Economic Evaluation

Despite the relatively large economic literature on the impact of malaria, especially at the microeconomic level, the volume of research has not produced many estimates of cost-benefit ratios. Recent economic analysis has focused almost exclusively on cost-effectiveness analysis (drawn on below) and cost-benefit analyses (CBAs) date from the 1960s and 1970s. Table 2.4 summarises the results based on a review quoted in Najera, Liese and Hammer (1993). These data are largely of historical interest, and are not used further here: no estimates relate to high-transmission settings in SSA, and all rely on control methods (largely residual spraying) which are not favoured today in high-transmission settings. However, the attractive cost-benefit ratios should be noted.

BCRs and ANBs were estimated for SSA, drawing on recent evidence. Three approaches were taken:

(1) *Macroeconomic evidence* was used to estimate the economic costs associated with the burden of malaria and the benefits of malaria

[11] http://www.who.int/ctd/whopes/.
[12] Medicines for Malaria Venture.

Table 2.5. Costs and Benefits of Malaria Control Estimated from Macroeconomic Models (2003 Int$)

Study used	Population benefiting	Total benefit ($ m, 2002–15)	Total cost ($ m, 2002–15)	Net benefit ($ m, 2002–15)	Annualised net benefit ($ m)	BCR
Gallup and Sachs (2001)	563,282,922	664,309	142,473	521,835	37,274	4.7
McCarthy, Wolf and Wu (2000)	563,282,922	275,948	142,473	133,475	9,534	1.9

Source: Population and GDP data taken from World Bank (2003a).

control, and related to recently estimated costs of control.

(2) The *intervention package* was evaluated based on intervention-specific estimates of cost-effectiveness.

(3) Calculations of costs and benefits were made for *KwaZulu Natal* in South Africa, which changed to an ACT in 2002.

Macroeconomic Approach

The Gallup and Sachs (2001) and McCarthy, Wolf and Wu (2000) models reviewed above predicted the additional amount that economies would have grown if malaria had been eradicated, the first predicting an additional 1.3 per cent per-person growth in annual GDP, and the second an additional 0.55 per cent. Based on the Abuja Declaration (WTO 2000b) and CMH Working Group 5 calculations (Jha and Mills 2002), we assume a target to halve the malaria burden in SSA by 2015. Assuming that incremental reductions in malaria elicit economic pay-offs at a constant rate, we extrapolated the economic benefits that would result if the target were achieved. This extrapolation was determined according to a linear function between current and predicted malaria levels.

Working Group 5 (WG5) of the CMH estimated the annual *per capita* cost at 'district' level[13] of a package of interventions that would be necessary to achieve high levels of coverage (Jha and Mills 2002). For adults, it included recurrent and annual equivalent capital costs of measures to prevent and treat malaria. The costs of treating childhood malaria were aggregated with other medical costs for childhood illness in this report, and we used these costs in their entirety. Costs were averaged across high and low estimates, and discounted into the future. Overall, the cost of

reaching the target would be Int$18 per person per year.

We calculated benefits by taking the difference between baseline and intervention scenarios of per-person GDP growth. A baseline scenario of economic growth with current levels of malaria was established based on the average annual GDP growth rate in SSA between 1990 and 2001 (2.15 per cent per person per year) (World Bank 2003b). From this baseline, we extrapolated the benefit of reducing the malaria burden by 50 per cent for the 563 million people living at risk. Results are shown in table 2.5.

The sensitivity analysis found that with a DCR of 6 per cent, the ANB of the Gallup and Sachs (2001) model decreased by 25 per cent, and the ANB of the model by McCarthy, Wolf and Wu (2000) decreased by 30 per cent.

In their analysis, Gallup and Sachs (2001) estimated further that a 10 per cent reduction in malaria would allow economies to grow an additional 0.3 per cent per person each year. Using this estimate as the lower limit of the function from which we extrapolated benefits, calculations showed that a 50 per cent reduction in malaria would result in a 0.74 per cent annual increase in *per capita* GDP. Total net benefit increased from $522 bn to $624 bn, and the BCR increased from 4.7 to 5.4.

If costs are decreased by 25 per cent to allow for the costs of non-malaria interventions included in the full child treatment package, the total net benefit in each scenario increases by $36 bn. The benefit-cost ratio increases from 4.7 to 6.2 using Gallup and Sachs (2001) estimates, and from 1.9 to 2.6 using McCarthy, Wolf and Wu (2000) estimates. If costs

[13] Including capital and recurrent costs of service delivery, plus training, management and supervisory costs at the local level.

are increased by an arbitrary 25 per cent, the BCR decreases to 3.7 for Gallup and Sachs (2001) and to 1.5 for McCarthy, Wolf and Wu (2000).

Package of Interventions

Evidence on the three interventions applied to SSA (ITNs for children under five years, IPTp for first pregnancies and ACTs to treat malaria) was taken from models constructed by teams at the LSHTM which used methods of probabilistic sensitivity analysis, thus allowing ranges of values to be used rather than single-point estimates (Goodman, Coleman and Mills 2000; Coleman et al. 2004). In these models, key determinants of cost-effectiveness were also included, such as drug resistance, intensity of transmission season, behavioural factors, price of key commodities and expected mortality. Costs were considered from a provider's perspective for all interventions except for ITNs, where the cost of community time was included. Benefits were measured in terms of DALYs calculated according to Mark II methods with no age weighting (Fox-Rushby 2002), except for IPTp which estimated YLLs. A standard West African life table was used for life expectancy (UN 1982).

The net benefits of ITNs and IPTp were calculated according to income strata, as used in the original models. Income strata were defined as having per capita GNIs of less than Int$1,300 for very low-income countries, between Int$1,300 and Int$3,000 for middle-income countries, and above Int$3,000 for higher-income countries. Variations in income strata affected staff salary and training costs in these models.

ITNs The model drew evidence of effectiveness from a Cochrane meta-analysis of large-scale trials (Lengeler 1998). Deltamethrin rather than permethrin was assumed to be the insecticide, since deltamethrin's unit cost is lower and it lasts twice as long. Costs in the model were drawn from the economic evaluations that accompanied the trials, published and unpublished literature and expert consultation. Trials have not been conducted in areas of low-transmission intensity in SSA, so results are relevant for areas of high and moderate transmission. The model measured effectiveness for children aged 1–59 months only.

Without any intervention, children aged 1–59 months in high-transmission areas experience 1–2.9 clinical episodes of malaria (Nájera and Hempel 1996). Although the ITN trials found a 19 per cent reduction in all-cause mortality in children aged 1–59 months (Lengeler 1998), effectiveness in practice can be expected to be lower than effectiveness in a trial. Households may not re-treat their nets, children may not sleep under them during periods of hot weather, other family members may use the nets and nets may be taken away, destroyed or sold. The average compliance reported in the trials was 65 per cent. Other studies have found that between 20 per cent and 80 per cent of nets are re-treated (Chavasse, Reed and Attawell 1999) and that 57–97 per cent of children use nets appropriately (Alonso et al. 1993; D'Alessandro et al. 1995; Nevill et al. 1996). The latter two estimates were averaged to estimate actual compliance. A linear relationship between compliance and effectiveness was assumed, such that zero compliance resulted in no effectiveness and 65 per cent compliance resulted in the reduction in mortality found in the meta-analysis. Effectiveness results from the meta-analysis were multiplied by the ratio of actual compliance to trial compliance to estimate effectiveness in a programme situation. Based on these assumptions, it can be expected that protected children will lose 0.19 fewer years due to malaria than unprotected children.

Costs included insecticide, staff, transport, other overheads, community time, a sensitisation and awareness campaign and the cost of mosquito nets, and were updated to 2003 values from Goodman, Coleman and Mills (2000). Although the programme was targeted at children aged 1–59 months, it was assumed that 2–3.9 nets would need to be supplied per household. The overall cost of the programme was Int$28.47, Int$29.02 and Int$33.50 per child with increasing income strata, with the cost of the net being the most important input.

We predicted the incremental economic returns of scaling up ITN coverage in SSA from 2 per cent to 70 per cent to protect an additional 61,143,375 children under five years old living in endemic areas. The ANB was Int$17 bn, with a BCR of 10. Table 2.6 shows the results by income strata.

The discount rate affects only the useful life span of the net, and has very little effect on ANB.

Table 2.6. Costs and Benefits of ITNs (2003 Int$)

Income strata (value of a DALY)	Additional children covered	Total benefit ($ m, per year)	Total cost ($ m, per year)	Annual net benefit ($ m)	BCR
Low-income (Int$850)	41,445,555	6,693	1,180	5,513	5.7
Middle-income (Int$1,863)	14,995,918	5,308	435	4,873	12.2
High-income (Int$7,250)	4,701,902	6,477	158	6,319	41.1

Source: Calculated from World Bank (2003a); Goodman, Coleman and Mills (2000); Jha and Mills (2002).

Increasing the discount rate from 3 per cent to 6 per cent lowers ANB by less than 1 per cent. Standardising the ceiling ratio to Int$3,830/DALY strongly affected the results, giving a ANB of Int$43 bn and a BCR of 25.1. For several reasons, the calculation of ANB given by this model may be an overestimate. Families may wash nets more frequently, reducing effectiveness. Overall child mortality may be lower than the predicted baseline in higher income countries, and thus benefits may be exaggerated.

On the other hand, the calculation of ANB may be an underestimate:

- The model considers benefits only for children, yet accounts for the cost of enough nets to protect entire families. If distribution were targeted so that only one net could be provided per child, the costs of the programme would be substantially reduced.
- The cost of nets was determined according to the price given for publicly administered programmes; privately managed social marketing programmes may be able to provide nets at lower cost (Armstrong-Schellenberg et al. 2001).
- A high community level of net use may protect families without nets living in the same area, through the 'mass effect' (Wiseman et al. 2003).
- Control households in epidemiological studies tend to have better outcomes than unobserved families due to the Hawthorne effect,[14] thus producing a lower estimate of the difference between intervention and control.

The mechanism used to deliver an ITN programme is of vital importance to its cost-effectiveness. If the cost structure of net provision is shifted from the government to the consumer, overall costs to government would be lower than those found in the trials used in this analysis. However, evidence from

the Gambia shows that effectiveness is likely to decrease substantially if this shift occurs, as demand for ITNs is price elastic (Hanson et al. 2000). Given that willingness-to-pay (WTP) for nets appears to be greater than WTP for insecticide treatment (Hanson et al. 2000), the imminent introduction of long-lasting nets which do not require re-treatment may increase the effectiveness of private purchases.

Prevention in Pregnancy   We based our estimates on the model of Goodman, Coleman and Mills (2001) that evaluated the cost-effectiveness of using SP to protect foetuses born to primigravidae. This study used evidence from a Cochrane review of strategies for preventing malaria during pregnancy, whose outcome measure was impact on low birth weight (Gülmezoglu and Garner 1998). In order to estimate impact in terms of deaths, Goodman, Coleman and Mills (2001) modelled the impact of low birth weight on child survival using a Wilcox–Russell mortality curve and distributions of birth weight for both protected and unprotected foetuses.

Under ideal conditions, this model predicts that 0.011 fewer babies born to primigravidae will die with IPTp. However, treatment failure can occur for several reasons. Women may not begin prophylaxis early enough in their pregnancy, they may not fully comply with the drug regimen and parasites may carry mutations that confer drug resistance. The model assumed that treatment was successful only if women made at least two visits per pregnancy before the end of their second trimester, took the correct doses at the appropriate times, and were

---

[14] http://pespmc1.vub.ac.be/ASC/HAWTHO_EFFEC.html, and http://www.accel-team.com/motivation/hawthorne_02. html.

Table 2.7. Costs and Benefits of IPTp (2003 Int$)

Income strata (value of a YLL)	Additional PG covered	Total benefit ($ m, 2002–15)	Total cost ($ m, 2002–15)	Net benefit ($ m, 2002–15)	ANB($ m)	BCR
Low-income (Int$850)	3,294,313	2,260	282,073	1,978	152	8
Middle-income (Int$1,863)	1,191,955	1,792	112,899	1,679	129	16
High-income (Int$7,250)	373,732	2,187	60,603	2,126	164	36.1

Source: Calculated from World Bank (2003a); Goodman, Coleman and Mills (2000); Jha and Mills (2002).
Note: PG = primagravidae.

not infected with resistant parasites. The effective reduction in neonatal mortality rate, D, was calculated as

$$(3) \quad D = d * (1 - s) * (1 - r)$$
$$* (g + [1 - g]z) * v_1 * v_2$$

where d is the maximum level of possible effectiveness, s is the stillbirth rate, r is parasite resistance, g is compliance to the correct drug regimen, z is the proportion of underdosed cases where treatment was still effective, v_1 is the probability of attending the antenatal clinic during the first or second trimester, and v_2 is the probability of returning for a second visit.

It can be expected that drug resistance, r, will change through time. Based on methods used by Coleman *et al.* (2004), we assumed that parasite resistance grows according to a sigmoidal trajectory using a logistic function. Longitudinal drug resistance studies in Eastern and Southern Africa suggest that the maximum rate at which resistance grows to SP, k_i, is between 30 per cent and 50 per cent per year (Roper *et al.* 2003). Current levels of resistance, $R_{i,0}$, were assumed to be 13 per cent according to the mean of thirty-nine 'sentinel sites' in East Africa (EANMAT 2004). The dynamic spread of drug resistance at time t was modelled using (4).

$$(4) \quad R_{i,t} = k_i \left[\frac{R_{i,0}}{R_{i,0} + (k_i - R_{i,0}) \exp^{-r_i t}} \right]$$

A thirteen-year time frame was used to be consistent with other calculations in this chapter. The model

predicted that an average of 0.062 YLLs would be averted each year per child born to primigravidae.

Costs were determined according to income strata and updated from Goodman, Coleman and Mills (2001). It was assumed that antenatal services already existed for women receiving this treatment, and that IPTp was added to the services currently provided. The mean incremental costs per primigravidae were Int$6.59 for very low-income strata, Int$7.29 for middle-income strata and Int$12.47 for higher-income strata.

This model predicts that the incremental net benefit of scaling up IPTp from 0 per cent to 90 per cent, to cover an additional 4,860,000 primigravidae,[15] will be Int$5,783 m between 2002 and 2015 (BCR of 13.7). Results according to income strata are given in table 2.7.

The DCR has a substantial effect on net benefits because it influences the weight of future treatment failure due to increasing resistance. Changing the DCR from 3 per cent to 6 per cent increases net benefit by 12 per cent. Standardising the ceiling ratio to Int$3,830/YLL strongly affects results, giving a total net benefit of Int$14,567 m for 2002–15 and a BCR of 33.0. Net benefits may be underestimated if IPTp has an impact on child mortality beyond twenty-eight days. In addition, the health benefit of IPTp for the mother in terms of reduced anaemia has not been included (Brabin, Hakimi and Pelletier 2001).

In other ways, the mortality associated with malaria may be overestimated. As in the ITN model, all-cause mortality can be expected to be lower in wealthier counties, which would reduce the incremental mortality averted between the intervention and comparator. Malaria affects birth weight through both pre-term births and retarded

[15] Based on estimates made by the US Bureau of the Census that the number of births in SSA would increase from 25 million in 1996 to 33 million in 2020.

interuterine growth during a full term. Mortality rates are higher for pre-term birth than retarded interuterine growth, but it is not clear which mechanism is influenced by SP. If IPTp affects only retarded interuterine growth, net benefits would be lower.

Switching to ACTs   Based on a previous model (Coleman *et al.* 2004), we evaluated the net benefit of a change in policy from SP to ACT, including the use of dipsticks for diagnosis to ration drugs more efficiently and combat the spread of resistance. To account for resistance and to be consistent with other models, we evaluated this model over a thirteen-year time frame.

A simple decision tree of the diagnosis and treatment of malaria was used to follow the possible costs and outcomes of a patient presenting with malaria and receiving first-line treatment. Costs were attached to the branches of the tree so that a cost could be estimated for each path that an outpatient could be expected to take. Cost per individual outpatient was calculated by multiplying the cost of each branch by the probability that it would be followed. The cost per adult treatment with ACT included an estimate of ACT drug costs (Bloland 2001; Kindermans 2002), and ranged between Int$3.57 and Int$8.57. The SP cost (which would be no longer incurred) was fixed at Int$0.50. We assumed that half of the patients presenting with malaria would be under five years old, and that they would receive a half-dose. As switching drug policy for people already receiving treatment is likely to use existing distribution and treatment systems, we assumed that no additional transport, administration, or overhead costs would be incurred.

The decision tree framework is useful because *gross costs* can be calculated for each strategy, as well as *net costs* between them. Net costs are particularly relevant for this analysis, as ACTs are expected to improve health outcomes significantly. Reductions in the number of persistent cases of uncomplicated malaria and the number of cases developing to severe malaria would lead to lower follow-on treatment costs for providers. As severe malaria can lead to hospitalisation, these cost savings can be substantial, heavily influencing net benefit. The annualised incremental cost of using ACTs instead

of SP over a period of thirteen years was calculated at Int$2.98 per malaria patient treated.

We evaluated outcomes according to treatment failure or cure, defined as adequate clinical response following WHO criteria (WHO 1996b). If treatment fails, the patient may develop severe malaria or continue to suffer from uncomplicated malaria. If severe malaria develops, they may seek inpatient care, where they will receive intravenous quinine. If they seek care with uncomplicated malaria, they may receive a second-line antimalarial.[16] The probabilities of full recovery or death were then estimated, as reported in Coleman *et al.* (2004).

The probability of treatment failure, F, with a given first line drug, i, at time t was defined as being dependent on three main inputs. First, the proportion of malaria parasites, R, resistant to drug i at time t. Second, the probability, m, that a patient complies at the recommended dose with drug therapy i. Third the probability, p, that therapy i is effective despite the patient not complying fully with the treatment regimen.

As SP can be treated with a single dose, it can be expected that a high proportion of patients will fully comply. However, ACTs must be taken in several doses, and it is possible that patients will abandon treatment before finishing the full regimen. In a Zambian study, 21.2 per cent of patients did not comply with drug regimens, and an additional 39.4 per cent probably did not follow them (Depoortere *et al.* 2004). We assumed that 85–95 per cent of patients complied to SP, and 60–80 per cent of patients complied to ACT. In some cases of non-compliance with combination therapy, only minor underdosing may have occurred and some therapeutic effect may be experienced. In the absence of drug resistance, it was expected that ACTs would be effective in 10–30 per cent of underdosed patients.

We assumed that all patients infected with resistant parasites experience treatment failure, regardless of whether or not they fully comply with the treatment regimen. Treatment with drug i at time

---

[16] It was assumed that amodioquine was the second-line drug to SP, and that ACTs would be re-administered if ACT was used as the first-line treatment.

Table 2.8. Costs and Benefits of Changing from SP to ACT (2003 Int$)

Intervention (value of DALY)	Malaria patients treated	Total benefit ($ m, 2002–15)	Total cost ($ m, 2002–15)	Net benefit ($ m, 2002–15)	ANB ($ m)	BCR
SP to ACT (Int$1,750)	168,000,000	251,297	6,510	244,787	18,830	38.6

Source: Calculated from World Bank (2003a); Jha and Mills (2002); Coleman *et al.* (2004).

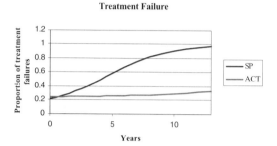

Figure 2.3. *Effect of resistance on treatment failure*
Source: *Coleman* et al. *(2004).*

t may be successful if the patient is not infected with resistant parasites and fully complies with the treatment regimen; the probability of this occurring is $(1 - R_{i,t})m_i$. Alternatively, the patient may be infected with susceptible parasites but, despite not complying with the treatment regimen, is still cured; the probability of this occurring is $(1 - R_{i,t})(1 - m_i)p_i$. Thus

$$(5) \quad F_{i,t} = 1 - \left[(1 - R_{i,t})\, m_i \right.$$
$$\left. + (1 - R_{i,t})(1 - m_i)\, p_i \right]$$

defines treatment failure, which simplifies to

$$(6) \quad F_{i,t} = 1 - (1 - R_{i,t})[m_i + p_i(1 - m_i)]$$

Levels of resistance were modelled using the same logistic function as in the IPTp model. The rate at which resistance will grow to ACTs has yet to be observed, and we assumed that it would grow at one-half the rate of SP based on the arguments outlined in section 3.2[17] (figure 2.3).

The decision tree was used to calculate the probabilities of surviving or dying, which were converted to expected DALYs per patient. Estimates

[17] The lower level of compliance to ACT makes treatment failure more likely at initial levels of resistance, despite its higher efficacy.

were made separately for patients over and under five years of age, and the total DALYs were calculated as a weighted average according to each group's share in the population. Overall, it can be expected that this policy change will avert 0.066 DALYs per case each year until 2015.

It has been estimated that children experience 200 million cases of malaria each year in SSA (D'Alessandro 2004). If half of malaria cases affect adults in endemic areas, it can be assumed that twice this number will occur in total (Coleman *et al.* 2004). Currently, only about 42 per cent of these cases receive an antimalarial, implying 168 million treatments needing an ACT. The incremental net benefit of switching to ACT is given in table 2.8.

Increasing the DCR to 6 per cent would decrease net benefits by 23 per cent. Standardising the ceiling ratio to Int$3,830/DALY would increase net benefits to Int$543 bn with a BCR of 84.5. The results are also relevant to countries still using CQ, as unit costs for CQ and SP are very similar and patients are more likely to adhere to SP than CQ (Goodman, Coleman and Mills 2000).

Scaling Up ACT Coverage   In order to halve the malaria burden by 2015 it will be necessary to scale up substantially the proportion of people who are treated for malaria (Jha and Mills 2002). Adapting the decision tree used to evaluate a change in first-line therapy, we evaluated the net-benefit of extending ACT treatment to currently untreated malaria cases, to reach a treatment target of 70 per cent, and including dipstick diagnosis in order to target treatment effectively.

Incremental costs of scaling up coverage can be expected to be much higher than for switching treatment policy since capacity expansion will be required. Costs include buildings and equipment, supervision and training, staff salaries, and costs

Table 2.9. Costs and Benefits of Scaling Up ACT (2003 Int$)

Intervention (value of a DALY)	Additional malaria patients covered	Total benefit ($ m, 2002–15)	Total cost ($ m, 2002–15)	Net benefit ($ m, 2002–15)	ANB ($ m)	BCR
SP to ACT (Int$1,750)	112,000,000	157,683	8,240	149,443	11,496	19.1

Source: Calculated from World Bank (2003a); Jha and Mills (2002); Coleman *et al.* (2004).

Table 2.10. Costs and Benefits of a Package of Malaria Control Measures (2003 Int$)

Intervention	Per capita costs (annualised) ($)	Total monetary benefit (annualised) ($ m)	Total cost (annualised) ($ m)	Net benefit (annualised) ($ m)	BCR
ITNs	28.99 per child	18,479	1,773	16,706	10.4
IPTp	7.21 per PG	480	35	445	13.7
Changing to ACT	2.98 per malaria case	19,331	501	18,830	38.6
Scaling up ACT	20.21 per malaria case	12,129	634	11,496	19.1
Total		**50,419**	**2,942**	**47,476**	**17.1**

incurred by individual patients. The incremental costs of scaling up ACT coverage were estimated at Int$20.21 per additional patient.

The health benefits of scaling up treatment will also be substantial. People with malaria that do not receive treatment can be expected to incur 0.310 DALYs, and patients treated with ACTs average 0.089 DALYs, over a 13 year time frame. An incremental 0.221 DALYs would be averted per patient.

Given that around 42 per cent of cases in SSA are currently being treated with a malaria drug (6), if the proportion of cases treated for malaria is scaled up to 70 per cent, it can be expected that an additional 112 million episodes will be treated each year. The incremental net benefits of this policy change are shown in table 2.9.

Increasing the discount rate to 6 per cent would decrease the net benefit by 17 per cent. Standardizing the ceiling ratio to Int$3,830/DALY would increase total net benefits to Int$337 bn with a BCR of 41.9.

Package of Interventions   Net benefits and BCRs for each of the three interventions are summarised in table 2.10 in annual terms. In the absence of evidence on synergies between interventions, costs and benefits have been simply summed to illustrate the costs and benefits of the package.

It should be noted that benefits in table 2.10 are valued using ceiling ratios specific to SSA. The value of benefits thus reflects the low incomes of SSA. We present results using a standardized ceiling ratio in the final section.

A notable feature of this analysis, largely neglected to date, has been the inclusion of considerations of *drug resistance*. Although this considerably complicates the analyses, not least because it requires analysis over time, it provides a more realistic estimate of costs and benefits. However, it should be noted that the costs of research into new drugs have not been included here.

Success Story: KwaZulu Natal

Evidence of the cost-effectiveness of different malaria treatment and control strategies was taken from the South East African Combination Antimalarial Therapy (SEACAT) study done in the Ingwavuma district in the KwaZulu Natal province of South Africa (Muheki, Barnes and McIntyre 2004), which has seasonal malaria. In 2000, this region suffered a particularly severe outbreak of malaria, with nearly 6,000 cases per month at its peak. The national malaria policy was deemed ineffective and immediately changed.

The programme existing in 2000 consisted of insecticide residual spraying (IRS) with deltamethrin and malaria case management with SP. In 2002, IRS with a combination of deltamethrin (60 per cent) and DDT (40 per cent) was introduced, and first-line drug treatment was changed to ACT. An economic evaluation was conducted to test the cost-effectiveness of this change in policy at one hospital and nine clinics between 2000 and 2002. The authors separated the effects of ACTs from those of IRS using a Delphi survey of ten international malaria experts.

The interventions were hugely successful, as the facilities saw 21,874 fewer cases of malaria between 2000 and 2002. The Delphi survey suggested that ACT was responsible for averting 36 per cent (range 25–50 per cent) of these cases. Assuming that people with malaria would otherwise be treated with SP, 0.002 YLLs would be avoided for each case averted (Coleman *et al.* 2004). Valuing each YLL according to the South African GNI (Int$10,910), the programme would have a monetary benefit of Int$202,798 (range $140,832–$281,664). Int$774,630 were saved due to fewer treatments being necessary, and the net benefit of the programme was Int$977,428 (range Int$915,462–Int$1,056,294). Lowering the ceiling ratio to Int$3,830/YLL gives a net benefit of Int$845,823.

In addition to being highly effective in averting malaria cases, this programme was cost-saving: South Africa has a relatively well-developed primary care system, where 69 per cent of people live within 5km of a clinic. Publicly provided health care is widely used – over 93 per cent of patients with malaria sought treatment from one of these clinics, which were backed by a well-regulated and reliable drug supply (Muheki, Barnes and McIntyre 2004). The findings of this study represent programme data, not a controlled trial. Cost-effectiveness may be overestimated if other factors, such as changes in climate and precipitation, contributed to the reduced prevalence of disease.

Feasibility

Feasibility can be examined according to a number of different dimensions, notably political, financial and managerial. Many aspects of feasibility are common to all three opportunities, most notably

because some of the malaria and HIV/AIDS interventions require a basic health service system. Hence the general discussion on feasibility is located on p. 101, and the discussion here and in the subsequent HIV/AIDS feasibility section concentrates on issues specific to these two diseases, including the extent to which interventions can be successfully delivered where basic health services are weak.

Political feasibility has changed markedly in recent years with respect to malaria. A coordinated effort at international level, including the creation of Roll Back Malaria (RBM), culminated in the Abuja Declaration (WTO 2000b). Malaria was included in the scope of the new Global Fund for AIDS, TB and Malaria. An external evaluation of RBM found it to have been highly successful in global advocacy, and in attracting attention to malaria control (Malaria Consortium 2002). The evaluation team estimated that international expenditures on malaria had doubled. However, there was lack of progress in demonstrating a significant reduction in the global burden of malaria. At country level, National Malaria Control Programmes and National Programme Officers were judged to be weak, and unable to advocate effectively. Political commitment thus remains an issue at the country level.

The Abuja Summit called for US$1 bn a year to help Africa tackle malaria; however, this request may be an underestimate of the actual resources needed to address the epidemic effectively. CMH Working Group 5 estimates, which sought to cost fully the provision of a package of malaria control measures at local level, estimated that to achieve high levels of coverage by 2015, $1.5–2.2 bn (US$2002) would be needed a year for prevention and treatment of adults in SSA, and a further $3.3–4.2 bn for a child treatment package which included malaria. Fighting malaria would be less costly than fighting HIV, which CMH Working Group 5 estimated to cost between $10.1 and 12.1 bn a year in SSA by 2015.

Managerial feasibility can be examined with respect to the three interventions evaluated. With respect to ITNs, feasibility is dependent on the *delivery strategy*. At one extreme, a strategy of free public distribution is dependent on the existence of an effective basic heath service network, and a well-managed supply pipeline from manufacturers to health centres. However, the Tanzanian experience demonstrates that, in some settings, relying on private sector distribution channels and individual willingness to pay, stimulated by publicly funded social marketing campaigns and encouragement to manufacturers, can achieve a marked increase in net coverage. From a relatively small base of 200,000 nets per year in 1994, there has been a dramatic increase to domestic sales of around 1.5 m nets in 2002.[18] Manufacturing capacity exceeds 4 m nets, and nets are being exported to other countries in Africa. The reasons for this expansion in net production include the positive impact of reductions in taxes and tariffs, and the effects of demand creation activities undertaken through a variety of small-scale projects, and more recent large scale social marketing activities. Retail prices have fallen dramatically, to US$ 1.8 *ex-factory*, presumably reflecting competition, and possibly also economies of scale operating at lower levels of the distribution system. There is anecdotal evidence that saturation of urban markets is leading to increased penetration into rural areas. The challenge currently faced is how to channel subsidies to those unable to pay the commercial price. While, as in Tanzania, nets can be bundled with the initial insecticide treatment, encouraging re-treatment has proved a major problem in many countries. This problem will be solved in the foreseeable future by the introduction of long-lasting nets.

IPTp delivery is dependent on an *antenatal care* (ANC) infrastructure. In most of SSA the percentage of primagravidae receiving ANC is high. Although historically the coverage of malaria prophylaxis of pregnant women in ANC has been very low, this has in part resulted from lack of attention to this intervention and low adherence to the previous drug, CQ. Intermittent treatment using SP improves adherence, which can also be improved by education of mothers. Thus except in countries with extremely weak ANC, this intervention is managerially feasible. In the future, development of resistance to SP will threaten this strategy, and research is urgently needed to identify anti-malaria drugs that are safe to give in pregnancy.

Malaria treatment for children and adults is accessed though both public and private sectors. In SSA, given the limited reach and often poor quality of government services, as much as 60 per cent of treatments may be purchased from the private sector, often local drug shops and general stores (Hanson *et al.* 2000). If the additional cost of ACT is to be matched by the benefits of reduction in the rate of growth of resistance, it is likely that coverage of ACTs must be high, and coverage of either of the component drugs given as monotherapy low.[19] This means that not only do public sector services need to be improved (considered on pp. 101ff. below), but also private sector dispensing practices must be addressed. Experiences of how this can be done are accumulating, and include a combination of consumer education, improved drug packaging and retailer training and support (Hanson *et al.* 2000). Franchising and contracting approaches can be used to structure the implementation of these specific measures, and provide incentives for good practice.

Control of HIV/AIDS

Identification and Description of Opportunity

Introductory Statistics

HIV/AIDS affects nearly every country in the world, with more than 90 per cent of infections occurring in developing countries (Ainsworth and Over 1999; CIA 2003). Between 2.5 and 3.5 m people died from HIV/AIDS in 2003, accounting for over 5.1 per cent of all deaths world-wide (WHO 2002; UNAIDS 2003). Current estimates are that more than 22 million people have died through the course of the epidemic (Alleyne and Cohen 2002), between 34 and 46 million people are currently living with HIV/AIDS and 5.3 million new infections occur each year (UNAIDS 2003).[20] The problem has reached such a magnitude that it is considered not just a health issue, but a development issue (Arndt and Lewis 2000), and most recently a global security threat (ICRG 2002). The Commission for

---

[18] Karen Kramer, personal communication.
[19] Otherwise, use of the monotherapy will increase the probability of resistance developing and spreading, and threaten the combination drug.
[20] http://www.whitehouse.gov/onap/facts.html.

Macroeconomics in Health argued that it is 'a distinct and unparalleled catastrophe' with the 'capacity to overturn economic development in Africa and in other regions for decades' (Gallup and Sachs 2001). There have been recent suggestions that prevalence is lower than had been thought – for example 22 m cases in SSA rather than 26.6 m (Anon 2004) – though this is still appallingly high.

Epidemiological Description

The distribution of HIV/AIDS is geographically diverse, and can be classified according to three stages of the epidemic: nascent, concentrated and generalized (Ainsworth and Over 1999). As large-population studies are expensive and problematic, these definitions rely on prevalence levels among women attending antenatal clinics and groups considered to be particularly at risk. These high-risk groups include sex workers, injecting drug users (IDUs), the military, homosexual and bisexual men and people already affected by another sexually transmitted infection (STI).

The HIV/AIDS epidemic can, as we have seen, be categorised as nascent, concentrated and generalised. The epidemic exists in its *nascent* stage where less than 5 per cent of individuals in high-risk groups are infected, and less than 1 per cent of the overall population is affected (UNAIDS 2003). Over 2.3 bn people live in these areas, which include China, Indonesia, Papua New Guinea, several central Asian republics, the Baltic states and parts of North Africa (Ainsworth and Over 1999). The epidemic is in its *concentrated* stage where it has become established among high-risk groups (over 5 per cent), but not among the general population. Concentrated epidemics exist in much of Latin America, several central Asian republics, SSA and around the heroin networks in Southeast Asia and Pakistan. The *generalised* form of the epidemic exists where over 5 per cent of the overall population is affected (Ainsworth and Over 1999). Southern and eastern Africa, along with a few countries in west Africa, are currently suffering this stage of the epidemic. In some areas, as in Botswana (UNAIDS 2003), the overall prevalence of infection may reach as high as 40 per cent.

While the HIV/AIDS epidemic has yet to be fully described, solutions lie in addressing the *risk factors* associated with its spread. A large proportion of HIV is transmitted through the sex industry, especially in areas where condom use is low. Without protection from condoms, individuals already infected by other STIs are particularly vulnerable to HIV infection. This risk factor is especially important in SSA, where 90 per cent of HIV infections are transmitted through heterosexual sex. Sex between men is another contributing factor to HIV spread, particularly in Latin America. IDU spreads the epidemic among users during the nascent stages of the epidemic; these individuals then spread the virus further by infecting their sexual partners (Ainsworth and Over 1999; UNAIDS 2003).

Microeconomic Impact

At the household level, HIV/AIDS can impose heavy cost burdens, undermine assets and livelihoods and be a cause of impoverishment. In many developing countries this is exacerbated by households' poor access to health services, and the high costs (both direct and indirect) of seeking treatment.

The costs of an adult death constitute the key microeconomic impact of the HIV/AIDS epidemic. Unlike malaria, HIV can affect poor and rich alike, though it might be expected that over time richer people would be more able and likely to adapt their behaviour. A number of household studies in subsistence economies have sought to measure the impact of an AIDS death, and to study how households cope (Pitayanon, Kongsin and Janjaroen 1997). The effects of HIV/AIDS are felt on two key farm parameters. First, *household labour quality and quantity* are reduced, initially as the infected person is less productive, and subsequently with their death. This is exacerbated when there is more than one infected person in a household, which is not unusual given the nature of transmission. In addition, household time is diverted to care for the sick person. For example, in the Thai study, 13 per cent of school aged children in families with an AIDS sufferer were withdrawn from school to support the family (Pitayanon, Kongsin and Janjaroen 1997); interruption of education, to care for parents, contribute to household income or food needs, or because of lack of money for school fees, was also found in the Ugandan study (Barnett and Blaikie

1992). Secondly, HIV/AIDS affects the availability of *cash income*. Financial resources have to be diverted to pay for medical treatment and funeral costs; since the disease is a chronic one, such costs can be very substantial and will often require sale of assets. In the Thai study, 60 per cent spent all their savings as a result of the AIDS infection, and on average out-of-pocket medical expenditure from the beginning of the illness until death amounted to six months of average total household income (Pitayanon, Kongsin and Janjaroen 1997). In the study in Tanzania, household medical expenses tended to be much higher for AIDS than for other causes of death (Ainsworth and Over 1999). Funeral expenses are also a substantial expense, in the Tanzanian study amounting to about as much as medical care. Such diversion of expenditure can be at the expense of food consumption, where resources are very limited. Shortage of labour may lead households to change the mix of crops, shifting from cash to subsistence crops, or reduce the area under cultivation (Barnett and Blaikie 1992). In the longer term, households may dissolve or be reconstituted as children are fostered, orphaned or die, and spouses remarry or migrate.

However, households do not all respond in the same way, or suffer the same level of costs. Studies demonstrate that the impact of AIDS varies according to three sets of characteristics: those of the *dead individuals*, such as age, sex and income; those of the *household*, such as composition, assets and source of livelihood; and those of the *community*, such as support systems and the availability of resources (Ainsworth and Over 1999). In general, studies have suggested that households can be surprisingly resilient to the costs of AIDS, precisely because of coping mechanisms: altering household composition (e.g. sending children to live elsewhere, or inviting adult relatives into the household); drawing down savings or assets (for example 41 per cent of households with a death in the Thai survey reported selling land; and 60 per cent of households in the Uganda study sold property to cover care costs); and drawing on assistance from other households (for example, local associations may be set up specifically to assist community members with AIDS). In an African context,

labour-intensive farming systems with a low level of mechanisation and agricultural inputs are said to be particularly vulnerable to the impact of AIDS (Barnett and Blaikie 1992).

As might be expected, the economic impact of AIDS is larger in poorer households. In the Thai study the lowest income and the least educated engaged in agricultural work were least able to cope (Pitayanon, Kongsin and Janjaroen 1997). In the Tanzanian study, *per capita* food consumption dropped by 15 per cent in the poorest 50 per cent of households during the six months following the death, which would be likely to increase levels of malnutrition (Ainsworth and Over 1999). Where the death was of a woman, children had lower school enrolment rates and were more likely to undertake activities normally done by women, such as cooking.

In addition to imposing costs on households, HIV/AIDS increases demands on government health care services, since it increases demand for health care among adults, usually a section of the population where health care demands are relatively low. In addition, several studies suggest that adults with AIDS use more health care prior to death than those who die of other causes (Ainsworth and Over 1999). Since HIV/AIDS also reduces the supply of health care, notably by reducing the supply of health care workers, the result is that health care facilities become swamped by chronic care patients. For example, the percentage of beds occupied by HIV-positive patients in six referral hospitals in developing countries with large epidemics was over 50 per cent in five of the six cases, and there was evidence that non-HIV positive patients were less likely to be admitted (Ainsworth and Over 1999).

The consequences of HIV/AIDS for the business community have recently attracted increased attention (Barnett and Whiteside 2002; Haacker 2002). AIDS not only increases absenteeism in people stricken by the virus, but also in those that must provide care for them. AIDS deaths increase staff turnover, and increase costs of re-assigning and training workers. Production processes become disrupted, and output of firms decreases as a result. Firms are required to allocate more resources towards medical benefits for the sick and pensions for their dependants after they die. These effects are discussed further below.

Macroeconomic Impact Mechanisms

The mechanisms through which HIV/AIDS affects national economies are as yet poorly understood, and the variety of approaches and assumptions have led to widely differing estimates of impact. Macroeconomic models, discussed later in this section, have sought to quantify the detrimental effect of the epidemic on productivity and economic growth, often summarised as the impact on total and *per capita* Gross Domestic Product (GDP). Making predictions about the effect of a hypothetical alternative to an existing scenario is a fundamental challenge of economic modelling. For areas where no intervention has been implemented, the *impact of intervening* must be estimated. Likewise, in areas where measures have been taken to combat HIV/AIDS, the disease burden in the *absence of these measures* must be approximated. Currently, no method for modelling the macroeconomic effects of HIV/AIDS has been agreed upon; however, a review of existing work can illustrate what progress has been made.

The question of how the costs and benefits of HIV/AIDS can be most appropriately quantified is fundamental in the macroeconomic modelling of the epidemic. The epidemic has a complex impact on economic growth since the majority of HIV-related deaths are among people of working age. In the medium term, the size and composition of the labour force is affected mainly through increased mortality rates, whereas in the long term, declining birth rates also contribute to the loss of workers (Haacker 2002). Early models assumed that the economy would sustain these losses, as increased mortality would relieve pressure on existing land and physical capital. The argument supporting this assumption was that unemployment levels are currently very high in Africa, and immigrants often fill vacant positions. As a result, models created between 1980 and 1992 found that mortality would have little effect on output per head (Alleyne and Cohen 2002; Bell, Devarajan and Gersbach 2003; McPherson 2003). However, more sophisticated approaches have recently been developed, and have

found that reductions in the labour force have a powerful impact on GDP (Haacker 2002; Robalino, Jenkins and El Maroufi 2002).

The decimation of the labour force has economic costs in itself in terms of productivity and training in all areas of the public and private sectors. Aside from the impact of higher mortality rates, surviving workers are less productive as they spend more time away from work either caring for the sick or coping with their own infection. As experienced workers are eliminated from the labour force, new staff must be recruited and trained. These effects are likely to be especially important in the education sector as education is a strong determinant of the productivity of future generations. On the supply side, fewer teachers are available. In Zambia, for example, the death rate of school teachers exceeds the annual capacity of teacher training colleges (McPherson 2003). Further, governmental funds allocated towards education are reduced. The demand for education is likely to become weaker, especially among vulnerable groups, as people become less certain about their future.

The structure of the household is another consideration that must be taken into account when measuring macroeconomic effects. The epidemic creates unprecedented numbers of full and partial orphans, disrupting traditional channels of community support and organisation. Bell, Devarajan and Gersbach (2003) evaluated these effects by constructing a model that considered two family structures, nuclear and 'pooling'. In a 'pooling' family structure, the extended family raises its children in a cooperative effort. Where this collective responsibility is not taken, transmission of knowledge vital for children to become productive members of society is weakened. When these children become adults, their capacity to raise their own children well is severely reduced.

Spending on HIV/AIDS prevention was found to be much more likely to reduce the impact of the epidemic on the South African economy if resources were pooled than if people were organized into nuclear families (Bell, Devarajan and Gersbach 2003). If society is structured around nuclear families, these losses can be alleviated somewhat by educational subsidies. However, these subsidies

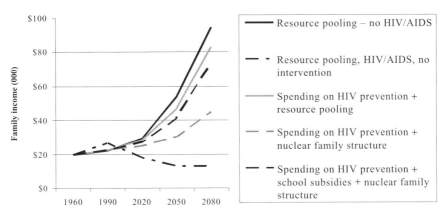

Figure 2.4. *Long-run economic costs of AIDS, South Africa, 1960–2080*
Source: Calculated from Bell, Devarajan and Gersbach (2003).

are not as effective as family reorganisation, as figure 2.4 shows.

From the perspective of government expenditure, fewer resources are available for investment in non-health-related sectors as they are directed towards strategies that attempt to manage the epidemic. Governmental revenue declines as individual productivity decreases and levels of taxable income drop. As people change their spending patterns, and have less disposable income to save and spend, tax revenues decline further.

Haacker (2002) demonstrated that the economic impact of HIV/AIDS is exacerbated when it is considered from the more realistic perspective of an *open economy*, as compared to a *closed economy* where the relationship to the rest of the world is ignored. In an open economy, the rate of return on domestic assets is linked to world interest rates, and foreign investors will be less inclined to risk ventures in that country as it becomes less productive. In addition, residents will have more incentive to invest abroad. Mortality is considered identically in each scenario, but reductions in the capital–labour ratio have greatest impact in the open economy. These assumptions have powerful effects on predictions about GDP. Depending on which perspective is taken, predictions about whether economic gains or losses can be expected are reversed. In Botswana, closed economy assumptions predict that national

GDP will rise by 9.6 per cent in the long term; open economy assumptions predict a 3.3 per cent loss (Haacker 2002).

McPherson (2003) has argued that the macroeconomic impact of HIV/AIDS predicted by current models is likely to be grossly understated. With the exception of Zerfu (2002), no model has considered effects from disruption to agricultural production and food security, yet maize production in northern Zambia decreased by 71 per cent in the 1990s, and 40 per cent of positions in the Malawian Ministry of Agriculture are vacant, so these disruptions can be expected to be severe (McPherson 2003). Further, current models assume an early peak in the epidemic, which is unlikely to occur given the already devastated condition of many affected countries (McPherson 2003).

Regional Impact Estimates

Middle East and North Africa   For the Middle East and North Africa, a macroeconomic model was coupled with an HIV diffusion model that considered spread through both STI and IDU. Three types of labour were considered: skilled, unskilled and unemployed. The model found that the most severe impact of the epidemic occurred on unskilled and unemployed groups. By 2025, it predicted that the epidemic will reduce the total GDP of North Africa by 35 per cent of today's GDP, compared to projections of what would occur in the absence

Table 2.11. Effects of HIV/AIDS on National GDP, 2000–2025

	2000 GDP ($ m)	(%) loss no intervention	Monetary loss ($ m)
Algeria	186,900	36.20	67,658
Egypt	222,190	44.30	98,430
Iran	364,400	33.60	122,438
Jordan	18,684	27.90	5,213
Lebanon	17,950	26.30	4,721
Morocco	97,991	33.20	32,533
Tunisia	58,574	45.50	26,651
Yemen	13,954	31.40	4,382

Source: Calculated from Robalino, Jenkins and El Maroufi (2002).

Table 2.12. Effect of HIV/AIDS on Long-Term GDP: No Action Taken

Country	% loss (per capita)
Botswana	3.2
Lesotho	2.1
Malawi	1.4
Mozambique	1.2
Namibia	1.8
South Africa	1.8
Swaziland	2.3
Zambia	1.8
Zimbabwe	2.3

Source: Calculated from Haacker (2002).

of HIV/AIDS (Robalino, Jenkins and El Maroufi 2002). The expected losses borne by nine countries in this region over this period are summarized in table 2.11.

Sub-Saharan Africa   Haacker (2002) devised a model for SSA that assumed that HIV prevalence remains in a steady state, in order to examine its impacts on the macroeconomy. This assumption can also be justified on the basis that the prevalence of HIV in many countries may be approaching its natural limit. The model used evidence on the demographic impact of HIV from UNAIDS and the US Bureau of the Census to predict the effects of the epidemic at end-1999 levels on companies and disaggregated areas of the public sector. Effects on GDP were measured from the perspective of both an open and a closed economy. From the perspective of an open economy, the losses to *per capita* GDP shown in table 2.12 could be expected in the long term.

Alleviation of the Challenge: Interventions

A complete package of services to alleviate the impact of the HIV/AIDS epidemic must include both *treatment* and *preventive interventions* (Jha and Mills 2002). While preventive measures are crucial as AIDS is currently an incurable disease, a strong moral argument has been put forward to justify the inclusion of measures to treat the

34–46 m people currently infected by the virus (UNAIDS 2003). However, as ARV prices are changing rapidly and the effects of ARV treatment in the developing world is highly uncertain, we have considered here primarily preventive interventions.

Nascent Epidemics

In countries where the epidemic is nascent, treatment measures are expected to be a negligible component of overall costs and benefits, as less than 5 per cent of people in high-risk groups will be infected and condom distribution and expanding safe access to needles are considered the major preventive measures (Robalino, Jenkins and El Maroufi 2002). However, the relative importance of IDU and STI as risk factors varies according to geography. Therefore, programmes need to be tailored to specific country needs.

Concentrated Epidemics

Concentrated epidemics require both treatment and preventive interventions to address the health crisis fully, most notably a set of interventions specifically targeted to high-risk groups (such as IDUs, sex workers and their clients). As an illustration, in 1989, the Ratchaburi province in Thailand introduced an initiative focused on prevention commonly known as the '100 per cent condom programme', which was expanded nationally by 1991 (Brown 2003). In this programme, condoms were provided free of charge to brothel workers, who were required to refuse sex to anyone who refused to wear them. If an infection was detected in any of these workers, police had the right to close the brothel. Further, information was obtained from men who presented to governmental health clinics with STIs to trace their infection back to its source. Non-governmental organizations (NGOs) provided training and empowered experienced sex workers to train younger ones to negotiate condom use by their clients. Public health checks were also provided free of charge to these workers. The initiative directed at brothels was supplemented by a TV and radio campaign to warn men of the dangers of visiting brothels and not wearing a condom.

Generalised Epidemics

A programme to address generalized epidemics would include many of the same interventions as in a concentrated epidemic, but they would be implemented on a wider scale. Creese *et al.* (2002) provide a standardised review of the effectiveness and cost-effectiveness of HIV/AIDS interventions in SSA (interventions are listed on p. 95).

Stover *et al.* (2002) designed a model to determine if the Declaration of Commitment, made by the UN General Assembly Special Session (UN-GASS) in June 2001, to reduce the prevalence of HIV/AIDS by 25 per cent by 2010, could be met. From a review of literature on effectiveness, they evaluated a general package of preventive interventions that should be implemented in low- and middle-income countries to combat the epidemic (table 2.13).

For some of these interventions (youth education programmes, social marketing schemes, workplace prevention programmes, harm reduction programmes, and outreach programmes for homosexual men) evidence on effectiveness is very limited.

Side Effects

Positive Side Effects

HIV/AIDS interventions include both those focused on the sick individual, and those aimed at changing sexual practices and lifestyles within the household, among IDUs, within society more

Table 2.13. UNGASS HIV/AIDS Recommendation, June 2001

Prevention interventions
School-based AIDS education
Peer education for out-of-school youth
Outreach programmes for commercial sex workers and their clients
Condom social marketing
Treatment for STIs
Public sector condom promotion and distribution
Voluntary counselling and testing
Workplace prevention programmes
Prevention of mother-to-child transmission
Mass media campaigns
Harm reduction programmes
Outreach programmes for homosexual men

Source: Stover *et al.* (2002).

generally and within the commercial sex trade. They are thus likely to have many beneficial side effects. Moreover, some of the interventions are not specific to HIV/AIDS, and provide protection against other diseases.

Examples of beneficial side effects include:

- Increased *control of fertility* through greater availability of condoms
- Reduced incidence of *other STIs*
- Better management of other *STIs and TB*
- Increased access to life-saving *blood transfusion*
- *Reduced transmission* of disease through blood transfusions
- *Reduced domestic violence* as result of improved education on sexual health and support to women (Shaw 2003)
- *Better-educated youth* as a result of school health education programmes
- Strengthened *disease surveillance and epidemiological capacity* at international and national levels.

Negative Side Effects

The comments made above on the adverse effects of medicines and vaccines apply here also. However, there are some concerns specific to HIV, particularly that of drug resistance, above all in countries where controls are lax and affordability is low. Supply and resource constraints have encouraged practices such as the use of single-dose nevirapine to treat pregnant women, which has been shown to cause resistance in as many as 75 per cent of women treated (Beckerman 2003). The Global HIV/AIDS programme of the World Bank has collaborated with other international bodies to make recommendations for how to rationally manage ARV programmes (World Bank 1993a) and several initiatives are showing success in lowering the price of drugs (Sharma 2003).

Economic Evaluation

Four approaches were taken to assess the costs and benefits associated with services proposed to address the HIV/AIDS epidemic:

1. Findings on the potential *macroeconomic impact* of preventive measures in the Middle East and North Africa are reported, to exemplify benefits for countries in the nascent stage of the epidemic.
2. The costs and benefits from *Thailand's response* are estimated, to represent a successful programme implemented in a country in the concentrated stage of the epidemic.
3. BCRs are calculated for the *interventions in SSA*.
4. The overall costs and benefits are estimated of the *package of interventions advocated by UNGASS* for low- and middle-income countries.

Nascent Epidemic Package

Robalino, Jenkins and El Maroufi (2002) found that expanding condom use by 30 per cent and access to safe needles for IDUs by 20 per cent in the Middle East and North Africa would prevent losses to the economy as high as 30 per cent of 2000 GDP between 2000 and 2025 (table 2.14).

However, if this intervention is delayed by as few as five years, the results could be disastrous. Hesitation could make as much as half of the economic decline unavoidable. Historical examples corroborate the benefits of acting early. For example, the gay population in the USA and the national initiative in Uganda have shown remarkable success in

Table 2.14. Net Benefit in Terms of 2000 National GDP by 2025 (2003 Int$)

Country	Implement immediately		Five-year delay	
	% loss averted	Monetary loss averted ($ m)	% loss averted	Monetary loss averted ($ m)
Algeria	20.40	38,128	14.70	27,474
Egypt	27.50	61,102	19.20	42,660
Iran	20.60	75,066	14.40	52,474
Jordan	15.50	2,896	11.20	2,093
Lebanon	16.80	3,016	11.80	2,118
Morocco	20.10	19,696	14.00	13,719
Tunisia	30.40	17,806	22.30	13,062
Yemen	2.20	307	−1.80	−251

Source: **Figures calculated from Robalino, Jenkins and El Maroufi (2002); World Bank (2003a).**

preventing the epidemic from spreading (Low-Beer and Stoneburner 2003).

Macroeconomic estimates of the impact of HIV/AIDS interventions are too uncertain for regions with higher prevalence, so we did not apply this approach elsewhere.

Concentrated Epidemic Package

Brown (2003) estimated the number of HIV infections that were averted in Thailand's 100 per cent condom programme. In the worst-affected areas in northern Thailand, the number of new HIV cases fell five times between 1991 and 1993, and the number of new STIs fell ten times between 1991 and 1995. While 4 per cent of new Thai military conscripts had HIV in 1993, only 0.5 per cent were infected in 2001. Overall, the number of new cases of HIV in Thailand fell from 142,819 in 1991 to 25,790 in 2001, ultimately even reducing the incidence in sex workers (Brown 2003; Low-Beer and Stoneburner 2003). Based on these figures, Brown (2003) estimated that 200,000 infections were averted between 1993 and 2000.

The costs of the programme were borne by both the private sector and by the government (Brown 2003). The private sector financed information campaigns broadcast through the media costing

Table 2.15. Costs and Benefits of Thailand's 100 per cent Condom Programme, 1993–2000 (2003 $Int)

	No. of cases averted	Total benefit ($ m)	Total cost ($ m)	Net benefit ($ m)	ANB ($ m)	BCR
100% condom programme	200,000	24,105	1,820	24,105	3,444	14.2

Source: Figures based on Brown (2003).

Int$160 m.[21] The cost of government programmes aimed at brothels rose from Int$3,396,437 in 1991 to Int$93,369,040 in 1996. We assumed this cost grew linearly during this period, and remained constant between 1996 and 2000. Discounted at 3 per cent, the programme cost Int$1,820 m in 1993–2000. The ANB and BCR are shown in table 2.15.

Increasing the discount rate to 6 per cent decreased the net benefit to Int$22,085 m. Standardizing the ceiling ratio to Int$3,830 reduced the net benefit to Int$14,118 m and the BCR to 8.8.

Interventions in SSA

Microeconomic studies have shown that most individual interventions for combating HIV are highly cost-effective (Creese *et al.* 2002). Table 2.16 demonstrates this, together with estimated benefit cost ratios.

Many of these figures are likely to underestimate the cost-effectiveness (and BCR) of the interventions. For example, none of the studies that evaluated preventive measures against vertical transmission considered the knock-on effects on *horizontal transmission*. The effects of ARV therapy may be underestimated, as transmission may be reduced through the reduction in viral loads; prices are also falling rapidly.

Several other interventions not included in this review show promise of being highly cost-effective measures against HIV. Microbicides are being developed that women could use discreetly to protect themselves in the absence of condom use, and may be available as soon as 2007. It has been shown that their benefits in terms of productivity gains and direct cost savings to the health system would be substantial, and are robust to wide variations in assumptions (Watts *et al.* 2002).

When interventions are packaged according to those that complement each other, the cost-

effectiveness improves further. A 2003 study shows that integrating TB and HIV services can be done for $1 per person under favourable assumptions (Terris-Prestholt *et al.* 2003). Further, the cost-effectiveness of many interventions has been shown to improve as programmes mature.

Overall Package for HIV Prevention

The model developed by Stover *et al.* (2002) estimated baseline HIV prevalence in countries with generalised and concentrated epidemics according to the size of risk group, current practice and degree of sexual mixing. With no intervention, they predicted that 45.4 million new infections would occur between 2002 and 2010. Evidence on the effectiveness of interventions (table 2.13) to limit the spread of the epidemic was taken from eighty-six studies found through a literature review. Their effectiveness was defined in terms of their impact on five behaviours: condom use, treatment seeking behaviour for STIs, number of sexual partners, age at first sexual intercourse and sharing of potentially infected needles. They then estimated costs and outcomes according to coverage levels, many of which varied with prevalence. In total, their model predicted that 63 per cent of infections would be averted if an expanded response costing Int$1.42 *per capita* were put in place.

We applied an estimate for the number of YLLs lost per HIV infection (23.08), and a monetary value per YLL lost for the countries included (Int$4,460), to calculate costs and benefits (table 2.17).

Table 2.17 shows that the implementation of the UNGASS package of HIV/AIDS interventions is substantially beneficial. When the value of a YLL is lowered to Int$3830, the net benefit decreases to Int$2.5 trillion, with a BCR of 42.9.

---

[21] We assumed that this programme cost $23.4 m each year.

Table 2.16. BCRs of Interventions, SSA

		Cost per DALY averted	
Prevention	BCR	Reported (2000 US$)	Adjusted (2003 Int$)
Condom distribution plus STD treatment for sex workers	466	$1	$4
Female condoms targeted to			
Sex workers	39	$12	$45
High-risk women	10	$48	$180
Medium-risk women	5	$99	$372
Blood safety			
Hospital-based screening	93–466	$1–$5	$4–$19
Strengthening blood transfusion services			
Defer high-risk donors	93–466	$1–$5	$4–$19
Test and defer high-risk donors	155–233	$2–$3	$8–$11
Rapid test	155	$3	$11
Improved transfusion safety with outreach	39–47	$10–$12	$38–$45
Improved blood collection and transfusion	11	$43	$162
Peer education of sex workers	67–116	$4–$7	$15–$26
Prevention of mother-to-child transmission			
Single-dose nevirapine (universal)	52	$9	$34
ZDV Petra regimen	52	$9	$34
ZDV CDC Thai regimen	6–14	$33–$75	$124–$282
Formula recommendation	4	$131	$492
Breastfeeding three months	3	$171	$642
Formula provision	2	$218	$819
Breastfeeding six months	1	$731	$2,748
Diagnosis and treatment of STIs	39	$12	$45
Voluntary counselling and testing	21–26	18–$22	$68–$83
Treatment and care			
Short-course TB treatment for new sputum-smear positive pulmonary patients			
TB ambulatory care			
Malawi, Mozambique, Tanzania (1991)	155–233	$2–$3	$8–$11
Uganda (1995)	116–233	$2–$4	$8–$15
South Africa (1997)	29–58	$8–$16	$30–$60
IUATLD model			
Uganda (1995)	116–155	$3–$4	$11–$15
Malawi, Mozambique, Tanzania (1991)	58–116	$4–$8	$15–$30
South Africa (1997)	7–14	$34–$68	$128–$256
Community-based DOT	22–33	$14–$21	$53–$79
Co-trimoxazole prophylaxis for HIV and TB patients	78	$6	$23
Home-based care for people with AIDS			
Community-based programme			
Tanzania	6	$77	$289
Zambia	5	$99	$372
Health facility-based programme			
Zambia (1994)	1	$681	$2,560
Tanzania (2000)	1	$786	$2,955
Zimbabwe (1998)	0.4–0.9	$469–$1230	$1,763–$4,624
Preventive therapy for TB			
Isoniazid six months	3	$169	$635
Rifampicin plus pyrazinamide two months	2	$282	$1,060
Isoniazid plus rifampicin three months	2	$288	$1,083
ARV for adults			
Senegal and Côte D'Ivoire (2000)	0.4	$1,100	$4,135
South Africa (2000)	0.3	$1,800	$6,766

Source: Figures based on Creese *et al.* (2002).

Table 2.17. Cost and Benefits of the UNGASS Package of Interventions, Middle- and Low-Income Countries (2003 Int$)

New infections baseline (2002–10) (m)	New infections package (2002–10) (m)	Infections averted (2002–10)	Benefits ($ m) (2002–10) (m)	Costs ($ m) (2002–10)	Net benefit ($ m) (2002–10)	ANB ($ m)	BCR
45.4	16.9	28.5	2,934,148	58,760	2,875,389	359,424	49.9

Source: Figures based on Stover *et al.* (2002); World Bank (2003a).

Stover *et al.* (2002) stress that the full impact of their programme is achievable only in the presence of strong care and support programmes, and with political commitment to its implementation. More infections are preventable epidemiologically in countries where the epidemic is growing rapidly, such as China and Cameroon, than in countries where it is stable or declining. With full effect, 33 per cent of global infections would be prevented in China and India alone, with 40 per cent prevented in SSA.

Feasibility

A successful battle against the HIV/AIDS epidemic requires political and social commitment at all levels. This has been developing slowly – as evidenced by the high levels of prevalence in much of SSA, and the relatively few countries which are known for their high commitment to control (such as Uganda and Senegal). HIV/AIDS confronts countries with a unique challenge, since major routes of transmission include those which are illegal, or at least judged morally unacceptable. To the extent that the transmission route has to be openly acknowledged in order for it to be addressed, this poses great challenges to countries reluctant to accept, for example, that homosexual relationships are widespread in prisons, or that all levels of society frequent sex workers. Commitment can take the form of government support to public health workers, such as meetings set up by the police between public health workers and brothel owners (Brown 2003), and clear public messages. It has been argued that the impact of these measures is greatest when the public is actively involved in spreading these messages through the community because people are more likely to internalise the message and change their behaviour (Low-Beer and Stoneburner 2003).

For the HIV/AIDS epidemic to be confronted effectively, financial resources from both higher- and lower-income countries must be increased. The total UNGASS package would cost US$9.2 bn annually by 2005 to provide the expanded response in low- and middle-income countries (Low-Beer and Stoneburner 2003). Currently, the Global Fund for AIDS, TB and Malaria provides most of the world's funding to fight AIDS, and has allocated US$2–3 bn towards efforts to control HIV (Jha and Mills 2002). Donor support has been increasing at an unprecedented level, with the Bill and Melinda Gates Foundation recently increasing its pledge to fight HIV/AIDS in India to US$200 m (Sharma 2003). Other organisations, such as the Clinton Foundation, are successfully negotiating lower prices for ARV medications (Sharma 2003). Since 2000, the cost of antiretroviral regimens has fallen from an annual US$10,000 per patient to US$300 (Anon 2003). Considering that the PPP adjusted GNI of OECD countries was $25.6 trillion in 2002, full support for the UNGASS package would require these countries to donate 0.04 per cent (World Bank 2004b), a share that has been judged feasible (Gallup and Sachs 2001; Potts and Walsh 2003).

Further investment is needed to improve technology to supplement available interventions. Currently, there is no cure or vaccine that would provide protection against the HIV virus. As previously mentioned, a microbicide that women could use secretly before sex to protect themselves against infection could be available by 2007.

Lines of responsibility must be drawn for intervention programmes to be effective. Placing local authorities in charge of promoting awareness and delivering services increases coverage to marginalised groups and raises awareness. Non-state providers have an important role in supplementing government health services. In Uganda,

NGOs such as TASO have been successful in promoting awareness through their work with faith-based organisations (Low-Beer and Stoneburner 2003). In India, autonomous AIDS control societies have been set up through which public funds for HIV/AIDS services are channelled (Ramasundaram *et al.* 2001). They appear to offer an efficient means of working around the often slow Indian state bureaucracy.

Countries and organisations need to ensure that information is continuously collected and analysed for intervention programmes, in order to learn from previous mistakes and improve effectiveness and efficiency. AIDS surveillance in Thailand and Uganda permitted these countries to monitor the status of their epidemics, and has been recognised as a major factor contributing to their successes (Brown 2003; Low-Beer and Stoneburner 2003).

General issues of feasibility of implementation are reviewed on pp. 101ff.

Strengthening Basic Health Services

Identification and Description

While the opportunity to scale up basic health services is inclusive of the first two, it provides a comprehensive perspective of the challenge posed by communicable disease in the developing world, as well as including other common conditions. The great majority of health interventions depend for successful and sustained implementation on an infrastructure of basic health services, consisting of community-based services, health centres and local hospitals offering inpatient care. Such a service infrastructure has also been referred to as *primary health care* (PHC), or a *district health system*. Relative to other forms of medical care, PHC can be argued to be the most accessible, least costly and best-equipped method to provide effective care for the conditions that most affect global health (Doherty and Govender 2004). Theoretically, it is estimated that PHC is able to address 90 per cent of health care

demands. Although recent international initiatives have tended to be disease- or programme-specific – e.g. RBM, the Global Fund for HIV, TB and Malaria GAVI (Global Alliance for Vaccines and Immunisation), 3 by 5[22]) – they all acknowledge their reliance on basic health services. Moreover, there are historical experiences where a strong public health role has been related to health outcomes that are much better than might be expected at low levels of income (for example Cuba and Sri Lanka) (Halstead and Walsh 1985; Mehrotra 2000).[23]

Two types of evidence are available on the costs and benefits of expanding health services: evidence from cross-country analyses of the relationship between health expenditure and health gains; and estimates of the costs and health benefits of packages of interventions. Regression analysis has been used to measure the effect of economic inputs on health sector outputs in terms of elasticities. To make this link, 'health' must be defined in quantitative terms, and a proxy measure is used such as under-five mortality, maternal mortality, underweight among children under five and disease-specific mortality. Public spending in the health sector is commonly used as an independent variable. An advantage of this approach is that it seeks to measure the link between expenditure and health while controlling for other factors that contribute to national health status, such as income and education. While an often-cited study found that government spending had a small and insignificant impact on under-five mortality (Filmer and Pritchett 1999), more recent analyses are beginning to find specific effects on population sub-groups (Rajkumar and Swaroop 2002). For example, Gupta, Verhoeven and Tiongson (2001) found that spending had a significant impact on child mortality, specifically benefiting population groups living on less than $2 per day.

There have been several efforts to identify a package of priority interventions to be delivered through local health services, using some mix of criteria including magnitude of the burden, availability of interventions and cost-effectiveness. These efforts include the 1993 *World Development Report* 1993 (World Bank 1993) (its list is reproduced in table 2.18, p. 99), *Better Health in Africa* (World Bank 1994), the 2000 *World Health Report* (WHO 2000a;

---

[22] Providing antiretrovirals to 3m people by 2005.
[23] Though good nutrition and education also contributed to these health gains.

Table 2.18. The 1993 *World Development Report* Minimum Health Package

Clusters of interventions	Main disease conditions addressed
Public health	
Expanded programme on immunisation	Measles, poliomyelitis, tetanus, whooping cough, yellow fever, hepatitis B
School health programme	Intestinal worms
AIDS prevention programme	STIs and AIDS
Tobacco and alcohol control programmes	Lung cancer, cardiovascular disease, cirrhosis, injuries associated with alcohol abuse
Other public health programmes (including family planning, health, and nutrition information)	These are not disease-specific
Clinical	
Short-course chemotherapy for tuberculosis	Tuberculosis in adults
Management of the sick child	Diarrhoeal diseases, pneumonia and other respiratory infections, malaria, measles, and severe malnutrition
Pre-natal and delivery care	Perinatal mortality and morbidity, complications of pregnancy and delivery, low birth weight, unwanted pregnancies and congenital syphilis and gonorrhea
Family planning	Perinatal and infant mortality and maternal mortality and morbidity
Treatment of STIs	AIDS, syphilis, gonorrhea, chlamydia and other STIs
Limited care (mainly for adults)	Pain control, infection and minor trauma treatment and advice to reduce chronic diseases

Source: World Bank (1993b).

Doherty and Govender 2004) and the CMH Working Group 5 (Jha and Mills 2002). In general, these efforts identify very similar packages.

Alleviation of the Challenge: Interventions

Studies estimating the relationship between increased health sector expenditure and improved health make no assumption on specific interventions: health expenditure is increased in proportion to current patterns.

For a package of interventions to strengthen basic health services, we have chosen to use the 1993 *World Development Report* package, because its DALY benefit was estimated and the package is still relevant. Table 2.18 lists the interventions in the package. In general, the interventions make few demands on high-level care, with the required hospital resources consisting of a capacity for emergency surgery, blood transfusion and treatment of the more severe cases.

Side Effects

Positive Side Effects

The existence of a well-functioning system of basic health services may have positive side effects in providing a visible demonstration of the effectiveness of government, and in improving relationships between the government and local people. Achieving the MDGs related to health will be vital for making gains in other MDGs. As outlined in Figure 2.2 (p. 67), health influences income, nutrition and access to resources, and can be expected to make an important contribution to halving the proportion of people who live on less than $1 per day.

Negative Side Effects

Comments in earlier sections on the adverse effects of drugs and vaccines apply also here. Drugs and vaccines used in basic health services have mostly been used for many decades, so their safety profiles are well known.

Table 2.19. Costs and Benefits of Increased Health Expenditure, 2002–2015 (2003 Int$)

Intervention	Under-five population	Total benefit ($ m)	Total cost ($ m)	Net benefit ($ m)	ANB ($ m)	BCR
Increased overall public spending on health in HIPC group (Int$ 1,470)	27,541,139	480,426	225,115	225,311	18,236	2.1

Source: Calculated from Gupta, Verhoeven and Tiongson (2002); World Bank (2003a).

Economic Evaluation

We estimated the costs and benefits of scaling up basic health services, drawing on the two sources of data mentioned above: evidence of the relationship between health expenditure and health gains; and estimates of the costs and health benefits of the package of interventions recommended in the 1993 *World Development Report*.

Increased Overall Health Expenditure

According to the elasticities in their model, Gupta, Verhoeven and Tiongson (2001) estimated the expenditures necessary for a cohort of countries to reach the International Development Goal (subsequently adopted as an MDG) to reduce child mortality by two-thirds by 2015. These countries were HIPCs approved for further aid from the International Monetary Fund (IMF) and World Bank in mid-2001, as they found that it would be especially crucial for these countries to increase preferential spending on the poor for the MDGs to be met. Assuming that income and education levels remained constant, they estimated that public spending on health would need to increase from an average of 2 per cent of GDP in 1999 to 12 per cent of GDP in 2015.

We quantified the expenditure for thirteen of these countries assuming that spending increased at a constant rate from levels of GDP.[24] Between 1990 and 2001, GDP grew by 3.4 per cent in low-income countries (World Bank 2002) and we assumed that this pattern would continue to 2015 (World Bank 2003b). Assuming that additional

health expenditures would increase linearly between 1999 and 2015, incremental expenditure was calculated and discounted.

We calculated benefits by projecting levels of child mortality into the future, decreasing linearly at an annual rate of 2.67 per cent from a rate of 157 deaths per 1,000 children in 1990, in order to reach the goal by 2015. Deaths avoided were calculated by subtracting this trajectory from a baseline scenario in which child mortality remained constant at 1990 levels. Each child death was associated with 28.41 YLLs, and valued in monetary terms according to the average GNI for these countries (Int$1,407) (World Bank 2003a). Costs and benefits are shown in table 2.19.

If a 6 per cent discount rate is used, ANB falls to Int$14,383 m, with little effect on the BCR of 2.1. If the ceiling ratio is increased to Int$3,830, ANB increases to $77,332 m, with a BCR of 5.8.

Results are highly sensitive to the trend of *baseline mortality* used to calculate deaths averted. If it is assumed that the annual decreases in child mortality (1.1 per cent) that occurred in the developing world during the 1990s continue to 2015 in the absence of intervention (Black, Morris and Bryce 2003), averted mortality is so reduced that total net benefit becomes negative (−Int$7.3 bn) (though it should be noted that if this trend does indeed occur, a greater than two-thirds reduction in child mortality might be expected from increased expenditure).

In interpreting these figures, several points should be noted. On the expenditure side, the calculations assume an overall expansion in current patterns of health expenditure. To the extent that expenditures can be better targeted, on high-return health interventions and on individuals with the worst health status, the returns are likely to be

[24] These countries included: Bolivia, Burkina Faso, The Gambia, Honduras, Madagascar, Mali, Mauritania, Mozambique, Niger, Rwanda, Senegal, Tanzania and Uganda.

Table 2.20. Costs and Benefits of the 1993 *World Development Report* Minimum Health Package (2003 Int$)

	Population	Annual benefits ($ m)	Annual costs ($ m)	ANB ($ m)	BCR
Low- and middle-income countries (Int$3,830)	5,173,100,000	871,158	337,073	534,084	2.6

Source: Figures based on World Bank (1993b, 2003a).

higher. Determinants of health other than expenditure, such as improvements in education and level of consumption, are not considered and are likely to have a synergistic impact. On the benefit side, the effects of the expenditure increase on child deaths only is included, although service expansion would be expected to benefit a range of population groups. Overall, the cohort of highly indebted countries in the analysis is expected to produce a modest estimate of the returns to investment. Health systems in financially constrained countries are notoriously weak, and are likely to require proportionally more investment to scale up health services than wealthier ones.

Package of Priority Interventions

Bobadilla *et al.* (1994) estimated that the 1993 *World Development Report* package would cost Int$65 per person in low- and middle-income countries and would reduce the disease burden by 25 per cent. Based on 2002 estimates from the Global Burden of Disease database, this package would be expected to avert 227,456,368 YLLs each year. The economic benefits of implementing such a package are outlined in table 2.20.

The favourable BCR is expected as the framers of this package selected clusters of interventions with strong consideration of their cost-effectiveness, targeted towards groups that were most likely to benefit. By clustering interventions and including those with synergies between them, costs were kept to a minimum. Applying a standard ceiling ratio has no effect, since the ceiling ratio is already that for low- and middle-income countries.

Feasibility

The growing literature on the relationship between public expenditure on health care and health outcomes (Filmer and Pritchett 1999; Gupta, Verhoeven and Tiongson 2001) cautions against easily assuming that increased public expenditure will be translated into improved health outcomes. Analysis of the relationship between public spending and child mortality finds results varying from statistical significance to insignificance (World Bank 2004a), for a variety of both methodological and policy-related reasons. With respect to the latter, public spending may not be well targeted on the poor who have the worst health outcomes; much of it may not reach the local service provider, being tied up at higher levels and in central hospitals; and service quality is often very poor. Failings may both be a reflection of the overall poor quality of the policy environment, and of more mundane difficulties in managing service provision in settings with very limited capacity, difficult communications and few trained staff.

The challenge of meeting the MDGs has led to a recent focus on the difficulties facing health service delivery, and on the constraints that need to be overcome to scale up the coverage of priority health services (Jha and Mills 2002; Ranson *et al.* 2003; World Bank 2004a). This body of work directly addresses the managerial challenges in strengthening basic health services. Although evidence is still quite limited on how best to address constraints (Oliveira-Cruz, Hanson and Mills 2003), it is good enough to make some suggestions on how best to improve health services, in both the most highly constrained countries (for example, those with very weak governments) and those which are somewhat less constrained. Table 2.21 both identifies constraints by level and suggests measures to address constraints in settings which are more or less constrained. A key difference between these settings is that the weaker the government system, the greater needs to be the reliance on working outside

Table 2.21. Relaxing Constraints: Priority Actions, By Type of Country

Level of constraint	Highly constrained countries	Least constrained countries
Community and household level	• Encourage community mobilisation through NGOs • Use social marketing and retail sector to make effective drugs available to households	• Use incentives to stimulate demand
Health services delivery level	• Build up health care delivery infrastructure through public services and/or agreements with NGO and church providers • Use outreach services and NGOs where public sector difficult to extend	• Improve human resource management policies in order to ensure better staff performance • Strengthen local management
Health sector policy and strategic management level	• Increase degree of management decentralisation • Strengthen drug supply and distribution system through public and/or private sector • Greater donor coordination	• Increase degree of management decentralisation • Greater donor coordination • Strengthen regulation of private sector
Public policies cutting across sectors		• Give greater autonomy to health sector
Environmental characteristics	• Prepare for possible scale up under improved conditions; maintain links with NGOs; support education and training	• Encourage more pluralist policy process

Source: Jha and Mills (2002).

government channels, using NGOs and the private sector, for example.

However, there are also issues of political and financial feasibility. At international level, there has been reluctance to envisage support for a health service development strategy. Political commitment appears to be easier to gain for specific disease control efforts, such as HIV/AIDS and malaria. It may be, however, that the current international focus on extending antiretroviral treatment to AIDS patients will help change this attitude, since of all priority interventions, ARV treatment is highly dependent on a health service infrastructure. The importance being given to improving service delivery and ensuring it serves the poor is indicated by its choice as the subject of the 2004 World Development Report (World Bank 2004a), which emphasises institutional changes to strengthen relationships of accountability between policy makers, service providers and citizens, as the key to improving service delivery.

Financially, this opportunity faces the most severe financial constraints, since it is the most costly of all three opportunities. There is substantial disagreement over how much countries need to spend to achieve high levels of coverage of priority interventions. The total annual costs estimated for the *World Development Report* 1993 package were US$12 *per capita* in low-income countries and US$22 *per capita* in middle-income countries (US$1993). The *Better Health in Africa* cost was $13 *per capita* (US$1990), in low-income African countries (World Bank 1994). The CMH report put great stress on adequately costing the full cost of scaling up, including adequate remuneration to health staff and expansion of training and management and supervisory capacity at all levels. It also included a more extended AIDS package, including treatment. It estimated a total of US$38 *per capita* (US$2002) for low-income countries (US$41 for least-developed countries, LDCs), to achieve the scaling up targets (CMH 2001). This level of expenditure implies on average 5.9 per cent of GNP devoted to health (11.4 per cent for LDCs), consisting of 2002 total health expenditure plus the additional costs of raising coverage and quality. It can be noted that the CMH figure for LDCs is consistent with Gupta, Verhoeven and Tiongson (2001), who estimated 12 per cent. The CMH report estimated that donor aid to LDCs would need to rise by an additional US$31 bn a year by 2015, if these country expenditure levels were to be achieved (CMH 2001).

Discussion and Conclusion

This chapter has reviewed the evidence on the economic benefits of good health, specifically in relation to communicable disease, and the economic costs of malaria and HIV/AIDS. It has also sought to estimate the benefits and costs of reducing the burden of communicable disease, considering separately malaria control, HIV/AIDS control, and strengthened basic health services. In order to do this, evidence was drawn from four main sources: studies of the economic cost of disease; microeconomic studies of the costs and health effects of health interventions; estimates of the efficiency of health expenditures with respect to health outcomes; and examples of successful programmes where some data were available on costs and health benefits.

All these sources of data have substantial shortcomings, which must inform the interpretation of the estimates of costs and benefits:

- The *macroeconomic literature* is quite inadequate. In the case of malaria, it is very sparse (two recent studies only) and has yet to generate a critical debate on methods and data. In the case of HIV/AIDS, the literature provides wildly differing estimates, ranging from a minimal impact to a massive impact on *per capita* income.
- The *interventions literature* is derived largely from epidemiological trials; evidence of costs and health effects in the context of large-scale programme implementation is rather limited. Furthermore, health effects have to be translated into a monetary value. We chose to apply the ceiling ratio of one times *per capita* GNI, but this decision is arbitrary; in sensitivity analyses we applied the GNI for low- and middle-income countries and fixed values per life in order not to disadvantage health gains in poor countries.
- The analysis of the *efficiency of health expenditure* relates all health expenditure to health

outcomes for a single population group, omitting benefits for others.
- Evidence from *successful programmes* is hard to interpret, since external factors may also have affected changes in health effects.

Macroeconomic estimates of benefits and calculations made from cost-effectiveness evidence cannot, of course, be assumed to reflect the same dimensions of benefits. Macroeconomic benefits allow for interactions over time – where improved health feeds, for example, into increased labour supply quantity and quality, and into changed savings and investment patterns. In contrast, the conversion of health gains into a monetary value reflects an assumption on the value of human life, not related only to its productive potential but rather to its broader value in terms of human welfare. Moreover, given the weakness of the evidential base, it would be unwise to read too much into differences between the evidence from these two different sources.

In addition, our estimates suffer from four other shortcomings:

- We would have preferred to have estimated costs and benefits over the same time periods, and discounted to *present values* or calculated an *internal rate of return* (IRR). Given the varied nature of the available data, this was not possible to do consistently
- Available costs were not necessarily consistent in the cost items included, and usually costs to the *provider*, excluding costs to users
- Savings in health care costs that would result from *preventive activities* were not included in the Thailand, HIV package or Gupta calculations (thus underestimating benefits)
- We would have liked to have been more explicit on *who would benefit* under each of the opportunities, and in particular on the extent to which the poorest would benefit. This is partly a question of which groups suffer most from the diseases in question, and partly an issue of the extent to which countries are able or willing to ensure that all population groups benefit from expanded disease control efforts.

This last point bears on the feasibility of the opportunities considered. Increased health expenditure

Table 2.22. Summary of Key Results (Int$ 2003)

Opportunity, source, geographic region	Per capita costs (annualised) ($)	Total benefit (annualised) ($ m)	Total cost (annualised) ($ m)	Net benefit (annualised) ($ m)	BCR 3% DCR	BCR 6% DR	BCR Rc = Int$3,830
Control of malaria							
Based on evidence from macroeconomic models	18.0 per capita	19,711–47,451	10,177	9,534–37,274	1.9–4.7	1.8–4.3	No ceiling ratio
Package of malaria interventions	n/a	50,419	2,942	47,476	17.1	23.4	38.9
Control of HIV/AIDS							
Thai programme of prevention	4.25 per capita	3,704	260	3,444	14.2	14.4	8.8
Package for prevention of HIV/AIDS; six regions (EAP, EAC, LAC, SEA, SAR, SSA)	1.42 per capita	366,769	7,345	359,424	49.9	DCR within model	42.9
Scaled up basic health services							
Increased health expenditure; thirteen HIPCs;	584 per child	34,316	16,080	18,236	2.1	2.1	5.8
1993 *World Development Report* minimum package; low- and middle-income countries	65 per capita	871,158	337,073	534,084	2.6	1 year	2.6

Note: n/a = not applicable.

will be translated into improved health outcomes only if the right policies are adopted and well implemented. Low- and middle-income country health systems often have shortcomings, which mean that they are less efficient at transferring expenditure into health gains than they could be. Considerable attention has thus to be paid to the structures through which health programmes are implemented, as well as to the preferences and knowledge of users. Moreover, the focus of two of the challenges on controlling specific communicable diseases should not be interpreted to indicate that their implementation can avoid the problems and inefficiencies of working through existing health systems. As made clear in the text, important components of both malaria and HIV/AIDS control are dependent on the health system.

Given all these caveats, we highlight and summarise our main estimates in table 2.22. A complete summary of all results is in appendix 1 (p. 106). On the basis of the earlier analyses, we have selected a sub-set of results to highlight, based on criteria of:

- Relevance to a range of countries
- Inclusion of a package of interventions.

It should be noted that the *per capita* costs apply to different populations; in some cases the general population and in others the target groups for particular interventions (as noted in the relevant column). The last two columns show the results of the sensitivity analysis on the DCR and ceiling ratio in terms of its impact on the BCR.

Table 2.22 suggests that many health interventions and programmes are highly cost-beneficial. There is a general pattern, as one might expect, that estimates based on cost-effectiveness data for specific interventions (packages of malaria and HIV interventions) show much higher BCRs than broader programmes. At least in part this is for methodological reasons – for example, underestimation of the necessary costs of system strengthening, and likely overestimation of benefits because of drawing evidence of effectiveness from trial data. However, it is noteworthy that the real-life example, that of HIV prevention in Thailand, shows substantial net benefits and a favourable BCR of 14.2. The WDR package has the highest net benefits of all (partly because it is applied to all low- and middle-income countries) and a favourable benefit-cost ratio, of 2.6. The estimate based on Gupta, Verhoeven and Tiongson (2001) also has a favourable BCR, of 2.1, despite three factors that might be expected to reduce it: the costs relate to increasing health expenditure overall but the benefits were estimated for child mortality only (excluding benefits in adult health); the increase in health expenditure represents an increase in the overall pattern of health expenditure, not the targeting to effective interventions; the countries in the analysis are some of the poorest, where it might be expected that the costs of achieving a given health effect are higher given the multiple disadvantages faced by their populations. However, the estimate is highly sensitive to assumptions on the underlying rate of child mortality change.

Despite uncertainties over the estimates, table 2.22 emphasises that there are likely to be high returns from investing in communicable disease control – BCRs substantially exceeding 1. Taken with the currently low coverage of malaria, HIV/AIDS and basic health care programmes in large parts of the developing world, especially SSA, they suggest that communicable disease control is substantially under resourced. Moreover, investments where health status is low will provide substantial benefits to the poorest populations of the world.

To support comparisons across other chapters in this volume, we estimated BCRs according to standard values for deaths averted. In our baseline calculations, where the value of benefits was linked to *per capita* GNI, the value attributed to each death averted ranged between US$39,977 and US$141,767 (appendix 2, p. 108). Standardising the value of life to the extremely low value of US$1,250 reduces the value of benefits substantially, resulting in values below 1 for the Thai HIV programme and strengthened health services. When the value of life is raised to US$100,000, BCRs become very attractive, increasing by an order of magnitude from baseline calculations.

To allow readers to interpret findings according to their own judgement about the value of life, baseline results are given in appendix 3 (p. 109) in terms of cost per life year averted and cost per death averted. Finally, the age of the group that benefits may influence prioritisation decisions, and these proportions are also given in appendix 3.

Given estimation and data difficulties, it remains unclear whether greater returns are achievable from focusing on a specific disease, such as malaria or HIV/AIDS, or from a broader (though still focused) basic health services strategy. Moreover, it cannot be emphasised enough that these three approaches are not completely independent – both malaria and HIV/AIDS control must include a substantial component of strengthening basic health services if they are to be successful. While costing sought to allow for this, it is probable that the system strengthening costs required for malaria- and HIV-specific interventions have not been adequately allowed for, suggesting that in practice there may be less of a difference between BCRs for disease-specific interventions and general health service interventions than suggested in table 2.22.

For reasons of space and focus, this chapter has not explored issues of the role of government in addressing communicable disease. However, a strong case can be made for public funding for controlling communicable diseases, on both poverty and efficiency grounds (given positive externalities and public goods arguments). Finally, it should be noted that the productivity of health expenditure is likely to be greater both in a *supportive policy environment*, and where *complementary investments* take place, such as in female education.

Appendix 1

Table 2A1.1. Complete Summary of Results (Int$ 2003)

Opportunity, source, geographic region	*Per capita* costs (annualised) ($)	Total annual benefit ($ m)	Total annual cost ($ m)	ANB ($ m)	BCR	BCR 6% DR	BCR Rc = $3,830
Control of malaria							
Based on macroeconomic models							
Gallup and Sachs (2001); Jha and Mills (2002)	18.0 *per capita*	47,451	10,177	37,274	4.7	4.3	No ceiling ratio
McCarthy, Wolf and Wu (2000); Jha and Mills (2002)	18.0 *per capita*	19,711	10,177	9,534	1.9	1.8	No ceiling ratio
ITNs for children under five, Goodman et al. *(2000)*							
SSA – LIC	28.47 per child	6,693	1,180	5,513	5.7	5.4	25.6
SSA – MIC	29.02 per child	5,308	435	4,873	12.2	11.5	25.1
SSA – HIC	33.50 per child	6,477	158	6,319	41.1	39.1	21.7
SSA – Total	**28.99 per child**	**18,479**	**1,773**	**16,706**	**10.4**	**9.9**	**25.1**
IPTp at ANC visits, Goodman et al. *(2000)[a]*							
SSA – LIC	6.59 per PG	174	22	152	8.0	7.5	36.1
SSA – MIC	7.29 per PG	138	9	129	15.9	14.8	32.6
SSA – HIC	12.47 per PG	168	5	164	36.1	34.0	19.1
SSA – Total	**7.21 per PG**	**480**	**35**	**445**	**13.7**	**12.8**	**33.0**
Switch from SP to ACTs, Coleman et al. *(2004)[a]*							
SSA	2.98 per malaria case	19,331	501	18,830	38.6	34.3	84.5
Scaling up ACTs, Coleman et al. *(2004)[a]*							
SSA	20.21 per malaria case	12,129	634	11,496	19.1	19.1	41.9
Switch from SP to ACTs in South Africa							
Muheki *et al.* (2004)	−98.37 per case averted	0.1	−0.4	0.5	Cost-saving	No DCR	Cost-saving
Control of HIV/AIDS							
Based on macroeconomic models, Robalino, Jenkins and El Maroufi (2002)							
Algeria	n/a	n/a	n/a	1,525	n/a	n/a	n/a
Egypt	n/a	n/a	n/a	2,444	n/a	n/a	n/a
Iran	n/a	n/a	n/a	3,003	n/a	n/a	n/a

Table 2A1.1. (*Cont.*)

Opportunity, source, geographic region	Per capita costs (annualised) ($)	Total annual benefit ($m)	Total annual cost ($m)	ANB ($m)	BCR	BCR 6% DR	BCR Rc = $3,830
Jordan	n/a	n/a	n/a	116	n/a	n/a	n/a
Lebanon	n/a	n/a	n/a	121	n/a	n/a	n/a
Morocco	n/a	n/a	n/a	788	n/a	n/a	n/a
Tunisia	n/a	n/a	n/a	712	n/a	n/a	n/a
Yemen	n/a	n/a	n/a	12	n/a	n/a	n/a
Country experience							
Thailand programme, Brown (2003)	4.25 *per capita*	3,704	260	3,444	14.2	14.4	8.8
Specific interventions, Creese et al. (2002), SSA							
Condom distribution	n/a	n/a	n/a	n/a	466–5	n/a	1,019–10
Blood safety	n/a	n/a	n/a	n/a	466–11	n/a	1,019–24
Peer education for sex workers	n/a	n/a	n/a	n/a	116–67	n/a	255–146
Prevention of MTC transmission	n/a	n/a	n/a	n/a	52–1	n/a	113–1.39
Treatment of STIs	n/a	n/a	n/a	n/a	39	n/a	85
VCT	n/a	n/a	n/a	n/a	26–21	n/a	57–46
Short-course treatment, TB	n/a	n/a	n/a	n/a	233–7	n/a	509–15
Co-trimoxazole prophylaxis	n/a	n/a	n/a	n/a	78	n/a	170
Home care	n/a	n/a	n/a	n/a	6–0.4	n/a	13–0.8
Tuberculosis preventive therapy	n/a	n/a	n/a	n/a	3–2	n/a	6–3.5
ARV	n/a	n/a	n/a	n/a	0.4–0.3	n/a	0.9–0.6
Package for prevention of HIV/AIDS, Stover et al. (2002)							
Six regions (EAP, EAC, LAC, SEA, SAR, SSA)	1.42 *per capita*	366,769	7,345	359,424	49.9	DCR within model	42.9
Scaled up basic health services							
Increased health expenditure, HPIC, Gupta (2001)	584 per child	34,316[b]	16,080	18,236	2.1	2.1	5.8
WDR (World Bank 1993) Minimum package, low- and middle-income countries	65 *per capita*	871,158	337,073	534,084	2.6	1 year	2.6

Notes: MTC: mother-to-child transmission; VCT: voluntary counselling and testing; STIs: sexually transmitted infections; ARV: antiretroviral therapy; LIC: low-income countries; MIC middle-income countries; HIC higher-income countries; IPT(p): intermittent treatment of pregnant women; SP: Sulfadoxine-pyrimethamine; PG: primigravidae (first pregnancy); ACT: artemisinin-based combination therapy; WDR: World Development Report.
[a] Adapted from original study.
[b] Gains in child health only included.

Appendix 2

Table 2A2.1. Baseline Value of Life and BCR from Sensitivity Analysis Applying Standard Value of Life (Int$ 2003)

Opportunity, source, geographic region	Value of death averted (baseline) Int$	Value of death averted (baseline) US$	BCR Int$4,127 per life (US$1,250)	BCR Int$330,172 per life (US$100,000)
Control of malaria				
Package of malaria interventions	44,021	13,333	1.57	125.9
Control of HIV/AIDS				
Thai programme of prevention	141,767	42,937	0.49	33.2
Package for prevention of HIV/AIDS, six regions (EAP, EAC, LAC, SEA, SAR, SSA)	102,953	31,181	2.00	160.1
Scaling up basic health services				
Increased health expenditure. 13 HIPCs	39,977	12,108	0.22	17.6
WDR (1993) Minimum package. Low- and middle-income countries	72,406	21,930	0.15	11.8

Notes: Purchasing power parity/Local currency unit (PPP/LCU) conversion factor of 0.3029 was revealed from the ratio of *per capita* GNI for low- and middle-income countries in terms of US$ and INT$ (2003 WDI CDRom); estimates derived from malaria macroeconomic models omitted here since benefits are expressed in terms of GNP.

Appendix 3

Table 2A3.1. Baseline Results Expressed as Cost-Effectiveness Ratios, and Proportion of Target Group Under Five Years Old

Opportunity, source, geographic region	Cost per YLL or DALY (Int$)	Cost per death averted (Int$)	% under 5: mortality	% under 5: YLLs
Control of malaria				
Package of malaria interventions	98	2,622	72	72
Control of HIV/AIDS				
Thai programme of prevention	437	9,953	0	0
Package for prevention of HIV/AIDS, six regions (EAP, EAC, LAC, SEA, SAR, SSA)	89	2,062	0	0
Scaling up basic health services				
Increased health expenditure. 13 HIPCs	659	18,732	100	100
WDR (1993) Minimum package. Low- and middle-income countries	1,482	28,017	12	22

Note: Estimates derived from malaria macroeconomic models omitted here since benefits are expressed in terms of GNP.

References

Aikins, M. K. S., 1995: Cost-effectiveness analysis of insecticide-impregnated mosquito nets (bednets) used as a malaria control measure: a study from the Gambia, PhD thesis, Department of Public Health and Policy, London School of Hygiene and Tropical Medicine, University of London

Ainsworth, M. and M. Over, 1999: *Confronting AIDS: public priorities in a global epidemic*, Oxford University Press, Oxford

Alleyne, G. A. O. and D. Cohen, 2002: Health, economic growth, and poverty reduction: Report of Working Group 1 of the Commission on Macroeconomics and Health, World Health Organization, Geneva, 114

Alonso, P. L., S. W. Lindsay, J. R. Armstrong *et al.*, 1991: The effect of insecticide-treated bed nets on mortality of Gambian children, *Lancet*, 337, 1499–502

Alonso, P. L., S. W. Lindsay, J. R. Armstrong Schellenberg *et al.*, 1993: A malaria control trial using insecticide-treated bed nets and targeted chemoprophylaxis in a rural area of The Gambia, west Africa: 2, Mortality and morbidity from malaria in the study area, *Transactions of the Royal Society of Tropical Medicine and Hygiene*, **2**, 13–17

Anon, 2003: AIDS: a mixed prognosis, *The Economist*, 115–17, 27 November

2004: Good news, apparently: building better models of the prevalence of HIV, *The Economist*, 78–9, 15 January

Armstrong-Schellenberg, J. R. M., S. Abdulla, R. Nathan *et al.*, 2001: Effect of large-scale social marketing of insecticide-treated nets on child survival in Tanzania, *Lancet*, **357**, 1241–7

Arndt, C. and J. D. Lewis, 2000: *The macro implications of HIV/AIDS in South Africa: a preliminary assessment*, Purdue University/World Bank, Geneva, 18

Attaran, A., K. Barnes, C. Curtis *et al.*, 2004: WHO, the Global Fund, and medical malpractice in malaria treatment, *Lancet*, **363**, 237–93

Audibert, M., J. Mathonnat and M. Henry, 2003: Social and health determinants of the efficiency of cotton farmers in Northern Côte d'Ivoire, *Social Science and Medicine*, **56**, 1705–17

Barlow, R., 1967: The economic effects of malaria eradication, *American Economic Review*, **57**(2), 130–48

Barnett, T. and P. Blaikie, 1992: *AIDS in Africa: its present and future impact*, Guilford Press, New York

Barnett, T. and A. Whiteside, 2002: *AIDS in the twenty-first century: disease and globalization*, Palgrave Macmillan, Basingstoke

Barro, R. J., 1991: Economic growth in a cross-section of countries, *Quarterly Journal of Economics*, **106**, 407–43

Beckerman, K. P., 2003: Long-term findings of HIVNET 012: the next steps, *Lancet*, **362**, 842–3

Bell, C., S. Devarajan and H. Gersbach, 2003: *The long-run economic costs of AIDS: theory and an application to South Africa* World Bank Working Paper, 3152

Black, R. E., S. S. Morris and J. Bryce, 2003: Where and why are 10 million children dying each year?, *Lancet*, **361**, 2226–34

Bloland, P., 2001: *Drug resistance in malaria*, WHO, Geneva, 27

Bloom, D. E. and D. Canning, 2000: The health and the wealth of nations, *Science*, **287**, 1207–9

Bobadilla, 1994: Design, content and financing of an essential national package of health services, *Bulletin of the World Health Organization*, 72, 653–62

Boissier, M., J. B. Knight and R. H. Sabot, 1985: Earnings, schooling, ability and cognitive skills, *American Economic Review*, **75**, 1016–30

Borts, G. H., 1967: Discussion of 'The economic effects of malaria eradication' by R. Barlow, *American Economic Review*, **57**(2), 149–51

Brabin, B. J., M. Hakimi and D. Pelletier, 2001: An analysis of anemia and pregnancy-related maternal mortality, *Journal of Nutrition*, **131** (Suppl), 604S–615S

Breman, J., 2001: The ears of the hippopotamus: manifestations, determinants, and estimates of malaria burden, *American Journal of Tropical Medicine and Hygiene*, **64**, 1–11

Brown, P., 2003: *Thailand curbs HIV and sexually transmitted diseases*, Center for Global Development

Chavasse, D., C. Reed and K. Attawell, 1999: *Insecticide treated net projects: a handbook for managers*, Malaria Consortium, London and Liverpool

Chima, R. I., C. A. Goodman and A. Mills, 2003: The economic impact of malaria in Africa: a critical review of the evidence, *Health Policy*, **63**, 17–36

CIA, 2003: *The world factbook*, Central Intelligence Agency, Washington, DC

CMH, 2001: *Macroeconomics and health: investing in health for economic development*, World Health Organization, Geneva, 200

Coleman, P. G., C. M. Morel, S. D. Shillcutt *et al.*, 2004: A threshold analysis of the cost-effectiveness of artemisinin-based combination therapies in sub-Saharan Africa, *American Journal of Tropical Medicine and Hygiene*, Forthcoming

Creese, A., K. Floyd, A. Alban *et al.*, 2002: Cost-effectiveness of HIV/AIDS interventions in Africa: a systematic review of the evidence, *Lancet*, **359**, 1635–42

D'Alessandro, U., 2004: Commentary: Treating severe and complicated malaria, *British Medical Journal*, **328**, 155

D'Alessandro, U., B. O. Olaleye, W. McGuire *et al.*, 1995: Mortality and morbidity from malaria in Gambian children after introduction of an impregnated bednet programme, *Lancet*, **345**, 479–83

Depoortere, E., J. P. Guthmann, N. Sipilanyambe *et al.*, 2004: Adherence to the combination of sulphadoxine-pyrimethamine and artesunate in the Maheba refugee settlement, Zambia, *Tropical Medicine and International Health*, **9**, 62–7

Devlin, N. and D. Parkin, 2004: Does NICE have a cost-effectiveness threshold, and what other factors influence its decisions?, *Health Economics*, **13**(5), 437–52

Doherty, J. and R. Govender, 2004: The cost-effectiveness of primary care services in developing countries: a review of the international literature, Background paper, Disease Control Priorities Project, 48

EANMAT, 2004: East African Network for Monitoring Antimalarial Treatment, http://www.eanmat.org/

Ettling, M. B. and D. S. Shepard, 1991: Economic cost of malaria in Rwanda, *Tropical Medicine and Parasitology*, **42**, 214–18

Ettling, M., D. A. McFarland, L. J. Schultz *et al.*, 1994: Economic impact of malaria in Malawian households, *Tropical Medicine and Parasitology*, **45**, 74–9

Filmer, D. and L. Pritchett, 1999: The impact of public spending on health: does money matter?, *Social Science and Medicine*, **49**, 1309–23

Folland, S., A. C. Goodman and M. Stano, 1997: *The economics of health and health care*, Prentice-Hall, Upper Saddle River, NJ

Fox-Rushby, J., 2002: *Disability-adjusted life years (DALYs) for decision-making? An overview of the literature*, Office of Health Economics, London, 172

Gallup, J. L. and J. D. Sachs, 2001: The economic burden of malaria, *American Journal of Tropical Medicine and Hygiene*, **64**, 85–96

Goodman, C. A., P. G. Coleman and A. J. Mills, 2000: *Economic analysis of malaria control in sub-Saharan Africa*, Global Forum for Health Research, Geneva, 185

Goodman, C. A., P. G. Coleman and A. J. Mills, 2001: The cost-effectiveness of antenatal malaria prevention in sub-Saharan Africa, *American Journal of Tropical Medicine and Hygiene*, **64**, 45–56

Gülmezoglu, A. M. and P. Garner, 1998: Malaria in pregnancy in endemic areas (Cochrane Review), The Cochrane Library, Issue 3: Oxford, Update Software

Gupta, S., M. Verhoeven and E. Tiongson, 2001: Public spending on health care and the poor, International Monetary Fund Working Paper

Haacker, M., 2002: *The economic consequences of HIV/AIDS in southern Africa*, International Monetary Fund, Washington DC, 40

Halstead, S. and J. A. Walsh, 1985: Good health at low cost, Rockefeller Foundation, New York

Hanson, K. G., C. G. Goodman, J. Lines *et al.*, 2000: The economics of malaria interventions, http://mosquito.who.int/cmc_upload/0/000/015/605/ea_ch2.pdf

ICRG, 2002: *HIV/AIDS as a threat to global security*, International Crisis Research Group, New Haven, CT, 69

International Artemisinin Study Group, 2004: Artesunate combinations for treatment of malaria: meta-analysis, *Lancet*, **363**, 9–18

Jha, P. and A. Mills, 2002: *Improving health outcomes of the poor*, Report of Working Group 5 of the Commission on Macroeconomics and Health (CMH), World Health Organization, Geneva, 175

Kindermans, J., 2002: ACTs: availability and prices, presentation at RBM Partners Meeting, Geneva

Klose, T., 1999: The contingent valuation method in health care, *Health Policy*, **47**, 97–123

Leighton, C. and R. Foster, 1993: *Economic impacts of malaria in Kenya and Nigeria*, Abt Associates, Health Financing and Sustainability Project, Bethesda, MD

Lengeler, C., 1998: Insecticide treated bednets and curtains for malaria control (Cochrane Review), The Cochrane Library, 3, update software, Oxford

Low-Beer, D. and R. L. Stoneburner, 2003: Behaviour and communication change in reducing HIV: is Uganda unique?, *African Journal of AIDS Research*, **2**, 9–21

Malaria Consortium, 2002: External evaluation of malaria, Final report

Marsh, K., M. English, J. Crawley *et al.*, 1996: The pathogenesis of severe malaria in African children, *Annals of Tropical Medicine and Parasitology*, **90**, 395–402

McCarthy, F. D., H. Wolf and Y. Wu, 2000: *The growth costs of malaria*, National Bureau of Economic Research Working Paper Series, Cambridge, MA, 31

McCormick, M. C., 1985: The contribution of low birth weight to infant mortality and childhood morbidity, *New England Journal of Medicine*, **312**, 82–90

McPherson, M., 2003: Macroeconomic models and the impact of HIV/AIDS

Mehrotra, S., 2000: Innocenti Working Paper, Integrating economic and social policy: good practices from high-achieving countries, UNICEF, Innocenti Research Centre, Florence

Molineaux, L., 1985: The impact of parasitic diseases and their control, with an emphasis on malaria and Africa, in J. Vallin and A. Lopez (eds.), *Health policy, social policy and mortality prospects*, Ordina Editions, Liège, 13–44

Muheki, C., K. Barnes and D. McIntyre, 2004: Artemisinin-based combination therapy reduces expenditure on malaria treatment in KwaZulu Natal, South Africa, Work in progress

Najera, J. A., B. H. Liese and J. Hammer, 1993: Malaria, in D. Jamison (ed.), *Disease Control Priorities Project*, Oxford University Press, Oxford, 281–362

Nájera, J. A. and J. Hempel, 1996: The burden of malaria, WHO CTD/MAL/96.10

Nevill, C. G., E. S. Some, V. O. Mung'ala *et al.*, 1996: Insecticide-treated bednets reduce mortality and severe morbidity from malaria among children on the Kenyan coast, *Tropical Medicine and International Health*, **1**, 139–46

Oliveira-Cruz, V., K. Hanson and A. Mills, 2003: Approaches to overcoming constraints to effective health service delivery: a review of the evidence, *Journal of International Development*, 15, 41–66

Oliveira-Cruz, V., C. Kurowski and A. Mills, 2003: Delivery of health interventions: searching for synergies within the vertical versus horizontal debate, *Journal of International Development*, **15**, 67–86

Over, M., R. P. Ellis, J. H., Huber *et al.* 1992: The consequences of adult ill-health, in R. G. A. Feachem, T. Kjellstrom, C. J. L. Murry, M. Over and M. A. Phillips (eds), *The health of adults in the developing world*, published for World Bank by Oxford University Press, Washington DC, 161–207

Pitayanon, S., S. Kongsin and W. Janjaroen, 1997: The economic impact of HIV/AIDS mortality on households in Thailand, in D. Bloom and Godwin, P. (eds.), *The economies of HIV and AIDS: the case of South and Southeast Asia*, Oxford University Press, Delhi

Pollitt, E., 1997: Iron deficiency and educational deficiency, *Nutrition Reviews*, **55**, 133–41

Pollitt, E., C. Saco Pollitt, R. L. Leibel *et al.*, 1986: Iron deficiency and behavioral development in infants and preschool children, *American Journal of Clinical Nutrition*, **43**, 555–65

Potts, M. and J. Walsh, 2003: Tackling India's HIV epidemic: lessons learned from Africa, *British Medical Journal*, **326**, 1389–92

Quattek, K., 2000: The economic impact of AIDS in South Africa: a dark cloud on the horizon, Konrad Adenauer Stiftung Occasional Paper,

HIV/AIDS, A threat to the African Renaissance? (originally an ING Baring Research Report)

Rajkumar, A. and V. Swaroop, 2002: Public spending and outcomes: does governance matter?, World Bank, Washington DC

Ramasundaram, S., K. Allaudin, B. Charles *et al.*, 2001: Working Paper, 25, HIV/AIDS control in India – Lessons from Tamil Nadu, Commission on Macroeconomics and Health, Working Group 5

Ranson, M. K., K. Hanson, V. Oliveira-Cruz *et al.*, 2003: Constraints to expanding access to health interventions: an empirical analysis and country typology, *Journal of International Development*, **15**, 15–39

Robalino, D. A., C. Jenkins and K. El Maroufi, 2002: Risks and macroeconomic impacts of HIV/AIDS in the Middle East and North Africa: why waiting to intervene can be costly, World Bank Policy Research Working Paper, 2874, 35

Roper, C., R. Pearce, B. Bredenkamp *et al.*, 2003: Antifolate antimalarial resistance in southeast Africa: a population-based analysis, *Lancet*, **361**, 1174–81

Ruger, J. P., D. T. Jamison and D. E. Bloom, 2001: Health and the economy, in M. Merson, R. Black and A. Mills (eds.), *Health and the economy*. Aspen, Gaithersburg, MD

Sachs, J. and P. Malaney, 2002: The economic and social burden of malaria, *Nature*, **415**, 680–5

Sauerborn, R., A. Adams and M. Hien, 1996: Household strategies to cope with the economic costs of illness, *Social Science and Medicine*, **43**, 291–301

Sharma, D., 2003: ARV prices nosedive after Clinton brokering, *Lancet*, **362**, 1467

Shaw, M., 2003: Before we were sleeping but now we are awake: the Stepping Stones workshop programme in the Gambia, Proceedings of the Global Fund for Health Research, Annual Meeting, Geneva

Shepard, D. S., M. B. Ettling, U. Brinkmann *et al.*, 1991: The economic cost of malaria in Africa, *Tropical Medicine and Parasitology*, **42**, 199–203

Shulman, C. E., W. J. Graham, H. Jilo *et al.*, 1996: Malaria is an important cause of anaemia in primigravidae: evidence from a district hospital in coastal Kenya, *Transactions of the Royal*

Society of Tropical Medicine and Hygiene, **90**, 535–9

Slutsker, L., L. Chitsulo, A. Macheso *et al.*, 1994: Treatment of malaria fever episodes among children in Malawi: results of a KAP survey, *Tropical Medicine and Parasitology*, **45**, 61–4

Snow, R. W., J. R. Armstrong, D. Forster *et al.*, 1992: Childhood deaths in Africa: uses and limitations of verbal autopsies, *Lancet*, **340**, 351–5

Snow, R. W., I. Bastos de Azevedo, B. S. Lowe *et al.*, 1994: Severe childhood malaria in two areas of markedly different falciparum transmission in East Africa, *Acta Tropica*, **57**, 289–300

Snow, R. W., M. Craig, U. Deichmann *et al.*, 1999: Estimating mortality, morbidity, and disability due to malaria among Africa's non-pregnant population, *Bulletin of the World Health Organization*, **77**, 624–40

Soemantri, A. G., E. Pollitt and I. Kim, 1985: Iron deficiency anemia and educational achievement, *American Journal of Clinical Nutrition*, **42**, 1221–8

Stevens, C. M., 1977: Health and economic development: longer-run view, *Social Science and Medicine*, **11**, 809–17

Stover, J., N. Walker, G. P. Garnett *et al.*, 2002: Can we reverse the HIV/AIDS pandemic with an expanded response?, *Lancet*, **360**, 73–7

Terris-Prestholt, F., L. Kumaranayake, R. Ginwalla *et al.*, 2003: The cost-effectiveness of the Zambian ProTEST project: integrating voluntary counselling and testing with tuberculosis activities

UNAIDS, 2003: *AIDS epidemic update*, UNAIDS and WHO, Geneva, 40

UNICEF, 2003: *State of the World's Children 2003*, United Nations, Geneva http://www.unicef.org/sowc03/

United Nations, 1982: Model life tables for developing countries, UN, New York

Wagstaff, A., 2002: Health spending and aid as escape routes from the vicious circle of poverty and health, British Association for the Advancement of Science, 22

Watts, C., L. Kumaranayake, P. Vickerman *et al.*, 2002: The public health benefits of microbicides in lower-income countries: model projections, The Rockefeller Foundation, New York, 55

WHO, 1993: *Implementation of the global malaria control strategy – report of a WHO Study Group on the implementation of the global plan of action for malaria control* 1993–2000, WHO, Geneva

1996a: Investing in health research and development, Report of the Ad Hoc Committee on Health Research Relating to Future Interrention Options, TDR/Gen/96.1, Geneva

1996b: Assessment of therapeutic efficacy of antimalarial drugs for uncomplicated falciparum malaria with intense transmission, WHO/MAL/96.1077, Geneva

2000a: *The world health report 2000: health systems: improving performance*, WHO, Geneva, 215

2002a: *Global burden of disease estimates 2002*, WHO, Geneva http://www3.who.int/ whosis/menu.cfm?path=evidence,burden

2002b: *The world health report*, WHO, Geneva

2002c: The African Summit on Roll Back Malaria: The Africa Declaration and plan of action, WTO, Geneva

2003a: *World health report 2003: Shaping the future*, WHO, Geneva, 182

2003b: *The Africa malaria report 2003*, UNICEF and World Health Organization, Geneva, 120

2003c: Assessment of the safety of artemisinin compounds in pregnancy, WHO, Geneva (document WHO/RBM/TDR/ Artemisinin/03.1)

Wiseman, V., W. A. Hawley, F. O. Ter Kuile *et al.*, 2003: The cost-effectiveness of permethrin-treated bed nets in an area of intense malaria transmission in western Kenya, *American Journal of Tropical Medicine and Hygiene*, **66** (Suppl. 4), 161–7

World Bank, 1993a: Provision of ARV therapy in resource-limited settings: the challenges of resistance and adherence: Global HIV/AIDS program of the World Bank, 17–18 June 1993, http://www.unaids.org/EN/other/functionalities/ search.asp

1993b: *World development report 1993*, World Bank, Washington, DC

1994: *Better health in Africa, experience and lessons learned*, World Bank, Washington DC, 261

2002: *World development report 2002*, World Bank, Geneva, 249

2003a: World Development Indicators CD-rom

2003b: *World Development Report 2003*, World Bank, Geneva, 250

2004a: *World Development Report 2004*, World Bank, Washington, DC, 271

2004b: World development indicators online, http://www.worldbank.org/data/dataquery.html

Worrall, E., S. Basu and K. Hanson, 2003: The relationship between socio-economic status and malaria: a review of the literature; background paper prepared for conference on 'Ensuring that malaria control interventions reach the poor', School of Hygiene and Tropical Medicine, London

Zerfu, D., 2002: The macroeconomic impact of HIV/AIDS in Ethiopia, Addis Ababa University, Addis Ababa

Alternative Perspectives

Perspective Paper 2.1

DAVID B. EVANS

Introduction

Cost-benefit analysis (CBA), as it has long been used in the sectors of the economy traditionally considered to be productive, can be characterized as having the objective of seeking to maximize the present value of a stream of consumption changes resulting from a decision to use resources (Ray 1984). Some types of social concerns have been incorporated from time to time, including giving greater weight to investment than consumption resulting from a project to allow for distortions in the capital market, or to introduce weights on the consumption benefits depending on who receives them, thereby incorporating equity concerns. This traditional approach has been applied extensively to health investments, and is related to the literature classified by in chapter 2 in this volume Mills and Shillcutt (hereafter, M&S) as the microeconomic impact of the disease and the macroeconomic approach to estimating costs and benefits.

At the same time, perhaps influenced by environmental economics, there is a strand of the literature which broadens the definition of welfare to incorporate the intrinsic value people place on health and on preventing death. This is clearly not totally separable from the consumption possibilities resulting from good health or a long life, but even if the net effect of improving health on consumption is non-positive (perhaps health care for the aged is an example), the investment in health could still lead to increases in welfare assuming that health is an argument in a social welfare function. This literature values health improvements in terms of the money value of the gain in welfare based on willingness-to-pay (WTP) (e.g. Weaver *et al.* 1996; Klose 1999; Onwujekwe *et al.* 2002). This approach is the essence of the cost-effectiveness evidence presented by M&S and categorized as the 'microeconomic approach'.

It should be noted at the outset that the two approaches have different maximands, and the numbers produced relate, therefore, to different concepts. Estimates of the impact of health investments on GDP should be smaller than those based on the money value of averting Disability-Adjusted Life Year (DALY). Using the first method to value health benefits will show very low or zero economic benefits for some health interventions, but the same intervention could look attractive using the second method.

This is important when it comes to comparing the results reported by M&S with the CBAs of various other types of interventions. Investments in the environment, and sometimes in water and sanitation, are commonly evaluated in terms of WTP (Alberini and Krupnick 2000; Bowland and Beghin 2001). Some environmental investments may well have non-positive impacts on economic growth, like some health investments. To compare the numbers produced by studies reported under the macroeconomic approach for malaria with those from the microeconomic (cost-effectiveness) approach for HIV/AIDS is not appropriate. To compare the numbers produced by the macroeconomic studies reported by M&S with the results from a CBA of environmental health interventions based on WTP is also not appropriate.

From the perspective of someone working with health policy makers, an additional concern is that the current global focus on the economic impact of health has been interpreted largely as the impact of health investments on GDP rather than on welfare (Commission on Macroeconomics and Health 2001). This makes health practitioners assume that if it is not possible to show that a particular intervention improves GDP, it is not worth doing from an economic perspective. It also encourages donors to fund yet more cost-of-illness studies.

I argue in the rest of this Perspective paper that the numbers summarized by M&S under the rubric of microeconomic impact and the macroeconomic approach to measuring benefits are not very reliable, partly because of questions about their quality and partly because they produce conflicting results. The information based on the microeconomic (cost-effectiveness) approach is more reliable and addresses some of the most important questions for policy makers in the health sector. I conclude with some suggestions on how to make the analysis even more useful to policy makers.

The Microeconomic Impact of Malaria and HIV/AIDS

This literature is based on the cost-of-illness (COI) methodology that separates costs into those linked to obtaining care, including the costs of treatment, transport, special foods, etc. (called direct costs) and the lost income associated with illness (called indirect costs). An industry of COI studies has developed over the last decades, and many of the weaknesses are well established (Drummond 1992; Maynard 1997; Koopmanschap 1998; Bloom et al. 2001). At the household level, direct costs represent the resources that could have been used for other types of consumption or investment had the disease or illness not occurred, although the impact on the present value of future consumption depends partly on whether the costs are funded from current consumption or savings.

Indirect costs of survivors are typically measured as an estimate of time loss multiplied by a wage rate,

and are added to the discounted future earnings of people who have died estimated in the same way – years lost multiplied by annual per capita income. For example, the studies summarised in Shepard, Etting and Brinkmann (1991) and used by M&S assumed that the self-reported duration of a malaria episode in adults equated with lost work time, and that one adult would lose 30 per cent of the duration of disease in children due to their caring functions. This loss was multiplied by an imputed daily wage rate that was apparently constant over the year. The discounted future earnings of children who died because of malaria was estimated as described above.

Agricultural communities, where much of malaria occurs, have developed various methods of coping with disease, some of which are described in M&S. The agricultural cycle means that there is great flexibility in the timing of labour inputs at some times of the year (e.g. weeding), less so at other times (e.g. planting or harvesting). Most COI studies in developing countries, including some of those reported by M&S, have ignored this and assumed that a day sick is a day of lost work (e.g. Shepard et al. 1991; for a critical review of studies related to malaria, see Chima, Goodman and Mills 2003). The appropriate method would be to compare the days worked by the sick person and their family compared to the counterfactual of what would have happened in the absence of the illness. Only a few studies have tried to assess this by comparing activity patterns of people with illness to those of people in the same community, with the same characteristics, without illness (Mills Nepal; Ramaiah et al. 2000), but this is rare and most of the studies reported by M&S for malaria and HIV/AIDS do not use this approach. The case-control approach suggests that the actual time lost due to illness is considerably lower than suggested by the cruder method.

On the other hand, many of the most important potential effects on households are not measured at all in COI studies. Few have measured the impact of ill health on productivity (output per unit of time input), likely to be lower for people with chronic conditions (Ramu et al. 1996), or the impact on long-term production through reductions in savings, changes in activity patterns, reduced educational investment, etc. (e.g. Kochar 2004). The end result is that most COI studies produce estimates of indirect costs that probably have little to do with the impact of illness on the discounted present value of household consumption, to the extent that even the direction of the bias is unclear. The data on direct costs is potentially more useful, in the sense of showing the immediate impact on a household's budget, although again the quality of the costing assumptions made in such studies leaves a lot to be desired (Adam, Evans and Koopmanschap 2003).

It is important to health policy makers to understand the impact – economic and social – of disease and ill health on households. COI studies are an imperfect estimate of the economic burden on households. They are even more misleading when they are aggregated across households and the results interpreted as a loss of GDP. Even in industrial countries, this does not hold. In Europe, relatively high levels of unemployment and imperfect labour markets mean that multiplying days lost by the wage rate for each person suffering illness, then aggregating across individuals, overestimates the impact of that time loss on GDP (Koopmanschap and van Ineveld 1992; Hutubessy *et al.* 1999). This is even more important in developing countries with large agricultural and informal sectors.

Assuming that the sum of direct costs is a loss of GDP is also incorrect, as the health sector is included in national accounts and contributes to GDP. The impact of direct costs on GDP would be through a drawdown of savings or similar mechanisms. This type of link is explored in some of the macroeconomic models discussed in the next section, but for the moment the conclusion is that many of the COI studies reported in the chapter do not show the impact of illness on the discounted present value of household consumption, and the aggregation of the costs across households bears an unknown relationship to the impact of malaria and HIV/AIDS on GDP.

That being said, the impact of malaria and HIV/AIDS on households is undoubtedly substantial and important for policy purposes. Health financing systems in the parts of the world where these diseases are most endemic rely relatively heavily on direct out-of-pocket payments by households; these payments are high for the two diseases but particularly for HIV/AIDS, and can push households into poverty or deepen the poverty of households that are already poor (Xu *et al.* 2003; Wagstaff and van Doorslaer 2003). The impact on lifetime consumption is less clear for malaria but is high for HIV/AIDS because it affects adults of working age while malaria deaths occur predominantly in children. In addition, as M&S state, the impact of HIV/AIDS can lead to the disintegration of households and family structures in countries where it is most endemic, and a generation of children is being raised without traditional social support mechanisms (Moatti *et al.* 2003; WHO 2004). Indeed, Friere (2003) argues that by focusing on the families directly touched by AIDS, the way other households have been forced to adapt and modify their economic activities as a result has been ignored. She claims that these effects can be substantial. This type of effect is difficult to quantify in money terms without relatively costly studies that trace households over time, but the destruction of households and the social fabric of societies is real, and of a different nature and order of magnitude of the types of estimates emerging from the COI studies (Moatti *et al.* 2003; WHO 2004).

Macroeconomic Studies

The macroeconomic studies reviewed by M&S for malaria differ to those reviewed for HIV/AIDS. The former rely on two studies using cross-country regressions that are not really production functions. Gallup and Sachs (2001), for example, explained the growth of *per capita* GDP as a function of initial GDP *per capita*, initial levels of health and education, and a variety of other country-descriptive variables such as the proportion of the land area in the tropics, quality of public institutions and a malaria index. The specification did not explicitly account for reverse causation, or changes in capital and labour. McCarthy, Wolf and Wu (2000) did account for reverse causation and suggest that the negative impact of malaria on growth was robust to many different specifications. The estimated impact of malaria on GDP *per capita* is far greater than would be estimated if the effect was limited to the impact on the size of the labour force (Gallup and Sachs 2001).

The most important health impact of malaria is on child mortality, which poses a dilemma. Bloom and Williamson (1997) have suggested, using similar cross-country regressions (although with a different set of countries), that the decrease of the dependency ratio linked to low fertility rates was a key to the success story of the East Asian countries. Reducing malaria would initially increase the dependency ratio which might be expected to reduce growth rates. Indeed, the mechanisms through which malaria might have retarded economic growth in Africa that were suggested by Gallup and Sachs – e.g. the suggested relationship between malaria severity and foreign investment flows – have not, to my knowledge, been tested in any way.

The impact of HIV/AIDS on the quantity of labour is now very substantial – the gains in life expectancy made through most of the twentieth century in SSA started to be reversed in the mid-1990s when life expectancy began to decline. Life expectancy at birth was forty-three years in Southern Africa in 2002 and would have been fifty-six years in the absence of the disease (WHO 2004). The macroeconomic approaches to assessing the impact of HIV/AIDS on GDP reported by M&S incorporate the reduced size of the labour force into computerized general equilibrium (CGE) models that also try to account for the impact of the disease through other mechanisms such as reduced labour productivity and savings. However, as M&S show, the results are confusing, with changes in assumptions showing a range of outcomes varying from increases in GDP *per capita* to economic catastrophe.

In any case, a general equilibrium model cannot capture the full impact of HIV/AIDS on a society or economy. Annual deaths from AIDS among nurses has represented around 40 per cent of the recent output of nursing schools in some countries and similar trends are observed in other sectors such as education (WHO 2004). When this is added to shortages caused by migration, natural attrition and absenteeism due to illness, the health and education systems in the most heavily endemic countries simply cannot function. They certainly cannot function to the extent necessary to support the recent scale-up in funds available for HIV/AIDS and malaria, something to which I shall return.

The Microeconomic Approach (Cost-Effectiveness)

Most estimates of health effects used in cost-effectiveness studies are based on observing what happens with the introduction of an intervention compared to settings in which the intervention is not introduced. This is in contrast to the modelling necessary to estimate the counterfactual in the general equilibrium models of the previous section. The set of interventions described by M&S for malaria reflect the currently available technologies and approaches, and the studies from which the estimates were taken generally use appropriate methods and assumptions. A few small technical questions can be raised. The analysis of the decision to switch from one anti-malarial to a new type of combination therapy was based on a time horizon of only thirteen years. This does not allow for consideration of the risk that a new anti-malarial will not be available by the time resistance to the combination therapy reduces its clinical effectiveness, something that has happened to all anti-malarials to date. This consideration is surely important in any decision to switch. The second problem concerns the assumption that the costs and benefits of the interventions undertaken singly can simply be added to obtain the costs and benefits of the package. Preventive interventions such as insecticide treated nets (ITNs) reduce incidence, thereby reducing the need for, and the cost of, the curative interventions. The number of people that M&S assume would be protected by nets would not change, nor would the cost. However, the number of people needing to be treated would be lower and so would the total costs and the benefits of treatment (though not necessarily the cost-effectiveness ratio). However, the net benefits reported by M&S should not change drastically.

The package M&S have chosen to report for the HIV/AIDS interventions does not include *care* – i.e. treatment using antiretrovirals – something that is now dominating resource allocation decisions internationally. The WHO has estimated that almost

$1 bn has been pledged, largely by the international community, for care in the forty most endemic countries over 2002–3, and the question of the return to this investment is important to consider. The WHO argues that in addition to keeping people at work and allowing systems such as health and education to function better than they do currently, the provision of care will also encourage people to present voluntarily for testing and counselling, thereby reducing transmission (WHO 2004).

The economic analysis of the package reported by M&S, unlike the malaria package, includes interactions between interventions in terms of effectiveness. In some cases it is difficult to understand the source of estimates of effectiveness – for example, the interventions used for the estimates of the effectiveness of something described as 'voluntary counselling and testing' included some focusing on female sex workers, some on their clients, some on serodiscordant couples, some on pregnant women and some on people with sexually transmitted infections. Many included condom distribution and health education, also evaluated separately as part of the package. However, reanalysis of some of this work suggests results of a similar order of magnitude (WHO 2002).

In my opinion, therefore, the studies reported under the microeconomic approach provide a reasonable assessment of the health effects and costs of key interventions against malaria and HIV/AIDS, with the exception of care. When the DALYs averted are multiplied by a monetary value of the health benefit, the result is, at least in theory, more akin to valuing outcomes in terms of the broader welfare gain than the narrower effect on GDP, as discussed earlier. The question is what value to place on a DALY averted. Viscusi and Aldy concluded that estimates of the value of a statistical life, based on workers' willingness to accept a greater risk of death in return for higher salaries, ranged from 100–200 times GDP *per capita*. This was based on studies from ten countries (Viscusi and Aldy 2003; Bloom, Canning and Jamison 2004). Even though this type of measure does not incorporate the impact of improved health on welfare, it suggests that the value of GNI *per capita* used by M&S as the value of averting a DALY is too low. If there are seventy years to the

average life, and years are undiscounted, the value of a year would be between 1.4 and 2.8 times GDP *per capita*. However, if the present value of a life is worth twenty-nine discounted years (at 3 per cent), each year would be worth approximately 3.4–6.9 times GDP *per capita*.

The important question, however, is to be consistent in this valuation *across interventions and challenges*, an issue considered again briefly in the conclusions. In any case, as shown by M&S, the benefits exceed the costs of the interventions by a considerable margin, even using the low value of a DALY averted. In addition, the discounted net benefits of a package focusing on HIV/AIDS are substantially greater than that for malaria given the nature of the HIV/AIDS epidemic. It should also be remembered that this way of valuing outcomes does not include the impact of interventions on maintaining family structures and the social fabric, nor the inability of the health, education and other sectors to function.

Strengthening Basic Health Services

M&S use two methods to examine the costs and benefits of strengthening health services. The first is based on cross-country regressions, where they show that some studies report that higher levels of government spending on health are associated with health outcomes, while others show no effect. Nevertheless, they feel that more recent studies find a positive impact and use the most recent (Gupta, Verhoeven and Tiongson 2001) as the basis for their valuation of the benefits of strengthening the health infrastructure. However, a more recent study, like that of Gupta Verhoeven and Tiongson from the IMF, again finds no significant impact of government expenditure on health (but a significant impact on health of expenditure on education) (Baldacci, Guin-Siu and de Mello 2002). This study used a MIMIC model so does not have the same problem of finding a single indicator to define health associated with the studies reported by M&S.

In any case, the specifications are wrong (except perhaps for the MIMIC model). Health services involve a complex interaction between government and non-government sectors in most countries, and the assumption that only government expenditure is important, or that the impact of government expenditure can be determined from regressions which omit private expenditure, is not appropriate. This literature is, at best, inconclusive.

The second approach was to base the estimates on the costs and effectiveness of a package of interventions reported in 1993 (Jamison *et al.* 1993). That study combined information on the costs and effects of interventions evaluated in different countries without trying to adjust for differences in epidemiology or costs. The individual studies also used different methods. Moreover the epidemiology of diseases, effectiveness of interventions and costs have changed since then. While the approach might be appropriate, the numbers are not very relevant today. Unfortunately, it remains the only attempt to compare a wide variety of interventions in terms of the costs and DALY gains, which is the reason why there are two current international activities designed to update and improve the evidence base (the WHO–CHOICE project, see Tan-Torres Edejer *et al.* 2003 and the Disease Control Priorities Project 2004).

I do believe, however, that the potential gains from the increases in expenditure described earlier for AIDS care, considerably higher if all recent funds allocated to HIV/AIDS, tuberculosis and malaria are considered, will not be fully realised without an intense effort to improve health systems. It requires not only building health centres and distribution networks, and providing drugs, testing facilities, community services and a set of key interventions, but it also requires developing new ways of interaction between the government and non-government sectors, and probably new ways of organizing and delivering services. It requires identifying any binding short run constraints to scale-up – the availability of human resources is one such constraint in many African countries where there are strong fears that it might not be possible to train enough skilled staff to fill the demand created by the additional funds for health. Strengthening of the health system is a fundamental requirement if the challenge set by HIV/AIDS and malaria are to be met.

Conclusions

Communicable diseases continue to be the major cause of death and illness in poor countries. With the advent of HIV/AIDS, the gains in health and life-expectancy experienced throughout the twentieth century are being eroded in much of SSA. The burden that HIV/AIDS, malaria and other communicable diseases such as TB imposes on households is substantial, partly because a significant proportion of health payments in poor countries are met out-of-pocket. Households are pushed into poverty, or their poverty deepened, as a result – something only partially captured by COI studies. The impact of HIV/AIDS is even more dramatic, destroying family structures and long-established mechanisms of caring for the sick and sharing the financial burden of doing so. The impact of these diseases on GDP *per capita* has yet to be demonstrated conclusively, but there is certainly reason to believe that many African countries are being fundamentally changed because of HIV/AIDS in ways that are only beginning to be understood. Similar changes could emerge in parts of South and East Asia without immediate action.

Effective, low-cost methods for preventing both diseases exist – they are among the most cost-effective interventions possible (WHO 2002). Treatment for malaria is still relatively low-cost, although the cost is rising because of the way the parasite relatively rapidly develops resistance to new pharmacological products. The cost of care for HIV/AIDS has declined rapidly since 2002 and can be expected to decline further. There are also strong grounds for believing that the availability of treatment will encourage people with the infection to present for treatment and counselling and will then decide to protect their sexual partners from infection.

The increase in funding is a good sign, but much more is needed. There remains a funding gap of between $3.4 and $4 bn if only a half of the estimated number of people requiring treatment for HIV/AIDS are to receive treatment before the end of 2005, and much more is needed if the associated problem of TB is to be tackled effectively, and if a basic package of interventions for malaria is to be made widely available. The numbers do not include the need for strengthening health systems, without which the current investments in health will not achieve their full potential. I agree with van der Gaag (2004) that much more could have been done by now, and much more needs to be done quickly, to meet these challenges.

The final question concerns the way in which health benefits are valued in money terms. Valuations based on willingness to accept risk or willingness to pay assume rational decisions and markets that work. Health economists almost universally accept that market failures in health are so great that governments must intervene, though the extent of this intervention is not necessarily agreed. One of the most important market failures is that of information, where the asymmetry between the information held by the provider and the patient means that the patient is not able to make their own rational decisions and must trust the provider to act as their agent. The use of WTP and willingness to accept valuations is troubling in that the assumption is that the same people can make informed decisions about accepting risks, or paying for interventions that would reduce their risk of ill health and death.

Moreover, the use of these measures for setting international priorities has fundamental ethical problems. M&S, by basing their valuation on GNI *per capita*, assign a lower value to saving life in the poorest parts of the world than in the less poor. Other studies have also shown that WTP and the value of a statistical life based on willingness to accept, not surprisingly, vary by such factors as country, race and age (Krupnick 2000; Bowland and Beghin 2001; Viscusi 2003). To set international priorities based on a value of life saved, or of a DALY averted, that is some multiple of national product, will give priority to diseases that are currently found predominantly in the richer countries, and in the rich in poor countries. On those grounds, it may well be that cardiovascular disease (CVD) interventions would show higher money benefits than investments to control HIV/AIDS as the highest burden of CVD is in rich countries, and in poor countries it currently affects predominantly the rich. Although it has been shown that people have an altruistic willingness to pay for some health interventions (Onwujekwe *et al.* 2002), something more is needed to resolve this dilemma. One possibility is to postulate the existence of a global welfare function, in which case there is a global WTP for saving life and improving health which can be applied across all interventions and societies for global decision-making.

References

Adam, T., D.B. Evans and M.A. Koopmanschap, 2003: Cost-effectiveness analysis: can we reduce variability in costing methods?, *International Journal of Technology Assessment in Health Care*, **19**(2), 407–20

Alberini, A. and A. Krupnick, 2000: Cost-of-illness and willingness-to-pay estimates of the benefits of improved air quality: evidence from Taiwan, *Land Economics*, **76**(1), 37–53

Baldacci, E., M. Guin-Siu and L. de Mello, 2002: More on the effectiveness of public spending on health care and education: a covariance structure model, IMF Working Paper, WP/02/90

Bloom, B. *et al.*, 2001: Usefulness of US cost-of-illness studies in healthcare decision making, *Pharmacoeconomics*, **19**(2), 207–13

Bloom, D., D. Canning and D. Jamison, 2004: Health, wealth, and welfare: new evidence coupled with a wider perspective suggest sizable economic returns to better health, *Finance & Development*, **41**(1), 10–15

Bloom, D. and J. Williamson, 1997: Demographic transitions and economic miracles in emerging Asia, NBER Working Papers, **6268**

Bowland, B. and J. Beghin, 2001: Robust estimates of value of a statistical life for developing economies, *Journal of Policy Modeling*, **23**, 385–96

Chima, R., C. Goodman and A. Mills, 2003: The economic impact of malaria in Africa: a critical review of the evidence, *Health Policy*, **63**(1), 17–36

Commission on Macroeconomics and Health, 2001: *Commission on macroeconomics and health: investing in health for economic development*, WHO, Geneva

Disease Control Priorities Project, 2004: www.fic.nih.gov/dcpp/gbd.html

Drummond, M., 1992: Cost-of-illness studies: a major headache?, *Pharmacoeconomics*, **2**(1), 1–4

Friere, S. 2003: HIV/AIDS affected households: status and temporal impacts, in J. Moatti, B. Coriat, T. Souteyrand *et al.* (eds), *Economics of AIDS and access to HIV/AIDS care in developing countries: issues and challenges*, National Agency for AIDS Research, Paris

Gallup, J.L. and J.D. Sachs, 2001: The economic burden of malaria, CMH Working Paper Series, WG1:10

Gupta, S., M. Verhoeven and E. Tiongson, 2001: Public spending on health care and the poor, International Monetary Fund Working Paper, 01/127

Hutubessy, R., M. van Tulder, H. Vondeling, *et al.*, 1999: Indirect costs of back pain in the Netherlands: a comparison of the human capital method with the friction cost method, *PAIN*, **80**, 201–7

Jamison, D., H. Mosely, A. Measham and J. Bobadilla (eds.), 1993: *Disease control priorities in developing countries*, Oxford Medical Publications, New York

Klose, T., 1999: The contingent valuation method in health care, *Health Policy*, **47**, 97–123

Kochar, A., 2004: Ill-health, savings and portfolio choices in developing economies, *Journal of Development Economics,* **73**(1), 257–85

Koopmanschap, M., 1998: Cost-of-illness studies: useful for health policy?, *Pharmacoeconomics*, **14**(2), 143–8

Koopmanschap, M. and B. van Ineveld, 1992: Towards a new approach for estimating indirect costs of disease, *Social Science & Medicine*, **34**(9), 1005–10

Krupnick, A., 2000: Age, health, and the willingness to pay for mortality risk reductions: a contingent valuations survey of Ontario residents, Resources for the Future Discussion Paper, 00/37, 41

Maynard, A., 1997: Economic evaluation techniques in healthcare: reinventing the wheel?, *Pharmacoeconomics*, **11**, 115–18

McCarthy, F.D., H. Wolf and Y. Wu, 2000: The growth costs of malaria, NBER Working Paper, W7541

Mills, A. and S. Shillcutt, 2004: Communicable diseases, chapter 2 in this volume

Moatti, J.,T. Barnett, Y. Souteyrand *et al.*, 2003: Financing efficient HIV care and antiretroviral treatment to mitigate the impact of the AIDS epidemic on economic and human development, in J. Moatti, B. Coriat, T. Souteyrand *et al.* (eds.), *Economics of AIDS and access to HIV/AIDS care in developing countries: issues and challenges*, National Agency for AIDS Research, Paris

Onwujekwe, O., R. Chima, E. Shu *et al.*, 2002: Altruistic willingness to pay in community-based sales of insecticide-treated nets exists in Nigeria, *Social Science & Medicine*, **54**(4), 519–27

Picard, J. and A. Mills, 1992: The effects of malaria on work time: analysis of data from two Nepali districts, *Journal of Tropical Medicine and Hygiene*, **95**(6), 382–9

Poullier, J., P. Hernandez, K. Kawabata *et al.*, 2003: Patterns of global health expenditures: results for 191 countries, in C.J.L. Murray and D.B. Evans (eds.), *Health systems performance assessment: debates, methods and empiricism*, World Health Organization, Geneva

Ramaiah, K., M. Radhamani, K. John *et al.*, 2000: The impact of lymphatic filariasis on labour inputs in southern India: results of a multi-site study, *Annals of Tropical Medicine & Parasitology*, **94**(4), 353–64

Ramu, K., K. Ramaiah, H. Guyatt *et al.*, 1996: Impact of lymphatic filariasis on the productivity of male weavers in a southern Indian village, *Transactions of the Royal Society of Tropical Medicine & Hygiene*, **90**(6), 669–70

Ray, A., 1984: *Cost-benefit analysis: issues and methodologies*, World Bank/Johns Hopkins University Press, Baltimore, MD

Shepard, D., M. Ettling and U. Brinkmann, 1991: The economic cost of malaria in Africa, *Tropical Medicine and Parasitology*, **42**(3), 199–203

Tan-Torres Edejer, T., R. Baltussen, T. Adam, R. Hutubessy, A. Acharya, D.B. Evans and C.J.L. Murray (eds.), 2003: *Making choices in health: WHO guide to cost-effectiveness analysis*, World Health Organization, Geneva

van der Gaag, J., 2004: Perspective paper 2.2 in this volume

Viscusi, W. K., 2003: Racial differences in labor market values of a statistical life, *Journal of Risk & Uncertainty*, **27**(3), 239–56

Viscusi, W. K. and J. Aldy, 2003: The value of a statistical life: a critical review of market estimates throughout the world, *Journal of Risk & Uncertainty*, **27**(1), 5–76

Wagstaff, A. and E. van Doorslaer, 2003: Catastrophe and impoverishment in paying for health care: with applications to Vietnam 1993–1998, *Health Economics*, **12**(11), 921–34

Weaver, M., R. Ndamobissi, R. Kornfield *et al.*, 1996: Willingness to pay for child survival: results of a national survey in Central African Republic, *Social Science & Medicine*, **43**(6), 985–98

World Health Organization (WHO), 2002: *World health report 2002: reducing risks, promoting healthy life*, World Health Organization, Geneva 2004: *World health report 2004: changing history*, World Health Organization, Geneva

Xu K., D.B. Evans, K. Kawabata, R. Zeramdini, J. Klavus and C.J.L. Murray, 2003: Understanding household catastrophic health expenditures: a multi-country analysis, *Lancet*, **362**, 111–17

Perspective Paper 2.2

JACQUES VAN DER GAAG

Introduction

In their chapter 2 in this volume, Mills and Shill-cutt (hereafter, M&S) give a good overview of what we know, given current drug availability, treatment protocols, etc. about the costs and benefits of an integrated health care intervention (primary health care, PHC), and preventing and/or treating two infectious diseases (malaria, HIV/AIDS). The existing literature is well covered, but I will argue that the existing literature is in some cases highly inadequate. Most studies are based on 'best-case' scenarios, where benefit-cost (B/C) analysis is done under 'laboratory' conditions. Little reference is made to the fact that in many countries primary health care facilities are lacking or are dilapidated. In other countries there is no political will to take proper action. Bilateral, multilateral and private donors too often seem to be more comfortable with the status quo, even when circumstances cry out for new and perhaps unconventional approaches. These issues can be addressed within the B/C framework of this chapter. It boils down to an effort to answer the question: why, when resources are available, technology exists and national and international awareness is high, is so little done in the light of so much human suffering and potential economic loss? Unless we are willing to address this question little use can be made of even the most sophisticated B/C analyses.

Control of Malaria

Every 2 minutes four people die from malaria in SSA alone. Three of those deaths are children

I would like to thank Jaap Goudsmit Joep M.A. Lange and Onno Schellekens for their inputs and useful discussions. All points of view and mistakes are my own.

[1] An additional four children die, every 2 minutes, from other, mostly preventable, diseases.

under five.[1] In addition to the human suffering associated with this high mortality, recent estimates suggest that a 10 per cent reduction in malaria can result in a 0.3 percentage point higher growth rate per year. Technology to deal with malaria exists. M&S evaluate a package of two preventive and one curative measure. The preventive measures are (1) insecticide treated mosquito nets (ITNs) and (2) intermittent treatment of pregnant women (IPTp). The treatment measure is a shift from existing therapies (CQ, SP) to artimisinin-based combination therapy (ACT). It would be easy to make the point, as I will do in the next two sections, that while in theory cost effective interventions exist, in practice current delivery systems fail to reach large number of patients. This suggests that important aspects of the total delivery chain (from laboratory to patient) are ignored in the B/C analysis. However, this section of the M&S chapter makes the strong case that effective interventions are not only possible in theory, but can be implemented on a (relatively) large scale.

The KwaZulu Natal example from South Africa is a case in point. A programme shift (including ACT) was found to be highly successful, leading to large net benefits. It should be noted though, that South Africa has a relatively well-developed primary care system, which made the effective implementation of the programme possible. Unfortunately, such success stories are scarce. The authors acknowledge that global initiatives as, for example, the 'Roll Back Malaria' programme, have contributed to the doubling of international expenditures on malaria, but there is no evidence of a significant reduction in the global burden of the disease. Full reliance on public (government) health care infrastructure may be one of the reasons progress is slow. Experience in Tanzania, mentioned by the authors, shows that an appropriate division of labour between the private sector (distribution channels, out-of-pocket contributions) and the government (social marketing, stimulation of manufactures), can achieve a significant increase in ITN coverage.[2]

The need is high, the technology exists, there are examples of successful implementation on a relatively large scale and B/C ratios (BCRs) are impressive, and the international community has pledged significant increases in resources to fight malaria. The question remains: why is progress against this disease so sluggish? Or, in order to stay within the framework of this chapter: are major obstacles (and thus costs), which prevent rapid expansion of coverage, being overlooked? Part of the answer to this question may be found in the failure of the Garki programme in Nigeria where, despite a huge effort to control malaria, and despite the successful reduction of the human-biting rate of mosquitoes by 90 per cent, no significant change in the parasite rate among villagers was found. A National Institute of Health report also concludes that currently available measures can probably cope with the malaria problem everywhere, except in the Afrotropical region.[3] If these technical constraints remain, BCRs for SSA will be much smaller than elsewhere.

Another possible constraint to successful implementation of proven remedies is a combination of government failure and donor failure. Since this is also the likely cause of any lack of progress against the HIV/AIDS pandemic, I will discuss this in the next section.

Control of HIV/AIDS

The numbers are staggering: between 2.5 and 3.5 m deaths in 2003 alone, for a total of more than 22 m up to now 34–46 m infected at the moment, and 15,000 more next week, and for every next week to come, into as far in the future as we dare to make projections. HIV/AIDS is a genuine global development disaster. While early (micro) impact studies found only modest effects on economic well-being (*per capita* GDP growth), recent and more realistic models[4] predict economic collapse unless there is an immediate and far-ranging response to the pandemic.

M&S provide a survey of what is known about economic losses that can be averted by a variety of preventive measures. For countries where the epidemic is in a nascent stage, the losses averted between 2000 and 2005 can amount to 27.50 per cent of 2000 GDP in Egypt, or even 30.40 per cent GDP in Tunisia, if action is taken now. The results are less impressive if action is taken five years from now. This conveys a sense of urgency that could have been underlined much more throughout the chapter. In countries in the concentrated epidemic stage, high BCRs can be achieved by aggressive programmes to promote condom use (as in Thailand), but here the chapter begins to miss the point: in such countries, preventive measures are not enough. This is particularly true in countries with generalized levels of infection – up to 20 per cent or even 40 per cent of the population. Unless treatment regimes are implemented in these countries, they are economically doomed. Unfortunately, the chapter is silent about treatment regimes.

Here is the situation in SSA: 26 million persons infected, and an estimated 70,000 persons receiving treatment, just about equal to the number of *new* infections in one week. M&S discuss the recent increase in available funding for HIV/AIDS, plus the dramatic decrease in the cost of drug regimes, and the increased awareness of the international community. Unfortunately, they fail to address the following question: how come, with billions of dollars available, proven technology and the apparent willingness of the international community to commit itself to addressing this issue, only one week's worth of new infections is currently receiving treatment? How come that, according to the Global Fund website, this number will be raised only threefold over the next five years (i.e. to three weeks' worth of new infections)? Trying to answer these questions within the context of this chapter is tantamount to asking: which enormous costs are apparently overlooked in the B/C analysis? The answer to this question has at least the following two components: government failure and donor failure.

---

[2] For additional examples of successful public/private partnerships in health see Van der Gaag (1995).
[3] Both examples are mentioned in Gallup and Sachs (2001).
[4] Notably Bell, Devarajan and Gersbach (2003).

All B/C calculations assume a more or less well-functioning health sector infrastructure and a committed government. In most SSA countries, neither exists.[5] As with basic health services (see below), governments have generally failed to provide even the most rudimentary health sector infrastructure that is needed to successfully address the HIV/AIDS epidemic, in terms of either prevention or treatment. Up to 75 per cent of the people currently receiving treatment in SSA depend on the private sector. Most of them receive either insurance or direct treatment from their employers.

International donors are generally reluctant to involve private insurers or private providers. NGOs are usually involved in development efforts, including the prevention and treatment of diseases. But the for-profit private sector is often ignored or excluded, especially when it comes to health care provision. The little bit of success in providing drug treatment for HIV/AIDS patients is largely a private sector story. This donor failure to try and do *everything thinkable* to bring this terrible epidemic to a halt is inexplicable in light of the gross discrepancy between what needs to be done and what is done (or only scheduled to be done).

The total problem is daunting, but more can be done if donors were willing to lift constraints that currently prevent a much larger role for the private sector. For instance, an HMO in Nigeria covers about 65,000 patients and has contracts with about 200 hospitals. This organisation exists, and the infrastructure exists. Unfortunately the organisation is under tremendous financial stress, up to the point that it is no longer capable of treating (in-hospital) end-stage AIDS patients. The same organisation could provide drug treatment for about 10,000 patients, if only someone would put up the money, for the drugs and for the work involved. But organisations that can be accused of trying to 'make money from AIDS' are not eligible for international financial support. Governments are supposed to deal with the problem, but fail to do so. Those who have the organisation and the infrastructure to, at the very least, provide a modest contribution, are not asked (and financed) to do so.

The potential for involving more of the private sector is real but, at least initially, relatively small.

Once successful programmes do exist, however, one might expect a 'supply response' when more private insurers and more private providers are attracted to this – dare I say it – emerging industry. Infrastructure is costly but needs to be built and maintained (many governments have shown themselves to be incapable of doing this). Physicians and nurses expect to earn a decent salary (many governments are too poor to pay decent salaries). When donors are willing to provide billions of dollars to address the problem, and donors and governments together fail to show adequate results, one should stop pursuing 'more of the same', and experiment with alternative delivery systems, such as those available in the private sector.

One major obstacle to greater private sector involvement is the fact that the private sector does not provide services to the poor. But HIV/AIDS is a democratic disease, hitting the poor and rich alike. Furthermore, international donors could provide the resources, treating poor patients will be as 'profitable' for the private provider as treating rich patients. In addition, the status quo – treating almost nobody – can hardly be considered ethically superior.

What does all this mean for the B/C analyses? It probably means that the cost of getting the HIV/AIDS epidemic under control is vastly underestimated. In countries where the epidemic is in the generalized stage, prevention needs to be supplemented with treatment. And both prevention and treatment need infrastructure (organisation, clinics, staff). If you add these requirements to the calculations, the BCRs will surely worsen. The alternative – i.e. the apparent inability of both governments and the international donor community to act effectively – will, according to the best available evidence, lead to economic collapse of unprecedented proportions, not to mention the certain death of the tens of millions of people currently infected. The chances are that, when more complete economic models become available, the total benefits of HIV/AIDS treatment and prevention will vastly exceed currently available estimates.

In sum, M&S do provide a good overview of what we currently know about the (sometimes only theoretical) highly beneficial impact of prevention measures for HIV/AIDS. They do not address treatment issues although they cannot be ignored in countries

---

[5] With notable exceptions (as, for example, in Uganda).

with concentrated, and especially with generalized, levels of infections. Most of all, they do not convey the gross inadequacy of current national and international efforts to get the epidemic under control. Unless new approaches are tried, more parties allowed to participate, old alliances replaced by new ones and – in general – old dogmas thrown out, the epidemic will not be brought under control. This is not the time to search for the cheapest fire fighter: the house is already on fire and the fire is spreading fast.

Strengthening Basic Health Services

The authors first provide a B/C analysis for an overall increase in health expenditure in HPIC countries. This analysis is based on a paper by Gupta, Verhoeven and Tiongson (2001), which shows that public spending on health in these countries needs to increase from 2 per cent of GDP in 1999 to 12 per cent in 2015 in order to reach the Millennium Development Goal (MDG) of reducing child mortality by two-thirds. Not only is such an increase highly unlikely, the rate of decline in child mortality that is assumed to be *caused* by such an increase is contrary to what is commonly found in the literature that tries to link health improvements to public spending on health. Filmer and Pritchett (1999) conclude, from a careful analysis of cross-national data, that 'the impact of public spending on health is quite small, with a coefficient that is typically numerically small and statistically insignificant'. These authors also show the relevance of such findings for B/C analysis. While most studies of the cost-effectiveness of preventive and curative interventions suggest that massive health gains can be achieved at low cost (e.g. $10 per death averted), estimates of the association between public health spending and health gains imply that *in practice* the cost of a child death averted (by spending on PHC) may be between $50,000 and $100,000.

M&S are well aware of the importance of factors other than health expenditures, such as income and education, in the production of health. These determinants are ignored in the analysis, although economic growth is projected to stay at 3.4 per cent annually during the period 2001–15. Filmer and Prichett (1999) report an income elasticity of child mortality of 0.6, in line with other literature on this topic. Together with a projected increase in GDP of 3.4 per cent, that alone will result in a 2 per cent annual decline of child mortality. When M&S include a much smaller autonomous decline in child mortality (1.1 per cent annually) they already find negative net benefits of increased health spending. Clearly, the results presented in table 2.3 (a BCR of 2.6) are not credible.

This leaves the main question still unanswered: millions of children die every year in developing countries from causes that can easily and cheaply be prevented by (often simple) PHC interventions. The relationship between public health spending and child mortality (or other health measures) is *in practice* virtually non-existent, however. To put it differently, based on the theoretical link between an intervention and its impact on health, PHC-type interventions are highly cost-effective. On the other hand, the empirical link between public spending on such interventions and health outcomes is so weak that net benefits can become negative. We must again conclude that in the theoretical analysis some huge costs are overlooked. M&S mention some possible causes for these costs: poorly managed public health facilities, lack of ability to translate expenditures into the actual delivery of drugs and goods to local service providers, preference for spending on tertiary facilities. Perhaps the biggest problem is that, in virtually all countries where governments try to run the health care system, the vast majority of publicly provided goods and services are consumed by the middle and upper middle classes, and do not reach the poor. Private health care providers are being crowded out, while those who would benefit most from publicly provided services, do not have access to such services.

The Commission on Macroeconomics and Health (Sachs 2001) correctly draws attention to the need to drastically increase spending on health in poor countries, with donors playing a major role. But 'more of the same' will not have the desired impact. Where governments fail, the role of private providers (of services and of insurance) should be given a larger role, even when public and donor financing will continue to provide the vast majority of resources. What is needed is a break with the traditional view that health is such a special commodity that the provision of health services should remain in the hands of the government. Nine million children in developing countries die every year from preventable causes. Higher incomes, better education (for women), access to safe water and sanitation have all been shown to greatly reduce child mortality. Public spending on health care has virtually no effect – or, rather, the current way of public spending on health care has no effect, despite the proven potential of PHC. The separation of finance and provision is essential to improve this situation. Governments and donors alike should actively stimulate a larger role for the private sector in health insurance and health care provision for the promises of modern health care to become reality for the world's poor.

Conclusion

In this Perspective paper I have tried to draw attention to the big gap between what is needed and what is actually being done (or even only scheduled to be done) to greatly reduce the burden of disease in developing countries. In doing this, I followed the three topics addressed by M&S: malaria, HIV/AIDS and PHC. Since the mid-1990s it has become abundantly clear that much more resources need to be devoted to health in the developing world, and not only out of humanitarian concerns; the impact of disease on the economic development of a country can be huge. Recent studies show that the choice between treatment and no treatment can be tantamount to the choice between economic development and economic collapse. National and international efforts to address these issues are grossly inadequate; the main question is 'why?'. Why, in light of all the evidence (and, let's not forget, all the human suffering) do we

collectively fail to get results at a sufficiently large scale?

I point to (well-known) government failure and to (less frequently acknowledged) donor failure. Current efforts can still be characterized as 'more of the same', with a heavy government role and too little attention given to what the private sector can do. In B/C terms that means that the costs of the prevention or treatment of diseases, in real-world situations, are severely underestimated. It remains to be seen whether the higher estimates of both the benefits and the costs will lead to higher or lower B/C estimates. But that uncertainty should not be cause for inaction. In current B/C analyses we do not address the most important question: why do we fail? As a result, these studies are likely to come up with the wrong answers.

References

Bell, C.S., S. Devarajan and H. Gersbach, 2003: *The long-run economic costs of AIDS: theory and an application to South Africa*,

Filmer, D. and L. Pritchett, 1999: The impact of public spending on health: does money matter? *Social Science and Medicine*, **49**, 1309–23

Gallup, J.L. and J.D. Sachs, 2001: The economic burden of malaria, *American Journal of Tropical Medicine and Hygiene*, **64**, 85–96

Gupta, S., M. Verhoeven and E. Tiongson, 2001: Public spending on health care and the poor, International Monetary Fund Working Paper, *Economic Development*, World Health Organization, Geneva

Sachs, J.D., 2001: *Macroeconomics and health: investing in health for economic development*, World Health Organization, Geneva

van der Gaag, J., 1995: *Private and public initiatives*, World Bank, Washington, DC

Conflicts

PAUL COLLIER AND ANKE HOEFFLER

Introduction and Overview

Definition of the Challenge

Large-scale violent conflict takes several forms. However, over time international conflict has tended to become less common, whereas civil war has tended to become more common. The two phenomena are radically different and cannot sensibly be analysed within the same study. Here we focus exclusively upon the challenge of reducing the global incidence of civil war. Much of what we will do is previewed in our book *Breaking the Conflict Trap: Civil War and Development Policy* (Collier et al. 2003). We should add that the main models we use to calculate the costs and benefits are our own. It would clearly strengthen the robustness of the analysis were a range of models to be used, but unfortunately the quantitative analysis of civil war risk is still at an early stage and so there is not yet a substantial literature.

Benefits

The benefits of a reduction in the global incidence of civil war are common to all successful deployments of instruments for conflict reduction. The next section attempts to establish credible lower-bound estimates of these benefits. They accrue at three levels: national, regional and global. The benefits at the national level are partly economic and partly social. The economic benefits of avoiding war in a country can be estimated from the effect of civil war on growth. The social benefits are more difficult, but some estimate in terms of Disability-Adjusted Life Years (DALYs) has been attempted. The regional benefits of avoiding war have also been estimated, at least in terms of economic growth; the social spillovers, though large, are more difficult to

quantify. The global benefits of conflict reduction are the most difficult to estimate. Three big global scourges – HIV/AIDS, drugs, and 'safe havens' for terrorism, have been attributed to civil war environments. We leave these unquantified, but include them as separate speculative benefits.

Opportunities

Within the challenge of reducing the global incidence of civil war, we focus on three opportunities. These are the prevention of civil war in currently peaceful environments; the shortening of conflicts in currently war-torn environments; and the reduction in the risk of the resumption of conflict in post-conflict situations. These opportunities are very different, both in terms of instruments and pay-offs. Probably the highest pay-off is from improved interventions in post-conflict situations. Post-conflict relapses into renewed violence account for around half of all global civil wars, and so they provide an opportunity for highly focused interventions. By contrast, prevention is a highly diffuse approach.

Conflict Prevention

In the third section we investigate the costs and benefits of two instruments of conflict prevention. While all large-scale violent conflicts have elements of internal politics, it is striking that the risk of conflict is much higher in countries with particular economic characteristics – low *per capita* income, negative growth and dependence upon natural resource exports. By contrast, social and political characteristics – such as ethnic and religious composition, and a lack of political rights, do not seem to have much if any predictive power as to conflict risk. This suggests that interventions that improve the *economic characteristics* can reduce proneness to conflict even if they do not directly address the political issues that are the ostensible triggers of violence. We look at two international interventions that have some potential to improve economic performance – enhanced aid to the poorest countries, and improved transparency of natural resource payments to governments. Of these, it is much easier to place the former into the context of costs and benefits.

Aid as an Instrument of Conflict Prevention
The costs of aid are straightforward, and the benefits depend upon the effects upon economic development, and then upon the effects of economic development upon conflict risk. There is a massive literature on the effect of aid on development. We use the methodology of Collier and Dollar (2002), partly because this is the most straightforward to link to the conflict reduction benefits. It is also currently probably the dominant model in policy circles.[1] The model can be used to forecast how incremental aid would raise growth, country by country. For assessing the risks of conflict, and the contribution of growth to conflict reduction, we use the model of conflict risk of Collier and Hoeffler (2004b). In combination, these two models generate estimates of the benefits of aid for conflict prevention in a way that can be compared with their costs.

Transparency in Natural Resources as an Instrument of Conflict Prevention   There is a useful literature (e.g. Sachs and Warner 2000; Ross 2000, 2002; Klare 2001; Bannon and Collier 2003), on the adverse effects of natural resource dependence on development. There are also practical proposals – discussed at the Evian meeting of the G-8 in 2003 – for greater transparency in the management of natural resource rents. Greater transparency is an important and cheap practical instrument.

Shortening Conflicts   In the fourth section we investigate the opportunity of shortening conflicts and focus on one particular instrument. To date, there do not seem to have been systematic effects of either economic or military interventions to shorten conflict. The most promising intervention is to improve

the tracking of natural resources, and this is the intervention on which we will focus.

Tracking the Natural Resource Trade   Many conflicts are sustained because rebel forces get substantial finance from plundering natural resources and selling the proceeds on the international market. Recent developments are trying to certify the origin of natural resources so as to curtail this trade. The best example is the Kimberley process in diamonds, but there is also a new initiative for timber. Using a new model of the duration of conflict (Collier, Hoeffler and Söderbom 2004) we show, at least tentatively, that reductions in the price of natural resource exports increase the chances that a conflict will end. In effect, schemes such as Kimberley are trying to create a price discount for rebel sales of natural resources 'conflict diamonds' by making them illicit, and this can be interpreted within the model as significantly shortening conflict. The benefits of shortening conflicts can be handled within the same framework as the benefits of conflict prevention.

Post-Conflict Policies

In the fifth section we investigate the opportunity of reducing the risk of a reversion to conflict in post-conflict situations. Improving post-conflict policies provides the biggest opportunities for reducing the global incidence of civil war. We focus on two interventions, aid and military expenditures.

Aid in Post-Conflict Situations   Aid in post-conflict situations has distinctive effects – different from aid in the more normal situations that will be discussed later. Here we rely upon our application of the Collier–Dollar model of aid in post-conflict situations (Collier and Hoeffler 2004a). The growth effects are then fed into model of conflict risk, to show how aid in post-conflict situations could reduce the risk of repeat conflict.

Military Intervention Post-Conflict   We compare and contrast the effect on conflict risk of military spending by the post-conflict domestic government with a post-conflict external military presence – e.g. the British military presence in Sierra Leone. According to a new model of the

---

[1] See, for example, Benyon (2003).

effect of military intervention on risk (Collier and Hoeffler 2002a, 2003a), military spending by post-conflict governments is highly dysfunctional. This intervention is all costs and no benefits. By contrast, external military peace-keeping interventions appear to be highly cost-effective.

Conclusion

To summarise, we look at the challenge of reducing the global incidence of civil war. We take three opportunities, one of which is much bigger than the others – reducing the risk that conflicts restart once they have ended. We take five interventions:

* Aid as conflict prevention
* Transparency in natural resource rents as conflict prevention
* Natural resource tracking as conflict shortening
* Aid post-conflict to reduce the risk of repeat conflict
* Military spending post-conflict to reduce the risk of repeat conflict.

In the sixth section, we pull the analysis together and attempt to rank the cost-effectiveness of these five interventions.

The Benefits of Reducing the Incidence of Civil War

The benefits of reducing the incidence of civil war accrue at three distinct levels – national, regional and global. We consider them in turn.

The most straightforward benefits to estimate are the economic costs of civil war at the national level. Collier (1999) estimates the costs of civil war in terms of the reduction in the rate of economic growth. For this he adapts the standard approach of empirical growth econometrics, taking as the dependent variable the growth rate during a decade, and introducing the number of months during which the country is at civil war as an explanatory variable. Unsurprisingly, during civil war the growth rate is significantly reduced. The estimate from this regression is that each year of civil war reduces the growth rate by around 2.2 per cent. The counterfactual takes into account the country's initial level of income but does not allow for the fact that countries

prone to civil war might in any case tend to have worse economic policies even in the absence of war. Other estimates have been made from aggregations of case studies, and these tend to propose rather higher growth costs of war. However, the case studies were not selected randomly and there may have been a tendency to select particularly costly wars. In what follows we will take 2.2 per cent as the best estimate of the opportunity cost of war for the economy during the conflict. It does not seem inherently unreasonable, and there are plenty of cases of civil war where the costs were clearly higher. The average civil war lasts for around seven years (Collier and Hoeffler dataset). Thus, by the end of a civil war the economy is approximately 15 per cent below its counterfactual level.

The next issue is to determine how long this persists. Collier and Hoeffler (2004a) study the growth pattern during the first post-conflict decade. We find that the typical pattern is that by the end of the decade the economy has more or less recovered its pre-conflict growth path. The growth rate during the decade is 1.13 percentage points above normal, and this is statistically significant. Hence, a reasonable approximation is that the typical conflict involves a cumulative decline of 2.2 per cent per year (relative to counterfactual income) for the seven years of the conflict, followed by a cumulative recovery over the following decade. If we extrapolate this recovery to the twenty-first year after the conflict started, GDP is back to its counterfactual level. Discounted at 5 per cent back to the year in which the conflict starts, this implies a NPV of 105 per cent of initial GDP. We will take this as the first cost of civil war.

We are able to get some sense of the robustness of this figure from the 90 per cent confidence intervals around the two growth rates from which it is generated. The confidence intervals define the bounds within which there is a 90 per cent chance of finding the 'true' growth rate. We will estimate the lower bound for the cost of a civil war as that generated by the *lower* bound on the loss of growth during the conflict and the *upper* bound on the additional growth after the conflict.[2] Conversely, the

---

[2] Although the bounds on the growth rates define the 90 per cent confidence interval for each growth rate, the bounds on the costs of conflict are likely to represent a wider confidence

upper bound for the cost is generated by the upper bound on the loss of growth during the conflict and the lower bound on the additional growth after the conflict. Applying precisely the same procedure as previously, the range generated by these bounds is 41 per cent–305 per cent of initial GDP. Evidently, while our cost estimate of 105 per cent used the central estimate of the growth rates, it is close to the bottom of the implied range of costs. Hence, there is reason to think that our cost estimate is conservative. Where it is feasible to do so, we will include analogous estimates of confidence intervals in our subsequent calculations.

The income loss from civil war is compounded by a change in the composition of expenditure. Specifically, the share of GDP spent on the military increases and this can reasonably be seen as a waste – not in the sense that it is necessarily foolish given the context of conflict, but in the sense that benchmarked against peace it constitutes a further lowering of welfare. It is a deterioration in the conversion of GDP into well-being. Our estimate of how civil war affects military spending is taken from Collier and Hoeffler (2002a). There we explain the share of GDP spent on the military in terms of various characteristics, including whether the country is engaged in civil war. We find, unsurprisingly, that during civil war military spending rises significantly, by around 1.8 per cent of GDP. In a further paper

(Collier et al. 2003) we investigate what happens to military spending post-conflict, and find that during the first decade governments tend to maintain it at much higher levels than prior to conflict – approximately, governments reduce spending by only around 0.5 per cent. Beyond the first decade there is no evidence and it seems best to make the conservative assumption that spending levels revert to normal, if only to avoid large but very speculative numbers. Hence, the additional waste on military expenditure as a result of civil war is 1.8 per cent of GDP for the seven years of the conflict, followed by 1.3 per cent of GDP for the next decade. Again discounting at 5 per cent to the first year of the conflict, this produces an NPV of 18 per cent of initial GDP.[3]

These economic benefits omit major effects that may well be more important. After all, civil war is not socially equivalent merely to a prolonged economic recession; civil war causes a severe deterioration in health states. Most of this does not arise from the direct casualties of combat, but from forced population movements and the collapse of basic preventative health services. There have been some estimates of this in terms of DALYs and others in terms of mortality rates, especially among infants. Ghobarah, Huth and Russett (2003) use data on twenty-three major diseases and find significant adverse effects of civil war. Using WHO data, they estimate that during 1999 then-current wars were causing the loss of 8.44 million DALYs, and that a further 8.01 million DALYs were lost as a legacy effect of the civil wars that had ended during the period 1991–7. On the basis of the first of these figures, the typical civil war incurs around 0.5 million DALYs a year of loss during the conflict.[4] These losses persist for some time after the conflict. There is some evidence that the health effects are more persistent than the economic effects, but to err on the side of caution we will taper the health costs out at the same rate as the economic costs – that is we assume that they decline to zero by the twenty-first year after the onset of the conflict. We taper the loss of DALYs out linearly from the end of the war after seven years of conflict to zero by the twenty-first year. The resulting estimate of DALYs lost post-conflict is a little less than that of Ghobarah, Huth and Russett (2003), and so is probably an

interval. At one extreme, the two growth rate effects are independent of each other, so that the chance of being 'lucky' in terms of both low growth losses during conflict and fast recovery post-conflict is the product of two one-in-ten events, i.e. one in a hundred. At the other extreme, the same circumstances which make growth losses low during conflict make recovery rapid, so that there is only one chance event, the odds being one in ten. Hence, our bounds for the cost of conflict represent at least the 90 per cent confidence interval and may represent the 99 per cent interval.

[3] Again we can assess the robustness of this figure from the 90 per cent confidence intervals on the additional military expenditure. As before, there are two apparently independent effects – the increases in spending during conflict and after conflict, which are nevertheless likely to be correlated. The estimated bounds – 12 per cent and 25 per cent – thus represent at least the 90 per cent confidence interval for the extra costs of military spending.

[4] There are typically around seventeen civil wars at any one time (Collier et al. 2003, chapter 4). Hence, the loss per war is 8.44/17.

underestimate. We then discount the loss of DALYs at 5 per cent and reach an NPV in terms of discounted DALYs of 5 million. To convert DALYs into an economic metric of income equivalent is not straightforward. Work by Becker, Philipson and Soares (2003) and Soares (2003) provides some basis for valuing a DALY, country-by-country, but unfortunately their evidence is fragmentary for precisely the low-income countries with which we are primarily concerned. Rather than leave DALYs hanging as an additional cost to bear in mind, we will assign the obviously arbitrary value of $1,000 to a DALY. This is approximately the 'purchasing power parity' (PPP) level of *per capita* annual income in many of the countries at risk of conflict, and is also within the ballpark implied by the analyses of Becker, Philipson and Soares and Soares. This yields a health cost of the typical civil war of around $5 bn.

There are other important costs of civil war that accrue to the nation directly affected. For example, forced migration is a bad in itself, over and above its adverse consequences for health and income. However, rather than aggregate a range of effects that are difficult to quantify, we will include only these two effects of civil war – health and economic costs. These are clearly underestimates of the full costs of civil war, but hopefully not such wild underestimates that they are worthless.

We now turn to the second layer of costs of civil war, namely those that accrue to neighbouring countries. There is no clear quantitative evidence that conflict in one country directly spills over into an increased risk of conflict in neighbouring countries. However, there are various estimates of the effect of conflict in one country on the economies of neighbouring countries. The first credible estimate was by Murdoch and Sandler (2001), who established rigorously that there were significant effects not just on neighbours, but on a much larger geographic area over a region. Chauvet (2003) also finds significant effects. Our own estimate is that a civil war in one country reduces the growth rate of neighbouring countries by around 0.9 percentage points.[5] There is as yet to our knowledge no research on the effects on neighbours post-conflict. We will assume that the recovery of the neighbourhood follows the same trajectory as that of the

country directly affected. Again taking a discounted NPV of these losses, the cost to the typical neighbour is 43 per cent of initial GDP. The average country has 2.7 neighbours (Collier and Hoeffler 2002a). Hence, the adverse growth effects of a conflict during the conflict are equivalent to a loss of 115 per cent of initial GDP of one country (ignoring any systematic differences in the size of war-affected countries and their neighbours). The growth loss to neighbours thus exceeds the loss to the country itself. The 90 per cent confidence interval on this estimate comes from that around the coefficient on neighbouring civil war in our growth regression.[6] The lower bound is 49 per cent and the upper bound 182 per cent.

A further cost to the neighbourhood is through neighbourhood arms races. Recall that during and after a civil war the government of the affected country substantially raises its military spending. Collier and Hoeffler (2002a) show that the military spending of neighbours is a powerful influence upon the level of spending that a country chooses. That is, there are neighbourhood arms races. An increase in military spending by a country affected by civil war triggers such an arms race, with the neighbourhood also significantly increasing its spending. The extent of this arms race effect – termed the 'arms race multiplier of neighbour's expenditure' – depends upon the number of neighbours. As the number of neighbours increases the multiplier declines sharply. We estimate that for the typical country – with 2.7 neighbours – an exogenous

[5] Our estimate, made for the purposes of the present study, regressed the annual growth rate over a five-year period, on the initial level of income, education, dummy variables for whether the country was landlocked, for time period and for region, and the number of months during which the country itself, and any of its neighbours were experiencing civil war. If a neighbour was at civil war for the full five years the reduction in the annual growth rate was 0.89 percentage points. This is larger than the effect found by Murdoch and Sandler (2001), but their growth regression includes investment as an explanatory variable so that any effects of neighbourhood civil war on growth via the investment rate are omitted. Results are available from the authors.

[6] We maintain the assumption that post-war the neighbour gradually recovers over the same period as the country that experienced the civil war.

1 percentage point increase in military spending by one country – due to civil war – would increase the average spending of neighbours by around 0.23 per cent.[7] Recall that during conflict spending by the conflict-affected country rises by 1.8 per cent of GDP and that for the decade after conflict spending is 1.3 per cent of GDP higher. The typical neighbour would thus raise its spending during its neighbour's conflict by around 0.4 per cent of GDP and during the post-conflict period by around 0.3 per cent.[8] The NPV of these extra expenditures is 4.3 per cent of initial GDP.[9] Since this occurs in each of the 2.7 neighbours, the total extra expenditure is equivalent to around 12 per cent of the GDP of one country (again ignoring size differences between countries).[10]

There are also indirect non-growth costs of civil war on neighbours. Perhaps the most important is that during forced migration out of the civil war country migrants pick up diseases to which they lack immunity, and then transmit these diseases to neighbouring populations. An estimate of the incidence of malaria by Reynol-Querol finds that each 1,000 civil war immigrants to a neighbouring country raise the number of cases of malaria in the recipient country by 1,400. It is not possible at present to quantify these effects into DALYs or some other equivalent. Hence, we will make no attempt to incorporate these costs.

Before continuing, it is useful to sum the various costs that we have so far considered. The cost of the loss of GDP to the country directly affected is 105 per cent of initial GDP. Onto this is added the loss of GDP to neighbours, being equivalent to 115 per cent of initial GDP, the diversion of spending into the military in the country directly affected, costing the equivalent of 18 per cent of GDP and finally the same diversion in neighbours, costing the equivalent of 12 per cent of GDP. Hence, the total cost is the equivalent of 250 per cent of initial GDP. To express this in dollars we need the GDP for pertinent countries. Our discussion of policy instruments will be designed to reduce risks in low-income countries, hence, the benefits will be proportionate to the GDP of conflict-affected low-income countries. In estimating the GDP of such countries we exclude India and China, even though they have both had relatively minor internal conflicts. The exclusion of these countries is because they are too large and *sui generis* to be pertinent to our policy instruments. Being so large, their inclusion would swamp the results. Thus defined, the average GDP of conflict-affected low-income countries just prior to conflict was $19.7 bn.[11] Thus, had a representative conflict been averted the benefit would have been around $49 bn.[12] To this must be added the health benefits, which we have already estimated directly in dollars to be around $5 bn. The total benefit of averting the typical civil war in a low-income country would thus be around $54 bn.

Having established a figure for the cost of a single civil war we must now introduce a further cost generated by the 'conflict trap'. That is, once a country has had a civil war it becomes much more likely to have a further war. Evidently, in econometric terms such a proposition is problematic unless due allowance is made for 'fixed effects': that is, it is easy to confuse an inherent proneness in a particular country to civil war for the legacy effects of war. However, it is possible to an extent to distinguish the two since the legacy effects fade over the course of around two decades. It is thus possible to exclude any highly persistent effects that make a country atypically prone to conflict. We may be

---

[7] We estimate this using the results of Collier and Hoeffler (2002a, equation (6)).

[8] That is, 0.23*1.8 = 0.4, and 0.23*1.3 = 0.3.

[9] As usual, we assume that the conflict lasts for seven years. We assume that the post-conflict increase in military spending persists for a decade. We discount at 5 per cent.

[10] We again estimate the confidence interval. Potentially there are now three components in the estimate, each with a confidence interval: the civil war country's increased military spending during and after conflict, and the degree of gearing in the response of the neighbours. However, the degree of gearing in the neighbours' response can reasonably be treated as independent of the other events and so our 90 per cent confidence interval on this component of cost incorporates only the confidence interval around the degree of gearing, namely 8 per cent and 16 per cent.

[11] We use here our comprehensive dataset for global conflicts, 1965–99. We take the average GDP of all conflict-affected low-income countries (excluding India and China) just prior to the conflict. Our dataset uses 1985 constant price dollars from the Penn World Tables 5.6. We convert this into current dollars using the US CPI.

[12] That is, 2.50*19.7 = 49.

misattributing to the legacy effects of civil war risk factors which actually cause both the first war and a subsequent relapse, but are not highly persistent. All that can be said here is that civil war is itself such a profound experience for a society that it is likely to dwarf other non-persistent events that precede it. With these caveats, we use the Collier–Hoeffler (2004b) model of the risk of civil war to estimate the additional risks faced by societies that have recently had a civil war, period by period. Here we take the twenty-one civil wars which both began and ended during the period 1965–99 and for which we have complete data both just prior to the commencement of the war and after its ending. We then consider a hypothetical country with characteristics that are the mean of this group and estimate the risk of conflict both just prior to the war and once it has ended. Even prior to war, the modelled five-year risk of war for this group of countries was high, at 22.3 per cent.[13] However, just after the end of the war the predicted risk had risen to 38.6 per cent. This increase in risk of 16.3 percentage points was thus a further legacy effect of the war. If the peace is maintained, the risk gradually fades: it takes around fifteen years for the risk to revert to its pre-conflict level. The cost of this legacy is then the enhanced risk of conflict, times the cost of a single war, discounted back to the beginning of the first conflict. Taking this approach yields a 'conflict trap' effect of around $10.2 bn.[14] This has to be added to the $54 bn, yielding a cost of $64.2 bn. In effect, in a probabilistic sense, the typical civil war persists for more than seven years. Again we estimate confidence intervals. The lower bound of the 90 per cent confidence interval is 10 per cent of GDP, and the upper bound is 26 per cent, the central estimate being 19 per cent (see table 3A4.2).[15]

The final layer of effects is global. These effects are too important to ignore but too speculative to quantify. Since the 1980s three massive world scourges have been linked to civil war. As will be obvious, at the most civil war has been a contributing factor to these scourges rather than their sole cause. The best-documented is the link to the production of hard drugs that are consumed predominantly in the OECD societies. Around 95 per cent of hard drugs production takes place in civil war

areas. The reason for this is straightforward: production basically needs territory outside the control of a recognised government, and this is inadvertently – and in some cases consciously – provided by rebel organisations (Brito and Intriligator 1992). The second scourge is HIV/AIDS. A reasonable, but not definitive medical case has been made that the origin of the present pandemic is a civil war. Civil war can vastly increase the spread of a new sexually transmitted disease (STD) because it combines mass rape with mass movements of populations. Hence, what might normally have been localised outbreaks that quickly died out might have been scaled up to the point of sustainability. The third scourge is international terrorism. As with drugs, it is highly convenient for such terrorists to have access to territory outside the control of any recognised government. Al Quaida located in Afghanistan, not because its members were Afghani, but because it was outside the control of a recognised government.

The global costs of these three scourges have been astronomic and huge resources are being deployed to contain them. International military interventions were eventually felt to be necessary in six civil wars where the interventions have been costed: Bosnia, Cambodia, El Salvador, Haiti, Rwanda and Somalia. The combined cost of external intervention was $85 bn.[16] For the moment, however, we will leave these benefits as a large but unknown

[13] The risk for the typical low-income country other than post-conflict countries is much lower at 13.8 per cent.

[14] We assume that the conflict occurs in the middle of the five-year period of prediction. Thus, during the first five year period the NPV of the additional risk of conflict is $(0.386 - 0.223)(54)/(1.05)^3$. During the second five-year period the risk falls to 31.9 per cent, and so the additional legacy cost is $(1 - 0.386)(0.319 - 0.223)(54)/(1.05)^8$. During the third five-year period the risk falls to 25.8 per cent so the additional legacy cost is $(1 - 0.386)(1 - 0.319)(0.258 - 0.223)(54)/(1.05)^{13}$. The post-conflict risk gradually falls due to three effects: the increased duration of peace, the higher rate of growth and the cumulative effect of growth upon income.

[15] The confidence interval is established from the coefficient on the duration of peace in the logit regression. We replace the central estimate for this coefficient with the lower and upper bounds in turn, and then repeat our estimates as set out above.

[16] See Brown and Rosecrance (1999).

residual. In effect, we will try to determine how large this residual would have to be before our various interventions started to look attractive in a cost-benefit sense.

So far, we have considered what a typical civil war might cost, and also what civil wars in aggregate do to global society. However, when we turn to opportunities for reducing civil war, to the extent that they work they reduce the global incidence of civil war – the number of countries at war at any one time. We thus need to convert our measures of the cost of a typical war into something that is commensurate with the effects of the opportunities. At present, on average two civil wars start each year. Thus, for opportunities which reduce the risk of war starts but leave the duration of war unaffected, the benefits are double the NPV of the cost of a civil war – i.e. $128.4 bn – multiplied by the reduction in the risk of war initiation. This then becomes the annual benefit from the opportunity. For example, an initiative which reduced the risk of war by a tenth would generate benefits of around $12.8 bn per year.

The opportunities which we discuss in the following sections do not, however, reduce the risks of all civil wars but rather focus on the two most salient sources. Here we rely on a simulation model of the global sources of civil war set out in Collier and Hoeffler (2003a). This model simulates the steady-state flows into and out of civil war with countries divided into five groups: high-income countries at peace; middle-income countries at peace; low-income countries at peace; post-conflict countries; and countries at civil war. According to this model, the most salient source of civil war starts

is post-conflict relapses. Typically, half of all civil wars are relapses into conflict during the first decade of peace following a previous conflict. We will be considering specific instruments to reduce this risk. The other salient source of civil war is from low-income countries (excluding post-conflict situations). Typically, 0.7 civil wars per year start in such countries.

For opportunities which shorten wars, the benefits need to be calculated differently. We simply repeat all the above calculations replacing the actual seven-year duration of civil war with an imagined six-year duration. Such a shortening has quite a large effect on the total cost of a war, reducing it from $64.2 bn to $53.5 bn.[17] This would be a gain to the two civil wars which on average start annually, representing an annual gain of $21.4 bn. However, in addition to this continuing gain, were existing civil wars to be shortened by one year there would be a once-and-for-all gain from this stock of ongoing wars. Typically, there are around seventeen significant civil wars going on at any one time. Were their average cost to be reduced by $10.7 bn this would constitute a gain of $181.9 bn. To get this one-off stock gain into a flow gain in order to make it comparable with our other figures we again apply a 5 per cent interest rate. The flow gain is thus $9.1 bn. Hence, an initiative which shortened civil wars by one year would generate an annual benefit of around $30.5 bn.[18]

At present these benefits are entirely hypothetical because we have yet to discuss instruments for achieving a reduction in the risk of war initiation and a reduction in war duration. These are the tasks of the next two sections. This will determine whether the potentially large numbers involved in the benefits of greater peace can actually be accessed.

Opportunities for Conflict Prevention

We now consider the first opportunity for reducing the incidence of civil war. This is to reduce the risk that conflicts will start. Here we exclude the circumstances in which a recently ended conflict restarts because we consider this separately later.

---

[17] Excluding the legacy effects, the cost of a civil war of six years duration is $36.8 bn compared with $45 bn for a seven-year war. Again we estimate the 90 per cent confidence interval. In the low-cost scenario (a smaller growth loss during the war and a faster recovery), shortening the war by one year reduces total costs by 27 per cent. In the high-cost scenario (a larger growth loss during the war and a slower recovery), shortening the war by one year reduces total costs by 13 per cent. In our central estimate, shortening the war by one year reduces costs by 18 per cent.

[18] That is, the $21.4 bn from shortening the two wars that start each year, plus the $9.1 bn which is the annual income from the one-off windfall from shortening the seven current civil wars.

To investigate the opportunities for conflict prevention we need a quantitative model of the risks of conflict. The Collier–Hoeffler (hereafter, CH) model was, we believe, the first such model, and we will use its latest version (see appendix 1). There are now several other such models and we will discuss the extent to which our model agrees with the findings of other models.

The CH model finds that *political and social characteristics* of a country prior to conflict are surprisingly unimportant in determining the level of risk. Whether a country is democratic or not seems to have no significant effect. This result is broadly echoed by the political science literature. Some scholars find a non-monotonic effect, such that partial democracies are actually more dangerous than dictatorships. Some authors also find a disturbing interaction with *per capita* income, such that in lower-income countries democracy is significantly more dangerous than dictatorship. Such results do not, of course, lead to the conclusion that dictatorship is preferable, but they do suggest that solutions purely in terms of the design of the political system may be less promising than one would have hoped. Similarly, but more hopefully, ethnic and religious diversity does not appear to be a very significant risk factor with the possible exception of 'ethnic dominance', in which the largest ethnic group constitutes a modest majority of the population. Fortunately, most low-income countries are too diverse to be characterised by such dominance.

By contrast, the CH model finds that three economic characteristics have significant and substantial effects on the risk of conflict. These are the *level of income*, its *rate of growth*, and the degree of *dependence upon primary commodity exports*. The effect of the level of income is well supported – it is evident that civil war is concentrated in the poorest countries. While potentially this could be due to reverse causality, during colonialism there was in effect an imposed peace. Countries came out of colonialism at very different levels of income, and on top of this had very different economic performance, before some of them succumbed to their first conflict. The relationship to the level of income is robust to the exclusion of cases of repeat conflict. The effect of the rate of growth of income is questioned by some scholars. However, unless the post-conflict phase is properly treated, analyses are liable to obtain spurious results: during the post-conflict phase there is both a high rate of growth – due to recovery – and a very high risk of further conflict, so that the two can appear to be positively associated. We will use the CH results because they seem to be both intuitively reasonable and to be predicted by simple theory. When an economy is growing rapidly the returns to expanding the cake are higher relative to fighting over how to divide the cake, and so one would expect a reduction in the risk of conflict.

We are going to focus here on low-income countries. These are the ones that according to the CH model are most at risk, and they are also the ones for which aid as an instrument is pertinent. Specifically, we will consider low-income countries excluding post-war situations (these will be considered later). We will also exclude both India and China from our data because they are too large for international interventions to make a credible difference. Our focus is therefore on relatively small, poor countries with a recent history of peace. Such countries are, according to our analysis, nevertheless living dangerously. During a five-year period, we estimate that the typical such country faces a risk of civil war of 13.8 per cent. This is based on average experience in 1965–99, but over that period there were no major trends in the risk of civil war, so it is a reasonable estimate to apply to present circumstances.

Raising the growth rate of such an economy thus has two beneficial effects on the risk of conflict – it reduces the risk directly through the growth rate effect, and it reduces it cumulatively through the income levels effect. We are going to take as an experiment an increase in the growth rate of 1 percentage point sustained for a period of ten years. According to the CH model, which analyses risk in five-year periods, this would have an impact effect during the first five-year period, through its effect on the growth rate. Specifically, the risk would decline from 13.8 per cent to 12.7 per cent. In the second five-year period there would be both a growth effect and an income level effect, since growth would cumulatively have raised income. Their combined effect on conflict risk would be to reduce it to 12.2 per cent. In the third and subsequent five-year periods the growth rate reverts to its previous level and the only effect is therefore due to the permanently higher level of income. This permanent effect is for the risk to be 12.7 per cent, rather than the 13.8 per cent that it would have been.

The benefits of the reduced risk of conflict can then be valued using our previous estimate of the cost of a conflict and the contribution of low-income countries to this risk. Recall that the cost of a civil war is $64.2 bn, and that 0.7 such wars occur in the typical year in low-income countries (excluding post-conflict situations). The 'impact' effect of faster growth, that is during the first five-year period, is to reduce the rate of conflict initiation by 8 per cent.[19] Hence, for each year of this five-year period, there is a gain of $3.6 bn.[20] Analogously, in the second five-year period the rate of conflict initiation falls by 12 per cent, and so the annual gain rises to $5.4 bn. Finally, in the third five-year period and all subsequent years there is a gain of $3.6 bn. The NPV of this income stream, discounted at 5 per cent, is around $79.2 bn. We should, of course, note that this is simply the gain due to *conflict* reduction in these societies. The main benefit of growth in these societies is likely to be poverty reduction. We are focusing only on the value of the additional benefits of enhanced security, which are normally omitted from the analysis of the effects of growth. This particular estimate has a wide confidence interval, the 90 per cent bounds being $29 bn and $127 bn.[21]

Having got some valuation of the effect of enhanced growth in low-income countries with a history of peace, we now consider instruments for achieving faster growth. The first such instrument that we will consider is an increase in aid.

The Instrument of Aid

The effect of aid on growth is controversial, although most scholars find it to be significantly positive. The main controversy is the extent to which the effect of aid on growth is contingent upon the policy, governance and institutional context. We will use the estimates of Collier and Dollar (2002), and combine them with the CH model of conflict. This was the approach taken in Collier and Hoeffler (2002b).

Collier and Dollar (2002) find that aid raises the growth rate but that it is subject to diminishing returns. Hence, at some point a country can become saturated with aid and no additional growth is achieved by further aid. They find that the capacity to absorb aid (as a percentage of GDP) is dependent upon the quality of economic policies, governance and institutions. They measure these using a detailed ordinal index compiled annually by World Bank staff for each country, the 'Country Policy and Institutional Assessment' (CPIA), So measured, they find that the CPIA itself powerfully influences the growth rate, and that it also influences the capacity to absorb aid.

Recall that for conflict prevention we are focusing on low-income countries that are not in post-conflict situations, and we are excluding India and China. Thus defined, we consider incremental aid as a means of raising growth rates. We abstract from issues of aid allocation by adding extra aid worth 2 percentage points of GDP (valued at PPP prices) to all such countries. We simplify by considering the effect on the 'representative' such country, with characteristics at the mean of the group. The extra 2 percentage points of aid raise the growth rate by 0.2 percentage points. This is a relatively modest gain – much smaller than the impact of existing aid flows – because of the problem of diminishing returns. We should also note that it abstracts from issues of improved aid delivery. With better delivery mechanisms and more selective allocation, the contribution of aid to growth could be considerably higher. However, our figure is a simple benchmark.

The benefits of such growth in terms of conflict prevention are approximately one-fifth of the benefits of those achieved by a 1 per cent faster growth rate, which we have just estimated. Hence, the benefits are approximately $16 bn.

The costs are simply the additional aid flows. There are thirty-two countries in the category of low-income, at peace, and not in their first decade

---

[19] That is, $1 - (12.7)/(13.8) = 0.08$.

[20] That is, $0.08*0.7*$64.2$ bn.

[21] The bounds come from the confidence interval on the growth coefficient in our logit of conflict risk.

post-conflict (excluding China and India). Their combined GDP is $1,200 bn (again valued at PPP prices but expressed in current dollars), so that the extra aid programme would cost $24 bn annually.[22] Over the decade, this would amount to an NPV of $195 bn.

Evidently, the conclusion of this estimate is that conflict prevention achieved purely by unselective aid programmes to low-income countries is not very cost-effective. The benefits amount to less than 10 per cent of the costs. The uncounted global costs of conflict would therefore have to be over ten times the included costs for this strategy to justify itself purely on security grounds. Recall that this is decidedly not a comment on the efficacy of additional aid, since the main purpose of such aid is poverty reduction rather than security. However, it does suggest that the addition of security considerations may not be central to the argument over additional aid for low-income countries.

The Instrument of Improved Governance of Natural Resource Rents

Natural resource rents are usually not successfully converted into growth. Indeed, they appear often to be detrimental (Lane and Tornell 1999, Sachs and Warner 2000). In addition to these adverse effects for growth, we find that revenue from primary commodities is a risk factor in civil war. While this specific econometric result has been challenged, at least for natural resource rents the result is supported by a considerable body of case study evidence. Such evidence is particularly useful because it can suggest the likely mechanisms by which natural resource rents increase the risk of conflict, and hence what policies might be appropriate.

There seem to be five routes by which natural resource rents increase the risk of conflict. The first is that such resources are prone to *price booms and busts*, and these episodes tend to destabilise the economy, producing both overall slower growth and phases of rapid economic decline. Both of these economic consequences would raise the risk of conflict. The second route is that because the government gets income from natural resources it does not need to *tax* the population so heavily, and some

political scientists suggest that this tends to distance the government from the population. In effect, the population is less concerned to hold the government to account and so spending becomes corrupt. This is compounded by a third effect, namely that natural resource rents tend to be associated with increased levels of *'grand' corruption*. Large contracts have to be negotiated, and there are enormous incentives for companies and politicians to enter into deals that are beneficial for each party at the expense of the country. This in turn tends to play into a fourth route, namely *regional secessions*. Natural resources tend to be located in the periphery of a country, where there will usually already be some romantic ethnic separatist movement even prior to the resource discovery. However, once valuable resources have been discovered this romantic secessionism can batten on to the robust cause of economic self-interest. If national-level politicians can plausibly be depicted as corruptly looting the resource rents then the secessionist party will of course do so. Finally, natural resource rents provide opportunities for *extortion rackets* on the part of rebel movements and these finance and sustain conflict even if they do not initially motivate it.

Where in this is there an opportunity for the international community? We suggest that there is an opportunity for collective action around the principles of how natural resource rents are managed. Specifically, international action could improve the *domestic governance of primary commodities* by establishing a 'template' for their proper use. Such a template could lay down two core principles. The first would relate to transparency of revenues. At present in many countries the rents from natural resources are not reported in the budget and so expenditures cannot be scrutinised effectively. A major campaign is currently being mounted, backed by a range of NGOs, G-8 governments and the international financial institutions (IFIs), known as the Extractive Industries Transparency

---

[22] Thinking the same costing through using prevailing exchange rates instead of PPP, the amount of aid needed would be around 6 per cent of GDP rather than 2 per cent, but there would be an offsetting reduction in the value of GDP itself.

Initiative (EITI). It aims to establish guidelines for both corporate and government disclosure of natural resource rents. The second would relate to *intertemporal revenue management*. While there is little rationale for low-income countries to establish funds for future generations, along the lines of Norway and Kuwait, there is a much stronger case for medium-term revenue smoothing. Poor management of revenue booms has been an important cause of slow growth in many resource-rich countries. International guidelines could encourage the adoption of either hedging or savings rules to cope with such shocks. For both transparency and smoothing mechanisms the advantage of international guidelines is that it makes it much easier for a reforming government to achieve change. For example, the President of Nigeria has publicly announced his intention of adopting the EITI transparency guidelines. Similarly, a government newly facing a resource discovery has a ready-made policy to adopt or reject. The EITI has already proved potent in the context of such a discovery in São Tomé and Principe. Finally, it makes it more costly for a government to persist with bad policies. Citizens can challenge their government as to why it is choosing to flout international guidelines, and the decision not to adopt them would constitute a negative signal to international markets. An analogy would be the widespread adoption of Basel guidelines in banking. An effective precursor to the EITI was the Chad–Cameroon pipeline initiative, which has substantially increased the ability of citizens of Chad to scrutinise how revenues are being used.

The cost of producing such guidelines is not financial. Rather its cost is the opportunity cost of achieving collective international action in some other sphere. Such action is difficult, and only a very few initiatives can be achieved. If, for example, a summit can reasonably discuss only three issues, the cost of the EITI is the gain from whichever issue it crowds out.

To estimate the gains from a successful initiative, we proceed as follows. We first establish that

[23] OLS regression results, *t*-statistics in parentheses, robust standard errors used, time dummies not reported. To reduce the problem of endogeneity *GDP* and *SXP* are lagged by five years. To reduce the problem of autocorrelation we use only five-year 'snapshots': 1975, 1980 . . . 1995.

there is indeed an adverse effect of natural resource rents upon policies, governance and institutions. For comparability we again rely upon the CPIA of the World Bank. We regress the CPIA on *per capita* GDP and upon the share of natural resource exports in GDP:[23]

$$
(1) \quad CPIA_t
$$
$$
= 0.463 + 0.320 \ln GDP_{t-5} - 0.513 SXP_{t-5}
$$
$$
\quad (1.44) \quad (7.16)^{***} \quad \quad (-2.53)^{***}
$$
$$
n = 465, R^2 = 0.12
$$

The effect of natural resource rents, as proxied by *SXP*, is indeed both highly significant and adverse: controlling for the level of income, the more dependent upon natural resources is a country, the worse is its policy, governance and institutions.

We have no way of telling how effective global guidelines on natural resource management would be. A fully successful effort to improve the management of natural resource rents would eliminate the adverse effect on the CPIA. We suppose that such an improvement would be beyond the bounds of the feasible, but imagine that by giving the issue sufficient prominence and promoting sound guidelines the adverse effects of natural resource rents could be halved. In terms of the above regression this would imply that the negative coefficient on *SXP* of –0.513 would be reduced to –0.257. This we take to be the feasible aspiration of an international effort. Some of the mismanagement of natural resource rents has indeed been so egregious that major improvements should be possible with little effort.

Our next task is to estimate the benefits for conflict prevention of such an improvement. We find that the CPIA has no direct effect on conflict risk (Collier and Hoeffler 2002b). However, following Collier and Dollar (2002), an improvement in the CPIA would raise growth. At the mean characteristics of the low-income countries at peace that we are considering in this section, halving the adverse effect of natural resources on policy would raise growth rates by 0.067 percentage points. In the case of aid we considered a ten-year programme. However, there is no reason to suppose that once international guidelines became effective their benefits would be only temporary. The goal is to produce a one-off permanent change in practices. The

NPV of the gain in reduced risk from this permanent higher rate is $12.1 bn.[24]

Recall that we find that in addition to the adverse effect on growth, there is a substantial direct effect of primary commodity dependence increasing the risk of civil war. This effect is controlling for the growth and level of income. Case study evidence suggests that one of the important routes by which this happens is that secessionist movements gain strength by being able credibly to suggest that resource rents generated in their region are being wasted or embezzled. Hence, transparency and scrutiny of revenue use can be expected to weaken the risks generated by a given level of natural resource rents. More generally, if natural resource rents flow transparently into the budget and out again for reasonable public expenditures, then there is less incentive for rebels to try to capture them, and less reason for them to expect to be successful in doing so. We have no way of knowing how large such an effect might be. For illustrative purposes, we assume that the EITI could reduce the direct contribution of natural resources to conflict risk by one-tenth of the overall risk that they generate. According to our model, natural resources are a major source of risk, although we cannot disaggregate among the various channels. A reduction in the risk from natural resources of one-tenth would reduce the overall risk for the typical low-income country from 13.8 per cent to 12.7 per cent. From this, we calculate the gains as above. That is, we take the proportionate reduction in risk, and multiply it by the annual cost of conflict generated by poor countries falling into conflict. The annual gain is around $3.9 bn. Since this is a permanent gain, the NPV would be around $77 bn.

Thus, the overall security gain from an effective implementation of the EITI would be the $12.1 bn from permanently faster growth, and $73 bn from a reduction in the direct risks of conflict. That is a total gain of $89.1 bn. These are, of course, highly speculative numbers. However, they are not necessarily overestimates. They assume that effective international action would halve the damage currently being done by natural resources to growth, and reduce by one-tenth their direct contribution to conflict risk. While the benefits of these improvements are considerable, the improvements themselves are not wildly ambitious.

Opportunities for Shortening Conflicts

Civil wars last far longer than international wars. The typical civil war lasts around seven years whereas the typical international war lasts around six months. The difference was dramatically illustrated in the case of the Eritrea–Ethiopia conflict. When this was a civil war it lasted for around thirty years and was ended only by a military victory on the part of the rebels. When it resumed after Eritrean independence, and hence as an international war, it lasted less than a month. Evidently, if civil wars could be shortened more to resemble the duration of international wars, their global incidence would be dramatically reduced. Worse, the duration of civil wars appears to be increasing. The average duration of wars in the period 1980–99 was around double that in the period 1960–79. Average duration in the 1990s was fortunately a little shorter than in the 1980s, but this probably reflected the one-off effect of the end of the Cold War, with a number of conflicts that had been funded by one or other of the superpowers coming to an end.

The long duration of civil wars reflects the much greater ability of the international community to put pressure on states to end international wars, to act even-handedly between the parties and to guarantee the terms of a settlement. With a civil war, the terms of a settlement often lack credibility: rebel forces are unable to guarantee that rival rebel groups will not emerge to continue the war, and governments have no way of binding themselves to their offers.

Collier, Hoeffler and Söderbom (2004) analyse the duration of civil wars econometrically. Using

[24] We estimate the effect of the increase in the growth rate on the risk of conflict for low-income countries at peace, period by period. Thus, in the first period there is only a growth rate effect, whereas in subsequent periods there is both a growth rate effect and an income-level effect. From this we calculate the proportionate reduction in risk, per period. This reduction is then multiplied by the cost of civil war generated annually by poor countries at peace falling into conflict. That is, 0.7 countries per year, multiplied by the cost of a civil war ($64.2 bn). The NPV of this stream of future gains is then calculated, discounting at 5 per cent.

a dataset on international interventions collected by Regan (2002) we test to see whether there has been any systematic effect of either economic or military interventions – whether on the side of the government or on the side of the rebels. We find that none of these types of intervention has had a significant effect on the duration of conflict. This has to be qualified. It was not possible to 'instrument' for international interventions. Hence, it may be that the interventions occurred in the most difficult environments where wars would otherwise have lasted longer than average. Further, even taken at face value, the result does not show that all interventions were ineffective, simply that no type of intervention was *systematically* effective. However, with these qualifications, the result is discouraging. It suggests that although the shortening of civil wars superficially looks to be an important opportunity for reducing the incidence of civil war, in practice the international community lacks effective instruments.

The fact that civil wars have been getting longer may give us some guidance as to how to shorten them. One of the important developments in civil war has been the emergence of commercial markets for both natural resources that can be extorted by rebel organisations, and for military equipment. Whereas in the 1960s a viable rebel movement generally needed some supportive government for funding and armaments, by the 1990s rebel movements could be entirely viable as private enterprises. This suggests that the greater control of these two international markets, with a view to curtailing access by rebel movements, might be effective instruments in shortening conflicts. Here we consider only the markets in natural resources, while noting that control of the trade in armaments is also worth serious effort.

The Instrument of Curtailing Rebel Access to Commodity Markets

Concern over rebel access to international commodity markets initially arose among NGOs – most notably by Global Witness – and was then taken up by the United Nations. The first market which attracted attention was that for diamonds. There was overwhelming evidence that two large rebel organisations – the RUF in Sierra Leone and UNITA in Angola – were generating much of their income from the sale of diamonds extorted from the territories under their control. A campaign of public awareness that introduced the concept of 'conflict diamonds' led to dramatic changes in industry practice. First De Beers withdrew from making purchases of diamonds on the open market, and then the industry in collaboration with NGOs and diamond-producing governments established the Kimberley process whereby diamonds were certified by governments as to having a legitimate source. The Kimberley process is new, and as such it is too early to determine its effectiveness. However, the change in the practice of De Beers preceded Kimberley, and given the dominance of that company in the market, this itself must have substantially impaired rebel access. Subsequent to the change in De Beers' policy, and to the radically greater scrutiny placed on diamond transactions, both of the diamond-financed rebel movements – RUF and UNITA – collapsed. The squeeze on their finances was most certainly not the only reason for this reversal in their fortunes. However, by the account of their own senior leadership, international actions had made their operations substantially more difficult. It is also worth noting that by the standards of rebel movements both the RUF and UNITA had been very large and successful.

The idea of certification of source has now been taken up in respect of timber, where there is also compelling evidence that rebel movements in both Asia and Africa have been using timber felling as a revenue-generating activity. There may also be a need for it in oil. For example, criminal – rebel groups in the Delta region of Nigeria are looting around $3 mn per day of oil by tapping into pipelines and selling the product on the international market. With such revenues they are well equipped militarily. Similar concerns are likely with the network of pipelines planned in Central Asia.

The basic idea behind certification is to create a two-tier market in which illegitimate supplies can be sold only at a deep discount. The analogy is with counterfeit goods where essentially the same physical product – such as watches or videos – is sold at radically different prices depending upon its provenance. The price discount indeed provides a good measure of the effectiveness of the certification process.

Other than the example of diamonds and the ending of the civil wars in Sierra Leone and Angola, is there any evidence that creating a price discount for rebel-supplied natural resources would shorten conflicts? Collier, Hoeffler and Söderbom (2004) investigate whether the prevailing world price of a country's export commodities has any bearing on the chance that a conflict will end. They utilise a price series for commodity exports constructed by Dehn (2000). They find that for those countries with large natural resource exports, the world price of their exports has a significant effect upon the chance of peace – and hence upon the expected duration of conflict. Specifically, as the world price falls the chances of peace significantly rise. For countries with large primary commodity earnings (30 per cent of GDP) a 10 per cent decline in the world price is associated with a shortening of the duration of conflict by 12 per cent. This is open to multiple interpretations. One interpretation is that the result is picking up effects analogous to those of a price discount for rebel-controlled resources. If so, this would be encouraging evidence supporting efforts such as the Kimberley process. A different interpretation would be that lower commodity prices squeeze the finances of both the rebels and the government, and so encourage them to find a settlement. On that interpretation, generating a price discount for rebel-controlled commodities would not necessarily be effective, since it would not encourage the government to reach a settlement.

Perhaps the most that can reasonably be said is that the case study evidence and the econometric evidence do not contradict each other, and both give some reason to hope that creating a price discount will tend to shorten some civil wars. Given that other initiatives for shortening wars appear not to have been systematically effective, and that the duration of wars is already long and appears to be lengthening, this new initiative may be worthwhile.

All certification procedures can be evaded at a cost. The purpose of certification is not literally to shut rebel supplies out of the market, but rather to create a deep discount in the price that rebels receive. The cost of certification procedures is negligible. The basic principle is the 'presumption of guilt' – that is, supplies are presumed to be illegitimate, and national-level certification procedures themselves are presumed to be ineffective, unless it can be demonstrated to internationally agreed and monitored standards that they are not. Policing the supply chain is already standard practice in products where there is a risk of counterfeiting, and the problems of 'conflict commodities' are not intrinsically different.

We have already discussed the case for such measures in diamonds, timber and oil. There is one further commodity strongly linked to conflict and that is illegal drugs. For example, all the main rebel groups in Colombia generate their major revenues from extortion rackets on the cultivation of hard drugs. Approximately 95 per cent of the world's supplies of hard drugs come from civil war environments. As discussed later, a key reason for this is that the cultivation of an illegal commodity essentially needs the connivance of the controlling authority. Thus, only territory outside the control of recognised governments is suitable for sustained cultivation.

While superficially curtailing rebel revenues from hard drugs may appear to be a very different problem from curtailing rebel revenues from diamonds, there are in fact important similarities. The certification approach seeks to create a two-tier market between a legitimate source and an illegitimate source. In the case of diamonds, until recently no source was treated as illegitimate; in the case of hard drugs, at present no source is treated as legitimate. As a result, illegitimate producers of hard drugs do not have to compete with legitimate supplies. It may seem fanciful to imagine a two-tier market in hard drugs, but this was, in fact, the policy in the UK during the 1960s. Once an individual because addicted to heroin they could become registered as an addict through the health services, and thereafter supplied with drugs paid for by the government. In turn, the government obviously purchased its supplies on the legitimate market. This approach – which yielded very low rates of addiction – had various advantages: for example, drug addicts did not resort to crime in order to finance their addiction. However, for our present focus, its big advantage was that during this period hard drug addiction in the UK provided no significant opportunity for rebel groups to acquire finance. The situation in the USA and Europe today is in dramatic contrast to the UK in the 1960s. Western drug addiction creates a massive demand for territory outside the control of recognised governments, and hence finances civil war.

Hence, the proposed instrument of international certification of the supply chain is meant to come into effect wherever rebel groups are getting significant finance from extortion rackets on commodity exports. The intention is always to create a two-tier market, with a legitimate source of supply competing with an illegitimate source of supply. The direct effectiveness of the instrument can be monitored by measuring the extent of this price discount. Obviously, the price of the illicit product is not quite as observable as that of the licit product. However, informed industry participants are aware of the illicit price. For example, in the case of diamonds, it is reported within the industry that as of 2002 the discount on the price of illicit diamonds was around 10 per cent. Since diamonds are a very difficult product to monitor, and since at the time of this discount the Kimberley process lacked any monitoring procedure and so was not yet operating on a 'presumption of guilt' basis, this scale of discount probably represents the minimum that could reasonably be expected from a certification process. As with the EITI, the costs are primarily in terms of the opportunity cost of international collective action in some other sphere.

We now attempt to quantify the benefits. Suppose, for illustrative purposes, that certification processes in the relevant commodities achieved a 10 per cent price discount for illicit commodities similar to that already achieved for diamonds. What might this achieve by way of benefits of reduced conflict?

The closest we have to a reasonable quantitative estimate, at present, is the contribution of a lower world price of exported commodities on the duration of conflict. Recall that a 10 per cent reduction in this price shortened conflict by around 12 per cent. A price discount might have larger or smaller effects

than an overall lowering in the world price. It is different in that it tilts the balance more clearly against rebel forces, but this might enhance or weaken pressures for an end to a conflict, depending on each situation. Assuming, however, that conflicts were on average shortened by 12 per cent, what would this imply for the incidence of conflict? Recall that an across-the-board shortening of conflict by one year would have an NPV of around $30.5 bn. For a country with primary commodity earnings at 30 per cent of GDP a 10 per cent reduction in export prices achieves a shortening of not far off this, namely 0.84 years. However, only a minority of countries at civil war are as dependent upon primary commodities as this. Specifically, when we allow for the proportion of civil war countries that are significantly affected, according to the analysis of Collier, Hoeffler and Söderbom (2004), the NPV of a successful price discrimination strategy would be around $5.9 bn.

Reducing the Risks Post-Conflict

During the first decade post-conflict there are very high risks of repeat conflict. According to the CH model, approximately half of these risks are inherited from the characteristics that already made a county prone to conflict and have not improved during it. The other half of the risk arises from changes brought about by the conflict. On the nature of these changes the econometric evidence is more or less non-existent. The case study evidence points to the build-up of armaments and military skills, the desensitisation of part of the population to violence, the creation of a rebel organisations with a financial interest and capabilities and the legacy of hatred and distrust.

Because of the high risk of conflict repeat, around half of all civil wars are due to a breakdown of peace during the first post-conflict decade. Yet at any one time relatively few post-conflict countries (in the sense of countries at peace but still in their first post-conflict decade). Typically, there are around twelve countries in this category at any one time, and so it is possible to focus resources with relatively little waste.[25] Compared with conflict prevention in countries with a long record of peace,

[25] The 'typical' number of conflicts, and other figures on the flow into and out of conflict are taken from chapter 4 of Collier and Hoeffler (2003a) which estimates a steady-state global model of the incidence of civil war.

interventions are much more precisely targeted. Obviously, compared to strategies for shortening conflicts by direct intervention at the country level, resources are less well-targeted since even without intervention some post-conflict countries will succeed in establishing a durable peace. However, as we have seen, there appears to be relatively little scope for shortening conflicts. By contrast, there is considerable scope for the international community to do a better job at *reducing post-conflict risks.*

Here we will focus on two instruments already widely used: aid and military spending. We will suggest that aid is particularly effective in post-conflict circumstances, but that to date both its scale and its timing has been flawed. Because of the high risk of repeat conflict, post-conflict governments naturally tend to spend a lot on the military. While this is natural, we will show that it is counterproductive. We accept that there is an important role for a stabilizing military force in post-conflict situations – even with ideal economic assistance and government policies the risk of repeat conflict is irreducibly high. We will argue that foreign military intervention is likely to be far more effective than domestic military forces. We will suggest that a condition for such intervention should be the swift reduction in domestic military spending.

The Instrument of Post-Conflict Aid

As discussed on pp. 136ff., aid reduces the risk of conflict by raising the growth rate. A higher growth rate directly reduces the risk of conflict and cumulatively, by raising the level of income, further reduces the risk. These effects also appear to apply in post-conflict situations. Using the CH model, Bigombe, Collier and Sambanis (2002) find that growth is slightly but significantly more effective in reducing the risk of conflict during the first post-conflict decade than it is in less-focused situations of conflict prevention. The issue to which we now turn is the effect of aid on the post-conflict growth rate. For this we rely upon the results of Collier and Hoeffler (2004a), summarised as appropriate in appendix 3.

During the first post-conflict decade growth is typically faster than normal. That is, there is some economic recovery. This is not surprising given the loss of growth during conflict. Recall that by the end of a typical seven-year civil war GDP is around 15 per cent lower than it would have been. By the end of the first decade this is more or less fully recovered.

However, the growth recovery is neither evenly spread through the decade, nor inevitable. In terms of timing, supranormal growth is concentrated in the middle years of the decade – approximately the fourth through the seventh post-conflict years. In analysing this growth we apply the model of Collier and Dollar (2002), which partitions growth into an exogenous component, a component determined by the quality of policies, institutions and governance and a component determined by the amount of aid received (partly a direct effect, and partly interacted with the quality of policies, institutions and governance). We find that growth during the post-conflict decade is distinctive within this framework. Specifically, supranormal growth is entirely determined by the volume of aid (and its interaction with policy). That is, aid is atypically effective in raising growth rates during the middle years of post-conflict recovery. To understand why this should be we have to rely upon case study experience. Evidently, in post-conflict conditions there are atypically high needs for aid. This was, indeed, the original rationale for establishing the World Bank – it was originally named the International Bank for *Reconstruction and Development* (IBRD). However, there is reasonable evidence that in the first few years after a civil war the quality of institutions is so low that, while needs are great, the capacity to use resources effectively is very limited, so that the returns to aid are no higher than normal. By the middle of the decade the ability to manage resources has usually increased, while needs remain great. Hence, purely from the perspective of maximising the impact on growth, donors should allocate atypically large amounts of aid to the middle years of the first decade of post-conflict societies. Clearly, growth has two types of pay-off. For aid donors the normal interest is that growth tends to reduce poverty, which for many donors is their prime objective. However, for our present purposes we are interested in the peace-building effects of growth. Hence, over and above its enhanced poverty-reducing effects, aid targeted in this way significantly reduces the risk of civil war in the category of countries most prone to lapse into conflict.

Are donors already taking this opportunity? At the end of the Second World War the USA mounted a major aid programme that was, in effect, targeted to the recovery of societies in the middle of their first post-conflict decade. But, more recently, donor allocation of aid has not followed this pattern. Over the entire course of the first post-conflict decade aid is no higher than were the society not post-conflict, while during the first couple of years of peace there is a flood of aid. Hence, aid typically tapers out just as it should be tapering in.

What would be the pay-off to increasing aid to post-conflict societies in the middle of the post-conflict decade? We take the average characteristics of post-conflict societies during the 1990s, and consider what would have been the costs and returns to increasing aid for five years in the middle of the first post-conflict decade by 2 percentage points of GDP (at PPP prices).

Typically there are around twelve such countries at any one time and, as previously, we evaluate the policy sustained for a decade. Given that the typical post-conflict country would receive additional aid

for only half of the decade, at any one time only six countries would be receiving it. The combined GDP of all twelve post-conflict countries is around $163 bn, so that the cost of the additional aid to the six would be around $1.6 bn a year. The NPV of this aid, discounted over the decade, would be $13 bn.

Following the same procedure as previously, we estimate that the gain in the growth rate during these years would be 1.1 percentage points – that is, around five times the effect of incremental aid in normal low-income situations.[26]

We now estimate the effect of faster growth on risk in post-conflict situations. For comparability with our previous estimates we first consider the effect of a sustained 1 percentage point addition to the growth rate. We evaluate the risk for the typical low-income country. Although the absolute level of risk is much higher for post-conflict countries, the proportionate effect of faster growth is very similar to that for other low-income countries. The only important difference in the calculation of the benefits is that the base for conflict prevention in low-income countries at peace is only 0.7 new conflicts a year, whereas the base for post-conflict countries is one new conflict a year. Hence, the benefits of an extra percentage point of growth in post-conflict countries are greater at around $5 bn per year during the decade.[27] In the third and subsequent periods countries that have not reverted to conflict cease to be 'post-conflict', and so become part of the group of low-income countries at peace. The gains here are therefore those of that category of country, proportionate to the number of countries being funded. That is, whereas our previous calculation of the benefits of aiding low-income countries at peace involved aiding thirty-two countries, it now involves aiding only twelve.[28] Hence, from the eleventh year on, the gains are equal to 12/32 of the gains from the conflict prevention aid programme.[29] The NPV of these gains is $56.9 bn.[30]

The gain from post-conflict aid targeted to the middle of the decade would be less than the gain from the 1 per cent additional growth sustained throughout the decade since the extra growth of 1.1 per cent would for be sustained only five years. The benefits are around $31.5 bn. The bounds of

---

[26] We use the growth regression reported in table 3A3.1, column (2), and the means for post-conflict countries.

[27] Specifically, the risks of conflict decline as a result of faster growth from 38.6 per cent to 36.3 per cent in the first five-year period, and from 31.9 per cent to 28.8 per cent in the second five-year period (when both growth and accumulated income effects are working). We approximate by taking the average proportionate reduction in risk during the decade, namely, 7.8 per cent. Since the category of post-conflict countries generates around one civil war per year, costing $64.2 bn, the gain from such a proportionate reduction in risk would be 0.078*$64.2 bn = $5.0 bn.

[28] Because the extra post-conflict aid is concentrated during only half the post-conflict decade, only six such countries would be receiving aid at any one time. However, since the effect of aid on growth is double its normal effects, the twelve five-year aid programmes achieve the same as twelve ten-year aid programmes in normal situations.

[29] Recall that the annual gains for the conflict prevention category of country were $3.0 bn, so that the gains from the smaller group of post-conflict countries would be (12/32)*$3.0 bn = $1.1 bn.

[30] That is, $5 bn for a decade, and $1.4 bn subsequently.

the 90 per cent confidence interval around this figure are \$20 bn and \$40 bn.[31]

At our central estimate of the benefits, the returns on post-conflict aid are more than double their costs. Further, even at the lower bound of our estimate of the security benefits, they still comfortably exceed the costs, generating a gain or around \$7 bn. We should stress that there are global security benefits that we have entirely omitted from quantification, and that we have omitted all the usual benefits of aid, namely poverty reduction. The security considerations are now large enough to be dominant in the case for aid, whereas in the case of more generalised conflict prevention they appeared to be only a marginal consideration.

The Instrument of Military Expenditure

In early post-conflict situations the risk of reversion to conflict is typically very high although it gradually declines if peace is maintained. Economic remedies eventually work to lower risk, but inevitably they take time. However rapid is growth, it cannot reduce risks to acceptable levels during the first few post-conflict years. Nor, it seems, can political design. There is some evidence that in cases where democracy has been introduced into post-conflict situations, the second election is actually a time of enhanced risk. This is not to say that democracy is inappropriate in post-conflict settings, but rather that in the short term it should not be expected in itself to solve the problems of violent conflict. Most governments in post-conflict settings appear to conclude that high military expenditure is needed to maintain the peace. During civil wars the typical level of military spending is around double peacetime levels, and during the first post-conflict decade it declines only modestly. Post-conflict military spending is much closer to wartime spending than to peacetime spending. Given the high risks of repeat conflict, it indeed seems likely that there is a need for some military force to keep the peace. However, such expenditures should be judged by their effectiveness.

Collier and Hoeffler (2003a) analyse whether military spending in post-conflict situations is effective in reducing risks. Naturally, there is a potential

endogeneity problem here since spending is likely to be highest where risks are highest. They therefore 'instrument' for military spending using the military spending of neighbours and the past history of international warfare, both of which are good predictors of spending. So instrumented, in normal conditions (i.e. other than in post-conflict settings) military spending has no significant effect on the risk of rebellion – it appears to be an ineffective deterrent. However, in post-conflict settings it is significantly counterproductive, increasing the risk of repeat rebellion. This result is broadly consistent with the case study literature which emphasises the low credibility of peace settlements. Rebels try to read signals of government behaviour to form a judgement as to whether the government intends to maintain its agreement or renege upon it. High military spending might well be read by rebels as a signal of an intention to renege.

The combination of a high risk of repeat conflict in post-conflict settings, and an understandably high, but counterproductive, level of government military spending, creates an opportunity for international military intervention designed to keep the peace. A condition of such an external military presence could be that the government itself makes deep cuts in its military budget, thereby reaping a peace dividend. Knight, Loayza and Villanueva (1996) estimate the costs to growth of military spending, conditional upon the maintenance of peace. Based on their figures, the reduction of post-conflict military spending to peacetime levels, maintained for a decade, would raise GDP by the end of the period by 2 per cent.

We will take as a concrete example the current British military presence in Sierra Leone. The intervention started in 2000 and is continuing. It is sanctioned under Article VII of the United Nations Charter and was a response to a request by the government of the country. It replaced a large but spectacularly ineffective UN military presence under Chapter VI rules of engagement, during which a large UN military force was held hostage by rebel

---

[31] The confidence intervals are generated from the coefficient on the post-conflict interaction term in table 3A3.1, column (2).

forces. During the period of British military engagement peace has been secured throughout the country and elections held. The future risks once external forces withdraw can only be estimated. We will assume that the risk reverts to the normal level of a post-conflict country that has maintained peace for however many years the British presence has been maintained, subject to one qualification. We will assume that during the external military presence, domestic military spending is reduced to normal peacetime levels. In turn, this lower level of military spending relative to most post-conflict situations delivers additional growth, which we estimate following the results of Knight, Loayza and Villanueva (1996). The actual conflict risk post-withdrawal could be higher or lower than this, but there is no evidence on which to choose between these possibilities.

The pay-off to the temporary external military presence can thus be estimated as the elimination of risk during the period of external military presence, which we will take to be ten years, plus the reduction in risk thereafter as a result of faster economic growth during the decade. In the first five-year period of post-conflict, the risk of reversion to war is typically around 38.6 per cent, and in the second five-year period it is typically around 31.9 per cent. Recalling that the cost of a civil war is around $64.2 bn, the NPV of the gains from eliminating these risks during the military presence is around $29.9 bn.[32] Onto this should be added the

gain after military withdrawal from the reduced risk consequent upon the 2 per cent higher level of income due to the reduced level of domestic military spending during the post-conflict decade. The NPV of this is $3.2 bn.[33] Hence, the overall gain is $33.1 bn.

The costs of an external military presence evidently depend upon its scale. An advantage of taking the concrete situation of Sierra Leone is that here the external military presence can be precisely costed, and it was of a scale that proved to be effective not only in maintaining peace, but in establishing it in the first place. Further, Sierra Leone is a pretty typical civil war situation – a low-income country, with a large rebel movement well-resourced by natural resource income. The costs per year of the British military presence in Sierra Leone for the four years of the present occupation were around $49 m; were the presence to be maintained for a decade at this rate of expenditure, the NPV of the cost would therefore be $397 m. The pay-off to such external military intervention is clearly massive relative to its cost. An outlay of less than half a billion dollars secures benefits in excess of $30 bn. Further, the benefits have been estimated on very pessimistic assumptions about risks after the withdrawal of external forces.

Typically, there are around twelve post-conflict situations and hence twelve opportunities for this sort of pay-off. Historically, these opportunities have not been taken – Sierra Leone marked the launch of a new, and at the time highly experimental strategy. Were the strategy applied in all twelve post-conflict situations the approximate costs and benefits would be $4.8 bn costs and $397 bn benefits, yielding a net gain of $392 bn. Again, this benefit omits all the global-level gains from reduced conflict.

---

[32] Thus, in the first five-year period there is a 38.6 per cent risk of a $64.2 bn loss, which we assume accrues in year 3. In the second five-year period, conditional upon there being no war in the first period, there is a 31.9 per cent risk, again of a $64.2 bn loss, which we again assume accrues in the middle of the period. The NPV of these losses is thus $(0.386*\$64.2 \text{ bn})/(1.05^3) + ((1 - 0.386)*0.319*\$64.2 \text{ bn})/(1.05^8) = \$29.9 \text{ bn}$.

[33] The 2 per cent higher level of income reduces the risk of the typical poor country at peace from 13.8 per cent to 13.6 per cent, a proportionate reduction of 1.6 per cent. Recalling that there are 0.7 civil wars per year generated from the 'poor-at-peace' category of countries, and that there are only twelve countries in the post-conflict category, rather than the thirty-two in the 'poor-at-peace' category, the annual gain is therefore $0.016*(12/32)*0.7*\$64.2$ bn. This sets in from the eleventh year after conflict. The NPV of this income stream is $3.2 bn.

Conclusion and Comparison of Instruments

All the estimates in this study are gross approximations. At best they provide guidance as to orders of magnitude. Nevertheless, this can be useful. Our estimates suggest that some instruments are radically uneconomic, whereas others offer remarkably large returns. This ranking of instruments is probably more robust than the assessments of individual instruments.

We started by estimating the costs of civil war. We have taken lower-bound estimates, and these figures are, we believe, reasonably well-founded when interpreted as a lower bound. That is to say, civil war may be much more damaging than implied by our estimate, but it is unlikely to be less costly. Even these lower-bound estimates suggest that the economic and social costs of civil war are enormous. As such the issue clearly deserves international attention. The question is not whether the problem is important, but rather whether there are instruments that can be used effectively to tackle the problem through international action. We have explored five of them.

The most disappointing instrument is, in a sense, the most obvious and the most readily available. This is aid for conflict prevention. We should at once make it clear that our estimates have been quite ungenerous to such a strategy. We have simply increased aid to all low-income countries (excluding India and China). No attempt has been made to target aid to countries at particularly high risk, and aid agencies may be able to do much better than our unselective simulation experiment. Nevertheless, if our numbers are within the right ballpark, selectivity would need to be pretty good before aid could be justified simply in terms of conflict prevention. Of course, additional aid can be justified on other grounds, notably poverty reduction. But our analysis suggests that the addition of security considerations is marginal rather than central to the benefits of aid in normal, peacetime situations. Even if our estimates are grossly and systematically wrong – notably by massively underestimating the cost of conflict – this would not significantly affect our ranking of interventions.

Aid does become an effective instrument in post-conflict situations. This is mainly because it is more effective in the growth process, but also because it is more precisely targeted on high-risk countries. The pure security gain is now sufficient by itself to warrant additional aid even at the lower bound of the 90 per cent confidence interval. Further, we have completely omitted the gains at the global level from reducing the incidence of civil war, some of the gains at the regional level, notably health effects, and all the poverty reduction benefits of aid. These considerations make higher aid for post-conflict situations look to be a good use of international public resources, as long as it is properly timed.

Our third instrument was to extend the initiative which began with diamonds and is now known as the Kimberley process. The objective is to partition the market in pertinent commodities that might provide revenue for rebel forces into a legitimate market and an illegal market on which produce can be sold only at a discount. We found that a 10 per cent discount for illegal produce, which seems a feasible international objective, might yield global benefits of around $6 bn. The costs of this initiative were almost entirely the opportunity cost of international collective action. There is a capacity for only a few international initiatives at any one time, and so only those initiatives should be undertaken which offer high pay-offs. An advantage of the proposed instrument is that, being virtually costless, the sign of the pay-off is robust. International action here is highly unlikely to be counterproductive, and there is a reasonable basis for expending a large, though not massive, return.

Our fourth instrument was to extend the current EITI. By improving the governance of natural resource rents, albeit not eliminating the problems associated with them, there are reasonable grounds to expect two security benefits: a direct one that reduces the risk of conflict initiation, and an indirect one through faster growth. We estimated the combined pay-off to this instrument as being very substantial at around $89 bn. Again, the cost of this instrument is the opportunity cost of international collective action, the direct costs being trivial. An advantage of this instrument is that because its benefits come through two distinct routes the prospect of some substantial returns are reasonably robust. The actual numbers we have suggested are speculative, but not biased. They are based on the idea that effective international action could reduce by half, but not eliminate, the adverse effects on growth that currently come from natural resource rents, and that it can reduce by one-tenth the adverse effects that directly increase the risk of conflict. By analogy with other international economic guidelines, such as in the sphere of banking, this does not seem to be an unreasonable goal.

Our fifth, and most effective, instrument is also the most problematic politically. This is external military intervention under Chapter VII of the United Nations Charter to enforce peace in an immediate post-conflict situation and to maintain it throughout the prolonged period – a decade – during which the risks of reversion to conflict are very high. The pay-off to this instrument we estimated using the example of Sierra Leone. This choice was not, however, a matter of picking a rare success, but rather a matter of investigating a new strategy. This was the first substantial Chapter VII intervention by a major power (as distinct from using UN forces under Chapter VI) for many years. It has recently been followed by similar French intervention in Côte d'Ivoire, and most recently (February 2004) by the creation of a Franco-British 'rapid reaction force' of 1,500 men. The pay-off to such a strategy adopted universally in post-conflict situations is massive, at around $392 bn, even on the rather pessimistic assumption that after withdrawal risks revert to what they would have been without the military presence. The pay-off is all the more remarkable given the relatively unpromising returns to some of the other interventions.

Appendix 1 The CH Model of Conflict Risk

Table 3A1.1. Determinants of the Outbreak of Civil War

Determinant	(1)
Primary commodity exports/GDP	16.773 (5.206)***
(Primary commodity exports/GDP)^2	−23.800 (10.040)**
ln GDP *per capita*	−0.950 (0.245)***
(GDP growth)$t-1$	−0.098 (0.042)**
Peace duration (months)	−0.004 (0.001)***
Geographic concentration (index 0–1)	−0.992 (0.909)
ln population	0.510 (0.128)***
Social fractionalisation (index 0–10,000)	−0.0002 (0.0001)***
Ethnic dominance (45–90%) (Dummy variable)	0.480 (0.328) p = 0.14
N	750
No. of wars	52
Pseudo R^2	0.22
Log likelihood	−146.84

Notes: Logit regressions, dependent variable is 'war start'. The regression includes time dummies. Standard errors in parentheses. ***, ** and * indicate significance at the 1, 5 and 10 per cent level, respectively.
Source: Collier and Hoeffler (2004).

Appendix 2 Relationship between the International Prices of Natural Resources and the Duration of Conflict

Table 3A2.1. Duration Analysis of Civil War: Econometric Estimates of Hazard Function Parameters

Hazard function	(1)
Income inequality	−0.1258 (0.0283)***
Missing inequality	−5.8717 (1.2689)***
Per capita income	0.4043 (0.1370)***
Ethnic fractionalisation	−0.0695 (0.0261)***
Ethnic fractionalisation^2	0.0007 (0.0003)**
ln population	−0.2860 (0.1225)**
1970s	0.1298 (0.4677)
1980s	−1.3830 (0.5256)***
1990s	−1.1810 (0.5405)**
3rd and 4th years of war (λ_2)	−0.8747 (0.5790)
5th and 6th years of war (λ_3)	0.0044 (0.5601)
7th year of war and beyond (λ_4)	0.7100 (0.4440)
Change in commodity price index (*CPI*)	1.7669 (1.0629)*
Primary commodity exports/GDP (*SXP*)	10.6114 (5.9267)*
*CPI*SXP*	−11.3237 (5.8518)**
Democracy	
Constant	5.2044 (3.0352)*
Log likelihood	−78.18
No. of observations	55

Notes: *z*-statistics are based on asymptotic standard errors.
Significance at the 10%, 5% and 1% level is indicated by *, ** and ***, respectively.
Source: Collier, Hoeffler and Söderbom (2004).

Appendix 3 Aid and Growth, Post-Conflict

Table 3A3.1. Aid, Policy and Economic Growth

Item	(1)	(2)
ln (*per capita* income)	0.629 (0.638)	0.712 (0.617)
Governance (ICRGE, index 1–6)	0.164 (0.160)	0.172 (0.155)
Policy (CPIA, index 1–5)	0.871 (0.418)**	1.021 (0.392)***
ODA * Policy	−0.329 (0.377)	0.127 (0.064)*
$(ODA/GDP)^2$	−0.023 (0.016)	−0.028 (0.012)**
South Asia (dummy variable)	0.228 (0.113)**	2.662 (0.620)***
East Asia (dummy variable)	2.563 (0.636)***	2.880 (0.660)***
SSA (dummy variable)	2.938 (0.668)***	−0.366 (0.809)
Middle East/North Africa Europe (dummy variable)	−0.535 (0.815)	1.606 (0.563)***
Central Asia (dummy variable)	1.537 (0.558)***	−0.365 (1.053)
Post-conflict dummy* (ODA/GDP) *Policy		0.186 (0.046)***
Observations	344	344
p.-conflict obs.	34	13
R^2	0.37	0.38

Notes: OLS regressions with robust standard errors, dependent variable is 'average annual *per capita* GDP growth'. All regression include a constant. Standard errors in parentheses. ***, ** and * indicate significance at the 1, 5 and 10 per cent level, respectively.
Source: Collier and Hoeffler (2004a).

Appendix 4 Estimating the Risk of a Civil War Outbreak

The figures and probability of civil war estimates presented in this chapter are based mainly on the logistic regression analysis reported in table 3A4.1. The dataset used is global, spans the years 1960–99, and covers 161 countries. We divide the data series into eight sub-periods, 1960–4, 1965–9, ..., 1995–9.

In our regressions we estimate the probability of a war breaking out during a five-year period, and the model can be written in the following general form:

$$(A4.1) \quad Y_{it} = a + bX_{it} + cM_{i,t-1} + dZ_i + u_{it}$$

where t and i are time and country indicators. The dependent variable is a dummy variable indicating whether a war broke out during the five-year period, so that Y_{it} is the log odds of war. The explanatory variables are either measured at the beginning of the period (for example, income *per capita*,

primary commodity exports/gross domestic product (GDP), population), or during the previous five-year period (for instance, *per capita* income growth, or are time invariant or changing slowly over time (for example, social fractionalisation).

The expected probability $\hat{p}_{it}$ of a war breaking out can be calculated by using the estimated coefficients obtained from (A4.1):

$$(A4.2) \quad \hat{a} + \hat{b}X_{it} + \hat{c}M_{i,t-1} + \hat{d}Z_i = \hat{W}_{it}$$

$$(A4.3) \quad \hat{p}_{it} = \frac{e^{\hat{W}_{it}}}{(1 + e^{\hat{W}_{it}})} \cdot 100$$

We calculate probabilities for hypothetical observations. For example, we find the average values for $\bar{X}_{it}, \bar{M}_{i,t-1}, \bar{Z}_i$ for a sub-group of countries and take this to be a typical country within the subgroup. We then calculate $\hat{p}_{it}$ by applying (A4.3). For the policy

Table 3A4.1. Estimating the Risk of a Civil War Outbreak

	(1) Coefficients from table A1	(2) Means for low income countries	(3) (1)*(2)
Primary commodity exports/GDP	16.773	0.164	2.751
(Primary commodity exports/GDP)^2	−23.800		−0.640
ln GDP *per capita*	−0.950	975	−6.541
(GDP growth)$t-1$	−0.098	0.248	−0.024
Peace duration (months)	−0.004	340	−1.292
Geographic concentration (index 0–1)	−0.992	0.57	−0.565
ln population	0.510	11,100,000	8.282
Social fractionalisation (index 0–10,000)	−0.0002	2964	−0.593
Ethnic dominance (45–90%) (dummy variable)	0.480	0.48	0.230
Sum of coefficient*mean $\hat{W}_{it}$			−1.830
Estimated probability $\hat{p}_{it}$			13.819

Note: For *per capita* income and population we take the natural logarithm of the average *per capita* income and total population and multiply these numbers with the corresponding coefficients.

Table 3A4.2. Confidence Intervals

	Lower confidence limit	Estimates	Upper confidence limit
Loss of GDP due to reduced growth (%)	41	105	305
Loss of GDP due to increased milex (%)	12	18	25
Loss of GDP due to the arms race multiplier (%)	8	12	16
Loss of GDP due to legacy effect (%)	8	19	27

simulations we used the probability for the average low-income developing country as a baseline.

References

Bannon, I. and P. Collier, P. (eds.), 2003: *Natural resources and violent conflict: options and actions*, World Bank, Washington DC

Becker, G. S., T. J. Philipson and R. R. Soares, 2003: The quantity and quality of life and the evolution of world inequality, paper presented at the WIDER conference September

Benyon, J. 2003: Poverty efficient aid allocations – Coller/Dollar revisited, ESAU Working Paper, 2, Overseas Development Institute and the Department for International Development, London

Bigombe, B., P. Collier and N. Sambanis, 2002: Policies for building post-conflict peace, *Journal of African Economies*, **9**(3), 322–47

Brito, D. L. and M. D. Intriligator, 1995: Arms races and proliferation, in K. Hartley and T. Sandler (eds.), *Handbook of Defense Economics*, 1, Elsevier, Oxford, 109–62

Brown, M. E. and R. Rosecrance (eds.), 1999: *The costs of conflict*, Rowman & Littlefield, Boulder, CO

Chauvet, L., 2003: Economie de l'aide dans un contexte d'instabilite socio-politique, Doctorat these, CERDI, Universite d'Auvergne Clermont-Ferrand 1

Collier, P., 1999: On the economic consequences of civil war, *Oxford Economic Papers*, **51**, 168–83

Collier, P. and J. Dehn,: Aid, shocks and growth, Policy Research Working Paper, 2688, World Bank, Washington DC

Collier, P. and D. Dollar, 2002: Aid allocation and poverty reduction, *European Economic Review*, **46**, 1475–1500

Collier, P., L. Elliot, H. Hegre, A. Hoeffler, M. Reynal-Querol and N. Sambanis, 2003: *Breaking the Conflict Trap: Civil War and Development Policy*, Oxford University Press, Oxford

Collier, P. and A. Hoeffler, 2002a: Military expenditure: threats, aid and arms races, Policy Research Working Paper, 2927, World Bank, Washington DC

  2002b: Aid, policy and peace: reducing the risks of civil conflict, *Defence and Peace Economics*, **13**, 435–50

  2003a: Military spending in post-conflict societies, Centre for the Study of African Economies, Oxford, mimeo

  2004a: Aid, policy and growth in post-conflict societies, *European Economic Review*, **48**, 1125–45

  2004b: Greed and grievance in civil war, *Oxford Economic Papers*

Collier, P., A. Hoeffler and M. Söderbom, 2004: On the duration of civil war, *Journal of Peace Research*, **41**, 253–73

Dehn, J., 2000: Commodity price uncertainty, investment and shocks: implications for economic growth, D Phil thesis, Oxford University

Ghobhara, H. A., P. Huth and B. Russett, 2003: Civil wars kill and maim people – long after the shooting stops, *American Political Science Review*, **97**(2)

Klare, M., 2001: *Natural resource wars: the new landscape of global conflict*, Metropolitan Books, New York

Knight, M., N. Loayza and D. Villanueva, 1996: The peace dividend: military spending cuts and economic growth, *IMF Staff Papers*, **43**(1), 1–37

Lane A. and P. R. Tornell, 1999: The voracity effect, *American Economic Review*, **89**, 22–46

Murdoch, J. C. and T. Sandler, 2002: Economic growth, civil wars, and spatial spillovers, *Journal of Conflict Resolution*, **46**, 91–110

Regan, P. M., 2002: Third-party interventions and the duration of intrastate conflicts, *Journal of Conflict Resolution*, **46**, 55–73

Ross, M. L., 2000: Does oil hinder democracy?, *World Politics*, **53**, 325–61

2002: Resources and rebellion in Aceh, Indonesia, Department of Political Science, University of California, Los Angeles, mimeo, http://www.polisci.ucla.edu/faculty/ross

Sachs, J. D. and A. M. Warner, 2000: Natural resource abundance and economic growth, in G. M. Meier and J. E. Rauch (eds.), *Leading issues in economic development*, Oxford University Press, Oxford

Soares, R. R., 2003: The welfare cost of violence, University of Maryland, mimeo

Alternative Perspectives

Perspective Paper 3.1

MICHAEL D. INTRILIGATOR

The Purpose of the Perspective Paper

The purpose of this Perspective paper is to provide a counterbalance to chapter 3 (hereafter, CH). It will evaluate the issues covered in CH and will reach some conclusions about these issues, some of which differ from the chapter or go beyond it. It will, in addition, discuss other issues involved in civil wars as well as issues involved in other types of conflicts that are not treated in the chapter.

The Focus of CH

The focus of CH is civil wars, especially those in Africa, which has been the area of concern of its authors. Their chapter is largely based on their book *Breaking the Conflict Trap: Civil War and Development Policy* (Collier 2003), which, in turn, is based on many past publications, particularly those of Paul Collier. The authors correctly note that international conflict has become less common while civil wars have become more common. This is true, but international conflicts do, of course, exist and some are of great importance, such as the US-led wars in Afghanistan and Iraq and their aftermaths that should also be addressed in a study of conflict and its avoidance.

Civil wars are, nonetheless, extremely important, particularly in Africa, where some of the biggest wars have been fought in recent years and up to the present (see Ali and Matthews 1999). Huge civil wars have been fought or are being fought in, among

other places, Angola, Congo and Sudan. Unfortunately these wars are largely unreported and, if they are reported in the press they are mostly confined to the back pages while they are largely unreported in the broadcast media. As a result, these wars are mostly unknown to the general public, and many specialists have not treated them in depth, with Paul Collier's work in this area being an important exception. The chapter concerns civil wars in Africa, such as those mentioned above but also those in Liberia, Sierra Leone, Somalia and Côte d'Ivoire. It also concerns civil wars on other continents, such as those in Asia (including Afghanistan and Cambodia), Europe (including Bosnia and Serbia) and Latin America (including Colombia, El Salvador and Haiti).

The Benefits of a Reduction in the Global Incidence of Civil War

CH attempts to establish credible lower-bound estimates of the benefits that would stem from a reduction in the global incidence of civil war. They note that these benefits accrue at three levels: national, regional and global, although one could also add the local level. At the national level, the authors state that the benefits are partly economic and partly social. One might add the political benefits of a stable national government versus the instability that would stem from civil war, with a change in government or many such upheavals that could lead to a failed state. There are also other benefits – health, environment, etc., some of which are discussed below. CH measures the economic benefits of avoiding civil war by the effects of civil war on growth, and it measures the social benefits in terms of Disability Adjusted Life Years (DALYs). The authors also estimate the regional benefits of avoiding war in terms of its effects on economic growth. Finally, the global benefits of conflict reduction, as the authors correctly note, are the most difficult to estimate and are left unquantified, although the chapter does discuss in general terms the global impacts of civil wars – of AIDS, drugs and safe havens for terrorists.

Three Opportunities Treated in CH

CH focuses on three opportunities: the prevention of civil war in currently peaceful environments, the shortening of conflicts in currently war-ridden environments and the reduction in the risk of the resumption of conflict in post-conflict situations. These so-called 'opportunities' are analogous to Schelling's canonical goals of arms control: to prevent war; to reduce the damage resulting from war, which in a civil war is related to the length of the war; and to reduce the cost of arming, which is related to the war resuming in the civil war context (see Schelling 1960, 1966; Schelling and Halperin 1961).

CH states that probably the highest pay-off is from the third of these opportunities – an improved intervention in post-conflict situations to reduce the risk of the war resuming – but this is questionable. Given the huge costs of civil wars in their first days and weeks (as seen, for example, in the genocide in Rwanda), a case can be made that the highest pay-off is from the first opportunity, simply preventing civil war in the first place. The chapter states that renewed violence accounts for around half of all global civil wars and argues that such resumptions of conflict provide an opportunity for 'highly focused interventions', while they refer to prevention as a 'highly diffuse approach'. In many cases, however, it is possible to foresee the outbreak of violence in a nation and to take steps to forestall it, while in others it might be able to contain it at an early stage, either of which

would yield a very high pay-off. Thus, the focus of international public policy should be on all of these opportunities, with a balanced approach to all three.

CH Instruments for Conflict Prevention: Aid, Transparency in Natural Resources and Some Others

CH investigates two instruments for conflict prevention: aid and transparency in natural resources. The former is based on their reasoning that the risk of conflict is much higher in countries with low *per capita* income, negative growth and dependence on natural resource exports, such as many of the nations in Africa that have suffered from civil war. They argue that interventions that improve the economic characteristics of nations can reduce their tendency to engage in civil conflict. The approach is based on their assumptions that a country receiving aid will experience higher growth and that this, in turn, will reduce the chance of conflict. Both of these assumptions are highly questionable, however. In many cases, particularly in SSA, aid funds have done little more than add to the offshore bank accounts of dictators through corruption and other criminal acts. Examples include Mobutu in Zaire and Taylor in Liberia. Such aid does not necessarily add to economic growth. This is also shown in the empirical findings of CH, where they estimate that an extra 2 percentage points of aid raises the growth rate by only 0.2 percentage points, which they admit is a 'relatively modest gain' and which they attribute to the problem of diminishing returns. As they note, 'conflict prevention achieved purely by unselective aid programmes to low-income countries is not very cost-effective. The benefits amount to less than 10 per cent of the costs'. This lack of effectiveness of aid in preventing conflict is reiterated in their conclusions as: 'The most disappointing instrument is, in a sense, the most obvious and the most readily available. This is aid for conflict prevention.' Probably more important than financial aid is *technical assistance* to help create the institutions of a modern economy that can facilitate growth and development. Establishing such an infrastructure could have substantial pay-offs, as seen in the literature on economic institutions (see North 1990).

As to the second part of CH's reasoning, higher growth does not necessarily lead to reduced conflict since economic resources may just feed the acquisition of arms and even make the country a more attractive target for expatriates who would like to take it over and commandeer these resources. In their empirical work the authors find that three economic characteristics have significant and substantial effects on the risk of conflict: the level of income, its rate of growth and the degree of dependence on primary commodity exports, but the effect of growth appears to be relatively small, a 1 per cent increase in the growth rate sustained over a period of ten years having the effect of reducing the risk of civil war over the first five-year period from 13.8 per cent to 12.7 per cent, a relatively small effect. Taking account of the income-level effect lowers the risk in the second five-year period to 12.2 per cent, but even this is still relatively small.

The other instrument that CH treats is greater transparency in natural resources, which they see as 'an important and cheap practical instrument'. They refer to the adverse effects of natural resource dependence on development but do not elaborate on why that is the case or how greater transparency in this area could prevent conflict. One argument might be that greater transparency would enable one to trace the use of natural resources to fund a continuing civil war, as in the case of so-called 'blood diamonds'. These are diamonds that are exported, where the proceeds of their sale are used to continue a civil war, as happened in Angola. If greater transparency could reduce the chance of this occurring then this instrument might be a useful way to prevent or shorten a civil war. A counterargument, however, would be that greater transparency would identify where a country is building up its capital, making it the target for a civil war. In any case, the mechanisms connecting greater transparency in natural resources to conflict prevention must be elaborated. In fact, there are countries that are heavily dependent on exports from extractive industries that have not had a civil war and, conversely, there are counties with no such dependence that have had a civil war. Thus, this issue must be studied more carefully, looking at the effects of

dependence on natural resources on corruption and the way revenues from sales of such resources have fuelled war in some countries but not in others.

CH does not consider other possible instruments to prevent conflict. Looking at the issue as an economist, one might treat both the supply and demand for conflict. As to the supply, conflict in civil wars requires arms, and most poor countries, such as those in Africa, do not have the indigenous capability to produce arms. Depriving these nations by cutting off their arms supply could be an effective means to reduce conflict from breaking out, continuing, or restarting. CH mentions that control of the trade in armaments is one worth serious effort. Oscar Arias, the former President of Costa Rica and the winner of the Nobel Peace Prize, has made a proposal along these lines (see Arias, 1996, 2002). His proposal was that the major industrial nations, particularly the permanent members of the UN Security Council (China, France, Russia, the UK and the USA), impose an embargo on all arms shipments to SSA. These are the major arms-exporting nations and if they would stop shipping weapons into the region it could go a long way to reducing conflict in this part of the world, a region that has suffered inordinately from civil wars, including some of the largest in recent years. A type of precedent for this Arias proposal is the Tripartite Agreement under which three of these major powers, France, the UK and the USA, agreed to limit the quantity and type of weapons they were shipping to the Middle East, which worked reasonably well until the Soviet Union started to ship weapons to Egypt in 1958, after which the agreement collapsed.

More generally, one of the best ways to prevent civil war is to reduce the *resources* of the people who would engage in such conflict, including not only their access to arms but also their access to financial resources, to personnel, to mercenaries, to training, etc. Such a reduced access could be achieved by concerted actions of neighbouring states in policing the borders and by the great powers and international organizations in monitoring of flows of arms, money and people to the nation at risk (Sandler 2002 argues that this is the best approach to fighting terrorism).

The other side of this approach is the demand for conflict. This is where the tools of diplomacy could be important in mediating conflicts, establishing a peace agreement, or installing troops to preserve or restore order. These types of instruments for preventing conflict would probably be more effective in preventing conflict than the two that are discussed in CH (see Stedman, Rothchild and Cousens 2002 on establishing peace agreements; see also President Jimmy Carter, 1984, 2001 about his experience in negotiating agreements to prevent war).

Another instrument to prevent conflict is the use of peace-keeping forces, whether from the UN or regional military groups, as happened in the case of Liberia, or even former colonial powers, as happened in the case of Sierra Leone. These peacekeepers can restrain the warring parties and preserve the peace, avoiding conflict whether before it starts or during a civil war or to prevent the repeat of such a war (see Klein and Marwah 1996; Brahimi 2000; Rotberg, *et al.* 2000).

An Instrument for Shortening Conflict: Tracking of Natural Resources and Some Others

CH considers only one instrument for shortening conflict: the tracking of natural resources, which they suggest is the most promising intervention. As the chapter notes, such tracking through a certification process has the potential of choking off those arms that are purchased with sales of oil, gold, diamonds and other natural resources. An example is the Kimberley process to limit sales of conflict diamonds, and CH notes that it played an important role in ending the civil wars in Sierra Leone and Angola. It also notes that the same approach has been applied to other natural resources, including timber, and could be applied to yet others, including oil and drugs, many of which originate in areas of civil conflict.

There are other instruments that could also be considered to shorten conflicts, including arms embargoes, diplomacy and peace-keeping troops, as discussed above. CH tested, using an econometric approach, whether there had been any systematic effects of either economic or military interventions on the duration of civil wars. They found that there was no type of intervention that was system-

atically effective and thus concluded that the international community lacked effective instruments. More detailed studies should be done along these lines, however, considering different types of economic or military intervention and evaluating their effectiveness, as well as considering other such instruments. For example, it appears that UN peace-keeping interventions have been successful when they are small missions in terms of funding and numbers of solders but less successful in the case of large missions. Other instruments might include economic sanctions that have worked in some cases despite the often-stated claim that they are never effective (see Hufbauer, Schott and Elliott 1997).

Instruments for Reducing the Chance of the Resumption of Conflict: Aid and Military Intervention

CH reports that about half of all civil wars are relapses into conflict during the first decade of peace following a previous conflict. The chapter thus concludes that the diplomatic and military resources of the world community should be focused on such situations to try to prevent such a relapse using whatever tools at its disposal – economic, political, diplomatic, military, etc.

CH considers only two instruments for reducing the risk of reversion to conflict in post-conflict situations: aid to promote economic growth and military expenditure. The chapter claims that aid is particularly effective in post-conflict circumstances but that both its scale and its timing have been flawed. Aid has the same problems in this situation as those discussed above, where the connections between both aid and growth and between growth and reduction of conflict are problematic. In fact, CH finds that on a cost-benefit basis such aid is ineffective, with the net present value (NPV) of the cost of post-conflict aid, at $12.4 bn, exceeding its benefits of $10.6 bn, although the chapter notes that other global benefits and benefits in terms of poverty reduction have not been treated. Aid by itself is probably not effective as when it feeds the resources of either side in the conflict, whether directly or through corruption, it provides them only with the wherewithal to resume the conflict. Where it can be effective is as part of a larger package of reform and institution-building that ensures that aid does not stimulate further conflict.

CH mainly treats military intervention in terms of military spending rather than the use of foreign or international military forces. It also considers military intervention only in this situation and not as a way of preventing war in the first place or as a way to shorten a conflict, even though it has this potential as well. The chapter argues that foreign military intervention is likely to be more effective than domestic military forces. This historical record also supports this view. Colonial powers used their military to accomplish both war prevention and the shortening of conflicts in their colonies, with armies used to prevent the outbreak of conflict and to shorten conflicts that did break out, a classic example being the French Foreign Legion in the French colonies in Africa. In the post-colonial world the UN peace-keeping forces here to some extent served this function of preventing war outbreak in potential conflict situations, of shortening conflicts and of preventing the resumption of conflict in post-conflict situations, the three situations treated in the chapter. In its conclusions, CH finds that the most effective instrument for preventing civil wars is external military intervention under Chapter VII of the UN Charter to enforce peace in an immediate post-conflict situation and to maintain it over a decade during which the risks of reversion to conflict are very high. They find that such external military intervention, if adopted universally in post-conflict situations, would have a massive pay-off of over $300 bn, even after assuming that after their withdrawal the situation reverts to what it would have been without the military presence.

Along these lines, CH suggests an opportunity for international military intervention designed to keep the peace. This opportunity is to combine an external military presence with the government making deep cuts in its military budget to obtain a peace dividend. This proposal makes sense, as a foreign military presence could be effective in preserving peace, but deep cuts in the government's military budget are valuable not as a way of obtaining a peace dividend, which is doubtful in any case in the short run. Rather this is a way of limiting their role in a potential resumption of the civil war and at the same time a way of signalling to the opposition forces that they are not intending to resume the conflict. CH illustrates an external military presence in the case of British troops in Sierra Leone and suggests that this might be a model for twelve other post-conflict situations (on the peace dividend and its different results in the long run and the short run, see Intriligator 1996).

Benefits of Reducing the Incidence of Civil War

CH treats the benefits stemming from a reduced incidence of civil war at the national, regional and global level. At the national level, they assert that the benefits stem from avoiding a reduction in the rate of economic growth. Surely civil war would lower the growth rate due to the diversion of resources from production and distribution to war fighting as well as the generally chaotic situation during such a war. Indeed the chapter finds that each year of civil war reduces the growth rate by around 2.2 per cent. At the same time, there are direct costs of lost lives, loss of infrastructure and many others that go beyond simply reduced growth. These costs should be considered in any study of avoiding civil wars.

CH estimates the costs of a typical civil war – or, equivalently, the benefit stemming from avoiding such a war – as $45 bn in NPV terms. This remarkable figure is obtained by their estimate of the loss of GDP to the country directly affected (amounting to 105 per cent of initial GDP), the diversion of spending into the military in the country directly affected (amounting to 18 per cent of GDP) and a similar diversion in neighbours (amounting to 12 per cent of GDP). The total cost is thus the equivalent of 202 per cent of GDP. The average GDP of conflict-affected low-income countries just prior to conflict is $19.7 bn, so the representative conflict cost around $40 bn. To this they add health costs of around $5 bn, leading to their estimate of $45 bn as the cost of a typical civil war in a low-income country. While this cost estimate is subject to many uncertainties, it is a huge amount that dwarfs the cost of potential ways of avoiding such a war, whether through diplomacy, military intervention, or other means. The implication is that the world as a whole should not ignore these wars but rather work assiduously to avoid them if at all possible. As the chapter properly notes: 'Even these lower-bound estimates suggest that the economic and social costs of civil war are enormous. As such the issue clearly deserves international attention. The question is not whether the problem is important, but rather whether there are instruments that can be used effectively to tackle the problem through international action.'

This conclusion on the importance of avoiding civil wars is reinforced by what the authors refer to as the 'conflict trap', namely the high chance that a country that has had a civil war that ended will have another war. Taking account of the higher probability of a civil war for a nation suffering such a war, which amounts to over 40 per cent as compared to around 14 per cent for a typical low-income country, discounting back to the beginning of the first conflict results in an additional cost of around $12 bn, yielding a total cost of $57 bn. Even this huge figure does not account for global effects that the authors note are important but difficult to quantify. These include drugs, AIDS and international terrorism, with added very large costs. Clearly, there are very high rewards to preventing, shortening, or stopping the resumption of civil wars. This much is clearly demonstrated in CH. What is less convincing are the instruments that they propose to deal with this issue, whether aid or transparency in natural resources. These are relatively weak ways of avoiding civil wars, and there are more potent instruments that could be used, including diplomacy and military intervention.

Other Dimensions of the Problem of Avoiding Civil Wars

There are yet other dimensions of the challenge of avoiding civil wars, including those of health, the environment, politics, psychology, international relations and others. It is a mistake to ignore these other dimensions, that can also have profound economic effects.

As to health, DALYs do not tell the entire story, given the cost of burdening the health system, given the fact that the wounded in a civil war must be treated and given the fact that as a result of a civil war people are not able to work or to harvest food, etc. These effects of war via loss of health should be treated. CH does refer to the deterioration of health as a result of civil war, including forced population movements and the collapse of basic health services, leading to the loss of millions of DALYs, which they compute (using an assumed value of $1,000 per DALY) as around $5 bn for a typical civil war. This is an underestimate, however, as it does not account for other health costs involved in a civil war.

As to the environment, wars, including civil wars, have a devastating effect, which imposes costs on the nation, including loss of agricultural land, loss of potable water, etc. These costs are acute during and after a war and some are long-term, lasting many years. They can also spill over to neighbouring countries.

As to politics, civil wars are sometimes fought to overthrow a brutal dictator, but the result is in some cases to lead to the takeover of the country by another dictator and a sequence of civil wars. These political factors also have economic consequences in terms of lack of an appropriate infrastructure for an economy to function, corruption that has the effect of diverting scarce resources, etc.

As to psychology, this is also part of the problem of civil wars and a challenge to stopping them or ending them. Belligerents during such a war argue: 'Why stop now?' They will also try to avoid any show of weakness, arguing against a settlement or even a negotiated end to the conflict by saying that 'We will look weak'. The idea of stopping fighting or not resuming a war will be met with 'We can't give them what they want, so we can't stop fighting', leading to unbridgeable divides, uncontrollable armies and an inability to stop the war. These factors must be overcome to stop civil wars, and they must be carefully studied (see Smith 1995; Berdal 1996).

As to international relations, it is often the case that other nations, particularly neighbouring states, or great power states, play a role in initiating or inhibiting a civil war, and they could play an important role in stopping it. There are usually both domestic causes and international factors at work in starting any particular civil war, and the international community can play an important role in stopping or shortening such wars.

Other Conflict Challenges

While there are certainly challenges stemming from civil wars, there are other conflict challenges stemming from international wars, from military interventions, from acts of terrorism, from the burden of spending on arms, from the issues of proliferation and arms control and from other related issues not addressed in CH. These might be addressed in future work dealing with the global challenge of conflict. Many significant problems of potential conflict exist today, and some specific areas that call for further study and analysis in this area include:

- The dangers of regional conflicts growing from local issues into wider conflagrations
- The potential role of international organizations, major powers, weapons of mass destruction, deterrence or other mechanisms in avoiding major conflicts
- Arms races, regional arms races, and the outbreak of war
- Arms sales, particularly to nations in unstable regions
- Accidental or inadvertent nuclear war
- Proliferation of nuclear weapons and of other weapons of mass destruction (WMD), including demand and supply factors
- Terrorism – and, in particular, the extremely dangerous potential acquisition of nuclear weapons or other weapons of mass destruction by terrorist groups.

References

Ali, T. M. and R. O. Matthews (eds.), 1999: *Civil wars in Africa: roots and resolution*, McGill–Queens University Press, Montreal and Ithaca, NY

Arias, O., 1996: International code of conduct on arms transfers Speech at the State of the World Forum, San Francisco, 5 October, http://www.hartford-hwp.com/archives/27a/004.html
2002: Peace and justice in the new century, Speech presented at the University of San Francisco, 17 September 17, http://www.usfca.edu/president/arias.html

Berdal, M. R., 1996: *Disarmament and demobilization after civil wars: arms, soldiers and the termination of armed conflicts*, Adelphi Paper **303**, Oxford University Press for the International Institute for Strategic Studies, New York

Brahimi, 2002: *Report of the panel on United Nations peace operations*, August

Carter, President J., 1984: *Negotiation: the alternative to hostility*, Mercer University Press, Macon, GA
2001: *Talking peace*, UCLA Burkle Center for International Relations, Bernard Brodie Distinguished Lecture on the Conditions of Peace, http://www.international.ucla.edu/article.asp?parentid = 2198

Collier, P., 2003: *Breaking the conflict trap: civil war and development policy*, Oxford University Press, New York

Copson, R. W., 1994: *Africa's wars and prospects for peace*, M. E. Sharpe, Armonk, NY

Hufbauer, G. C., J. J. Schott and K. A. Elliott, 1997: *Economic sanctions reconsidered: history and current policy*, revised edn., Institute for International Economics, Washington, DC

Intriligator, M. D., 1996: The peace dividend: myth or reality?, chapter 1 in N. P. Gleditsch, O. Bjerkholt, O. Cappelen, R. P. Smith and J. P. Dunne (eds.), *The peace dividend*, Elsevier, Amsterdam

Klein, L. R. and K. Marwah, 1996: Economic aspects of peacekeeping operations, in N. P. Gleditsch, O. Bjerkholt, O. Cappelen, R. P. Smith and J. P. Dunne (eds.), *The peace dividend*, Elsevier, Amsterdam

North, D. C., 1990: *Institutions, institutional change, and economic performance*, Cambridge University Press, Cambridge and New York

Rotberg, R. I. *et. al.*, 2000: *Peacekeeping and peace enforcement in Africa: methods of conflict*

prevention, World Peace Foundation, Cambridge, MA, Brookings Institution Press, Washington, DC

Sandler, T., 2002: Fighting terrorism: what economics can tell us, *Challenge*, **45**

Schelling, T. C., 1960: *The strategy of conflict*, Harvard University Press, Cambridge, MA

1966: *Arms and influence*, Yale University Press, New Haven

Schelling, T. C. and M. H. Halperin, 1961: *Strategy and arms control*, Twentieth Century Fund, New York

Smith, J. D. D., 1995: *Stopping wars: defining the obstacles to cease-fire*, Westview Press, Boulder, CO

Stedman, S. John, D. Rothchild and E. M. Cousens, 2002: *Ending civil wars: the implementation of peace agreements*, Lynne Rienner, Boulder, CO

Perspective Paper 3.2

TONY ADDISON

Introduction

Violent conflict is a major challenge for the global community. In 2002 there were twenty-one major armed conflicts in nineteen locations across the world (Eriksson, Sollenberg and Wallensteen 2003, 109). Most occur in the developing world, particularly in the poorest countries. In chapter 3, Paul Collier and Anke Hoeffler (hereafter CH) focus on the challenge of reducing the global incidence of civil war, and estimate the net benefits of doing so. CH present three opportunities to meet this challenge, as well as some instruments for doing so:

- Preventing civil war in *currently peaceful environments* (two instruments: aid and transparency in natural resources).
- Shortening conflicts in *currently war-torn environments* (one instrument: curtailing rebel access to commodity markets).
- Reducing the risk of the *resumption of conflict* in post-conflict situations (two instruments: aid and military intervention).

The purpose of this Perspective paper is to provide an assessment and constructive criticism of chapter 3.[1] The structure of my note mirrors that of the chapter. The next section discusses the estimates of the costs of civil war and, therefore, the benefits of reducing its incidence. The next three sections discuss each of the CH opportunities in turn, starting with a brief summary of CH's argument, followed by an evaluation. The final section concludes and suggests one further opportunity: reducing the *intensity* of civil wars that have already begun.

The Benefits of Reducing the Incidence of Civil War

There are many benefits from reducing the occurrence of civil war. CH calculate the cost of a typical civil war in a low-income country. The net present value (NPV) of the total cost is estimated to be 250 per cent of the initial pre-war GDP, comprising GDP loss in the conflict country (105 per cent), GDP loss in neighbouring countries (115 per cent), higher military spending in the conflict country (18 per cent) and higher military spending in neighbouring countries (12 per cent) (all NPVs are calculated using a discount rate of 5 per cent). Thus given that the average initial GDP of a conflict-affected low-income country is US$ 19.7 bn, the cost of a typical civil war is US$ 49 bn (i.e. US$ 19.7 bn multiplied by 250 per cent). To this they add the NPV of health costs measured in lost disability adjusted life years (DALYs), which is US$ 5 bn. The total cost of a typical civil war in a low-income country is therefore US$ 54 bn, and the value of the enhanced risk of conflict in a country that has been through conflict is a further US$ 10.2 bn. This

I thank Paul Collier and Michael Intriligator for their comments, and discussions with Tun Lin, George Mavrotas and Mark McGillivray were also helpful.

The views expressed in this Perspective paper are those of the author alone, and should not be attributed to UNU-WIDER.

[1] The expert group of the Copenhagen Consensus will consider the ten challenge papers (chapters 1–10 in this volume) together with the associated Perspective papers. Authors of Perspective papers are provided with the following guidelines: (i) Have results relevant to the challenge and the opportunities been left out of the chapter and are the issues presented in a balanced way? (ii) Could other models have been chosen? (iii) Are key assumptions reasonable? In addition, Perspective paper writers may include one new opportunity.

gives a combined total of US$ 64.2 bn (Collier and Hoeffler 2004).

Although there are a few case studies that value the cost of war, the CH estimate is the most comprehensive to date.[2] There are other costs – for instance, forced migration – but the monetary value of these is largely speculative, and CH therefore exclude them. There remain, however, two problems with the CH methodology.

The first is with the way that CH place a monetary value on the DALYs lost to war. I have no ethical objection to placing monetary values on DALYs (such a step is essential to make health costs commensurate with the other costs of war). My problem is with the CH approach, which simply sets the value of a lost DALY at US$ 1,000, the purchasing power parity (PPP) level of *per capita* income in many of the countries at risk of conflict (Collier and Hoeffler 2004). This basically amounts to valuing the *livelihood* rather than the *life*. The former reflects the largely discredited human capital approach to valuing life which uses earned income as a measure of a person's marginal product, and therefore the loss or gain to society of a life which is ended or saved. In contrast, 'willingness-to-pay' approaches to valuing life – the preferred method in most recent cost-benefit analyses (CBAs) of health and safety – typically yield monetary valuations of a life that are five times greater than the human capital approach. There is also a downward bias in applying the human capital approach to civil war countries since their presently low *per capita* income is partly a result of their conflict history.

The method chosen to value lives has important implications for any economic CBA of military interventions by developed countries in the civil wars of developing countries. The lives lost by military personnel will have a much higher value than a life saved in the local population if the human capital approach is used, since there is a large gap in *per capita* income between developing and developed countries and therefore a large difference in human capital measures of life. This can lead to tactics which preserve military lives but increase the dangers to civilian lives – for example, the high-altitude bombing used in Afghanistan and Kosovo.

The second problem concerns the discount rate used by CH to calculate the NPV of the GDP loss, the extra military spending and the loss of life. No reason is given for the choice of a 5 per cent discount rate.[3] It is also by no means self-evident that DALYs should be discounted at all, given the uniqueness of life and health compared to other goods and, if discounted, whether the rate should be the same as that applied to monetary costs; empirical evidence shows that individual rates of time preferences often differ for health versus money (Dolan, 2000; Smith and Gravelle, 2000).

Finally, given that the Copenhagen Consensus will attempt to rank opportunities *across* challenges, it is important for each challenge paper to apply the same approach to valuing changes in human life and health (resulting from civil war, global climate change and disease, for example) and to apply the same discount rate in calculating NPVs of costs and benefits. Otherwise the ranking will be biased by inconsistencies in the methodologies across challenge papers.

In summary, CH provide a set of rigorously derived estimates of the costs of civil war, and thus the benefits of reducing it. However, there is an ambiguity in their use of the discount rate, and their valuation of health and life is downwardly biased because it values a person's livelihood and not their life. And, relatedly, there is a need for consistency in methodologies across challenges if a ranking of opportunities is to be achieved.

---

[2] Individual case studies that value the cost of war include Harris (1997), Arunatilake, Jayasuriya and Kelegama (2001) and Abadie and Gardeazabal (2003).

[3] There is very little discussion of the discount rate in the literature on contemporary conflict. One exception is the study by Davis, Murphy and Topel (2003) which applies a discount rate of 2 per cent in their economic CBA study of US strategies towards Iraq.

Conflict Prevention

Instrument: Aid and Conflict Prevention

CH argue that aid can reduce conflict if it raises growth since: 'When an economy is growing rapidly the returns to expanding the cake are higher relative to fighting over how to divide the cake and so one would expect a reduction in the risk of conflict' (Collier and Hoeffler 2004). The merit of the CH focus is that growth is a variable over which national policy makers and international donors have some traction. Even if countries do not manage to optimise their growth strategy, they can at least strip out the worst inhibitors (weak property rights, overtaxation of smallholder agriculture and chaotic fiscal management, to name but three). If aid helps them to do this, then aid is an effective peace instrument. This is in contrast to democratisation, a highly desirable objective in itself, but one whose effect on conflict is more uncertain (an empirical study by Goldstone *et al.* 2003 finds that new democracies have a higher risk of conflict).

Nevertheless CH may be underestimating aid's *potential* with respect to peace for four reasons:

(1) Access to a slice of a growing economy depends on how people make their livelihood as well as their access to productive assets (such as land, water and other 'natural capital'), infrastructure and their stock of human capital (Shorrocks and van der Hoeven 2004). These variables determine how they connect to the growth process and whether some groups (with ethnic, regional and religious characteristics) are marginalized from its benefits. If aid directly improves the livelihoods of disadvantaged groups – via financing community projects and encouraging pro-poor expenditure reform – then it will *raise their participation in growth*, and aid will reduce conflict by more than CH allow for.

(2) Growth raises the *tax base* and, thereby, potentially, public spending to redress the grievances of disadvantaged groups. In mineral-rich countries, growth is enclave in nature and generates little employment, and therefore most people's slice of the pie depends on how the state distributes the revenue (a theme we return to later). The *fiscal effect* of growth is additional to growth's income effect, but it depends on effective institutions to collect revenue – which in resource-poor countries mainly originates in sales taxes and customs duties – and to manage

the resulting public expenditures. Aid can support national efforts to build those institutions (a point we return to later on the post-conflict opportunity).

(3) Aid can be used as a *tactical* instrument to influence the behaviour of actual or potential belligerents. In pre-genocide Rwanda, aid financed a significant amount (up to 50 per cent) of the budget, and threatening to suspend it could have modified the behaviour of Hutu extremists in government and bolstered diplomatic and military action. In Sudan, the UN and other donors are today attempting to head off a worsening crisis (and a potential genocide) by applying pressure on the Khartoum government.

(4) In Collier and Hoeffler (1998) income inequality is insignificant as a determinant of conflict risk. But this result has been challenged, notably by Nafziger and Auvinen (2002) in a study which uses a larger inequality dataset; they find that income inequality increases conflict risk. For Nepal, Murshed and Gates (2003) find that regional human development indicators and landlessness are important determinants of regional variation in support for the country's Maoist insurrection. If aid successfully improves the livelihoods of disadvantaged groups, either directly or through fiscal policy, then it will improve the chances of peace.

In summary, *well-designed* aid can do more for conflict than CH allow, and therefore their valuation of the benefit may be an underestimate. Note, however, my emphasis on 'well-designed'. Aid can do major damage to peace when it bolsters dictatorships that use natural resources and the fiscal system for gross patronage, thereby slowing growth, and raising inequality. This is especially so in Africa. During the Cold War superpower aid flowed to dictatorships in Angola, Ethiopia, Liberia, Somalia and Zaire (now the Democratic Republic of the Congo), and dictators (and rivals) became adept at manipulating geopolitical rivalries to access assistance. Moreover, some donors have used bilateral aid to ruthlessly pursue commercial and foreign policy advantage, particularly in Burundi, Rwanda and Zaire. Under pressure from powerful rich countries, the IMF and the World Bank were encouraged to lend to client states beyond the point of economic rationality, leaving them crippled by large and unserviceable foreign debts (Addison and Rahman, 2004).[4] A former World Bank chief economist, Nicholas Stern, puts this well:

> Underlying all of these instruments should be one guiding principle: the international community should provide finance for change, not finance for not changing. We must recognise that the international community has in the past, often for political reasons, financed the cost of not changing – in Mobutu's Zaire, for example. (Stern 2002, 29)

Instrument: Transparency in Natural Resources

CH highlight five mechanisms through which natural resource rents increase conflict risk. First, the macroeconomic difficulties inherent in managing large and fluctuating resource rents lower growth and *per capita* income, both of which raise conflict risk. Second, resource-rich governments become politically disconnected from an increasingly resentful populace. Third, 'grand' corruption and resource rents often go together, encouraging a 'winner-takes-all' politics at the expense of growth. Fourth, regions endowed with natural resources are often the least likely to benefit, and are therefore prone to secede. Fifth, resource rents provide an incentive, and a means, for criminal networks to finance conflict (Collier and Hoeffler 2004).

CH accordingly argue for international action to improve the domestic governance of resource revenues through two mechanisms. First, encourage *greater transparency of resource use* in budgets together with corporate and government disclosure of resource revenues through the Extractive Industries Transparency Initiative (EITI). Second, improve the intertemporal smoothing of revenues so that they become less destabilizing to growth.

---

[4] Of the forty-one Heavily Indebted Poor Countries (HIPCs) eleven are classified by the IMF and the World Bank as conflict-affected, and owe some US$ 63 bn, much of it to the donors themselves (IMF and World Bank 2001, 21).

CH first estimate the effect of natural resources on policy performance, which they find negative, and then simulate the growth effect of an improvement in the management of resource revenues (they assume that better resource rent management halves the adverse effect of rents on policy). In addition to the effect of higher growth on conflict risk, there is a direct effect of commodity dependence on conflict. For the two effects, CH estimate a total gain of US$ 89 bn from effective implementation of the EITI.

CH are right to emphasise the need for more transparency in the flows and use of resource rents. The sums are large: for example in a leaked unpublished report in 2002 the IMF estimated that Angola could not account for US$ 4.3 bn of revenues from oil (Hoyos and Reed 2003) and at least US$ 3 bn was stolen from the public purse under the military dictatorship of Nigeria's General Sani Abacha.

Nevertheless there are three problems with the CH line of argument:

(1) In a pre-conflict situation, resource revenues are largely under the control of states (but as conflict develops they fall increasingly under the control of non-state actors). To effectively prevent conflict EITI must encourage state actors towards *revenue transparency*. CH argue that this will happen in two ways: 'citizens can challenge their government as to why it is choosing to flout international guidelines, and the decision not to adopt them would constitute a negative signal to international markets' (Collier and Hoeffler 2004). This is more likely to work in Nigeria – which has developed a vibrant democracy and an independent media since the end of the Abacha regime and which has large international commercial debts – than in Equatorial Guinea (sometimes described as the 'Kuwait of Africa') which has a strongly authoritarian regime and little need to maintain its reputation in the international financial markets.

(2) Even if a government commits itself to an EITI framework, translating the revenues into the effective *public spending* that lowers grievances remains a formidable task given the often chronic state of public expenditure

management. Consequently, even when the political will exists in central government, public money intended for local services can still be diverted along the way (see Reinikka and Svensson 2004). It is effective service *delivery*, not transparency itself, which is critical to reducing grievances – particularly in long-neglected regions.

(3) Foreign bribery subverts national transparency efforts. But despite their rhetoric, rich-country governments have taken little action. For example, the UK signed the OECD's anti-bribery convention, and in 2002 a new law came into effect which makes it easier to prosecute bribery and corruption by UK nationals and companies overseas. Yet not a single prosecution has been brought in a UK court, and no additional funds have been allocated to the authorities to pursue prosecutions.[5] Clearly there are powerful externalities between the separate challenges of civil war and corruption in the agenda of the Copenhagen Consensus.

In summary, CH may overstate EITI's effectiveness as a conflict-prevention measure, and therefore overestimate the value of its benefits (an NPV of US$ 89 bn). Nevertheless, as they point out, it is relatively cheap to implement and so the net benefit is still large even if we reduce their estimate of the gross benefit. And its chances will be strengthened if: (1) more aid and domestic resources are committed to improving fiscal management and service delivery and (2) rich countries act more vigorously to prosecute corruption by their nationals.

Shortening Conflicts

Instrument: Curtailing Rebel Access to Commodity Markets

There are many instruments that could potentially shorten conflicts. These include reducing supplies of mercenaries and weapons; external military intervention (which CH discuss instead as a *post-conflict* instrument); and reducing the profitability to rebels of selling valuable minerals, timber and drugs. It is the latter instrument which CH focus on. They note the success of the Kimberley process in creating a two-tier market in which illegitimate diamonds sell at a discount to legitimate (certified) diamonds, thereby reducing the value of 'blood diamonds'. And as they suggest, a two-tier market in drugs (with registered addicts able to obtain legal government supplies) would reduce some of the flow of finance from the drugs trade to conflict zones.

These proposals are eminently sensible, and in the case of 'blood diamonds' some success has already been achieved. The drugs problem is more difficult given the very large and growing market in rich countries (and sizeable markets in poor countries as well). One additional way to address the problem is to provide alternative livelihoods for farmers who grow opium and other drug-producing plants.

Take the case of Afghanistan. Opium is a high-value crop, and is the country's main source of foreign exchange, aside from foreign aid and remittances. Opium revenues finance the country's warlords, and indeed provide them with more revenue than the central government can command through its weak powers of taxation. The incentive of farmers to grow opium depends on its *relative* price to other crops. One suitable export crop for Afghanistan is cotton, which was produced in significant amounts before the war. But like all cotton producers, Afghanistan faces an international price which is depressed by large US subsidies to farmers. Hence, the relative world price of cotton to opium would be raised by the elimination of the US$ 3.4 bn subsidy which 25,000 American cotton farmers presently enjoy.[6] The profitability of legal crops such as cotton could be further raised by transferring the subsidy savings into agricultural research for smallholder farmers in Afghanistan and elsewhere in the developing world, particularly

---

[5] 'Claims of UK bribery abroad higher than published data', *Financial Times*, 23 March 2004.

[6] Similarly, the elimination of the EU's US$ 1.5 bn subsidy to European sugar producers would help the sugar farmers in the post-conflict countries of Ethiopia, Mozambique and Uganda.

farmers in environmentally stressed areas, who receive too little help at present.

In summary, it is highly desirable to shorten the *duration* of conflicts, and CH offer a practical way forward, and I suggest that agricultural trade liberalisation is a further instrument. Shortening the average duration of civil wars will save lives. But equally it is desirable to reduce conflict's *intensity* – i.e. the number of deaths that occur per year of conflict, whether combatant deaths from military action, civilian deaths at the hands of combatants, or deaths caused by the hunger and ill-health associated with war (IFRC 2003). I return to this point in the Conclusion, where I suggest that this is an additional opportunity for the Copenhagen Consensus to consider.

Reducing Post-Conflict Risks

CH rightly highlight the risks of conflict returning to 'post-conflict' countries. Peace agreements to end civil wars collapse more often than agreements to end inter-state wars (Walter 2002). And belligerents find it increasingly difficult to credibly signal commitment to peace since their reputation declines as the number of broken agreements rises (Addison and Murshed 2002).

Instrument: Aid in Post-Conflict Situations

For CH, aid is more effective in supporting post-conflict recovery than in preventing conflict. Based on the Collier and Dollar (2002) model, CH make a case for altering the time-profile of post-conflict aid, specifically: 'aid is atypically effective in raising growth rates during the middle years of post-conflict recovery' (Collier and Hoeffler 2004). And given the CH growth-to-conflict mechanism, aid targeted in this way significantly reduces the risk of civil war returning. This leads them to criticise the present timing of aid flows since 'while during the first couple of years of peace there is a flood of aid . . . . aid typically tapers out just as it should be tapering in' (Collier and Hoeffler 2004). Their argument is based on the view that: 'in the first few years after a civil war the quality of state institutions

is so low that, while needs are great, the capacity to use resources effectively is very limited, so that returns to aid are no higher than normal' (Collier and Hoeffler 2004).

However, the CH approach is potentially misleading as a policy guide, precisely because, as they say, the quality of state institutions is often low in the immediate post-conflict years. Finance to rebuild those institutions is required, but they generally need reform as well, involving a restructuring of their operations, the payment of wage arrears and, most often, an increase in salaries to recruit the necessary skills. All of this is expensive. But unless the state enjoys generous natural resource revenues, its funds will be limited by low revenues from sales taxes and customs duties. These usually account for the largest shares of domestic revenue in low-income countries, and typically contract along with economic activity and trade during civil war. Revenues become more buoyant as the economy recovers. But the strength of the revenue recovery will not match the strength of the economic recovery if tax and customs institutions remain weak. These institutions are often in a chronic condition after prolonged civil war, and frequently corrupt. A complete and early overhaul of taxation and the customs service is essential but governments typically lack the resources to do it. Moreover, the central government may not fully control revenue collection – the situation in Afghanistan today – and political (and perhaps military action) will be necessary to wrest control of revenue raising from warlords.

As a result of low domestic revenues, the government must either limit its reconstruction expenditures or resort to inflationary finance of its budget, neither of which is desirable. Aid in the form of budgetary support can finance not only capital spending but also a proportion of recurrent spending – and associated institution-building – and will enable the government to raise total reconstruction spending while maintaining macroeconomic stability. A larger share of the budget is eventually funded by domestic revenues as these rise with economic recovery and as newly reformed tax and customs services become effective. From a *fiscal perspective*, an aid dollar therefore has a higher marginal value in the early years of recovery (when domestic revenues are low) than in later years (when domestic revenues are higher). This is the exact reverse of the CH conclusion. Indeed, if donors did allocate more of their aid to the middle years of recovery, as CH suggest, then the return will be low – since the institutions to effectively use it will most likely never have been built.

There is also a case for early and generous aid from a *poverty perspective.* One of the main dangers for post-conflict reconstruction is not growth failure (Mozambique and Uganda enjoy high and sustained post-war growth) but the failure of the poor to recover (Addison 2003). Refugees must resettle, primary education and basic health services need to be provided, safe water and sanitation established, rural roads repaired, livestock herds recreated and smallholder farms and micro enterprises put back into business. And it is not just a question of rebuilding what was there before: the pre-war distribution of infrastructure and services is often skewed away from the poor (and may reflect ethnic discrimination as well). Regions that never had much in the first place need special assistance – in particular environmentally fragile regions where poverty is typically high.

Considerable resources exist within communities to do all of this. But their labour time needs substantial external supplies of materials and technical skills, and this requires aid. National and international NGOs do much to deliver this, and to help poor communities when state institutions are weak. And in some conflict countries, there are pockets of strength within state institutions that are capable of effective delivery. In Mozambique, for example, the health ministry was very pro-active in the immediate years of peace, in part reflecting the country's early and pioneering primary health care strategy. In Angola, a social fund financed by the World Bank and bilateral donors had some success operating in cooperation with the country's better local governments. Assisting such institutions has important demonstration effects for the rest of government and yields vital, often experimental, lessons, on how to achieve wider institutional reform within government.

Finally, there is a *tactical case* for front-loading aid. In Mozambique, the promise of generous aid in the immediate post-war years was one factor

encouraging the rebel movement, RENAMO, to come to the negotiating table. When the private discounts rates of government and rebel leaders are high – as they are in conflict countries – the promise of aid in the middle years of recovery is worth much less than at the moment the peace deal is signed. When government resources are too thin to make a credible transfer to rebels as part of a peace deal, then aid provides a partial substitute (by financing infrastructure and service delivery in rebel areas for example). And aid can substitute for the missing 'peace dividend' in public spending when post-war insecurity keeps domestic military-spending high.

In summary, in reaching their conclusion on the timing of post-war aid, CH overemphasise the growth objective, and underemphasise aid's fiscal dimension, its poverty dimension and its use as a tactical instrument to secure peace. Their general point on aid policy is an important one – donors have to commit to countries for the long haul and are too ready to declare victory and go home – but the time profile of aid should not just be governed by its growth effects. A spokesperson for the Afghan government recently summarized the urgency of the issues as follows: 'If the international community . . . fails to grasp the importance of continuity to help Afghanistan stand on its feet within a short period of time and rebuild its infrastructure, then the cost might be much higher down the road for all of us . . . We do not want to repeat the mistakes of a decade or so ago, when Afghanistan was left at the mercy of destiny' (quoted in Philips 2004).

Instrument: military intervention post-conflict

Given the high frequency with which peace deals crumble, CH advocate external military intervention to secure a post-conflict country. This will permit a reduction in government military spending, since otherwise: 'High military spending might be read by rebels as a signal of an intention to renege' (Collier and Hoeffler 2004). They cite the UK military intervention in Sierra Leone as an example (although it is debatable whether Sierra Leone was in a conflict or 'post-conflict' situation at the time). And they estimate a substantial net gain: at least US$ 392 bn.

The cost of external peacekeeping varies with who does the peacekeeping (and the scale of the insecurity). CH cite a figure of US$ 49 m per year for the UK military presence in Sierra Leone. However, Sierra Leone is not the most expensive war by any means. It costs the USA about US$ 800 m per month to keep 13,000 troops in Afghanistan. A further 8,000 troops are supplied by other nations. If they cost as much as US peacekeepers, then the additional monthly cost is US$ 490 m but they are likely to be cheaper than US forces, so assume for argument's sake that they cost US$ 200 m per month. Adding this to the US expenditure, implies that the total cost of external military forces in Afghanistan is roughly US$ 1 bn per month, or US$ 12 bn per year. So the cost of an external military intervention in a country such as Afghanistan is substantially more than in a 'small' African war such as Sierra Leone.

The cost of external intervention can be reduced if militaries from developing countries are used since their labour cost is substantially lower than those of rich-country forces (for US peacekeeping operations, the US Congressional Budget Office assigns average personnel costs of about USD 250,000 per person-year). Many of the 50,000 'blue helmets' currently deployed in seventeen UN peacekeeping operations around the world are from developing countries. Unfortunately, the effectiveness of developing country forces in civil wars is sometimes limited, especially when they are undertrained and underequipped. The UN forces held hostage in Sierra Leone were mainly from developing countries.

One way forward is to create a highly trained rapid reaction force at the disposal of the UN Security Council, a suggestion that has often been made – most recently by former UN Under-Secretary General Brian Urquhart who was involved in many of the early UN peacekeeping operations (Urquhart 2003). One of the main benefits would be speed – for rapid intervention in situations such as Rwanda in 1994, Liberia in 2003 and western Sudan today. Another way forward is to

accelerate the EU's ability to deploy forces globally: this was done for the first time, and relatively successfully, in Bunia (north-eastern DRC) in 2003 and may shortly occur in the Sudan.

In summary, the CH proposal for greater military involvement by external forces is worthwhile and has large benefits as the swift end to the carnage in Sierra Leone demonstrates. But greater attention should be given to using the forces of developing countries themselves which means greater assistance to them in training and equipment. The latter should be factored into aid programmes; development practitioners are often rightly sceptical of military aid and budgetary support to the security sector. But if such aid enables democratic countries, particularly in Africa, to contribute to effective peacekeeping, then it will be money well spent.

Conclusions

Chapter 3 addresses a vital global challenge. The chapter itself is methodologically sound, and innovative in its use of the sparse data which are available. Although some of their policy conclusions are questionable, the chapter's great merit is the way in which it highlights the role of development in reducing the risk of conflict.

The Copenhagen Consensus permits authors of Perspective papers to offer one more opportunity to meet the assigned challenge. I would therefore like to end by proposing the *reduction of conflict intensity* as an extra opportunity (where intensity is measured by the annual number of battlefield deaths and civilian deaths). Although CH address duration, this is not the same as intensity: long wars may be low-intensity affairs, while short wars can be very bloody. Space precludes a detailed discussion of instruments but a list of viable instruments must include: reducing the flow of weapons and mercenaries to conflict countries; revision of the Geneva Conventions to fully encompass war crimes committed during civil wars (including the proper treatment of prisoners of war); increased effort to bring perpetrators of war crimes to international justice (including the International Criminal

Court); protecting IDPs and refugees from harm by belligerents (i.e. preventing a repeat of Srebrenica and other massacres); and better humanitarian and medical assistance to civilian populations (Gutman and Rieff 1999; IFRC, 2003). War is the ultimate modern horror, but much can still be done to lessen its impact while striving to end it completely.

References

Abadie, A., and J. Gardeazabal, 2003: The economic costs of conflict: a case study of the Basque Country, *American Economic Review*, **93**(1), 113–32

Addison, T. (ed.), 2003: *From conflict to recovery in Africa*, Oxford University Press for UNU–WIDER, Oxford

Addison, T. and S. M. Murshed, 2002: Credibility and reputation in peacemaking, *Journal of Peace Research*, **39**(4), 487–501

Addison, T. and A. Rahman, 2004: Resolving the HIPC problem: is good policy enough?, in T. Addison, H. Hansen and F. Tarp (eds.), *Debt relief for poor countries*, Palgrave Macmillan for UNU–WIDER, Basingstoke 1105–20

Arunatilake, N., S. Jayasuriya and S. Kelegama, 2001: The economic cost of the war in Sri Lanka, *World Development*, **29**(9), 1483–1500

Collier, P. and D. Dollar, 2002: Aid allocation and poverty reduction, *European Economic Review*, **46**, 1475–1500

Collier, P. and A. Hoeffler, 1998: On the economic consequences of civil war, *Oxford Economic Papers*, **50**(4), 563–73
    2004: Conflicts, chapter 3 in this volume

Davis, S. J., K. M. Murphy and R. H. Topel, 2003: War in Iraq versus containment: weighing the costs, University of Chicago, 20 March 2003, mimeo; available at: http://gsbwww.uchicago.edu/fac/steven.davis.research

Dolan, P., 2000: The measurement of health-related quality of life for use in resource allocation decisions in health care, in A. J. Culyer and J. P. Newhouse (eds.), *Handbook of Health Economics: 1B*, North-Holland, Amsterdam, 1723–60

Eriksson, M., M. Sollenberg and P. Wallensteen, 2003: Patterns of major armed conflicts,

1990–2002, in SIPRI (ed.), *SIPRI yearbook 2003: armaments, disarmament, and international security*, Oxford University Press for the Stockholm International Peace Research Institute, Oxford, 109–21

Goldstone, J. A., T. R. Gurr, M. Marshall and J. Ulfelder, 2003: Beyond democracy, 28 February, mimeo

Gutman, R. and D. Rieff, 1999: *Crimes of war: what the public should know*, W. W. Norton, New York

Harris, G., 1997: Estimates of the economic cost of armed conflict: the Iran–Iraq war and the Sri Lankan civil war, in J. Brauer and W. G. Gissy (eds.), *Economics of conflict and peace*, Avebury, Aldershot

Hoyos, C. and J. Reed, 2003: Angola forced to come clean, *Financial Times*, 2 October

IFRC, 2003: *World disasters report 2003: focus on ethics in aid*, International Federation of Red Cross and Red Crescent Societies, Geneva

IMF and World Bank, 2001: Assistance to post-conflict countries and the HIPC framework, Washington DC; available at: www.imf.org

Murshed, S. M. and S. Gates, 2003: Spatial–horizontal inequality and the Maoist insurgency in Nepal, Paper prepared for the UNU-WIDER Project Conference on Spatial Inequality in Asia, United Nations University Centre, Tokyo, 28–29 March

Nafziger, E. W. and J. Auvinen, 2002: Economic development, inequality, war and state violence, *World Development*, **30**(2), 153–63

Philips, M. M., 2004: Afghan financial assistance likely to fall short of request, *Wall Street Journal*, 26–28 March

Reinikka, R. and J. Svensson, 2004: Efficiency of public spending: new microeconomic tools to assess service delivery, in T. Addison and A. Roe (eds.), *Fiscal policy for development: poverty, reconstruction, and growth*, Palgrave Macmillan for UNU–WIDER, Basingstoke, 218–36

Shorrocks, T. and R. van der Hoeven (eds.), 2004: *Growth, inequality, and poverty: prospects for pro-poor development*, Oxford University Press for UNU–WIDER, Oxford

Smith, D. H. and H. Gravelle, 2000: The practice of discounting in the economic evaluation of health care interventions, Centre for Health Economics, University of York

Stern, N., 2002: The challenge of Monterrey: scaling up, ABCDE Oslo Keynote Speech, 17 December, Washington, DC; available at: http://econ.worldbank.org/view. php?id=30289

Urquhart, B., 2003: A force behind the UN, *New York Times*, 7 August

Walter, B., 2002: *Committing to peace: the successful settlement of civil wars*, Princeton University Press, Princeton, NJ

Access to Education

CHAPTER 4

LANT PRITCHETT

Introduction

This chapter is part of the Copenhagen Consensus process, which aims to assess and evaluate the opportunities available to address the ten largest challenges facing the world. One of these ten challenges is the 'lack of education'. As a challenge paper this chapter intends to:

- Describe the scope of the global challenge of 'lack of education' in enrolments, attainments and learning achievement
- Provide an analytical framework for assessing opportunities to address this challenge
- Review the existing literature to produce estimates of the costs and benefits of five classes of feasible opportunities for addressing this challenge.

As grappling with this Herculean task in the limited space available leads to an extremely dense document, I want to highlight the main conclusions up front, and in particular stress how they differ from (at least some strains of) the current international conventional wisdom:

Scope

Defining the scope of the problem of 'lack of education' must begin with the *objectives* of education – which is to equip people with the range of competencies (which includes both cognitive and

non-cognitive skills, knowledge and attitudes) necessary to lead productive, fulfilling lives fully integrated into their societies and communities. Many of the international goals are framed exclusively as targets for universal enrolments or universal completion. But getting and keeping children 'in school' is merely a means to the more fundamental objectives and while schooling is necessary, it is by no means sufficient. The challenge of the lack of education must remain focused on creating competencies and learning achievement.

Framework

The analytic framework for evaluating options must consider both the demand for education by parents and children and the supply of educational services.

Demand

The choices made by parents and children about schooling are based on objectives, constraints and information. Since the vast majority of those not receiving adequate education are children from poor households, it has to be acknowledged that their choices are difficult ones that trade off additional spending on necessities and additional help and labour from children in needed tasks versus more spending on and time devoted to education today. Their choices are also based on the information they have about the benefits to education generally: the abilities, aptitudes and preferences of their children, the quality of the available schooling options.

Supply

A key element that is missing from nearly all existing analysis of the lack of education is a coherent, general, positive theory of government action. Typically in policy discussions and international forums it is simply assumed that the variety of *normative*

With assistance from Michal Shwarzman. I would like to thank, without implication, Barbara Bruns, Michael Clemens, Alex Schlegel and Miguel Urquiola for comments. I would also like to thank Paul Schultz and Ludger Wößmann for their insightful Perspective papers 4.1 and 4.2. I would like particularly to thank Luis Crouch to whom, as usual, I am indebted for seeing clearer and writing clearer than I dared.

reasons why a government *ought* be involved in schooling (e.g. 'externalities' or credit constraints or a concern for inequality) are actually the *positive* explanation of government action. This is simply untenable as a theoretically or empirically adequate explanation of what governments actually do. Assuming perfect governments is as unrealistic as assuming perfect markets. Some plausible positive model of government action is necessary to answer the question of what is an 'opportunity' – a realistic discussion of opportunities must address not just the question of *what* should be done but also *who* should do it and *why* it is not already being done.

Teachers

Teachers are the core of any system of schooling. Learning requires millions upon millions of individual interactions between teachers and students every day. These interactions are effective in generating learning achievement when teachers:

- Know what it is they are trying to accomplish
- Have command over the necessary knowledge themselves
- Are competent in at least one (and preferably multiple) ways of teaching
- Are motivated to perform
- Have adequate facilities and instructional resources with which to teach.

Any discussion of the supply of education has to have a positive model of how it will do this.

Opportunity 1: Physical Expansion

A quantitative expansion of existing school facilities is far from sufficient for addressing the lack of education – and in the majority of country cases will have almost no impact at all. Nearly all of the global lack of education is due to (a) children not attending available schools, (b) children dropping out of available schools too early and (c) low levels of learning achievement while in school. While there are certainly situations in which school availability is a key constraint (e.g. sparsely populated rural areas, junior secondary in some countries), system expansion ('building more schools') as an opportu-

nity for addressing the lack of education tends to be vastly overrated.

Opportunity 2: Improve Quality

Radial Expansion in Budgets

There is almost no evidence that 'more of the same' or 'business as usual' expansions in expenditures per pupil will be capable of improving learning achievement. This is not to say that increases in expenditure *cannot* improve quality or that increases in expenditure will not be necessary, but only that there are many ways in which expenditures have increased without improvements in learning achievement. Expanding the budget is not the solution – it is only a part of a broader solution – and more money in isolation in systems with entrenched and pervasive problems may even make matters worse.

Expand Specific Interventions

While nearly everyone engaged in the debate about schooling acknowledges that more resources are not a panacea – the question is whether budgets can be expanded on specific items in a way that would increase the efficacy of schooling. Nearly every empirical study in developing countries that can establish any relationship between schooling inputs and outputs finds that, starting from the existing pattern of expenditures, more spending on elements of infrastructure, recurrent inputs and learning materials are more cost-effective than raising teacher wages or reducing class sizes. But whether or not sustained changes in the composition of expenditures is feasible in the absence of systemic reforms and within a reasonable total budget is an open question.

Techniques to be Discovered

A second possibility is that there exist techniques or interventions that would substantially improve learning but that these are not known because there has been too little rigorous evaluations of education options. Expanding the scope of rigorous evaluation is certainly a key opportunity because the current level is so low the marginal returns to additional research are high. However, as with selective budget expansions, the problem is how improved knowledge will translate into action.

Opportunity 3: Expand Demand for Schooling through Increased Income or Raising Returns

Since parental income and education are key determinants of child enrolment, expanding education has a cumulative effect which leads to further improvements. Increases in *per capita* incomes will typically increase schooling. This is only worth stressing because, while education sector-specific solutions are often what is under direct policy consideration, government actions that improve living standards generally are almost certainly the surest route to expanded educational attainment.

Government policies that increase the returns to schooling will be key to raising the demand for education. It is plausible that one of the major reasons for the low (and declining) enrolments in many parts of the world is that a stagnant economy has meant low and declining returns to education.

Opportunity 4: Reductions in the Cost of Schooling to Increase Demand

There is no question that educational choices respond to costs and three types of actions have been shown to increase enrolments: (a) reductions in fees, (b) either targeted or non-targeted cash or non-cash inducements to attend school (e.g. school lunches) and (c) making cash transfers from poverty reduction programmes conditional on school attendance (e.g. PROGRESA in Mexico). The key question is whether these programmes are cost-effective, which depends critically on their design characteristics – in particular the extent to which the programme can be targeted to avoid 'infra-marginal' transfers. If infra-marginal benefits – those going to students who could have enrolled without the transfer – are high then these programmes cannot be justified on their educational expansion benefits alone.

Creating the Conditions for Effective Policy Action: Systemic School Reform to Increase Accountability

After evaluating the four policy action opportunities I will suggest that in many cases the key constraint is that the problem in many countries with low levels of education is the way in which the production of schooling is organised – the relationship of accountability and performance simply does not exist. Currently schooling systems are entirely *input oriented* and systemic reform is necessary to create a *performance orientation*.

The key opportunity for remedying the lack of education in the world are actions that simultaneously create:

- Clear objectives for the schooling system
- Adequate financing to achieve those objectives
- Greater producer autonomy to manage for results
- Greater producer accountability for results, which implies a need for transparent, consistent, measures of progress towards the objectives.

There are many ways to do this (in particular, one does not need 'markets' or 'vouchers'). All of the innovative reform agendas:

- Public sector reforms
- School autonomy (e.g. 'charter' schools)
- 'Community' control
- Use of non-government providers
- Market-based ('voucher') programmes
- Public sector reforms
- Political decentralisation

are all ways of changing the system to produce these objectives.

A key difference is between those who believe that the lack of education can be addressed only with 'policy action' – actions taken within more or less the existing structures for organising the production of schooling – and those who believe that 'systemic reform' is the one opportunity that rules them all.

Current Initiatives

The EFA/FTI is what there is, and it is the best there is. The key will be to keep the innovative components and its general well-designed structure from being overwhelmed by the tendency to revert to an 'input oriented' and 'nation-state centric' approach. That is, EFA/FTI can be a force for building elements of output orientation, performance management, autonomy and accountability into schooling systems. It will take enormous force to resist the usual pressures to lapse into the donor-driven 'business as usual' of funding more inputs.

A final two notes of explanation about this chapter. First, this is not a 'review of the literature' in the usual academic sense that the document will describe the literature and the results, the differing methodologies. There simply is not space to cover the broad agenda in this depth. Rather, after reviewing the literature I try and present tables and figures which best convey the key general findings and results – in many instances one could have chosen any number of examples or papers that have the same or similar findings. So the tables and figures I present are typically not the evidence for the arguments I am making: they convey the sense of the evidence for the arguments that I make.

Second, since many of the readers of this document will have no direct experience living or working in the poorer countries of the world in which the lack of education is most pressing I would ask them to abandon now any assumptions based on their personal experience. Citizens of the developing world cannot take for granted what every resident of a rich industrial country does. In particular, many of the same words are used in discussions – but they convey problems of different orders of magnitude:

- When 'poor pedagogical approaches' are discussed it is usually taken for granted the children are not being hit with by the teacher with a stick – not always so.
- When teachers are 'undermotivated' it is usually assumed they at least show up – not always so.
- When 'poor facilities' are discussed it is usually assumed there is at least a classroom – not always so.
- When 'political patronage' is discussed it is usually assumed that teaching positions are not openly sold as patronage – not always so.
- 'Low-quality teachers' is not assumed to *not* mean 'cannot read and write at a fourth grade level' – not always so.

The challenge is the lack of education in the rural areas of India, China, Indonesia, Nigeria, Pakistan, Bangladesh (to name the largest developing countries), the stark reality that parents, children and teachers in these countries grapple with day in and day out that needs to be addressed.

The Scope of the Challenge and a Framework

The 'lack of education' as a global challenge must be understood as a failure to master the many distinct competencies – decoding, cognitive skills, factual information, socialisation – necessary to thrive in a modern economy and society.[1] Basic schooling is a means to acquiring the skills and competencies that contribute to a fuller, more humane, and productive human existence.[2] Remedying a 'lack of education' implies that each individual has *sufficient exposure to learning opportunities to achieve mastery of the basic competencies needed in her*

---

[1] The chapter will not review the justification or benefits of quality basic education (e.g. growth externalities, fertility reduction benefits, enhanced democracy, reduced crime). It will be assumed that the lack of quality basic education is a major social challenge and a legitimate social objective. In particular, I will not assume that there is or is not any particular 'externality' or 'public good' aspect to schooling.

[2] Tertiary education will not be covered except insofar as it relates to basic education. While there are legitimate arguments that tertiary education is increasingly important as the scope of the market expands and as the market for talent is increasingly international, there are three justifications for not addressing tertiary education. First, tertiary presupposes quality basic schooling, as unless a sufficient number of high-quality prospects emerge the tertiary system cannot function. Second, Heckman and Carneiro (2003) have demonstrated that, in the USA, public sector interventions at early stages of learning have much higher pay-offs than either educational interventions at later stages (e.g. college financing) or direct labour market interventions (e.g. job training). Third, pragmatism – I could do either a challenge paper on tertiary education or on basic education – but the issues are sufficiently distinct that attempting to cover both in the space and time available is impossible.

Table 4.1. Estimates of Primary School Enrolment and Repetition, by Regions: While Gross Enrolment Rates are High Nearly Everywhere, Universal *Net* Primary Enrolment is more Rare

Data Income	Gross enrolment (2000)	Net enrolment (2000)	Repetition (2000)	On-time enrolment (2000)
Low-income	102	85	4	55
Middle-income	110	88	10	61
High-income	102	95	2^a	73^b
Region				
SSA	77	56	13	30
South Asia	98	83	5	–
Middle East/North Africa	97	84	8	64
East Asia	111	93	2	56
Latin America	127	97	12	74
East Europe/FSU	100	88	1	67^a
OECD	102	97	2^a	91^a

Notes: Countries with populations of less than 1 million are excluded.
[a] Data are based on between 25 per cent and 50 per cent of the total population of the country group or region
[b] Data are based on between 10 per cent and 25 per cent of the total population of the country group or region
Source: Glewwe and Kremer (2004).

society and economy.[3] What level of schooling is 'sufficient' will vary: some countries may consider completion of a five-year cycle of primary schooling sufficient, others a longer primary cycle, still others have extended 'basic' schooling to include primary plus a cycle of junior secondary. I will use the term 'basic' schooling to encompass any of those definitions.

This first section examines enrolment, grade attainment and learning to document the lack of education, with a special emphasis on the low learning achievement of those in school.

Enrolment

Official data on *enrolment* rates in primary schooling show a varying magnitude of 'out-of-school' children across countries and regions of the world (table 4.1). Sub-Saharan Africa (SSA) lags all other regions of the world with only 56 per cent of primary school aged children enrolled in school. South Asia and the Middle East/North Africa also have well under 100 per cent net enrolment ratios.

The nearly exclusive use of enrolment data in discussions of education is unfortunate as these data

mask three key features – (a) the difference between gaps in *attainment* that are due to 'never enrolment' versus 'drop-out', (b) the *gaps* in educational attainment by categories other than gender and (c) the actual *learning achievement*. The next three sub-sections address these in turn.

Attainment Profiles and their Patterns

The Demographic and Health Surveys (DHS) are a comparable set of over fifty nationally representative household surveys that have been carried out in a large number of developing countries. The advantage of these household surveys over administrative data on enrolments is threefold. First, they have self-reported enrolment which does not rely on administrative data that can often overstate actual enrolment. Second, they have data on grade attainment – the highest grade completed – which is the result of enrolment, repetition, etc. Third, they

---

[3] For instance, the Millennium Development Goals (MDG) target for the universal completion of a primary cycle cannot be taken literally as a goal that children sit in a building called a 'school' for a given number of years. The goals of Education For All include a stipulation that each child complete a primary cycle of 'good quality' (UNESCO 2002).

Proportion of 15–19-year olds who have completed each grade

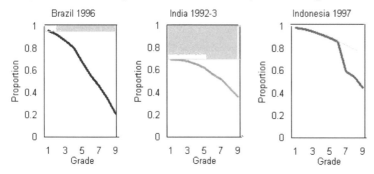

Figure 4.1. *Attainment profiles reveal different patterns of enrolment and progress as differing amounts of the deficit from universal completion are due to children who never enrol (e.g. India), children who abandon schooling within a cycle (e.g. Brazil) and students who do not progress across a cycle (e.g. transition to junior secondary in Indonesia), 1990s*

can be linked with household characteristics such as wealth and residence to give a clearer picture of socio-economic differences in education.

Patterns in Attainment   The data on attainment from the DHS can be used to generate 'attainment profiles' as in figure 4.1, which shows the fraction of the cohort aged 15–19[4] which has completed a given grade or higher.[5] The fraction of children who did not complete even grade 1 – those who 'never enrolled' – is shown as the gap between 1 and the 'intercept' of the graph. The slope of the attainment profile shows the fraction of children who do not progress across any given year. This includes both 'drop-out' within a level of schooling (e.g. primary), including drop-out after repeating a grade, and not making a transition to the next level of schooling (e.g. primary to junior secondary). If the goal is universal completion through some specified grade (say, grade 9), then the total deficit in school years attended relative to the goal is the trapezoidal area.

[4] The ages 15–19 are chosen to balance the relevance of the information to current conditions (the older the cohort the longer ago educational decisions were taken) versus the censoring problems of those still in school. One can produce estimates adjusted for the censoring – all of the basic patterns observed are the same.
[5] All of the attainment profile figures come directly from a World Bank web site maintained by Deon Filmer that contains over 90 datasets, http://www.worldbank.org/research/projects/edattain/edattain.htm

The attainment profiles permit a decomposition of the problem of low *grade attainment* into that due to 'never enrolment' and that due to 'failing to complete a minimal level conditional on enrolment', and show at least three distinct patterns represented by the three countries shown:

- Brazil (cohort aged 15–19 in 1996) shows the pattern of high initial enrolment with high drop-out both within and across levels of schooling. Nearly all of the deficit from grade 9 completion is due to those who once enrolled but did not persist.
- India (1992–3) shows the pattern of low ever enrolment. Of this cohort, only about 65 per cent ever enrolled in schooling – but of those that did enrol, most persisted. Astoundingly, grade 9 completion was *higher* in this period in India than in Brazil.
- Indonesia shows that pattern of high initial enrolment, persistence through primary school and a large drop-off in enrolment across the transition from primary to junior secondary.

Table 4.2 shows the relative role of 'drop-out' versus 'never enrolment' in explaining the deficit from universal completion of basic schooling (defined as either grade 5 or grade 9) across various regions of the world. The very poorest countries in West Africa and South Asia show a substantial fraction of children who never enrol in

Table 4.2. Decomposition of the total years of schooling attainment deficit from either universal grade 5 or grade 9 completion into the fraction due to children 'never enrolled' and those who 'drop out': 'Drop-out' within the primary cycle (prior to grade 5) typically accounts for more of the deficit from universal primary completion that does 'never enrolment' – and even more so for 'basic' (grade 9) completion

Region (unweighted average of available countries)	Never enrolled (%)	Completing grade 5 (%)	Deficit from universal grade 5 completion due to 'drop-out' (%)	Completing grade 9 (%)	Deficit from universal grade 9 completion due to 'drop-out' (%)
West and Central Africa	43.7	41.6	15.3	13.3	33.4
East and South Africa	17.1	55.7	46.8	12.9	69.7
South Asia	27.9	59.7	16.4	27.0	39.5
Central America	9.7	65.6	52.9	25.3	74.7
MENA	17.8	69.8	21.8	30.8	57.1
East Asia and the Pacific	9.1	73.5	53.2	30.5	78.5
South America	1.9	83.4	76.3	42.9	92.0
Europe and Central Asia	0.5	99.2	24.1	83.3	79.6
Representative countries from the above regions					
Nigeria	21.5	73.1	8.5	37.8	37.2
Kenya	3.5	84.3	54.5	18.9	87.4
India	21.6	69.6	13.7	39.0	38.6
Guatemala	14.1	57.4	48.5	23.6	68.0
Turkey	4.4	92.2	25.7	40.0	82.8
Philippines	1.4	92.2	63.0	52.4	90.6
Brazil	3.8	67.8	75.2	21.6	89.2
Kazakhstan	0.5	99.1	32.4	92.7	72.6

Source: Based on Filmer and Pritchett (1998) and Filmer (2004).

school and, hence, a large fraction of the deficit from even grade 5 completion is due to 'never enrolment'. In contrast, even in quite poor regions, such as Central America, East and Southern Africa, and East Asia (this sample does *not* include the richer 'Tigers') almost half of the deficit from completion of grade 5 is due to children who begin schooling but then drop out before completing even grade 5.

Socio-Economic Characteristics and Attainment   The enrolment data can reveal differences in enrolment by residence and by sex. Without links to the household, however, the enrolment data cannot provide evidence on the attainment differentials by socio-economic condition of the households. Filmer and Pritchett (2000) have demonstrated that questions in the DHS on asset ownership (e.g. does the household own a radio, bicycle?) and housing characteristics (e.g. does the household have a separate kitchen, toilet facilities?) are adequate for the construction of an asset index as a proxy for long-run household wealth. As figure 4.2 indicates, there are large gaps in attainment between children from richer and poorer households.

In addition to the gaps by household wealth it is also the case that, conditional on wealth, children with more educated parents are more likely to be enrolled and that rural children are less likely to be enrolled.

Proportion of 15–19-year olds who have completed each grade

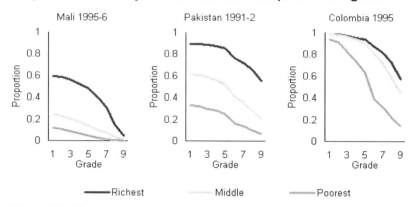

Figure 4.2. *The gaps in attainment between richer and poorer households are substantial in every country of the world, sometimes driven by low ever enrolment of poorer children (e.g. Mali, Pakistan) and sometimes by higher drop-out rates (e.g. Colombia): (attainment profiles of the poorest 40 per cent, middle 40 per cent and richest 20 per cent ranked by an index of household wealth based on asset ownership and housing characteristics*

In some (though not all) regions of the world, girls are also significantly less likely than boys to attend school and to complete basic education.[6] Figure 4.3 shows the attainment profiles from three countries in SSA which show how varied the experiences are, as all three show different attainment profiles, different wealth gaps and different gender patterns. In South Africa it is boys who drop-out much earlier than girls; in Nigeria both poor and rich girls are less likely to enrol but once enrolled their attainment profiles are similar; in Malawi the patterns of boys and girls are nearly identical. In spite of the tremendous importance of gender issues in society in general and within educational systems in particular, I will not address gender issues in any depth here (except in the section on demand-side transfers) because I have very tight space constraints and no value to add to the already enormous literature on this issue.

---

[6] It is worth noting that this appears to be more a *regional* than a *country* issue – that is, the gender gap in education within India varies as much across states as the gender gap varies across countries in the world, and within regions within other countries (e.g. the Sahelian countries) the gender gap varies enormously. It is also worth nothing that there are many countries and regions of the world in which there either is no gender gap or girls receive more schooling than boys.

Low Levels of Learning Achievement

The completion of primary schooling or higher in itself, however, does not guarantee that a child has mastered the needed skills and competencies. In fact, all of the available evidence suggests that in nearly all developing countries the levels of learning achievement are strikingly low.

Figure 4.4 shows the results of all the available recent (since 1984) internationally comparable assessments of achievement in reading, mathematics and science. The examinations have often used widely different approaches to testing and measuring learning achievement and so the figure displays the both the regional distribution and the results separately for each participating country on each of the nine examinations. The figure shows each country's average score, for each assessment, scaled by calculating the standard deviation of scores across all participating OECD countries. Consequently, the figure reports how many 'OECD standard deviations' each country was above or below the OECD mean. In addition a box-plot shows the regional average, 25th, 75th, 90th and 10th percentile using that same metric. These examinations have all been population-based schooling and are cover populations aged 9–10 or 13–15. Obviously, by testing only children in school these results understate both the differences in *population*

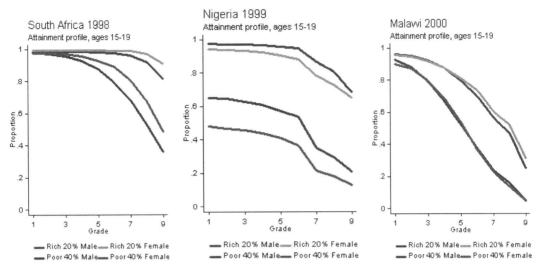

Figure 4.3. *Three countries from SSA illustrating the different combinations of enrolment profiles, wealth gaps and gender differences in attainment: attainment profile by wealth and gender*

achievement – between countries where schooling is universal at these ages, and countries where not all children are still enrolled – and the differences in *school quality*.

Except for two 'regions' – Eastern Europe (EE) and the Former Soviet Union (FSU), and the four 'tigers' in East Asia – the developing countries lag far behind the OECD in learning achievement. Latin American countries are 4.8 OECD standard deviations below the OECD median, countries in SSA 6.7, countries in the Middle East and North Africa 4.7 and countries in East Asia 3.1. These astoundingly large differences imply that the developing countries are not just the lower tail of the OECD, but have performance far below the poorest performing OECD countries. For instance, on the recent PISA, Greece, which was the poorest performing major OECD country, with an average score of 447, scored roughly 2 OECD standard deviations (of 31 points) below the OECD mean of 505. Most of the non-tiger non-FSU/EE developing countries are well below the *worst* OECD country. Thailand at 433 may not be so far behind, but Argentina (388), Mexico (387) and Chile (384) are roughly 60 points (two OECD standard deviations) behind, Indonesia at 367 is 80 points behind, and Brazil at 334 is 113 points behind. Peru at 292 is an astounding 155 points – 5 OECD standard deviations – below Greece, the

worst-performing OECD country, and 265 points behind Japan.[7]

These large differences in country average performance translate into large differences in performance at the top and bottom end of the spectrum. For each of the three subject areas in the recent PISA – reading, mathematics and science – figure 4.5 compares the distribution of student scores between the typical (median) OECD country and a developing country. In assessments of reading competence only 3.1 per cent of Indonesian students scored above the *average* French student. Conversely, the average Indonesian student performed at the 7th percentile of French performance.

---

[7] The low level of achievement is perhaps illustrated by a concrete question. In the TIMSS, the question was asked: 'Three-fifths of the students in a class are girls. If 5 girls and 5 boys are added to the class, which statement is true of the class?' (a) There are more girls than boys, (b) There are the same number of girls are there are boys, (c) There are more boys than girls, (d) You cannot tell whether there are more girls or boys from the information given'. The correct answer is (a). One would be tempted to say 'obviously'. But while 82 per cent of Japanese eighth-graders and 62 per cent of US eighth-graders answered this question correctly, only 31 per cent of South African and only 30 per cent of Colombian students answered this question correctly – when random guessing would produce 25 per cent correct on average!

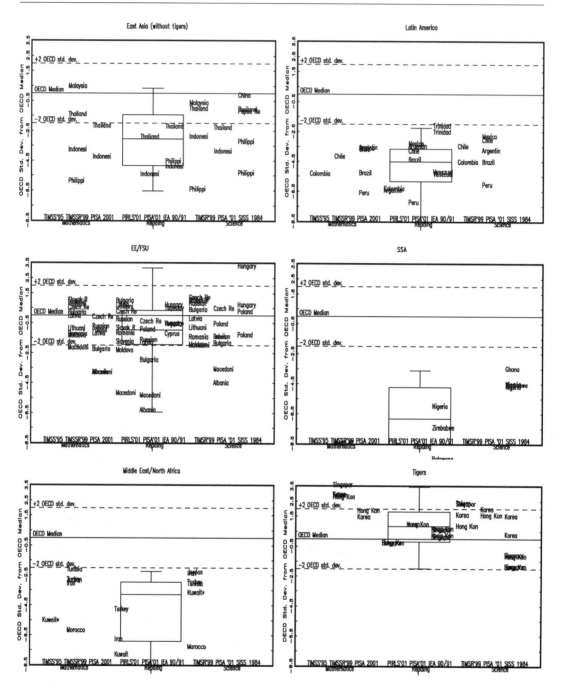

Figure 4.4. *Performance on internationally comparable assessments of learning achievement in maths, reading and science show most developing countries strikingly behind the OECD: performance on all existing international comparisons (IEA, SISS, PISA, PIRL) scaled as 'OECD cross-national standard deviations below the OECD mean'*

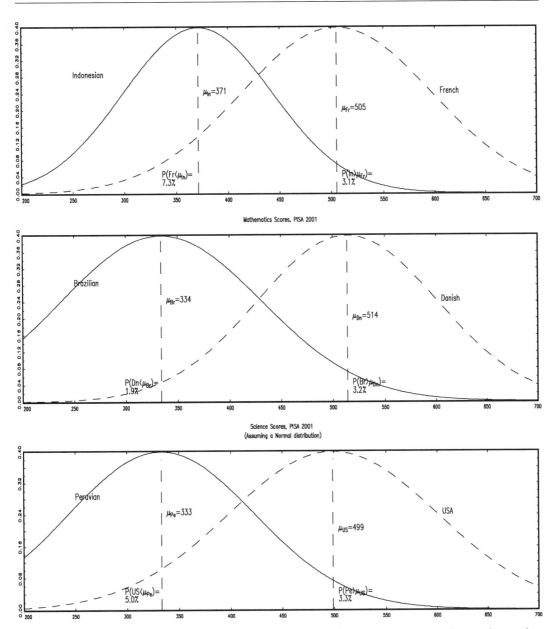

Figure 4.5. *Low average country scores imply that the average developing country student ranks very low in a typical OECD country distribution and that even the best students rank only at about the average OECD student: comparisons of two countries' distributions of scores for maths, reading and science, showing the fraction of students from the OECD below the developing country and the fraction of students from the developing country above the OECD country mean*

In mathematics only 3.2 per cent of Brazilian students could outperform the average Danish student while the average Brazilian student would find himself at the same level of only 2 per cent of Danes.

In science, the poor and lagging performance of US students has been a major concern of educators and policy makers. The fact that US students lag behind Japanese and Korean students has raised serious concerns about the nation's competitive position and ability to maintain a technological lead and has mobilised efforts at increasing expenditures and a variety of education reforms. But according to the PISA results, the gap between US (499) and Peruvian (333) students, is more than three times as large as the gap between US students and their Japanese counterparts. Only 3.3 per cent of Peruvian students can perform at or above even the average the performance of US students which is generally regarded as unimpressive, at best.

There are many reasons not to rely exclusively on international examinations. One might believe that these paint an unfairly negative picture of developing country student performance because the examinations are not based on the curriculum covered, or because 'Western' students are more adept at these type of examinations, or because the exams are 'biased' in one way or another. However, since participation in international assessments is voluntary (based on interest on the part of the country) and requires substantial technical capacity to implement, these results may *overstate* typical developing country performance if the learning achievement in countries that do participate is higher than in those that do not.

The available evidence from other types of assessments of student learning – school leaver examinations, individual assessments and tests done for research – is patchy and hard to compare, but is consistent with very low levels of learning. In an assessment of competencies in Bangladesh, Greaney, Khandker and Alam (1998) found that two-thirds of those who had completed primary school failed to achieve the minimal level. School leaver examinations in many African countries (which rarely appear in international assessments) suggest that, relative to the curriculum objectives, learning achievement is low (table 4.3). Finally, a common problem in research into the determinants of learning outcomes done by economists is that the original tests designed to test student competence are designed based on the curriculum. However, when representative samples of students are given these 'age and grade appropriate' examinations, the results cluster around scores that are consistent with random guessing (making research difficult).[8]

No one who has spent much time in and around classrooms in developing countries would be surprised by the findings of low learning achievement since in most, though not all, countries in the world nearly every aspect of the schooling system is seriously deficient:

- *Infrastructure* is lacking – schools lack sufficient classrooms and necessary facilities
- Even the most basic *instructional materials* (pencil, paper, chalk) and textbooks are often in short supply, and more advanced materials (libraries, science supplies) that would allow 'hands-on learning' are almost entirely absent
- The entire system of recruiting, training, assigning, supervising, and monitoring teachers is '*badly designed*' in nearly every regard.[9]

Part of all of these problems is that within the public sector there is no system at all for managing for performance. The system is entirely *input*-driven. To the extent that the management of the education system works at all, it works to deliver exclusively *logistical* targets – Was money spent? Were schools constructed? Are bodies in place? Often, even this logistical information is not actively used in management. The result of this is that, even though

---

[8] This fact, however, rarely makes it into the published literature because the test results cannot be used econometrically. This is based on conversations with economists who have encountered this problem in Ghana, Kenya and Pakistan.

[9] Actually 'badly designed' is in quotes because this assumes that the design features must be a technical 'mistake' because a benevolent and rational government would never do anything like this. But one view is that the system does exactly what it was designed to do: maximise bureaucratic power over communities and maximise union and bureaucratic leader control over teachers and communities. It is very hard to avoid the habit of assuming that the fault is a mistake in technical rationality.

Table 4.3. Examples of low test performance of children, even after years of schooling

Study	Country/Year	Age/Grade	Description of test	Findings
Greaney, Khandker and Alam (1998)	Bangladesh (1998)	Age 11+ in rural areas	A test of basic learning skills in reading, writing, written mathematics and oral A professional panel specified minimal acceptable levels of performance for each areas based on minimum skills considered necessary to function in the market place	About two-thirds of those who had *completed primary school* failed to achieve the minimum competency level in all four basic skill areas
Banerjee, *et al.* (2003)	India (2000)	Sample of schools in Vadodara and in standards 3 and 4	Pre-test and post-test were administered for schools with and without remedial education assistance The test included a maths section and language section testing competencies prescribed by the Vadodara Municipal Corporation	The raw scores on the exam exhibited a basic lack of knowledge with only 5.4% (Vadodara) and 14% (Mumbai) of *third standard* children able to pass the minimum competencies for maths scoring
National Examination Council of Tanzania	Tanzania (1998–2000)	Grade 7	Primary School Leaving Certificate (PSLC) testing skills in language, maths and general knowledge	In 1998–2000 only 21.3% (language), 19.32% (maths) and 21.95% (general knowledge) of students who sat the exam passed the PSLC
Glewwe and Jacoby (in Lavy 1996)	Ghana (1994)	Primary school	Raven's Progressive Matrices test, which measures abstract thinking ability, reading and mathematics	The mean scores on the simple reading test show scores equivalent to random guessing after *six years of primary schooling*

nearly all teachers are sincere and well-meaning – and many are heroic in their efforts – the front-line providers do not get any support or incentives to produce high learning achievement.

Scope of the Challenge of 'Lack of Education'

The scope of the challenge of the lack of basic education should be conceived as the failure of children to achieve mastery of the basic cognitive and non-cognitive competencies necessary to thrive in a modern economy. Figure 4.6 illustrates the connections between competencies and schooling. The vertical axis represents any measure of a basic competency (e.g. literacy, numeracy, abstract reasoning skills). A horizontal line indicates the threshold minimal target for that competency. The slope of the line indicates the speed of learning (gain in competency per unit time). While most of the discussions of the 'lack of education' suggest that 'years of schooling' are the target, it is useful to stress that the true goal is achievement and that 'years of schooling' are only a proxy. The true targets are *competencies*.

Children come into school with very different levels of school readiness (children A and B begin lower than children D and E) and figure 4.6 illustrates the four dimensions of the challenge of basic education:

- Some children, represented by child A, never enrol in school
- Some children, represented by child B, enrol in school but drop out before completing all of the grades in the basic cycle
- Some children, represented by child C, complete the entire basic cycle but the combination of their

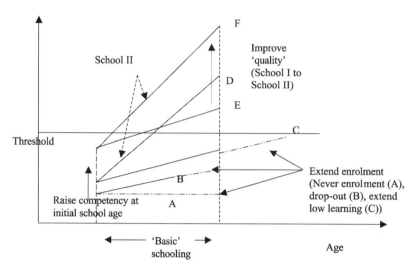

Figure 4.6. *How to raise the levels of competence through schooling: the proximate determinants of learning achievement*

initial level and the low learning achievement in school leaves them below the threshold even after completing basic schooling.[10]

• Other children do achieve the threshold, either because they begin the schooling cycle with high levels of preparation (children E and F) or because they are in a high-quality school (School II for child D).

---

[10] Figure 4.6 can help interpret the apparent deficiencies in learning achievement documented in the international comparisons above. For example, the TIMSS examinations in 1994–5 were given in seventh and eighth grade classrooms. The median gain across this grade for the OECD and 'tigers' was 33 points in mathematics and 41 points in science. For the average Colombian eighth-grader at 385 to reach the OECD median of 500 at the OECD rate of progress would take 3.5 years (= 115/33) of additional schooling. But the gain from seventh to eighth grade in Colombia a gain of gives only 16 points (369 to 385) so to reach the OECD median performance at the Colombian rate of progress would take more than *seven additional years of schooling* (7.2 = 115/16).

[11] If scores are normally distributed, then about 16 per cent of students are 1 standard deviation below the median. I think few would argue that those in the 16th percentile of the achievement distribution among 14–15-year-olds in American schools (which are usually near the median on international comparisons) are not seriously deficient in basic skills and at serious disadvantage in a modern economy.

Table 4.4 shows estimates of the lack of education decomposed into those never enrolled, those who enrolled but did not complete grade 5, who enrolled and completed grade 5 but did not complete grade 9, and finally an estimate of those who were enrolled at age 15 (roughly grade 9) but had not achieved a 'minimal' level of learning achievement. Of course, establishing a 'minimal' level of skills or competence will always be arbitrary, but no more arbitrary than setting up completion of 'primary' school as a target – 'primary' school of five years in some countries, six in others and eight in yet others. Presumably the basis of setting up any given level of grade attainment as the target is the presumption that the threshold level of competencies are acquired in that span (On average? For all who complete?) but judging progress just by grade attainment with no indicator of learning achievement or mastery of competencies is hollow. To construct estimates of the lack of learning achievement I will assume that students more than 1 standard deviation below the performance in the median OECD country 'lack education'.[11]

The framework in figure 4.6 illustrates the *proximate* determinants of increased mastery of basic competencies:

• Increase levels of competency on enrolling in school – 'early childhood' interventions

Table 4.4. Estimates of the 'lack of education' among a cohort of 15–19-year-olds in various lower-middle and middle-income developing countries: In lower-middle and middle-income countries there is an enormous lack of education – almost none of which is due to children not enrolling in school

Country	Cohort aged 15–19 in year	Never enrol (%)	Did not complete grade 5 (%)	Did not complete grade 9 (%)	% completing grade 9 with 'inadequate' learning achievement[a] (more than 1 std dev. below the OECD mean) (%)	Total fraction of cohort that 'lacks education' (either did not complete grade 9 or inadequate learning achievement) (%)
Colombia	2000	1.5	12.5	50.4	73.4	86.8
Indonesia	1997	1.6	10.3	55.2	48.8	77.1
Morocco	1992	34.8	49.5	83.1	75.6	95.9
Philippines	1998	1.4	7.8	47.6	71.5	85.1
Turkey	1998	4.4	7.8	60.0	36.8	74.7

Notes: [a] This uses the TIMSS-R scores for eighth graders on mathematics in 1999. To calculate the fraction of students with scores below 400 (1 standard deviation (100 points) below the OECD median of 500) we use the country mean and standard deviation and assume a normal distribution. This makes a number of heroic assumptions: (a) that scores are roughly constant over time so that the 1999 test represents the cohort 15–19 in the survey year, (b) that eighth- and ninth-grade competencies would be roughly similar.

- Increase learning achievement by lengthening the time (and/or grade progression) in school by:
  - Reducing the number of children who never enrol in school, or
  - Reducing late enrolment (to the extent this extends years completed), or
  - Raise grade attainment by increasing the number of years a child who does enrol completes
- Increase the competency gain per year of schooling.

Analytical Framework for Evaluating Opportunities

What opportunities are available for addressing the lack of education? None of the *proximate determinants* are under the *direct* control of any given international or national or regional policy maker. Rather, the levels of these proximate determinants of competency – early childhood preparation, enrolment, persistence, learning achievement – are all the outcome of the decisions taken by millions of households (parents and children) and by millions of educators.

An 'opportunity' is a *feasible 'intervention'* that affects outcomes. An 'intervention' just means some change – somebody does something differently – which could be anything from greater ex-

penditures, to increased teacher training, to adopting a new textbook, to lower school fees, to systemic changes in the 'rules of the game' in the way schools are run. Any assessment of the 'opportunities' must invoke a plausible model in which the 'intervention' changes the previous decisions made by parents and teachers in a way that leads to more learning (through any of the channels in figure 4.6 – new enrolment, less repetition, longer persistence, or greater learning) in the post-intervention situation.

To evaluate an 'opportunity' one has to specify a *complete, coherent causal chain* from the action to the desired outcome. That complete coherent causal chain has to include a *plausible positive behavioural* model for each agent (parent, child, teacher, headmaster, politicians, analysts) whose actions are on the critical path from policy action to outcome. Simply put, one needs to be able to answer the question 'Why will they do that?' for everyone involved. If one claims that building more schools will increase enrolment, one needs to be able to say *why* the children will show up. If one claims that expanding the budgets will raise learning, one needs be able to say *why* those using the additional resources will use them to increase learning. If one claims that rigorous evaluation will improve outcomes, one needs to be able to say *why* the new knowledge will be adopted. And, if one claims teacher training will improve learning, one needs to be able to say *why* the training will change teacher behaviour.

The analytical framework used to evaluate opportunities will be *demand* – to understand the education choices of parents and children – and *supply* – to understand the decisions of those engaged in the provision and production of education:

Demand

The schooling a child receives depends on decisions taken by the parents and the child. This decision balances at the margin all of the anticipated private benefits against all of the costs. The benefits of schooling include pecuniary benefits from higher expected levels of income and non-pecuniary benefits which include improved well-being (e.g. health) and may include other psychological benefits (e.g. a greater sense of personal worth). The benefits depend on the quality of the available schooling options as well as the current academic inclinations and capabilities of the student – which are affected by previous decisions.

The marginal benefits of additional schooling are balanced against the marginal costs of additional schooling options. The costs include both opportunity costs of the student time devoted to travel – to and from school, in class time, homework – and all of the incremental money costs of enrolment in school – tuition, fees, books, supplies and uniforms. Credit constraints may affect schooling decisions such that investment choices depend not just on increment to discounted lifetime benefits versus costs, but also on current income.

Supply

The supply of education depends on both schooling and non-schooling inputs into a child's education (education is *not* synonymous with formal schooling). The *supply* of formal schooling could come from public, private-religious, private non-religious non-profit (e.g. NGOs), or private for-profit firms.

It is perhaps provocative, but not unreasonable, to think of 'basic schooling' as one segment of a much larger market for 'instructional services'. There is a market for instruction for both children and adults in a wide array of activities – foreign languages, sports, music, dance, religion and trade skills (such as computer training). It is impossible to walk down the street of any even medium-sized city in a growing economy and not be struck by just how many of the small businesses are related to instruction of one kind or another. The typical 'primary school' produces a package of instructional services as a graded, sequenced curriculum delivered through some type of classroom guided instruction involving lectures, exercises, readings from texts, homework, feedback, etc.

It is assumed, as a first approximation, that instructional services are a 'perfectly competitive' industry in the economist's sense and that the industry supply curve of primary schooling is roughly infinitely elastic. Schooling is not particularly capital-intensive, the economies of scale are not particularly large and costs of entry and exit are small.[12] The markets for all other child-related instructional and care services are dominated by small providers, with large firms almost completely absent.[13]

Moreover, instructional services do not rely on factors that are in fixed supply in the long-run, so the long-run elasticity is likely quite large.[14] There

---

[12] The costs per student obviously rise as students per teacher rise. So when the total of students is very small then costs are high. But primary schools with a few hundred students are cost-effective, and there are some arguments that schools above a few thousand students are arguably 'too large' so economies of scale will not make any single school 'large' as a fraction of the market. While there are economies of scale in some inputs into schooling – e.g. textbooks, instructional materials, test development – these can be provided by separate firms.

[13] In the USA the market for child care and other child oriented instructional services – e.g. music, dance, religion, sports – and for tutoring are dominated by small suppliers – for example, no large firm has been able to make significant inroads into the substantial market for piano lessons. Even in universities, where one might suspect some substantial economies of scale, in the USA where there is a competitive market. There are roughly 2 m students enrolled in higher education in the USA, while the highest quality schools have remained quite small.

[14] The major input into instruction is people with sufficient education to become teachers. In very low-income environments teaching may absorb a substantial fraction of the educated population, and hence make the supply of people into teaching modestly upward sloping.

is often a great deal of confusion about schooling being 'supply constrained'. What is 'constrained' is the supply of schooling services at less than their full cost, at a price equal to the long-run marginal cost (equal to long-run average cost since the cost curve is flat) the supply of schooling is almost certainly enormously (if not infinitely) elastic and analogy and historical experience suggest that in the absence of any government intervention primary schooling would be provided by thousands of small enterprises. Schooling is unlikely to be limited by a lack of suppliers of educational services.

Of course, in practice nearly all primary schooling is carried out by producers who provide these services at less than their full cost, including governments and religious groups. The principal lacuna in the economics of education is that, while the bulk of basic education around the world is carried out by the government directly, *there is no empirically plausible, general, positive behavioural model of the public sector production of schooling*.[15] That is, there are a variety of perfectly coherent 'market failure' or 'equity' justifications that normatively justify *some* public action in education. However, assuming that 'normative is positive' – that the reason governments do what they do is because of the market failures or equity rationales for public sector intervention – does not have even surface plausibility as a general model.

One needs a positive model of schooling, not just a general model of political economy, because the features of schooling span a variety of types of governments. I have developed this argument at length elsewhere (Pritchett 2004a) but there are four obvious empirical points that argue against 'normative as positive' (NAP) as even a useful first approximation to a general positive model. First, as has been pointed out by economists from at least Milton Friedman to Caroline Hoxby (2000), 'anything public production can do a voucher and private production can do better'. That is, while NAP can justify some public action, it cannot explain why the chosen instrument of public sector intervention has, nearly everywhere and always, been the direct production of schooling services by a public sector agency. Second, even if NAP could explain some production, it cannot explain why this is – nearly everywhere and always – the only support

for education. Third, using NAP to explain public schooling is not a coherent general model of public sector action, as governments, especially in developing countries, produce schooling even when they are not democracies and do a range of very nasty, corrupt, abusive, or just grossly indifferent to human welfare actions as well. Invoking one model to explain why governments do 'good' things and another to explain why they do 'bad' things is more than just a little ad hoc. Fourth, NAP has a hard time explaining the actual behaviours of government in the allocation of expenditures, either across levels of schooling, or across inputs.

Therefore it cannot be simply assumed – because it is frequently plainly counterfactual – that (a) governments produce schooling because they are intrinsically benign, (b) governments are other than rhetorically committed to universal enrolment, (c) governments are deeply interested in quality schooling, or (d) the public sector produces schooling services efficiently. As with any other actors, the actions, efficiency and efficacy of public sector officials (politicians and policy makers) and producers in the public sector – as suppliers of schooling – will depend at least, in part, on the incentives they face, and on ideologies that have little to do with education as an enterprise for the delivery of cognitive development services, but rather with the control of education as a key for the transmission of socialisation.

What are the Opportunities and how Can They be Assessed?

With the field prepared – delineating the problem as a lack of learning (for which enrolment in school is the means) and delineating a framework of the determinants – we are ready to discuss the specific opportunities often proposed in various literatures in a piecemeal way within an overall coherent scheme. In assessing opportunities there are two

---

[15] A key qualification here is 'general': while there are many theories of why particular governments produce education (e.g. economists who work on 'median voter' models to explain government production – Kremer and Sachryvev 1998; Gradstein and Justman 2002) these suffer from the defect that (a) median voter models are not particularly robust even in the best of cases and (b) it is not obvious median voter models are at all relevant in non-democratic settings.

Table 4.5. Proposed Policy Actions to be Considered as Opportunities to Address the Lack of Education

Supply		Demand	
Quantity	Quality	Cost reductions	Raising returns
Physical expansion	• Expansion in spending per student • Expansion in specific, known, pedagogical interventions (e.g. increased instructional materials, textbooks, teacher training) • Expansion in the evaluation of pedagogical innovations, which are then taken to scale.	• Vouchers • Gender • Conditional transfer • School feeding/health • Late enrolment • School fees	Policy reform *Interactive growth*

fundamentally different alternatives, depending on whether one endogenises the behaviour of the government or not: *policy action* or *systemic reform*.

Four Policy Actions

The approach which is nearly always taken is to assume a government that is motivated to remedy the lack of education and examine the question: 'What policy interventions should a government, which is willing and politically able to acts take to address the lack of education?' This approach assumes that governments *produce* schooling and hence control the supply side directly as a matter of policy and can decide to build more schools or train more teachers or raise class sizes or lower class sizes, etc. Table 4.5 delineates the four classes of policy actions (with alternatives in each class) that will be considered.

• Supply side, expanding the quantity: building or expanding schools
• Supply side, improving quality: (a) increase expenditures radically, (b) increase expenditures on specific interventions, (c) expand rigorous evaluation of interventions
• Demand side: direct (targeted) support to households that lowers the cost of schooling
• Demand side: raising the benefits of schooling.

Systemic Reform: The Fifth Element

The approach of evaluating supply-side policy actions that assume direct government production is unusual for economists. In nearly all other markets economists consider government interventions as taking the form of setting the rules of the game

and of affecting the relative prices by taxes and subsidies or mandates. They then examine the outcomes that emerge from the decisions of consumers and producers. Economists rarely pretend to superior sector-specific knowledge about the technology of production that would allow them to argue for more of this or that particular input into the production process. Imagine how odd the equivalent of the 'class-size debate' would be in other contexts – economists recommending how much labour Dell Computer should hire in computer assembly or the temperature at which steel producers should anneal or the mix of car colours GM should produce. Even with education-related areas such as private firms' on-the-job training, economists assume that firms – as demanders of education – choose the privately optimal amount of training and that competition in the market for training (including the possibility of in-house production) leads suppliers to be productively efficient.

One possibility that needs to be seriously considered is that the desirable policy actions discussed above are not adopted when governments as direct producers of education face the wrong incentives. In this case, the 'wrong' policy action is not a 'mistake' but an endogenous *outcome* of the existing rules of the game and incentives. If existing public sector actions are in fact the stable result of the existing institutional design (a word to describe the formal and informal 'rules of the game') then 'recommending' new policy actions might be pointless. If teachers have been hired by local politicians as a means of providing political patronage, then 'recommending' these politicians hire fewer teachers is itself an odd behaviour.

Alternatively, one could make government actions in the education sector partially or wholly endogenous and focus on 'how reforms of institutional conditions for the provision of education would impact the level of education by changing the opportunities facing demanders and suppliers of education'. I want to stress up front that I am not saying that existing deficiencies mean public sector education is 'unreformable' or that a private market with vouchers is a panacea. After all, as one examines the high-performing countries in education in any given dimension – coverage, equity, learning achievement – one will find countries with a public sector producing education. Teachers are just as much employees of the government in high-performing Hungary, Korea, or Singapore as they are in low-performing Morocco, Nigeria, Peru or the Philippines.

The question is how the system of responsibilities and accountabilities for production are structured. A 'market' is one way of structuring responsibilities – individual firms control all of the production decisions (what mix of products to produce, what production techniques to use, what factors and inputs to hire) and are held accountable by the decisions of consumers to buy (or not buy) their products. A 'centralised hierarchical organisation' is another way to structure responsibilities and accountabilities (internal, top-up reporting).

The question which we address is: 'What pattern of responsibilities and accountabilities and set of policy induced relative rewards will produce high levels of education as the *endogenous outcome* of the decisions of individual producers of educational services and parents and children?' This takes the role of analyst from direct recommendations about production decisions (e.g. class sizes should be higher/lower) to recommendations about the structure of responsibilities accountabilities and incentives from which the correct decisions about class size will emerge.

But once policy actions are endogenous, 'recommendations' about opportunities become problematic. To tackle the question of the opportunities available to address the lack of education, one must ask: The opportunity for *who*? For a national government? For a parent? For an individual teacher? For a headmaster? For a researcher/policy analyst? For an NGO? For a bilateral or multilateral donor?

Evaluating the Four Opportunities for Policy Action

This section evaluates the four classes of policy actions with the question: 'Are there policy actions with high returns in addressing the lack of education'?

Opportunity 1: Supply Side, Expanding the Quantity of Schools

The expansion of education has always had a high priority in development efforts.[16] Clemens (2004) reviews the long history of commitments to universal primary education from at least the Universal Declaration of Human Rights in 1948 to the Dakar Declaration of the World Education Forum and Millennium Declaration of the Millennium Summit in 2000. These rhetorical international commitments to education all implicitly adopt a similar conceptual framework – 'needs are *the* problem, direct government supply is *the* solution, and available financing is *the* constraint' – that pervaded much of the approach to development assistance (Scott 1999; Pritchett and Woolcock 2004). Since schooling is a 'need', the demand side is not considered a key issue and the 'opportunity' most prominently on the international agenda to address the lack of education is an expansion in the supply of government-produced school places. With the assumption that low-income governments are doubly constrained by both low income and low capacity for revenue mobilisation, the key constraint on expansion is financing – so that external financing can play a key role.

This conceptual approach is reflected in some answers to the question: 'What is the cost of meeting the Millennium Development Goal (MDG) for

---

[16] It is a pernicious myth that recent economic research on economic growth has 'discovered' or even 'emphasised' the role of human capital more than earlier approaches to development. While the Solow model had no formal role for education all of the major development theorists (e.g. Lewis, Myrdal) acknowledged the key role of education and knowledge acquisition at least as early as late 1950s – early 1960s.

Table 4.6. Summary of Additional Annual Spending at Constant Average Costs to Reach Universal Primary Enrolment

Estimate method	Average cost per student (No. students)	$110.6 per out of school student (100 m)	Delamonica, Mehrotra and Vandermoortele (2001) 13% of GDP PC spent on all school age children (100 m)	Regional median-level spending (100 m)	Devarajan, Miller and Swanson (2002) Country-level spending (100 m)	% of *per capita* income (country level) (120 m)
SSA	4.94	1.27	2.63	2.15	2.90	
South Asia	2.69	1.58	2.24	1.80	2.20	
East Asia and Pacific	0.89	10.4	0.89	0.38	0.40	
Middle East and North Africa	0.90	5.73	0.87	2.18	2.20	
Latin America and Caribbean	0.73	8.10	1.45	3.23	0.90	
E. Europe and Central Asia	0.30	0.46	0.47	0.63	0.60	
Total	**11.4**	**27.6**	**14.9**	**10.4**	**9.1**	

universal primary completion?' The most straightforward calculation is to estimate the sum, across all countries, of the number of children/years of schooling to reach the goal, times an estimate of the average cost:

$$1) \quad \text{Total cost} = \sum_j (\text{Additional school years})_j *$$
$$(\text{Average cost of a year of schooling})_j$$

Table 4.6 summarises some of the existing estimates for total additional annual resources necessary to put every child who is out of school through primary education. There are different studies available regarding the number of children of primary school age who are currently 'out of school' which provide totals between 100 m (Devarajan, Miller and Swanson 2002) and 120 m (Delamonica, Mehrotra and Vandermoortele 2001) children. The major

discrepancies in these estimates are the different methodologies employed in calculating the average cost per student. Delamonica, Mehrotra and Vandermoortele (2001) use actual average costs (public expenditures divided by enrolment) country by country. The Devarajan, Miller and Swanson (2002) estimate uses four methods: an average cost per student per year of $110.6 for all countries, assuming the average in each country is equal to the regional median, assuming existing country averages, or assuming the average cost is 13 per cent of GDP *per capita* in each country. The range of estimates is from US$9.1 bn – to US$27.6 bn to put an additional 100–120 m children through primary school.[17]

But it is not immediately obvious how to interpret these estimates, as they are only the answer to the question: '*If* children who are not currently attending school *were* to decide to attend school *and* each of those children could be accommodated with an expansion of the current system with marginal cost assumed equal to average cost *then* how much would additional spending be?' But this is not the answer to the question: 'How much will it cost to attain universal primary completion?' unless one believes that the causal mechanism whereby universal primary completion will be achieved is, more or less: 'If you build it they will come'. That is, another

[17] The different assumptions have the obvious implications – if constant costs are assumed across countries it is expensive (US$4.94 bn) in Africa (where actual costs are lower and many children out of school) and cheap (US$730 m) in Latin America (where costs are higher but few students are not in school). Alternatively, if costs are a fixed fraction of GDP *per capita* the estimated incremental cost is higher (US$8.1 bn) in Latin America (which has (relatively) high GDP *per capita*) and low (US$1.27 bn) in SSA (where GDP *per capita* is low).

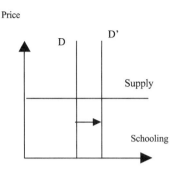

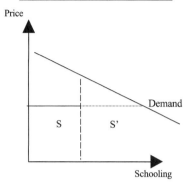

Figure 4.7. *Interpreting the use of current average cost to 'cost' the achievement of the MDGs of universal primary completion: is the casual interpretation* A *or* B*?*

way to interpret this approach is that the supply of public education (e.g. school buildings and class-rooms) is *fixed* and that the demand for education by the household is *constrained* – in the sense that the number of people who would like to be enrolled at the given price of schooling is far higher than the provided capacity – and hence are 'rationed out' in some way or another (figure 4.7). Therefore an expansion in the government-produced supply of education will translate one for one into increases in enrolment and attainment.

What is the evidence about the costs and benefits of an *expansion of the educational facilities (primary and secondary schools) as a means of addressing the lack of education?* Filmer (2003) examines the correlates of child enrolment using the (nearly) identical datasets from the DHS from twenty-one different countries (twenty-four datasets as India, Bangladesh and Niger have two) including child, household and cluster level covariates. These DHS datasets included a 'community'-level questionnaire that included information about the distance from the sampling cluster (a very small unit – usually a census tract) to a variety of facilities – primary or secondary schools, a post office, a market, a paved road, etc. His findings suggest two points very strongly. First, in sixteen (fourteen) of the twenty-four datasets the distance from the clus-

ter to a primary school is statistically significant at the 10 per cent (5 per cent) level as a correlate of child enrolment, with similar findings for a binary variable for whether there was a primary school in the cluster (figure 4.8).

Second, the estimated effects of school construction, while positive, are small, *very* small. The median enrolment of children aged 6–14 in this sample of country datasets (which are by no means an estimate of 'global' totals) is 53.2 per cent. Reducing the distance to a primary school to zero raises the median enrolment to 54.7 per cent – 1.5 percentage points. Alternatively, the use of estimates from a binary variable to simulate the enrolment impact of having a primary school in each cluster raises the median enrolment rate from 53.2 to 55.4 per cent – 2.2 percentage points.

There are methodological pluses and minuses of relying on studies that implement exactly the same regression across a number of datasets which represent a variety of circumstances. The plus is that it increases the generalisability of the reported results, in two senses. First, there is probably enormous publication bias – since a 'failure to reject' is often treated as less interesting that a 'rejection' – so a review of the published literature might overstate the typical correlation substantially. Second, there is clearly a good deal of variability to the

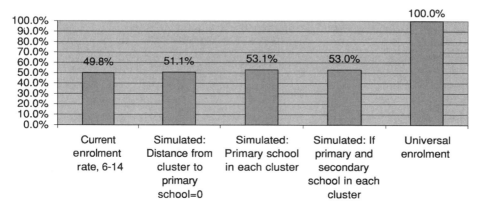

Figure 4.8. *Using the estimated relationship between enrolments and distances suggests only modest progress in enrolments from building more schools: actual and predicted average enrolment rates of children aged 6–14 in the twenty-one countries using estimates in table 4A.1*

results – the linear probability coefficient ranges from 3.1 per cent to 0 (or even positive in the case of Senegal) and a selective review of the literature which emphasised the largest findings could overstate the 'typical' response by a factor of 4, or more.[18]

[18] These points are consistent with the existing literature that finds a mix of strong and small or no effects of distance to facilities on enrolments. Lavy (1993) found that the elasticity of the probability of enrolling in primary school with respect to the distance to middle and primary school is 0.30 and 0.07, respectively. In a study evaluating the relative importance of supply and demand factors in determining primary school enrolment in rural Ghana, Handa (2002) found that increasing school coverage by decreasing the travel time to school (i.e. more school buildings) would have a larger impact on enrolment (13 per cent increase) than income changes (2–4 per cent increase). Based on these studies in Ghana alone, one has no idea whether these results are large or small relative to the typical result. Other studies, such as Holmes (1999) in Pakistan and Burfey and Ifan (2000) in a number of countries find little or no impact of distance.

[19] In his study Filmer (2004) uses fixed effects for the two countries with repeated surveys and common clusters and finds substantially smaller fixed effect than cross-sectional OLS estimates – suggesting that, if anything, the cross-sectional estimates in table 4.6 are too large. Pitt, Rosenzweig and Gibbons (1993) used fixed effects to eliminate the impact of selective placement based on geographically fixed characteristics and find that their fixed effect estimates are different. Duflo (2001) identifies the impact of additional school construction using data from Indonesia that combines the geographic distribution of a large-scale school construction programme in Indonesia (1973–8) with information about individuals' location of birth. She found substantial

The minus is that datasets which are cross-nationally comparable on a large scale typically do not contain data sufficient to address the 'identification' problem. Hence, the step from a reported multivariate correlation – which is perfectly valid only as a descriptive statistic – to treating the coefficient on distance as representing a reliable estimate of an exploitable causal impact which any simulations impact must assume cannot be taken. The bias of the OLS regressions as estimates of causal impact is impossible to predict *a priori* – it could be positive or negative. If schools are located in villages with characteristics that are not included in the regression equation that are positively correlated with the (net) demand for education then OLS will *over*estimate the causal impact. Conversely, if the placement of schools were determined by some deliberately compensatory approach and schools were more likely to be present where enrolments would otherwise have been low then the OLS estimates will *under*estimate the impact of additional construction.[19]

Evaluations of specific interventions are another means of assessing the responsiveness of enrolments. The District Primary Education Project (DPEP) in India has spent 1.62 bn dollars since 1994 to expand schooling, and improve the quality of schooling, in India. Implemented in a phased manner in 242 districts in India – chosen because they had low female literacy – the project is much more than a 'build schools' project. The project

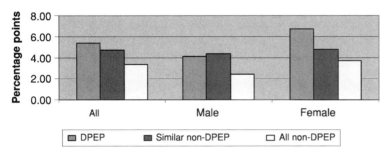

(Change in enrolments of children aged 6-10, 1993/94 to 1999/2000)

Figure 4.9. *Evaluation of a large-scale intervention in India (the District Primary Education Project) in forty-two low female education districts 1994–2000, shows positive, but modest, impacts on enrolment rates*

had many components including financing for non-teaching inputs, teacher training, formation of village committees and mother–teacher associations. Therefore the impact should be much *larger* than a 'build schools' approach. Jalan and Glinskaya's (2003) evaluation finds that enrolments in the DPEP districts did improve but the 'before and after', if one compares the performance of DPEP to either (a) all non-DPEP districts or, (b) similar non-DPEP districts, or (c) uses propensity matching scores, shows the impact of DPEP on enrolments as, at most, about 1–2 percentage points. Figure 4.9 from Jalan and Glinskaya's paper shows the evolution of enrolment in DPEP districts non-DPEP districts and in non-DPEP districts that had below-average female literacy. The improvement in the DPEP districts is very difficult to distinguish from the progress in the non-DPEP districts.[20]

Summary of Opportunity 1: Expansion

On the opportunity of raising schooling through supply-side expansion, the international consensus is in a strange position. Although much of the international rhetoric has a 'if you build it they will come' flavour and the reporting 'costing' exercises of international targets make assumptions that seem to be consistent with this view, almost no international expert on education believes this is literally true (except perhaps in a few of the world's poorest countries). Rather, it is now generally accepted that success depends on *increasing the demand for schooling* through either (a) increases in

quality (opportunity 2), (b) raising returns (opportunity 3), or lowering costs (opportunity 4). What divides opinion is primarily whether these are possible through policy actions or require systemic reform (the fifth element).

Opportunity 2: Improving Quality, Supply-Side Policy Actions

Given the enormous progress most countries in the world have already made in expanding the basic

impacts – children aged 2–6, when a school was constructed, received 0.12–0.19 more years of schooling for each school constructed per 1,000 children. The fact this is compelling, well-identified, evidence about the causal impact of school construction, but that there was *some* impact at least in *some* places, was never in doubt and this does not address whether the OLS are overstated or understated.

[20] Jalan and Glinskaya (2003) use the econometric technique of propensity score matching to identify the counterfactual by asking essentially: 'How much more did enrolments increase in DPEP districts than in districts that were otherwise comparable but did not participated in DPEP?' Across a variety of indicators of performance she finds that the naïve 'before and after' approach dramatically overstates programme impact and the 'differences in differences' estimates of either DPEP and non-DPEP districts. Her best estimates of the programme impact are mixed: (a) the impact on enrolment rates is either small (1.3 per cent increase in enrolment rates due to the programme or, strangely, negative), (b) the impact of girls, who were a special focus, is uniformly small or negative, (c) the impacts were much more positive in one state, Madhya Pradesh, which also implemented two other educational programmes in tandem so, if anything, the estimates *over*state the pure DPEP impact.

physical and human infrastructure of the schooling system, improving the quality of schooling is almost certainly a key to addressing the lack of education, for two reasons. First, as shown above, the fact that a large fraction of the children do not complete basic schooling is due to children who begin schooling and fail to progress and/or abandon school. The *low perceived quality of school* is one factor behind low progression and high dropout rates. Raising the quality of schooling therefore raises the demand for schooling. Second, many children are completing the primary and/or basic education cycle with astoundingly low levels of learning achievement. Raising the learning achievement per year of schooling will benefit not only those at the margin, but also all those who are currently enrolled.

A key debate in education today is between those who believe that increasing expenditures per student (perhaps generally, perhaps devoted to some key input) is key to improving learning achievement and those who believe that without serious systemic reform increases in expenditure are unlikely to be effective in raising learning achievement. As with any starkly stated sides in any debate the vast majority believe some combination of 'both' – that improving learning achievement which is will require both more money and more 'performance accountability' (one of the key slogans of systemic reform). But 'both' is not really an answer, as the *proportions* and *sequencing* in the mixture of money and reform are both crucial – is the mix 90–10? 50–50? Or 10–90? Should money lead reform or vice versa?

A Framework for Reviewing the Literature, and the Example of the 'Class-Size' Debate

Reviewing the empirical literature relevant to this question requires some basics, which are presented in figure 4.10.[21] Suppose there is some connection between learning achievement and inputs, as pictured in figure 4.10a between two inputs – 'teaching services' and 'instructional materials' – where the surface represents the *maximum achievable* learn-

ing achievement from any combination of factors. To maximise learning achievement subject to a budget constraint and the relative price of teaching services to instructional materials producers should be on the surface (that is, be productively efficient for any combination of inputs) and the particular point on the surface should equalise the marginal learning achievement gain per dollar of additional input. This is represented in figure 4.10b by the equalisation of the slope of the budget constraint – which is the relative price of the two inputs – and the slope along the level sets of the learning achievement surface (combinations of teaching services and instructional materials that produce equivalent outputs). For instance, for this particular functional form of the learning achievement surface and the given parameters, the optimal combination of inputs for a learning achievement of 20 is 25.2 units of teaching services (TS) and 12.6 units of instructional materials (IM) (all on arbitrary scales).

Figure 4.10b also illustrates that as the budget available expands, the optimal amounts of the two inputs increase and the maximum achievable learning achievement at the optimal allocation increases.

Figure 4.10c illustrates two common assumptions about the 'education production function' – that the productivity of additional teaching services depends on the level of teaching services and illustrates *declining marginal productivity*, and that the productivity of teaching services is higher the more instructional material inputs are available. Figure 4.10d illustrates that the relative marginal product of the two inputs varies widely. For instance, if inputs are at their optimum for producing 20 (12.6 of IM, 25.2 of TS) then the marginal products are equalised. If, however, at that same level of TS one were only using 20 per cent of the optimal instructional materials the marginal product of additional IM would be five times higher than additional teaching services, and at only 10 per cent of the optimal IM the marginal product would be ten times as high. This means that, away from the optimum, the increment to learning achievement from additional budget can depend completely on how that additional budget is spent.

This simple analytic concept of an 'educational production function' can combined with the

---

[21] Everything about this example is kept as simple as possible to illustrate the points – but everything could easily be generalised in nearly any way, with the basic points still holding true.

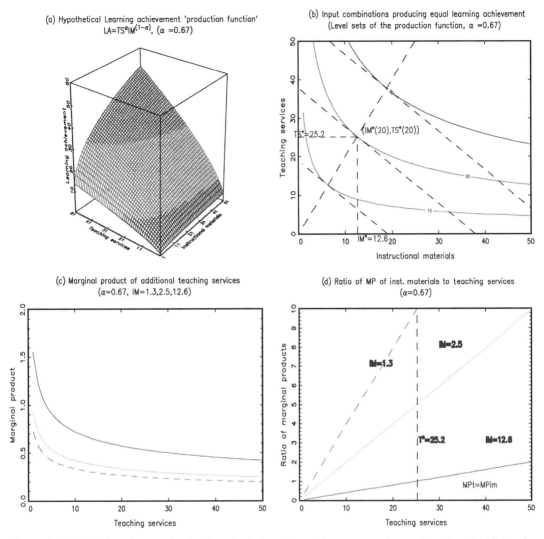

Figure 4.10. *An 'education production function': learning achievement as the productivity of additional inputs*

enormous empirical literature estimating the impact of class-size reductions to illustrate four fundamental points about the methodology and empirical findings:

- Uniformly 'zero' marginal products is rarely an interesting hypothesis
- The 'identification' problem – statistical associations do not estimate 'treatment effects'
- School 'value added' accounts for only a small fraction of total differences

- The observed 'treatment effect' will vary widely, hence a positive model of producer behaviour is needed for interpretation.

Uniformly zero marginal product is not an interesting hypothesis   There is an enormous literature estimating the relationship between class size (or, more broadly, teaching services per child) and learning achievement. A central paper in this literature is a review by Hanushek (1986) which claimed that the bulk of the evidence suggested that the typical impact of reductions in class size on improving learning achievement (usually as measured by some type of standardised test) was statistically insignificantly different from zero. However, no one ever seriously suggested the effect of class size was everywhere and always zero. An analogy would be investigations into rice yields. If the effect of additional applications of fertiliser is non-linear and displays diminishing returns – or even negative returns past a certain point – then the impact of additional increments of fertiliser will depend on the rate from which the increases are made. One can imagine finding that if current rates of fertiliser application are high the impact of additional applications on yield would be quite near zero (or even negative). But this would not be interpreted as 'the impact of fertiliser on rice yields is *everywhere and always* zero'. In contrast, someone might suggest that playing Wagner operas while the rice was growing would increase yields. In this case it is a meaningful hypothesis that the impact of Wagner operas on rice yields is zero at all rates of application (volumes, durations, pieces).

The first interesting question about class size and learning achievement is properly framed as the question of the *magnitude* of 'treatment effects' of class-size reductions, starting from existing levels relative to the cost and relative to the marginal products of other inputs. The debate about 'statistical significance' of a test of zero is therefore misguided from two points of view. First, a 'failure to reject' can either be because the estimated magnitude of the coefficient is small or because of low statistical power. Second, the only reason zero is interesting

is that zero is almost certainly a 'small' effect from any point of view – but the converse is not true – one could easily reject that the class size was zero but also be able to reject that the class size was of sufficient magnitude to make class size reductions cost-effective.[22]

The Identification Problem: OLS Regressions do not Necessarily Identify Treatment Effects

As a statistical technique multivariate OLS uses the covariances in the data to estimate the partial correlations between achievement and class size. However, as economists have long recognised, if the data are generated by purposive choices then it is not clear how to interpret these partial correlations. For instance, if there are good teachers and bad teachers within a school and parents–students are allowed to choose teachers and good students choose good teachers then good teachers will have large class sizes with high-performing students and bad teachers will have small class sizes and the data will suggest a negative link between class size and performance – even though for any given teacher a reduction in class size would improve student performance. Another possibility (Lazear 2001) is that if students are assigned to classes purposively by school administrators then they may choose to place disruptive students in small classes and these students may detract from learning of others so that smaller class sizes may again be associated with lower learning achievement – even though the 'treatment effect' of lower class sizes is positive.[23]

The empirical solution is to use variation in class sizes that is 'exogenous' – that is, that component of the variation in class sizes that is *not* caused by choices of parents–students or administrators – to identify the 'treatment effects'. This has been done in three ways: using exogenous variation in class sizes caused by demographic fluctuations (and/or classroom assignment rules), using experimental variation – or, most recently, using within-school variation in class size across grades.

The use of demographically induced variation in class sizes has tended to produce mixed results. Angrist and Lavy (1999) using the 'Maimonides' rule in Israel, which limits class sizes, find statistically significant and modestly sized impacts in

---

[22] Therefore increasing refinements on what the existing studies show, either from 'meta-analysis' (e.g. Hedges, Laine and Greenwald 1994) or from differing weights on different studies, would be interesting only to the extent they are framed around whether the evidence suggests the marginal product per dollar is higher or lower than other feasible policy actions.

[23] Of course, merely because it is possible to construct a behavioural model in which choices cause the OLS to understate the LATE, does not mean it is plausible that any proposed behavioural model does affect the observed partial correlations and hence that OLS does, in fact, understate the LATE. Moreover, estimation bias is not an 'all or nothing' phenomenon – the behaviour-induced biases of OLS coefficients for LATE may be large or small relative to the application of interest.

some grades and some subjects. Case and Deaton (1999) essentially use the *apartheid* restrictions on residential mobility in South Africa to identify class-size effects (as this eliminates people being able to move to good schools) that are statistically significant and substantial, in a situation in which class sizes were on average large and also quite variable. Urquiola (2001) finds substantial class size impacts in Bolivia using exogenous demographic variation. In contrast, Hoxby (2000) uses administrative data from Connecticut and class-size variation induced by demographics and finds 'high-powered' rejections of zero – that is, she fails to reject zero impact and can reject even modest-sized positive impacts. While this literature produces some positive and statistically significant results the reported results are 'hit and miss' – there are class-size effects in some grades and subjects and not others – with no particular pattern. Moreover, this literature is subject to enormous potential 'publication bias' at every stage of the research.

The use of true experimental variation is much more rare, so that an experimental study that has gotten considerable attention is the Tennessee STAR (Student Teacher Achievement Ratio) Project in which class sizes were reduced to very small sizes (Krueger and Wh˙ .nore 2001). This study found that there were large impacts at the very early grades, particularly for disadvantaged students. An issue we return to in the next section is that randomised experiments in education are not necessarily compelling identification of treatment effects because they are not 'double blind' – the subjects know they are participating in a study. This leads to three types of bias. First, there are potential 'Hawthorne' effects, in which performance might improve just because it is the subject of study. Second, there are potential 'management' effects, in which the involvement of those administering a study assists in the solution of problems. Third, as pointed out by Hoxby (2000), if teachers know that if the experiment 'proves' that the impact of class sizes is large this will lead to lower class sizes and if small class sizes are good for teachers, then teachers will be motivated to work extra hard during the experiment. All of these will lead the 'experimental' treatment effects to be larger than the treatment effects of widespread implementation.

Wößmann (2002) has used a new approach which addresses several of these limitations. He uses the fact that the TIMSS examinations tested students from one class in two different grades in the same school and recorded both the class size of the class tested and the average class size in the grade in the school. This allows him to use both school fixed effects (which should eliminate the bias of school sorting) and also use the grade average class size as an instrument for actual class size (which should eliminate the bias of within-school sorting of students into classes). The TIMSS data allow him to produce school fixed effect instrumental variables estimates for eighteen different countries and implement the same methodology for a number of countries and report all of the results, which reduces 'publication' bias.

These results are clear that (a) there is a large bias in the weighted OLS (WLS) results but that (b) the statistical procedure to address the OLS bias (school fixed effects with instrumental variables (SFE-IV)) produces estimates that are quite small (or the SFE-IV have huge standard errors). These two propositions can both be true because the WLS results give results that are mostly of the 'wrong' sign as they suggest that smaller class sizes are associated with *worse* performance (only 11 per cent in maths and 22 per cent in science are negative). By reducing the bias SFE-IV therefore makes a negative effect of class size into a small positive effect.

The final SFE-IV are consistent with class-size impacts that are typically quite small (figure 4.11). In the TIMSS results, the international standard deviation is 100. The estimated median of the coefficients suggest that a reduction in class size by five students (which is about a 20 per cent reduction from a typical class size of twenty-five) would increase maths scores by about 0.5 point (5*0.12) and increase science scores by 1.5 points.[24] Wößman (2002) uses the calculations of Krueger (2000) to estimate that an improvement of 3 points for each one-student reduction in class size would be large

[24] In elasticity terms, from the averages of twenty-five students and the mean test score of 500, a 10 per cent reduction in class size would cause maths scores to increase by 0.29 point (0.06 of 1 per cent) for an elasticity of 0.0059 and science scores to increase by 0.90 point (0.18 of 1 per cent) for an elasticity of 0.018.

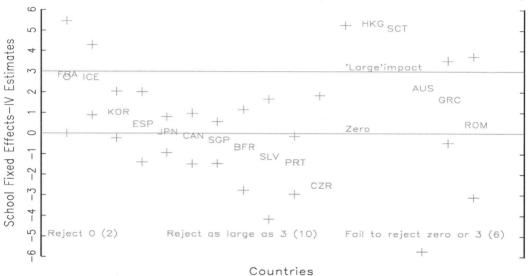

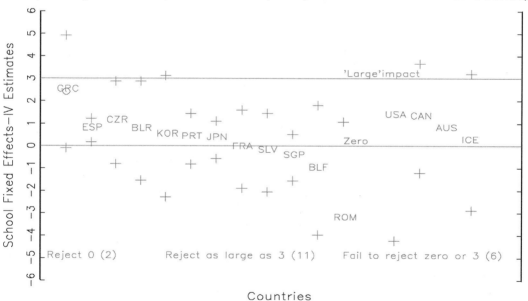

Figure 4.11. *The estimates of the size effect of class size reduction on test performance are usually positive, but quite small: school fixed effect, instrumental variable (SFE-IV) estimates*

enough to justify the cost.[25] The results for the thirty-six combinations of countries and subjects divide into three groups. First, there are four of thirty-six country–subject estimates that are statistically significant and of the 'right' sign – but none of these has a magnitude as large as 3. Second, there are twenty-one of the thirty-six that fail to reject a zero impact but are sufficiently precise to *reject* an impact as large as 3. Third, there are twelve cases in which the estimation technique is essentially uninformative, in that the standard errors are too large to reject either a zero impact or a large impact.[26]

Schools Account for Only a Fraction of Variation in Learning Achievement   A third basic fact that is learned from the class-size debate is that part of the reason it is difficult to establish a clear association between factors at the school level and student performance is that (a) measured learning achievement varies so much across students within schools and (b) so much of school-specific variation depends on the fact that student household background characteristics vary across schools (since children with similar income and parental education tend to attend similar schools). So, for instance, in the PISA examinations in Brazil 55 per cent of the total variation in child performance was within schools. Of the remaining 45 per cent that was due to differences in averages across schools, 25 percentage points were due to the fact that student background varied across schools. This means that the *maximum* amount of student performance that could be explained by *everything* about the schools is 20 per cent of the observed variation in student scores.[27] This poses large problems for the researcher in trying to disentangle the causes of higher student performance, as modest amounts of sorting by parents and students into schools can lead to large bias in estimates of the relationship between school factors such as class size and learning outcomes (table 4.7).

Interpreting the Observed 'Treatment Effects' for Policy Implications Requires both a Model of Instruction and a Positive Model of Producer Behaviour – and the Usual One Won't Do   There are two reasons why moving from observed 'treat-

ment effects' to policy implications requires a positive model. First, almost certainly the magnitude of effects varies as the level of the treatment varies. Second, the treatment effect almost certainly varies widely from situation to situation in ways that depend on other choices of producers.

First, *if* one applies the standard economic model to schooling and *assumes* that producers are choosing inputs and production techniques to maximise learning achievement, then the observed levels of class size should be consistent with equalisation of marginal products per dollar. *But there is absolutely no reason to adopt this positive model of the behaviour of the producers of schooling when they are in the public sector.* That is, suppose that decisions about inputs are affected by lobbying, negotiations and political pressure on the public sector and suppose that teachers are able to mobilise more effectively than the representatives of other inputs (or – more crudely put – teachers strike and books don't). Then one might expect that teaching services will be overused relative to the cost-minimising optimum allocation so that, evaluated around existing levels the marginal product per dollar will be low. The effects of class size on achievement could

[25] This is likely to be extremely generous towards finding that class size is effective as even with all of the assumptions the internal rate of return (IRR) to class size reductions was 5.5 per cent – well below most investment thresholds. Moreover, in their commentary Carneiro and Heckman (2003) characterise Krueger's cost-benefit analysis (CBA) as 'whimsical' (345).

[26] The large standard errors are not particularly surprising as both fixed effects and IV reduce the total variation used, and hence tend to increase standard errors.

[27] It is perhaps worth noting that at least some the motivation of the research into school impacts in the USA in the 1960s was the question of how large a role compensatory school spending in schools attended by African-Americans could play in reducing existing racial inequalities. What made the Coleman Report (1966) so shocking was that he found not just that there was no association between school spending and performance – which implies that no amount of spending will equalise outcomes – but that there were no school-specific effects at all. In many ways these findings have structured all future research: (a) are there school-specific effects?, (b) are those effects associated with observable (and controllable) levels of inputs (e.g. Hanushek 1986), and (c) are those effects associated with other characteristics of the school (e.g. vision–mission, school management practices, pedagogical practices)?

Table 4.7. Schools Account for only a Small Part of Variance in Student Learning Outcomes (Results from Analysis of the PISA Examinations)

	Share of total variance across students due to:			Maximum variation *possibly* attributable to school-specific factors (2)–(3) (4)
	Students within schools (1)	Total across schools (2)	Across schools due to school student background (3)	
Brazil	55	45	25	20
Russian Federation	63	37	17	20
Czech Republic	48	52	4	18
Korea, Republic of	62	38	14	24
Mexico	46	54	32	22
OECD average	**66**	**34**	**20**	**14**

Source: OECD (2001), annex B1, table 2.4.
Note: Share of total variation in student test performance that is (a) school-specific and (b) not attributable to student background differences across schools.

be non-linear so that class-size reductions could be enormously important for learning starting from very high levels – but the effect tapers off and political factors may end up with class sizes that are either much too large or much too small relative to the efficient size.

Second, the effects of class-size reductions are almost certainly heterogeneous in many ways: the 'class-size effect' is not a physical constant. For instance, the empirically observed impact of class-size reductions almost certainly varies by the motivation of teachers for students to perform better. Suppose a teacher usually has thirty students but by demographic chance one year happens to have twenty. If the teacher applies constant effort then one would expect higher performance. But what if the teacher reduces total effort and does not take advantage of smaller class sizes to change learning technology or provide more group work? Then the expected empirical impact of class size reductions is small. Without a behavioural model for teachers, it is impossible to know what to expect.

Another example is that almost certainly the impact of class sizes depends on teacher competence and on the capability of teachers to take advantage of smaller class size to apply superior teaching methods. If learning achievement is low because the teacher does not know the material (as has been shown in Pakistan) then reducing class size is unlikely to matter much. Also, it may well be that reductions of class sizes to very small facilitates the application of 'student-centred' learning in which teachers tailor the teaching to the individual student's learning style. This could lead to large improvements in performance at small class sizes with very highly capable teachers but no impact at small class sizes with poorly trained teachers. So, for instance, it would not be contradictory to observe the highest quality education choosing small class sizes (e.g. expensive private schools in the USA) and still find no impact of small class sizes resulting from low attendance in rural areas of Pakistan.[28] There is no reason to believe that the existing observations on learning achievement and

[28] As a final note, there is a slogan which is popular among some economists that: 'one rigorous study trumps a thousand bad regressions' but which is just so deeply unscientific as to be ridiculous. A fundamental of the *physical* sciences are 'invariance' principles – that physical laws are invariant with respect to 'translations' (Feynman 1989). If the slogan were applied to estimates of some physical constant such as the charge of the proton or the gravitational constant is the best estimate. But *none of this applies to schooling* and especially not schooling *undertaken by public sector, about which there is no widely accepted positive behavioural model.* Suppose one accepted the STAR experiment results that reductions in class sizes (a) to very small levels, (b) in early grades, (c) in Tennessee (with all that implies about availability of school infrastructure, class materials, quality of teachers) and about the overall quality of public sector governance had

class size are on the 'education production function' so the *empirically observed* treatment effect may have nothing to do with the *possible* treatment effect.

Opportunity 2A: Radial Budget Expansion

As with supply-side expansion, international policy discussions of options for improving quality tend to be dominated by assumptions that expanding budgets is necessary and sufficient for quality expansion – even though no one actually believes that to be true. There are countless examples of countries' 'commitment' to education measured by the share of GDP devoted to spending and the 'quality' of schooling proxied by crude indicators such as class size. Economists are predisposed to believe that expenditures are positively related to outputs because of their positive theory of producers. If producers are maximising cost, expenditures must expand to increase output. However, this simple theoretical intuition does not apply for the relationship between public sector schooling costs and learning achievement for so many reasons.

This section asks the question: 'When and where does expanding the budget *alone* – in the absence of changes in the composition of expenditures, system reform, or demand shifts – constitute an opportunity for remedying the lack of education?' The combination of (a) the facts on measured learning achievement and schooling expenditures from time series, cross-national, cross-regional, across schools and (b) a review of the educational production function literature suggest this is only rarely a promising activity.

Expenditures and Learning Achievement

There are four literatures that examine different aspects of the covariation between learning achievement (almost always as measured by student learning achievement on standardised tests) and expenditures per pupil: over time, cross-national, cross-regional and across schools.

Time Series Hanushek (1995a) details two major trends in schooling from the 1970s to the 1990s – rising per-pupil expenditures and stagnant test scores as measured by the intertemporally comparable, national representative National Assessment of Economic Progress (NAEP). This implies that the ratio of 'test question correct per [real] schooling expenditure per pupil' (TQC/SEP) was falling sharply.[29] While this kicked off a sharp debate in the USA about the explanations for these trends, most of this debate focused on US-specific explanations.

Wößmann and Gundlach (1999) and Wößmann, Gundlach and Gmelin (1999) combine a clever insight with one new set of data to produce a striking finding that the TQC/SEP decline is general in the OECD and East Asian countries examined. Their clever insight was that if the USA has an intertemporally consistent evaluation of learning achievement and if the USA has participated in multiple internationally comparable assessments of learning achievement, then estimates for the evolution of the learning achievement of a large number of countries can be recovered by linking the two datasets. The new set of data are calculations of the 'real' expenditures per pupil – where the deflator for schooling expenditures is based on the price of 'productivity-resistant services' so that these real expenditures

substantial effects primarily on (d) disadvantaged students. How does this empirical knowledge inform decisions to reduce class size from fifty to forty at for median income students in grade 4 in a province of Pakistan? If one adopts equal methodological scepticism about generalisability as economists have adopted about identification then a rigorous experiment tells *absolutely nothing* outside the conditions and ranges in which the experiment is done. There is simply no scientific reason to believe the experimental STAR estimates in Tennessee or the well-identified 'Maimonides' rule estimates in Israel are better predictors of the impact of a reduction in class size in Pakistan than the simplest possible OLS regression done on Pakistani data, since there are two fundamentally different reasons why the two methods might misestimate the 'treatment effect.' While a good study trumps a better study *of the same thing*, rarely do we have such luxury to pick and choose, and a review of the literature has to do its best to incorporate all existing findings. That said, given the bias in simple OLS regressions it does make sense to pay careful attention to identification in assessing the implications of any study.

[29] While some would refer to this as a 'productivity shock' this presupposes that the test measure is the desired 'product' of schooling – which is far from obvious – so I will use the deliberately awkward TSC/SEP to be clear this is a descriptive statistic which does not presuppose any given explanation nor normative conclusion.

Table 4.8. Real Expenditures per Pupil have Risen Enormously while Measured Learning Achievement has Stagnated...

Country	Estimated change in the assessment of maths and science learning achievement (1970–94) %	Estimated change in real expenditures per pupil (1970–94) %	Estimated change in 'test questions correct per school expenditures per pupil' %
Sweden	4.30	28.50	−23.20
USA	0.00	33.10	−33.10
Netherlands	1.70	36.30	−34.10
Belgium	−4.70	64.70	−72.80
UK	−8.20	76.70	−92.50
Japan	−1.90	103.30	−107.20
Germany	−4.80	108.10	−118.60
Italy	1.30	125.70	−122.80
France	−6.60	211.60	−233.70
New Zealand	−9.70	222.50	−257.20
Australia	−2.30	269.80	−278.50

Source: Adapted from Wößman (2002, tables 3.3, 3.4).

already take into account that the costs of services rise relative to manufactures because of slow productivity growth (the Baumol effect). The striking finding produced is that TQC/SEP decline is not a US-specific phenomena, rather the opposite – the fall in the USA is second smallest of all OECD countries.

As shown in table 4.8, the rise in real per-student expenditures (where 'real' uses a services deflator that already accounts for a general service sector-specific Baumol effect) is enormous. At the same time, no country shows a large increase in measured learning achievement. By these estimates maths and science learning declined modestly in France – while expenditures tripled. Although, as discussed above, Japan leads the USA in the *level* of learning achievement the *gap* has not widened, which implies the growth of achievement is about the same – even though expenditures per pupil have doubled in Japan.

While the time-series evidence is specific to the OECD – and a few high-performing East Asian countries – the general point that expenditures per pupil *can* expand enormously with very little impact on measured learning achievement is probably true elsewhere as well.

Cross-National/Cross-Regional   There are large differences in the performance of countries on the international examinations but very little of that variation is associated with differences in expenditures per pupil – or any other physical indicator of educational systems such as pupil–teacher ratios or teacher wages – either unconditionally or after conditions for basic background factors. Hanushek and Kim (1995) and Hanushek and Kimko (2000) find no statistically significant correlation of test scores and pupil–teacher ratios, current expenditures per pupil, or expenditures on education as a fraction of GDP. Barro and Lee (1997) also conduct cross-national estimates of the correlates of cross-national examination performance and find that the pupil–teacher ratio, expenditure per pupil or average teacher salary are not correlates of maths or science score performance, while for reading scores there were positive associations with pupil–teacher ratios and teacher salary but not with education expenditures per pupil.

There is also very little connection between spending and enrolment and attainment outcomes. Just to mention two of many studies, Jayasuriya and Wodon (2002) find no connection between net primary enrolments and education expenditures

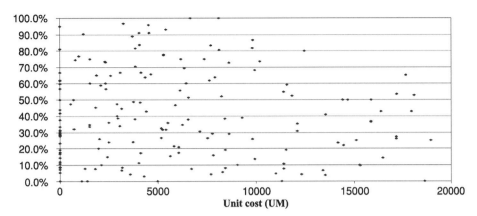

Figure 4.12. *Primary school success varies hugely, despite similar unit costs: pass rate (per cent) at the end of primary education exam (vertical axis) versus unit cost (horizontal axis)*
Source: Mingat (2003).

per capita (controlling for adult literacy); Roberts (2003) finds no connection between gross enrolment rates or primary completion rates and either primary spending as a percentage of income or primary spending per pupil as a fraction of *per capita* income.

Of course, the methodological problems are so overwhelming that it would be hardly worth mentioning these type of results if these same crude indicators that show no correlation with learning outcomes (e.g. 'class size' or 'spending per pupil') were not constantly used as if they were reliable proxies for school quality.

Cross-Schools Wößmann (2002) uses the massive dataset (over a quarter of a million observations) from the TIMSS to examine child, school and country-specific factors associated with performance. He finds that none of the standard measures of school inputs – expenditures per child, class size – is associated with improved performance. There are an enormous number of studies that relate performance to school-level factors, almost none of which find that expenditures are an important independent determinant of school performance (particularly once student background characteristics, which tend to be strongly correlated with school expenditures are controlled). On one level, it is hardly worth saying that *total* school expenditures have little correlation with performance in public sector systems, for three reasons.

First, schools are not managed at any level to think of cost-effectiveness as a *performance measure* – it is actually rare for schools to even know unit costs, much less manage to minimise the cost of a given performance (or maximise performance for a given cost). Second, in standard public sector systems individual schools do not typically have control over their total expenditures, which are mainly driven by teacher wages that are typically beyond the managerial control of the schools themselves. Third, since student background accounts for so much of the variability in performance the school effect itself is typically quite small, the amount that can be empirically attributed to any school-specific features at all is necessarily even smaller, and the fraction of the variance attributable to one factor like total expenditures smaller still (figure 4.12).

Equalisation of Marginal Learning Achievement Gain per Dollar Spent across Inputs The strongest case for a budget expansion is if schools are already both productively efficient and have allocated their expenditures efficiently. Otherwise, it makes sense to allocate any available incremental expenditures to inputs with higher marginal product per dollar (table 4.9).

Summary on Budget Expansion There is an obvious contradiction between the surface interpretation of the rhetoric in the development community

Table 4.9. Implications of Productive Efficiency in the Allocation of Inputs

Implication of allocation of inputs for productive efficiency	Source of test	Findings (Caveats)
Marginal product per dollar should be equalised across all inputs	Rigorous evaluation of interventions	No rigorous evaluation in a developing country has failed to reject equal marginal product per dollar (e.g. Harbison and Hanushek 1992 in Brazil) (So few have been done)
	Cost-effectiveness calculations from econometric studies	Typical finding is that the marginal product of teacher-related inputs is small and non-teacher-related inputs have cost-effectiveness between one and three orders of magnitude higher. (Identification across different inputs difficult to impossible)
	Non-experimental variation, 'confirmation frequencies'	Reviews of the literature that do counts find that measures of infrastructure adequacy and availability of learning materials are much more likely to have 'right sign/statistically significant' associations with learning achievement than expenditures, class size, teacher wages, or teacher formal qualifications (Hanushek 1986; Fuller and Clark, 1994) (Most of the studies reviewed had no plausible identification strategy)
If resources are used efficiently then only total expenditures should matter – not sources	Variations in degree of finance from local sources	Financing from local sources has more impact on performance than centrally provided financing. (e.g. Birdsall and Orivel 1996 in Mali James, King and Suryadi 1996 in Indonesia). The composition of inputs financed by central and local sources differs systematically – with central sources providing teachers and local sources providing other inputs. (Inputs from communities could easily be correlated with other community characteristics that promote high-quality learning)
If resources are used efficiently in both public and private sector then input allocation should be equal and performance per dollar equal.	Comparisons between private and public schools	Even after controlling for selection effects private schools tend to produce higher learning achievement with fewer resources (e.g. Jimenez and Lockheed 1995 on five countries) Public and private schools tend to have very different input mixes (Alderman, Orazem and Paterno 1996 in Pakistan). (Very difficult to control for selection of students into private or public schools)

Source: Based on Filmer and Pritchett (1997, tables 1–6).

and the existing evidence. The conventional wisdom seems to be inputs, inputs, inputs: a country's 'commitment' to education can be judged by *spending* (as a fraction of GDP or total government expenditures); educational spending should be '*protected*' during budget adjustments; *debt relief* is important because it will allow more spending on education; *international goals* for education are crucial because they will allow more donor finance for spending on education. Yet I say that this 'seems to be' the conventional wisdom because my perception is that no one actually engaged with education actually believes that spending *per se* is sufficient to raise the level of education. Everyone is aware that

none of the available evidence supports the view that the major, or even a sizeable, portion of the existing variation in schooling performance (either in attainment or learning achievement) – across time, countries, regions, schools – is accounted for by differences in spending. No study has ever tested any implication of the hypothesis that public sector production is productively efficient and failed to reject it. There is agreement that in many countries they are far from the 'frontier' in either productive or allocative efficiency.

The current conventional wisdom among practitioners is that additional spending will be necessary, but that it will serve to raise attainment and learning

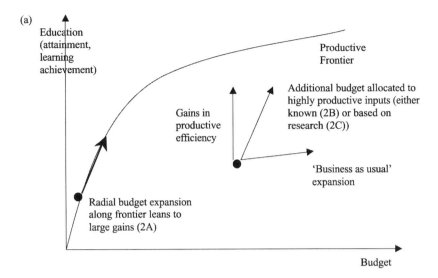

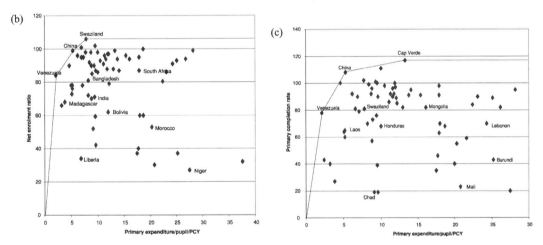

Figure 4.13. *If countries are on (or near) near the efficiency frontier and spending is low, then radial budget expansions can have substantial impact: but if countries are not efficient then 'business as usual' expansion is of indeterminate impact and improvements in productivity or allocative efficiency are more promising*
Source: Robert (1993).

outcomes only if:

(a) it is devoted to categories of expenditure that are *highly productive* – including either better productive efficiency or better allocation across inputs (opportunity 2B)
(b) if it is devoted to, or combined with, *new* techniques and pedagogical approaches (opportunity 2C)
(c) it is accompanied by *systemic reform*.

Opportunity 2B: Quality Improvements, Supply-Side: Expanding Chosen Known Specific Elements

I will devote only a relatively short space to what most might regard as the single most important element of improving education: identifying and expanding the particular actions that lead to increased *learning achievement*. That is, while most will admit that budget expansion will not necessarily improve performance, nearly everyone has a 'favourite' input, action, or activity that if the incremental resources were devoted to it then budget increases would lead to greater attainment and learning achievement. There are three classes of inputs that are frequently identified as promising in the voluminous empirical literature relating measures of student learning to inputs (see reviews of the 'education production function' literature by Fuller and Clark 1994; and Hanushek 1996 and, on a slightly different tack, the literature in Pritchett and Filmer 1997):

- *Instructional materials*   Many studies find that some measure of instructional materials in either the classroom (presence or absence of textbooks, for instance) or school (having a library) is associated with higher test scores. Many education projects and programmes build on those findings and focus on increasing those identified inputs.
- *Key infrastructure*   Many studies find that some measure of infrastructure (e.g. having desks, having latrines, having running water, having windows) is an important determinant of progress. Again, many education projects and programmes are structured around not just school construction but school upgrading of one type or another.
- *Teacher training*   Many studies find that some measure of teacher knowledge of the content and/or pedagogical practices is associated with higher test scores. Nearly every educational project or programme has some component for pre-service or in-service 'teacher training' that attempts to improve teacher content or knowledge.

Conclusion on Expanding Known Quality Improvements

I will not even attempt to review this literature; rather I will go straight to four points:

- First, there are almost certainly interventions in each of these dimensions, which, if successful in their intermediate objectives (e.g. raising textbook availability, improving teaching) will have substantial, cost-effective, impacts on attainment and learning achievement.
- Second, what the particular interventions are will vary across countries, regions, schools, etc. Since

the 'learning achievement' function is so complex and depends on the presence of a variety of inputs, the *impacts will vary*.

- Third, while 'associations' are easy to establish using the data at hand the question of *causal* impact has been underplayed and the findings from studies using randomisation find that the usual methods (OLS or HLM) would produce estimates that were quite wrong as predictors of programme impact (see p. 213 on Kenya). This goes back to the issue that, since most of the observed variation in the data is the result of choices made by parents or producers, without a positive model and 'identification' the associations are consistent with a very wide range of underlying causal models. For instance, lack of key inputs may just be a proxy for a dysfunctional school situation. Take the example of textbooks. Suppose in the data there is a strong correlation of textbook availability and scores in a cross-section of schools. This could be because the schools that did not have textbooks were dysfunctional in a variety of other ways. If this is the case, then a programme that gave textbooks to all schools might have no impact on performance – even if it saturated the school with books – in spite of the strong positive association of textbooks and performance because the incremental textbooks would all be used in a still dysfunctional school and hence might have little or no impact.
- Fourth, the key pragmatic objection is whether programmes designed at eliminating 'bottlenecks' to learning by devoting incremental resources to high-productivity activities can be successfully implemented. For instance, the world is littered with projects and programmes for teacher training that had no impact on subsequent teacher classroom practices (see box 4.1 for a particularly depressing example from Pakistan).

In examining the claims that incremental spending on this or that activity would increase scores enormously, one needs to ask the question: 'Then why is this not happening already?' Convincing evidence that some inputs have incredibly high marginal products relatively to other inputs is at the same time convincing evidence that existing producers are not efficient (since the implication of efficiency is equalisation of marginal products

Box 4.1 The Dismal State of Teacher Training, Pakistan, early 1990s

Teacher training in this province is a mockery. We should close down the teacher training institutes and stop this nonsense. I have been teaching in a BA/BEd program for many years and see no signs that I have any impact on the students I teach. (University education instructor quoted in Warwick and Reimers 1995)

Most inmates of this system [two teacher training institutes] have no respect for themselves, hence they have no respect for others. The teachers think the students are cheats, the students think the teachers have shattered their ideals. Most of them are disillusioned. They have no hopes, no aims, no ambitions. They are living from day to day, watching impersonally as the system crumbles around them. (Nauman 1990)

A national survey of Pakistan's primary schools suggests that these anecdotal accounts are only too true. Survey data on teaching practices 'provide no basis for statements that . . . teacher training makes a substantial difference to how teachers teach'. A 1998 study of teacher training suggests that 'staff and faculty are professionally untrained, political interference is common, resources and facilities are poor and badly utilised, motivation and expectations are low and there is no system of accreditation to enforce standards'. Embedded in an education system that was fundamentally unaccountable and lacked any outcome orientation, teacher training reflected worst practice.

Sources: **Warwick and Reimers (1995); Kizilbash (1998, p 45); Adapted from World Bank (2004)**

per dollar). But if the system is such that there are no built-in tendencies towards *productive efficiency* then why will a particular intervention to raise efficiency with no changes in systemic incentives succeed? I am not arguing that such a case can *never* be made – there are numerous successful piecemeal initiatives to act as counterexamples – but it cannot simply be assumed that piecemeal policy action can be effective as the many failures attest.

Opportunity 2C Quality Improvements, Supply-Side: Experimentation with Rigorous Evaluation

A third opportunity is to improve the quality of schooling through empirical research which investigates the impact of interventions, better establishes the determinants of learning and evaluates new techniques for raising learning. If successful in raising quality, this would increase the learning achievement of students currently enrolled and probably increase retention of students who now enrol but abandon early.

Rigorous evaluations of the impact on learning achievement of a variety of actions – both the proximate determinants of learning and the institutional/incentives determinants of the proximate determinants – are notable by their almost complete

absence in nearly all countries. Work has begun to apply randomised evaluations to educational interventions, including a series of experiments in rural Kenya led by Michael Kremer involving the effect of subsidies (free uniforms), textbooks, teacher incentives, class size and health interventions (deworming). These evaluations confirm almost none of the 'conventional wisdom' about education. In fact, in a paper that summarises almost a decade of experience Kremer, Moulin and Namanyu (2003) concludes that (a) fees are too high, (b) class sizes are *too small*, (c) school 'choice' practised by parents has perverse incentives for headmasters, and (d) most programmes that provide additional inputs for 'poorly performing' schools are wrongheaded – and that all of these outcomes are *endogenous* to the institutional conditions for the production of education in rural Kenya (Kremer, Moulin, and Namanyu 2003).

Evaluations often find that what 'everyone knew' would work – doesn't. They also sometimes identify actions that have enormous impacts. A randomised evaluation of a tutoring programme created by a local NGO and targeted at students who are lagging behind in early grades is enormously effective and cost-effective (Banerjee, Duflo and Linden 2003). In addition to evaluating specific techniques, there have been increasing attempts to

[30] There is an ongoing debate among US academic economists. One group seems to believe the identification problem is so severe that essentially only randomisation can produce clean estimates as otherwise the 'instruments' will be weak or strong 'structural' assumptions will need to be made. Another group believes the estimate of structural models is both possible and essential to understanding the economics of the intervention in any case.

[31] There are many ways in which 'false positives' could be produced, particularly in complex experiments that alter incentives (e.g. school autonomy). For instance, if talented managers are attracted into managing the experiments they might also, in the course of implementing the experiment, have impact on improving the 'treatment' schools through their contacts. Or, as Hoxby (2000) argues may be true for the Tennessee STAR class-size experiments, teachers–administrators might make extra temporary effort to make an experiment succeed if its success serves their long-run interests.

[32] I would like to quote at length from a comment from one reader of an earlier draft, as it is a succinct expression of a valid objective to a bandwagon of randomised evaluation:

> I just don't think economists should be production engineers for state monopolies. The idea behind all this stuff is that if we can discover the 'magic bullets' that work, then we can make everyone take the magic bullet. But that's a really, really naïve view of how anything, at any point in history, has ever improved. In fact, things improve because of Schumpeterian innovation and destruction. Even good bureaucracies improve that way. Good bureaucracies, including effective private ones like McDonald's, observe what effective real administrators do, and then force others to do it. The market does it via the pressure of competition, and because in good markets entrepreneurs can imitate the technology other entrepreneurs discover (including the organisational technology). We tend to forget the lesson that the information that has to exist is not just about the quality of what is produced, so that consumers can make wise decisions, but about production technology, so that entrepreneurial rents are bid away. Note that you have to have a real feel for the actual technology and human interaction for how this happens. Entreprenerial information is often diffused through employees. They often do this by poaching employees from each other. Observe how technique (say, a better filing system, or a better way to make proposals) spreads from firm to firm, by the interchange of employees. Production technologies in one firm are always set up by someone who either discovered it or, more often, brought it from another firm. Anyway, a good (public or private) bureaucracy forces principals to adopt practices by laterally disseminating what it observes works, not by making grandiose experiment to discover what works. And a good bureaucracy ratchets things up by allowing enough mavericks to do things a little differently, so that they can learn from them

investigate the impact of other innovations such as greater school autonomy in Nicaragua (King and Ozler 1998), 'vouchers' to secondary school students in Colombia (Angrist et al. 2002).

Not all evaluations need be randomised to be rigorous. The key is to have a research method that is capable of identifying the *true causal impact* of a particular intervention or policy action. The comparison of 'before and after' is simply inadequate to estimate the 'with and without' impacts that are needed.[30]

There are, however, four questions about the use of rigorous evaluation as a key to improving education: two methodological and two about impact. First, there is a *methodological problem* even with 'randomised' experiments, which is the lack of a true 'double blind' control that allows for a control of 'placebo' or 'Hawthorne' effects, which tend to find false positives of *any* intervention.[31]

Second, the results of randomised evaluations cannot be applied with any confidence *outside the range of the experiment*. If the effect under study is plausibly homogeneous across time and space, and one rigorous study can be extrapolated to a variety of contexts, then the benefit-cost ratio (BCR) for evaluation is enormous. If, however, the impact of specific interventions varies widely from place to place, then the benefits of any given study are smaller – potentially dramatically smaller. The mixed evidence reviewed above about one seemingly simple determinant of learning – class size – suggests large heterogeneity in its effects. If reducing class size is essentially a different 'treatment' depending on a host of other factors – teacher quality and motivation, availability of complementary inputs, etc. – then the cost-effectiveness of evaluation is more difficult to defend.

Third, the principal costs of randomisation are *political* and *organisational* risk. Few governments have proved willing to participate in randomised experiments. Nearly all of the experiments to date have been carried out either with NGOs (e.g. Kenya, India) or implemented outside of mainstream agencies (e.g. Colombia). Moreover, reform agendas tend to be promoted by those who are truly convinced of the desirability of their idea and hence hesitate to run the risk of being disproved.[32]

Box 4.2 Randomised Experiments in Schooling: Busia District, Kenya

Since 1996 a group of researchers has been working with a Dutch non-profit (International Christelijk Steunfonds) supporting schools in rural Kenya to estimate the impact of various interventions. Through random selection, some schools were chosen to implement the interventions first, with the other schools to follow. This allowed the researchers to test a number of ideas:

- *Textbooks* Everybody knows that textbooks are important and that their lack is a major constraint on effective instruction. Yet the first study found 'no evidence that the provision of textbooks in Kenyan primary schools led to a large positive impact on test scores, nor is there any evidence that it affected daily attendance, grade repetition, or dropout rates'. Does this mean that textbooks don't matter? No. Although textbooks did not increase the performance of the *typical* (median) student, they did improve performance for students who did the best on the pre-test. This suggests that because the textbooks in this instance were too difficult for the typical student, the books did not matter.
- *Teacher incentives* Everybody knows that teacher incentives are crucial since teachers are under motivated. Yet a study on incentives for teachers based on student test scores found that 'teacher responded to the programme primarily by seeking to manipulate short-run test scores . . . [T]eachers' absence rates did not de-

cline, homework assignments did not increase, teaching methods did not change'. Does this mean that teacher incentives don't matter? No. Teachers did change their behaviour – they 'conducted special coaching sessions and encouraged students to take the test'. This suggests that you get what you pay for – whether you like it or not.

- *Deworming* Deworming does not feature widely in the education effectiveness literature. Yet a randomised trial of an inexpensive medical treatment for hookworm, roundworm, whipworm and schistosomiasis found that it reduced absenteeism by a quarter. Does this mean that health is all that matters? No. While attendance improved, test scores did not.

Three observations. First, things that everybody 'knows' to be important did not work as planned, whereas the intervention with lower expectations had large impacts. Second, these results from 100 schools in an isolated area of Kenya have been getting enormous academic attention because there are so few rigorous, randomised evaluations of schooling interventions. Third, the findings from each intervention do not reveal universal, immediately generalisable results, but they reveal that specifics matter and that learning about what works needs to be *local to be useful*.

Sources: **Glewwe, Kremer and Moulin (1997); Miguel and Kremer (2001); Glewwe, Ilias and Kremer (2003)**

Fourth, the question is one of the diffusion of information and adoption, and the fact that *knowledge itself is potentially endogenous*.[33] If what limits adoption is not knowledge or even the perceived reliability of knowledge, but rather deep incentive problems then the BCR of new knowledge conditional on an endogenous lack of adoption, is small.[34] Many observers have concluded from the observation of many waves of reform initiatives that knowledge is not the problem. Let me quote at length a passage from the introduction to a excellent introduction to education reform in Africa:

There is a particular irony to education reform. Pockets of good education practice (such as enlightened and effective classroom management, novel curricula, and innovative instructional

and spread it to the non-mavericks. But some bureaucracies get really good at what they do, and the norms are really effective, so they ossify. This happens all the time, which is why firms go broke: Schumpeterian destruction. In my view, the public sector, and education, need to work more or less this way, and that is how in fact they do work, when they work well. This randomised experimentation stuff seems, to me, to ignore how social change and social improvement works, and hence is sort of barking up the wrong tree. In short, if experimentation and then Stalinist diffusion of 'what works' could work in education, it would have worked for Stalin in tractor production. It didn't.

[33] See Pritchett (2003) for a simple political economy argument explaining the lack of rigorous evaluation.

[34] The constraints to adoption can result in ideological arguments deeply tied up with interests as well. There are some who argue it is no coincidence that 'progressive' notions of how to teach get interpreted by many teachers and teacher organisations in ways that imply less individual accountability for effort and results.

Box 4.3 Randomised Experiments in Radio Instruction, Nicaragua

Randomised evaluations are not a new technique. Jamison *et al.* (1981) report on an experimental study of the impact of textbook availability on the mathematics achievement of students in Nicaraguan first-grade classes. The evaluation compared control classes in which textbooks are relatively rare with two treatments: textbooks alone and with textbooks plus a radio-based instructional programme. The evaluation revealed that while both the textbooks and the radio treatments had significant effects on achievement, the radio group improved at a substantially higher rate than the textbook group. Since the incremental cost of the radio instruction was low, this was an enormously cost-effective innovation.

What was the impact of this rigorous demonstration of a cost-effective technique? While there was a wave of adoption of radio-based instruction in some countries in the 1980s it has not become widespread and Glewwe (2002) doubts whether the results of randomised evaluation played any role.

Interestingly, Jamison *et al.* (1981) originally predicted that the results on textbooks proved more popular as they were easier to implement logistically. In addition, the political economy is more favourable to textbooks which are clear complements to teacher inputs than to radio instruction, which is a clear possible substitute.

---

technologies, many of them cost-effective) can be found almost anywhere, signifying that good education is not the result of arcane knowledge ... Yet the rate of uptake of effective practices is depressingly low. As a result, these innovations exist on a very small scale and many soon sputter out ... Most projects that introduce innovations are in one sense or another meant to be demonstration projects. They are supposed to yield and disseminate practical information about good pedagogical practice. Yet reality contradicts the 'information' assumption on which such projects are based. Effective practices are often found in areas far from the world's information centers. And effective schools are often found just a few blocks from dysfunctional ones. (Crouch and Healey 1997)

Summary on Evaluation

It is almost certainly the case that the amount currently invested in rigorous investigation into the impact of educational projects and into the conditions for promoting learning is far less than the 'optimal'. Since the amounts of money involved in rigorous research are typically small (relative to budgets) and since the potential returns in improvements are large, expanding rigorous impact evaluation is a promising opportunity. In particular, there is no reason to not demand much greater attention to impact evaluation in donor-financed projects. The problem is to insist that attention be paid to the counterfactual – while nearly every donor-financed project has 'monitoring' and nearly every project

now does some impact assessment, they are almost always simply estimates of outcomes 'before and after' rather than a serious attempt to measure 'with and without'.

The opportunity is mainly limited by two factors. First, whether the results will actually *change actions* – obviously the returns to rigorous evaluations which are ignored in future planning is near zero. In many countries of the world, the slow diffusion and adoption of innovations is due to existing institutional incentives and hence is a reform issue and without the fifth element of system reform the payoff to increased knowledge will be small. Secondly, careful attention to the viability and 'scalability' of the proposed intervention – again, obviously devoting expensive and scarce high-quality researcher attention to investigating 'pilot' programmes that cannot be replicated to scale is a waste of resources.

Conclusion on Supply-Side Policy Actions to Improve School Quality

This long and complex section is perhaps best summarised as a decision tree (figure 4.14).

- *Are producers already optimizing* and is the *marginal product high?* If this is so, then key to improving education will be to mobilise financing to *increase expenditures per child* in roughly the way that expenditures are currently allocated. I judge this state of affairs to be extremely rare precisely in those situations in which education is

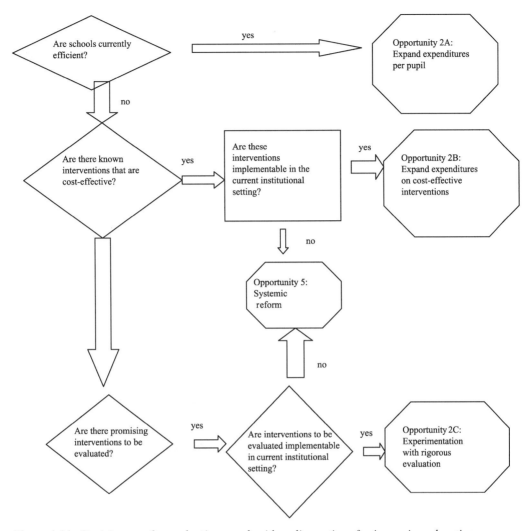

Figure 4.14. *Decision tree for evaluating supply-side policy actions for improving education*

the most lacking. In fact the on-going empirical debate is not so much whether countries are at, or would move along, the production frontier (for which there is no evidence), but whether a 'business as usual' expansion in expenditures (e.g. class-size reductions, higher teacher wages with same structure of incentives, modestly more inputs) would have roughly zero impact (my view) or a positive impact that is high enough to be justified.

- Are there *inputs with higher learning achievement gain per dollar* in existing conditions? And can these be implemented in the *existing institutional structures*? If this is so, the key to

improving quality is to adopt better *expand expenditures on cost-effective inputs* – those that improve productive efficiency (e.g. teacher training) or allocative efficiency (e.g. more spending on instructional materials, key infrastructure deficits).
- Are there *promising alternatives* to be evaluated? And would demonstration of the superiority of these techniques lead to their adoption? If this is so, then *rigorous research into alternatives* is key.
- Is the *lack of productive and allocative efficiency* the endogenous result of the incentives created by the existing institutional organisation of the production of schooling?

- Is the *lack of widespread adoption of existing innovations* and the lack of rigorous research into alternatives and the lack of rigorous impact evaluation the endogenous result of existing incentives for the producers of schooling? If the latter is the case then the only option is some type of *systemic reform* – which could be either entirely within the public sector or could involve non-public sector providers either on their own or with government support via contracts or demand-side financing.[35]

Again, this is the essence of the current debate. The debate is not principally about the *proximate determinants* of learning – nearly everyone agrees that exposure to school is essential and there is broad agreement on the fundamentals of learning while in school. The debate is not even principally about what policy actions by producers of education that could lead to improvements – nearly everyone agrees that better teaching practices and better instructional material inputs could lead to better outcomes. The debate is also not about whether it is possible for public sectors to produce high-quality schooling – of course they can, and do. The key question is whether in any given country the current institutional conditions lead to a public sector that is *motivated to* and *capable of* implementing the required actions.

My personal view of the decision tree in figure 4.14 is that in nearly all developing countries the path through the decision will lead to systemic reform. The existing failures are almost entirely the endogenous outcome of the existing incentives of the public sector (which is unconcerned about quality and unresponsive to citizen demands for higher-quality schooling) and of public sector producers who are given no support in increasing quality.

However, I will be the first to admit there are many informed and well-meaning analysts who disagree and believe that policy actions – to improve

teaching practices (content knowledge and pedagogy), to raise the quality and availability of instructional materials and to improve infrastructure are possible within the existing institutional structures for the production of schooling. Moreover, the problems with schooling are so pressing and the damage to children of not having access to quality schooling are so irreversible it is very difficult to 'give up' and simply do nothing even in environments which all acknowledge are not promising, such as Nigeria.

This debate comes back to the key question of a *positive* model of public sector producers. Everyone who advocates the adoption of some policy action that promises to dramatically improve educational outcomes should be able to answer the question: If what is being proposed has the benefits claimed then why is the public sector currently not doing it already?

Opportunity 3: Demand-Side: Raising the Benefits of Schooling

There are two key opportunities to address the lack of education that are indirect, but which may be far and away the most powerful empirical correlates (and perhaps determinants) of increases in education. First, since the most important determinants of a child's educational attainment appear to be *household income* and *parental education*, generalised increases in productivity and/or income – from whatever sources – that raise the incomes of parents will increase schooling, and increases in education will beget future increases in education. Second, are *policy or institutional reforms* that raise the returns to education. However, while there are, in all likelihood the most powerful determinants of education, I will not explore them in much depth because they are not education-specific.

The Effect of Income on Education

Filmer (2000) uses the DHS datasets to investigate the factors associated with child (age 6–14) enrolment. Using a probit regression that controlled for child age and age[2], urban versus rural residence, wealth of the household, education of the adult females and males in the household and child biological sex, he finds that the effects of parental

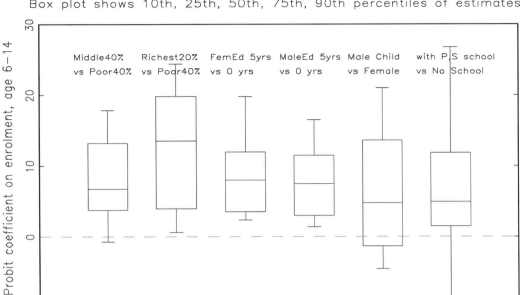

(Probit regression results, 57 developing country HH datasets
Box plot shows 10th, 25th, 50th, 75th, 90th percentiles of estimates)

Figure 4.15. *The estimated association in household datasets between child enrolment, household wealth and parental education is consistently large and significant, while the association with school availability is much less consistent*

income and parental education are consistently empirically large and nearly always statistically significant. The median estimated marginal effect of living in a middle-wealth versus poor household is 8.8 percentage points, the richest 20 per cent versus the poorest 40 per cent had a median 13 percentage point effect, having a mother with five years of schooling versus no years had a median impact of 8.0 percentage points, while having a father with five of schooling versus no years had a 7.5 percentage point effect. One would expect a child from a rich household with father and mother with five years of schooling to have an enrolment rate 28 percentage points higher than a poor child with parents with no education. The median association with having both a primary and secondary school in the cluster is 6.9 per cent (figure 4.15).

These strong correlations at the household level are also apparent in cross-country comparisons and in comparisons over time. The same studies that find only weak impact of public spending on enrolment and achievement outcomes tend to find quite strong correlations with adult education–literacy and *per capita* income. Similarly studies that trace out the impact of income changes over time find a large role for improvements in income. One example is Edmonds' (2003) examination of the rapid growth in Vietnam in which he finds that 80 per cent of the reduction in child labour observed in households that emerged from poverty can be accounted for by increases in *per capita* expenditures (as a proxy for income increases).

Clemens (2004) emphasises that in spite of decades of focus on the 'supply side' of public action the primary determinant of progress towards universal education has appeared to be principally *demand determined* and that very little that countries have done on the supply side has significantly altered progress. One implication of this is that since the demand-side factors – particularly parental education – tend to evolve slowly in most countries the transition from modest levels of education (50 per cent primary enrolment) to near-universal

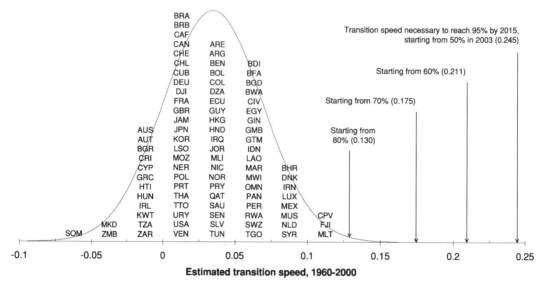

Figure 4.16. *The distribution of observed transition speeds to universal primary enrolment shows that even the most rapid are far slower than the rates needed the meet the MDGs in 2015 in countries starting from anything less than 80 per cent enrolment in 2004*

levels has been steady but slow. In fact, Clemens points out that the rate of progress necessary for countries to meet the currently Millennium Development Goals (MDG) by 2015 are wildly beyond the bounds of any observed rates of progress (figure 4.16).

The Effect of Raising the Returns to Education

There is no question that returns to education vary widely and that in stagnant technological and economic conditions the returns to education can be very low – sufficiently low that *if* current labour market conditions are expected to persist then *not* attending school may well be the *optimal* decision from a narrowly drawn economic calculation. I would recommend adopting this narrow view as the view that basic education is a human right and

an essential element of well-being in the modern world is pretty compelling. But it is worth pointing out that when returns are low the economic calculation and the human rights desires may be at odds.

There is powerful evidence that certain types of *technological shocks* raise the returns to schooling.[36] There is also pretty strong evidence that parents–students respond to perceived returns to schooling. In an important paper Foster and Rosenzweig (1996) show three important things. First, the technological shock of the introduction of High Yielding Varieties caused returns to education to be higher in those regions conducive to these changes than in other regions – so the return to primary schooling in regions with a technological shock to farm profits a standard deviation above average was estimated at 7.8 per cent (figure 4.17). Second, the returns in regions that did not have a positive technological shock were very, low – only around 2 per cent. Third, in regions in which returns were higher the growth in schooling was much higher.

In Latin America there has been an enormous expansion in the returns to schooling (figure 4.18).

[36] There is, of course, the enormous literature on the rise in the wage premia to education in the USA (and to a lesser extent, Europe) in spite of rising supplies of educated workers that attempts to determine the sources of the rise.

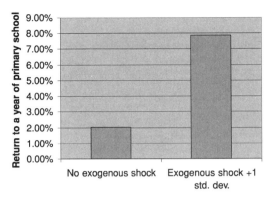

Figure 4.17. *The returns to primary schooling (from increased farm profits) were much higher in regions conducive to the adoption of 'Green Revolution' technologies, India, 1970s*

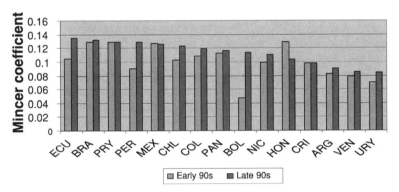

Figure 4.18. *Returns to schooling typically increased during the 1990s in Latin America: coefficient on schooling in Mincer regression, with datasets from the early versus the later 1990s*

Behrman, Birdsall and Szekely (2001) show that policy changes affect technological progress, which then creates higher returns to education in the 'adaptation to disequilibria'. This is the macroeconomic counterpart of the effects seen in the 'Green Revolution'. In contrast, in economies that are stagnant the demand for educated labour will be stagnant and the dramatic expansions in the supply of educated workers will drive down the wage gains from education.

It is not impossible to imagine that one reason that the expansion of schooling has stagnated in SSA is that there have been neither large positive shocks to agricultural technologies (*à la* some regions of India) nor has there been a large expansion in employment in industry or general economy-wide increases in productivity. Almost certainly the returns to education in most of Africa today are much lower than they could be.

Conclusion on Raising Incomes and Benefits

Even if one accepts that reforms that raise the general level of income raise demand for education and that raising economy-wide returns to skills acquired through schooling are key to expanding educational attainments, the question remains: 'What is the "opportunity"?' It is 'policy reform'? And if so, what are the costs and benefits? Is it investing in technological innovations that raise returns

Table 4.10. The Variety of Demand-Side Transfers

			Cash (or equivalent)	Non-cash
Untargeted			Fee waivers (Malawi, Uganda, Kenya)	
Targeted	Pure education	'Need'	Scholarships/vouchers (Colombia)	School feeding (e.g. Tamil Nadu)
		'Ability'		
	Social transfers conditioned on education		PROGRESA (Mexico)	FFE in Bangladesh (Vermeersh 2002)

to schooling? If so, what are the costs and benefits of investing in innovations?[37] Generally, reforms that raise output are desirable on their own terms (without taking into account the feedback to improved education) and so 'should' be adopted in any case.

The main point is that there is a tendency by education analysts to overstate the importance of sector-specific measures (a natural tendency, since this is what they might control or influence) and understate the importance of economy-*wide* factors. Generalised increases in *per capita* income are an enormously important route for improvements in 'human development' indicators of all types, and should not be ignored.

Opportunity 4: Demand-Side: Direct (Targeted?) Support to Households that Lower the Cost of Schooling

The second demand-side opportunity to be considered is mechanisms to increase enrolment, attainment, or learning by lowering the *(relative) costs of schooling*. The reduction in costs can either be untargeted (as in fee waivers) or targeted on some criteria (gender, location, caste) and can either be reducing costs or a positive reward,

such as a scholarship or conditional cash transfer (table 4.10).

Costs of Raising Enrolments by Lowering Relative Prices

To an economist, there is no question that lowering relative prices will raise the quantity of schooling demanded – the only question is whether this is 'cost-effective' as a means of addressing the lack of education. A helpful way of thinking about that question is table 4.11, which distinguishes the *incremental* enrolment from the transfer and the total cost of the transfer plus the additional cost of schooling.

Obviously the two key aspects of the cost-effectiveness is the ratio A/C, which depends on two elements: the price elasticity of demand for schooling and the ability to target so that A/C is low.

Price Elasticity of the Demand for Schooling and Universal Reductions in Cost

If enrolments are to be increased by lowering the price of schooling universally – say, reducing or eliminating school fees across the board – then the cost per additional student enrolled is a function of the elasticity of the aggregate demand for schooling. If enrolments are already high and the elasticity is low then the costs per additional student enrolled are astronomical.

Most of the available evidence suggests the demand for schooling is quite price inelastic. Schultz (2001) found that the school subsidy offered by the PROGRESA programme – which provides education grants for poor families in rural Mexico – reduced the private costs of school by more than half,

---

[37] This is particularly striking as many of the 'opportunities' that would raise the returns to schooling would also be beneficial in their own right and, in fact, the impact on raising schooling would be only a tiny part of the overall benefits. This implies that if these could be justified on schooling grounds alone the total BCR would be spectacularly large, which raises the question of why they have not already been done – that is, what is the 'market' for income–human capital return-raising economic reforms that it is so inefficient?

Table 4.11. Illustration of the Implications for Cost-Effectiveness of Targeting Transfers

	Do receive the transfer	Do not receive the transfer
Enrol with or without the transfer of magnitude T	**A** ('Type II' error-transfer where it has no impact)	*B*
Would enrol with the transfer T but not without transfer	**C**	*D* ('Type I error' – transfer where it would have an impact)
Would not enrol even with the transfer	**E** ('Type II' error-transfer where it has no impact)	*F*

Examples of alternative policies

	Incremental cost	Incremental enrolment	Cost per incremental enrolment
Reducing fees from f to zero with cost of schooling c	$A*f+C*c$ (**A = all previously enrolled**)	C	$(A/C)*f+c$
Targeted transfer of t to 'poor' households with cost of school of c.	$(A+C)*t+C*c$ (**A = just 'poor' who would have enrolled**)	C	$(A/C)*t+t+c$

but increased the educational attainment by only 10 per cent, hence the implied demand elasticity was around −0.2. The evidence from the distance regressions reported (plus many assumptions) allows a calculation of the price elasticity implied by the enrolment response to reduced travel time. These calculations suggest an elasticity of around −0.3 and that above −0.5 is substantially too high.

In contrast, the experience with the elimination of fees followed by huge increases in enrolments in Africa suggests that aggregate demand for *enrolment* is quite elastic (e.g. Deininger 2001). There are, however, three aspects to the experience that makes one slightly cautious about a policy of universal fee waivers. First, by making the fee waiver universal the revenue forgone per additional student enrolled is quite high.

Second, the evidence is mixed of the impact on *attainment* as, at least in Malawi, there is some evidence that the reductions have increased ever enrolment but that persistence is lower (perhaps because quality is lower) and attainment has not been influenced nearly as much (figure 4.19). The attainment profile of those aged 15 in 1992 (unaffected by the elimination of fees in 1994) and in 2000 suggests that while completion of the early grades has

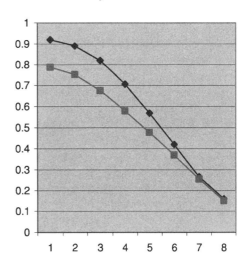

15-yrs attainment

Figure 4.19. *Attainment profiles after the elimination of fees in Malawi show unchanged grade attainment*

increased, the fraction of 15-year-olds completing the 6th, 7th or 8th grade is nearly unchanged.

Third, unless there is the political willingness to replace the revenue forgone in a sustained way, reductions in budgets may lead to reductions in learning achievement for all students so that the net impact on learning achievement could actually be negative. One hint of these problems is that repetition rates in the 1st grade have increased from 20 per cent in 1992 to 45 per cent in 2000.

Conditional Cash Transfers

Morley and Coady (2003) review the experience with 'cash for education' (CFE) or conditional cash transfer schemes such as Mexico's PROGRESA, Food For Education (FFE) in Bangladesh, Bolsa Escola in Brazil (taken nation-wide in 2001) and others. It is clear that these programmes have substantial impact on enrolments. The PROGRESA scheme had a built-in randomised evaluation and hence has about as reliable estimates as one could hope – which suggest that grade 8 completion was roughly 12 percentage points higher for PROGRESA recipients than non-recipients.

Whether CFE schemes are 'cost-effective' all depends on whether one views the programme as a social transfer programme with the additional benefit of increasing enrolment – that is, the transfer would have been made anyway and the education benefits are attributed only to the incremental costs – or whether all of the transfer is attributed to the education objective. The basic point is illustrated with the cost-effectiveness calculations in Morley and Coady (2003). They calculate that the transfers produced an additional 393 years of schooling for a cohort of a 1,000 with a total transfer of 3.43 m pesos in grants for that same cohort for an incremental cost per extra year of education generated of 8,727 pesos – this is 15 per cent of GDP *per capita* per year of additional schooling. A rough estimate of the cost of per year of schooling in Mexico in 2002 is about 8,800 pesos. This means that the total public sector cost of an additional year of schooling via PROGRESA was about double the current average cost per student. It is hard to believe that is the most cost-effective way to increase schooling.[38]

---

[38] Morley and Coady (2003) compare that to the cost-effectiveness of raising enrolments via school construction and, needless to say given the weak connection between school construction and enrolments noted above find the cost eleven times higher via construction.

Targeted Transfers

The key questions for these types of interventions as a means of expanding education are design questions:

- At what age–stage of education? There is evidence from the USA that 'the earlier the better', although many scholarship programmes focus only on retention or progression.
- The key issue is the trade-off between cost-effectiveness of targeting. This is a function of the cost and feasibility of distinguishing the enrolment of various groups (the attainment profiles on pp. 182 and 183 give some indication of how much the enrolment differences vary across easily identifiable characteristics in a given country). On the downside sharp targeting to maximise cost-effectiveness may miss many who are not enrolled. So if the groups with low achievement are small (e.g. poor girls in remote villages) then cost-effective targeting will still leave many out of school.
- One key issue that has not been sufficiently addressed is *targeting on late enrolment* (figure 4.20). There is increasing evidence that late enrolment also an important determinant of total attainment. This would suggest that targeting the age group where the enrolment rates are the most different would have the least 'leakage' to inframarginal (these would attend in any case) – but targeting can have high administrative or political costs.

Finally, a large issue is targeting ability versus some combination of ability and need. This is typically not even addressed.

Conclusions on Demand-Side Transfers

This brief review suggests the following conclusions:

- *Conditional cash transfers:* if the government is going to make cash transfers to individuals/households that are part of a poverty programme, there is little reason to not make these transfers conditional on the children of recipients enrolling in school. In this sense, conditional cash transfers are 'cost-effective' in raising enrolment because most of the cost of the programme – the

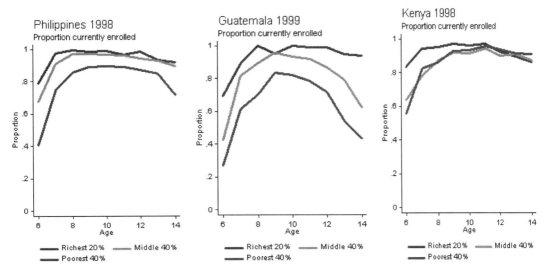

Figure 4.20. *Late enrolment implies much larger differences in enrolment rates by household wealth at early ages than later*
Source: Filmer and Pritchett (1999x) and website.

financial transfer – is a cost that would be incurred in any case and hence the education gains need to be judged only against the incremental costs of making the transfer conditional.

By this same logic it is almost inconceivable that most conditional cash transfer programmes could be justified exclusively (or even primarily) by their education benefits as, in nearly any setting capable of implementing such a programme, nearly all of the transfer will be inframarginal (that is, go to families whose children would have enrolled anyway). There is some hope for transfers sharply targeted on stages of the cycle – e.g. to reduce late enrolment, repletion in early grades and transitions across levels of schooling

- *Untargeted reductions in fees:* while most are favourable about the experience with fee waivers in Africa, I would be much more cautious.
- *Targeted programmes:* There is no question that targeted programmes such as in-kind transfers such as meals in school can have substantial enrolment impacts. The cost-effectiveness question hinges on the ability to target to make the enrolment increase per dollar spent substantial.
- *Why not portable demand-side transfers?* One large question is whether 'demand-side' transfers should be limited exclusively to public sec-

tor producers. If there is the capability of providing a cash transfer, an in-kind benefit to targeted groups, or a scholarship, the logic of limiting the use only to public producers escapes me.

The Fifth Element: Systemic Reform to Create Performance Management and Producer Accountability

The World Bank's *World Development Report 2004: Making Services Work for Poor People* (World Bank 2004) documents the problems with public production of schooling – low levels of budget commitment, high levels of teacher absenteeism, teachers hired for political patronage, low technical quality, misallocation of resources by level of education and across inputs, ineffectiveness of teacher training, stagnant productivity.[39] More importantly, it argues that these failures are *endogenous* and *systemic*. It proposes what is essentially an extended principal–agent analysis in which the relationship between the principal and agent is called

[39] I was a member of the 2004 *World Development Report* and had responsibility for chapter 7 on education and hence, naturally, believe that the analysis presented there is largely correct.

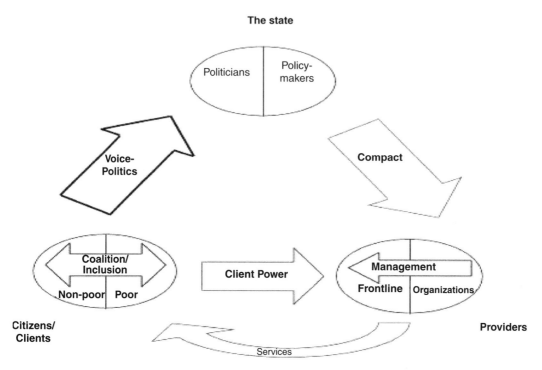

Figure 4.21. *An illustration of the four (potential) relationships of accountability involved in the provision of services via the public sector: voice-politics (between citizens and the state), compact (between the state and producers), management (between organisations and front-line producers) and client power (between citizens/consumers and producers)*
Source: World Bank (2004).

a 'relationship of accountability'. The primary thesis is that to a large extent the currently observed poor educational outcomes are the result of failures of the relationships of accountability (figure 4.21).

[40] One would think that analysing education policy in terms of the incentives it created would be second nature to economists, but not so. One conjecture of mine is that the 'externality' version of the 'normative as positive' (NAP) model had such a powerful attraction as a formal apparatus that economists could easily assume that if welfare maximising governments had a rationale for intervention in the market for education and governments did in fact produce schooling then the *reason* governments produced schooling was to maximise welfare. If that is the case then all that needs to be worried about are issues such as the allocation of the budget as, after all, if governments are producing schooling to maximise welfare then they are doing so efficiently. But, since not all (any?) governments produce schooling to maximise citizen welfare then it also goes without saying there is no particular reason to assume productive or allocative efficiency.

This implies that the key problem is not applying the discrete policy actions (opportunities 1–4) that attempt to directly affect the 'proximate determinants' of learning even when it is clear there are 'off-the-shelf' innovations that would substantially improve the quality of schooling. The key problem is that within the current institutional conditions for government production of schooling, there are too few incentives to create *performance oriented* management – in either the government or market sectors. The problem is that the choices are the outcome of the *existing incentives* (or lack thereof) for producers to raise the quality of learning. Where the key constraint is that the system does not produce incentives for producers to be effective, then neither budget increases nor new knowledge are likely to be effective.[40]

In order for (near-exclusively) publicly produced education to be effective *either* an authoritarian nation-state has to create powerful incentives for performance without either the 'voice' of citizens or direct 'client power' on providers (which the high levels of learning achievement in Cuba, for instance, prove is possible) *or* the 'long route' accountability has to operate. The 'long route' is that citizens have to make demands felt via the political system, and those demands have to translate into clear signals to public sector producers (via 'compact' and 'management') with or without a great deal of direct 'client power'. Of course, a country can also provide education without direct production by transferring resources directly to citizens and allowing direct client power to operate via their choice of schooling (with, of course, oversight of content and quality) to discipline producers. But systems in which the only form of government support for basic education is the direct production of schooling can become dysfunctional if any of these key links breaks down.[41]

This is *not* an ideological case for 'vouchers' or wholesale 'privatisation' – some of the world's best schooling systems rely on direct public production and many of the worst schools in the world are 'private'. Nor does 'performance management' mean slavish reliance on standardised tests or simple-minded proposals for teacher pay. But much of the world's population is not well-served by existing systems.

A well ordered system for schooling has to solve four key problems simultaneously:

- Create clear *objectives* for the schooling system
- Provide sustained, adequate, *financing* to 'line producers' – principals and teachers – to achieve those objectives
- Give – 'line producers' – sufficient *autonomy* to manage for results
- Maintain producer *accountability* for results – which implies transparent, consistent, measures of progress towards objectives.

There is no unique, universally applicable, way to accomplish these desiderata. The industrial economies have all found different ways to create systems that are reasonably effective (if not efficient or dynamic) – the Dutch have almost complete choice of publicly subsidised, privately produced schooling, the USA has historically relied on extremely decentralised control of school districts,[42] France has maintained quite tight centralisation of schools at every level. By the same token, the basic structures of the educational system in Singapore and Nigeria are similar – as descendents of the British system – and yet have almost polar opposite outcomes.

At the same time, while discussions, especially in international forums, tend to focus almost exclusively on government production of schooling, the provision of basic schooling outside the traditional public sector model has been demonstrated to be feasible at scale in a wide variety of formats and in a wide variety of settings (table 4.12). A variety of alternatives to traditional public production has emerged in a wide range of settings in response to conflict (community-controlled schools in El Salvador), lack of government alternatives (BRAC non-formal education in Bangladesh), changing demands in the labour market (English as medium of instruction schools in Mumbai), parental demands for religious education (*Fe y Alegria* in Venezuela), or simply a collapse in government schools (Cameroon). This is, of course, in addition to the usual alternative of 'vouchers' that allow students to attend private schools that has been demonstrated as workable system for the provision of education in Chile and the Czech Republic.

Centralised, monoposonistic production of basic schooling has a tendency to blur everything. Since everything is within 'the government' the roles of government as financer of schooling, as regulator, as monitor and as producer are all conflated. This can lead to a lack of clear objectives. But if there are no clear objectives (which, of course, includes the case of having many objectives which cannot be measured) then, as the literature on principal–agent

---

[41] A key limitation of many international efforts to improve education is precisely that they are inter*national* – that is, the key agents are representatives of nation-states (or agglomerations of nation-states, such as the UN or World Bank), and hence tend to assume the perspective of the nation-state, which may have very different interests in schooling than the typical citizen.

[42] But with a high degree of centralisation within school districts so that principals are perhaps even more constrained in this 'decentralised' system than in a 'centralised' system like that in the UK.

Table 4.12. Alternatives to the Traditional Organisation of Government Production of Schooling – Examples of Different Types of Arrangements, at Scale

	Description of organisation, performance
NGO	The Non-Formal Primary Education (NFPE) provides basic education in small one-room mud structures, located within the village, for 8- to 10-year-olds in rural Bangladesh with an emphasis on girls' schooling – of the 1.1 m students currently enrolled, 70% are girls. **Teachers** are mostly local married women, part-time workers. They must have at least nine years of schooling, and undergo intensive training. There is decentralised management, active parent and community involvement including in determining the location of the school, assisting in construction, setting schedules, hiring and supervision of teachers. Parent–teacher meetings are held regularly. BRAC students have equal or better performance on national exams to test mastery of basic education, over 50% of BRAC graduates passed, compared with 20% of government students.
Community control (EDUCO)	EDUCO schools in El Salvador are community-managed schools which receive a per-student subsidy from the government. Community committees have complete control over finances, including the hiring and firing of **teachers** who are on one-year, renewable, contracts. Evaluation of performance finds that, controlling for student background, EDUCO schools do no worse (and arguably better) than government-organised schools.
Religious	Schools run by the Catholic church aimed at disadvantaged students in Venezuela (among other countries). Evaluations suggest that performance is higher, costs are lower and, in spite of much lower salaries, teachers are more satisfied.
Private for-profit – without support	As a response to changing economic conditions English as medium of instruction schools have emerged spontaneously in Mumbai. These schools now account for a large percentage of all enrolment.

and compensation (e.g. Holmstrom and Milgrom 1997; Milgrom and Roberts 1997) shows there is no clear basis to *manage* or to *create incentives* within organisations, which almost inexorably leads to 'input'-based management and 'rules-based' behaviour.

That said, the tasks are difficult and the challenges of making any system of education work formidable:

- *Clear objectives:* schools are not machines for teaching facts – schools are the mechanism *whereby societies replicate themselves.* This means that while learning achievement is obviously a key element of schooling the objectives for schools are much broader. Since 'what gets measured gets done' one cannot produce a set of educational goals that include lists of desired outcomes but then set about measuring only enrolments or physical targets that measure 'quality' like pupil–teacher ratios. By the same token, one cannot set education goals for creativity and measure only standardised tests.
- *Sustained adequate financing:* the financing of schools is an issue that is, in many ways, inde-

pendent of the structure of production – as one can always finance schools from general revenue irrespective of who produces. But any system has to face a series of challenges – particularly the issue of financing teachers.

- *Autonomy to manage for results:* once there is a clear statement of the objectives of using tax revenues for basic schooling and a source of financing then one can create a mechanism that allows producers to make decisions as how those goals can be most effectively met. Accountability for performance requires *autonomy* to act. In general, this means pushing responsibility and power for decision making to the lowest feasible level which, depending on the function, could be the region, the school system (public or private), the school headmaster or the classroom teacher. This doesn't mean each that school invents a curriculum. Wößmann (2002) addresses nicely the issue of which functions should be allocated to which level.
- *Accountability*: Perhaps the key element is a centralised system of *creating and disseminating* information to parents–students about school performance. This function of the school system

Table 4.13. Conclusions: Likely Returns to Improving Education

	The returns to devoting additional public resources are high if:	Frequency of the *possibility* of high pay-offs
1 System expansion	Demand under existing conditions exceeds supply, as evidenced by: high class sizes (especially in upper grades), students willing to long travel distances Schools of adequate quality can be provided, as evidenced by high retention in existing schools	Rare
2(a) Radial expansion of budgets	Producers are (reasonably) efficient, as evidenced by: cost ratios near norms, active management for effectiveness, ability to measure resource use, measurement of quality	Rare
2(b) Selective expansions of inputs	Educational system capable of managing and implementing programmes for expansion of high impact of inputs, as evidenced by: measurement of quality (to monitor quality improvement), capability of active management, teaching force capable of implementing new techniques–utilising new inputs.	Rare to uncommon in poorest settings, common in middle-income countries
2(c) Rigorous evaluation of impact	Knowledge about effectiveness is scarce Some possibility of impact on decisions	Common (since this capability can be 'cocooned')
3 Economic reforms to stimulate demand	Existing returns to education are low Reforms are possible that will raise economic growth and returns to schooling	Common in SSA, uncommon elsewhere Common – feasibility case by case
4 Demand-side transfers/cost reduction	Existing school is of adequate quality, as evidenced by low repetition, high persistence, and preferably by measurement Administrative capability of targeting at reasonable cost Alternative sources to generate revenue	Rare to uncommon in poorest, more common in middle income
5 System reform	Improve the definition of learning objectives Financing Expand producer autonomy Expansion of availability of information about performance Expand accountability in some mode	Everywhere Rare/uncommon Common (at the margins) Common Common

needs to be centralised because the schooling system creates a *common system of core objectives* against which all schools (which receive public funds) are to be gauged and against which progress over time can be measured. There are substantial economies of scale in developing a proper way to do this.

Given the sufficient relevant information (e.g. about comparative features, costs and expenditures and performance (adjusted)) there are a variety of *mechanisms* to pressure schools for better performance. Public organisations do that in one way, private non-profit organisations do it another, choice-based systems do it another, community management in another. The key is that accountability should be based on adequate information. 'Choice' without reliable information is not a happy recipe.

Bringing All Opportunities Together in an International Programme: Education for All/Fast Track Initiative (EFA/FTI)

The most prominent intervention on the international (particularly donor) agenda is the *Education for All/Fast Track Initiative.* This set of proposals follows up on the Dhakar 'commitments' to Education for All (EFA) and the Millennium Development Goals (MDGs). The basic idea is that donors will provide incremental budget support to countries that provide 'credible' plans for meeting the

EFA targets (or at least improving performance on the targets). The people behind the EFA/FTI understand the depth of the problem and that meeting the targets is about much more than 'building schools' and that improving quality is about much more than 'increasing spending'. The EFA/FTI is the 'cutting-edge' approach to the problem of the lack of education. In the descriptions of what the country plans should include it has has attempted to grapple with how to integrate all four opportunities for policy action plus elements of systemic reform into a coherent package (and particularly a coherent package that could be supported with international financial assistance).

One of the striking and innovative features about the EFA/FTI, for instance, is that financing gaps are based on a move towards 'efficient' expenditures. Based on an empirical analysis of the expenditure allocations of countries which have been successful in reaching the goals of primary completion they establish indicative ratios for teacher wages/GDP and class size. If a country has high unit costs of primary schooling this does not imply a higher financing gap to meet the MDG that donors have to meet. Rather, it implies that unit costs should be reduced (or the country should finance the 'excess' expenditure themselves).

As a conclusion, I assess the likely returns in improving basic education from the opportunities considered (table 4.13). Obviously assessing a credible plan for progress in any given country requires consideration of the existing conditions and the likely outcomes from policy action and the 'fit' of various systemic reform alternatives with existing conditions (including political situations).

References

Alderman, H., P. Orazem and E. Paterno, 1996: School quality, school cost, and the public/private school choices of low income households in Pakistan, Impact Evaluation of Education Reform Working Paper Series, 2 PRDPH, World Bank, Washington, DC

Angrist, J., E. Bettinger, E. Bloom, E. King and M. Kremer, 2002. Vouchers for private schooling in Colombia: evidence from a randomized natural experiment, *American Economic Review*, **92**(5), 1535–58

Angrist, J. D. and V. Lavy, 1999: Using Maimonides' rule to estimate the effect of class size on scholastic achievement, *Quarterly Journal of Economics*, **144**, 533–75

Association for the Evaluation of Educational Achievement, 2003: PIRLS 2001 International report, IEA's Study of Reading Literacy Achievement in Primary Schools in 35 Countries,

Banerjee, A., S. Cole, E. Duflo and L. Linden, 2003: Remedying education: evidence from two randomized experiments in India, unpublished manuscript

Barro, R. J. and J.-W. Lee, 1993: International comparisons of educational attainment, *Journal of Monetary Economics*, **32**(3), 363–94

Behrman, J. R., S. Khan, D. Ross and R. Sabot, 1997: School quality and cognitive achievement production: A case study for rural Pakistan, *Economics of Education Review*, **16**(2), 127–42

Birdsall, N. and F. Orivel, 1996: Demand for primary schooling in rural Mali: should user fees be increased?, *Education Economics*, **4**(3)

Bredie, J. W. B. and G. K. Beeharry, 1998: School enrolment decline in Sub-Saharan Africa: beyond the supply constraint, Discussion Paper, **395**, World Bank, Washington, DC

Bruns, B., A. Mingat and R. Rakotomalala, 2003: A chance for every child: achieving universal primary education by 2015, World Bank, Washington, DC

Burney, N. A. and M. Irfan, 1995: Determinants of child school enrolment: evidence from LDCs using the choice-theoretic approach, *International Journal of Social Economics*, **22**(1), 24–40

Canagarajah, S. and H. Coulombe, 1997: Child labour and schooling in Ghana, Policy Research Working Paper, **1844**, World Bank, Washington, DC

Carneiro, P. and J. Heckman, 2003: Human capital policy, National Bureau of Economic Research, Working Paper, **9495**

Case, A. and A. Deaton, 1999: School inputs and educational outcomes in South Africa,

Quarterly Journal of Economics, **114**(3), 1047–84

Castro-Leal, F., 1996: Who benefits from public education spending in Malawi? Results from the recent education reform, Discussion Paper, 350, World Bank, Washington, DC

Clemens, M. A., 2003: The long walk to school: development goals in historical perspectives, Center for Global Development, unpublished manuscript

Colclough, C. and S. Al-Samarrai, 2000: Achieving schooling for all: budgetary expenditures on education in Sub-Saharan African and South Asia, *World Development*, **28**(11), 1927–44

Comber, L.C. and J. P. Keeves, 1973: *Science education in nineteen countries*, John Wiley, New York

Crouch, L. and F. H. Healy, 1997: *Education reform support, I: overview and bibliography*, Office of Sustainable Development Bureau of Africa, US Agency for International Development,

Deininger, K., 2003: Does cost of schooling affect enrolment by the poor? Universal primary education in Uganda, *Economics of Education Review*, **22**, 291–305

Delamonica, E. S. Mehrotra and J. Vandermoortele, 2001: Is the EFA affordable? Estimating the global minimum cost of 'Education for All', Innocenti Working Paper, **87**, UNICEF Innocenti Research Centre, Florence

Devarajan, S., M. Miller and E. Swanson, 2002: Goals for development: history, prospects and costs, Policy Research Working Paper, **2819**, World Bank, Washington, DC, April

Duflo, E., 2001: Schooling and labour market consequences of school construction in Indonesia: evidence from an unusual policy experiment, *American Economic Review*, **91**(4), 795–813

Elley, W. B., 1992: How in the world do students read?, Hamburg: International Educational Association

Feynman, R., 1989: *The Feynman lectures on physics*, Addison-Wesley, Reading, MA

Filmer, D., 2004: School availability and school participation in 21 developing countries, World Bank, Washington, DC

Filmer, D. and L. Pritchett, 1999a: What education production functions really show: a positive theory of education expenditure, *Economics of Education Review*, **18**(2), 223–39

1999b: The effect of household wealth on educational attainment: evidence from 35 countries, *Population and Development Review*, **25**(1)

Foster, A. D. and M. R. Rosenzweig, 1996: Technical change and human-capital returns and investments: evidence from the Green Revolution, *American Economic Review*, **86**(4), 931–53

Fredriksen, B., 2002: Education for all African children by 2015: what will it take to keep the promise?, paper prepared for the Annual Bank Conference on Development Economics – Europe, Oslo, 24–26 June

Fuller, B. and P. Clarke, 1994: Raising school effects while ignoring culture? Local conditions and the influence of classroom tools, rules, and pedagogy, *Review of Educational Research*, **64**(1), 119–57

Glewwe, P., 2002: Schools and skills in developing countries: education policies and socioeconomic outcomes, *Journal of Economic Literature*, **40**, 436–82

2004: Schools, teachers, and education outcomes in developing countries, in *Handbook on the economics of education*, forthcoming

Glewwe, P., N. Ilias and M. Kremer, 2003: Teacher incentives, Working Paper, 9671. National Bureau of Economic Research

Glewwe, P. and M. Kremer, 2003: Schools, teachers, and education outcomes in developing countries, in *Handbook on the Economics of Education*, forthcoming.

Glewwe, P., M. Kremer and S. Moulin, 1997: Textbooks and test scores: evidence from a prospective evaluation in Kenya, unpublished manuscript

Glewwe, P., M. Kremer, S. Moulin and E. Zitzewitz, 2000: Retrospective vs. prospective analyses of school inputs: the case of flip charts in Kenya, Working Paper, **8018**, National Bureau of Economic Research

Glewwe, P. and H. Jacoby, 1994: Student achievement and schooling choice in low-income countries: evidence from Ghana, *Journal of Human Resources*, **29**(3), 843–64

Gradstein, M. and M. Justman, 2002: Education, social cohesion and growth, *American Economic Review*, **92**, 1192–1204

Greany, V., S. Khandker and M. Alam, 1998: Bangladesh: assessing basic learning skills,

Gundlach, E. and L. Wößmann, 1999: The fading productivity of schooling in East Asia, Working Paper, **945**, Kiel Institute of World Economics

Gundlach, E., L. Wößmann and J. Gmelin, 1999: The decline of schooling productivity in OECD countries, Working Paper **926**, Kiel Institute of World Economics

Handa, S., 2002: Raising primary school enrolment in developing countries: the relative importance of supply and demand, *Journal of Development Economics*, **69**, 103–28

Hanushek, E. A., 1986: The Economics of Schooling: Production and Efficiency in Public Schools. *Journal of Economic Literature*, **24**, 1141–77.

1995a: Outcomes, costs, and incentives in schools, in Board on Science, Technology, and Economic Policy, National Research Council, *Improving the performance of America's schools*, National Academy Press, Washington, DC, 28–51; reprinted in E. A. Hanushek and D. W. Jorgenson (eds.), *Improving America's schools: the role of incentives*, National Academy Press, Washington, DC, 1996

1995b: Interpreting recent research on schooling in developing countries, *World Bank Research Observer*, **10**, 227–46

1995c: Some findings from an independent investigation of the Tennessee STAR experiment and from other investigations of class size effects, *Educational Evaluation and Policy Analysis*, **21**, 143–63

1996: School resources and student performance, in G. Burless (ed.), *Does money matter? The effects of school resources on student achievement and adult success*, The Brookings Institute, Washington, DC

1999: The evidence on class size, in S. E. Mayer and P. Peterson (eds.), *Earning and learning: how schools matter*, Brookings Institution, Washington, DC, 131–68

Hanushek, E. and D. Kim, 1995: Schooling, labour force quality, and economic growth, Working Paper, **5399**, National Bureau of Economic Research

Hanushek, E. A. and D. D. Kimko, 2000: Schooling, labour-force quality, and the growth of nations, *American Economic Review*, **90**(5), 1184–1208

Harbison, R. and E. A. Hanushek, 1992: *Educational performance of the poor: lessons from northeast Brazil*, Oxford University Press, Oxford, for the World Bank

Harmon, C., H. Oosterbeek and I. Walker, 2003: The returns to education: microeconomics, *Journal of Economic Surveys*, **17**(2), 115–55

Heckman, and Carneiro, 2003

Hedges, L. V., R. D. Laine and R. Greenwald, 1994: Does money matter? A meta analysis of the effects of differential school inputs on student outcomes, *Educational Researcher*, **23**(3), 5–14

Holmes, J., 1999: Measuring the determinants of school completion in Pakistan: analysis of censoring and selection bias, *Economics of Education Review*, **22**, 249–64

Hoxby, C. M., 2000: The effects of class size on student achievement: new evidence from population variation, *Quarterly Journal of Economics*, **115**, 1239–85

Jacoby, H., 1994: Borrowing constraints and progress through school: evidence from Peru, *Review of Economics and Statistics*, **76**(1), 151–60

Jalan, J. and E. Glinskaya, 2003: Improving primary school education in India: an impact assessment of DPEP – phase I, unpublished manuscript

James, E., E. King and A. Suryadi, 1996: Finance, management, and costs of public and private schools in Indonesia, *Economics of Education Review*, **15**(4), 387–98

Jamison, D., B. Searle, K. Galda and S. P. Heyneman, 1981: Improving elementary mathematics education in Nicaragua: an experimental study of the impact of textbooks and radio on achievement, *Journal of Educational Psychology*, **73**(4), 556–67

Jimenez, E. and M. E. Lockheed, 1995: Public and private secondary education in developing countries, Discussion Paper, **309**, World Bank, Washington, DC

Jayasuriya, and Wodon, 2002:

King, E. and B. Ozler, 1998: What's decentralisation got to do with learning? The case of Nicaragua's autonomy reform, Working Paper Series on Impact Evaluation of Education Reforms, 9, Development Economics Research Group, World Bank, Washington, DC

Kremer, M., Moulin and Namanyu, 2003: Randomized evaluations of education program in developing countries: some lessons, *American Economic Review Papers and Proceedings*,

Kremer, M. and A. Sarychev, 1998: Why do governments operate schools?, mimeo

Krueger, A. B., 2000: Economic considerations and class size, Working Paper, **447**, Princeton University, Industrial Relations Section

Krueger, A. B. and D. M. Whitmore, 2001: The effects of attending a small class in the early graduation college-test taking and middle school test results: evidence from Project STAR, *Economic Journal*, **111**, 1–28

Lavy, V., 1996: School supply constraints and children's educational outcomes in rural Ghana, *Journal of Development Economics*, **51**, 291–314

Lazear, E., 2001: Educational production, *Quarterly Journal of Economics*, **116**(3), 777–803

Lee, J.-W. and R. J. Barro, 2001: School quality in a cross section of countries, *Economica*, **68**, 465–88

Lockheed, M. E., A. M. Verspoor *et al.*, 1991: Improving primary education in developing countries, Oxford University Press for the World Bank, Oxford

Medrich, E. and J. Griffith, 1992: International mathematics and science assessment: what have we learned?, Research and Development Report, National Center for Education Statistics, January

Miguel, E. and M. Kremer, 2001: Worms: identifying impacts on education and health in the presence of treatment externalities, Working Paper, **8481**, National Bureau of Economic Research; forthcoming in *Econometrica*

Morley, S. and D. Coady, 2003: From social assistance to social development: targeted, education subsidies in developing countries,

Munshi, K. and M. Rosenzweig, 2003: Traditional institutions meet the modern world: caste, gender, and schooling choice in a globalizing economy, MIT Department of Economics Working Paper, **03–23**

National Examination Council of Tanzania,

National Center for Education Statistics, 2000: Pursuing excellence: comparison of international eighth-grade mathematics and science achievement from a US perspective, 1995 and 1999

Newman, J., L. Rawlings and P. Gertler, 1994: Using randomized control design in evaluating social sector programs in developing countries, *The World Bank Research Observer*, **9**(2), 181–202

Nwaerondu, N. G. and G. Thompson, 1987: The use of educational radio in developing countries: lessons from the past, *Journal of Distance Education*, **2**(2), 43–54

OECD, 2001: Reading for change: performance and engagement across countries, Results from PISA 2000, Paris

Pitt, M., M. Rosenzweig and D. Gibbons, 1993: The determinants and consequences of the placement of government programs in Indonesia, *World Bank Economic Review*, **7**(3), 319–48

Pritchett, L., 1996: Where has all the education gone?, *World Bank Economic Review*, **15**(3)
2002a: Ought ain't is: midnight thoughts on education,
2002b: When will they ever learn: why all governments produce schooling,

Pritchett, L. and M. Woolcock, 2004: Arraying the disarray in development, forthcoming in *World Development*

Ravallion, M. and Q. Wodon, 1999: *Does child labour displace schooling? Evidence on behavioural responses to an enrolment subsidy*, Working Paper, **2116**, World Bank, Washington, DC

Roberts, J., 2003: Poverty reduction outcomes in education and health: public expenditure and aid, Working Paper, **210**, ODI, UK

Robitaille, D. and R. Garden (eds.), 1989: *The International Association for the Evaluation of Education Achievement (IEA) study of mathematics*, II: *Contexts and outcomes of school mathematics*, Pergamon Press, Oxford

Scott, J. 1999: *Seeing like a state: how certain schemes to improve the human condition have failed*, Yale Agrarian Studies

Schultz, P. T., 2001: School subsidies for the poor: evaluating the Mexican PROGRESA poverty program, Center Discussion Paper, 843, Economic Growth Center, Yale University, New Haven

UNESCO, 2002: Education for All: is the world on track?, EFA Global Monitoring Report

Urquiola, M. 2001: Identifying class size effects in developing countries: evidence from rural schools in Bolivia, Policy Research Working Paper, **2711**, World Bank, Washington, DC

US Department of Education, 2000: *Mathematics and science in the eighth grade: findings from the Third International Mathematics and Science Study*,

Vermeersch, C., 2002: School meals, educational achievement and school competition: evidence from a randomized evaluation, unpublished manuscript

World Bank, 2004: *World development report 2004: making services work for poor people*, World Bank, Washington DC

Appendix 1

Table 4A.1. Estimated Impact of Reducing Distance to Schools in Rural Areas in Twenty-One Countries is Typically Statistically Significant but Quantitatively Small…

Country	Year	Avge Dis-tance (km)	Avge enrol-ment ages 6–14 (%)	Linear prob. model coeff. on cluster distance to primary school[a] (%)	Sig. (%)	If distance to primary school = 0 for all clusters (%)	If distance to primary *and* secondary school = 0 for all clusters (%)	If a primary school in each cluster (%)
Chad	1998	7.2	27.0	−0.8	**	32.8	40.4	36.5
Mali	1995–96	6.6	16.1	−0.8	**	21.4	21.4	28.4
Senegal	1992–93	5.0	18.2	0.5	**	15.7	15.7	16.8
CAR	1994–95	3.9	46.4	−0.9	**	49.9	45.5	51.3
Niger	1992	3.4	10.3	−0.5	**	12.0	12.0	16.0
Zimbabwe	1994	2.5	83.6	−0.6	*	85.1	87.3	87.4
Cameroon	1991	2.5	62.0	−1.3		65.2	80.2	66.5
Niger	1998	2.4	14.5	−0.3	*	15.2	18.2	19.7
Burkina Faso	1992–93	2.4	19.5	−0.7	**	21.2	21.2	23.9
Morocco	1993–94	2.0	36.4	0.0		36.4	36.4	39.5
Haiti	1994–95	1.5	66.8	−1.7	**	69.4	69.4	69.3
Uganda	1995	1.4	67.9	−0.5		68.6	71.4	67.8
Côte d' Ivoire	1994	1.1	41.7	−0.1		41.8	45.3	43.3
Tanzania	1991–92	1.0	45.5	−0.3	*	45.8	45.8	46.5
Nigeria	1999	0.9	59.3	−0.2		59.5	61.8	59.9
Benin	1996	0.9	33.7	−1.4	**	34.9	44.7	36.4
Madagascar	1992	0.9	52.2	−2.3	**	54.2	54.2	55.3
Bolivia	1993–94	0.8	83.1	−0.8	+	83.7	85.5	85.4
Dom. Rep.	1991	0.5	54.2	−2.2	*	55.3	55.3	55.6
Philippines	1993	0.4	75.2	−0.1		75.2	75.2	76.5
India	1998–99	0.4	76.0	0.0		76.0	76.4	76.6
India	1992–93	0.2	62.9	−0.1		62.9	63.4	65.0
Bangladesh	1992–93	0.2	73.2	−3.1	+	73.8	74.0	75.9
Bangladesh	1996–97	0.2	70.3	−2.2	*	70.6	73.1	73.4
Average		2.0	49.8	−0.9		51.1	53.1	53.0
Median		**1.3**	**53.2**	**−0.7**		**54.7**	**54.7**	**55.4**

Notes: [a]Based on a linear probability model regression of enrolment for each child in a regression that, in addition to schooling availability included variables for the child (age, age^2, gender), household (dummy for top half of households by an asset index, highest schooling of males in the household, highest schooling of females in the household, gender of household head, schooling of the household head) and cluster (distance to facilities – e.g. post office, local market, bank, cinema).
Source: Filmer (2003).

Table 4A.2. Achievement (Positive means Smaller Class Sizes Raise Achievement) Using School Fixed Effects and Instrumental Variables to Identify the Class-Size Effect

Country	Mathematics			Science		
	Weighted least squares	School fixed effects	SFE-IV	WLS	SFE	SFE-IV
Australia	−4.33	−4.30	2.08	−3.65	−1.46	0.70
Belgium–Flemish	−2.18	−0.82	−8.09	−1.47	−0.48	−1.08
Belgium–French	−1.51	0.53	−0.80	0.58	1.70	0.67
Canada	−0.76	−0.20	−0.25	−0.09	−0.17	1.22
Czech Rep.	−2.37	1.10	−2.67	−1.43	1.82	1.03
France	−2.59	−1.60	2.73	−0.55	−0.10	−0.14
Greece	−0.46	0.88	1.53	−0.29	−0.05	2.41
Hong Kong	−5.47	−4.06	5.22	−5.47	−3.50	12.98
Iceland	−0.16	0.44	2.59	1.01	0.47	0.16
Japan	−3.81	0.29	−0.07	−2.59	0.44	0.26
Korea	0.15	0.21	0.90	−0.19	−0.07	0.42
Portugal	−0.77	−0.85	−1.54	−0.17	−0.07	0.31
Romania	−2.14	−0.30	0.30	−1.43	−0.70	−3.31
Scotland	−2.52	−2.92	4.98	0.66	0.63	−31.58
Singapore	−4.69	−3.10	−0.45	−5.03	−3.47	−0.52
Slovenia	−0.52	0.05	−1.25	0.39	−0.13	−0.29
Spain	−0.17	0.10	0.31	−0.19	−0.10	0.70
USA	0.16	0.00	−20.26	−0.04	−0.15	1.28
Median	−1.82	−0.10	0.12	−0.24	−0.10	0.36
Fraction positive (%)	11.1	44.4	55.6	22.2	27.8	72.2
Number positive, reject zero			2			2
Number fail to reject 0, reject effect as large as 3			10			9
Number fail to reject either 0 or effect as large as 3			6			6

Alternative Perspectives

Perspective Paper 4.1

T. PAUL SCHULTZ

There are three interrelated issues involved in the design of an efficient and equitable educational system for the world. First, the *productivity* of similar workers with different levels of schooling must be assessed, from which the *productive benefits* of schooling can be inferred, and in combination with the costs of producing this schooling, the *private and social rates of return* to schooling can then be approximated. Second, public subsidies of educational services should not only raise the average welfare, but also reduce *economic inequalities* in personal economic opportunities, if possible. Third, schooling, given its quality, should be produced at the *lowest possible private and public cost* at every level.

Lant Pritchett's chapter 4 in this volume focuses primarily on the third issue and concludes that school system reforms are his top priority. He argues that reforms should lower the cost of producing educational services and represent the most cost-effective means for expanding and improving the educational systems in low-income countries, and thus respond to the challenge of a 'lack of education' in the world. No empirical evidence is presented that documents precisely what the recommended system reforms in education could accomplish at a specified cost. Nor is evidence marshalled from randomised evaluation studies which might demonstrate the proposed reforms increase the quantity and quality of education. If reforms involved no social cost, and they achieved an increase in the output of educational services, they would, of course, be attractive and presumably cost-effective

responses to the 'lack of education'. But it would be naïve not to recognise the political and economic resources expended to implement reforms of the scope recommended, in which powerful groups who have vested interests in current arrangements and would stand to lose. Evaluation methods could be devised to clarify the conditions under which such reforms are likely to produce gains in enrolments and school quality, and how large the restructuring costs can be expected to be to accomplish such reforms in more and less favourable circumstances. Since the proposed reforms are entirely hypothetical, it is understandable that Pritchett deals with the reforms in only the most general conceptual terms in the last few pages of his chapter.

But the first two issues – the market for education and the distributional consequences of educational systems and subsidies – also warrant analysis; the efficiency and equity of public educational policies should be analysed together, and they are not confronted together or separately in Pritchett's chapter. In early human capital studies conducted in the 1960s and 1970s, it was common to assume that private wage returns to education tended to decrease at higher levels of schooling (e.g. Becker 1975, 108–49). When public subsidies for education are added to the private costs to approximate social returns to schooling, social returns are lower than private returns, and probably social returns decline more rapidly than private returns at higher levels of schooling in a society. Although the social externalities of education creating benefits beyond the family have attracted theoretical interest, empirical measurement of these social externalities has proven difficult, suggesting that they may be relatively small, even though some specific areas of education, research and development are combined to deal with local problems in agriculture and public health, and are thought to be associated with societal returns which cannot be readily appropriated by the producer of the education.

International agencies gradually adopted the view in the 1980s that education should be seen as a *social investment*, and the public sector in low-income countries should coordinate this sector and establish its priorities, rather than leave the private sector to set them. The conclusion was reached that the social returns to education are highest for primary education, and the public sector should therefore concentrate its resources in low-income countries on the basic levels of education to maximise social returns. This assignment of priority to the objective of efficiency in coordinating the sector was reinforced by the presumption that public subsidies for primary and then basic secondary schooling would narrow the personal differences in education, and thus beneficially reduce inequality in earnings within a society.

But there are growing empirical indications that private returns to education are often higher at more advanced levels of schooling, although social returns may still be moderated because of the large public subsidies per student at the level of secondary and tertiary schooling in many low-income countries. But with the new emerging structure of wages by education, in which the ratio of wages of college graduates to primary school graduates has increased, the goals of promoting an efficient (i.e. high social returns) and an equitable pattern of public educational investments may conflict, and tradeoffs between these general goals should be evaluated with care. Pritchett does not comment on the consequences for educational policy or priorities on social or private returns, or on the equitable personal distribution of public subsidies due to the educational system.

If the highest private returns to education are associated with post-secondary schooling, for which the benefits of public subsidies are often most unequally distributed across the population, further tensions arise between achieving efficiency and equity in determining public sector priorities for education. Correspondingly, the lowest private returns are today often empirically observed at the primary school level, and yet public investments at this level are nonetheless expected to reduce inequalities. These issues of how educational priorities will be set when efficiency and equity objectives conflict is an emerging issue for the Copenhagen Consensus panel to address before deciding what the most promising opportunities are to remedy the 'lack of education' in the world.

What does Pritchett's chapter argue? It is a broad and cogent review of a large literature on efficiently producing educational services, with a focus on policy opportunities in low-income countries that would increase the number of years of schooling completed by youth and improve the quality of that schooling. In brief, the chapter considers five strategies or policy opportunities: (1) expanding existing school operations, such as building more schools and hiring more teachers; (2) improving the quality of schools by traditional approaches, such as increasing teacher wages or reducing class size; (3) increasing the private demand for schooling, by either adding to household income or increasing the private returns to schooling; (4) increasing the private demand for schooling by reducing the private cost of schooling, either by cutting school fees or by increasing cash or in-kind transfers to parents whose children go to school; (5) reforming the entire school system to increase accountability for using resources to accomplish clearly measured school objectives.

The chapter argues that opportunity (1) and (2) are not generally cost-effective for increasing the quantity or quality of schooling. Increasing household income in order to augment the private demand for schooling, as in (3), is promoting a universal welfare goal, growth in income, to foster a small increase in expenditures on schooling, and policy measures which would predictably increase the private returns to schooling are not well understood, except that returns appear to increase and enrolment rates to rise in conjunction with more rapid technological change, openness of the economy to international trade, and a lack of natural resource endowment to otherwise bolster exports (Schultz 2003b).

In his review of the policy opportunities to reduce private costs of schooling (4), Pritchett adopts a more cautious stance. He concludes that the policy innovations in this area may prove productive, but our evaluations of these experiences are currently mixed, and do not provide a foundation to recommend specific policy measures. The two critical features of such a school subsidy approach are, first, how much do parents respond to a subsidy by increasing their children's enrolment in school and, second, how efficient are programmes in targeting parents who would not otherwise send their children to school? Unless the programme can identify in a socially acceptable way those parents who are on the 'margin' of educating their children, and then concentrate the school subsidy on these segments of the population, the schooling subsidy becomes for many parents an ineffectual 'rent' paid to those who would be sending their children to school without the subsidy. If the school subsidy is partially justified on other grounds than 'lack of education,' such as 'alleviating poverty' in the target population, then the costs of the programme must be divided between the multiple objectives, making the school subsidy a more cost-effective policy instrument to remedy the lack of education. However, experience with targeted school subsidy policies is limited, and only a few countries have evaluated these programs with the aid of randomised social designs, such as the Mexican PROGRESA programme which started in 1998 (Schultz 2001). How should mechanisms be designed to reward only parents who are likely to enrol their child if and only if the parent is eligible for the targeted transfer? More evaluation studies could aid in the design of efficient and socially acceptable approaches, which may not be the same in all countries.

For many years, societies have sought institutions to extend to the poor and unlucky a safety net to sustain a minimum level of consumption, but they should be designed in a manner which does not encourage beneficiaries from altering otherwise productive behaviour. Knowledge has accumulated on many possible designs for these social welfare programmes and how they affect welfare and work, but no miracle has emerged which does not dull the incentives for the beneficiaries to work. Household models of school enrolment have received only recent study, and can be expected to improve their capacity to identify parents who, given their initial conditions, are not likely to send their children to school. Can programmes strengthen the impact on enrolments by targeting these identified 'types' of parents with transfer payments to enrol their children? How might such an incentive system 'distort' parent effort to educate their children, or influence their migration or other forms of household behaviours among persons potentially eligible for the school subsidy programme? Will society view such a conditional transfer scheme as fair? This is a new challenge to redesign social policy to increase the level and reduce the variance in schooling in society, which may prove to be more cost-effective than opportunities (1), (2) or (3) in so far as they increase the resources allocated to the children of the poor and poorly educated parents. Is the decision not to enrol children in school occurring because parents cannot borrow to invest in the schooling of their children, they fail to appreciate the returns to schooling, they are less effective in helping their children's progress through school, or they are simply less altruistic toward their children? Whatever the combination of mechanisms which explain the disparities in school enrolments, the targeted school subsidy holds promise as a new and distinctive policy tool for increasing enrolments in the low-income world, and I would expect it to achieve this objective at less cost than would traditional funding of opportunities (1)–(3).

If you set aside all the traditional means to expand education in poor countries because they are cost-ineffective ((1)–(3)), and conclude that targeted transfers are as yet unproven as a reliable policy instrument ((4)), then Pritchett is left grasping for the only remaining option ((5)), systemic school reform. The chapter states that school systems should be reformed to produce their public services more efficiently by (a) establishing clear objectives, (b) publicly financing producers who should have autonomy to manage how they operate and (c) measuring their accomplishments in a manner which will be transparent to inform private consumers and public regulators, who both will need to evaluate outputs and inputs. Accountability for the educational system is attractive, of course, but where are the case studies which document that implementing a specific set of school system reforms in the many regions of the low-income world will have the promised cost-effective impact of expanding and improving the educational systems?

Many evaluation studies have concluded that policies listed under (1)–(3) have not performed satisfactorily, and the few available studies of (4) indicate that costs may vary when subsidies are poorly targeted across households. But on the other hand, these targeted programme subsidies are likely to achieve a more equitable distribution of schooling and economic resources than will the other policy options. I do not know where there are peer-reviewed studies confirming that a generalised package of school reforms has achieved more, or less, than school subsidies for the poor. There are probably case studies showing that reforms can work, though I expect most will not rely on an experimental design, or sound matching methodology: they are also likely to measures of school outcomes differently, and focus on incomparable policy inputs. Only a few final pages of Pritchett's chapter are devoted to guidelines on how the school reforms should be structured, and only then is the reader referred to the 2004 *World Bank Development Report* (World Bank 2004).

What gains in schooling can be confidently attributed to (1) introducing more autonomy for local school administrators or teachers, or (2) decentralizing monitoring and decision making to parents at the community level, or (3) transparently measuring school outcomes (e.g. test scores or repetition rates), or (4) accounting for progress in achieving clearly stated educational objectives? Where are the testing grounds for the proposed components of the educational system reform? The set of goals for school system reforms is plausible. Yet the political economy of a low-income country would likely resist such changes and modify them to advance the objectives of other involved parties, including teachers, administrators, bureaucrats and politicians who control public sector patronage or access to employment in schools. If there is little agreement on how to evaluate educational achievements or improve the performance of schools in high-income countries, one can be sceptical whether the systemic reforms outlined in this chapter would effortlessly increase school quality

and quantity in the different political economies of SSA, the gender-imbalanced schools of rural South Asia, the poor or rich Middle Eastern countries, or many of the poorer countries of Central and South East Asia where democratic institutions are not yet well rooted.

I agree with Pritchett that reforms that improve the accountability of schools could be an important step in accelerating the expansion of education in many low-income countries. It is unclear to me, however, that systemic school reform as advocated in this chapter will occur without broader political reforms, and I am not confident that we understand how to introduce a self-sustaining reform of political systems for schools any more than we have a proven blueprint for building democracy in societies where it does not now exist. The school system reforms outlined in Pritchett's chapter provide no more than a conceptual framework to guide more concrete thinking about the institutional conditions that would help schools function more efficiently. Implementing these reforms would require creating and empowering groups who want the public service of schooling for their children and family members, and are willing to share them and pay for them. Some experiments with decentralisation of schooling systems which encourage local area parents to monitor performance may work as reformers imagined. Yet, I would expect that many decentralisation reforms have not worked much better than the earlier more centralised regimes, because school resources are coopted by local elites who favour their own constituents rather then the educationally disadvantaged. If Pritchett is understandably cautious in recommending evaluation of policy experiments to demonstrate that targeted school subsidies are effective among the least educated and poorest parents, the same cautious approach should be applied to evaluation of systemic school reforms, until these reforms have been rigorously shown to achieve both the expected increases in the quantity and quality of schooling, and to distribute those educational benefits at a moderate cost across the poorer segments of society.

Pritchett hypothesises that school systems perform inefficiently because the structure of incentives leads agents who are involved in operating schools to promote their own objectives. These claims that existing policies are endogenous and not perverse is eminently plausible, but do not provide much insight into how to enact the proposed reforms. What incentive structures which can be enacted would foster the reforms and how does one create the coalitions to sustain momentum once the reforms get under way? The policy maker can rarely dictate the entire package of reforms outlined in the chapter, and for this reason many second-best solutions are introduced with the hope that they will create pressures to consider more fundamental reforms. Charter schools may allow diversity and autonomy to express the heterogeneous preferences of parents within large, otherwise inflexible, metropolitan school systems, and may thereby foster experimentation with different teaching routines, specialisation and even using auxiliary teaching assistants or tutors who can be recruited at low cost from local women. School vouchers permit private schools to compete for public school subsidies to provide lower cost schooling, and thereby pressure urban public schools to be more flexible and cost-effective in allocating their resources, as well as encouraging teachers and unions to reconsider restrictions on work routines and to introduce pay bonuses to reward teaching accomplishments. These types of second-best partial reforms are noted in passing at the outset of Pritchett's chapter, but they may ultimately provide the needed institutional mechanisms to start systemic reforms on a small scale. Pritchett's chapter should illustrate his global systemic reforms with specific case studies from which he might extract key features associated with their success or failure.

This brings me back to my initial criticism of Pritchett's chapter. It ignores the mounting evidence of an inversion of private returns to schooling by school level, first observed in the USA in the 1980s, but increasingly documented in the other high-income countries, and now observed in a growing number of low-income countries. Specifically, when a Mincerian wage function is estimated from representative household survey data, in which the wage returns are allowed to vary by level of schooling, the percentage increases in wages associated with an additional year of secondary and tertiary schooling tends to be larger today than the percentage increases in wages associated with a year of primary schooling. This suggests that many poor parents, who are marginally considering whether to keep their child in primary schooling, may face lower marginal returns than do rich parents, who are considering whether to keep their child in secondary school or to send them on to post-secondary school. In contrast with the economic intuition that the marginal percentage wage returns to schooling would tend to decrease at more advanced levels of schooling, private returns to school appear today often to increase at more advanced levels of schooling, even in regions with very low levels of education, as in SSA (Schultz 2003a). This empirical regularity may be a short-run disequilibrium due to slow macroeconomic development or distortions in the labour market, but it poses a dilemma for educational policy makers today that should be addressed by the Consensus Panel. If school reforms are successful, the increasing private returns to secondary and post-secondary schooling may induce increased enrolments by the middle class at these levels of schooling whereas the poor will have little incentive to enrol more of their children in the primary school system. Polarisation in educational attainments, rather than convergence, within poor countries may occur unless new educational policies are introduced.

Moreover, when public subsidies per student year for post-secondary schooling are often ten times larger than public subsidies per student year for primary schooling, as they are in many low-income countries, it may be argued that higher education could be more efficiently produced and more equitably distributed if the children of relatively well-educated parents paid more of the public costs of their children's higher education, and these public tuition revenues could then be reallocated toward the expansion of targeted transfers to the poor and less educated parents to encourage them to enrol their children in secondary school. In short, Pritchett's chapter does not deal with the mounting evidence that private returns to primary schooling are declining. In Africa, for example, where barriers to international trade remain high, political stability is a serious problem, foreign direct investment (FDI) is low and resulting economic growth is slow, supplies of primary-educated workers may satisfy current aggregate demands for these types of workers.

The difficult question for the experts assessing the Consensus on the Global Challenge of the Lack of Education is whether world labour markets are already supplying enough primary-educated workers to meet current economic demands in many large labour markets, from Nigeria, to Ghana, and even from India to China. Is the Millennium Development Goal (MDG) of universal primary schooling no longer justified on the grounds of the economic scarcity of primary educated workers or their enhanced labour productivity, or is the MDG of universal primary schooling merely a rhetorical target, or should universal primary enrolment be justified because of its impact on economic and social inequality?

References

Becker, G. S., 1975: *Human capital: a theoretical and empirical analysis with special reference to education*, 2nd. edn., University of Chicago Press, Chicago; addendum, pp. 108–49, originally published as a Woytinsky Lecture at the University of Michigan, 1967

Schultz, T. P., 2001: School subsidies for the poor: evaluating the Mexican Progresa poverty program, Economic Growth Center Discussion Paper, **843**, Yale University, August; http://www.econ.yale.edu/~egcenter/EGCdp4d.htm; forthcoming in the *Journal of Development Education*, **74**, 199–250

2003a: Evidence of returns to schooling in Africa from household surveys: monitoring and restructuring the market for education, Economic Growth Center Discussion Paper, 875, Yale University, December; http://www.econ.yale.edu/~egcenter/EGCdp4d.htm

2003b: Is globalization associated with advancing schooling, health, and gender equality? Paper prepared for a conference on The Future of Globalization, Yale University, 10–11 October

World Bank, 2004: *World Bank Development Report*, Washington, DC

Perspective Paper 4.2

LUDGER WÖßMANN

This Perspective paper is meant to provide critical comments on Lant Pritchett's chapter 4 in this volume. As I will argue, I think that the chapter does a wonderful job of defining the challenge and of discussing relevant opportunities to address it. I do not see major omissions, nor do I think that there are gross imbalances in the chapter's assessments. What I would like to add is some additional details and cost-benefit discussions on the opportunity constituted by systemic school reform, as well as a more positive view on the cost-benefit assessment (CBA) of the opportunity of increasing demand for education by eliminating primary-school fees. The note closes with some concluding comments. The appendix has two more specific remarks, less related to the Copenhagen Consensus assessment.

General Assessment

Pritchett (2004) defines the challenge of lack of education as one of 'creating competencies and learning achievement' rather than just formal school enrolment. It seems obvious that the chosen one is the preferable definition, which is worth stressing only because unfortunately, many policy discussions do not make the same choice. The definition is particularly appropriate because it places a focus on the *quality* as well as quantity of schooling, which has been shown to be of key relevance in much recent research.

Pritchett also provides a very useful framework for choosing and structuring the most important opportunities to alleviate the challenge of lack of education. I wholeheartedly agree with the chapter's main thrust of argument and general assessment of the costs and benefits of the different opportunities to tackle the education challenge. When Pritchett (2004) states that there may be a divide of opinion in the literature as to whether policy actions will be sufficient to meet the challenge or whether this will require systemic reform, for example, I think that evidence forces me to be firmly on his side of the divide, stressing the need for institutional reforms in addition to resource policies.

The chapter discusses the opportunities most often considered in public debates, and shows that many of the 'usual suspects' have been shown to give rise to only small benefits. Therefore, it has to be doubted that these would substantially alleviate the challenge of lack of education. On the supply side, for example, overwhelming evidence has shown that simple physical expansion (opportunity 1) and increased spending per student (opportunity 2) generally do not seem to lead to substantial increases in children's competencies and learning achievement. On the demand side, Pritchett stresses that increased income and education of parents as well as increased returns to schooling (opportunity 3) would probably be very effective ways to alleviate the lack of education. However, these features are not subject to easy policy control, so that unfortunately, this again is not a clear practical 'opportunity' to address the challenge. I agree with all these assessments.

The other opportunity on the demand side is to reduce the cost of schooling for households (opportunity 4). Much evidence shows that actions in this direction have the potential to alleviate the challenge of lack of education. However, Pritchett sounds a cautionary note on this opportunity as well, stressing that the costs of such actions can easily be so large as to not warrant the benefits. While this cautionary note is clearly warranted, I will give a more optimistic assessment of one opportunity in this class, namely the eradication of fees for primary schooling.

Finally, Pritchett stresses that probably the most important opportunity to address the education challenge is systemic performance-focused school reform (opportunity 5, or Pritchett's 'fifth element'). Such systemic reform would set clear objectives and hold producers accountable for achieving them, while at the same time giving producers the autonomy required to do so. I could not agree more.

The 'bad news' from the point of view of the Copenhagen Consensus project is that systemic reform is not really a simple 'project' where you can put money into and see what benefits this money brings about. This is not about having $50 bn and wondering where to spend it, because the very behaviour of government is endogenised in this model of how to face the challenges of the world. This is somewhat disillusioning for the Copenhagen Consensus effort, as it is difficult to place this key opportunity in the framework of applied welfare economics, attaching a net present value (NPV) of costs and benefits to it. Still, some sort of quantification does not seem impossible, at least on the benefit side. Much research over recent years has shown that institutional reforms that focus on altering the incentives of the people involved by increasing accountability, choice and autonomy have very large benefits indeed. This leads into a discussion of feasibility, asking why it is that there is a lack of education in the first place. Arguably, it is the opposing interests of many actors in the field that have prevented an alleviation of the challenge so far – and, without systemic reform, will keep preventing it in the future, whatever budget-relevant policy action is implemented. Systemic reform has thus to be considered the binding constraint on the global challenge of lack of education. Given that the discussion in the chapter gets a bit thin on this topic, I will add some additional aspects and CBAs on this opportunity in the following section.

[1] For a positive model of why and how institutions such as central exams and school autonomy affect behaviour and ultimately students' learning achievement, see Bishop and Wößmann (2004).

Additional Aspects on Institutions and Incentives

While Pritchett (2004) emphasises institutional reform as the key opportunity to alleviate a lack of education, the final part of the chapter discussing this opportunity is a little flimsy, sometimes lacking concreteness, justification and an assessment of costs and benefits. The reader is left wondering, for example, if and how measurement of different outputs can be achieved, which concrete functions should or should not be decentralised, where the recommendation list for a 'well ordered system for schooling' is derived from, which positive theory it is based on, and what the returns to specific reforms may be. The following brief notes try to fill some of these gaps.

Some Additional Concrete Elements of Successful Systemic Reform

One concrete systemic element focusing on introducing accountability that has been shown to be strongly related to superior student learning is *curriculum-based exit exams* that are external to schools (e.g. Wößmann 2003a; Bishop 2004). Another means to increase accountability is explicit school-focused *accountability systems*, which have been shown to increase students' learning achievement in the USA (Carnoy and Loeb 2003; Hanushek and Raymond 2004).

In terms of *school autonomy*, using data from international student achievement tests Wößmann (2003a) finds that students learn more in schools that have autonomy in process and personnel decisions and in schools whose teachers have both incentives and powers to select appropriate teaching methods. By contrast, in curricular and budgetary decision making areas, *centralised control mechanisms* are related to better student learning.[1] In addition, there are important interaction effects between external exams and school autonomy, in that school autonomy is more beneficial in systems that have external exit exams (Wößmann 2003b). External exams thus are a precondition for decentralised education systems to function properly, just as centrally provided currencies are for decentralised economic systems. Systemic school reforms should thus combine central exams with school autonomy, setting and testing standards externally but leaving it up to schools how to pursue them.

Jimenez and Paqueo (1996) find that *local financial contributions* increased the productivity of public schools in the Philippines relative to central financing, and Jimenez and Sawada (1999) show that enhanced community and *local involvement* improved student learning in El Salvador. Another systemic feature that introduces performance orientation focuses on the *incentives of teachers*. Lavy (2002, 2003) shows that monetary incentives for teachers based on their students' performance immensely improved student learning in Israel. Finally, Colombia ran a programme that provided vouchers for the attendance at *private schools*, which can be argued to be more subject to performance-focused incentives than public schools due to market forces. The benefits of this programme have been found to clearly exceed its cost, which was similar to providing a place in public schools (Angrist *et al*. 2002). Similarly, James, King and Suryadi (1996) and Bedi and Garg (2000) find that privately managed schools in Indonesia are more efficient and effective than public schools.

The Costs and Benefits of Systemic Reform

It seems hard to perform a meaningful CBA of systemic reforms. This is particularly true for the cost side. What are the costs of systemic reform? These are probably mainly not directly budget-related, but tend to lie in the political realm of breaking opposing interests. I am unaware of any study trying to quantify such costs in monetary terms; however, it seems fair to say that any such implementation costs are probably similar for meeting most other challenges and not restricted to education. In contrast to the political costs, the direct costs of most systemic reforms in education seem to be minuscule (see Hoxby 2002 for evidence in the case of accountability programmes).

Likewise, quantifying the benefits of systemic reform is difficult, albeit not impossible. To get economic estimates of the large benefits found in recent research in terms of student learning, the easiest

way would be to focus on effects on later earnings in the labour market. There are probably also significant non-market benefits to increased student learning, but these are much harder to measure. Thus, one can at least estimate the benefits of systemic reforms in terms of additional (quantity and/or quality of) education, and then try to link them to estimates of how they translate into additional earnings. In this sense, it seems somewhat unfortunate that Pritchett (2004) chose not to review the benefits of quality basic education, as these should probably be the foundation stone for any CBA of educational opportunities, as well as for their comparison to opportunities that address other global challenges.

Given limited concrete developing country evidence on effects of institutional variation on student learning, as well as of learning achievement on earnings, much of this evidence will have to come from cross-country and developed country evidence. The estimates presented have therefore to be treated with considerable caution. Still, for example in the case of curriculum-based external exit exams, cross-country evidence from at least five different international student achievement tests (SATs) and cross-regional evidence from Canada, Germany and the USA all show that such exam systems are a powerful accountability device that yields benefits in terms of students' learning achievement that dwarf any effect found for resource-related policies (cf. Bishop 2004). The effects found in these studies are often as large as a whole grade-level equivalent and more, or roughly some 40 per cent of an international standard deviation in test scores (Wößmann 2003b). The different systemic features analysed in Wößmann (2003a) combine to a total effect that equals about two international standard deviations in test scores.[2]

Unfortunately, not much is known about how exactly such gains in educational achievement translate into economically quantifiable benefits, particularly in developing countries. However, to give

---

[2] One caveat is that all these estimates were based on secondary rather than primary education, so that they could serve only as a rough estimate of how large the benefits of systemic reforms in primary education might be.

a rough assessment, one might refer to Krueger's (2003) estimate that a plausible assessment of the existing evidence might be that an improvement in test-score performance by 1 standard deviation is associated with an 8 per cent improvement in annual earnings in Britain and the USA. External exit exams might thus increase annual earnings by more than 3 per cent and, combined with autonomy effects, the total effect might be as large as 16 per cent. Given that these increases in annual earnings accrue throughout the lifetime for each individual who is taught in the reformed system, the total benefits of the reform would be immense. Whether taking the narrow external exam estimate or the broader institutional reform estimate, this rough back-of-the-envelope calculation suggests that the total benefit of these systemic reforms would equal 3–16 per cent of the total NPV of all lifetime earnings of all students.[3] This is astoundingly large, compared to whatever the cost of such a reform may be in the end, and it does not even consider additional promising systemic reforms such as performance-related teacher incentives and choice-based reforms.

Effects and Cost-Effectiveness of Fee Waivers

Dropping Out of School Versus Never Enrolling in School

Before getting concretely to the fee issue, I would like to briefly downplay the emphasis that Pritchett

(2004) lays on the difference between insufficient education due to dropping out of school and insufficient education due to never enrolling in school. Pritchett stresses that the problem of dropping out is much more important than the problem of never enrolling. First, based on the evidence that he presents, my feeling is that this assertion is valid only for middle-income countries at best. In those regions of the world where the challenge of lack of education is strongest (SSA and South Asia), the problem of not enrolling actually seems to be more important than the problem of dropping out. According to Pritchett's table 4.2 (p. 181), only 15 per cent (16 per cent) of the deficit from universal completion of grade 5 in West and Central Africa (South Asia) is due to dropping out, and as many as 44 per cent (28 per cent) of children never enrol in school. Furthermore, the lack of education is most severe for those who never enrol, so this latter group presents a very important margin for action.

Second, the difference between dropping out and never enrolling is probably not an utterly crucial one anyway. This is because both problems are probably mainly due to similar reasons (high costs relative to household income, low quality of schools, low rate of return) and susceptible to similar policy remedies. Thus, if a main constraint is high school fees, then this will probably lead some households to decide that they cannot afford to enrol (some of) their children at all, and at the same time lead other households to decide that they can afford to enrol (some of) their children for, say, three years, after which they will have to drop out of school.

The Impact of Primary-School Fees

In situations of insufficient public budgets, user fees have been cautiously advocated as a means to increase enrolment (e.g. Mingat and Tan 1986), and most developing countries today impose some type of user fees in primary education (World Bank 2002b, 12).[4] However, school fees that might seem rather low to outside observers prove to be prohibitive for people living in extreme poverty. Even though parents might be well aware of potentially substantial future benefits of education

---

[3] To give a general idea of how large this is in monetary terms, one could make the following assumptions. First, assume that the benefits apply to all children of primary-school age (6–11) in the developing world, which are 623 m (Delamonica, Mehrotra and Vandemoortele 2001). Second, assume that the relevant average income is the simple mean of low- and lower-middle-income countries, which is US$ 770 (gross national income *per capita* in purchasing power parity (PPP), World Bank 2002a). Third, assume that the benefits accrue for an average working life of twenty-five years and that the relevant discount rate is 5 per cent. Then, the total NPV of a 3 per cent increase in earnings would equal US$ 213 bn and US$ 1.1 trillion for a 16 per cent increase.

[4] While the discussion here focuses only on primary-schools fees, it should be noted that due to significant cross-price elasticities (cf. Lavy 1996), fees in secondary schools will also have negative effects on decisions to enrol in primary schools.

for their children, the mere necessity to obtain the means to survive inhibits them from financing school fees for their children. If poor people in developing countries are credit- or even cash-constrained, fees may lead to sub-optimally low education. In such a situation, a feasible positive model might indeed predict, 'if you make schooling free, they will come!' (compare to Pritchett 2004). This has certainly proved to be the case in Malawi and Uganda, where direct primary-school fees were abolished in the mid-1990s and school enrolment shot up immediately and substantially (cf. Al-Samarrai and Zaman 2002; Deininger 2003).[5] Kremer (2003) presents additional evidence that school participation is quite elastic to cost, and Spohr (2003) reports noteworthy effects of an extension of tuition-free education from six to nine years in Taiwan. Still, the potential importance of school fees seems to be largely neglected in current policy initiatives, such as Education for All (EFA).

Pritchett (2004) raises three points of caution in the chapter against a policy of primary-school fee waivers. First, the revenue forgone might be substantial. However, I will argue below that it might still be easily dwarfed by the potential benefits. Second, evidence from Malawi seems to suggest that the attainment and persistence response to the fee waiver was not nearly as large as the enrolment response. To some extent, this point is well taken, as it shows only that complementary, mainly systemic, reforms as well as a commitment to replacing the fees by public funds are needed for a sustained effect, both of which are largely missing in Malawi. Pritchett shows that attainment of 15-year-olds in grade 6–8 in Malawi was not substantially higher in 2000 than in 1992, arguing that this shows a lack of sustained attainment effect. This is quite misleading, however, because the fee waiver was introduced only in 1994, and the children entering school in that year would have reached only grade 6 at best in 2000. Given that attainment in grades 1–5 has increased substantially, one may be more optimistic on this example. Third, the revenue forgone by waiving fees will have to be replaced by public funds, as otherwise the learning achievement of all students may suffer, a point which is certainly correct.

CBA of Fee Waivers

Ultimately, the decisive question comes down to one of comparing the costs and benefits of waiving fees. At first sight, this does not seem to be promising for fee waivers, because they are untargeted and thus particularly prone to Pritchett's (2004) cost-effectiveness caveat with respect to infra-marginal transfers. For the costs and benefits of a targeted poverty reduction programme in Mexico that made transfers contingent on children attending school, Schultz (2004) estimates an internal rate of return of 8 per cent in terms of the educational outcomes, which are in addition to the main poverty-alleviation objective pursued by the programme. Unfortunately, no explicit CBA of fee waivers is available in the literature. Still, using available information from the Uganda case, we might get a rough idea of in which ballpark the costs and benefits lie. In 1997, Uganda eliminated primary-school fees, which until then had been a major contribution to school financing, for up to four children per household. Using data from two household surveys, Deininger (2003) shows that the primary-school attendance rate increased dramatically, from 62.1 per cent (in 1992) to 83.6 per cent (in 1999) on average.[6] According to World Bank (2002c) data, total primary-school enrolment increased from 3.4 m children in 1996 to 6.9 m in 2001.

The costs of this fee waiver policy are both the forgone fees of those students who would have attended school anyway and the full additional cost of schooling for the new students. Direct data on fees are not available, but we have estimates of the total costs of primary education per student per

[5] Note that public school fees generally do not vary within countries at a given point in time, so that cross-sectional studies of student enrolment in individual countries, such as Nielsen (2001) and Handa (2002), cannot analyse the impact of public school fees because there is no variation. Those schooling costs which they can analyse are not necessarily exogenous to educational enrolment in a cross-sectional setting, as they are mainly the outcome of endogenous parental choices to pay voluntarily.

[6] These household survey-based figures may be more reliable than official enrolment statistics, which in 1999 had the gross enrolment rate at 140.9 and the net enrolment rate at 108.9 (UNESCO 2002a, 2002b).

year. These might overestimate the fee by a wide margin. Delamonica, Mehrotra and Vandemoortele (2001) report that the costs of primary education per student per year in Uganda are US$13. Based on this estimate, paying for the total costs of primary education for all students in school after the fee waiver costs US$89.7 m per year. However, the cost figure that Delamonica, Mehrotra and Vandemoortele (2001) report for Uganda is relatively low, even among SSA countries. The costs of primary education per student per year in the median SSA country are more than three times as large, at US$45. Using this figure, the total costs of primary education for all students in school after the fee waiver would be estimated at US$310.5 m per year.

What are the benefits of the Ugandan fee waiver, which created an additional 3.5 m individual years of schooling each year, in monetary terms? Taking the mean of the available estimates across SSA countries surveyed in Psacharopoulos and Patrinos (2004), each additional year of schooling increases individuals' earnings by 11.7 per cent (based on the coefficient on years of schooling in standard Mincer equations).[7] Using the mean SSA *per capita* income and years of schooling to which this estimate applies, this means that increasing a person's years of education from none at all to five years would raise her annual income by US$321.[8] If we simply divide this by the five years, this gives a rough estimate of an additional annual income per additional year of schooling of US$64.2. Assuming that, on average, people might get this additional annual income for maybe twenty-five years, and using a

discount rate of 5 per cent, this is equivalent to a NPV of additional lifetime earnings of US$950 for each additional year of schooling. Multiplying this by the 3.5 m additional years of schooling created each year by the fee waiver, a rough estimate of the total benefits in Uganda stands at US$3.3 bn.[9]

Comparing this to the cost estimate of US$89.7 m, we get a stunning BCR of 37! Even with the overrated cost estimate of US$310.5 m, the BCR would be larger than 10. That is, even though infra-marginal transfers may be high, they seem to be dwarfed by the generated benefits. Clearly, these estimates have to be taken with extreme caution, as a lot of very imprecise measures entered the calculations. Furthermore, increasing enrolment so quickly and dramatically will probably have a negative effect on the quality of schooling – because, for example, there may simply not be enough trained teachers around, which may reduce the total benefits of the policy. Also, with the ensuing substantial increase in the supply of workers who have primary education, the rate of return might be lowered (although evidence from more developed countries does not really suggest this). Thus, the cost-benefit estimates presented may surely be wide of the true value. However, in choosing the values entering the estimation, I tended to choose to overestimate the costs and underestimate the benefits. Also, while the infra-marginal transfers do not directly cause additional education, they relieve constraints on the infra-marginal households. At least part of the relieved resources may well be spent on more advanced educational goals. There are thus also good reasons to consider the presented BCRs as rather conservative estimates. If they roughly fall in the right ballpark, then the fee waiver policy seems like an incredibly attractive opportunity to address the challenge of a lack of education, in precisely those countries and for those people where the challenge is greatest.

Concluding Comments

In conclusion, it should be noted that there are also many non-market benefits of increased education that have not been considered here and that might tilt the CBAs even more to the positive side

---

[7] No Mincer estimate is available for Uganda. However, the social rate of return to investment in primary education in Uganda was estimated as high as 66 per cent in 1965 (cf. Psacharopoulos and Patrinos 2004), which is the highest among all reported estimates. Compared to this, using the mean SSA Mincer estimate of 11.7 per cent seems extremely conservative.

[8] Using Ugandan *per capita* income (gross national income *per capita* in PPP in 2000, from World Bank 2002a) and average years of schooling (from Barro and Lee 2001) instead of SSA means, the estimate would be 89 per cent higher at $607.

[9] Using alternative discount rates, the total benefits would stand at US$4.5 bn for a discount rate of 2 per cent and at US$2.2 bn for a discount rate of 10 per cent.

(cf. Haveman and Wolfe 1984; Glewwe 2002). As one example, Lochner and Moretti (2004) show that education substantially lowers criminal behaviour, which adds 14–26 per cent to the private return to high-school graduation in the USA. Furthermore, there are substantial complementarities between addressing the education challenge and addressing other major global challenges. Education has been shown to be positively related to political awareness, stability of democratic systems and social cohesion. Achieving better education will no doubt have alleviating effects on such challenges as malnutrition and hunger, health and armed conflicts. Bettering the education of one generation has also been shown to have strong intergenerational effects on the education and well-being of the next. Similarly, alleviating challenges such as bad governance and corruption, armed conflicts and poor health will no doubt help in alleviating the education challenge, as will general improvements in the economic well-being of the population (cf. Pritchett's opportunity 3; Glewwe and Jacoby 2004).

One cautionary note should be raised on Pritchett's (2004) positive assessment of the current international policy initiative, the Education for All/Fast Track Initiative (EFA/FTI). While this initiative clearly has several laudable features, and while I do not doubt that 'the people behind EFA/FTI understand the depth of the problem', it is less clear whether the same can be said for the responsible people in the countries. More importantly, EFA/FTI is likely to suffer from the general problem of foreign aid, well documented in Pritchett's chapter, that most initiatives are undermined by the divergent interests of the relevant actors in the countries. The crucial task is probably not one of providing 'plans', but one of how to change interests to overcome dysfunctional systems. It is thus not too clear whether in the end the EFA/FTI initiative will be substantially more effective than the many previous national and foreign aid initiatives with their disappointing results (cf. Pritchett 2004, for one example).

To conclude on the economic costs and benefits of the opportunities to address the global challenge of lack of education, all estimates suggest that the potential benefits would be immense, but also that there is no easy way to get the improvements implemented in practice. The most promising opportunity by far seems to be systemic reforms that introduce performance oriented incentives for all the people involved. The benefits of such institutional changes have been shown to be very large, and the direct costs low – the problem being that the 'costs' of breaking interfering interests might be high. In addition to systemic reform, I am also cautiously optimistic on demand-focused policies in many circumstances, particularly in the most severely affected situations. There will always be shortcomings to initiatives such as universal waivers of primary-school fees, but the potential benefits are very large in all but the most pathologic circumstances. Most of these benefits will occur only in the relatively long run, raising future productivity and having additional positive effects on subsequent generations. But they appear to be more than worth the cost.

Appendix

This appendix makes two further comments which may help Pritchett in finalizing his thoughts, but which are not central to the assessments of the Copenhagen Consensus and may thus not be of specific interest to the panellists.

As one example of the possibility of effect heterogeneity of class size, Pritchett (2004) suggests that class sizes might matter much with high-capability teachers, but not with low-capability teachers. Evidence in Wößmann and West (2003) suggests that the effect of class size on student performance indeed depends on teacher capability, but in precisely the opposite way: smaller classes have an observable beneficial effect on student achievement only in countries where the average capability of the teaching force, as measured by average teacher pay and teachers' education levels, appears to be low. This suggests a positive theory of educational production where capable teachers are able to promote student learning equally well regardless of class size – i.e., they are capable enough to teach well in large classes. Less capable teachers, however, while perhaps doing reasonably well when faced with small classes, do not seem to be up to the job of teaching large classes.

In calculating the share of students completing grade 9 but with 'inadequate' learning achievement in his table 4.4, Pritchett (2004, 189) uses the somewhat arbitrary assumptions that (1) 'students more than one standard deviation below the performance in the median OECD country 'lack education' and that (2) in calculating the fraction of students in a country falling below this threshold, we can use the country mean and standard deviation and assume a normal distribution. Both are actually quite reasonable assumptions, but I think that there would be preferable choices and justifications in both cases. (1) For the threshold value, it would seem advisable to use the 'International Benchmarks of Student Achievement' developed in the TIMSS-R study 'in order to provide meaningful descriptions of what performance on the scale could mean in terms of the mathematics that students know and can do' (Mullis *et al.* 2000, 38). Preferably, to depict students who lack education, it would seem sensible to use the 'Lower Quarter Benchmark' for lower-achieving students, because these generally could not even demonstrate 'computational facility with whole numbers' (Mullis *et al.* 2000, 39, cf. 42). This benchmark is at 396 test-score points, which – incidentally – is very close to Pritchett's (2004) choice of 400, but has a preferable justification to it. (2) To derive the share of students not achieving this threshold, it would seem straightforward to go for direct student information to compute the correct share, rather than basing it on the assumptions mentioned. Actually, the share of students not meeting the 'Lower Quarter Benchmark' are also reported for each country in Mullis *et al.* (2000, 43): Indonesia 52 per cent, Morocco 73 per cent, the Philippines 69 per cent and Turkey 35 per cent.[10] These numbers are close to Pritchett's, thus showing the sensibility of his assumptions, but maybe they carry a bit more rigour.[11]

---

[10] Colombia did not participate in TIMSS-R in 1999, but only in TIMSS 1995, where the comparable benchmark is not directly available.

[11] It would also help interpretability of the results in table 4.4, as well as in table 4.2, if the numbers were presented in a way so that they sum to 100 per cent across each row – i.e. each number would report which share of the total cohort would lack education because of each specific reason.

References

Al-Samarrai, S. and H. Zaman, 2002: The changing distribution of public education expenditure in Malawi, Africa Region Working Paper, **29**, World Bank, Washington, DC

Angrist, J., E. Bettinger, E. Bloom, E. King and M. Kremer, 2002: Vouchers for private schooling in Colombia: evidence from a randomized natural experiment, *American Economic Review*, **92**(5), 1535–58

Barro, R.J. and J.-W. Lee, 2001: International data on educational attainment: updates and implications, *Oxford Economic Papers*, **53**(3), 541–63

Bedi, A.S. and A. Garg, 2000: The effectiveness of private versus public schools: the case of Indonesia, *Journal of Development Economics*, **61**(2), 463–94

Bishop, J.H., 2004: Drinking from the fountain of knowledge: student incentive to study and learn, in E.A. Hanushek and F. Welch (eds.), *Handbook of the Economics of Education*, North-Holland, Amsterdam, forthcoming

Bishop, J.H. and L. Wößmann, 2004: Institutional effects in a simple model of educational production, *Education Economics*, **12**(1), 17–38

Carnoy, M. and S. Loeb, 2003: Does external accountability affect student outcomes? A cross-state analysis, *Educational Evaluation and Policy Analysis*,

Deininger, K., 2003: Does cost of schooling affect enrollment by the poor? Universal primary education in Uganda, *Economics of Education Review*, **22**(3), 291–305

Delamonica, E., S. Mehrotra and J. Vandemoortele, 2001: Is EFA affordable? Estimating the global minimum cost of 'Education for All', UNICEF Innocenti Research Centre, Innocenti Working Paper, **87**, Florence

Glewwe, P., 2002: Schools and skills in developing countries: education policies and socioeconomic outcomes, *Journal of Economic Literature*, **40**(2), 436–82

Glewwe, P. and H.G. Jacoby, 2004: Economic growth and the demand for education: is there a wealth effect?, *Journal of Development Economics*, **74**(1), 33–51

Handa, S., 2002: Raising primary school enrollment in developing countries: the relative importance of supply and demand, *Journal of Development Economics*, **69**(1), 103–28

Hanushek, E.A. and M.E. Raymond, 2004: The effect of school accountability systems on the level and distribution of student achievement, *Journal of the European Economic Association*, **2**(2–3), 406–15

Haveman, R.H. and B.L. Wolfe, 1984: Schooling and economic well-being: the role of nonmarket effects, *Journal of Human Resources*, **19**(3), 377–407

Hoxby, C.M., 2002: The cost of accountability, NBER Working Paper, **8855**, National Bureau of Economic Research, Cambridge, MA

James, E., E.M. King and A. Suryadi, 1996: Finance, management, and costs of public and private schools in Indonesia, *Economics of Education Review*, **15**(4), 387–98

Jimenez, E. and V. Paqueo, 1996: Do local contributions affect the efficiency of public primary schools?, *Economics of Education Review*, **15**(4), 377–86

Jimenez, E. and Y. Sawada, 1999: Do community-managed schools work? An evaluation of El Salvador's EDUCO program, *World Bank Economic Review*, **13**(3), 415–41

Kremer, M., 2003: Randomized evaluations of educational programs in developing countries: some lessons, *American Economic Review*, **93**(2), 102–6

Krueger, A.B., 2003: Economic considerations and class size, *Economic Journal*, **113**(485), F34–F63

Lavy, V., 1996: School supply constraints and children's educational outcomes in rural Ghana, *Journal of Development Economics*, **51**(2), 291–314

2002: Evaluating the effect of teachers' group performance incentives on pupil achievement, *Journal of Political Economy*, **110**(6), 1286–1317

2003: Paying for performance: the effect of teachers' financial incentives on students' scholastic outcomes, CEPR Discussion Paper, **3862**, Centre for Economic Policy Research, London

Lochner, L. and E. Moretti, 2004: The effect of education on crime: evidence from prison inmates, arrests, and self-reports, *American Economic Review* **94**(1), 155–89

Mingat, A. and J.-P. Tan, 1986: Expanding education through user charges: what can be achieved in Malawi and other LDCs?, *Economics of Education Review*, **5**(3), 273–86

Mullis, V.S. *et al.*, 2000: *TIMSS 1999 international mathematics report: findings from IEA's repeat of the third international mathematics and science study at the eighth grade*, Boston College, Chestnut Hill, MA

Nielsen, H.S., 2001: How sensitive is the demand for primary education to changes in economic factors?, *Journal of African Economies*, **10**(2), 191–218

Pritchett, L., 2004: Access to education, chapter 4 in this volume

Psacharopoulos, G. and H.A. Patrinos, 2004: Returns to investment in education: a further update, *Education Economics*, forthcoming; originally Policy Research Working Paper, **2881**, World Bank, Washington, DC, 2002

Schultz, T.P., 2004: School subsidies for the poor: evaluating the Mexican Progresa poverty program, *Journal of Development Economics*, **74**(1), 199–250

Spohr, C.A., 2003: Formal schooling and workforce participation in a rapidly developing economy: evidence from 'compulsory' Junior High School in Taiwan, *Journal of Development Economics*, **70**(2), 291–327

UNESCO, 2002a: *World education indicators*, UNESCO Institute for Statistics; http://www.uis.unesco.org/en/stats/statistics/indicators/i_pages/indic_2.htm (10/16/02)

2002b: *UIS education data: statistical tables*, UNESCO Institute for Statistics; http://portal.unesco.org/uis/ev.php (10/16/02)

World Bank, 2002a: *The 2002 world development indicators*, CD-ROM, Washington, DC

2002b: Education for dynamic economies: action plan to accelerate progress towards Education for All, Development Committee, DC2002-0005/Rev1, World Bank, Washington, DC; http://wbln0018.worldbank.org/DCS/devcom.nsf/(documentsattachmentsweb)/April2002EnglishDC20020005Rev1/$FILE/DC2002-0005-1.pdf (10/14/02)

2002c: EFA: the lessons of experience – the impact of policy in 20 case studies, Draft for discussion, prepared for the Acceleration Action Towards EFA Conference, World Bank, Washington, DC; http://www1.worldbank.org/education/pdf/efa_lessons.pdf (10/14/02)

Wößmann, L., 2003a: Schooling resources, educational institutions, and student performance: the international evidence, *Oxford Bulletin of Economics and Statistics*, **65**(2), 117–70

2003b: Central exams as the 'currency' of school systems: international evidence on the complementarity of school autonomy and central exams, *DICE Report – Journal for Institutional Comparisons*, **1**(4), 46–56

Wößmann, L. and M.R. West, 2003: Class-size effects in school systems around the world: evidence from between-grade variation in TIMSS, Ifo Institute for Economic Research at the University of Munich and Harvard University, mimeo; revised version of IZA Discussion Paper, 485, Institute for the Study of Labor, Bonn, 2002.

Financial Instability

BARRY EICHENGREEN

Introduction and Motivation

Financial instability matters. Table 5.1, drawn from Dobson and Hufbauer (2001), shows some representative estimates of annual average output losses per year from currency and banking crises. Losses like these are of first-order importance. 2.2 percentage points of growth per year – which is what Latin America lost as a result of financial instability in the 1980s – makes incomes and living standards two-thirds higher in a generation.[1] Raising *per capita* incomes to this extent transforms a society's living standards, providing the resources to address critical social problems. For developing countries as a class, Dobson and Hufbauer's estimates suggest that since 1975 financial instability has reduced the incomes of developing countries by roughly 25 per cent. Back-of-the-envelope calculations like these can reasonably be questioned.[2] But they nonetheless show how profoundly financial instability matters.

Economies without financial markets cannot have financial crises.[3] This is a pointer to what sorts of countries suffer most from financial instability. Generally, these are not the poorest countries, which have relatively rudimentary financial markets. In these countries, households are only loosely linked to the financial economy and feel only indirect effects when financial markets malfunction or collapse. It is in the next tier of developing countries and emerging markets where the costs of financial instability are greatest.[4]

Thus, ameliorating problems of financial instability may not meet the immediate needs of the poorest countries. But it will enhance the welfare of several billion residents in the next tier of developing countries. In addition, of course, a solution to this problem will also benefit the poorest countries

over time as they develop and become more vulnerable to financial instability.

Insofar as countries without financial markets cannot have financial crises, one conceivable response to the problem of financial instability is to suppress domestic financial markets and transactions, thereby eliminating the problem of banking and financial crises, and international financial markets and transactions, thereby eliminating the problem of currency and exchange rate crises. Banks that are not permitted to borrow and lend will not fail; more generally, if banks are very tightly regulated, the scope for risk taking by their managers will be limited. Similarly, if strict capital and exchange controls limit purchases and sales of foreign exchange, then there will be limited scope for speculating against a currency. Thus, China, despite the presence of significant financial problems, has not experienced an overt banking or currency crisis in recent years.[5] The obvious explanation for this fact

This chapter is based on a paper written on behalf of the Copenhagen Consensus. It draws on some of my previous work with Ricardo Hausmann, whose collaboration is acknowledged with thanks. I also thank Henrik Meyer for helpful comments and Peter Henry and Charles Wyplosz for their reactions.

[1] A generation of twenty-five years.

[2] Many of the grounds on which they can be questioned are enumerated on pp. 253ff.

[3] If there is no finance, in other words, there can be no financial problems.

[4] Thus, Dobson and Hufbauer (2001), in the same sections of their work from which table 5.1 is drawn, also consider financial crises in Sub-Saharan Africa (SSA). While there have been some major and devastating crises in this region, overall they reach conclusions consistent with the assertions in this chapter.

[5] That is, it has not experienced a severe disruption to financial markets leading to a significant fall in output, which is how an actual crisis can be defined for present purposes. The definition of financial crises is discussed at greater length below.

Table 5.1. Annual Average Output Loss From Banking and Currency Crises, 1980s and 1990s

	1980s	1990s
Asia	0.1	1.4
Latin America	2.2	0.7

Source: Dobson and Hufbauer (2001).

is that the country maintains strict controls on both its banks and capital account transactions.

These observations point to the question of why more countries do not respond to financial instability by suppressing financial markets and transactions. The answer is that policies that stifle financial development have *economic costs*. Financial development relaxes borrowing constraints, thereby enabling new firm formation, intensifying competition and facilitating the adoption of new technologies. There is overwhelming evidence of the positive association of financial development with productivity growth (Guiso, Sapienza and Zingales 2002). Well-developed financial markets disseminate information about profitable and productive investment opportunities, enhancing the efficiency with which capital is allocated. They help with monitoring managers and strengthening corporate control, positively influencing the efficiency with which resources are allocated within the firm. They mobilise savings, facilitate specialisation and encourage exchange.

How important are these effects? Financial development that raises financial depth, as measured by the ratio of domestic credit to GDP, from 0.25 to 0.55 – that is, from the levels typical of financially underdeveloped countries to that typical of their more financially well-developed counterparts – raises the rate of economic growth by a full percentage point per annum according to the widely cited estimates of King and Levine (1993).

These numbers are large. Raising growth by a percentage point a year raises incomes by a third in a generation.[6] This suggests that the benefits of financial development may be as large, or even larger, than the costs of financial instability. Thus, the costs of a policy that limits financial instability by

limiting financial development may be even greater than its benefits. Additional calculations consistent with this conclusion are presented below. Revealingly, not just economists but also policy makers acknowledge the practical importance of these arguments. To continue with the preceding example, it is revealing that we see China moving gradually in the direction of domestic financial liberalisation and capital account decontrol despite the existence of significant financial vulnerabilities. Evidently, the country's policy makers, who are hardly free market ideologues, see benefits from increased financial development as well as potential costs from increased financial vulnerability. Their view is that if the transition is carefully managed, the former can exceed the latter.

To be sure, there is less than full agreement on the best strategy for stimulating financial development. In particular, there is no agreement on how far the deregulation of domestic financial markets and transactions should proceed, and on whether it is also necessary at some point to deregulate the capital account of the balance of payments. In particular, not everyone agrees that there is a trade-off between policies that limit financial instability by tightly regulating domestic financial markets and international financial transactions, on the one hand, and policies to encourage domestic financial development, on the other. Even among those who do, there is less than full consensus on the terms of trade.

This chapter evaluates responses to the problem of financial instability in this light. The next section describes the challenge, asking questions such the following:

• Has crisis frequency been rising or falling?
• Have crises been growing more or less severe?
• What is their impact on poverty and other social ills?

It then examines what we know about the causes of currency and banking crises and reviews additional estimates of their costs. It critically scrutinises the case for domestic and international financial liberalisation and asks whether the evidence lends support the relevant theory.

The next section considers alternative treatments for the problem of financial instability and presents

---

[6] The basis for these estimates is described below.

some estimates of their costs and benefits. It discusses two 'opportunities' with the capacity to diminish the prevalence of financial instability but at significant cost in terms of growth and economic development forgone. It then goes on to describe two more unconventional treatments that would offer similar benefits at lower costs but subject to different degrees of political feasibility.

Before proceeding, a few comments on methodology are irrestistible. The organisers of this meeting seem to have in mind a specific template of how a discussion of policy interventions to address social and economic issues, including financial crises, should be framed.[7] Policy options should be referred to as 'opportunities.' Experts should assign numerical values to their costs and benefits. Results should be derived by assembling and crunching lots of numbers. Large simulation models are presumably best for these purposes. Panellists can then simply turn to the last page of the computer printout and read which number for 'net benefits' is largest.

Several decades of social science research have taught us the importance of making our assumptions explicit and of unambiguously describing the logical apparatus used to move from assumptions to conclusions. It is important to clearly specify the model underlying a particular piece of analysis and to provide clear justifications for its assumptions. But this does not mean that a more complicated model is better. Large models have advantages, but large simulation models of the extent, costs and benefits of a problem, whether the latter is financial instability, global warming, population ageing or any other issue that might be considered by the experts assembled by the Copenhagen Consensus, will be full of assumptions of varying degrees of reliability. The larger the model, the more such assumptions are heaped one on top of the other, and the harder it is to understand which assumptions are critical for the results. The assumptions are sometimes so numerous that it is impossible to even mention them all, much less discuss them.

Not only does this make the source of a 'finding' hard to identify, but it encourages a false sense of precision. If a variety of other assumptions about parameter values and structural relationships are equally plausible, so too are a variety of other estimates. In large models, this point cannot be met simply by constructing confidence intervals, since so many parameters and structural relationships can be varied and these interact in poorly understood but clearly high non-linear ways. The point applies equally to the simulation models built by natural scientists to explain physical phenomena and to the simulation models built by economists to explain social phenomena; natural scientists will readily admit that these same points apply to studies of, *inter alia*, the determinants of global warming or the spread of disease vectors. For some applications, the costs of this approach may exceed its benefits.[8] The more general point is that there are reasons to question an approach that encourages all authors, regardless of the problem with which they are concerned and the literature on which they build, to adopt a common template.

The Challenge

A foundation of recent research on financial liberalisation is the observation that the policy has both *benefits* and *costs*. The benefits of well-developed, freely functioning financial markets are familiar if difficult to quantify. These include the ability for individuals and households to smooth their consumption by borrowing and lending, to share risk by diversifying their portfolios of assets and liabilities, to undertake profitable investment opportunities that would otherwise be inhibited by liquidity constraints, and more generally to achieve faster growth, greater returns on investment and higher incomes. The costs take the form of volatility in markets that respond sharply to new information – volatility with which the affected economies can find it difficult to cope.

It is important to emphasise that volatility is intrinsic to financial markets. The more efficient are markets, they more decisively they will react to new information, and the more volatile they are likely to be, other things equal. Volatility cannot – indeed, should not – be eliminated. It is a mechanism for

---

[7] Here I am drawing conclusions both from the instructions given to the authors of expert papers for the Consensus and personal communications from the organizers.
[8] To use the organizers' preferred language.

conveying information relevant to resource allocation decisions.

But excessive volatility can be disruptive and costly. A sudden decline in asset valuations can erode the value of collateral on which access to external finance depends. When credit and leverage are widely utilised, the result may be a 'domino effect' of bank failures and distress among non-bank financial intermediaries (NBFIs). The consequences can include a cascade of cancelled investment projects, leading to a sharp drop in output. The challenge of coping with financial instability is thus not to eliminate volatility but to limit it and its negative effects.

A recent analysis of this tradeoff is Ranciere, Tornell and Westermann (2003) in an NBER Working Paper that received prominent coverage in *The Economist* (Economist 2003). The authors show that countries where credit growth is relatively volatile, because financial markets are allowed to operate more freely, tend to grow more quickly. The authors even find that countries where credit growth is more negatively skewed – where relatively steady growth rates are interrupted by occasional sharp drops, presumably associated with financial crises – grow more quickly than those where credit growth is slow and smooth. Thus, even though volatility may cause periodic sharp drops in credit output, the benefits for growth of having free if also volatile financial markets may still exceed the costs.[9]

The net benefits would be even greater, of course, if the occasional, disruptive drops in credit growth associated with crises could be eliminated without also eliminating the positive impact on growth. The

next section of this chapter considers some possible ways of going about this.

On the Costs of Financial Instability

A moment's reflection reveals why there exists a range of estimates of the costs of financial crises. First, there is disagreement about what constitutes a 'crisis'. Analytically, a crisis can be defined as a sharp change in asset prices that leads to distress among financial markets participants.[10] In practice, unfortunately, it is not clear where to draw the line between sharp and moderate price changes or how to distinguish severe financial distress from financial pressure.

Even if crises can be identified, there is still the problem of quantifying their effects. As a first cut, one might attempt to measure the induced fall in GDP. But simply taking the difference between growth rate in crisis and non-crisis periods may not be an appropriate way of going about this. Crises may result from recessions rather than or in addition to causing them. In other words, the entire fall in output may not be properly attributable to the crisis. Similarly, crises may be more likely following periods of unsustainably rapid economic growth; in this case, simply taking the difference between growth rates before and after the event will exaggerate its effects.

Bordo *et al.* (2001) attempt to take the preceding observations on board in estimating output losses due to crises for a consistent sample of twenty-one middle- and high-income countries over the last 120 years, as well as for a larger sample of emerging markets over the shorter period starting in 1973. Over the entire period, the loss from the average crisis approaches 9 per cent of GDP, and the probability of a randomly selected country experiencing a crisis in a random year averages 8 per cent. Thus, at slightly less than 1 per cent per annum, their estimates of average annual output losses are close to those presented by Dobson and Hufbauer (2001) for emerging markets and developing countries in the 1980s and 1990s (and, again, generated using an entirely different approach). A range of other empirical studies reach similar conclusions.[11]

Averages like these tend to conceal the diversity of country experience. Some financial crises

---

[9] Some calculations below, using an entirely different methodology, reach essentially the same conclusion.

[10] This definition is due to Eichengreen and Portes (1987).

[11] To cite to of the more authoritative studies, Caprio and Klingebiel (1996) estimate that banking crises cost 2.4 per cent of output per year for each year of their duration. Goldstein, Kaminsky and Reinhart (2000) estimate that currency crises cost 3 per cent of output per year of their duration in low-inflation countries and 6 per cent of output per year of their duration in high-inflation countries. To get annual averages like those in the text and table 2.1, it is then necessary to multiply these output losses by the corresponding crisis frequencies. Mulder and Rocha (2000) provide a critical review of the empirical literature.

Table 5.2. Korean Social Indicators Following the Crisis, 1996–1999

	Divorces	Crimes	Crimes per 100,000	Drug addicts per 100,000	Suicides
1996	79,895	1,494,846	3,282	6,189	5,777
1997	91,159	1,588,613	3,454	6,947	5,957
1998	116,727	1,765,887	3,803	8,350	8,496
1999	118,014	1,732,522	3,697	10,589	7,014

Source: Lee (2004).

produce relatively limited output losses, while others, such as those of Indonesia in 1997–8 and Argentina in 2001–2, precipitate a full-scale economic collapse, in which output falls by upwards of 20 per cent and living standards, further eroded by the collapse of the country's exchange rate and the terms of trade, fall by even more.

Statistical analyses also provide a sanitised sense of the social consequences. To remind oneself of the immediacy of there effects, it is necessary only to observe that Indonesia and Argentina experienced larger falls in output and real incomes than that suffered by the USA in the Great Depression, an event that produced a revolution in social and economic policy. This is another way of saying that the social impact of financial crises can be enormous. Chen and Ravallion (2001) have estimated that the Asian Financial Crisis in 1997 increased the incidence of poverty in the region by 22m individuals. In South Korea alone, the total number of poor rose from 6 million in 1997 to more than 10 million in 1998. (Table 5.2 shows the associated changes in social indicators ranging from divorce to crime to drug addiction to suicide.) To put these figures in perspective, recall that Korea was not even a case where the Asian crisis was relatively severe (largely because recovery from the crisis was unusually rapid). In Indonesia (where the crisis was severe), poverty increased from 7–8 per cent in the second half of 1997 to 18–20 per cent in September 1998 (Suryahadi *et al.* 2000). Atinc and Walton (1999) show that women and girls generally suffered the most from the decline of living standards. If the goal of the Copenhagen Consensus is to address social ills such as gender inequality, crime, drug addiction, poverty and suicide in a broad range of countries, then an 'opportunity' that successfully addresses the problem of financial instability would seem to be a priority.

There is little evidence in the Bordo *et al.* study just cited that the output costs of banking or currency crises have been rising or falling. What does seem to have changed is crisis frequency, which was greater in the 1970s, 1980s and 1990s than over the entire twentieth century and the 1950s and 1960s in particular (see figure 5.1). This increase in frequency is mainly due to an greater incidence of currency crises and of twin crises (instances where currency and banking crises coincide and reinforce one another). This is turn points to a change in the mix of financial crises, with a growing incidence of twin crises, the most costly type.[12]

On the Causes of Financial Instability

Recommendations for action should logically start from an analysis of the causes of these problems. Contributors generally distinguish four classes of explanations for financial instability and crises.[13]

---

[12] Thus the incidence of twin crises is the immediate explanation for recent episodes in which countries suffered double-digit output losses and very serious economic distress.

[13] Here I consciously avoid the first-generation, second-generation and third-generation terminology that is commonly used (and frequently misused, causing no end of confusion) to distinguish different theories of balance of payments crises (an author's prerogative when the author in question coined this terminology).

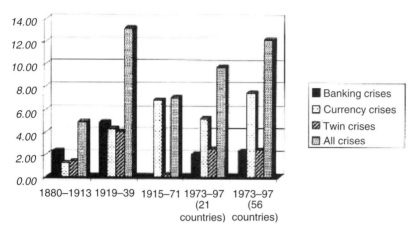

Figure 5.1. *Crisis frequency, 1880–1997, per cent probability per year*
Source: Bordo et al. *(2001).*

Unsustainable Macroeconomic Policies

This was the focus of early crisis models such as Krugman (1979).[14] Countries suffer currency crises in these models because they run inconsistent and unsustainable policies. In the classic case, monetary and fiscal policies are too expansionary to be consistent with the currency peg. Countries experience banking crises because their governments treat the banks as a captive market for the public debt issues that they desperately must place in order to finance their deficits.[15] Macroeconomic imbalances are the fundamental cause of crises, in this view, although the proximate triggers may be contagion effects or imprudently low levels of foreign exchange reserves.

This leaves open the question of why governments run unsustainable and contradictory macroeconomic policies in the first place. Increasingly, scholars point to weaknesses in policy making processes. In some cases, the central bank lacks a clear mandate and independence from political pressures. In others, the excessive decentralisation of fiscal institutions allows spending ministries and provincial authorities to spend now and appeal later to the central government for the necessary finance,

creating common-pool problems for the fisc. Politicians in unstable political systems may spend and borrow excessively, without worrying about the intertemporal consistency of their fiscal plans, in order to increase their probability of staying in power. These theories thus point to the development of stronger policy making processes as the fundamental prerequisite for financial stability.

Fragile Financial Systems

A number of recent crises were not obviously rooted in macroeconomic factors. Macroeconomic imbalances were not particularly prominent in the Asian crisis, for example.[16] At the same time, financial weaknesses seemed to play a larger role there than in previous crises. In countries such as South Korea, the banks' dependence on short-term debt rendered them vulnerable to investor panic. More generally, balance-sheet vulnerabilities put banks and non-bank financial institutions (such as finance companies) at risk when confidence eroded and capital began to haemorrhage out of the financial system.

Recent work (e.g. Goldstein and Turner 2003) has emphasised the prevalence of currency mismatches in the financial system as a key source of financial fragility. When banks have assets in local currency but liabilities in dollars, fears of a crisis that lead to the exchange rate to weaken can become self-fulfilling, since at the now weaker exchange rate assets will no longer be sufficient to service or

---

[14] It continues to be the theme of authoritative analyses of recent crises, such as Mussa's (2003) treatment of the Argentine case.
[15] See Serven and Perry (2003).
[16] The case of Thailand notwithstanding to the contrary.

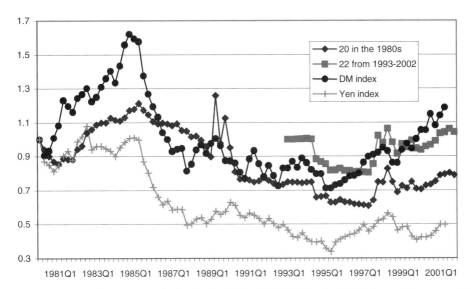

Figure 5.2. *Exchange rates* vis-à-vis *the dollar, 1980–2001: the EM indexes, the yen and the mark.*

redeem liabilities (figure 5.2).[17] Even when banks match the currency composition of their assets and liabilities, lending as well as borrowing in dollars, their clients, with incomes in pesos but debts in dollars, will be thrust into bankruptcy if the currency declines, bringing the financial system crashing down.

This view consequently emphasises strengthening prudential regulation and supervision as the key to reducing financial instability. Governments should distance themselves from the financial system, resisting the temptation to use domestic banks as instruments of development policy. Responsibility for supervision and regulation should be assigned to an independent central bank or regulatory agency. Special attention should be paid to limiting currency mismatches, not just on bank balance sheets but on the balance sheets of corporations and other borrowers as well. Again, however, this leaves open the question of why some countries regulate their financial systems so poorly in the first place.

Institutional Weaknesses

This question has given rise to a literature emphasising weaknesses in domestic governance structures as the ultimate cause of financial instability. Bank managers and corporate CEOs who are

inadequately accountable to their shareholders may have inadequate incentive to prudently manage financial risks. Short-sighted governments, for their part, may be reluctant to distance themselves from financial institutions and may deny regulatory agencies the autonomy needed for their effective operation.

In this view, weak corporate and public sector governance allows excessive risk taking, resulting in vulnerable corporate financial structures (specifically, too much reliance on debt as opposed to equity and excessive dependence on short-term borrowing). The corresponding treatment is to strengthen shareholder and creditor rights, improve corporate governance and financial transparency and place clear and credible limits on the official safety net extended to financial institutions.

Flaws in the Structure of International Financial Markets

A final strand of analysis links financial instability, in emerging markets in particular, to the structure and operation of the international financial system, and specifically to aspects of that structure largely

[17] Leading to further sales of domestic claims in anticipation of default, which in turn produces a further fall in the exchange rate.

beyond the control of individual countries.[18] Scholarly statements of this view emphasise the pervasiveness of asymmetric information in international financial markets, which encourages herding by investors and gives rise to sudden stops and capital flow reversals that can cause crises independently of conditions in the afflicted economies.[19] Capital mobility is the problem, in this view. Capital flows can be unstable due to the prevalence of other distortions.[20] The corresponding solution is retaining controls on capital flows.

A different statement of this view harks back to explanations for financial crises emphasising weaknesses in financial systems, and currency mismatches in particular. It suggests that emerging markets are vulnerable to crises because of the reluctance of international investors to hold debt securities denominated in emerging-market currencies. Thus, countries that borrow abroad will inevitably have currency mismatches on their national balance sheets. Solving the problem of financial instability therefore requires an international initiative that will enhance the ability of emerging markets to borrow in their own currency.

Contributions to this literature, starting with Eichengreen and Hausmann (1999), observe that the global portfolio is concentrated in the currencies of a few large countries and international financial centres.[21] Although it is tempting to blame weak policies and institutions for the difficulty emerging markets face when attempting to borrow abroad in their own currencies, even countries with admirably strong policies and institutions (Chile and Singapore are a good examples) find it difficult to borrow abroad in their own currencies. The one country characteristic that is robustly associated with the ability to borrow abroad in the local currency is country size (large countries can, small countries can't).

Transactions costs in a world of heterogeneous economies can explain this bias toward a small number of currencies issued by a handful of large countries. These observations are related to the literature on the determinants of key currency status (Kiyotaki, Matsuyama and Matsui 1992), which explains the dominance of a small number of currencies in international markets as a function of network externalities and transactions costs. They suggest that the global portfolio is concentrated in the currencies of a few countries for reasons largely beyond the control of those which are excluded.

The Empirical Literature

The empirical literature on explanations for financial instability is too extensive to be adequately summarised here. Suffice it to say that recent empirical studies suggest that these explanations for financial vulnerability are complementary rather than competing and that they can interact in mutually reinforcing ways.[22] For example, the same macroeconomic imbalances are more likely to precipitate a crisis when the financial system is weak, since the authorities will be less able to raise interest rates in order to prevent capital from haemorrhaging out of the economy, reflecting the fear that weak banks will be unable to cope with higher interest rates, bringing the financial system crashing down. Similarly, characteristics of the international financial system that make it difficult for emerging markets to borrow abroad in their own currencies make all the more imperative careful macroeconomic management and rigorous supervision and regulation to limit the vulnerabilities of the financial system. More attractive than attempting to run a horse-race between these explanations, in other

---

[18] This interpretation has roots in Keynes (1933) and Nurkse (1944), who generalised from the Great Depression about the destructive effects of destabilising international speculation. A famous restatement of this view is the speech of then Malaysian Prime Minister Mahathir at the IMF – World Bank meetings in Hong Kong in 1998, in which he blamed hedge funds and other 'international speculators' for destabilising fundamentally stable emerging-market economies. For the academic version of this argument see de Brouwer (2001).

[19] See Devenow and Welch (1996).

[20] See Bhagwati (1998).

[21] Of the nearly $5.8 trillion in outstanding securities placed internationally in the period 1999–2001, $5.6 trillion was issued in five major currencies: the US dollar, the euro, the yen, the pound sterling and Swiss franc. While residents of these countries issued $4.5 trillion dollars of debt over this period, the remaining $1.1 trillion of debt denominated in their currencies was issued by residents of other countries and by international organisations. Since these other countries and international organisations issued a total of $1.3 trillion dollars of debt, it follows that they issued the vast majority of it in foreign currency.

[22] See for example Ghosh and Ghosh (2003).

words, is attempting to identify the appropriate treatments for each and estimating the costs and benefits of the latter.

On the Benefits of Financial Liberalisation

By tightly controlling financial markets and transactions, governments can limit financial instability. But if doing so was costless, then we would regularly see countries that experience financial crises slapping on tight controls. That we do not suggests that policies of financial repression have costs as well as benefits.

A large literature, going back to at least Schumpeter (1939) and Goldsmith (1969), documents the importance of financial development for economic growth. Recent research has focused on disentangling cause and effect, showing that the correlation does not reflect the operation of a third omitted variable, and quantifying the impact. Macroeconomic estimates using time-series techniques and dynamic panel estimators, as well as microeconomic and sectoral evidence, all point to independent effects running from financial development to economic growth. Khan (2000), in a review of the relevant literature, shows that raising a country's level of financial development (as measured by the sum of stock market capitalisation and domestic bank credit as a share of GDP) from the levels of India to the levels of Singapore can raise its growth rate by 2 per cent per annum.[23]

The question for present purposes is whether policies that restrict domestic and international financial transactions also discourage financial development.[24] That statutory restraints on domestic financial transactions limit financial development is uncontroversial; indeed, that regulatory limits on domestic financial transactions limit such transactions is all but tautological. Empirically, authors like Demetriades and Luintel (1996) report econometric estimates that banking sector controls have negative effects on domestic financial deepening.[25] Others like Henry (1998) have provided evidence for financial markets as well as financial institutions, showing that liberalisation is associated with an increase in capitalisation, valuation and turnover on equity markets.[26]

More controversial is the link between capital account liberalisation and financial development. De Gregorio (1998), in what is perhaps the first

systematic study of this question, finds that domestic financial development is negatively impacted by capital controls. Klein and Olivei (1999) extend this analysis to a larger sample of countries and again find that financial development is negatively affected by the maintenance of capital controls. However, they find that this relationship is significant only for the developed countries in their sample. Chinn (2001), on the other hand, finds that some of the largest effects on activity in equity markets (as measured by the total value of equities traded and equity market turnovers) are for developing countries.[27]

Some authors bypass the link from specific liberalisation measures to financial development and from there to economic growth and to ask whether there is evidence that the removal of restraints on international financial transactions impacts growth directly. An early and widely cited econometric study by Rodrik (1998) lent no support to this hypothesis. Subsequent investigators have reproduced

[23] Other reviews of the relevant literature include Levine (1997) and Khan and Senhadji (2000). Singapore is a small country that has attempted to specialise as a financial centre; consequently, it has unusually high levels of stock market capitalisation and domestic bank credit as shares of GDP. Biasing this example in the other direction is the fact that India has a higher ratio than other developing countries (Pakistan and Bangladesh, for example). More modest estimates are used in the cost-benefit analysis (CBA) exercises below.

[24] Alternatively, one could look at the impact of domestic financial liberalisation on the efficiency of domestic resource allocation directly without forcing the effects to go through financial deepening (analogously to studies, considered below, that look at the direct impact of capital account liberalisation on resource allocation growth). Abiad, Oomes and Ueda (2003) construct comprehensive indicators of domestic financial liberalisation and show, using firm-level data, that countries with freer domestic financial markets are characterized by a lower dispersion of Tobin's q, which is an indicator of more efficient resource allocation.

[25] The one policy that does not obviously have this effect is lending rate ceilings, but the effect of all other banking sector controls is strongly negative.

[26] Which in turn has positive effects on investment and growth. Some of Henry's work, discussed further below, suggests larger effects of some forms of financial market liberalisation (those affecting equity flows) than others (those affecting debt flows).

[27] As the author notes, it is the same forms of financial activity that exhibit the strongest connection to economic growth (in, *inter alia*, Henry 2002) that are evidently most likely to be stimulated by financial liberalisation.

his results, with some prominent exceptions (see table 5.3).[28] At the same time, the fact that the advanced industrial countries all have open capital accounts suggests the existence of a threshold above which the removal of capital controls is viewed as advantageous. This has led to a recent literature seeking to estimate thresholds above which capital account liberalisation has favourable effects but below which it does not (for example, Ferreira and Laux 2003, Klein 2003, Prasad *et al.* 2003). In the most widely cited of these studies, Klein places this threshold at a *per capita* income of US$2,000.

Other authors have attempted to distinguish different aspects of capital account liberalisation. For example, Henry (2003) looks at the effects of liberalising the access of foreign investors to domestic equity markets. He finds that the growth rate of the capital stock increases by an average of 1.1 percentage points per year following such liberalisations, while the growth rate of output per worker rises by 2.3 percentage points per year. Henry concludes that since the cost of capital falls, investment accelerates, and the growth rate of output per worker increases when countries liberalise the stock market, 'the increasingly popular view that capital account liberalisation brings no real benefits seems untenable'.[29]

Related to this is recent work considering the impact of capital account liberalisation not on growth but on volatility. Kose, Prasad and Terrones (2003) find that in the 1990s capital account liberalisation is associated with an increase in the volatility of consumption. Gavin and Hausmann (1996) similarly find a positive association between the volatility of output and the volatility of capital flows. O'Donnell (2001) also finds that a higher degree of financial integration leads to a higher level of output volatility in developing countries (in contrast to the results for OECD countries, where more financial integration leads to less output volatility).

This association of capital account liberalisation with volatility helps to explain why positive connections to growth are difficult to detect. If capital account liberalisation increases the likelihood of costly crises and output losses, or if crises lead to larger output losses when the capital account is open, then it is not surprising that it is hard to distinguish the positive effects of capital account liberalisation on growth. This is the finding of Eichengreen and Leblang (2003), who show that capital account liberalisation slows growth when it is undertaken by countries that are crisis-prone but accelerates it when it is undertaken by countries that are not.[30]

Summary

A growing body of evidence shows that financial liberalisation is a two-edged sword. Liberalisation facilitates financial deepening and development, which has strong positive impacts on economic growth, other things equal. At the same time, liberalised financial markets can be volatile, and extreme instances of volatility can result in sharp dislocations (financial crises) that result in costly output losses. There is some dispute about how significantly capital account liberalisation stimulates financial development and economic growth and about whether it has different effects on countries at different levels of economic and institutional development. But the general point is that policies that limit financial instability by limiting financial transactions are likely to have costs as well as benefits. It would be preferable, the implication follows, to find ways of limiting costly financial instability without at the same time discouraging financial development.

---

[28] The reason for these disagreements is of course straightforward enough. Analytically, it is always possible for a policy that removes one distortion to reduce rather than increase welfare and growth if other distortions are present. Thus, Hellman, Murdock and Stiglitz (2000) present a model in which the removal of ceilings on domestic interest rates may be welfare-reducing because of asymmetric information that gives rise to moral hazard in banking. Other authors have provided analytical demonstrations that the removal of controls on capital inflows and outflows can be welfare-reducing rather than welfare-increasing when other distortions are present. A classic demonstration is Brecher and Diaz-Alejandro (1977). These results are not surprising; they are straightforward applications of the theory of the second best.

[29] In subsequent work (Henry and Lorentzen 2003), he argues that some forms of liberalisation (those affecting equity flows) have more favourable effects than others (those affecting debt flows).

[30] Other studies reach similar conclusions, as shown in table 5.4.

Table 5.3. Macroeconomic Effects of Capital Account Liberalisation

Author	Impact on	Controls	Measured as	Countries	Period	Findings
Alesina, Grilli and Milesi-Ferretti (1994)	Growth, debt, inflation, real interest rates	Government stability, majority government, central bank independence, exchange rate regime, government turnover	Binary	20 industrial	1950–89	Less debt, lower real interest rates, higher inflation, possibly faster growth
Garrett (1995)	Budget deficit, government spending, capital taxation, interest rates	US interest rates, Left–labour power, unemployment, inflation, trade openness	Four-point scale, with a point each for capital account restrictions, bilateral payments to IMF members, bilateral payments to members, and foreign deposits	15 industrial	1967–90	Lower government spending, budget deficits and interest rates except where Left–labour is powerful
Grilli and Milesi-Ferretti (1995)	Growth, investment	Central bank independence, trade openness, democracy, black market premium, *per capita* income, government consumption	Binary plus measure of separate exchange rates for capital account transactions and for current account restrictions	61 industrial and developing	1966–89	Higher inflation, lower real interest rates, possible positive impact on growth from capital account restriction; negative effect of current account restrictions on growth
Lewis (1997)	Risk sharing	Theoretical restrictions	Binary	72 industrial and developing	1967–92	Greater risk sharing
Quinn (1997)	Growth, inequality, corporate taxation, government expenditure	*Per capita* income, population growth, primary and secondary education, investment, socialist economy, revolutions/coups, regional dummies	Quinn (1997)	21 industrial and 43 developing	1959–88	Positive impact on corporate taxation, government spending income inequality, growth
Bordo and Eichengreen (1998)	Growth, public debt, inflation, real interest rates, export growth, current account, investment	*Per capita* income, government consumption, trade openness, democracy, turnover of central bankers, central bank independence	Binary	63 industrial and developing	1959–89	Weaker current account, some evidence of faster (slower) growth in industrial (developing) countries, higher inflation in industrial countries; lower real interest rates, higher investment

(*cont.*)

Table 5.3. (*cont.*)

Author	Impact on	Controls	Measured as	Countries	Period	Findings
Garrett (1998)	Growth, budget deficit, interest rates, unemployment, inflation	Old age population, central bank independence, Left–labour power, oil dependence, labour market institutions, trade openness	Quinn (1997)	15 industrial	1966–90	Larger budget deficits, lower interest rates, lower unemployment and slower growth except where Left is powerful
Kraay (1998)	Growth, investment, inflation, maturity of debt	*Per capita* income, secondary education, population growth, regional dummies	Quinn (1997) Binary, Actual inflows and outflows	117 industrial and developing	1985–97	No impact except when openness is interacted with rate of return; positive impact on share of short-term debt.
Levine and Zervos (1998)	Stock market size, liquidity, volatility and integration	Theoretical	Binary (alternative sources)	16 emerging markets	1980–93	Stock markets become larger, more liquid, more volatile and more integrated
Rodrik (1998)	Growth, investment, inflation	*Per capita* income, secondary education, quality of government, regional dummies	Binary, per cent of years capital account was restricted	100 industrial and developing	1975–89	No impact on growth investment or inflation
Swank (1998)	Corporate taxation, payroll taxation	Inflation, trade openness, profitability, investment, GDP growth, election year, Left cabinet members, government spending	Quinn (1997)	17 OECD	1966–93	Positive, not negative, impact on level of business taxation
Klein and Olivei (1999)	Financial depth	Government spending, regional controls	Binary, and per cent of years capital account was restricted	92 industrial and developing	1986–95	Positive impact on liquid liabilities and claims on non-financial private sector for OECD countries only
Tamirisa (1999)	Volume of trade	*Per capita* income, population, distance, tariffs	Three-way categorisation of controls on current payments, capital movements, and both	40 industrial, developing and transition	1996	Capital controls reduce trade for developing and transition economies; restrictions on current payments have negligible effect

Table 5.3. (*cont.*)

Author	Impact on	Controls	Measured as	Countries	Period	Findings
Wyplosz (1999)	Interest rate levels and volatility, budget surplus	Credit ceilings, exchange rate regime, US interest rates	Binary	9 European	1957–97	Lower and more volatile interest rates, larger primary deficits
Montiel and Reinhart (1999)	Volume and composition of capital inflows	US interest rate, Japanese interest rate, domestic financial depth, sterilisation policies	0–2 index of intensity of capital account restrictions	15 developing	1990–96	Some estimates suggest that controls reduce share of portfolio and short-term flows, increase share of FDI, in total inflows
Edwards (2001)	GDP growth, growth of total factor productivity (TFP)	Investment, schooling, GDP *per capita*	Binary (per cent of years capital account was restricted) and Quinn (1997)	20 industrial and 45 emerging	1980s	Capital account liberalisation raises (lowers) growth in high-(low)-income countries
Garrett (2000)	Government spending, budget deficit, capital tax rate, labour tax rate, consumption tax rate	Trade openness, unemployment, growth, dependency ratio, exchange rate regime	Quinn (1997)	21 OECD	1973–94	Smaller budget deficits, lower rates of labour taxation when currency is pegged; higher government spending and capital taxation but no impact on budget deficit when it floats
Garrett and Mitchell (2000)	Public spending, taxation	Unemployment, growth, dependency ratio	Quinn (1997)	18 OECD	1961–94	Rates of capital taxation not lower where capital account is open, though public spending is lower

Opportunities

This section considers four options ('opportunities') for addressing the problem of financial instability.

There is of course a fifth option, which is simply to continue to encourage economic development and growth. As noted above, financial instability is often seen as a consequence of weaknesses in policies and institutions symptomatic of economic underdevelopment. While advanced countries also experience financial turbulence, full-blown crises there are now exceptional.[31] Economic and financial development and maturity have thus led to increased financial resiliency, allowing the

[31] Prasad *et al.* (2003) document the lower levels of volatility in these countries. Again, the fact that all of the advanced industrial countries have chosen to deregulate their domestic financial markets and capital accounts in order to reap the efficiency advantages of financial liberalisation is evidence that the negative side effects, in the form of increased volatility and financial instability, have been reduced to acceptable levels. Historically, the USA is a clear example of a country that has undergone this transition. In the nineteenth century it was regularly battered by financial instability (see Sprague 1910). Although it still experiences financial disturbances (like the Savings & Loan (S + L) problem of the 1980s and the all-but-failure of Long-Term Capital Management (LTCM) of the 1990s), these events generally do not have the highly disruptive output effects evident in emerging markets.

Table 5.4. Crises and Capital Account Liberalisation

Author	Impact on	Controls	Measured as	Countries	Period	Findings
Eichengreen, Rose and Wyplosz (1995)	Currency crises	Political events, lagged inflation, growth, employment, budget and current accounts	Binary	20 OECD	1959–93	Controls increase (reduce) likelihood of failed (successful) attack
Rossi (1999)	Currency crises and banking crises	GDP *per capita*, growth, real interest rate, change in terms of trade, domestic credit, M2 to reserves, openness, current account balance, government consumption, corruption, strength of supervision	Separate indices of intensity of inflow and outflow controls	15 developing	1990–7	Inflow controls reduce currency crisis risk. Some specifications suggest outflow controls associated with greater risk of both banking and currency crises
Eichengreen and Arteta (2000)	Banking crises	Reserves, current account balance, budget balance, overvaluation, domestic credit, M2, *per capita* growth, OECD growth, OECD interest rate	Binary, sum of capital inflows and outflows	122 developing	1972–97	Binary measure suggests no effect, while gross flows suggest negative (positive) effect when domestic markets are not (are) liberalised
Glick and Hutchinson (2000)	Currency crises	Export growth, M2 to reserves, credit growth, current account ratio, recent banking crisis, exchange rate regime	Binary, plus measure of current account restrictions and export surrender requirements	69 developing	1975–97	Capital market liberalisation appears to reduce crisis likelihood
Leblang and Bernhard (2000)	Currency crises	Current account balance, inflation, trade openness, real overvaluation, Left power, changes in unemployment, shift in government orientation	Binary, Quinn (1997)	16 industrial	1973–95	No impact
Leblang (2000)	Currency crises	International reserves, domestic credit growth, debt service, openness, US interest rates, contagion proxy, prior attacks, political variables	Binary	90 developing	1985–98	Presence of capital controls appears to raise crisis risk but also increase the likelihood of a successful defence
Wyplosz (2000)	Currency crises/pressure	Domestic financial liberalisation, current account convertibility, export surrender requirements	Four-point scale	61 industrial and developing	1966–98	Following initial inflows, capital account liberalisation intensifies pressure on the exchange rate

high-income countries to obtain a superior point on the tradeoff between financial development and volatility.

Those who see financial instability as just another symptom of economic underdevelopment, one conceivable response is simply to continue with the current approach of encouraging economic development and growth. As rule of law – and shareholder and creditor rights in particular – becomes more firmly established, market participants will be able govern financial markets more effectively. The public sector will develop an enhanced regulatory capacity. Problems of financial instability will then find a natural solution, as they have in the high-income countries. The international policy community, led by the multilateral financial institutions, can remind emerging markets of the need to enhance financial transparency, strengthen shareholder and creditor rights, and improve prudential supervision and regulation, and by exerting peer pressure for the adoption of such measures. The recent push to promulgate international standards for financial best practice is an illustration of this international role.[32] But beyond this they need not go.

There is much merit in this point of view, and the policy agenda that flows from it should continue to be pursued whether or not, in addition, one or more of the 'opportunities' listed below is also pursued. Adopting one of the innovative treatments for financial stability detailed below will produce few benefits if it is taken as an excuse to slack off on ongoing efforts to strengthen economic and financial institutions and policies. At the same time, building stronger policies and institutions is easier said than done. It may take many years for the natural process of 'growing up' to reduce financial instability to socially acceptable levels.[33] As Reinhart, Rogoff and Savastano (2003) emphasise, emerging markets have made only painfully slow progress in this direction. And, as poor countries grow less poor and their development becomes more financially intensive, they may experience more financial instability before they experience less, unless additional steps are taken to address the problem. This creates a certain impatience with the standard diagnosis and conventional, if not unimportant, treatment.

The question is what additional steps to take. I now consider four options ('opportunities') for addressing the problem of financial instability.

Re-Regulate Domestic Financial Markets

A long line of work, starting with the literature on narrow banking, advocates strict regulation of domestic financial institutions and markets in response to problems of financial instability.[34] Such measures would limit the growth of bank credit to the economy and bond and equity market capitalisation relative the benchmark in which domestic financial markets and institutions are lightly regulated. The more comprehensive the relevant regulations (and the more effective they therefore are in limiting financial instability), the more certain one can be that the growth of credit to the private sector would be constrained. Less financial instability would be attained at the cost of less financial depth and development.

To be clear, not all regulation discourages financial development or efficient financial intermediation. Given the prevalence of asymmetric information leading to adverse selection and moral hazard in financial markets, the argument for some regulation to enhance market efficiency and development is incontrovertible. Conceptually, one can imagine a continuum stretching from zero to one, where zero denotes no regulation and one denotes draconian financial repression. From the point of view of financial development, the optimal intensity of financial regulation lies somewhere in the middle. The

---

[32] The most notable of these standards is the Basel standard for capital adequacy of internationally active banks. This standard-setting agenda received an additional push from Goldstein's (1997) proposal for an international banking standard. On the subsequent expansion of the standard-setting process, see IMF and World Bank (2001).

[33] To return to the previous illustration, it took the USA half a century and more; recall the devastating financial crises of the 1930s.

[34] In today's world, such regulatory measures would be effective only if they were comprehensive. Narrow banking would not be enough, for intermediation would simply shift from banks to near-banks (such as finance companies, as was the case in South Korea after 1997) and securities markets, and the result would be no significant reduction in financial instability.

current thought experiment involving asking what happens when the intensity of regulation is moved significantly beyond this point.

Some simple cost-benefit calculations run as follows.[35] Assume that re-regulation of domestic financial markets eliminates banking but not currency crises.[36] Banking crises are less frequent and costly in terms of output losses than currency crises, according to Dobson and Hufbauer, on whose estimates I draw.[37] The average output loss per year from a banking crisis is 53 per cent as large as the average output loss per year from a currency crisis, and a banking crisis in randomly selected country in a randomly selected year is 66 per cent as likely as a currency crisis. The result is to attribute 30 per cent of the total cost of financial crises to their banking crisis component. Given a ballpark estimate of a 1 per cent loss in developing GDP growth per annum due to financial crises, a 0.3 per cent per annum loss of GDP is eliminated by this policy intervention.

The costs of the intervention depend on the elasticity of economic growth with respect to financial development and on how drastically financial regulation hinders the development of financial markets. Demetriades and Luintel (1996, table 3) provide detailed estimates of the impact on financial development for one country, India; their estimates suggest that moving from deregulated to highly

regulated financial markets results in a 30 per cent decline in financial depth at the mean (where the financial intermediation ratio is computed relative to GDP). King and Levine (1993) show that reducing financial depth by this amount will cut *per capita* growth by 1 per cent a year.

Putting these pieces together, the net benefits of this first 'opportunity' are −0.7 per cent of developing country GDP per annum. To express this as a share of global GDP, recall that developing countries account for slightly less than one-half of global GDP (42.9 per cent in 2000) when the latter is computed at PPPs. The result is a loss of just above $100 bn per annum in 2003 US dollars as an annual flow, an amount which will rise as the world economy continues to expand.[38]

As noted above, it would be silly to attach an unrealistic degree of confidence to such estimates. For example, some readers may object to King and Levine's estimates of the impact of financial development on economic growth as too large.[39] But it is straightforward for the reader to scale down this parameter and then the estimates of the gross costs of this initiative proportionately. That a specific number is presented for this estimate in the text and table 5.5 (as per the organizers' instructions) should not lead one to pay undue attention to this one-point estimate. But a more general analysis would not change the key conclusion that this treatment for financial instability would have significant costs that would in large measure offset its benefits.

Re-impose Capital Controls

This recommendation responds to the view that the volatility of capital flows and international financial markets is at the root of financial instability. The experience of countries such as Malaysia suggests that the maintenance of strict capital controls can limit the risk of currency crises, but at some cost in terms of domestic financial development. Since the share of the costs of financial crises that is not attributable to banking crises is attributable to currency crises, the calculations of the preceding sub-section lead immediately to the conclusion that benefits of this intervention are 0.7 per cent of developing country GDP.

---

[35] For this option, I also assume no change in international financial regulation. Goldstein and Turner (2003) explicitly make the point that it is then possible to open the capital account and enjoy the benefits of international financial transactions if the banking system is adequately regulated to limit currency and maturity mismatches (and complementary steps are taken on the corporate governance front).

[36] Since currency crises can and have occurred for a variety of reasons not related to instability in the banking system (see pp. 253ff. above), there is no reason to think that they too would disappear as a result of this approach to the problem.

[37] As noted above, a variety of other estimates (like those of Bordo *et al.* 2001) for the post-1973 period are compatible and would lead to very similar results.

[38] $107 bn, to be precise. This figure is derived by grossing up IMF estimates of global GDP in 2000 by 9 per cent to account for growth in the interim, taking the developing country share of this total (at PPP exchange rates), and multiplying the result by 0.007.

[39] Or too small.

Table 5.5. Summary of Costs and Benefits

Opportunity	Annual gross benefits, 2003 ($)	Annual gross costs, 2003 ($)	Annual Initial benefits – costs ($)	Remarks
Re-regulate financial markets	46 bn	153 bn	−107 bn	Note that costs exceed benefits[a]
Re-impose capital controls	107 bn	153 bn	−46 bn	Again, costs exceed benefits[a]
Create a single world currency	107 bn	16 bn	91 bn	Political feasibility is seriously questionable
Have IFIs borrow and lend in emerging-market currencies	107 bn	0.5 bn	106 bn	Not surprisingly, the author's preference

Note: [a] Which is the point of the analysis.

Estimating the costs of this intervention requires an estimate of the impact of capital account restrictions on financial depth and development. Widely cited estimates by Klein and Olivei (1999) suggest that the financial intermediation ratio (calculated as liquid liabilities as a share of GDP) is 28 per cent lower in countries that continuously maintain capital controls than in countries that eliminate them.[40] Note that this effect is very slightly smaller than the effect of strict domestic financial regulation on financial deepening and development. King and Levine's (1993) work on the connections between financial development and growth again suggests that reducing the financial development ratio by this amount will lower *per capita* income growth by 1 per cent per annum.

The net benefits of this second 'opportunity' are then −0.3 per cent of developing country GDP. Again, to express this as a share of global GDP, recall that developing countries account for slightly less than one-half of global GDP when the latter is computed at PPPs. The resulting total, computed as above, is a net loss per annum of $42 bn in 2003 US dollars, an amount that will again rise as the world economy continues to expand.

Again, sensitivity analysis of this point estimate is straightforward. Some observers will question whether the impact of capital account liberalisation on the financial intermediation ratio is as large as estimated by Klein and Olivei. It is straightforward to scale down this parameter and scale down the estimated gross costs of this initiative proportionately. Others will doubt whether measures to re-regulate capital account transactions will eliminate all currency crises, since even the tightest capital

controls can sometimes be evaded and when there are other potential sources of financial instability, the incentive to do so will be strong. Again, it is straightforward to assume that strict regulation of capital flows eliminates only some fraction of currency crises and to scale down the estimate of gross benefits proportionately.

Be that as it may, the preceding analysis suggests that re-regulating domestic financial markets and re-imposing strict capital controls are unattractive. While these measures can limit the incidence of banking and currency crises, these gains come at significant cost. In both cases, representative estimates from the mainstream economic literature suggest that those costs, which take the form of limiting financial development, may actually exceed the benefits, in the form of limiting financial instability.[41] It can be argued that the preceding

[40] These are their instrumental variables estimates, which seek to control for simultaneity. Klein and Olivei's (1999) results suggest, intuitively enough, that this effect is most robust for developing countries. That is the way that they are applied in the current exercise, since the calculations of the costs and benefits of capital account regulation presented here are for developing countries only.

[41] Thus, focusing on these policy options sits uneasily with the organisers' notion that expert papers should concentrate on 'opportunities' whose benefits presumably exceed their costs. But proposals for financial re-regulation and the re-imposition of capital controls have been – and remain – the starting point for the policy debate, and no analysis which neglects them would be regarded as definitive. If I have convinced my readers that these widely cited options have costs as well as benefits and that the former might even dominate, then focusing on two 'opportunities' whose net returns are estimated as negative has served its purpose.

exaggerates the negative impact of strict domestic financial regulation and capital controls on domestic financial deepening and development or the positive effects of financial development on economic growth. But other authors have reached similar conclusions on the basis of independent, and often very different, analyses.[42] And even if such effects are arguably subject to exaggeration, there is no doubt that they exist. As such, net gains will be smaller than gross gains. In turn this creates an understandable wish to look to other opportunities for limiting financial instability.

Adopt a Common Currency

Currency mismatches are widely implicated in financial crises in developing countries. As noted above, developing countries that borrow abroad do so in foreign currency, virtually without exception. Countries that accumulate a net foreign debt, as capital-scarce developing countries are expected to do, therefore incur a currency mismatch. This mismatch is a source of currency instability, insofar as even limited exchange rate depreciations significantly increase the domestic currency cost of servicing external debts, in turn precipitating the kind of large depreciation that is the defining feature of a currency crisis. Currency mismatches are also a source of banking sector instability insofar as exchange rate depreciation then has adverse

balance-sheet effects for the banking sector, as well as for the corporate sector that is the banks' principal lending-side clientele.

Some commentators insist that the inability of developing countries to borrow abroad in their own currencies reflects weaknesses in their domestic policies and institutions that can only be remedied by developing stronger policies and institutions.[43] Since strengthening policies and institutions takes time, in the meantime developing countries face the Hobson's choice of either suffering these vulnerabilities or limiting net foreign borrowing (since net foreign borrowing means net foreign currency borrowing) and domestic financial development through the policies described in previous subsections.[44]

But insofar as the cause of financial vulnerability is currency mismatches, currency unification provides another opportunity for remedying it. If borrowing and lending countries have the same currency, currency mismatches are eliminated, by definition, and they no longer create vulnerabilities in financial systems. This has led authors like Mundell (2000) to envisage a single world currency as a solution to the financial instability problem.[45] The experience of the euro area illustrates how this response can eliminate the currency crisis problem; just contrast the prevalent of currency crises in Europe in the 1980s and 1990s with their absence from the euro area today.

Eliminating currency crises produces a benefit to emerging markets of 0.7 per cent of developing country/emerging market GDP per year (as calculated in the preceding subsection). Generalising from the experience of the euro area, the changeover costs of replacing national currencies with a single world currency would be no more than 0.1 per cent of GDP. Together these figures suggest an initial annual gross flow benefit of $107 bn, a nearly 600 per cent annual return on an investment of $16 bn, or a net gain of $91 bn per annum.[46]

An appeal of this proposal is that the single-currency solution would not enhance financial stability at the cost of financial development. To the contrary, Europe's experience with a single currency suggests that adoption of a single currency may have positive implications for financial depth. Witness the rapid growth of a pan-European

---

[42] See Dobson and Hufbauer (2001, 69) and *passim.*

[43] See for example Reinhart, Rogoff and Savastano (2003).

[44] Reinhart, Rogoff and Savastano (2003) thus argue that developing countries should solve this financial-fragility problem by limiting foreign borrowing, notwithstanding the possible negative implications for their sustainable rates of growth.

[45] Early analyses recommended currency boards and unilateral dollarisation as possible solutions to the problem (see e.g. Eichengreen 1994; Eichengreen and Hausmann 1999), but recent experience, notably in Argentina, suggests that such arrangements would not be sufficiently durable to rule out the possibility of re-issuance or additional issuance of the national currency, and that they would therefore be unlikely to provide a durable solution to the mismatch problem.

[46] With the share of developing countries in world GDP again calculated at PPPs, the net gain of $91 bn falls to $50 bn when that share is calculated at market exchange rates.

corporate bond market following the elimination of currency risk premia by the euro.

One question about this proposal is how *banking crises* will be affected by a move to a single world currency. Insofar as banking crises result from vulnerabilities associated with the presence of currency mismatches on the balance sheets of financial and non-financial firms, their incidence and costs will be reduced (along with the incidence and costs of currency crises), raising the gross benefits from the policy by as much as an additional 40 per cent.[47]

On the other hand, one can argue that a policy initiative that eliminates currency volatility without otherwise modifying the underlying sources of volatility may only cause the same volatility to show up elsewhere, for example in banking systems rather than currency markets. For example, if macroeconomic volatility increases as countries forsake the option of an independent national monetary policy that can be tailored to local needs, this increase in amplitude of business cycles may limit the reduction in banking crises, or even lead to more banking sector instability, not less.[48] Unfortunately, there is no consensus on how useful an independent monetary policy is for damping cyclical fluctuations.[49]

The other question that must be posed concerns the *political feasibility* of a world currency. For many countries, the national currency has symbolic value matched only by the national flag and national airline. At the same time, it is tempting to argue that if monetary unification is possible for Europe, then there is no reason that it should not be possible for the world as a whole. But in Europe monetary integration is part of a larger integrationist project with political as well as economic aspects. In Europe, there exists a European Parliament (EP) to hold the European Central Bank (ECB) politically accountable for its policy actions. In contrast, there exists no body with analogous powers at the global level and little prospect of creating one for the foreseeable future.

Thus, the lack of a mechanism for political accountability is a serious obstacle to the creation of a single world currency. This is why many observers regard this option as politically unrealistic over the time frame relevant for practical policy making.

Pursue an International Solution to the Currency Mismatch Problem

A fourth approach is to address the distortions in international financial markets that make it difficult for developing countries to borrow abroad in their own currencies. This would help to limit financial instability by eliminating the problems that saddle net foreign debtors with costly currency mismatches. It would allow them to borrow abroad to smooth consumption and finance their investment needs. It would not enhance financial stability at the cost of financial development.

As explained on pp. 253ff. some analysts view the difficulty that developing countries have in borrowing abroad in their own currencies as related to the limited appetite of international investors for emerging-market currencies. Eichengreen and Hausmann (2003) show that the global portfolio is concentrated in the currencies of a few large countries and international financial centres. The explanation, they suggest, is that for other more 'exotic' currencies the management costs incurred by international investors exceed the associated benefits in the form of additional portfolio diversification. In addition, they show that markets in the currencies of the select few emerging economies that have managed to escape this problem have tended to develop through debt issuance by non-residents, who then swap their debt service obligations into their currency of choice, allowing residents on the other side of the swap to offload their currency risk as if they had borrowed in local currency.

---

[47] Recall that three-tenths of the total costs of financial crises are attributable to banking crises according to the studies underlying the preceding calculations, while seven-tenths are attributable to currency crises. Three to seven is approximately 40 per cent. This is an upper bound on the additional benefit, of course, insofar as banking crises also occur for reasons not related to currency mismatches.

[48] This is also a caveat to the notion that currency unification would encourage financial development, insofar as additional macroeconomic volatility due to the abandonment of the stabilisation role of national monetary policy would negatively impact the development of financial markets.

[49] The latest IMF analysis of this question (Rogoff *et al.* 2003) suggests that it has been of little, if any, value in practice for the developing countries that are the subject of the present analysis.

The authors therefore propose the creation of a synthetic unit of account in which claims on a diversified group of emerging-market economies can be denominated, together with steps by the international financial institutions (IFIs) to develop a liquid market in claims denominated in this unit. They propose that the non-concessional windows of the World Bank and IFIs should issue debt in this index. Their AAA rating allows the IFIs to place debt with institutional investors. The historical properties of the underlying bonds suggests that claims denominated in this unit would exhibit trend appreciation, relatively low volatility and a negative correlation with consumption in the countries in which they are

marketed, all of which would make them attractive to international investors.

To be sure, such claims would be less attractive initially insofar as the market in them would be relatively illiquid. However, given the mandate of the IFIs to foster economic growth and stability, it can be argued that the IFIs should subsidise issuance until sufficient liquidity develops to make the new bonds easily tradable. The G-10 countries should then follow by issuing sovereign debt denominated in the EM index (see below). As a liquid market develops, developing countries will be able to do the same. The result will be the more efficient international diversification of risks and a reduction in financial fragility.[50]

The proposal described in Eichengreen and Hausmann (2003) has four components. Step 1 is to define an inflation-indexed basket of currencies of emerging and developing countries (the 'EM index'). Step 2 is for multilateral institutions such as the World Bank to issue debt denominated in this index. To avoid incurring a currency mismatch, they would convert a portion of their existing loans into claims denominated in the inflation adjusted currencies of each of the countries included in the index so as to replicate the index in their pattern of lending. Step 3 would broaden and deepen the EM market by having G-10 sovereigns issue debt in this instrument and swap their currency exposure with countries whose currencies are included in the EM index. Step 4 would then encourage institutional investors and mutual funds to create products that add credit risk to the index as a way of further encouraging the development of the market. The details of this proposal are described in the appendix.

It is important to emphasise that this proposal does not envisage additional official lending. It does not entail an expansion in the scale of the World Bank's lending operations.[51]

The benefits of this initiative would be similar to those of the single-currency option described above. Eliminating the risk of currency crises by no longer forcing developing countries that are net foreign debtors to incur currency mismatches again produces a benefit of 0.7 per cent of developing country/emerging-market GDP per year. This amounts to an initial annual flow benefit of $107 bn.

---

[50] This is not the only proposal for increased international risk sharing as a response to problems of macroeconomic and financial instability. The World Bank has attempted to promote the development of insurance markets for terms of trade risk. Shiller (2003) has proposed that governments issue derivative securities that would permit GDP *per capita* swaps between countries as a way of diversifying country-specific macroeconomic risks. Caballero (2003) has advocated the development of instruments indexed to the prices of the principal commodity exports of emerging-market borrowers. Berg, Borensztein and Mauro (2002) have promoted the idea of GDP-linked bonds, the coupons on which would fluctuate with the growth of real GDP. The Eichengreen–Hausmann proposal is one more attempt, in this spirit, to help to complete incomplete financial markets.

[51] An expansion of IFI lending may or may not be desirable for general development purposes, but it is not integral to the present initiative. Neither does the proposal imply that developing countries should issue debt in EMs. This would not help to solve the currency mismatch problem since it would just substitute exchange rate risk *vis-à-vis* the EM for exchange risk *vis-à-vis* the dollar. Currency risk would not be significantly diminished, because any one emerging market currency would account for only a fraction of the EM basket. Rather, the proposal is designed to allow countries to denominate their obligations in constant units of their domestic consumption basket. That is, they would become able to issue domestic currency-denominated bonds indexed to their consumer price indices. The World Bank (and possibly the regional development banks) would aggregate the loans of the countries making up the EM index in order to create a basket of loans with the same currency composition as the EM bonds that they themselves issue. Institutional investors would not do this for them because private markets would initially be lacking in liquidity. But by taking steps to render the market more liquid, they would be paving the way for private financial institutions to take over the task.

Again, insofar as only some currency crises are eliminated by this initiative, one will want to scale down this estimate. On the other hand, insofar as banking crises result from vulnerabilities associated with the presence of currency mismatches on the balance sheets of financial and non-financial firms, their incidence and costs will be reduced (along with the incidence and costs of currency crises), one may want to raise one's gross benefits (by up to an additional 40 per cent).[52]

The costs of this initiative will depend on the yield that investors demand on EM-denominated World Bank bonds.[53] This will differ from the yield on dollar-denominated World Bank bonds, for three reasons. First, it will depend on the expected change in the exchange rate between the dollar and the EM index over the life of the bond.[54] Second, it will depend on the risk premium that foreign investors require in order to hold EM currency risk. Third, it will depend on the liquidity premium that investors demand to compensate them for the more limited liquidity of the new instrument.

It is hard to estimate the magnitude of these costs. The reduction in risk associated with making the world a safer financial place and the expected appreciation of the EM might in fact result in no additional interest rate cost for the World Bank. On the other hand, new instruments often have to be priced at a discount until investors gain familiarity with them and liquid secondary markets develop. The World Bank could choose to absorb this cost on the grounds that it has an interest in solving currency mismatch problems that threaten the stability of the international financial system.

The World Bank's reported loans outstanding in FY 2003 were US$116 bn; its own borrowings outstanding were US$109 bn.[55] Discussions with market participants suggest that, in order to issue EM-denominated debt, the Bank might have to pay from 0 to 50 additional basis points to compensate investors for the initially limited liquidity of these issues (in addition to a current cost of borrowing of approximately 3.25 per cent). This is comparable to the premium demanded by investors for private placements on international bond markets – private placements similarly differing from other bond issues by their lesser liquidity. Taking the upper bound of 50 basis points suggests a net cost of the initiative of US $545 m per annum (until a liquid market develops and the need for a liquidity premium disappears).[56] This is a small figure relative to the annual flow benefit of $107 bn estimated above.

Concluding Remarks

Table 5.5 summarises the costs and benefits of these four 'opportunities.' Since that speaks for itself, I use this conclusion for some additional remarks.

In his memoirs, Robert Rubin emphasizes the importance of probabilistic thinking for policy making.[57] Policy is made in an uncertain world. Given the complexity of social systems and the imperfect predictability of human behaviour, the impact of a policy is unavoidably uncertain. Those responsible for policy decisions and advice must therefore consider a range of probable outcomes. The point applies equally to policies toward financial instability, disease, hunger, corruption, global warming, demographic change and any other challenge confronting the world today. Whatever the problem,

[52] Again, this is an upper bound on the additional benefit insofar as banking crises also occur for reasons not related to currency mismatches.

[53] In principle, the additional balance sheet risk assumed by the World Bank might be included. In practice, however, it is not obvious that the Bank and its regional counterparts would be assuming additional balance sheet risk. The effect of the initiative would be to repackage currency risk already on their books and place it with international investors through the issuance of EM-denominated debt. Emerging markets that borrow from the World Bank, for their part, would be able to offload the currency risk currently associated with their debt service obligations. Insofar as the result is an improvement in the capacity of countries borrowing from the Bank to keep current on their external obligations, the credit risk in the World Bank's loan portfolio could in fact decline, other things equal. In addition, there would be no additional convertibility risk as countries' payments would be made in the same currencies used at present.

[54] As explained in the appendix, since the EM should have a tendency to appreciate against the dollar due to the Balassa–Samuelson effect, on average this factor should reduce the interest cost to the World Bank.

[55] World Bank (2003, 3).

[56] Calculated as $109 bn * 0.005.

[57] See Rubin and Weisberg (2003).

it is dangerous and even potentially counterproductive to base policy decisions on a false sense of certainty and precision.

In the present context, this means that one should not be misled by confidently presented estimates of the costs and benefits of policy options based on spuriously rigorous models. In discussing the costs and benefits of different responses to financial instability, it would have been possible to offer much more complex calculations and present the results with many more decimal points. It would have been possible to obtain estimates of these magnitudes by simulating one of the popular global macroeconomic models or by building a general equilibrium model of the world economy expressly for this purpose. But the resulting estimates would have been contingent on dubious assumptions, many of which would even not have been apparent to the naked eye. Very detailed calculations of this sort, whether

they estimate the costs and benefits of interventions to control financial instability, disease, hunger, or global warming, have a tendency to look deceptively precise. Basing evaluations on spuriously precise estimates that do not acknowledge intrinsic uncertainty runs the risk of producing bad policy.

The advantage of the simpler approach to such calculations taken here is that the underlying assumptions are explicit. The uncertainty to which they are subject is clear. Readers wishing to re-do those calculations subject to some assumptions can do so freely, following the examples provided in the text. In reality, of course, the same uncertainty surrounds estimates of the key parameters underlying models of AIDS diffusion, malaria propagation, poverty reduction, global warming and so forth. Thoughtful readers of the material prepared for this project would do well not to allow themselves to be lulled by a false sense of scientific precision.

Appendix

This appendix provides more detail on the four steps of the Eichengreen–Hausmann proposal.[58]

Step 1: Develop an Index Based on a Basket of Emerging-Market Currencies

For developing countries to be able to borrow abroad in local currency, foreign investors will have to take a long position in those currencies. But it is hard to imagine foreign investors managing portfolios that include the currencies of many small, poorly diversified economies. The authors therefore propose the creation of a unit of account made up of a portfolio of emerging-market and developing country currencies.[59]

To deal with the temptation to debase the currency faced by net debtors borrowing in their own currencies, the underlying debt instruments would be indexed to the consumer price index (CPI) of each country. Indexing to the CPI, like indexing to the dollar, allows countries with limited credibility to lengthen the maturity of their obligations. But indexing to the CPI has better properties from the point of view of macroeconomic stability: it is similar to indexing to the real exchange rate, which is a relative price.[60] Thus, if the real exchange rate is stationary, the index will display long-run stability. Averaging over twenty countries enhances this stability still further. In addition, since the real exchange rate tends to appreciate in good times and depreciate in bad times, debt service payments on these obligations are positively correlated with capacity to pay, which is the opposite of dollar debts. Finally, to the extent that late-developing countries grow faster than advanced economies, this generates domestic inflation not offset by depreciation of the exchange rate (the Balassa–Samuelson effect), strengthening the real exchange rate and thereby raising the compensation received by foreign investors.[61] This gives the index a long-run tendency to appreciate.

Eichengreen and Hausmann consider two such baskets, one that includes the twenty largest countries for which the IMF publication *International Financial Statistics* conveniently provides quarterly data on exchange rates and consumer price indexes since at least 1980, and another that includes the largest twenty-two countries with the same continuous data since 1993.[62] Figure 2A.1 shows the value of the two indexes along with the yen–dollar and deutschemark–dollar exchange rates.[63] Historically, the two EM inflation adjusted currency baskets are less volatile against the dollar than are the

---

[58] The text is drawn, with some modifications, from Eichengreen and Hausmann (2003).

[59] As argued by Shiller (2003), new markets typically need new indexes to synthesise relevant information, whether it is the S&P 500, the CPI or the Lehman Bond Index.

[60] While indexing to the CPI may be necessary to create a demand by foreign investors to hold claims denominated in the currencies of emerging markets, it is not obviously sufficient, given that many emerging markets already issue CPI-indexed claims which have not found their way into the portfolios of foreign investors. This is the problem that the remainder of the proposal seeks to address.

[61] The EM index appreciates *vis-à-vis* the dollar over time if the sum of the real exchange rate appreciation of the underlying currencies plus US inflation is positive. This means that the index will appreciate, even if the real exchange rate depreciates, as long as this depreciation is less than US inflation.

[62] They weight the constituent countries by GDP at PPP in order to avoid setting weights in a manner that favours countries that do not behave prudently, as would happen if the indices were weighted by the market dollar value of GDP or the value of foreign debt.

[63] The indexes are presented on a per-dollar basis so that increases in the index imply depreciations.

yen and the mark. For example, it is striking that in the period of the Asian and Russian crises the EM index actually depreciated against the dollar by less than the deutschemark. This low volatility suggests, other things equal, that claims denominated in the EM index should be attractive to international investors.

Note that the reduction in volatility associated with moving from a single emerging-market currency to a portfolio of such currencies is related to more than pure diversification.[64] In addition, there are structural reasons why one should expect negative correlations among the real exchange rates of the countries constituting the index. Many of the countries in question are on opposite sides of the same markets. While some export oil or coffee, others import those commodities. Therefore a positive shock to one is a negative shock to another. Even when different countries export the same commodities, they are affected in opposite ways when shocks are to commodity supply. A frost in Brazil's coffee growing regions is a negative shock to Brazil but a positive shock to other coffee producers. An aggregate of emerging market real exchange rates is thus more stable than the individual components.[65]

In sum, the EM index has three characteristics – trend appreciation, low volatility and a negative correlation with consumption growth in industrial countries – that should make it attractive for global investors. The question is how to create a liquid market in claims denominated in this index. The answer begins with Step 2.

Step 2: Have the World Bank and Other IFIs Issue Debt Denominated in the EM Index

By borrowing in the currencies that comprise the EM index, the IFIs would gain the ability to extend loans to the countries issuing those currencies in inflation adjusted local currency terms without incurring balance sheet mismatches themselves. And by issuing high-grade debt securities denominated in a basket of EM currencies, the IFIs would provide investors with a claim on a more stable unit than could be achieved by issuing in an individual currency.[66]

In practice, the process by which a select number of countries has acquired the ability to issue external debt denominated in their own currencies has been led not by residents but by foreigners and often by IFIs issuing obligations denominated in the currencies of these countries. This pattern reflects the need to separate credit risk from currency risk and the difficulty that the residents of countries with original sin have in doing so themselves. Foreigners, in contrast, can issue instruments with currency risk that is uncorrelated with credit risk.

Eichengreen and Hausmann therefore propose that the non-concessional windows of the World Bank and other international financial institutions should issue debt in the index described above.[67] Their AAA rating allows them to access institutional investors, as noted in the main body of the text. These bonds would be attractive as a result of the trend appreciation of the EM index, its relatively low volatility and its negative correlation with consumption in the countries in which they are marketed. To be sure, they would be less attractive initially insofar as they would be

---

[64] That is, it is related to more than offsets in random, uncorrelated shocks to real exchange rates.

[65] The more countries that are included, other things equal, the more stability one would expect. In the limit (when all countries are included), the real exchange rate would not fluctuate, since the real exchange rate of the world as a whole is constant, by definition. Moreover, the inflation-indexed local currency is just the value of the domestic consumption basket which is itself much more diversified than the export basket, hence is also more stable.

[66] In a world of costless transactions, an investor could create an implicit index by herself. Individuals could in theory create an S&P or a Nasdaq- based portfolio by themselves. In practice, transaction costs imply that it is more efficient for somebody to create the portfolio and sell shares in it. In addition, an attempt to replicate the EM index privately by purchasing the underlying instruments in the market would involve buying securities that have much more credit risk than the AAA-rated IFIs, as no EM member is AAA rated.

[67] IFIs usually operate through two main windows: a *non-concessional* window that is funded by borrowing in international capital markets using their capital base as collateral and a *concessional window* that is funded with fiscal resources of donor governments. In the case of the World Bank, the non-concessional window is known as the International Bank of Reconstruction and Development (IBRD) and the concessional window is called the International Development Agency (IDA).

relatively illiquid. However, given the mandate of the IFIs to foster economic growth and stability, not to mention their self-interest in the development of this market, it can be argued that the IFIs should subsidise issuance until sufficient liquidity develops to make the new bonds easily tradable.[68]

The argument that it is in the self-interest of the IFIs to develop the capacity to lend to their clients in local currency inflation-indexed terms runs as follows. Currently the World Bank and other IFIs lend in dollars to finance projects relevant to the borrowers' development needs. All lending by the World Bank and the regional development banks (RDBs) is in dollars, other major currencies, and Special Drawing Rights (SDRs which are themselves a basket of major currencies).[69] This means that IFI lending creates a currency mismatch in the balance sheets of the corporations whose investment projects are funded by these institutions. They similarly create a mismatch for governments by loaning in dollars to fund schooling, transport, water and energy projects whose costs are ultimately paid through local currency-denominated taxes and service charges.

For non-concessional lending, the practice of dollar lending has a clear explanation. The development banks borrow on international capital markets in the major currencies. By lending in those same currencies, they neatly match the currency denomination of their assets and liabilities.[70]

However, the concessional windows of these institutions – the IDA and the Poverty Reduction and Growth Facility (PRGF) of the IMF and its equivalent in the RDBs – are not financed by borrowing on capital markets but by grants from the high-income countries.[71] This makes it hard to argue that the reason for denominating these loans in dollars is to permit the development banks to avoid incurring currency mismatches. In this context, lending in dollars and SDRs is more difficult to rationalise.

Hausmann and Rigobon (2003) show that one result of the practice of denominating concessional loans in dollars is that repayments to the IDA have undesirable cyclical characteristics. IDA loans become more burdensome precisely when it is harder for countries to pay – i.e. when the dollar value of the GDP of the borrowing countries declines significantly. Compare this with a situation in which

IDA lending is denominated in inflation-indexed local currency units of each country. In this case, the dollar value of debt service would decline (rise) when exchange rate depreciates (strengthens). Occasions on which a borrowing country was forced to suspend its repayment to IDA might then become less frequent because the tendency for the exchange rate to collapse at the same time output fell (making it doubly difficult to repay dollar debts) would no longer be relevant for debt servicing capacity. This improved outcome might even be achieved without any additional subsidisation of concessional loans, insofar as its improved risk characteristics caused the net present value (NPV) of the IDA portfolio to rise rather than fall.[72]

---

[68] Moreover, since the World Bank would calculate the index, it would have a fiduciary responsibility to its investors in assuring that there is no opportunistic manipulation of the estimates of exchange rates or the CPI by member countries. This would impart more credibility to the index.

[69] In the interest of simplicity, the text that follows refers to these alternatives as dollar lending.

[70] To put the point another way, they lend in dollars because, absent an initiative of the sort we develop here, original sin prevents them from issuing debt in the currencies of their borrowers.

[71] They are then supplemented by reflows from their own lending operations.

[72] Hausmann and Rigogon (2003) show that the currency risk of the portfolio of inflation-indexed local currency IDA loans between 1985 and 2000 would have been low, given the low and often negative correlations among real exchange rate movements of IDA countries. This is the same pattern that holds for our EM index, as noted above. In addition they show for IDA that the inflation-indexed local currency portfolio would exceed the value of the dollar portfolio if the sum of the US inflation plus the real appreciation of the IDA basket of currencies exceeds 1.37 per cent. US inflation has been running at approximately 2 per cent. If this rate is maintained going forward, there would be scope for some long-run real depreciation of the basket while still generating a larger NPV. However, if developing countries' income levels exhibit a trend towards convergence – as has been the case in China, India, East Asia and Eastern Europe – the Balassa–Samuelson effect would imply that they should also exhibit some trend appreciation. In this case, the move to local currency inflation-indexed lending should generate an even larger expected repayment stream, even better risk characteristics and an even lower volatility in the total dollar value of the portfolio (given the low volatility of the basket).

Note that foreign currencies would maintain their function as means of payment. Borrowing countries would still receive loans and repay the World Bank in dollars. The only difference is that the unit of account on which those payments were based would now be inflation-indexed local currency.[73]

Hausmann and Rigobon propose that the concessional window of the World Bank (the IDA) should move rapidly in this direction by converting all dollar- and SDR-denominated loans into inflation-indexed local currency. Our proposal is directed to the non-concessional window of the World Bank (the IBRD) and would imply moving in the same direction, albeit more gradually. The problem with moving quickly is that, as just noted, the Bank finances its non-concessional lending by borrowing on international capital markets. If the Bank were to redenominate its loans into inflation-indexed currencies of emerging markets while continuing to borrow in dollars, it would incur a currency mismatch. The solution to this is for the IBRD to be-

gin funding itself by issuing bonds denominated in EMs. Because this market would be relatively illiquid initially, this part of the adjustment would take time. Hence there is an argument for moving more gradually.

Note that the World Bank would not be required to take on additional currency risk if it funded itself by issuing EM-denominated debt. By converting some of its already outstanding loans to EM members into inflation-indexed local currency loans, it could match the currency composition of the asset and liability sides of its balance sheet.

RDBs such as the Inter-American Development Bank, the European Bank for Reconstruction and Development (EBRD), the Asian Development Bank (ADB) and the African Development Bank lend only to sub-sets of the countries whose currencies are included in the EM index, as the latter is a globally balanced index. This would make it more difficult for them to align the currency composition of the asset and liability sides of their balance sheets if they started borrowing in EMs. But it would still be relatively straightforward for them to offload the currency exposure associated with not lending to members of the EMs basket that are not in their region. They could do so by swapping currency exposures among themselves or with the World Bank. Each RDB would then have nicely matched EM-denominated debts and EM-denominated assets.[74] They would thereby eliminate the currency mismatch generated by their own lending, and at the same time become part of the solution to the financial-instability problem.[75]

Once issuance by the World Bank and the RDBs reached significant levels, claims denominated in the EM index would form part of standard global bond indexes. This would then increase the demand for EM bonds by institutional fixed income investors with a mandate to form portfolios that track the index.

Step 3: Have G-10 Countries Issue Debt Denominated in the Index

If this effort succeeds in creating space in the global portfolio for EM debt, there will then be an

---

[73] In other words, while dollars and other foreign currencies would be delivered, the amount of the obligation would be related to the inflation indexed-local currency value of the debt.

[74] Conceivably, if the issuance of EM debt by the World Bank is very large, the Bank might be unable to hedge the resulting currency exposure by converting some of its old loans into the member currencies of the index because the required amounts would exceed the volume of loans in its books to at least some of the EM members. But the Bank could still hedge its excess exposure to that currency by arranging a swap with another IFI – say a RDB – that would similarly wish to convert its dollar loans to local currency. Alternatively, the World Bank could purchase inflation-indexed local currency government obligations or ask an investment bank to offer it a hedge. All these operations would have the beneficial effect of reducing the currency mismatch of the respective countries.

[75] Hausmann and Rigobon (2003) simulate the impact on the IDA portfolio of converting IDA loans into inflation-indexed local currency in the 1985–2000 period. They find that diversification implies a very large reduction in the overall currency risk of the portfolio of IDA. In addition, debt service becomes less procyclical and less correlated with the real exchange rate, moving the debt burden to states of nature where the capacity to pay is larger. Monte Carlo simulations show that under the counterfactual the same shocks to output, inflation and the real interest rate are associated with a more predictable evolution of the debt–GDP ratio than under dollar-based lending.

opportunity for other high-grade non-residents to develop the market further. The governments of the USA, Euroland, Japan, the UK and Switzerland, the issuers of the five major currencies, are natural candidates to do so.[76] The debt denominated in their currencies is significantly greater than the debt issued by their residents. They are at the opposite end of the currency of denomination spectrum from emerging markets, which should make some portfolio diversification toward EMs relatively attractive. More broadly, they are not immune from the systemic consequences of original sin, giving them an interest in solving the problem.

Thus, these countries could issue EM debt in order to further transform the structure of the global portfolio. Following issuance, they would presumably wish to swap out of some or all of the EM currency exposure in order to avoid adding an inconvenient currency mismatch to their own fiscal accounts.[77] To do this, they would negotiate currency swaps with the countries whose currencies make up the index. In turn, this would allow emerging markets to swap out of (to hedge) their dollar exposures. Eventually, these swaps could be intermediated by the investment banks, although in the initial stages the World Bank might have to organise them.[78]

The net cost of borrowing for the G-10 countries, after taking into account the swap, might actually be less than borrowing in their own currencies. The swap would entail a transfer of resources from the country that is most anxious to pay in order to hedge its currency exposure to the country that is most indifferent about the transaction. In other words, the first country would be especially willing to pay for the privilege of concluding the transaction, while the second one would be relatively indifferent and could therefore negotiate more favourable terms. Since countries suffering from original sin would be particularly anxious to pay for the privilege of offloading their currency exposures, the G-10 countries could presumably obtain relatively attractive terms.

However, the swap may be expensive to organise. If the cost of the swap exceeds the benefit to EM member countries of hedging their currency exposures, then the transaction may not take place. Anticipating this outcome, G-10 countries may not be willing to issue EM debt in the first place. A solution to this problem would be for EM member countries to commit to swap their exposures with G-10 countries at a pre-announced price. G-10 governments could then exercise this *de facto* put option in the event that they did not find a more attractive swap alternative in the market.

The development of a private market in swaps will depend on the existence of liquid long-term fixed rate bond markets in local currency. These exist in some emerging markets and not in others. While this initiative would facilitate the development of local markets, the regional development banks could accelerate the process further, by issuing instruments denominated in the (inflation-indexed) currencies of individual member countries in order to help create a benchmark long-term bond that would be devoid of sovereign and convertibility risk. The existence of a market in these claims would encourage investment banks to create and price the relevant swaps.

[76] In what follows these countries are referred to as the 'G-10'.

[77] That is to say that may not want debt service denominated in EMs when their tax revenues were denominated in domestic currency.

[78] In particular, the Bank's AAA rating would allow it to provide greater assurances to the treasuries of developed countries. It is useful to consider the performance risk associated with these swaps. Emerging markets would pay into the swaps when their currencies were strong while getting money from them when their currencies were weak. Since real appreciation (depreciation) tends to occur in good (bad) times, the performance risk will be concentrated in good times. In times of crisis, when their currencies weaken significantly, emerging markets would be receiving net income from their swaps. This minimises the relevance of ability to pay for performance risk, which is the opposite of what happens with dollar debts. A swap can be thought of as an exchange of bonds between the two final parties to the transaction. Hence, if the emerging market were to default on its swap obligation – i.e. on the bond that it issued – then the industrial country would simply take back the bond that it had committed to the swap. Default risk would be limited to the change in value of the two bonds since the time they were issued. Again, performance risk would be limited.

Step 4: Further Develop the EM Index Market

Imagine that as a result of the preceding steps there develops a market in claims denominated in the EM index. It is reasonable to think that institutional investors and mutual funds will then create products that add credit risk to the index. They will be able to do so by buying local currency debt of the countries in the index. This will facilitate the development of these markets, further helping to erode original sin. It is conceivable that once the market has developed sufficiently, the role of industrial country governments and international institutions can be scaled back, as has happened with the issuance by non-residents of debt denominated in the currencies of the Czech Republic, Hong Kong, Poland, Slovakia and South Africa.

References

Abaid, A. de G. N. Oomes and K. Ueda, 2003: The quality effect: does financial liberalisation improve the allocation of capital?, unpublished manuscript, International Monetary Fund, New York

Alesina, Grilli and Milesi-Ferretti, 1994:

Atinc, Tamar Manuelyan and Michael Walton, 1999: *Social consequences of the East Asian financial crisis*, World Bank, Washington, DC

Berg, Andrew, Eduardo Borensztein and Paulo Mauro, 2002: Reviving the case for GDP-indexed bonds, IMF **Working Paper, 02-211**, December

Bordo, M. and B. Eichengreen, 1998:

Bordo, Michael, Barry Eichengreen, Daniela Klingebiel and Soledad Maria Martinez Peria, 2001: Is the crisis problem growing more severe?, *Economic Policy*, **32**, 51–82

Brecher, Richard and Carlos Diaz-Alejandro, 1977: Tariffs, foreign capital and immiserizing growth, *Journal of International Economics*, **7**, 311–22

Caballero, Ricardo, 2003: On the international financial architecture: insuring emerging markets, NBER Working Paper, **9570**, March

Caprio, Gerald and Daniela Klingebiel, 1996: Bank insolvencies: cross country experience, Policy Research Paper, 1620, World Bank Washington, DC

Chen, Shaohua and Martin Ravallion, 2001: How did the worlds poorest fare in the 1990s?, *Review of Income and Wealth*, **47**, 283–300

Chinn, Menzie D., 2001: The compatibility of capital controls and financial development: a selective survey and empirical evidence, unpublished manuscript, UC Santa Cruz, December

De Brouwer, Gordon, 1991: *Hedge funds in emerging markets*, Cambridge University Press, Cambridge

De Gregorio, Jose, 1998: Financial integration, financial development, and economic growth, unpublished manuscript, University of Chile, July

Demetriades, P.O. and K.B. Luintel, 1996: Financial development, economic growth, and banking sector controls: evidence from India, *Economic Journal*, **106**, 359–74

Devenow, Andrea and Ivo Welch, 1996: Rational herding in financial economics, *European Economic Review*, **40**, 603–15

Dobson, Wendy and Gary Hufbauer, 2001: *World capital markets: challenge to the G-10*, Institute for International Economics, Washington, DC

Economist, 2003: Economics focus: no pain, no gain, *Economist Magazine*, 13 December, 77.

Edwards, 2001:

Eichengreen, Barry 1994: *International monetary arrangements for the 21st century*, Brookings Institution, Washington, DC

Eichengreen, B. and Arteta, 2000:

Eichengreen, Barry and Ricardo Hausmann, 1999: Exchange rates and financial fragility, in Federal Reserve Bank of Kansas City, *New Challenges for Monetary Policy*, Federal Reserve Bank of Kansas City, Kansas City, MO, 329–68

2003: Original sin: the road to redemption, in B. Eichengreen and R. Hausmann (eds.), *Other people's money: debt denomination and financial instability in emerging market economies*, University of Chicago Press, Chicago

Eichengreen, Barry and David Leblang, 2003: Capital account liberalisation and growth: was Mr. Mahathir right?, *International Journal of Finance and Economics*, **8**, 205–24

Eichengreen, Barry and Richard Portes, 1987: The anatomy of financial crises, in R. Portes and A. Swoboda (eds.), *Threats to international financial stability*, Cambridge University Press, Cambridge, 10–57

Eichengreen, B., Rose and Wyplosz, 1995:

Ferreira, Miguel A. and Paul A. Laux, 2003: Portfolio flows, volatility and growth, www.ssrn.com

Guiso, Luigi, Paola Sapienza and Luigi Zingales, 2002: Does local financial development matter?, NBER Working Paper, **8923**, May

Gavin, Michael and Ricardo Hausmann, 1996: Sources of macroeconomic volatility in developing countries, unpublished manuscript, IADB

Ghosh, Swati R. and Atish R. Ghosh, 2003: Structural vulnerabilities and currency crises, *IMF Staff Papers*, **50**, 481–506

Goldsmith, Raymond, 1969: *Financial structure and economic development*, Yale University Press, New Haven

Goldstein, Morris, 1997: The Case for an international banking standard, Policy analyses in International Economics, 47, Institute for International Economics, Washington DC

Goldstein, Morris, Carmen Reinhart and Graciela Kaminsky, 2000: *Assessing financial vulnerability: an early warning system for emerging markets*, Institute for International Economics, Washington, DC

Goldstein, Morris and Philip Turner, 2003: Controlling currency mismatches in emerging market economies: an alternative to the original sin hypothesis, unpublished manuscript, Institute of International Economics, August

Hausmann, Ricardo and Roberto Rigobon, 2003: IDA in UF: on the benefits of changing the currency denomination of concessional lending to low-income countries, unpublished manuscript, World Bank

Hellman, Thomas, K. Murdock and J. Stiglitz, 2000: Liberalisation, moral hazard in banking, and prudential regulation: are capital requirements enough?, *American Economic Review*, **90**, 147–65

Henry, Peter, 1998: Do stock market liberalizations cause investment booms?, Graduate School of Business, Stanford University, Research Paper, 1504, November; published in *Journal of Financial Economics*, **58**(1–2), 301–34

2003: Capital account liberalisation, the cost of capital, and economic growth, *American Economic Review*, **92**, 91–6

Henry, Peter and Peter Lorentzen, 2003: Domestic capital market reform and access to global finance: making markets work, in R. E. Litan,

M. Romerleano and V. Sundararajan (eds.), *The future of domestic capital markets in developing countries*, Brookings Press, Washington, DC

IMF and World Bank, 2001: Assessing the implementation of standards: a review of experience and next steps, www.imf.org, 11 January

Keynes, John Maynard, 1933: National self sufficiency, in D.E. Moggridge (ed.), *The collected works of John Maynard Keynes*, Cambridge: University Press, Cambridge

Khan, Aubhik, 2000: The finance and growth nexus, *Business Review of the Federal Reserve Bank of Philadelphia*, January–February, 3–14

Khan, Mohsin S. and Abdelhak S. Senhadji, 2000: Financial development and economic growth: an overview, IMF Working Paper, **00/209** December

King, R.G. and Ross Levine, 1993: Finance and growth: Schumpeter might be right, *Quarterly Journal of Economics*, **108**, 717–37

Kiyotaki, Nobu, Kiminori Matsuyama and Akihiko Matsui, 1992: Toward a theory of international currency, *Review of Economic Studies*, **60**, 283–307

Klein, Michael, 2003: Capital account openness and the varieties of growth experience, NBER Working Paper, 9500, January

Klein, Michael and Giovanni Olivei, 1999: Capital account liberalisation, financial depth, and economic growth, NBER Working Paper, **7384**, July

Kose, M. A., E. S. Prasad and M. E. Terrones, 2003: Financial integration and macroeconomic volatility, *IMF Staff Papers*

Krugman, Paul, 1979: A model of balance of payments crises, *Journal of Money, Credit, and Banking*, **11**, 311–25

Lee, Joung-Woo, 2004: Social impact of the crisis, in D.-K. Chung and B. Eichengreen (eds.), *The Korean economy beyond the crisis*, Edward Elgar, Cheltenham

Levine, Ross, 1997: Finance development and economic growth: views and agenda, *Journal of economic perspectives*, **35**, 688–726

Mulder, Christian and M. Rocha, 2000: The soundness of estimates of output losses in currency crises, unpublished manuscript, IMF

Mundell, Robert, 2000: A reconsideration of the 20th century, *American Economic Review*, **90**, 327–40

Mussa, Michael, 2003: *Argentina and the Fund: from triumph to tragedy*, Institute for International Economics, Washington, DC

Nurkse, Ragnar, 1944: *International currency experience*, League of Nations, Geneva

O'Donnell, Barry, 2001: Financial openness and economic performance, unpublished manuscript, Trinity College

Prasad, Eswar, Kenneth Rogoff, Shang-Jin Wei and M. Ayhan Kose, 2003: Effects of financial globalisation on developing countries: some empirical evidence, unpublished manuscript, IMF

Ranciere, Romain, Aaron Tornell and Frank Westermann, 2003: Crises and growth: a reinterpretation, NBER Working Paper, **10074**, December

Reinhart, Carmen, Kenneth Rogoff and Miguel Savastano, 2003: Debt intolerance, *Brookings Papers on Economic Activity*, **1**, 1–74

Rogoff, Kenneth, Aasim Husein, Ashoka Mody, Robin Brooks and Nienke Oomes, 2003: The evolution and performance of exchange rate regimes, IMF Working Paper, **03/234**, December

Rodrik, Dani, 1998: Who needs capital account convertibility?, in P. Kenen (ed.), *Should the IMF pursue capital account convertibility?*, Princeton Essays in International Finance, 207, May

Rubin, Robert and Jacob Weisberg, 2003: *In an uncertain world*, Random House, New York

Schumpeter, Joseph, 1939: *Business cycles*, McGraw-Hill, New York

Serven, Luis and Guillermo Perry, 2003: Argentina's macroeconomic collapse: causes and lessons, unpublished manuscript, The World Bank, September

Shiller, Robert, 2003: *The new financial order: risk in the 21st century*, Princeton University Press, Princeton

Sprague, O.M.W., 1910: *History of crises under the national banking system*, Government Printing Office, Washington, DC

Suryahadi, A., S. Sumarto, Y. Suharso and L. Pritchett, 2000: The evolution of poverty in Indonesia, 1996–99, unpublished manuscript, Country Economics Department, World Bank, Washington, DC

World Bank, 2003: *Annual report: management's discussion and analysis*, World Bank, Washington, DC

Alternative Perspectives

Perspective Paper 5.1

CHARLES WYPLOSZ

Eichengreen's chapter 5 in this volume provides a masterly overview of our understanding of financial instability. It advances four proposals, three of which serve as strawmen to provide support for the fourth, previously presented in Eichengreen and Haussman (2003, hereafter EH). Given the impressive costs of financial instability presented in the early part of the chapter, support for the EH proposal should be nothing else but enthusiastic. My assessment will be less enthusiastic, however. I will argue that the EH proposal is a good idea, one of many similar recent proposals to 'complete incomplete markets', but that it is not the panacea that Eichengreen makes it. In particular, I will argue that the benefits of the proposal are lower, the costs higher and the net benefits considerably more uncertain than asserted. I will also provide an alternative that shares with the EH proposal the intention of creating a missing market – an insurance market – as well as the use of CPI-indexed bonds.

Methodology

The chapter provides numerous estimates of the costs of financial instability and of the net benefits of proposed remedies. These estimates are based on existing studies rather than on new purpose-built models. This is a sensible strategy. Eichengreen correctly notes that large-scale models unavoidably rest on an unknown but large number of assumptions that cannot be assessed. He might have added

that when these models are statistically estimated, the estimating procedures are usually open to serious criticisms that force us to be highly sceptial; as a result, the standard errors of the estimates are usually very large, in fact larger than their authors indicate (when they report any standard error at all). This is why a tendency is not to estimate models but to calibrate them, using 'plausible' numbers; unfortunately it is impossible to evaluate the relevance of these numbers and the associated standard errors. The results may look precise, but we know they are not.

Eichengreen's approach is to draw on the literature to obtain estimates used for simple calculations. This procedure has three advantages: it is transparent (in a limited sense, see below), it does not pretend to be precise and it allows us to scan the range of plausible estimates. These advantages should not be exaggerated, though. Its transparency is limited; unless we carefully read the relevant papers, we do not know which assumptions are made by the primary estimate authors. Nor do we know how precise the estimates are when several studies are combined, as is the case in Eichengreen's chapter. The solution would be to provide upper and lower bounds of the estimates found in the literature. Eichengreen instead selects those estimates that he regards as reasonable. In the end, therefore, the chapter falls in the trap that he wants to avoid, giving a misleading sense of precision even though, to his credit, he does not present many decimals. This is specially the case for the crucial net benefits/costs of various proposals, obtained by netting out estimates, each of which is subject to sizeable standard errors.

The Costs of Financial Instability

Principles

The chapter correctly notes that instability is part and parcel of financial markets. It briefly discusses the reasons for the phenomenon, essentially the fact that financial markets are necessarily forward-looking. This features puts uncertainty at centre stage, including the volatility of expectations, moral hazard and adverse selection, all of which result in phenomena such as herding and bank runs or crises, credit rationing and 'original sin', multiple equilibria that result in self-fulfilling crises and gambling for resurrection.

These observations provide a fundamental rationale for public intervention. Eichengreen correctly notes that such interventions can either improve or worsen the situation. This is a ubiquitous consequence of the second-best theory: removing some failures while others exist, in both financial and other markets, does not necessarily result in an improvement. But then he tends to forget the lesson when mooting his own proposal.

These observations are not controversial. They set the ground for the hard part: how bad is financial instability and what is to be done about it? The answer has to be informed by empirical estimates, which is where many controversies lie.

The Empirics of Financial Markets

Dealing with financial market failures calls either for the suppression of financial markets or for their regulation. Many developing countries have suppressed financial markets – as did many developed countries between 1945 and the early 1980s. The question is whether the cure is worse than the symptoms – i.e. whether man-made policy distortions hurt growth more than the market distortions that they intend to suppress or attenuate.

The literature on this question is voluminous, yet it does not yield clear-cut answers. Eichengreen provides an almost exhaustive overview of the literature on the effects of capital account restraints, some of which is summarized in tables 5.3 and 5.4. He correctly breaks down the question into two parts: what are the effects of policy restraints on financial market development? And what are the effects of financial development on growth performance? His own assessment is that capital account restraints do prevent financial market development, which can be restated as saying that these policies are effective, and that financial development boosts growth. I find this conclusion too sharp, for five reasons that Eichengreen in fact acknowledges:

(1) Studies that bypass the development of financial markets – for example, those that try to estimate the effect of financial liberalisation on growth – disagree greatly on whether the effect is positive or negative, as a quick look at the chapter's table 5.3 readily confirms.

(2) Eichengreen slips from financial liberalisation to capital account liberalisation – i.e. to the external component of the process. However, capital account liberalisation is often part of a larger liberalisation move, a change in domestic politics which includes not only domestic financial liberalisation but also goods market liberalisation, possibly associated with similar moves on the labour markets. Few studies are careful enough to attempt to disentangle the effects of these simultaneous moves, so that it is not clear what is the source of enhanced growth – and, at any rate, the effect of capital liberalisation can be exaggerated.[1]

(3) The results, quoted by Eichengreen, that tend to show that the benefits from financial liberalisation mostly accrue to already relatively well-off countries further underline the importance of taking into account a broad array of policies and of being very careful with causality as distinct from simultaneity. Economic growth tends to cause the development of domestic financial markets, which in turn raises the likelihood that capital account liberalisation will boost growth. Put differently, is it capital account liberalisation that causes growth or growth that makes it

---

[1] Among those that do, see Bekaert, Campbell and Lundblad (2001); and Arteta, Eichengreen and Rose (2003).

possible to dismantle capital controls? The empirical literature is obviously concerned with the causality question but the verdict is not yet available.

(4) Much of the literature on capital account liberalisation shows that such a move is often followed by a currency crisis, sometimes also including a banking crisis, before favourable effects set in. Timing thus matters a great deal in passing judgement. Long-run effects may indeed be favourable but the early costs can be huge, as documented in Eichengreen's chapter.

(5) Crisis episodes are typically associated with huge income and wealth redistribution and with widespread increases in poverty. Inequality is a topic too often overlooked in aggregate studies. In the present case, beyond their traumatic implication for well-being, sudden and widespread increases in poverty may lead to long-lasting effects, including deep political opposition to liberalisation.

Financial Instability and Crises

The main theme of the chapter is that reducing financial stability is a big-ticket item that ought to be on the Copenhagen Consensus. Yet, it quickly restricts its attention to the need to eliminate banking and currency crises, shown to involve large costs. Eichengreen is well aware, of course, that crises are just one symptom of financial instability, which suggests that overall instability is even costlier.

Focusing on one aspect of financial stability is understandable. Some degree of instability is, as previously noted, unavoidable; indeed, the function of financial markets is to absorb and price unavoidable pre-existing uncertainty. Not only it is impossible to eliminate this amount of unavoidable volatility, it is also undesirable. Indeed, countries that lack financial markets usually exhibit a high level of output volatility that affects the population at large while financial market volatility, when moderate, affects agents that are better equipped to deal with its consequences. Since we are unable to separate out unavoidable and intrinsic volatility, and therefore to draw a border between unavoidable and excessive volatility, focusing on banking and currency crises may make sense. This will be the case under two

conditions: (1) that crises reflect intrinsic financial market instability; (2) that it entails the bulk of the costs of financial instability. Unfortunately, neither condition is met in practice.

Eichengreen identifies four classes of explanations for crises: (1) unsustainable macroeconomic policies, (2) fragile financial systems, (3) institutional weaknesses and (4) financial market failures. Explanations (1) and (3) refer to policy mistakes and are unavoidable as far as financial markets are concerned; explanations (2) and (4) are generated by the markets themselves. How many crises and how much cost is explained by policy mistakes has not been studied. A ballpark guess is that mistakes lie behind most crises but not necessarily the costlier ones. Eichengreen's focus on crises may thus be a poor proxy for financial instability as far as frequency is concerned, while capturing a significant share of the costs.

Overall Comments

In assessing the net benefits of the proposals, the chapter uses estimates of the effects of financial restraints on financial market development, and the effects of financial market development on growth. The literature finds both effects to be significant, but it also finds that the direct effects of financial restraints on growth are ambiguous.[2] This high degree of imprecision should be reflected in the calculations – for example, by presenting a range of estimates drawn from the extensive survey of the literature that is presented.

In assessing the costs of financial instability, Eichengreen focuses on banking and currency crises, partly because it is impossible to draw a border between unavoidable and avoidable instability, partly because this is where the literature provides estimates. While reducing the frequency and impact of crises is certainly an opportunity to provide the world with massive welfare and economic gains, this focus directs attention to only part of the policy challenge that financial instability poses. In so doing, it may lead us to mis-estimate the net benefits

---

[2] As noted by Eichengreen, these findings are not necessarily contradictory. The second-best theory provides a quite plausible interpretation.

of the four suggested proposals and, quite possibly, to ignore other proposals. For example, the first two proposals (re-regulate financial markets, re-impose capital controls) stand to bring more benefits and more costs than suggested in the chapter, with an uncertain impact on the balance.[3]

The Eichengreen–Hausmann Proposal

The Currency Mismatch Problem

The EH proposal addresses the currency mismatch problem. There is no doubt that the developing countries' inability to borrow in their own currencies is a major source of financial and economic instability. Not only is currency mismatch the source of many currency and banking crises, its impact is pervasive throughout developing countries.[4] It leads many countries to accumulate huge amount of unproductive foreign exchange reserves, in effect preventing them from becoming net borrowers, thus wiping out a key benefit from financial liberalisation. Eliminating currency mismatch is therefore a serious challenge candidate for the Copenhagen Consensus.

There is some debate on the causes of the currency mismatch problem. One view, defended by Reinhart, Rogoff and Savastano (2003), is that markets have learned to be cautious with countries that have a history of inflating away their debts, an easy way of *de facto* defaulting. A related view, pre-

sented by Goldstein and Turner (2003), is that poor public and private governance provides insufficient protection to international investors contemplating lending in the domestic currency. These views imply that solving the currency mismatch problem is a matter best left to the developing countries: they should adopt sound institutions and be patient. In a series of papers, Eichengreen and Hausmann have developed an alternative interpretation. They argue that the problem lies instead in a *market failure*. Characterized by entry costs and network externalities, financial markets limit their attention to a handful of international currencies. The others are simply kept out, with no chance of overcoming their late-comer and small-size handicaps. The EH view implies that a public intervention is justified, that it is desirable given the size of the expected benefits and that their proposal is one way of dealing with the problem.

It is too early to determine which side of this fledgling debate is right. In fact the two views are not mutually exclusive and each may hold some explanatory power. To borrow an example provided by EH, it is troubling that a country like Chile, which has put in place solid domestic institutions and has built up an impressive record of good policy-making, still cannot borrow in its own currency. On the other side, many countries are just bad risks with poor rating; they are barred from market access, in any currency, like any other bad risk. The currency mismatch problem therefore affects a limited number of emerging market countries with proper governance structures. Table 3 in Eichengreen and Hausmann (2003) provides a list of the twenty-two largest countries whose currencies would be promoted by their proposals[5]: it is doubtful whether countries such as Argentina, Indonesia, Turkey or Venezuela, to name a few, would be able to borrow even in the absence of a market failure.

In addition, the EH interpretation, plausible at it may be, needs detailed scrutiny. Are fixed costs and network externalities large enough to explain the currency mismatch problem? Two counterexamples spring to mind. First, most currencies that are not subject to strict capital controls are freely traded on exchange markets. These markets many not have the depth and breadth of those of the major currencies, yet they are reasonably efficient. Second, stock

---

[3] In estimating the net benefits of re-regulation, Eichengreen looks only at the gross benefits of eliminating banking crises while he looks at the overall costs of financial repression. The same applies for the re-imposition of capital controls, except that Eichengreen's calculation of the gross benefits is based on the elimination of currency crises.

[4] For instance, Brazil faced a rapid currency depreciation and a massive increase in its interest rates in anticipation of the late 2002 election of Ignazio Lula da Silva to the presidency. The 'original sin' translated these understandable market reactions into a sudden increase of the public debt that forced the newly elected administration to adopt tight fiscal and monetary policies, avoiding a crisis but bringing the Brazilian economy to a standstill for more than one year.

[5] The twenty-two countries are, by declining GDP weight: Brazil, Korea, India, Mexico, Argentina, Indonesia, Turkey, South Africa, Thailand, Poland, Singapore, Malaysia, Israel, Colombia, the Philippines, Chile, Venezuela, Pakistan, Peru, Czech Republic, Hungary and Uruguay.

markets deal in thousands of large and medium-sized firm shares with no apparent difficulty. The key in these markets is that floating shares is subject to strict rules edicted by the local regulator. Even firms from 'exotic' countries are able to raise resources on US exchanges through the specially created American Depository Receipts (ADR) facility. Nothing prevents regulators in the major markets from specifying a set of rules that borrowers would have to fulfil to issue debt in their own currencies. That this has not happened yet, in spite of the potential for a large market, could be due to fixed costs and network externalities, as EH argue, but suspicions about policy management in the developing countries must also loom large.

The Proposed Solution

Under the assumption that the currency mismatch problem is a symptom of a missing market due to fixed costs and network externality, the policy objective is to jump start this market. The task requires defining the product that will be traded and finding willing market participants, possibly offering a temporary subsidy to overcome the fixed costs. This is precisely how Eichengreen frames his fourth option.

The EM Index

The asset to be dealt with is a synthetic unit of account, the Emerging Market (EM) index. This index would be a weighted average of some twenty countries' exchange rates corrected for the CPI (P_i/E_i where E_i is country i's dollar exchange rate and P_i its CPI).[6] The EM index has a number of important advantages:

- From the lender's viewpoint, the dollar value of the debt is protected from inflation in the borrowing countries as long as the exchange rate depreciates proportionally (P_i/E_i remains constant). Inflating away the debt is therefore impossible unless the national authorities are able to sustain an overvalued exchange rate for a long time. Since exchange rate overvaluation is costly for trade reasons, the incentive to do so is weak.
- From the borrower's point of view, the debt is fixed in real terms, which means that the

instability associated with exchange rate fluctuations – the main problem associated with currency mismatch – is eliminated.
- Bad policies that lead to long-term real exchange rate depreciation (P_i/E_i decreases) reduce the dollar value of the index, providing incentives to lenders to closely monitor their customers, much as shareholders do with the firms that they own.
- The Balassa–Samuelson effect implies a long-term real appreciation (P_i/E_i increases), allowing lenders to share in productivity gains in the developing countries, again setting the incentives right.
- As a weighted average of some twenty countries indices, the EM is bound to be more stable than any single-country index. This is partly the result of the law of large numbers, but EH claim that it also follows from complementarities between developing countries. At any rate, the relative stability of the index means less risk for the lenders and therefore a lower interest charge, another benefit to the borrowers.

EH also claim that the index has nice cyclical properties. This would be the case indeed under the assumption that the real exchange rate appreciates during expansions and depreciates during recessions. They do not provide evidence, however, that this is the case.

Creating the Market

The proposal is that the international financial institutions (IFIs), especially the AAA-rated World Bank, kick starting the market. The Bank would acquire a portfolio of national real bonds in the proper (GDP weights) proportion and simultaneously borrow in the synthetic bond that corresponds to the EM index. The Bank would thus not incur any currency mismatch, it would act only as an intermediary. It would incur a country risk, but that is already the case when it borrows and lends in dollars. The currency risk would be borne by the international investors who acquire the Bank's synthetic bonds

---

[6] Let b_i be the local currency real debt. Its local currency nominal value is $b_i P_i$ and its dollar nominal value is $b_i P_i/E_i$. The dollar real value is $(P_i/E_i P*)b_i$. Note that the nominal exchange rate E_i is defined as the number of local currency units needed to purchase 1 US dollar.

but, as argued by EH, these bonds are quite diversified. The EM-indexed bonds issued by the World Bank would be traded. Over time, the market would grow, possibly supported by the G-10 countries, until the private sectors take over.

Conceivably, therefore, breaking the currency mismatch problem could be done at no cost to the World Bank. Indeed, this is what one would expect from the creation of a missing market; it creates opportunities that did not exist previously – it is all benefits, no cost. Yet, prudently, EH suggest that the World Bank might initially subsidise the market as they suspect that its initial shallowness might lead to an interest premium of up to 500 basis points. Fully absorbing this premium, in order to avoid punishing the borrowers would still amount to a small cost relative to the gain of eliminating currency crises.

Limits

There is hardly any better economic action that can be done than creating *ex nihilo* a missing market. Economists do not usually believe in finding bank notes in the street, because they know that someone will have picked them up beforehand – i.e. they usually assume that markets will have taken care of any potential opportunity of improving the needs of economic agents. Missing markets are of a different nature, but why are they missing? The economists' gut reaction is that there must some good reason and that creating a missing market can be an expensive and risky undertaking. Is this presumption verified in the present case?

Higher Costs and Smaller and Smaller Benefits

The proposal's value critically depends on EH's interpretation of the currency mismatch problem. Let us suppose that they are wrong, that the reason for

the missing market is that lenders fear that borrowers will succumb to perverse incentives and inflate away their local currency debts. This becomes impossible once the debt is indexed to the CPI. Indeed, many emerging market governments already issue domestic currency CPI-indexed debt precisely for this reason. Typically, these debt instruments are of a very short maturity and limited to local markets, a reflection of international lenders' fears of implicit default through inflation.[7]

That is not the end of the story, however. The case of Argentina, long a darling of the IFIs and of financial markets – a country that came close to adopting Eichengreen's third proposal – serves as a useful reminder that poor governance and policy mistakes must be factored in. As markets indeed factor in the perceived risk of default, the interest premium on the EM-indexed bonds will be large. This will have two unpleasant effects. First, it will restore much financial instability, in effect undermining the purpose of the scheme.[8] Second, should the World Bank actually carry on with the subsidy proposal, the costs could easily escalate by a considerable amount, even though the country risk premium is economically efficient and should not be subsidized. Worse still, since the proposal concerns a basket of country debts, doubts about a few important countries would affect the whole index, hitting all the other countries and becoming a channel of crisis contagion.

If the costs might be larger than Eichengreen allows for, what about the benefits? Eichengreen computes the benefits by assuming that the proposal would eliminate crises. But not all crises are due to currency mismatch, which means that the benefits are overestimated. Crises are bound to continue to be a feature of the world economy, with or without the EH proposal. The possibility of contagion via the index, suggested above, further erodes the magnitude of the benefits that one should reasonably expect.

The risk of contagion may be even worse. So far, I have assumed that all borrowing countries intend to dutifully fulfil their debt obligations, but let us assume that one important country included in the index defaults outright. What will happen to the index? Its value will decline and the interest rate will increase, which is likely to dampen the borrowers'

---

[7] This begs the question of why a *domestic* market for CPI-indexed debt exists. The answer can either be EH's view that international markets are concentrated in a few currencies, or credit rationing by large investors (a classic case of adverse selection).

[8] In the case of Brazil mentioned in n. 4, interest rates on CPI debts rose as much as interest on exchange rate debts, by more than 1,200 basis points.

incentive not to misbehave. As the markets follow this logic, the risk premium is bound to further rise, in turn affecting borrowing countries' incentives, in effect opening up the very kind of 'vicious circle' that the currency mismatch creates. Being involved in the scheme, the IFIs – and the G-10 governments that will have followed step 3 in Eichengreen's proposal – will feel the need to intervene and dish out emergency support to the countries in the index, a group that represents 10 per cent of world GDP. This, again, is bound to provide borrowers with perverse incentives.

Most Countries Left Out

The proposal envisages starting with an index that covers twenty–twenty-two developing countries, chosen for being large, in line with EH's preoccupation with network externalities. Implicitly, therefore, the proposal will leave out the more than 100 other smaller developing countries not in the list.[9] The logic must be that decreasing returns to scale limit the ability of the IFIs to lend in local currencies to all countries. It may also reflect the observation that financial liberalisation has positive effects on growth only in countries that have achieved a sufficient level of development.

One way out, suggested by Eichengreen, is that the regional development banks will follow the World Bank's lead and cook up their own indices, thus issuing local currency loans to more countries. Another possibility is that some of the currently emerging market countries will eventually break out of the 'original sin' syndrome and be able to borrow directly in their own currencies, making room for the next layer of emerging market countries.

One difficulty with that view is that the countries left out will feel discriminated against and may object to the proposal. It is easy to anticipate arguments to the effect that the World Bank helps only the richest of the developing countries. Passing over their case to the regional development banks (RDBs) is unlikely to solve the problem. The network externality interpretation suggests that there might not be room for several EM indices. This reasoning means that drawing the border between the countries that benefit from the scheme and those that are left out, unavoidably an arbitrary

decision, may be so contentious as to scupper the proposal.

An Alternative: The Creation of an Insurance Market

Dealing with the currency mismatch problem is undoubtedly a worthy effort. Eichengreen's proposal is interesting and could make a useful contribution, but it rests on the view that the main source of the problem is a market failure. The alternative view emphasizes the perception by lenders that the risk involved in buying local currency bonds is excessive. Those who defend this second interpretation hasten to conclude that there is no market failure and, therefore, no justification for a public intervention. Which interpretation is correct is currently being debated but it is worth noting that the conclusion that there is no market failure involved in the currency mismatch misses the fact that credit rationing is a feature of any credit market. Thus it may be that the adverse selection phenomenon associated with the perception of risk has shut down the market for local currency loans.

Assuming that both interpretations have some merit suggests a different approach, one which has already been advanced by the World Bank. Risk is normally dealt with through insurance. Yet, there is no private insurance market for developing country lending, even though many governments offer insurance for trade credit. Following Eichengreen's logic that the problem lies in a missing market suggests an alternative proposal: the public creation of an *insurance market for local currency loans to developing countries*. Under this scheme, local currency loans would be provided by the private sector but lenders would purchase insurance against non-performing loans. That such an insurance scheme has not arisen spontaneously indicates that the risks are perceived too high. An international subsidy would therefore be needed to bring the cost down.

---

[9] It may be surprising that size is the criterion chosen by EH. An alternative criterion, which takes into account the alternative interpretation of the currency mismatch problem, could be the quality of national institutions, both public and private.

The insurance could be provided by an international agency or by private insurers with access to subsidies (the World Bank could finance these subsidies). Evaluating the cost of such a subsidy is beyond the scope of this Perspective paper, but diversification could hold the tab down.

The weakness of this alternative proposal arises from the familiar moral hazard associated with any insurance scheme. Countries might overborrow, and lenders would be willing to oblige given that they would not bear the costs of borrower misbehaviour. If misbehaviour takes the form of inflation and currency depreciation, the EH idea of debts indexed to the CPI can be put to another good use: insurance would be available only for CPI-indexed loans. This would leave the borrower misbehaviour to the case of overborrowing followed by default. In this case, the solution is the usual one, the imposition of a deductible component that would encourage lenders to act with prudence.

This proposal would eventually fulfil the central aim of the EH proposal, the emergence of a market for local currency loans. Once much of Brazil's debt, for instance, is issued under the proposed scheme, the insured debt instrument would amount to a size large enough for a market to emerge. A side benefit of the emergence of such a market is that it could be used as a guide for deciding when to terminate the insurance programme: the elimination of a significant market-set risk premium would clearly show that the country has graduated to the rank of a regular local currency borrower.

Conclusion

Eichengreen's chapter makes a strong case that financial instability ought to be part of the challenges adopted by the Copenhagen Consensus. Its most visible manifestation alone, currency and banking crises, exacts a massive economic and human toll. Its less visible manifestations, including excessively restrictive macroeconomic policies and

booms followed by busts, probably add an equivalent amount to the total cost.

Eichengreen envisages four approaches to lessen financial instability. Re-regulating financial markets and re-introducing capital controls look bad under the assumption that financial liberalisation raises growth. This assumption is popular but the empirical backing is still controversial, which means that estimates of the size of the effect are subject to large standard deviations. It would be desirable to provide a range of estimates of both the benefits – beyond reducing the incidence of crises – and the costs. Adopting a single world currency would eliminate currency crises but not banking crises and other manifestations of financial instability. The benefits are therefore less than those suggested by Eichengreen. Anyway, I fully concur with his judgement that this is an option whose time has not come, for a host of political and institutional reasons that a study of the European Monetary Union (EMU) well illustrates.[10]

The fourth proposal is a novel idea, pretty much in line with current thinking and other proposals[11]: EH propose that the World Bank, followed by the G-10 countries and assisted by the RDBs, promote the creation of a market for bonds indexed to the price indices of some twenty emerging market countries. The aim is to eliminate the currency mismatch problem which has been found to lie at the root of many recent currency and banking crises in these countries. The proposal is ingenious and well-crafted.

The immediate natural question is: why such a market has not been developed by the private sector? One view is that international lenders are suspicious of borrowers who have long story of poor repayment performance, largely because their public and private institutions suffer from poor governance. The solution would seem to be to encourage these countries to put their house in order. The other view starts from the observation that many countries with excellent institutions and a 'clean' history of foreign borrowing still cannot borrow in their own currencies. This points to a market failure, and the EH proposal addresses this by having the IFIs create a missing market.

Eichengreen's evaluation of costs and benefits is inevitably subject to considerable uncertainty. To

---

[10] In a nutshell: if the UK, Denmark and Sweden feel that they cannot join the euro area, how could they join a world monetary union?

[11] For references, see n. 47 in Eichengreen's chapter 5.

start with, under his own assumptions, it is hard to put precise numbers on the costs and the benefits of the proposal. In addition, he tends to overestimate the benefits and to underestimate the costs. Overestimation stems from the fact that eliminating the currency mismatch problem will not get rid of all currency and banking crises. It will only make them less frequent and probably less lethal. In addition, currency mismatch is not the whole story as far as financial instability is concerned. On the cost side, Eichengreen ignores a number of adverse side effects of the EH proposals. These side effects include high country risk premia that would be subsidized and contagion risk that would call for large-scale interventions in an effort to salvage the market. In addition, the proposal would concern only a relatively small number of comparatively already well-off countries, making its political acceptance uncertain and certainly controversial.

An alternative proposal does not attempt to choose between the two competing explanations of the currency mismatch problem. It also observes the absence of a market, one that would provide insurance for local currency debts. This proposal is for the provision of subsidies to such insurance. Interestingly, it borrows from the EH proposal the idea that the countries affected by the currency mismatch would issue CPI-indexed bonds, thus eliminating the incentive to inflate away their debts.

References

Arteta, C., B. Eichengreen and C. Wyplosz, 2003: When does capital account liberalisation help more than it hurts?, in E. Helpman and E. Sadka (eds.), *Economic policy in the international economy*, Cambridge University Press, Cambridge

Bekaert, G., H. Campbell and C. Lundblad, 2001: Does financial liberalisation spur growth?, NBER Working Paper, **8245**, National Bureau of Economic Research, Cambridge, MA

Eichengreen, B. and R. Hausmann, 2003: Original sin: the road to redemption, in B. Eichengreen and R. Hausmann (eds.), *Other people's money: debt denomination and financial instability in emerging market economies*, University of Chicago Press, Chicago

Goldstein, M. and P. Turner, 2003: Controlling currency mismatches in emerging market economies, Institute of International Economics, Washington, DC, unpublished monograph

Reinhart, C., K. Rogoff and M. Savastano, 2003: Debt intolerance, *Brookings Papers on Economic Activity*, **1**, 1–74

Wyplosz, C., 1999: International financial instability, in I. Kaul, M. Stern and I. Grunberg (eds.), *International development cooperation and global public goods: towards sustainable development in the 21st century*, Oxford University Press, Oxford

Perspective Paper 5.2

PETER BLAIR HENRY

Introduction

Barry Eichengreen deserves a hero's tribute. The twelve labours of Hercules are mere child's play in comparison to the task that the Copenhagen Consensus set before him. While anyone who has been reading the newspaper for the past twenty years knows that financial crises can be highly disruptive to developing countries, proposing a series of policy options to combat financial instability and producing a cost-benefit analysis (CBA) of each option is an altogether different matter. Eichengreen's chapter 5 is an excellent piece of work. It summarizes a vast amount of material in a lucid and compelling manner; the discussion of the literature is balanced; and the costs of financial instability are forcefully established but not overstated.

The chapter identifies three sources of financial instability: banking crises currency crises and twin crises (the simultaneous occurrence of a banking crisis and a currency crisis). The chapter calculates the cost of each type of crisis by surveying the empirical literature on financial crises and performing simple back-of-the-envelope calculations. The chapter then presents four potential policy options for reducing financial instability. The four policy options are: (1) Re-regulation of domestic financial markets to address the problem of banking crises; (2) Re-imposition of capital controls to address the problem of currency crises; (3) Creation of a single global currency; (4) Pursuit of an international solution to the currency mismatch problem.

The CBA of the four options reaches the following conclusions: (1) Each of the first two options

I thank Manuel Amador, Anusha Chari, Nan Li, Paul Romer, Owi Ruivivar and Andrei Shleifer for helpful comments. Peter Lorentzen provided stellar research assistance.

entails costs that are larger than their benefits; (2) the benefits of the third option outweigh the costs but a single-global currency is politically infeasible; (3) the fourth option is feasible and it offers the largest positive net benefits. Importantly, the chapter warns the reader, especially the organizers of the conference, not to focus too narrowly on the final cost-benefit numbers and instead to keep in mind the bigger picture.

From that bigger picture, three central messages emerge: (1) Financial instability is costly – on average, financial instability reduces GDP growth in developing countries by 1 percentage point per year; (2) any attempt to reduce financial instability must begin with an examination of the causes of financial instability; (3) policy options to limit financial instability have costs as well as benefits; some instability may be the natural by-product of structural changes that improve a country's ability to exploit growth opportunities; attempts to curb this kind of instability may come at the cost of lower future growth rates. I am in broad agreement with all three messages, but I disagree with some of the details.

My objections are not methodological. Eichengreen's decision to perform simple, transparent calculations is surely the most helpful approach for this forum. As he emphasizes, the calculations are meant to focus attention on the fundamental trade-offs that are at stake and the calculations certainly accomplish that goal.

Nor are my objections philosophical. The chapter emphasizes the power of markets, but also acknowledges their limitations. In Eichengreen's view, markets generally work best, but policy interventions can be welfare-improving when externalities and information asymmetries are present. No reasonable economist could object to such a characterisation.

Rather, my concerns lay with the way in which the chapter frames the analysis of the policy options. For example, the chapter describes the first policy option, re-regulation of domestic capital markets, as tantamount to financial repression. Similarly, the analysis of capital controls considers only the most draconian of measures – a complete prohibition of any cross-border capital flows. While policies that restrain financial markets have costs as well as benefits, the tradeoffs need not be so stark. Prudential oversight and supervision of domestic financial markets are not the same thing as financial repression. Similarly, there is a continuum of sensible policy options that lie between completely unfettered capital flows, on the one hand, and the re-imposition of strict capital controls, on the other. A more nuanced view of domestic and international financial policy – monitoring and surveillance as opposed to re-regulation and prohibition – delivers a more sanguine (and accurate) picture of the potential for banking and capital account policies to reduce the frequency and severity of crises.

Second, I don't think that the benefits of the proposal to solve the currency mismatch problem of developing countries would be as large as the estimates in the chapter. The CBA of the proposal assumes that the proposal would eliminate currency crises. I am not so sure. The validity of the assumption hangs critically on the notion that developing countries are unable to issue debt in their own currency because of a variety of factors that are completely beyond their control. An equally plausible explanation is that countries have not been able to issue local currency-denominated debt because they suffer from weak institutions. The Eichengreen–Hausmann (2003) proposal for allowing countries to issue debt in their own currency is a remarkable intellectual construction, but it focuses too little attention on the more fundamental changes that are needed to reduce financial instability in developing countries.

Finally, and it is not an objection *per se*, the policy options that Eichengreen presents in chapter 5 need not be regarded as mutually exclusive. For example, policies directed at the capital account and the banking system interact with one another. As

such, they have to be viewed as part of a broader package of policies that try to reduce financial instability by strengthening domestic institutions. If one accepts the argument that measured and deliberate steps toward capital account liberalisation along with prudential regulation and oversight of the domestic financial system can yield positive net benefits, then there is no reason not to implement multiple policy options in parallel.

How Large Are the Costs of Financial Instability?

Eichengreen estimates the cost of financial crises in two steps. First, he notes that the average output loss associated with a financial crisis is approximately 9 per cent of GDP, or 0.09 (Bordo *et al.* 2001). Next, he documents that the probability that a randomly selected country experiences a crisis in a given year is 8 per cent, or 0.08. Finally, he argues that the expected output loss associated with financial crises can be computed by multiplying the two numbers. The resulting figure is 0.0072, or roughly seven-tenths of a percentage point of GDP growth per year.

Other authors have reached similar conclusions using different methodologies, so there is little doubt that the average cost of a financial crisis is large. For example, table 5.1 (Dobson and Huffbauer 2001, 68) reports that the average annual loss of GDP in emerging markets due to financial crises in the 1990s was about 0.7 percentage points of growth per year. After surveying the literature more broadly, Eichengreen concludes that a reasonable estimate of the cost of a financial crisis is roughly 1 percentage point of GDP growth per annum.

The 1 percentage point number is the cost of all financial crises lumped together – banking crises, currency crises and twin crises. In order to compute the cost of a stand-alone banking crisis, the chapter performs another series of calculations. The cost of a typical banking crisis is 53 per cent of the cost of the typical currency crisis and, in any given year, a banking crisis is 66 per cent as likely as a currency crisis. The chapter thus argues that multiplying

53 per cent by 66 per cent gives the fraction of the financial crisis-induced reduction in output that is attributable to banking crises alone – roughly 30 per cent, or 0.3 percentage points of GDP growth per year. The cost of a currency crisis is taken to be the remainder of the financial crisis-induced reduction in GDP – 0.7 percentage points of growth per year. I have one minor question of clarification about this calculation. It seems to assume, contrary to discussion elsewhere in the chapter, that the probability of a twin crisis is equal to zero.

To see the point, recall that the expected cost of a financial crisis is equal to 1 percentage point of GDP growth per year. Since there are three types of crises – banking, currency and twin – it seems that conditional on the occurrence of a crisis, the following relationship must hold:

$$1 = \textit{Expected cost of a financial crisis}$$
$$(1) \qquad = B \cdot P_B + C \cdot P_C + T \cdot P_T$$

Where B, C and T are the costs of banking, currency and twin crises, and P_B, P_C, and P_T are the associated probabilities of occurrence. Using the observation that $B = 0.53C$ and $P_B = 0.66P_C$, we can rewrite (1) as

$$1 = \textit{Expected cost of a financial crisis}$$
$$(2) \qquad = 1.35C \cdot P_C + T \cdot P_T$$

If $P_T = 0$ we get Eichengreen's result that the expected cost of a banking crisis $C \cdot P_C$ is equal to roughly 0.3 percentage points of GDP growth. If P_T is not equal to zero, then the costs will be somewhat different. Now, none of the final rankings of the policy options are altered by this observation and I may be grabbing at the wrong end of the stick, but it would be helpful to state the assumptions that went into the calculation a bit more explicitly.

Are the Calculations Reasonable?

Eichengreen takes the most transparent approach to the task at hand. He surveys the empirical literature to ascertain consensus estimates of the effects of financial development and financial crises on economic growth. He then uses these estimates to perform simple expected value calculations. There are many grounds on which to question the validity of such calculations, because even the most careful estimates come with a laundry list of caveats. For example, there is much evidence that financial development is associated with higher growth, but a reasonable reader of this literature could still come away unpersuaded about the direction of causation (Zingales 2003).

Issues of causality notwithstanding, the organizers of the conference have imposed the discipline of coming up with an answer. Economists who want to be helpful sometimes have to step outside the pristine environs of the university seminar room and carefully feel their way through the murky empirical reality of the policy world (McMillan 2003). Still, a balance must be struck. Rules of thumb and simple calculations provide points of reference around which to organise constructive discussion and disagreement, not immutable truths.

Eichengreen's chapter gets this balancing act right. The methodology is careful yet practical. The estimates of the costs of financial instability are conservative. In fact, they may be too conservative. There are two costs of financial instability. The first cost is direct – financial crises induce collapses in actual output. The second is indirect – weak economic institutions that lie at the heart of financial instability may also contribute to poor resource allocation, thereby reducing potential output. The estimates in the chapter capture the first effect but not the second. I am not suggesting that Eichengreen should have tried to measure the second effect; his task was difficult enough. The point is that the economic consequences of financial instability may be even greater than the already large effects suggested by Eichengreen's conservative approach.

What Causes Financial Instability?

Addressing financial instability requires an examination of its root causes. The chapter identifies four potential causes from the literature: unsustainable macroeconomic policy, fragile financial systems, institutional weaknesses and flaws in the structure of international financial markets. Since the chapter's preferred policy option focuses on the last of these four causes, I shall begin there.

One flaw of international financial markets that plays a central role in the analysis is the idea that financial markets are *incomplete*. Markets for developing countries are incomplete because there are contingencies for which they would like to write financial contracts, but are unable to do so for a host of reasons. One particularly salient example is the absence of a market in which developing countries are able to raise external financing with debt contracts denominated in their own currency. In other words, developing countries can raise external financing only by issuing dollar-denominated debt. In other work, Eichengreen and Hausmann have dubbed this phenomenon 'original sin' (Eichengreen and Hausmann 2003). For Eichengreen and Hausmann, original sin is completely exogenous; developing countries' inability to issue local currency-denominated debt stems from external factors completely beyond their control.

The problem with issuing dollar-denominated debt is that it creates a *currency mismatch*. The country's flow of income is largely denominated in domestic currency while its liabilities are denominated in dollars. Suppose that a country with a currency mismatch is hit by a real shock – a worsening of its terms of trade, for example – that requires a devaluation of the currency. At the same time that the country's income is falling, its repayment burden is rising due to the devaluation. If, in addition to the government, firms have also borrowed in dollars then the problem is even worse. As the dollar value of assets fall, some firms find themselves in a position of negative net worth.[1] Since many of these firms will also have loans through the domestic banking system, a currency crisis may precipitate a spate of non-performing loans and an attendant banking crisis (Krueger, 2000; Mishkin, 2003).

The Eichengreen–Hausmann Proposal for Curbing Financial Instability

If currency mismatches are the fundamental source of financial instability, it follows that one way to reduce instability is to help countries borrow in local currency-denominated debt. Since developing countries seem unable to raise financing in their own currency, the chapter proposes that the World Bank and other international financial institutions (IFIs) step in to complete the market.

Specifically, the chapter proposes a three-step international solution to the currency mismatch problem. First, the IFIs would define a synthetic index called the EM, comprising a basket of emerging market currencies. Second, the IFIs would issue debt denominated in EMs (their AAA rating would allow them to avoid original sin) and, at the same time, convert their concessional loans into claims denominated in the inflation-indexed currency of the countries comprising the index. Converting their concessional loans in this fashion would allow the IFIs to avoid a currency mismatch. Third, G-10 countries would issue debt in EMs. In order for the G-10 issuers to avoid a currency mismatch, they would swap their EM-denominated liabilities with the countries whose currencies comprise the EM index. By engaging in these swaps, the developing countries would reduce their currency mismatches by passing their dollar-denominated debt obligations to the G-10 countries in exchange for inflation-indexed local currency-denominated liabilities.

What would be the net benefits of such a policy initiative? The chapter's calculation goes as follows. The gross benefit of the policy initiative is simply the negative of the cost of the type of crisis it helps avert. The chapter assumes that having the IFIs borrow and lend in local currencies would eliminate currency crises by helping countries avoid currency mismatches. From the earlier calculation, the expected cost of currency crises is a loss of 0.7 per cent of developing country GDP, so the benefit is a gain of 0.7 per cent of GDP or an initial flow

---

[1] In principle, borrowing in dollars creates a liability mismatch only for firms whose revenues are in *local currency*. Firms whose revenues are in dollars (such as exporters) may actually see their profitability rise when a devaluation occurs. Of course, if there is a financial crisis in the banking system, those firms may still be adversely affected if a panic arises or if financially stricken banks are no longer able to extend them credit.

benefit of $107 bn. The financing cost of the initiative is the rounding error relative to the size of the gain, so the net benefits of the policy initiative would be large.

Would the Eichengreen–Hausmann Proposal Work?

Currency mismatches can certainly exacerbate crises, and it is a little ironic that the loan structure of the world's largest development institution exacerbates its clients' currency mismatch. So, the suggestion that the World Bank denominate concessional lending to its clients in local currency-denominated inflation-indexed debt has a sensible ring to it (Williamson 2003a, 2003b). Having said that, I have several concerns about the ability of the broader proposal to deliver the kinds of benefits the chapter envisions.

The broader proposal, specifically the third step, presumes that transactions costs are the principal obstacle to developing countries being able to issue debt in their own currency. The transactions-cost argument says that developing countries are 'forced' to issue dollar-denominated debt because global financial portfolios are concentrated in the currencies of a few large countries. Outside of these large countries, the transactions costs associated with borrowing and lending in an additional currency exceed the marginal benefit that would accrue to developed country investors. Consequently, they refuse to do so.

But the swaps envisioned in the third step of the proposal would involve precisely the kinds of transactions costs that Eichengreen sees as the leading explanation of original sin. The only difference is that under the Eichengreen–Hausmann proposal the transactions costs are shifted from institutional investors to the G-10 governments. To the extent that transactions costs are the obstacle to local currency lending, it is not obvious that G-10 governments – who don't need to issue EM debt in the first place – have a greater incentive to bear these costs than do institutional investors. More generally, it seems to me that the transactions cost argument has two weaknesses.

First, developed country managers of developing country investment portfolios also face currency-related transactions costs when they buy stocks in developing countries. Yet the fraction of developing country stocks in developed country portfolios has been increasing over time (Stulz 1999). Why should transactions costs deter managers from buying local currency bonds but not stock? Now, it is true that stock returns and bond returns have different stochastic properties. So, it is possible that the diversification benefits of developing country stocks are large enough to offset the currency-related transactions costs that inhibit investment in local currency bonds. But in order for the transactions cost argument to stand, the superior diversification benefits of emerging market stocks over bonds would have to be demonstrated empirically – no such evidence is presented in the chapter.

Second, purchasing dollar-denominated debt may also entail substantial expected transactions costs. Many countries default on their dollar-denominated debt as a matter of course (Shleifer 2003, Reinhart and Rogoff 2004). When defaults occur, bondholders incur transactions costs in the form of debt negotiations and restructurings. It is not obvious that the transactions costs associated with managing a bond portfolio of multiple domestic currencies are significantly larger than the expected renegotiation costs associated with purchasing dollar-denominated debt from countries that are prone to default.

Furthermore, currency swaps cannot get around the risk that arises from the possibility that the counterparty – in this case, the developing country governments – will renege on their obligations. If developing country governments do not uphold their end of the swap, the G-10 governments will be stuck with the legal responsibility for servicing the EM debt. Knowing this up front, the G-10 governments may charge a swap fee that raises the cost of the swap to developing country counterparties. Potential investors in EM bonds are also forward-looking. They realise that after these swaps take place they will effectively be left holding local currency-denominated claims on developing country governments. To the extent that the original sin argument is valid, potential investors might also require a premium for bearing the risk of potential debt servicing disruption in the case of counterparty default. The point is that swaps are not a free lunch. We cannot evaluate the feasibility of the Eichengreen–Hausmann proposal without addressing the basic question: why can't developing countries issue debt in their own currency?

An alternative view to that of original sin says that financial market incompleteness is endogenous. Developing countries are unable to issue debt in their own currency because they have weak economic institutions – lax fiscal policy, profligate monetary policy and poor creditor rights, to name but a few. Weak institutions make investors reluctant to hold a country's debt. For example, a country that has no legal separation of fiscal and monetary policy may print currency in order to meet its fiscal obligations. Doing so inevitably generates inflation. From 1970 to 1999 inflation in Argentina averaged over 300 per cent per year (Rogoff 2003). Nominal bonds are not a good investment in such an environment.

While poor institutions may leave investors vulnerable to moral hazard, original sin advocates might counter that poor institutions can't explain countries' inability to borrow in local currency, because financial markets have short memories. Countries that default on their debt regain access to international capital markets in relatively short order. If financial markets have short memories of default, then they should also possess short memories about institutional weaknesses that have generated inflation and other macroeconomic problems in the past.

Financial markets may be quick to re-lend to defaulters, but that does not mean default is irrelevant. Countries with a history of default may suffer from lower credit ratings, higher borrowing costs and debt intolerance (Reinhart, Rogoff and Savastano 2003). Just as banks charge higher interest rates to risky customers, requiring countries to borrow in dollar-denominated debt may simply be the lenders' way of insuring against the possibility that sovereign borrowers will attempt to inflate away the real value of their payment obligations.

If inflation risk is the problem, then why don't countries simply issue inflation-indexed debt? Well, inflation-indexed debt protects investors against inflation risk, but they still bear the risk that the government will default on its obligations outright. If a government has weak fiscal institutions – a poor tax collection system, for example – then it simply may not have the capacity to raise the real resources that it needs to service its debt and the risk of default may be significant. The central issue here is *credibility*. Whether debt contracts are written in dollars or inflation-indexed local currency terms, the question is: do markets believe that the government has the ability to collect, and the will to deliver, the real resources that are necessary to honour its debt obligations? No amount of financial engineering can circumvent this reality.

Broadly speaking, fiscal and monetary policy institutions have been improving in developing countries. In comparison with the 1970s and 1980s, fiscal deficits today are smaller, central banks more independent and monetary policies more conservative (Rogoff 2003). The impact of stronger fiscal and monetary institutions is evident in the data. For example, in Latin America the average annual rate of consumer price inflation from 1980 to 1999 was roughly 130 per cent; from 2000 to 2004 that figure dropped to 7.9 per cent (Rogoff 2003). If inflation is lower and deficits are smaller, then why are governments, in particular Latin American ones, still resorting to dollar-denominated debt? There are at least three possible answers.

First, credibility does not come overnight. It is easy to forget in what is now a low-inflation environment that things were not always so. In the USA, the Federal Reserve had to engineer a massive recession – the prime rate hit 21 per cent at one point in 1979 – under Chairman Paul Volcker in order to reduce inflation. The Fed's inflation-fighting credibility today is the hard-won prize of two straight decades of a vigilant anti-inflationary stance. In contrast, lower inflation in Latin America is a much more recent phenomenon.

Second, although fiscal deficits are smaller, many developing countries still have less efficient tax collection systems than their developed country counterparts. Historically, taxes on trade-related items have comprised the largest fraction of tax revenue in developing countries. Consequently, trade liberalisation during the 1980s significantly decreased their trade-related tax intake and led to a decline in total tax revenue as a fraction of GDP (Reinhart, Rogoff and Savastano, 2004). Again, at the end of the day, the government must be both able and willing to service its debt, irrespective of the currency in which that debt is denominated.

Finally, countries may simply have not tried hard enough to avoid dollar-denominated debt. Politicians in search of the next election victory may find it in their narrow self-interest to issue dollar-denominated debt, ignoring the obvious externalities it imposes on the populace (Rajan 2004). Issuing dollar-denominated debt is certainly easier than trying to implement the more fundamental changes that would make the issuance of local currency debt a feasible alternative. Again, it makes sense for the World Bank and other IFIs to index the repayment of their concessional loans to the real-local currency value of the countries to which they are lending. But instead of having the World Bank serve as an intermediary between developing countries and G-10 lenders, why not let the developing countries issue inflation-indexed debt to them directly?

In fact, local currency markets bond markets are developing and some countries have begun to issue local currency-denominated debt (Del Valle and Ugolini 2003; Turner 2003). To be sure, these are fledgling developments. Continued and perhaps increased commitment to sustainable macroeconomic policy is a necessary condition for success, but other challenges are certain to arise as well. In spite of the difficulties that lie ahead, it may ultimately be best to let countries develop their bond markets in a way and at a pace that is most appropriate to their country-specific context. While resorting to local currency-denominated bond issues would almost surely reduce debt-raising capacity in the short run, this may not be a bad thing. Arguably, the greatest challenge facing developing countries is not how to borrow more but how to use what they borrow more effectively (Bulow 2002).

Other Options for Dealing with Financial Instability

The rules and regulations that govern a country's domestic and international financial flows can have a large impact on the frequency and severity of financial crises. Accordingly, Eichengreen's chapter presents policy options that consider alternative institutional arrangements for a country's domestic financial system and its capital account.

Re-Regulation of Domestic Financial Markets

Financial liberalisation, broadly defined as the deregulation of banking activities, is often followed by financial crises (Diaz Alejandro 1985; Mishkin 2003). This raises an important question. Would countries be better off under re-regulation – that is, without financial liberalisation? Eichengreen tells us that in order to answer this question we must recognise that financial liberalisation brings benefits as well as costs.

The gross costs of re-regulating domestic financial markets are equal to the negative of the benefits of financial liberalisation. Liberalizing domestic financial markets permits banks and non-bank financial institutions (NBFIs) to engage in a wider range of intermediation activities than in a non-liberalized environment. Greater financial intermediation leads to greater financial depth (McKinnon 1973; Shaw 1973). There is also evidence that financial depth and GDP growth are positively correlated (Levine 1997; Levine and Zervos 1998). For instance, the chapter cites a study which shows that increasing the ratio of domestic credit to GDP from 0.25 to 0.55 raises growth by approximately 1 percentage point per annum. If re-regulation erases such gains in financial depth, then it follows that re-regulation could reduce GDP growth by as much as 1 percentage point per annum.

The gross benefits of re-regulation, on the other hand, are simply equal to the negative of the gross costs of a banking crisis. Recall that Eichengreen's estimated cost of a banking crisis is 0.3 percentage points of GDP growth per year. Hence, the net effect of re-regulation is to reduce GDP growth by an average of 0.7 percentage points per annum.

Re-imposition of Capital Controls

Just as some authors have argued that financial liberalisation causes banking crises, others have argued that capital account liberalisations can cause currency crises (Bhagwati 1998). Would abolishing free capital flows solve the problem? Eichengreen addresses this question by applying the same logic he uses to compute the net benefits of re-regulating financial markets.

The gross benefits of re-imposing capital controls are the negative of the cost of currency crises. The cost of a currency crisis is 0.7 percentage points of GDP growth per annum. If we accept Eichengreen's assumption that imposing capital controls eliminates currency crises but not banking crises, then the maximum benefit of imposing capital controls is 0.7 per cent of GDP per annum.

Re-imposing capital controls has costs for similar reasons that re-regulating domestic banks have costs. Capital account liberalisation tends to reduce the cost of capital, increase financial deepening and raise economic growth in the liberalizing countries.[2] Re-imposing controls might reduce financial depth and economic growth along with it. Marrying the literature on capital account liberalisation and financial depth with the literature on financial depth and growth, the chapter concludes that reimposing capital controls would reduce GDP growth by about 1 percentage point per annum. Hence the net effect of reimposing capital controls would be to reduce economic growth by about 0.3 percentage points of GDP growth per annum.

Discussion

Given Eichengreen's framing of the policy choices, his numbers make sense. If we must choose either completely unregulated financial markets or financial repression, then unregulated markets are preferable. Similarly, unfettered international capital flows are preferable to none at all. My objection is that the framing of the choices is too stark. Unlike

Odysseus, we do not have to choose either Scylla or Charybdis – safe passage in between is a viable option.

For example, sound banking supervision need not stunt financial development. A long-run increase in the ratio of domestic credit to GDP that represents genuine financial deepening is probably good for growth. A short-run spike in domestic credit in the immediate aftermath of financial liberalisation may not be as auspicious (Krueger 2000). Similarly, there may be sensible policy options that allow capital to flow largely unencumbered but keep a watchful eye on the build-up of short-term dollar denominated debt (Summers 2000; Fischer 2003). If the dollar lending goes primarily to firms whose revenues are in local currency, then it may be sowing the seeds of a future crisis rather than laying a foundation for higher long-run growth rates. On the other hand, if the lending goes to firms whose revenues are in dollars, the situation is less worrisome.

History tells us that the presence of a fixed exchange rate tends to raise the probability that the bad scenario will prevail. When the exchange rate is fixed, borrowing in dollars is typically cheaper than borrowing in local currency – so long as the fixed exchange rate holds. Consequently, firms and banks may be tempted to gamble, all the while failing to internalise the externalities that their individual and collective behaviour will impose on the rest of the economy if and when a devaluation occurs (Akerlof and Romer 1994).

The Policy Options Are Complementary

If one accepts the argument that a more nuanced policy towards the domestic financial system and capital account can yield positive net benefits, then the largest welfare gains might come from a policy option that combines elements of proposals (1), (2) and (4). In order to provide adequate supervision and prudential oversight of their financial systems, many developing countries will require a significant increase in the number of people sufficiently skilled to perform such duties (Krueger 2000). At

---

[2] See Henry (2000a, 2000b, 2003) and the references therein.

the margin, money spent to help countries train and retain such individuals might yield greater long-run benefits than implementing a policy that tries only to circumvent the currency mismatch problem without addressing the more fundamental causes of financial instability.

Other institutional changes that developing countries can undertake themselves include the following: (1) Fiscal reform: governments should run countercyclical fiscal policy – surpluses during booms and deficits during downturns. At present, we see governments doing exactly the opposite (Williamson 2003). (2) Exchange rate reform: fixed exchange rates have been the impetus for and the exacerbating factor in a number of recent crises. Adopting a more flexible exchange rate policy might help reduce countries' vulnerability (Krueger 2000; Fischer 2003). (3) Address the debt bias: financial flows to developing countries are biased to debt over equity. Developing countries can begin to reduce the internal bias in favour of debt financing by altering the institutions that skew incentives in that direction – permitting greater foreign investment in portfolio equity while simultaneously increasing domestic protection of minority shareholders' rights would be a good start (Henry and Lorentzen 2003; LaPorta *et al.* 1997, 1998). G-7 countries can begin to reduce the external bias in favour of debt by altering the incentives in their legal systems that drive developed country lenders toward debt and away from equity (Obstfeld, 1998; Rogoff, 1999; Krueger, 2000; Dobson and Huffbauer 2001).

Although institution-building is never easy, I am more optimistic than chapter 5. Its primary argument against institution-building as a strategy for reducing financial instability is that the process would take too long. But all proposals would take time, and effort to build stronger institutions would focus attention on the fundamental causes of instability unrelated to currency mismatches *per se.*

Conclusion

The financial crises of the 1990s were spectacular events, ostensible signals of the evils of globalisation writ large. Yet nearly a century of evidence suggests that globalisation, world-wide trade in goods and capital, is the surest means of raising living standards over long periods of time. In recognition of this evidence, countries all over the world – rich and poor alike – have been reforming their economies in an attempt to reap the benefits of globalisation. No one set of policies is right for all countries, and almost two decades of reform have delivered less than stellar results (Rodrik 2003a, 2003b; McMillan, 2004).

Nevertheless, there are far fewer examples of countries that have built successful economies by eschewing markets and closing themselves off from international trade in goods and capital than there are of the other kind (Fischer 2003). Reforms can work when they are designed in a country-specific context and the domestic political system gives them a chance to work. When financial markets break down, they disrupt societies and weaken popular support for changes that have the power to raise long-run living standards. That in the end may be the greatest cost of financial crises.

References

Akerlof, G. and P. M. Romer, 1994: Looting: the economic underworld of bankruptcy for profit, *Brookings Papers on Economic Activity*, **2**, 1–74

Bhagwati, J., 1998: The capital myth, *Foreign Affairs*, May–June, 7–12

Bordo, M., B. Eichengreen, D. Klingebiel and S. M. Martinez Peria, 2001: Is the crisis problem growing more severe?, *Economic Policy*, **32**, 51–82

Bulow, J., 2002: First world governments and third world debt, *Brookings Papers on Economic Activity*, **1**, 229–55

Del Valle, C. and P. Ugolini, 2003: The development of domestic markets for government bonds, in R. E. Litan, M. Pomerleano and V. Sundararajan (eds.), *The future of domestic capital markets in developing countries*, Brookings Press, Washington, DC

Diaz-Alejandro, C. F., 1985: Goodbye financial repression hello financial crash, *Journal of Development Economics*, **19**, 1–24

Dobson, W. and G. C. Huffbauer, 2001: *World capital markets: challenge to the G-10.*, Institute for International Economics: Washington, DC

Eichengreen, B. and R. Hausmann, 2003: Original sin: the road to redemption, in B. Eichengreen and R. Hausmann (eds.), *Other people's money: debt denomination and financial instability in emerging market economies*, University of Chicago Press, Chicago

Fischer, S., 2003: Globalisation and its challenges, *American Economic Review*, **93**(2), 1–30

Henry, P. B., 2000a: Do stock market liberalisations cause investment booms? *Journal of Financial Economics*, **58**(1–2), 301–34

　2000b: Stock market liberalisation, economic reform, and emerging market equity prices, *Journal of Finance*, **55**(2), 529–64

　2003: Capital account liberalisation, the cost of capital and economic growth, *American Economic Review*, **93**(2), 91–6

Henry, P. B. and P. L. Lorentzen, 2003: Domestic capital market reform and access to global financial markets: making markets work, in R. E. Litan, M. Pomerleano and V. Sundararajan (eds.), *The future of domestic capital markets in developing countries*, Brookings Press, Washington, DC

Krueger, A. O., 2000: Conflicting demands on the International Monetary Fund, *American Economic Review*, **90**(2), 38–42

LaPorta, R., F. Lopez-de-Silanes, A. Shleifer and R. Vishny, 1997: Legal determinants of external finance, *Journal of Finance*, **52**, 1131–50

　1998: *Journal of Political Economy*, **106**, 1113–55

Levine, R, 1997: Financial development and growth: views and agenda, *Journal of Economic Literature*, **35**(2), 688–726

Levine, R. and S. Zervos, 1998: Stock markets, banks, and economic growth, *American Economic Review*, **88**(3), 537–58

McKinnon, R. I., 1973: *Money and capital in economic development*, Brookings Institution, Washington, DC

McMillan, J., 2003: Market design: the policy uses of theory, *American Economic Review*, **93**(2), 139–44

　2004: Avoid hubris: and other lessons for reformers, *Finance and Development*, forthcoming.

Mishkin, F. S., 2003: Financial policies and the prevention of financial crises in emerging market countries, in M. Feldstein (ed.), *Economic and financial crises in emerging market countries*, University of Chicago Press, Chicago, 93–130

Obstfeld, M., 1998: The global capital market: benefactor or menace?, *Journal of Economic Perspectives*, **12**(4), 9–30

Rajan, R., 2004: How useful are clever solutions?, *Finance and Development*, 56–7

Reinhart, C. M. and K. S. Rogoff, 2004: Serial default and the 'paradox' of rich to poor capital flows, *American Economic Review*, **94**(2)

Reinhart, C. M., K. S. Rogoff and M. A. Savastano, 2003: Debt intolerance, Brookings Papers on Economic Activity, **1**, 1–62

Rodrik, D., 2003a: What do we learn from country narratives? in D. Rodrik (ed.), *In search of prosperity*, Princeton University Press, Princeton

　2003b: Growth strategies, NBER Working Paper, 10050

Rogoff, K., 1999: International institutions for reducing global financial instability, *Journal of Economic Perspectives*, **13**(4), 21–42

　2003: Globalisation and global disinflation, *Federal Reserve Bank of Kansas City Bulletin*, **88**(4), 45–81

Shaw, E. S., 1973: *Financial deepening in economic development*, Oxford University Press, New York

Shleifer, A., 2003: Will the sovereign debt market survive?, *American Economic Review*, **85**(2), 85–90

Stulz, R. M., 1999: International portfolio flows and security markets, in M. Feldstein (ed.), *International capital flows*, University of Chicago Press, Chicago, 257–93.

Summers, L., 2000: International financial crises: causes, prevention, and cures, *American Economic Review*, **90**(2), 1–16

Turner, P., 2003: Bond market development: what are the policy issues?, in R. E. Litan M. Pomerleano and V. Sundararajan (eds.), *The future of domestic capital markets in developing countries*, Brookings Press, Washington, DC

Williamson, J. 2003a: Domestic versus global responsibilities for curbing financial instability in Latin America, Speech delivered to The Inter American Development Bank, 20 July http://www.iadb.org/res/publications/pubfiles/pubS-174.pdf.

2003b: Comments on Debt Intolerance Brookings Papers on Economic Activity, **1**, 66–70

Zingales, L., 2003: Commentary on more on finance and growth: more finance more growth?, *Federal Reserve Bank of St. Louis Review*, **85**(4), 47–52

Governance and Corruption

SUSAN ROSE-ACKERMAN

Introduction

All political systems need to mediate the relationship between private wealth and public power. Those that fail risk a dysfunctional government captured by wealthy interests. Corruption is one symptom of such failure with private willingness-to-pay trumping public goals. Private individuals and business firms pay to get routine services and to get to the head of the bureaucratic queue. They pay to limit their taxes, avoid costly regulations, obtain contracts at inflated prices and get concessions and privatised firms at low prices. If corruption is endemic, public officials – both bureaucrats and elected officials – may redesign programmes and propose public projects with few public benefits and many opportunities for private profit. Of course, corruption, in the sense of bribes, pay-offs and kickbacks, is only one type of government failure. Efforts to promote 'good governance' must be broader than anti-corruption campaigns. Governments may be honest but inefficient because no one has an incentive to work productively, and narrow elites may capture the state and exert excess influence on policy. Bribery may induce the lazy to work hard and permit those not in the inner circle of cronies to obtain benefits. However, even in such cases, corruption cannot be confined to 'functional' areas. It will be a temptation whenever private benefits are positive. It may be a reasonable response to a harsh reality but, over

time, it can facilitate a spiral into an even worse situation.

'Corruption' is a term whose meaning shifts with the speaker. It can describe the corruption of the young from watching violence on television or refer to political decisions that provide narrow benefits to one's constituents in the form, say, of a new road through the district. In short, speakers use the term to cover a range of actions that they find undesirable. Because my topic includes both corruption and poor governance, I omit both morally corrupting activities, on the one hand, and run-of-the-mill constituency-based politics, on the other. I use the common definition of corruption as the 'misuse of public power for private or political gain', recognizing that 'misuse' must be defined in terms of some standard. Many corrupt activities under this definition are illegal in most countries – for example, paying and receiving bribes, fraud, embezzlement, self-dealing, conflicts of interest and providing a *quid pro quo* in return for campaign gifts. However, part of the policy debate turns on where to draw the legal line and how to control borderline phenomena, such as conflicts of interest, which many political systems fail to regulate. As I outline below, one of the most important debates turns on the issue of 'state capture' or the problem of creating open democratic-market societies in states where a narrow elite has a disproportionate influence on state policy. In those countries outright bribery may be low, but the system is riddled with special interest deals that favour the few over the many.

Researchers at the World Bank estimate that world-wide bribery totals at least $1 trillion per year, just over 3 per cent of world income in 2002. The Bank staff extrapolated from firm- and household-level data contained in their own country-level surveys so the number represents an

I am grateful to Madiha Afzal and Dionysia-Theodora Avgerinopoulou for very useful research help. In parts of this chapter I draw on Rose-Ackerman (1999). I am grateful to Daniel Kaufmann, David Nussbaum, Benjamin A. Olken, Luccio Picci, Martin Raiser and Jong-Song You for helpful comments and current references.

order of magnitude with a large margin of error.[1] It is an estimate of the volume of bribes, not the impact of corruption on economic growth and global income. If used to measure the costs of corruption, it assumes that the volume of pay-offs is a good proxy for their economic effects. This, of course, need not be true. In economic terms, bribes are transfers from one pocket to another and are not an accurate measure of corruption's impact. Rather, the economic costs are the distortions induced by these transfers. Those costs may be many orders of magnitude higher than the volume of bribes themselves, or they may, under some conditions, be lower. Bribes may be small in some countries because bribe payers have bargaining power and do not need to pay much to get large benefits. In other countries, public officials may be able to extort large pay-offs that represent most of the benefits of the corrupt transaction. The estimate also ignores the role of corruption in increasing inequality and undermining support for democracy. Nevertheless, it provides a starting point from which to develop more fine-grained estimates.

Pointing to the magnitude of the problem, however, does not determine solutions. Because of the diversity of circumstances that produce corruption and poor governance, it is difficult to propose global approaches. Nevertheless, in what follows I make an effort, recognizing that improving governance in individual countries will require carefully tailored policies carried out with the hard work and personal commitment of those on the ground. Estimates of costs and benefits are obviously only rough guesses. However, it is important not to overlook reform possibilities in this area. Some reforms, if well designed and implemented, would have large benefits and very low costs. Unfortunately, they also have serious distributive effects, and those who gain from the status quo are frequently powerful economic and political actors capable of blocking reforms.

Cost-benefit ratios (CBRs) for other types of reforms will be distorted if they do not take corrup-

tion, self-dealing and incompetence into account. The risks of corruption and weak administration thus need to be considered in assessing proposals, for example, to limit hunger, reduce violence, or improve education and health.

The options that I discuss fall into five categories: voice and accountability, procurement, revenue raising, regulation of business and efforts to limit high-level corruption in international business.

First, I summarise many successful examples of programmes that *improve accountability at the grass roots*, and argue that these cases provide lessons that can be applied elsewhere. Some cases, such as school financing in Uganda and public works construction in Nepal, suggest that relatively simple, inexpensive reforms can have large benefits if the political will exists.

Second, I recommend efforts to develop *benchmark cost estimates* that can help constrain procurement fraud and corruption. This would require coordinated data gathering efforts, but given the large cost distortions in contracting – sometimes up to 30–40 per cent – the gains could be large. Under some conditions, a state could combine benchmarking and citizen control to constrain waste and malfeasance.

Third, I consider reform of revenue collection through *tax simplification and incentive-based reforms*. Once again the net benefits of a well-designed programme can be large, but the mixed record of past efforts suggests caution.

Fourth, I recommend the *streamlining of business regulations* based on data indicating the economic costs of 'red tape'. However, past work has looked only at the gains to business and has failed to consider the costs to society of eliminating regulations that provide social benefits. Policy must thus balance the benefits and costs of regulations.

Finally, I discuss international initiatives to *increase transparency* in international concession contracts for natural resources and efforts to track down the assets of corrupt officials. The former option is also recommended in Paul Collier and Anke Hoeffler's (2004) chapter 3 in this volume on civil war. They estimate that it could provide multi-billion dollar benefits with minimal costs. Like the other options on my list, however, there is a dearth of actual experience in putting this

---

[1] Correspondence with Daniel Kaufmann, World Bank Institute, February 2004. The World Bank Institute is preparing a document explaining the derivation of this figure and considering the relationship between the volume of bribes and the social costs of bribery.

idea into practice. One should follow an experimental approach to see what works and what does not.

This chapter focuses on empirical evidence. It does not discuss theoretical work on the causes and consequences of corruption and poor governance. Those who want to pursue these issues further should consult Rose-Ackerman (1978, 1999), a review article by Pranab Bardhan (1997) and the framework presented in Shleifer and Vishny (1993). These sources also include extensive references to the literature. To access current work, the World Bank Institute maintains a website (http://www. worldbank.org/wbi/governance) as does Transparency International (TI), an international non-governmental organization (NGO) committed to fighting corruption (http://www.transparency.org). Several recent literature reviews are at the website of U4 Utstein Anti-Corruption Resource Centre (http://www.u4.no).

Research on the Causes and Consequences of Corruption

Several strands of literature demonstrate the benefits of corruption control and government reform. I begin with cross-country studies that try to explain the consequences of corruption and poor governance for economic growth and well-being. The next section considers firm-level surveys that explore the consequences of corruption for firm behaviour. Next, I summarise surveys that provide a window onto individual attitudes toward and experiences with corruption and dysfunctional government. Then I turn the causal link around and review studies that seek to determine the causes of poor government and corruption. Finally, I introduce distinctions between administrative corruption, 'state capture', and what Michael Johnston calls 'power chasing wealth' (2002).

The Consequences of Corruption and Poor Governance: Cross-Country Research

Cross-country research on corruption and governance is part of a growing body of research that looks for the institutional bases of economic growth. Measures of corruption and poor governance are correlated with *per capita* income and with the United Nations Human Development Index (HDI). Richer countries, on average, have less reported corruption and better functioning governments.[2] The same holds true for countries with high levels of the HDI, a measure that includes estimates of health and educational attainment as well as a logarithmic measure of income. Figure 6.1 shows the relationship between the HDI and the index of corruption developed by TI. Very high levels of human development are associated with low levels of corruption (high numbers on the TI index). However, high levels of corruption (between 1 and 4 on the TI index) are associated with a wide range of middle to low levels of human development.[3]

These two stylised facts raise the possibility that policy makers should forget about governance and just focus on stimulating growth though standard economists' prescriptions. Under that view, marginal improvements in governance are of questionable benefit to poor and corrupt countries, and good governance is a 'luxury good' that citizens will demand once they are rich enough to care. However,

---

[2] Kaufman (2003, annex 2, figures 1A, 1B and IC) presents three figures showing the postive correlations between the log of real GDP *per capita* and corruption, the rule of law, and voice and accountability, respectively. The governance measures are derived from survey evidence mostly based on the perceptions of business people and country experts.

[3] The corruption measure is an ordinal index derived from surveys, not a cardinal measure. Thus, a move from 2 to 3 on the index might imply a greater increase in integrity on some cardinal measure, such as level of bribes *per capita*, compared with a move from 8 to 9. One should not give a cardinal interpretation to indices of corruption. If a country's index fall from 6 to 3, this does not mean that corruption has been halved. However, if one compares countries at any CPI score between 2 and 4 with those between 8 and 9, there is a greater spread in the HDI levels in the former case than in the latter. There is, however, another aspect of the data that deserves mention because it determines the curvilinear shape in figure 6.1. The HDI uses a logarithmic scale for the income portion of the index, a technique that compresses the scale for wealthy countries. A similar graph with *per capita* income on the *y*-axis instead of the HDI shows a more dispersed pattern of income at higher levels of the (somewhat different) corruption index (Kaufmann 2003, figure 1A). However, at low levels of the index (that is, in highly corrupt environments) the data points continue to appear more dispersed than at high levels.

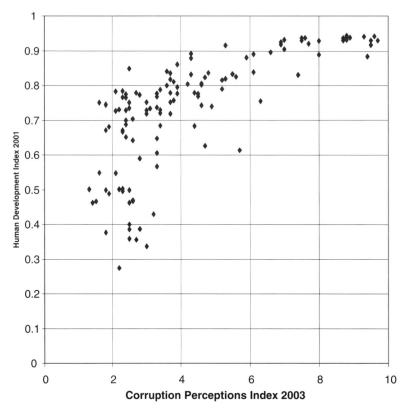

Figure 6.1. *Human development index and corruption perception index*
Source: Calculated from UNDP and TI data.

the available statistical evidence suggests that, correcting for other factors, poor governance is itself one of the reasons that some countries are poor and have low or negative growth rates. Kaufmann and Kraay (2002) confirmed this result and, in addition, found no positive feedback from higher incomes to improved governance. However, the issue remains contested. It seems plausible that both directions of causation hold. Demands for greater democracy, transparency and integrity in government often become more insistent as *per capita* income rises. However, to the extent that corrupt rulers recognise this possibility, they have an incentive to limit prosperity to constrain such demands. Those who benefit from a corrupt status quo will try to impede reform. Improvements in human well-being seldom occur spontaneously but, instead, require government actions to complement private efforts.

Governments that waste resources through malfeasance or inadvertence are a drag on growth and undermine the achievement of other goals.

As Mancur Olson (1996) demonstrated, economic measures alone do a poor job of explaining the divergence in growth rates. This finding spurred research on the importance of institutions. At around the time of the publication of that article, cross-country data ranking countries' institutional quality began to be available, and researchers interested in economic development began to use existing political science measures of democratisation. This spawned a large literature showing that 'institutions matter'. I cannot summarise that literature here except to say that I am sympathetic to Dani Rodrik's (2003) view that first-order economic principles do not map onto unique policy packages; furthermore, as he argues, igniting growth and sustaining it over the long term are two different things and may require different polices. I focus here on work that incorporates a measure of corruption, recognizing that these indices reflect not just the level and frequency of bribes but also capture the general quality of state–business–society relations.

TI has published cross-country data on corruption since 1995. It collects data from a number of different surveys that mostly report business and expert perceptions of corruption in various countries. Some of the underlying data sources also include questions concerning the overall business environment – asking about red tape, the quality of the courts, etc. Respondents rank the countries on a scale from 'excellent' to 'poor'. The annual TI indices are a compilation of corruption scores that average three years of data. They are ordinal rankings and do not provide measures of the volume of bribes, the incidence of corruption, or its impact. Because the underlying surveys included in the index vary from year to year, the data can not be used for time series studies. The World Bank has made use of the underlying indices that make up the TI index and has produced its own 'graft' index using a different aggregation method and including more countries. It is highly correlated with the TI index. Most studies use one or the other of these indices. Although some countries change position from index to index and have different rankings in the TI and World Bank datasets, there is an overall stability to the rankings. Furthermore, if a country's score differs from survey to survey, one cannot tell if this is because of the use of different sources, changed underlying conditions, or shifts in perceptions. Thus, these indices are a rough measure of the difficulties of doing business across countries, but they should not be used to make precise bilateral comparisons between closely ranked countries.

Studies using these data have found that high levels of corruption are associated with lower levels of investment and growth and that corruption discourages both capital inflows and foreign direct investment (Mauro 1995; Wei 2000; Graf Lambsdorff 2003a). According to Wei, an increase in the corruption level from relatively clean Singapore to

relatively corrupt Mexico is the equivalent of an increase in the tax rate of over 20 percentage points. The statistical result holds for East Asian countries as well as for the others in his sample. Acemoglu, Johnson and Robinson (2001) find that when the risk of expropriation is high, growth rates tend to be low. Most measures of institutional quality are correlated, and in this case, expropriation risk and corruption go hand in hand so that the same association holds for corruption. Countries perceived as more corrupt pay a higher risk premium when issuing bonds (Ciocchini, Durbin and Ng 2003). Corruption lowers productivity, reduces the effectiveness of industrial policies and encourages business to operate in the unofficial sector in violation of tax and regulatory laws (Ades and Di Tella 1997; Kaufmann 1997; Graf Lambsdorff 2003b). Graf Lambsdorff (2003a, 2003b) finds that an improvement in a country's TI corruption score by 1 point increases productivity by 4 per cent of GDP and increases net annual capital inflows by 0.5 per cent of GDP. This means that if a country such as Tanzania could achieve the corruption score of the UK, its GDP would increase by more than 20 per cent and net annual *per capita* capital inflows would increase by 3 per cent of GDP. Of course, such extrapolations are not to be taken strictly literally because the corruption score reflects all sorts of complex underlying conditions, but they do suggest the importance of the institutional environment to the achievement of economic success.

Highly corrupt countries tend to underinvest in human capital by spending less on education, to overinvest in public infrastructure relative to private investment and to have lower levels of environmental quality (Mauro 1997; Esty and Porter 2002; Tanzi and Davoodi 2002a). High levels of corruption produce a more unequal distribution of income under some conditions, but the mechanism may be complex – operating through lower investments in education and lower *per capita* incomes (Gupta, Davoodi and Alonso-Terme 2002; Gupta, Davoodi and Tiongson 2000). One study hypothesises a U-shaped relationship. If corruption is very low or very high, inequality is low. However, in the high-corruption case, everyone is equally poor. The empirical work, which omits the most impoverished countries, suggests that higher levels of corruption lead to increases in inequality, but the effect reaches a plateau at very high corruption levels associated with low levels of *per capita* income. Corruption levels help explain Gini differentials within Latin America, the OECD and Asia, but they do not explain the large Asia–Latin American differences in Gini coefficients or the intercontinental differences in growth rates (Li, Xu and Zou 2000). Corruption can undermine programmes explicitly designed to help the poor. For example, Ben Olken (2003) shows how corruption and theft undermined a rice distribution programme in Indonesia. At least 18 per cent of the rice disappeared; in the one third of the villages that suffered losses, 43 per cent of the rice was missing on average. Under reasonable assumptions, corruption and theft turned a welfare-improving programme to one that was welfare-reducing.

Corrupt governments lack political legitimacy (Anderson and Tverdova 2003). However, political supporters of corrupt incumbent governments, not surprisingly, express more positive views of the government. Presumably, this difference depends upon the individualised benefits that flow to these supporters. Surveys carried out in four Latin American countries (El Salvador, Nicaragua, Bolivia and Paraguay) in 1998 and 1999 showed that those exposed to corruption had both lower levels of belief in the political system and lower interpersonal trust (Seligman 2002). In Nicaragua, respondents were asked if the payment of bribes 'facilitates getting things done in the bureaucracy'. Interestingly, those who agreed that corruption gets things done were *less* likely to believe in the legitimacy of the political system (Seligman 2002, 429). Surveys of firms in countries making a transition from socialism provide complementary findings. Firms with close connections with the government did better than other firms, but countries where such connections were seen as important for business success did worse overall than those where political influence was less closely tied to economic success (Fries, Lysenko and Polanec 2003).

In circumstances of low government legitimacy, citizens try to avoid paying taxes and firms go underground to hide from the burden of bureaucracy,

including attempts to solicit bribes. Using data from the World Values Survey and Transparency International, Uslaner (2003) shows that high levels of perceived corruption are associated with high levels of tax evasion, with countries falling into two distinct groups. His survey data from Romania show that those who believe that one has an obligation to pay taxes have more trust in government. Similarly, Torgler's (2003) study of attitudes toward tax evasion in Central and Eastern Europe (CEE) shows that when individuals perceived that corruption was high, they were less likely to say that people have an obligation to pay taxes. Thus, one indirect impact of corruption is to persuade people that it is acceptable not to pay taxes because government has been captured by corrupt officials and those who support them. As a consequence, corrupt governments tend to be smaller than more honest governments, everything else equal (Friedman *et al.* 2000; Johnson *et al.* 2000). Thus in corrupt governments, the individual projects are excessively expensive and unproductive, but the overall size of the government is relatively small.

Business Surveys on the Consequences of Corruption

More nuanced results come from surveys that questioned businesses about the costs of corruption, red tape and other constraints on doing business. The World Business Environment Survey (WBES), carried out between the end of 1998 and the middle of 2000 under World Bank auspices, questioned several thousand enterprises in eighty countries (Batra, Kaufmann and Stone 2003). Figure 6.2 indicates the way that constraints on business differ between OECD members and emerging economies. In the statistical work using firm-level data, a high frequency of corruption, financing difficulties, high taxes and lack of government–business consultation each had significant negative impacts on firms' sales growth over 1997–9. In countries with negative scores on all four measures, the average growth of sales of existing businesses was more than 10 percentage points less than in countries on the positive side on all four. Investment growth was affected by four factors as well, with policy predictability

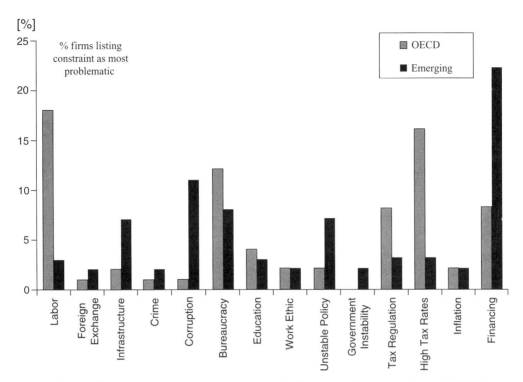

Figure 6.2. *Key business environment constraints to the firm: emerging economies and OECD*
Note: Executive Opinion Survey (2003) – question 13.01: 'From the following list, please select the five
most problematic factors for doing business in your country, and rank them between 1 (most problematic)
and 5.' Figure 6.2 shows the percentage of firms ranking the constraint as the most *problematic among the*
fourteen items on the list.
Source: Kaufmann (2004).

replacing lack of consultation. The same was true for the four significant variables in the investment equation.[4] As the authors conclude: 'While it may be difficult and take years to reform taxes, financing, corruption, and policy predictability, the evidence suggests that higher growth and investment are associated with such improvements.'[5]

Other less comprehensive research studied countries as diverse as those in Asia, SSA, and CEE. Most of this work is broadly consistent with the WBES survey. Survey work in Asia by the World Bank demonstrates the way that government effectiveness affects the investment climate and hence both the level of foreign investment in a firm and the firm's export orientation. In Bangladesh, China, India and Pakistan firm export levels and foreign investment were higher where hassles and delays were low. Given the evidence

that endemic corruption is 'sand' not 'oil', that is another way of saying that corrupt pressures are low. To help one understand the magnitude of the effects, the authors report 'that if Calcutta could attain

[4] Neither predictability of bribe requests nor positive views of government on other questions (a 'kvetch' effect) affected that conclusion and no measure of these effects was significant (Kaufmann, Mastruzzi and Zavaleta 2003, 372–7).
[5] Batra, Kaufmann and Stone (2003, 14). The survey results were converted to binary zero/one codings with zero indicating the desirable outcome for business (Batra, Kaufmann and Stone 11). A related study by Fries, Lysenko and Polanec (2003, 40) using only data from Eastern Europe and the Former Soviet Union (FSU) produced similar results. Qualitative perceptions of corruption, crime, judicial quality, regulatory constraints, taxes and financing constraints significantly affected GDP *per capita* in 2001, real GDP growth from 1997 to 2001 and real GDP growth in 2002, all in the expected direction.

Shanghai's level of investment climate, the share of firms ... exporting would nearly double from the current 24 per cent to 47 per cent, comparable to the coastal Chinese cities. Similarly, the share of foreign-invested firms would increase by more than half, from the current 2.5 per cent of firms, to 3.9 per cent' (Dollar, Hallward-Driemeier and Mengistae 2003, 7).

Svensson (2003) surveyed firms in Uganda. The level and incidence of bribery were positively associated with a firm's contact with the public sector for such matters as foreign trade, tax collection and regulatory compliance. The level of bribes was a function of both a firm's ability to pay and of the expected cost of relocation. More corrupt firms had lower growth rates on average than others. This research suggests how corruption imposes differential costs on different types of firms and demonstrates how it is connected to the underlying policies of the government.

The most comprehensive survey work has been done in CEE. The World Bank's two waves of surveys of the business environment in that region document the specific ways that corrupt officials and intrusive rules affect businesses and show how corrupt environments impose costs (Johnson *et al.* 2000; Hellman, Jones and Kaufmann 2003, 2004). There are broad differences in corruption and protection payments between Russia and the Commonwealth of Independent States (CIS), on the one hand, and Central Europe, on the other. Formally organised firms in Russia and Ukraine are much more likely to admit to hiding sales and salaries than firms in Central Europe (Johnson *et al.* 2000, table 1). Wholly off-the-books enterprises are more common in Russia and Ukraine and such firms hide all of their output from the authorities. Furthermore, firms in

Russia and Ukraine reported spending more time on government and regulatory matters than elsewhere (18 per cent and 25 per cent, compared with about 10 per cent for the other countries; Johnson *et al.* 2000, table 2). This may be a rough measure both of the degree of extortion to which firms are subject and of the degree to which firms can be exempted from rules if they curry favour with authorities. In Russia and Ukraine almost all firms that answered the question reported making illicit payments, and they hide a high proportion of their sales. In Central Europe, a group of firms also operates both corruptly and partly off-the-books, but the practice is not so widespread.

Surveys demonstrate how firms manage to cope when the legal system is weak. Informal relationships built on trust and private sanctions exist but cannot easily bear the entire burden of maintaining business deals. Weak states produce widespread corruption, private protection rackets and the flouting of regulatory and tax laws. The CEE countries vary in the security of property rights. Those countries with more secure property rights have higher levels of new investment by established firms (Johnson, McMillan and Woodruff 2000, 2002).[6] The security of property rights is measured by the ability of the state to enforce its own rules impartially. In other words, the benchmark is not a libertarian state but one that provides services, regulates behaviour, levies taxes and operates an impartial court system. Property rights are less secure if bribery and protection payments are common and if the courts do not enforce contracts. Thus, corruption is not a route to a secure relationship with the state but opens up possibilities for extortion. Furthermore, if firms pay for protection, either to private mafias or to the police, this reduces the security of rights as well (Johnson, McMillan and Woodruff 2002, table 1). Trust in the state as a *reliable actor* seems important. Firms appear willing to substitute legal and impartially administered taxes for the uncertainties of bribe payments and the dangers of relying on private protection services (Friedman *et al.* 2000).[7]

Household Surveys

Surveys of individuals sometimes ask about attitudes toward corruption and bribery. The results provide a counterweight to those who claim that

[6] Entrepreneurs with the least secure property rights invest 40 per cent less than those with the most secure property rights. At the time of the survey in 1997, the absence of bank finance did not prevent firms from investing because they were profitable enough to satisfy their investment needs internally (Johnson, McMillan and Woodruff 2002). Although employment growth is unrelated to property rights, high sales growth is significantly associated with more secure property rights (Johnson, McMillan and Woodruff 2000).

[7] See also Graf Lambsdorff (2003a), who concludes, using cross-country data, that legal reform, directed at the improvement of property rights and the maintenance of law and order, is crucial for attracting foreign capital.

Table 6.1. Citizens' Feelings about Giving Money or a Present

	Czech Republic		Slovakia		Bulgaria		Ukraine	
Q103 'Suppose people gave money or a present to an official and got what they wanted, would they be most likely to feel …' **Q104** 'But if they thought very few other people gave such things to officials, would they then be most likely to feel …'	Q 103 (%)	Q 104 (%)	Q 103 (%)	Q 104 (%)	Q 103 (%)	Q 104 (%)	Q 103 (%)	Q 104 (%)
Happy	50	15	63	18	66	36	55	22
Angry	25	36	23	37	13	20	11	24
Worried	7	15	5	14	11	16	18	34
Ashamed	18	34	8	31	11	29	16	20

Note: 'Don't know', 'Mixed/Depends', etc. answers were recorded if given spontaneously, but never prompted; they have been excluded from the calculation of percentages.
Source: Miller, Grødeland and Koshechkina (2001).

entrenched corruption is acceptable to ordinary citizens. Interviews in a range of countries have found widespread popular disapproval of entrenched corruption (e.g. Pasuk and Sungsidh 1994; Anderson, Kaufmann and Recanatini 2003).

One particularly detailed study of four CEE countries provides some nuance (Miller, Grødeland and Koshechkina 2001, 2002). The research revealed that people disapprove of corruption even if they report engaging in it themselves. The authors conducted surveys and focus groups in four countries that cover the spectrum of transitional democratic and market institutions – from the relatively far-advanced Czech Republic, through Slovakia and Bulgaria, to Ukraine. Although experience with corruption varied markedly across the countries, the public's underlying values and norms did not differ greatly. A majority in each country expressed strong moral disapproval of pay-offs but, at the same time, a plurality of citizens in every country except the Czech Republic said they would pay a bribe if asked. The authors conclude that the basic problem is not a weakness in the underlying values of citizens and public officials but an excess of *corrupt opportunities*. Because of a concentration of corrupt opportunities in some areas of public life, the officials most likely to receive gifts or bribes are hospital doctors, traffic police and customs officials. One hopeful finding – reproduced in table 6.1 – was that people's attitudes toward bribery were affected by their perceptions of others' actions. Attitudes are not deeply entrenched but depend on situation-specific variables, such as one's perception about whether or not others are paying.

A second type of household survey is a part of the International Crime Victimization Survey

(ICVS) compiled by the United Nations Inter-regional Crime and Justice Research Institute (http://www.unicri.it/icvs). Individuals are asked if during the past year any government official had asked them or expected them to pay a bribe in return for services. Naci Mocan (2004) used this data, which is available for 49 countries, to show that both personal and country characteristics determine the risk of exposure. Those of higher wealth and education reported more frequent requests, presumably because they interact more frequently with public officials and have a greater ability to pay. Low levels of reported corruption are related to high levels of institutional quality, uninterrupted democracy, and an absence of war. Poor institutional quality leads to both high perceptions of corruption under the TI or World Bank indices and high levels of victimization. The study confirms the claim that corruption is a symptom of underlying institutional weaknesses. Law enforcement policies that target corruption alone without touching the underlying institutional weaknesses are unlikely to be effective either in changing perceptions or in improving growth. Holding other things constant, 'a one-half standard deviation increase in the quality of institutions (e.g. from the level of Indonesia to the level of India), generates an additional 0.7 percentage point increase in … average annual *per capita* GDP growth. For a developing country with $2,500 *per capita* income in 1975 this translates into an additional $500 *per capita* income by 1995' (Mocan 2004, 28).

In diagnostic exercises the World Bank has used household surveys to narrow down anti-corruption efforts to areas of most concern to the population. However, although these surveys isolate pressure points where corruption is widespread, they do not measure the cost of bribery in terms of the inefficient or unfair allocation of public services or burdens. The ICVS does not provide this kind of information either. It simply reports the proportion of people who were asked for a bribe in four areas: The next step in the diagnostic exercise, therefore, should be an estimate of the relative costs of tackling different types of corruption that affect daily life.

Causes of Corruption and Poor Governance

Given the costs of corruption and poor governance, reformers need to isolate the causes of these phenomena. Cross-country data permit one to obtain a broad overview of the underlying causes of corruption and weak governance. I have already mentioned the role of income and wealth as both a cause and a consequence of corruption. However, the simultaneity often is not well handled in the empirical work. Nevertheless, it seems possible to conclude, first, that poor governance contributes to low growth and to the other harmful outcomes noted above, and that weak underlying economic conditions facilitate corruption. The exception is a very poor country with weak institutions that is so badly off that there is little for anyone to steal.

Some studies find that trade openness and other measures of competitiveness reduce corruption (Ades and Di Tella 1999; Sandholtz and Koetzle 2000; Blake and Martin 2002), suggesting that societies with fewer rents to share are less corrupt. However, once again the causation is unclear; countries that do not favour corrupt firms may be able to establish a policy of open and competitive markets. Graf Lambsdorff (2003a), for example, finds that weak law and order and insecure property rights encourage corruption which in turn discourages foreign capital inflows.

Inequality contributes to high levels of corruption. In democracies in particular, inequality facilitates corruption, a result consistent with the state capture variant of corruption. The negative effect of inequality on growth may be the result of its impact on corruption taken as a proxy for government

weakness (You and Khagram 2004). Here, too, the causal arrow goes both ways.

Historical and social factors help explain cross-country differences. For example, Acemoglu, Johnson and Robinson (2001) use the mortality rates of European settlers as an instrument for the type of colonial regime put in place by the imperial power and find that it does a good job of predicting expropriation risk (and corruption levels) at the end of the twentieth century. La Porta *et al.* (1999) consider legal origin, religion, ethnolinguistic fractionalisation, latitude and *per capita* income as determinants of a range of features of economic, social and political life. Corruption, as well as other measures of institutional weakness, is worse in countries with higher ethnolinguistic fragmentation, few Protestants, and Socialist or French legal origins. (See also Sandholtz and Koetzle 2000; Treisman 2000.)

Colonial heritage, legal traditions, religion and geographical factors seem associated with corruption and other measures of government dysfunction, but these are not policy variables that present-day reformers can influence. The key issue is whether these historical regularities directly affect government quality or whether they help determine intermediate institutions and attitudes that present day policies can affect. In La Porta *et al.* (1999) the historical variables are not always significant and become entirely insignificant when they add income and latitude. These historical patterns may thus operate through their impact on underlying *institutional structures*, not as direct determinants of corruption. If so, that may be good news for reformers so long as there are alternative routes to the creation of institutions that facilitate economic growth and high income (cf. Rodrik 2003). Latitude and history need not be destiny.

The impact of democracy on corruption is complex. High levels of economic freedom and lower levels of corruption go together, as does an index of democratisation (e.g. Sandholtz and Koetzle 2000; Blake and Martin 2002; Kunicova and Rose-Ackerman 2005). Governments with more female participation in politics are less corrupt and this is consistent with survey evidence suggesting that women are more disapproving of corruption than men (Crook and Manor 1998, 42; Swamy *et al.*

2001). Within the universe of democracies, features of government structure, such as presidentialism, closed-list proportional representation and federalism, facilitate corruption (Treisman, 2000; Kunicova, 2002; Kunicova and Rose-Ackerman, 2005).[8] Presidential systems that use proportional representation (PR) to elect their legislature are more corrupt than other types of democracies. Many parliamentary democracies that elect legislatures by plurality rule have a heritage of British colonial rule, and many PR systems had French or Spanish rulers. Present-day levels of freedom also have historical roots. However, if constitutional form, protection of rights, women's rights and electoral institutions are important determinants in and of themselves, then countries have policy levers available even if they cannot change their histories.

A World Bank survey permits one to see how one country compares with others on a range of different factors (Kaufmann, Mastruzzi and Zavaleta 2003, 363–4). Although measures of corruption, government quality and informal sector activity are strongly correlated, more fine-grained analysis often shows pockets of strength and weakness. For example, a study of Bolivia, using this survey, showed that it ranked poorly on several measures of corruption, judicial quality and property rights, but rather well on standard macroeconomic variables such as inflation, the exchange rate and the quality of the central bank. Because Bolivia has had a low growth rate, the results suggest that getting the macroeconomics fundamentals right is not sufficient. *Institutional reforms* are needed and within Bolivia itself some public institutions score better than others and may provide reform models (Kaufmann, Mastruzzi and Zavaleta 2003, 364–5).

'Crony Capitalism' and the Links between Political and Economic Power

The World Bank distinguishes between administrative corruption and what its calls 'crony capitalism' or 'state capture'. Country-specific research on such countries as Russia, Albania, Indonesia and Malaysia confirms the importance of the distinction. *Administrative corruption* includes the use of bribery and favouritism to lower taxes, escape

regulations and win low-level procurement contracts. '*State capture*' implies that the state itself can be characterised as largely serving the interests of a narrow group of business people and politicians, sometimes with criminal elements mixed in. Even if the group with influence changes when the government changes, most of the citizens are left out. Michael Johnston (2002) proposes a richer taxonomy that includes political systems that manipulate private firms for personal gain. He calls this 'power chasing wealth' as opposed to 'wealth chasing power'. The World Bank would probably put both types in the 'state capture' category, but they may have different implications. For example, Russia may be moving from a case where private wealth controlled public power to one where political power dominates private wealth.

Favoured firms may not have secure property rights in the legal sense but may be able to obtain favoured treatment because of their insider status (Hellman, Jones and Kaufmann 2003). This can promote economic growth at least for a period of time. Rock and Bonnett (2004) conclude that between 1984 and 1996 the large East Asian countries (China, Indonesia, Korea, Thailand, Japan) were in a different category from the rest of the world. They argue that, during their study period, these countries were characterised by strong centralised governments with long time horizons that were able to control corrupt networks. Rulers promoted growth by providing privileges to capitalists in return for kickbacks. These are very special cases that appear to store up problems for the future. The main risk is a change in the political leadership. For example, in a study of Indonesia under President Suharto, Fisman (2001) used an index of the political connectedness of firms listed on the Jakarta Stock Exchange, dubbed the Suharto Dependency Index. He demonstrates that rumours about Suharto's health problems between 1995 and 1997 had a more negative impact on the share prices of firms with

---

[8] Fjeldstad (2003) provides a literature review on decentralisation and corruption that cites studies that contradict the results for federalism found in the sources listed in the text. In any case, it is important to distinguish between federalism and explicit policies designed to empower those at the grassroots. I discuss the latter below.

high levels of this index and that the differential impact was greater the worse the rumours.[9]

Because sustained corruption undermines political legitimacy, corruption can itself undermine the rulers' long time horizon, leading to regime change (Rose-Ackerman 1999, 32). However, the more democratic regimes that emerged in several of the countries studied by Rock and Bonnett (2004, 1101) have had to confront corrupt network that now work to undermine growth.

More detailed research has been done on the former Communist states in Europe and Central Asia. The World Bank and the European Bank for Reconstruction and Development (EBRD) show that, although administrative corruption is a problem throughout the former Communist states, state capture is a particularly serious problem in the countries of the former Soviet Union (FSU). In such situations the firms that do the capturing perform well, but overall economic growth suffers (Hellman, Jones and Kaufmann 2003). Fries, Lysenko and Polanec (2003, 31–2) document the differences between 'captor' firms with insider status and 'non-captor' firms. The former have higher growth rates of fixed capital, revenue and productivity. Slinko, Yakovlev and Zhuravskaya (2004) obtain similar results using data from the Russian provinces.

If top political figures themselves exploit their position for private gain, the effectiveness of government programmes and the impact of foreign aid and lending suffer. Even if those with good political connections are also good economic managers, there is a long-term risk that they will exploit their dominant positions to squeeze out potential competitors (Acemoglu 2003). This inequality of influence can extend beyond special treatment by the executive and the legislature to include the courts as well.

[9] Of course, Suharto did actually resign from office in May 1998 but, as Fisman points out, this is a difficult event to study within his framework because so many other things were happening at the same time: the 'event window' was several months long, the successor was a Suharto ally and trading volumes were exceptionally low by the end of 1997. Perhaps for these reasons, the relationship did not hold in the beginning of 1998 except for steep declines in the shares of firms controlled by Suharto's children (Fisman 2001, 1100, n. 9).

World Bank researchers define 'crony bias' as the difference between the reported influence of one's own firm and business association, on the one hand, and the influence of those with close ties to political leaders, on the other. In a study using firm-level data from the 2002 Business Environment and Enterprise Performance Survey on former socialist countries (BEEPS), Hellman and Kaufmann (2004) find that firm managers who believe that the state is unduly influenced by a narrow set of 'cronies' are more likely to withhold taxes, pay bribes and avoid using the courts. These actions then help keep state institutions weak. Bribery and extortion are mostly a problem for medium-sized businesses. Large dominant firms have close relationships with top political leaders so that mutually beneficial deals are possible. These deals are often harmful to the overall growth and prosperity of the country and undermine efforts to establish the legitimacy and trustworthiness of the state.

In the geographically broader WBES survey of eighty countries there is a marked relationship between this measure of crony bias and survey responses on the size of the unofficial economy and the decree of democratic voice and accountability. A large unofficial economy indicates that the regulatory and taxation powers of government are low and that many firms cannot obtain outside financing because they are off-the-books. Low levels of voice and accountability suggest that the state is not responsive to its citizens' interests. Figures 6.3 and 6.4 present these results.

Reform Proposals

Research on the causes of corruption suggests ways to think about reform. First, the simultaneity between *income* and *poor governance* implies that purely economic prescriptions, taken alone, will not succeed either in promoting growth or in improving government performance. If, as Kaufmann and Kraay (2002) argue, causation flows mostly from corruption to low levels of income and growth, that conclusion is strengthened. Macroeconomic policy prescriptions presuppose a well-functioning government, which is just what is lacking in corrupt

% firms unofficial

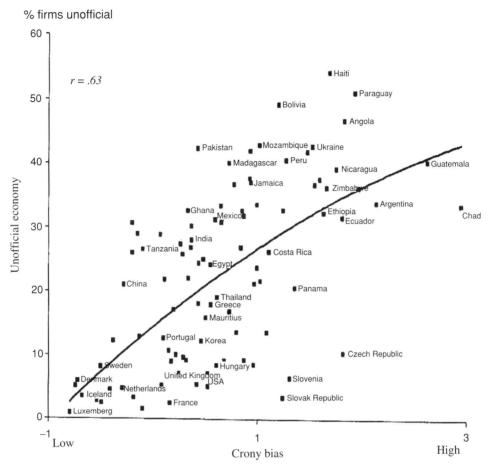

Figure 6.3. *The unofficial economy and crony bias (data from World Bank Worldwide Survey)*
*Note: Only selected countries among the 102 in the worldwide survey are labelled, owing to space
limitations. Unofficial economy data are drawn from firms' responses to the following question: 'What
percentage of business in your country would you guess are [sic] unofficial or unregistered?' (categorical,
converted using minimum within each range). Crony bias is constructed based on data from the 2003
worldwide survey of firms in 102 countries, calculated as the difference between influence by firms with
political ties and influence by the firm's own business association.*
Source: Kaufmann (2004).

countries. Similar problems of simultaneity exist for trade openness and inequality. Proposals
to improve governance by concentrating on economic growth, trade openness, and reductions in
inequality thus beg the question of how weak states
could accomplish such fundamental changes. Second, history and latitude may be important, but they
are givens, not policy tools. One needs to determine what they are instruments for and whether

present-day institutions are subject to reform whatever a country's history. Third, some features of
political systems seem to promote honest and effective government: high levels of economic freedom,
parliamentary structure, certain types of electoral
institutions and avoidance of private capture of the
state and of state capture of the economy. Some
of these statistical associations could be translated
into particular policy proposals, but most of them

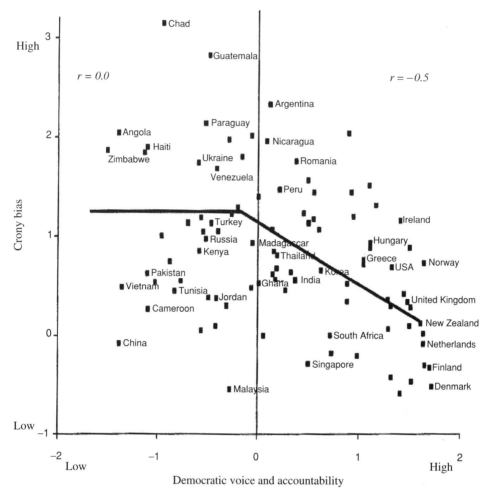

Figure 6.4. *Crony bias, voice and accountability*
Note: Data from Executive Opinion survey (2003) and World Bank Institute's calculations; 'crony bias' is defined in the note to figure 6.3; the voice and accountability variables are from Kaufmann, Kraay and Mastruzzi (2003).
Source: Kaufmann (2004).

are at a level of abstraction that is not easy to op-erationalise. Because the associations are statistical regularities based on cross-country research, I am reluctant to translate them into concrete proposals. My own emphasis is on middle-range proposals that concentrate on particular sectors and deal with gov-ernment accountability from the bottom up. They are consistent with the broad empirical regularities outlined above, but they have a more selective focus.

The net benefits from some specific anti-corruption reforms seem to be quite high. Weighting benefits and costs more highly if they are experi-enced by the poor would only enhance the value of most policies (cf. Olken 2003). The problems are, first, setting priorities for a long-term response and, second, overcoming the resistance of those who benefit from the status quo. Often even if the net benefits are large, the beneficiaries of the status quo are very powerful (Fries, Lysenko, Polanec 2003; Krastev and Ganev 2004).

The priorities I establish are based on my belief in some stylised facts and obviously depend on the truth of the following empirical hunches:

(1) To the extent that low corruption is associated with beneficial outcomes – stronger growth, higher incomes, more equal income distribution – the explanation is not corruption taken in isolation but rather the close correlation between *corruption and other measures of the way government functions.*[10]

(2) From this, it follows that policies to improve government functioning should not primarily focus on enforcing criminal laws against corrupt dealings. These laws are a necessary background condition but will mean little unless accompanied by more *systemic reforms.*

(3) Instead, one must consider the underlying *institutions and habits of behaviour* that make corruption endemic in some countries and in some sectors but not others.

(4) Although norms of behaviour with historical and social roots influence the level of corruption, corruption is also a *crime of opportunity* that requires willing participants on both sides of the transaction. Variations in corruption within a country suggest that this is so. Thus, a country's legacy of corruption and poor governance need not be accepted as somehow determined for all time. The situation can be improved on a case-by-case basis.

(5) Political and bureaucratic corruption occurs where *greed and self-interest interact with government institutions.* However, different factors create corrupt incentives in each case, and hence they need different policy responses.

Corruption, standing alone, is not comparable to hunger, disease and violence among the world's problems. However, if the weak government capacities of which it is a symptom persist, targeted policies will fail in weak and dysfunctional states. This is especially so when a central state is under the control of a narrow group that does not operate in the interest of most of the population. Government may

also be dysfunctional because it is excessively decentralised so that lower-level government officials can establish local monopolies free of oversight from higher levels of government. Rather than deal with the problem of concentrated political power head on, my options focus on ways to constrain and limit such power while at the same time acknowledging the value of a competent, well-functioning state.

The largely negative finding of a study of reform efforts in Eastern and Central Europe provides support for my approach (Steves and Rousso 2003). The World Bank and the EBRD carried out surveys of businesses in that region in 1999 and 2002. These are not panel studies, but they do shed some light on changes in the business environment over time. The survey results were matched with country level measures of anti-corruption initiatives that took the form of an index combining: (1) domestic legal reforms designed to increase transparency and accountability, (2) ratifications of anti-corruption conventions and (3) specific anti-corruption actions such as publication of an anti-corruption strategy and action plan and the establishment of an anti-corruption commission. In general, those countries that were least corrupt in 1999 adopted more of these reforms during the time period, partly in response to EU pressure. Scoring high on the index, however, was not a reliable predictor of reductions in reported corruption and, unfortunately, was also associated with a perceived increase in the problem. These results need to be interpreted with caution because they cover only a short period of time and one region of the world. They do, however, suggest that policies that simply raise awareness will not have the desired effect unless they are accompanied by more concrete, substantive changes in state–society relations.

Based on existing research and my own view of the way the parts of the good government puzzle fit together, I have isolated the following policies for further discussion. They are complements, not substitutes. Where possible I discuss studies that highlight successful policies and analyse failures. Some states are so dysfunctional that none of these reforms makes sense. My candidate for the most misguided World Bank project was one designed to improve President Mobutu's tax collection capacity

[10] See, for example, table 2 in La Porta *et al.* (1999, 240–1). High levels of corruption are highly correlated with bureaucratic delays and low levels of tax compliance on a country-by-country basis.

in Zaire. Obviously, such a 'reform' would not have improved social welfare. Leaving such deeply dysfunctional states to one side, the policies I discuss are: (1) improved oversight and participation by citizens and greater government transparency; (2) procurement reform; (3) improved revenue raising capacity; (4) improvements in the business environment by cutting unnecessary red tape; and (5) international efforts involving multinational firms and international organisations with a focus on asset recovery and greater transparency in international natural resource contracts.

Some reforms could, in principle, produce measurable improvements in productivity and economic growth; others, however, enhance government legitimacy and accountability and have no straightforward financial counterpart. However, as I demonstrate below, quantitative studies in individual countries demonstrate that empirical work can provide strong guides to policy. Thus, all of my specific policy proposals are accompanied by ideas for improving the quantitative bases for policy making. This research will usually require primary data gathering efforts, but in highly corrupt environments, the pay-offs can be substantial.

In some countries corruption of the police and the army reflects the role of organised crime in society. That kind of 'state capture' is obviously a major problem for the states involved and for those harmed by illegal businesses such as drugs and trafficking in humans and weapons. However, because it raises a host of issues specific to the control of organised crime and illegal businesses, I will not discuss this type of corruption here.[11]

Oversight, Participation, and Transparency

[C]orruption is an institutional system in which *rights are dissolved in exchange for gifts*. (Robbins 2000, 440)

Survey data from eighty countries suggest an association between low levels of voice and accountability and low levels of *per capita* income

(figure 6.5). Furthermore, as figure 6.4 indicates, when voice and accountability are high, 'crony bias' tends to be low. However, that relationship does not hold when a country moves from very low to low levels of voice and accountability. Thus, if reforms raise expectations through pure participatory strategies, they may produce disillusionment if not coupled with more fundamental changes. At this level of aggregation, however, one cannot make specific policy proposals. Instead, I move down a notch and consider the benefits of a particular type of citizen oversight and government transparency: local citizen involvement both in monitoring programmes and in direct provision of services.

The benefits of moving to more local control depend both on the effectiveness of such control and on how bad things are at present. There are two prongs to the development of a strategy. First, one must find programmes and governments that are very wasteful in providing services or managing aid flows and second, within that universe, one must select countries and projects suitable for managed decentralisation. By this I mean, decentralisation of either monitoring or service provision along with centralised information flows and the enforcement of anti-corruption and anti-fraud laws.

Several detailed studies have examined the way local involvement in public programmes can enhance efficiency and increase benefits. They show that it can be done, but also provide numerous cautionary tales of poorly designed programmes. I concentrate on the conditions for successful decentralised programmes, recognizing the need to guard against the capture of state structures by those seeking illegal enrichment. Careful studies of individual programmes suggest that the benefits of improved integrity in local aid projects and public service delivery ranged from 100 per cent to 400 per cent in the cases studied. However, the more anthropologically informed work suggests limits to participatory models in hierarchical rural societies. Decentralisation can be an invitation to local corruption and self-dealing if not managed effectively.

In Latin America reformers have made numerous attempts both to involve rural people in the design and monitoring of agricultural development programmes and to increase the participation of city

---

[11] For an excellent collection of articles that focus specifically on failed states see Rotberg (2003, 2004). For more on the establishment of the rule of law in weak states see Rose-Ackerman (2004, in Rotberg 2004).

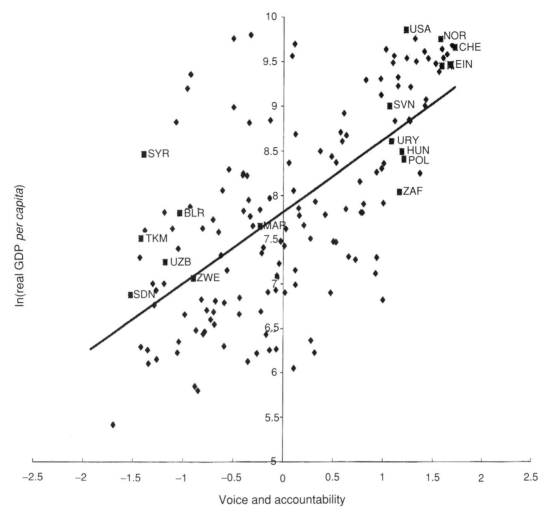

Figure 6.5. *Voice, accountability and* per capita *income*
Note: *Figure 6.5 plots a measure of voice and accountability in 2000–1 (horizontal axis) against real* per
capita *GDP in 1995 (vertical axis). The governance ratings on the horizontal axis are based on subjective
assessments from a variety of sources and are subject to a substantial margin of error.*
Source: *Kaufmann (2003).*

dwellers in government decision making. The rural development programmes sought to improve the
targeting of programmes to the needs of farmers and
to increase accountability to beneficiaries (Parker
1995; Das Gupta, Grandvoinnet and Romani 2000).
The urban cases, of which the most famous is Porto
Alegre, Brazil, had the explicitly political goal of
increasing democratic participation in opposition
to existing clientelistic structures (Abers 1998; de

Sousa Santos 1998). The successful cases in both
settings gave citizens better information about what
to expect from government and developed their capacity to hold public officials to account. The result
was a reduction in corruption and self-dealing.

The World Bank's surveys of public officials
in Bolivia provide some statistical backing for
the view that low corruption and high levels of
transparency and 'voice' are beneficial to the actual

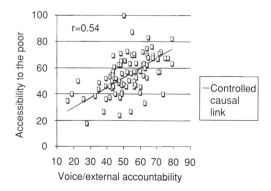

Figure 6.6. External accountability and feedback improve access of the poor to public services (Bolivia GAC diagnostic)
Note: Based on Kaufmann, Mehrez and Gurgur (2002). The sample of institutions includes forty-four national, departmental and municipal agencies that provide services to the poor. Each point depicts an institution.
Source: Kaufmann (2003).

performance of government and help the poor (Kaufmann, Mastruzzi and Zaveleta 2003, 380–8). A study based on 1,200 interviews with public officials in many different national agencies and local governments demonstrated wide interagency and intergovernment variation. Using simultaneous equation techniques, the study found that public service delivery is negatively associated with corruption and positively associated with the external voice of users and with transparency. Bribery and corruption are higher in more politicised units of government and in those with lower transparency and less meritocracy. Transparency is affected positively by voice and negatively by corruption and politicisation. Municipal governments perform worse than central government agencies on average but do sometimes provide better access for the poor. Measures of civil service management and individual ethical commitments had no independent impact although they may obviously be associated with some of the other variables (Kaufmann, Mastruzzi and Zaveleta 2003, 383). Figure 6.6 illustrates one result – the finding that higher levels of voice and accountability are associated with greater accessibility of the poor to public services (Kaufmann 2003, 24).

Survey evidence and case studies of participatory programmes suggest that they require a long-term commitment from established governments along with technical and organisational help. For example, case studies of USAID Community Partnership Grant Programmes in South Africa found that successful programmes had broad-based involvement combined with support from the incumbent local government. The one clear failure was when USAID worked with a defeated politician whose efforts were undermined by those in power (Adams, Bell and Brown 2002). Trevor Brown (2001) documented the importance of technical assistance in developing local government capacity in Ukraine and cites other supportive results from around the world. People who are not used to political power need time to learn how to exercise it responsibly. A 1998 study reports that over eighty Brazilian cites have begun to adopt some form of participatory budgeting (de Sousa Santos 1998). This suggests that one could review these efforts to see which ones worked and which failed.

One positive example comes from work by Ritva Reinikka and Jakob Svensson (2002, 2004a, 2004b). They document the severe leakage of central government funds meant for local primary schools in Uganda: $1 of central government funds produced $0.20 in budget for local schools. Their study led to a simple, information-based reform that had positive results. Reform focused on publicity combined with better monitoring. After its introduction, $1 expended by the centre produced $0.80 of local school funds, a 400 per cent increase. Nearly 75 per cent of the improvement in the targeting of funds can be explained by a newspaper campaign to publicise funding levels so that parents would know what funds their children's schools were due to obtain (Reinikka and Svensson 2004a, 2004b). Importantly, parents were already organised and able to exert pressure. Mere publicity will not work in isolation. The study gives no estimate of the cost of newspaper advertisements and notice boards, but they must have been minimal. The most substantial costs were increased official monitoring and the time spent by parents in checking on the school budgets. Because 20 per cent is still lost, the returns on a dollar of actual education spending would need to be at least 12.5 per cent for the returns to the central government on the programme to be 10 per cent. Before the reform, however, the returns would have needed to be 50 per cent! Thus, the programme appears to be cost-effective although it also has an upper bound – losses will never go to zero. A key feature of the Uganda case, however, is the existence of parent–teacher groups at the village level that can perform monitoring. In countries where such groups do not exist or where powerful local or regional actors can steal with impunity, more costly and complex interventions will be necessary. Even in Uganda, education may be a special case because it is a service used by school-aged children on a daily basis, unlike, say, health care where demand is more episodic, and sick and injured users are vulnerable to exploitation.

Uganda provides a 'best'-case scenario. Conditions were very bad *ex ante* and once research revealed the shortfall, a centralised information provision policy combined with better enforcement reversed the percentages. This reform does not answer the question of how much a country ought to spend on education but suggests that, with the reform, education spending will appear to be more productive. This result may lead to an increase in the budget. Suppose, just for the sake of illustration, that the extra costs of the anti-corruption programme are $0.10 for every dollar of appropriated funds, then every $100 of budget would produce $100 − $10 − 0.2($90) = $72 of education spending, up 360 per cent from before the reform. Of course, as noted above, these are only pecuniary gains so one would also want to know how many resources were wasted hiding the fraud and the rate of return on education compared to the use of the diverted funds. At the very least, however, the distributive impact of the reform is in favour of children, many with low income. The gains are very large if one takes as given the share of the government budget going to education.

To perform a CBA of this reform, one would need an estimate of the rate of return to primary education spending in Uganda. Unfortunately, such data are not available. However, in wealthy countries returns to an added year of education are in the range of 8–12 per cent in increased earnings for individuals. Because these estimates ignore public benefits from an educated citizenry, social benefits ought to

be larger. Recent attempts to measure the impact of education on economic growth have produced disappointing results in the developing world, suggesting that years of education are not a good predictor (Easterly 2001, 71–84). Jere Behrman (2003), in a review article, argues that older studies showing high returns to education in poorer parts of the world overstate the private and public returns to schooling. Perhaps the disjunction between the results for individuals in developed countries and cross-country studies lies in the fact that a year of schooling in a poor country may not mean much in terms of actual learning if corruption and self-dealing lead schools to operate poorly. Easterly refers to absent teachers and school officials who sell school supplies for person gain. Literacy levels would surely be higher if these illegal practices could be curtailed. The study in Uganda suggests that simple theft of resources by regional officials was the reason for underfunded schools. If theft is high, years in school may be a poor proxy for learning.[12]

Other instructive cases concern the devolution of authority in Nepal, India, Bangladesh and Indonesia. In Nepal and Karnataka researchers estimated that the productivity of external aid funds doubled as a result of more local control. The programmes were of direct benefit to local people – roads, irrigation projects. Thus, they had a reason to assure that funds were used effectively. However, research in Rajasthan, Tamil Nadu, Bangladesh, and Indonesia highlights the need to give careful consideration to local conditions to avoid failure.

In Nepal, a pilot programme involved local people in the direct administration of a food-for-work programme through information diffusion and a

---

[12] Careful work at the country level is sometimes possible. For example, Esther Duflo (2001) estimated the economic returns to a school construction programme in Indonesia in the seventies. She found that each school constructed per 1,000 children led to a average increase of 0.12 to 0.19 years of education and a 1.5 to 2.7 per cent increase in wages. This implies economic returns of 6.8 to 10.6 per cent. Duflo also performed a cost/benefit analysis that found internal rates of return of 8.8 to 12 per cent. The high values partly depend upon Indonesia's solid growth rate. Notice that if the cost estimates include kickbacks, the value of the programme would have been substantially increased if the kickbacks had been eliminated.

workable structure of monitoring. Standard practice involved national government guidelines for paying workers that were far above market wages. As a result, contractors with the national government paid market wages and pocketed the difference. When control was transferred to a sample of villages in an experiment, they paid market wages and built twice as many miles of roads with the same budget. The result was a dramatic increase in the cost-effectiveness of aid programmes and a large increase in client satisfaction. The costs were the time spent by the villagers in administering the programme as well as the cost of technical assistance to establish the system. However, presumably there are corresponding savings at the national level where bureaucratic inputs could be reduced. The main issue in such cases is how to generalise the positive experience in an experiment to the country as a whole. Key questions about the relationship between local authorities and the national administration are not answered by positive experiences in a few villages. In fact, in Nepal efforts to expand the programme failed as national-level officials and private contractors mounted resistance (Meagher, Upadhyaya and Wilkinson 2000).

In Karnataka, decentralisation improved government performance and limited corruption according to fieldwork done between 1978 and 1981 (Crook and Manor 1998, 22–84). Public sector workers, especially teachers, worked harder because they were, in the words of one person interviewed, 'under the supervision of the questioning public mind' (Crook and Manor 1998, 60). Absenteeism continued to be a problem, but those who did come to work performed better. Although the number of people involved in corrupt acts increased, they siphoned off fewer resources (Crook and Manor 1998, 61). Before decentralisation 'a large fraction' of funds was diverted. The Indian decentralisation policy increased the number of officials (elected and otherwise) from over a score to 3,000, this increased the number of potential bribe takers. However, the greater transparency of the political process limited the overall level of pay-offs. A vigilant press, an active two-party system and effective voluntary organisations contributed to transparency. For a given level of funding from the centre, there was a large increase in micro-level infrastructure projects. The authors conclude that this increase resulted both from the preferences of local political actors for such projects and from a decline in corruption. Under the decentralisation policy corruption took 5–25 per cent of local government funds, with most districts falling in the 5–10 per cent range. Only in two–three remote districts was the share 25 per cent. This was a major improvement over the past. However, although overall corruption decreased, most people believed that it had increased because of the greater transparency of government operation (Crook and Manor 1998, 79).

On the downside, increases in local control do not necessarily increase transparency and accountability but might instead promote locally based corruption and even facilitate organised crime influence (Das Gupta, Grandvoinnet and Romani 2000; Gong 2002; Anderson, Kaufmann and Recanatini 2003, 11). In a worst-case scenario, devolution enhances the power of local patrons and entrenched interests. For example, an interview-based study of forest management in the Indian state of Rajasthan demonstrated the way a *de jure* institution transformed into a stable system of extra-legal exchanges (Robbins 2000). Robbins reports the range of *de facto* prices for various uses of the forest and explains how personal connections interacted with pay-offs to favour some individuals and families over others. As a result, many of the national conservation goals were unmet with some species of trees and wildlife becoming particularly endangered. Households lost the ability to complain because of their own complicity. Increased 'oversight' would have been ineffective. According to Robbins, nothing will change without a change in local power relations (Robbins 2000, 434–5, 439–40).

Consider also an experiment in Bangladesh (Crook and Manor 1998, 85–135). Here an effort to decentralise political decision making increased corruption and increased the inefficiency of public works spending. According to the authors, 'corruption assumed major proportions, so that the councils would need to receive huge injections of funds if significant amounts were to be left over for development after profiteering' (Crook and Manor 1998, 112). Based on interviews and their own observation, the authors estimate that perhaps 30–40 per cent was stolen (Crook and Manor 1998, 119). Notice that if the funder wants a rate of return of 10 per cent on its money, then the underlying project would have to earn 14–17 per cent. The authors attribute the high rate of corruption and theft not only to the venality of local leaders but also to the permissive attitude of higher authorities.

In Tamil Nadu in the 1980s and 1990s investments in tank irrigation systems were supported by overseas aid through procedures that encouraged the formation of local Water User Associations (WUAs). The WUAs were to contract for work, organise construction and manage the improved systems using resources from new community rights over local resources. An outside team supported each WUA including a technical assistant, an institutional organiser and a process documenter (Mosse 1997, 268). Mosse details the caste and other conflicts in the WUAs and the way that the WUAs were embedded in local social structures. They became a locus for conflict, not a site for reform. The actions of the WUAs were, according to Mosse, driven by the priorities of outsiders as much or more than the wishes of village residents.

Finally, in Indonesia, another study documents how resources were wasted through corruption and self-dealing in village-level aid projects and suggests some ways of involving the beneficiaries in monitoring the programmes using existing local institutions such as local Muslim prayer groups (Woodhouse 2002). A further study of the way local communities and the state dealt with allegations of corruption in Indonesia stresses the interactions between local processes and the state. Local procedures to recover corruptly obtained funds were successful in many cases, but often only because of the threat of going to the courts. Outside actors involved in the administration of aid programmes or willing to provide legal help for free were often essential to persuade local people to pursue a case against powerful local individuals. Even in such cases, however, court judgements were difficult to enforce and even if an official went to jail, the lost funds were not recovered. Because of the distance of the courts from remote villages, once a case entered the formal legal system it lost salience at the village level (World Bank 2003). Benjamin Olken, an economist who has done fieldwork in Indonesia, echoes some of

these concerns. He observed villagers who feared retaliation from elites if they reported corruption. If such pressures are powerful, the only place to turn is to more well-organised national civil society groups. Olken also stresses the importance of combining devolution with centralised monitoring and information gathering, as in the Uganda case, and he stresses the need to include the opportunity cost of people's time before recommending devolution over more centralised control.[13]

In evaluating these cases, one must, of course, recognise that money lost to corruption and self-dealing is not burned up: it is used for something. Individual officials and their families are better off with more money in their pockets. A pure CBA is agnostic about who obtains the benefit and looks only at net total gains. The analyst would compare the marginal productivity of the corrupt transfers with the marginal productivity of the public project before recommending reform. However, this is, in my view, a fundamentally misguided way to approach the issue. If, indeed, funds are more productive in private hands, then the government should simply discontinue the programme, not condone corruption. At the very least corruption and self-dealing require wasteful efforts to keep malfeasance secret, skew the distribution of benefits and costs and encourage the use of resources to compete for rents, rather than to engage in productive activity (Krueger 1974; Rose-Ackerman 1999, 9–15, 213–15). If one cannot locate feasible anti-corruption strategies for very ineffective programmes, simply cancelling the programme is always an option.

The cases suggest that there are two ways for grassroots involvement to limit corruption, both of which appear promising. First, local households can monitor the use of central government or foreign aid funds and report to the government when they observe misuse. This can produce very large gains if the status quo is characterised by large leakages at the centre. Second, local people can actually provide the services themselves under contract with an aid agency or a higher-level government. Both of these options require that the public service be one that is actually desired by the local people; otherwise the benefits will be limited to jobs and supplies

[13] Email from Benjamin A. Olken, 11 March 2004.

and few services may be provided as people accept sinecures and walk off with materials. The options also require local organisational structures that are relatively effective and egalitarian. Even if these two conditions hold, the interaction between the grassroots and higher levels of government needs to be analysed to be sure that empowering the local level is actually a sustainable goal. In short, these encouraging successes are not capable of mindless generalisation, although one can surely find other cases beyond those outlined above where they can work well.

The rich variety of experience is both encouraging and humbling. The cases indicate which factors need to be considered but can hardly produce the 'blueprints' or 'best practices' preferred by the international lending organisations. Existing research suggests that a number of factors must come together before government reform can succeed. Transparency and publicity are powerful tools, but only if combined with grassroots organisations with the incentive and the competence to use the information provided. Outsiders can help both in providing information and in helping construct functioning local organisations. These strategies will not work, however, if state officials use intimidation and threats to keep ordinary people from engaging in oversight and political action. Formal state institutions such as the courts, the Ombudsman, a functioning Freedom of Information Act and an independent Audit Office, need to form a backstop for efforts to make government more transparent and accountable to ordinary citizens. It does not do people much good to know what the government is doing if they are too intimidated to act on this

information or if the routes for protest are blocked or ineffective. An outline for reform in this area would include both efforts to improve accountability at the grassroots in small towns and urban neighbourhoods and the strengthening of central government institutions that provide accountability. However, even if effective programmes can be designed, they cannot deal with corruption that is not subject to monitoring by individuals. I turn now to two areas where grassroots efforts are not sufficient: procurement and revenue collection.

Procurement Reform

Business executives world-wide believe that corruption in public procurement contracts is prevalent although there is considerable interregional and cross-country variation. The 2002 Executive Opinion Survey of the World Economic Forum shows the proportion of those surveyed who report that bribery is high/very high in various areas of business life including corruption in procurement (figure 6.7). Some business people report that they avoid government business for that reason (Anderson, Kaufmann and Recanatini 2003, 11–13; Kaufmann 2003, 8–9). Of course, corruption in contracting occurs in every country – even those at the high end of the honesty index such as Scandinavia, Singapore and New Zealand – but it appears more widespread and harmful in some countries than in others.[14] This is partly a function of the share of business in government hands. Two countries might have corruption in 20 per cent of all public construction contracts, but if the public sector accounts for 80 per cent of construction in one state and 10 per cent in another, the private construction sector's perception of the level of bribery will probably be affected by this difference.

'Grand' corruption involving major construction projects can increase costs and distort priorities. If the cost of a project is inflated by 10 per cent as a result of corruption, the rate of return on many projects will fall so low as to make the project not worth pursuing. Furthermore, some projects would not be worthwhile with zero corruption; they are only on the government's agenda because of the kickbacks provided. In other cases, the project provides net benefits if pay-offs are zero, and

[14] TI issues a cross-country index of corruption that is a compilation of others' rankings based mostly on perceptions of the level of corruption in business dealings. New Zealand and Singapore are near the top of the list along, with the Scandinavian countries, Canada Australia and the Netherlands. The 2003 Transparency International Corruption Perception Index is available at http://www.transparency.org/surveys/index.html#cpi. The United States Department of Justice (DOJ) prosecutes cases of corruption at all levels of government. Over the decade 1993–2002, the DOJ obtained 20,497 convictions (9,821 of federal officials, 5,782 of state and local officials and 4,894 of private citizens involved in public corruption offences) (DOJ 2003). Obviously some convictions were associated with the same underlying corrupt practices.

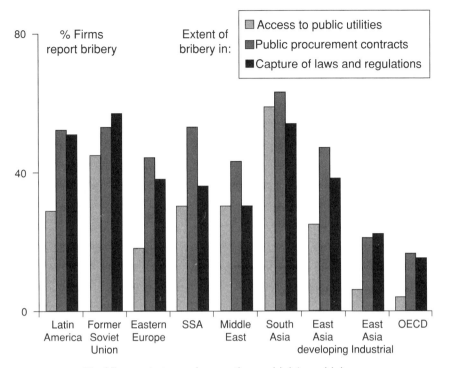

Figure 6.7. *Unbundling corruption (Executive Opinion survey (GCR), regional averages, 2002)*
Source: *Kaufmann (2003)*.

the important issue is the link between bribe payments and the rate of return on the project. Do the
bribes just lower the profits earned by contractors in
oligopolistic markets, or are they shifted to taxpayers? We have no good estimates of the incidence of
bribes, but only under extreme conditions will contractors bear the full burden. Systemic corruption
of this kind reduces competitiveness by limiting the
number of bidders, favouring those with inside connections over the most efficient candidates, limiting
the information available to participants and introducing added transactions costs. If top officials, including the head of state, are concerned primarily
with maximizing personal gain, they may favour
an inefficient level, composition and time path of
investment. Investors' decisions may also be affected by the fact that they are dealing with political
leaders.

Consider the officials' decision calculus. The impact of high-level corruption goes beyond the mere
scale of public investment and lost revenue for

the public budget. Top officials select projects and
make purchases with little or no economic rationale. For example, if kickbacks are easier to obtain
on capital investments and input purchases than on
labour, rulers will favour capital-intensive projects
irrespective of their economic justification. One
empirical study demonstrates that high levels of corruption are associated with higher levels of public
investment as a share of GDP, less productive public investment and lower levels of total investment
(Tanzi and Davoodi 2002b). Corrupt rulers favour
capital-intensive public projects over other types of
public expenditures and will favour public investment over private investment. They will frequently
support 'white elephant' projects with little value in
promoting economic development.[15] The demand

[15] See Tanzi and Davoodi (2002a) for a review of empirical
work on corruption, growth and public finance. A study of
structural adjustment lending in seven African countries concluded that much investment spending was of dubious worth.
'"White elephant" projects, inflated contracts, flight capital

for cement is one tip-off and might be used as a rough measure of excess public construction. For example, in Italy the annual *per capita* consumption of cement has been double that of the USA and triple that of Germany and Britain. A review of the 'Clean Hands' corruption cases in Italy reveals that many construction projects were poorly conceived, overpriced and had little or no justification beyond their ability to produce kickbacks (della Porta and Vannucci 1999).

Using an Italian case, Miriam Golden and Lucio Picci (2004) demonstrate that more precise measurement is possible. They use a study that finds that, across the Italian regions, corruption has a negative effect on economic growth by reducing private investment and reducing the efficiency of public investment (Del Monte and Papagni 2001). Golden and Picci provide evidence on one important type of inefficiency – excessively costly public investment projects. They combine measures of physical public capital stock in the Italian regions with measures of cost to produce estimates of the relative efficiency and inefficiency of public spending throughout Italy. Building on research that finds that corruption and waste go together, they assume that corrupt officials encourage wasteful projects as a way of generating rents. The physical data cover a range of government capital investments in 1997, including roads, railroads, hospital beds and number of school classrooms, combined into an index that is expressed as a ratio to the national average. They use a perpetual inventory model that adds up past capital formation and deducts assets when they reach the end of their service lives. The financial measures are then corrected for inter regional cost differences and normalised so that the country mean is set at one.[16] Overall, the physical index favours the northern part of the country and the financial index favours the south. The ratio of the two indices is a rough

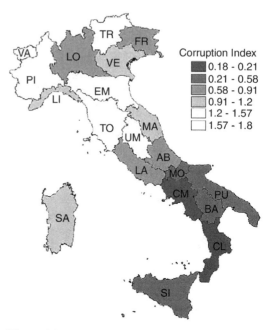

Figure 6.8. *Map of proposed level of corruption, by region, Italy, c. 1997*
Source: Golden and Picci (2004).

measure of the relative levels of corruption and inefficiency. Figure 6.8 is a map of Italy with the regions shaded from dark to light, with darker regions representing lower values of this measure. The index has a 0.82 correlation with Robert Putnam's (1993) measure of regional governments' institutional performance and a correlation of −0.66 with legal charges of high-level legislative malfeasance.

Of course, these are just indices that range from 1.7 to 0.2. They do not translate directly into a cost-benefit ratio (CBR). However, if the statistical work has corrected for other reasons for interregional variation, these results indicate that there are large potential gains either from reducing waste and corruption in the poorly performing regions or from transferring funds to the high-performing regions. Unfortunately, the poorly performing regions also tend to be the poorer regions (figure 6.9). Hence, a shift of funds would be regressive. Nevertheless, within the group of low *per capita* income regions the state might announce its willingness to allocate future funds on the basis of past performance. Because the ratios are based on stocks, not flows, the state would also need to be able to calculate flows

and other associated ills became rampant before – and eventually contributed to – the [government fiscal] crisis in each case. A major aim of adjustment programmes has been to weed out these undesirable investments (particularly in the public sector) and to improve overall efficiency' (Faruqee and Husain 1994, 6).

[16] For more details see Golden and Picci (2004) who report that the overall index of physical capital is not very sensitive to the method of aggregation.

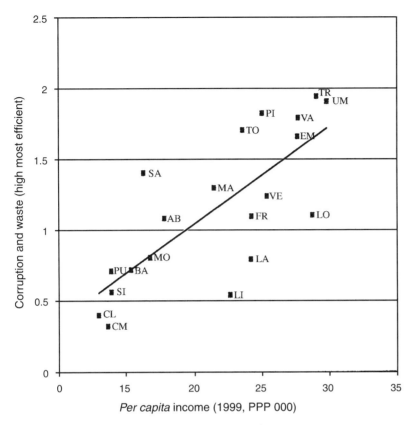

Figure 6.9. *Corruption and* per capita *income, Italy*

over a two- or-three year period. Within individual countries such estimates could help national policy-makers see where the pressure points are. In Italy, regions that are more efficient (less corrupt) than expected given their income are above the regression line in figure 6.9.

As a thought experiment, suppose that we interpret the data as measuring productivity in the sense that $1 spent in the region with the mean score produces $1 worth of output. (Of course, it is possible that the mean represents either a higher or a lower level of absolute output per dollar of input.) Suppose we take the goal of raising the ten lowest regions up to the mean. If productivity in all these regions could be improved to equal the present country mean, this would imply that a $100 invested in these regions would yield $100 of output instead of $53.90, an increase of 86 per cent. Even if omitted variables related to real resource costs

explain half the difference, the increase would be over 40 per cent. Of course, the same caveat applies as with the education example above. A full CBA would need an estimate of the social benefits of spending on infrastructure. However, once again, for a given infrastructure budget, output could be increased either by relocating the funds or by reforming the production process in weak regions.

Given the work of Golden and Picci for Italy, one might replicate this work in other parts of the world to permit rough estimates of the variation over regions, states, or metropolitan areas in the productivity of public spending. These results can then be used to allocate public funds in a way that gives sub-national governments an incentive to use funds efficiently. Such a policy, however, leaves the actual reforms to the sub-national governments. Thus, we also need to consider reforms of the *procurement system.*

Procurement reform is a basic component of an anti-corruption strategy. It should be viewed as an opportunity to rethink *what* the government buys as well as *how* it goes about making purchases. Government purchasing specifications should take account of the risk of corruption. When possible, goods sold in international markets where benchmark prices exist should be favoured over custom made or state-of-the-art products. Under decentralised systems, regional and local governments can favour goods and services sold in national market. In such cases, the state can look to private market prices as benchmarks and state its specifications in terms of standard off-the-shelf items (Rose-Ackerman 1978, 132–5; Kelman 1990).

Benchmarking can have an international dimension. Countries and sub-national governments that are small relative to the markets in which they operate can make purchases of standard products in the international market. Market prices are excellent benchmarks here because the small government's own demand is unlikely to affect prices.

One way to obtain rough estimates is through data on US trade. The Trade Research Institute calculates average prices and variances for goods using US trade statistics and estimates the tax revenues lost to the USA from overinvoicing and under-invoicing (Pak and Zdanowicz 1994, 2002; Paul *et al.* 1994). Because of product differentiation even within quite detailed categories, these price estimates are guesses, but they could give developing countries a starting point for negotiating with suppliers.

Benchmarking is in some tension with International Competitive Bidding (ICB) procedures, whose sealed bidding process is often taken to be the presumptive standard of fairness and economic efficiency. The World Bank requires ICB, under which the lowest 'evaluated' bidder must be accepted, for its infrastructure loans and these standards have

influenced the development of procurement codes world-wide.[17] The process does permit non-price factors to be weighed in the final decision but requires these factors to be specified and quantified if possible. It is appropriate for a project, such as a dam, that is capital-intensive, self-contained and uses known and tested technology. However, if followed mechanically, it can lead to low-quality work and collusive bid rigging. Instead, for small aid-dependent countries, the reputation of bidders could be drawn from the international arena. An international organisation might keep a roster of contractors with information on their past performance. To avoid controversy, however, such a system should focus on a few key variables that are measurable and comparable across countries. Relevant indicators might include evidence of fraud, corruption, cost overruns and time delays. The World Bank could integrate such a roster into its revised Procurement Guidelines (1999) which state that the Bank will declare firms ineligible for Bank contracts 'either indefinitely or for a stated period of time' if it determines that the firm has engaged in corrupt or fraudulent practices in connection with Bank-financed projects section 1.15(d). Thus one could imagine something similar to Golden and Picci's estimates for Italy, although obviously these estimates would be less precise if applied internationally.

In correspondence with the author, Lucio Picci suggested an intriguing connection between benchmarking in public procurement and citizen oversight. He pointed to the way internet services, such as eBay, provide feedback on the reputation of buyers and sellers. The feedback is entirely voluntary and is a decentralised mechanism with broad reach. Although there are obvious risks – for example, a seller with a low reputation can re-enter the system under a new name – and reputations can be influenced by self-interested buyers and sellers praising themselves (Dellarocas 2003), nevertheless, such a feedback mechanism might have applications to government contracting. Picci suggested that a benchmarking system organised by the central government in a country like Italy or internationally by the World Bank could provide information on the costs of various standardised infrastructure activities under different contracts. Citizens who use the services or observe the work

[17] See World Bank (1999, 25–8) at http://web.worldbank. org/WBSITE/EXTERNAL/PROJECTS/ PROCUREMENT/0,contentMDK:20060840~pagePK: 84269~piPK:60001558~theSitePK:84266,00.html.   The World Trade Organization (WTO) Agreement on Government Procurement and related documents are available at http://www.wto.org.

being done could post opinions on the internet with respect to particular public works. There are obvious design problems that would have to be overcome to make such a system operational, but it seems worth study for countries with reasonably high levels of both literacy and internet access. It is not a viable option for the people at the bottom of the income ladder in some of the case studies outlined above.

Civil service reform can complement procurement reform by providing incentives to officials to perform effectively and avoid corruption. Bonuses earned by officials who achieve procurement goals could substitute for illegal pay-offs. However, civil service reforms that simply raise wages to competitive levels are unlikely to be sufficient. One study, based on data from thirty-five countries, found that meritocratic recruitment was associated with measures of good bureaucratic performance, but that the role of competitive salaries was unclear (Rauch and Evans 2000). A study that examines the impact of a specific reform effort suggests a reason for the ambiguity. The study deals with a very narrow issue: hospital procurement of standardised supplies – saline solution, ethyl alcohol, iodine povidine and hydrogen peroxide – by hospitals in Buenos Aires (Di Tella and Schargrodsky 2002). The authors studied the impact of a crackdown in which the central authorities checked the prices paid at twenty-eight hospitals and used information of high relative prices as evidence that pay-offs might have occurred. Prices decreased during the crackdown, especially in the early months. Wage levels and enforcement intensity had complementary impacts except at high levels of enforcement where enforcement appeared to be a substitute for high wages. One cannot tell if these results generalise, but they do suggest that a policy of paying high wages to officials needs to be combined with a credible enforcement effort for optimal deterrence.

However, civil service reforms and enforcement against lower-level officials are only necessary, not sufficient, for success in combating corruption in procurement. Scandals frequently have implicated top government leaders who profited from their inside knowledge and connections. The above proposals are not much help in dealing with such 'grand corruption,' they focus instead on middle-level procurement decisions under the control of professional civil servants. They are, however, consistent with reforms that shift procurement decisions to career officials and tender boards. If rulers wish to insulate themselves from the demands of political supporters, they should create impartial bodies with independent procurement authority.

The basic reorientation of reforms efforts away from perfecting the bidding process toward making the overall purchasing environment more efficient and effective is a fundamental shift in perspective spearheaded by Kelman's work (1990, 2002). It seems an especially valuable innovation for developing countries with limited capacity to carry out complex bidding procedures. Although competitive bidding sounds like a good idea, bidding does not play a role in a truly competitive market. Instead, the market price is set through the multiple interactions of many buyers and sellers. The World Bank does permit what it calls 'shopping' for off-the-shelf purchases so long multiple suppliers exist (World Bank 1999, section 3.5). My point is simply that countries should try to design their projects to favour 'shopping' over sealed bidding as a way of limiting corruption.

Of course, frequently governments do need to make special purpose deals using a well-organised bidding process to minimise costs. Developing countries will be making large investments in special-purpose infrastructure for years to come. These projects are unlikely to require sophisticated new technology, but they are one of a kind. Thus the effectiveness of competitive bidding procedures will remain a central concern. Accepting the validity of the basic principles of ICB procedures for such projects, countries still need to assure robust competition among bidders. The same is true for competitive systems that make use of pre-screening processes. There are two problems – the possibility of collusion and the difficulty of attracting bidders. If contractors are willing to use violence to silence critics, the challenge to democratic state authority is greatest. The first order of business is then protection for whistleblowers and a willingness to follow up on allegations in a way that removes the impunity of officials. These procedures, however, must be designed to avoid encouraging people to use corruption scandals as a way to undermine one's political opponents.[18]

Developing countries could experiment with benchmarking, experience-rating for contractors, the adoption of more transparent processes and civil service reform. In countries with a scarcity of skilled procurement experts and weak public accountability, the case for benchmarking and the purchase of standard items is strong. The cost-benefit calculus here requires a balance between reductions in flexibility and reductions in costs. The reduction in corruption is gained at the cost of a poorer fit between procurement specifications and the government's 'needs'.

Customs and Tax Administration

States cannot function if they are unable to collect taxes. A few countries rely heavily on outside grants and loans from international financial institutions (IFIs), and a few still obtain considerable revenue from publicly owned enterprises. Most countries, however, require a functioning tax system. A legitimate democratic state appears to require that the state be able to collect taxes from its own citizens, not rely on outside sources of revenue. If citizens are not taxed, they have little incentive to hold the state accountable (Moore 1998). Many poor and emerging economies have very low capacities to collect taxes from their own citizens and from businesses and tend to collect taxes in arbitrary and unfair ways. In nearly every developing or transitional country where diagnostic surveys have been conducted, customs and tax administration are cited as loci of frequent and large unofficial payments (Anderson, Kaufmann and Recanatini 2003, 10). One consequence of an arbitrary and corrupt revenue system is to drive firms to operate at least partly off-the-books. The 2002 BEEPS survey in Eastern Europe and the FSU found a negative association

[18] As an example, see 'Treacherous Roads', *The Economist*, 20 December 2003, 56. The article reports on the murder of a young engineer employed by the state of Bihar in India to manage part of a highway project. He sent a letter to the Indian Prime Minister outlining a list of 'dodgy practices'. The letter was leaked to the relevant contractors and the engineer then received threats. The authorities did not respond, and the engineer was eventually shot and killed.

between the percentage of sales reported to tax authorities and the proportion bribing tax authorities (Fries, Lysenko and Polanec 2003, 15). Dissatisfaction with the quality of public services becomes a justification for underpayment, and underpayment produces low-quality services. (See Fjeldstad and Sembola's survey in Tanzania: 2001, 2069.) Thus limiting corruption in procurement and service provision can help limit tax avoidance. However, independent corrupt incentives exist in the collection of taxes and duties and reduction in those incentives is the theme of this section.

Businesses and individuals frequently collude with tax collectors and customs agents to lower the sums collected and expedite services. As a result, revenue collection may be both inadequate and distributed unfairly. Taxpayers and corrupt officials divide the savings in taxes and duties. The costs are borne by those taxpayers who are poorer and less well-connected and by the general public in the form of reduced services.

Take just a few examples. A recent scandal in China revealed that state and party officials in a major port in southern China had been entirely corrupted by smugglers with a huge loss in customs revenue (Gong 2002). In Pakistan, one study estimated that if the leakages caused by corruption and mismanagement could be reduced by 50 per cent, the tax–GDP ratio would increase from 13.6 to over 15 per cent (Burki 1997, 16). In Bolivia, a highly politicised tax administration is also viewed as very corrupt and is estimated to lose millions in tax revenues through a mixture of corruption, smuggling and informal, off-the-book businesses (Kaufmann, Mastruzzi and Zaveleta 2003, 355). A study of efforts to reform tax administration in Mexico and Argentina points to the costs of corruption and inefficiency in the revenue system as an underlying cause of the fiscal crises of the early 1980s. The weak and arbitrary aspects of the tax system in both countries contributed to a poorly functioning public sector and inefficiencies in the private sector as well. The resulting crisis persuaded political elites of the need for reform (Berensztein 1998).

The experience of a number of African countries illustrates the magnitude of the problem. In some studies the revenue shortfall was about 50 per cent (Stasavage 1999, 71). In Gambia, in the early

1990s, forgone revenue from customs duties and the income tax amounted to 8–9 per cent of GDP (six–seven times the country's spending on health). Income tax evasion alone was 70 per cent of revenue due. Only 40 per cent of small and medium-sized enterprises (SMEs) paid taxes, and many individuals did not file returns. Underpayment of customs was facilitated by the lack of clear guidelines and of published tariffs. The extensive discretion of officials encouraged corrupt pay-offs designed to evade tariffs. Of course, a well-functioning system would have been able to reduce tax and tariff rates, but the distortions introduced by such a high level of evasion are clear (Dia 1996, 46–7, 94–100). A study of tariff exemptions in Zambia, Tanzania and Mali estimated that exemptions, both justified and unjustified, produced a revenue shortfall of close to 50 per cent (Low 1995). In Mozambique in 1995, the customs service collected 49 per cent of the revenue it would have collected if no exemptions had been given. Officials added extra delays, overestimated the value of goods and applied higher rates in an attempt to extract pay offs (Stasavage 1999). In Zaire, much of the country's output was smuggled out with the complicity of customs officials. Corruption was also pervasive in evading import duties and controls (MacGaffey 1991). Studies of the Gambia, Mozambique and Ghana suggest that corruption permits the rich to avoid taxes (Dia 1996; Stasavage 1999). Tax avoidance in the Philippines reputedly means that the poor contribute twice as much as the rich, and 63 per cent of imports pay no duty.[19]

Corruption in tax and customs is not just a transfer from one pocket to another. In addition, tax burdens are distributed unfairly, and resources are lost keeping the illegal behaviour secret. A corrupt tax and customs system that favours some groups and individuals over others can destroy efforts to put a country on a sound fiscal basis and discredit reform. For example, in Mozambique interviews carried out in 1996 indicated that corruption had grown since the beginning of reform efforts ten years earlier. Overall taxes fell from 20 per cent of GDP in 1993 to 17.6 per cent in 1994 with import taxes falling from 5.1 per cent to 3.9 per cent of GDP (Stasavage 1999). Corruption and other forms of evasion are especially common when nominal tax and tariff rates are very high (Webster and Charap 1993;

De Melo, Ofer and Sandler 1995; Fisman and Wei 2004). High nominal tax rates lead to bribes and other types of tax avoidance which lead to even more avoidance and on in a vicious spiral.

One response is to repeal certain taxes that are difficult to collect and to lower overall rates. Tax reform frequently involves simplifying taxes and levying them on bases that are difficult to hide or underestimate. For business taxes, presumptive taxes can be levied that are fixed independently of a firm's actual profitability. The reduction in corruption and tax evasion is traded off against the reduction in fairness. For example, Mexico introduced an alternative minimum tax of 2 per cent on the real value of firm assets. A firm pays the maximum of the value of this tax and the corporate tax otherwise due. Small businesses pay a lump-sum tax per person employed, and medium-sized businesses are taxed on turnover. All these reforms raised additional revenue through reductions in tax evasion and in corruption (Das Gupta and Mookherjee 1998, 311–12). Such reforms are, however, unlikely to be sufficient if officials have no incentive to work effectively and if the state does not punish the underpayment of tax. For example, tax simplification in the Philippines apparently provided few benefits because there were no improvements in the incentives facing tax collectors and taxpayers (Das Gupta and Mookherjee 1998, 410).

Reforms may produce a win–win situation where administrative costs are reduced because of tax simplification and revenue collections rise. Successful reform of a country's system of revenue collection should permit a reduction in nominal rates of tariffs and taxation. This may permit an escape from the trap where high rates lead to evasion and evasion leads to higher nominal rates and even more evasion. A case study of India provides a classic case. Despite an increase in rates, total revenue declined both because of an increase in corruption and a shift into off-the-books activity. In such cases, nothing short of a thoroughgoing reform of the structure and administration of the tax system will allow a breakthrough. Simply raising the wages of tax collectors and increasing surveillance are unlikely to be sufficient (Das Gupta and Mookherjee 1998, 101–2).

---

[19] *Far Eastern Economic Review*, 20 April 1996.

In contrast, Russia has simplified its income tax system by introducing a flat 13 per cent rate for residents and introducing credible enforcement measures; tax revenues have increased (Rabushka 2002, 2004).

Incentive schemes have sometimes had positive effects. These can provide incentives for both tax collectors and for tax payers. Das Gupta and Mookherjee (1998, 257) report on efforts that combined the creation of a relatively autonomous bureaucracy with a budget linked, in part, to its success at collecting revenue. Reforms of revenue collection services in several African countries had similar features (Dia 1996). For example, in the 1980s Ghana tried an enclave approach to tax and customs reform by creating a new National Revenue Service (NRS). Prior to the reform, tax revenues were 4.5 per cent of GDP. Under the reform, the most corrupt existing officials were dismissed or retired, and pay and working conditions were improved. Increased salaries were accompanied by incentive systems to reward strong performance by individuals and by the agency as a whole. Revenue targets were established, and the NRS was given a bonus of 3.5 per cent of tax revenue and 2.5 per cent of customs revenue. Between 1984 and 1988 tax and customs revenue rose from 6.6 per cent to 12.3 per cent of GDP. Thus as long as the cost of the programme did not exceed 5.7 per cent of GDP, the programme was a net revenue-generator. The reforms illustrate the importance of combining improved base pay with incentives for good performance. Furthermore, rank-and-file officials must believe that corruption is rare at senior levels. The programme was a relative success, but it was not without problems. The rest of the civil service chafed at the special treatment afforded tax collectors. After all, the bonuses received by the NRS increased not

only if effort increased but also if taxes rose because of an exogenous increase in GDP. Furthermore, the Ministry of Finance objected to its loss of authority. In 1991 revenue collection was again placed under the authority of the Ministry of Finance, although it retained some of its independence. Corruption reportedly increased (Chand and Moene 1999). The strengths and weaknesses of several African experiments with revenue authorities are summarised by Devas, Delay and Hubbard (2001).

In an instructive study of a failure, Fjeldstad (2002) analysed an unsuccessful effort to reform the Tanzanian Revenue Authority along the same lines as the Ghana case. Before reform, lost revenues were high because of illegal behaviour. Up to 70 per cent of the value of imports did not appear in official statistics, and domestic businesses underreported production volumes and profits and falsified deductions. The reform focused on the control of discretionary tax exemptions, reform of the high and complex rate structures, improved pay and working conditions for tax officials and strengthened enforcement. As in Ghana, a semi-autonomous agency was set up with local leaders of known integrity, and most staff were fired and had to re-apply and take a test. The first year, 1996–97, was a seeming success with a 30 per cent increase in revenue collected. However, between 1997 and 2001 corruption re-emerged and revenue collection fell. The dismissed officials became 'tax experts' who facilitated corrupt tax avoidance deals. Improved salaries did not deter officials. Fjeldstad points to the partial nature of reform: the tax system remained complex, non-transparent and unclear.[20]

One proposal is a contract with a private preshipment inspection (PSI) service that assesses duties before goods leave their port of origin and then earns a fraction of the value of the imports. In general, the PSI firm receives about 1 per cent of the value of the imports inspected with a minimum charge per shipment of about $250 (Yang 2004, 6). The actual duties are collected by customs officials in the importing country on the basis of the information supplied by the PSI service (Low 1995, Yang 2004). Over 50 developing countries have hired PSIs over the last two decades (Yang 2004: 3).

Unfortunately, cross-country evidence suggests that these programmes have little effect.[21] There

---

[20] The problem of short term gains turning to long term losses seems a more general problem. Introducing a new set of officials may reduce corruption, at first, simply because they have not yet figured out the new system. Over time the gains may erode unless the underlying incentives have been changed. Benjamin Olken stressed this point in an email on 11 March 2004.

[21] Yang (2004: 6–7, appendix A.3) found that the 'import capture ratio' was not affected by PSI programmes. This is the ratio of a country's self-reported imports to the sum of trade partner's reported exports to that country.

are two ways in which importers can undermine such contracts. First, customs inspectors can be bribed, although this type of corruption ought to be fairly easy to detect. Second, and more important, imports are diverted into exempt categories or smuggled outright. Dean Yang (2004) looked at this phenomenon in detail for Colombia and the Philippines. PSI services are so expensive that countries, such as Colombia and the Philippines, do not employ them for all imports. As a result, firms divert imports into exempt categories that are not checked by the PSI service. In the Philippines, where more detailed data were available, Yang concludes that the use of PSI led to significant net losses for the Philippine government. The Philippines only used PSI for imports from nine Asian countries. During the study period, it reduced the minimum threshold for shipments being inspected from $5,000 to $2,500 and eventually to $500. As a result, imports shifted to exempt methods, and Yang estimates that the net loss to the government was over $46 m over the period December 1990 to February 1992 (2004, 20–57). Note that the size of the bribes themselves does not figure into this calculation. The bribe is a transfer from the taxpayer or importer to the official. The social cost is the distortion introduced by the bribe in the form of reduced tax collections from bribe payers and a distorted incidence of taxes.

As another example consider Mozambique that has experimented with such a system for customs revenues. In 1997 revenues jumped by 40 per cent (Hubbard, Delay and Devas 2001). Revenue collection has increased each year. In 2000 the contract was extended and is now set to expire at the end of 2004 (http://www.crownagents.com/). The contract is also meant to be a step toward a reformed and locally operated customs service, but that aspect of the project is behind schedule.[22] The contractor obtains 3.5 per cent of revenues collected but, in addition, Mozambique covers the costs of the expatriate staff. In 2003 there were thirteen expatriate consultants and two short-term specialists. Overall the contract cost over 20 per cent of projected revenues although net costs were presumably lower because the government saved money on its own bureaucracy (Hubbard, Delay and Devas 2001). No

study has been done of this case comparable to Yang's research, but this appears to be an expensive programme that is yielding, at least, short-run benefits.

Nevertheless, Yang's research suggests that PSI is not a panacea and may often be a cost-ineffective policy. If it is not comprehensive, many importers will find ways to avoid it. If it is comprehensive, the cost to the importing country may not be worth the benefit. In any case, the long run solution must be a reform of the local customs service combined with simplified and reduced restrictions on trade.

Durable reform should deal with the *underlying incentives for tax evasion*. In some countries, the nominal level of taxes and duties is so high that citizens and businesses justify their evasion on the grounds that they cannot survive if they obey the law. In addition, tax laws are often complicated and unclear, giving tax collectors leeway to make exceptions. These factors can produce a situation where a high proportion of households and businesses are law breakers. This gives the incumbent government a tool for controlling dissent and undermining political opponents. The goal should be a tax system with rates that can realistically be paid and with simple and clear standards. In addition, the rules must be transparent to the public and systems of accountability must exist. If they do not, simple clear rules can simply permit a ruler to extract pay-offs more effectively. Furthermore, governments can give taxpayers incentives to pay on time. The government of Mexico City, for example, is encouraging people to pay their taxes on time by giving them a discount if they file early.

Some reforms in the collection of state revenue are, in principle, costless. The goal is to limit bureaucratic discretion, a policy that ought to both reduce bribes and bureaucratic inputs. The problem is political will, and the political power of those who pay and receive bribes. However, if personnel are deeply corrupt, simply changing the rules may not be sufficient. The state may need to replace officials, and new employees may need to

---

[22] For example, a 2002 report pointed to problems in achieving this goal. See http://www.u4.no/projects/projects.cfm?id=103.

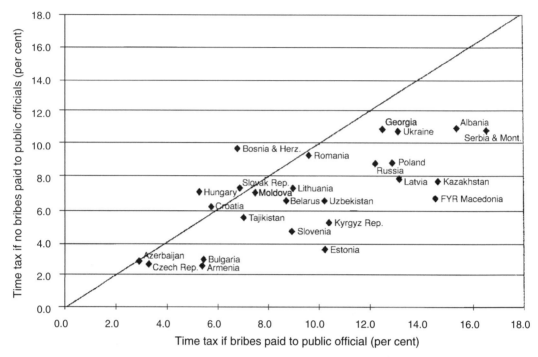

Figure 6.10. *Average time tax for firms paying bribes to public officials and for firms not paying bribes, by country*
Note: *The time tax is calculated for each country as an unweighted average of individual firms' responses on the proportion of senior managements' working time spent dealing with public officials. The time tax is calculated separately for those firms that bribe frequently and for those that do not.*
Source: *Fries, Lysenko and Polanec (2003).*

earn higher salaries, have better working conditions and get bonuses for good performance. Costly oversight and auditing may be necessary. One option is to contract with a PSI service based in a developed country. This may increase revenue collection, but it is an expensive option and is unlikely to be a feasible long-term solution.

Business Regulation

A high proportion of firms surveyed in the Executive Opinion Survey in 2002 reported that the illicit purchase of laws, policies, and regulations was high/very high (see figure 6.7). These results appear to include both the outright purchase of general rules and corruption in the administration of existing policies. Bribery to obtain access to public utilities was also a prevalent in some regions.

Corruption appears to take time. Data on Eastern Europe and the FSU indicate that the larger the share of firms that bribe public officials, the greater the proportion of senior managers' time spent dealing with public officials (Fries, Lysenko and Polanec 2003, 16–17). The data indicate that corrupt firms usually spend more, not less, time dealing with authorities. Figure 6.10 shows that in most countries in the region, corrupt firms average more time dealing with authorities than firms that report paying few or no bribes. This result suggests that corrupt officials may well create red tape and vague rules as spurs to the payment of bribes.

Corruption occurs both at the time a business is established and later as it seeks to survive. The World Bank has pioneered studies of the hurdles facing those seeking to establish and maintain business firms throughout the world. One part of this research focuses on the costs in time and money of establishing a new business legally. Building on Hernando de Soto's (1989) research in Peru, these studies show how entrepreneurship is discouraged and how those who persevere are pushed into corrupt and off-the-books operations by the tediousness and expense of complying with the law. The second strand of research begins with measures of the shares of managers' and employers' time spent dealing with government officials. This research deals only with registered companies but it, of course, indicates one reason why firms operate in the informal or 'gray' economy seeking to avoid official notice.

A simple conclusion from this research is that firms would be much more productive if the government removed the rules and regulations that make entry and operation costly. This looks like a costless reform. Firm managers and employees redirect their time to productive activities, and more firms enter the market, thus increasing competitive pressures and benefiting consumers with lower prices. Some of the studies of this phenomenon take this viewpoint, and see obstacles to firm entry and operation as pure costs. Unfortunately, this conclusion is too glib. Although reformers should examine the existing rules and regulations in most countries to determine if some can be eliminated, some business–government interactions can be socially beneficial. The proper response is then not to eliminate the programme but to reform it in ways that limit corrupt incentives. However, even with such reforms some costs will remain. I have already discussed two important examples in my discussions of tax collection and procurement and their reform. In addition, rules regulating environmental pollution, waste generation and disposal, worker health and safety, unionisation, the issuance of securities, consumer fraud and product safety and so on have solid public policy justifications even if the details of a state's actual laws are far from ideal. Some countries may have such dysfunctional state institutions that it is better not to take on some regulatory tasks until conditions improve. Others, however, may be able to institute reforms that suit their level of capacity – similar to the simplified tax system discussed above.

This leads to a basic recommendation: expand the diagnostic work already done to more countries but also include a more nuanced policy response that tries to sort out valuable from useless public programmes. However, if reform is selective, the result may simply give the remaining officials more power to extract bribes. It is quite possible that the actual level of pay-offs may increase as the transaction costs of corruption fall. This can still be beneficial, as less time is wasted by the firm and by public officials, but remaining corrupt officials still have an incentive to facilitate market monopolisation to maximise rents. The 'one-stop-shops', much touted by development agencies, may simply be efficient bribe collection agencies. Thus, in streamlining business–government relations, governments need to decide what public functions are really necessary and then construct bureaucratic procedures that limit corrupt opportunities through such devices as impersonal procedures; simple, transparent rules; interbureaucrat competition; effective complaints and appeals procedures; etc. (Rose-Ackerman 1999, 39–68, 146–9).

There appear to be some win–win possibilities here where dysfunctional rules and regulations can simply be repealed. The main cost is an expansion of the diagnostic work already being done by organisations such as the World Bank to include more countries and a modification of existing work to highlight the benefits of government programmes that impose financial and time costs on business.

International Efforts

Multinational firms are involved in many deals with developing countries and emerging economies. If corruption is involved, the result may bring few benefits to the host country and impose costs on the multinational. This has led to international treaties to control corruption – most notably at the Organization for Economic Cooperation and Development (OECD), the Organisation for American States (OAS), the Council of Europe and, most recently, the United Nations. These documents all reflect the salience of the issue of global corruption, but none of them is very powerful as a law enforcement tool. Their impact will depend upon their ability to *change the discourse* inside member countries and in the international business communities in ways that also change behaviour. These treaties have so far not had much concrete impact although they do seem to have changed the dialogue over corruption in ways that have a real impact on firms that care about their reputations. However, to go further, these treaties will have an impact only when combined with strong domestic efforts in both home and host countries. I will not describe these efforts here. Those with a deeper interest in the current status of these treaties can consult the relevant websites maintained by each organisation.[23] I discuss several possibilities that are related to current debates and to some aspects of these international agreements. My main focus is on alternative forms of information disclosure and accountability in extractive industries. I conclude with a discussion of asset recovery initiatives.

Extractive industries (e.g. oil, minerals) are a current focus because considerable empirical evidence suggests that, when the state is weak or venal, there can be a 'resource curse' in which the presence of such resources hurts economic growth by diverting energy into rent-seeking instead of productive activity (Rose-Ackerman 1999, 213–15). Paul Collier and Anke Hoeffler (2004) point to the link between natural resource dependence and civil war (see also chapter 3 in this volume). The management of such resources is of great importance especially in SSA which is on the verge of an oil boom and has many poor resource-dependent countries. According to *The Economist*, 'a handful of states are expected to receive $200 bn in the next decade' as a result of oil and gas exploitation (6 December 2003, 39).

One initiative is a campaign backed by a coalition of non-governmental and civil society organisations called 'Publish What You Pay.' The campaign's goal is an international regime that requires disclosure of net taxes, fees, royalties and other payments made by natural resource companies to developing country governments. The aim is to help citizens of these countries hold their governments responsible for the use of revenues from these investments (http://www.publishwhatyoupay.org). Of course, if the country's government is not dependent on the support of its own citizens, this can be an empty gesture that simply informs helpless citizens that their rulers are benefiting at their expense.

The second proposal is an international, multi-stakeholder effort called the Extractive Industries Transparency Initiative (EITI). The EITI includes host countries in the mix and seeks to have both sides of the transactions make public reports of legal payments. Part of the motivation for this initiative is to permit outsiders to check if there is any discrepancy between the figures reported by firms and by governments. At this point, the EITI is working toward a voluntary pilot programme involving a few resource-dependent countries. The pilot countries are likely to be drawn from the following list: East Timor, Azerbaijan, Ghana, Trinidad and Tobago, Democratic Republic of the Congo, Indonesia and Nigeria. One idea is to use a 'trusted third party', perhaps the World Bank, to develop a standardised process and to receive reports (details and updates at http://www.dfid.gov.uk). As a background report prepared for a February 2003 meeting makes clear, there are a number of problems in making the data comparable and in dealing with contracting issues, including confidentiality. Furthermore, presumably a programme could go forward only if all the multinational and domestic contractors and concessionaires in an industry agree on the procedure. Thus even a 'voluntary' procedure would have to have mandatory aspects as participating countries make disclosure a condition for doing business. Collier and Hoeffler discuss EITI in chapter 3 as a promising option to reduce the risk of civil conflict and to fuel growth. They estimate the total discounted present value of benefits at roughly $29 bn with trivial costs. Even if

---

[23] OECD Convention on Combating Bribery of Foreign Public Officials in International Business Transactions, 11 December 1997, http://www.oecd.org/document/21/0,2340,en_2649_34859_2017813_1_1_1_1,00.html. Council of Europe, Criminal Law Convention on Corruption, 27 January 1999, E.T.S. 173 (entered into force 2002), http://conventions.coe.int/Treaty/EN/Treaties/Html/173.htm and http://www.greco.coe.int/docs/ResCM(1999)5E.htm. Inter-American Convention Against Corruption, 29 March 1996, 35 I.L.M. 724 (entered into force 6 March 1997, available at http://www.oas.org/main. United Nations Convention Against Corruption, 9 December 2003, available at http://www.unodc.org/unodc/crime_convention_corruption.html.

those benefit numbers are much overstated, the potential net gains look large although they are a very small share of the discounted present value of world income.[24] The main problems are the difficulty of specifying exactly what EITI requires, and of being sure that its terms are followed. This is one example of a programme with small social costs but that will impose massive losses on those in favourable positions to extract rents. Thus it will not be easy to implement.

Third, efforts are underway to monitor host-country use of the funds from oil and mineral extraction. For example, the World Bank, which helped finance the Chad–Cameroon pipeline, has set up an International Advisory Group (IAG) to make periodic reports on the institutional capacity of Chad and Cameroon and on the ways funds are being used (http://www.gic-iag.org). The Bank also required Chad to set up an independent watchdog Revenue Oversight Committee to scrutinise how the oil money is spent. The Committee has rejected over half of the government contracts and insisted on open bidding. However, it has some weaknesses of its own with low staffing levels and tight deadlines that limit oversight (*The Economist*, 6 December 2003, 39). The World Bank has made this project a test case in the effort to be sure that natural resource revenues benefit a nation's citizens. Its successes and failures are worth monitoring as project revenues begin flowing in.[25] However, making natural resource payments from multinationals contingent on a country's own institutional oversight is possible only in very poor, aid-dependent countries such as Chad. Other countries can simply refuse to accept loans from IFIs.

Nevertheless, these efforts seem worth pursuing. The initiatives are related to the OECD Treaty outlawing overseas bribery. Multinationals may hope that by supporting greater transparency, they can avoid having payments that they record as royalties or taxes end up in the personal bank accounts of leaders. They may also hope that transparency will limit the financial demands of host-country officials. However, the leaders of countries that have only weak democratic institutions may not be deterred by transparency which, although necessary for corruption control and good governance, is not sufficient. If civil society is weakly organised

in the host country and lacks the expertise to understand company and country reports, transparency may have little impact inside the country. Its main role may be in putting international pressure on both firms and country leaders. This suggests that the NGOs behind the 'Publish What You Pay' initiative have a point in pushing for a mandatory disclosure system managed by an international organisation. The mandatory aspect of such a plan could take the form of making such disclosure by firms and governments a condition for receiving favourable investment guarantees and subsidies from home countries or from the international aid and lending organisations such as the World Bank Group, including the International Finance Corporation (IFC) and MIGA.

The international business community is beginning to recognise the costs of corruption to the global investment environment. Insofar as this is true, it suggests that international businesses themselves could contribute to the effort by providing funds and technical assistance to countries interested in reform. This is already being done through professional associations such as the American Bar Association, but the aid and lending organisations might explore the possibility of collaborative projects. For example, one aspect of the EITI is a plan to provide technical assistance to developing countries to improve their public budgeting procedures and reports. Such assistance could be underwritten by the firms that invest in the countries in question although, of course, they ought not play a direct role in the administration of such programmes.

Although a wide range of options have been proposed to deal with corruption at the international level (Rose-Ackerman 1999, 177–97), I conclude with just one additional possibility, asset recovery – an important part of the new United Nations treaty. One key requirement is to make corruption a predicate offence to the application of money laundering

[24] World income in 2002 was estimated to be $32.2 trillion. Even supposing no growth in the total, the discounted present value of a 10-year stream at this level, discounted at 5 per cent is $248.6 trillion. The estimated benefits of EITI are 0.012 per cent of that total.

[25] 'Greasing the Engines of Change in Chad', *New York Times*, 18 February 2004.

requirements. This broadening of the definition was included in the United States Patriot Act in 2001, but it is not a universal provision of such laws. A second issue is the grounds under which assets can be frozen and ultimately turned over to the government of the country of the corrupt official. The process is often cumbersome, if it works at all. Thus the Congo has had little success in retrieving Mobutu's overseas riches, and Nigeria has only recently obtained substantial sums from overseas banks that hold funds deposited in them by Sami Abacha, its former ruler. Kenya's new government has decided not to prosecute its former president, in part because of the difficulty of recovering assets.[26] Enhanced asset recovery appears to depend not so much on a willingness to bear large costs as on changes in entrenched modes of operation. Reform would require a difficult and controversial rethinking of present practices.

Options for Improving Governance and Reducing Corruption

The operation of the state and its interaction with the public are key challenges facing the world. If government performance does not improve in many states, programmes designed to help the poor, improve the natural environment and stimulate economic growth will have little impact and risk inflicting harm.

Estimating the costs and benefits of specific reforms is difficult even if cross-country research indicates that the gains from reducing corruption and improving governance are large. The main problem is tracing specific links from particular, concrete policies to desirable outcomes. Even the World Bank, which has been a leader in quantifying the costs of the corruption, has been unwilling to organise the data in that fashion. However, some options are almost costless. Hence, even if the benefits cannot be precisely measured, the rates of return are large. This is, of course, not to say that there are no losers. Obviously, individuals and firms, many

with political power, benefit from the status quo and will oppose change. A major challenge for governance reform is to overcome or coopt entrenched interests.

Unresolved empirical issues limit the estimates of the relative cost-effectiveness of different strategies and the ways in which distinct alternatives interact. Thus an option may be better than the status quo but not necessarily better than another proposed reform. Furthermore, some of the options have never been tried on a large scale and have never been subject to systematic efforts to measure their effectiveness. Thus, reformers need to design experiments and pilot programmes to test the value of options that appear promising. Based on my collection of reform options, there are several promising options (box 6.1).

I conclude with a few thoughts about the relationship between these policy proposals and the international environment. Consider aid and lending: there is presently an ongoing debate about the value of conditionality in the provision of aid. 'Conditionality' in some broad sense is inevitable. International donors must choose where to put scarce funds, and they will consider where the funds will have some positive pay-off. A weak state or one with high levels of corruption will be unlikely to manage aid well and so will get less. A state that does receive aid must comply with financial reporting requirements to assure that the funds are not lost to corruption and waste. Such conditionality, however, is less directly intrusive than aid that comes with explicit requirements for institutional reform. This latter type of conditionality has not been notably successful. An alternative is to organise projects that are directly focused on improved governance. For example, the Chad Revenue Oversight Committee and International Advisory Group for the Chad/Cameroon pipeline are cases in point that deserve to be carefully studied to isolate their strengths and weaknesses.

I have documented some successes and some failures, but projects that improve governance and oversight can benefit from external resources so long as they are designed eventually to be self-sustaining. A condition of such projects should be a *research component* that measures progress (or its opposite) by

[26] 'Kenya joins nations pursuing funds stolen by ex-leaders', *New York Times*, 21 December 2003.

Box 6.1   Options for Reform

Option 1

Grassroots monitoring and service delivery with technical assistance and information provision provided centrally by government or non-governmental organisations.

Benefits

Cost savings on existing programmes that have ranged as high as 400 per cent. Better overall economic performance and access of the poor to public services.

Costs

Opportunity cost of people's time; costs of consultants and central government officials to help design programmes and provide information. Demoralisation costs if government does not respond to citizen complaints

Note

Assuming the underlying programme is beneficial, net benefits for successful programmes are likely to be large with high BCRs, but more needs to be learned about what works and is sustainable.

Positive Model Cases

Brazilian urban democracy, monitoring of Uganda school funding, Nepalese local public works, South Africa Community Participation Programmes.

Option 2

Procurement reform. Develop benchmarks and use them to reward efficient providers of public services. Consider integrating benchmarking with web-based reputation system based on public input. Role for international institutions, regional bodies, or central governments in providing benchmarking cost estimates and setting up interactive public comment systems. Encourage competition in providing goods and services to the state through use of more open procedures. More purchase of standardised products sold in international markets.

Benefits

Cost saving on public contracts that may total 30–40 per cent according to some estimates.

Costs

Costs of gathering benchmarking information and creating a system to use it.

Note

Once again, assuming the underlying project is worthwhile, net benefits and BCRs will be large with benefits many multiples of costs. The main problem is a 'technical' one – no one really knows exactly how to design a viable system.

Model Cases

Golden and Picci's work on Italy, Pak and Zdanowicz's estimates of overinvoicing and underinvoicing in the USA, US procurement reforms in the 1990s spearheaded by Kelman.

Option 3

Reform of revenue collection through tax simplification, incentives to collectors and tax-payer monitoring. Short-term use of private firms from outside the country to assure integrity.

Benefits

Increased revenue collection in the best cases was close to 100 per cent.

Costs

Increased pay and bonuses for collectors or fees paid to outside contractors, but these seldom total more than 50 per cent of the revenue collected. Because the costs apply to all revenue, the existing situation must be quite dire to justify these expenses. But the costs and revenue gains can be checked *ex post* so the policy is self-correcting. A further cost is demoralisation costs imposed on other government employees who see the benefits flowing to the tax office.

Box 6.1 (continued)

Note

Net benefits and BCRs will be high in many cases. Either the state can lower taxes or raise the level of service provision, but either way the productivity of public spending rises.

Negative Model Cases: Tanzania
Mostly Positive Model Cases: Ghana, Mozambique

Option 4

Reduction in the state-imposed costs of establishing a new business and in the costs associated with ongoing business–government relations. Regulatory cutbacks tempered with concerns for valid goals of some public regulations.

Benefits

Encourages formation of new businesses and increases economic value of existing businesses. Less managerial time spent dealing with public officials.

Costs

Close to zero for pure 'red tape', but reformers also need to evaluate any benefits forgone from programmes with some social value.

Note

If reforms are designed with care, there are very high BCRs and net benefits.

Option 5

International options. Technical assistance to develop monitoring and transparency initiatives as in the Chad–Cameroon pipeline and the EITI. Enhanced asset recovery.

Benefits

More of the benefits of extractive industry projects would flow to developing countries. Given the leakage in some past projects, this could increase host-countries' benefits substantially. Increased likelihood of asset recovery could reduce the incentives to engage in corruption. These are transfer or pecuniary benefits that shift resources from multinationals and key political insiders to ordinary citizens in poor countries. However, research on the costs of corruption suggest that there are also efficiency gains as well. For example, chapter 3 in this volume estimates that the total discounted present value of a successful EITI initiative could be $29 bn.

Costs

Administrative costs of setting up such systems which should be only a few percentage points of the value of any project.

Note

Although the net benefits of EITI appear large, some technical issues have not been resolved so this is not an 'off-the-shelf' option. A range of experiments could be carried out in this area involving pilot programmes in vulnerable countries.

providing information on background conditions, tracking the design and implementation of the reform and measuring outputs. Donors and country partners would try to quantify inputs and outputs in terms such as the speed and effectiveness of government activities, the satisfaction of citizens and the distribution of benefits. Sometimes, as in a tax or procurement reform, the benefits can be quantified in terms of additional dollars collected or cost savings but in other cases, such as more transparent government, the benefits take the form of greater citizen satisfaction and better government

accountability. These factors are valuable in their own right and are associated with higher levels of growth and individual well-being, but the precise links from specific policy interventions to outcomes are not well specified.

Recent discussions of how to allocate foreign assistance to developing countries sometimes conclude that some countries have such poorly functioning institutions that no external aid should be provided because so much of it will be lost. This represents not, as some say, an end to conditionality but is instead conditionality writ large – at the level of the country as a whole, rather than at the level of the programme. The best mixture seems to be broad-based decisions about which countries to support with some share of aid taking the form of grants to improve government performance. Outsiders would not micro-manage individual projects, for example, to build roads, support education and provide health care. Instead, they would supply technical assistance that could lead to a quite deep involvement with the details of government operations. In contrast, policies which try to isolate corrupt countries and individuals from the international community encourage their rulers to descend into paranoia and isolation and are ineffective ways to help the citizens of these countries who are the real victims of corruption. Real reform requires *systemic policy initiatives*. Corruption is a problem of *institutional failure*. A 'clean hands' policy in which wealthy countries hold themselves aloof from tainted countries and individuals without doing anything actually to address the underlying problems will simply further divide the world into rich and poor blocs.

References

Abers, R., 1998: From clientalism to cooperation: local government, participatory policy and civic organizing in Porto Alegre, Brazil, *Politics and Society*, **26**, 511–37

Acemoglu, D., 2003: The form of property rights: oligarchic vs. democratic societies, Department of Economics, MIT, Cambridge MA, September, draft

Acemoglu, D., S. Johnson and J. A. Robinson, 2001: The colonial origins of comparative development: an empirical investigation, *American Economic Review*, **91**, 1369–1401

Adams, C. F., M. E. Bell and T. Brown, 2002: Building civic infrastructure: implementation community partnership grant programmes in South Africa, *Public Administration and Development*, **22**, 293–302

Ades, A. and R. Di Tella, 1997: National champions and corruption: some unpleasant interventionist arithmetic, *Economic Journal*, **107**, 1023–42

1999: Rents, competition and corruption, *American Economic Review*, **89**, 982–3

Anderson, C. J. and Y. V. Tverdova, 2003: Corruption, political allegiances and attitudes toward government in contemporary democracies, *American Journal of Political Science*, **47**, 91–109

Anderson, J., D. Kaufmann and F. Recanatini, 2003: service delivery, poverty and corruption – common threads from diagnostic surveys, background paper for the 2004 *World Development Report*, World Bank, Washington DC, 27 June, www.worldbank.org/wbi/governance/capacitybuild/d-surveys.html

Andvig, J. C., 1995: Corruption in the north sea oil industry: issues and assessments, *Crime, Law, and Social Change*, **28**, 289–313

Anechiarico, F. and J. B. Jacobs, 1996: The pursuit of absolute integrity: how corruption control makes government ineffective, University of Chicago Press, Chicago

Bardhan, P., 1997: Corruption and development: a review of issues, *Journal of Economic Literature*, **35**, 1320–46

Batra, G., D. Kaufmann and A. H. W. Stone, 2003: The firms speak: what the world business environment survey tells us about constraints on private sector development, chapter 9 in G. Fields and G. Pfefferman (eds.), *Pathways out of poverty: private firms and economic mobility in developing countries*, Kluwer Academic Publishers, Amsterdam, http://www.worldbank.org/wbi/governance/pubs/firmsspeak.html

Behrman, J., 2003: Labor markets in developing countries, chapter 43 in O. Ashenfelder and D. Card, *Handbook of labor economics*, 3B,

Blake, C. H. and C. G. Martin, 2002: Combating corruption: reexamining the role of democracy, paper presented at the Annual Meeting of the Midwest Political Science Association, Chicago, 25–28 April

Brown, T., 2001: Contracting out by local governments in transitioning nations: the role of technical assistance in Ukraine, *Administration and Society*, **32**, 728–55

Burki, S. J., 1997: Governance, corruption and development: the case of Pakistan, paper presented at the Workshop on Governance Issues in South Asia, Yale University, New Haven, 19 November

Buscaglia, Jr., E. and M. Dakolias, 1996: Judicial reform in Latin American courts: the experience in Argentina and Ecuador, World Bank

Technical Paper, 350, World Bank, Washington, DC

Chand, S. K. and K. O. Moene, 1999: Controlling fiscal corruption, *World Development*, **27**, 1129–40

Ciocchini, F., E. Durbin and D. T. C. Ng, 2003: Does corruption increase emerging market bond spreads?, *Journal of Economics and Business*, **55**, 503–28, available at http://www.sciencedirect.com

Collier, P. and A. Hoeffler, 2004: The challenge of reducing the global incidence of civil war, Oxford University, Oxford, January, draft; see chapter 3 in this volume

Crook, R. C., and J. Manor, 1998: *Democracy and decentralization in South Asia and West Africa: participation, accountability and performance*, Cambridge University Press, Cambridge

Das Gupta, A. and D. Mookerjee, 1998: *Incentives and institutional reform in tax enforcement: an analysis of developing country experience*, Oxford University Press, Delhi

Das Gupta, M., H. Grandvoinnet and M. Romani, 2000: State–community synergies in development: laying the basis for collective action, World Bank, Washington, DC, draft

Dellarocas, C., 2003: The digitalisation of word of mouth: promise and challenges of online feedback mechanisms, *Management Science*, **49**, 1407–24

Del Monte, A. and E. Papagni, 2001: Public expenditure, corruption, and economic growth: the case of Italy, *European Journal of Political Economy*, **17**, 1–16

Della Porta, D. and A. Vannucci, 1999: *Corrupt exchange*, Aldine, New York

De Melo, M., G. Ofer and O. Sandler, 1995: Pioneers for profit: St Petersburg entrepreneurs in services, *World Bank Economic Review*, **9**, 425–50

De Soto, H., 1989: *The other path: the invisible revolution in the third world*, Harper & Row, New York

De Sousa Santos, B., 1998: Participatory budgeting in Porto Alegre: toward a redistributive democracy, *Politics and Society*, **26**, 461–510

Devas, N., S. Delay and M. Hubbard, 2001: Revenue authorities: are they the right vehicle for improving tax administration?, *Public Administration and Development*, **21**, 211–22

Di Tella, R. and E. Schargrodsky, 2002: The role of wages and auditing during a crackdown on corruption in the City of Buenos Aires, in D. Della Porta and S. Rose-Ackerman, (eds.), *Corrupt exchanges: empirical themes in the politics and political economy of corruption*, Nomos Verlag, Frankfurt; a longer version is in *Journal of Law and Economics*, **46**, 2003

Dia, M., 1996: Africa's management in the 1990s and beyond: reconciling indigenous and transplanted institutions, World Bank, Washington, DC

Dollar, D., M. Hallward-Driemeier and T. Mengiste, 2003: Investment climate and international integration, draft paper prepared for Conference on the Future of Globalization, Yale Center for the Study of Globalization, World Bank, Washington, DC, 11 October

Duflo, E., 2001: Schooling and labor market consequences of school construction in Indonesia: evidence from an unusual policy experiment, *American Economic Review* **91**, 795–813

Easterly, W., 2001: *The elusive quest for growth: economists' adventures and misadventures in the tropics*, MIT Press, Cambridge, MA

Esty, D. and M. Porter, 2002: National environmental performance measurement and determinants, in D. Esty and P. K. Cornelius (eds), *Environmental performance measurement: the global report 2001–2002*, Oxford University Press, New York

Fisman, R., 2001: Estimating the value of political connections, *American Economic Review*, **91**, 1095–1102

Fisman, R., and S.-J. Wei, 2001: Tax rates and tax evasion: evidence from 'missing imports' in China, National Bureau of Economic Research Working Paper **8551**, Cambridge MA: NBER, October

Fjeldsted, O.-H., 2002: Fighting fiscal corruption: the case of the Tanzania Revenue Authority, Chr. Michelsen Institute Working Paper, **2002**: 3, Bergen

2003: *Decentralization and corruption: a review of the literature*, U4 Report, Chr. Michelsen Institute, Bergen

Fjeldsted, O.-H. and J. Semboja, 2001: Why people pay taxes: the case of the development levy in Tanzania, *World Development*, **29**, 2059–74

Friedman, E., S. Johnson, D. Kaufmann and P. Zoido-Lobaton, 2000: Dodging the grabbing hand: the determinant of unofficial activity in 69 countries, *Journal of Public Economics*, **76**, 459–93

Fries, S., T. Lysenko and S. Polanec, 2003: The 2002 Business Environment and Enterprise Performance Survey: results from a survey of 6,100 firms, Working Paper, **84**, European Bank for Reconstructions and Development, London, November, http://www.ebrd.com/pubs/econ/workingp/84.pdf

Golden, M. and L. Picci, 2004: Proposal for a new measure of corruption illustrated using Italian data, draft 4, UCLA and University of Bologna, March; available at http://www.spbo.unibo.it/picci/article.pdf

Gong, T., 2002: Dangerous collusion: corruption as a collective venture in contemporary China, *Communist and Post-Communist Studies*, **35**, 85–103

Graf Lambsdorff, J., 2003a: How corruption affects persistent capital flows, *Economics of Governance*, **4**, 229–43

2003b: How corruption affects productivity, *Kyklos*, **56**, 457–74

Gupta, S., H. R. Davoodi and R. Alonso-Terme, 2002: Does corruption affect income inequality and poverty?, *Economics of Governance*, **3**, 23–45

Gupta, S., H. R. Davoodi and E. R. Tiongson, 2001: Corruption and the provision of health care and education services, in A. K. Jain (ed.), *The political economy of corruption*, Routledge, London

Hellman, J. S., G. Jones and D. Kaufmann, 2003: Seize the state, seize the day: state capture, corruption and influence in transition, *Journal of Comparative Economics*, **31**, 751–73

Hellman, J. S. and D. Kaufmann, 2004: The inequality of influence, in J. Kornai and S. Rose-Ackerman (eds), *Building a trustworthy state in post-socialist transition*, Palgrave, New York, 100–18

Hubbard, M., S. Delay and N. Devas, 1999: Complex management contracts: the case of customs administration in Mozambique, *Public Administration and Development*, **19**, 153–63

2001: Revenue authorities: are they the right vehicle for improving tax administration?, *Public Administration and Development*, **21**, 211–22

Johnson, S., D. Kaufmann, J. McMillan and C. Woodruff, 2000: Why do firms hide? Bribes and unofficial activity after communism, *Journal of Public Economics*, **76**, 495–520

Johnson, S., J. McMillan and C. Woodruff, 2000: Entrepreneurs and the ordering of institutional reform: Poland, Slovakia, Russia and Ukraine compared, *Economics of Transition*, **8**, 1–36

2002: Property rights and finance, *American Economic Review*, **92**, 1335–57

Johnston, M., 2002: Comparing corruption: participation, institutions and development, prepared for a conference on Corruption: Public and Private, John Jay College of Criminal Law, New York, August

Kaufmann, D., 1997: The missing pillar of growth strategy for Ukraine: institutional and policy reforms for private sector development, in P. K. Cornelius and P. Lenain (eds.), *Ukraine: accelerating the transition to market*, IMF, Washington, DC, 234–75

2003: Rethinking governance: empirical lessons challenge orthodoxy, Discussion draft, World Bank, Washington DC, http://www.worldbank.org/wbi/governance/pdf/rethink_gov_standford.pdf

2004: Governance redux: the empirical challenge, discussion draft, World Bank Institute, Washington DC, http://www.worldbank.org/wbi/governance/pdf/govredux.pdf

Kaufmann, D. and A. Kraay, 2002: Growth without governance, *Economia*, **3**, 169–229

Kaufmann, D., A. Kraay and M. Mastruzzi, 2003: Governance matters III: governance indicators 1996–2000, discussion draft, World Bank, Washington DC, http://www.worldbank.org/wbi/governance/pdf/govmatters3.pdf

Kaufmann, D., M. Mastruzzi and D. Zaveleta, 2003: Sustained macroeconomic reforms, tepid growth: a governance puzzle in Bolivia, in D. Rodrik (ed.), *In search of prosperity: analytic narratives on economic growth*, Princeton University Press, Princeton

Kaufmann, D., G. Menvez and T. Gurgur, 2002: Voice or public sector management? An empirical investigation of determinants of public sector performance based on a survey of public officials, discussion draft, World Bank, Washington DC

Kelman, S., 1990: *Procurement and public management: the fear of discretion and the quality of government performance*, AEI Press, Washington DC

2002: Remaking federal procurement, *Public Contract Law Journal*, **31**, 581–622

Krastev, I. and G. Ganev, 2004: The missing incentive: corruption, anticorruption, and reelection, in J. Kornai and S. Rose-Ackerman (eds.), *Building a trustworthy state in post-socialist transition*, Palgrave, New York

Krueger, A., 1974: The political economy of a rent-seeking society, *American Economic Review*, **64**, 291–303

Kunicova, J., 2002: Are presidential systems more susceptible to political corruption? California Institute of Technology, Pasadena, CA, draft

Kunicova, J. and S. Rose-Ackerman, 2005: Electoral rules and constitutional structures as constraints on corruption, *British Journal of Political Science*, forthcoming

La Porta, R., F. Lopez-de-Silanes, A. Shleifer and R. Vishny, 1999: The quality of government, *Journal of Law, Economics, and Organization*, **15**, 222–79

Li, H., L. C. Xu and H.-F. Zou, 2000: Corruption, income distribution, and growth, *Economics and Politics*, **12**, 155–82

Li, W., 2002: Corruption and resource allocation: evidence from China, in D. Della Porta and S. Rose-Ackerman (eds.), *Corrupt exchanges: empirical themes in the politics and political economy of corruption*, Nomos Verlag, Frankfurt

Low, P., 1995: Preshipment inspection services, World Bank Discussion Paper, 278, Washington, DC

MacGaffey, J., 1991: *The real economy of Zaire: the contribution of smuggling and other unofficial activities to national wealth*, University of Pennsylvania Press, Philadelphia

Manzetti, L., 1999: *Privatization South American style*, Oxford University Press, Oxford

Mauro, P., 1995: Corruption and growth, *Quarterly Journal of Economics*, **110**, 681–712
1997: The effects of corruption on growth, investment, and government expenditure: a cross-country analysis, in K. A. Elliott (ed.), *Corruption and the global economy*, Institute for International Economics, Washington: DC, 83–108

Meagher, P., K. Upadhyaya and B. Wilkinson, 2000: Combating rural public works corruption: food-for-work programmes in Nepal, IRIS Center Working Paper, **239**, University of Maryland, College Park, MD, February;

available at http://www.iris.umd.edu/publications.asp

Miller, T., 1997: Kelman's latest proposal and past performance explored, *Federal Computer Market Report*, 21(11), 7 (9 June)

Miller, W. L., A. Grødeland and T. Y. Koshechkina, 2001: *A culture of corruption: coping with government in post-communist europe*, Central European University Press, Budapest
2002: Values and norms *versus* extortion and temptation, in D. Della Porta and S. Rose-Ackerman (eds.), *Corrupt exchanges: empirical themes in the politics and political economy of corruption*, Nomos Verlag, Frankfurt

Mocan, N., 2004: What determines corruption? international evidence from micro data, NBER Working Paper 10460, Cambridge MA: National Bureau of Economic Research, April

Moore, M., 1998: Death without taxes: aid dependence, democracy, state capacity and aid in the fourth world, in M. Robinson and G. Whites (eds.), *The democratic developmental state: politics and institutional design*, Oxford University Press, Oxford

Mosse, D., 1997: The ideology and politics or community participation, in R. Grillo and R. Stirrat (eds.), *Discourses of development: anthropological perspectives*, Berg, Oxford, 255–91

Nichols, P. M., 2001: The fit between changes in the international corruption regime and indigenous perceptions of corruption in Kazakhstan, *University of Pennsylvania Journal of International Economic Law*, **22**, 863–973

Olken, B. A., 2003: Corruption and the costs of redistribution: micro evidence from Indonesia, draft, Harvard University, July

Olson, M., 1996: Big bills left on the sidewalk: why some nations are rich and others poor, *Journal of Economic Perspectives*, **10**, 3–24

Pak, S. J. and J. S. Zdanowicz, 1994: A statistical analysis of the US merchandise trade data base and its uses in transfer pricing compliance and enforcement, *Tax Management Transfer Pricing Report*, **3**, 50–7, 11 May
2002: US trade with the world: an estimate of 2001 lost US federal income tax revenues due to over-invoiced imports and under-invoiced exports, Trade Research Institute, Miami

Parker, A. N., 1995: Decentralization: the way forward for rural development?, Policy Research Paper, 1475, World Bank, Agriculture and Natural Resources Department, Washington, DC, June

Pasuk P. and P. Sungsidh, 1994: *Corruption and democracy in Thailand*, The Political Economy Centre, Faculty of Economics, Chulalongkorn University, Bangkok

Paul, K., S. Pak, John Z. and P. Curwen, 1994: The ethics of international trade: use of deviation from average world price to indicate possible wrongdoing, *Business Ethics Quarterly*, **4**, 29–41

Putnam, R., 1993: *Making democracy work: civic traditions in modern Italy*, Princeton University Press, Princeton

Rabushka, A., 2002: The flat tax at work in Russia, Hoover Institution Public Policy Inquiry, The Russian Economy, February http://www.russianeconomy/org/comments/022102.html

2004: The flat tax at work in Russia: year three, Hoover Institution Public Policy Inquiry, The Russian Economy, April, http://www.russianeconomy/org/comments/042604.html

Rauch, J. E. and P. B. Evans, 2000: Bureaucratic structure and bureaucratic performance in less developed countries, *Journal of Public Economics*, **75**, 49–71

Reinikka, R. and J. Svensson, 2002: Measuring and understanding corruption at the micro level, in D. Della Porta and S. Rose-Ackerman (eds.), *Corrupt exchanges: empirical themes in the politics and political economy of corruption*, Nomos Verlag, Frankfurt

2004a: Local capture: evidence from a central government transfer program in Uganda, *Quarterly Journal of Economics*, **119**(2)

2004b: The power of information: evidence from a newspaper campaign to reduce corruption, Policy Research Working Paper Series, World Bank, Washington, DC

Robbins, P., 2000: The rotten institution: corruption in natural resource management, *Political Geography*, **19**, 423–43

Rock, M. T. and H. Bonnett, 2004: The comparative politics of corruption: accounting for the East Asian paradox in empirical studies of corruption, growth and investment, *World Development*, **32**, 999–1017

Rodrik, D., 2003: Growth strategies, *Handbook of Economic Growth*, Kennedy School of Government, Harvard University, Cambridge MA, draft; available at http://ksghome.harvard.edu/~.drodrik.academic.ksg/growthstrat10.pdf

Rose-Ackerman, S., 1978: *Corruption: a study in political economy*, Academic Press, New York

1999: *Corruption and government: causes, consequences and reform*, Cambridge University Press, Cambridge

2002: Grand corruption and the ethics of global business, *Journal of Banking and Finance*, **26**, 1889–1918

2004: Establishing the rule of law, in R. Rotberg (ed.), *When states fail: causes and consequences*, Princeton University Press, Princeton, 182–221

Rotberg, R. (ed.), 2003: *State failure and state weakness in a time of terror*, The Brookings Institution, Washington, DC

2004: *When states fail: causes and consequences*, Princeton University Press, Princeton

Sandholtz, W. and W. Keotzle, 2000: Accounting for corruption: economic structure, democracy, and trade, *International Studies Quarterly*, **44**, 31–50

Seligman, M., 2002: The impact of corruption on regime legitimacy: a comparative study of four Latin American countries, *Journal of Politics*, **64**, 408–33

Shleifer, A. and R. Vishny, 1993: Corruption, *Quarterly Journal of Economics*, **108**, 599–617

Slinko, I., E. Yakovlev and E. Zhuravskaya, 2004: Effects of state capture: evidence from Russian regions, in J. Kornai and S. Rose-Ackerman (eds.), *Building a trustworthy state in post-socialist societies*, Palgrave, New York, 119–32

Stasavage, D., 1999: Causes and consequences of corruption: Mozambique in transition, *Commonwealth and Comparative Politics*, **37**, 65–97

Stella, P., 1992: Tax farming – a radical solution for developing country tax problems?, IMF Working Paper, WP/92/70, IMF, Washington, DC

Steves, F. and A. Rousso, 2003: Anti-corruption programmes in post-communist transition countries and changes in the business environment, 1999–2002, Working Paper, **85**, European Bank for Reconstruction and Development, London

Svensson, J., 2003: Who must pay bribes and how much? Evidence from a cross section of firms, *Quarterly Journal of Economics*, **118**, 207–30

Swamy, A., S. Knack, Y. Lee and O. Azfar, 2001: Gender and corruption, *Journal of Development Economics*, **64**, 25–55

Tanzi, V. and H. Davoodi, 2002a: Corruption, growth, and public finance, in G. T. Abed and Sanjeev (eds.), *Governance, corruption and economic performance*, IMF, Washington, DC, 197–222

 2002b: Corruption, public investment and growth, in G. T. Abed and Sanjeev (eds.), *Governance, corruption and economic performance*, IMF, Washington, DC, 280–99

Torgler, B., 2003: Tax morale in central and eastern European countries, paper prepared for the Conference on Tax Evasion, Trust, and State Capacity, University of St Gallen, St Gallen, 17–19 October

Treisman, D., 2000: The causes of corruption: a cross-national study, *Journal of Public Economics*, **76**, 399–457

United States, Department of Justice (DOJ), Criminal Division, Public Integrity Section, 2003: *Report to Congress on the activities and operations of the public integrity section for 2002*, Washington, DC

Uslaner, E. M., 2003: Tax evasion, trust and the strong arm of the law, paper prepared for the Conference on Tax Evasion, Trust, and State Capacity, University of St Gallen, St Gallen, 17–19 October

Van Rijckeghem, C. and B. Weder, 2001: Bureaucratic corruption and the rate of temptation: do wages in the civil service affect corruption, and by how much?, *Journal of Development Economics*, **65**, 307–31

Webster, L. M. and J. Charap, 1993: The emergence of private sector manufacturing in St Petersburg, World Bank Technical Paper, 228, World Bank, Washington, DC

Wei, S.-J., 2000: How taxing is corruption on international investors?, *Review of Economics and Statistics*, **82**, 1–11

Woodhouse, A., 2002: Village corruption in Indonesia: fighting corruption in the World Bank's Kecamatan development program, report to the World Bank, Washington DC, June

World Bank, 1997: *Helping countries combat corruption: the role of the World Bank*, Poverty Reduction and Economic Management Network, Washington, DC

 1999: Guidelines procurement under IBRD loans and IDA credits, World Bank, Washington, DC, January, http://web.worldbank.org/WBSITE/ EXTERNAL/PROJECTS/PROCUREMENT/ 0,contentMDK:20060840~pagePK:84269~ piPK:60001558~ theSitePK:84266,00.html

 2003: Village justice in Indonesia: case studies on access to justice, Jakarta, draft, September

Yang, D., 2004: Can enforcement backfire? crime displacement in the context of a common customs reform, working paper, Gerald R. Ford School of Public Policy and Department of Economics, University of Michigan, Ann Arbor MI, April

You, J.-S. and S. Khagram, 2004: Inequality and corruption, Working Paper, RWP04–001, Kennedy School of Government, Harvard University, Cambridge MA

Alternative Perspectives

Perspective Paper 6.1

JENS CHRISTOPHER ANDVIG

The challenge raised by poor governance and corruption to be emphasised here is a challenge of *tools*: Do we have the ability to meet any global challenge if our basic tools for dealing with them, the formal organisations, are populated with a large number of leaders and ordinary members who shirk, embezzle or engage in corrupt transactions? The very same tools have to be applied when solving the problems of governance and corruption. Hence, if corruption is a key problem, do we have any way of solving it?

Rose-Ackerman (2004, chapter 6 in this volume) underlines a different side of corruption: skewed distribution of purchasing power based on private wealth induces illegal buying of influence. That undermines legitimate political power, particularly when based on voting power. This illegal buying of political and judicial decisions by private business, is nowadays called 'state capture' and recent research has been able to capture some of its possible quantitative dimensions (e.g. Hellman *et al.* 2000). I think this return to old Marxian fields of inquiry has already become fruitful. There are also important spillover mechanisms from the political game to the day-to-day behaviour of formal organisations. Still, I consider the consequences of corruption for that behaviour to be the key challenge.

Rose-Ackerman addresses five options, five roads of attack in chapter 6: Voice and accountability, procurement reforms, tax reforms, changes in systems of business regulation and international efforts to limit high-level corruption in

business. For reasons of space I will focus on the last option.

Data: Do We Have Sufficiently Precise Knowledge of the Governance Challenge?

Looked at from outside, chapter 6 may appear somewhat peculiar by classifying both the consequences and causes of corruption according to their sources of statistical information. A rather heterogeneous picture of seemingly unrelated phenomena and measures is presented. This is not, however, a flaw in the chapter as such, but reflects in an interesting way some inherent characteristics of the corruption and poor governance challenge itself and, to some degree, temporary limitations of current state of relevant research. It has not yet quite digested the large amount of recently available data in the field.

In the following I will mainly discuss corruption, not because I believe that corruption and the other aspects of poor governance are synonymous phenomena, or always strongly linked, but because I have not found any option where tradeoffs between the different dimensions of governance are both essential and possible to determine. With the more precise weighing of forces implied by such

I am grateful to Nick Duncan and Arne Melchior for helpful comments and to Eilert Struksnes for comments and minor language editing.

tradeoffs, the problem of 'noisiness' in the different governance indicators becomes acute.[1]

With exceptions, such as Gunnar Myrdal (1968), few economists believed until recently that corruption was a researchable phenomenon. It was not researchable partly because no interesting model had been constructed but, more importantly, no quantitative data were available. Not least due to the early efforts of the author of chapter 6 (Rose-Ackerman 1978), interesting models were soon constructed, but quantitative data were missing until the mid-1990s. The publication of such data, beginning with the Corruption Perception Index (CPI) of Transparency International (TI), was part of the political process that has made corruption and poor governance available as a public challenge where quantitative cost-benefit analyses (CBAs) of measures at least are thinkable.

Nevertheless, I will argue that corrupt transactions remain in many ways as unobservable as before. The quantitative information is not based upon direct observation, with the exception of a few case studies that still are extremely scarce. The information is rather based on questionnaires that differ widely in how they relate to observable action. Since the different sources of quantitative information reflect the various forms of corruption and poor governance at different distances from the actual acts, it is reasonable to build different kinds of empirically based models around them. When closer to the actual corrupt acts, the wide variety of situations, reflected now also in the data, cries out for specific empirically based models to analyse the set of normally small-scale options tailored to that particular challenge.

Most quantitative research has been cross-country studies based on the most aggregate data. TI's CPI index has been most frequently used, but another developed in the World Bank, roughly using the same sources of information, but applying different principles of aggregation, is likely to become as important.[2] These indexes now allocate numbers for the average corruptibility of almost every country in the world of some economic significance, stimulating both political discussion and research. That research is of great potential value in assessing the economic dimensions of the challenge of poor governance and corruption. The quantitative specification of the negative effects of corruption on growth has been paradigmatic (Mauro 1995), but many other effects have been studied, some of which have been dealt with in chapter 6. Since the corruption level is not a policy instrument, however, models where corruption plays the role as dependent or intermediate variable are more immediately relevant. For example, in Ades and Di Tella (1999) the degree of economic openness impacts corruption, and corruption influences growth. Since it is possible to influence the degree of openness by a large number of policy instruments, including tried methods of trade policy, the implications for the search of policy options are obvious.[3]

The informational core of the TI's and World Bank's governance indexes is assessments made by experts and businessmen collected by different organisations. When constructing the indexes both the TI and the World Bank economists have, of course,

---

[1] With regard to the problem at hand, one may, for example, believe that the long periods of relatively high degree of political stability in Kenya with relatively low-scale political violence are related to the high level of corruption. But are we in this case dealing with processes that are so predictable that we may, for example, settle for an option that reduces corruption by 20 per cent at the cost of increasing the probability of civil war by 10 per cent? With such mixes of data 'noise' and difficult-to-predict situations, I believe it is reasonable to restrict the range of options considered to situations where all the good things go together – less interesting for economists, but less demanding for the quality of the governance indicators. That is, I shall in the following treat 'corruption' and 'poor governance' as synonymous.

[2] The aggregation principles of the World Bank index are explained in Kaufmann, Kraay and Zoido-Lobaton (1999). They allow information from sub-series covering only a few countries when constructing the aggregate index covering most countries in the world. By being able to include data from more countries and through the fact that the World Bank researchers have built up other, easy to access, governance indicators of bureaucratic quality, voice and the rule of law, using the same aggregation methodology, it is safe to predict that it will become the database for much research into corruption and poor governance in the future.

[3] As pointed out in chapter 6, many explanatory variables in the corruption equations are past events, historical or geographical givens, impossible to influence today and useless in option search. It is difficult to take authors seriously here when discussing the counterfactual of how much less corruption one might observe in parts of present-day Russia if it had been colonised by England (Treisman 2002)!

noted many of the problems which arise through the aggregation of these heterogeneous data sources and devised two different econometric solutions.

Both solutions, however, assume that the stochastic errors across sub-indicators are independent. The assumption is crucial and difficult to relax, as noted by Kaufmann, Kraay and Zoido-Lobaton (1999, 10). Without it, the gains in precision by aggregation become indefinite.[4] How reasonable is it that the strong correlation between the sub-indexes is due to correlation of errors, and not to independent observations of the same government characteristics? Several of the sub-indicators with the strongest intercorrelation are based on respondents' answers to very general and vague questions about their perceptions of corruption levels in country *A*, *B* or *C*. The questions are not leading the respondents to focus on their own experience. At least in countries where the citizens have no daily, individual experience of corruption, the assessments have to be based on the process through which information about corruption reaches the public domain. What is that process?

As far as I know, little precise, empirically based knowledge is available. As a first approximation, however, I would expect strong correlation and spillover effects: the experts read the same reports and gauge other experts' statements. Since the assessments are often not based on individual experience, when expert *X* claims that corruption in country *A* is very high, expert *Z* has no clear evidence to the contrary, so when knowing *X*'s statement it may be optimal to make an assessment close to hers. Informational cascades may easily develop in this context.[5] The fact that the TI index in particular is widely published reinforces the argument. The case of expatriate businessmen is somewhat different, but they are not likely to base their assessments only on their own, independent experience either. Most will be based upon other businessmen's communication. The degree to which that will contain private information, will at best depend on how much genuine information other expatriates reveal.[6] The striking way that corruption has moved from being perceived as a sideline issue in the public mind to a major challenge today may in part reflect this emperor-has-no-clothes informational structure (Andvig 2002).

The work under the auspices of the World Bank since 1996 to develop more detailed and focused information about corruption, such as the size and frequency of bribes paid by enterprises and other parts of public administration, is one of the most interesting and important expansions of statistical information since the development of national accounting. The thrust of this research is reflected in Kaufmann's (2003) strong headline: 'The power of data: governance can be measured, monitored, and rigorously analysed.' It is now possible to construct reasonably comparable (across countries) measures of different forms of corruption, whether corrupt deals are honoured and so on, for a large and increasing number of countries, all seen from the enterprises' point of view.

For some countries that information may be compared with the private households' and public officials' experience or perceptions in so-called diagnostic surveys.[7] In another line of research

[4] Another reason Kaufmann, Kraay and Zoido-Lobaton (1999) do not emphasise this problem is that the relaxing of the assumption would result in a greater variance in the country estimates and that would only support their polemics against TI's use of its index to publish a precise ranking of countries in terms of their (perceived) corruptness. An important ingredient in the World Bank aggregation procedure is that it (endogeneously) gives greater weights to those sub-indexes that are more strongly intercorrelated with the others. If that intercorrelation is due to intercorrelation of errors, however, this property of the aggregation procedure may not be of any advantage.

[5] Many of the conditions for of such cascades to develop are fulfilled in this case (see, for example, Bikhchandani, Hirschleifer and Welch 1992).

[6] The main reason why most information about corruption remains private (except the daily demand for bribes in high-corruption areas) is, of course, that corrupt transactions usually are criminal and the agents performing them are interested in keeping them secret. Furthermore, the agents most likely to discover corrupt transactions, the public or private bureaucracies directly involved, are also normally interested in keeping the acts secret from the public. In the case of private enterprises the economic losses when such information is revealed, may prove significant, around 5 per cent of stock values in more serious cases (Karpoff and Lott 1995). At this level, the information game may at best have a prisoner's dilemma structure. It may be better for all enterprises if everyone told about her experience; if only you reveal it, you will lose.

[7] See: http://www.worldbank.org/wbi/governance/ capacity-build/diagnostics.html.

guided by somewhat different theoretical presump-
tions, the World Bank has focused on the different
branches of public government and asked different
groups of officials about their perception and experience of governance issues, including corruption.[8]
For a few Latin American countries Seligson (2002,
2003) has also collected a set of corruption data
where households are asked about their direct experience.

So far, however, most micro-based research has
relied on the more widely collected business perception data, mentioned above, such as the World
Business Environment Survey (WBES), but the results of these surveys are interpreted as if they
report the officials' or enterprises' own experience.
In many cases, this may be misleading. Sensibly,
in order to gain answers from the enterprises about
their experience of sensitive corruption, the questions had to be 'phrased indirectly about the corruption faced by "firms in your line of business"'
(Hellman *et al.* 2000, 20). Despite the precautions
taken, this is not the same as reporting experience.
Given the informational nature of corrupt transactions, these perceptions are also likely to be strongly
influenced by the other agents' communication of
their perceptions, which may or may not be based
on their own experience.

An important example of possible ambiguity
is the World Bank group's paper on multinational companies' behaviour in transition countries
(Hellman, Jones and Kaufmann 2002). Here they
find that enterprises from low-corruption countries
roughly behave as corruptly as the locals even in the
most corrupt countries. It is an interesting hypothesis, to which I return when dealing with the international efforts option, but a more straightforward
interpretation is that the multinationals simply per-

ceive the corruption problem roughly in the same
way as the locals, they share the same 'folklore of
corruption' (Myrdal 1968, 940).

Chapter 6 does not discuss the weak observa-
tional basis of most quantitative measures used in
this field. The result is that one may believe this
challenge to have more precise dimensions than
are warranted. Despite all the progress and insights
and hypotheses made through the quantitative perception data, the challenge of corruption as a field
of empirical research is still its secret nature. In
order to gain a more precise idea about the size
of the corruption and poor governance challenges,
more detailed analysis of data sources is needed. In
particular, we should know more about how the perceptions about them are formulated and, eventually, how these perceptions may influence the performed actions. A few suggestive observations have
been made,[9] but to my knowledge few concentrated research efforts. Cábelková's (2001) study
from Ukraine is an interesting exception. It models the impact of actual experience, the impact
of media and friends on perceptions and the impact of perceptions on the reported incidence of
corrupt transactions at a number of public institutions.

Options: Do We Have the Tools to Deal with the Corruption Challenge?

As pointed out by World Bank researchers (Huther
and Shah 2000) we have two rather different corruption challenges. In one case we have an honest principal, a government willing to deal with corruption
and other forms of poor government, and where corruption is not a dominant form of behaviour among
politicians and most branches of public administration. In this situation one may often simply create
new, working tools that may repair the defective
ones: working anti-corruption agencies, reorganisation of public auditing and hiring agencies and
so on. Corruption and poor governance certainly
may also prove important and difficult to handle issues in this case since corruption implies that people
try to collect potential economic rents attached to
their positions in difficult-to-monitor situations. As
crime, it is difficult to detect. We may also have

---

[8] In the case of Bolivia, see Manning, Mukherjee and
Gokcekus (2000). So far, only a few countries are covered.

[9] For example PriceWaterhouseCoopers (2001, 6) compares
the distribution of different forms of *experienced* economic
crime with their *perceived* prevalence among about 3,400
European organisations, mostly business enterprises. While
embezzlement constituted 63 per cent of the actual economic
crime incidence, but 29 per cent of the perceived prevalence,
corruption constituted only 11 per cent of the actual incidence, but 23 per cent of the perceived prevalence. The sample space is defined by a list of possible types of economic
crime.

strong positive spillover effects in this case: if you make a corrupt transaction it becomes easier for me to do the same.

It is the other challenge, however – the situation where the principal is dishonest or too weak to deal with a public apparatus permeated with corruption – that is really the serious one. Given the present level of cross-country information and concern, the resulting large pockets of mismanagement and deep poverty represent a major global challenge. The option of simply creating new bureaucratic tools is not likely to be available here, they are also likely to be tainted. The tools available to deal with such situations are either too weak or too harsh.

This is also the answer I read from chapter 6. Since the harsh tools of outside military interventions or internal revolutions are both extremely risky and costly with too uncertain benefits, they will remain outside our scope of attention. To transform, let us say, the World Bank into a kind of activist, anti-establishment type of organisation is not an option either. We have to focus on the weaker instruments. Hence, chapter 6's outline of options deal with a combination of fairly weak measures that may have some positive effects on the second situation and some measures that may mainly work as a response to the first.

As noted in the Introduction, in the deep corruption situation the national authorities are unlikely to have regular tools available since they are all likely to become corrupt. Note that this proposition assumes that the spillover mechanisms across different sectors of the public apparatus inside a country are much stronger than cross-country spillovers within the same sector of administration, such as customs. While probably realistic in most cases, the assumption is left unexplained. Nevertheless, closer cross-country interaction at sector level, such as the international anti-corruption movement in customs administrations, may assist in reducing corruption in the customs in high-corruption countries (or, eventually, stimulate corruption in low-corruption administrations). In outlining international measures Rose-Ackerman has not sufficiently underlined the possibilities through cross-country interaction at sector level. More generally, interactions between a thoroughly corrupt public apparatus and some outside agencies or interests

have to be established to release internal pressures in corruption-decreasing directions.

This is clearly the central part in the first 'oversight and transparency' option in chapter 6. Here Rose-Ackerman reports several cases where the combination of publication of precise information of local programmes reaching locals with strong interests in them has succeeded in mobilising groups of locals to become effective monitors of them, sometimes drastically reducing the corrupt waste involved. Due to the painstaking research made at the World Bank (Reinikka and Svensson 2004) it has been possible to determine the pre- and post-experiment waste in the school transfer programme in Uganda. While 80 per cent of funds, according to chapter 6, were wasted before the experiment, only 20 per cent were wasted afterwards. In addition to its scientific interest the example indicates the size of the waste involved in countries with high embezzlement and corruption propensities.

If it is true that public expenditures in these countries are deliberately moved away from education to large infrastructure projects due to the even larger corruption possibilities there, an obvious conclusion is that most foreign aid projects based on cost-benefit analysis (CBA) need to be killed before leaving the drawing board. That is a conclusion I, like most others, am unwilling to draw, but here we have a major challenge. If we calculate the value of resources spent on bribing to be zero, as Rose-Ackerman does, the return on the original programme needs to be 50 per cent in order to have a 10 per cent return on the whole programme.[10]

---

[10] I find Rose-Ackerman's proposal here for how to do a CBA of anti-corruption projects very reasonable. The more valuable the original projects are, the more costly will the corruption waste be, and for given anti-corruption project expense, the higher the rate of return of that project. In general, a person who believes that no foreign aid project is likely to be of value should not be so worried about corruption. The funds should not be transferred in any case. Another person, believing in the value of many of the original projects, may reach the same conclusion if corruption waste is very high, but for her the potential rate of return on corruption projects will be very high, if they work. If no efficient anti-corruption project is possible to formulate, we have a very difficult ethical situation, in many ways analogous to peace-keeping operations.

Since unpaid local mobilisation may be difficult to sustain in the long run, and international support is short-run in nature, one may doubt if anti-corruption programmes of this kind will be sustainable. In particular, in the Uganda case, the anti-corruption project may have been so successful in the first place because the rent collectors here were among the less powerful.

Presumably, most formal organisations located in the rich countries are comparatively low-corrupt and external to the system of formal organisations of the highly corrupt countries. May they, either through designed or uncontrolled interaction, become tools for improving the workings of the governance of high-corruption countries? Since I consider chapter 6 to be somewhat unsystematic here in both its choice of issues and choice of options, I will focus on this matter.

International Efforts

North–South Interactions: Multinational Companies

May the strong governance systems of the large multinational companies somehow induce lower corruption in high-corruption countries? The companies will be involved in three major type of activities: (1) regular exports with modest involvement with public authorities, (2) delivery on public construction and consultancy projects (public procurement) which implies denser interaction and the even tighter involvement implied by (3) foreign direct investment (FDI).

The international pressure towards opening the trade regime may induce less corruption here than before, but in public procurement and FDI activ-

ities there are no obvious system-wide changes with clear impact on corruption tendencies. Data collected about multinationals' behaviour give few grounds for optimism. For example, World Bank research into multinational bribing activities in the post-communist countries may indicate that their bribing – connected to regular sales, in public procurement and FDI-related capture activities – are roughly on the same scale as the locals', although differing in detail (Hellman, Jones and Kaufmann 2002). While not so clear-cut in this respect, the TI index of corruption propensity in major exporting countries does not clearly contradict this result.

One result of this research is that the corruption behaviour of US multinationals is not among the best in the transition countries. It may support Rose-Ackerman's neglect of the OECD convention against bribing and the other treaties that intend to apply stronger judicial systems in the home country to reduce their involvement in corrupt transactions in poor, highly corrupt countries. This conclusion appears to follow since the USA has applied its judicial apparatus this way since the introduction of its Foreign Corrupt Practices Act in 1977. The low probability of being caught supplies an explanation of why this may be the case.

Nevertheless, this may be too rash a conclusion. The companies involved deny vehemently that they are engaged actively in corrupt activities abroad but, more importantly, the data may, as argued before, be interpreted as reflecting *perceptions*, not behaviour. Furthermore, in certain bribe situations created under experimental conditions, low-probability but high-value punishment is surprisingly effective in mitigating some forms of corruption (Abbink, Irlenbusch and Renner 2002).[11] It will be misleading to translate the effects of strong punishment in the experiment into real-world conditions by minor jail sentences or similar punishment directed against individuals. Long-lasting international bid denials better simulate these experimental conditions, particularly so for large, multinational companies. To develop the OECD and the UN conventions in this direction may make them a more potent option in fighting cross-country corruption. The fact is that the World Bank's list of companies not allowed to bid because of their violation of no-corruption conditions of the Bank, so far (to

---

[11] Rose-Ackerman does not use any of recent experimental evidence. Given the difficulty of transferring the results to real-world conditions, that may be reasonable, but since it is so difficult to observe corrupt transactions, the experiments may be more useful than in most other fields of economics but sometimes even more difficult from an ethical point of view. At present experiments may shed light on such issues as whether stricter monitoring may increase corruption, the role of transparency in certain situations, the effectiveness of appointed versus elected monitors, the preventive effects of rotation of officials and so on.

my knowledge) does not contain any major, multi-national company and this surely undermines the credibility of the list.[12]

I still believe more may be achieved along this road to make the multinational companies contribute less to corruption in high-corrupt countries than the voluntary 'Publish What You Pay' and EITI initiatives recommended in chapter 6. While increased information and transparency are certainly to be welcomed, I believe the NGO interests are too muddled and transient to become any external force that may make the kind of pressure performed by the parent–teacher groups in Uganda. With regard to the interest groups internal to the harmed country, I expect their pressure to also be weak in this case, since the potential increase in tax income resulting from the initiatives is likely to be widely spread.

North–South Interactions: Foreign Aid

Another important arena for transactions between high- and low-corrupt organisations is foreign aid. May such meetings result in the low-corrupt public and semi-public NGO organisations transferring their standards to the high-corrupt public apparatuses, or may the transfer of standards go in the opposite direction? After all, corrupt transactions are profitable for the individuals involved.

Again, we have few direct observations. To my knowledge there has been no systematic collection of evidence, although in a number of countries with a tradition of investigative journalism, such as Kenya, the number of documented stories are large. So far, we have to rely on more indirect evidence. Alesina and Weder (1999) show that, unlike private FDI, there is no indication that most foreign aid organisations until then had systematically tried to avoid highly corrupt countries, which may not be so surprising since these countries on average are also among the world's poorest. Nevertheless, there is also, according to the World Bank and TI indexes, a wide variation in the corruption propensities and governance quality inside this group of countries.

One of the most hotly debated options is whether one may use the information in the governance indexes to systematically direct foreign aid away from the most corrupt and into the poor countries with better governance. In addition to the direct effects such a scheme may give, it may yield disincentives for behaving corruptly, giving politicians directing highly corrupt bureaucracies less resources for patronage. Following this line of approach, recent evidence has shown that even inside highly corrupt countries there are wide variations in the quality of the public sub-sectors (e.g. as documented for Bolivia in Manning, Mukherjee and Gokcekus 2000). Might not this information also be used in even more fine-grained aid allocation?

Rose-Ackerman (2004) touches upon this option at the end but, believing that the countries with the worst governance would then tend be isolated, probably sinking into even deeper poverty, she does not discuss it systematically. Svensson (2001) suggests a more careful application of the idea: to give programme and fungible forms of aid to countries with good results on governance indicators (and good macroeconomic policies), while limiting aid to poor-governance countries to non-fungible projects or projects implemented by well-working NGOs, but within the framework of a country plan drawn up by the aid giver. To some degree the allocation of foreign aid has recently been influenced by governance considerations, but to my knowledge no study of the effects of the policy shift on corruption has been made.

Rose-Ackerman's objections are reasonable, but since it is an option that goes to the core of the problem of corruption as a global challenge, I miss a more extensive discussion. The option deals, after all, directly with the transmission mechanism from the ideas for solving a major global economic or social challenge, to their possible implementation. It is also evident that if, let us say, 80 per cent of aid funds may reach its destination under a system of good governance but only 20 per cent with bad governance, very few projects will give any positive

---

[12] This list has already had an important impact on the bidding outcomes of other public organisations. The impending case of Acres International now being considered by the World Bank's sanction committee may become an exception and improve the credibility of the list (*Guardian*, 16 March 2004).

internal rate of returns (IRRs) in the last case, so to scrap projects up front may make good economic sense.

As pointed out in this context by Kaufmann and Kraay (2002), the margin of error of the government indexes is so large, that if aid could be given only to countries that are among the 50 per cent least corrupt (and at least in the best half among half of the other indicators (which is the so-called Millennium Challenge Account conditions)), only two of the seventy-four aid candidacy countries would be certain not to qualify and only eight would certainly do so.

If the errors in the sub-indexes are correlated, the confidence intervals would become even wider (Kaufmann, Kraay and Zoido-Lobaton 1999). I think we have good reason to believe that the indicators are likely to be influenced by country opinion fashions in the aid industry. It is striking that in 2002 countries such as Rwanda, India and Mozambique were among the eight aid-worthy countries.[13] For countries where there are observations from only one sub-index, the 90 per cent confidence interval is so wide that in most cases the outcome – to be aid-worthy or not – would almost be determined by pure chance. The same would naturally apply to the thirteen countries where data are completely missing. Hence, it is not possible to apply the policy in any rigorous manner.

Moreover, if any index were allowed to determine the aid given, all kinds of manipulation of the index, so well-known from the former Soviet system, are likely to be tried, undermining the information value of the index itself. This said, the indexes of country corruption combined with bits of less perception-based indicators represent an improvement on the purely anecdotal-based fashions which may otherwise rule the aid industry. Sometimes that fashion is so strong that it overrules the governance indicators. As pointed out by Cooksey

(1999), Uganda has been able to collect an unreasonable share of foreign aid by projecting a good governance image although being at least as corrupt as its neighbours according to several corruption indicators.

Among the reasons why there appear to be few, if any positive spillover effects from the low-corrupt administrations to the high-corrupt ones, is that some are deeply entrenched and difficult to do anything about. For example, a large number of informal feedbacks about the execution of a public project internal to a democratic country are likely to reach citizens and taxpayers. Some are collected by relevant pressure groups and put into effective use. No similar mechanisms exist with regard to foreign aid. While some multilateral organisations such as the World Bank try to compensate by having more professional evaluation procedures than the bilateral aid organisations, their projects are one step further away from the ultimate aid giver. The potential monitors of foreign aid such as NGOs and researchers will not have the capacity for informal monitoring that home-country projects are exposed to. Moreover, they usually receive their main support from the same organisations they may monitor. Here is, of course, some possibility of reform by financing monitoring differently. In particular cases, such as the Uganda school case, it may even be possible to stimulate pressure groups in the receiving country.

Some corruption-stimulating aspects of cross-country aid interactions are in principle easy to reform. As noted by Svensson (2001), the pressure on aid administrations to disburse loans and grants before the end of the year and the incentives for disbursing funds in both the bilateral and multilateral aid organisations are strong disincentives against strict monitoring and stimulate collusion with highly corrupt officials in poor countries.

In research on corruption in high-corruption countries, low administrative wages are often emphasised. That sometimes is a problem, but a neglected problem in the cross-country aid interactions is rather that wages for tasks performed for foreign aid agencies often are way above regular government pay. Two widely different price levels for the same good or service are well known to be a clear stimulant to corruption. Here, collusion

---

[13] As pointed out in Seligson (2003, 6) the decline in Argentina's status on the TI index from 5.2 in 1995 (the second best in Latin America) to the bottom half (2.8) in 2002, is remarkable. Such drastic change is difficult to explain, except through noting that Argentina in 1995 was considered very 'successful', while after the Financial Crisis of 2001–2 it was considered a 'failure' among experts, and probably also among the experts who judged its corruption rate.

among donor agencies may bring down expert wage levels closer to government levels and thereby reduce the level of rent-seeking and corruption in the aid agency–country official interactions.

So far, we have little information about the spillover from highly corrupt countries into aid agencies. Participating experts claim that the difference between the corruption propensities in the aid-giving and receiving countries persists in the aid interactions while corruption in multilateral organisations is somewhere in between (Cooksey 1999). If not for other reasons, to make the anti-corruption work initiated recently by many different aid agencies credible, more systematic information should be collected and published.

South–North Interactions: The Migration Pressure

Another major challenge – migration, in this case international migration – is also tied to the existence of two prices for the same service, labour performed in rich or poor countries (see chapter 8 in this volume). This situation is driving bribes in the opposite direction in the cross-country agency interactions; bribes are paid by citizens in poor countries to international agencies and formal organisations located in rich countries.

In TI (Kenya)'s first corruption survey (2002) 'Embassies and international organisations' were ranked as 10 among 52 public organisations taxing Kenyan households through bribes. In early 2002, the UN Office of Internal Oversight Services released a report (UNOIOS A/56/733) which showed that part of the UNHCR staff had colluded with large gangs in refugee camps in Kenya, taxing each successfully receiving refugee status for between US$2,000 and US$5,000. Local, international and foreign embassy organisations were involved.

Focusing on what might be done about global challenges, including corruption, the tools of cross-country agency interactions are clearly important. I have discussed and outlined a set of reforms based on Rose-Ackerman's suggestions. Alas, I believe that, so far, research-based analysis has not discovered any sufficiently strong instrument to really meet the challenge of corruption and bad governance.

References

Abbink, K., B. Irlenbusch and E. Renner, 2002: An experimental bribery game, *Journal of Law, Economics and Organization*, **18**(2), 428–54

Ades, A. and R. Di Tella, 1999: Rents, competition and corruption, *American Economic Review*, **89**, 982–93

Alesina, A. and B. Weder, 1999: Do corrupt governments receive less foreign aid?, NBER Working Paper, **7108**, Cambridge, MA

Andvig, J.C., 2002: Globalization, global and international corruption – any links?, *The globalization project, report no. 6*, Norwegian Ministry of Foreign Affairs, February

Bikhchandani, S., D. Hirshleifer and I. Welch, 1992: A theory of fads, custom and cultural change as informational cascades, *Journal of Political Economy*, **100**(5), 992–1026

Cábelková, I., 2001: Perceptions of corruption in Ukraine: are they correct?, CERGE-EI Working Paper, **176**

Cooksey, B., 1999: Do aid organizations have comparative advantage in fighting corruption in Africa?, Paper delivered at the 9th International Anti-Corruption Conference, 10–15 October, Durban

Hellman, J. S., G. Jones and D. Kaufmann, 2002: Far from home: do foreign investors import higher standards of governance in transition economies?, World Bank Institute, August

Hellman, J. S., G. Jones, D. Kaufmann and M. Schankerman, 2000: Measuring Governance, corruption and state capture, World Bank Policy Research Paper, 2312, April

Huther, J. and A. Shah, 2000: Anti-corruption policies and programmes: a framework for evaluation, World Bank Policy Research Working Paper, **2501**, December

Karpoff, J. M. and J. R. Lott, 1995: The reputational penalty firms bear from committing criminal fraud, in G. Fiorentini and S. Peltzman (eds.), *The Economics of Organised Crime*, Cambridge University Press, Cambridge, 199–250

Kaufmann, D., 2003: Rethinking governance: empirical lessons challenge orthodoxy, Discussion Draft, World Bank, Washington, DC, 11 March

Kaufmann, D. and A. Kraay, 2002: Governance indicators, aid allocation and the Millennium Challenge Account, World Bank Institute, December, draft

Kaufmann, D., A. Kraay and P. Zoido-Lobaton, 1999: Aggregating governance indicators, World Bank Policy Research Paper, **2195**, October

Lambsdorff, J. G., 2003: Framework document 2003, Transparency International, September

Manning, N., R. Mukherjee and O. Gokcekus, 2000: The experience of public officials in Bolivia, World Bank (unpublished 2nd draft), May

Mauro, P., 1995: Corruption and growth, *Quarterly Journal of Economics*, **110**(2), 681– 712

Myrdal, G., 1968: *Asian drama*, vol. II, Pantheon, New York

PriceWaterhouseCoopers, 2001: European economic crime survey

Reinikka, R. and J. Svensson, 2004: Local capture: evidence from a central government transfer program in Uganda, *Quarterly Journal of Economics*, **119**(2),

Rose-Ackerman, S., 1978: *Corruption: a study in political economy*, Academic Press, New York

2004: Governance and corruption, chapter 6 in this volume

Seligson, M. A., 2002: The impact of corruption on regime legitimacy: a comparative study of four Latin American countries, *Journal of Politics*, **64**(3), 408–33

2003: Corruption and democratisation in Latin America, University of Pittsburgh Latin American Public Opinion Project, Department of Political Science

Svensson, J., 2001: Bistånd: Fungerar det? Kan det fungera (Foreign aid: does it work? May it ever?), Report, May; available at www.iies.su.se/~svenssoj/

Treisman, D., 2002: Postcommunist corruption, Department of Political Science, UCLA, May

TI (Kenya), 2002: The Kenya urban bribery index

UN-OIOS, 2002: Report(A/56/733) on investigation into UNHCR branch office, Nairobi, January

Perspective Paper 6.2

JEAN CARTIER-BRESSON

Susan Rose-Ackerman's chapter 6 perfectly charts the current state of the literature in economics on corruption and governance in countries undergoing development or transition. It deals less with the issue of corruption in market democracies. The chapter responds to three traditional questions: (1) What are the causes of corruption? (2) What are its consequences? (3) What are the available means for an efficient and credible campaign against this very old and universal phenomenon? A fourth question has emerged out of the framework of the Copenhagen Consensus: (4) What are the stakes of the fight against corruption for the other challenges considered by the conference?

To a large extent, we share Rose-Ackerman's approach, as summarised in the following four points:

- Institutionalised corruption is a symptom of a *dysfunctional state* that must be understood within a larger conceptual framework than that of poor governance. In effect, this concept enables a broadening of the subject by integrating problematics concerning: (a) the nature of the political regime, (b) the processes of the exercise of power and of exchanges between the public and private spheres, (c) the capacity of governments to prepare, formulate and administratively implement social and economic policy (World Bank 1997). This approach is clearly institutional and proposes reforms enabling state-(re)building (Abed and Davoodi 2002).
- It is impossible to propose a *global, empirical cost-benefit analysis* (CBA) for at least two reasons. First, the illegal nature of the transactions (corruption) or acts (misappropriation of funds, extortion), as well as the character of the actors concerned (mainly elites in the case of high-

stakes corruption), seriously limits access to the kind of hard data needed to determine the direct costs of specific phenomena (the sums in question) and their subsequent distortions; without such data, it is impossible to ascertain the marginal benefits of a reduction in such phenomena. What was the contribution of poor governance or exchange rate policy to the Asian Financial Crisis? Was a small bribe paid to inspectors the cause of the Chernobyl disaster? Moreover, in regard to the second part of the calculation, the widely shared hypothesis that the battle against corruption involves a multi-pronged approach (World Bank 2000a, 154) precludes any rigorous accounting of the very diverse costs involved in the improvement of governance. What is the cost of implementing deregulation, democratisation, and efficiency wage within an administration? In the case of a state reform agenda, or even one of political regime change, one encounters the problem of imputing costs related to a wide range of objectives. Secondly, it is necessary to take into account the distortions that lead to these forced transfers which, in turn, encourage agents to adapt (flight to the informal sector, brain drain, disappearance of innovative entrepreneurs) and it is impossible to stick to the traditional rent-seeking approach focused on the waste of time and money.
- Methodologically, Rose-Ackerman (1999, 3–4) remains sceptical on the pertinence of using *cross-country research* for overcoming problems of data. She privileges, instead, 'bottom-up' analyses and case studies.
- Theoretical and empirical analyses of the causes and consequences of, as well as the means of fighting against, corruption have reached a certain level of maturity. The functionalist currents,

which viewed corruption as a system that lubricates the cogs of the bureaucratic machine, have disappeared. Economists have reached a consensus on the very negative effects of the phenomenon and on its primary importance for a number of development projects (namely, the challenges elaborated in this conference). Unfortunately, this maturity has still not paved the way for a meaningful advance in the *improvement of governance*, for the political barriers erected by the losers of such reforms are formidable.

Despite these points of concurrence, chapter 6 tends to understate some significant areas of disagreement that continue to persist among economists on the causes of corruption and the means of combating it. These dissensions parallel two classic debates. The first opposes the partisans of state failures to those of market failures, the second opposes proponents of universalist policies to adherents of institutional compromises specific to each environment. While we share Rose-Ackerman's disappointment concerning both the lack of political will for waging the anti-corruption battle and the consequent lack of results, analysis of the obstacles to international coordination and of the national barriers to state reform is progressively becoming the new challenge. Our Perspective paper thus takes shape around two issues that are essential to the political feasibility of the battle at hand: (1) the obstacles to global governance, (2) the fragility of various models of institutional transition, as well as uncertainty as to their relative costs.

Good Governance: A Global Public Good

It seems important to review briefly the international origins of the agenda for good governance (Glynn, Korbrin and Naim 1997), its stakes and the actors that have promoted it. Until the 1990s, corruption was a taboo subject for international organisations and the vast majority of political and economic observers underestimated the ways in which the phenomenon undermined democratisation, competition, microeconomic and macroeco-

nomic policies and international exchanges. Four factors explain international mobilisation since 1995:

- Globalisation has forced the establishment of international norms guaranteeing the *security of transactions* for international firms
- The new role of the USA, which seeks to harmonise the *agreed-upon terms of competition* between American and either European or Japanese firms, the latter of whom are reputed to be the most corrupt
- The willingness of the World Bank and the IMF to *reconstruct political institutions* capable of applying structural adjustment policies (SAPs), and improving the productivity of their loans in order to prevent international aid donors from becoming discouraged
- The *end of the Cold War and the triumph of the Western model* have led to both the reduction of aid resource allocation based on geopolitical considerations and the universal affirmation of the market democracy model.

The fight against corruption is thus a question on the agenda of global governance, insofar as: (1) The central issue is the stability and security of international economic transactions (trade and direct foreign investments) and the risks arising from the spread of problems are systemic; (2) It involves a common structure for negotiation, decision making and policy implementation. The fight against corruption can thus be defined as a public imperfectly global good (see Kaul, Grunberg and Stern 1999) that poses the typical problems of collective action (free-rider and prisoner's dilemma). It is imperfectly global since, while it tends to be universal over the long term, it creates winners and losers in the short term: countries, politico-economic regimes, generations and social groups. If the international process is geared towards the harmonisation of norms for the benefit of all concerned, in reality, the reformers (see below for further explanation of the importance of this concept) of the less powerful countries in the field of international relations have the feeling that international cooperation is inequitable and tends only to reinforce the power of the wealthier countries. These reformers usually complain that the wealthier countries continue to defend their own national self-interest. Therefore, within the sectors symbolizing international corruption structured by multinational firms (arms, oil, aerospace, public works, etc.), two constants prevail. To begin with, multinational firms, always linked to a particular country, have not concretely demonstrated a strong willingness to leave behind a system that still seems to serve them well. They seek primarily to maintain their traditional clientele (even through illegal payments). Moreover, the governments of the 'North' continue to support their 'strategic' firms with all the resources at their disposal (diplomacy, restrictive standards, informally conditional forms of aid). In actuality, these governments continue to tolerate international and national corruption, failing to set an example of sound governance and have been reluctant to undertake diagnostic studies on international and national corruption, as developing countries have done. Even if they have little scientific reliability, the appearance over the past few years of indices ranking the most corrupt countries (TI 2001) has at least managed to open the debate on the culpability of developing countries in major international corruption. In the same sense, the corporate accounting and stock market scandals of the 1990s reoriented perceptions of unethical behaviour and the costs of these fraud cases towards developed countries. These fraudulent acts are always accompanied by corruption – or, at the least, exchanges of favours to advance shadowy lobbying practices. On this point, the agenda intersects with that of corporate governance.

The questions of international political economy are thus: (1) Who profits from international anti-corruption conventions? (2) Given that their application brings about an improvement in local governance, who should finance these programmes? (3) Who negotiates the options and controls their implementation?

A CBA at the international level is thus indispensable. Cross-country analyses, we should also note, also run the risk of giving a distorted image. The wealthy, democratic countries facing lower costs in terms of investment and growth would thus have little motivation to finance this fight. On the other hand, in adopting a broader but less rigorous perspective, it is easy to see how the collapse of states and widespread poor governance pose risks for the functioning of the world economy.

International cooperation requires the effectiveness of strategies of *reciprocity*. The key to success rests in the exchange of reliable information making it possible to foresee the concrete effects of this cooperation. In developing countries, despite a display of enthusiasm for new governance, the reality is completely different for socio-political reasons. Whether they are dictators – kleptocratic or well-intentioned – or reformers, the leaders in these countries achieve their power through clientelist relations that tend to be arbitrary. The fight against corruption and poor governance is thus either in conflict with their mode of domination or very risky. Perhaps most alarming is the fact that the actors comprising this movement are few and that hidden agendas are always present (the fight against corruption as a means for eliminating competitors, for example). It is for this reason that Rose-Ackerman favours prevention (reform) over repression. The withdrawal of international organisations and NGOs supporting this cause, however, would diminish any chance of progress. In effect, the governments of the 'South' have not yet been convinced that they will receive an equal share of the fruits of cooperation. In the absence of any guarantee of the assistance required for state reform, the fight against corruption will remain political suicide (Klitgaard 1988).

As Rose-Ackerman argues (pp. 335–6), the jurisdictional deficit tends to diminish (for example, due to the proliferation of conventions), but deficits in participation and motivation remain very important since moral and economic arguments do not carry much weight in the field of politics. The impact of such arguments is all the more weak since the system of power legitimation is not primarily based on the performance of and respect for the law (as in the case of a non-democratic regime). These arguments are further weakened in regimes undergoing democratic transition, when results are deteriorating in the initial period following reforms, before

they have the chance to make a turnaround. For example, it is, unfortunately, possible that the application of the OECD Convention could, by limiting
corruption in international contracts, have effects
quite contradictory to those intended. The reduction of illegal rents paid by multinational firms
to the leaders of developing countries may diminish the clientelist redistribution that these leaders
engage in, without the official system necessarily
being capable of replacing them. The cunning of
reason could, then, bring about a moralisation of
international flows, but also a deterioration of living conditions for the most vulnerable populations
linked to clientelism and, ultimately, to a situation
of political instability that would limit the possibility of future growth.

When dealing with non-democratic regimes, *ex
ante* conditionality (aid in exchange for governance
reforms) remains a possibility, even though, as
Rose-Ackerman reminds us, the poorest countries,
and especially the marginalised people within those
countries, will bear the burden of it. For countries
experiencing a process of democratisation, reformers must be able to draw clear-cut advantages from
international cooperation to show their electorates.
What is more, they must be able to demonstrate
that the results constitute new conditions of fairness and that their point of view, which most often diverges from that of the major powers, was
heard and taken into account in the final compromise. Indeed, only national governments themselves are up to the task of finding solutions adapted
to a range of environments. From our perspective,
the inability of international organisations to consider the feasibility of reform constitutes the first
obstacle to this governance agenda. There can be
no improvement of national governance without
an improvement in global governance, more sensitive to the diversity of internal political processes.
One final remark must be made. We must stop the
strategic and diplomatic use of governance norms
(for instance, the arbitrary designation of rogue
states) or else the programme risks losing its ethical
dimension.

In conclusion, the collective mobilisation of international NGOs and institutions gave rise to the
good governance agenda. The local relays, however, are still fragile. In order to strengthen these
local relays, global governance must prove that it
serves the interests of developing countries, and the
model of local governance must be adapted and
made credible. The cost of this evolution (or the
benefit, depending on one's point of view) is the
development of a new balance in favour of developing countries.

The State, Social Capital and the Costs of Institutional Transition

If international institutions understand that improving governance entails improving world governance (fairer negotiations), they are often unaware that their proposed governance agenda would
amount to political suicide for many ruling governments. An underestimation of the stability of
clientelism and the potential costs of transition
to market democracy (the cost of disillusionment
for Rose-Ackerman) detracts from the credibility of the current discourse. Besides, the governance programme gives a restrictive definition and
a very specific view, of state-(re)building, which
is not necessarily adapted to fragile institutional
environments and situations of acute distributive
conflicts.

There has been an excessive use of cross-country
analysis to demonstrate the negative effects of corruption and the need to undertake reforms which
would address its causes. The method was to present
the results of dozens of studies (World Bank 2000b,
103–9) in the form of lists. This aggregative method
did not reflect divergences in the microeconomic
basis of the studies, the discrepancies between their
results and, finally, the persistent disagreements
over recommended policies.

For instance, some of the studies suggest that
protectionist and certain industrial policies favour
the creation of rents and therefore rent-seeking and
hence corruption, whereas others demonstrate that
structural adjustment policies are faulty. The decrease in civil service salaries, the rise of inequalities, the degradation of social services, as well as
the opening to international competition, the reduction of industrial policies and privatisation are

seen as encouraging the agents' adaptation to the new constraints through corruption. Trade liberalisation, in itself, is not seen as having reduced corruption, but as having fostered growth. In the cases where openness reduced performance, corruption often increased. In this sense, Harris-White and White (1996) have demonstrated how, in many countries, democratisation and liberalisation have led to more disorganised and destructive forms of corruption, according to the Shleifer and Vishny typology (1993). There is, thus, an older corruption (issuing from rents) and a new form of corruption (stemming from liberalisation), which unfortunately often coexist (Cartier-Bresson 1998). It is, therefore, necessary to determine, on a case-by-case basis, the credibility of the recommendations for fighting corruption in light of the institutional context, and to verify whether the necessary conditions are present to enable an improvement in governance, in the short term, through democratisation and liberalisation. In general, the answer depends primarily on the *objectives* of elites and the *norms* that structure their negotiations. Since redistributive conflicts figure prominently in the stakes of governance and since the evolution of these conflicts has potentially dramatic consequences for certain vulnerable segments of the population, political economic analyses are essential. As in the literature on conflicts and civil wars, the contributions of sociology, history and political science must be addressed and confronted (Andvig *et al.* 2000; Cartier-Bresson 1992), as the necessary complements to economic formalisation.

The ruling political regimes in many developing countries articulate, to varying degrees, forms of neo-patrimonialism and clientelism. Order is based on personalised transactions, the overlapping of both public and private spheres and formal and informal positions. Strategies for accumulation of economic and political resources are conjoined and, according to some political scientists, this is unavoidable over the medium term (Hibou 1999). The scope of analysis should not be limited to studies of bribery, but rather should extend to the networks of clientelist redistribution (Wade 1985; Cartier-Bresson 1997) with their multiple resources

(bribes, patronage, favours, public service employment, ballots, rents). Poor governance is therefore a form of government that rests on *micro legitimacies*, and the stability of the system could significantly increase economic performance, if the dictator maximises his utility function over over the long rather than the short term (plunder). This explains why so many studies have recorded a negative correlation between democratisation and growth. There are, roughly, two models of market democracy transition that continue to coexist: public choice and neo-institutionalism (Cartier-Bresson 2000).

According to Public Choice theory, political powers trade rents to pressure groups in exchange for political support. The classic typology distinguishes between: (a) autonomous states (guardian or predator) who, because they are deeply rooted, can pursue their objectives without being subjected to pressure from an opposition and (b) factional states (democratic or authoritarian) which must, in order to make decisions, engage in collective processes with pressure groups. The latter's decisions are constrained by the need to satisfy the demands of its supporters according to an Olsonian logic. The democratic faction state limits predation, but often leads to state paralysis. According to this logic, in countries where the private sector is too weak to counterbalance the state, only an autonomous state of technocrats can 'force' the implementation of shock therapy (like that of an anti-corruption fight). This hypothesis holds that shock therapy (the liberalisation of all markets at once) is the only means to avoid triggering the perverse collateral effects linked to the liberalisation of only a single market. Its application entails either rapid growth and more or less immediate adherence (an unlikely scenario), or a situation in which the short-term costs (decreased growth, increased taxes and decreased subsidies) do not compensate for future uncertain benefits (growth and employment). In the latter case, social resistance will block the implementation of further reforms. This hypothesis lends relative support to certain kinds of pro-market dictatorships and sees all democratisation as accentuating the power of factions. The solution is a strong and autonomous political regime and the drastic reduction of state intervention in the economy.

The main limitation of the rent-seeking approach is that the results of exchanges between the political and economic spheres vary considerably, depending on public policies that are: (a) only the outcome of the influence of powerful pressure groups; (b) the outcome of state power alone; or, finally, (c) the outcome of an interaction between these two components combined with their multiple sub-components (Meier 1991). If rents have not had a negative effect in Korea, as compared with Pakistan, it is because the political-economic networks that managed the transfers in Korea possessed a kind of legitimacy in a minimally polarised society, the rents were offered to capitalist sectors and the state was powerful and autonomous enough to demand efficiency (Khan 1998). The objectives of elites and mediators, then, become a determining factor, and it becomes counterproductive not to take into account the diversity of exchanged resources and their more or less contradictory effects in the joint construction of the state and the economy. As Bardhan (1997) has remarked, the mistake of studies of rent-seeking and the predatory state is that they do not explain the differences in *levels of corruption* between similar countries, and why identical levels of corruption allow for different levels of performance. Some African states have become predatory after being weakened, whereas strong states in East Asia with interventionist policies and networks mixing private and public sectors have not prevented administrations from functioning relatively efficiently. This finding calls for an explanation of how social order and trust (resolution of the Hobbesian conflict) can emerge in countries with no democratic traditions and where Weberian norms are not rooted. In any case, it is necessary to make exchanges between political and economic powers (since it is indeed power we are dealing with) more efficient (virtuous?) and not to stigmatise them in a model that axiomatically reduces the effectiveness of the political sphere. In many countries, the reduction of rents will not result in a spontaneous emergence of innovative entrepreneurs, and state intervention in the productive system will remain necessary.

According to the neo-institutional analysis of governance (Coase and Williamson), the state is both the problem and the solution. The state is too big for small problems and too small for big ones. Thus decentralisation, regional integration and private ordering offer means to circumvent the bureaucratic state through tripartite negotiations (state, NGO and private sector). At the international and regional levels, one must add to this framework international organisations and 'soft' law procedures. This strategy, which requires the adhesion of all parties, can only be incremental. The legal system (to be reformed first and foremost) must provide guarantees for the execution of contracts, including those coming from private negotiations and which involve compensatory transactions. Increasing social capital (for instance, through peer pressure) reduces transaction costs and improves the efficiency of the system. The feasibility of such a scenario requires a civil society mature enough to not highjack the network coordination of negotiations for the purposes of fraud and corruption. The potential dangers are similar to those of decentralisation. This post-Weberian logic requires an institutional architecture few developing countries possess. Furthermore, for the transaction costs of negotiations to be low and, thus, for consensus to be quick, one would need an understanding, which does not exist, of the redistributive effects of political choices. The social polarisation of developing countries does not favour the success of the governance scenario, since it has not yet been demonstrated that Coasian negotiation can be applied to political stakes while respecting the ability of the weakest parties.

Therefore, it seems to me that public choice offers an analysis of political conflict without a sufficiently refined institutional framework, and that the neo-institutionalists offer an institutional framework without politics. The improvement of 'governance' (state-building) nonetheless requires maintaining these two dimensions simultaneously.

Conclusion

The five alternatives proposed by Rose-Ackerman in chapter 6 seem to me to move in the right direction. They are well chosen, necessary and economically – or 'technically' – credible. However, their political feasibility is uncertain, the short-term secondary social effects are very ambiguous in the absence of a significant increase (that is not misappropriated!) of international aid and the right timing is difficult to determine. The pessimistic tone of this chapter on the feasibility and credibility of policies aiming at the improvement of governance should not cause us to overlook the fact that the stakes are as big as the challenge at hand. Indeed, the state often remains both the problem and the solution, and the difficulties involved in its reform are both political and financial. If rigorous, global CBAs are impossible, it is still essential to continue to quantify – sector by sector – the potential costs and benefits of the reforms to be implemented, and to evaluate the initial results of implemented policies. The diagnostic inquiries being undertaken by the World Bank move in this direction (World Bank 2000b), but must now be used as the basis for local discussions on state reform.

The funding of democratisation (of which no evaluation currently exists to my knowledge), will have to pave the way for an improvement in public services sufficient to making clientelist relations less attractive or necessary. It is only under such conditions that the power and legitimation of reformers will no longer come simply from their words (charisma), but will result from concrete transformations in the relationship between society and the state. This relationship will finally offer a certain security to citizens in exchange for their confidence and their loyalty to the new rules. We are currently in a period of experimentation, and only over the medium term will the empirical evidence become available to distinguish the good from the bad economic recipes.

References

Abed, G. T. and H. R. Davoodi, 2002: Corruption, structural reforms, and economic performance in the transition economies, in G. T. Abed and S. Gupta (eds.), *Governance, corruption and economic performance*, IMF, Washington, DC, 489–537

Andvig, J. C., O.-H. Fjeldstad, I. Amundsen, T. Sissener and T. Soreide, 2000: *Research on corruption: a policy oriented survey*, Chr. Michelsen Institute & Norwegian Institute of Internal Affairs, Oslo

Bardhan, P., 1997: Corruption and development: a review of issues, *Journal of Economic Literature*, **35**, 1320–46

Cartier-Bresson, J., 1992: Eléments d'analyse pour une économie de la corruption, *Revue Tiers Monde*, **131**, 581–609

1997, Corruption network, transaction security and illegal social exchange, *Political Studies*, **45**(3), 463–76

1998: Présentation and Les analyses économiques des causes et des consequences de la corruption: quelques enseignements pour les PED, *Mondes en Développement*, **102**, 9–11, 25–40

2000: Corruption, libéralisation et democratization and La Banque mondiale, la corruption et la gouvernance, *Revue Tiers Monde*, **161**, 9–22, 165–92

Glynn, P., S. J. Korbrin and M. Naim, 1997: The globalization of corruption in K. A. Elliott (ed.), *Corruption and the global economy*, Institute for International Economics, Washington, DC, 7–27

Harris-White, B. and G. White, 1996: Corruption, liberalization and democracy: editorial introduction, *IDS Bulletin*, **27**(2), 1–5

Hibou, B., 1999: *La privatization des états*, CERI, Karthala

Kaul, I., I. Grunberg and M.A. Stern, 1999: *Global public goods, international cooperation in the 21st century*, UNDP and Oxford University Press, Oxford

Khan, M., 1998: Patron–client networks and economic effects of corruption in Asia, in M. Robinson, Corruption and Development, *European Journal of Development Research*, **10**(1), 15–39

Klitgaard, R., 1988: International cooperation against corruption, *Finance & Development*, **35**(1), IMF, Washington, DC, 3–6

Meier, G. M., 1991: *Politics and policy making in developing countries*, International Centre for Economic Growth, ICS Press,

Rose-Ackerman, S., 1999, *Corruption and government: causes, consequences and reform*, Cambridge University Press, Cambridge

Shleifer, A. and R. Vishny, 1993: Corruption, *Quarterly Journal of Economics*, **108**, 599–617

Transparency International (TI), 2001: 1999 Bribe Payers Index, in *Global Corruption Report*, Berlin, 237–9

Wade, R., 1985: Market for public office. Why the Indian state is not better at development, *World Development*, **13**(4), 467–97

World Bank, 1997: *The state in a changing world*, World Development Report, Washington, DC

2000a: *The quality of growth*, Oxford University Press, Oxford

2000b: *Helping countries combat corruption. Progress at the World Bank since 1997*, PREM Network, Washington, DC

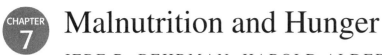

Malnutrition and Hunger

JERE R. BEHRMAN, HAROLD ALDERMAN
AND JOHN HODDINOTT

Introduction: The Challenge of Malnutrition and Hunger

While episodes of severe hunger such as famines receive considerable press coverage and attract much public attention, chronic hunger and malnutrition is considerably more prevalent in developing countries. It is estimated that at least 12 m low-birth-weight (LBW) births occur per year and that around 162 million pre-school children and almost a billion people of all ages are malnourished. In poorly nourished populations, reductions in hunger and improved nutrition convey considerable productivity gains as well as saving resources that would otherwise be used for the care of malnourished people who are more susceptible to infectious diseases and premature mortality. While reducing hunger and malnutrition is often justified on intrinsic grounds, it is these potential gains in productivity and reductions in economic costs that provide the focus of our challenge paper.[1]

Poverty, hunger and malnutrition are linked. Strauss and Thomas (1995, 1998) and Hoddinott, Skoufias and Washburn (2000) document the empirical literature relating dimensions of access and intakes of calories to household consumption levels. A reasonable reading of these studies suggests an income–calorie elasticity of around 0.2–0.3, though careful studies have also found estimates both higher and lower than this range. Behrman and Rosenzweig (2004) report that cross-country variation in GDP per worker in PPP terms is inversely related to the percentage of LBW (< 2.5 kg) births among all births and is consistent with almost half of the variation in the percentage of births that are LBW across countries.[2] Haddad, *et al.* (2003) estimate that the cross-country elasticity of pre-school

underweight rates with respect to *per capita* income for 1980–96 is -0.5, virtually the same as the mean for the elasticity from twelve household datasets. These relationships have two important implications: that nutritional objectives such as the Millennium Development Goal (MDG) of halving the prevalence of underweight children by 2015 are unlikely to be met through income growth alone[3] and that successful efforts to reduce most forms of malnutrition are likely to have incidences of benefits concentrated relatively among the poor. These implications, in part, motivate our choice of the

The authors thank Simon Appleton, Henrik Jacob Meyer, Peter Svedberg and other commentators for their reactions and suggestions.

[1] We understand the focus of the Copenhagen Consensus to be on productivity gains from intervention. In his Perspective paper 7.2, however, Appleton (2004) suggests that we underestimate the returns from the interventions considered in this chapter in part because we do not include the gains in the form of (a) intrinsic health and nutrition or (b) use distributional weights. But with regard to (a) we do include the resources saved from dealing with morbidity if nutrition were better, which presumably reflects the value that people and societies place on intrinsic health and nutrition. And with regard to (b), as we note, the types of hunger and malnutrition on which we focus are primarily experienced by the poor.

[2] Their estimates suggest, however, that only a small part of this association between LBW and GDP *per capita* is due to the causal effects of LBW on productivity.

[3] Svedberg (2004), in his Perspective paper 7.1, reports inverse associations between real *per capita* income and child stunting and wasting that is consistent with about half of the variance in aggregated data for forty-eight countries in 1988–92 and sixty-seven countries for 1998–2002. He emphasises the important role of income growth in improving child nutrition, but expresses doubt that income growth alone will lead to achievement of the MDG on nutrition.

following opportunities:

- Opportunity 1 – Reducing the prevalence of low birth weight
- Opportunity 2 – Infant and child nutrition and exclusive breastfeeding promotion
- Opportunity 3 – Reducing the prevalence of iron deficiency anaemia and Vitamin A, iodine and zinc deficiencies
- Opportunity 4 – Investment in technology in developing country agriculture.

We begin in the next section by setting the stage, discussing the nature and measurement of hunger and malnutrition, the current levels and trends in the geographical distribution among developing countries of some important types of hunger and the nature of the benefits from reduced malnutrition in terms of both productivity and of direct resource use. This is essential to avoid repetition because many of the measurement issues, including those pertaining to impacts of improved nutrition over the life cycle, are somewhat parallel among the various challenges and opportunities. The next section outlines a general framework for considering these opportunities. For each opportunity, we discuss: (1) the definition and description of the opportunity, (2) how this opportunity partially solves the challenge and (3) economic estimates of the benefits and costs and how they relate to distributional and efficiency motives for policies. Our conclusion summarises these opportunities, noting that there are potentially considerable gains in the sense of estimated benefit-cost ratios (BCRs) exceeding one or relatively high internal rates of return (IRRs) to investing in some programmes or policies to reduce hunger and malnutrition, particularly those directed towards increasing micronutrients in populations with high prevalences of micronutrient deficiencies – in addition to the intrinsic welfare gains to the individuals who would be affected directly by reduced hunger and malnutrition. Such investments may be relatively easily justified on anti-poverty grounds, because the poor tend to be relatively malnourished. There also are some plausible efficiency grounds for such interventions due to the role that malnourishment plays, for example, in the spread of contagious diseases, but the available estimates do not permit very satisfactory iden-

tification of social versus private rates of return, as would be required to assess the efficiency motive for subsidies.

Essential Background to the Challenge and Opportunity of Hunger and Malnutrition: Nature and Measurement, Geographical Distribution and Potential Benefits

This section provides background material for understanding the opportunities in the following section. It discusses the nature and measurement of hunger and malnutrition, current levels and trends in the geographical distribution of dimensions of hunger and malnutrition and the nature of the benefits from reduced hunger and malnutrition, which are similar over the lifecycle for several of the opportunities.

The Nature and Measurement of Hunger and Malnutrition

Both hunger and malnutrition reflect the interaction of purposive actions of individuals given preferences and constraints together with biological processes. In behavioural models, an individual's nutritional status often is treated as an argument in the welfare function of individuals or the households in which they reside (Behrman and Deolalikar 1988; Strauss and Thomas 1995), a reflection of the intrinsic value placed on nutritional status. Typically, welfare is assumed to increase as nutritional status improves, but possibly at a diminishing rate, and increases in certain measures of nutritional status, such as body mass, may be associated with reductions in welfare beyond a certain point. In allocating resources, household decision makers take into account the extent to which these investments will make both their children and themselves better off in the future as well as currently. These allocations are constrained in several ways. There are resource constraints reflecting income (itself an outcome because nutritional status can affect productivity) and time available as well as prices faced by households. There is also a constraint arising from the production process for health outcomes, including nutritional status. This constraint links nutrient intakes – the physical consumption of macronutrients (calories and protein) and micronutrients (minerals and vitamins) – as well as time devoted to the production of health and nutrition, the individual's genetic make-up and knowledge and skill regarding the combination of these inputs to produce nutritional status. There are interdependencies in the production of nutritional status and other dimensions of health; for example, malaria limits haemoglobin formation.

But while hunger and malnutrition are manifestations of such actions given preferences, constraints and biological processes, they are not synonymous.

Hunger

Hunger can be defined as 'A condition, in which people lack the basic food intake to provide them with the energy and nutrients for fully productive lives' (Hunger Task Force, 2003, 33). It is measured in terms of availability, access or intake of calories relative to requirements that vary principally by age, sex and activities. Table 7.1 describes measures of hunger important to this chapter.

The most widely cited data on the number of persons considered hungry come from the UN Food and Agriculture Organisation (FAO). On an ongoing basis, FAO constructs estimates of mean *per capita* dietary energy supply (production + stocks – post-harvest losses + commercial imports + food aid – exports). Assumptions regarding the distribution of this supply are made based on data on income distribution, the distribution of consumption or, in some cases inferences based on infant mortality (Naiken 2003). The constructed distribution is compared against minimum *per capita* energy requirements (Weisell 2002) and, from this, the proportion of persons whose access to food is below these requirements is estimated. FAO calls this the 'prevalence of undernourishment'.

Criticisms of this approach are widespread. First, there are serious concerns about the quality of the underlying data on food supply (Devereux and Hoddinott 1999). Second, the absence of good data on the distribution of food consumption means that estimates of the prevalence of hunger are highly sensitive to changes in the shape of the distribution around the minimum requirements threshold.

Third, Aduayom and Smith (2003) show that in many cases the FAO approach significantly understates hunger prevalence when compared to those derived from household consumption surveys.

Despite these valid concerns, the FAO approach provides the only data available on a global basis over a relatively long time period. FAO (2003) estimates that over the 1990s, the number of people undernourished in the developing world declined slightly from 816 to 798 m, while population increased from 4,050 to 4,712 m persons. Overall, the proportion of persons undernourished fell from 20 to 17 per cent between 1990–2 and 1999–2001. The hungry are found predominantly in Asia and the Pacific (505 m) and secondarily in sub-Saharan Africa (SSA) (198 m); these two regions account for nearly 90 per cent of the world's hungry. However, these two regions exhibit different trends. In Asia, both the number and prevalence of undernourishment fell during the 1990s. The fall in the number of undernourished is almost entirely attributable to a fall in the number of undernourished in China; elsewhere, the number of undernourished stayed relatively constant while population grew, leading to a decline in prevalences. In Africa, the number of malnourished increased with prevalences rising in some countries and falling in others. Despite these shifts, in the near future over twice as many of the hungry will be in Asia than in Africa. The distribution of the hungry *within* countries and by socio-economic groups is even less well documented. Preliminary work by the Hunger Task Force (2003, p. 27) suggests that on a *global* basis:

• Approximately 50 per cent of the hungry are in farm households, mainly in higher-risk production environments
• Approximately 22 per cent are the rural landless, mainly in higher-potential agricultural regions
• Approximately 20 per cent are urban
• Approximately 8 per cent are directly resource-dependent (i.e. pastoralists, fishers, forest-based).

Malnutrition

Nutrients provided by food combine with other factors, including the health state of the person consuming the food, to produce 'nutritional

Table 7.1. Measures of Hunger and Malnutrition

Indicator	Interpretation	Most common means of reporting
1 Measures of hunger		
Proportion of undernourished persons in a population	An indicator of inadequate food availability, access or intake; reducing this is an MDG indicator	% of individuals with food availability, access or intake of food below some threshold
2 Anthropometric measures of malnutrition		
Prevalence of LBW	An indicator of intrauterine growth retardation resulting from short maternal stature, poor maternal nutrition before or during pregnancy, infection and smoking	% of children with birth-weights below 2,500 gs

Prevalence of low height-for-age (stunting)	Children's skeletal (linear) growth compromised due to constraints to one or more of nutrition, health, or mother–infant interactions; this is an indicator of chronic nutritional deprivation	Expressed as a Z-score or as the % of individuals stunted
		    Z-scores are calculated by standardizing an individual's height-given-age and sex against an international standard of well nourished people[a]
		    Individuals with Z-scores below –2 are classified as stunted; with Z-scores below –3 are classified as severely stunted

Prevalence of low weight-for-height (wasting)	People suffer thinness resulting from energy deficit and/or disease-induced poor appetite, malabsorption, or loss of nutrients; this is an indicator of transitory nutritional deprivation	Expressed as a Z-score or as the % of individuals wasted
		    Z-scores are calculated by standardizing an individual's weight-given-height and sex against an international standard of well nourished individuals[a]
		    Individuals with Z-scores below –2 are classified as wasted; with Z-scores below –3 are classified as severely wasted

Prevalence of low weight-for-age (underweight)	This is a composite measure of nutritional status, reflecting both chronic and transitory nutritional deprivation. This is an MDG indicator	Expressed as a Z-score or as the % of individuals underweight
		    Z-scores are calculated by standardizing an individual's weight-given-age and sex against an international standard of well nourished individuals[a]
		    Individuals with Z-scores below –2 are classified as underweight; with Z-scores below –3 as severely underweight

Prevalence of low body mass index in adults or adolescents	Adults suffer thinness as a result of inadequate energy intake, an uncompensated increase in physical activity, or (severe) illness	Expressed as Body Mass Index (BMI) BMI is calculated by dividing weight in kgs by the height^2 in ms Individuals are considered to be chronically energy deficient if they have a BMI below 18.5, overweight if they have a BMI greater than 25 and obese if they have a BMI greater than 30

Table 7.1. (*cont.*)

Indicator	Interpretation	Most common means of reporting
	3 Measures of micronutrient deficiency	
Prevalence of iodine deficiency	Iodine deficiency results from low intake of iodine in the diet	Expressed by clinical inspection of enlarged thyroids or in terms of iodine concentrations in urine (μg/L) The benchmark for the elimination of iodine deficiency is to have less than 20% of the population with levels below 50 μg/L
Prevalence of low haemoglobin (anaemia) in pre-school, school-aged children, non-lactating or non-pregnant women	Children suffer from anaemia, either as a result of low iron intakes or poor absorption, or as a result of illness Severe protein-energy malnutrition and vitamin B12/folate deficiency can also lead to anaemia Women suffer from anaemia as a result of low iron intakes, poor absorption, illness, or excessive losses of blood Severe protein-energy malnutrition and vitamin B12/folate deficiency can also lead to anaemia Anaemia is rare in adult men except in cases of extreme iron-deficient diets	Expressed as gs of haemoglobin per litre of blood Cutoffs to define anaemia are 110 g/L for children aged 6–59 months, 115 g/L for children aged 5–11 years and 120 g/L for children aged 12–14 years Cutoffs to define anaemia are 120 g/L for non-pregnant women, 110 for pregnant women and 130 for adult men
Prevalence of vitamin A deficiency	Vitamin A deficiency results from low intake of animal products containing high amounts of absorbable retinal or plant products high in beta-carotene Diarrhoea, fevers and some infections can interfere with the absorption or Vitamin A or utilisation of retinal	Clinical deficiency is estimated by combining night blindness and eye changes – principally Bitot's spots to form a total xerophthalmia prevalence Sub-clinical deficiency is assessed as prevalence of serum retinal concentrations below 0.70 μmol/L.

Sources: **Gibson (1990); ACC/SCN (2000a); Allen and Gillespie (2001); Morris (2001); Hunger Task Force (2003); Alderman, Behrman and Hoddinott (2004).**
Note: [a] A *z*-score of −1 indicates that given age and sex, the person's characteristic (e.g. height, weight-for- height, weight) is 1 standard deviation below the median person in that age/sex group.

status'.[4] Indicators of nutritional status are measurements of body size, body composition, or body function, reflecting single or multiple nutrient deficiencies. Table 7.1 also summarises measures of nutritional status important to this chapter.

Many poor nutritional outcomes begin *in utero*. A number of maternal factors have been shown to be significant determinants of intrauterine growth retardation (IUGR), the characterisation of a newborn who does not attain their growth potential. Most important are mother's stature (reflecting her own poor nutritional status during childhood), her nutritional status prior to conception as measured by her weight and micronutrient status and her weight gain during pregnancy. Diarrhoea disease, intestinal parasites and respiratory infections may also lead to IUGR

and where endemic (such as in SSA), malaria is a major determinant. In developed countries, smoking is also a significant contributor to IUGR. IUGR is measured as the prevalence of newborns below the 10th percentile for weight given gestational age (ACC/SCN 2000b). Because gestational age is rarely known, IUGR is often proxied by LBW. As

---

[4] While food can relieve hunger through providing macronutrients such as calories and proteins and provide nutrients that lessen the forms of malnutrition characterised as 'undernutrition' with respect to the nutrients that the food provides, more food does not relieve all forms of malnutrition. Some forms of malnourishment are relieved by reducing calories (e.g. obesity), others by reducing debilitating health stresses such as parasites. Undernutrition with regard to macronutrients and micronutrients historically has been, and continues

of 2000, it is estimated that 16 per cent of newborns, or 11.7 m children have LBW (ACC/SCN 2000b, 2004).[5] LBW is especially prevalent in south Asia, where it is estimated that 30 per cent of children have birth-weights below 2,500 g (ACC/SCN 2004).

In pre-school and school-aged children, nutritional status is often assessed in terms of anthropometry. 'The basic principle of anthropometry is that prolonged or severe nutrient depletion eventually leads to retardation of linear (skeletal) growth in children and to loss of, or failure to accumulate, muscle mass and fat in both children and adults' (Morris 2001, 12). A particularly useful measure is height-for-age, as this reflects the cumulative impact of events affecting nutritional status that result in stunting. As of 2000, it is estimated that 162 m children – roughly one child in three – are stunted (ACC/SCN 2004). While stunting prevalences are highest in South Asia and SSA, in South Asia, numbers and prevalence have been declining since 1990 whereas in SSA, prevalence has remained largely unchanged and numbers have increased.

Multiple factors contribute to poor anthropometric status in children. One is LBW; a number of studies show a correlation between LBW and subsequent stature though, in the absence of any subsequent intervention, not between LBW and growth (Ashworth, Morris and Lira 1997; Hoddinott and Kinsey 2001; Ruel 2001; Li *et al.* 2003). Another is reduced breastfeeding. Indeed, the first two years of life pose numerous nutritional challenges. Growth rates are highest in infancy, thus adverse factors have a greater potential for causing retardation at this time. Younger children have higher nutritional requirements per kg of body weight and are also more susceptible to infections. They are also less able to make their needs known and are more vulnerable to the effects of poor care practices such as the failure to introduce safe weaning foods

to be, the dominant nutritional problem in developing countries, but other forms of malnutrition – in particular those that lead to obesity and diets heavy in fats – are an increasing public health concern. In middle-income countries such as Egypt, Mexico and South Africa, obesity levels among adults are rapidly growing, and in some cases the obese already exceed one-quarter of the population.

[5] Other estimates are higher. Ceesay *et al.* (1997) claim that there are over 22 m LBW children per year.

in adequate quantities. Evidence from numerous studies clearly indicates that the immediate causes of growth faltering are poor diets and infection (primarily gastrointestinal) and that these are interactive.

For these reasons, almost all the growth retardation observed in developing countries has its origins in the first two–three years of life (Martorell 1995). Indeed, our choice of opportunities is conditioned, in part, by the growing recognition that many nutritional outcomes are the consequence of cumulative lifecycle processes. Specifically, a growing body of evidence indicates that growth lost in early years is, at best, only partially regained during childhood and adolescence, particularly when children remain in poor environments (Martorell, Khan and Schroeder 1994). Martorell (1995, 1999), Martorell, Khan and Schroeder (1994) and Simondon *et al.* (1998) all find that stature at age three is strongly correlated with attained body size at adulthood in Guatemala and Senegal. Hoddinott and Kinsey (2001) and Alderman, Hoddinott and Kinsey (2003) find that children who were initially aged 12–24 months in the aftermath of droughts in rural Zimbabwe in 1994–5 and 1982–4, respectively were malnourished relative to comparable children not exposed to this drought. However, older children did not suffer such consequences; this is consistent with evidence that child development has 'sensitive' periods where development is more receptive to influence, and that during such periods some shocks may be reversible while others are not.

Further, severe malnutrition in early childhood often leads to deficits in cognitive development (Pollitt 1990; Grantham-McGregor, Fernald and Sethuraman 1999a). Though many studies from developed countries fail to show difference in developmental levels for children with LBW, there are few longitudinal studies from developing counties from which to generalise (Hack 1998). Moreover, recent studies indicate that the relationship between birth weight and cognitive function carries into the range of normal weights even in developed countries (Matte *et al.* 2001; Richards *et al.* 2001). Reduced breastfeeding – an effect of LBW as well as a common cause of childhood malnutrition – also has well-documented influences on cognitive development, even in developed countries (Grantham-McGregor, Fernald and Sethuraman 1999a). Malnourished children score more poorly on tests of cognitive function, have poorer psychomotor development and fine motor skills, have lower activity levels, interact less frequently in their environments and fail to acquire skills at normal rates (Lasky *et al.* 1981; Johnston *et al.* 1987; Grantham-McGregor *et al.* 1997; Grantham-McGregor, Fernald and Sethuraman 1999). Controlled experiments with animals suggest that malnutrition results in irreversible damage to brain development such as that associated with the insulation of neural fibres (Yaqub 2002). This is in keeping with the prevailing view that very young children are most vulnerable to impaired cognitive development.[6]

A further dimension of malnutrition is that of micronutrient deficiencies. Particularly important are deficiencies in iron, iodine, Vitamin A and zinc, all of which have both immediate and long-term consequences. Iodine deficiency adversely affects development of the central nervous system. A meta-analysis indicates that individuals with an iodine deficiency had, on average, 13.5 points lower IQs than comparison groups (Grantham-McGregor, Fernald and Sethuraman 1999b). ACC/SCN (2004) reports that globally approximately 2 bn people are affected by iodine deficiency, including 285 m children aged 6–12 years. Adequate iron intake is also necessary for brain development. More than 40 per cent of children aged 0–4 in developing countries suffer from anemia (ACC/SCN 2000a); further, anaemia in school-aged children may also affect schooling whether or not there had been earlier impaired brain development. Vitamin A deficiencies, which are estimated to affect 140 m pre-school children, are associated with increased risk of infant and child mortality (see below); zinc deficiencies may be a cause of slowed physical growth.

Undernutrition, particularly foetal undernutrition at critical periods, may result in permanent changes in body structure and metabolism. Even if there are not subsequent nutritional insults, these changes can lead to increased probabilities of chronic non-infectious diseases later in life. The hypothesis that foetal malnutrition has far-ranging consequences for adult health is bolstered by studies that track LBW infants into their adult years and document increased susceptibility to coronary heart disease, non-insulin-dependent diabetes, high blood pres-

sure, obstructive lung disease, high blood cholesterol and renal damage (Barker 1998). For example, while the various studies on the impact of the Dutch famine indicate few long-term consequences on young adults, more recent evidence shows that children whose mothers were starved in early pregnancy have higher rates of obesity and of heart disease as adults (Roseboom *et al.* 2001). In contrast, children of mothers deprived in later pregnancy – the group most likely to be of LBW – had a greater risk of diabetes (Ravelli, van der Meulen and Michels 1998).

The nutritional status of adults reflects in substantial part their nutritional experience since conception with, as noted, a number of possible long-run effects of early nutritional insults. But, in addition to such longer-run effects, there also may be important consequences of adult diets – for example, low energy or iron intakes or chronic diseases related to obesity, hypertension and high cholesterol.

Lastly, malnutrition may have long-term consequences through the intergenerational transmission of poor nutrition and anthropometric status. Recall that stature by age three is strongly correlated with attained body size at adulthood. Taller women experience fewer complications during childbirth, typically have children with higher birth weights and experience lower risks of child and maternal mortality (World Bank 1993; Ramakrishnan *et al.* 1999).[7]

The Nature of the Benefits from Reduced Malnutrition

We now turn to micro-evidence about productivity impacts of improved nutrition in developing

---

[6] One exception is provided by Glewwe and King (2001), who find that malnutrition in the second year of life had a larger impact on the IQs of Philippine school children than that in earlier periods. This may reflect the fact that risks increase with weaning.

[7] However, Behrman and Rosenzweig (2004) find that intergenerational birth weight effects are primarily genetic, not due to better nutrition in the womb, based on their analysis of identical twins in the USA. It is not clear whether this result generalises to developing countries because there may be important compensating investments for LBW in developed societies that are not common in developing countries (and that may be reflected, for example, in the evidence noted suggesting stronger effects on cognitive development in the latter).

countries – from conception through infancy and childhood and into adolescence and adulthood.[8] The many channels through which these gains may operate are grouped as follows: saving of resources that are currently directed to dealing with diseases and other problems related to malnutrition; direct gains arising from improvements in physical stature

and strength as well as improved micronutrient status; and indirect gains arising from links between nutritional status and schooling, nutritional status and cognitive development and subsequent links between schooling, cognitive ability and adult productivities.

Resource Savings

One significant cost of malnutrition is higher mortality. The probability of infant mortality is estimated to be significantly higher for LBW than for non-LBW infants. Conley, Strully and Bennett (2003) conclude that intrauterine resource competition – and, by inference, nutrition – explains a substantial portion of excess mortality of LBW children in the USA. In their study, an additional pound at birth led to a 14 per cent decrease in mortality in the period between twenty-eight days and one year for both fraternal and identical twins. In contrast, the risk of death in the first twenty-eight days was elevated by 27 per cent for each pound difference in weight for fraternal twins compared to only 11 per cent for identical twins, implying a large role for genetic factors. Ashworth (1998) reviews twelve datasets, including two from India and one from Guatemala, and concludes that the risk of neonatal death for term infants 2,000–2,499 gs at birth is four times that for infants 2,500–2,999 gs and ten times that of infants 3,000–3,499 gs. Relative risks of post-neonatal mortality for LBW compared to the two respective groups were two and four times as large (not controlling for other factors). These risk ratios translate into fairly large differences in mortality rates given the relatively high mortality rates in many developing countries (see the discussion of opportunity 1).

When the impacts of poor pre-schooler nutrition are added to the effects of LBW, Pelletier *et al.* (1995) venture the widely cited estimate that 56 per cent of child deaths in developing countries are attributable to malnutrition (83 per cent of this due to the more prevalent mild to moderate malnutrition rather then the severe cases most commonly monitored). More recently, WHO (2002) has claimed that malnutrition contributed to 3.4 m child deaths in 2000 (60 per cent of child deaths).[9]

The availability of experimental evidence on the use of micronutrient supplements provides

[8] There are aggregate or macro-alternatives, such as to define benefits in terms of an investment's impact on economic growth, typically measured in terms of growth in GNP *per capita*. This approach was used in the pioneering study by Coale and Hoover (1958) of the economic benefits of fertility reduction and more recently in combination with other methods to estimate the economic benefits of a broad strategy to improve health in developing countries (Commission on Macroeconomics and Health 2001). The latter's estimates of the relationship between cross-country economic growth rates, indicators of population health and a set of additional explanatory variables indicate that each 10 per cent improvement in average life expectancy at birth is associated with an increase in the rate of economic growth of 0.3–0.4 percentage points per year. However, the associations found in cross-national analysis are unlikely to represent unbiased estimates of the causal effects of investments due to non-trivial omitted variable and endogeneity bias. For example, Behrman and Rosenzweig (2004) explore the relation between birth weight and productivity across countries: aggregate estimates indicate an association with over 40 per cent of the variance in product per worker across countries, but estimates that control for micro-endowments suggest that less than 1 per cent of cross-country differences can be attributed to differences in birth weight distributions. Further, most of the available cross-national data are not sufficiently disaggregated to disentangle the effects of the types of investments being considered by the Copenhagen Consensus from similar broader investments in the population.

[9] Pelletier and Frongillo (2003), using data on changes in national malnutrition rates and mortality to get a different perspective on this association, also find an association of mortality and malnutrition. However, these associations do not control for changes in infrastructure or income that may both affect mortality directly as well as influence nutrition nor can they indicate a counterfactual of the impact of improved nutrition on expected mortality. Guilkey and Riphahn (1998) use longitudinal data on Filipino children with controls for the endogeneity of nutrition and other health care choices. Their simulations indicate that children with two months without weight gain in the first year of life (about 10 per cent of their sample) have 50 per cent higher mortality risk. The scenarios similarly show that if a mother is unable or unwilling to adopt standard recommendations on breastfeeding, the hazard of child mortality increases markedly. Care has to be taken, however, in interpreting the last association as causal because mothers may be less likely to be able to breastfeed infants who are at high risk.

unambiguous data on the relationship of mortality and vitamin intakes in many environments, including those that show few clinical symptoms of deficiencies. The potential to reduce child deaths by distributing Vitamin A on a semi-annual basis is particularly dramatic; meta-analysis of field trials indicates that such provision of Vitamin A can reduce overall child mortality by 25–35 per cent (Beaton, Martorell and Aronson 1993). Among adults, anaemia is a particular concern for the health of women of child bearing age, not only because of elevated risk of adverse birth outcomes but also because the risk of maternal death is substantially elevated for anaemic women: over a fifth of maternal deaths are associated with anaemia (Ross and Thomas 1996; Brabin, Hakimi and Pelletier 2001).[10]

Beyond the issue of increased mortality, malnutrition increases the risk of illnesses that impair the welfare of survivors. This relationship between nutrition and both infections and chronic diseases can be traced through different parts of the lifecycle. Children with LBWs – reflecting a range of causes, not all of which are due to dietary deficiencies – stay longer in hospitals in circumstances where births occur in such settings and have higher risks of subsequent hospitalisation (Vitoria *et al.* 1999). In addition, they use outpatient services more frequently than do children with normal birth-weights. For young children, in general, malnutrition, including micronutrient deficiencies, leads to a vicious cycle, with impaired immunity leading to infection with attendant loss of appetite and increased catabolism and, thus, increased likelihood of additional malnutrition.

Increased morbidity has direct resource costs in terms of health care services as well as lost employment or schooling for the care givers. The magnitudes of these costs differ according to the country's medical system, markets and policies. In developed countries, the costs for the survivors can be substantial. Lightwood, Phibbs and Glanz (1999) calculate the excess direct medical costs due to LBW in the USA attributed to one cause – maternal smoking – to be $263 m in 1995. Similarly, 75 per cent of the $5.5–6 bn of excess costs due to LBW in the USA estimated by Lewit *et al.* (1995) is due to the costs of health care in infancy. A further 10 per cent

of these costs are attributed to higher expenditures for special education as well as increased grade repetition. Such expenditures for special education or for social services are substantial in developed countries (Petrou, Sach and Davidson 2001). While these costs may be far less in low-income countries where, for example, the majority of births occur outside a clinical setting, these lower medical costs associated with LBW come at the expense of higher mortality. In the absence of an educational system that can recognise and accommodate the individual needs of students, moreover, some of these costs are not incurred during childhood but rather in the form of reduced productivity in adulthood.

The evidence for the foetal origins of chronic diseases described above is still being assessed. The fact that some consequences may not be observed until the affected individuals reach middle age is an important consideration for interpreting the range of evidence being assembled. There are few longitudinal studies that follow cohorts this far, and extrapolation from shorter panels or from cohorts with different life histories is problematic. In addition, there are at least two other explanations for the association between LBW and adult diseases. LBW may be an indicator of poor socioeconomic status (SES). Low SES may have a causal impact on adult disease probabilities via other variables such as poor nutrition later in life, or higher rates of smoking. If so, LBW may only be a correlate and not a causal variable. A different possibility is that LBW may be due to a genetic predisposition to insulin resistance. This would tend to account for a higher predisposition for adult diabetes and coronary heart diseases that reflect genetics rather than aspects of the uterine environment that may be influenced by medical and nutritional interventions.[11] Finally, even if there are the effects proposed in the

---

[10] As with associations of child mortality and nutrition, it is difficult to prove causality with these associations.

[11] An additional aspect of the hypothesis of subsequent costs stemming from biological adaptation to deprivation *in utero* has a bearing on the estimation of the consequences of LBW. That is, the implications will be different if the consequences are a direct result of the deprivation compared to the possibility that they manifest themselves only if the deprivation is followed by relative abundance (Lucas, Fewtrell and Cole 1999; Cameron 2001).

foetal origins hypothesis, due to the long lags the present discounted value of improvements due to pre-natal interventions to offset them is not likely to be very large (Alderman and Behrman 2004; also see opportunity 1).

Direct Links between Nutrition and Physical Productivity

There is fair amount of evidence of direct links between nutrition and productivity. Deolalikar (1988), Behrman and Deolalikar (1989), Haddad and Bouis (1991), Behrman (1993), Foster and Rosenzweig (1993b), Schultz (1997), Strauss and Thomas (1998) and Thomas and Strauss (1997) (though not Glick and Sahn 1998) find, after controlling for a variety of characteristics, that lower adult height – as described above, a consequence in part of poor nutrition in childhood – is associated with reduced earnings as an adult.[12] Thomas and Strauss (1997) estimate the direct impact of adult height on wages for urban Brazil, while the elasticity varies somewhat according to gender and specification, for both men and women who work in the market sector a 1 per cent increase in height leads to a 2–2.4 per cent increase in wages or earnings.[13] While their study is relatively sophisticated in the methodology used to account for labour selectivity and joint determination of health, this result is similar to others reported in the literature.

Low energy intakes can reduce productivity, creating a vicious circle in which poor workers are unable to generate sufficient income to obtain sufficient calories to be productive. This relationship, sometimes dubbed the 'efficiency wage hypothesis', has been the object of considerable theoretical work since Leibenstein (1957). Strauss and Thomas' (1998) review of the empirical literature

notes that efforts to test this relationship empirically have been dogged by a number of problems: unobservable heterogeneity, measurement error and observability issues. They note, 'It is not obvious how to interpret a result that additional calories are associated with higher productivity if higher productivity workers are stronger and consume more calories' (1998, 806). While individual fixed effects specifications can address unobservable fixed heterogeneity, they are especially susceptible to problems derived from measurement error. Thomas and Strauss (1997) lessen the latter problem by drawing on micro-data in which caloric intakes were measured directly over a seven-day period; in the Brazil data, they find that wages of workers in urban areas were positively and significantly affected by calories at low intake levels. Foster and Rosenzweig (1993, 1994) find that calorie intakes have a significant affect on piece rates (but not time rates) in the Philippines, where some workers engage in both time rate and piece rate activities so it is possible to control for unobserved individual heterogeneities.

Micronutrient status also has important productivity effects. Vitamin A deficiency can cause blindness, with obvious consequences for productivity. Anaemia is associated with reduced productivity in both cross-sectional data and in randomised interventions (Basta, Karyadi and Scrimshaw 1979; Li et al. 1994; Thomas et al. 2004). The magnitude may depend on the nature of the task. For example, piece work may have greater incentives for effort while heavy physical labour may show greater increases in productivity, though anaemia is nevertheless a factor in productivity with relatively light work (Horton and Ross 2003).

Indirect Links: Nutrition, Cognitive Development, Schooling and Productivity

Poorly nourished children tend to start school later, progress through school less rapidly, have lower schooling attainment and perform less well on cognitive achievement tests when older, including into adulthood. These associations appear to reflect significant and substantial effects in poor populations even when statistical methods such as instrumental variables are used to control for the behavioural determinants of pre-school

---

[12] As Appleton (2004), notes, however, this literature generally (for an exception, see Alderman et al. 1996) considers height as predetermined in a statistical sense, though possibly, even if height is determined primarily in infancy and early childhood, the determining factors also have direct effects on adult wages and productivity (e.g. though genetic endowments).

[13] From a different perspective, Margo and Steckel (1982) found that the value of an American slave prior to the US Civil War fell by roughly 1.5 per cent for every reduction in height of 1 inch.

malnutrition. In productivity terms, the magnitudes of these effects are likely to be substantial, easily exceeding the effects of height on productivity even if the indirect effect of height on wages mediated by the relationship between height and schooling is included.[14]

There are at least three broad means by which nutrition can affect education. First, malnourished children may receive less education. This may be because their care givers seek to invest less in their education, because schools use physical size as a rough indicator of school readiness or because malnourished children may have higher rates of morbidity and thus greater rates of absenteeism from school and learn less while in school. While delayed entry, the second way by which nutrition may influence schooling, does not necessarily lead to less completed schooling – although under standard models of the returns to schooling this would be an expected consequence of delayed enrolment if the opportunity cost of schooling increases with age – late enrolment leads to lower expected lifetime earnings. In order to maintain total years of schooling with delayed entry, an individual has to enter the workforce when older. As Glewwe and Jacoby (1995) illustrate, for each year of delay in entry to primary school in Ghana a child in their study loses 3 per cent of lifetime wealth. The third pathway from malnutrition to educational outcomes is via the capacity to learn, a direct consequence of the impact of poor nutrition on cognitive development described above. Additionally, a hungry child may be less likely to pay attention in school and, thus, learn less even if she has no long-term impairment of intellectual ability.[15] These three pathways clearly interact; a child with reduced ability to learn will probably spend less time in school as well as learn less while in class.

While there are many studies that document associations between nutrition and schooling (see Pollitt 1990 and Behrman 1996 for reviews), there are far fewer studies that persuasively portray the *causal* impact of child health and nutrition on school performance. Many of the observable factors that affect nutrition, such as family assets and parental education, are also ones that affect education. Similarly, unobservable attitudes about investment in children and intra-family equity influence heath provision and schooling decisions in a complex manner. Four recent studies represent the most complete efforts to date at distinguishing the distinct contributory role of nutrition on education from associations. Glewwe, Jacoby and King (2001) track children from birth through primary school and find that better-nourished children both start school earlier and repeat fewer grades. A 0.6 standard deviation increase in the stature of malnourished children would increase completed schooling by nearly twelve months. Using longitudinal data from rural Pakistan where school enrolment is much lower, Alderman et al. (2001) find that malnutrition decreases the probability of ever attending school, particularly for girls. An improvement of 0.5 standard deviations in nutrition would increase school initiation by 4 per cent for boys, but 19 per cent for girls. As the average girl (boy) in the villages studied who begins school competes 6.3 (7.6) years of schooling, improvements in nutrition will have a significant effect on schooling attainment. Alderman, Hoddinott and Kinsey (2003) track a cohort of Zimbabweans over two decades finding that *both* delayed school initiations and fewer grades completed for those malnourished as children. Extrapolating beyond the drought shocks used for identification, the study concludes that had the median pre-school child in the sample achieved the stature of a median child in a developed country, by adolescence she would be 3.4 cm taller, would have completed an additional 0.85 grades of schooling as well as started school six months earlier. Finally, Behrman et al. (2003) investigate the impact of community-level experimental nutritional interventions in rural Guatemala

---

[14] Strauss and Thomas (1998) point out that an illiterate man would need to be 30 cm taller than his literate coworker to have the same expected wage.

[15] A few studies have attempted to investigate the tie between hunger and classroom performance using experimental designs. Available results, however, are not conclusive regarding long-term consequences perhaps, in part, because controlled studies are hampered by difficulties in running experiments for an appreciable duration as well as the difficulty of encouraging parents to conform to the protocols of research design and the inability to use a placebo. Moreover, as shown in Grantham-McGregor, Chang and Walker (1997), while feeding children may improve attention, the impact on learning depends on the classroom organisation. See also Powell et al. (1998).

on a number of aspects of education, using the well-known INCAP longitudinal dataset dating back to the initial intervention in 1969–77 (when the subjects were 0–15 years of age) with the most recent information collected in 2002–3 (when the subjects were 25–40 years of age). They find that being exposed to a randomly available nutritional supplement when 6–24 months of age had significantly positive and fairly substantial effects on the probability of attending school and of passing the first grade, the grade attained by age 13 (through a combination of increasing the probability of ever enrolling, reducing the age of enrolling, increasing the grade completion rate per year in schooling and reducing the drop-out rate), completed schooling attainment, adult achievement test scores and adult Raven's test scores.

It is may seem straightforward to infer from the impact of nutrition on schooling attainment to the productivity lost due to early malnutrition using the substantial literature on wages and schooling. There are hundreds of studies on the impact of schooling attainment on wages – many of which are surveyed in Psacharopoulos (1994) and Rosenzweig (1995). But there is considerable controversy regarding to what extent these estimates are biased due to frequent failures to control for the endogeneity of schooling and the impacts of unobserved factors such as ability and motivation endowments and some aspects of family background (e.g. Card 1999 and the references therein; Behrman and Rosenzweig 1999). Wages, moreover, are also directly influenced by cognitive ability, as well as by the appreciable influence of cognitive ability on schooling achieved. Poor cognitive function as a child is associated with poorer cognitive achievement as an adult (see Martorell, Rivera and Kaplowitz 1989; Martorell, Khan and Schroeder 1994; Martorell

1995, 1999; Haas *et al.* 1996; Behrman *et al.* 2003). A series of studies shows that reduced adult cognitive skills (conditional on grades of schooling completed) directly affect earnings (Boissiere, Knight and Sabot 1985; Psacharopoulos and Velez 1992; Alderman *et al.* 1996; Altonji and Dunn 1996; Glewwe 1996; Lavy, Spratt and Leboucher 1997; Cawley, Heckman and Vytlacil 2001).[16] It is possible to use these studies to estimate the magnitude of the productivity costs of poor nutrition. Alderman, Hoddinott and Kinsey (2003) use the values for the returns to education and age/job experience in the Zimbabwean manufacturing sector provided by Bigsten *et al.* (2000) to infer the costs associated with poor nutrition in Zimbabwe. The loss of 0.7 grades of schooling and the seven-month delay in starting school there translates into a 12 per cent reduction in lifetime earnings. Behrman and Rosenzweig (2004) take a more direct approach. They study a sample of adult identical twins in the USA and determine that with controls for genetic and other endowments shared by such twins (which would not be affected by programmes to increase birth weight), the impact of LBW on schooling or wages is far larger than it appeared without such controls (e.g. the impact on schooling attainment is estimated to be twice as large, with a pound increase in birth weight increasing schooling attainment by about a third of a year).

Four Opportunities for Reducing Hunger and Malnutrition

In this section, we set out four opportunities for reducing hunger and malnutrition. These are: reducing the prevalence of LBW; improving infant and child nutrition and exclusive breastfeeding; reducing the prevalence of iron, iodine, Vitamin A and zinc deficiencies; and investments in developing country agriculture. Having done so, we then assess the strengths and limitations of the framework we use to represent these opportunities.

Opportunity 1: Reducing the Prevalence of LBW[17]

Many of the 12 m LBW infants born each year die at young ages, contributing significantly to neonatal mortality, which makes up the largest proportion

[16] In addition, studies such as Behrman and Rosenzweig (2004) and Strauss (2000) estimate the total impact of LBW on earnings, including the indirect schooling effect, the direct impact of ability and any influence of stature.

[17] Because this opportunity is based on substantial work that we have undertaken that is summarised in Alderman and Behrman (2004), we begin with it as a more extensive illustration of the assumptions that underlie estimates of benefits and costs and the sensitivity of such estimates to alternative assumptions. We discuss the subsequent opportunities somewhat more briefly.

Table 7.2. Base Estimates of PDVs of Seven Major Classes of Benefits of Shifting One LBW Infant to Non-LBW Status, 5% Discount Rate

	PDV ($)	% of column
1 Reduced infant mortality	92.86	16
2 Reduced neonatal care	41.80	7
3 Reduced costs of infant/child illness	38.10	7
4 Productivity gain from reduced stunting	99.34	17
5 Productivity gain from increased ability	239.31	41
6 Reduction in costs of chronic diseases	23.29	4
7 Intergenerational benefits	45.12	8
Sum of PDV of seven benefits ($)	579.82	100

Source: Alderman and Behrman (2004, Table 2).

of infant mortality in many developing countries. Unfortunately, rates of LBW have remained relatively static in recent decades. Because LBW infants are 40 per cent more likely to die in the neonatal period than their normal-weight counterparts, addressing LBW is essential to achieve reductions in infant mortality. Moreover, many of the LBW children who survive infancy suffer cognitive and neurological impairment and are stunted as adolescents and adults. Thus, in addition to contributing to excess mortality, LBW is associated with lower productivity in a range of economic and other activities. LBW also may be important in light of new evidence that shows that LBW infants may have an increased risk of cardiovascular disease, diabetes and hypertension later in life. LBW may also be an intergenerational problem because LBW girls who survive tend to be undernourished when pregnant, with relatively high incidence of LBW children. Table 7.2 reproduces Alderman and Behrman's (2004) estimates of the PDV of seven different benefits of shifting one infant from LBW to non-LBW status for a discount rate of 5 per cent in developing countries.

Reducing Infant Mortality

The probability of infant mortality is estimated to be significantly higher for LBW than for non-LBW infants. The studies by Ashworth (1998) and Conley, Strully and Bennett (2003) reviewed on p. 00 show

an elevated risk of infant mortality associated with LBW that translates into fairly large differences in mortality rates given the relatively high mortality rates in many developing countries. The Indian and Guatemalan samples that Ashworth summarises, for example, have neonatal mortality rates of from 21 to 39 per 1,000 births and post-neonatal mortality rates per 1,000 neonatal survivors of from 25.3 to 60.0. The mid-point of these ranges, together with the mid-point of the percentage LBW in these samples (21.2–39.0 per cent) and Ashworth's summary that for term infants weighing 2,000–2,499 gs at birth the risk of neonatal death is four times as high and the risk of post-neonatal death is twice as high as for term infants weighing 2,500–2,999 gs implies that the probability of an infant death (either neonatal or post-neonatal) drops by about 0.078 for each birth in the 2,500–2,999 gs range instead of in the 2,000–2,499 gs range.[18]

How to value a life saved is a big question, about which there is a range of views. (We return to this issue later.) One possibility is to use the resource costs of alternative means of saving a life. Summers (1992) suggests that World Bank estimates of the cost of saving a life through measles immunisation were of the order of magnitude of $800 per life saved in the early 1990s. Adjusting this cost for inflation in the next decade, and for the distortion costs of raising these revenues, the alternative resource cost of saving an infant's life is estimated to be about $1,250. The advantage of this approach is

[18] Ashworth (1998) does not provide all the information necessary to make this calculation. As an approximation, Alderman and Behrman (2004) assume that the mid-point of the neonatal death rate (30.1) is the weighted average of infants with LBW (at the mid-point of that range, 32.5 per cent) and of those non-LBW, and that all LBW are in the 2,000–2,499 gs range and all non-LBW are in the 2,500–2,999 gs range. Given the fourfold risk for the former, this implies that the neonatal mortality rate of LBW is 61.0 and that for non-LBW is 15.2, so the difference is 45.8, or a probability of 0.046. A parallel calculation for the twofold risk of mortality for the 2,000–2,499 gs range versus the 2,500–2,999 gs range among neonatal survivors with an overall mortality rate at the midpoint of 42.7 and a midpoint of the birth weight range of 32.5 per cent implies that the post-neonatal mortality rate for LBW infants is 64.4 and for non-LBW infants 32.2, so the difference is 32.2, or a probability of 0.032. Together, these calculations imply that a shift of an infant from LBW to non-LBW status reduces the probability of mortality in such a population by about 0.078.

that it uses the resources actually used in a society to avert a death to estimate that value that the society places on averting a death. Therefore, based on this approach the estimated monetary benefit of reducing the infant mortality associated with LBW is about $97.50. This is, the $1,250 benefit times the excess probability that a LBW would have died in infancy. Alderman and Behrman (2004) assume that on average this benefit is obtained one year after the intervention so that the discount rate does not greatly affect the PDV of this benefit (see table 7.2, row 1).

Reducing the Additional Costs of Neonatal Medical Attention due to LBW

This is the sum of the extra neonatal care in hospitals as well as the additional costs of outpatient care. The former is the product of the costs of a day of a hospital stay times the number of additional days on average for children born weighing less than 2.5 kg and who are born in hospitals. Given that the share of children born in hospitals is small in most developing countries, under the assumption that these costs are incurred only for children born in hospitals, the contribution of this component to the total may be small, even though its costs are not discounted over many years.

Alderman and Behrman were not able to find any recent studies indicating the average length of neonatal stay for LBW children compared to children with normal weights in low-income countries. As an initial estimate based on experience in Bangladesh, Alderman and Behrman assume

that duration of hospitalisation for a normal-weight baby with normal delivery is one–two days and for LBW babies (between 1,500 and 2,500 gs) it is five–seven days. For very-low-birth-weight (VLBW) babies (below 1,500 gs) the length of stay is seven–ten days.[19] Using 2,000 Taka per day at private hospitals inclusive of medicine as the opportunity cost of care (governmental hospitals charge 200–300 plus medicine, but the cost of beds is subsidised) the extra direct hospital-related resource cost of hospitalisation for a LBW child is $155, taken at the mid-point of the difference in days.[20] The extra total direct resource cost also includes the extra cost of time for the parents and the distortion costs from raising governmental revenues to finance the subsidised hospitalisation and from inducing inefficient use of resources through their subsidised hospitalisation. Under the assumption that the distortion costs are about 25 per cent of the hospitalisation costs, as above, and that the time cost of the parents for the extended hospital stay is $15, the resource cost for longer hospitalisation for a LBW baby is $209, which Alderman and Behrman assume is incurred close enough to the intervention so that no discounting is needed. However, in many low-income countries the majority of babies are born at home, and not in hospitals. While there may be some parallel costs for LBW babies born at home, they are likely to be much less. For their base estimates in table 7.2, row 2, therefore, Alderman and Behrman assume that 90 per cent of the babies are born at home and the additional initial resource costs for those LBW babies are only 10 per cent of those born in hospitals.

Reducing the Additional Costs of Subsequent Illnesses and Related Medical Care for Infants and Children Due to LBW[21]

Ashworth (1998) reports a regular pattern of increased morbidity with lower birth-weights, particularly in the first two years of life. For example, days with diarrohea among LBW children 0–6 months increase 33 per cent compared to normal birth weight children in Brazil and 60 per cent for children aged 0–59 months in Papua New Guinea. Barros *et al.* (1992) show a doubling of the rate of hospitalisation for dehydration in Brazil and a 50 per cent increase in hospitalisation for pneumonia.

---

[19] Dr Mohammed Shahjahan of the Micronutrient Institute and former Medical Director of Save the Children Foundation's Children's Nutrition Unit in Dhaka provided this information.

[20] The extra hospitalisation direct resource costs for a VLBW child are $240, or $300 in total resource costs if the distortion costs are 25 per cent.

[21] ACC/SCN (2004, 2–13) claims that: 'Overall, malnutrition is the main contributor to illness and disease in the world (Essati, et al. 2002), comprising risk factors related to undernutrition, excess consumption of certain diet components . . . and low components of others. Childhood and maternal underweight alone are responsible for 138 million disability-adjusted life years (DALYS) lost or about 9.5 per cent of the global burden of disease . . . , mostly in the high-mortality countries.'

Victora *et al.* (1999) report similar magnitudes of increases of pneumonia and acute respiratory disease for a number of countries. Such increased morbidity has direct and immediate costs, as well as indirect costs due to the associated stunting (see below). However Alderman and Behrman were not able to find estimates of the resource costs of such illnesses and related medical care. Estimates of out-of-pocket costs can be obtained from some household surveys, but these are likely to be substantial understatements of resource costs because in most developing economies medical care is subsidised and such costs do not include the opportunity costs of care givers who are likely to be diverted from other activities because of children's illnesses. For their basic estimates, therefore, Alderman and Behrman assume that the additional total direct resource costs for such illnesses of LBW infants are $40, centred at the end of one year (table 7.2, row 3).

The Expected Discounted Loss of Lifetime Productivity Due to Stunting

The first component of this benefit from increasing the birth weight of a LBW baby to normal birth weight can be derived from the product of an estimate of the impact of LBW on adult height times an estimate of the difference in earnings attributed to low stature, under the maintained assumption that the impact on earnings reflects the impact on productivity. A second component comes from the fact that, as discussed on p. 364, stature also affects the timing and amount of school attended. Long-term follow-up studies in the UK (Strauss 2000) indicate a loss of 0.5 Z-scores in height for children born small for gestational age who average 1 kg difference from the normal controls. In a study of identical twins, Behrman and Rosenzweig (2004) also show a lasting impact of height of a similar magnitude; a difference of 1 kg in birth-weights for a full-term baby leads to a 1.6 cm difference in adult heights. This is roughly a 1 per cent difference. Li *et al.* (2003) followed a cohort whose mothers received supplementation in a randomized experiment. They found that a 1 standard deviation difference in birth weight (0.5 kg for boys and 0.4 kg for girls) led to 1.8 and 0.6 cm differences, respectively, in adult heights. What do differences of this magnitude mean for productivity? Thomas and Strauss

(1997), as noted on p. 372, estimate the direct impact of adult height on wages for urban Brazil. This result is similar to others reported in the literature. The direct effects on schooling of the nutritional shock studied by Alderman, Hoddinott and Kinsey (2003) were estimated to lead to a 7 per cent reduction in lifetime earnings. The impact of lifetime earnings in rural Pakistan from the impact on the probability of school enrolment from a 0.5 Z-score improvement in nutrition was estimated at 1.6 per cent (Alderman *et al.* 2001). This study considered only age of school enrolment and not the full impact of nutrition on school achievement. Based on these studies, Alderman and Behrman assume for their basic estimates that the impact on productivity through stunting of increasing the birth weight of a LBW infant to above 2,500 gs is about 2.2 per cent of annual earnings that Alderman and Behrman assume to be $500 per year in constant prices over an assumed work life from 15 of age to 60 years old (table 7.2, row 4).

The Expected Discounted Increase in Lifetime Productivity Due to Increased Ability with the Reduction of LBW

Earnings are based not only on school attended and on direct anthropometric effects, but also on learning within school (Alderman *et al.* 1996). This learning may be affected by the impairment of cognitive development that is associated with LBW, so reducing LBW may increase productivity through this channel.

What is the range of cognitive loss that may be a consequence of LBW? Bhutta *et al.* (2002) report a range of 0.3–0.6 standard deviation decrease in IQ, a range that includes the decline in cognitive ability in the sample followed by Ment *et al.* (2003) even after that cohort had improved over time. Extrapolation to the task at hand, however, is subject to a set of caveats additional to those discussed below. In particular, the two studies mentioned above investigate children whose birth-weights reflect prematurity. Potentially offsetting this is the fact that Ment *et al.* also noted that the improvements over time were associated with higher socio-economic status. By inference, these improvements may be less likely among low-income families with little education or access to quality pre-schools. The mental impairment, however, may not be only for extreme cases or for pre-maturity. Sorensen *et al.* (1997) study the relation of birth weight and IQ over the normal range of birth-weights and found the score of intelligence increased until a birth weight of 4,200 gs. The difference between the LBW group and the children born at 4 kg was roughly half a standard deviation of the score. Although Matte *et al.* do not report standard deviations for their study of siblings with normal gestation, the magnitude of the increase in IQ is consistent with Sorensen *et al.* (1997).

Whatever the magnitude of impairment, the impact of this change on subsequent earnings must be estimated. Altonji and Dunn (1996) provide one such estimate of the impact of IQ on earnings, conditional on years of schooling using data from the USA. For men, the impact of half a standard deviation decline in IQ on the logarithm of wages was 0.05, or slightly more than the impact of an additional year of post-secondary schooling.[22] Using the same dataset, but a different measure of ability, Cawley, Heckman and Vytlacil (2001) show that the estimated impact on wages of ability is substantially smaller conditional on levels of schooling. For example, in the cases of black males or females, the coefficients of a general measure of ability decline by a third when schooling is included in the model. For their purposes, the net impact of ability is both the direct impact on wages and the impact that works through schooling choices.[23] Using the models in Cawley, Heckman and Vytlacil (2001), disaggregated by gender and ethnic group as well as including other background variables but without

schooling, half a standard deviation decline in cognitive ability leads to 8–12 per cent lower wages.

Alderman *et al.* (1996) use a different measure of cognitive ability – performance on Raven matrices – in their study of wages in rural Pakistan. They find that half a standard deviation decline in this measure leads to a 6.5 per cent reduction in wages in estimates that do not include schooling in the regression. The point estimate drops by two-thirds in estimates that include both years of schooling as well as achievement in school. One can also infer the relation between scores on Raven matrices and household income in Ghana by looking at the product of the impact of ability on school achievement in Glewwe and Jacoby (1994) and the impact of achievement on household income from the same data source in Jolliffe (1998). In this case, half a standard deviation decline leads to a 5 per cent decrease in total income.

While Boissiere, Knight and Sabot (1985) do not find a direct impact of Raven scores on wages in their study of Kenya and Tanzania, they do find that this measure of ability influences schooling as well as learning conditional on years of school. Taking these pathways into account, half a standard deviation decline in ability would lead to a decline in wages of 8 and 5 per cent, respectively.[24] Similarly, Psacharopoulos and Velez (1992) find a modest direct effect of reasoning ability as measured by Raven matrices on wages in Colombia, together with a large impact of this measure of ability on wages through its impact of schooling. Thus, half a standard deviation change leads to a 3.5 per cent direct change in wages (holding schooling constant) and a *total* impact on wages of 11.6 per cent. This is also in the range of results from Chile reported by Selowsky and Taylor (1973). Their results imply that one half a standard deviation decline in child IQ leads to reduced earnings between 3 and 5 per cent.[25]

An alternative approach that combines the fourth and fifth components of the seven LBW benefits being considered is to look directly at the earnings of individuals as a function of their birth weight. That is, instead of summing the impact of low stature on wages with the impact of reduced cognitive function times an expectation of this type of impairment, simply compare directly earnings of

---

[22] This result is based on a family fixed effects model. The estimated response is 40 per cent less without fixed effects. Curiously, although the coefficient of IQ in the non-fixed effects model for women is larger than the corresponding coefficient for men, the fixed effects coefficient for women is negative, but not statistically significant.

[23] Hansen, Heckman and Mullen (2003) also point out that many measures of ability are affected by schooling.

[24] Based on table 6 of Boissiere, Knight and Sabot (1985), and assuming that the coefficient of variation for ability is 0.3, the same as in both the Ghana and Pakistan studies.

[25] Selowsky and Taylor (1973) actually found that malnutrition reduced IQ by one standard deviation, but they were addressing childhood malnutrition, not LBW.

children with similar opportunities at birth but different birth-weights. The impact of birth weight on earnings in this case is the sum of the impacts on stature, on school investments and on cognitive ability, although the relative contribution of each is not elucidated.

Strauss (2000) finds that individuals aged 26 who were born small for gestational age (SGA) earned 10 per cent less than individuals who had normal birth-weights. The birth-weights of the SGA group differed on average from the normal group by a kg. However, the difference in cognitive abilities on standard tests ranged from 0.13 to 0.37 standard deviations in follow-up measures between the ages of 5 and 16. Thus, even with a modest difference in measured ability and no difference in average years of schooling, Strauss observed a significant difference in wages of the same magnitude – indeed greater – than with the assumption of half a standard deviation of cognitive ability and the range of wage effects of such a deficit derived from wage equations that include cognitive ability. Similarly, using the within twins estimates in table 2 of Behrman and Rosenzweig (2004), a 1 kg difference in birth weight (0.98 ounces a week foetal growth) implies a difference of 18.6 per cent in wages for adults.

Overall, considering either the total impact of LBW on wages or the sum of the impacts due to stunting, impaired cognitive development and schooling, the consequences on earnings of an infant moving from LBW to non-LBW can be assumed to be bracketed as between 5 and 10 per cent per year.[26] Alderman and Behrman use 7.5 per cent for their basic estimates, which – given their use of 2.2 per cent for the expected productivity benefit from reduced stunting for the fourth benefit – implies about 5.3 per cent for the expected productivity benefit from improved ability. They again assume annual earnings or productivity of $500 in constant prices for a working life from age 15 through age 60 (table 7.2, row 5).

Reduced Costs of Chronic Diseases Associated with LBW

There has been considerable attention given in recent years to these possible impacts of LBW in the 'foetal origins' hypothesis described on pp. 371–2. Given the heterogeneity of the chronic illnesses associated with foetal malnutrition it is difficult to assign costs to this array of diseases. Moreover, as noted, there are still relatively few studies that have been able to trace long-term impact and to assign them to nutritional deprivation in a particular trimester of pregnancy. As mentioned above, some consequences of foetal malnutrition that may affect adult health may not manifest themselves in LBW, nor are all cases of LBW directly attributable to malnutrition. Moreover, the contribution of LBW to chronic disease may depend on the degree of deprivation in the rest of the individual's life, adding an additional dimension to any assumption. We further do not know how many SGA children will survive to ages at which chronic diseases are likely in current developing country conditions.

One study that does attempt to calculate the costs of LBW, as well as those of subsequent nutritional and dietary patterns on chronic disease, is Popkin, Horton and Kim (2001). Their estimates consider the cost of diet-related chronic disease, to two economies – China and Sri Lanka. For China, all diet-related factors are estimated to account for costs totalling 2.1 per cent of GNP in 1995. For Sri Lanka, these costs are estimated to be 0.3 per cent. In both countries costs are projected to rise appreciably over the next generation, though the share of these costs attributable to LBW (compared to, say, obesity) is projected to decline.

In their basic estimates for illustration Alderman and Behrman make two broad assumptions (table 7.2, row 6). First, they assume that the cost in terms of lost productivity and increased medical care is equivalent to ten years of earnings in a low-income population ($5,000) and is experienced on average at age 60. Second, they assume that the probability of experiencing these chronic diseases is reduced by 0.087 by moving a LBW baby to a non-LBW status.[27]

---

[26] This assumes that this differential remains constant over a worker's lifetime. Altonji and Pierret (2001) note that the impact of ability may increase over time as workers obtain more information by observation, and that conversely the impact of schooling on wages may decline.

[27] Their reasoning for this approximation is as follows. For the illustrative stereotypical low-income developing countries, they assume that about 10 per cent of adult deaths are due to these diseases under the assumption that the share of

Cross-Generational Impacts of LBW

Alderman and Behrman also include an estimate of the second-generation impacts of the children born to women who were themselves LBW children. Since many women begin having children in their teens or early twenties, some of the costs on the second generation actually may occur before all of the direct costs to the earlier generation – for example, the reduced earnings of older adults and the costs of chronic illnesses for adults who themselves were LBW.

They were not able to find much persuasive evidence on the causal impact of mothers' LBW on that of their children. Indeed, as noted on p. 363, Behrman and Rosenzweig (2004) report that in data for the USA the significant positive correlation disappears if there is control for all endowments (including genetic endowments) using data on identical twins (which are a LBW population). Their findings suggest that the intergenerational correlations in birth-weights between mothers and children are due to genetic influences and not to the nutritional status of mothers when they were in the womb, which presumably is what is of interest from a policy perspective. On the other hand, as also noted on p. 369, Ramakrishnan *et al.* (1999) find a small significant effect in the low-income context of rural Guatemala using the INCAP data in which mothers

of current mothers were exposed to nutritional supplements made available in an experimental design at the community level. Therefore, in their basic estimates (table 7.2, row 7). Alderman and Behrman illustrate some possible effects under the following assumptions: (1) these effects are only for mothers who were LBW, not fathers, and thus for about half of LBW infants; (2) on average these mothers have four children, born when the mother is 17, 20, 26 and 35; (3) For a mother who was LBW, the probability for each of her children of being LBW is one in five; (4) this probability is reduced to one in ten if she was not LBW; and (5) the benefits of reducing LBW for the children over their lifecycles are the same as the benefits for the mothers/fathers, but lagged in time and therefore discounted more, with such possibilities over three generations of children.

Summary of Basic Estimates of PDV of Benefits of Shifting One Infant from LBW to Non-LBW

The final row of table 7.2 gives the bottom line for Alderman and Behrman's basic estimates, subject to the many caveats and assumptions made above. For their basic estimates, the PDV of reduction of LBW per infant is about $580. That means that from a social point of view in purely economic terms it would be desirable to reduce the incidence of LBW infants in low-income populations as long as the true resource cost of doing so is less than $580 per affected infant.[28] The last column gives the percentage contributions, among these seven individual benefits, in this overall benefit. The overall benefits are dominated by the estimated impacts on productivity through reducing stunting and increasing cognitive ability (working in part through its effects on schooling), with these two benefits accounting for over half (58 per cent) of the total. While there are considerable delays in receiving these benefits, they persist over the many years of the working life, with the result that their cumulative effects are considerable even when discounted to the time of the intervention at a 5 per cent discount rate. The next largest PDV among the seven benefits is for reduced infant mortality (16 per cent), with reduced neonatal care and cost of infant/child illness together (14 per cent) and intergenerational benefits (8 per cent) next. Though the estimated

---

annual deaths will be the same as share of eventual cause of death (the information in Popkin, Horton and Kim suggests about 18 per cent for China, but China has a much older population than do most low-income countries), that about 15 per cent of the adult population was LBW (which is much higher than China and a number of low-income countries, but lower than other low-income countries primarily in South Asia and SSA) and that the odds ratios for having these chronic diseases are twice as high for LBW as for non-LBW babies (consistent with information in Popkin, Horton and Kim). Let X be the probability of having these chronic diseases for non-LBW babies (and $2X$ for LBW babies), where $X = 8.7$ per cent is the solution to 10 per cent $= 0.85*X + 0.15*(2X)$. Since the odds ratio for adults who were LBW babies is twice that for adults who were not LBW babies, the reduction in the probability of having these chronic diseases by moving a baby from LBW to non-LBW status is 0.087.

[28] The estimated benefits are much larger with the alternative of valuing an averted death at $100,000 that is discussed below and summarised in appendix table 7A.4 – $8,535, with the value of the averted life accounting for 87 per cent of the benefits.

benefits from reduced infant mortality and reduced neonatal care and costs of infant/child illness are not huge, their relative contribution is appreciable because the benefits occur very early in the life-cycle. There is thus not much of a lag before they are reaped after an intervention and the benefits are not discounted greatly. The intergenerational bene-fits are fairly large in some cases, but spread over a number of years and are assumed to start only after seventeen years. The PDV of the reduction in costs of chronic diseases, even though at the time they occur they have fairly large constant dollar values per year, are fairly small (4 per cent) because they are discounted for so many years.

Cost Estimates

Many interventions to address LBW problems have been proposed, including:[29]

- Anti-microbial treatments
- Anti-parasitic treatments
- Insecticide-treated bednets (ITNs)
- Maternal health records to track gestational weight gain
- Provision of iron/folate supplements
- Targeted food supplements
- Social marketing regarding birth spacing or tim-ing of marriage.

While some of the recommended interventions fo-cus solely on LBW, a number of other programmes to reduce LBW also address other goals – for ex-ample, campaigns against smoking or consump-tion of other drugs during pregnancy – with ben-efits in terms of LBW possibly secondary. Ideally, one would sum the expected PDV from all antic-ipated outcomes to estimate the benefits of such interventions. In any case, most lists of possible interventions provide little guidance regarding pri-orities, either for using scarce public resources for the general purpose of alleviating problems related to LBW or for deciding which interventions have relatively high returns in which situations.[30]

Under the assumptions in table 7.2, any interven-tion that costs less than $580 per LBW birth averted in a low-income country is a suitable candidate in terms of a BCR greater than one. Rouse (2003) presents a brief review of the cost-effectiveness of interventions to prevent adverse pregnancy out-comes, including LBW. He indicates that it costs $46 per LBW infant averted with treatments for asymptomatic bacterial infections. In a specific ex-ample, based on treating over 2,000 women in Uganda for presumptive sexually transmitted dis-ease, a reduction of 2 per cent of LBW infants was reported (Gray et al. 2001). As the therapy was re-ported as costing $2 per treatment, this resulted in an estimate of $100 per LBW averted. This is con-trasted with a much smaller intervention targeted to pregnant women in Kenya with a poor obstet-ric history that reduced LBW by 14 per cent. With drugs costing $2, this is presented as costing $14 per LBW averted. These studies did not report the costs of the delivery system that could identify the high-risk women and target the services and the distor-tionary costs of raising and using public resources for such programmes. But the fact that the costs of medicine in these examples are substantially below the expected benefits in table 7.3 suggests that these possibilities are promising.

Table 7.3 summarises the implied BCRs for vari-ants on these three interventions with costs of medicine, respectively, of $100, $46 and $14 per LBW birth averted. For each of these costs of medicine there are three alternative multiplicative factors – two, five and ten – to represent the total costs – e.g. the costs of screening women, staff costs and distortionary costs of obtaining the resources to fund the programmes and for their implementation. Finally, alternatives for the same six discount rates are presented. While each of the BCRs for these in-terventions is subject to a number of strong assump-tions, the ranges of BCRs in table 7.3 are suggestive. At a 5 per cent discount rate, all but one of the BCRs are greater than one – in many cases, much greater than one. The single exception is for the most expen-sive intervention in terms of the costs of medicine

[29] See, for example, Merialdi, et al. (2003) for a review of a number of interventions related to LBW that have been under-taken. ACC/SCN (2000b) contains a summary of a workshop on LBW held in 1999.

[30] The lack of apparent priorities probably means that advo-cates of using scarce public resources to alleviate problems related to LBW are much less effective in their advocacy than they might be, and that there is likely to be a lack of agree-ment regarding how any additional resources should be used, even among those who agree that LBW is a major problem that warrants increased public resources.

Table 7.3. Estimates of BCRs for Alternative Costs for Three Different Treatments to Move One LBW Infant to Non-LBW Status, Different Discount Rates[a]

	Annual discount rate (%)					
	1	2	3	5	10	20
$100*cost factor of two	10.19	6.89	4.93	2.90	1.37	0.86
$46*cost factor of two	22.15	14.98	10.71	6.30	2.97	1.87
$14*cost factor of two	72.77	49.22	35.20	20.71	9.76	6.14
$100*cost factor of five	4.08	2.76	1.97	1.16	0.55	0.34
$46*cost factor of five	8.86	5.99	4.29	2.52	1.19	0.75
$14*cost factor of five	29.11	19.69	14.08	8.28	3.91	2.45
$100*cost factor of ten	2.04	1.38	0.99	0.58	0.27	0.17
$46*cost factor of ten	4.43	3.00	2.14	1.26	0.59	0.37
$14*cost factor of ten	14.55	9.84	7.04	4.14	1.95	1.23

Note: [a] The three different treatments are described in the text. The costs provided from the studies cited there (i.e. $100, $46, $14) are the estimated direct costs of medicine per LBW birth averted. The multiplicative cost factors (2, 5, 10) used in this table are illustrative possibilities for the direct staff and non-medicinal material costs of screening and administering these medicines, the direct bureaucratic costs of running the programmes and the distortionary costs of raising revenues to run these programmes and of implementing these programmes.
Source: Alderman and Behrman (2004, table 6).

($100 per LBW averted) with a multiplicative cost factor of ten. With higher discount rates, of course, the BCRs decline. Table 7.3 suggests that these interventions might have attractive BCRs for a range of non-medicine costs and discount rates – but certainly not for all reasonable non-medicine costs and discount rates. It would therefore be valuable to attempt to refine the cost estimates to narrow down the probable estimates.

While there is less evidence on the impact of treatment for helminths on LBW (Steketee 2003), given the body of information on the costs of delivery mechanisms it should be possible to convert information on impact evaluations to estimates of costs per LBW birth averted. Similarly, while evidence on the relationship of malaria and LBW points to the strong contribution of malaria to poor birth outcomes and evidence on the feasibility of interventions is being accumulated, the complexity of programmes to reduce malaria add to the

challenge of assigning a marginal cost to these efforts. For example, the use of ITNs is estimated to reduce LBW by 28 per cent in Kenya (Ter Kuile *et al.* 2003), with externalities to neighbouring villages. The benefit per LBW averted, nevertheless, was modest because the rate of LBW, even in the untreated population, was less than 10 per cent. Adverse outcomes including SGA and pre-term births, however, occurred in 32 per cent of births in the control group and 24 per cent in the treatment group. Generalisation of costs per LBW averted is also limited since only one of four previous controlled trials of ITNs – in the Gambia, and then only in the rainy season – had similar results. Even in the study on Kenya, wider inference is limited because overall adherence to the use of the nets was affected by knowledge of the vector (and fears of the insecticide) as well as age, temperature and number of household visitors. Moreover, even after two years, few individuals were willing to pay for the full costs of re-treatment, a condition for full effectiveness of the nets from a private perspective (Alaii *et al.* 2003).[31]

Micronutrient supplementation may represent a cost-effective means of reducing LBW. For

[31] Though from a social perspective the use of such nets may be desirable even if individuals are not willing to pay the full marginal resource costs of the nets, because there apparently are positive externalties (though not well measured) to their use.

example, an extensive field trial in a community in Nepal characterized both by high rates of LBW and of maternal anaemia, supplementation with iron and folate was found to reduce LBW significantly (Christian *et al.* 2003). Similar marked decreases in LBW were observed with iron supplementation for low-income women in the USA (Cogswell *et al.* 2003). Additional micronutrients were not found to affect birth weight in this study (though Vitamin A has been shown to affect maternal mortality in such an environment). The authors found that eleven women would need to be reached to prevent one case of LBW. The programme required daily intakes of the supplementation and twice-weekly visits by health staff. While no cost data were provided in the published study, Christian and West (personal communication) estimated that the experimental costs of $64.3 per pregnant woman reached could be reduced to $13.14 in an ongoing programme. Due to economies of scope, such a cost would also allow provision of Vitamin A at little marginal cost and, thus, might reduce both infant and maternal mortality. We return to micronutrient supplementation below.

Estimating the marginal costs of adverting one LBW birth by means of balanced protein energy supplementation is hampered, in part, by the modest gains reported in the literature (Kramer 1993). Nevertheless, Merialdi *et al.* (2003) claim that this is the one nutritional intervention for which a practical recommendation might be made (2003, S1626). In a study designed to address criticisms of earlier encouraging (but seasonal) results from the Gambia, Ceesay *et al.* (1997) found that the provision of supplements to pregnant women reduced the prevalence of LBW by 6 percentage points. Concerns explicitly addressed in the design include the complexity and expense of the initial intervention and the need for intense experimental conditions. This was tackled by the use of a simple peanut and flour fortified biscuit baked in village clay ovens, though the protocol of having women consume the biscuits in the presence of birth attendants does set a high standard for full-scale projects. In principle, then, the reported reduction in LBW combined with table 7.3 as well as the cost of the intervention could provide a BCR; unfortunately, however, costs do not appear to have been published.

Summary

The basic substantive bottom line is that the economic benefits from reducing LBW in low-income countries are fairly substantial, under plausible assumptions including a discount rate of 5 per cent, on the order of magnitude of a PDV of $580 per infant moved from the LBW to the non-LBW category. This means that there may be a number of interventions that are warranted purely on the grounds of saving resources or increasing productivity. With a 5 per cent discount rate, the gains are primarily estimated to be from increases in labour productivity, in important part through inducing more education, with the gains from avoiding costs due to infant mortality and morbidity together secondary in importance. If the appropriate discount rate is higher than 5 per cent, then the relative gains would increase for the latter relative to the former. The estimated gains from reducing chronic diseases, a topic of considerable interest in recent years, are much less for any reasonable discount rate simply because the gains – even if large when they occur – arise decades after any interventions that might reduce the prevalence of LBW and subsequently of these associated diseases.

Opportunity 2: Improving Infant and Child Nutrition and Exclusive Breastfeeding Promotion

The nutritional literature emphasizes that undernutrition is most common and severe during periods of greatest vulnerability (Martorell 1997; UNICEF 1998). One such period is *in utero*. Opportunity 1 addresses that period. A second vulnerable period is the first two years or so of life. Young children have high nutritional requirements, in part because they are growing so fast. Unfortunately, the diets commonly offered to young children in developing countries to complement breast milk are of low quality (i.e. they have low energy and nutrient density), and as a result, multiple nutrient deficiencies are common. Young children are also very susceptible to infections because their immune systems are both developmentally immature and compromised by poor nutrition. In poor countries, foods and liquids are often contaminated and are thus key sources of frequent infections which both reduce appetite and increase metabolic demands. Furthermore, in many societies, sub-optimal traditional remedies for childhood infections, including withholding of foods and breast milk, are common. Infection and malnutrition thus reinforce each other. Opportunity 2 is thus directed towards improving the nutrition of infants and young children.

Opportunity 2 differs from opportunity 1 more with regard to the type of interventions that may be promoted than in potential benefits. To a fair degree the expected gains from improved child nutrition are the same as those for changes in LBW. In both cases, there are immediate benefits in terms of reduced mortality and health care costs as well as subsequent benefits in improved productivity from associated cognitive development and increased stature. Even intergeneration transmission of nutritional shocks in childhood is perceived to be similar to those from LBW. Of the seven categories of benefits listed for opportunity 1, perhaps the two that differ most from the current opportunity are numbers (2) Reduced neonatal care and (6) Reduced costs of chronic diseases associated with LBW. Neonatal care is obviously not relevant for children who are older than the neonatal phase, though childhood nutrition and feeding patterns also are believed to influence subsequent chronic disease. But, as noted in the discussion of opportunity 1, with a 5 per cent discount rate, these two benefits are only about a tenth of the overall benefit.

Infant and child nutrition is often depicted as the outcome of the combination of appropriate food and health inputs mediated through child care practices. Several implications follow from this observation. First, a number of other chapters in this volume address issues important for the reduction of malnutrition in infant and pre-school children. For example, repeated bouts of diarrohea are associated with growth faltering; improvements in water and sanitation are thus expected to convey benefits in terms of reduced malnutrition. Investments in women's education may also convey benefits in terms of reduced child malnutrition. Second, dietary quality – particularly access to micronutrients – is important for nutrition for children in this age group and these are covered under opportunity 3. Third, increasing dietary quality and quantity can be achieved, in part,

by investments in agricultural research, the focus of opportunity 4. Fourth, some of the most promising interventions related to infant and child nutrition do not aim to increase the amount of food available or consumed, but rather to change how it is *provided* to the infant. Those are the focus of this discussion.

Breastfeeding promotion and improved knowledge about the timing and composition of complementary foods are examples of this opportunity. The importance of exclusive breastfeeding in low-income environments is well established.[32] Horton *et al.* (1996) provide a study of the cost-effectiveness of breastfeeding promotion in hospital settings in Latin America and find cost per death averted (\$133–\$266 when the norm had been formula feeding in hospitals and \$664–\$1,064 when less dangerous practices were promoted in the hospital)[33] were similar to those for measles immunisation and less than for oral rehydration therapy, a widely supported programme. In terms of DALYs, the study concluded that the promotion was nearly as cost-effective as Vitamin A supplementation, one of the most cost-effective programmes among a wide range in the literature. While the relative risk of mortality – the study does not consider benefits other than reduction of mortality as well as diarrhoea morbidity in the first six months of life – differs from those in poorer countries, as does the alternative to formula feeding of early weaning with family diets, as is common in Asia and Africa, this study provided underpinnings for a key element of child growth promotion strategies. However the study focuses only on the first, and to a limited extent, the third of the benefits that are discussed with regard to opportunity 1 – which are a little less than a quarter of the overall benefits. In particular, this

---

[32] This is the case despite some confusion in some of the literature about the direction of causality since some sick children will not breastfeed. To some degree, HIV/AIDS complicates this once relatively unambiguous understanding about the benefits of breastfeeding, but the importance of breastfeeding promotion and advice remains valid even if the optimal strategy depends on the costs and availability of substitutes as well as of antiretroviral therapy.

[33] These values incorporate an adjustment of the reported \$100–\$200 in 1992 when the norm had been formula feeding in hospitals and \$500–\$800 when less dangerous practices were promoted in the hospital for changes in the US cost of living index between 1992 and 2002.

study ignores the relatively large productivity gains from reduced stunting and increased ability. If the proportional value of these other gains relative to measured mortality and infant/child illness gain are roughly the same for opportunity 2 as for opportunity 1, then the BCR with a 5 per cent discount rate is about 5.6–44.8 and with a discount rate of 3 per cent is about 8.4–67.1.[34] This is thus a relatively attractive opportunity.

The results of the Horton *et al.* study also feed into the 'food versus care' debate. When cash or in-kind transfer programmes are linked to attendance at health clinics or supplementary feeding programmes, the value gained is arguably as much the services provided at the centres as the food or cash itself. An early review of supplementary feeding programmes documented the range of costs in causing net increment in consumption using inframarginal take-home rations due to substitution as well as the high cost and irregular service delivery with on-site feeding (Beaton and Ghassemi 1982). The Integrated Child Care programme in Honduras (*Atencion Integral al Ninez-Comunitara*), one of the most cost effective community nutrition programmes (Fiedler 2003), made an explicit decision to avoid reliance on supplementary food. The programme aims to improve child care practices at home as well as to provide a simple diagnostic decision tree to identify causes of inadequate child growth. More than three-quarters of the total costs – inclusive of the imputed opportunity costs of volunteers, but not of participating mothers – is for preventative rather than curative care. Fiedler (2003) estimates that the annual long-term incremental recurrent costs were $4 per child. With initial estimates of more than 50 per cent reduction of moderate and severe malnutrition in a country where malnutrition rates were estimated to be about 40 per cent when the programme began (Judith McGuire, personal communication), this is in the neighbourhood of $20 per child prevented from becoming malnourished. Even if the programme proves half as cost-effective, and using only rows 3–5 of table 7.2 and any but the largest discount rates under the maintained assumption that the effects of moving from being undernourished to nourished are the same for infants and young children as those at birth, this type of investment generates a favourable

BCR – 9.4 for a discount rate of 5 per cent and 16.2 for a discount rate of 3 per cent.

Other infant and child nutrition programmes combine supplementary food with other inputs in ways that do not make it possible to identify the impacts of the individual components of the programme, yet are thought to be successful. One example is the well-known Mexican rural anti-poverty human resource investment programme, PROGRESA, that provides nutrition and health information to parents in addition to micronutrient supplements for infants and young children and income transfers to poor families. The combination is estimated by Behrman and Hoddinott (2004) to lead to a 1.2 per cent increase in child height (with control for unobserved fixed effects), which in itself is estimated to lead to a 1–3 per cent increase in lifetime earnings based on the estimates in Thomas and Strauss (1997). Information is not available with which to measure the costs of this intervention on its own (in part because PROGRESA provides a package of benefits), but back-of-the-envelope calculations suggest that the BCR is likely to be greater than one.[35] For another example, Behrman, Cheng and Todd (2004) estimate a BCR of an early child development programme in Bolivia that achieved increases in growth as well as in measures of cognitive development using marginal matching methods to control for selection into the programme on unobserved characteristics. Based on their estimated programme effects and extrapolating what these changes mean for schooling and subsequent earnings on the basis of studies in the literature (and used in opportunity 1), they find BCRs well above one (2.9 for a discount rate of 3 per cent; 1.4 for

---

[34] This estimate is based on the following logic. The costs are in the range $133–$1,064 and the benefits of $1,250 per death averted (as in opportunity 1) are assumed also to include the benefits from reducing infant/child mortality, and these two benefits are assumed to be about 0.21 of the total benefits (0.14 in the case of a discount rate of 3 per cent) as in table 7.2.

[35] Because PROGRESA provides a bundle of benefits – scholarships, nutrient transfers in kind for infants and young children, cash transfers, health and nutrition information – it is not possible to identify with confidence a BCR for the in-kind nutrition supplement in itself. As noted on pp. 364 ff., moreover, there is some ambiguity about what is the appropriate treatment of in-kind provision of goods and services.

a discount rate of 5 per cent), even when assuming incremental costs to raising revenue as is done above.[36]

Opportunity 3: Reducing the Prevalence of Iron, Iodine, Vitamin A and Zinc Deficiencies

Benefits from Reducing Micronutrient Deficiencies

Iodine   The benefits from reducing iodine deficiency are conceptually similar to those from reducing LBW – indeed, an important means of reducing the LBW is to reduce iodine deficiencies in populations in which the prevalence of such deficiencies is high. Both for reducing LBW and reducing iodine deficiency, the main concerns are infant mortality and irreversible impairment of mental capacities that are manifested in lower productivity later in life. That is, although iodine is a required nutrient throughout life, most documented consequences of deficiencies are from pre-natal and early-child deficiencies (Dunn 2003). This evidence comes from epidemiological studies such as the 13.5 difference in IQ between deficient and normal individuals cited above as well as maternal supplementation studies (reviewed in Grantham-McGregor, Fernald and Sethuraman 1999b and Black 2003). The evidence on whether the effects of iodine deficiencies *in utero* can be reversed or whether supplementation or fortification to children can improve performance is less conclusive than the evidence on interventions before birth; though some recent evidence is encouraging (Von den Briel, West and Bleichrodt 2000) it is generally recognized that the earlier an

iodine deficiency can be addressed the greater the impact.

In addition to its influence on cognitive development, iodine deficiencies have been linked to increased child mortality with two randomised trials of intramuscular injections in extreme iodine-deficient areas showing that treatment reduced infant and child mortality by 30 per cent (Rouse 2003). Similarly, a trial using iodine-treated irrigation water reduced infant mortality by half in three villages in China (DeLong *et al.* 1997). In addition, deficiencies lead to lower birth weight or subsequent weight-for-age; Mason *et al.* (2002) present cross-sectional evidence that iodation of salt and or capsule distributions can account for as much as a 40 per cent reduction in LBW.

Because the largest and most assured gains from reducing iodine deficiencies are similar to those for reducing LBW – that is, they manifest in terms of birth outcome and cognitive functions – benefits are estimated along the lines discussed with regard to opportunity 1. We assume that infant and child mortality is reduced by 3 percentage points and the average gain in cognitive development in previously iodine-deficient areas is similar to the average gain in preventing a LBW child. As the costs are expressed per woman, we assume five births per woman. For a 5 per cent discount rate if the cost is less than $130 per deficient women reached, the BCR is greater than one.

Vitamin A   Prior to the 1980s Vitamin A supplementation campaigns were mainly advocated for communities with clinical symptoms indicating risk of blindness. However, in light of meta-analysis of field trials of mass supplementation to children 6–59 months of age that indicated an overall reduction in child mortality by 25–35 per cent (Beaton, Martorell and Aronson 1993, Fawzi *et al.* 1993) Vitamin A promotion is now routine in low-income countries. These and subsequent trials were less consistent in the rates of reduction in morbidity, with greater reduction in severity than incidence of illness (Villamor and Fawzi 2000).[37] Impacts on morbidity are also mediated by presence or absence of other deficiencies – for example, zinc. As with morbidity, the evidence on Vitamin A interventions and growth is mixed, with little impact

---

[36] This study counts the costs of meals provided – a significant share of the total costs – as programme costs and not as transfers with offsetting benefits. If the food were counted only as transfers, the BCR would increase. However as noted on pp. 364 ff., there is some ambiguity about what is the appropriate treatment of in-kind provision of goods and services.

[37] We concentrate here on benefits from the prophylactic provision of Vitamin A or its precursors. Additional therapeutic benefits have regularly been noted in clinical settings. For example, it is now standard practice to provide Vitamin A to children suffering from measles and to use Vitamin A to treat clinical signs of xerophthalmia.

Table 7.4. Estimates of PDVs of Two Classes of Benefits of Vitamin A Intervention, Different Discount Rates

	Annual discount rate (%)					
	1$	2$	3$	5$	10$	20$
1 Reduced mortality	40.94	30.64	30.34	29.76	28.41	26.04
2 Productivity gain due to reduced blindness	26.63	18.88	13.65	7.53	2.17	0.32
Sum of PDV of these two benefits	67.57	49.52	43.99	37.29	30.58	26.36

Source: See text.

of supplementation on growth of moderately deficient children. Children who are severely malnourished or who also have serious infections, however, may benefit more from supplementation (Rivera *et al.* 2003).

While initial evidence on prophylactic supplementation was based on provision to children 6 months or older, targeting of newborn children may have as significant an impact on infant mortality with significant impact on infant mortality reported with supplementation as early as the first two days after delivery (Rahmathullah *et al.* 2003). Moreover, although current recommendations for post-partum supplementation of mothers are aimed at improving the Vitamin A status of the child, one large trial supplementing pregnant women with weekly low doses of Vitamin A showed a marked decrease in maternal mortality in Nepal (West *et al.* 1999). Additional trials are under way. In addition to concerns for the Vitamin A status of young children, there are recommended intakes of Vitamin A for older children as well as adults. Indeed, supplements are regularly provided to school-age children, for example, in school feeding programmes. However, while the cost of this supplementation may be low at the margin, there is little evidence on the economic returns to such programmes in terms of reduced clinical costs or increased productivity.

Changes in rates of Vitamin A deficiency do not correlate well with changes in mortality. For example, improvements in control of xerophthalmia – and, presumably, mortality – in Nepal and Bangladesh have not been accompanied by reduction in Vitamin A deficiencies using serologic cutoffs (West 2002). The estimates of benefits of prophylactic provision of Vitamin A or its precursors used here will thus be phased in terms of an illustrative benefit of reaching an at-risk individual in a programme rather than in terms of a reduction in a deficiency *per se*. This approach differs slightly from how we estimate benefits in the case of LBW (measured in terms of LBW prevented), mainly affecting how to interpret the cost per unit of benefit. These benefits are usually thought to be mainly from changes in mortality. While, as noted, a commonly cited figure for reductions in child mortality is 25–30 per cent, it is also likely that the children missed in any wide-scale programme are also likely to have higher than average risk of mortality (and also that the marginal costs of reaching these children are higher than average costs). Hence, we use a conservative 10 per cent reduction in expected mortality. This reduction will be for infant-plus-child mortality for programmes reaching newborns or their mothers and for incremental child mortality (only) for children reached after 1 year of age. We do not assume any reduction in costs of outpatient or clinic care for survivors. Fiedler (2000) reports one case of blindness prevented for every seven deaths averted in the Vitamin A prophylactic programme in Nepal. This ratio may be higher then elsewhere so we assume a one-to-ten ratio below to estimate the impact on lifetime productivity of reducing blindness.

Table 7.4 gives estimates of the benefits from reducing mortality and from increasing productivity for different discount rates. The basic assumptions underlying these estimates include that infant-and-child mortality rates drop by 25 per cent from 0.10

to 0.075 with the drop concentrated among infants, the prevalence of blindness drops by 0.0025 and productivity of a blind person is a third of the average productivity of a person who is not blind.[38] (The assumptions regarding the value of reducing mortality and the lifetime path of productivity of a person who is not blind are the same as for Opportunity 1 above.) The estimated benefit with a 5 per cent discount rate is $37, with a fifth of that benefit coming from increased lifetime productivity for persons who are not blind but would have been blind without the intervention. In contrast to LBW, under these assumptions the benefits from the productivity gains over decades of work are relatively small in comparison with benefits from reducing early mortality.

Iron   The estimation of the benefits of reducing iron deficiencies must incorporate the fact that iron-deficiency anaemia can affect adult worker productivity directly, as discussed on pp. 364 ff., as well as through its impairment of child development. We have indicated the gains to iron supplementation in terms of LBW in the discussion of opportunity 1. Regardless of birth weight, iron deficiency of young children appears to have irreversible consequences on development; Grantham-McGregor, Fernald and Sethuraman (1999b) find inconclusive evidence that subsequent treatment of young children can offset the consequences of earlier deprivation though prophylactic treatment may be beneficial. However, the inconclusive evidence is, in part, a consequence of ethical considerations that limit long-term interventions. In a review similar to our study, Horton and Ross (2003) find that half a standard deviation reduction in IQ due to iron deficiency anaemia is consistent with the overall evidence (indeed, the most detailed long-term intervention they cite implies a one standard deviation diminution).

In addition to reduced cognitive capacity, iron deficiency can also affect schooling, and hence future productivity, by lowering effort and attendance;

Miguel and Kremer (2004) found that treatment for worms reduced primary school absenteeism by 25 per cent in Kenya. Similarly, productivity in adults can be affected by reduced capacity for effort. Based on their review of published studies – and so they do not include the very recent study of benefits by Thomas, *et al.* (2004) – Horton and Ross assume this productivity loss is 5 per cent for blue-collar workers and 17 per cent for heavy manual labour. They note that this is lower than other assumed losses reported in the literature.

For our benefit estimates, we assume a 5 per cent across-the-board loss of labour productivity due to current anaemia in addition to the gains already discussed in opportunity 1 through reducing LBW. This implies a total benefit of $815 with a 5 per cent discount, which is about 30 per cent above the estimate in table 7.3 for the benefit through reducing LBW alone. However increased benefits come at increased costs, because to obtain these additional ongoing productivity gains, there must be an ongoing flow of interventions over the worklife in addition to the one-time intervention working through birth-weights.

Zinc   Evidence from meta-analyses indicate that zinc supplementation of young children has an appreciable impact on growth with incremental increases in height or weight averaging over 0.3 standard deviations (Brown *et al.* 2002). Poorer growth at the baseline was associated with increased response to treatment. The studies reviewed in this analysis excluded premature or hospitalized children, though supplementation to mothers may also reduce LBW. Moreover, one intervention targeted at SGA children and motivated, in part, by evidence that zinc deficiency is associated with increased infectious disease morbidity indicated that daily supplementation at home reduced infant mortality by 70 per cent (Sazawal *et al.* 2001). While zinc deficiencies are not strongly linked with cognitive development (Black 2003), the results on growth and mortality indicate potential benefits from targeted programmes. However, trials in the literature do not generally provide experience on delivery mechanisms suitable for large-scale interventions (except, perhaps, with multiple fortification). The potential benefits are, nevertheless,

---

[38] We have no basis other than casual observations for this assumption. For the contexts that we are considering in which manual labour is predominant, our intuition is that this is conservative.

important when considering plant breeding for increased bioavailability, as discussed further in opportunity 4.

Key Interventions and Costs for Reducing Micronutrient Deficiencies

Broadly speaking, approaches to reducing micronutrient deficiencies can be categorized as either *supplementation* or *food-based*. The latter are further divided into fortification of foods commonly consumed and encouragement of increased consumption of micronutrient-rich foods through either social marketing or horticulture. Often programmes to increase production include social marketing since increased production does not by itself guarantee increased consumption. Successful programmes may increase income and shift preferences as well as modify techniques of home food preparation.

The costs of supplements *per se* as well as fortificants are easily documented; the costs of delivery systems as well as their efficacy are somewhat harder to obtain. Unfortunately, it is harder still to derive meaningful costs from the sizable literature on social marketing or horticultural approaches – in part because the opportunity costs of, say, home or school gardens are often not considered nor, when costs of any type are provided, is it standard to distinguish start-up from recurrent costs. Few studies that document a significant increase in micronutrient consumption following a food-based intervention assess whether the success is self-replicating or whether recurrent investments are necessary to maintain progress. Proponents of such interventions often indicate that, in addition to impacts on micronutrient status, such projects generate intangible benefits in terms of social capital or empowerment. This potential is not considered in the discussion that follows because we are unaware of persuasive empirical evidence of such possibilities. Finally, it may be possible to reduce micronutrient deficiencies by increasing the bioavailability of nutrients through agronomic research without significantly changing their perceived properties (and, thus, not altering consumer demand) or adding to the cost of production. As the stream of costs and benefits with such approaches differs substantially from other food-based approaches, they are addressed separately below.

These potential micronutrient interventions have both biological synergies and programmatic synergies. For example, utilisation of food sources of Vitamin A or its precursors is influenced by zinc status as well as the presence of intestinal helminths (Jalal *et al.* 1998) while iron absorption is improved when Vitamin C is taken in the same meal. In turn, iron status may complement iodine utilisation. Programmatic synergies occur when the delivery system for one micronutrient lowers the marginal costs for the provision of others. Home gardens to increase the availability of Vitamin A precursors, for instance, also provide other nutrients and the logistics and promotion of dual fortification generates economies of scope.

Costs of Reducing Iodine Deficiencies   The addition of potassium iodine or iodate to table salt is a widespread practice in both developed and developing countries and has been estimated to add no more than US $0.02–0.07 per kg, roughly 5 per cent of the retail cost of salt (Goh 2002). Impacts of successful interventions can be rapid and striking; China with an estimated 40 per cent of the world's at-risk population more than doubled the percentage of individuals consuming salt with at least 20 parts per m (ppm) in a five-year period. In that period, the share of school children with low iodine status (as measured by urine excretion) was reduced by 75 per cent (Goh 2002). Madagascar went from no iodated salt in 1992 to 98.3 per cent coverage by 1999, with a corresponding elimination of low urinary iodine in school children.

These impressive programmes do not imply that fortification is problem-free; industry compliance requires monitoring. Many programmes for fortification in Latin America in the 1950s and 1960s failed for this reason (Dunn 2003). Where quality control is imperfect, reductions in goitre rates are less (Goh 2002). When iodation is not mandatory, consumers need to be made aware of the benefits from using the more expensive fortified alternative. Moreover, a number of remote areas produce their own salt from mines or lake beds. An alternative or supplementary approach is thus to distribute iodated oil capsules or provide intramuscular injections to pregnant women in high-risk underserved areas.[39] Two trials using the latter approach reduced one child death for every eighteen women reached (Rouse 2003). Capsule distribution to women may be similarly effective where fortified salt is not commonly used, although it is redundant or even deleterious where iodine is regularly consumed in salt (Mason *et al.* 2002). Indeed, it may be possible to reach newborn children with capsule distribution with up to a 72 per cent reduction in infant mortality (Cobra *et al.* 1997). Capsule distribution is relatively expensive, however, compared to fortification and may not be suited to preventing damage to children in the first trimester unless supplements are targeted to women of child bearing age rather than to pregnant women or newborn children. Oil injections are also more expensive than fortification, although Levin *et al.* (1993, table 19–7) point out that when the five-year protection provided by this intervention is considered it provided benefits of $13.8 discounted $1,987 for every dollar expenditure on protection. Regular supplementation is also possible, and the costs of supplements have been estimated to be comparable to fortification ($0.05 a year, reported in Alnwick 1998), but this excludes the likely appreciable costs of distribution.

Costs of Reducing Vitamin A Deficiencies
There is over two decades of experience with the provision of prophylactic Vitamin A supplementation, little of it available when Levin *et al.* (1993) illustrated that the intervention was one of the most cost-effective medical interventions, with a BCR of 146. With the safety of the dosage confirmed, the cost of screening within an age cohort is not cost-effective (Loevinsohn, Sutter and Costales 1997). Coverage of supplementation has generally been high during national immunisation days against polio. It has been estimated that the average cost for reaching a child in such immunisation days is about $1 and that the inclusion of Vitamin A in such campaigns adds 2–10 per cent to these costs (Goodman

et al. 2000). However, polio campaigns do not provide regular (twice-yearly) contact and in many countries these have been wound up. Consequently a more sustainable approach may be to add Vitamin A to routine immunisation schedules or to conduct child health days or similar camps to provide services outside of routine clinic visits. As coverage in inoculations generally declines with age, targeting during these procedures offers a particularly effective window of opportunity to reach at-risk populations (Ross 2002). The International Vitamin A Consultative Group recommends that 50,000 international units (IU) of Vitamin A be provided at the same time as infant vaccines. The marginal costs of the supplement remain low for services connected with immunisation programmes; it is more problematic to attribute shares of the costs of community mobilisation (including volunteer effort) to any of the various interventions provided. It is also difficult to determine the increased effectiveness of immunisations due to the adjuvant nature of Vitamin A Ching *et al.* (2000) attempt to translate the costs of supplementation in immunisation campaigns into a cost per life saved, assuming a 23 per cent reduction in mortality when two doses are given annually and half that with one dose.[40] These estimates take into account the coverage rates; as over half the programmes in the years studied achieved more than 80 per cent coverage, the coverage rates used are high. The estimates also depend on the child mortality rates of the different countries. Using incremental costs of Vitamin A of $0.10 and average costs of distribution of $0.43, Chung *et al.* found that the cost per death averted in 1999 was $64 and $294, respectively. While the assumed cost of delivery was constant across countries, costs per death averted varied per country depending on the variables mentioned above; overall, costs per death averted tended to decline as child mortality rates increased. Chung *et al.*, also observe that the relatively few countries that have integrated supplement delivery into routine health services have lower rates of coverage than do national immunisation campaigns.

Fiedler (2000) reports costs of $1.25 per child receiving two doses in Nepal's national programme of distribution through community health workers. He estimates that this programme cost $1.7 m but saved 1.5 m in costs of reduced incidence of diarrhoea and

---

[39] DeLong *et al.* (1997) claim that adding iodine to drinking water or to irrigation is a less expensive alternative than adding it to salt. However, little additional information on the efficacy of this strategy is available.

[40] This is based on Beaton, Martorell and Aronson (1993) although they present more recent cases from Vietnam and the Philippines that are consistent with the earlier study.

measles under the assumption that it costs $3.12 per disease incidence. Moreover, he estimates that the cost per life saved ranged between $289 and $489, depending on assumptions of coverage. In Uganda, it cost $1 to $1.33 per child reached in child health days with a set of services including inoculations, growth monitoring and Vitamin A supplementation (Nutrition and Early Child Development Project, personal communication). In addition, demonstrations and songs were presented to provide information about child care as well as about food production and income-generating possibilities. These costs, however did not include the opportunity cost of time of community volunteers.

While there is evidence that smaller more frequent dosages may be more effective than supplementation at four- or six-month intervals, this requires a different delivery system than commonly provided with immunisations. Similarly, the recommendation from the International Vitamin A Consultative Group that 400,000 IU be provided to mothers within the first six weeks of delivery implies a distinct intervention from those directly aimed at pre-school children. Likewise, the delivery mechanism for addressing maternal mortality with weekly doses is different than that for providing mega-doses to either mothers or their children and may not provide appreciable economies of scale. On the other hand, the costs of this potential intervention can be easily shared with a programme to reduce LBW with regular supplementation of iron. While Rouse (2003) indicates that with reductions of death and costs similar to those observed in the Nepal study cited above it would cost $193 per death averted, it is also acknowledged that this study needs to be replicated. As the benefits from these interventions occur shortly after the costs, there is little sensitivity to assumptions on discount rates.

There also exist a number of promising vehicles for fortification to reduce Vitamin A deficiency (Dary and Mora 2002). Given the role of fat in absorption, cooking oil and margarine are particularly promising, although flour and sugar have been used and MSG-piloted.

To our knowledge, only one study has directly compared the costs of supplementation, fortification and promotion of home gardening to prevent Vitamin A deficiency in the same programme environment (Phillips *et al.* 1996). Using various outcome measures in terms of persons or adequacy reached, the study found that sugar fortification was generally less expensive than alternatives for the same outcome in Guatemala. For example, at medium levels of fortification the cost of achieving Vitamin A adequacy for high-risk groups (i.e. women and children) was half as expensive as capsule distribution and one-quarter as expensive as encouraging home gardens under various assumptions about the drop-out rate following discontinuation of input subsidies.

Fiedler *et al.* (2000) make a similar comparison of the costs of supplementation and a hypothetical fortification of wheat flour in the Philippines in order to ensure intake of at least 70 per cent of recommended levels. They note that the opportunity costs of volunteers constituted 30 per cent of supplementation costs, while the capsules themselves comprised only 3 per cent of the costs. They find that it cost roughly twice as much per child year of adequate intake achieved using supplementation as fortification. Their estimate of the full costs of supplementation was approximately $10 per year of adequacy achieved. They also note that the cost per year of adequacy achieved with supplements rises as parallel efforts of fortification increase. They also note that although fortification is more cost-effective, it would miss more children than the supplementation programme was able to reach. Implicitly, then, the greater coverage with higher costs points to rising marginal costs of coverage.

Some qualifications are needed before generalizing on the relative effectiveness of fortification in these studies. In particular, fortification may be effective in urbanized Latin America or in Asian economies where even rural markets are penetrated by processed foods, yet not be as promising in rural Africa. While particular attention has been given to the local dietary role of the food to be supplemented, technical considerations also include the loss or potency during shipping and storage and the potential for discoloration that may reduce consumer acceptance. Moreover, when close substitutes are not fortified, even small increases in costs may not be easily passed on. Fortification programmes in both the Philippines and Guatemala have been intermittently halted due to shortages of imported ingredients or the lack of interest of producers. Similar marketing issues have prevented programmes such as the MSG pilot in the Philippines from being brought to scale. On the other hand, Fiedler *et al.* (2000) indicate that ten products marketed in the Philippines were fortified with Vitamin A at the time of their study.

Moreover, with a few exceptions such as Muhilal *et al.* (1988) and English *et al.* (1997), studies that indicate the effectiveness of fortification or other food-based approaches use changes in consumption or changes in serum levels of Vitamin A as outcome measures rather than either morbidity or mortality. Using changes in consumption is particularly problematic when assessing the promotion of gardens, since plant-based sources, particularly green leafy vegetables, may be less effective for improving Vitamin A status than previously assumed (de Pee, Bloem and Kiess 2000). A review of food-based strategies noted that a number of recent evaluations have shown an impact of strategies to modify cooking and storage or cultivate home gardens on consumption of Vitamin A rich foods, generally when linked with social marketing or nutrition education. However, few of these studies measure nutritional status and none reviewed by Ruel (2001) were designed to assess changes in morbidity or mortality. Moreover, most studies that focus on changes in intake do not contain information on costs. Pant *et al.* (1996), however, are able compare the effectiveness of nutrition education to mega-dose supplementation in Nepal. They found that both achieved similar reductions in the risk of mortality (by 36 per cent and 43 per cent, respectively) although the capsule distribution programme was more economical. The education programme, however, was more effective at reducing cases of xerophthalmia.

Costs of Reducing Iron-Deficiency Anaemia
Supplementation to address iron-deficiency anaemia is more difficult than for iodine or Vitamin A deficiency since it is not possible to provide mega-doses. Thus, with the exception of providing supplements to school children or other groups that assemble regularly, a health worker cannot easily administer the desired treatment and must rely on patient compliance. Small-dose supplements have

fewer side effects and greater biological effectiveness when taken regularly, but this increases the cost of treatment. However, as mentioned above, the costs of regular monitoring of compliance may be less than the benefits when targeting pregnant women in high-density populations of South Asia where rates of both anaemia and LBW are high. The evidence cited pertains to child survival but it is likely that similar programmes will reduce maternal mortality although prospective studies are limited by ethical considerations as well as sample-size requirements (Allen 2000).

Due to problems of compliance, an intermittent schedule has been recommended, often in terms of weekly instead of daily supplements. Some of these studies have found little difference in efficacy as measured by serological indicators (Galloway and McGuire 1996, Beard 2000). However, meta-analysis of twenty-two trials concluded that weekly doses were less efficacious than daily doses (Beaton and McCabe 1999). While the authors of this analysis acknowledged that it is not known what the relative cost implications were of designing delivery systems to reach the target groups, they concluded that weekly supplementation was not advisable for pregnancy.

There are many vehicles for fortification of iron, either as single nutrients or in combination with others. This includes home-based fortification with sachets to be sprinkled on food as well as industrial fortification of flours, rice and salt (Mannar and Gallego 2002). Horton and Ross (2003) provide an estimate of a BCR using the costs of $0.12 *per capita* derived from the early experience of compulsory fortification of corn flour and voluntary fortification of wheat flour in Venezuela and benefits estimated from ten countries. The median value using productivity gains only was 6.3:1 and 35.7:1 when estimates of increased cognitive development were also included. Unfortunately, while initial survey data in Venezuela following the fortification showed a halving of anaemia, rates returned to pre-fortification levels in subsequent years (Garcia-Casal and Layrisse 2002). This may, perhaps, reflect declining economic conditions, but no confirmation is available. Using a different set of assumptions and programmes to extrapolate from probable increases in haemoglobin to work productivity, Levin *et al.*

(1993) estimated that fortification could provide a BCR of 84 and supplementation could achieve a ratio of 25.

Promotion of home gardening is not generally promoted as a strategy to reduce iron-deficiency anaemia; although iron absorption is enhanced when Vitamin C is taken at the same meal, overall iron absorption from plant sources is low. Other food-based strategies include increased frequency of consumption of animal-based foods and changes in food preparation. An example is the provision of iron cooking pots in Ethiopia. A pilot trial found that the provision of pots (costing about $3 per pot) was less costly than providing supplements to the same population for a year (Ruel 2001); no toxicity was noted.

In addition to supplementation and fortification, the mass provision of deworming medicine may affect anaemia. Miguel and Kremer (2004) found that it cost $3.50 to increase school participation one child year via deworming of children in Kenya, presumably partially mediated through reduced anaemia (though this was not assessed). Similarly, a combined programme of deworming and supplementation was found to increase pre-school participation in Delhi. Using a range of plausible assumptions this was extrapolated to the estimated impact on earnings with an additional $29 expected for a cost of $1.70 per child (Bobonis, Miguel, and Sharma 2003). A similar intervention – a combination of deworming and daily supplementation – was found to improve motor and language development of pre-school children in Zanzibar (Stolzfus *et al.* 2001). It is possible that iron supplementation to non-anaemic populations can have detrimental impact for women with reasonable iron stores; these risks are relatively small compared to the potential benefits (Allen 2000). An additional potential cost recognized in the literature is the risk of increased infection. However, a meta-analysis of supplementation trials failed to find a significantly elevated risk of overall incidence of infections in children (Gera and Sachdev 2002).

Summary of Benefits and Costs for Reducing Micronutrient Deficiencies

The available evidence suggests that the BCRs may considerably exceed one for best practices for reducing micronutrient deficiencies related to iron-deficiency anaemia and iodine and Vitamin A deficiencies in a number of developing country contexts. Such potential is limited, of course, to areas in which the prevalence of such deficiencies is relatively high due to natural conditions and past market and policy developments.

Opportunity 4: Investment in Technology in Developing Country Agriculture

Definition and Description of Opportunity

Approximately 798 m people are considered hungry. Further, inadequate access to food – in terms of both macronutrients and micronutrients – is associated with malnutrition among children and adults. Technological improvements in developing country agriculture may have important effects on reducing hunger and malnutrition. In this opportunity, we focus on technological change embodied in improved cultivars – improved genetic material in seeds that permits increased grain yield; higher levels of micronutrients; greater responsiveness to other inputs such as fertilizers or water; reduced need for complementary inputs such as pesticides and herbicides; greater tolerance to pests, droughts or other stresses; shorter maturity times; improved post-harvest qualities (e.g. greater resistance to disease or pests when stored), and improved taste. A broader definition of technological improvements would add to this improved agronomic practices such as integrated pest management whereby pests are controlled through crop rotation and the careful use of natural predators and the use of trees for shade, green fertilizer and nitrogen fixation in soils; and improvements in complementary inputs such as fertilizers and pesticides (Kerr and Kolavalli 1999).

How Does this Opportunity Partially Solve the Challenge?

From Malthus (1817/1992) to the early 1980s, hunger was seen as a consequence of inadequate food production, or increases in production in a world characterized by rapidly growing population. However, the since 1980 years have seen a recasting of the problem of world hunger in terms of access or 'entitlement' to food. Formalized most famously by Sen (1981, 1999), hunger results when the resources of individuals and households – reflecting the *assets they hold and the returns on those assets* – are inadequate to acquire sufficient food conditional on prices.

Investing in research, in technological improvements to developing country agriculture, provides the opportunity to reduce hunger and malnutrition through four channels: increasing net returns on assets – land and labour – by farm households in areas where hunger is endemic; increasing labour demand in rural areas, thereby increasing the incomes of landless labourers; reducing the costs of food which benefits net food consumers in both rural and urban areas; and improving access to micronutrients.

Increasing Net Returns on Assets – Land and Labour – By Farm Households in Areas where Hunger is Endemic   There is overwhelming evidence, surveyed in Lipton with Longhurst (1989), Kerr and Kolavalli (1999) and Runge *et al.* (2003) that improved cultivars have been associated with dramatic increases in yields. It is important to note, however, that technological change in agriculture extends well beyond the development and dissemination of hybrid varieties of rice and wheat that became known as the 'Green Revolution'. Byerlee (1996), cited in Kerr and Kolavalli (1999), notes that most farmers have replaced their varieties at least twice since the introduction of high-yielding rice and wheat in the late 1960s. These second-generation modern varieties contribute yield gains of about 1 per cent annually. Whether these increases in yields lead to increases in incomes, particularly among poor households, is less clear-cut. The answer depends on the pattern of adoption over time, the ability to obtain and use complementary inputs such as water and fertilizer, as well as changes in input and output prices. In turn, these are affected by market and institutional arrangements such as access to credit and market structure and market policies.

Increasing Labour Demand in Rural Areas, Thereby Increasing the Incomes of Landless Labourers   Improved cultivars have the potential to increase the demand for labour through several channels. Increased yields imply that additional labour is needed for harvesting and processing. The prospect of higher yields may also encourage farmers to weed more intensively, which also increases labour demand, as does the introduction of short-duration varieties that make it possible to increase the number of crops planted and harvested over a given period and cultivars with increased drought resistance that permit food to be grown in more marginal areas. Incomes, particularly those of landless labourers, will rise if wages increase, if the amount of employment rises, or if both occur. The increase in wages and employment depends critically on the elasticity of labour supply. In the short run, wages will rise if labour supply is highly inelastic and employment will rise if labour supply is highly elastic. In the longer run, labour supply may become more elastic if higher wages induce inmigration and labour demand may fall, or grow less rapidly, if labour costs rise relative to labour-substituting inputs such as machinery. While it is possible that increased profitability as well as the time demands of multiple cropping may encourage mechanisation, the bulk of the evidence indicates that the introduction of improved cultivars increased wages and employment in Bangladesh, India, Nepal, Pakistan, the Philippines and Thailand, though the effects were uneven within and across these countries (Pinstrup-Andersen and Hazell 1985; Alauddin and Tisdell 1986; Anderson, Herot and Scobie 1988; Abler, Tolley and Kriplani 1994; David and Otsuka 1994; Goldman and Smith 1995).

Reducing the Costs of Food that Benefit Net Food Consumers in Both Rural and Urban Areas   Increases in output can lead to reductions in food prices, thus benefiting net food consumers in both rural and urban areas. Even modest price changes can generate significant welfare gains where food purchases, especially staples, comprise a large share of household budgets. The magnitude of the price fall will depend on the price elasticity of demand, the existence and extent of price controls on food, and the extent to which local food markets are integrated into regional, national and global food markets. It will also be affected by changes in demand brought about by population and income growth.

Again, there is considerable evidence from Asia (Bangladesh, India, the Philippines) that food prices have gradually declined as higher-yielding cultivars have spread (Quizon and Binswanger 1986; Byerlee and Moha 1993; Warr and Coxhead 1993). In China, Fan, Fang and Zhang (2001) estimate that investment in agricultural research led to higher output and, in turn lowered food prices that account for 30 per cent of the reduction in urban poverty between 1992 and 1998. In India, expenditures on agricultural research are associated with higher outputs and higher outputs are associated with a reduction in food prices, with an elasticity of 0.23. In turn, a 10 per cent decline in food prices is associated with a reduction in urban poverty of 3.5 per cent (Fan 2002).

Improving Access to Micronutrients   As explained on pp. 364 ff. and in opportunity 3, micronutrient deficiencies are costly. Traditionally, such deficiencies have been addressed via efforts to diversify diets and through the fortification of foods during processing. However, plant breeding work undertaken in the 1990s – using both conventional crop-breeding and biotechnology – shows that it is possible to breed rice and wheat plants that are more dense in iron, zinc and Vitamin A.

There are several possible constraints that would prevent such an approach – commonly refereed to as 'biofortification' – from being successful. First, farmers might be reluctant to adopt such varieties if they compromised yields or incomes. Second, consumers might not be willing to eat such foods. And third, micronutrient intakes might not be increased very much (Bouis 2002a). With respect to the first question, Graham, Welch and Bouis (2001) and Welch's (2002) reviews suggest that these nutritionally enhanced cultivars are more resistant to disease and environmental stress. Their roots extend more deeply into the soil, by tapping more sub-soil moisture and nutrients, they are more drought resistant and require less irrigation. Their roots release chemical compounds that unbind trace minerals present in most soils, and thus they require fewer chemical inputs. Lastly, nutritionally enhanced seeds produce seedlings with higher survival rates and more rapid initial growth (Bouis 2002a).

Regarding consumer preferences, in the case of iron and zinc mineral micronutrients comprise less than 10 ppm in milled rice, so it is unlikely that such amounts will affect the taste, appearance or texture of rice or wheat in a manner that affects consumer demand. However, this may not be the case for Vitamin A; higher levels of beta-carotene turn light-coloured varieties of rice to dark yellow, producing 'golden rice'. Consumers also may resist 'golden rice' since it is a product of genetic modification through gene splicing. However, in many cases, nutritional enhancement can be achieved through conventional crop breeding.

Research on the third question is ongoing. Preliminary results from Bangladesh, however, suggest that a 50 per cent increase in iron intakes derived from fortified rice would reduce anemia by as much as 6 per cent (Bhargava, Bouis and Schrimshaw 2001) and that 'golden rice' would increase provitamin A by 79–90 per cent in women and pre-school children (Bouis, 2002a).

Economic Estimates of the Benefits and Costs

There are a number of specific issues associated with assessing the benefits and costs of improved agricultural technologies. First, there is the issue of the appropriate assessment of costs. As a general guide, it takes about seven–ten years to develop a new variety with reliably improved attributes along some dimensions. But as Runge *et al.* (2003, p. 85) point out, 'New crops not only carry forward the genes of earlier varieties, they also carry the crop breeding and selection strategies of earlier breeders.' It is not always clear whether measured costs include the marginal costs of the development of a particular variety or some combination of marginal and fixed costs such as those associated with basic research and development (R&D). Second, there is no guarantee that crop breeding will be successful, so there is a legitimate question as to whether discount rates should include a risk premium. Third, estimated returns will be sensitive to assumptions regarding demand and supply elasticities, whether markets are open or closed to trade, whether prices are endogenous or exogenous, whether environmental effects are included and the unit of analysis (e.g. local or regional assessments) may omit spillover effects into other regions or to other commodities (Alston, *et al.* 2000). Fourth, two-thirds of estimates of rates of return on technological investments in developing country agriculture that have been produced since 1958, and 80 per cent of those published since 1990 are found in the 'gray literature' rather than as formal journal articles. 'Gray literature' estimates could potentially be lower than those found in journal articles if 'publication bias' discourages the publication of 'non-results' or may be more error-prone if they are dominated by work that was not considered sufficiently rigorous for journal articles.

Alston *et al.* (2000) provide the most comprehensive survey of returns to investments in agricultural R&D. The average estimated social rate of return (SRR) across the 1,700-odd studies they considered is high, 79.3 per cent, but there is significant variation around this mean. The median estimated SRR is approximately 44 per cent. This can be translated into a BCR by noting that $SRR \approx BCR(i)$ where i is the discount rate (Alston *et al.* 2000). Under this formula, the BCR is 14.7 using a 3 per cent discount rate and 8.8 using a 5 per cent discount rate.[41] Median estimated rates of return by geographical region are 34.3 per cent in SSA, 49.5 per cent in Asia and the Pacific and 42.9 per cent in Latin America and the Caribbean. Alston *et al.* also undertake a meta-analysis to determine whether these estimates are sensitive to characteristics of the research or the researchers. These suggest that rates of return have not declined over time, nor do they appear sensitive to the inclusion of spillover effects or market distortions. However, reported results do appear to be sensitive to a number of characteristics: specifically, they are lower when a longer gestational period for research is assumed or specified, when the principal researcher is based at a university, or when the results are published in a non-refereed publication.

There are a number of additional reasons to be cautious about these estimates. First, there are important issues relating to the assumed distributions over time of both costs and benefits. While some

attention is paid to the distribution over time of benefits,[42] it is not always clear how costs are distributed across time. Given the nature of discounting, assuming that costs are spreadout evenly as opposed to being largely 'up-front' can significantly increase the BCR. Second, a number of studies appear to estimate benefits based on data taken from experimental plots. Actual increases in farm yields may be lower, especially where water control is imperfect and where there are difficulties obtaining inputs on a timely basis – characteristics that apply especially in much of SSA. Third, while assumptions are often stated about the extent of adoption, it is less clear whether the distributions of *adopters* – particularly by farm management skills – are taken into account. Bourdillon *et al.* (2003) illustrate this in their analysis of the impact of new maize hybrids introduced in Zimbabwe in the mid-1990s. Unconditional comparisons of means suggested that adopters enjoyed considerable gains in gross incomes, of the order of 50 per cent. However, when controls for household characteristics were included as well as taking into account the endogeneity of the adoption decision, the increase in gross incomes was considerably less, of the order of 10 per cent.

Lest these caveats appear too negative, we again note the core reasons for including investment in agricultural technologies as one of our opportunities. In our view, these represent the single most effective means of increasing incomes of those groups across and within developing countries who suffer from hunger. While these caveats suggest that returns may not be as high as is sometimes claimed, they are likely to be sufficiently high to justify increased investment – and because the social returns to increasing knowledge are likely to exceed the private returns, public subsidies are likely to be warranted on efficiency grounds.

Because improved cultivars that are more dense in iron, zinc and Vitamin A are still being developed, there are no *ex post* assessments of rates of return to these investments. There are, however, a number of *ex ante* assessments. In addition to being somewhat speculative, these assessments of benefits depend critically on three assumptions. The first relates to the increase in micronutrient density within these improved cultivars. The second relates to coverage or take-up amongst those with micronutrient

---

[41] Note that this approximation assumes that benefits flow in perpetuity; relaxing this assumption will lower the estimated BCR.

[42] In particular, new varieties break down over time. For example, Byerlee (1993) notes that mutation of rust pathogens means that new varieties of hybrid wheat typically have a life span of seven years before they need to be replaced.

deficiencies. Take-up could be relatively high, but if it is concentrated among populations where deficiencies are limited or non-existent, they will have little impact. The third relates to bioavailability or bioconversion – the ability of the human body to use the micronutrients found in these improved grains. Even if density within the grains is greatly increased and even if take-up amongst affected populations is high, impact will be minimal if these micronutrients are not bioavailable.

Bouis (2002a, 2002b) provides estimates of the BCRs of the dissemination of iron and zinc dense varieties of rice and wheat in India and Bangladesh. He assumes a twenty-five-year time period. There are no benefits in the first ten years, only costs associated with plant breeding and dissemination. Using a 3 per cent discount rate, and incorporating an allowance for maintenance costs over the following fifteen years, the present value of these costs is estimated at $35.9 m. Benefits accrue from years eleven to twenty-five. Conservatively, it is assumed that these improved varieties are adopted in only 10 per cent of the area devoted to rice and wheat, and that they reduce anaemia rates by only 3 per cent, averting 44 m cases of anaemia annually. The present discounted lifetime value of a case of anaemia averted is $27.50, as calculated by Horton and Ross (2003). Using these assumptions, the total PV of nutrition benefits is $694 m, giving a BCR of 19 or an internal rate of return of 29 per cent.[43] In addition to using conservative assumptions and omitting the beneficial impact of higher zinc intake or the impact on individuals who increase iron intake but remain anaemic, these calculations omit the fact that these iron and zinc dense varieties produce higher yields. Table 7.5 shows the impact on benefit-cost ratios of relaxing these assumptions.

Zimmerman and Qaim (2003) provide *ex ante* BCRs for the dissemination of 'golden rice' in the Philippines. They ignore the costs of the basic research undertaken on these varieties, focusing only on the marginal costs associated with adapting, testing and disseminating these biofortified rice varieties over a seven-year period. They take into account the need for public information campaigns to encourage consumers to eat this new rice and also assume that there will be recurrent costs for maintenance research and monitoring. Using the cost figures they provide, the PDV of these costs

over a twenty-five-year period with a 3 per cent discount rate is $9.5 m. They consider only benefits to three target groups: pre-school children, pregnant women and lactating mothers. These are calculated in terms of averted DALYs from reduced mortality, and reduced incidence of temporary or permanent disability resulting from blindness. Each DALY is assumed to carry an opportunity cost of current *per capita* income, $1,030.[44] A variety of scenarios are presented. Assuming benefits occur in years eight to twenty-five, under the 'pessimistic scenario', a 25 per cent coverage rate, low density of beta-carotene (1.6 μG/G), processing loss of betacarotene of 25 per cent and poor bioconversion, 'golden rice' produces a present discounted value of $135.8 m. The BCR is 14.3.[45] Under the optimistic scenario, with 100 per cent coverage, higher density of beta-carotene (3.0 μG/G), no losses of betacarotene during processing and better bioconversion, 'golden rice' produces a PDV of $753.9 m and a BCR of 79.3.

Strengths and Limitations Associated with this Framework for Considering Opportunities

To identify which of the areas of interest for the Copenhagen Consensus present real opportunities in the sense of having high expected BCRs or high IRRs, information is required on time patterns of expected resource costs and benefits and prices, uncertainties for each of these time paths and the appropriate discount rate. It is also important to identify the relevance of opportunities in terms of basic policy motives of distribution (e.g. alleviating poverty) and efficiency (e.g. narrowing the difference between private and social rates of return to an action). To have a realistic perspective about what

---

[43] Bouis presents only estimates for a discount rate of 3 per cent. Under the assumption that the benefits are distributed evenly over the eleven–twenty-five-year period, with a discount rate of 5 per cent the BCR is 11.6.

[44] As noted above, these gains would probably be reduced considerably if each DALY were evaluated at the least-cost alternative of obtaining a DALY.

[45] These estimates only use a 3 per cent discount rate. Again assuming that the benefits are distributed evenly over the eight–twenty-five year period, a 5 per cent discount rate produces a BCR of 8.5.

Table 7.5. Simulated Discounted Costs and Benefits of Iron and Zinc Dense Rice, India and Bangladesh, Assuming 3% Discount Rate

	Variety adoption rate (%)			
	10		20	
	Anaemia reduction rate (%)			
	3	8	3	8
Total costs	35.9	35.9	43.7	43.7
Total nutrition benefits	694.2	1851.2	1388.4	3702.4
Total agricultural benefits	2142.7	2142.7	4285.3	4285.3
Nutrition benefits/costs	19.3	51.5	31.8	84.7
(Nutrition + agricultural) benefits/costs	79.0	109.6	129.8	182.8

Notes: All monetary amounts are in $ million.
Source: Bouis (2002b).

underlies the BCRs or IRRs on which the Copenhagen Consensus Experts have to make their ranking, it is useful to review here some of the major components of such calculations.[46]

Discount Rates and Time Horizons

Impacts often are spaced over time, with different time patterns for different impacts. Because there is an opportunity cost in terms of waiting, the benefits must be discounted; the choice of the discount rate can make a considerable difference for investments for which there are considerable lags (e.g. the impact of improved *in utero* nutrition on adult health five or six decades later). Appendix table 7A.1 provides some illustrations of the PDVs of an impact of $1,000 over different time horizons and alter-

native discount rates. The PDV of $1,000 received fifty years later is $608.04 with a discount rate of 1 per cent, $371.53 with a discount rate of 2 per cent, $228.11 with a discount rate of 3 per cent, $87.20 with a discount rate of 5 per cent, and $8.52 with a discount rate of 10 per cent. For impacts with lags of this duration, the benefit (and thus the BCR) can be tripled by changing the discount rate from 5 per cent to 3 per cent or increased by ten by changing the discount rate from 10 per cent to 5 per cent. Thus whether a project with this benefit is a great choice or a lousy choice may depend critically on the discount rate that is used. For lags that are less long, the PDVs vary less with the discount rates, but they still may vary substantially even with lags of five–ten years. Where possible, we have used two discount rates, 3 per cent and 5 per cent; nevertheless, because there does not seem to be agreement on what discount rate is appropriate, any effort to compare opportunities across challenges may end up only reflecting the different discount rates that different analysts choose rather than the true merits of the alternatives.

While the mathematics of discounting are well understood, there is a further implication worth noting. Many of the interventions we describe convey multiple benefits but these are obtained over different time periods. Different discount rates not only generate different PDVs, they also alter the proportion of benefits received from different sources. We use our work on the benefits of reducing

---

[46] Knowles and Behrman (2003) discuss these issues at some length. The health issues we consider are often addressed using DALYs. The approach can be adapted to accommodate assumptions on discount rates and to consider changes in productivity conceptually the same as with disabilities. While the DALY approach is generally used for cost-effectiveness comparisons, it can be converted to a CSA with assumptions similar, but not identical to those used here. See, for example, Levin *et al.* (1993). There are basic questions about how best to evaluate DALYs that are parallel to the questions discussed in the text for mortality. That is, what we argue is the preferred alternative for evaluating a DALY due to a particular intervention is to use the least-cost alternative means of attaining one DALY, but in some studies (e.g. discussion of opportunity 4), DALYs are evaluated by *per capita* income, which leads to much larger estimated benefits.

low birth weight (LBW) to illustrate this. The BCRs were based on a discount rate of 5 per cent. Appendix table 7A.2 summarizes estimates that are identical to those in table 7.3 with the single exception that the same range of discount rates as in appendix table 7A.1 is used, including 5 per cent for easy comparison.

The overall effect of these alternative discount rates is a sum of PDV of benefits that ranges from 30 per cent to 351 per cent of that in table 7.2 (bottom row of appendix table 7A.2).[47] This is a considerable range. But the discount rates also vary in the table, from 1 per cent to 20 per cent. But even with small changes in discount rates the PDVs may vary considerably. For example, the sum of the PDV for all seven benefits with a discount rate of 3 per cent is 170 per cent as large as that with 5 per cent. The sum of the PDV for all seven benefits with a discount rate of 10 per cent is 47 per cent as large as that with a discount rate of 5 per cent. And many studies use discount rates within the 3–10 per cent range. It certainly is not known that the 'right' discount rate is 5 per cent and not 3 per cent, or vice versa. But, to illustrate, with 3 per cent an intervention costing almost $1,000 ($986) per infant moved from LBW to non-LBW would be warranted, while with 5 per cent the maximum that would result is a favorable BCR would be $580. Further, the relative importance of different classes of benefits also varies widely. Using a 2 per cent discount rate, the reduction in costs of chronic diseases and the intergenerational benefits contribute just over 25 per cent to the total PDV, a substantial contribution. Using a 10 per cent discount rate, these two benefits contribute only 3 per cent of total PDV. In other words, whether one perceives that these two benefits are important depends critically on the discount rate used.

Costs The PDV of the costs should equal the marginal resources needed for the intervention. Since a significant share of the total costs of an intervention is typically incurred at the time of the intervention, the question of what discount rate is appropriate is not likely to be as important for the costs as for the benefits. Nevertheless, discounting still may be of some importance because the initial costs may be spread over some time and because there may be important recurring costs. Three

other points about the relevant costs are important to mention because they are not always followed in the literature. First, the relevant costs are *resource costs* that do *not* include transfers, even though transfers may be important parts of public sector budgetary costs.[48] Second, the relevant costs are those *experienced by society*, not only by the public sector. The private costs often include, for example, the time costs for members of society and the distortionary costs of raising revenues for interventions and of making the interventions. Both may be considerable. For instance, a major share of the costs of time-intensive interventions such as schooling or training is often the opportunity cost of time not spent in productive activities. For another example, it has been estimated that the distortionary cost (often called the 'deadweight loss') of raising a dollar of tax revenue in the USA and in other countries ranges from $0.17 to $0.85, depending on the type of tax used (e.g. Ballard, Shoven and Whalley 1985; Feldstein 1995; Van der Gaag and Tan 1997). Third, costs may vary by *scale of intervention*, the *duration* over which it takes place and the *prevalence* of the problem. It is difficult to say, *a priori*, how these will affect costs. Larger-scale interventions may benefit from economies of scale or scope (for example, where it is possible to make purchases in bulk) but may be more likely to suffer from managerial inefficiencies. As interventions are implemented, learning-by-doing may drive down implementation costs but as the 'easier' cases of malnutrition or hunger are addressed, the costs of reaching the 'harder' cases (e.g. individuals found in remote areas) may rise.

---

[47] The PDVs of all of the benefits (except reduced neonatal care, which is not discounted) decline as the discount rate increases. But they decline at very different rates because of the different lags for the different benefits. As the discount rate increases, the benefits that are early in the lifecycle (reduced infant mortality, reduced neonatal care and reduced costs of infant/child illness) become relatively more important.

[48] Operationalizing the point about transfers, however, may be difficult in many circumstances. Transfers in terms of money are fairly straightforward. In-kind transfers are more ambiguous. Goods such as food provided in-kind typically are (appropriately) considered transfers, but in-kind provision of services (e.g. subsidised schooling or health clinics) often are not considered transfers, though the real distinction is not clear.

Benefits

Estimating the PDV of benefits due to an intervention is difficult for many reasons. Most interventions have multiple impacts, some positive and cutting across the different challenges considered here and some negative, because they affect the basic

constraints under which entities such as households and firms and farms are making their decisions – thus resulting in what Rosenzweig and Wolpin (1982) call 'the unintended consequences' of programmes and policies. Most economic evaluations of the magnitudes of impacts must be made on the basis of imperfect non-experimental data, which raises problems of estimation due to endogeneity of right-hand-side variables, unobserved heterogeneity and selected sub-samples.[49] Though there are a number of studies that provide evidence that controlling for such estimation problems can change impact estimates substantially (and even, in some cases, reverse the signs!), far too often associations in micro or in aggregate data are interpreted as if they reflect causal effects. Most impact estimates, moreover, do not relate well to the basic policy motives of efficiency and distribution.[50] In particular, the efficiency policy motive pertains to differences between private and social impacts due, for example, to positive externalities, for which reason there may be an efficiency argument for public subsidies for an action. But most micro-estimates present only private impacts and most aggregate estimates present only total impacts, so neither provides a basis for judging the efficiency case for interventions.

Further, estimated benefits will vary due to country-specific conditions. For example, a greater share of births in hospitals and higher costs of medical care will increase the second benefit from reduced LBW, while higher average productivity will change the fifth benefit. Changes in the return to schooling will increase the benefits of averted low birth-weights, reduced pre-schooler malnutrition and certain micronutrient deficiencies. To illustrate the implications of these uncertainties and intercountry differences in the case of birth weight, Alderman and Behrman present a set of seven simulations, each of which starts with the base estimates in table 7.2, still with a 5 per cent discount rate,[51] but increases one of the seven benefits by 50 per cent (appendix table 7A.3).[52] These simulations permit the examination, for example, of what difference it would make for the estimates of the PDV of overall benefits if the probability of infant mortality fell by 0.117 instead of by 0.078, if the lowest alternative cost of preventing such mortality were $1,875 instead of $1,250, if the resource

[49] Some of these issues also may be problems with experimental data, depending on the details of the experiments. There are a relatively few cases in which impact evaluations in developing countries are based on what appear to be good experiments such as those associated with the PROGRESA programme (e.g. Gertler *et al.* 2003; Behrman and Hoddinott 2004; Behrman, Sengupta and Todd 2004) or smaller-scale experiments such as in NGO schools in Kenya (e.g. Miguel and Kremer 2002, 2004) or differential nutritional supplements among four rural Guatemalan communities (e.g. Martorell 1995; Behrman *et al.* 2003) or with random assignment of vouchers among poor student applicants in urban Colombia (e.g. Angrist *et al.* 2002).

[50] While some of the nutrition literature discusses possible market failures that might lead to inefficiencies, the discussion is not always clear. For example, ACC/SCN (2004, 4–3) states:

> *Market Failure:* The principles of cost-conscious public spending demand that governments contribute to the cost of services only if individuals are unwilling to pay for these services themselves. In the health sector, fees have been introduced for curative health services and products because sick people are highly motivated to pay for treatment. For the same reason, these services can be privatized. But preventive nutrition services such as micronutrient supplementation and breastfeeding promotion are much more difficult to market on a willing-to-pay basis, even though they may offer much better value for money.

Standard analysis of economic efficiency, however, suggests only public subsidies if the social rates of return exceed the private ones (and taxes if they are below), which is *not* the same as inferring that neither taxes nor subsidies would be efficiency-enhancing for curative health care because people pay positive prices, nor that they would be efficiency-enhancing for micronutrient supplementation because people are not willing to pay very high prices.

[51] Appendix table 7A.3 indicates what would happen if there were changes that increased each of the benefits. The implications of changes that reduced each of the benefits, of course, would be similar in spirit but opposite in sign.

[52] Under any assumed discount rate, a proportional (decrease) increase in the estimates of future benefits has an equal proportional change in the discounted benefit. Thus, one can vary the assumptions used in any column of table 7.2 to explore other variations of the core assumptions in a manner parallel to that illustrated here.

costs for the extended hospital stay for LBW infants were $314 instead of $209, if the additional resource costs for LBW infants and children averaged at $60 instead of $40, if the gain in annual earnings due to reduced stunting were 3.3 per cent instead of 2.2 per cent, if the relevant baseline earnings were $750 rather than $500, if the gain in ability were 8.0 per cent rather than 5.3 per cent, if the reduced lost productivity and medical care cost from chronic diseases averaged fifteen rather than ten years of low-income earnings, or if the intergenerational effects were 50 per cent larger than assumed in table 7.2.

Each of these changes, of course, increases the total PDV of benefits with estimates that range from $591 (chronic illnesses) to $699 (productivity effects of ability) as compared with $580 from table 7.2. This means, not surprisingly, that under each of these alternative assumptions somewhat higher-cost interventions would be warranted. But, because there are multiple benefits, increasing any one of the benefits by 50 per cent increases the PDV of the sum of benefits by much less than 50 per cent – indeed by from 2 per cent to 21 per cent. The estimates in appendix table 7A.3 also illustrate the obvious point that it is much more important to pin down the magnitudes of some of the benefits than others. With a 5 per cent discount rate it would appear most important to lessen uncertainty about the estimates of the impact on economic productivity and secondly on early life mortality and morbidity costs than on, at the other extreme, the costs and probabilities of chronic diseases.[53]

[53] With a higher (lower) discount rate, the value of improved estimates would shift somewhat towards events earlier (later) in the life cycle.

[54] For other examples of such use, see Summers (1992, 1994), Van der Gaag and Tan (1997), Behrman and Knowles (2003) and Knowles and Behrman (2003). This strategy requires the identification of the least-cost alternative action that has exactly the same effects as the one being valued. This is a strong requirement. But the alternatives also require strong assumptions. While there are examples in the literature of basing such assessments as the value of reducing mortality on expected lifetime earnings, for example, this methodology is fraught with pitfalls, including the implicit ranking of the value of life as a function of wages within and across countries. In addition, assigning a value in proportion to earnings does not net out consumption from these earnings.

In addition to these caveats, even where impacts are well measured and even where there is agreement regarding discount rates and time horizons, not all benefits are monetary or in easily monetized terms. But they must be expressed in such terms in order to be made comparable to the costs and to the impacts of other changes. There are various means of doing so that are used in the literature. For example, options that are used to address the vexing problem of assigning a value to postponing mortality include the PDV of the estimated productivity of the individual that is forgone due to early mortality or, as in the approach taken, the resource cost of the most effective alternative means of postponing such mortality.[54] However, there are legitimate criticisms associated with such an approach. For example, it tends to value averting a death less in poorer societies than in richer societies, since poorer societies typically devote fewer resources to averting deaths at the margin than do higher *per capita* income societies. In part for this reason some, including Appleton (2004) and Mills and Shillcutt (2004), advocate using a value of averting a death that is independent of the level of *per capita* income, so this value is the same across societies. To illustrate the implications of this alternative assumption, and to permit direct comparison with studies such as Mills and Shillcutt (2004), we examine the implications of following the recommendation of the Copenhagen Consensus Experts to consider the alternative of valuing averting a death at $100,000. Under this assumption, for example, the estimated monetary benefit of reducing the infant mortality associated with LBW is about $7,800 – about 80 times larger than the alternative used on p. 00. But this alternative is also not without its problems. It implies, for example, that a saving a child from death is worth many more years of average adult earnings in a poor country than in a middle-income country. To be explicit, if the average annual adult earnings are $500 (as we use to represent a low-income country), 2000 adult years of earnings equals the value of one death averted – but if average annual adult earnings are $5,000 (as in some middle-income countries), only twenty adult years of earnings equals the value of one death averted. It also may have what would seem to be peculiar implications for evaluating life avoided due to fertility control (with a forgone benefit of $100,000 per birth averted). Finally, if $100,000 is interpreted to be the PDV of earnings that the deceased would have earned had there not been the death – a measure that often is used in the literature to value the cost of a death – under conservative assumptions this implies annual average earnings of $10,893 with a 5 per cent discount rate and $5,907 with a 3 per cent discount rate – roughly twenty-two times and twelve times the assumed average adult earnings of $500 per year in low *per capita* income countries that we use in our illustrative calculations.[55] Therefore while we present estimates of BCRs using the value of an averted death at $100,000 for some sub-components of the first three opportunities in appendix table 7A.4, we stress that we are much more comfortable with the more conservative estimates we present in the main body of the paper.[56]

Benefits and Costs

Three further points, finally, are common to both benefits and costs. First, both are *context-dependent*. They both may depend importantly, for example, on relative prices, the state of the economy and the nature of the health environment and broader aspects of the environment. High return policies in a society with high prevalence of a particular disease, for example, may not be very effective in a society with low prevalence of that disease. Second, for both benefits and costs there may be *aggregate effects* that have important feedbacks through changing relative scarcities, market prices and governmental policies, particularly in economies that

are more closed to international trade. Third, serious assessments of impacts and of costs must incorporate *aspects of behaviour* of individuals, collective units such as households (with intrahousehold distribution possibly affecting distribution by gender and by generation), and other entities – including governments (due to the endogeneity of policy choices).

In a nutshell, evaluation of opportunities is very difficult and is not likely to lead to a set of recommendations that are universally applicable in all developing country contexts. Claims that there are such interventions are likely to be misleading and costly in terms of their use of scarce resources. Our discussion of opportunities is subject to these important caveats and it is for this reason that we have explored how sensitive some of the estimates are to underlying assumptions to illustrate some of these points. But it should be noted that these qualifications and problems are not unique to this chapter, but are pervasive for all the chapters in this volume.

Conclusions

Reducing hunger and malnutrition, endemic in many parts of the developing world, is intrinsically important. But so, too, are many of the other challenges considered at the conference. Our focus here has been on the *economic* case for investing in activities that reduce hunger and malnutrition. We have focused on four opportunities:

- Reducing the prevalence of LBW
- Infant and child nutrition and exclusive breast-feeding promotion
- Reducing the prevalence of iron-deficiency anaemia and Vitamin A, iodine and zinc deficiencies
- Investment in technology in developing country agriculture.

While the opportunities described here represent our current view of the most promising approaches, several other opportunities, in part covered by other chapters in this volume, have important implications for reducing hunger and malnutrition, in that successes in these other challenges will affect nutrition and, conversely improvements in nutrition

---

[55] These numbers are conservative because we assume a long worklife, starting at a relatively young age from fifteen through sixty-five years of age and assume that earnings are constant over this worklife rather than increasing. All of these assumptions bias downward the average earnings in comparison with alternatives of starting work when older, having a worklife that is shorter and having increasing earnings over the initial part of the work cycle. It also implies that interventions that reduce mortality will have higher BCRs than interventions that reduce DALYs, since the monetary value of DALYs is usually expressed in terms of forgone earnings or country *per capita* income.

[56] Note, too, that we do not have information to permit us to include directly the value of averting a death for opportunity 4, nor for some of the alternatives for opportunities 2 and 3.

will influence the other challenges.[57] For example:

- *Women's education and status.* Numerous studies show strong correlations between maternal education and reductions in undernutrition amongst pre-school children. While some of this work is subject to caveats (for example, maternal education may be correlated with unobserved family background characteristics), progress on the challenge relating to low education is likely to produce benefits in terms of reduced malnutrition.
- *Addressing infectious diseases such as malaria and the HIV/AIDS pandemic.* For example, HIV/AIDs increases hunger and malnutrition directly by reducing the income and food security of affected households, and by interfering with the intergenerational transmittal of agricultural and other productive skills. In addition, young orphans and children with chronically ill care givers risk higher rates of malnutrition. HIV also imposes a dilemma in assessing the increased risks of breastfeeding against the risks of not breastfeeding. Conversely, nutrition affects HIV/AIDS, since nutritional status is a major factor influencing a person's risk of infection. Well-nourished HIV positive individuals live longer and respond more positively to treatment. Moreover, the efficacy of certain antiretroviral drugs is diminished when they are not taken on a full stomach (Stillwaggon, 2002; Castleman *et al.* 2003; ACC/SCN 2004).
- *Improving infrastructure to reduce possibilities of famine or chronic hunger.* Famines and chronic undernutrition typically currently do not reflect food shortages in the aggregate so much as inadequate access to food for poorer segments of the population – due either to short-run shocks or chronic conditions. Inadequate food access, in turn, reflects limited purchasing power in the short run or longer run, often exacerbated by food price shocks in partially segmented markets. Communication and transportation infrastructure investments can serves to lessen localized price shocks that may be an important factor in famines, and may lead to increased growth and therefore lessened chronic undernutrition.
- *Effective improvements in water and sanitation* lead to reductions in diarrhoea. As noted in oppor-

tunity 2, repeated diarrhoeal infections are correlated with growth faltering, particularly for children less than three years of age.
- *Trade barriers impose considerable costs on developing countries.* The majority of hungry and malnourished people in developing countries are poor. The majority of poor people in developing countries live in rural areas and depend directly or indirectly on agriculture for their livelihoods. Changes in the returns to agriculture in developing countries may thus have a major impact on hunger and malnutrition in developing countries through affecting the income of the poor and the prices that the poor pay for basic staples and other foods. These changes, in turn, may have impacts throughout the lifecycle, from conception onwards, since changes in the resources that households have and the prices that they face may trigger nutritional changes over the lifecycle with effects such as are reviewed on pp. 372–3.
- Lessening conflicts and improving governance, as long emphasized by Sen (1981, 1999) and others, are likely to lessen problems of transitory localized food shortages that result in extreme hunger and famine.[58]

We have estimated BCRs for four opportunities to directly address hunger and malnutrition. These estimates suggest attractive opportunities from: resource saving arising from reduced mortality; resource saving arising from reduced morbidity; direct links between nutrition and physical productivity; and indirect links between nutrition, cognitive development, schooling and productivity. While we have drawn upon recent evidence of project impacts and costs, we note that our main conclusions about the high returns to investing in nutrition and in agricultural technology repeat general observations that have been made earlier in the literature and yet, to a fair degree, the potential investments remain to remain underresourced. Indeed the high estimated BCRs raise important questions

---

[57] ACC/SCN (2004) discusses at some length the synergies between improving nutrition and some of these other challenges.

[58] Svedberg (2004) suggests that extensive corruption accounts for limited success in improving child health and nutrition, perhaps in part because corrupt governments have high discount rates.

Table 7.6. Summary of Benefits and Costs for Opportunities Related to Hunger and Malnutrition[a]

Opportunities and targeted populations	Benefits ($) (1)	Costs ($) (2)	Benefits/ costs (3)	Discount rates (%) (4)	Size of targeted populations[d] (5)	Annual costs in ($ bn if coverage of targeted population were (%)) 25 (6)	50 (7)
1 **Reducing LBW for pregnancies with high probabilities LBW (particularly in S. Asia)**					12 m LBW births per year		
1a Treatments for women with asymptomatic bacterial infections	580–986	200–2,000	0.58–4.93	3–5		0.1–0.6[e]	0.1–1.2[e]
1b Treatment for women with presumptive STD	580–986	92–460	1.26–10.71	3–5		0.03–0.1[e]	0.06–0.3[e]
1c Drugs for pregnant women with poor obstetric history	580–986	28–280	4.14–35.20	3–5		0.01–0.1[e]	0.02–0.2[e]
2 **Improving infant and child nutrition in populations with high prevalence of child malnutrition (fairly widespread in poor populations in developing countries)**					162 m stunted children 0–5 years old		
2a Breastfeeding promotion in hospitals in which norm has been promotion of use of infant formula	5,952–8,929	133–1,064	5.6–67.1	3–5		0.1–0.9[e]	0.2.–1.7[f]
2b Integrated child care programmes	376–653	40	9.4–16.2	3–5		1.6	3.2
2c Intensive pre-school programme with considerable nutrition for poor families			1.4–2.9	3–5			
3 **Reducing micronutrient deficiencies in populations in which they are prevalent[b]**							
3a Iodine (per woman of child bearing age)[c]	75–130	0.25–5.0	15–520	3–5	2 bn people (285 mn children 0–6) with iodine deficiencies)	0.1–1.3[g]	0.25–2.5[g]
3b Vitamin A (pre-school child under six years)	37–43	1–10	4.3–43	3–5	140 million pre-school children	0.04–0.4	0.07–0.7

Table 7.6. (*cont.*)

Opportunities and targeted populations	Benefits ($) (1)	Costs ($) (2)	Benefits/ costs (3)	Discount rates (%) (4)	Size of targeted populations^d (5)	Annual costs in ($ bn if coverage of targeted population were (%)	
						25 (6)	50 (7)
3c Iron (*per capita*)	44–50	0.25	176–200	3–5	3.5 billion people	0.5	0.9
3d Iron (pregnant women)^c	82–140	10–13.4	6.1–14	3–5	67 million	0.2	0.3–0.4
4 Investment in technology in developing agriculture					800 million undernourished who would benefit from price reductions, about 0.7 of whom would benefit from any income increases due to productivity gains.		
4a Dissemination of new cultivars with higher yield potential			8.8–14.7	3–5%			
4b Dissemination of iron and zinc dense rice and wheat varieties			11.6–19	3–5%			
4c Dissemination of Vitamin A dense 'golden rice'			8.5–14	3–5%			

Notes: ^{a} These estimates are based on extensive assumptions that are discussed in the text and in the underlying studies, are subject to considerable uncertainties and cannot be understood without reference to those discussions. The estimates are all of total (private plus social) benefits relative to total (private plus social) costs – and therefore do not provide information about the differences between social and private BCRs (or IRRs) that would be necessary to assess the efficiency case for public subsidies. For these (and for all other interventions being considered by the Copenhagen Consensus) the marginal costs are likely eventually to increase as there is expansion to attempt to cover those most difficult to reach. For that reason columns (6) and, (7) give the costs for a quarter and a half of the target populations, respectively, for which it would seem that the assumption that the average costs in column 2 are constant would be more likely.
^{b} Under opportunity 3 on micronutrients, we assume fortification is not targeted but that supplements are.
^{c} Benefits and costs in opportunity 1 are in terms of LBW prevented while opportunities 3a and 3d are per woman, though both interventions result in more favourable birth outcomes.
^{d} Sources given in text (ACC/SCN 2000a, 2003, 2004; FAO 2003; Hunger Task Force 2003; UNICEF 2001).
^{e} Assumes that 10% of the mothers have the indicated condition and are treated (1.2 m mothers).
^{f} Assumes that 10% of children below 12 months of age are exposed (3.2 m children).
^{g} Assumes all people (not just women of childbearing ages) who are treated are treated at the indicated cost.

as to why such opportunities have not been seized.[59] Are there upward biases in the estimated impacts? Would induced price and policy changes counter the benefits? Are discount rates used by governments much higher than used in our illustrations? Do the beneficiaries – primarily infants and children in poor households – have too little voice to be weighed sufficiently heavily in the welfare functions that are dictating intrahousehold allocations and policies? Do marginal costs rapidly increase if interventions are scaled up? Do important market failures preclude private exploitation of sufficient gains? Investigating such questions should be given high very priority.

But, subject to such caveats and questions, the estimates discussed on pp. 374–97 and summarized in table 7.6 suggest considerable possible gains to be had in investing in these opportunities, in the sense of BCRs exceeding one or relatively high IRRs to investing in programmes or policies to reduce hunger and malnutrition – in addition to the intrinsic welfare gains to the individuals who would be effected directly by reduced hunger and

[59] These questions are much stronger for the much larger BCRs that result if the value of an averted death is $100,000 as in appendix table 7A.4.

malnutrition.[60] The estimated BCRs in table 7.6 are particularly large for reducing micronutrient deficiencies in populations in which prevalences are high and for investments in technology for developing agriculture. The people who are likely to benefit from these four opportunities tend to be relatively poor, so such investments are likely to have important gains in terms of the objective of reducing poverty as well as in terms of increasing productivity. While the available studies generally do not distinguish well between private and social rates of returns to these interventions, on the basis of limited studies and casual observations it would appear that there are important aspects of the potential gains that are social beyond the private gains due to externalities related to contagious diseases and to education – so there is likely to be a case for the use of some public resources for such interventions on efficiency grounds in addition to the case on poverty alleviation grounds. Finally the annual costs of such opportunities under the assumptions that the average costs in the second column of table 7.6 apply to a quarter or alternatively to a half or the population at risk (with increasing costs possible for the remaining population) are of the order of magnitude of only a tenth or a fifth of $US 50 bn that is being mentioned as a benchmark for the discussions of the Copenhagen Consensus, suggesting that these opportunities could be undertaken together with a number of others that are under consideration.[61]

---

[60] The BCRs are much higher for the first three opportunities (again, we do not have information with which to explore the effect of such a chance for opportunity 4) if an averted death is valued at $100,000 (see appendix table 7A.4).

[61] We are able to estimate these costs only for the first three opportunities. Our estimates are given in the last two columns of table 7.6.

Appendix

Table 7A.1. PDV of $1,000 Gained, Different Years in the Future, Different Discount Rates

Years in future	Annual discount rate (%)					
	1($)	2($)	3($)	5($)	10($)	20($)
5	951.47	905.73	862.61	783.53	620.92	401.88
10	905.29	820.35	744.09	613.91	385.54	161.51
20	819.54	672.97	553.68	376.89	148.64	26.08
30	741.92	552.07	411.99	231.38	57.31	4.21
40	671.65	452.89	306.56	142.05	22.09	0.68
50	608.04	371.53	228.11	87.20	8.52	0.11
60	550.45	304.78	169.73	53.54	3.28	0.02

Table 7A.2. Estimates of PDVs of Seven Major Classes of Benefits of Shifting One LBW Infant to Non-LBW Status, Different Discount Rates

	Annual discount rate (%)					
	1	2	3	5	10	20
1 Reduced infant mortality ($)	96.53	95.59	94.66	92.86	88.64	81.25
2 Reduced neonatal care ($)	41.80	41.80	41.80	41.80	41.80	41.80
3 Reduced costs of infant/child illness ($)	39.60	39.22	38.83	38.10	36.36	33.33
4 Productivity gain from reduced stunting ($)	351.46	249.20	180.17	99.34	28.61	4.28
5 Productivity gain from increased ability ($)	846.71	600.35	434.06	239.31	68.91	10.32
6 Reduction in costs of chronic diseases ($)	239.45	132.58	73.83	23.29	1.43	0.01
7 Intergenerational benefits ($)	421.99	219.53	122.26	45.12	7.61	0.84
Sum of PDV of seven benefits ($)	2,037.54	1,378.27	985.61	579.82	273.36	171.83
Sum as % of that for 5%	351	238	170	100	47	30

Source: Alderman and Behrman (2004, table 3).

Table 7A.3. Impact of Increasing Each Benefit One at a Time by 50% Relative to Table 7.2, 5% Discount Rate

		1	2	3	4	5	6	7
1	Reduced infant mortality ($)	**139.29**	92.86	92.86	92.86	92.86	92.86	92.86
2	Reduced neonatal care ($)	41.80	**62.70**	41.80	41.80	41.80	41.80	41.80
3	Reduced costs of infant/child illness ($)	38.10	38.10	**57.15**	38.10	38.10	38.10	38.10
4	Productivity gain from reduced stunting ($)	99.34	99.34	99.34	**149.01**	99.34	99.34	99.34
5	Productivity gain from increased ability ($)	239.31	239.31	239.31	239.31	**358.97**	239.31	239.31
6	Reduction in costs of chronic diseases ($)	23.29	23.29	23.29	23.29	23.29	**34.93**	23.29
7	Intergenerational benefits $	45.12	45.12	45.12	45.12	45.12	45.12	**67.68**
	Sum of all seven benefits ($)	626.25	600.72	598.87	629.49	699.48	591.46	602.38
	Sum relative to that in table 7.2 (%)	108	104	103	109	121	102	104

Source: Alderman and Behrman (2004, table 5).

Table 7A.4. Alternative Summary if Value of Averting a Death is $100,000

Opportunities and targeted populations	Benefits ($)	Costs ($)	Benefits/costs	Discount rates (%)
1 Reducing LBW for pregnancies with high probabilities LBW (particularly in S. Asia)	8.535			
1a Treatments for women with asymptomatic bacterial infections	8,535–9,523	200–2,000	4.3–47.6	3–5
1b Treatment for women with presumptive STD	8,535–9,523	92–460	18.6–103.5	3–5
1c Drugs for pregnant women with poor obstetric history	8,535–9,523	28–280	30.5–340.1	3–5
2 Improving infant and child nutrition in populations with high prevalence of child malnutrition (fairly widespread in poor populations in developing countries)				
2a Breastfeeding promotion in hospitals in which norm has been promotion of use of infant formula	114,943–125,000	133–1,064	108.0–939.8	3–5
3 Reducing micronutrient deficiencies in populations in which they are prevalent[b]				
3a Iodine (per woman of childbearing age)	3,115–3,347	0.25–5.0	622.6–13,388	3–5
3b Vitamin A (per per-school child under six years)	2,389–2,441	1–10	238.9–2,441	3–5
3d Iron (pregnant women)	8,535–9,523	10–13.40	636.9–952.3	3–5

Note: [a] This table is identical to table 7.6 except, for those opportunities for which we have data that make it possible, the value of an averted death is assumed to be $100,000. We do not have such data for opportunities 2b, 2c, 3c and 4 in table 7.6, though since these opportunities have some impact on mortality their BCRs would probably also increase (probably not as much as for the opportunities for which we have data) were the data available to permit us to undertake the estimates.

References

Abler, D. G., G. S. Tolley and G. K. Kriplani, 1994: *Technical change and income distribution in Indian agriculture*, Westview Press: Boulder, CO

ACC/SCN (Administrative Committee on Coordination/Sub-Committee on Nutrition), 2000a: *4th report on the world nutrition situation*, United Nations, New York, in collaboration with the International Food Policy Research Institute, Washington DC

2000b: *Low birth Weight: a report based on the international low birth weight symposium and workshops Held on 14–17 June 1999 at the International Centre for Diarrhoeal Disease Research in Dhaka, Bangladesh* (eds.) J. Pojda and L. Kelley, ACC/SCN, Geneva, in collaboration with ICDDR,B, Nutrition Policy Paper 18

2003: *5th report on the world nutrition situation*, United Nations, Geneva, draft

Adair, L., 1999: Filipino children exhibit catch-up growth from age 2 to 12 years, *Journal of Nutrition*, **129**, 1140–48

Adato, M., R. Meinzen-Dick, L. Haddad and P. Hazell, 2003: Impacts of agricultural research on poverty reduction: findings of an integrated economic and social analysis, IFPRI: Washington, DC

Aduayom, D. and L. Smith, 2003: Estimating undernourishment with household expenditure surveys: a comparison of methods using data from three sub-Saharan African countries, in, *Proceedings: measurement and assessment of food deprivation and undernutrition*, FAO, Rome

Ahn, N. and A. Shariff, 1995: Determinants of child height in Uganda: a consideration of the selection bias caused by child mortality, *Food and Nutrition Bulletin*, **16**(1), 49–59

Alaii, N. *et al.*, 2003: Perceptions of bed nets and malaria prevention before and after randomized controlled trial of permethrin-treated bed nets in Western Kenya, *American Journal of Tropical Medicine and Hygiene*, **68** (Suppl), 142–48

Alauddin, M. and C. Tisdell, 1986: Market analysis, technical change and income distribution in semi-subsistence agriculture: the case of Bangladesh, *Agricultural Economics*, **1**, 1–18

Alderman, H. and J. R. Behrman, 2004: Estimated economic benefits of reducing LBW in low-income countries, HNP Discussion Paper, World Bank, Washington, DC

Alderman, H., J. R. Behrman and J. Hoddinott, 2004: Nutrition, malnutrition, and economic growth?, in G. López-Casasnovas, B. Rivera and L. Currais (eds.), *Health and economic growth findings and policy implications*, MIT Press, Cambridge, MA

Alderman, H., J. Behrman, V. Lavy and R. Menon, 2001: Child health and school enrollment: a longitudinal analysis, *Journal of Human Resources*, **36**(1), 185–205

Alderman, H., J. Behrman, D. Ross and R. Sabot, 1996: The returns to endogenous human capital in Pakistan's rural wage labor market, *Oxford Bulletin of Economics and Statistics*, **58**(1), 29–55

Alderman, H., J. Hoddinott and B. Kinsey, 2003: Long term consequences of early childhood malnutrition, World Bank, Washington, DC, mimeo

Allen L., 2000: Anemia and iron deficiency: effects on pregnancy outcome, *American Journal of Clinical Nutrition*, **71**(5): 1280S–1284S

Allen, L. and S. Gillespie, 2001: What works? A review of efficacy and effectiveness of nutrition interventions, Asian Development Bank, Nutrition and Development Series, 5, Manila

Alnwick, D., 1998: Weekly iodine supplements work, *American Journal of Clinical Nutrition*, **67**(6), 1103–5

Alston, J., C. Chan-Kang, M. Marra, P. Pardey and T. J. Wyatt, 2000: A meta-analysis of rates of return to agricultural R&D, *IFPRI Research Report*, 113, International Food Policy Research Institute, Washington, DC

Altonji, J. and T. Dunn, 1996: The effects of family characteristics on the returns to education, *Review of Economics and Statistics*, **78**(4), 692–704

Altonji, J. and C. Pierret, 2001: Employer learning and statistical discrimination, *Quarterly Journal of Economics*, **116**(1), 313–50

Anderson, J. R., R. W. Herdt and G. M. Scobie, 1988: *Science and food: the CGIAR and its partners*, World Bank, Washington, DC

Angrist, J., E. Bettinger, E. Bloom, E. King and M. Kremer, 2002: Vouchers for private schooling in Colombia: evidence from a randomized natural experiment, *American Economic Review*, **92**(5), 1535–59

Appleton, S., 2004: Perspective paper 7.2 in this volume

Ashworth, A., 1998: Effects of intrauterine growth retardation on mortality and morbidity in infants and young children, *European Journal of Clinical Nutrition*, **52** (Suppl), S34–S42

Ashworth, A., S. Morris and P. Lira, 1997: Postnatal growth patterns of full-term low birthweight infants in Northeast Brazil are related to socioeconomic status, *Journal of Nutrition*, **127**, 195–6

Aylward, G., 2003: Cognitive function in preterm infants: no simple answers, *Journal of the American Medical Association*, **289**(6), 747–50

Aylward, G., S. Pfeiffer, A. Wright and S. Verhulst, 1989: Outcome studies of low birth weight infants published in the last decade: a meta-analysis, *Journal of Pediatrics*, **115**, 515–20

Ballard, C., J. Shoven and J. Whalley, 1985: General equilibrium computations of the marginal welfare costs of taxes in the United States, *American Economic Review*, **75**(1), 128–38

Barker, D. J. P. (ed.), 1992: Fetal and infant origins of adult disease: papers written by the Medical Research Council Environmental Epidemiology Unit, University of Southhampton, *British Medical Journal*

1998: *Mothers, babies and health in later life*, 2nd edn., Churchill Livingstone, Edinburgh, London and New York

Barrera, A., 1990: The role of maternal schooling and its interaction with public health programs in child health production, *Journal of Development Economics*, **32**(1), 69–92

1992: The interactive effects of mother's schooling and unsupplemented breastfeeding on child health, *Journal of Development Economics*, **34**(1/2), 81–98

Barro, R. and X. Sala-i-Martin, 1995: *Economic growth*, McGraw-Hill, New York

Barros, F. C., S. R. Huttly, C. G. Victoria, B. R. Kirkwood and J. P. Vaughan, 1992: Comparison of the causes and consequences of prematurity and intrauterine growth retardation: a longitudinal study in Southern Brazil, *Pediatrics*, 2 (part 1), 238–44

Basta, S., D. Karyadi and N. Scrimshaw, 1979: Iron deficiency anemia and the productivity of adult males in Indonesia, *American Journal of Clinical Nutrition*, **329**, 16–925

Beard, J., 2000: Effectiveness and strategies of iron supplementation during pregnancy, *American Journal of Clinical Nutrition*, **71**(5), S1288–S1294

Beaton, G. and H. Ghassemi, 1982: Supplementary feeding programs for young children in developing countries, *American Journal of Clinical Nutrition*, **34**, 864–916

Beaton, G., R. Martorell and K. Aronson, 1993: *Effectiveness of vitamin A supplementation in the control of young child morbidity and mortality in developing countries*, United Nations: New York

Beaton, G. H. and G. P. McCabe, 1999: *Efficacy of intermittent iron supplementation in the control of iron deficiency anaemia in developing countries, an analysis of experience: final report to The Micronutrient Initiative*, The Micronutrient Initiative, Ottawa

Becker, G., 1967: *Human capital and the personal distribution of income: an analytical approach*, University of Michigan, Ann Arbor, Woytinsky Lecture, republished in G. Becker, *Human Capital* 2nd edn., NBER, New York, 94–117

Behrman, J., 1993: The economic rationale for investing in nutrition in developing countries, *World Development*, **21**(11), 1749–72

1996: Impact of health and nutrition on education, *World Bank Research Observer*, **11**(1), 23–37

Behrman, J., Y. Cheng and P. Todd, 2004: Evaluating preschool programs when length of exposure to the program varies: a nonparametric approach, *Review of Economics and Statistics*, February

Behrman, J. R. and A. Deolalikar, 1988: Health and nutrition, in H. B. Chenery and T. N. Srinivasan (eds), *Handbook on economic development*, 1, North Holland, Amsterdam, 631–711

1989: Wages and labor supply in rural India: the role of health, nutrition and seasonality, in D. Sahn (ed.), *Causes and implications of seasonal variability in household food security*, Johns Hopkins University Press, Baltimore, MD, 107–18

Behrman, J. R., A. Foster and M. Rosenzweig, 1997: The dynamics of agricultural production and the calorie–income relationship: evidence from Pakistan, *Journal of Econometrics*, **77**(1), 187–207

Behrman, J. R. and J. Hoddinott, 2004: Program evaluation with unobserved heterogeneity and selective implementation: the Mexican *Progresa*

impact on child nutrition, University of Pennsylvania, Philadelphia, mimeo

Behrman, J. R., J. Hoddinott, J. A. Maluccio, Agnes Quisumbing, R. Martorell and Aryeh D. Stein, 2003: The impact of experimental nutritional interventions on education into adulthood in rural Guatemala: preliminary longitudinal analysis, University of Pennsylvania, IFPRI, Emory Philadelphia, Washington, DC and Atlanta, mimeo

Behrman, J. and J. Knowles, 1998a: Population and reproductive health: an economic framework for policy evaluation, *Population and Development Review*, **24**(4), 697–738

1998b: The distributional implications of government family planning and reproductive health services in Vietnam, prepared for the Rockefeller Foundation, University of Pennsylvania, Philadelphia, mimeo

1999: Household income and child schooling in Vietnam, *World Bank Economic Review*, **13**(2), 211–56

2003: Economic evaluation of investments in youth in selected SEE countries, University of Pennsylvania, Report prepared for the World Bank Europe and Central Asia Region – Social Development Initiative, Bangkok and Philadelphia, mimeo

Behrman, J. R. and M. Rosenzweig, 1999: 'Ability', biases in schooling returns and twins: a test and new estimates, *Economics of Education Review*, **18**, 159–67

2004: Returns to birthweight, *Review of Economics and Statistics*, **86**(2), 586–601

Behrman, J. R., P. Sengupta and P. Todd, 2004: Progressing through PROGRESA: an impact assessment of Mexico's school subsidy experiment, University of Pennsylvania, Philadelphia, mimeo

Behrman, J. and B. Wolfe, 1987: How does mother's schooling affect family health, nutrition, medical care usage and household sanitation? *Journal of Econometrics*, **36**, 185–204

Bhargava, A., H. Bouis and N. Schrimshaw, 2001: Dietary intakes and socioeconomic factors are associated with the hemoglobin concentration of Bangladeshi women, *Journal of Nutrition*, **131**, 758–64

Bhutta, A., M. Cleves, P. Casey, M. Cradock and K. J. Anand, 2002: Cognitive and behavioral outcomes of school-aged children who were born preterm, *Journal of the American Medical Association*, **288**(6), 728–37

Bigsten, A. *et al.*, 2000: Rates of return on physical and human capital in Africa's manufacturing sector, *Economic Development and Cultural Change*, **48**:801–28

Black, M. 2003: Micronutrient deficiencies and cognitive functioning, *Journal of Nutrition*, **133**(11), S3927–S3931

Bobonis, G., E. Miguel and C. Sharma, 2003: Child nutrition and education: a randomized evaluation in India, University of California, Berkeley, unpublished working paper

Boissiere, M., J. Knight and R. Sabot, 1985: Earnings, schooling, ability and cognitive skills, *American Economic Review*, **75**, 1016–30

Bouis, H., 2002a: Plant breeding: a new tool for fighting micronutrient malnutrition, *Journal of Nutrition*, **132**: S491–S494

2002b: Appendix to: Productivity losses from iron deficiency: the economic case, by Joseph Hunt, *Journal of Nutrition*, **132**, S794–S801

Bourdillon, M., P. Hebinck, J. Hoddinott, B. Kinsey, J. Marondo, N. Mudege and T. Owens, 2003: Assessing the impact of HYV maize in resettlement areas of Zimbabwe, FCND Discussion Paper, 161, International Food Policy Research Institute, Washington DC

Boyle, M. G. Torrance, J. Sinclair and S. Horwood, 1983: Economic evaluation of neonatal intensive care of very low birth-weight infants, *New England Journal of Medicine*, **308**, 1330–7

Brabin, B., M. Hakimi and D. Pelletier, 2001: An analysis of anemia and pregnancy-related maternal mortality, *Journal of Nutrition*, **131** (2S-2), S604–S614

Brown K., J. Peerson, J. Rivera and L. Allen, 2002: Effect of supplemental zinc on the growth and serum zinc concentrations of prepubertal children: a meta-analysis of randomized controlled trials, *American Journal of Clinical Nutrition*, **75**, 1062–71

Byerlee, D., 1993: Technical change and returns to wheat breeding research in Pakistan's Punjab in the post-Green Revolution period, *Pakistan Development Review*, **32**, 69–86

1996: Modern varieties, productivity and sustainability, *World Development*, **24**, 697–718

Byerlee, D. and P. Moya, 1993: *Impacts of international wheat breeding research in the*

developing world, 1960–90, CIMMYT, Mexico City, DF

Cameron, N., 2001: Catch-up growth increase risk factors for obesity in urban children in South Africa, *International Journal of Obesity*, **25** (Suppl.), S48

Card, D., 1999: The causal effect of education on earnings, in O. Ashenfelter and D. Card (eds.), *Handbook of labor economics*, Elsevier Science BV, New York

Castleman, T. *et al.*, 2003: Food and nutrition implications of antiretroviral therapy in resource limited settings, FANTA Technical Note, 7, Washington, DC

Caulfield, L., N. Zavaleta, A. Shankar and M. Merialdi, 1998: Potential contribution of maternal zinc supplementation during pregnancy to maternal and child survival, *American Journal of Clinical Nutrition*, **68**, S499–S508

Cawley, J., J. Heckman and E. Vytlacil, 2001: Three observations on wages and measured cognitive ability, *Labor Economics*, **8**, 419–42

Ceesay S., A. Prentice, T. Cole, R. Ford, E. Poskitt, L. Weaver and R. Whitehead, 1997: Effects on birth weight and perinatal mortality of maternal dietary supplements in rural Gambia: 5 year randomised controlled trial, *British Medical Journal*, **315**, 786–90

Ching, P., M. Birmingham, T. Goodman, R. Sutter and B. Loevinsohn, 2000: Childhood mortality impact and costs of integrating vitamin A supplementation into immunization campaigns, *American Journal of Public Health*, **90**(10), 1526–9

Christian *et al.*, 2003: Effects of alternative maternal micronutrient supplements on low birth weight in rural Nepal: double blind randomised community trial, *British Medical Journal*, **326**

Coale, A. and E. Hoover, 1958: *Population growth and economic development in low-income countries: a case study of India's prospects*, Princeton University Press, Princeton

Cobra, C., K. R. Muhilal, D. D. Rustama, S. Suwardi, D. Permaesih, S.M. Muherdiyantiningsih and R. Semba, 1997: Infant survival is improved by oral iodine supplementation, *Journal of Nutrition*, **127**, 574–8

Cogswell, M. E, I. Parvanta, L. Ickes, R. Yip and G. M. Brittenham, 2003: Iron supplementation during pregnancy, anemia, and birth weight: a randomized controlled trial, *American Journal of Clinical Nutrition*, **78**(4), 773–81

Commission on Macroeconomics and Health, 2001: *Macroeconomics and health: investing in health for economic development*, World Health Organization, Geneva

Conley, D. and N. Bennett, 2000: Is biology destiny? Birth weight and life chances, *American Sociological Review*, **65**(2), 458–67

Conley, D., K. Strully and N. Bennett, 2003: A pound of flesh or just proxy? Using twins differences to estimate the effects of birth weight on (literal) life chances, NYU Department of Sociology, New York, mimeo

Corman, H. and S. Chaikind, 1993: The effect of low birth weight on the health, behavior and school performance of school-aged children, Working Paper, 4409, National Bureau of Economic Research, Cambridge, MA

Currie, J. and R. Hyson, 1999: Is the impact of health shocks cushioned by socioeconomic status? The case of low birth weight, *American Economic Review*, 89(2), 245–50

Czeizel, A and I. Dudas, 1992: Prevention of the first occurrence of neural-tube defects by periconceptional vitamin supplementation, *New England Journal of Medicine*, **327**, 1832–5

Dargent-Molina, P., S. James, D. Strogatz and D. Savitz, 1994: Association between maternal education and infant diarrhea in different household and community environments of Cebu, Philippines, *Social Science and Medicine*, **38**(2), 343–50

Dary, O. and J. Mara, 2002: Food fortification to reduce vitamin A deficiency: International vitamin A Consultative Group recommendations, *Journal of Nutrition*, **132**, S2927–S2933

David, C. and K. Otsuka, 1994: *Modern rice technology and income distribution in Asia*, Lynne Rienner, Boulder, CO

Dawe, D., R. Robertson and L. Unnevehr, 2002: Golden rice: what role could it play in alleviation of vitamin A deficiency? *Food Policy*, **27**, 541–60

DeLong, G., P. Leslie, S.-H. Wang, X.-M. Jiang, M.-L. Zhang, M. abdul Rakeman, J.-Y. Jiang, T. Ma and X.-Y. Cao, 1997: Effect on infant mortality of iodination of irrigation water in a severely iodine-deficient area of China, *Lancet*, **350**, 771–3

Deolalikar, A., 1988: Nutrition and labor productivity in agriculture: estimates for rural South India, *Review of Economics and Statistics*, **70**(3), 406–13

De Onis, M., M. Blossner, and J. Villar, 1998: Levels and Patterns of Intrauterine Growth Retardation in Developing Countries, *European Journal of Clinical Nutrition*, **52**(S1), S5–S15

De Pee, S., M. Bloem and L. Kiess, 2000: Evaluating food-based programmes for the reduction of vitamin A deficiency and its consequences, *Food and Nutrition Bulletin*, **21**(2), 232–8

Deutsch, R., 1999: How early childhood interventions can reduce inequality: an overview of recent findings, Inter American Development Bank, Washington, DC, mimeo

Devarajan, S., L. Squire and S. Suthiwart-Narueput, 1997: Beyond rate of return: reorienting project appraisal, *World Bank Research Observer*, **12**(1), 35–46

Devereux, S. and J. Hoddinott, 1999: Improving food needs assessment methodologies, International Food Policy Research Institute, Washington, DC, mimeo

Dunn, J., 2003: Iodine should be routinely added to complementary foods, *Journal of Nutrition*, **133**, S3008–S3010

English R. M., J. C. Badcock, T. Giay, T. Ngu, A.-M. Waters and S. A. Bennett, 1997: Effect of nutrition improvement project on morbidity from infectious diseases in preschool children in Vietnam: comparison with control commune, *British Medical Journal*, **315**, 1122–5

Ezzarti, M., A. Lopez, A. Rodgers *et al.*, 2002: Selected major risk factors and global and regional burden of disease, *The Lancet*, **360**(9343), 1–14

Fan, S., 2002: Agricultural research and urban poverty in India, EPTD Discussion Paper, 94, International Food Policy Research Institute, Washington, DC

Fan, S., C. Fang and X. Zhang, 2001: How agricultural research affects urban poverty in developing countries: the case of China, EPTD Discussion Paper, 83, International Food Policy Research Institute, Washington, DC

FAO (United Nations Food and Agriculture Organization), 2003: *The state of food insecurity in the world, 2003*, FAO, Rome

Fawzi, W. W., M. G. Herrera, W. C. Willett, A. el Amin, P. Nestel, S. Lipsitz, D. Spiegelman and K. A. Mohamed, 1993: Vitamin A supplementation and dietary vitamin A in relation to the risk of xerophthalmia, *American Journal of Clinical Nutrition*, **58**, 385–91

Feldstein, M., 1995: Tax avoidance and the deadweight loss of the income tax, National Bureau of Economic Research Working Paper, **5055**, Cambridge, MA

Fiedler, J., 2000: The Nepal national vitamin a program: prototype to emulate or donor enclave?, *Health Policy and Planning*, **15**(2), 145–56

2003: A cost analysis of the Honduras community-based integrated child care program, World Bank, Health Nutrition and Population Discussion Paper, Washington, DC

Fiedler, J., D. Dado, H. Maglalang, N. Juban, M. Capistrano and M. Magpantay, 2000: Cost analysis as a vitamin A program design and evaluation tool: a case study of the Philippines, *Social Science and Medicine*, **51**, 223–42

Foster, A. and M. Rosenzweig, 1993: Information, learning, and wage rates in low-income rural areas, *Journal of Human Resources*, **28**(4), 759–79

1994: A test for moral hazard in the labor market: effort, health and calorie consumption, *Review of Economics and Statistics*, **76**(2), 213–27

Galloway, R. and J. McGuire, 1996: Daily versus weekly: how many iron pills do pregnant women need?, *Nutrition Reviews*, **54**(10), 318–23

Garcia-Casal, M. and M. Layrisse, 2002: Iron fortification of flour in Venezuela, *Nutrition Reviews*, **60**(7), S26–S29

Gera, T. and H. P. S. Sachdev, 2002: Effect of iron supplementation in incidence of infectious illness in children: systematic review, *British Medical Journal*, **325**, 1142–54

Gertler, P., J. Rivera, S. Levy and J. Sepulveda, 2003: Mexico's PROGRESA: using a poverty alleviation program as an incentive for poor families to invest in child health, *Lancet*, Principles of nutritional assessment, Oxford University Press, Oxford

Gibson, R., 1990: *Principles of nutritional assessment*, Oxford University Press, New York

Glewwe, P., 1996: The relevance of standard estimates of rates of return to schooling for education policy: a critical assessment, *Journal of Development Economics*, **51**(2), 267–90

1999: *The economics of school quality investments in developing countries: an empirical study of Ghana*, St Martin's Press, New York

Glewwe, P. and H. Jacoby, 1994: Student achievement and schooling choice in low-income countries: evidence from Ghana, *Journal of Human Resources*, **29**(3), 843–64
   1995: An economic analysis of delayed primary school enrollment and childhood malnutrition in a low income country, *Review of Economics and Statistics*, **77**(1), 156–69
Glewwe, P., H. Jacoby and E. King, 2001: Early childhood nutrition and academic achievement: a longitudinal analysis, *Journal of Public Economics*, **81**(3), 345–68
Glewwe, P. and E. King. 2001: The Impact of early childhood nutrition status on cognitive achievement: does the timing of malnutrition matter?, *World Bank Economic Review*, **15**(1), 81–113
Glick, P. and D. Sahn, 1998: Health and productivity in a heterogeneous urban labor market, *Applied Economics*, **30**(2), 203–16
Goh, C., 2002: Combating iodine deficiency: lessons from China, Indonesia and Madagascar, *Food and Nutrition Bulletin*, **23**(3), 280–91
Golden, M.H., 1994: Is complete catch-up growth possible for stunted malnourished children?, *European Journal of Clinical Nutrition*, **48**, S58–S70
Goldman, A. and J. Smith, 1995: Agricultural transformation in India and northern Nigeria: exploring the nature of green revolutions, *World Development*, **23**, 243–63
Goodman, T., N. Dalmiya, B. de Benoist and W. Schultink, 2000: Polio as a platform: using national immunization days to deliver vitamin A supplements, *Bulletin of the World Health Organization*, **78**(3), 305–14
Graham, R. D., Welch, R. M. and Bouis, H. E., 2001: Addressing micronutrient malnutrition through enhancing the nutritional quality of staple foods: principles, perspectives and knowledge gaps, *Advances in Agronomy*, **70**, 77–142
Grantham-McGregor, S., S. Chang and C. Walker, 1997:
Grantham-McGregor, S., L. Fernald and K. Sethuraman, 1999a: Effects of health and nutrition on cognitive and behavioural development in children in the first three years of life, Part 1. low birth weight, breastfeeding and protein-energy malnutrition, *Food and Nutrition Bulletin*, **20**(1), 53–75
   1999b: Effects of health and nutrition on cognitive and behavioural development in children in the

first three years of life, Part 2, Infections and micronutrient deficiencies: iodine, iron and zinc, *Food and Nutrition Bulletin*, **20**(1), 76–99
Grantham-McGregor, S., C. Walker, S. Chang and C. Powell, 1997: Effects of early childhood supplementation with and without stimulation on later development in stunted Jamaican children, *American Journal of Clinical Nutrition*, **66**, 247–53
Gray, *et al.*, 2001: Randomized trial of presumptive sexually transmitted disease therapy during pregnancy in Rakai, Uganda, *American Journal of Obstetrics and Gynecology*, **185**, 1209–17
Guilkey, D. and R. Riphahn, 1998: The determinants of child mortality in the Philippines: estimation of a structural model, *Journal of Development Economics*, **56**, 281–305
Haas, J., S. Murdoch, J. Rivera and R. Martorell, 1996: Early nutrition and later physical work capacity, *Nutrition Reviews*, **54**, S41–S48
Hack, M., 1998: Effects of intrauterine growth retardation on mental performance and behavior: outcomes during adolescence and adulthood, *European Journal of Clinical Nutrition*, **52**, S65–S71
Hack M., D. Flannery, M. Schluchter, L. Cartar, E. Borawski and N. Klein, 2002: Outcomes in young adulthood for very-low birth weight infants, *New England Journal of Medicine*, **346**(3), 149–57
Haddad, L., H. Alderman, S. Appleton, L. Song and Y. Yohannes, 2003: Reducing child malnutrition: how far does income growth take us?, *World Bank Economic Review*, **17**(1), 107–31
Haddad, L. and H. Bouis, 1991: The impact of nutritional status on agricultural productivity: wage evidence from the Philippines, *Oxford Bulletin of Economics and Statistics*, **53**(1), 45–68
Hansen, K., J. Heckman and K. Mullen, 2003: The effect of schooling and ability on achievement test scores, University of Chicago, mimeo
Harberger, A., 1997: New frontiers in project evaluation? A comment on Devarajan, Squire and Suthiwart-Narueput, *The World Bank Research Observer*, **12**(1), 73–9
Heckman, J. J., 1997: Instrumental variables: a study of implicit behavioral assumptions in one widely used estimator, *Journal of Human Resources*, **32**(3), 441–62

Heckman, J. J., H. Ichimura and P. Todd, 1997: Matching as an econometric evaluation estimator: evidence from evaluating a job training program, *Review of Economic Studies*, **64**, 4

1998: Matching as an econometric evaluation estimator, *Review of Economic Studies*, **65**, 261–94

Henriksen, T., 1999: Foetal nutrition, foetal growth restriction and health later in life, *Acta Paediatrica*, **429**, S4–S8

Hoddinott, J. and B. Kinsey, 2001: Child growth in the time of drought, *Oxford Bulletin of Economics and Statistics*, **63**(4), 409–36

Hoddinott, J., E. Skoufias and R. Washburn, 2000: The impact of PROGRESA on consumption, International Food Policy Research Institute, Washington, DC, mimeo

Horton, S. and J. Ross, 2003: The economics of iron efficiency, *Food Policy*, **28**(1), 51–75

Horton, S., T. Sanghvi, M. Phillips, J. Fiedler, R. Perez-Escamilla, C. Lutter, A. Rivera and A. Segall-Correa, 1996: Breastfeeding promotion and priority setting in health, *Health Policy and Planning*, **11**, 156–68

Hunger Task Force, 2003: *Halving hunger by 2015: a framework for action*, Interim Report, Millennium Project, UNDP, New York

2004: *Interim report*, Millennium Project, UNDP, New York

Jalal, F., M. Neisheim, Z. Agus, D. Sanjur and J.-P. Habicht, 1998: Serum retinol concentrations in children are affected by food sources of B-carotene, fat intake and anthelmintic drug treatment, *American Journal of Clinical Nutrition*, **68**, 623–9

Jefferis, B., C. Power and C. Hertzman, 2002: Birth weight, childhood socioeconomic environment, and cognitive development in the 1958 British Birth Cohort Study, *British Medical Journal*, **325**, 305–10

Johnston, F., S. Low, Y. de Baessa and R. MacVean, 1987: Interaction of nutritional and socioeconomic status as determinants of cognitive achievement in disadvantaged urban Guatemalan children, *American Journal of Physical Anthropology*, **73**, 501–6

Jolliffe, D., 1998: Skills, schooling and household income in Ghana, *World Bank Economic Review*, **12**(1), 81–104

Kerr, J. and S. Kolavalli, 1999: Impact of agricultural research on poverty alleviation,

EPTD Discussion Paper, 56, International Food Policy Research Institute, Washington, DC

Knowles, J. C. and J. R. Behrman, 2003: Assessing the economic returns to investing in youth in developing countries, University of Pennsylvania, Bangkok and Philadelphia, mimeo

Kramer, M., 1998: Socioeconomic determinants of intrauterine growth retardation, *European Journal of Clinical Nutrition*, **52**(81), S29–S33

1993: Effects of energy and protein intakes on pregnancy outcomes: an overview of the research evidence from controlled clinical trials, *American Journal of Clinical Nutrition*, **58**, 625–35

Lasky, R., R. Klein, C. Yarborough, P. Engle, A. Lechtig and R. Martorell, 1981: The relationship between physical growth and infant development in rural Guatemala, *Child Development*, **52**, 219–26

Lavy, V., J. Spratt, and N. Leboucher, 1997: Patterns of incidence and change in Moroccan literacy, *Comparative Education Review*, **412**

Lechtig, A. and R. Klein, 1980: Maternal food supplementation in infant health: results of a study in the rural areas of Guatemala, in H. Aebi and R. Whitehead (eds.), *Maternal nutrition during pregnancy and lactation*, Hans Huber, Berne, 285–313

Lewit E., L. Baker, H. Corman and P. Shiono, 1995: The direct costs of low birth weight, *The Future of Children*, **5**(1), 35–56

Li, R. X. C., H. Yan, P. Deurenberg, L. Graby and J. Hautvast, 1994: Functional consequences of iron supplementation in iron-deficient female cottonmill workers in Beijing, *American Journal of Clinical Nutrition*, **59**, 908–17

Li, H., A. Stein, H. Barhhart, U. Ramakrishnan and R. Martorell, 2003: Associations between prenatal and postnatal growth and adult body size and composition, *American Journal of Clinical Nutrition*

Leibenstein, H., 1957: *Economic backwardness and economic growth*, John Wiley, New York

Levin, H., E. Pollitt, R. Galloway and J. McGuire, 1993: Micronutrient deficiency disorders, in D. Jamison, H. Mosley, A. Measham and J. Bobadilla (eds.), *Disease control priorities in developing countries*, Oxford University Press, Oxford

Lightwood, J., C. Phibbs and S. Glanz, 1999: Short-term health and economic benefits of smoking cessation: low birth weight, *Pediatrics*, **104**(6), 1312–20

Lipton, M., 2001: Reviving global poverty reduction: what role for genetically modified plants?, *Journal of International Development*, **13**, 826–46

with R. Longhurst, 1989: *New seeds and poor people*, Unwin Hyman, London

Loevinsohn, B., R. Sutter and M. Costales, 1997: Using cost-effectiveness analysis to evaluate targeting strategies: the case of vitamin A supplementation, *Health Policy and Planning*, **12**(1), 29–37

Low, J., T. Walker and R. Hijmans, 2001: The potential impact of orange-fleshed sweetpotatoes on Vitamin A intake in sub-Saharan Africa, Centro Internacional de la Papa, Lima, mimeo

Lucas, A. Fewtrell and T. Cole, 1999: Fetal origins of adult disease – the hypothesis revisited, *British Medical Journal*, **319**, 245–9

Malthus, T. R., 1817/1992: *An essay on the principle of population*, 5th edn., John Murray, London

Mannar, V. and E. Gallego, 2002: Iron fortification: country level experiences and lessons learned, *Journal of Nutrition*, **132**, S856–S858

Margo, R. and R. Steckel, 1982: The heights of American slaves: new evidence on slave nutrition and health, *Social Science History*, **64**, 516–38

Martorell, R., 1995: Results and implications of the INCAP follow-up study, *Journal of Nutrition*, **125** (Suppl), S1127–S1138

1997: Undernutrition during pregnancy and early childhood and its consequences for cognitive and behavioral development, in M. E. Young (ed.), *Early child development: investing in our children's future*, Elsevier, Amsterdam, 39–83

1999: The nature of child malnutrition and its long-term implications, *Food and Nutrition Bulletin*, **20**, 288–92

Martorell, R., K. L. Khan and D. G. Schroeder, 1994: Reversibility of stunting: epidemiological findings in children from developing countries, *European Journal of Clinical Nutrition*, **48** (Suppl.), S45–S57

Martorell R., U. Ramakrishnan, D. G. Schroeder, P. Melgar and L. Neufeld, 1998: Intrauterine growth retardation, body size, body composition and physical performance in adolescence, *European Journal of Clinical Nutrition*, **52** (S1), S43–S53

Martorell, R., J. Rivera and H. Kaplowitz, 1989: Consequences of stunting in early childhood for adult body size in rural Guatemala, Stanford University, Food Research Institute, Stanford, CA, mimeo

Martorell R., J. Rivera, D. G. Schroeder, U. Ramakrishnan, E. Pollitt and M. T. Ruel, 1995: Consecuencias a largo plazo del retardo en el crecimiento durante la niñez, *Archivos Latinoamericanos de Nutricion*, **45** (1S), S109–S113

Mason, J., M. Deitchler, A. Gilman, K. Gillenwater, D. Hotchkiss, K. Mason, N. Mock and K. Sthuraman, 2002: Iodine fortification is related to increased weight-for-age and birthweight in children in Asia, *Food and Nutrition Bulletin*, **23**(3), 292–308

Matte, T. M. Bresnahan, M. Begg and E. Susser, 2001: Influence of varition in birth weight within normal range and within sibships on IQ at age 7 years: cohort study, *British Medical Journal*, **323**, 310–14

Ment, L., B. Vohr, W. Allan, K. Katz, K. Schneider, M. Westerveld, C. Duncan and R. Makuch, 2003: Change in cognitive function over time in very low birth weight infants, *Journal of the American Medical Association*, **289**(6), 705–11

Merialdi, M., G. Carroli, J. Villar, E. Abalosi, M. Gulmezoglu, R. Kulier and M. de Onis, 2003: Nutritional interventions during pregnancy for the prevention or treatment of impaired fetal growth: an overview of randomized controlled trials, *Journal of Nutrition*, **133**, S1626–S1631

Miguel, E. and M. Kremer, 2002: Why don't people take their medicine: experimental evidence from Kenya, Harvard University and University of California, Berkeley, mimeo

2004: Worms: identifying impacts on health and education in the presence of treatment externalities, *Econometrica*,

Morris, S., 2001: Measuring nutritional dimensions of household food security, in J. Hoddinott (ed.), *Methods for rural development projects*, International Food Policy Research Institute, Washington, DC

Mills, A. and S. Shilcutt, 2004: Communicable diseases, London School of Hygiene and Tropical Medicine, London: see also chapter 2 in this volume

Muhilal, P., Y. R. Idjradinata, Muherdiyantiningsih and D. Karyadi, 1988: Vitamin A fortified monosodium glutamate and health, growth and survival of children: a controlled field trial, *American Journal of Clinical Nutrition*, **48**, 1271–6

Myers, R., 1995: *The twelve who survive: strengthening programmes of early childhood development in the third world*, 2nd edn., High/Scope Press, Michigan

Naiken, L., 2003: FAO methodology for estimating the prevalence of undernourishment, in, *Proceedings: measurement and assessment of food deprivation and undernutrition*, FAO, Rome

Pant, C., G. Pokharel, F. Curtale, R. Pokharel, R. Grosse, M. Lepkowski, M. Bannister, J. Gorstein, S. Pak-Gorstein, Atmarita and R. Tilden, 1996: Impact of nutrition education and mega-dose vitamin A supplementation on the health of children in Nepal, *Bulletin of the World Health Organization*, **74**, 533–45

Pelletier, D. L., E. Frongillo, D. Schroeder and J.-P. Habicht, 1995: The effects of malnutrition on child mortality in developing countries, *Bulletin of the World Health Organization*, **73**, 443–8

Pelletier, D. L. and E. Frongillo, 2003: Changes in child survival are strongly associated with changes in malnutrition in developing countries, *Journal of Nutrition*, **133**(1), 107–19

Petrou, S., T. Sach and L. Davidson, 2001: The long-term costs of preterm birth and low birth weight: results of a systematic review, *Child: Care, Health and Development*, **27**(2), 97–115

Phillips, M., T. Sanghvi, R. Suarez, J. McKigney and J. Fiedler, 1996: The costs and effectiveness of three vitamin A interventions in Guatemala, *Social Science and Medicine*, **42**, 1661–8

Pinstrup-Andersen, P. and P. Hazell, 1985: The impact of the Green Revolution and prospects for the future, *Food Review International*, **1**, 1–15

Pitt, M. M., M. R. Rosenzweig and D. Gibbons, 1993: The determinants and consequences of the placement of government programs in Indonesia, *The World Bank Economic Review*, **7**(3), 319–48

Pitt, M. M., M. R. Rosenzweig and M.N. Hassan, 1990: Productivity, health and inequality in the intrahousehold distribution of food in low-income countries, *American Economic Review*, **80**(5), 1139–56

Pollitt, E., 1990: Malnutrition and infection in the classroom, UNESCO, Paris

Popkin, B., S. Horton and S. Kim, 2001: The nutritional transition and diet-related chronic disease in Asia: implications for prevention, IFPRI, FCND Discussion Paper, 105, Washington, DC

Powell, C. A., S. M. Grantham-McGregor, S. P. Walker and S. M. Chang, 1998: School breakfast benefits children's nutritional status and school performance, *American Journal of Clinical Nutrition*, **69**, 873–9

Prada, J. and R. Tsang, 1998: Biological mechanisms of environmentally induced causes in IUGR, *European Journal of Clinical Nutrition*, **52**(51), S21–S28

Psacharopoulos, G., 1994: Returns to investment in education: a global update, *World Development*, **22**(9), 1325–44

Psacharopoulos, G. and E. Velez, 1992: Schooling, ability and earnings in Colombia, 1988, *Economic Development and Cultural Change*, **40**, 629–43

Quisumbing, A. R. and J. A. Maluccio, 1999: Intrahousehold allocation and gender relations: new empirical evidence, *Policy Research Report on Gender and Development*, Working Paper Series, 2, World Bank, Washington, DC

Quizon, J. and H. Binswanger, 1986: *Modeling the impact of agricultural growth and selected government policies on the distribution of income in India*, World Bank, Washington, DC

Rahmathullah, L., J. Tielsch, R. Thulasiraj, J. Katz, C. Coles, S. Devi, J. Rajeesh, P. Karthik, A. V. Sadanand, N. Edwin and C. Kamaraj, 2003: Impact of supplementing newborn infants with vitamin A on early infant mortality: community based randomised trial in Southern India, *British Medical Journal*, **327**(2), 254

Ramakrishnan U., R. Martorell, D. Schroeder and R. Flores, 1999: Intergenerational effects on linear growth, *Journal of Nutrition*, **129**(2), 544–9

Ravelli A., H. P. van der Meulen, R. P. Michels and C. Osmond, 1998: Glucose tolerance in adults after prenatal exposure to famine, *The Lancet*, **351**(9097), 173–7

Richards, M., R. Hardy, D. Kuh and M. Wadsworth, 2001: Birth weight and cognitive function in the British 1946 birth cohort: longitudinal population based study, *British Medical Journal*, **322**, 199–203

2002: Birth weight, postnatal growth and cognitive function in a national UK birth cohort,

International Journal of Epidemiology, **31**, 342–8

Rivera, J., C. Hotz, T. González-Cossío, L. Neufeld and A. García-Guerra, 2003: The effect of micronutrient deficiencies on child growth: a review of results from community-based supplementation trials, *Journal of Nutrition*, **133**, S4010–S4020

Roseboom, T., H. P. van der Meulen, A. Ravelli, C. Osmond, D. Barker and O. Bleker, 2001: Effects of prenatal exposure to the Dutch famine on adult disease in later life: an overview, *Molecular and Cellular Endocrinology*, **185**, 93–8

Rosenzweig, M. R., 1995: Why are there returns in schooling?, *American Economic Review*, **85**(2), 153–8

Rosenzweig, M. R. and T. P. Schultz, 1982: Child mortality and fertility in Colombia: individual and community effects, *Health Policy and Education* 2, 305–348

Rosenzweig, M. R. and K. J. Wolpin, 1982: Governmental interventions and household behavior in a developing country: anticipating the unanticipated consequences of social programs, *Journal of Development Economics*, **10**(2), 209–26

  1986, Evaluating the effects of optimally distributed public programs, *American Economic Review*, **76**(3), 470–87

Ross, J. S., 2002: Recommendations for vitamin A supplementation, *Journal of Nutrition*, **132**, S2902–2906

Ross, J. S. and F. L. Thomas, 1996: Iron deficiency anemia and maternal mortality, Academy for Education Development, Profiles, 3, Working Notes Series, 3, Washington, DC

Rouse, D., 2003: Potential cost-effectiveness of nutrition interventions to prevent adverse pregnancy outcomes in the developing world, *Journal of Nutrition*, **133**, S1640–S1644

Ruel, M., 2001: Can food based strategies help reduce vitamin A and iron deficiencies? A review of recent evidence, Food Policy Review, 5, IFPRI, Washington, DC

Runge, C., B. Senauer, P. Pardey and M. Rosegrant, 2003: *Ending hunger in our lifetime: food security and globalization*, Johns Hopkins University Press, Baltimore, MD

Sahn, D. and H. Alderman, 1988: The effect of human capital on wages, and the determinants of labor supply in a developing country, *Journal of Development Economics*, **29**(2), 157–84

Saigal, S., L. Hoult, D. Streiner *et al.*, 2000: School difficulties at adolescence in a regional cohort of children who were extremely low birth weight, *Pediatrics*, **105**(2), 325–31

Sastry, N., 1996: Community characteristics, individual and household attributes, and child survival in Brazil, *Demography*, **33**(2), 211–29

Sazawal S., R. E. Black, V. P. Menon, D. Pratibha, L. Caulfield, U. Dinghra and A. Bagati, 2001: Zinc supplementation in infants born small for gestational age reduces mortality: a prospective, randomized, controlled trial, *Pediatrics*, **108**, 1280–6

Schultz, T. P., 1993: Investments in the schooling and health of women and men: quantities and returns, *Journal of Human Resources*, **28**(4), 694–734

  1997: Assessing the productive benefits of nutrition and health: an integrated human capital approach, *Journal of Econometrics*, **77**(1), 141–57

Selowsky, M. and L. Taylor, 1973: The economics of malnourished children: an example of disinvestment in human capital, *Economic Development and Cultural Change*, **22**(1), 17–30

Sen, A., 1981: *Poverty and famines*, Clarendon Press, Oxford

  1999: *Development as freedom*, Alfred A. Knopf, New York

Shiono, P. H. and R. E. Behrman, 1995: Low birth weight: analysis and recommendations, *The Future of Children*, **5**(1), 4–18

Simondon, K., F. Simondon, I. Simon, A. Diallo, E. Benefice, P. Traissac and B. Maire, 1998: Preschool stunting, age at menarche and adolescent height: a longitudinal study in rural Senegal, *European Journal of Clinical Nutrition*, **52**, 412–18

Sorensen H., S. Sabroc, J. Olsen, K. Rothman, M. Gillman and P. Fischer, 1997: Birth weight and cognitive function in young adult life: historical cohort study, *British Medical Journal*, **315**, 401–3

Stein, Z. *et al.*, 1975: *Famine and human development: the Dutch hunger winter of 1944–5*, Oxford University Press, New York

Steketee, R., 2003: Pregnancy, nutrition and parasitic disease, *Journal of Nutrition*, **133**, S1661–S1667.

Stevenson, R., C. McCabe, P. Pharoah and R. Cooke, 1996: Cost of care for a geographically determined population of low birth weight infants to age 8–9 years, *Archives of Disease in Childhood*, **74**, F114–F117

Stillwaggon, E., 2002: AIDS in Africa: fertile terrain, *Journal of Development Studies*, **38**(6), 1–22

Stoltzfus, R., J. Kvalsvig, H. Chwaya, A. Montresor, M. Albonico, J. Tielsch, L. Savioli and E. Pollitt, 2001: Effects of iron supplementation and anthelmintic treatment on motor and language development of preschool children in Zanzibar: double blind, placebo controlled study, *British Medical Journal*, **323**, 1389–93

Strauss, J., 1986: Does better nutrition raise farm productivity?, *Journal of Political Economy*, **94**, 297–320

1990: Households, communities and preschool children's nutrition outcomes: evidence from rural Côte d'Ivoire, *Economic Development and Cultural Change*, **38**(2), 231–62

Strauss, J. and D. Thomas, 1995: Human resources: empirical modeling of household and family decisions, in J. R. Behrman and T. N. Srinivasan (eds.), *Handbook of development economics*, 3A, North-Holland, Amsterdam, 1883–2024

1996: Wages, schooling and background: investments in men and women in urban Brazil, in N. Birdsall and R. Sabot (eds.), *Opportunity foregone: education in Brazil*, Johns Hopkins University Press for the Inter-American Development Bank, Baltimore, MD, 147–91

1998: Health, nutrition, and economic development, *Journal of Economic Literature*, **36**(2), 766–817

Strauss, R., 2000: Adult functional outcome of those born small for gestational age, *Journal of the American Medical Association*, **283**(5), 625–32

Summers, L. H., 1992: Investing in all the people, *Pakistan Development Review*, **31**(4), 367–406

1994: Investing in all the people: educating women in developing countries, World Bank, Economic Development Institute Seminar Paper, 45, Washington, DC

Susser, E., H. Hoek and A. Brown, 1998: Neurodevelopmental disorders after prenatal famine, *American Journal of Epidemiology*, **147**, 213–16

Svedberg, P., 2004: Perspective paper 7.1 in this volume

Ter Kuile, F. *et al.*, 2003: Reduction of malaria during pregnancy by permetethrin-treated bed nets in an area of intense perennial malaria transmission in western Kenya, *American Journal of Tropical Medicine and Hygiene*, **68** (Suppl. 4), 50–60

Thomas, D., V. Lavy and J. Strauss, 1996: Public policy and anthropometric outcomes in the Côte d'Ivoire, *Journal of Public Economics*, **61**: 155–92

Thomas, D. and J. Strauss, 1992: Prices, infrastructure, household characteristics and child height, *Journal of Development Economics*, **39**(2), 301–31

1997: Health and wages: evidence on men and women in urban Brazil, *Journal of Econometrics*, **77**(1), 159–87

Thomas, D. *et al.*, 2004: Iron deficiency and the well-being of older adults: early results from a randomized intervention, RAND, Santa Monica, CA, mimeo

Todd, P. and K. Wolpin, 2003: Using a social experiment to validate a dynamic behavioral model of child schooling and fertility: assessing the impact of a school subsidy program in Mexico, University of Pennsylvania, Philadelphia, mimeo

United Nations Children's Fund (UNICEF), 1998: The *state of the world's children 1998*, Oxford University Press, New York

2001: LBW database at http//www.childinfo.org/eddb/lbw/database.htm

Vallamor, E. and W. Fawzi, 2000: Vitamin A supplementation: implication for morbidity and mortality in children, *Journal of Infectious Diseases*, **182**, S122–S133

Van der Gaag J. and J. P. Tan, 1997: The benefits of early child development programs, an economic analysis, Human Development Network, The World Bank, Washington, DC

Verhoeff, F. H., B. J. Brabin, S. van Buuren, L. Chimsuku, P. Kazembe, J. M. Wit and R. L. Broadhead, 2001: An analysis of intra-uterine growth retardation in rural Malawi, *European Journal of Clinical Nutrition*, **55**, 682–9

Victoria, C., B. Kirkwood, A. Ashworth, R. E. Black, S. Rogers, S. Sazawal, H. Campbell and S. Gove, 1999: Potential interventions for the prevention of childhood pneumonia in developing countries: improving nutrition, *American Journal of Clinical Nutrition*, **70**, 309–20

Villar, J. and J. M. Belizán, 1982: The relative contribution of prematurity and feral growth retardation to low birth weight in developing and developed societies, *American Journal of Obstetrics and Gynecology*, **143**, 793–8

Von den Briel, T., C. West and N. Bleichrodt, 2000: Improved iodine status is associated with improved mental performance of schoolchildren in Benin, *American Journal of Clinical Nutrition*, **72**(5), 1179–85

Warr, P. and I. Coxhead, 1993: The distributional impact of technical change in Philippine agriculture: a general equilibrium analysis, *Food Research Institute Studies*, **22**, 253–74

Weisell, ? 2002: ?

West, K., 2002: Extent of vitamin A deficiency among preschool children and women of reproductive age, *Journal of Nutrition*, **132**, S2857–S2866

West, K. P., J. Katz, S. K. Khatry S. C. LeClerq, E. K. Pradhan, S. R. Shrestha, P. B. Connor, S. M. Dali, R. P. Pokhrel and A. Sommer, 1999: A double blind, cluster randomised trial of low dose supplementation with vitamin A or beta carotene on mortality related to pregnancy in Nepal., The NNIPS-2 Study Group,

British Medical Journal, **318** (7183), 570–5

Welch, R. M., 2002: Breeding strategies for biofortified staple plant foods to reduce micronutrient malnutrition globally, *Journal of Nutrition*, **132**, S495–S499

World Bank, 1993:

1995: *Vietnam: poverty assessment and strategy*, Report 13442-VN, East Asia and Pacific Region, The World Bank, Washington, DC

World Health Organisation (WHO), 2002: *The world health report*, Reducing risks, Promoting healthy lives, WHO, Geneva

Yaqub, S., 2002: Poor children grow into poor adults: harmful mechanisms or over-deterministic theory, *Journal of International Development*, **14**, 1081–93

Young, M., 1995: Investing in young children, World Bank Discussion Papers, 275, Washington, DC

Zimmerman, R. and M. Qaim, 2003: Potential health benefits of Golden Rice: a Philippine case study, Center for Development Research (ZEF), University of Bonn, Bonn, mimeo

Alternative Perspectives

Perspective Paper 7.1

PETER SVEDBERG

Introduction

Jere Behrman and his co-authors in chapter 7 in this volume summarise and discuss results from a large number of micro-level experimental programmes aimed at reducing low birth weight (LBW) and child malnutrition through the dissemination of knowledge about improved breastfeeding practices and supplementation of micronutrients (i.e. iron, iodine, Vitamin A and zinc). Almost all the evaluations of the trial programmes suggest that they are not only efficient in reducing child malnutrition; they also have high benefit-cost ratios (BCRs). Benefits are measured in monetary terms at alternate discount rates. The costs are mainly those associated with providing new drugs and therapies, while the expenses for the infrastructure required to disseminate new knowledge and medicines are not directly included. Behrman, Alderman and Hoddinott (2004, chapter 7 in this volume) nevertheless exude optimism when it comes to challenging inadequate child nutritional status through an array of micro-level interventions.

Two other developments since the late 1980s and early 1990s add optimism regarding opportunities for reducing the prevalence of (child) malnutrition and undernutrition in poor developing countries – in addition to improvements following from economic growth. First, improved vaccines and extended immunisation, and also cheap and efficient curing methods, have become more readily available during the 1990s. There is a host of other instruments – old and new – for reducing child ill health, such as

immunisation against TB, DPT, polio and measles, and more lately, Hepatitis B. Also oral rehydration therapy and other child disease control practices have been developed recently (e.g. malaria insecticide-treated bed-nets (ITNs) and improved drugs). Since child health and malnutrition are intimately treated interrelated, any reduction in child morbidity following from the application of such vaccines, cures and technologies should help alleviate undernutrition and malnutrition – to the extent that they have been adopted on an increasing scale during the 1990s.

Second, there has been a notable change of policy instruments used by government for alleviating undernutrition and malnutrition. During the 1970s and 1980s, governments in many developing countries provided food at subsidised prices to large sections of the population. Common to all these interventions in the food market were that they were ill-targeted (some by intention), corruption was rampant and the fiscal burden excessive. The most well-documented cases are Bangladesh, Egypt, India and Sri Lanka.[1] In the late 1980s or early 1990s, these broad-based programmes were abolished or scaled down considerably. In most instances, they were replaced by various more narrowly targeted nutrition-cum-health programmes (Allen and Gilliespie 2001). A similar transition

[1] For evaluations of these broad-based programmes see, among many recent studies, Adams (1998, 2000); Chowdhury and Haggblade (2000); McClatterty (2000); Löfgren and El-Said (2001); Ahmed and Bouis (2002); Gutner (2002); Ramaswami and Balakrishnan (2002).

took place in many other countries, for example in Tunisia, Jamaica and Costa Rica (Adams 2000).[2]

In this Perspective paper, I will first provide a simple test of the extent to which the various 'technological developments' helped to reduce malnutrition world-wide during the 1990s, as measured at the macro level by the overall prevalence of child stunting and underweight.[3] This I will do by examining whether the statistical relationship between child malnutrition and real *per capita* income across countries changed from 1990 to 2000. The second objective is to test whether the prevalence of child stunting and underweight are correlated to LBW, exclusive breastfeeding and the micronutrient content in national diets across countries. There are large intercountry variations in these three variables, which should be reflected in the prevalence of stunting/underweight if they are as important as suggested by the micro-level investigations covered by Behrman, Alderman and Hoddinott (2004).

Child Malnutrition and *per capita* Income

An extensive empirical literature shows that poverty (low income) is the crucial determinant of hunger and undernutrition. This has been demonstrated in numerous cross-country (as well as cross-household) studies.[4] *Per capita* income affects child nutritional status in two main ways. The first is that with higher *per capita* income, households can (on average) exert stronger effective demand for essen-

tial private consumption goods, including more and nutritionally richer food. The second is that higher GNI/C means higher government revenues and expenditures. To the extent that these expenditures finance public investment and consumption in health- and nutrition-related services, child nutritional status should be positively affected (Svedberg 2000; Smith and Haddad 2002; Haddad *et al.* 2003).

Hypothesis and Data

The basic hypothesis to be tested is whether the relationship between malnutrition (child stunting and underweight) and real income has changed during the 1990s. Behind this hypothesis lies a presumption that the technological improvements mentioned above have been spread widely among and within the poor countries, that targeting instruments have been refined and the intervention methods have become more efficient. Since knowledge travels slowly and application takes time, it is important that we have the most recent anthropometric data available (up to 2002–3).

The WHO (2004) *Global Database on Child Growth and Malnutrition* provides the data needed to undertake the tests. This database contains what is claimed to be nationally representative data on the prevalence of child stunting and underweight for varying years in the late 1980s up to 2003 from more than 100 developing countries. After some filtering (Svedberg 2004c), I ended up with a dataset comprising 115 anthropometric surveys, forty-eight for years close to 1990, and sixty-seven surveys for years close to 2000. For thirty-seven countries we have anthropometric observations at both points in time, which enable intertemporal comparisons for a given set of countries. Income in both sub-periods is measured by GNI/C, valued in 2000 constant international dollars (PPP), derived from World Bank data sources (Svedberg 2004c).[5]

The data to be used are summarised in table 7.1.1. In the full samples, the average (unweighted) prevalence of stunting fell from 31.5 to 28.0 per cent, or by 11.1 per cent in relative terms. The prevalence of underweight declined from 21.8 to 20.4, or by 6.4 per cent. In the thirty-seven overlapping countries, the average incidence of stunting fell from 33.2 to 27.9, and underweight from 23.5 to 20.3.

---

[2] The more narrowly targeted programmes that flourished during the 1990s are of various types. Some rely on means-testing (income or assets) and various incentive-based screening methods (school attendance), others on self-selection (food for work or education) and still others on administrative fiat (selection at health clinics or by place of residence).

[3] These are the only reasonably reliable indicators of malnutrition that are available for most countries. The food-supply based indicators from the FAO are biased and not very relevant for assessing nutritional status (see Svedberg 1999, 2000, 2002).

[4] For a recent contribution to the large literature based on cross-household data, see Haddad *et al.* (2003).

[5] For an assessment of the reliability and inter-temporal comparability of the anthropometric data in the WHO database, see Svedberg (2004b, forthcoming).

Table 7.1.1. Summary Statistics on GNI *per capita* and Prevalence of Stunting and Underweight in Children aged 0–5 years, 1990 and 2000

	GNI *per capita*[a]			Height-for-age[b]			Weight-for-age[b]		
	1990	2000	Diff. (%)	1988–92	1998–2002	Diff. (%)	1988–92	1998–2002	Diff. (%)
All countries	3190	3890	700	31.5	28.0	−3.5	21.8	20.4	−1.4
(N)	(140)	(150)	*21.9*	(45)	(67)	*−11.1*	(48)	(66)	*−6.4*
Overlapping	2525	2975	450	33.2	27.9	−5.3	23.5	20.3	−3.2
countries (N)	(37)	(37)	*17.8*	(36)	(37)	*−16.0*	(37)	(37)	*−13.6*

Sources: Data on GNI *per capita* from World Bank (2002); height- and weight-for-age data from WHO (2004), as reported for all developing countries in ACC/SCN (2004).
Notes: [a] GNI *per capita*, unweighted averages, valued in international $ (PPP) at 2000 prices for low- and middle-income countries in World Bank (2004).
[b] Percentage of children below − 2 sd of the WHO/NCHS norm; unweighted averages.

In relative terms, these drops correspond to 16.0 and 13.6 per cent, respectively. The annual average (unweighted) growth of real GNI/C over the 1990s in the thirty-seven overlapping countries was a notch above 1.6 per cent, signifying a cumulative *per capita* real income growth of about 18 per cent.

Estimation Model and First Results

The model used to test the hypothesis of a changed relationship between 1988–92 and 1998–2002 has the following property:

$$(1) \quad HA_T = \alpha_T + \beta_{T1}\ln GNI/C_T$$
$$+ \beta_{t2}\ln GNI/C_{88-92} + \beta_{t3}D_{88\ 92} + \varepsilon$$

We have 115 pooled observations for prevalence of height-for-age failure, HA_T, and $\ln GNI/C_T$ ($T =$ 1988–92 and 1998–2002) and also for the alternate dependent variable, weight for age (WA_T). Adding $\ln GNI/C_{88-92}$ as an additional independent variable, means that we can check whether the regression slope has changed between the two points in time (or short sub-periods). The dummy variable $(D_{88-92}) = 1$ for 1988–92 and 0 for 1998–2002, is aimed to pick up changes in the intercept.

The results of the estimations are presented in table 7.1.2. In all four regressions reported, the coefficient for the pooled income variable is statistically significant at the 0.000 level, and the adjusted R^2 are in the 0.49–0.61 range. About 60 per cent of the variation in child stunting across the countries is 'explained' by the income variable alone. For

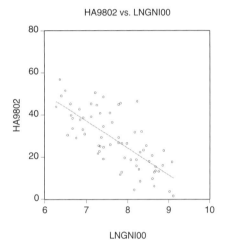

Figure 7.1.1. *Plot of proportion of stunted children 1998–2002 and lnGNI/C$_{2000}$; N = 67*

underweight, the corresponding number is a little below 50 per cent. (I will come back to the problem with reverse causality.) For the entire set of countries and observations (115), the dummy (D_{88-92}) turns out statistically significant at the 0.10 level ($\rho = 0.0986$) in the regression for height-for-age. In the other regressions, the dummy variable, as well as the coefficients for $\ln GNI/C_{88-92}$, are insignificant. Figure 7.1.1 shows the correlation between the prevalence of child stunting and $\ln GNI/C$ in the 1998–2002 period and figure 7.1.2 displays the analogous relationship ten years earlier.

There is hence not much evidence of a dramatic impact of 'technological improvements' on

Table 7.1.2. Estimated Change in the Relationship Across Countries between Real *per capita* Income and Child Stunting/Underweight 1988–92 and 1998–2002

	Dependent variables (OLS regressions)			
	All countries (48 + 67 = 115)		Overlapping (2 × 37 = 74)	
	Height-for-age ($<-2sd$)	Weight-for-age ($<-2sd$)	Height-for-age ($<-2sd$)	Weight-for-age ($<-2sd$)
Independent variables	(1)	(2)	(3)	(4)
$\ln GNI/C_{88-92,98-02}$ (pooled)	−12.79 [8.65]*	−13.10 [7.81]*	−13.64 [7.03]*	−12.82 [5.52]*
$\ln GNI/C_{88-92}$	−3.47 [1.49]	−0.56 [0.22]	−1.93 [0.68]	−0.64 [0.19]
$DUMMY_{88-92}$	30.00 [1.67]***	5.95 [0.30]	17.96 [0.83]	6.34 [0.24]
R^2 adj.	0.59	0.49	0.61	0.45
N	111	114	72	74

Source: Author's calculations.
Notes: absolute *t*-values in square brackets. *, ** and *** indicate statistical
significance at the 0.01, 0.05 and 0.10 levels, respectively.

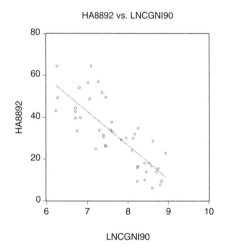

HA8892 vs. LNCGNI90

Figure 7.1.2. *Plot of proportion of stunted children, 1988–92 and lnGNI/C$_{1990}$; N = 48*

the prevalence of child stunting and underweight over the 1990s. That the incidence of stunting has declined over and above that predicted by income growth alone in the full sample is encouraging, although the relevant coefficient is barely significant. Moreover, the fact that partly different countries are included in the full samples from 1988–92

and 1998–2002 may have influenced this result. For the thirty-seven overlapping countries, only the coefficient for the pooled income variable turns out significant in the regressions for both stunting and underweight; the coefficients for $\ln GNI/C_{88-92}$ and the dummy D_{88-92} are insignificant throughout.

Correlation of Changes in Stunting/Underweight and Income

The fact that we have anthropometric data from thirty-seven countries for both periods makes it possible to correlate *changes* in stunting/underweight to *changes* in GNI/C over the 1990s. In these regressions we include two additional variables: initial income (GNI/C_{1990}) and income distribution (as measured by the share of total income/expenditure that accrues to the 40 per cent poorest in respective country). The initial income is included to test for the possibility that there is a tendency for the poorest to catch up with the less poor countries (or fall further behind). The income-distribution variable is included to check whether more growth is required for alleviating malnutrition in countries with uneven income distribution (cf. the poverty-reduction-cum-growth literature).[6]

The results are reported in table 7.1.3. The negative association between the relative *changes* in

[6] For an assessment of trends in world income distribution, both relative and absolute, see Svedberg (2004a).

Table 7.1.3. Correlation between Relative Change in Stunting/Underweight and Change in $GNI/C_{1990-2000}$**, with Controls for Initial Level of Income (**GNI/C_{1990}**) and Income Distribution. OLS**

| | Dependent variables (relative change over period 1990–2000) | | | |
| | Height-for-age (<-2sd) | | Weight-for-age (<-2sd) | |
$N = 37$	(1)	(2)	(3)	(4)
Growth of $GNI/C_{1990-2000}$	−0.38 [2.89]*	−0.39 [2.85]*	−0.26 [2.03]**	−0.25 [2.59]*
GNI/C_{90} (initial income)	–	−0.000 [0.44]	–	−0.008 [5.08]*
Income distribution[a]	–	−0.003 [0.34]	–	−0.018 [2.46]**
R^2 adj.	0.17	0.14	0.08	0.49
N	36	34	37	35

Notes: [a] **Income distribution measured as the share of total income or expenditures accruing to the 40 per cent poorest in respective country.**
Absolute t**-values in square brackets; * and ** indicate significance at the 0.01 and 0.05 levels, respectively.**

stunting/underweight and income growth is statistically significant throughout.[7] The coefficients (elasticities) are significant at the 0.01 level in most of the regressions. The size of the estimated elasticity for underweight (−0.25) is lower than reported in a previous study on the basis of pooled data from the 1970–95 period (Haddad *et al.* 2003). This may have to do with the fact that the estimates here are the first to have been derived for a given set of countries.

The initial income and the income distribution variables turn out insignificant in the regression for stunting, while being significant in the regression for underweight. The initial income variable is negative, indicating that, in countries with relatively high *per capita* income in 1990, underweight declined relatively more. The income distribution variable is also negative, suggesting that in countries where the 40 per cent poorest have a relatively large share of total incomes, underweight declined more for given *per capita* income growth than in countries with more uneven distribution.[8]

Extending the Model

According to the results presented in table 7.1.2, more than half the cross-country variation in the prevalence of child underweight is *not* explained by differences in *per capita* income. For stunting, the equivalent number is about 40 per cent. That there can be large differences in stunting between

countries at similar income levels is clear from figure 7.1.1. In Jamaica, for example, only 4.4 per cent of the children are stunted, while 25–45 per cent are stunted in Albania, Guatemala, Peru and the Philippines, countries in the same *per-capita* income bracket. To identify the reasons for such variations, not related to income, has been a main preoccupation of empirical economists in the field. Various proxy variables for parental education status, public provision of services and demographic characteristics have been added on the right-hand side of the estimations.

Variable Extensions

In the extension of the model here, I will focus on the variables that are analysed from a micro-perspective by Behrman, Alderman and Hoddinott (2004) – LBW, exclusive breastfeeding up to six months (EBF-6) and the content of micronutrients in the diet. Data on the prevalence of LBW and EBF-6, albeit not very accurate (Allen and Gillespie 2001), are readily available for most countries (UNICEF 2004). The micronutrient content in the

---

[7] We also measured the change in stunting and underweight in absolute terms, and the results are quite similar.

[8] The inclusion of additional explanatory variables had little impact on the results and was statistically insignificant (not reported). The reason for this is probably that there are seldom large changes in adult female literacy rates, the provision of communal services, or in demographic composition, in individual countries over a ten–year period.

national diets will be proxied by the share of calories that originates from animal sources (FAO 2002). In addition to these variables, I will include female (mother) literacy rate.[9]

The Importance of Meat and Other Animal Foods

An explanation for the choice of the proxy variable for micronutrients may be warranted. The main animal products are meat (including fish and poultry), eggs and milk. Meat contains various proteins, which 'are composed of different combinations of 20 amino acids' and '[in] order for protein to be used for [child] growth, rather than for energy, all the essential amino acids must be present in adequate amounts. Generally speaking, foods of animal origin supply needed amino acids in approximately the required proportions, and foods of plant origin are relatively deficient in one or more essential amino acids' (Jamison, Leslie and Musgrove 2003, 152).[10] Animal products also contain many essential minerals (e.g. riboflavin, calcium, iron and zinc) and are rich in vitamins (A, B_2, B_{12}, D and E), all most probably important for child growth.

Behrman, Alderman and Hoddinott emphasise Vitamin A, iron and zinc, which are essential according to the nutritionists, but so are many other micronutrients. There are also synergistic bioavailability effects among the various micronutrients (Bhargava 2003). Moreover, some minerals are several times more absorbable by the human body when supplied from animal sources than from plants (Allen and Gillespie 2001, 33). All this suggests that supplementation of poor diets with one or two micronutrients may have limited effects when other essential nutrients are lacking.

Animal foods, especially meats, seem to be close to perfect 'packages' of most of the proteins and micronutrients needed for full genetic-potential growth in children. According to the FAO (2002), there are large differences across countries in the share of calories in the national diets which emanate from animal sources. In some African countries, especially in West Africa, but also in Bangladesh and Indonesia, the estimated share is less than 5 per cent; in India, the share is about 8 per cent. In several other developing countries, including China, the share is 20 per cent or more, with Mongolia at the top of the list (at 45 per cent). There is hence enough variation across countries to expect that the 'animal-origin' factor could play a role in explaining differences in child stunting (and underweight).

Regression Model and Results

The simple regression model to be run is the following:

$$(2) \qquad CHILD\text{-}MAL_{it} = \alpha_t + \beta_{kt} \ln GNI/C_{it} + [X_{kit}][\delta_{kt}] + \varepsilon_{it}$$

where $i = 1 \ldots n$ (number of countries), $t = 1$, 2 are the two time periods and $k = 1 \ldots K$ are the number of control variables; $[X_{kit}]$ is a vector of these controls and ε_{it} is the random error term. Child malnutrition (CHILD-MAL) will alternately be measured by the share of children who are stunted and underweight.

Results from regressions of the prevalence of stunting in 1998–2002 against the incidence of LBW, EBF-6 and the share of calories obtained from animal sources in the national diets (ANIM), are reported in table 7.1.4, section A (OLS regressions). Real per capita income is, as before, highly significant in all regressions (i.e. robust). The female literacy rate (FLR) and LBW come out (in separate regressions) with a significant coefficient (and expected signs) for underweight, but not for stunting. This result hence only partly corroborates the evidence from micro-level studies reported by Behrman, Alderman and Hoddinott (2004) and others.

The perhaps surprising result shown in table 7.1.4., section A, relates to EBF-6. The coefficient for this variable is positive throughout and, in some of the regressions, also statistically significant. At

---

[9] The role of mother education for child nutrition has been emphasised in several recent studies; see, among others, Senauer and Kassouf (1996): Glewwe (1999); Handa (1999); Schultz (2002).

[10] See Allen and Gillespie (2001, 33–4) for a concise discussion of the importance of foods originating from animal sources for ensuring that the essential micronutrients needed for normal child growth are provided. Also see several comments on the article by Jamison et al. (2003) in *Food and Nutrition Bulletin*, 24(2).

Table 7.1.4. Summary of Regression Results for Extended Variable Set

N = 67 Indep. variab.	A OLS estimations				B Instrument variable estimations			
	Height-for-age		Weight-for-age		Height-for-age		Weight-for-age	
	(1)	(2)	(3)	(4)	(5)	(6)	(7)	(8)
lnGNI/C (ln)^a	−9.72 [5.28]**	−10.02 [5.84]**	−8.13 [3.96]**	−9.05 [5.41]**	−0.36 [3.11]**	−0.48 [4.57]**	−0.21 [1.66]***	−0.39 [3.73]**
FLR	−0.02 [0.38]	– –	−0.14 [2.15]**	– –	−0.11 [1.52]	– –	−0.23 [3.13]**	– –
LBW	– –	0.25 [1.43]	– –	0.67 [3.92]**	– –	0.68 [2.67]**	– –	1.16 [4.66]**
EBF-6	0.10 [1.97]***	0.08 [1.59]	0.03 [0.45]	0.04 [0.72]	0.18 [2.61]**	0.19 [2.97]**	0.08 [1.11]	0.13 [2.03]**
ANIM	−0.45 [2.19]**	−0.32 [1.74]***	−0.33 [1.51]	−0.35 [1.97]**	−0.60 [2.42]**	−0.45 [2.16]**	−0.47 [1.82]***	−0.44 [2.15]**
R^2 adj.	0.58	0.57	0.56	0.63	0.48	0.51	0.47	0.56
N	61	64	61	64	55	58	55	58

Source: Author's calculations.
Notes: Absolute *t*-values in square brackets, ** and *** indicate statistical significance at the 0.05 and 0.10 levels, respectively.
^{a} In the OLS regressions with LnGNI/C as the sole regressor, the R^2 adjusted is 0.54 in the regressions for stunting and 0.52 in that for underweight.

the macro-level, there is hence no vindication of the WHO proposition that exclusive breastfeeding up to six months leads to less stunting, rather the opposite.[11] This result may be due to weak data, but it is not altogether implausible that it reflects reality (a short discussion will be provided later).

The variable measuring the animal-source content of the national diet (*ANIM*) is significant throughout, at a probability in the 0.02–0.07 range, and with the expected negative sign (robust). There is hence support at the macro level for the findings that micronutrients are essential for child growth, as suggested by the studies conducted at the levels of individuals, and reported by Behrman, Alderman and Hoddinott (2004). This is not to say, however, that the supplementation of one or two essential minerals/vitamins is effective in reducing child stunting in environments where many other crucial micronutrients are deficient in the mainly vegetarian diets of poor households.

The dominance of the income variable in explaining intercountry variations in child stunting and underweight is underscored by the fact that adjusted R^2 increases by only a few points with the inclusions of the other variables in table 7.1.4 (see note *a* to the table). This result squares with earlier studies.[12]

Multicollinearity

FLR turns out insignificant in many regressions. Whether this is due to the fact that FLR is highly correlated to income (and also to LBW), or is reflecting real phenomena, is hard to tell. The high degree of multicollinearity makes it difficult to disentangle the separate effects of these explanatory variables. (In appendix table 7.1.A (p. 432), a partial correlation matrix of the variables is presented.) It also means that estimates become very sensitive to the inclusions or exclusion of other variables, and to the specification of the regression model.[13] In a longer version of this chapter (in progress), I also discuss the uncertainty inflicted by unobservable, but potentially important, omitted variables, such as the relative price of food and the disease

[11] The WHO strongly recommends exclusive breastfeeding up to six months, but this recommendation is not universally accepted (Allen and Gillespie 2001).
[12] Cross-country studies include Osmani (1997), Klasen (1999/2003), Svedberg (2000), Smith and Haddad (2002) and Haddad *et al.* (2003).
[13] An illustrative example is the different results for the education proxy (female secondary school enrolment) in Smith and Haddad (2002) and Haddad *et al.* (2003), respectively. In the former study, this variable is found to be statistically significant, while not in the latter.

environment.[14] In that version, a battery of robustness tests are carried out as well.

Checking Simultaneity

In most earlier related empirical cross-country investigations, the possibility of reverse causality between stunting/underweight and *per capita* income was ignored (Osmani 1997; Klasen 1999; Svedberg 2000; Haddad *et al.* 2003). The predominant view thus seems to be that simultaneity is not a major

problem when it comes to the association between the nutritional status of young children and national *per capita* income. Only one of the related studies attempts to test for simultaneity through the use of instrument variables (Smith and Haddad 2002). They found little evidence of reverse causality, but some doubts remain about the validity of the chosen instruments.[15]

Why Simultaneity?

Even though it is difficult to find valid instruments for the *level* of income, the simultaneity problem cannot be dismissed offhand. If the prevalence of undernutrition in children is a marker of undernutrition in the population as a whole, and poor nutritional status has negative effects on labour productivity,[16] this may stifle economic growth and, in the longer term, keep *per capita* income at a low level.[17] The 'marker' hypothesis is not altogether implausible considering the close correlation (R^2 adjusted $= 0.79$) between the prevalence of underweight children and of adult women across forty-five countries for which data are available (Svedberg 2004c).[18]

Another plausible hypothesis is that 'third' factors explain both low income levels and child undernutrition. This is basically the question why some countries have had little (or no) economic growth over their entire history, reflected in very low *per capita* incomes today, as well as miserable social conditions in all respects, including the nutritional status of the population.[19] Perhaps self-evident, but nevertheless central to recall, the high incomes in the contemporary richest countries are the outcomes of an accumulation of physical and human capital, and also rival technological innovations, over a very long period – more than 200 years (Maddison 1995). Why this long-term accumulation of productive assets has taken place in some countries, while not in others, is perhaps the most important question in development-cum-growth economics. In recent years, a broad consensus has emerged on the notion that long-term growth depends on 'institutional arrangements: on the legal systems that enforce contracts and protect property rights and on political structures, constitutional provisions, and the extent of special-interest lobbies and cartels' (Olson 1996).

---

[14] In previous work I focused on relative food prices as a main determinant of differences in child stunting and underweight. I worked with ICP data from the World Bank (World Bank 2001), which indicated huge differences in the relative price of food across countries (by a factor of three). However, the more I dug into this dataset, the more confused I became. After I had contacted the World Bank, I was told that the relative price data they had produced were so unreliable that they had stopped publishing them in recent *World Development Indicators*.

[15] In a paper by Pritchett and Summers (1996), aimed at estimating the extent to which 'wealthier is healthier' on the basis of cross-country data, the ratios of (1) investment and (2) Foreign direct investment (FDI) to GDP, are used as instruments for income growth. Smith and Haddad (2002) use the same instruments, making reference to Pritchett and Summers, for the *level* of *per capita* GDP. That the variation in the level of income across countries should be a function of the contemporary investment ratios has no support in the empirical growth literature (Sala-i-Martin 1997; Temple 1999).

[16] According to the calculations by Behrman, Alderman and Hoddinott (2004), the largest benefit from reducing LBW stems from future higher labour productivity. Numerous investigations of the link from poor nutrition (status or calorie intake) to low labour productivity have been made, although in most cases the simultaneity problem is not satisfactorily resolved. See Svedberg (2000, chapter 4 for references and a discussion of studies using calorie intake as the nutrition variable, and Strauss and Thomas 1998 for references to studies based on anthropometric indicators for adults (e.g. height)).

[17] In some of the cross-country regressions aimed at identifying the determinants of growth, longevity (a marker of health-cum-nutrition status) comes out as a significant and robust explanatory variable in growth regressions (Bhargava *et al.*, 2001). Bloom, Canning and Sevilla (2004) provide summaries of results from more than a dozen such studies as well as own estimates.

[18] This close correlation has also been documented on older data (Svedberg 2000; Nubé 2001).

[19] In constant international dollars, the poorest countries today, with a *GNI/C* below US$1,000 (PPP) in 2000 price levels, are almost as poor as they were in 1900 (see Maddison 1995 and Jones 1997 for further discussion).

Table 7.1.5. Regression of $GNI/C_{2000/01}$ **on Indexes of Quality of Institutions, Base Sample and the World, OLS**

Sample	Dependent variables			
	GNI/C_{2000}	$\ln GNI/C_{2000}$	$\ln GNI/C_{2001}$	
	Base sample (1)	Base sample (2)	World (3)	World (4)
Indep. variab.[a]	IICR	IICR	IICR	ECCWR
	131.55 [9.67]*	0.043 [8.19]*	0.038 [21.73]*	0.044 [22.10]*
R^2 adj.	0.61	0.52	0.79	0.78
N	61	61	128	138

Source: Author's calculations (regressions-CH-04-03-30 in computer printout).
Notes: [a] IICR = Institutional Investor Credit Rating; ECCWR = Euromoney Country Credit-Worthiness Rating, as reported by the World Bank (2003, table 5.2).
Absolute t-values in square brackets.
*Indicates statistical significance at the 0.000 level.

The Instrument

As an instrument for *per capita* income, I will use an index of the quality of countries' institutions. The choice of this instrument is inspired by findings in the recent growth literature, not the least by the results obtained by Hall and Jones (1999) and Acemoglu, Johnson and Robinson (2001).[20] The latter found current bad institutions to be a function of historically (c. 1900) bad institutions and *per capita* income today to be closely associated with present institutions (after several robustness tests). My assumption is hence that the persistence of bad institutions over a long time explains both low levels of *GNI/C* and high prevalence of stunting/underweight in children. There may well be reverse causation between poor nutrition and income (growth), but concurrent child malnutrition can hardly explain the historic – and hence the present – bad institutions.

Correlation Between GNI/C and Instruments

The correlations between GNI/C_{2000} and the Institutional Investment Credit Ratings (IICR) instrument are reported in table 7.1.5 for different sets of countries. All regressions show a very strong correlation, significant at the 0.000 level throughout. For all 128 countries for which data are obtainable, the adjusted R^2 is 0.79. Considering unavoidable mismeasurements, this is a remarkable number: 79 per cent of

the variation in countries' real *GNI/C* today, ranging from less than US$1,000 (PPP) to well above US$35,000, is explained by this index of the quality of institutions. Moreover, this result is not dictated by the choice of one particular index. Practically identical results emerge when an alternative index (ECCWR) is used.

Effects on Main Results

Replacing *GNI/C* in our regressions with the IICR index as the instrument does not alter the main results. The cross-country bivariate correlations between stunting/underweight and this instrument are intact, although the adjusted R^2s drop (table 7.1.4, section B). The statistical significance for the income instrument remains at the 0.000 level throughout. The fact that most results tend to be less strong with the instrument variable than with OLS is an indication that there is reverse causality between prevalence of stunting (and underweight) and *per capita* income.[21]

---

[20] Other relevant references are Knack and Keefer (1995), Collier and Gunning (1999) and Rodrik (1999).

[21] Institutions may, in addition to be an appropriate instrument for income levels, have an independent effect on child malnutrition. Good institutions probably mean that the *quality* of public health and education services, as well as of sanitation facilities, are higher than when institutions are faltering.

Discussion

Technological Improvements?

When it comes to 'technology improvements' for abating child malnutrition, it is not straightforward to say whether a weakly significant, and not very large, reduction in stunting, unrelated to *per capita* real income growth, is a development that merits optimism or not.

A positive interpretation is that micro-level interventions with supplementation of vitamins and minerals, iodine fortification and improved vaccines, and also better targeting instruments, have had an impact large enough to make a dent in the statistics at the macro-level. If so, our results suggest, such interventions are more important for enhancing child growth in stature, while less so for stifling underweight. The latter condition is probably determined more by provision of sanitation facilities, the disease environment and the quantity of food (calories) rather than the quality (micronutrients).

Although more efficient targeting instruments and new nutrition-enhancing technologies, available at little cost, may have emerged during the 1990s, constraints on implementation remain in many poor economies. In countries where the administrative capacity and physical infrastructure is highly underdeveloped, even free-of-charge knowledge may take considerable time to implement on a substantial scale. The scarcity of adequately trained personnel (doctors and health workers) needed to disseminate free-to-obtain knowledge and improved drugs is also a constraint. It should be recalled that results obtained in controlled trial tests, based on micro-data, and results from macro-data are not always consonant, for real reasons. An oft-mentioned such reason is that most macro-

investigations take into account dynamic and indirect effects, and also externalities and synergies, which most micro-level investigations fail to capture (Mills and Shillcutt 2004, see chapter 2 in this volume).

Moreover, most of the successful micro-level interventions analysed by Behrman, Alderman and Hoddinott (2004) are experimental trials, aimed at gathering information rather than real-life policy programmes. That small-scale, tightly controlled and well-managed and operated programmes yield results that are far better than those obtained in fully-fledged policy programmes is well known. As noted by Gillespie (2001), 'The failure – or limited achievements – of many large-scale nutrition programmes is very often a function of insufficient sustainable capacities within communities and organisations responsible for implementing them.' The list provided of the prerequisites needed for policy programmes to become efficient is very long and detailed (Gillespie 2001, 78). In fact, it includes most of the achievements that development is all about, and that can be accomplished in the long run only through equitable economic growth.[22]

There are no comprehensive and detailed estimates of the extent to which new 'technologies' actually have been applied throughout the developing countries. Scattered evidence suggests, however, that many programmes reach only a fraction of the population in their respective country (Allen and Gillespie 2001). It may thus be that the new 'technologies' have yet to be applied on a scale that leaves significant marks in the aggregate statistics. This could be the reason for the apparent micro–macro paradox (which has frequently been observed for foreign aid projects).[23]

In many of the countries included in our dataset, corruption is endemic. According to the assessment made by Transparency International (TI) (2002), only three of the sixty-seven countries in our sample for 1998–2002, Botswana, Chile and Trinidad and Tobago, score more than 5 in its index – where a 'clean score' is 10. Incidentally, the latter two countries had the lowest incidence of stunting and underweight out of the sixty-seven countries in the 1998–2002 sub-period. Botswana, also a middle-income country but with a relatively high incidence of stunting and underweight, may be special because it has

---

[22] The targeting efficiency, usually evaluated as the share of the explicit or implicit income transfer going to the poorest quintile group, is often low (e.g. Gabremedhin and Swinton, 2001; Jayne *et al.*, 2001).

[23] In its own evaluations of World Bank aid projects in Sub-Saharan Africa (SSA), the Bank finds about two-thirds to be efficient, and many bilateral donors report similar numbers. Despite this, and the fact that most African countries are heavily aid-dependent, many have minuscule or even negative growth in their macroeconomies.

the highest prevalence rate of HIV/AIDS in the world, estimated at 39 per cent of the adult population (UNICEF 2004, table 4). Not all countries in our sample are covered by TI, but more than two dozen of these countries are included, and score less than 3. Such low scores reflect deep-rooted and widespread corruption at most levels in society.

There is also the uncomfortable question whether governments in many of the countries covered here actually have improved child health and nutrition on their short list of priorities. As clearly demonstrated by Behrman, Alderman and Hoddinott (2004, table 7.6), the high benefit-cost ratios (BCRs) for some trial interventions are derived on discount rates that could be relevant in high-income, democratic countries (say 5 per cent). In countries with autocratic, non-elected, unaccountable and unstable governments, one may suspect that investments in social welfare programmes for the poor are discounted at much higher rates. Since most of the benefits are very long-term (decades), high discount rates make many investments unattractive in such political environments.

On the Causes of Child Malnutrition

The cross-country regression analysis produced two results that merit some comment. The first was that exclusive breastfeeding up to six months is associated with *higher* levels of stunting and underweight. This result goes against the WHO's findings and is also at odds with many small-scale experimental tests (Behrman, Alderman and Hoddinott 2004). The WHO recommendation is not universally accepted, however. In some countries, the official recommendation is exclusive breastfeeding for three or four months, based on the conviction that older infants need some solid food after that age.

In the poor-country context, considering sanitation, I can find only one plausible reason for why EBF-6 should not be beneficial for child growth: malnutrition in mothers. If mothers are anaemic and have a diet which is poor in most micronutrients, milk quality may be low. This is a matter in which I have no expertise, but the very close association between underweight in adult women and children

aged 0–5 years across the forty-five countries for which we have data (R^2 adjusted $= 0.79$), is an indication pointing in that direction.

The other notable result is the close association between child stunting/underweight and the share of calories emanating from animal sources. Animal foods, especially meat, contain almost all the micronutrients needed for child growth in well-balanced combinations. This seems to suggest that propagation (and subsidies) for more animal products in young children's food is warranted. Supplementation (or fortification) of normal poor diets with one or two micronutrients, when many others are lacking, may be insufficient to bolster normal growth in children.

Summary and Conclusion

We have long known that economic growth reduces child undernutrition (and most other deprivations, including LBW prevalence), although very high growth rates are required if notable reductions are to be forthcoming over a decade or two. Considering that *per capita* economic growth is *de facto* very low in most developing countries, and even negative in some cases, there is a desperate need for methods and policies that reduce the plight of children which are not primarily dependent on high *per capita* incomes.

In this Perspective paper, I have examined what, besides economic growth, could contribute to a notable reduction of child undernutrition. The results are not totally encouraging. The relationship between stunting and *per capita* real income drifted downwards somewhat during the 1990s, indicating that non-income factors helped to reduce stunting. The impact is not very large, however, and there is no similar effect when it comes to underweight. The search for improved micro-level interventions and targeting methods must continue, but in the absence of higher economic growth rates in the poor countries, there is scant hope for realising the Millennium Development Goal (MDG) of halving the prevalence of child undernutrition by 2015.

Appendix

Table 7.1.A. Partial Correlation Matrix, data from 2000 (N = 67 in sample)

	GNI/C	LBW	EBF-6	FLR	ANIM	Water	Sanitation
GNI/C[a]	1.00	–	–	–	–	–	–
LBW	−0.29	1.00	–	–	–	–	–
EBF-6	−0.24	−0.05	1.00	–	–	–	–
FLR	**0.56**	**−0.53**	−0.07	1.00	–	–	–
ANIM	0.34	**−0.49**	0.20	**0.54**	1.00	–	–
Water[b]	**0.47**	0.14	0.08	0.19	−0.21	1.00	–
Sanitation[b]	−0.19	0.11	0.11	0.13	−0.37	0.30	1.00

Notes: [a] Log of GNI *per capita*. [b] Share of population in rural areas using improved drinking water and adequate sanitation facilities, respectively (data from UNICEF 2004, table 3).

References

ACC/SCN 2004: *5th report on the world nutrition situation*, Geneva

Acemoglu, D., S. Johnson and J.A. Robinson 2001: The colonial origins of comparative development: an empirical investigation, *American Economic Review*, **91**(5), 1369–1401

Adams, R.H., Jr., 1998: The political economy of the food subsidy system in Bangladesh, *Journal of Development Studies*, **35**(1), 66–88
   2000: Self-targeted subsidies: the political and distributional impact of the Egyptian food subsidy system, *Economic Development and Cultural Change*, **49**(1), 15–36

Ahmed, A.U. and H.E. Bouis, 2002: Weighting what's practical: proxy means tests for targeting food subsidies in Egypt, *Food Policy*, **27**(5–6), 519–40

Allen, L. and S. Gillespie, 2001: What works? A review of efficacy and effectivness of nutrition interventions, *ACC/SCN Nutrition Policy Paper*, 19

Behrman, J.E., H. Alderman and J. Hoddinott, 2004: Hunger and malnutrition, chapter 7 in this volume

Bhargava, A., 2003: Comment on malnutrition and dietary protein, *Food and Nutrition Bulletin*, **24**(2), 160–1

Bhargava, A., D.T. Jamison, L.J. Lau and C.J.L Murray, 2001: Modelling the effects of health on economic growth, *Journal of Health Economics*, **20**(3), 423–40

Bloom, D.E., D. Canning and J. Sevilla, 2004: The effect of health on economic growth: a production function approach, *World Development*, **32**(1), 1–13

Chowdhury, T. and S. Haggblade, 2000: Dynamics and politics of policy change, in R.T. Ahmed, T. Chowdury and S. Haggblade (eds.), *Out of the Shadow of Famine: Evolving Food Markets and Food Policy in Bangladesh*, Johns Hopkins University Press, Baltimore, MD

Collier, P. and J.W. Gunning, 1999: Why has Africa grown slowly?, *Journal of Economic Perspectives*, **13**(3), 3–22

FAO, 2002: *Food balance sheets*, FAO, Rome

Gabremedhin, B. and S.M. Swinton, 2001: Reconciling food-for-work projects with food aid targeting in Tigraay, Ethiopia, *Food Policy*, **26**(1), 85–95

432

Gillespie, S., 2001: Strengthening capacity to improve nutrition, Discussion Paper, **106**, IFPRI

Glewwe, P., 1999: Why mothers' schooling raises child health in developing countries. Evidence from Morocco, *Journal of Human Resources*, **34**(1), 124–59

Gutner, T., 2002: The political economy of food subsidy reform: the case of Egypt, *Food Policy*, **27**(5–6), 455–76

Haddad, L., H. Alderman, S. Appleton, L. Song and Y. Yohannes, 2003: Reducing child undernutrition: how far does income growth take us?, *World Bank Economic Review*, **17**(1), 107–31

Hall, R.E. and C.I. Jones 1999: Why do some countries produce so much more output per worker than others?, *Quarterly Journal of Economics*, **114**(1), 83–116

Handa, S., 1999: Maternal education and child height, *Economic Development and Cultural Change*, **47**(2), 421–40

Jamison, D.T., J. Leslie and P. Musgrove, 2003: Malnutrition and dietary protein: evidence from China and international comparisons, *Food and Nutrition Bulletin*, **24**(2), 145–54

Jayne, T.S., J. Strauss, T. Yamano and D. Molla, 2001: Giving to the poor: targeting food aid in Ethiopia, *World Development*, **29**(5), 887–910

Jones, C.I., 1997: On the evolution of world income distribution, *Journal of Economic Perspectives*, **11**(3), 19–36

Klasen, S., 1999/2003: Malnourished and surviving in South Asia, better nourished and dying young in Africa: what can explain this puzzle?, University of Munich, draft

Knack, S. and P. Keefer, 1995: Insitutions and economic performance: cross-country tests using alternative measures, *Economics and Politics*, **7**(3), 207–27

Löfgren, H. and M. El-Said, 2001: Food subsidies in Egypt: reform options, distribution and welfare, *Food Policy*, **26**(1), 65–83

Maddison, A., 1995: *Monitoring the world economy 1820–1992*, OECD, Paris

McClafferty, B., 2000: Ensuring food security in Egypt: food subsidy, income generation and market reform, *Food Policy*, **25**(2), 219–24

Mills, A. and S. Shillcut, 2004: Communicable diseases, chapter 2 in this volume

Nubé, M., 2001: Confronting dietary energy supply with anthropometry in the assessment of undernutrition prevalence at the level of countries, *World Development*, **29**(7), 1275–89

Olson, M., 1996: Big bills left on the sidewalk: why some nations are richer and others poor, *Journal of Economic Perspectives*, **10**(2), 3–24

Osmani, S.R., 1997: Poverty and nutrition in South Asia, *Nutrition Policy Paper*, 16, ACC/SCN, World Health Organisation

Pritchett, L. and L.H. Summers, 1996: Wealthier is healthier, *Journal of Human Resources*, **31**(4), 841–68

Ramaswami, B. and P. Balakrishnan, 2002: Food prices and the efficiency of the public distribution system in India, *Food Policy*, **27**(5–6), 419–36

Rodrik, D., 1999: Where did all the growth go?, *Journal of Economic Growth*, **4**(4), 385–412

Sala-i-Martin, X., 1997: I just ran one million regressions, *American Economic Review*, **87**(2), 178–83

Schultz, T.P., 2002: Why governments should invest more to educate girls, *World Development*, **30**(2), 207–25

Senauer, B. and A.L. Kassouf, 1996: Direct and indirect effects of parental education on malnutrition among children in Brazil: a full income approach, *Economic Development and Cultural Change*, **44**(4), 817–37

Smith, L.C. and L. Haddad, 2002: How potent is economic growth in reducing undernutrition? What are the pathways of impact? New cross country evidence, *Economic Development and Cultural Change*, **51**(1), 55–76

Strauss, J. and D. Thomas, 1998: Health, nutrition, and economic development, *Journal of Economic Literature*, **17**, 766–815

Svedberg, P., 1999: 841 million undernourished?, *World Development*, **27**(12), 2081–98

2000: *Poverty and undernutrition: theory, measurement, and policy*, Oxford University Press, Oxford

2002: Undernutrition overestimated, *Economic Development and Cultural Change*, **51**(1), 5–36

2004a: World income distribution: which way?, *Journal of Development Studies*, **40**(5), 1–32

2004b: Has child malnutrition declined over the 1990s: a re-assessment of the evidence, *International Journal of Epidemiology*, 33(6) (forthcoming, December 2004)

2004c: Has the relationship between child undernutrition and income changed?: A cross-country investigation IIES, in progress, mimeo

Temple, J., 1999: The new growth evidence, *Journal of Economic Literature*, 17, 112–56

Transparency International (TI), 2003: *The corruption perceptions index 2001*, http://www.transparency.org

UNICEF, 2004: *The state of the world's children, 2004*, UNICEF, Geneva

World Bank, 2001: *World Development Indicators, 2001*, World Bank, Washington, DC

2002: *World development report, 2002*, World Bank, Washington, DC

2003: *World development indicators, 2003*, World Bank, Washington, DC

World Health Organisation, 2004: *Global database on child growth and malnutrition*, WHO, Geneva

Perspective Paper 7.2

SIMON APPLETON

Introduction

Chapter 7, by Jere Behrman, Harold Alderman and John Hoddinott provides a valuable survey of academic literature on the subject as well as a thought-provoking evaluation of the economic returns to public investments in that field. The range and volume of literature surveyed – much of it original research by the authors themselves – is a testament to the chapter's scholarly contribution while the exceptionally high benefit-cost ratios (BCRs) produced show its interest for policy. Consequently, the chapter is one beneficial outcome of the Copenhagen Consensus exercise. The literature surveyed spans a variety of fields, ranging from econometric to medical journals, and is very up to date. The chapter's review of the literature is characterised by an acute awareness of the empirical problems involved and, although often circumscribed by the quality of the evidence available, at times shows a formidable degree of rigour in interpreting data. The four opportunities evaluated are all major ones, of great importance and concern to policy-makers, although – perhaps because they are so fundamental – difficult subjects for cost-benefit analysis (CBA).

The chapter is wide-ranging and comprehensive, so this Perspective paper does not propose any new opportunity. Nonetheless, it is noteworthy that the chapter does not address the more general issue of poverty reduction, which is intimately linked to malnutrition, nor does it formally evaluate any interventions to deal with the most extreme case of hunger, namely famine. The omission of the former is understandable, as the topic of poverty reduction may be too broad, intractable and less subject to high-return interventions. The topic of famine may be already be partly addressed by the opportunities for reducing civil conflict considered in chapter 3, since famine appears increasingly to be a corollary to conflict, or even a weapon of war. Nonetheless, interventions to reduce the risk of famine – such as contingencies for emergency food-for-work schemes – could well have been the basis for a fifth opportunity within this chapter.

However, rather than try to broaden the discussion, this Perspective paper addresses three aspects of chapter 7. First, it questions some of the assumptions that underlie the chapter's estimates of BCRs. Here, the general thrust is that the authors' assumptions may lead them to *underestimate* the benefits to the opportunities they evaluate. Second, this Perspective paper provides a 'second opinion' on the relevant empirical evidence. It is argued that the evidence base for much of the chapter is rather fragmentary and partial, often drawing on developed country data rather than developing country data and frequently subject to serious methodological limitations. Moreover, the derivation of figures for benefits and costs in the chapter from the evidence is sometimes opaque or merely reflects the authors' judgements. The implication is not that the chapter necessarily overstates the returns to the opportunities it presents, but that the uncertainty surrounding the evidence implies that they should be subject to a discount for uncertainty. Of course, these two sets of comments are to a degree offsetting. The fact the authors' assumptions lead them to tend to underestimate the returns to the opportunities is mitigated by the fact that these returns should be discounted due to the uncertainty over the empirical estimates. It is not clear whether, on balance, the chapter underestimates or overestimates the returns to interventions, and for this reason, it would seem unwarranted to try to 'second guess' it. Consequently, the final part of this Perspective paper takes the chapter's estimates at face value and addresses the question of aggregation that arises. The chapter provides a range of BCRs for three–four interventions per opportunity rather than a single median cost-benefit estimate for each opportunity. Consequently, we conclude by discussing the problem of aggregation the Consensus Experts will face in assigning an overall rate-of-return to each opportunity.

Assumptions Used in Return Calculations

As required by the Copenhagen Consensus procedure, the chapter focuses on the estimates of the benefit and costs for various opportunities. Some of the assumptions underlying these estimates can be questioned, although some criticisms are dependent on one's value judgements.

First, too narrow a view of what constitutes costs and benefits is taken.[1] The focus is on productivity effects and resource costs of malnutrition. No value is placed on the intrinsic importance of *nutrition* or, indeed, *health*. For example, when considering the effect of low birth weight on the illnesses of infants, only out-of-pocket costs of illness are computed – the suffering of the infants (and their parents) is given no weight. Ascribing some monetary value to instances of illness – for example, analogous to the 'severity index' used in computations of QALYs and DALYs – would appear warranted. Other things being equal, this point is likely to mean that the returns to the nutritional interventions presented in the chapter are underestimates.

Second, the benefits of opportunities that do not operate via *nutritional pathways* are often not valued (the main exception being for opportunity 4, agricultural research and development (R&D), which is valued in terms of general economic returns). For example, the interventions to raise birth weight operate by increasing the welfare of the mother (e.g. by treating presumptive STD). However, only the benefits for the child are quantified. This comment implies that the returns to Opportunity 1, in particular, are underestimated.

[1] This is signalled on p. 0 by the statement 'While reducing hunger is often justified on intrinsic grounds, it is these potential gains in productivity and reduction in economic costs that provide the focus of our chapter.'

Third, distributional weights are not used in evaluating the benefits of interventions. The implicit assumption is that '*a dollar is a dollar*' and dollar gains are equally valuable whoever receives them. The implicit social welfare function appears to be a simple 'utilitarian' one, but with no allowance for the utilitarian argument for equality (diminishing marginal utility of income). However, this assumption appears particularly questionable given the intimate link between hunger and poverty. If, as is widely agreed among those concerned with global poverty reduction, greater weight should be assigned to benefits accruing to the poor then this may have a number of implications. Within this particular challenge, it may increase the importance of Opportunity 3 – if micronutrient deficiencies are concentrated amongst the poorest – and reduce the importance of the fourth – if better-off farmers benefit more from agricultural research and development. Perhaps more importantly, distributional weighting will increase the importance of the nutritional interventions compared to some of the other Challenges (e.g. financial or trade liberalisation) which are less intimately connected with poverty.

Fourth, the approach taken to the value of life is curious. It is based on a figure, $800, given by Summers (1992) as the *cost* of saving a statistical life (specifically, the estimated cost of saving a life through measles inoculation in the early 1990s). The first observation here is that this appears to make life extremely cheap (even after the authors' upward revaluation to $1,250). For example, it can be compared with $4,515, the present discounted value of the lifetime stream of $500 annual earnings taken in the chapter as the benchmark earnings of people in developing countries. The implicit assumption is that we are indifferent between an intervention that saves a statistical life and one that increases a person's productivity by 28 per cent. Noting this feature helps understand why the productive benefits of the nutritional opportunities are often estimated to be larger than the benefits in terms of mortality reduction. Further, the rationale for the Summers' approach to valuing life seems curious – wishing to avoid the thorny issue of putting a value on life, it merely calculates the opportunity cost. This approach seems of questionable use in evaluating some interventions – presumably, it would imply that the benchmark intervention of measles inoculation had zero net benefit. Moreover, to be morally persuasive it would have to be the case that the life being valued would in fact be saved (through measles inoculation), when obviously this is a fiction. Like 'compensation tests' in welfare economics, it seeks to avoid making valuations but does this only by positing hypothetical conditions that are arguably morally irrelevant. A preferable approach would be to confront the issue of valuing life more directly – for example, by looking at what people appear willing to pay to avoid risks of death.

If, understandably, one wishes to avoid the difficulties with such direct approaches to valuing statistical life, the admittedly arbitrary approach used in chapter 2 on communicable diseases (Mills and Shillcutt 2004) may have wider appeal than that proposed by Summers. This simply values a year of life lost at *per capita* Gross National Income (GNI).[2] Using the mean GNI *per capita* for low- and middle-income countries (PPP$3,830 or US$1,160) might have the widest appeal, since it would be unlikely to be internationally acceptable to assign a lower value to the lives of those in poorer countries. Under this approach, the present discounted value (at 5 per cent) of a life expectancy of sixty-five years is US$22,227 or PPP$73,387, exceeding the Summers' valuation by factor of 18 (or 59, using the PPP figure). This implies that the estimated benefits of opportunities 1–3 in the chapter are substantially underestimated.

More generally, given the subjective and controversial judgements involved in valuing life, it might be useful if the outcomes of interventions in terms of lives saved and other benefits were presented separately. Aggregation into a single monetary value – as required by the Copenhagen Challenge – appears to be a rather old-fashioned application of welfare economics and does not seem to take seriously the multi-dimensionality of welfare and poverty now widely acknowledged (Sen 1999; World Bank 2000). While lives saved may be the dominant benefit from some opportunities (e.g. communicable diseases, see chapter 2 in this volume), they may be negligible for others (e.g. financial or trade reform, see chapter 5 in this volume). Prioritisation between these different kinds of opportunities will

depend heavily on the valuation of life and aggregation into single benefit-cost indicators will mask this. The argument here parallels the criticism of composite welfare indicators (e.g. the Human Development Index) for masking information and applying arbitrary weights.

Fifth, the approach taken in the chapter might be criticised as being 'top-down' and technocratic, rather than 'bottom-up'. It represents experts evaluating technical interventions that are delivered to people by public servants (via fortification, supplements, injections, etc.). However, such criticism would seem to be misplaced. Primary health care and nutrition seem to be one area where simple mass technical interventions (e.g. immunisations) can yield enormous benefits. Moreover the delivery of many interventions is likely to require participation of many primary health workers working at the 'grass-roots' – as, for example, was done with the Chinese 'barefoot doctors'. Mobilising political support for the interventions, and involving local communities in their delivery, may be required to overcome some of the problems of implementation discussed in the chapter.

Empirical Evidence on Benefits and Costs of Interventions

Perhaps the main strength of the chapter is the wealth of empirical literature it has uncovered and draws upon. There are sometimes slips in the presentation of the evidence,[3] but the authors' mastery

---

[2] The authors assert in n. 16 that this has the 'pitfall' of implicitly valuing life in terms of wages. However, the appeal of valuing a year of life at income *per capita* is *not* that this measures the economic contribution of the life, as it would indeed be bizarre to value people as if they were income-generating machines. One could say that since income consumed has value, it provides a minimum bound on the value of the consumer's life (minimum since one should also include the value of leisure and non-marketed goods, services and activities). On such grounds, there would be no reason to 'net out consumption from . . . earnings' as suggested in n. 16. More generally, using income *per capita* may appeal on egalitarian grounds, as it could be taken as implying that each person has a claim on – or entitlement to – an equal share of total income.

[3] For example, on p. 375 it is stated that 'LBW infants are 40 per cent more likely to die in the neonatal period than their

of the technical issues in empirical analysis is apparent in the chapter. However, a careful reading of the chapter and some of the sources it reviews shows the often fragmentary and partial nature of the evidence base upon which it rests. This section illustrates this limitation, focusing on the evaluation of Opportunity 1, to which the chapter also devotes the most space and which raises a number of key issues common to some of the other Opportunities.

---

normal weight counterparts'. Presumably, what is meant is 400 per cent rather than 40 per cent, since the benefit calculations follow Ashworth's (1998) summary that for LBW 'the risk of neonatal death is four times as high'.

[4] Rouse (2003) provides a cautionary note here: 'even for the archetypal and nearly universally recommended pregnancy nutrition supplements folate and iron, compelling evidence of effectiveness in reducing the occurrence of adverse maternal or fetal and neonatal outcomes is not available'.

[5] Many interventions may raise the adult height and cognitive ability of those children who would not have LBW without the intervention. In such a case, looking at only the benefits for children who would have LBW would seriously underestimate the total benefits of the intervention.

[6] This likely upwards bias is explicitly acknowledged by Ashworth (1998). 'If families with LBW (or IUGR) infants are more disadvantaged in terms of income, housing, parental education, etc. than families of ABW infants, then they may be more exposed to infection postnatally and have inferior medical care when ill. Consequently higher mortality in LBW or IUGR infants could be due, at least in part, to their environment, rather than birth weight per se.' Only two studies reviewed by Ashworth included confounders. In the one for a developing country (Lira in Brazil), controlling for confounders reduced relative risk of death aged 0–6 months by around a third.

[7] In this context, Ashworth (1998) makes the interesting observation that the LBW appears to be less associated with adverse outcomes among black Americans than their more affluent white countrymen. Of the ten studies that are used to generate the median fourfold risk of neonatal death due to LBW, only three are from developing countries – the rest are from the USA. The three developing country studies show very varied relative risks (1.4, 3.4 and 4.5); none are nationally representative and two are for urban areas only. The twofold risk of postnatal death due to LBW appears particularly questionable given that the three developing country studies show risk factors of 0.8, 1.1 and 2.3 (the two available American studies show a twofold risk). Ashworth's evidence also appears rather dated – the developing country studies all relate to the end of the 1960s and the beginning of the 1970s.

Opportunity 1: Reducing Prevalence of Low Birth-Weights

The chapter covers in most detail the benefits and costs of the first opportunity considered, interventions to avoid low birth weight (LBW). It devotes most attention to quantifying the benefits of avoiding an instance of LBW *per se* rather than the benefits of specific interventions to reduce low birth weight. In particular, there is relatively little critical examination of the *effectiveness* of interventions to reduce low birth weight.[4] Instead, various alternative kinds of intervention are reviewed and assigned rough costs per LBW avoided. It should be noted that this approach will underestimate even the nutritional benefits of some interventions to the extent that the interventions benefit children who would not anyway have had LBW.[5]

Considerable uncertainty surrounds the estimates of the two major sources of benefits to reducing LBW – lower mortality and higher productivity. The mortality benefits are questionable because they are based on Ashworth's (1998) summary of studies of bivariate associations, which in turn were largely driven by studies of the USA. These studies made no control for confounders and as such are likely to overestimate the beneficial effect on mortality.[6] The authors' reliance on such evidence contrasts with the rigour espoused in some of their own studies where they try to factor out the effect of genetic factors unobserved by the researchers as well as observable ones (e.g. Behrman and Rosenzweig 2004). The reliance on developed country data introduces additional uncertainty, because it is not clear that results from areas where there are not serious problems of malnutrition can be generalised to developing countries, where there are. It is possible that low birth weight in an affluent society often reflects more serious medical conditions than it commonly does in poor countries. However, this is hard to test for precisely the reason that the authors were forced to rely on developed country evidence – because the developing country studies available appear so few and rely on small, not nationally representative, samples.[7]

The authors find the largest source of main benefit from avoiding LBW to be higher future productivity. However, unlike the clearly derived mortality benefit, the 7.5 per cent productivity benefit assumed reflects a judgement rather than being something mathematically computed from estimates in the literature. Only two studies that directly relate birth weight to wages are reviewed – Strauss (2000) and Behrman and Rosenzweig (2004). These imply around 9 per cent and 16 per cent productivity gains from avoiding LBW, respectively. The studies are of the UK and USA, not developing countries, but do control for some confounders and even, in the US study, for genetic differences.[8] In addition to this rather limited direct evidence, the chapter also reviews indirect evidence, looking at the effects of birth weight on height and cognitive ability, and then the effects of height and cognitive ability on wages. The non-economic evidence reviewed on the links between low birth weight, height and cognitive ability is largely drawn from studies of developed countries. The economic evidence of a link between height and wages is somewhat less voluminous than the authors assert.[9] The evidence on the link between cognitive ability and wages is stronger, in terms of both volume and the implied quantitative effects. Nonetheless, the economic studies typically take height and cognitive achievement as exogenous and so estimates of their effects may be contaminated by the impact of factors unobserved by the researcher. One may also question the extent to which evidence on wage differentials applies to productivity outside the wage sector, particularly to the majority of adults in low-income countries who are engaged in agricultural self-employment or other work for their households. Furthermore, since no studies simultaneously control for both height and cognitive ability, it would not be valid to simply add together estimated returns to LBW via these two pathways. Taken together these issues imply considerable uncertainty around the assumed 7.5 per cent productivity benefit, although the figure does not appear unreasonable in view of the available evidence.

There also appears to be considerable uncertainty around the costs of each LBW averted: the authors consider a range of costs from $28 to $1,000 per LBW. Part of the variation is driven by differences between studies of specific interventions. However, since the studies tend only to cost the medicines, the authors also consider a range of assumptions about the ratio of medicine costs to total costs – specifically, various multiplicative costs of 2, 5 and 10. No guidance is given as to what ratio is more plausible, which is disappointing given that in this context determining costs seems in principle more straightforward than determining benefits.

What this short discussion of the evidence on Opportunity 1 implies is, not that the chapter necessarily overestimates the returns to interventions to reduce LBW, but that considerable uncertainty prevails over the particular figures presented.

Opportunity 2: Improving Infant and Child Nutrition

This opportunity is discussed by reviewing the costs and benefits of four different interventions. It is assumed that such interventions will have comparable productivity benefits similar to those posited for Opportunity 1. However, the calculations here sometimes have what the authors concede to be a 'back-of-the-envelope' nature. While it is plausible that qualitatively similar benefits may be expected, it is not established that magnitudes of these effects will be similar. Furthermore the derivation of some of the results is often opaque.

Opportunity 3: Reducing Micronutrient Deficiencies

The evidence for the returns to interventions to reduce micro-nutrient deficiencies is arguably the strongest of all four opportunities. This is partly on account of the persuasiveness of the evidence on the benefits of the interventions – often based on experimental trials. However, it is also a reflection of

---

[8] Berhman and Rosenzweig (2004) control for genetic factors by using a sample of identical twins and, perhaps surprisingly, find that this *increases* the apparent returns to birth weight. Although the authors consider whether twin studies are generalisable, one possibility they do not consider is whether birth weight may be particularly important for twins as it affects which one is dominant and hence confidence, which may be important in future lifetime success.

[9] Although nine studies are reported on p. 372. as giving evidence of the impact of height on earnings, the first four cited do not appear to provide original research on this question.

the extremely low cost of some interventions, such as fortification. Nonetheless, the quantification of the benefits and costs in the chapter is sometimes unclear. Consider, for example, the case of the intervention to offset iron deficiency – the highest-return intervention discussed in the chapter (according to table 7.9). It is not clear how the *per capita* cost of $0.25 was arrived at, nor why the BCRs are in the range 176–200 when the highest benefit ratio reported in the text was 84 (Levin *et al.*, 1993) cited on p. 390.

Opportunity 4: Agricultural R&D

This opportunity is discussed partly in terms of the general return to agricultural research and development, highlighting the 44 per cent average return found in meta-analysis by Alston *et al.* (2000). This figure is not straightforwardly comparable with the returns estimated for the other opportunities, since it implicitly incorporates a range of benefits wider than the purely nutritional impacts evaluated for other interventions. Moreover these benefits are likely to be much more widely spread in developing countries and less focused on the disadvantaged (especially when disadvantage is assessed in nutritional terms). The benefits do not include large effects on mortality and this may reduce the relative priority assigned to this opportunity if life is valued more highly than is done in the chapter.

However, the discussion of Opportunity 4 also includes estimates of *ex ante* returns to disseminating staples rich in micronutrients. Arguably, these interventions should be included within Opportunity 3 as they are essentially concerned with reducing micro-nutrient deficiencies rather than the general benefits to agricultural research *per se*.

In summary, considering all four opportunities, although the chapter reviews a substantial and varied amount of literature, one is struck by the fragmentary and partial nature of the evidence base used to assign BCRs to various interventions. The derivation of some of the key figures is often unclear and sometimes reflects assumptions based on judgement. It is not that these judgements appear flawed or biased in a particular direction; however,

the tentative nature of the empirical evidence and consequent uncertainty over key magnitudes may warrant discounting the estimates by some arbitrary 'risk premium'. The general implication that the chapter *overstates* the returns to the opportunities considered must, however, be set against the argument of the previous section that it tends to *understate* the returns by virtue of some of its key assumptions.

Aggregation

Although the chapter does provide estimates of costs and benefits for interventions within opportunities, it stops well short of assigning an overall rate of return to each opportunity. Costs and benefits are given in table 7.9, but it is stated that these cannot be understood without reference to the text and it is not clear that they meant to be taken as strictly comparable. Moreover, a range of estimates are given for three–four interventions in each opportunity with no median value provided or attempt to aggregate to provide a single BCR per opportunity. Furthermore there is little discussion of the scale of the possible interventions – for example, if one had $50bn to spend, could it all be spent iron fortification and still achieve the extraordinarily high BCRs presented? However, none of the interventions are likely to be one-off opportunities, but instead warrant recurrent expenditures each year for the foreseeable future. Consequently, even a very large sum of money could be usefully allocated to each intervention, provided that it did not all have to be disbursed in a single year (some could, instead, be set aside in a trust fund for used in future years).

This authors' reluctance to provide overall BCRs for each opportunity is understandable given the varied nature of possible interventions and the fragmentary quality of the evidence on their returns. The authors may well have concluded that assigning an overall rate of return to each opportunity is going further than the available data will support and left such assignment to the panel of ten experts chosen by the Copenhagen Challenge. However, as a spur to discussion and aid to the deliberation of the expert panel, it may be useful to conclude this note by providing a tentative assignment based on the evidence in the chapter.

Looking at the summary table 7.9, it is hard to avoid the conclusion that the third opportunity – reducing micro-nutrient deficiencies – offers the highest rate of return. (As stated earlier, it seems more coherent to bundle interventions 4b and 4c into this opportunity – as dissemination of new varieties of staples appears an attractive way of dealing with micro-nutrient deficiencies.) For almost all interventions considered, the lower bounds on the BCRs presented are higher for this Opportunity than for others while the upper bounds (and hence mid-points) are often incredibly high. Furthermore, interventions within this category are likely to have benefits in terms of reduced mortality – which this Perspective paper has argued may be undervalued in the chapter and should be presented as distinct from benefits which can be more easily be given a monetary value. Given the extreme range of values presented, assigning a single BCR for Opportunity 3 seems an impossible task. However, the ratio of 36 put forward for iron fortification by Horton and Ross (2003) does not seem atypical of the estimates considered in the chapter.

Of the other opportunities, the returns to agricultural R&D appear to have the highest BCR (a median of 15 when the discount rate is 3 per cent, if the meta-analysis of Alston *et al.* 2000, is believed). However, given the much weaker likely linkages with poverty and mortality, those who assign higher values to life and/or have more progressive distributional weights may wish to prioritise the other two remaining opportunities. Of these, the impression gained from the chapter is that returns from the two opportunities are comparable, with perhaps interventions to avoid LBW having slightly higher benefits (particularly, if benefits for the mother were to be incorporated into the calculations). For Opportunity 1, it would seem churlish not to accept the estimate of benefits put forward by Alderman and Behrman (1993, 2003). The benchmark to be taken for costs is less obvious, so arbitrarily one could take the middle of the range used by Alderman and Behrman, leading to a BCR of 4.3. For Opportunity 2, one might take as representative one of the

Table 7.2.1. Summary BCRs

Opportunity	BCR
1: Reducing prevalence of LBW	4
2: Improving infant and child nutrition	3
3: Reducing micro-nutrient deficiencies	36
4: Agricultural R&D	15

more in-depth published studies for a programme in Bolivia by Behrman, Cheng and Todd (2004), which estimated a BCR of 2.9. Consequently, this Perspective paper concludes by tentatively proposing the summary BCRs for each opportunity shown in table 7.2.1.

References

Alderman, H. and J. Behrman, 1993, 2003: Estimated economic benefits of reducing LBW in low-income countries, University of Pennsylvania, Philadelphia, PA

Alston, J., C. Chan-Khang, M. Marra, P. Pardey and T. J. Wyatt, 2000: A meta-analysis of rates of return to agricultural R&D, IFPRI Research Report, **113**, International Food Policy Research Institute, Washington DC

Ashworth, A., 1998: Effects of intrauterine growth retardation on mortality and morbidity in infants and young children, *European Journal of Clinical Nutrition*, **52** (Suppl.), S34–S42

Behrman, J., Y. Cheng and P. Todd, 2004: Evaluating preschool programs when length of exposure to the program varies: a non-parametric approach, *Review of Economics and Statistics*, February

Behrman, J. and M. Rosenzweig, 2004: Returns to birthweight, *Review of Economics and Statistics*,

Glick, P. and D. Sahn, 1997: Gender and education impacts on employment and earnings in West Africa: evidence from Guinea, *Economic Development and Cultural Change*, **45**(4), 793–823

  1998: Health and productivity in a heterogeneous urban labor market, *Applied Economics*, **30**(2), 203–16

Horton, S. and J. Ross, 2003: The economics of iron efficiency, *Food Policy*, **28**(1), 51–75

Levin, H., E. Pollitt, R. Galloway and J. McGuire, 1993: Micronutrient deficiency disorders, in D. Jamison, H. Mosley, A. Measham and J. Bobadilla (eds.) *Disease control priorities in developing countries*, Oxford University Press, Oxford

Mills, A. and S. Shillcutt, 2004: Communicable diseases, London School of Hygiene and Tropical Medicine, mimeo; chapter 2 in this volume

Rouse, D., 2003: Potential cost-effectiveness of nutrition interventions to prevent adverse pregnancy outcomes in the developing world, *Journal of Nutrition*, **133**, 1640S–1644S

Sen, A., 1999: *Commodities and capabilities*, Oxford University Press, Oxford

Strauss, R., 2000, Adult functional outcome of those born small for gestational age, *Journal of the American Medical Association*, **285**(5), 625–32

Summers, L. H., 1992: Investing in all the people, *Pakistan Development Review*, **31**(4), 367–406

World Bank, 2000: *World development report 2000/01: attacking poverty*, Oxford University Press, New York

Migration

PHILIP MARTIN

Description of the Challenge

Migration and Economic Efficiency

In an ideal world, there would be few migration barriers and little unwanted migration. For most of human history, there were few governmental barriers to migration, and the challenge of too many people for available resources and technologies meant that people migrated from one place to another in response to famine, war and displacement in traditional economies. However, migration was often limited by nascent communication and transportation networks as well as institutions and rules from slavery to serfdom.

There was migration in the pre-industrial world, including the great migration of 60 million Europeans to the Americas in the nineteenth and early twentieth centuries. During the twentieth century, the world's population increased fourfold, and sharply different rates of population and economic growth emerged between the world's nation-states, whose number quadrupled to about 200 in the twentieth century.[1] Most nation-states have more workers than formal sector jobs, and young people who know that wages are ten or twenty times higher in another country are especially eager to cross national borders, putting international migration 'close to the center of global problems' (Bhagwati 2003a, 82).

If people were goods, the solution to different wage and employment levels would be obvious: encourage the transfer of 'surplus' people from poorer to richer nation states, which should benefit individuals whose incomes rise, increase global GDP and promote the convergence in wages and opportunities between sending and receiving areas that eventually reduces migration pressures. If we knew how to ensure that economically motivated migration effectuated convergence between areas, migration would truly be the proverbial 'free lunch' among global challenges, and lowering migration barriers would be first priority among the global challenges.

However, we do not know how to ensure that economically motivated migration sets in motion 'virtuous circles' that yield convergence in wages and opportunities between sending and receiving areas. Indeed, in some cases migration sets in motion 'vicious circles' that increase the motivation to migrate, so the migration challenge in a world of nation-states is to ensure that migration promotes convergence between them. This chapter tackles this challenge in three parts: explaining why the migration of professionals from developing to developed countries may lead to divergence rather than convergence, how to provide incentives for employers and unskilled migrants to abide by the rules of guest worker programmes so that richer countries open their doors to migrant workers, and how to use the '3 Rs' associated with migration – recruitment, remittances and returns – to accelerate economic development in migrant countries of origin. The concluding section discusses the costs of measures to be implemented to allow more migration.

There is significant international migration from poorer to richer nation-states: about 175 m people – 3 per cent of the world's residents and equivalent to the world's fifth most populous country were migrants living outside their countries of birth or

I am indebted to Henrik Jacob Meyer and other commentators for their reactions and suggestions.

[1] There were forty-three generally recognised nation-states in 1900, and 191 in 2000, when the CIA factbook listed 191 'independent states', plus one 'other' (Taiwan), and six miscellaneous entities, including the Gaza Strip, the West Bank and the Western Sahara (www.cia.gov/cia/publications/factbook/index.html).

citizenship for a year or more in 2000, including 6 per cent classified as refugees who are unable or unwilling to return because they would face persecution at home.[2] The number of migrants roughly doubled between 1975 and 2000, while the world's population increased by 50 per cent. Most migrants move from poorer to richer countries, and some 60 per cent of world's migrants are in the more developed countries, which have 15 per cent of the world's residents. Most of the remaining 40 per cent of the world's migrants have moved from poorer to richer developing countries, as from Burma to Thailand or Nicaragua to Costa Rica.

Far more people would like to move from lower- to higher-income countries, as is evident in the daily reminders of migrants detected by ever-larger migration control agencies or by reports of migrants dying en route to or in their destinations. However, opinion polls suggest that most residents of richer destination countries oppose additional immigration, and instead support increased governmental efforts to curb illegal or irregular migration. After the 11 September 2001 terrorist attacks, fears of economic competition and cultural change due to immigration were joined by security fears, and many governments responded with new checks and restrictions on arriving migrants.

Most economists welcome migration from lower- to higher-wage countries, since voluntary migration from lower- to higher-wage areas increases allocative efficiency, allowing the world to make the most efficient use of available resourses and thus maximise production. The overall economic gain from migration in receiving countries is the sum of net income gains to migrants plus

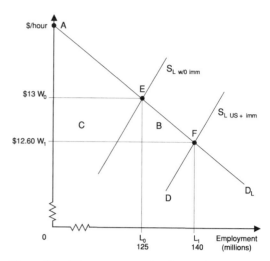

Figure 8.1. *The net economic effects of migration*

a (small) dividend. The migration of workers has two major economic effects in receiving areas: it increases the supply of labour and reduces wages or the growth in wages, and the increase in employment raises national income. The wage and employment changes due to migrant workers are illustrated in figure 8.1 for the USA in the mid-1990s. If there were no migrant workers at E, the USA would have 125 million US-born workers earning an $13 an hour. Total national income is the rectangle AEL_0 – the wages paid to workers plus the triangle above, which is the share of national income going to owners of capital and land. The USA had 15 million migrant workers in the mid-1990s, which shifted the labour supply to the right, to 140 million at F, and lowered average hourly earnings by 3 per cent to $12.60. The movement from E to F creates two rectangles, C and D, as well as triangle B. Rectangle C represents reduced wages paid to US workers; they do not disappear into thin air, but are transferred to the (US) owners of capital and land in the form of higher profits and rents. Because of immigration, the US economy expands by rectangle D and triangle B, with migrant workers getting most of the benefits of this expansion in the form of their wages (D).

The net gain from immigration is triangle B, and its size can be estimated in percentage-of-national-income terms as $1/2 \times$ (estimated 3 per cent decrease in US wages due to immigration $\times$ 11 per

[2] The 1951 Geneva Convention on refugees obliges signatory countries not to refoul or return to danger persons who are outside their countries because of a well-founded fear of persecution because of race, religion, nationality, membership in a particular social group, or political opinion. In 2003, there were 10.4 million refugees, 1 million asylum seekers, 2.4 million refugees who had recently returned to their countries of origin and almost 7 million internally displaced and stateless persons, a total of 20.6 million persons 'of concern' to UNHCR (UNHCR 2003). As the number of asylum seekers – foreigners who arrived in industrial countries and asked not to be returned because they faced persecution at home – rose in the 1990s, the industrial countries spent an estimated $10 bn a year to care for and process asylum seekers.

cent immigrant share of US labour force × 70 per cent share of labour in US national income or 1/2 × 0.002 = 0.001, which means that US national income was about 1/10 of 1 per cent or about $8 bn higher in 1997 (Smith and Edmonston   1997).[3] To put this economic gain due to immigration in perspective, if the US economy grows by 2 per cent a year, it expands by $160 bn, so the immigrant economic gain is equivalent to about 20 days of 'normal' economic growth. If there are positive externalities – if immigrants are entrepreneurial or if their dedication to work inspires Americans to work more productively, the economic gains due to immigration are larger. If there are negative externalities – if immigration is associated with crime or crowding in schools, for example, the gains are smaller.

Most of the economic gains from migration accrue to migrants whose incomes rise. Roughly every 1 m foreigners moving over borders and achieving a net income gain of $10,000 increase global income by $10 bn.[4] Using this approach, Hamilton and Whalley (1984) estimated that global GDP could more than double with migration that equalised the marginal productivity of labour (and wages) between 179 countries grouped into seven world regions, adding $5 trillion–$16 trillion to global GDP of $8 trillion in 1977.[5] Even small increases in migration can significantly raise global GDP in such models, since the first migrants face the largest gaps in marginal productivity or wages, and thus gain the most by moving.

This basic logic – migration increases allocative efficiency – raises a fundamental question: why don't the richer countries to which migrants want to move open their doors? It is especially surprising that migration controls are high and rising when we remember that the benefits of migration tend to be immediate, measurable and concentrated, since migrants who go to work abroad have higher wages measurable in monetary terms.[6] The costs of migration, if any, tend to be deferred, diffused and harder to measure, as when wages in destination areas rise slower due to the presence of migrants, or if settled migrants send for their families and increase schooling and health care costs. There are also more difficult integration questions, ranging from bilingual education, distributing scarce resources

such as housing and maintaining unity with growing diversity.

Cost-benefit analyses (CBAs) require a common metric, a time horizon and a discount rate to compare present and future. The metric is usually money, the time horizon puts benefits and costs on a time continuum and low discount rates mean that current benefits can offset costs that are far in the future. If each migrant moving from poorer to richer countries increases her income from the poor-country average to the rich-country average, and if country averages are not changed significantly by migration, the sum of the individual gains represents the global gain plus the dividend in the form of increased returns to capital and land.

This exercise produces enormous potential gains from migration, and prompts assertions such as that of economist Dani Rodrik that 'even a marginal

---

[3] The increase in national income due to immigration – triangle B – will be larger if (1) there are more migrant workers and/or (2) if the wage-depression effect of migrant workers is larger. For example, if the migrant wage-depression impact doubled to 6 per cent, and the migrant share of the workforce doubled to 22 per cent (as in California in the late 1990s), the income increase due to migration is 1/2 × 0.06 × 0.22 × 0.7 = 0.005, or 5/10 of 1 per cent, four times larger.

[4] In a similar exercise, the 1992 UNDP *Human Development Report* estimated that, if an additional 2 per cent of then 2.5 billion strong labour force of developing countries migrated to industrial countries, there would be 50 m additional migrants. If each migrant earned an average $5,000 a year or a total $250 bn, and remitted 20 per cent of foreign earnings or $50 bn a year to countries of origin, the extra remittances would be equivalent to ODA.

[5] Hamilton and Whalley (1984) assumed that the world's labour supply was fully employed producing a single output and used CES production functions to estimate differences in the marginal productivity of labour across seven multi-country regions – these differences were assumed to be due to migration restrictions. They estimate the efficiency gains that would result from labour moving until MPs and wages were equalised – that is, they assume factor-price convergence via migration, with workers losing and capital owners gaining in receiving areas and workers gaining and capital owners losing in sending areas. There are many problems with such estimates. For example, the full employment assumption is necessary to assume that wages are determined by marginal productivity; it is assumed that the ratio of wages to profits is one in both rich and poor countries before migration barriers are lifted, and that capital does not move even as labour migrates.

[6] Owners of capital in receiving areas also benefit.

Table 8.1. Migration: Economic Impacts, 2001

Countries	World	Low	Middle	High
Population (m)	6,133	2,511	2,667	955
Ave GDP($/year)	5,140	430	1,850	26,710
Total GDP ($bn)	31,500	1,069	4,922	25,506
Moving 100 m people from low to high, same per capita averages				
Population (m)		2,411		1,055
Ave GDP($/year)		5,566	430	26,710
Total GDP ($bn)		34,138	1,037	28,179
Change in ave/tot.	8			
GDP(%)				

Source: Work Bank and own calculation.

liberalization of international labour flows would create gains for the world economy' far larger than prospective gains from trade liberalisation. For example, moving 100 m migrants from low- to high-income countries, and not changing average GDPs in sending and receiving countries, could raise average and total global GDP by 8 per cent (table 8.1).

However, migration does not lend itself to easy CBA because there is little agreement on benefits and costs. There are losers from migration in the destination country, especially for workers similar in skill, location, etc. to the arriving migrants, whose wages may fall or not rise as fast – or, if labour markets are rigid – whose unemployment rates rise. On the other hand, workers made more productive by the presence of migrants, such as skilled workers who now have more unskilled helpers as well as owners of capital, gain from migration. In receiving countries, the existence of triangle *B* means that the overall net economic gain from migration is positive, and that the receiving country would still be better off if the losers from migration were compensated. In this sense, the analysis of migration is much like trade analysis, and points to the solution of educating protectionists about the virtues of free trade and compensating losers to overcome their opposition to freer trade.

However, the economic results of migration are more ambiguous for sending countries, so that, if we take nation-states as the unit of analysis, it is not clear that sending countries benefit. Economist

Harry Johnson in the 1960s asserted a 'cosmopolitan liberal' position that put priority on the individual and global impacts of migration. Johnson argued that voluntary migration 'like any profit-motivated international movement of factors of production – may be expected to raise total world output … [except] when the migrant's private calculation of gain from migration excludes certain social costs that his migration entails' (Johnson 1968, 75). Johnson believed that there were relatively few negative externalities associated with migration for sending countries, and that those could easily be dealt with, such as changing the way education is financed in countries concerned about a brain drain.

Economist Don Patinkin, on the other hand, took a 'nationalist' approach, rejecting the argument that 'the "world" should be considered as a single aggregate from the welfare viewpoint – and that the welfare of this unit is maximized by the free flow of resources between countries' (Patinkin 1968, 93). Instead, Patinkin argued that developing countries require a critical mass of talent, and that too much emigration can prevent their economic take-off. Reflecting the times, Patinkin argued that some of the 1960s 'brain drain' was due to demand created by nationalistic forces in the developed countries, such as 'US government defense and space programmes' and the 'nationalistic war in Vietnam' (Patinkin 1968, 106).

The overall goal of those who study the welfare implications of migration is the same – a world of few migration barriers and little economically motivated migration. However, there is little agreement on the role that migration can play in getting to this ideal world. Unlike most of the other challenges being considered in Copenhagen, in which the desired direction of change is clear – less disease and less hunger, and more education and more financial stability – there is no agreement on whether more or less migration speeds us toward a world of few migration barriers.

One reason for this ambiguity is that the effects of migration on sending countries can vary. There can be 'virtuous circles' in which the '3Rs' speed up growth in sending countries, accelerating convergence, and there can be 'vicious circles' in which the '3 Rs' increase the gaps that motivate migration. The virtuous circle appears to have played out in the case of Indian IT workers, whose emigration led to the creation of a significant service export industry that improved IT services in India and created jobs there. The vicious circle seems to be playing out in some African countries that train medical personnel to first-world standards, and then see their doctors and nurses emigrate for higher wages just when they face the health challenges associated with AIDS. In extreme vicious circle cases, some nation-states could wind up as long-term labour exporters, and countries acting as nurseries and nursing homes for others raise complex economic and human rights issues. The shift from individual to national government perspectives highlights the difficulty of finding consensus on the benefits and costs of migration. If an individual doctor or nurse achieves higher earnings by migrating, but there are negative externalities in the home country's health care system, can the national government legitimately impose restrictions on emigration in the name of the greater national good? What if nationals abroad are mistreated? In the past, some countries have gone to war to protect their nationals abroad, and there were 1990s conflicts marked by 'ethnic cleansing', or removing particular groups.

Since there are enormous economic gains to be achieved from more and orderly migration, the challenge and opportunity is cooperative management of migration for the mutual benefit of individual migrants and nation states. Achieving such mutual benefits requires three major steps:

- Reducing fears of immigration in rich countries with active selection systems that pick the foreigners most likely to succeed, which in turn enables new and wider entry channels to be opened for professionals and skilled workers
- Widening legal entry channels for unskilled guest workers who are encouraged to return to their countries of origin by aligning migrant and employer incentives with the purpose of guest worker programmes, adding workers temporarily to the labour force, but not settlers to the population
- Using the '3 Rs' of the migration that occurs to ensure that migration helps to reduce economic differences between nation-states over time.

It should be emphasised that people are different from goods. A car crossing borders remains a car,

with foreseeable economic and environmental impacts. People change their intentions, status and impacts, as when migrants intending to be temporary sojourners become permanent residents and then seek to change socio-political conditions in their new countries of residence, highlighting the fact that importing workers also means importing new languages, cultures and ideas, and the means to reproduce them. The fact that migrant intentions and status may change means that the benefits and costs of migration are not always predictable, as Max Frisch noted when he wrote that European countries in the 1960s 'asked for migrant workers, but got people.' Clarifying benefits and costs, and overcoming the fear of irreversible (negative) change because of migration is a high hurdle, as illustrated by the undoubtedly apocryphal story of the dying North American Indian chief who lamented that failure to stop the arrival of European boat people ended a centuries-old way of life.

Population and Labour Force

At the dawn of agriculture, about 8000 BC, the population of the world was about 5 m. The world's population rose to 300 m in AD 1, was 500 million in 1650, reached the 1 bn mark in 1800, the 2 bn mark in 1930, 3 bn in 1960, 4 bn in 1974, 5 bn in 1987 and 6 bn in 1999. The most important demographic trends today are slower, but continued, population growth in developing countries and ageing and declining populations in more developed countries. The world's population is projected to grow to 9 bn by 2050, with almost all of the growth in what are currently developing countries.

About half of the world's population is in the labour force, including 1.3 bn or 43 per cent of the world's 3 bn workers in agriculture. The most important global labour trends[7] are:

---

[7] The World Bank's 2003 *World Development Indicators* (p. 44) reported that the global labour force in 2001 was 3 billion, including 2.5 billion in low- and middle-income countries and 470 million in high-income countries. The projected growth in the low- and middle-income countries is 40 million a year to 2010, and projected growth in high-income countries is one million a year.

- Rapid labour force growth in developing countries that is adding 40 m workers annually, while rural–urban migration reduces the share of workers in agriculture
- Slow labour force growth in developed countries, where two-thirds of workers are employed in service industries; labour costs are a high share of production costs in most service industries, encouraging some employers to turn to migrants to hold down costs and others to offshore or outsourced jobs.

If current trends continue, many developed countries will have shrinking workforces, while many developing countries will have high levels of unemployment and underemployment. To maintain the labour supply in developed countries, workers could work more hours, more women could be induced to join the work force, retirement could be delayed to reflect longer lives, or migrants could be admitted to stabilise workforces at current levels despite below-replacement fertility levels. There is a debate over the role that migration should play in the mix of policies available to stabilise labour forces and social security systems that were created during past periods of rapid population and labour force growth, especially in Europe and Japan.

In developing countries, unemployment and underemployment could be reduced with faster industry and service sector job growth, a seemingly endless quest. Thus, most developing countries welcome the opportunity to export some of their 'excess' workers, generating remittances, learning new skills and acquiring new ideas that may speed up development at home. The overarching questions include how much migration between developing and developed countries is optimal, in whose interest international migration for employment should be managed and whether migration management should be bilateral, regional, or global.

Differences and Migration

Migration is a response to differences. Rising differences between nation states in demographics,

Table 8.2. Europe and Africa, Demography, 1800–2050

	Share of world population-%		
	1800	2000	2050
Africa	8	13	20
Europe	20	12	7
World pop. (bn)	1	6	9

economics and security, plus revolutions in communications, transportation and rights that facilitate movement over borders, promise ever-more international migration for employment. It is important to remember that most people do not migrate over borders despite growing differences that encourage migration because of the desire to remain with family and friends. In addition, there are active government efforts to control who enters and stays in their territory. For these reasons, the migrant share of the global population has risen only slowly, from 2 per cent in 1975 to 3 per cent in 2000.

However, migration pressures are expected to rise with growing demographic and economic differences. The demographic 'weight' of world regions and nation states has and will continue to shift, increasing migration pressures, with one of the most dramatic examples the contrast between Europe and Africa. Europe had 20 per cent of the world's residents in 1800, when Africa had 8 per cent.[8] Today, Europe and Africa have about equal population shares, but by 2050 Africa is projected to have 20 per cent of global residents and Europe 7 per cent, a reversal of each continent's global demographic weight within 250 years. Demographic heavyweight Europe was the major source of migrants in the nineteenth century and, if history repeats itself, Africa could be a major source of migrants in the twenty-first century (table 8.2).

Economic differences between nation-states are widening, increasing the motivation for international labour migration. The world's GDP was $30 trillion in 2000, making average *per capita* income $5,000 a year, but there was significant variation – the range was from $100 per person per year in Ethiopia to $38,000 in Switzerland. When countries are grouped by their *per capita* GDPs, the gap between high-income countries (with $9,300 or

---

[8] Europe's share of the global population (including Asian Russia) peaked at 25 per cent between 1910 and 1920.

Table 8.3. Global Migrants and Incomes, 1975–2000

	Migrants millions	World Pop billions	Migrants World Pop	Yr change millions	Countries grouped by ave *per capita* GDP ($)			Ratios	
					Low	Middle	High	High-low	High-middle
1975	85	4.1	2.1%	1	150	750	6,200	41	8
1985	105	4.8	2.2%	2	270	1,290	11,810	44	9
1990	154	5.3	2.9%	10	350	2,220	19,590	56	9
1995	164	5.7	2.9%	2	430	2,390	24,930	58	10
2000	175	6.1	2.9%	2	420	1,970	27,510	66	14

Source: UN Population Division and World Bank Development Indicators; 1975 income data are 1976.
Note: 'Migrants' are defined as persons outside their country of birth or citizenship for twelve months or more.
The migrant estimate for 1990 was raised from 120 m to 154 m, to reflect the break-up of the USSR.

more per person per year), versus low- (below $750 per person per year) and middle- (between $750 and $9,300 per person per year) income countries has been widening, and very few low- and middle-income countries able to climb into the high-income ranks over the past quarter century.[9] For example, *per capita* GDPs in the high-income countries in 1975 were on average forty-one times higher than in low-income countries, and eight times higher than in middle-income countries. By 2000, high-income countries had *per capita* GDPs that were sixty-six times those in low-income countries and fourteen times those in middle-income countries (table 8.3).

There is a second dimension to increasing economic differences that adds to international migration pressures. Agriculture remains the world's major employer and, in the poorer countries in which farmers are a majority of workers, farmers who are often taxed have below-average incomes, while the relatively few farmers in rich countries are often subsidised in a manner that contributes to their above-average incomes. Low farm incomes in developing countries encourage rural–urban migration as well as international migration, in part because trade barriers for farm products maintain a demand for migrants in more developed countries while reducing farm prices and farm employment in developing countries.

The great migration off the land in developing countries provides a ready supply of workers willing to accept so-called '3-D' (dirty, dangerous, difficult) jobs inside their countries, as in China, or abroad, as when Mexicans migrate to the USA. The International Labour Organisation (ILO) estimated

Table 8.4. ILO Estimates of Migrant Workers, by Region, 2000

	m	Per dist (%)
Africa	5.5	7
Asia	22.1	27
Europe	27.0	33
Latin America[a]	2.5	3
North America	20.8	26
Oceania	2.9	4
Total	**80.7**	**100**

Notes: Applying regional labour force participation rates to UN migrant estimates
[a] Latin America and Caribbean.

that 60 per cent of the world's 81 million migrant workers in 2000 were in the more developed countries of Europe and North America (table 8.4).

The third major difference that prompts migration involves security and human rights. After the global conflict between capitalism and communism ended in the early 1990s, local conflicts erupted in many areas, leading to separatist movements, conflicts, new nations and more migrants, as in ex-Yugoslavia and ex-USSR. Creating new nations is almost always accompanied by conflict and migration, as populations are reshuffled so that the 'right' people are inside the 'right' borders. In some cases,

[9] For example, Portugal and South Korea moved from the middle- to the high-income group between 1985 and 1995, while Zimbabwe and Mauritania moved from the middle- to the low-income group (World Bank, *World Development Reports*, various years).

past migrations that brought migrants into an area result years later in situations in which those migrants and their descendents are considered foreigners in a newly independent country, such as Russians considered foreigners in the newly independent Baltic states.

Demographic, economic and human rights differences encourage individuals to migrate, but it takes networks or links between emigration and immigration areas to enable people to cross borders. Migration networks are a broad concept, and include factors that enable people to learn about opportunities abroad as well as an infrastructure that enables migrants to cross national borders and remain abroad (Massey, *et al.*, 1998). Migration networks have been shaped and strengthened by three major revolutions in the past half century: in communications, transportation, and rights. The communications revolution helps potential migrants to learn about opportunities abroad. The best source of information comes from migrants established abroad, since they are in a position to provide family and friends at home with information in a context they understand. Even without anchor migrants abroad, many people in developing countries see movies and TV shows produced in high-income countries, and some believe that, if they can get into countries that have such wealth, they can share it – which is one reason why it is sometimes said that the TV shows *Dallas* and *Dynasty* spurred migration toward the USA from all corners of the world.[10]

The transportation revolution highlights the declining cost of travel. British migrants unable to pay passage to the colonies in the eighteenth century often indentured themselves, promising to work from three–six years to repay one-way transportation costs to the Americas. Migrants would sign contracts before departure, and settlers looking for workers would meet the ships, pay the fare and obtain an indentured worker. Today transportation costs, even for unauthorised movements, are far less, typically less than $2,500 to travel anywhere in

the world legally, and $1,000–$20,000 for unauthorised migration. Most studies suggest that payback times for migrants are much quicker, so that even migrants who paid high smuggling fees can repay them within two or three years.

The 'rights revolution' refers to the spread of individual rights that allows some foreigners to stay abroad. Many countries have ratified UN, ILO and UNHCR conventions that commit them to providing all persons with basic rights such as due process. As a result, foreigners are not summarily removed and, in many countries, they have additional rights, such as not being returned to their countries of origin to face persecution. Most destination countries extend some eligibility for at least basic services to all residents, regardless of legal status, making it easier for migrants who are abroad to stay abroad.

There is little that countries experiencing 'unwanted immigration' can do in the short term about the demographic, economic and security differences that promote migration, and they have little power or desire to reverse the communications and transportation revolutions that, as a by-product of connecting the global village, inform migrants about opportunities abroad and make it less costly for them to travel. However, governments create and enforce rights, and the default policy instrument to manage migration has become new or modified laws that restrict the rights of migrants. For example, the USA in 1996 enacted laws that restricted the access of unauthorised as well as many legal immigrants to social assistance programme benefits, and many European countries revised their laws to define when and where foreigners had to apply for asylum to receive housing and support while their applications for asylum were considered. Middle-income countries also restrict rights in an effort to manage migrants, often tolerating the presence of migrants in economic booms, and then stepping up enforcement efforts when there is recession or complaints about the migrants' presence.

There is general agreement that manipulating the rights of migrants is not the optimal way to manage economically motivated migration. The challenge and opportunity is to find better ways to manage economically motivated migration in the twenty-first century to reduce the differences

---

[10] Even if migrants know that movies and TV shows portray exaggerated lifestyles, some of the migrants who find themselves in slave-like conditions abroad sometimes say that they did not believe that things in rich countries could be 'that bad'.

between nation-states that encourage people to cross borders.

Managing Migration

The two extremes of migration management – no borders and no immigrants – are neither desirable nor sustainable. Virtually all countries participate in international migration as countries of origin, transit, or destination, and many are all three (e.g. Thailand sends migrants to Taiwan and Singapore, has Burmese and other migrants who are transiting to Malaysia and receives migrants from Burma, Cambodia, and Laos).

The challenge is to manage migration in a way that allows the major actors involved – individuals and employers as well as sending and receiving countries – to reap *sustainable benefits* that reduce inequalities between countries. Moving people over borders in a way that reduces rather than increases inequalities is not easy. Over 200 years ago, Adam Smith observed that 'of all sorts of luggage [people are] the most difficult to be transported' over borders.

Assessing the Opportunities

The three opportunities laid out below would improve the migration system in a way that would raise the benefits for the major parties involved. Each opportunity could be implemented within the next five–fifteen years, and each could raise the benefits and reduce the costs of migration:

- Policies to select migrants most likely to be *economically successful* in the new country and thus reduce the opposition of host country residents to migration.
- Guest worker policies that can come closer to achieving their temporary worker goals by using *economic instruments* such as taxes and subsidies that align the incentives of employers and migrants with programme goals, such as increasing the levies charged to employers if they want to extend the work permits of migrants and refunding social security contributions to migrants to encourage them to return as required by their contracts.

- Managing migration to ensure that developing countries benefit by structuring the '3 Rs' in a manner that *speeds up economic and job growth* and *narrows economic differences* between labour senders and receivers.

The starting point for this chapter is to assume that the interests of both migrants and nation-states are important (Ellerman 2003),[11] and that the goal is to create a world in which people do not feel they must migrate over national borders. Unless there is a radical change in migration policies and flows, most of the world's residents will not be able to raise their incomes via migration; instead, they will enjoy higher incomes only if their own countries prosper. The challenge is to ensure that the migration of the exceptional few who cross national borders also improves conditions for those who do not migrate.

Active Immigration Policies

Identification and Description

International migration in the past meant moving a long distance and never or rarely returning to the country of origin. The cost of migration was high, so that those taking the uncertain and expensive journey often believed that 'anything abroad' must be better than what they had at home. There were dangers of disease and storms en route to distant shores, and there were dangers associated with settling in areas with antagonistic natives and ill-defined property rights.

Migration today is different. Much contemporary migration involves a temporary move abroad as a tourist, student, or guest worker and, for those who settle abroad, an 'adjustment' to immigrant or long-term resident status. Instead of a plunge into the dark from which there was assumed to be no return, migration today is often a 'testing' or 'filtering' process, with the result that about two-thirds of

---

[11] The motivation for migration is differences, but the international regime that has evolved, such as ILO conventions and recommendations, calls for equal treatment for migrants. The best protection for migrants – the best assurance that migrants will be treated equally – is if they are in an economy and labour market in which employers who do not pay minimum wages or offer adequate working conditions cannot find workers.

US immigrants are 'adjusters', persons already in the USA when their immigrant visas become available. Immigrant adjusters can and do shuttle or circulate between homes and jobs abroad and their countries of origin before and after they have a secure permanent residence status, enabling today's migrants to maintain close personal as well as economic ties with their countries of origin.

'Adjustment' means that many migrants today select their destinations, rather than destinations selecting migrants. The fact that many settlers and circulators were 'not supposed to stay' raises fears of 'migrant invasions'. Helping receiving countries to select the 'right migrants' can open or enlarge immigration doors, increasing migration flows and benefiting migrants, host and sending countries.

Alleviation of the Challenge

The common perception in most industrial countries is that they are getting too many of the 'wrong type' of migrant, including asylum seekers not found to be in need of protection or the unauthorised workers demanded by small segments of the host country population, such as farmers. The overall net economic benefits of migrants arriving in industrial countries are estimated to be positive but small, on the order of $1–$10 bn in the US economy in the mid-1990s, when GDP was about $7 trillion.

The economic benefits of immigration could be increased with active policies that selected the migrants likely to generate maximum economic benefits to the destination country. Canada, with 32 million residents, has an active selection system aimed at increasing its population 1 per cent a year via immigration,[12] as well as high levels of public satisfaction with immigration. There are several reasons for this exceptionalism: Canada does not border on a major emigration country, and has very flexible policies and admits most immigrants under a points system designed to ensure that they

Table 8.5. Canadian Immigration, 2002

Category	Number (m)	Dist (%)
Family	65,277	28
Economic principals	58,906	26
Dependents-Con	79,600	35
Refugees	25,111	11
Other	164	
Total	**229,058**	**100**

Source: www.cic.gc.ca/english/monitor/issue03/02-immigrants.html (7 January 2004).

are an economic asset to Canada. Canada admitted 229,000 immigrants in 2002, close to the average annual intake during the 1990s, which was 221,500. The leading countries of origin were China (15 per cent of immigrants), India (9 per cent) and Pakistan and the Philippines (5 per cent each) and most immigrants go to three cities – Toronto, Montreal and Vancouver.

Canada's 1976 Immigration Act established a points system to select economic or independent immigrants, half the flow, that assesses potential immigrants against nine criteria on which an applicant can score a maximum 107 points, and must score at least 75 points. For example, language skills (knowing English and/or French) can earn an applicant a maximum 15 points, while education beyond a BA can earn a potential immigrant up to 16 points. By most measures, the Canadian point system is working. In 2002, almost half of 178,000 principal immigrants and their dependants aged 15 and older had post-secondary (tertiary) schooling, such as college or advanced degrees, and over half spoke English or French.[13]

Points systems are *supply-based*, aiming to select migrants based on the personal characteristics most closely associated with economic success in the destination country, such as education and language. An alternative migrant-selection system is *demand-based*, making the entry of migrants dependent on receiving-country employers – if the employer says that the migrant is the best person to fill the job, the migrant is allowed entry. Supply- and demand-based selection systems can converge if points are awarded in supply-systems for having a job offer (as in Canada), or if only migrants with

---

[12] Then-Prime Minister Jean Chrétien said in July 2002 that Canada's 'population is not growing as fast as it should. And it's why we have a very open immigration policy. We're working to reform it because we don't achieve as many immigrants as we would like to have in the Canadian economy.'

[13] In 2002, of 229,000 immigrants, 43 per cent spoke English, 5 per cent French and 6 per cent both English and French: CIC (2002).

certain educational qualifications can be selected by employers (as the US H-1B system does by (usually) restricting entries to foreigners with a college degree or higher).

Demand-based selection systems are the norm in industrial countries, and they tend to be cumbersome and often adversarial. Most US employers who ask the Department of Labor (DOL) to approve their request to hire a foreigner do not want to go through an economic needs test for local workers, which requires DOL-supervised recruitment of local workers at DOL-set wages, since they have already identified the foreigner they want to employ.[14] The result in the USA is an infrastructure of lawyers and consultants who help employers to write job descriptions and develop recruitment strategies that satisfy DOL requirements but rarely result in the hiring of local workers.

The tension between employers and labour departments reflects the tradeoffs inherent in migration policies, in this case between employer access to foreign workers and first priority for local workers. The key to reducing the rules and regulations associated with economic needs tests are minimum age, education and language standards that migrants must meet, and economic instruments that allow employers to hire migrants if they are willing to pay for the privilege. The US Commission on Immigration Reform in the mid-1990s recommended that employers pay a $10,000 fee and then have easy access to immigrant visas for needed foreigners with BA degrees or more – paying the fee would be deemed to have satisfied the labour market test.[15] Alternatively, a fixed number of visas could be made available and auctioned among employers seeking foreign workers, with the market determining the price of each visa.

Supply-side selection systems could also auction immigrant visas. Countries could set minimum standards for immigrant visa applicants and allow applicants to bid for the available visas.[16] Auctioning immigration visas to the highest bidder has been proposed by several economists, including Gary Becker, but has not been fully implemented by any country.[17] However, the principle of using the economic instruments of fees rather than rules and regulations to balance access to immigrant visas while protecting local workers could

increase the efficiency of the migration system and reduce opposition to immigration, allowing doors for immigrants to open wider.

Side Effects and Uncertainties

There are two major side effects and uncertainties associated with economic instruments to select migrants. First, switching from they-pick-us to we-pick-them migration management is likely to require more efforts to curb unauthorised migration, and perhaps changes in asylum and related policies. Since it is costly to enlist employers in the fight against unauthorised migration, or to hire more staff to speed up the processing of asylum applicants and remove those not in need of protection, for example, enforcement costs may rise in the short term. However, without stepped-up enforcement that draws a clearer line between legal and illegal, employers and migrants may bypass the migration selection system.

The cost of curbing unwanted and unlawful immigration is high. In 2002 five industrial countries – Canada, Germany, the Netherlands, the UK and the USA – spent at least $17 bn on the enforcement of

[14] Labor Secretary Robert Reich testified in 1995 that 'Of the current employment-based immigrants who are subject to the Department of Labor-administered permanent labor certification process, we estimate that over 90 per cent are already in the US and about two-thirds are already working – sometimes illegally – for the employer which files the petition on his behalf.' Quoted in High-tech foreign workers, *Migration News*, 10, 1997.

[15] Hewlett-Packard testified in May 1996 that labour certification cost to obtain an immigrant visa for an H-1B worker cost an average $15,000 and took twenty-two months: CIR Commissioners Robert Hill and Bruce Morrison, Give me your skilled workers, *Legal Times*, 5 August 1996.

[16] The USA has diversity immigrant visas for persons who are nationals of countries that sent fewer than 50,000 immigrants to the USA in the previous five years. In most years, 10 m or more foreigners apply, and about 100,000 (or 1 per cent) are selected in the first round, since not all of those who apply satisfy the education requirement (at least a high-school education) and some decide that they do not want to immigrate.

[17] The closest auction-type immigration visa available is the investor visa, offered by Canada, the USA, and many developing countries, which allows foreigners to obtain immigration visas in exchange for investments, usually investments that create or preserve jobs. These programmes are often marred by fraud.

immigration laws and to care for asylum seekers, about two-thirds as much as they provided in ODA to the countries from which many of the migrants involved came (Martin 2003). Despite sharply higher enforcement costs and asylum expenditures, these countries had stable or growing stocks of illegal, irregular or unauthorised migrants.

Second, selection systems that facilitate the entry of the 'best and brightest' from developing countries could accelerate the 'brain drain' in a manner that leads to vicious circles, divergence and more migration pressures.[18] In order to prevent this, there should be compensation or human capital replenishment assistance from labour receivers to labour senders. This could be accomplished in several ways, including having emigration countries levy exit taxes on migrants or collecting income or other taxes on their nationals abroad. Alternatively, immigration countries could divert some of the taxes paid by migrants, or levy a surcharge on migrants' incomes to their countries of origin or a UN development agency. For example, Bhagwati proposed a 10 per cent surtax on migrant incomes during their first ten years abroad, collected by receiving countries and returned to the migrants' countries of origin (Bhagwati 1976; Bhagwati and Partington 1976).[19]

When compensation for the brain drain was discussed in the 1960s and 1970s, critics emphasised that a nationalist perspective that weighed both individual and nation-state welfare was required to argue that migrants enjoying windfall gains in the form of higher incomes abroad should share some of these gains with fellow citizens left behind. However, even with a nationalist perspective, most emigration countries cannot successfully tax their nationals abroad. Eritrea has since 1993 imposed a tax

of 2 per cent on the incomes of expatriates, and enforced collections by making it hard to keep or buy land in Eritrea or renew passports unless the tax is paid. Countries such as the USA tax the world-wide income of residents, but exempt from taxes the first $75,000 in income of those living overseas, which exempts most of the 3.2 million Americans abroad from paying US income taxes.

Most recommendations to deal with the brain drain suggest government-to-government transfers, with the amount of the transfer some fraction of the increased earnings of migrants abroad. Another option is to have the employers provide Human Capital Replenishment Assistance to migrants' countries of origin. This Replenishment Assistance could be an up front fee of perhaps 10 per cent of the migrant's first-year salary, which is what many employers pay to a local recruitment agency to find workers. This raises the possibility that sending- and receiving-country government agencies could cooperate to handle the recruitment of migrant workers, displacing private recruiters and providing Human Capital Replenishment Assistance at no additional cost to employers or migrants.

Economic Evaluation

In most of the industrial countries with ageing populations that 'need' immigrants to stabilise workforces and pension systems, most residents oppose additional migration. Migration systems that select those likely to succeed economically could reduce this opposition and thereby open new channels for migrants.

The best single predictor of a person's earnings is her level of education, and years of education is often the threshold characteristic to determine if a foreigner will be granted an immigrant visa in we-pick-them selection systems. However, a nation's stock of human capital is critical to its economic growth, especially in the endogenous growth theories that make technological progress and thus long-term growth rates dependent on the creation and implementation of new ideas. If immigrants on average have more education than residents, they can raise the average educational level of the workforce in destination countries and accelerate long-term growth. As newcomers, immigrants may play a special role in increasing productivity because of their

---

[18] Todaro (1980) observed that 'Migrants typically do not represent a random sample of the overall population. On the contrary, they tend to be disproportionately young, better educated, less risk-averse, and more achievement oriented and to have better personal contacts in destination areas than the general population in the region of out-migration.'

[19] Bhagwati proposed a brain drain tax in *Daedalus* in 1972, and the two 1976 volumes were the outcome of conferences to discuss compensation for the brain-drain. Legal scholar Partington emphasised that taxing migrants abroad on behalf of their country of origin could best be justified if the migrants were still considered members of their countries of origin.

different experiences and perspectives, as when the 'new blood' associated with the risk taking needed for migration raises innovation and growth.

Selective migration systems can also increase inequality between countries, an outcome that can be mitigated with some kind of compensation system. The case for brain drain compensation has been challenged by a new literature that reaches the seemingly counterintuitive conclusion that some emigration can accelerate economic growth in migrant countries of origin. This is not likely to occur in practice, but deserves a brief mention.

A 'brain drain' can be turned into a 'brain gain' by assuming a sequence of events. Imagine a developing country with no emigration that suddenly allows professionals to emigrate and earn higher incomes abroad. This raises the average return to education in the home country, which should induce more people there to get more schooling. However, not all of those obtaining more education will emigrate, which produces the paradox that opening emigration doors can *increase* the human capital in an emigration country (Mountford 1997; Beine, Docquier and Rapoport 2001). The very plausible result is that the 'optimal level of brain drain' from any country is not zero, and that richer countries should not close their doors to professionals to accelerate economic development.[20]

Feasibility

The fastest growth in international migration is at the top and bottom of the education ladder, involving well-educated professionals and uneducated farm workers. Among professionals, there appears to be a sharp contrast between the side effects of IT specialists emigrating from India and nurses emigrating from South Africa, highlighting the importance of conditions in both labour-sending and labour-receiving countries in evaluating migration's benefits and costs.

In the Indian IT industry, the positive externalities or 'spillover effects' of what began as an island of 7,000 IT specialists in the mid-1980s have been significant. In 2003, India had 700,000 IT workers and about $10 bn in revenues from exports of computer-related products, including services provided to foreign firms in India (outsourcing). The 'virtuous circle' that began with exporting IT workers include

higher enrolments in science and engineering and the availability of world-class IT services to private firms and government agencies in India – meeting global standards for foreign customers has raised the quality of services provided to local customers.

In South Africa, by contrast, the emigration of doctors and nurses is associated with vicious circles of fewer health care workers at a time when the need for health care is growing because of AIDS and recent initiatives to improve immunisation. The emigration of health personnel trained to developed country standards can leave especially rural areas with few medical staff, increase the workload on remaining staff and discourage change in bureaucratic, top-down and often staff- and patient-unfriendly health care systems. In many countries, health care graduates who have received government support for their education must serve several years in rural and other health care need areas before receiving their licences, but their experience in often unsupervised and poorly equipped and staffed clinics reinforces the desire to emigrate as soon as possible for better working conditions and higher wages to repay debts.

The response has been an agreement by the UK National Health Service to avoid 'aggressive recruitment', especially of nurses in South Africa and several other African countries. But stopping the emigration of health care workers would not necessarily solve the problem of worker shortages, as can be seen in South Africa, where there were about 32,000 unfilled nursing jobs in 2002, an estimated 7,000 South African nurses abroad, but 35,000 nurses in South Africa who are not working as nurses, so that, even if all South African nurses abroad returned, there would be unfilled nursing jobs. The large number of non-working nurses suggests a solution closer to home.

Countries such as the Philippines and India take the opposite approach, seeking to 'market' their health care professionals abroad. In both countries,

---

[20] For example, a study making heroic assumptions, including that the 1994 level of education in a country was a function of the average number of migrants from that country who arrived in OECD countries between 1988 and 1994, concluded that 'migration prospects seem to play a significant role in education decisions' (Beine, Docquier and Rapoport 2001, 288).

many health care workers are trained in private, tuition-charging schools, with students taking out loans to get their education and private recruitment firms finding jobs abroad for graduates. In the Philippines, about 15,000 nurses emigrated in 2003, there were 7,500 nursing graduates and some doctors were reportedly retraining as nurses in order to increase their opportunities to go abroad.

There are many contrasts between IT and health care. IT is often perceived as a private sector 'luxury', while health care is often considered a public sector necessity. Second, the costs of IT services have declined over time, while the cost of health care services has tended to rise over time. Third, there seem to be fewer issues with privately financed professionals who emigrate than with those whose professional education was subsidised by taxpayers, even if tax funds paid for the basic education of migrants. The migration of professionals from developing to developed countries is likely to increase, but it appears that flows must be evaluated separately to determine its effects on development, and the cases of Indian IT specialists and South African doctors and nurses may represent the two extremes of a very wide spectrum of cases.

The migration of professionals refers to persons who have completed their education before they cross borders. There is an associated issue involving students from developing countries who study in developed countries, and policies that permit them to settle as immigrants. In many ways, foreign student programmes are ideal 'probationary immigrant' systems, since foreign students can generally stay in the country only if they successfully complete their studies, which requires learning the host-country language and becoming familiar with host-country ways of study and work. If foreign students find an employer to hire them after graduation, more countries are permitting them to remain as guest workers or settlers.

In 2000, there were 2 m foreign students in the OECD countries, half from outside the OECD, including 34 per cent in the USA, 16 per cent in the UK, 13 per cent in Germany, 11 per cent in France and 8 per cent in Australia (OECD 2002, 52). Foreign students tend to study subjects that impart skills transferable internationally (e.g. science and engineering rather than law), and many institutions

of higher education have become dependent on the revenues from foreign students.

Teitelbaum (2003) argues that the high percentage of foreign students in USA doctoral programmes reflects labour market deficiencies and student desires for immigrant visas, not a 'national need' for more PhDs in basic sciences. In many basic sciences, six or more years of graduate study is followed by five–ten years of low-paid postdoctoral research, so that graduates do not get 'real jobs' until aged 35 or 40. According to one study, bioscientists can expect to earn $1 m less than MBAs graduating from the same university in their lifetimes, and $2 m less if stock options are taken into account, suggesting one explanation for the very different composition of students in MBA programmes and graduate science programmes.

Guest Worker Policies

Identification and Description

Guest worker programmes aim to add workers temporarily to the labour force. Most guest workers are unskilled, and they usually fill '3-D' (dirty, difficult, dangerous) jobs in labour-receiving countries. Guest worker programmes tend to become larger and to last longer than planned, and many migrants settle in the countries in which they are 'temporarily employed' despite programme rules that envision them rotating in and out of the country, with recruitment stopping when unemployment rises.

Guest worker programmes suffer from distortion and dependence. 'Distortion' refers to the fact that labour markets are flexible, adjusting to the presence or absence of migrants. If some businesses make investment decisions that assume migrants will (continue to) be available, they resist efforts to stop recruitment. 'Dependence' means that migrants and their families come to depend on earnings from foreign jobs. If legal channels to go abroad are blocked, migrants may turn to smugglers or traffickers to find foreign jobs.

The failure of past macro or economy-wide guest worker programmes to live up to their promise has discouraged the resumption of large-scale guest worker recruitment of unskilled workers. If distortion and dependence could be minimised with economic instruments, new channels for migrants to cross national borders could be opened.[21] Requiring employers to pay levies to hire migrants and refunding the social security tax contributions of migrants can thus minimise both distortion and dependence.[22]

Alleviation of the Challenge

Migrants generally move from lower- to higher-wage countries, and most developed and many middle-income developing countries are destinations for migrants seeking jobs and higher wages. Countries hosting unskilled migrants range from traditional immigration countries such as the USA, most of the Western European nations that recruited guest workers and Asian countries from Japan and Korea[23] to Singapore and Malaysia. The Gulf oil-exporting nations have some of the highest percentages of migrants in their work forces, and migrant workers are significant among a diverse set of countries that are richer than their neighbours, from South Africa to Côte d'Ivoire and from Argentina to Costa Rica. However, there are no universally accepted best practices for minimising the distortion and dependence associated with guest workers.

During the heyday of guest worker programmes in the 1960s and early 1970s in Western Europe, millions of migrant workers were recruited in southern Europe and Northern Africa to fill jobs in construction, mining and manufacturing. Most labour-importing countries had only one programme, and guest worker admissions were influenced by the macroeconomic policies that affected the unemployment rate, including fiscal policies as well as interest and exchange rates. In the early years of the programmes, the migrant work force was flexible, since workers who were laid off within a year of their arrival usually had to return to homes in Italy or other southern European countries. In this manner, the unemployment rate stayed low in northern European countries as unemployed guest workers returned home.

During the 1960s there was a close relationship between the number of foreigners in a country and the number of employed foreign workers. However, by the time that recruitment was stopped in Western Europe in 1973–4, most migrants had 'earned' permanent resident rights, and many unemployed migrants elected not to return to their countries of origin despite return bonuses as well as policies meant to discourage family unification. For example, in many countries spouses and older children could not work for a year or two, which meant that the breadwinner's earnings had to stretch further, but many guest worker families nonetheless unified and the result was that some newcomers had trouble finding jobs once they received work permits.

Contradictory policies that aimed to 'strengthen the will of migrants to return' while 'promoting the integration of migrants who nonetheless decided to stay' left European guest worker countries with the worst of all worlds – and a growing gap between the number of foreigners and the number of employed foreigners. Newly arrived foreigners with little education and few language skills found it hard to get first jobs and legal work experience, especially since high wages and high unemployment allowed employers to select non-migrant workers. Many countries made it far easier for new arrivals to obtain social benefits than jobs, and foreigners soon became associated with joblessness and welfare dependency. For example, adding 100 non-EU males increased employment by 73 per cent in 2000, while adding 100 EU nationals increased employment by 86 or 20 per cent more, and the gap was larger for women (table 8.6).

---

[21] Even if economic mechanisms ensured that guest workers arrived and departed according to programme rules, there could be opposition to guest workers on the grounds that guest workers have restricted rights in their host countries, since they normally lose the right to be in the country if they lose their jobs, for example. A leading study concluded that: 'restrictions on the employment and residential mobility of legally admitted aliens appear anachronistic and, in the long run, administratively unfeasible' (Castles and Miller 1998, 286).

[22] Sending countries can also benefit if the migration abroad is temporary. Ellerman (2003, 12) noted that the return of 'forced labour' from Slovenia to Germany during the Second World War helped to create electrical and electronics companies that led to the the *Iskra* (Spark) group and the modern high-technology industry in Slovenia.

[23] In Japan and (until recently) Korea, migrant workers are considered trainees and thus not covered by minimum wage and other labour laws. Trainees receiving below minimum wages often 'run away' from their employers and earn more as unauthorised workers.

Table 8.6. Non-EU Foreigners in the EU: Employment and Unemployment, 2000

Employed, 25–39	Men (%)	Women (%)
Non-EU foreigners	73	44
Nationals	86	68
Ratio–Non-EU/nationals	0.8	0.6
Unemployed, 25–39 (%)		
Non-EU foreigners	15	19
Nationals	6.5	10
Ratio–non-EU/nationals	2.3	1.9

Source: Thorogood and Winqvist, (2003).

Lagging employment–population ratios among foreigners helped to set the stage for the new guest worker programmes of the 1990s, each carefully aimed at filling jobs in particular industries or occupations. Unlike the macro guest worker programmes that could be likened to shotguns spraying migrant workers throughout the labour market, the new micro programmes are more like rifles aiming to provide workers to particular labour markets or segments of labour markets. Macroeconomic policies thus have far less impact on the demand for migrants, whether they admit computer programmers or farm workers. Despite a proliferation of micro programmes, there are far more irregular workers than before. The presence of these unauthorised workers distorts labour markets, leads to protection gaps and complicates the quest for a new migration management system in which migrants are legal. Irregular workers can give advantages to employers who hire them, and push particular types of employers toward hiring unauthorised workers, as with the spread of labour contractors and irregular workers in US agriculture.

Micro guest worker programmes are not likely to go away, but governments can expand their number

only if they find ways to deal with distortion and dependence. Taxes and subsidies can align employer and migrant incentives with rules by requiring employers to pay usual payroll taxes on the wages of guest workers (in some countries migrant wages are exempt), for example. To encourage worker rotation, employers could face additional charges to renew a migrant's work permit, and employer-paid taxes and fees could be used to raise subsidise R&D efforts aimed at raising productivity in migrant sectors that often have low profit margins and few organisations to facilitate cooperation to mechanise or restructure work in a way that reduces long-term dependence on migrants.

An example of one of the most successful 'mechanisation-replacing-migrants' cases shows the importance of a governmental coordinating mechanism. In the early 1960s, over 80 per cent of the workers who hand-picked the processing tomatoes used to make catsup (ketchup) in California were Mexican Bracero guest workers. Without them, the argument went, the US industry would move to Mexico and catsup would become a luxury product. The Bracero programme was nonetheless ended in 1964 during the War on Poverty and the quest for civil rights because of concerns that the presence of Braceros was slowing the economic progress of Hispanics. And the result was the opposite of what was predicted: instead of moving to Mexico, California today produces about five times more tomatoes at a fraction of Bracero-era costs.

There were two keys to the transformation of the processed tomato harvest: cooperative research and government grading. Plant scientists asked engineers what kind of tomato they needed to make it amenable to mechanical harvesting and bulk handling, and developed tomatoes that ripened uniformly and had an oblong shape. Engineers developed a machine that cut the plant, shook off the tomatoes and then used electronic 'eyes' to separate red from green tomatoes and other plant material. Mechanical harvesting eliminated 90 per cent of the hand-harvesting jobs, but its quick adoption required the establishment of state-run grading stations that took random samples of tomatoes to determine their quality and resolve the perennial price–quality issue between growers and processors.[24] The funds for transforming the tomato industry

[24] Hand-picked tomatoes were sold by farmers in 60-lb lugs and, with a current value of about $50 a ton or 2.5 cents a pound, there would be a relatively small loss of $1.50 if a lug was rejected by the processing plant because it had too many green tomatoes or too many dirt clods. Mechanical harvesting brings tomatoes to processing plants in 25 ton loads, so rejecting a load means a loss of $1,250 (Martin and Olmstead 1985).

were supplied by government, not by the employers of Braceros, but it is clear that employer-paid taxes and fees could substitute for government funds in such cases. For example, farmers already themselves assess fees to fund research on crop diseases and for product promotion.

The labour market distortion that accompanies migrant workers can be reduced with employer-paid taxes and fees, while migrant dependence on foreign jobs can be tackled with refunds of the social security and other taxes paid by migrants. Migrants (and their employers) contribute 20–40 per cent of their earnings in payroll taxes in most OECD countries, and refunding these social security and unemployment insurance contributions would encourage voluntary returns. Providing the refund to the migrant in her country of origin would also provide a convenient way to match a portion of returned migrants' savings that are invested in job-creating development projects. Labour-sending governments may be able to collect taxes on foreign earnings if returned workers receive credits in local social security systems for their work abroad in exchange for tax contributions made upon return, for example.

Dependence-reducing schemes should rely on incentives rather than coercion. Some Caribbean countries require guest workers leaving legally to sign contracts that deduct 10–30 per cent of wages and forward them from the foreign employer to a government institution at home that converts them into local currency for the migrant's family or holds them until the migrant returns. These forced-savings schemes have been prone to abuse: there are often unexplained deductions, and some workers and families complain they do not receive the monies due them.

For example, there is still litigation over the 10 per cent forced-savings programme in the first phase of the 1942–64 Mexico–US Bracero programme. The 256,000 Mexicans who received contracts to work as Braceros in the USA between 1942 and 1949 had 10 per cent of their US wages withheld by US employers and forwarded via the Wells Fargo Bank and Union Trust Company of San Francisco to the Bank of Mexico and then to the Banco de Credito Agricola in Mexico. A total of $34 m was deducted from Bracero earnings between 1942 and 1946, and some was not returned to the workers

to whom it was owed. Several class-action suits were filed in the USA in 2001–2 seeking to recover the World War II-era forced savings, plus $500 bn in punitive damages. Mexico's Foreign Relations Ministry says that there are no records of what happened to the forced Bracero savings. Nonetheless, the Mexican government in November 2003 offered each of the ex-Braceros who registered $5,000 or $10,000.

Side Effects and Uncertainties

It is very difficult to keep guest worker programmes true to their purpose, prompting the aphorism that 'there is nothing more permanent than temporary workers'. Taxes and subsidies can help to align employer and worker incentives with programme rules, but employers may still find it better to prolong the stay of experienced workers rather than recruit and train new migrants, and migrants may not be induced to return to their countries of origin voluntarily by the promise of a social security refund, especially if there are few jobs at home. If employers and migrants believe that migrant adjustment to settler status is an option, then a 'once-abroad, stay-abroad' mentality can make it difficult to enforce worker rotation despite taxes and subsidies.

There are two major challenges to expanding channels for legal guest workers: currently high levels of illegal or irregular migration, and the tension between numbers and rights in developing countries. With many employers and migrants already accustomed to operating outside of the tax system and in violation of immigration and labour laws, stepped up enforcement is necessary to persuade them to operate in the mainstream labour market rather than the underground economy. Simply opening more doors for guest workers without bringing employers and migrants in the underground economy out of the shadows may increase rather than reduce unauthorised migration.

Many countries have had legalisation programmes, offering regular immigrant status to unauthorised foreigners who satisfied residence, work and other criteria. However, one legalisation is usually followed by another, as the enforcement side of the grand bargain does not deter continued illegal migration, while talk of another amnesty encourages more migration. Given large and growing numbers of irregular migrant workers, the ends of the policy option spectrum are marked by two extremes – guest workers and legalisation. The guest worker option allows irregular foreign workers who find regular jobs to have their employers register them in exchange for work permits valid for one, two, or more years (as in Italy, Spain and Thailand), while the legalisation option allows irregular foreigners who satisfy residence or work requirements to receive immigrant or permanent residence visas, which puts them on a path to naturalisation.

The in-between option is earned legalisation, which means that unauthorised foreigners who satisfy work requirements receive a temporary legal status, and then they are allowed to 'earn' an immigrant status with continued employment, tax payments and crime-free records. One example is the 2003 Agricultural Job Opportunity, Benefits, and Security Act (AgJOBS), pending in the US Congress would allow unauthorised foreigners who did at least 100 days of farm work in a twelve-month period to register for a six-year Temporary Resident Status (TRS) that permits work in the USA and travel in and out of the US. While in TRS status, workers would have to do at least 2,060 hours or 360 days of any kind of farm work over six years, including at least 1,380 hours or 240 workdays during the first three years following adjustment to earn

an immigrant status, which their spouses and minor children would receive when the migrant qualified. Earned legalisation in this case aims to prevent currently employed illegal workers from leaving for better jobs with legal status.[25]

The USA has 6–8 m unauthorised foreign workers, and President George Bush in January 2004 proposed an earned guest worker programme to deal with them. Under the Fair and Secure Immigration Reform (FSIR) proposal, US employers would acknowledge that they hired irregular workers by giving them letters to show that the migrant had a US job. To become a legal guest worker, the migrant would take the employer's letter to a US government agency, pay a registration fee of $1,000–$2,000 and receive a three-year renewable visa. However, 'there is no linkage between participation in this programme and a green card [immigrant visa]... one must go home upon conclusion of the programme' unless the US employer has applied for an immigrant visa on behalf of the worker. The number of green cards or immigrant visas available for US employers who cannot find US workers – currently 140,000 a year for workers and their families – would increase by some undetermined number to make an immigrant visa a more realistic option, but there could still be long waits for visas.[26]

The second issue is the tension between numbers and rights, and it is often played out in sending-countries' policies toward particular groups, such as women. Countries such as Bangladesh and Pakistan ban the emigration of unskilled female migrants, under the theory that they will be vulnerable to abuse overseas, while Indonesia, the Philippines and Sri Lanka allow women to go abroad as domestic helpers, but try to educate them at home and protect them abroad. The result is a pendulum that sometimes swings toward numbers and sometimes toward rights. For example, in March 1995, Singapore hanged a Filipina maid for killing another maid and the child in her care, sparking massive demonstrations in the Philippines and a government-imposed ban on Filipinas going to Singapore to work as maids. The ban was short-lived, especially because women who had gone into debt to obtain contracts to work in Singapore protested when their opportunities to go abroad were restricted.[27]

---

[25] Earned legalisation represents another grand bargain between those with opposing views. Farmers want a workforce that is required to do farm work, and worker advocates are willing to exchange a few years of 'indentured status to agriculture' for the right of farm workers to eventually earn full immigrant status, which would mean they no longer had to work in agriculture.

[26] For example, if 5 m unauthorised workers register, and the government adds 100,000 employment-based immigrant visas a year, it would take fifty years to convert all of the temporary workers to immigrants – excluding families.

[27] A similar fight is playing out in Indonesia. Nahdhatul Ulama, the largest Muslim organisation in the country, asked the government in October 2003 to halt the emigration of women, saying: 'The sending of migrant workers to work as baby-sitters, domestic helpers, waitresses and the like will only disgrace the whole nation.' Advocacy groups estimate there are 4 m Indonesians working overseas legally and illegally, 70 per cent of them women, However, as pressures for a ban on women working overseas mounted, some 3,000 women scheduled to go overseas staged a demonstration demanding the right to emigrate.

Economic Evaluation

The purpose of using economic instruments to regulate guest worker admissions, employment and returns is to open more doors for unskilled workers to find jobs in higher-wage countries. Decisions to hire migrants and to migrate abroad are economic decisions, so guest worker programmes that regulate the entry, employment and stay of guest workers are more likely to achieve their goals if they include economic mechanisms that align employer and worker incentives with programme rules. One way to align employer incentives with programme rules that require employers to seek local workers first and then rotate guest workers in and out of the country is to require employers to pay a levy for the privilege of employing a migrant worker. Employer-paid levies could encourage an honest search for local workers and serve to minimise distortion by being used to mechanise or restructure work.[28]

To reduce migrant worker dependence on foreign jobs and to encourage returns, the social security taxes paid by migrants could be refunded to migrants returning home, which would encourage voluntary returns and provide a convenient way to match a portion of returned migrants' savings that are invested in job-creating development projects. Charging migrants social security taxes helps to level the playing field with local workers, and refunding their contributions helps to align migrant incentives with programme rules, making enforcement easier.

There are many examples of how *not* to use economic instruments to manage migration. Most Middle Eastern oil exporters have large foreign worker populations, and require foreigners to have local sponsors (*kafeels*). Sponsors often charge migrants a fee for sponsoring their stay in the country, and thus have an incentive to sponsor too many migrants. The result is a low-wage, low-productivity economic system that leaves local workers unemployed or underemployed. Gulf governments are trying to 'nationalise' their labour forces, but are discovering that nationals do not want to accept the low-wage private sector jobs now filled by migrants.

Refunding social security contributions to migrants who return is more common. In the 1980s several countries provided refunds of social security contributions to induce migrant returns, including the French and German governments.[29] In Germany, a migrant family could get a departure bonus of up to $5,000, plus the employee's contributions to social security, and the departure bonus scheme reduced the number of foreigners in Germany from 4.7 m in 1982 to 4.4 m in 1984–5. However, most studies concluded that the foreigners who took departure bonuses would have left in any event, so that Germany merely bunched normal emigration during the two years that bonuses were available (Hönekopp 1990).

Moving more workers over borders raises the more general issue of the economic impacts of migrants on countries receiving them. The economic impacts of immigrants on most industrial receiving countries is small but positive, making the most important economic issues surrounding migration distributional. In 1986, the President's Council on Economic Advisors (CEA) summarised the labour market effects of immigrants as follows: 'Although immigrant workers increase output, their addition to the supply of labour ... [causes] wage rates in the immediately affected market [to be] bid down ... Thus, native-born workers who compete with immigrants for jobs may experience reduced earnings or reduced employment' (CEA 1986, 221).

Most research interest and policy concern focuses on how immigrants affect those in the bottom half of the labour market. Governments have long protected vulnerable low-wage workers by establishing minimum wages and regulating hours of work; there are also education and training programmes to help workers improve their job skills and thus their earnings. Economists and other social scientists have used three kinds of studies to examine the labour market effects of immigrants in detail: case studies econometric studies and economic mobility or integration studies.

---

[28] The US H-1B programme, which admits foreign professionals for up to six years, charges employers a $1,000 per worker fee to generate funds that provide, *inter alia*, scholarships to US students interested in high-tech careers.

[29] The 1982 election in Germany was won by the 'rightist' CDU–CSU–FDP parties in part because they promised to 'do something' about out-of-control immigration. The newly elected government copied the French return bonus programme of 1981.

Case Studies   These examine a particular industry or occupation. Many of the first immigration studies were case studies that were undertaken after a strike by US workers resulted in their replacement by immigrants. When farm workers in southern California went on strike for a wage increase in 1982, for example, many lost their jobs. There was no direct competition between new migrants and established workers, however. The unionised workers were displaced in a competition between employers. The unionised harvesting association lost business to farm labour contractors (FLCs) who hired non-union and often unauthorised workers. The harvesting association went out of business, and the union workers lost their jobs (Mines and Martin 1984).

Case studies show that immigration can displace established workers and depress wages by adding vulnerable workers to the labour supply. This scenario conforms to accepted labour market theory, but the actual effects on wages and employment are indirect and hard to measure (GAO 1988). Once employers begin hiring newly arrived workers through FLCs, for example, hiring and supervision can change. Local workers may not learn about job vacancies if the FLCs find additional workers by asking current employees to bring in their friends and relatives. Such 'network hiring' helps explain why many garment shops in New York or Los Angeles have Mexican, Chinese, or Thai seamstresses, but not a mixture of the three. Network hiring also explains how the owners of office buildings in Los Angeles in the 1980s came to replace unionized US-born black janitors with immigrants hired by cleaning contractors.

Econometric Studies   These consider how immigration, wages, and employment interact in a city labour market, or they compare labour markets among cities. They begin with the assumption that, if immigrants depress wages or displace workers, then the more immigrants there are in a city, the greater the observed wage depression or job displacement, especially in comparisons across

cities with different shares of immigrant workers. Econometric studies might study the influence of immigration on the wages and unemployment rates of blacks, Hispanics and women in Los Angeles by comparing them with similar groups in Atlanta, which has a relatively small immigrant population.

In the 1980s, to the surprise of economists, such studies found few wage or labour market effects related to immigration. In 1990, George Borjas summarised the research literature by saying 'modern econometrics cannot detect a single shred of evidence that immigrants have a sizable adverse impact on the earnings and employment opportunities of natives in the United States' (Borjas 1990, 81). One well-known econometric study concluded, for example, that the 1980 influx of Cuban immigrants to Miami in the Mariel boatlift had no measurable negative effect on the wages and employment of local workers (Card 1990).[30] The best-known 1990s review concluded that the 'weight of the empirical evidence suggests that the impact of immigration on the wages of competing workers is small' (Smith and Edmonston 1997, 220).

As more data became available in the 1990s, however, it became clear that workers who competed with migrants tended to move away from areas with more newly arrived migrants – presumably to avoid competing with them in the labour market. The effects of immigration on wages and unemployment in Los Angeles or Houston were thus dissipated throughout the USA in a process that demographer William Frey called 'the new white flight' (1994). Many of the workers assumed to compete with newcomers may not (as with government employees whose wages are set at federal or state levels), and the earnings of many union workers are determined by national or regional collective bargaining agreements. Borjas reversed his earlier conclusion in 2003, finding that 'immigration reduces the wage and labour supply of competing native workers, as suggested by the simplest textbook model of a competitive labour market' (Borjas 2003, 1370).

Borjas concluded that an 11 per cent increase in the US labour force due to immigration between 1980 and 2000 reduced the wages of the average US-born worker by 3.2 per cent (Borjas 2003, 1370). But the wage depression was almost 9 per cent for US-born workers who had not completed

[30] During the four months of the boatlift, Miami's labour force increased by 7 per cent, but there were no significant differences in wage and job opportunities for native-born workers in Miami and in other US cities.

high school, suggesting significant wage effects in particular industries, such as agriculture, probably the US industry most dependent on immigrant workers. In 2000, about 90 per cent of hired workers on US farms were believed to be immigrants, including half who were unauthorised, despite the legalisation of over 1 m illegal farm workers in 1987 and 1988. Farm workers who were legalised moved on to non-farm jobs, which created a vacuum that drew in more unauthorised workers and helped keep farm worker wages and benefits among the lowest in America.

Economic mobility or Integration Studies

These investigate how immigrants and their children are faring in the USA. Their starting point is the fact that 'immigrants on average earn less than native workers [and] this gap . . . has widened recently . . . [as] the skills [years of education] of immigrants have declined relative to those of the native-born' (Smith and Edmonston   1997, 5–33). The average educational level of immigrants has been rising, but the educational level of US-born residents has risen faster, which explains the widening education gap. Because education is the best predictor of a person's earnings, the fact that the US-born residents have more years of schooling helps to explain the growing inequality of income among people living in America, in particular between foreign-born and US-born Americans and within the foreign-born population.

One of the most important issues for society and the economy is whether those who immigrate are so energetic and ambitious that their earnings will quickly catch up to and even surpass those of their native-born counterparts. Barry Chiswick conducted research in the 1970s that found just such a catch-up pattern for immigrants who arrived in the 1950s and 1960s (Chiswick 1978). The immigrant men Chiswick studied initially earned 10 per cent less than did similar US-born men. But the drive and ambition that prompted them to migrate enabled the migrants to close the earnings gap after an average of thirteen years in the USA, and to earn 6 per cent more than similar US-born men after twenty-three years in the USA.[31] The immigrants' motivation and ambition, it seemed, could expand the US economy and raise average earnings.

George Borjas, however, contended that Chiswick's study captured a unique set of circumstances: the influx of highly skilled Asian immigrants after 1965 policy changes and a booming US economy. In 1970, the average immigrant earned 1 per cent more than the average US-born worker. However, not all immigrants caught up in earnings, including Mexican and Central American immigrants. During the 1970s and 1980s, the proportion of Mexicans and Central Americans among immigrants rose, and so did the earnings gap – Mexican and Central American immigrant men had 25–40 per cent lower earnings than similar US-born men in 1970, and 50 per cent lower earnings in 1990. Instead of catching up to Americans in earnings, Borjas concluded that immigration could expand the low-income population.[32]

Feasibility

The number of guest worker programmes is increasing, with most targeted at providing migrant workers to particular niche labour markets – farm workers, seasonal hotels and restaurants and construction, for example. Most of these new programmes are unilateral, begun and administered by the labour-receiving country, and demand for migrants in these micro guest worker programmes is generally unaffected by larger economic trends. Levies and refunds to align employer and worker incentives with programme rules can minimise distortion and dependence.

Making the transition from the current widespread employment of irregular workers to a world of legal migrants may be the most difficult challenge. Experience shows that, in a world of growing inequality, it is hard to avoid sending the signal that there are brighter lights over the border, so that many policy actions in receiving countries are accompanied by more irregular migration. The obvious solution would be for the '3Rs' to

---

[31] The immigrant men were compared to US-born men of the same age and education (Chiswick 1978).

[32] Between 1970 and 1990, the proportion of the US male labour force who had not completed high school by age 25 fell from about 40 per cent to 15 per cent, while the proportion of immigrants without a high-school diploma fell only from 48 per cent to 37 per cent.

accelerate economic development so that emigration pressures decline over time.

Migration for Development

Identification and Description

Migration can be a tool for development, and development can affect migration patterns. Migration can speed up development if the '3 Rs' accelerate job and economic growth, while development can increase emigration if opening a previously closed economy to trade and changing economic policies to deregulate and privatise displaces workers in previously protected sectors. The result of freer trade can be a 'migration hump', or temporarily more migration in the short term, even as the stage is set for less migration in the long term.

Development should reduce economically motivated international migration by reducing its 'root causes'. These root causes are many and complex but, in contrast to studies of trade, investment and aid and their relationship to development, 'migration is the most under-researched of the global flows' (World Bank 2002, 82). Economists generally view voluntary migration as an investment: most migrants make sacrifices now in the hope that they and their families will have a better future in another place. Individuals who move voluntarily are better off, as are the employers abroad who hire them. The issue is whether individual and employer benefits spread to sending and receiving societies, and by how much.

There is a large and growing stock of migrants and a new interest in so-called Diaspora-led development, or using the '3 Rs' to narrow differences between sending and receiving countries. The second half of the challenge is development and

migration – how to manage migration cooperatively during the 'migration hump,' so that the prospect of unwanted migration does not slow economic integration. Concretely, the challenge is how to have more examples of NAFTA-type agreements, with the US government arguing that economic integration with Mexico would eventually reduce unauthorised migration, and fewer Turkey–EU dilemmas, in which fears of mass migration slow economic integration.

Alleviation of the Challenge

The current focus of migration research and policy is make better use of the '3 Rs' among the world's 175 m migrants to accelerate development in the migrants' countries of origin. The challenge is how to ensure that economically motivated migration in fact benefits migrant countries of origin, but most of the literature deals with with the 'architecture' of the international migration system rather than how to ensure that migration reduces inequalities between nation states. The most common prescription is for a World Migration Organization (WMO) to develop a 'new international regime for the orderly movements of people'(Ghosh 2000, 6).[33] Bhagwati (2003b) says that a WMO 'might realistically begin to fill the last remaining gap in the institutional architecture that covers our interdependent world'.

The WMO is meant to be an analogue to the World Trade Organization (WTO), and implicit in most recommendations for a WMO is the suggestion that, just as the WTO is credited with freeing trade, so a WMO could set rules that increase migration. However, there is no clear theoretical basis for more migration, or even a consensus on a theoretical framework to estimate an optimal level of migration. Thus, how can the development impacts of current levels of migration be maximised? The three major aspects of the migration process are recruitment, remittances and returns. Recruitment refers to who emigrates, and the concern is that if the best and brightest of a poor country's brains and brawn emigrate, economic development in countries of origin may be slowed. There is no easy answer to the recruitment dilemma, since employers in higher-wage countries want to hire the best workers, who are also the most likely to

[33] Ghosh calls for 'regulated openness' with participating countries sharing 'common objectives', a 'harmonized normative framework', and a 'monitoring mechanism' Ghosh 2000, 227). Regulated openness, according to Ghosh, means that migration policies should be comprehensive, transparent and predictable, should not alter the existing refugee regime, and should facilitate the migration that accompanies increasing trade in services (2000, 222–4). Ghosh lays out the three pillars of the new regime (2000, 227) – shared objectives, harmonised goals and new institutions – but does not specify what they would be.

be useful to the development of their countries of origin.

The keys to resolving the recruitment dilemma when professionals emigrate lie in remittances and some form of compensation to replenish the human capital that moves over borders. Maximising the benefits of unskilled migrants, on the other hand, rests on promoting remittances and returns. There is almost unanimous agreement that developing country efforts to restrict the emigration of all or some 'key workers' are not likely to be effective. However, if migrants moved over borders under bilateral agreements, and if employment services in sending and receiving countries could match workers and employers, there would be a potential for government services to substitute for the current migration infrastructure, which includes smugglers and traffickers.

Remittances from migrants abroad,[34] and the return of migrants with new skills and ideas, can help launch economic take-offs in the regions and countries from which migrants come. Meanwhile, new or strengthened 'people connections' or transnational communities can also facilitate trade and investment. Remittances, the portion of migrant incomes abroad that are sent home, can reduce poverty and reduce incentives to migrate. Remittances have risen with number of migrants, and surpassed ODA in developing countries in the mid-1990s.

Remittances to developing countries more than doubled between the late 1980s and the late 1990s, after experiencing drops in 1991 (Gulf War) and in 1998 (Asian Financial Crisis). Remittances surpassed ODA in the mid-1990s, and surged after 2000, perhaps reflecting a higher percentage of migrant savings transferred via the banking system as the costs of bank transfers fell and the 11 September 2001 terrorism curtailed informal transfer systems. Banks have begun to compete aggressively for the relatively high margin business of transferring funds in relatively small sums over borders, which should reduce transfer costs over time (figure 8.2).[35]

A handful of developing countries receive most remittances. The three largest recipients, India, Mexico and the Philippines, received a third of remittances in recent years, and the top six countries

(these three plus Morocco, Egypt-and Turkey) received half of all remittances to developing countries. Remittances are most important in smaller and island nations, where they can be equivalent to 20–40 per cent of GDP (in 2001, remittances were 37 per cent of GDP in Tonga, 26 per cent in Lesotho, 23 per cent in Jordan, and 15–17 per cent in Albania, Nicaragua, Yemen and Moldova). The major sources of remittances were the USA ($28 bn in 2001), Saudi Arabia ($15 bn) and Germany, Belgium and Switzerland ($8 bn each) (table 8.7).

The World Bank's *Global Development Finance* (GDF) report estimated that remittances to developing countries reached $80 bn in 2002 and emphasised two issues: how to increase the *access of workers to official banking channels*, which can allow governments to borrow against expected remittances,[36] as well as how to lower fees, which average 13 per cent of the amount transferred; and how to increase the *development impact of remittance spending* in the areas that receive it. Many countries are taking steps to make it easier for migrants to open bank accounts, which has the side effect of increasing competition in the money transfer business, a sector with high fixed and low marginal costs. Research to maximise the development impacts of remittances is in its infancy.

Studies demonstrate convincingly that the best way to maximise the volume of remittances is to

[34] The IMF estimates remittances for each country, and publishes them in its *Balance of Payments Statistics Yearbook* under several categories. The two major categories are worker remittances, which are the wages and salaries that are sent home by migrants abroad for twelve or more months and listed under current transfers, and compensation of employees (called labour income until 1995), which are the wages and benefits of migrants abroad for less than twelve months and included as income in a country's current account. Many countries do not know how long the migrants remitting funds have been abroad, so most analyses combine workers remittances and compensation of employees. For example, Mexico reports under worker remittances, while the Philippines reports under compensation of employees.

[35] Ratha (2003, 165), reports that the average remittance to Latin America is $200, and that transfer fees range from 13 to 20 per cent.

[36] When the risk premium for borrowing funds abroad is very high, some countries have been able to float bonds secured by the anticipated future flow of remittances, as Brazil did in 2001.

Table 8.7. Remittances to Selected Countries, 1995–2001

	1995	1996	1997	1998	1999	2000	2001
Developing countries ($bn)	48	53	63	60	65	65	72
India	6.2	8.8	10.3	9.5	11.1	9.2	10
Mexico	4.4	5	5.5	6.5	6.6	7.6	9.9
Philippines	5.4	4.9	6.8	5.1	6.9	6.2	6.4
Morocco	2	2.2	1.9	2	1.9	2.2	3.3
Egypt	3.2	3.1	3.7	3.4	3.2	2.9	2.9
Turkey	3.3	3.5	4.2	5.4	4.5	4.6	2.8
Sub-total	**24.5**	**27.5**	**32.4**	**31.9**	**34.2**	**32.7**	**35.3**
Share of total (%)							
India	13	17	16	16	17	14	14
Mexico	9	10	9	11	10	12	14
Philippines	11	9	11	9	11	10	9
Morocco	4	4	3	3	3	3	5
Egypt	7	6	6	6	5	4	4
Turkey	7	7	7	9	7	7	4
'Big 6' share	**51**	**52**	**52**	**54**	**53**	**51**	**49**

Source: www.worldbank.org/prospects/gdf2003/gdf_statApp_web.pdf (p. 198).

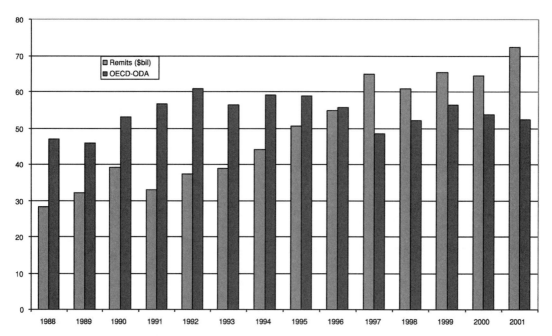

Figure 8.2. *Remittances and ODA to developing countries, 1988–2001, $ bn*
Source: IMF and OECD.

have appropriate *exchange rate and economic policies* that promise growth (Ratha 2003). Regardless of how much migrants remit, since the 11 September 2001 terrorism attacks many governments have tried to reduce transfer through informal channels and shift them to formal channels, such as via banks. Migrants have demonstrated a willingness to transfer money via official channels, especially if it is easy and cheap to so, but this usually requires banking outlets in migrant communities at home and abroad and competition to lower transfer costs.

There has been considerable progress on both fronts in some areas. In one of the largest transfer markets, that between the USA and Mexico, there were 25 million consumer money transfers in 2000, averaging about $300 each, and the Mexican government has been very active in increasing access to formal banking channels and lowering the cost of transferring funds.[37] Costs and services associated with the transfer vary widely. For example, on 23 April 2001, when the interbank exchange rate was $1 = 9.3 pesos, the fee charged by most money transfer firms in Los Angeles was $8–$15 and the exchange rate varied from 8.9 to 9.2 pesos per dollar, making the total costs of transferring $300 range from $5 to $20, or 2–7 per cent. Western Union, the largest firm, had two services, each with different charges, while Moneygram, the second-largest transfer firm, also had two services with different fees. Several of the transfer services offer a free three-minute telephone call so that those who send funds can advise the recipient.

The US–Mexico remittance market is unregulated, in the sense that Mexicans in the USA decide how and how much to remit. Several Asian countries, by contrast, have specified both the amount of remittances migrants must send and the form in which they are remitted. For example, many Korean migrants in the Middle East in the late 1970s and early 1980s were considered employees of their Korean construction company, and had their Korean currency earnings sent to their families in Korea while receiving a stipend in local currency abroad. Many Chinese and Vietnamese migrants today go abroad as employees of Chinese and Vietnamese firms, and their wages are paid in a similar way – most go to the migrant's family or bank account in

local currency. The Philippines, in a policy unpopular with migrants, attempted to specify how much should be remitted in the 1980s, but later abandoned the policy.

Remittances can reduce poverty and improve the lives of recipients, and can also accelerate development that reduces poverty for non-migrants. Most remittances are used for consumption, helping to explain their stability[38] even as exchange rates and investment outlooks change.[39] In an effort to, *inter alia*, attract remittances, many developing countries made their exchange rates more realistic in the 1990s, and presidents in Mexico and the Philippines acknowledged the important contributions that remittances make to development.[40] Automatic stabilisers in developed countries, such as unemployment insurance, help to stabilise the flow of remittances to developing countries (even jobless migrants sometimes remit), and can help to stabilise economies in migrant sending and receiving countries if they are at the same point in the economic cycle.

Remittances clearly improve the lives of the households that receive them, and can also improve the lives of non-migrant neighbours as they are spent, creating jobs via multiplier effects. Most studies suggest that each $1 in remittances generates a $2–$3 increase in local GDP, as recipients buy locally produced goods and services (Taylor

[37] Since December 1998, Mexico's federal consumer protection agency, Profeco, has compared the cost of transferring $300 from the USA to Mexico weekly in six US cities: Chicago, Los Angeles, New York, Dallas, Miami and Houston, http://www.profeco.gob.mx/enviodinero/ enviomnu.htm. The costs vary by city or origin and destination, as well as by the services provided with the transfer.

[38] Automatic stabilisers in developed countries, such as unemployment insurance, help to stabilise the flow of remittances to developing countries that have the same economic cycles as the countries in which their migrants work.

[39] Ratha (2003) noted that remittances to high-debt and less-transparent countries were more stable than those to middle-income open economies, because the latter included more remittances destined for investment.

[40] The World Bank's 2003 *Global Development Finance* speculated that remittances to high-debt and less-transparent countries tend to be more stable than those to middle-income open economies because the latter include more remittances destined for investment, and investment remittances fluctuate with variables such as interest rates and exchange rates.

and Adelman 1996). A study of seventy-four low- and middle-income developing countries found that a 10 per cent increase in the share of remittances in a country's GDP was associated with a 1.2 per cent decline in the share of people living on less than $1 per person per day (Adams and Page 2003).

Classical theories of migration suggested that the emigration of men in the prime of their working lives would reduce economic output in migrant areas of origin, or leave it unchanged in Lewis-type economic development models.[41] Empirical research suggests that, while emigration may initially reduce output in local economies, remittances can lead to adjustments that maintain output, as when migrant families shift from crops to less labour-intensive livestock or hire labour to continue to produce crops. If agricultural productivity in migrant areas of origin has been constrained by the unavailability of credit to buy machinery or construct irrigation, the remittances from migration can overcome the missing credit market constraint.

Remittances have many other effects in the communities in which they arrive. A very visible effect of remittances is to allow families receiving them to build or improve their housing. Many migrant families build more housing than they need,

introducing rental housing in areas that previously had none, a development that with socio-economic consequences, as when newlyweds began to live away from in-laws in rural Turkey as rental housing became available (Martin 1991). Women often assume new roles in the absence of migrant husbands, and some became moneylenders in their villages, a remarkable change in often traditional areas. There is a growing literature on the risk and relativity of remittances, as when a farmer is more likely to try planting new seeds or crops if he is receiving remittances from abroad that will cushion crop failure, or emphasising that, with one family using remittances to buy a TV and satellite dish, there is pressure on other families to keep pace.

The third 'R' in the migration and development equation is returns. Ideally, migrants who have been abroad provide the energy, ideas and entrepreneurial vigour needed to start or expand businesses at home. Migrants are generally drawn from the ranks of the risk takers at home, and if their new capital is combined with risk taking behaviour, the result can be a new push for economic development. On the other hand, if migrants settle abroad and cut ties to their countries or origin, or if they return only to rest and retire, there may be limited development impacts of returning migrants. There is also the possibility of back-and-forth circulation, which can under some conditions contribute to economic growth in both countries.

There are several cases of Diaspora-led development,[42] sometimes fostered by government programmes and policies that planted the seeds that led to the return of migrants and investment and job creation at home. For example, Taiwan invested most of its educational resources in primary and secondary education in the 1970s, so Taiwanese seeking higher education often went abroad for study, and over 90 per cent remained overseas despite rapid economic growth in Taiwan.[43] During the 1980s, even before the end of martial law, more Taiwanese graduates began to return, while others maintained 'homes' in North America and spent so much time commuting that they were called 'astronauts' because they spent so much time on planes.

The Taiwanese government made a major effort to attract home professional migrants, establishing

[41] Lewis (1954) assumed that the traditional agricultural sector of developing countries had an unlimited supply of labour that could be absorbed in an expanding modern industrial sector with no loss of farm output. Ranis and Fei (1961) extended the Lewis model so that, once the marginal product of labour and wages are equal in the traditional and modern sector, rural–urban migration stops; Johnson (1967) noted that rural–urban migrants could take capital with them. Todaro (1969) took a micro perspective, showing that rural and urban wages did not converge as expected in Lewis-style models because, with high and rigid urban wages, rural migrants continued to pour into cities despite high unemployment because their expected earnings (higher wages times the probability of employment) were higher in the cities. Todaro argued that the solution to unwanted rural–urban migration was urban wage subsidies and migration restrictions; Bhagwati and Srinivasan (1974) showed that tax and subsidy schemes could yield optimal migration levels without migration restrictions.

[42] 'Diaspora' is a Greek word first applied to Jews dispersed outside of Israel in the 6th century BC, after Nebuchadnezzar of Babylon destroyed the first Jewish temple.

[43] These students were highly motivated to pursue advanced studies. Before they could go abroad, they had to complete two years of military service and obtain private or overseas financing.

the Hinschu Science-Based Industrial Park (HSIP) in 1980 with the goal of creating a concentration of creative expertise as in Silicon Valley. The government provided financial incentives for high-tech businesses to locate in Hinschu, including subsidized Western-style housing (Luo and Wang 2002). By 2000, the park was a major success, employing over 100,000 workers in 300 companies that had sales of $28 bn. About 40 per cent of the companies were headed by returned overseas migrants, and 10 per cent of the 4,100 returned migrants employed in the park had PhD degrees.

The Taiwanese experience suggests that investing heavily in the type of education appropriate to the stage of economic development, and then tapping the 'brain reserves overseas' when the country's economy demands more brainpower can be a very successful development strategy. Chinese leader Premier Zhao Ziyang seemed to approve this strategy when he called Chinese abroad 'stored brainpower overseas', and encouraged Chinese cities to offer financial subsidies to attract them home, prompting the creation of 'Returning Student Entrepreneur Buildings'.[44] However, most Chinese who studied abroad remain abroad: 580,000 went abroad since 1979, but only 25 per cent had returned by 2002.

The poorest countries pose the largest return challenges. The International Organisation for Migration (IOM) operates a return-of-talent programme for professional Africans abroad, providing them with travel and housing assistance and wage subsidies if they sign two-year contracts that require them to work in the public sector of their country of origin. The United Nations Development Program (UNDP) has a similar Transfer of Knowledge Through Expatriate Nationals (TOKTEN) programme that subsidises the return of teachers and researchers.

However, most professionals under these programmes have an immigrant or long-term secure status abroad, and are in their country of origin only while receiving the subsidy. Subsidising the return of African professionals is expensive, prompting Sussex University's Richard Black to call subsidised return-of-talent programmes 'expensive failures', since they bring temporary return, but not the 'investment that [return] should bring'.[45]

Side Effects and Uncertainties

If migration is to be a tool for more rapid development, economically motivated migration should decline over time. The keys to more rapid development are globalisation to integrate economies into world markets and using markets to set prices and allocate scarce resources. But the same policies that can reduce economically motivated migration in the long run can increase it in the short run. This means that if there is a pre-existing migration link between areas with workers displaced by freer trade and labour markets abroad there can be a 'migration hump'. In a worst-case scenario, prospects for more migration can slow the integration necessary for faster growth.

The 'migration hump' is pictured in figure 8.3, where the straight line represents the status quo migration flow and the 'hump' line depicts the volume of migration – first rising and then falling. The number of migrants is on the Y-axis and time is on the X-axis, and the additional migration associated with economic integration is represented by A. However, the economic and job growth that economic integration facilitates leads to migration falling to the status quo level at B. C represents the migration avoided by economic integration and D represents the previously emigration country being a destination for migrants. The critical policy parameters are A, B, and C – how much additional migration results from economic integration (A), how soon does migration return to the status quo level (B), and how much migration is avoided by economic integration and other changes (C)?

The US Commission for the Study of International Migration and Cooperative Economic Development concluded that '*expanded trade* between the sending countries and the United States *is the single most important remedy*' for unwanted migration (1990, xv, emphasis added). However, the Commission warned that 'the economic

---

[44] Shanghai reportedly has 30,000 returned professionals, 90 per cent with MS or PhD degrees earned abroad, who are employed or starting businesses (Jonathan Kaufman, China reforms bring back executives schooled in US, *Wall Street Journal*, 6 March 2003; Rone Tempest, China tries to woo its tech talent back home, *Los Angeles Times*, 25 November 2002).

[45] Quoted in Alan Beattie, Seeking consensus on the benefits of immigration, *Financial Times*, 22 July 2002, 9.

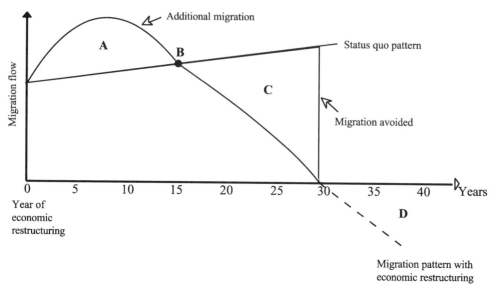

Figure 8.3. *The 'migration hump'*

development process itself tends in the short to medium term to *stimulate* migration'. This migration hump presents a 'a very real short-term versus long-term dilemma' for the USA when considering a free-trade agreement (FTA) billed as a long-term means to curb unauthorised immigration from Mexico (1990, xvi, emphasis added).

Martin (1993) examined NAFTA's likely impacts on Mexican and US agriculture, examining how 'demand-pull' factors in the USA and 'supply-push' factors in Mexico were likely evolve under NAFTA. He concluded that the flow of Mexicans to the USA, running at 200,000 settlers and 1–2 m sojourners a year in the early 1990s, would increase by 10–30 per cent for five–fifteen years, producing a 'hump' when Mexico–US migration was viewed over time. The upward slope of the 'hump' in the 1990s was due primarily to previous demographic growth and insufficient job growth in Mexico, as well as strong US demand for Mexican workers. The downward slope of the 'hump' was projected to occur when the number of new entrants to the Mexican labour market fell and economic growth created more and better-paid jobs in Mexico.

Fears of the migration 'hump' can slow the economic integration needed to accelerate development, as may be the case with Turkey's applica-

tion to join the EU. There are 3.5 m Turks living abroad, 5 per cent of persons born in Turkey, including 3 m in Europe. Turks are only partially integrated into many European societies, and there are fears that freedom of movement rights for Turks would lead to another wave of migration. Between 1961 and 1973, some 1.5–2 m Turks went abroad for employment, equivalent to 10–12 per cent of Turkey's 1970 workforce and 40 per cent of the Turkish men aged 20–39 in the Turkish workforce in 1970. Current estimates are that 20–30 per cent of Turkish youth would emigrate to seek higher wages in Europe if they could, although it is not clear how many would stay abroad if there were no jobs for them (Teitelbaum and Martin 2003).

The keys to minimise the size and duration of the migration 'hump' include careful phasing of policies that can promote displacement, and cooperation to manage any resulting migration. In the Mexico–US case, it is clear that it is far easier to displace workers in agriculture than to create new jobs for ex-farmers with foreign and local investment. Furthermore, the new jobs created may not be in areas with displaced workers, and displaced workers, may not be first in line to be hired even if there are jobs, as when male farmers are displaced but assembly-line factories prefer women. In some low-income countries, such as those in SSA, trade liberalisation alone can increase emigration pressures because the exchange rate falls, making overseas work more attractive (Faini, Grether and de Melo 1999).

There is another side effect of emigration that is rarely discussed. Migrants leave for many reasons, including because they have fundamental disagreements with their country's leaders. Diasporas can also finance civil wars and unrest, as in Sri Lanka and other countries (Collier 2000), so that migrant remittances can prevent the economic take-off needed for stay-at-home development.

Economic Evaluation

The new economics of labour migration moves the locus of migration decision making from individuals to families, and imagines families making decisions about who should emigrate in order to maximise family income, reduce risk and overcome constraints, such as absent markets for credit and insurance (Taylor and Martin 2001). Familial decision making is associated with sending some household members to domestic labour markets and some to foreign labour markets, as when households in rural Mexico send girls to *maquiladora*-type assembly plants and boys to the USA to work in agriculture, construction and services, for example.

Migrants tend to be positively selected from the general population with respect to human capital characteristics, and their exit can lead to a 'brain drain' that has effects similar to those of capital flight – that is, lower productivity and wages of complementary labour in migrant-sending areas. However, non-migrants can benefit from emigration if the remittances spent in the area at least equal to the value of the production migrants would have produced had they stayed behind (Djajic 1986). Emigration benefits all those who stay behind if it results in an overall increase in the capital–labour ratio within the migrant-sending economy (Wong 1983).

Instead of more migration, trade could be a substitute for migration, as occurred in countries such as Korea, that have gone through the migration transition from labour senders to receivers. Between 1950 and 2000, world GDP increased fourfold to $30 trillion, while world trade in goods increased

seventeenfold to $13 trillion, or 40 per cent of the value of global output.[46] Increased trade was stimulated by economic growth and reductions in the average tariff on manufactured goods, from 40 per cent in 1950 to 4 per cent in 2000. Most global trade involves goods, which means that a good is produced in one country, taken over borders and consumed in another.

Trade and investment often seem to be the slow road to stay-at-home development, but there is no other path that promises sustained economic and job growth. The 'new globalizers', as the World Bank (2002) terms the Chinese and Indian states that attracted foreign investment to produce manufactured goods for export, have had the fastest rate of poverty reduction and often attract internal migrants. Thus, at least parts of developing countries with about 3 billion residents have experienced substantial poverty reduction as a result of trade and investment, but other developing countries with about 2 billion residents seem to be falling further behind, 'in danger of becoming marginal to the world economy' except as sources of migrants (World Bank 2002, x).

Migrant-receiving nations could reduce migration pressures by liberalising trade in farm commodities. The World Bank (2002, 131) asserted that 'Industrial countries spend more than $300 bn a year in agricultural subsidies, more than six times the amount they spend on foreign aid'. If developing countries had unrestricted access to industrial country markets, their GDPs would rise 5 per cent, according to the World Bank, versus the 1 per cent gain from remittances.

In most developing countries, 40–60 per cent of the labour force is employed in agriculture, and farm goods are a major export. Most migrant-receiving countries protect their farm sectors, generally by guaranteeing their farmers higher than world prices for the commodities they produce, and then sometimes donating or subsidising the sale of the surplus in world markets, which depresses world prices for farm commodities. Between the late 1980s and late 1990s, the producer support equivalent (PSE) level of subsidy for the farm sector

---

[46] Average world *per capita* GDP doubled from $2,500 to $5,000 per person per year between 1950 and 2000.

Table 8.8. ODA and Farm Subsidies, 1990s

	ODA($bn) (2000)	Farm support (PSE $bn)	
		(1999)	(1986–88)
DAC/OECD	56	252	221
US	10	54	42
Japan	13	59	54
EU	28	114	95

Notes: DAC = Development Assistance Committee, member of the OECD.
PSE = producer support equivalent.
PSE = the value of transfers from taxpayers (payments) and consumers (higher prices) to farmers.
Source: OECD *data*.

in the USA, Japan and the EU rose from about four times ODA to five times ODA. In the late 1990s, when global exports of manufactured goods were about $3.5 trillion a year, global exports of farm goods were less than $500 bn a year, including a third from developing countries (table 8.8).[47]

Feasibility

Most of the world's workers are in lower-wage developing countries. The industrial countries, with 12 per cent of the world's workers and 60 per cent of the world's migrants, have labour forces that would shrink without immigration. The movement of migrants from south to north seems like a natural fit, but the question is whether south–north migration will speed or slow the convergence of wages that will bring the end to large-scale migration that governments in the south and north desire. The question is how to overcome fears of out-of-control migration in industrial countries that may slow the economic integration that fosters stay-at-home development. For example, here is little doubt that the presence of partially integrated Turks in Europe has made some EU countries reluctant to embrace full Turkish entry into the EU, and the US justified intervention in Haiti in 1994 to slow emigration to the USA.

[47] Another comparison is with global arms sales, some $26 bn in 2001, down from $40 bn in 2000. About two-thirds of global arms sales are to developing countries – they bought an average of $20–$22 bn worth of arms a year in the 1990s.

From the perspective of the industrial countries, the starting point must include more effective policies to reduce unauthorised migration and guest worker programmes that minimise distortion and dependence. Once such policies are in place, industrial countries are more likely to open doors to legal migrants, and cooperation between sending and receiving countries can set the stage for cooperative efforts to use the '3Rs' to reduce migration pressures over time.

Conclusions

Migration is as old as humans wandering in search of food, but regulated international migration is a relatively recent phenomenon: it was only in the early twentieth century that a system of passports and visas developed to regulate the flow of people across the borders of nation-states. International migration was widespread across the Atlantic before the First World War and government regulation reduced it, and international migration did not resume across the Atlantic in the 1950s and 1960s because economic convergence made economically motivated migration unnecessary. Fast-growing European countries instead recruited guest workers from southern Europe, many of whom settled. Most migrants move from lower- to higher-wage areas and achieve higher incomes, and the sum of these individual gains increases global GDP. Immigrant-receiving countries also receive a small immigration dividend which, for the USA in the mid-1990s, when about 10 per cent of workers were migrants, was estimated to be 0.1 of 1 per cent, or equivalent to about two weeks of normal economic growth.

The migration challenge is how to use existing migration flows to *reduce inequalities and thus migration pressures* in a globalising world. Many of the potential economic gains from migration are not realised, largely because the richer countries to which migrants want to move are raising their border controls in the face of fears that range from terrorism to the association of some migrants and their children with high rates of unemployment and welfare dependency. Most economic analyses suggest

Table 8.9. Migration: Economic Impacts, 2001 data

Countries	World	Low	Middle	High
Population (m)	6,133	2,511	2,667	955
Ave GDP($/year)	5,140	430	1,850	26,710
Total GDP ($bn)	31,500	1,069	4,922	25,506
Moving 100 million people from low to high, same *per capita* averages				
Population (m)		2,411		1,055
Ave GDP($/year)	5,566	430		26,710
Total GDP ($bn)	34,138	1,037		28,179
Change in ave/tot GDP%	8			
Moving 10 million people from low to high, same *per capita* averages				
Population (m)		2,501		965
Ave GDP($/year)	5,706	430		26,710
Total GDP ($bn)	31,760	1,065		25,773
Change in ave/tot GDP (%)	1			

Source: World Bank and own calculations.

that the economic costs of immigration in the form of lower wages, higher unemployment, or higher social welfare costs in receiving countries are easy to overestimate, but it is harder to assess the costs of terrorism or the costs of diversity, as when current residents fear that 'different' newcomers will change local languages and cultures.[48]

Migration Benefits

Disagreements on which items associated with migration are benefits and which are costs, and the complexity assessing potential costs such as terrorism, make it very hard to conduct a CBA exercise on migration. The exercise in table 8.9 is illustrative of the gains that could be realised from more migration. For example, doubling the number of migrants in the rich countries *if there were no change in GDP per capita in sending and receiving countries as a result of the migration* could increase global GDP by $2.6 trillion or 8 per cent, with all of the gain in the high-income countries.[49]

This economic gain in the high-income countries is immediate as they get jobs, measurable in higher earnings and a larger GDP, and concentrated in the hands of migrants and the local owners of capital. More realistic migration numbers, and efforts to take account of costs, would lower these economic gains. The movement of 10 m migrants, for example, would raise world GDP by $260 bn or 1 per cent, which is smaller but still almost five times the annual amount of ODA.[50]

The costs of migration tend to be deferred, especially if the first migrants are workers whose families arrive later. Nation-states have been likened to redistributive clubs, so that 'affluent and free countries are, like elite universities, besieged by applicants . . . as citizens of such a country, we have to decide: whom should we admit?' (Walzer 1983, 32). Costs, and perceptions of costs, rise with economic and non-economic factors, including unemployment and 'differences' between newcomers and established residents. Costs also tend to be dispersed widely and are much harder to measure; there can easily be disagreement over whether 'increased diversity' should be considered a benefit or cost.

Most of the gains of economically motivated migration accrue to migrants in the countries of destination, which raises the question of how and how much of these economic benefits to share with countries of origin. This chapter assumes that labour-sending and labour-receiving nation-states have legitimate interests in the economic consequences of migration. Instead of attempting to restrict emigration, it seems better to allow and in some cases facilitate emigration, but labour-receiving and labour-sending nations also need to cooperate to ensure that the '3Rs' maximise the benefits of migration for countries of origin.

---

[48] In one sense, the case for more migration is very analogous to the case for free trade – that is, overcoming the tendency of losing producers and their supporters to organise, and for winning producers and their supporters to attribute their success to their own abilities, not to freer trade (Summers 1999, 9).

[49] If an additional 100 m migrants moved from low- to high-income countries, and they on average gained $26,280 a year, the difference between average *per capita* GDPs in low and high income countries in 2001, the world's GDP would rise by $2.6 trillion or 8 per cent.

[50] The benefits of migration tend to fall over time if migration accelerates convergence between rich and poor countries.

Benefit-Cost Analysis

The major challenge in destination countries is to open entry doors wider, which means overcoming obstacles to more migration by selecting settlers or immigrants in systems that ensure their economic success and ensuring that guest workers and their employers have incentives to behave in accordance with rotation rules. Overcoming opposition to migration in destination countries does not lend itself readily to CBA, unless one assumes that more studies and education can convince sceptical publics that the migration they oppose is good for them.

A typical CBA asks whether a particular government intervention will be worthwhile – will a government-built dam generate more benefits than costs. In such analyses, costs usually come first and are relatively easy to measure, and the major challenge is to measure benefits, determine when they will occur and use an appropriate discount rate to compare costs and benefits. Migration poses different challenges – the benefits usually come first and are more readily measurable, while the costs come later and are far more difficult to measure. This makes it very hard to find an appropriate discount rate and to compare benefits and costs.

Suppose we take the simple approach of summing net individual gains to obtain the global gain from more migration, so that the global gain is simply the individual gain times the number of migrants. In such a scenario, gains very quickly mount unless benefits fall, as might be expected if there is a convergence in incomes. For example, if 1,000 migrants move and have no impacts on incomes in sending or receiving countries, and each experiences an income gain of $25,000, the aggregate gain is $25 m. However, if 10,000 migants move, the net gain may fall to $20,000; the total gain is greater at $200 m, but the gain per migrant falls with more migration (table 8.10).

The hard question in a migration CBA is *costs*. Do migration-related costs increase with migrant numbers because of difficulties in integrating more newcomers, or do they decrease with numbers

Table 8.10. Benefits and Costs of More Migration

Number	Net Individ. gain ($)	Aggregate gain ($)
1,000	25,000	25,000,000
10,000	20,000	200,000,000
100,000	15,000	1,500,000,000
1,000,000	10,000	10,000,000,000

Source: See text discussion.

because there are economies of scale in providing services to newcomers, or because the ambitions that motivated migration inject new entrepreneurial spirits into host countries?

If we assess costs according to opinion polls, the costs of migration appear high. For example, US public opinion surveys conducted between 1965 and 1993 consistently found that a majority of Americans wanted both legal and illegal immigration reduced, and fewer than 10 per cent of agreed that immigration should be increased (Simon 1989, 350).[51] Perhaps more striking is the gap between elites and masses: a summer 2002 US poll found that 55 per cent of the public believed legal immigration should be reduced, compared to 18 per cent of opinion leaders (Chicago Council on Foreign Relations 2002). There is no easy way to quantify the costs of migration perceived by the public, which makes it hard to reduce them. However, the unique aspect of migration as a global challenge is that *benefits exceed costs* as long as there is voluntary movement.

Prioritising Migration

Migration is playing out on a global stage in which demographic, economic and security differences are widening between many nation-states, encouraging more economically motivated migration. The challenge and opportunity is to manage the migration that is occurring, and the additional migration that could occur, in a manner that reduces these differences, and so that convergence between nation-states reduces migration over time.

Lowering migration barriers should rank very high on the global agenda. Most studies suggest

[51] The year 1953 was the only year in which more than 10 per cent of Americans favoured increasing immigration.

Table 8.11. Migration Benefits and Costs: A Summary

Opportunity	Benefit	Cost	BCR	Remarks
Select successful migrants	Open wider/new entry channels for migrants	Distortion in receiving/ brain drain in sending	Depends on numbers and extent of distortion etc.	
Guest workers	Open wider/new entry channels for migrants	Distortion in receiving/ dependence in sending	Depends on numbers and abilities of levies/refunds to align incentives/rules	
Migration for development	Convergence between nation-states that reduces migration pressures over time	May need changes in policy in both sending and receiving countries		

that the economic benefits of more migration are very high, and the costs are low. The trick is to lower resistance to more migration in destination countries, which can be accomplished by:

- *Selecting migrants* in a manner that ensures they will be successful, and then compensating their countries of origin so that inequalities between countries are reduced
- Opening wider channels for *less skilled migrants* by using economic instruments to align the incentives of employers and migrants with guest worker programme rules
- Ensuring that the '3 Rs' narrow economic differences between sending and receiving areas (table 8.11).

References

Adams, R. and J. Page, 2003: International migration, remittances and poverty in developing countries, World Bank, Working Paper, 3179

Beine, M., F. Docquier and H. Rapoport, 2001: Brain drain and economic growth: theory and evidence, *Journal of Development Economics*, **64**(1), 275–89

Bhagwati J. N. (ed.), 1976: *The brain drain and taxation: theory and empirical analysis*, North-Holland, Amsterdam

2003a: Borders beyond control, *Foreign Affairs*, **82**(1), 98–104

2003b: The world needs a new body to monitor migration, *Financial Times*, 24 October

Bhagwati, J. N. and M. Partington (eds.), 1976: *Taxing the brain drain: a proposal*, North-Holland, Amsterdam

Bhagwati, J. N. and T. N. Srinivasan, 1974: On reanalyzing the Harris–Todaro model: policy rankings in the case of sector-specific sticky wages, *American Economic Review*, **64**(3), 502–8

Borjas, G. J., 1990: *Friends or strangers: the impact of immigrants on the US economy*, Basic Books, New York

1994: The economics of immigration, *Journal of Economic Literature*, **32**(4), 1167–77

2001: *Heaven's door: immigration policy and the American economy*, Princeton University Press, Princeton

2003: The labour demand curve is downward sloping: reexamining the impact of immigration on the labour market, *Quarterly Journal of Economics*, November, 1335–74

Card, D., 1990: The impact of the Mariel boatlift on the Miami labour market, *Industrial and Labour Relations Review*, **43**, 245–57

Castles, S. and M. Miller, 2003: *The age of migration: international population movements in the modern world*, Guilford Press, New York

Chicago Council on Foreign Relations, 2002: World views, www.worldviews.org/ detailreports/usreport/html/ch5s5.html

Chiswick, B., 1978: The effect of Americanization on the earnings of foreign-born men, *Journal of Political Economy*, **86**, 897–921

Citizenship and Immigration Canada (CIC), 2002: Facts and figures: immigration, www.cic.gc.ca/english/pub/index-2.html# statistics

Collier, P., 2000: Economic causes of civil conflict and their implications for policy, World Bank; see chapter 3 in this volume

Cornelius, W. P. Martin and J. Hollifield (eds.), 2004: *Controlling immigration: a global*

perspective, Stanford University Press, Stanford, CA, www.sup.org

Council of Economic Advisors (CEA), 1986: *The economic effects of immigration*, Council of Economic Advisors, Washington, DC

Djajic, S., 1986: International migration, remittances and welfare in a dependent economy, *Journal of Development Economics*, 21, 229–34

Economist, 2002: Do developing countries gain or lose when their brightest talents go abroad?, 26 September

Ellerman, D., 2003: Policy research on migration and development, World Bank, Mimeo

Faini, R. G. J. M. and J. de Melo, 1999: Globalization and migratory pressures from developing countries: a simulation analysis, in R. Faini, J. de Melo and K. F. Zimmermann (eds.), *Migration: the controversies and the evidence*, Cambridge University Press, Cambridge

Feenstra, R., 1998: Integration of trade and disintegration of production in the global economy, *Journal of Economic Perspectives*, **12**(4), 31–50

Frey, W., 1994: The new white flight, *American Demographics*, April, 40–8

General Accounting Office (GAO), 1988: Illegal aliens: influence of illegal workers on the wages and working conditions of legal workers, General Accounting Office, PEMD-88-13BR, Washington, DC

Ghosh, B. (ed.), 2000: *Managing migration: time for a new international regime?*, Oxford University Press, Oxford

Grubel, H. and A. Scott, 1966: The international flow of human capital, *American Economic Review*, **56**(1/2), 268–74

Hamilton, B. and J. Whalley, 1984: Efficiency and distributional implications of global restrictions on labour mobility, *Journal of Development Economics*, 14, 61–75

Hönekopp, E., 1990: *Zur beruflichen und sozialen reintegration türkischer Arbeitsmigranten in Zeitverlauf*, Bundesanstalt für Arbeit, Institut für Arbeitsmarkt und Berufsforschung, Naremberg

IOM, 2003: *World migration 2003: managing migration – challenges and responses for* people on the move, www.iom.int/en/archive/pr861_en.shtml

Johnson, H. G., 1967: Some economic aspects of the brain drain, *Pakistani Development Review* 7, 379–411

1968: An 'internationalist' model, in W. Adams, (ed.), *The brain drain*, Macmillan, New York, 69–91

1972: Labor mobility and the brain drain, in G. Ranis (ed.), *The gap between rich and poor nations*, Macmillan, London

Lewis, W. A., 1954: Economic development with unlimited supplies of labour, *Manchester School of Economic and Social Studies*, **22**, 139–91

Luo, Y.-L. and W.-J. Wang, 2002: High-skill migration and Cluaese Taipei's industrial development, in OECD, *International mobility of the highly skilled*, OECD, Paris

Martin, P. L., 1991: The unfinished story: Turkish labour migration to Western Europe, with special reference to the Federal Republic of Germany, International Labour Office, Geneva

1993: Trade and migration: NAFTA and agriculture, Institute for International Economics, Washington, DC

2003: Bordering on control: a comparison of measures to combat irregular migration in North America and Europe, International Organization for Migration, Geneva, http://www.iom.ch/iomwebsite/Publication/ServletSearch Publication?event=detail&id=2251

Martin, P. and A. L. Olmstead, 1985: The agricultural mechanization controversy, *Science*, **227**(4687), 601–6

Massey, D. S., J. Arango, G. Hugo, A. Kouaouci, A. Pellegrino and J. E. Taylor, 1998: *Worlds in motion: understanding international migration at the end of the millennium*, Oxford University Press, New York

Mattoo, A. and A. Carzaniga, (eds.), 2002: *Moving people to deliver services: labour mobility and the WTO*, World Bank and Oxford University Press, Oxford

Migration News, monthly since 1994: http://migration.ucdavis.edu

Mines, R. and P. L. Martin, 1984: Immigrant workers and the California citrus industry, *Industrial Relations*, **23**(1), 139–49

Mountford, A., 1997: Can a brain drain be good for growth in the source economy?, *Journal of Development Economics*, **52**(2), 287–303

OECD, 2000: *Globalization, Migration, and Development*, OECD, Paris

2002: *International mobility of the highly skilled: from statistical analysis to the formulation of policies*. OECD, Paris annual: *Trends in International Migration*, OCED, Paris, www.oecd.org

Patinkin, D., 1968: A 'nationalist' model, in W. Adams (ed.), *The brain drain*, Macmillan, New York, 92–108

Ranis, G. and J. C. H. Fei, 1961: A theory of economic development, *American Economic Review*, **51**, 533–65

Ratrha, D. 2003: Workers' remittances: an important and stable source of external development finance, in *Global Development Finance 2003*, World Bank, Washington, DC

Simon, J., 1989: *The economic consequences of immigration*, Blackwell, New York

Skeldon, R., 1997: *Migration and development: a global perspective*, Addison-Wesley, Reading, MA

Smith, J. and B. Edmonston (eds.), 1997: *The new Americans: economic, demographic, and fiscal effects of immigration*, National Research Council, Washington, DC

Stalker, P., 2000: *Workers without frontiers: the impact of globalization on international migration*, Lynne Rienner, Balder, CO

Straubhaar, T., 2000: International mobility of the highly skilled: brain gain, brain drain or brain exchange, HWWA Discussion Paper, 88

Summers, L., 1999: Reflections on managing global integration, *Journal of Economic Perspectives*, **13**(2), 3–18

Taylor, J. E. and I. Adelman, 1996: *Village economies: the design, estimation and application of village-wide economic models*, Cambridge University Press, Cambridge

Taylor, J. E. and P. L. Martin, 2001: Human capital: migration and rural population change, in Bruce Gardener and Gordon Rausser (eds.), *Handbook of Agricultural Economics*, V I, Elsevier Science, Amsterdam, http://www.elsevier.nl/

Tcha, M., 1996: Altruism and migration: evidence from Korea and the United States, *Economic Development and Cultural Change*, **44**, 859–78

Teitelbaum, M. S., 2003: Do we need more scientists?, *The Public Interest*, **153**, 40–53

Teitelbaum M. S., and P. L. Martin, 2003: Is Turkey ready for Europe?, *Foreign Affairs*, **82**(3), 97–111

Thorogood, D. and K. Winqvist, 2003: Women and men migrating to and from the European Union, Eurostat, *Statistics in Focus* 2/2003

Todaro, M. P., 1969: A model of migration and urban unemployment in less-developed countries, *American Economic Review*, **59**, 138–48

UNHCR, 2003: *Refugees by numbers, 2003 edition*, UNHCR, Geneva, http://www.unhcr.ch

UN Population Division, 2002: *International Migration Report 2002*, ST/ESA/SER.A/220 www.un.org/Pubs/whatsnew/e03040.htm
  2003: *World Population Prospects*, esa.un.org/unpp/

US Commission for the Study of International Migration and Cooperative Economic Development, 1990: *Unauthorized migration: an economic development response*, Government Printing Office, Washington, DC

Van Hear, N. and N. Nyberg Sorensen (eds.), 2003: The migration–development nexus, IOM

Wong, K. Y., 1983: On choosing among trade in goods and international capital and labor mobility: a theoretical analysis, *Journal of International Economics*, **14**, 223–50

Walzer, M., 1983: *Spheres of justice*, Basic Books, New York

Winters, C. A., T. Walmsley, Z. Kun Wang and R. Grynberg, 2002: Negotiating the liberalization of the temporary movement of natural persons, University of Sussex, DP **87**, October

Wong, K.Y., 1983: On choosing among trade in goods and international capital and labour mobility: a theoretical analysis, *Journal of International Economics*, **14**, 223–50

World Bank, 2002: *Globalization, Growth, and Poverty*, World Bank, Washington, DC

Perspective Paper 8.1

MARK R. ROSENZWEIG

Introduction

In Philip Martin's chapter 8 in this volume, the opportunity for expanding world output substantially and reducing disparities in income *per capita* across countries by expanding the movement of labour from low- to high-productivity areas is presented and discussed. Estimates are presented that moving 100 m persons would raise world output by 8 per cent. According to Martin, there are two related main challenges: the first is to minimize the opposition of populations in potential receiving countries to expanded immigration. The second is to use the gains from expanded cross-border migration to compensate those whose welfare is reduced.

Martin presents a three-component plan to meet the dual challenges. The first component is to expand the flow of 'permanent' immigrants, but with improved selection criteria to maximize the 'success' of the immigrants. Martin suggests that this would entail placing much greater weight on the schooling of immigrants and host-country language skills. He thus envisages an expansion in the permanent cross-border movements of skilled workers. Presumably, 'successful' migrants pose less of a cost to host-country populations, as they create smaller demands on transfer systems. A key issue here is how to pick migration 'winners'.

The second component of the proposal is to expand the flow of unskilled immigrant workers. These workers would, however, be 'temporary', permitted to stay in host countries for short periods of time and then repatriated. The idea is that temporary migrants are less threatening to host-country populations, because they cannot have permanent influences on culture and institutions, a view also expressed by Winters *et al.* (2003) in their analysis of the economic impact of temporary expanded migration. The key challenge here is not only how to select who joins the pool of temporary workers, but how to enforce their *exit*, given the alleged enormous private returns from permanent migration.

The third proposal is to redistribute the gains from migration. Most of the gains from the movement of peoples accrues to those who move. Martin discusses a number of mechanisms to redistribute the gains, including special taxes on migrant earnings, and proposes some uses for the funds, including for investment in mechanization in host countries.

Martin's chapter presents a useful overview of the migration experiences of many countries, of analyses that have been carried out on immigration and of the many alternative mechanisms for selecting immigrants and enforcing repatriation. Unfortunately, the immigration literature and the chapter are deficient in providing a suitable framework or credible empirical evidence for evaluating the costs and benefits of expanded global migration and the alternative mechanisms for selecting immigrants. In this Perspective paper I will discuss first the calculation of the global benefits of migration, showing that Martin's analysis (and that of others) is a long way from that which is appropriate. I will present some new findings from new data to shed light on what the benefits might be, showing that Martin's calculations lack any theoretical foundation and substantially overstate the benefits from expanded migration, which are still large. Second, I will discuss and provide more reliable evidence on aspects of the distribution of the global gains from increased immigration, discussing briefly some of Martin's ideas about the use of expropriated gains from migration. Third, I will briefly discuss the issue of selection mechanisms, arguing that Martin's emphasis on schooling as a criterion for immigrant success is simplistic. Finally, I will discuss the permanent–temporary dichotomy, arguing, and presenting evidence that Martin and most other researchers have an exaggerated perception that migrants selected in permanent migration systems are permanent and migrants selected as part of 'guest' worker programmes are temporary, and undervalue the long-term costs of temporary worker programmes and the ease by which costs of enforcing temporariness can be enforced. I will also argue against the proposition that creating a large permanent population of temporary workers makes immigration more palatable to the host-country population. In my conclusion I raise issues about the root causes of global disparities in factor prices.

Calculating the Global Benefits from Increased Migration

The existence of cross-country wage differences among workers with the same skills suggests that there are global gains from moving labour to high-wage areas from low-wage areas. The gain is the difference between the contribution of the added worker in the host country less the output lost in the sending country. To calculate the gain from any proposal to expand cross-border movement of labour, we need to know both who will cross borders – which skill group – and the host-sending-country wage differences for these specific workers. To simplify, let us defer the issue of selection and assume that migration will take place through a random selection mechanism, so that migrants are the average (-skill) workers in sending countries. The global migration gain is thus the host-sending-country

wage difference for the *average worker in sending countries*.

Martin presents no data on gaps in skill-specific wages across countries. Instead, he uses the difference between rich and poor countries' total output per person to gage the gains from immigration. Output *per capita* is probably correlated with the wage of the average worker, but is a poor measure. Output *per capita* can differ across countries in which prices of skills are the same, for two main reasons: differences in the share of the population in the labour force and differences in the skill composition of workers. The use of *per capita* GDP to measure migration gains is a step backward from the earlier analysis by Hamilton and Whalley (1984) and the recent study by Walmsley and Winters (2003) on the global benefits of migration. Neither of these studies, however, uses the appropriate cross-country skill price differences.

Hamilton and Whalley use the wage bill per labourer to measure cross-country wage gaps. Information on average wages is obviously not sufficient to identify skill price differences – wages can differ either because skill prices differ or skill compositions differ. Hamilton and Whalley do not have data on skill differences across countries, so they examine the sensitivity of the estimates to assumptions about the skill gap between host-and sending-country labour forces. Walmsey and Winters use cross-country data on wages to measure the skill of migrants from different sending countries. They assume that immigrants from high-wage countries are more productive than immigrants from low-wage countries. Again, however, if skill prices differ across countries, which is the whole basis for the proposition that increased migration enhances global welfare, then the sending-country wage composition of emigrants cannot be used to measure their skill composition. Moreover, as I show below empirically, it is not even clear in theory that countries that have higher skill levels will have emigrants with higher skills. Assumptions about skill differences across counties matter for gains conclusions. Hamilton and Whalley show that the estimates of the global gains from migration using *per capita* GDP can be reduced by an order of magnitude when differences in labour force shares and worker skills are taken into account. However, the effects

Table 8.1.1. Alternative Measures of the Origin-Country Wage of Migrants to the USA

Group	Mean origin-country (PPP$) GDP *per capita* (1)	Mean origin-country wage bill (PPP$) per *worker*[a] (2)	Pre-immigration origin-country (PPP$) earnings[b] (3)	Post-immigration mean US earnings[b,c] (4)
All	8,158	12,687	17,470	32,345
<12 years of schooling	7,347	12,449	11,322	18,885
High-school graduate	7,522	11,778	17,936	26,887
College graduate and above	9,334	13,657	22,126	39,356

Source: Heston, Summers and Aten (2002).
Notes: [a] Mean origin-country GDP multiplied by the labour factor share (0.67).
[b] New Immigrant Survey, 1996 US employment principal and spouse visa holders.
[c] Immigrants with an average of three years of residence in the USA.

of differences in cross-country skills are based on guesses. In any case, Martin's analysis ignores both labour force share and skill composition.

How badly do differences in *per capita* GDP or in average wage rates across countries measure the gains from increased global migration? I use the methodology in Jasso, Rosenzweig and Smith (2002) to compute the actual cross-country wage gains of US immigrants and compare these with the cross-country gap between the aggregate country-level averages used by Martin and other researchers. The analysis is based on data from the New Immigrant Survey Pilot (NIS-P), a panel survey based on a random sample of new 'green card' recipients (permanent resident aliens) who obtained their visas in August through November of 1996.[1] The analysis concentrates on two groups of immigrants – those given visas based on skills and getting a job offer and those who married either a US citizen or a permanent resident alien ('green card' holder). These groups, in contrast to those who obtain visas because they have blood relatives in the USA, conform more closely to migrants in models in which migrants optimize based on wage differences. The survey obtained information on pre-immigration earnings in the last job in the home country and post-immigration earnings in the USA in each of the four rounds of the survey, which covered a period of about two years. I use information

on earnings in the final round of the survey, when the immigrants had been in the USA for approximately three years on average (1.6 years prior to becoming a permanent resident alien).

Table 8.1.1 presents alternative measures of the home-country wages of the immigrants, classified into three skill groups – less than a high-school education (twelve years), high-school graduate, and college graduate (sixteen+ years). Column (1) uses Martin's wage measure – *per capita* GDP – and is the average over the sending countries for the specific skill group of immigrants; column (2), computed by applying a wage share of 0.67 to per-worker GDP, is the wage bill per worker (the average wage).[2] Column (3) reports the actual annualized wage of the immigrants in their home-country job based on the NIS-P. The figures show that sending-country *per capita* GDP substantially understates the actual sending-country wage for the immigrants in all three education groups, by 54% even for the lowest skill group. The per-worker wage bill is about right for that group, but underestimates the home-country wage for higher-skill immigrants increasingly as immigrant skill increases. This latter result illustrates the problem with using even the wage bill estimate of the skill price – higher-education immigrants have education levels that are greater than the average worker in their home counties, and the country's average wage, as measured by the wage bill per worker (or *per capita* GDP), does not reflects a country's skill composition. Second, the variation in either average *per capita* GDP or the aggregate wage

[1] For details, see Jasso *et al.* (2000).
[2] These aggregate country statistics come from Heston, Summers and Aten (2002) and refer to 1996 (in 1996 PPP dollars).

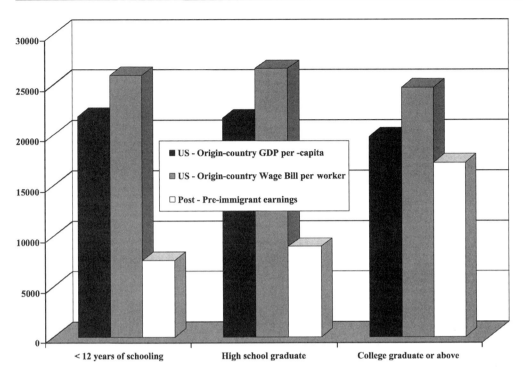

Figure 8.1.1. *Alternative measures of earnings gain from immigration, by immigrant schooling level*

of the home countries of the immigrants, used in Walmsley and Winters (2003) to proxy productivity differences among immigrants, understates substantially the skill differences among immigrants. This is because many high-skill immigrants come from low-average skill counties (e.g., India, China). Column (4) of table 8.1.1 reports the US earnings of the same immigrants, from which the actual wage gain of the immigrants can be calculated.

Figure 8.1.1 presents alternative measures of the wage gains from migration based on the two sending-country aggregate measures in table 8.1.1 and US GDP *per capita* ($57,259) and the actual cross-country wage gains of the immigrants, again by education level. Note that the cross-country wage gain for an immigrant holds constant her skill and thus reflects only the cross-country difference in skill price or marginal skill productivity, and any non-transferability of skill. The first bar in each education category is the measured gain based on the difference between the average *per capita* GDP of the sending countries of the immigrants reported in table 8.1.1 and *per capita* GDP in the USA in 1996.

The second bar is the difference in the per-worker wage bill in the USA and the average sending country of the immigrants, and the third bar is the actual cross-country wage gain at about three years of US experience of the immigrants. The figures show that measures of wage gaps based on average country-specific wages overestimate substantially the gains from migration. The *per capita* income-based measure of the gain used by Martin is almost double the actual gain for the lower-skill migrants whose immigration Martin wishes to expand. Moreover, the average-country wage gap of the countries of origin of the immigrants does not pick up the fact, evident in figure 8.1.1, that absolute wage gains are higher for higher-skill immigrants. Martin's measure of gain, as well as those used by other researchers based on average cross-country wage gaps, therefore substantially overestimates the true gain from immigration.

The gains calculated based on aggregate wage measures also evidently cannot identify an important fact – that the increased migration of higher-skill immigrants has a larger gross beneficial effect per migrant on world output than does the migration of the low-skilled. The absolute gain for the college graduates is more than double that for those migrants who had not completed twelve years of schooling ($17,230 versus $7,563). There is thus some evidence to back up Martin's call for increased high-skill immigration, but the case for an even greater expansion of low-skill immigration based on global gains is not supported.

The exaggerated gains based on average wage or *per capita* differences across countries is due in part to the fact that the average skill levels of the workers in sending countries are below those of the receiving countries. The average number of years of schooling in the origin countries of the US immigrants is about seven years; this compares with an average of about fourteen years of schooling in the USA. Despite the higher level of schooling, the US labour force is also likely more experienced than those in sending countries, where workers are substantially younger. It is thus not surprising that the average wage gap between the USA and the average sending country overestimates the gap in skill-specific prices and thus the potential immigration gain.

Although cross-country wage differences overstate by 100% or more the gains from a marginal increase in international labour mobility, the actual gains attained by the immigrants are large – $14,000 per year on average in the first few years after immigration, and even $8,000 per year for the low-skill immigrants, the latter one-year gain figure comparable to the average *per capita* incomes of the sending countries! Increasing immigration of the low-skill by 1 m workers thus adds $8 bn to the world economy; increasing the same number of high-skill immigrants (college graduates) adds over $17 bn. Are the actual wage gains of US immigrants a good measure of the global gains from increased migration? The wage gains obviously well characterize the initial gains for those persons who immigrated to the USA in 1996, although information is needed on both the lifetime trajectories of their US earnings

and the forgone earnings in the home country to compute the total gains. The question is whether the observed gains of immigrants predict the marginal gains for expanded future immigration. This will clearly depend on selection mechanisms that are used – as, indeed, the figures indicate that wage gains vary by schooling. The observed gains probably overstate the gain for a randomly selected resident of a home country, as we would expect those with the highest expected gains to migrate first.

The Global Distribution of Migration Gains

Martin's chapter does not go into the international distribution of the gains from increased labour mobility in a systematic way, either analytically or with non-anecdotal empirical evidence. There are three main avenues of redistribution that do not entail direct governmental intervention. First there are general equilibrium effects. Large flows of persons between countries affect the country-specific prices of labour or skills. Assessing these effects requires a general equilibrium model, and that is the contribution of the exercises by Hamilton and Whalley (1984) and Walmsley and Winters (2003), which use computable general equilibrium (CGE) models to assess, by skill group and country of residence, who gains and who loses from increased international labour mobility. One important caveat of those models is that capital is assumed to be completely immobile internationally, an assumption implicitly used by Martin in his more casual analyses of general equilibrium effects. Of course, increased capital mobility is an alternative means of achieving the same goals as enhanced international labour mobility. A complete assessment of the cost and benefits of encouraging increased immigration would compare any immigration scheme to those enhancing international flows of capital. In any case, the assumption of complete international capital immobility seems too strong, and more attention to capital mobility is needed to achieve a more accurate assessment of the level and distribution of the benefits and costs of international labour mobility.[3]

---

[3] Foster and Rosenzweig (2003) show that a large component of the wage gains in rural areas of India in the past thirty years was due to flows of capital into rural areas rather than through outmigration.

Table 8.1.2. Earnings and remittances: male employment and spouse immigrants, 1996^a

Group	Mean US earnings (1)	Mean remittances (2)	$((2)/(1)) \times 100$ (3)	Pre-immigration origin-country (PPP$) earnings (4)	$((2)/(4)) \times 100$ (5)
All	37,242	1,545	4.2	17,383	8.9
<12 years of schooling	20,813	612	2.9	8,028	7.6
High-school graduate	29,949	1,945	6.5	17,520	11.1
College graduate and above	52,794	2,100	4.0	30,597	6.9

Note: ^{a}New Immigrant Survey, 1996 US male employment principal and spouse visa holders with an average of three years of residence in the USA.

A second way in which the gains to immigrants are redistributed back to sending countries without international coordination or cooperation is via remittances. The role of remittances in the distribution of immigration gains is emphasized by Martin and incorporated into the Walmsley and Winters general equilibrium model. Data on remittances are incomplete at best, so again most researchers make assumption about the magnitudes of voluntary transfers. For example, Walmsley and Winters assume that remittances back to the home countries are 20 per cent of the earned wages of the immigrants. Is this a realistic assumption? The NIS-P data permit a look at remittance behaviour. Respondents were asked how much financial assistance they provided to relatives, friends and others not living in the USA in the year preceding the final round of the survey: 59 per cent of the male migrants with earnings sent remittances abroad. Table 8.1.2 provides the average US earnings and remittances by schooling group among male migrants in the sample in the last round of the survey. The data indicate that on average remittances were only 4 per cent of the US earnings of immigrants, a figure one-fifth that assumed in Walmsley and Winters.

Reasonably reliable data on remittances thus suggest that researchers may be considerably overestimating the promise of remittances as a redistributional mechanism for immigration gains, but from the perspective of the sending countries the contribution of remittances is at least not trivial. One way to gauge this is to look at remittances as a proportion of origin-country earnings. Based on the origin-country earnings of the immigrants as a proxy for incomes of the workers in the original country of origin, displayed in column (4), remittances add from 7 to over 11 per cent to incomes in the countries sending the immigrants. Temporary migrants are likely to send a much greater proportion of their earnings home in the few years they are immigrants, but then their gains are also smaller as their skills and incomes are lower and they do not accumulate host-country labour market experience. The data do show that higher-skill immigrants send a greater amount of remittances, although remittances make up a smaller proportion of income among the highest-skill groups.

A third market mechanism by which immigration gains accrue to sending countries that is highlighted by Martin is through the (voluntary) return migration of skilled immigrants. Martin provides no information on what return rates are or who returns, although there are anecdotes about returning Taiwan and Indian entrepreneurs. The benefits to sending countries from return migration derive from the skills acquired by the migrants in the host country. Thus, this redistributional mechanism is associated with Martin's 'permanent' migration flow – the immigrants need to be in the host country more than the few years envisiaged by Martin for temporary workers. The enforced rapid turnover of unskilled migrants does not have any significant benefit for the sending countries other than perhaps pleasing the families of the return migrants who are barred from emigrating under Martin's scheme. Thus, only if permanent migrants are not 'too' permanent does this redistributional mechanism have any salience (and if workers are 'too' temporary, then it has no effect).

The evidence suggests that 'permanent' migrants are by no means completely permanent. Jasso and Rosenzweig (1982) matched US Immigration and Naturalization Service immigration and naturalization records along with annual address reports of permanent resident aliens to compute cumulative emigration rates at ten years after immigration for permanent resident aliens who had received 'green cards' in 1971. The data indicated emigration rates on the order of 30%, with rates considerably higher than that for many countries. That data for that analysis did not permit an assessment of return rates by skill. However, preliminary results from the baseline round of the New Immigrant Survey (a national survey of a stratified random sample of all (permanent) US legal immigrants admitted between April 2003 and January 2004) indicate that a substantial fraction of more-skilled immigrants do not intend to stay in the USA permanently. Over 15 per cent of the new immigrants aged 23 through 59 with college degrees or higher said that they did not intend to remain in the USA, compared with just under 10 per cent for those with less education. More impressively, of the new male immigrants admitted with an employment visa, and thus screened for skills, over 21 per cent indicated they expected not to stay in the USA.[4]

The uncoerced return of skilled immigrants thus represents a real gain to sending countries, at least among those sending countries that provide an environment in which skills and entrepreneurship are rewarded. The irony, of course, is that if immigrant sending countries were characterized by high returns to skill, there might be few high-skill emigrants. Most of the stories about the recent successes of return skill migration – Taiwan, China, India pertain to countries that had a change in policies.

Martin appears to favour special taxation of the gains to high-skill migrants. He has a number of ideas for how to spend the proceeds. One of these is to remit the revenues to sending countries to compensate those losing from the migration. This seems at odds with the international trade literature, in which taxation based on the skill content of goods is eschewed as well as direct transfers to those taking losses, in favour of taxation uniformity and help in job training. A tax on high-skill immigration is like a tax on high-skill content goods, and should be looked at in that way – what exactly is special about immigration in terms of dealing with compensation issues, except that, as we have seen, it is possible to identify the individuals who reap a large part of the initial gains from immigration? In any case, if one views pressures for immigration as arising in part from incompetent economic management and dysfunctional institutions in sending countries, providing such governments with additional monies does not appear to be an effective way of spurring development. Indeed, it is a subsidy to mismanagement. This issue also pertains to the value of private remittances. Remittance income is no different from any other income from the perspective of families making savings and investment decisions. Thus, whether remittances help sending countries develop depends on the economic environment in those countries.

Another idea Martin advocates for reallocating the private gains from immigration is to subsidise research and development (R&D) in mechanisation in host countries. This seems peculiar – optimal subsidies are non-zero when there are market distortions. In this case the distortion is an artificial barrier to the immigration of labour. This raises the price of labour, which induces investment in labour-saving technologies. Martin provides an example of mechanised tomato harvesting (and a reshaping of the tomato) as a response to the difficulty of tomato growers in obtaining human tomato harvesters.[5] Lowering the barriers to immigration reduces the distortion. The economic case for subsidizing investment in mechanisation is not obvious, except as a distortion-creating mechanism for compensating those in the business of developing labour substitutes when immigration barriers are eased.

---

[4] These results, and those reported below, from the NIS are preliminary and are taken from early rounds of the survey, which is still in the field at the time the chapter is being written.

[5] The tasteless, rock-hard American tomato is evidently the direct result of immigration barriers.

Choosing Among Immigrants

Martin favours a selection system that places the most weight on schooling in selecting permanent migrants. He also distinguishes between demand- and supply-based immigration selection systems, where the former are defined in terms of demand by firms and are said to be prevalent in OECD countries. He neglects the fact that most legal immigration to the USA is sponsored by a US resident, but few US immigrants are screened for skills or obtain a visa because they have a job. Indeed, the largest category of legal immigrants, making up a third or more of non-refugee/asylees immigrants obtained a visa by marrying a US citizen.[6] Family-based immigration is a demand-based system, too. The issue is which selection rules yield the highest returns. Martin presents no evidence on this, noting only that the Canadian points system, which does emphasize schooling and jobs, 'is working' (Martin, 2004). The statistics he supplies to support this assertion are that over half of the Canadian immigrants selected in 2002 spoke either of the 'native' languages of Canada and almost half had some post-secondary education. Well, the NIS reveals that among the new 2003 US immigrants, almost half (43%) chose to conduct the interview in English (a stricter criterion than merely 'speaking' English) and over half (51%) had schooling beyond high school. Thus a points system is not necessarily superior to the family/sponsor-based US system by Martin's criteria.

The NIS data indicate that different selection rules do yield different qualities of immigrants. We can divide up US immigrants into three categories of selection: employer demand for high-skill immigrants, random selection ('diversity' visas) based on a lottery with a high-school or above requirement, and family, including marriage, sibling, parent and adult child as criteria but no schooling screen. Not surprisingly, as indicated in figure 8.1.2, the high-skill requirement visa yields immigrants with the highest level of schooling, and the category with a schooling floor yields immigrants with an average schooling level above that of family immigrants. The family immigrants, however, have a mean schooling level above twelve years.

What family-based immigration provides, however, is native-born assistance in finding a job.

Figure 8.1.3 indicates for each visa category the proportion of the immigrants who had a job lined up prior to immigrating and the proportion receiving job help from relatives. Not surprisingly, a large proportion (31%) of the employment-based immigrants had received a job offer before arriving and the family immigrants had the smallest proportion of those receiving pre-immigration job offers. But, the family-based immigrants were more than three times more likely to have received assistance from family members in finding a job compared with employment-based immigrants (13.9% versus 3.7%). The diversity immigrants have a surprisingly high proportion (12.2%) of immigrants receiving family help and having a pre-immigration job offer, considering that most had no experience in the USA and no family member who could help them obtain a visa (by definition). However, note that a large proportion of lottery visa winners chose not to come to the USA; those who did may have been those with job offers or some resident family members. The job assistance, however, may not have been very successful. Figure 8.1.4 shows that unemployment rates in the first few months after immigration among men aged 23–59 are over 40% for the diversity visa holders, more than double that of the family migrants, despite their lower schooling level. Thus schooling alone, contrary to Martin's view, is not sufficient to ensure immigrant success. Family networks help, too.

Permanent versus Temporary Immigration

We have already seen that a substantial fraction of immigrants entitled to stay without time limits leave or plan not to stay. Exits by the permanent migrants,

---

[6] Following some of Martin's arguments, he would support compensating the spurned native-born suitors of those who chose to marry an immigrant or compensating native-born single women who were crowded out of the marriage market by immigrant women (who are 55 per cent of marriage-visa immigrants).

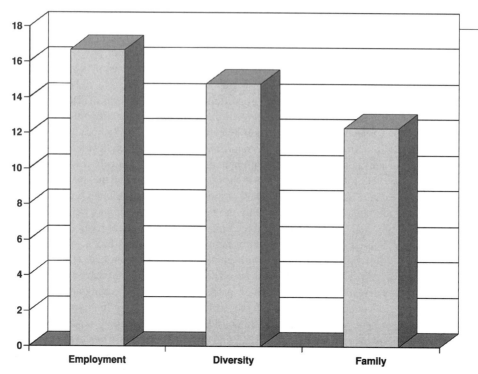

Figure 8.1.2. *Years of schooling completed, by visa category, immigrant men aged 23–59*

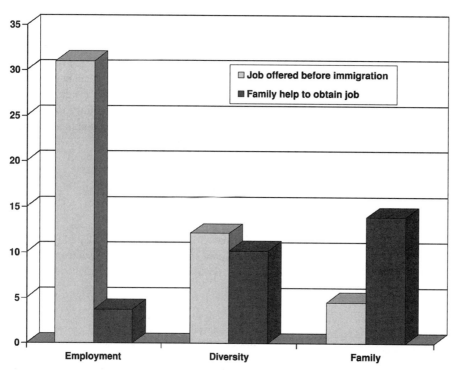

Figure 8.1.3. *Percentage receiving a job offer prior to immigrating and receiving job help from relatives, by visa category, immigrant men aged 23–59*

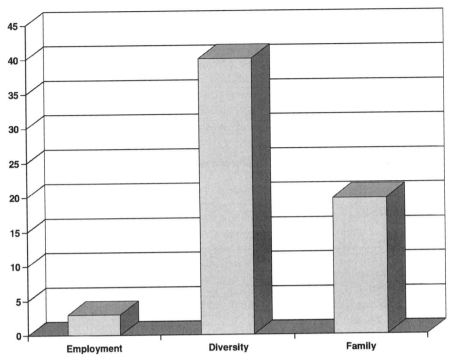

Figure 8.1.4. *Percentage unemployed, by visa category, immigrant men aged 23–59*

especially those with high skill, can have substantial benefits for their home countries. It is also well known, as cited by Martin, that a large proportion of immigrants not entitled to stay do not leave. Martin promotes a massive temporary immigration programme for unskilled workers in which immigrants must leave after very short periods of employment. No rationale or evidence is provided for why unskilled immigrants should not be allowed to remain in the host country. It is clearly not that they can then provide jobs or technical know-how in their home country. Winters *et al.* (2003) make the political economy argument that temporary workers do not affect the host economy's culture and do not make demands on its support or educational systems and thus a programme allowing only temporary workers, who cannot live with their families nor stay, would be politically acceptable. However, it is doubtful that creating a large, *permanent* population of temporary, unincorporated immigrants, who would have no incentive to learn the host-country language or adopt its cultural practices, would engender support for immigration. Indeed,

it is likely the opposite. Many of the jobs in which the unskilled are in demand are in the service sector, where such workers interact with native-born persons. A common objection to immigration is that immigrants do not learn the language. Martin's plan to expand the population of unassimilated immigrants who never learn the host-country language does not appear to have any benefits compared with a plan that does not attempt to impose stay limits.

Although Martin does a poor job of motivating the placement of restrictions on unskilled immigrants stay in host countries, he does a good job of discussing the difficulties of enforcing temporary worker programmes. But these costs understate the problems. Enforcement is not only costly, it is unlikely to be effective. As a consequence there will be a pool of workers who stay but who are separated from their families or who must use social services in an illegal status, thus alienating further the native population. A plan to provide 'temporary' workers with 'earned' entitlements to stay after a number of years as temporary migrants does not deal with the issue of investment in the children of immigrants.

Suppose that a male worker who is married comes to the host country and works for eight years. His children in the home country meanwhile are deprived of their father and obtain schooling in a system that may even be inferior to that in the USA. After eight years, the children can come, but they then have to learn the host-country language later in their life, which makes it more difficult to eliminate accents, and have had inferior schooling compared to their similarly aged cohorts in school. Much more attention needs to be paid to the longer-term costs of imperfectly enforced stay-restricted immigration.

Conclusion

There is a case to be made for expanding migration, particularly flows of skilled migrants, to developed countries based on global efficiency gains and the inability of trade in goods, even under a very liberal trading environment, to equalize cross-country factor prices, although Martin's chapter does not make the case well. There does not appear to be any good reason presented to limit the stay of immigrants in host countries as he proposes. There is also the issue of 'compensation' to those who lose from expanding immigration. Such compensation, if any, should be carried out in a manner that minimizes deadweight loss. Moreover, the notion that countries that lose immigrants, whatever their skill level, should be compensated raises important issues about the causes of skill price disparities across the world and the reasons for emigration pressures. To the extent that these arise from bad institutions and policies in sending countries, such compensation would slow reform and therefore not accelerate development. However, some pressures for migration are due to exogenous factors such as location and geography. There are areas of the world in which it would be inefficient even under optimal governmental regimes to support the large populations that reside there. Perhaps immigration

selection schemes in host countries should be attentive to the root causes of immigration pressures in specific countries, conditioning country-specific visa ceilings on institutional reforms in sending countries. Finally, the extent to which international capital flows interact with migration flows needs more attention to fully assess the costs and benefits of expanding immigration.

References

Foster, A. D. and M. Rosenzweig, 2003: Agricultural development, industrialization and rural inequality, Harvard University, September

Hamilton, B. and J. Whalley, 1984: Efficiency and distributional implications of global restrictions on labour mobility, *Journal of Development Economics*, **14**, 61–75

Heston, A., R. Summers and B. Aten, 2002: Penn World Table Version 6.1, Center for International Comparisons at the University of Pennsylvania (CICUP), October

Jasso, G., D. Massey, M. Rosenzweig and J. P. Smith, The new immigrant survey pilot: overview and new findings about legal immigrants at admission, *Demography*, February

Jasso, G. and M. Rosenzweig, 1982: Estimating the emigration rates of legal immigrants using administrative and survey data: the 1971 cohort of immigrants to the United States, *Demography*, August

Jasso, G., M. Rosenzweig and J. P. Smith, 2002: The earnings of US immigrants: world skill prices, skill transferability and selectivity, Harvard University

Martin, P., 2004: Migration, chapter 8 in this volume

Walmsley, T. L. and L. A. Winters, 2003: Relaxing the restrictions on the temporary movements of natural persons: a simulation analysis, CEPR Discussion Paper, 3719

Winters, L. A., T. L. Walmsley, Z. K. Wang and R. Grynberg, 2003: Liberalising temporary movement of natural persons: an agenda for the Development Round, *World Economy*, **26**, 1137–61

Perspective Paper 8.2

ROGER BÖHNING

Introduction

Stripped to its bare essentials, Phil Martin's three-pronged and interlocking proposals in chapter 8 in this volume suggest that migrant-receiving countries should (1) pursue an active selection policy of the 'best and brightest' but compensate migrant-sending countries for brain-drain losses; (2) temporarily admit other foreign workers with employers paying extra payroll taxes for extensions of their contracts and the refunding of social security contributions to workers when they return to their home country; and (3) operate a public recruitment, return and remittance system ('3Rs') that contributes to the development of migrants' countries of origin.

Martin's chapter is the best-informed and most comprehensive exposition of facts, figures, analyses, models and proposals in the field of OECD countries' international migration problems that I am aware of. His depiction of demographic trends, rural–urban migration, widening income disparities and growing migration pressures can be taken as valid as long as one can see ahead. I would agree with his characterisation of most OECD countries' policies in this field as 'cumbersome, ... often adversarial' (p. 453) and perpetuating employers' 'need' for fresh supplies of migrant workers. That his broad cost-benefit analysis (CBAs) is perhaps not what the organizers of the Copenhagen Consensus had in mind does not trouble me. The outcomes of international migration are not shaped by economic factors alone; private and social costs and gains often diverge; and pinpointed CBAs suffer from having to assume away crucial determinants.

My problem with the chapter lies in a key assumption that is glossed over, namely the general capacity of today's State to control migration, and its interplay with different types of enterprises. Economists traditionally view the State as a neutral, benign or facilitative background factor (or a distorter of markets). However, the shift induced by contemporary globalisation 'from equity to efficiency and from development to growth' (Nayyar 2003, 17) has caused countries to diminish regulatory labour market interventions and public functions that are crucial to the success of Martin's policy recommendations. Besides, the State happens to be made up of politicians and administrators who are human beings with all their strengths and failings. Given that 'the most difficult challenge' identified by Phil Martin (p. 463) is to make the 'transition from the current widespread employment of irregular workers to a world of legal migrants', I shall examine the three opportunities he elaborates in the light of what they would require the State to do, effectively and efficiently, in relation to the kind of employers who are prone to using (im)migrant workers unlawfully. In addition, I shall pick up the idea of establishing a World Migration Organization (WMO). Chapter 8 dismisses this idea too lightly. I believe that it constitutes an opportunity in the sense that a WMO could contribute significantly to alleviating the challenges so well identified.

What State and Which Enterprises Are We Concerned With?

One public function central to the repression of unlawful employment is *labour inspection*. Under conditions of contemporary globalisation, however, labour inspection is in danger of being hollowed out because employers dislike it, because it is an easy target of public expenditure cuts and because today's State prefers to see inspectors in more a counselling than a policing role. While this might not cause many economists to shed more than crocodile tears, Martin (p. 459) points to stepped-up

489

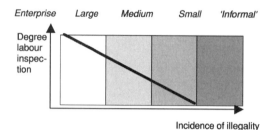

Figure 8.2.1. *Scheme 1: type of enterprise, incidence of illegality and degree of labour inspection*

enforcement of labour and immigration law as an indispensable tool in fighting the unlawful employment of (im)migrant workers. What makes matters worse is the uneven distribution of unlawful employment in the economy (see figure 8.2.1). The *x*-axis visualises the incidence of illegality, which is negligible in large enterprises, small in medium-size enterprises (SMEs), quite extensive in small enterprises and high in the informal economy, especially in ethnic niches. The *y*-axis represents the degree to which labour inspectors visit different types of enterprises: they visit large enterprises regularly, medium-size enterprises almost as frequently, small enterprises occasionally and the informal economy practically never. Their presence is inverse to the requirements of a policy of flushing out the unlawful employment of (im)migrants – or of nationals, for that matter.

Does the rise in post-11 September security concerns make up for the absence of labour inspector? Not yet, because all the attention is on border controls.

The second State function that impinges on Martin's proposals is a factor exogenous to migration, effective control of corruption. I carried out a 'quick and dirty' correlation between two sets of dummy variables in eighty-five countries: my estimate[1] of the incidence of unlawful migration for employment (high/medium/low) and the degree of corruption according to the Corruption

Perceptions Index (CPI) of Transparency International (TI) (2003).[2] As one might fear, there is a high correlation: the Pearson product moment correlation coefficient is +0.93, significant at the 1% level. Low-corruption countries such as Denmark, Canada or Singapore have few unlawful (im)migrants – in contrast to medium-corruption countries such as Germany, the USA or Malaysia. Migrant-sending countries tend to be afflicted by high degrees of corruption (Haiti, Indonesia, Bangladesh . . .). The story this tells is that, in order to make the 'transition from the current widespread employment of irregular workers to a world of legal migrants' that Martin sees as indispensable (p. 463), the world had better consist of nothing but virtuous Danes (or, even better, Finns) – or do something more effective in terms of repressing unlawful migration and employment.

A third element concerns the recruitment of (im)migrants – a role the State rarely assumes today. The USA abolished its *bracero* programme with Mexico in 1964; European countries ended public recruitment at the time of the first oil crisis in 1973. The vacuum was taken up by *coyotes* in Mexico and by a variety of private intermediaries in Europe who supplied employers with few legal and many unlawful migrants. The presence of illegals undermined the general acceptability of (im)migrant workers. Canada, by contrast, remains actively involved in the recruitment process of Mexican and West Indian workers for its agriculture, suffers little from unlawful migration and employment and enjoys high domestic approval of its (im)migration system (see Martin 2003).

Opportunity 1: Attracting the 'Best and Brightest' with Brain Drain Compensation

The chapter's first proposal is seductive, persuasively argued and can be applied flexibly. Unfortunately, it is of limited acceptability to migrant-receiving countries today, and it is unrealistic as far as the compensation of migrant-sending countries is concerned.

Like his other proposals, Martin's idea of an active, points-based admission system that selects those who are potentially of greatest value and who

---

[1] Based on Böhning (1996) estimates of legal and illegal (im)migrant workers in major migrant-receiving and migrant-sending countries.

[2] Countries' corruption scores were graded as *high* if they were in the 0–6 range of the Index, *medium* in the 6.1–8 range and *low* in the 8.1–10 range.

fit in easily seems to be aimed primarily at European countries. Its underlying philosophy corresponds to Australian, Canadian, New Zealand and US permanent immigration regimes that have no constraining post-entry restrictions or controls and where overall admissions are held in check by limits on the number of refugees. This philosophy has few followers in Europe and practically none elsewhere (though Singapore seeks to attract professionals). Europe's most important migrant-receiving country, Germany, had a commission of politicians and experts recommend such a policy, more particularly a Canadian-type points system (Deutschland, Bundesministerium des Innern, 2001). But little more than a tiny 'green-card' system for IT workers was acceptable in practice. I fear that permanent immigration policies in Europe will not pass national parliaments for many years to come. They would also require a shift in the open-ended refugee policies of European countries towards the low-level caps on the number of refugees practised by current immigration countries.

Chiefly due to the continued restriction on admissions and the development of networks, legal systems of immigration inevitably entail some degree of illegal immigration. The incidence of illegality will vary roughly in line with corruption levels. If one goes by TI's CPI (2003), this augurs well for Scandinavian countries, not so well for central European countries and not at all well for Greece and Italy or the eastern European countries, for example, thus posing a problem of harmonizing policies in the EU.

That being said, the proposal to set up a selective system for permanent immigration purposes designed to attract the 'best and brightest' warrants to be put on policy agendas throughout Europe alongside a discussion of the contingent changes in refugee admission policies. (The latter will be highly contentious in Scandinavian countries.) What I find especially attractive in Martin's proposal is his focus on *educational qualifications* rather than the – in Europe – widespread longing for an immigration-driven demographic fix to the problems of ageing in general and of social security in particular. The demographics of making good the ageing of the population very quickly sum to such numbers that they portend electoral suicide.

Education is a more promising basis for recasting Europe's admission policies without incurring frightening numbers. Education greases the wheels of the economy. Mere bodies may be dead-weights.

As regards compensating countries of origin for any losses they might suffer as a result of rich countries' immigration policies, I appreciate the well-meaning nature of the idea but fear that it reflects standard economics which contents itself with the *potential* of compensation for a proposal to pass muster. I believe that one should be honest rather than dangle the mirage of a compensation carrot in front of migrant-sending countries' eyes. As migrant-receiving countries can pick and chose from a growing supply of brains around the world, they feel no compunction – nor are they subject to notable political pressures – to pay for something that is available free. Proposals of this kind (including Böhning 1977) briefly floated around during the heyday of the 'New International Economic Order' (NIEO), but nothing came of them. Some of today's developing countries will increasingly tap into the international market for highly qualified workers, which will not endear them to the idea of compensating the workers' countries of origin. To be frank and honest, migrant-sending governments have no option other than to oversupply their countries with publicly or privately educated workers – in the hope of seeing some of them find suitable employment abroad, remit some of their savings to family members staying behind and return to some extent with new skills and motivations.

In the context of the fourth opportunity that I envisage in terms of creating a WMO, a rather different scheme is proposed to transfer a share of guest workers' income taxes to their countries of origin, which – although of different inspiration – could be likened to the idea of compensation.

Opportunity 2: A Functioning Guest Worker Scheme by Levying Taxes on Employment and Refunding Migrants' Social Security Contributions

The chapter adds a temporary employment component, presumably mainly for brawny rather than brainy work, to the range of desirable policies. In light of the failure of most previous guest worker programmes to rotate all migrants in and out of the country – notably in Europe and the USA (though Singapore fared better in that respect) – Martin envisages dissuading employers from reliance on cheap foreign labour by having them pay a fee if and when they renew guest workers' contracts, and he suggests enticing migrants back to their countries of origin by paying out accumulated social security contributions to them on their return.

Taxes on employers, which one may expect in the first instance to dampen their enthusiasm for employing workers,[3] can take the form of fees upon initial engagement or of a bond that is redeemed upon departure from the country or forfeited if the migrant worker goes underground. Greece, Israel, Malaysia, Singapore and Taiwan are the main migrant-receiving countries that practise such schemes, which shifts the enforcement of the migrants' departure from the government to the employers – all of which lack administrative enforcement authority and most of which lack the practical means to carry out such a responsibility. Theoretically, it is rather doubtful that employers would be prepared to shoulder an additional burden when they have other opportunities. One is to pass the costs on to the worker, which is apparently what happens in Asia. The other is to hire less costly illegal entrants or to hire unlawfully migrants who are already in the country (see Epstein, Hillman and Weiss 1999). What does reality show? Israel's measures since the early 1990s come closest to Martin's ideas and are the only ones known to have been investigated. Estimates show that the proportion of illegal to legal foreign workers, which was 84% in 1995, jumped to 118% or so within a couple of years (see Brücker et al. 2002, table 6.2). Greece

and Malaysia are other examples of countries with high proportions of illegally employed foreigners. The cases of Singapore and Taiwan are not well studied.[4] At any rate, inflation of illegal employment is what one should anticipate, which defeats the very purpose of setting up a truly rotating guest worker system.

One should not blind oneself to the fact that little protest and much collusion occurs in the kind of enterprises that, in the contemporary world, look to employ guest workers. Trade unions are practically inoperative in small enterprises; labour inspectors are rare visitors; and in the informal economy, anything goes and nothing holds. Not only are there pools of willing non-national workers present in many European countries who would rather work illegally than not at all, there are also national and international networks (ranging from single-person gangs to organized crime syndicates) which readily provide fresh supplies of work-hungry labourers from abroad, some 500,000 apparently each year in Europe (Brücker et al. 2002). A key characteristic of shady intermediaries is their willingness and capacity to bribe anybody, from border guards to local officials.

I believe a more effective policy of weaning small-scale and informal employers from using unauthorized workers would be a *blanket prohibition to hire foreigners not admitted as full immigrants*, of which the whole population would be regularly informed. The only future guest worker scheme that I can see having a reasonable chance of sailing close to its intentions would be limited to truly seasonal work. In practically all countries today that means seasonal agriculture, because construction and tourism are year-round activities with highs and lows like any other non-seasonal employment. As a complementary measure, labour inspection would have to be retooled on the lines foreseen in figure 8.2.2, with traditional policing functions being retained and applied intensively in respect of the kind of the small and informal employers who are inclined to use workers unlawfully. Ethnic niches would probably require repeated raids combining labour inspectors and special police forces. At any rate, the marginal value added generated by small employers, ethnic niches and the informal economy does not warrant being handed a public

[3] However, industry-level simulations for Germany (1977–94) concluded that, 'contrary to the public discussion, … the impact of payroll taxes, such as social security contribution rates, on employment is minimal' (Riphan and Bauer 1998, 2). This research is admittedly not differentiated by the size of enterprises in the way migration-related studies should be and, therefore, does not reflect well the cost-benefit context of small enterprises – and the informal economy – where labour costs assume a comparatively higher importance.

[4] The ILO has unsuccessfully approached Singaporean economists for an evaluation of the variable taxes paid there by employers for foreign workers.

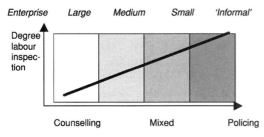

Figure 8.2.2. *Scheme 2: type of enterprise, desirable degree of labour inspection and form of inspection*

subsidy in the form of access to fresh migrants from abroad.

The effective repression of the illegal employment of migrant workers – and of nationals for that matter – is a touchstone of any future guest worker policy, indeed of any successful policy of admitting non-nationals.[5] It would warrant a share of the research funds that the Copenhagen Consensus might be able to mobilize.

I can go along with Martin's proposal to withhold and then refund social security contributions as an incentive for workers to return to their countries of origin. Although there are legitimate concerns that employers' and workers' payroll deductions for contingencies such as employment injury, illness and old age should be used for no other purpose – because such contingencies are unlikely to be catered for in any other way – even the ILO's Recommendation on Migrant Workers (Supplementary Provisions), 1975 (No. 151), paragraph 34(c)(ii), and the UN's International Convention on the Rights of All Migrant Workers and Members of Their Families, Article 27(2), allow such refunding up to a point. Forfeiture of such forced savings in the event of the migrant staying on unlawfully makes a switch into the underground economy a little less attractive. But long-term cost-benefit calculations discount this loss and anticipate adjustment to legal status after some time.

The understandable but counterproductive adjustment policies of migrant-receiving countries that enable workers who were not supposed to stay forever to gain residence entitlement hollows out legal (im)migration. As the chapter recalls (pp. 451–2), this accounts for some two-thirds of all legal

immigrant admissions in the USA and a large portion in Europe, too. This kind of policy would have to be dropped or its scope of application would have to be limited drastically so that no more than marginal numbers of adjustments would occur on strictly humanitarian grounds. Such a change would, however, be difficult politically given the power of ethnic and humanistic lobbies in Europe and North America.

Opportunity 3: Recruitment, Return and Remittance to Induce Development

The relationships between migration and development are multi-faceted (see Böhning 1982) and include, in the first instance, the relief of unemployment and of the need to house, feed, etc., the people who leave. Still, if one looks at the '3Rs', as Martin calls them, two of them (recruitment and return) form part of the opportunities set out previously. There is nothing I need to add to my preceding comments except to highlight Martin's starting point for 'government services to substitute for the current migration infrastructure, which includes smugglers and traffickers' (p. 465). I would entirely agree with him but, for the reasons indicated in the Introduction, find this unrealistic under the conditions of contemporary globalisation. Remittances are the new component. I agree with what has been stated. The most urgent practical question here is how to reduce the hefty margins that go into the pockets of formal and informal intermediaries.[6]

As regards the migration 'hump', its height and duration do not reflect some natural law but the concrete conditions of particular countries. The 'hump'

---

[5] Including in the USA. As Bertola commented: 'Enforcement of immigration constraints by inland inspection...is clearly the most effective means of enforcing any regulation...such enforcement is almost comically non-existent in the US' (quoted in Hanson *et al.* 2003, 289). By contrast, Bhagwati has consistently called for less internal enforcement and more policing of the borders, though he mischievously adds that it is futile to keep illegals out of advanced countries (see, e.g., Bhagwati 1998, 331, 335, 341, 346 and 373–5).

[6] Western Union made a profit in 2002 of one-third of its turnover based on usurious charges. In France, for instance, it lops off 21% from migrants' small remittances compared with 3.5% for large transfers.

can be anticipated to be low and short in duration in, for instance, countries scheduled to join the EU (see Brücker *et al.* 2002, figure 4.4). But the picture would be drastically different for, say, Russia and Ukraine relative to the EU, China relative to Japan or Egypt relative to Saudi Arabia.

Opportunity 4: A World Migration Organisation to Tackle the Key Challenges

There have been rising calls for the establishment of a WMO, as recounted by Ghosh in the Introduction to his book.[7] In 2003, UN Secretary-General Kofi Annan decided to launch a Global Commission on Migration to deliberate on improvements in the field of international migration and, when he lectured at Jagdish Bhagwati's university in November, lent his weight to the idea of setting up a migration agency under UN auspices. The Global Commission commenced work in early 2004 in Geneva. At the same time, the ILO's World Commission on the Social Dimension of Globalization published its findings and recommendations that strongly supported a multilateral framework in this field (ILO 2004a, 96).[8]

Two major hurdles must be overcome before one can usefully bring together sovereign States to

negotiate a WMO. The first refers to what Martin sees as the lack of a 'clear theoretical basis for more migration, or even a consensus on a theoretical framework to estimate an optimal level of migration' (p. 464). I believe there is no need for an analogy with theoretical bases such as those of trade liberalisation that inspired the GATT, GATS and WTO. In actual fact, migrant-receiving countries would object to any explicit or hidden objective that a global migration organisation would promote *more* or *free* cross-border flows of people.[9] Politically, it suffices to give WMO one or two self-evidently consensual overarching aims that permit the derivation of more detailed migration principles concerning economically productive movements and the protection of refugees. Refugees must be an integral part of a comprehensive regime, otherwise political migration threatens to undercut economic migration, as in Europe's recent past. For example, one could charge a future WMO with the 'promotion of desirable migration' and envisage an 'economically desirable migration' pillar and a 'politically desirable migration' pillar (see figure 8.2.3). I would eschew formulations such as 'orderly', 'better managed', 'sustainable' or 'regulated openness'. 'Orderly' and 'better managed' migration lack substantive reference points or ethical values – even slaves can be moved in an orderly fashion, and desperate job-seekers can easily be managed to perform efficiently and cost-effectively under exploitative conditions. 'Sustainable' opens the field wide to an open-ended array of subjects, competing claims and tradeoffs, which adds uncertainty rather than reassurance. Ghosh's 'regulated openness' may appear attractive to migrant-sending countries in that it appears to promise inflows abroad and some form of outflow control; but it lacks a counterpoint ('unregulated closure'?) and is an empty notion.

Of course, my own formulation begs the question of *what* is desirable and *for whom* specific forms of migration may be desirable. This brings me to the second major hurdle, i.e. the divergent or even opposed interests of migrant-receiving and migrant-sending countries (see figure 8.2.4).[10] These questions actually go still deeper. Any international regime entails some loss of countries' sovereignty (and budgets) in exchange for some expected value added. It must be able to share the costs and benefits

---

[7] Ghosh, though, left out Thomas Straubhaar's contribution in a 1991 ILO Working Paper and Jagdish Bhagwati's repeated suggestion to set up a WMO, which he first put forward in a 1992 article in the *Christian Science Monitor* (reprinted in Bhagwati 1998, 315–17) and barely changed since (see, e.g., Bhagwati 2003).

[8] A report by the ILO on migrant workers due to be discussed at its annual conference in June 2004 endorses, somewhat lamely, a new comprehensive international migration framework (ILO 2004b).

[9] Martin does not hide his view of seeing *more* migration come about as a result of *better* migration on the lines of his proposals. This will hardly endear his ideas to migrant-receiving countries.

[10] For simplicity's sake, I leave aside the fact that most countries today are both migrant-receiving and migrant-sending countries and that quite a number are important transit countries. I also leave aside the GATS Mode 4 service providers, which are considered to remain part of the economic sphere of the country where the service enterprise comes from. The same reasoning applies to project-tied migrants.

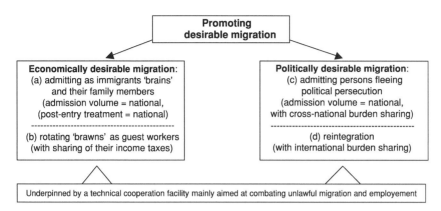

Figure 8.2.3. *Scheme 3: principal components of a WMO adding value to the international system*

	Migrant-receiving countries				Migrant-sending countries			
	Economic migrants			Refugees*	Economic migrants			Refugees*
	Lawful inflows and length of stay*		Unlawful		Lawful outflows and length of absence		Unlawful	
	Volume	Duration	Volume	Volume	Volume	Duration	Volume	Volume
Brains	Many	Permanent	Nil	} As few as possible	Few	Temporary	Few	} As many as possible
Brawns	Few	Temporary	Nil		Many	Permanent	Many	

* Including family members.

Figure 8.2.4. *Scheme 4: Basic interests of migrant-receiving and migrant-sending countries in the contemporary world*

of its existence relatively equally among States – unless it is imposed by a hegemon, which is undesirable in principle and unrealistic at present.[11]

Enlightened self-interest on the part of migrant-sending countries could theoretically lead them to agree to tackle seriously, and jointly with migrant-receiving countries, the unlawful movements that span the globe. Nayyar, for example, expresses enlightened self-interest when he stamps smuggling and trafficking of people as *public bads*, wants a 'regime of discipline to be imposed on intermediaries' (Nayyar 2002a, 170), and observes that 'in a world where the pursuit of self-interest by nations means uncoordinated action or non-cooperative behaviour, suboptimal solutions, which leave everybody worse off, are a likely outcome ... Such outcomes can be prevented only by evolving institutional mechanisms for cooperation ... which facilitate coordinated action and cooperative behaviour' (Nayyar 2002b, 374).

Beyond enlightened self-interest, I perceive the need for strong incentives to entice migrant-sending countries to join the WMO and the fight against undesirable migration. A revenue-sharing arrangement would seem to constitute an appropriate incentive, which I would pitch at migrant workers not admitted on a permanent basis (i.e. guest workers), as practised by several Swiss cantons towards neighbouring communes sending frontier workers. There are two possible justifications for splitting income taxes (on, say, a 50/50 basis). One is that, prior to departure, the migrant workers themselves will generally have paid income taxes, which go missing when they are abroad. The second justification is that guest workers' families almost invariably stay

[11] In effect, today's hegemon, the USA, may be a rather reluctant participant in the gestation of a WMO, not least because of the influence of humanitarian and ethnic lobbies on Congress.

behind and consume costly infrastructure, such as schools, roads, etc. with the burden of providing it falling exclusively on the shoulders of the migrant-sending countries.

The advantages of my proposal over Martin's are threefold: (1) mine would not inflict taxes on employers that they will seek to avoid by unlawful hiring; (2) there is no risk that the migrants will have to bear any burden; and (3) the revenue loss in migrant-receiving countries, which may be quite marginal, provides an incentive for governments to try and wean employers from using guest workers.

I should like to make clear that I do not see a WMO assuming collective enforcement and dispute settlement functions, let alone sanctions. I would not even go along with Bhagwati's suggestion that a WMO should study countries' migration practices so as to put pressure on those with bad practices through WMO publications and NGOs using the research results. Research will certainly be needed but not for the single purpose of handing out good or bad marks. The WMO should be a facilitator and coordinator, not a policeman or incriminator – otherwise there won't be a WMO. A WMO would stand little chance of being established at present unless it focused its activities, at least initially, on the flip side of the desirable migration coin, i.e. unlawful movements. Its constitution should, *inter alia*, oblige all member States to enable the prosecution of identified smugglers, traffickers and other perpetrators of both illegal movements and unlawful employment to take place irrespective of where they may find themselves at any point of time. And it would have to give migrant-sending countries an incentive to play by the rules. Thus, the WMO that I see as useful would:

- Organise the fight against unlawful cross-border flows as well as against the unlawful employment of (im)migrant workers in receiving countries. This would entail beneficial spin-off effects with

respect to a related undesirable phenomenon, the unlawful employment of national workers.
- Operate a strong technical cooperation facility to help countries lacking capacity to build up their migration administration so that out-flows from migrant-sending countries and in-flows into migrant-receiving countries conform to the ideals of 'desirable migration'.[12] A special technical cooperation fund should be established within the WMO that would not merely be a small fraction of the organisation's regular budget. The WMO's constitution could, for instance, oblige its 25 or 50 per cent richest member States to double their assessed contributions, with half of the money feeding the special technical cooperation fund; or the rich countries' extra contributions could be assessed according to other criteria or a mix of factors. Technical cooperation contributions should be pooled and thereby de-linked from funders' preferences. Actual assistance programmes should blend objectively determined needs with beneficiary countries' willingness to take decisive steps in the realisation of the WMO's principal aims. Additional voluntary contributions by member States' governments, other authorities, NGOs, Foundations, etc. could be added to the pool but need not be de-linked from preferences donors might have. Steps of this kind would enable the WMO to oversee a sizeable technical assistance operation with predictable funding aimed at helping countries battling with undesirable forms of international migration.
- Agree on the principle of sharing the income taxes paid by guest workers in migrant-receiving countries with their countries of origin.

Why should migrant-receiving countries be interested in and willing to fund a new UN agency covering all forms of international migration?[13] Because it promises value added in relation to unlawful migration and the three opportunities identified by Martin, and by bringing economic and political movements into a common policy-making framework. Since this field of population questions is quintessentially international in nature, solutions to most problems cannot stop at the border but require international cooperation. Bilateral solutions are decreasingly effective because of the fact that

---

[12] The promotion of remittance flows could equally be facilitated through technical cooperation as also their productive use in migrants' countries of origin.

[13] The WMO would, no doubt, absorb the existing International Organization for Migration (IOM) and UNHCR as well. Many countries would not have to shoulder additional costs.

increasing numbers of migrant-sending and transition countries are involved. A global intergovernmental organisation can do things that individual countries cannot achieve. The time has come to move from endorsing the desirability of setting up a WMO to the elaboration of possible models on what its functions should be and how it should operate in practice.

References

Bhagwati, J. N., 1998: *A stream of windows: unsettling reflections on trade, immigration and democracy*, MIT Press, Cambridge, MA

2003: Borders beyond control, *Foreign Affairs*, January–February

Böhning, W. R., 1977: Compensating countries of origin for the out-migration of their people, World Employment Programme Working Paper, ILO, Geneva

(ed.), 1982: Special issue: international migration and development, *International Migration Review*, **16**(4)

1996: *Employing foreign workers*, ILO, Geneva

Brücker, H., *et al.*, 2002: Managing migration in the European welfare state, in T. Boeri, G. Hanson and B. McCormick (eds.), *Immigration policy and the welfare system*, Oxford University Press, Oxford, 1–168

Deutschland, Bundesministerium des Innern, 2001: Bericht der Unabhängigen Komission 'Zuwanderung', http:www.bmi.hund.de/dokumente/Artikel/ix_46876.htm

Epstein, G. S., A. L. Hillman and A. Weiss, 1999: Creating illegal immigrants, *Journal of Population Economics*, **12**, 3–21

Gosh, B. (ed.), 2000: *Managing migration: time for a new international regime?*, Oxford University Press, Oxford

Hanson, G., *et al.*, 2003: Immigration and the US economy: labour market impacts, illegal entry, and policy choices, in T. Boeri, G. Hanson and B. McCormick (eds.), *Immigration policy and the welfare system*, Oxford University Press, Oxford, 169–309

ILO, 2004a: *A fair globalization: creating opportunities for all*, World Commission on the Social Dimension of Globalization, Geneva

2004b: *Towards a fair deal for migrant workers in a global economy*, ILO, Geneva.

Martin, P. L., 2003: *Managing labour migration: temporary worker programs for the 21st century*, mimeo

Nayyar, D., 2002a: Cross-border movements of people, in D. Nayyar, *Governing globalization: issues and institutions*, Oxford University Press, Oxford, 144–73

2002b: The existing system and the missing institutions, in D. Nayyar, *Governing globalization: issues and institutions*, Oxford University Press, Oxford, 365–84

2003: Work, livelihoods and rights, Presidential address to the 44th Conference of the Indian Society of Labour Economics, *Indian Journal of Labour Economics*, **46**(1), 3–13

Straubhaar, T., 1991: Migration pressure, in W. R. Böhning, P. V. Schaeffer and Th. Straubhaar, Migration pressure: what is it? What can be done about it?, World Employment Programme Working Paper, ILO, Geneva, 35–62

Riphan, R. T. and T. Bauer, 1998: Employment effects of payroll taxes: an empirical test for Germany, Institute for the Study of Labour Discussion Paper, 11, IZA, Bonn

Transparency International (TI), 2003: Deutsches chapter e.V.: Corruption Perceptions Index, http://www.transparency.de/index.php?id=280 (accessed 3.3.2004)

Sanitation and Access to Clean Water

FRANK RIJSBERMAN

Characteristics of the Water Challenge

There has been much talk about a 'world water crisis' among water experts for several decades now and among policymakers and the public at large for the last five to ten years. What is this crisis? Is the world running out of water? Has there not been enough investment to make water available to people? In the twentieth century there has been massive investment in water resources development.[1] The world population tripled in the last century, but water use[2] grew sixfold. The governments of the United States and Australia, for example, con-

The author thanks his IWMI colleagues for their contributions to the chapter. Many of the results cited, and the analysis provided, is based on the work and insights of Tushaar Shah, leader of the IWMI–Tata Water Policy Programme based in Gujarat, India. Data on Africa were provided by Arlene Innocencio, IWMI's leader of an ongoing water investment strategy study for Africa, a collaborative project of the World Bank, African Development Bank, IFAD, FAO and IWMI. Data on drip irrigation in Nepal were provided by Madhu Bhattarai. Data on irrigation multipliers were provided by Madar Samad. The author is grateful for comments and suggestions on earlier drafts received from Mark Giourdano, Meredith Giordano, Hugh Turral, Sanjiv de Silva and Jonathan Woolley and for the critical review by John Boland and Henry Vaux, authors of Perspective papers 9.1 and 9.2.

[1] A rough estimate of the annual investments in the water sector around the turn of the century was US$ 70–80 bn year (Cosgrove and Rijsberman, 2000). That was estimated to be considerably below the high point of irrigation sub-sector investments in the 1970s and 1980s.

[2] That is, the use of renewable water resources (i.e. the water flowing in rivers plus the annual recharge into groundwater aquifers which is roughly 40 per cent or $40,000 \, \text{km}^3$ of annual rainfall) for human purposes grew to about $4,000 \, \text{km}^3$ in the year 2000.

[3] In monsoon Asia up to 90 per cent of the annual rainfall comes in several large rainstorms in less than 100 hours – leading to the risk of floods at some periods and severe drought during a large part of the year.

structed some $5,000 \, \text{m}^3$ of water storage infrastructure for each and every one of their citizens. Most of this infrastructure is meant to produce hydro-electricity and to irrigate farm land, while some is meant to control floods and store water for domestic water supply for urban areas. Even more money has been invested in water distribution infrastructure, treatment plants, sewerage and wastewater treatment. Water resources development has been a major part of the investments in developing countries – a key component of bilateral aid, World Bank lending, and domestic investment – and the subject of a water supply and sanitation investment drive called 'the water decade' in the 1980s. With all this investment, why is there still a crisis?

For many people 'the water crisis' is defined by the lack of access to safe and affordable water for over a billion people and lack of access to safe and affordable sanitation for close to half the world population. As a result poor people suffer diarrhoeal diseases that kill some two million people each year, over 90 per cent children under the age of five. For others, the crisis is that poor and malnourished people in rural areas do not have access to water to grow their food and sustain their livelihoods. Some three-quarters of the 1.2 bn poor and the 800 m malnourished people in the world live in rural areas, with agriculture as their sole or primary source of food and income.

It is argued here that there is enough water in the world for domestic purposes, industry and even to produce food, but these water resources are distributed very unevenly and there are large, densely populated areas that have either scarce water resources, or water falling very unevenly during the year.[3] In these areas, making water available often requires considerable investments in infrastructure or reform of the institutions that allocate water. For domestic water supply, the problem is not so much that there are no water resources, but that the unserved do not have access to capital (financial or political) to make it available to them. Even for agriculture, while there clearly are areas where water is in short supply, and people experience water scarcity, the cause is economic or institutional scarcity rather than physical scarcity in the large majority of cases.[4] In short, both urban and rural poor people that do not have access to safe and affordable drinking water and sanitation are exposed to severe health risks, and people in rural areas that do not have access to water for productive purposes tend to be poor and malnourished. Providing access to poor people for domestic and productive purposes is the challenge addressed in this chapter.

The total amount of water required for domestic purposes is small, compared to the water required for other basic needs. Poor people that do not have washing machines, cars to wash or gardens to water need 20–50 litres of water per person per day for domestic purposes. People in Europe generally use some 200 litres per person per day while in the USA the figure is about 400 litres. In addition, all people require thousands of litres of water per day to produce their food, depending on their diet and lifestyle. To produce 1 kg of cereal grains requires about 1 m^3, or 1,000 litres, of crop evapotranspiration.[5] However, 1 kg of meat requires much more water to produce – depending on how much feed[6] is given to the animals versus animals that graze on rainfed pastures. In California for example, about 13.5 m^3 of water is used to produce 1 kg of beef. Renault and Wallender (2000) estimate that a typical diet of a person from the USA requires about 5.4 m^3 water in the form of evapotranspiration. On the other hand a vegetarian diet with approximately the same nutritional value is responsible for the consumption of 2.6 m^3 of water per day. On average, it takes roughly seventy[7] times more water to grow food for people than people use directly for domestic purposes.[8] In addition, the large majority (up to 90 per cent) of the water provided to people for domestic purposes is returned after use as wastewater and can be recycled, while most of the water (40–90 per cent) provided to agriculture to grow food is consumed (evapotranspirated) and cannot be re-used.

The water supply and sanitation challenge has everything to do with providing reliable and affordable 'water services', but for all but the largest cities and their immediate environment, it has little to do with the development of water resources. Physical water scarcity is not the issue for all but the largest cities in dry areas.[9] The water for productive purposes challenge, or water for food as the main productive use we shall focus on, has the potential to dry up rivers.

There is, in this author's view, no real competition for water between domestic water supply and other uses, both because the amounts involved are

---

[4] Physical water scarcity has been defined by IWMI (1999) as shortage of supply to meet demands even when all policies to use water efficiently and effectively have been implemented. Economic water scarcity has been defined (IWMI 1999) as an inability to meet demand because the resources have not been developed (i.e. lack of infrastructure). Institutional water scarcity can be similarly defined as a failure of institutions to allocate available water supplies equitably or to the highest value user.

[5] Evapotranspiration is a measure of the amount of water consumed during the growing process of plants, either transpired through the plants' stomata or evaporated directly from the soil.

[6] For instance, animal fodder grown under irrigated conditions.

[7] Based on a domestic requirement of 50 litres per person per day and a food requirement of 3,500 litres per person per day.

[8] And roughly 1,000 times more than people need to drink. What complicates matters is that roughly 60 per cent of the world's food grains are grown under rainfed conditions. This also uses water, but since this is rainfall that enters into the soil and is directly evapotranspirated back into atmosphere without entering the surface water (rivers) or groundwater – this water is not counted in the traditional definitions of the world's water resources. For this reason some authors prefer the term 'blue water' to describe the renewable resources in rivers and groundwater and 'green water' for the rainfall that is evapotranspirated directly back into the atmosphere. Blue water is 40 per cent or 40,000 km^3 of the total hydrological cycle, while green water forms the other 60 per cent.

[9] Such as Los Angeles, where the development of the city was intricately linked to the development of water supplies over large distances, see Kahrl (1982). For large cities, if they are wealthy and situated on the coast, the water challenge can potentially be largely solved by the development of desalination technologies that are affordable for developed country economies. Cities such as Singapore and Tampa Bay, Florida, have awarded large contracts for desalination plants in recent years that have effectively put the provision of water in the same category as the provision of electric energy.

small and because water for domestic purposes is of such high value and the clear the priority that it takes precedence over other uses.[10] Cities do tend to have a major impact on the water sources in their immediate vicinity. Rivers running through cities often come out severely polluted. An environmental success story in developed countries is that the investments in wastewater treatment have by and large solved this problem, but most cities in developing countries still cause massive water pollution.

There is real competition in quantitative terms for water resources among other uses than do-

mestic water supply, particularly water for agriculture and water for the environment. The enormous investments in water resources development, in developed countries and in Asia, have led to rivers running dry or not reaching the sea any more and to groundwater levels falling as much as 50–100 m in key aquifers. The water resources that are 'developed' for agriculture were not 'wasted' before their development.[11] Inland water systems, such as wetlands lakes and river floodplains, forests, grazing lands and coastal ecosystems all provide environmental good and services in their natural state that are highly dependent on water. Environmental goods and services have only recently been more widely recognised as having high values. In some areas, such as California, where the awareness of the value of environmental goods and services is highly developed, water is re-allocated out of agriculture and back to ecosystems in a number of cases. In Australia, too, total agricultural diversions have been capped in the country's major food producing river basin and the remaining flows reserved for the environment.[12] Conversely, the fall in groundwater levels, particularly in China and India, threatens the livelihoods of the farmers in these areas as well as the food supply for a significant share of the world population. The assessment of values produced by natural systems has been hampered by lack of data and comparative analysis, but there have been a few famous documented cases (e.g. Acreman 2000) where large public investments in the development of irrigated agriculture created a system that produced lower values than the wetlands it replaced.

In the challenge to provide water for productive purposes – food and livelihoods – the effective and efficient *delivery of services* also plays a key role, but the focus (compared with water supply and sanitation) is primarily on the *management* of the resource. In short, the water challenge has two crucial dimensions: one is the aspect of service delivery comparable to that of other utility services and the other is the aspect of (renewable) natural resources management. Both aspects are important and they are linked in most every real-life situation, but they should be recognised as distinct, with distinct solutions. Instead in the popular discussion of 'the water crisis' they are often confused.[13] In summary, the water crisis is not so much a crisis of physical water

[10] Globally, roughly 10 per cent of all water diverted for human purposes is used for domestic purposes, 20 per cent for industrial uses and 70 per cent for agriculture. In the developed countries the amount used for industry is higher (up to 50 per cent in Europe) both because agriculture plays a smaller role in the economy and because agriculture in temperate zones needs less irrigation, i.e. uses more green water and less blue water. The water used for industrial purposes is dominated by cooling water for thermal power plants and process water. Only a small portion is incorporated in products (e.g. food and drinks) – the remainder turns out to be highly price-elastic (i.e. can be reduced drastically as water gets more costly). Water used for industry is generally not considered a problem and not discussed here. It is clear, however, that industry does cause a considerable share of the urban water pollution.

[11] A popular expression (or myth) among agriculturalists and engineers when discussing the water resources available for development is that 'X amount of water is running to the sea wasted.' In fact, all water in the hydrological cycle supports ecosystem services, from wetlands to inland and coastal fisheries, and none of it is wasted. While awareness of environmental functions and services has increased in recent decades, the concept of 'wasted water' remains prevalent in some parts of the world.

[12] As recently as November 2003 the first decisions to reduce water to agriculture and re-allocate water to restore ecosystem functions have been taken for the Murray–Darling basin too.

[13] The most widespread confusion is probably the highly controversial case of 'water pricing'. What is proposed by proponents of water pricing is in almost all cases the pricing of the *water services*, not the resource. While pricing of the scarcity value of the resource is theoretically desirable, most water pricing proposals aim to achieve cost-recovery for the services. Those against 'water pricing' usually argue that the water (resource) should be free (because it is provided free by God, as is held in many Islamic countries) or should not be commoditised (but held as a public good by governments for the benefit of all and not the profit of a few, as is the argument of many environmentalists in developed and developing countries).

scarcity as one of economic and institutional water scarcity. By and large the crisis is a crisis of governance and management: lack of access to safe and affordable water supplies for poor people for domestic and productive use. Solutions to the crisis should focus on improved service delivery responsive to user needs and institutional mechanisms to (re-) allocate water to domestic use, or higher-value uses in general, from agriculture where necessary. Solutions for water for food and livelihoods will need to make more water available to poor people, but where additional resources are developed the water needs of ecosystems need to be accounted for and the emphasis should generally be on increasing water productivity rather than allocating more water.

The Case for Government Involvement in Water

Throughout history, water resources development as well as water service provision has generally been treated as a government task.[14] Water is viewed by many as a critical resource with partial public good characteristics and various arguments have been put forward to justify government investment and management:

1. A certain amount of water for drinking and domestic purposes is considered a basic need and has been recognised as a human right,[15] requiring governments to make it available to their citizens
2. Potential net benefits to society, e.g. provision to users who cannot afford to pay for the service, would not be captured by private investors, i.e. the government would invest as a social welfare function, which has been argued for water supply and sanitation as well as irrigated agriculture
3. Investments in surface water developments also require large or lumpy investments, beyond the capacity of private investors, which provide an additional rationale for public investments (often local, municipal government, rather than national government) in development projects such as dams, large canals, treatment plants or distribution systems

4. Surface water resources such as streams and lakes are often managed by communities as common property resources because of the partial public good nature of the resource, allowing to some degree (non- or partially consumptive) use by one individual upstream that does not impair the ability of individuals downstream to enjoy the same use (apart from the degradation in quality that often is associated with various forms of use)[16]
5. Provision of piped water services often has characteristics of a monopoly[17] and this provides a rationale for governments to be involved in service provision, or management of the water services as well
6. Water development and use often imposes significant externalities on other users downstream, either in reduced availability of the resource or in terms of reduced quality, requiring government regulation or control.

[14] There are numerous examples of major public investments in water projects, from the Roman aqueducts to the irrigation works developed 1,500 years ago by Sri Lankan kings, closely linked with the development of major cities and the development of civilisations throughout history.

[15] The General Comment on the right to water, adopted by the United Nations Covenant on Economic, Social and Cultural Rights (CESCR) in November 2002, is the first time water is explicitly recognised as a fundamental human right. The 145 countries which have ratified the CESCR will now be compelled to progressively ensure that everyone has access to safe and secure drinking water, equitably and without discrimination. The General Comment states that 'the human right to water entitles everyone to sufficient, affordable, physically accessible, safe and acceptable water for personal and domestic uses'. It requires governments to adopt national strategies and plans of action which will allow them to 'move expeditiously and effectively towards the full realisation of the right to water'. These strategies should be based on human rights law and principles, cover all aspects of the right to water and the corresponding obligations of countries, define clear objectives, set targets and goals to be achieved and the timeframe for their achievement and formulate adequate policies and corresponding indicators.

[16] Groundwater resources, by contrast, are often treated as private resources belonging to the owner of the land where the well is situated. Given that in many groundwater aquifers the use of one well-owner can lead to the drawdown of the groundwater level on a neighbour's land, or for a neighbour's well, it is clear that there are limitations to this approach.

[17] As opposed to tankered or bottled water services, obviously, where competitive markets exist.

That water is a public good, or has public good characteristics, does not imply that it ought to be a free good – only that there is reason for government involvement in its development and management. Some countries have changed the law (e.g. South Africa) to ensure that all water resources are public property and users have only use rights. How governments finance the services they provide is obviously a source of considerable debate, in the water sector as much as for various other areas of government involvement from education to health care to other utilities, and is not the subject of this chapter. Suffice it to say that in the water sector there is an ongoing, and often quite emotional rather than rational, debate on whether or not individuals should be charged for the amount of water they use.[18]

The investments in the water sector have not always generated the benefits they were expected to produce. An important lesson learned from past mistakes is that successful water resources development and management for all but the largest projects, in developed and developing countries, have been managed by governments or communities at local or municipal levels.[19] Users that are involved directly in these investments through water user associations, irrigation districts, farmer cooperatives, urban water districts, or as municipal taxpayers, have a stake in the projects and are more likely to hold the managers accountable. Users that pay for the water services that they use have an incentive to use the resource wisely and demand quality services. The more removed the investment

decisions are from the user, the higher the risk that resources are misallocated and mismanaged. The more removed the users are from paying for the services, and the managers respond to national budget allocations, rather than fees paid by the users they serve, the higher the risk that service quality is low. That initiates a well-known and often observed downward spiral where users refuse to pay the fees or charges, service providers do not recover their costs, operation and maintenance funding falls short, service quality declines further, etc. A general trend observed in the evolving government policies since the mid-1980s is to decentralise government responsibility for water and to introduce water charges.[20]

The counter argument against charging users, particularly farmers, for the amount they use, rather than a fixed fee, is that for surface water irrigation systems the transaction costs of metering and charging large numbers of small users are very high (Perry 2001; De Fraiture and Perry 2002). Shah *et al.* (2003) argue, for instance, that rational systems of rationing may be more efficient than individual charges.

As for the provision of other services provided by governments, from transport to education to health to electricity, the arguments for government involvement are not without counter argument. There can be private, or semi-private, large-scale investments in the water sector, as some countries such as France have demonstrated successfully, and there are many forms of service provision by various forms of semi-private (publicly held companies, parastatals) or private companies, either under a public charter or through long-term contracts with government. Wherever water services are privatised, there will still be a strong case for government involvement in, for example, setting (public health) quality standards and regulating monopolies and externalities. In most forms of water-related investments where the scale of the investment is limited, private investments are common, as is the case for groundwater used for domestic or agricultural purposes.

A further complication is that while many argue that water ought to be a social good, at least part of the use of water is as an economic good. That the use of water for industry or commercial-scale

[18] Whereas 'water experts' have by and large recommended charging for water to various degrees and under various systems, for financial and economic reasons, as laid down in the Dublin Principles (Dublin Statement 1992) or the report of the World Water Commission (2000), NGOs and citizen groups in many countries have strongly lobbied against charging for water.

[19] Assuming some form of organisation is necessary; development of groundwater has to a large extent been undertaken by private investors (farmers) individually, or in small groups.

[20] Governments decentralise water through: (1) establishing water user associations; and (2) establishing river basin management authorities. Governments often introduce water charges for financial reasons (i.e. because they can not afford to maintain the services) rather than for the economic reasons advanced by the experts.

agri-business has private, economic good characteristics will be disputed by few. The key remaining argument for government involvement is then: (a) to regulate external costs imposed by the private use; (b) to capture economies of scale; or (c) to stimulate regional economic development or to create jobs. The discussion above is germane to this chapter on the water challenge because in the following sections on costs and benefits of investments in the water sector, estimates of future benefits that differ from observed benefits will need to be based on a sound understanding of past performance. Particularly, this chapter will argue that future investments should not be focused on a narrow technology-based approach implemented primarily through national government. Instead, the focus should be on a combination of interventions that combine technology, institutions and (social) marketing, implemented through decentralised organisations closely linked to, or directed by, the users.

Specifically, the case for public investments in the water sector today will rest on how much these investments can improve public health as well as reduce poverty and hunger. If so, do they generate public benefits beyond those likely to be captured by private investors. Past public investments, it is argued here, were overly focused on providing technology and infrastructure and insufficiently targeted on the poor segments of the population. As a result of the one-sided focus on technology and insufficient user involvement, investments have underperformed and not produced enough revenue to cover their operation and maintenance costs, leading to a downward spiral of deteriorating service. As a result of the lack of pro-poor targeting, sizeable sections of the population have been marginalised by the development process, even where that development process was successful.

Rijsberman (2003) reviewed the trickle-down assumption of the 1960s and 1970s, that expected that infrastructure and technology provision for the relatively better off would trickle-down to the poorest sections of society, and concluded that this has not worked in the water sector. In agriculture the focus on better farmers in fertile lands has benefited the target group in large parts of Asia, but left aside the poorest farmers in marginalised areas. In

water supply and sanitation the public investments, or subsidies, have been effectively captured by the relatively better off in urban areas, leaving aside large sections of slum dwellers. In both cases access to water has been monopolised by the better off and this has marginalised the poor. Access to water resources is increasingly recognised as an important tool for rural poverty alleviation, however, if it is targeted and 'pro-poor'.

The Cost of Managing Water Resources and Services Badly

In this section an effort is made to assess the costs of managing water badly, that is, to assess the key elements of the costs to society of the current 'water crisis'. Without trying to be exhaustive, the following key costs are dealt with:

1. Health impacts of the lack of access to safe and affordable water supply and sanitation for domestic purposes, combined with unhygienic behaviour
2. Damage and deaths due to water-related natural hazards
3. Poverty and malnourishment due, in part, to lack of access to water for productive purposes, primarily in agriculture
4. Environmental impacts due to reduced water availability and pollution.

Water Supply and Sanitation

Lack of access to basic water supply and sanitation services has a broad range of impacts at the household level for what are generally referred to as 'the unserved'. These range from the high costs the urban unserved pay to water vendors for minimal amounts of water,[21] to large amounts of time spent carrying water in rural areas, or time not spent by adults on productive activities while caring for sick children suffering from water-related diseases. The water-related health impacts are well established. They can be divided into three classes:

---

[21] It is well documented that the price poor people in urban areas pay for drinking water purchased from private vendors is often at least a factor ten higher than what their better off neighbours pay for the tap water piped into their homes.

1. Some diseases are closely correlated with the lack of access to water supply and sanitation combined with unhygienic behaviour, particularly diarrhoeal diseases.
2. Other diseases are water-related because the habitat for the vector transmitting the disease is closely linked to water or live in water, e.g. malaria, filariasis, schistosomiasis, guinea worm.
3. Finally, health impacts can also be caused by natural or anthropogenic low-quality water or pollutants, e.g. arsenic, fluoride, heavy metals, persistent organic pollutants or endocrine disruptors.

An overview of water-related health impacts reported by the UN Task Force on Water and Sanitation (2003) provides an indication of the scale, for example:

• At any given time, close to half the population in the developing world are suffering from one or more diseases associated with inadequate provision of water and sanitation services: diarrhoea, ascaris, dracunculiasis (guinea worm), hookworm, schistosomiasis (bilharzias, or snail fever) and trachoma
• Over 2 billion people are infected by schistosomiasis and soil-transmitted helminths, of whom 300 million suffer serious illness
• There is a 77 per cent reduction in schistosomiasis from well-designed water and sanitation interventions
• Arsenic in drinking water affects 50 million people in Asia that drink water from deep wells.

The most complete, recent assessment of water-related health impacts was carried out by Prüss

et al. (2002). They conducted a study based on WHO health statistics that analysed deaths and the burden of disease (in Disability Adjusted Life Years, DALYs) due to water, sanitation and hygiene risks. They show that diarrhoeal diseases form the bulk of the health risk, with a total of some 4 bn cases per year that result in between 1,085,000 and 2,187,000 deaths per year and between 37,923,000 and 76,340,000 DALYs, with 90 per cent of deaths occurring among children under five. Adding impacts of other water-associated diseases (schistosomiasis, trachoma and intestinal helminth infections) led to a total estimate of water-, sanitation- and hygiene-related ill health of 2,213,000 deaths and 82,196,000 DALYs per year, not including malaria impacts.

According to the United Nations World Water Development Report (UNWWDR 2003), this study was innovative in that it systematically analysed transmission pathways in fourteen regions against six exposure scenarios. Combining the data on current levels of water and sanitation services in the WHO/UNICEF Joint Monitoring Programme then allows analysis of the potential decrease in morbidity and mortality for intervention scenarios, for an assessment of the cost-effectiveness of specific measures. The Prüss *et al.* (2002) study has significantly improved the global methodology of the water related health impacts and also (UNWWDR 2003):

• Confirms with stronger evidence than before that water, sanitation and hygiene are key determinants of health, with substantial mortality and morbidity occurring as a result of lack of access to water and sanitation and of inadequate hygiene behaviour
• Underlines how diseases related to water, sanitation and health disproportionately affect the poor
• Illustrates the high potential for disease reduction by simple methods such as safe drinking water storage and disinfection at the household level.

While assessment of the economic cost of DALYs is controversial, if we apply a cost of US$500 per DALY,[22] a low ballpark estimate of the *per capita* annual income of the poor in the poorest of developing countries, as a low boundary estimate, then

---

[22] It is noted that other chapters in this volume also use estimates for the value of a DALY, e.g. Mills and Shillcutt (2004) in their chapter 2 on communicable diseases propose to use the annual *per capita* Gross National Income (GNI) of the region in which the health impacts occur, expressed in 2003 Purchasing Power Parity (PPP) adjusted 'international dollars' – which yields a range of Int$2,000 to Int$10,000. Adoption of this estimate across all chapters, for comparison's sake, would increase the corresponding benefits estimated here by a factor of 4–20. During the Copenhagen Consensus some of the experts expressed a preference for using an average of US$1,250 per DALY.

Table 9.1. Impacts of Floods and Droughts, 1990s and 2000

Drought in Zimbabwe during early 1990s was associated with 45 per cent decline in agricultural production, and 11 per cent decline in GDP and a 60 per cent decline in stock markets.

El Niño floods in Kenya in 1997–98 caused economic losses estimated at US$1.7 bn.

Floods in Mozambique in 2000 led to a 23 per cent decline in GDP.

Drought in Brazil in 2000 led to halving of projected economic growth in that year.

El Niño floods in Peru in 1998 cost US$2.6 bn in public infrastructure damages or 5 per cent of GDP.

Landslides in Venezuela in 1999 cost losses of US$10 bn, or 10 per cent of GDP.

Hurricane Mitch in Honduras in 199X caused damages equivalent to 79 per cent of GDP.

Source: Hansen and Bhatia (2004, 17).

the annual health costs attributed to low access to water and sanitation are on the order of US$40 bn.

The other major water-related disease is malaria. The disease is the leading cause of deaths in young children in Africa, where 90 per cent of the over 1 m deaths from malaria occur. In 2001, the estimated global burden of disease of malaria amounted to 42.3 m DALYs (WHO 2002). The difference between diarrhoeal diseases and malaria is that there is no known, simple, affordable and effective measure to reduce or eliminate malaria, as there is for diarrhoeal diseases. The bulk of the efforts to reduce malaria focus on providing people with insecticide treated bednets (ITNs) and the development of a malaria vaccine. More limited efforts are underway at the research level to attempt to develop environmental management methods to reduce malaria, but the potential for water-related measures for the key area of the disease, Africa, appear limited.[23]

Natural Hazards

An analysis of macroeconomic impacts of natural disasters carried out for the UNWWDR (2003 12) showed that between 1991 and 2000 over 665,000 people died in 2,557 natural disasters, of which 90 per cent were water-related events and with 97 per cent of the victims from developing countries. While such impacts are considerable, and can be catastrophic in the locations concerned, as shown in table 9.1, the overall scale of impacts is assessed to be an order of magnitude lower than the impacts of lack of access to water supply and sanitation.

The impact of natural hazards such as floods and droughts is reviewed here because they are the most visible and reported forms of 'water crisis', but as the evidence reviewed here shows, the impact of the less visible lack of safe water supply and sanitation is much more devastating.

Agriculture

Lipton, Litchfield and Faures (2003) conclude in an overview paper that the high inverse correlation between poverty in rural areas and the percentage of the agricultural land that is irrigated is no coincidence. In other words, lack of access to water for productive purposes in agriculture is a key determinant of rural poverty[24] and malnutrition. Lipton, Litchfield and Faures (2003) also conclude that despite the irrigation's 'bad press', it remains an important tool for poverty reduction. The main impacts of irrigation on poverty are via increased employment and lower food prices.[25] There is ample evidence that irrigation has contributed significantly to poverty reduction. Shah

[23] The potential impact of environmental management (i.e. mosquito habitat reduction) is limited in Africa, compared to Asia, because the malaria transmission rates are so much higher in Africa that massive reductions in habitats would still yield only marginal impact.

[24] Of the 1,200 m people defined as dollar-poor (i.e. with a *per capita* household income of less than 1US$/day in 1985 PPP) three-quarters live in rural areas.

[25] A majority of the rural poor are not farmers, i.e. they are not net food producers, but they generate their income from employment and are net food purchasers. That makes them beneficiaries of lower food prices.

and Singh (2003) show that sub-districts in India with high irrigation density (irrigated area/net sown area) have significantly smaller numbers of households below the poverty line. Research carried out in India (Bihar and Madhya Pradesh/ Chattisgarh region), Myanmar, Philippines, Thailand and Vietnam suggests that the incidence, depth and severity of income poverty were substantially lower in irrigated and agriculturally developed areas compared to rainfed and less-developed areas in all these case studies except for Myanmar (Garcia, *et al.* 2000; Hossain, Sen and Rahman 2000; Hossain and Janaiah 2000; Isvilanonda, *et al.* 2000; Janaiah, Bose and Agarwal 2000; and Thakur, *et al.* 2000). Hussain and Hanrja (2003) analysed 120 published studies on the irrigation–poverty nexus, and conducted additional household surveys in Sri Lanka and Pakistan and similarly concluded that public irrigation investments reduced poverty. At the same time they conclude that there remains considerable poverty, not only in the rainfed, marginal lands, but also within irrigation systems due to inequitable distribution of benefits. Generally speaking, where the land distribution is inequitable, the benefits to irrigation will be inequitably distributed as well.

More land is irrigated, however – and more agrarian wealth created – in India by privately owned small groundwater pumps than by public irrigation systems (Shah 1993). Ownership of wells is highly scale-biased, however, and most marginal farmers were denied the gains of 'Green Revolution' farming since they would be unable to invest in their own wells and pumps. Over the past several decades, a spontaneous rise of groundwater markets has opened access for South Asia's rural poor to groundwater or pump irrigation. This was facilitated by the introduction of cheaper and smaller Chinese engines, and micro-credit schemes such as those developed by the Grameen Bank and other NGOs (van Koppen and Mahmud 1996).

In India alone surveys show that the 20 m private pump owners serve over 60 m smallholder farmers (Shah 2000). This accounts for more area irrigated than the entire public irrigation system in the country. The scale of informal trade in pump irrigation service in India and Bangladesh might well be of the order of US$ 3–5 bn per year during mid-1990s. The drawback of the groundwater boom has been that it has been fuelled by subsidised electricity, and the state electricity boards are by and large collecting insufficient revenue to be sustainable, so energy prices are going up and are affecting the use of groundwater for irrigation. The second side-effect is that the largely uncontrolled expansion of groundwater extraction has led in both India and China – the two countries with by far the largest area under irrigation – to severe drawdowns of groundwater levels in key groundwater aquifers. The lowering of the groundwater table significantly increases the (energy) cost of the groundwater and eventually makes the activity uneconomical.

The development of small-scale irrigation technology such as drip and micro-sprinkler irrigation systems, like groundwater, also increase the control farmers have over their water application and tends to significantly increases the value added of the water applied. The low cost varieties of the micro irrigation technology,[26] originally developed for capital-intensive commercial farming in places such as Israel and California, are highly labour-intensive and have shorter life spans but are affordable for small farmers. Particularly suited for vegetables, fruits and other high-value crops that are also labour-intensive, capital investments of only one to several hundred dollars can generate significant increases in family income that pay back for the investment in one to several years.

A key part of the challenge is that the evidence of the poverty reduction impact of irrigation (including 'traditional,' groundwater and micro-irrigation) comes primarily from Asia and to some extent from South America, while there are far fewer success stories from Africa. There is more evidence and data from Asia that community-based, small-scale interventions that improve the access of water for productive purposes to poor people have significant impacts on poverty and malnutrition – and may have positive impacts on the environment as well. To date there is only scant evidence from Africa but the subject is currently under intense study.

It is clear that lack of access to water is not the only cause of poverty in the rural areas. It is also

---

[26] E.g. bucket drip kits, low grade plastic 'Pepsee' drip lines, treadle pumps.

clear that simply providing irrigation infrastructure is by itself far from a guarantee that there will be a reduction in rural poverty and malnutrition. The argument advanced here and worked out below is that providing access to water for productive purposes is one of the key opportunities in the water sector to alleviate poverty for a considerable share of the three-quarters of the world's 'dollar poor' that live in rural areas.

Environmental Impacts

All irrigated land is potentially prone to waterlogging and salinisation if not managed carefully. All agriculture on sloping or steep lands is also potentially prone to soil erosion. The resulting decline in land productivity is very hard to assess but most estimates show very high shares of all land in use being affected. Hansen and Bhatia (2004) report a decline of land productivity affecting 30 per cent of world's irrigated areas, 40 per cent of rainfed agriculture and 70 per cent of rangelands. Wood *et al.* (2000) estimated that as much as 40 per cent of the agricultural area in the world is moderately degraded and a further 9 per cent is strongly degraded, which may have reduced global crop yield by as much as 13 per cent. It is clear that large areas of land are converted from natural ecosystems to agricultural use, are then more or less seriously degraded, often irreversibly, and then left. Various global (and by their very nature inaccurate) estimates of the areas of wetlands and natural grasslands that have been destroyed over the twentieth century come up with high numbers such as 50 per cent reduction in area. Only relatively recently have estimates been made of the values of the goods and services that ecosystems provide in their natural, healthy state.[27] All these estimates come up with very high estimates of the values of the natural capital that the ecosystems represent – and as a consequence very high costs to society when these systems get degraded or permanently converted into agriculture or urban use. Estimates of the cost of remediation of environmental damage due to degradation also come up with very high numbers. Jalal and Rogers (1977), for example, estimated the annual cost of remediation of environmental damage in Asia alone at US$35 bn.

Not all is grim on the environmental front, however. The major clean-up of rivers in Western Europe and North America, that began with building proper sewerage systems for large cities in the nineteenth century and continued with major investments in wastewater treatment plants from about the 1970s, has resulted in notably healthier rivers that are once again 'fishable and swimmable'. This is an environmental success story. This chapter has not identified opportunities for large-scale investments in water-related environmental remediation measures that would yield benefits on the scale of opportunities related to water supply and sanitation or water for food and livelihoods. For environmental issues, preventing damage makes more economic sense than remediation.

Estimating Benefits of Improved Water Management

Water is an intermediate input to achieve desired outcomes such as health, nutrition and income and the relationship between input and outcomes is complex. In addition the dynamic nature of water, which makes its value highly dependent on timing, location and quality, poses problems for any attempt to value its contribution. Rogers, deSilva and Bhatia (2002) propose a framework for valuation that includes the following components:

1. Direct value to the user
2. Net benefits of return flows, i.e. value to subsequent users from the fraction returned by the previous user
3. Net benefits from indirect use, e.g. the multiple use made of water in an irrigation system, not only for the primary purpose of irrigating the scheme, but for drinking, washing, fishing, watering household garden farm plots, etc.
4. Adjustment for societal objectives such as employment generation, poverty alleviation, or national food security

---

[27] Notably a well-known paper by Costanza *et al.* (1997) that estimated the value of the total global flow of environmental goods and services at US$5.254 trillion per year.

5. Intrinsic value of the resource, to account for environmental, social and cultural values that are otherwise not accounted for (e.g. stewardship and bequest values).

While the framework serves as a reminder of the complexity of doing complete valuations, there are very few studies available that follow this or a similarly complete framework to arrive at total values at any but a microeconomic case-study scale. In short, the economic literature on the benefits of improved water management is rather sparse. The bulk of the material available addresses cost-effectiveness analysis of specific measures, assuming a set objective for the level of the service. This is the standard approach for water supply and sanitation. In addition there is an extensive literature on project-level cost-benefit analysis (CBA), specifically to justify investments in irrigation and hydropower projects. An expert workshop convened by the United Nations on water economics and financing in 1998 concluded (UNDESA, 1998) that: 'The economics of water resources rarely influence water policy, even in water-short regions. As a result, the principal asset of the water resource base remains highly undervalued and readily used without much concern for its value to others, the structural role of water in the economy and its in situ value as an environmental asset.'

While the above quote at least expresses the belief that the disregards of economics is something to be lamented, there is also a large school in the water sector that bases itself on a human rights approach. As expressed by a report of the Task Force on Water and Sanitation of the UN Millennium Project[28]: 'expanding access to water and sanitation is a moral and ethical imperative rooted in the cultural and religious traditions of societies around the world and enshrined in human rights instruments' (UN Task Force on Water and Sanitation 2003, 18). It goes on to note that 'many services run on a shoe-string of

hope by volunteers, religious groups or dedicated, poorly paid officials succeed because they mobilise the enthusiasm and engagement of their communities, while other projects backed by extravagant budgets and massive expertise turn to dust in a bureaucratic desert that stifles individual and community spirit'.

At the very least, this illustrates the difficulty of producing reliable economic assessments.

Opportunities

This section discusses the opportunities in the water sector, in terms of specific interventions or intervention packages that, in the opinion of the author, have large potential net benefits for society. It presents the supporting evidence in terms of benefits and costs, and net benefits (in terms of net present value, NPV) where possible. There is unfortunately not a neat single methodological or modelling framework to assess the costs and benefits, as these are drawn from different sources of (partial) estimates available in the literature.

The opportunities discussed in detail in the following sections are:

1. **Community-managed low-cost water supply and sanitation**
2. **Small-scale water technologies for livelihoods.**

These are two important opportunities for which costs and benefits are known to a degree that estimates can be made as required for this chapter. They are not the only opportunities related to the sector, however. Other key opportunities, in the author's opinion, are the following:

3. **Re-using waste water for peri-urban agriculture**, which addresses a key aspect of the sanitation challenge as it turns the challenge of dealing with the urban wastewater into an opportunity, a resource, for livelihood generation. It also addresses the poverty and malnutrition challenge for one of the most vulnerable groups of very poor people, those living in the peri-urban areas, the slums, of medium to large cities in developing countries. It even has high relevance for the health and environment challenges. It has been estimated by FAO (UNWWDR 2003, 219) that 20 m hectare is directly or indirectly[29] irrigated

---

[28] Established by the UN Secretary General to develop strategies to implement the Millennium Development Goals (MDGs).

[29] 'Direct irrigation' refers to wastewater streams being applied directly, undiluted- and often untreated, to agricultural land. Indirect irrigation with wastewater takes place when wastewater is discharged in streams or irrigation canals, mixed with fresh water and used for irrigation.

with wastewater in fifty countries – close to 10 per cent of the total irrigated area. A national survey of Pakistan showed that one-third of all wastewater produced in the country is used directly, undiluted and untreated for irrigation[30] and an estimated quarter of all vegetables grown in the country are irrigated with wastewater (Ensink *et al.* 2004). The opportunity would refer to re-using wastewater in those medium to large cities in developing countries where low-cost sewerage needs to be installed to increase access to sanitation. Domestic wastewater from roughly every thousand people could sustain a farmer (therefore the number of farmers potentially affected could not be much higher than between 1 and 2 m). Costs would refer to minimal treatment to make the use of the wastewater biologically safe to use for producers and consumers. The costs of treatment would be medium (high),[31] but the potential returns could be very high, both for the farmers in terms of direct income and for the environment due to prevention of the pollution that would result from the untreated discharge of the wastewater. Consequently the benefit-cost ratio (BCR) is potentially very high.

4. **Developing sustainable smallholder agriculture in wetlands**, as a way to maintain ecosystem services associated with wetlands (as opposed to draining them and turning them into regular arable land) while providing livelihood opportunities for poor farmers – an opportunity particularly relevant for Africa where there are small scale wetlands ('dambos') that lend themselves for agricultural production without complete reclamation.[32] If successful, it would allow a critical type of ecosystem to be maintained, with services that are estimated to generate annual ecosystem services that are valued up to several thousand US$ per hectare. The total area of dambos in Africa, for example, is not well mapped but is estimated to cover several thousand hectares. The total number of farmers that could derive direct income from this opportunity is relatively small; the larger share of the benefits from this opportunity would be associated with the maintenance of the environmental services of the wetlands.

5. **Research to increase the productivity of water for food production**, thereby decreasing the total water required to produce food and rural livelihoods, as a way to accommodate the rapidly increasing needs for urban and industrial water supply without further penalizing the environment. This is an intervention aimed at the heart of the bulk of the water used for human purposes, i.e. increasing the crop per drop, the jobs per drop and the nutrition per drop of water used to produce food and rural livelihoods. This opportunity has recently been recognised as a top priority for the international system for agricultural research.[33] The investment costs are relatively low – in the order of US$300–400 m over a period of ten–fifteen years while the potential benefits are very high.[34] The benefits are hard to estimate – but earlier evaluations of the impact of the system of international agricultural research have estimated BCRs of 15–20.[35]

A further opportunity that was considered but rejected is desalination. Since it is often assumed that, with rapidly falling costs of desalination, the water challenge can be met by desalination of brackish or saline water, the following provides some perspective. The global market for desalination in 2002 stood at about US$ 35 bn (UNWWDR 2003, p. 89). In 2002 there were about 12,500 desalination

---

[30] The use of untreated sewage bring considerable health risks, both in increased helminth infection of producers and diarrhoea of consumers, but farmers – aware of the health risks – adopt the practice because of the high economic returns.

[31] Medium (or average) on a simple 5-point scale of 'very small', 'small', 'medium', 'high' and 'very high', compared to the costs and benefits of other opportunities.

[32] As has been the norm in Asia, where wetlands have been turned in to paddyfields.

[33] The CGIAR Challenge Programme on Water and Food, see www.waterandfood.org. It must be noted that the author, as the chief architect of this Programme, is not an independent source on the matter.

[34] The perception, at least, of the high potential benefits of the Programme is confirmed through the commitment of seven donors that have underwritten the Programme with, to date, about US$55 m for the first six-year phase.

[35] See, for example, the discussion on this issue in Behrman, Alderman and Hoddinott's chapter 7 in this volume.

plants in 120 countries (70 per cent in the Near-East, mostly Saudi Arabia, Kuwait, United Arab Emirates, Qatar and Bahrain) producing 14 million m^3 per day, or less than 1 per cent of global use. Energy costs are very high, i.e. 6 kWh per cubic meter of water desalinated for reverse osmosis technology and 80–150 kWh/m^3, mostly in the form of (waste) heat, for multistage flash technology. Costs have come down rapidly from several dollars per m^3 for most of the installed capacity to 0.5–1.0 US\$/m^3 for technology currently available, and are projected to fall further to possibly around 0.2 US\$/m^3 over the next ten–fifteen year (Cosgrove and Rijsberman 2000). This makes it an attractive option for domestic and industrial use through large plants for large, wealthy seaside cities from Singapore and Tampa Bay (Florida) to Santa Barbara (California) and in small units for tourism developments on small islands from the Caribbean to the Maldives. Small desalination units have become widely available off-the-shelf technology that has been shown to offer opportunities even for rural communities of relatively well off farmers in dry parts of India where the only alternative source of water is deep groundwater that contains high levels of fluoride or arsenic. The price indicates, however, that it is not a large-scale option for water supply for the rural poor or for poverty reduction through agriculture. In addition, both the high energy costs and the environmental problem of disposing of the brine, that is the unavoidable by-product of the process, reduce the attractiveness of the option for anything but 'niche' use.

For Opportunities 3–5 above sufficient data are unfortunately lacking to provide estimates of total costs and benefits. They are nevertheless important opportunities in the opinion of the author and can also be seen as important supporting elements of

the first two opportunities. It should be recognised that while the challenges and opportunities are discussed here as discrete, or even isolated, phenomena, they are of course highly interrelated.

Community-Managed Low-Cost Water Supply and Sanitation

The intervention proposed in this section is a package of community-managed low-cost water supply, sanitation and hygiene education. Low-cost water supply implies standpipes and low-cost sanitation refers to latrines (ventilated, improved) in rural areas and to low-cost sewerage in urban areas. Communities are assumed to be involved in the design, implementation and management of the systems, and contribute labour to reduce costs. Investment in infrastructure is linked to hygiene education, as part of a social marketing effort, and combined with micro-credit Programmes that increase the ability of the poor to pay (part of) the investment costs.

It is estimated that in the year 2000, 1.1 billion people lacked access to safe water and 2.4 bn lacked access to basic sanitation.[36] The MDG for water and sanitation, that sets out the target to halve the number of people unserved by 2015, has provided estimates of the number of people unserved by region, in both rural and urban areas (see table 9.2). Since this is the number to gain access by 2015 it contains both the currently unserved and the population growth between 2000 and 2015. Just to complete the picture, reaching complete access for all of the population by 2015 would then add another 550 m people to those to whom access to water supply must be extended and another 1,200 m to whom sanitation must be extended.

It is customary in the development literature to calculate the total cost of extending service to the unserved, compare this to the current investment levels, conclude that there is a financing gap and call for increased development aid to meet the perceived needs (i.e. close the gap). The UNWWDR (2003) reviews these approaches, and the global estimates of funding for the water sector required in the range of US\$110–180 bn, and concludes that there is 'a massive investment gap and that the sources of

---

[36] The data on the levels of access to water supply and sanitation are generally sourced from the Joint Monitoring Project (JMP), a partnership between UNICEF and WHO, that is generally acknowledged as the best, if not perfect, source of data available. The JMP data used to be based on reports provided by national governments, with all the problems that entail, but as of the assessment over the year 2000 (WHO–UNICEF 2000) and updated in 2001 (available at www.wssinfo.org/en/welcome.html) the basis for the assessment has shifted to household surveys.

Table 9.2. Number of People, in Millions, to Whom Access Must be Extended by 2015 in Order to Meet MDG Targets

Regions/Country categories	Number of people to gain access to improved water supply by 2015			Number of people to gain access to improved sanitation by 2015		
	Urban	Rural	Total	Urban	Rural	Total
SSA	175	184	359	178	185	363
Middle East and North Africa	104	30	134	105	34	140
South Asia	243	201	444	263	451	714
East Asia and Pacific	290	174	465	330	376	705
Latin America and Caribbean	121	20	141	132	29	161
CEE/CIS and Baltic States	27	0	27	24	0	
Total	**961**	**609**	**1,570**	**1,032**	**1,076**	**2,108**

Source: UN Task Force on Water and Sanitation (2003, 47).

finance are inadequate' (UNWWDR 2003, 335). It is worth noting, though, that at least one of those global estimates reviewed (Cosgrove and Rijsberman 2000) in an – admittedly also crude – analysis concluded that the bulk of both current and future financing comes, and will have to come, from domestic public and private funding, not international financing through development aid. It estimated that 80–90 per cent of current funding in the water sector comes from domestic funding, with the bulk coming from public investments (Cosgrove and Rijsberman 2000; GWP 2000).

In this respect, possibly the best news for the current unserved populations is that roughly half the people without access to sanitation live in China and India alone; countries whose sustained high economic growth rates makes it likely that the sources of finance necessary to 'fund the gap' may be available in the national economy. The 2002 and 2003 *Human Development Reports* analyse the progress towards achieving the water and sanitation targets. The overall conclusion is that countries that have some 40 per cent of the world population, and that are primarily situated in Asia, have either achieved the target or are on track towards achieving it. Another group of countries with some 30 per cent of the world population, primarily situated in Africa, show either stalled, or reversing, progress. The conclusion is that external funding should focus on, and

probably be more effective, in the countries where progress is slow or stalled.

A somewhat similar approach by the UN Task Force on Water and Sanitation attempted to analyse areas where the cost-effectiveness would be greatest by identifying where current low levels of access.[37] are combined with high prevalence of diarrhoeal diseases.[38] For water supply the list of high priority countries then includes Angola, Burkina Faso, Chad, Congo, Ethiopia, Eritrea, Guinea, Mauritania and Afghanistan; for sanitation the list consists of Angola, Benin, Burkina Faso, Central African Republic, Chad, Congo, Ethiopia, Eritrea, Mauritania, Mozambique, Namibia, Niger, Togo, Afghanistan and Bangladesh. These may, however, not be the countries where the opportunities for achieving impact are greatest, as the list clearly shows a high number of countries that are, or have been, engaged in conflict and the conditions may not be in place to achieve impact. This is an area where this challenge links in with chapter 3 in this volume on conflicts and arms proliferation. It must be noted that even though countries may be on the way to achieving the MDG target, i.e. halving the number of people without access, that still leaves considerable parts of the population unserved.

[37] Less than 50 per cent.
[38] Prevalence of 20–40 per cent.

Table 9.3. Improved versus Non-Improved Water Supply and Sanitation

	Improved	Non-improved
Water supply	• Household connection • Public standpipe • Borehole • Protected dug well • Protected spring water • Rainwater collection	• Unprotected well • Unprotected spring • Vendor-provided water • Bottled water[a] • Tanker-truck provided
Sanitation	• Connection to a public sewer • Connection to a septic system • Pour-flush latrine • Simple pit latrine • Ventilated improved pit latrine	• Service or bucket latrines[b] • Public latrines • Latrines with open pit

[a] Considered as 'non-improved' because of quantity rather than quality of supplied water.
[b] Latrines from where excreta are manually removed.
Source: UNWWDR (2003, 113).

The estimates reported in table 9.2 are only relatively rough estimates for several reasons. First, while the analysis in table 9.2 assumes that all people born between 2000 and 2015 need to be served with new infrastructure, Hutton and Haller (2004, cited in Evans, Hutton and Haller 2004, n. 13) assume that the percentage coverage in 2000 applies to the new population as well and arrives at an estimate of the total population to be served with sanitation to meet the MDG of 1.47 bn. Second, one must also analyse what is implied in the various definitions of 'access'. The data in the WHO–UNICEF Joint Monitoring Programme (as reported in table 9.2 above) report access to 'improved' water supply and 'improved' sanitation. This is a definition based on the availability of infrastructure (see table 9.3), not on the outcome in terms of access to water and sanitation. For this reason UN-HABITAT prefers to define the number unserved in terms 'adequate' access to water and sanitation (e.g. UNWWDR 2003). It concludes that for urban areas, particularly, improved water and sanitation does not need to imply adequate access. In its analysis of the number unserved in urban areas, on the basis of the 'adequate' definition, the numbers go up. The MDGs, on the other hand, speak about access to 'safe' water (without defining 'safe') and access to basic sanitation. The latter is understood to be a definition that focuses more on the outcome of sanitary conditions that include hygienic behaviour and focus less on the technology used. An important problem with the focus on the availability of infrastructure is that past experience shows that the availability of infrastructure is poorly correlated with the level of service provided.

Investments in infrastructure have often not led to the intended increase in access because, particularly, inadequate levels of operation and maintenance in rural as well as urban systems have led to large amounts of installed infrastructure being de-facto non-operational or functioning poorly. Reasons for the poor performance of these investments are: (a) donor-driven, top-down and technology focused projects, that failed to involve the users directly, tend to be poorly maintained and break down after a limited period of use; this has been the fate of a very large number of hand-pumps installed in rural areas; (b) low levels of financial recovery in urban systems, not covering operation and maintenance, sooner or later lead to badly functioning and badly managed systems with low service and high losses.

The widely accepted lessons learned from this past experience, based also on an analysis of success stories, is that successful water supply projects should be community managed. They should involve the community from the start of the project, mobilise community resources in terms of labour contributed and pay attention to the development of institutions that will manage the infrastructure once in place.

While past projects often focused on providing improved water supply systems as stand-alone projects, the benefits in terms of improved public health are only partially realised by providing access to clean water in sufficient amounts alone. A review of 144 studies linking sanitation and water supply with public health found that the 'role [of water quality] in diarrhoeal disease control was less important than that of sanitation and hygiene' (Esrey, *et al.* 1991). The greatest impact is obtained when water supply, sanitation and hygiene education are combined, however. The opportunity discussed here is therefore to combine water supply and sanitation in a single investment.

While Esrey's findings suggests that sanitation may be more important to achieving health impacts than water supply, Evans, Hutton and Haller (2004) report that JMP data suggest that sanitation investments make up only 20 per cent of the total water and sanitation sub-sector investments in developing countries (12 per cent in Africa, 15 per cent in Asia, 38 per cent in Latin America). While these data may under-report the household expenditures, the number does suggest why the lack of access to sanitation facilities is so much greater than that to water supply. Given findings from a multi-country study, also conducted by Esrey (1996), that providing access to improved sanitation facilities to an unserved population leads to an observed reduction of 37.5 per cent in diarrhoeal disease, investment in low-cost sanitation presents a major water investment opportunity. In other words, to capture some of the key benefits of providing water supply-related health benefits, it is necessary to provide water supply *and* sanitation, together with a basic hygiene public awareness campaign.

Low-cost sanitation for rural populations consists essentially of pit latrines, costing US\$30–60 *per capita* in initial investment (Evans, Hutton and Haller 2004). Low-cost sanitation for dense urban areas, where latrines are not an option, may consist of septic tanks or shallow, small-bore sewerage[39] combined with low-cost treatment, costing US\$60–140 *per capita* in initial investment, with so-called simplified or condominial sewer costs starting as low as US\$30 *per capita* (Evans, Hutton and Haller 2004; Mara, personal communication 2004).

To assess the overall benefits of extending access to water supply and sanitation there are two approaches available, both reported in Evans, Hutton and Haller (2004):

1. A micro-scale intervention analysis conducted by Hutton (reported in Evans, Hutton and Haller 2004) of the costs and benefits of meeting the MDG on sanitation by 2015, scaled up to global coverage. This involves an analysis of the costs of initial investment and recurrent costs *per capita* for a range of low-cost technologies, with costs varying for Africa, Asia and Latin America[40] and the benefits in terms of (a) health sector treatment cost avoided; (b) patient health seeking costs avoided; and (c) the annual value of time gained.

2. A macro cost-effectiveness analysis conducted by WHO that maps transmission pathways of faecal–oral diseases, and offsets the six WHO regions[41] distinguished in the global burden of disease statistics against six globally important exposure scenarios. It assesses exposure risks as derived from literature-based intervention reports, to arrive at relative risks for different scenarios, constructed on the basis of the WHO–UNICEF JMP data. It then assesses the cost of moving from one scenario to another and the benefits, in terms of reductions in DALYs, of moving from exposure scenarios with lower levels of safe access to water supply and sanitation to higher level scenarios. The analysis then reports the cost-effectiveness of each of the scenarios, in terms of the cost per DALY averted.

For the first approach, the detailed costs and benefits analyses (Evans, Hutton and Haller 2004) are reported in appendix 1. The conclusions are provided in table 9.4. The strategy is based on providing access to low-cost technologies, generally speaking public standpipes for water supply and pit latrines in rural areas and low-cost sewerage in urban areas for sanitation. The costs refer to both the costs of providing low-cost water supply, through community managed projects (i.e. assuming considerable

---

[39] Also referred to as low-cost sewerage.

[40] Costs adapted by Evans, Hutton and Haller (2004) based on UNEP/GPA Financing Domestic Wastewater Collection and Treatment in Relation to the WSSD Target on Water and Sanitation (forthcoming) and the WHO–UNICEF (2000) global assessment of water and sanitation.

[41] Sub-divided into fourteen regions on the basis of child and adult mortality levels.

Table 9.4. Costs and Benefits of meeting the MDGs on Water and Sanitation through Community-Managed Low-Cost Water Supply and Sanitation (US$ m)

Region	Water Supply annual investm. and recurrent cost	Sanitation annual investm. and recurrent cost	Sanitation benefits	Cost Benefit Ratios san. ben. over total costs	NPV (5%)	NPV (10%)
SSA	491	1,531	16,183	8.0	130,000	102,000
Latin America	171	617	7,325	9.3	60,000	47,000
East Mediterranean & North Africa	57	206	5,865	22.3	51,000	40,000
Central & Eastern Europe	60	198	2,508	9.7	21,000	16,000
South and S.E. Asia	403	3,692	11,104	2.7	64,000	50,000
West Pacific developing countries	566	3,056	11,619	3.2	74,000	57,000
Total	**1,748**	**9,300**	**54,604**	**4.9**	**400,000**	**312,000**

Source: Adapted from Evans, Hutton and Haller (2004).

contributions through the community and low implementation costs) and the cost of providing low-cost sanitation in a similar manner. These costs are in line with (and based on) estimates made by the Water Supply and Sanitation Collaborative Council in their Vision 21 process, and by the UNEP GPA Programme – but they are considerably lower than other estimates that assume 'conventional' technologies and implementation.

The benefits included in table 9.4 are benefits assessed in detail for sanitation by Hutton as reported in Evans, Hutton and Haller (2004),[42] assumed to be responsible for the lion's share of the reduction in diarrhoeal diseases. As there are obviously other benefits associated with better water supply, such as the reduced time spent to obtaining the water, which are not assessed, this can be considered a lower boundary of the overall benefits. At the same time it is worth noting that the bulk of the benefits reported in table 9.4, are associated with estimated annual value of time gained. Time is gained due to: (a) closer access to sanitation services; and (b) fewer days off work and school due to diarrhoea averted,[43]

valued at the minimum wage in each country; and (c) less days lost caring for sick babies (valued at 50 per cent of the minimum wage in each country). Benefits associated with 'health sector costs avoided' and 'patient health seeking costs avoided' were also estimated but amounted to only about 10 per cent of total benefits.

The strategy evaluated in table 9.4 assumes that water and sanitation is provided to 50 per cent of the people currently unserved, as well as the growth in population, between 2004 and 2015 (which is the MDG target). For the analysis of NPV the annual costs and benefits have been taken into account for that period (discounted at 5 and 10 per cent). This is also a lower estimate as it can be assumed that the benefits continue, while the investment costs would diminish; recurrent costs would remain, however, and the low-cost technologies assumed to be used do not have a very long life time and would need to be replaced at some point, therefore neither costs nor benefits are projected beyond 2015.

The BCR is highest in the East Mediterranean and North African region because the value of time gained is higher here (because minimum wage is higher in the region). The total number of cases of diarrhoea averted is estimated to be highest in South and South-East Asia, while the

[42] And updated by Hutton for the paper by Evans, Hutton and Haller (2004).
[43] An estimated total of 391 m cases of diarrhoea avoided per year, out of a total 5,388 m, see appendix 1.

overall NPV is highest for Africa because of both low current service rates and high prevalence of diarrhoea.[44]

This analysis shows that global welfare would be increased by US$300–400 bn through provision of low-cost, community managed water supply and sanitation to about 50 per cent of the people currently unserved. It would also leave another 550 m people without access to safe water supply and 1.2 bn people without access to basic sanitation. If providing water and sanitation is as beneficial as suggested in table 9.4 then it would make good sense to provide universal access – and that would, by simple extrapolation,[45] increase the total NPV by roughly half as much again – or up to US$ 450–600 bn. In practice, this is not a linear process, of course, as there are locations where providing the service is easier and therefore cheaper and there are areas where current diarrhoea prevalence is high and the benefits are therefore higher. Finally there are areas that are troubled by civil war, or very remote, etc., where costs would be so high that economic benefits, as estimated here, would not arise.

In practice, of course, the water supply and sanitation challenge cannot be divorced from the other challenges. Living in Sri Lanka, as the author does, it is all too clear that an end to civil war, and a stable institutional and financial system, is a pre-condition for making progress on many other fronts. Solid economic growth, that is then more likely to follow, is then the basis for dealing with many other challenges, including water supply and sanitation. That is why universal access, domestically funded, is more likely to be a realistic medium-term goal in e.g. China and India,[46] presuming their economic growth holds. If the case is a prioritisation of external assistance, in the absence of stability and economic growth, if that can be sustainable at all, then a target of making 'significant progress' – such as the MDG target to reduce by 50 per cent – may be a more useful goal.

The second approach is based on WHO-led cost-effectiveness analysis (see appendix 2) to reduce the burden of disease. As discussed earlier, the total burden of disease associated with water is estimated at about 82 m DALYs annually. If we assume a value per DALY of US$500, and discount at 10 and 5

per cent, then the NPV of that burden of disease is US$400–800 bn, respectively. This is roughly in line with the NPV of providing universal access arrived at above. Assuming a higher value per DALY, as done elsewhere in the chapters in this volume, obviously increases this value. The WHO analysis shows that chlorination of water at the point of use was most cost-effective with a cost of US$25–150 per DALY averted. Assume for a moment that all water-related disease could be resolved through this method, then the maximum NPV associated with this, at US$500 per DALY and discounted 10 and 5 per cent, would be in the range of US$280[47] to 760[48] bn.

The method with the highest chance to actually reduce the burden of disease to close to zero is to provide universal access (assumed to be 98 per cent) to piped water and sewerage connection, but the estimated cost of this strategy is US$850–US$7,800 per DALY averted. In other words, for an assumed value of US$500 per DALY there would not be any NPV, or no gain in welfare. This is not surprising, since it is another way of saying that for the dollar-poor, for whom the US$500 per DALY is assumed as an estimate of the income lost per DALY, conventional piped water supply and sewerage connections are not affordable. Or, in other words, it suggests that for conventional piped water supply and sewerage connections to have any economic benefit on improved health, income levels would have to be above US$850–US$7, 800.[49]

The intermediate option in the WHO analysis is to provide low-cost technologies (standpipes and

---

[44] And note that these are also, by and large, where the high-priority countries are located as identified by the UNDP Human Development Report (2003).

[45] Presuming here, for simplicity, that all services would be provided in the same period – even though it is not likely that that can be implemented.

[46] Or, for that matter, Asia as a whole. *The Human Development Report 2003*, UNDP 2003) reports satisfactory progress towards reaching the MDG on water and sanitation in Asia.

[47] A cost of US$150/DALY, benefits discounted at 10 per cent.

[48] A cost of US$25/DALY, benefits discounted at 5 per cent.

[49] Note that in chapter 2 on communicable diseases a range of Int$2,000–Int$10,000 is used as the value per DALY averted; the same approach would yield net benefits for piped water supply and sewerage connections.

latrines, as opposed to individually piped water sewerage connections) at a cost of US$650–5,600 per DALY averted. It is interesting to note that according to this WHO study the cost-effectiveness of this strategy improves to US$280–2,600 per DALY averted if disinfection (chlorination) at the point of use is added in.[50] It is also worth noting that – contrary to what is concluded in the WHO analysis that is discussed here – experience with low-cost (condominial) sewerage in Brazil has shown that individual (low-cost) house sewerage connections become more efficient (cheaper) than latrines at relatively low levels of density.

Small-Scale Water Technology for Livelihoods

The second opportunity assessed here is the dissemination of small-scale water technology for productive purposes, primarily to provide livelihoods to small and landless farmers. There is a range of technologies available that can be used depending on the agro-climatic and socio-economic conditions, ranging from rainwater harvesting in dry areas to the use of manual pumps to access shallow groundwater. As for the first opportunity, what needs to be recognised is that successful adoption by a large number of people depends less on the technology than on: (a) the social marketing of the technology; (b) the availability of micro-credit programmes; or (c) the institutional support through NGO networks or community-based

organisations to provide training and technical support.

The target group consists of the 800 m dollar poor in the rural areas, as well as a sub-set of the poor in peri-urban areas, whose livelihoods depend on agriculture (growing crops as well as tending livestock), fisheries, agro-forestry and aquaculture and for whom access to water for productive purposes is a key constraint, if not the key constraint.

The main public investments have been in large-scale publicly managed infrastructure, particularly large dams[51] for hydropower and irrigation. While these currently suffer from a rather bad press, and have certainly underperformed in a number of cases, national governments in key countries[52] maintain a high priority for these investments. Carruthers (1996), as discussed in Lipton, Litchfield and Faures (2003), reviewed 192 World Bank-funded irrigation projects implemented between 1950 and 1993 and concluded that 67 per cent performed satisfactorily at evaluation with an average internal rate of return[53] of 15 per cent. A World Bank review (2004) of eleven Brazilian publicly funded irrigation schemes in the semi-arid areas, with a total public investment of about US$2 bn in 200,000 hectares of irrigated land, showed an economic rate of return of 14–25 per cent, with four out of the eleven projects exceeding a social discount rate of 16–19 per cent.[54] The study also concludes that the main poverty impact of the projects is their job-generation or employment effect, with each job created in the irrigation sector costing US$5,000–6,000, compared to an average of US$44,000 in other sectors (World Bank 2004, 11).[55]

More recently, there has been an upsurge in the adoption of water technologies for smallholders such as low-cost small electric and diesel pumps, manual devices such as treadle pumps, low-cost bucket and drip lines, sustainable land management practices such as low or zero-till agriculture, supplemental irrigation, groundwater recharge and water harvesting systems. Emerging evidence suggests that access to water for agriculture through these technologies has a major potential to improve the livelihoods of the poorest farmers. Identification and promotion of these technologies therefore

---

[50] This increases costs by a relatively small amount, but is estimated, according to the WHO, to more than double the impact on the reduction in diarrhoeal diseases.

[51] Defined as dams higher than 15 m, of which there are now over 48,000, with a total value of some US$ 2 trillion.

[52] Notably China, India, Turkey and Brazil.

[53] That is, the discount rate that would result in a zero NPV.

[54] The social discount rate is defined in this study as reflecting the opportunity cost of capital in the economy at the time the capital was used, in the study area ranging from an average high of 19 per cent in the 1970s to about 16 per cent in the 1990s.

[55] The projects in semi-arid Brazil focused on labour-intensive high-value crops, primarily fruits, with a significant share for export markets.

offers significant opportunities for poverty reduction. The technologies are particularly suited to smallholders, poor and even landless households as they self-select the poor and have a strong land-and water-augmentation effect. Here, two examples are given of low-cost drip irrigation and treadle pumps.

Drip irrigation is promoted to help farmers in water scarce areas. The advantages of drip systems are that they minimise water losses and increase yields. Drip irrigation is part of the family of precision irrigation technologies that aim to deliver the right quantity of water at the right time (IWMI 2000). It can increase yields from 20 per cent to 70 per cent, while using less water than traditional methods (IWMI 2000). Water savings are reported to be around 60 per cent over flood irrigation (Shah and Keller 2002).

Drip irrigation is usually applied by commercial farmers who cultivate larger land areas than possessed by a typical smallholder farmer and are too expensive for poor farmers. Cheap, small-scale bucket-and-drip kits (e.g. the Chapin bucket-kits in Kenya) have been developed, however, for vegetable cultivation on small plots that do have potential for poor smallholders. (Shah and Keller 2002; Sijali and Okuma 2002). Research by IWMI in Nepal evaluated the economic impact of drip irrigation kits for small farmers (RITI consultants 2001). The cost of each drip kit promoted by IDE in mountain range of Nepal is US$13, with a life cycle of three years. The IWMI study shows that for a small farmer producing vegetables, one set is adequate for irrigation of 125 m^2. A farmer can irrigate 1,000 m^2 of land with eight such drip kits at a total cost of US$104. The total net benefits, subtracting all costs except labour, obtained by each farm household were US$210 per 1,000 m^2 per year by growing two crops of cauliflower and cucumber (RITI 2001). Thus, the total NPV for three years (at a 10 per cent discount rate) would be US$570 per farmer.

The costs of these systems are dropping dramatically. An innovation introduced in India , for example, is the 'Pepsee' kit, a locally developed 'disposable'[56] micro-irrigation kit made of low-grade plastic tubes. The technology was introduced in 1998–9. Initially, it was confined to the cotton growing areas of Madhya Pradesh and Maharashtra. Over the years its use has spread to grow other crops such as sugarcane and vegetables. The popularity of the Pepsee system is its low cost. The initial investment in a Pepsee system to irrigate an acre of cotton is estimated to be US$ 93 which, is about half the investment required for micro-tubes (US$ 158) and nearly 25 per cent of the capital required for conventional drips (Verma, Tsephal and Jose 2003). Farmers who adopted the technology claimed that it led to significant water savings at the farm level. An IWMI study in two districts in Madhya Pradesh (West Nimar) and Maharashtra (Jalgaon) showed that the cotton yield realised by farmers who had adopted Pepsee irrigation was comparable to yields obtained by farmers using conventional drip irrigation systems and was almost double the yield of non-adopters (Verma, Tsephal and Jose 2003). The same study showed that farmers were able to increase the area under irrigation and also enabled them to cultivate crops in the dry (Rabi) season. The growing popularity of the Pepsee technology clearly demonstrates the tremendous scope for appropriate, low-cost, grass-root level technologies that are within easy reach of poor farmers. IWMI research in India shows that farmers use the low-cost technology as a stepping stone to switch to more conventional technology after several seasons.

Another example is the treadle pump, a foot-operated device that uses bamboo or flexible pipe for suction to pump water from shallow aquifers or surface water bodies. Since it can be attached to a flexible hose, a treadle pump is useful for lifting water at shallow depths from ponds, tanks, canals or catchment basins, tubewells and other sources up to a maximum height of 7 m. It performs best at a pumping head of 3.0–3.5 m, delivering 1.0–1.2 l/s.

IWMI research found that treadle pump technology has had a significant impact in improving the livelihoods of the poor in eastern India, the

---

[56] 'Disposable', in this context, refers to the fact that the cost of the drip system is so low that the farmers can afford to use it for a single cropping season only; instead of an investment it becomes a consumable, much like fertilizer.

Nepal Terai and Bangladesh (the heartland of the Ganga-Brahmaputra-Meghna basin), South Asia's, so-called 'poverty square' (Shah *et al.* 2000). This region, which contains 500 m of the world's poorest people and is characterised by tiny land holdings, is underlain by one of the world's best groundwater resources, available at a depth of 1.5–3.5 m.

The treadle pump is cheap and affordable, with costs ranging from US$12–30, is easy to install, operate and maintain and has no fuel costs. The labour-intensive treadle pump self-selects the poor that have under-utilised time to work the pumps. Shah *et al.* (2000) suggest that: (1) for poor small holders constrained by limited land, treadle pump technology works as a land-augmenting intervention, enabling users to raise crops in both summer and winter thereby increasing overall cropping intensity; (2) treadle pump technology enables farmers to grow high-yielding and high-value crops (such as china rice, a high-yielding variety, and high-value crops such as vegetables); and (3) the technology increases crop yields.[57] The study estimates that farmers using treadle pump technology see an average increase of US$ 100 per year in annual net income with gross incomes of US$300–400 per acre quite common. Net incomes did vary across households and regions, however. International Development Enterprise (IDE), a US-based NGO that developed and promoted the technology,

estimates to have sold 1.3 m pumps since the mid-1980s in Bangladesh, and 200,000 in eastern India and the Nepal Terai since the mid-1990s. IDE indicates that 'eastern India and the Nepal Terai have an ultimate market potential for some 10 m treadle pumps'.

Assuming average investment costs of US$20 for low-cost treadle pumps, with a life of three years, and an average annual gain in net income of US$100, the total NPV for a treadle pump adopter, assuming the person will stick with the technology indefinitely, is US$900–1,900 (discounted at 10 and 5 per cent, respectively) For the 1.5 m adopters of the treadle pump technology the total NPV then is US$1.4–2.8 bn and for the estimated market in Eastern India and the Nepal Terai the NPV amounts to US$9–19 bn.

In addition to drip irrigation and treadle pumps (often combined with low-cost sprinkler or drip) there is a host of small-scale technologies that aim to conserve rainfall, either in the field directly, or in small structures.[58] Collectively referred to as 'rainwater harvesting', they have been actively promoted by NGOs and civil society organisations in India, particularly, but elsewhere as well. Contrary to large-scale public investments that often take ten–thirty years to get from the drawing board to implementation, the rainwater harvesting technologies have seen astounding adoption rates, on the order of several hundred thousand villages over several years in parts of India.

IWMI has conducted research over the last three–four years to evaluate the impact of these technologies. Since these technologies are evolved by local NGOs or 'barefoot hydrologists' to suit each socio-ecological context, one finds enormous variety in type, scale, costs, benefits, adoption rates and management approaches, making it difficult to work out economics that represent all of them. In India, for instance, these range from farm ponds – whose costs and benefits are concentrated on each small holder – to individual check dams or tanks benefiting a section of a village to a network of check dams built by a basin or sub-basin community. Construction costs range from US$0.4–0.5/m³ for earth structures (such as farm ponds in Gujarat's *Sujalam Sufalam* scheme or the so called '5 per cent technology' popular in the East Indian plateau[59]) and

---

[57] In Uttar Pradesh and north Bihar, treadle pump users had potato yields of 16–17 ton per hectare, 60–70 per cent higher than diesel pump users.

[58] Technologies range from creating small ridges along the contour line (by placing stones) or creating tiny basins of, say 2 by 2 m, to concentrate rainfall towards the roots of a single plant or tree, as practiced in the dry areas, to technologies such as digging a pond on 5 per cent of the land to store water within a farmer's field, to recharging groundwater wells with excess rainfall, creating underground barriers to create underground storage, to building small check-dams that create small reservoirs or tanks at village level. Some of these technologies hark back to traditional, indigenous technologies such as practiced in South-Asia over centuries, while others are based on, or combined with, modern technology.

[59] 5 per cent technology, popularised by PRADAN, an Indian NGO involves making a 3.5 feet deep pit over an area equal to 5 per cent of the farm size on its upstream end to capture run off and store water to save the main monsoon crop from the dry spell.

US$ 0.7–0.9/m^3 when bricks, cement and concrete structures are involved. Some of the larger structures can support some winter crop irrigation; however, the key benefit that drives India's rural communities to invest in these is to ensure one or two life-saving irrigations to the main monsoon crop during frequent dry spells that ruin standing crops. The value of irrigation water during these dry spells is very high and varies from US$0.1–0.8/m^3 depending on the losses the dry spell imposes on the farmer. For average construction cost taken at US$0.5/m^3 of storage, implicit value productivity of water at US$0.2/m^3 of dry-spell supplemental irrigation and average life of the structure at ten years, the NPV for a water harvesting structure of 1,000m^3 costing US$500 works out to around US$800 at a social discount rate of 10 per cent/year.

Numerous local studies suggest investment in small water harvesting structures far more attractive (see, e.g. Raju 2004). Most of these refer to a village or a small area but analysis of large regional programmes suggests high rates of return as well. In an evaluation of Gujarat Government's Sardar Patel Participatory Water Conservation Programme under which 10,708 check dams were constructed in Saurashtra and Kutch regions, Shingi and Asopa (2002) noted that 'within a period of three years, an initial investment of Rs. 1,58,000 (US$3511)[60] on an average check dam fetched total benefits worth Rs 251,582 (US$5591.)' And that 'The investment becomes more attractive if one recognises that the government had to in fact invest only 60 per cent of the average figure of Rs 1,58,000 under the 60:40 scheme'. Of Gujarat's 4.2 m ha of cultivated land, 2.2 m is rainfed and critically dependent upon supplemental irrigation sustained by small water harvesting and recharge structures. According to M. S. Patel, Gujarat's Secretary for water resources, the value of the main monsoon crop on these 2.2 m ha can increase from Rs10–15 billion now (US$0.22–33 bn) to Rs50bn (US$1.1bn) provided there is a check dam per km^2 (Shah 2003). India as a whole has over 80 m ha of rainfed farming area which can benefit greatly from crop-saving supplemental irrigation in terms of increase in the value of monsoon crop output from US$36–54 bn/year to US$180bn/year; but this would re-quire creating small water harvesting capacity and storage equivalent to some 2 m check dams costing US$7 bn.

IDE and Winrock estimated a global potential of 31 m smallholder families, or about 200 m people, who could potentially benefit from the adoption of low-cost, affordable water control systems, essentially 'micro-irrigation'[61] (Winrock–IDE, 2001). For SSA, using the total (1999) population of 625 million for the forty-six SSA countries, 65 per cent of this is rural. Using a 1998 rural poverty threshold, about 59 per cent of the rural populations in SSA were estimated to be poor families, i.e. about 240 m people or 50 m families. The Winrock–IDE project estimates that at least 4 m small holder families in SSA would have the basic pre-condition to engage in high-value crop production through small holder irrigation. Similarly, Postel *et al.* (2001) estimate that drip irrigation could bring a US$3 bn annual benefit to 150 m people.

In summary, the potential for adoption of small-scale water technology[62] in Africa and Asia is estimated at about 100 m farmers (or families), with an average annual direct net benefit[63] of US$100[64] per farmer. Discounted at 10 and 5 per cent, respectively this yields an NPV estimate of US$100 (C − B = 150 − 50) to 200 (C − B = 300 − 100) bn in terms of direct benefit to the users.

On top of the direct benefits to farmers there are indirect benefits, particularly in terms of employment downstream in the economy. A number of studies have reported multipliers (the ratio of total, i.e. direct plus indirect, over direct benefits) ranging from 2–6. An irrigation impact

---

[60] US$ = Indian Rs45 in early 2004.
[61] Projections made for the Winrock–IDE Smallholder Irrigation Market Initiative (SIWI) project.
[62] Combining rainwater harvesting potential in India alone of 80 m ha, with the estimate of 30 m farmers that have micro-irrigation potential, the 100 m farmer, or half a billion people, estimate is considered a low estimate, given the potential for rainwater harvesting in the global arid and semi-arid belt circling the globe from Brazil to North Africa, Central Asia, South Asia and Western China.
[63] That is, the increase in income minus the costs of the technology, both investment and recurrent.
[64] Assuming annualised investment plus recurrent costs of US$50 per farmer, yielding an increase in income of US$150.

Table 9.5. Estimates of Irrigation Multipliers

Project (source)	Irrigation multiplier (total / direct effects)
Muda, Malaysia (Bell, Hazell and Slade 1982)	1.83
NSW, Australia (Powell, Jenson and Gibson 1985)	6
Alberta, Canada (AIPA, 1993)	5
Senegal project (Delgado, *et al.*, 1994)	1.3–4.6
Bhakra project (World Bank 2004)	2
All-India (Bhattarai, Barker and Narayanamoorthy 2003)	3–4

study in Alberta province of Canada reported that only about 20 per cent of the total benefits of irrigation development have been captured by the farming sector in termed of increased agricultural production with the remaining incremental benefits accrued to the wider sections of the Canadian society (AIPA 1993; Hill and Tollefson 1996). These widespread benefits of irrigation included rural employment impact, and induced economic activities in the region. Powell, Jenson and Gibson (1985) have reported irrigation multiplier values of 6 for irrigation in New South Wales, Australia. A comprehensive economic impact study (Bell, Hazell and Slade 1982) reported that the Muda irrigation project, Malaysia, had produced substantial indirect effects through expansion of other sectors of the regional economy e.g. it had contributed over 95 per cent in agricultural machinery, over 70 per cent in construction, over 70 per cent in the financial sector and about 60 per cent in the trade sector in the region affected by the project. The study reported that for every dollar of direct benefits, another 83 cents were generated in the form of downstream or indirect effects (i.e. a multiplier of 1.83). Likewise, Bhattarai, Sakthivadivel and Hussain (2003) study in India shows an irrigation multiplier value of 3 at all-India level impact of irrigation development.

[65] Excluding 40 m DALY that is the annual burden of malaria.

Bell, Hazell and Slade (1982), Powell, Jenson and Gibson (1985), and AIPA (1993) have all used a project-level accounting framework of analysis such as an I-O (input–output) and SAM (Social Accounting Matrix)-based accounting framework. However, the 'irrigation multiplier' derived from constant coefficient assumptions of the accounting framework of I-O and SAM are short-run values of irrigation multipliers operating in a regional economy. The value of 'irrigation multipliers' derived from Computable General Equilibrium (CGE) models (or from regression based analyses) as used by Bhattarai, Sakthivadivel and Hussain (2003) is an estimation of the long-run value of the irrigation multiplier operating in the economy as these incorporate the societal substitution behaviour in resources use decisions (table 9.5).

Taking such indirect effects into account with an assumed multiplier of 3 would increase the total NPV of the widespread adoption of small-scale water technology to US$300 bn (discounted at 10 per cent) to US$600 bn (discounted at 5 per cent).

Conclusions

The lack of access to safe and affordable water for domestic purposes, lack of access to safe and affordable sanitation and lack of access to water for productive or livelihoods purposes has a major impact on the 1.2 billion dollar poor people in the world today. At any given time close to half the population in developing countries suffers from one or more water-related discases. The total annual burden of water-related disease is about 80 million DALY.[65] Three-quarters of the dollar poor live in the rural areas with agriculture as their only way out of poverty and water as one of the key constraints to obtaining a higher return on their labour.

Providing community managed access to low-cost water supply and sanitation is a major opportunity to increase global welfare. This requires an integrated approach to water supply, sanitation and hygiene education. The focus should be on service delivery rather than on infrastructure – and sanitation should receive at least as much attention as,

Table 9.6. Costs and Benefits of Water-Related Opportunities (bn US$)

Water Opportunities	Total Benefits	Total Costs	Annualised B/C	Discount rate/ remarks
Community managed low-cost water supply and sanitation[1]	392 502	80 102	4.9 4.9	10% 5%
Small-scale water technology for livelihoods[2]	350 700	50 100	7 7	10% 5%
Re-use of waste-water for peri-urban agriculture	Very high	Medium	Very high	
Sustainable agriculture in wetlands	Medium	Small	High	Focus on Africa
Research to increase water productivity in food production	Very high	Very small	Very high (15–20)	

[1] **Annualised costs, for the period 2004–2015.**
[2] **Multiplier for indirect benefits assumed as 3.**

and more funding, than water supply. Social marketing and micro-credit programmes are key ingredients of the package. The benefits to society range from improved health, particularly a reduction in diarrhoeal diseases and reduced loss of time engaged in gaining access to water and sanitation, but particularly reduction of time lost to disease. The total net benefits of making a significant progress towards increasing access, defined as MDG target 10, or halving the people without access by 2015, are estimated to be US$300–400 bn. Total benefits of providing universal access by 2015 based on the same package, although not likely to be a practical or realistic goal, could be extrapolated to US$450–600 bn.

Providing access to small-scale water technology for livelihoods purposes to smallholder and landless farmers is another major opportunity in the water sector. There is a wide variety of technologies available that range from rainwater harvesting, to small-scale electric pumps, manual treadle pumps to low-cost drip irrigation kits. The key impact of the tech-

nology is that it substitutes labour inputs for land and capital. Again, the focus should not be on development or provision of the technology, but rather on social marketing and micro-credit Programmes. For an estimated 100 m farmers that could adopt this technology, the direct total net benefits can be estimated to be US$100–200 bn at 10 and 5 per cent discount rate, respectively. When including indirect benefits in the economy, with a multiplier of 3, the total net benefits (NPV) can increase to US$300–600 bn.

There are more water-related opportunities for which there are insufficient data to attempt estimates of total benefits, particularly: (a) re-use of urban wastewater for peri-urban agriculture; (b) sustainable agriculture in wetlands; and (c) research to increase the productivity of water in food production. For these opportunities the costs and benefits have been assessed as small, medium, high and very high based on the expert judgment of the author.

Table 9.6 provides an overview of costs, benefits and BCRs.

Appendix 1: Costs and Benefits of Meeting the MDG on Sanitation

Table 9A1.1. Sanitation Technology Cost Estimates (US$ 2000)

| | Initial investment cost *per capita* | | | | Recurrent Costs | |
| | JMP Estimates | | | Other Estimates | | |
Improvement	Africa	Asia	LA&CN		Level	Source
Sewer and WWT				450[*1]	v. high	User fees/subsidy
Sewer connection	120	154	160	150–260[*2]	High	User fees/subsidy
Small bore sewer	52	60	112	120[*3]	Medium	User fees/household
Septic tank	115	104	160		High	Household
Pour-flush	91	50	60		Med/low (lumpy)	Household
VIP	57	50	52		Low (lumpy)	Household
Simple pit latrine	39	26	60		Low (lumpy)	Household
Improved trad.practice + hygiene promotion				10[*4]	Low (US$0.60 per annum)	Household

Source: adapted from UNEP/GPA *Financing Domestic Wastewater Collection and Treatment in Relation to the WSSD Target on water and sanitation.*

Notes:

[1] Adapted from *Global Water Supply & Sanitation Assessment 2000 Report* (www.who.int/docstore/water_sanitation_health/ Globassessment/Global3.3.htm). Unless states, figures are based on the average construction cost of sanitation facilities for Africa, Asia and Latin America and the Caribbean for the period 1990–2000 and include a small charge to account for inflation and currency fluctuations. These data were provided by member states as per of the JMP data collection exercise.

[2] Taken from Water: *A World Financial Issue* (PricewaterhouseCoopers, March 2001). The figure is based on a per head cost of $20/year multiplied by 13 years to reflect the timescale required for meeting the MDGs.

[3] This figure is quoted by Suez in the publication *Bridging the Water Divide* (Suez/Ondeo, March 2002) and is based on a one-off connection cost for households in poor neighbourhoods in the Aguas Argentinas concession area and assumes the bartering of local labour in exchange for connection to a network. However, no data is given for the number of persons per household.

[4] From *Sustainable Local Solutions, Popular Participation and Hygiene Education* (Richard Jolly) writing in *Clean Water*, Safe Sanitation: *An Agenda for the Kyoto World Water Forum and Beyond* (Institute of Public Policy Research, February 2003). Based on the Vision 21 estimate of average external costs per person for sanitation and hygiene promotion.

Table 9A1.2. Total Annual Benefits of Meeting Sanitation MDG in Natural Units

World/Region	Pop'n (m.)	Current annual diarrhoea cases (millions)	Meeting sanitation MDG (annual figures, in millions)				
			Diarrhoea cases averted	Hours gained per year due to closer access	Productive days gained (15+ age group) due to less illness	Nr of school days gained (5–14 age group)	Baby days gained due to less illness (0–4 age group)
SSA	968	1,239	115	38,616	78	1,700	330
Latin America	624	552	25	9,306	52	956	92
East Mediterranean & North Africa	373	286	9	4,156	28	426	100
Central & Eastern Europe	460	130	3	3,818	8	42	16
South and S.E. Asia	2,162	1,795	135	28,445	110	1,150	270
West Pacific developing countries	1,673	1,317	102	39,929	203	708	95
Developed regions	923	69	2	2,253	47	89	44
All regions	**7,183**	**5,388**	**391**	**126,523**	**527**	**5,071**	**947**

Source: Hutton (as quoted in Evans, Hutton and Haller 2004) – calculations updated by Hutton for the Evans, Hutton and Haller paper.

Table 9A1.3. Some Economic Benefits of Meeting Sanitation MDG, and Cost-Benefit Ratios

World Region	Population (m.)	Meeting sanitation MDG (annual figures, in US$ million)				
		Health sector treatment costs avoided	Patient health seeking costs avoided	Annual value of time gain	Total benefits*	Cost-benefit ration*
SSA	968	1,130	72	12,873	16,183	10.6
Latin America	624	514	16	5,695	7,325	11.9
East Mediterranean & North Africa	373	148	6	5,157	5,865	28.5
Central & Eastern Europe	460	60	2	2,381	2,508	12.7
South and S.E. Asia	2,162	1,378	84	8,112	11,104	3.0
West Pacific developing countries	1,673	1,645	64	8,905	11,619	3.8
All regions (incl. developed regions)	**7,183**	**4,955**	**244**	**51,525**	**63,269**	**6.6**

Source: Hutton (as quoted in Evans, Hutton and Haller 2004) – calculations updated by Hutton for the Evans, Hutton and Haller paper.
Note*: Total benefits includes time savings due to closer sanitation facilities, productive and educational time gain due to less ill from diarrhoea, and health sector and patient savings due to less treatment for diarrhoeal disease. Time savings per person were days from closer access to sanitation services was assumed to be 30 minutes. Days off work and school were assumed to be two and three days per case of diarrhoea, respectively, which were valued at the minimum wage for each country. A baby was assumed to be ill from a case of diarrhoea for five days, at a value of 50% of the minimum wage to take into account the opportunity cost of the carer. The economic benefits of reduced mortality were not included in the calculations of total economic benefit.

It is important to note that health sector costs are not actual costs saved, as the calculations includes health sector infrastructure and staff time, which are not saved in a real sense when a diarrhoeal case does not show up. This figure reflects the opportunity cost: in settings where services are used to 100% capacity, if someone does not show up with diarrhoea, then someone else with another disease can be treated.

Appendix 2: WHO Cost-effective Analysis of Improved Water Supply and Sanitation

Table 9A2.1. Average CER by WHO Region (US$ per DALY averted)

	AFRO D	AFRO E	AMRO D	SEARO B	SEARO D	WPRO B
Halve pop. without access to improved WS	338.8	498.3	954.9	3,362.0	427.4	2,611.1
Halve pop. without access to improved WS&S	686.0	822.5	1,898.4	5,654.0	1,117.0	5,618.6
Disinfection at point of use to pop. currently w/o improved WS	23.5	26.0	94.3	156.8	25.7	156.8
Universal access (98%) to improved water supply and improved sanitation (Low technologies)	648.5	718.9	1,886.6	5,251.2	1,116.1	5,618.5
Universal access (98%) to improved water supply and improved sanitation plus disinfection at point of use	283.8	332.7	736.6	1,484.1	471.4	2,552.2
Universal access (98%) to piped water supply and sewer connection (High technologies)	852.9	943.6	1,693.7	7,765.0	1,121.7	4,693.2

Source: Haller, as quoted in Evans, Hutton and Haller (2004).
Notes:
AFRO   D   Algeria, Angola, Benin, Burkina Faso, Cameroon, Cape Verde, Chad, Comoros, Equatorial Guinea, Gabon, Gambia, Ghana, Guinea, Guinea-Bissau, Liberia, Madagascar, Mali, Mauritania, Mauritius, Niger, Nigeria, Sao Tomé And Principe, Senegal, Seychelles, Sierra Leone, Togo.
AFRO   E   Botswana, Burundi, Central African Republic, Congo, Côte d'Ivoire, Democratic Republic Of The Congo, Eritrea, Ethiopia, Kenya, Lesotho, Malawi. Mozambique, Namibia, Rwanda, South Africa, Swaziland, Uganda, United Republic of Tanzania, Zambia, Zimbabwe.
AMRO   D   Bolivia, Ecuador, Guatemala, Haiti, Nicaragua, Peru.
SEARO   B   Indonesia, Sri Lanka, Thailand.
SEARO   D   Bangladesh, Bhutan, Democratic People's Republic of Korea, India, Maldives, Myanmar, Nepal.
WPRO   B   Cambodia, China, Lao People's Democratic Republic, Malaysia, Mongolia, Philippines, Republic of Korea, Viet Nam.

References

Acreman, M., 2000: Background study for the World Commission of Dams, reported in WCD (2000)

Alberta Irrigation Projects Association (AIPA), 1993: *Accomplishments and opportunities: AIPA's response to the Irrigation Impact Study.* Report prepared by Alberta Irrigation Projects Association, 7 vols; *Irrigation Impact Study*, volume 1. vol. 7, 43, is a summary of all the six component-wise reports of irrigation impact study

Bell, Clive, P. Hazell and R. Slade, 1982: *Project evaluation in regional perspective: a study of an irrigation project in northwest malaysia*, The World Bank and The Johns Hopkins University Press, Baltimore and London, 326

Bhattarai, M., R. Sakthivadivel and I. Hussain, 2003: *Irrigation impacts on income inequality, and poverty alleviation: policy issues and options for improved management of irrigation systems, IWMI Working Paper 39*, International Water Management Institute, Colombo, Sri Lanka, available at http://www.cgiar.org/iwmi/pubs/working/index.htm

Bhattarai, M., R. Barker and A. Narayanamoorthy, 2003: *Who benefits from irrigation investments in India? Implication of irrigation multiplier estimates for cost recovery and irrigation financing*, workshop paper presented at the ICID regional meeting in Taipei, Taiwan, 10–12 November, 2003, Published in the *Proceedings* (Shiang-Kueen, ed.), vol. 1. 285–96

Carruthers, I., 1996: Economics of irrigation, in *Sustainability of irrigated agriculture, proceedings of the NATO Advanced Study Institute*, Vimeiro, Portugal, March 21–26, 1994, Kluwer Academic, Boston, 35–46

Cosgrove, W. and F. Rijsberman. 2000: *World water vision: making water everybody's business*, Earthscan, London

Costanza, R., R.d'Arge, R. de Groot, S. Farber, M. Grasso, B. Hannon, K. Limburg, S. Naeem, R. O'Neill, J. Paruelo, R. Raskin, P. Sutton and M. van den Belt, 1997: The value of the world's ecosystem services and natural capital, *Nature*, 387, 253–60

De Fraiture, C. and C. Perry, 2002: Why is irrigation water demand inelastic at low price ranges? Paper presented at the conference on irrigation water policies: micro and macro considerations, 15–17 June, Agadir, Morocco

Delgado, C.L., P. Hazell, J. Hopkins and V. Kelly, 1994: Promoting inter-sectoral growth linkages in rural Africa through agricultural technology and policy reform, *American Journal of Agricultural Economics*. 76, 1166–71

Dublin Statement, 1992: Official outcome of the Conference on Water and the environment: Development Issues for the 21st Century, 26–31 January, 1992, Dublin. WMO, Geneva

Ensink, J., T. Mahmood, W. van de Hoek, L. Raschid-Sally and F. Amerasinghe, 2004: A nation-wide assessment of wastewater use in Pakistan: an obscure activity or a vitally important one? *Water Policy*, in press.

Esrey, S.A., J.B. Potasch, L. Roberts and C. Schiff, 1991: Effects of improved water and sanitation on ascariasis, diarrhoea, dracunculiasis, hookworm infection, schistosomiasis and trachoma, *Bulletin of the World Health Organisation*, 69(5), 609–21

Evans, B.G. Hutton and L. Haller, 2004: Closing the sanitation gap – the case for better public funding of sanitation and hygiene, paper prepared for the Roundtable on Sustainable Development, 9–10 March 2004, OECD, Paris

Garcia, Y.T., A.G. Garcia, M. Oo and M. Hossain, 2000: Income distribution and poverty in irrigated and rainfed ecosystems: The Myanmar case, *Economic and Political Weekly*, December 30, 4670–76

Hansen, S. and R. Bhatia. 2004: Water and Poverty in a Macro-economic Context. Paper commissioned by the Norwegian Ministry of the Environment in preparation of CSD12, April 19–30, United Nations, New York

Hill, Harry and Laurie Tollefson, 1996: *Institutional Questions and Societal Challenge*. 1996. In Pereira L. S., R. A. Fedds, J. R. Gilley, B. Lesaffre, 1996 (eds). *Sustainability of irrigated Agriculture*. Dordrecht/London: Kluwer Academic Publishers

Hossain, M., B. Sen and H.Z. Rahman, 2000: Growth and Distribution of Rural Income in Bangladesh; Analysis Based on Panel Survey Data. *Economic and Political Weekly*, December 30:4630–4637

Hussain, I. and M.A. Hanrja. 2003. Does Irrigation water matter for rural poverty alleviation?: Evidence from South and South-East Asia. *Water Policy*. 5(5/6):429–442

Jalal, K. and P. Rogers. 1997: IWMI (1991):

Janaiah, A., M.L. Bose and A.G. Agarwal 2000: Poverty and Income Distribution in Rainfed and Irrigated Ecosystems; Village Studies in Chhattisgarh. *Economic and Political Weekly*, December 30:4664–4669

Kahrl, W.L. 1982: *Water and Power*. University of California Press, Berkeley

Lipton, M., J. Litchfield and J-M Faures. 2003: The effects of irrigation on poverty: a framework for analysis. *Water Policy* 5(2003):413–427

Mills, A. and S. Shillcutt, 2004: Communicable Diseases, chapter 2 in this volume

Perry, C.J. 2001: Charging for Irrigation water: The Issues and Options, with a case study from Iran. *IWMI Research Report No 52*. International Water Management Institute, Colombo, Sri Lanka

Postel, S, P. Polak, F. Gonzales and J. Keller. 2001: Drip Irrigation for Small Farmers: A New Initiative to Alleviate Hunger and Poverty. *Water International*. 26(1):3–13

Powell, R.A., R.C. Jenson and A.L. Gibson, 1985: *The Economic Impact of irrigated Agriculture in NSW*. NSW, Australia: New South Wales Irrigators' Council Limited

Prüss, A.K. Day, L. Fewtrell, J. Bartram, 2002: Estimating the Global Burden of Disease from Water, Sanitation and Hygiene at a Global Level. *Environmental Health Perspectives.* **110**(5):537–542

Raju, KCB., 2004: 'Importance of Rainwater Harvesting to Improve the Rural Livelihoods in Kutch district', presented in National Conference on Hundred years of Rural development in India on 17th–19th March 2004, Guntur, Andra Pradesh

Renault, D. and W. Wallender, 2000: Nutritional Water Productivity and Diets. *Agricultural Water Management.* **45**(2000):275–296

Rijsberman, F, 2003: Can development of water resources reduce poverty? *Water Policy* **5**(2003), 399–412

RITI consultants, 2001: Poverty Focused Small Holder Water Management Technologies: Assessment of IDE-Nepal Low Cost Drip Irrigation Technology. A project report submitted to IWMI, Colombo Sri Lanka

Rogers, P., R. deSilva and R. Bhatia, 2002: Water is an economic good: how to use prices to promote equity, efficiency and sustainability. *Water Policy* **4**(2002):1–17

Shah, T., 1993: *Groundwater Markets and Irrigation Development: Political Economy and Practical Policy.* Oxford University Press, Bombay, India

2000: Wells and Welfare in the Ganga Basin: Public policy and Private initiative In Eastern Uttar Pradesh, India. *IWMI Research Report No. 54.* International Water Management Institute, Colombo

2003: Decentralised Water Harvesting and Groundwater Recharge: Can These Save Saurashtra and Kutch from Desiccation?', Anand, India: IWMI-Tata Water Policy Programme

Shah, T, M. Alam, M.D. Kumar, R.K. Nagar and M. Singh, 2000: Pedaling Out of Poverty: Socio-economic Impact of a Manual Irrigation Technology in South Asia. *IWMI Research Report 45.* International Water Management Institute, Colombo

Shah, T. and J. Keller, 2002: 'Micro-irrigation and the Poor:Livelihood Potential of Low-cost Drip and Sprinkler Irrigation in India and Nepal', in: H. Sally and C. Abernethy, eds.

Private irrigation in sub-saharan Africa. FAO/IWMI., IWMI, Colombo, p. 165–183

Shah, T., C. Scott, A. Kishore and A. Sharma, 2003: Energy-Irrigation Nexus in South-Asia: Groundwater Conservation and Power Sector Viability. *IWMI Research Report 70.* International Water Management Institute, Colombo

Sijali, I.V. and R.A. Okuma, 2002: New Irrigation Technologies, In Blank, H.G., C.M. Mutero and H. Murray-Rust, eds, *The Changing face of Irrigation in Kenya: Opportunities for Anticipating Change in Eastern and Southern Africa.* International Water Management Institute, Colombo

Thakur, J., M.L. Bose, M. Hossain and A. Janaiah, 2000: Rural Income Distribution and Poverty in Bihar; Insights from Village Studies. *Economic and Political Weekly*, December 30:4657–4663

UNDESA (United Nations Department of Economic and Social Affairs), 1998: Expert Group Meeting Report of Working Group 3: Economic and Financing Issues. UN, New York

UNDP, 2003: *Human Development Report 2003.* UNDP, New York

UN Task Force on Water and Sanitation, 2003: Achieving the Millennium Development Goals for water and Sanitation: What will it take? Interim Full Report, December 2003

UNWWDR (United Nations World Water Development Report), 2003: *Water for People, Water for Life.* UNESCO, Paris

Van Koppen, B. and S. Mahmud, 1996: *Women and water pumps in Bangladesh. The impact of participation in irrigation groups on women's status.* Intermediate Technology Publ., London

Van Koppen, B, R. Parthasarty and H. Joshi, 2002: Poverty Dimensions of Irrigation Management Transfer in Large-Scale Canal Irrigation in Andhra Pradesh and Gujarat, India. IWMI Research Report **62**

Verma, S., S. Tsephal and T. Jose, 2003: Pepsee Systems: Grassroots Innovation under Groundwater Stress, Anand, India: IWMI-Tata Water Policy Programme

WHO (World Health Organisation), 2002: *World Health Report 2002.* WHO, Geneva

WHO–UNICEF, 2000: *Global Water Supply and Sanitation Assessment Report 2000*. WHO, Geneva

Winrock–IDE, 2001: Smallholder Irrigation Market Initiative. Study on the Dissemination Potential of Affordable Drip and Other Irrigation Systems and the Concrete Strategies for their Promotion. Report by Winrock International and International Development Enterprises (IDE) to the World Bank, March 31, 2001

World Bank, 2004: Irrigated Agriculture in the Brazilian Semi-Arid Region: Social Impacts and externalities. Volume 1: Main Report. Brazil Country Management Unit. World Bank, Washington DC

Alternative Perspectives

Perspective Paper 9.1

JOHN J. BOLAND

The Water and Sanitation Challenge

It is customary to begin discussion of water and sanitation issues with multiple citations to claims of a 'global water crisis.' Chapter 9 (Rijsberman 2004), properly and expertly decomposes these claims, pointing out which aspects of the 'crisis' are truly global and which are, in fact, aggregations of specific and local problems. The reader's attention is then directed to what are arguably the most urgent of the many water crises: (1) the problem of ensuring access to safe and affordable water and sanitation for nearly half the world's population and (2) the problem of providing 'dollar-poor' communities with access to water for productive purposes (primarily food production).

Chapter 9 makes a detailed case for government involvement in water and sanitation provision, noting that (1) some uses of water have been recognised as a 'human right'; (2) private sector organisations will under-invest in water supply and sanitation; (3) there may be capital barriers to entry by private sector firms; (4) some water resources may be common property, or at least open access, resources; (5) some water services are natural monopolies; and (6) water development and use involves significant externalities. The counter argument, also presented, is that private provision of water services has worked well in some situations and in some places. There is some additional discussion of the difficulty of applying user charges to certain water services.

However water and sanitation are to be managed, the costs of managing them badly are unacceptable. Going well beyond the kinds of lost surplus usually associated with economic inefficiency, poor management of water and sanitation leads to significant and pervasive health impacts, damage and deaths due to water-related natural hazards, poverty and malnourishment and major environmental degradation. These factors point to both the importance of exploiting opportunities for successful interventions, and to the difficulty of fully evaluating the probable outcome of such interventions.

After briefly describing three candidate but not quantified opportunities, the chapter presents two proposed interventions which appear to be justified on strictly economic terms. These are briefly commented on below.

Community Managed Low-Cost Water Supply and Sanitation

The intended actions designed to bring about community managed provision of water supply and sanitation are not described in detail, but they apparently consist of (low-cost) technology transfer, community organizing, education, etc. The resulting water and sanitation systems would be community managed and financially and operationally self-sustaining.

For evaluation purposes, the end point is defined as achievement of the UN Millennium Development Goals (MDGs) for water and sanitation: to halve, by the year 2015, the proportion of people without access to safe drinking water or to basic sanitation.[1] This goal is generally interpreted as requiring provision of access to 'improved' water supply and sanitation to some 1.57 and 2.11 bn people, respectively. The chapter follows a UN World Water Development Report (UNWWDR 2003) in defining 'improved' water supply as ranging from rainwater harvesting to household connections, and in defining 'improved' sanitation as ranging from simple pit latrines to connection to public sewers. These changes may be, then, very modest improvements. Still, the public health literature predicts significant beneficial effects from even rudimentary provision of water services. Also, any changes that move water sources closer to living areas have the further potential to increase the amount of time available for other household duties or for productive employment.

The chapter considers the initial investment as well as recurrent costs of providing improved water and sanitation services, but it addresses only the health-related benefits of these services. Following the work of Esrey et al. (1991), it is further assumed that most health-related benefits derive from the provision of improved means for the disposal of human waste, although the cost of the water supply improvements is included in the benefit cost analysis (CBA). This is consistent with another interpretation of Esrey's findings, which is that access to safe water is a necessary, but not sufficient condition for health-related benefits. Sanitation, broadly defined (including personal hygiene and other activities which require water), is the sufficient condition (NRC 1996). The chapter estimates the effectiveness, costs and benefits of the proposed interventions on the basis of studies reported in Evans, Hutton and Haller (2004).

These and other assumptions lead to regional estimates of benefit-cost ratios (BCRs), ranging from 2.7 (South and Southeast Asia) to 22.3 (East Mediterranean and North Africa). The global BCR is stated as 4.9. These results are described as lower bound estimates, due to the omission of any benefit from increased availability of household labour.

A second approach to evaluation relies on the use of Disability Adjusted Life Years (DALYs) as a metric for health-related benefits. The estimates used are based on work by WHO, as reported in Evans, Hutton and Haller (2004). Because the DALYs consider both mortality and morbidity, this method allows for a relatively comprehensive form of cost effectiveness analysis. In this case, an economic value has been applied to the DALY measure: $500/DALY, roughly based on income levels in developing countries and certainly a lower bound on the value of a year of healthy life. It is noted that this valuation of the DALY produces a net present benefit roughly comparable to that obtained through the prior method, given discount rates in the range of 5–10 per cent.

Small-Scale Water Technology for Livelihoods

The second opportunity proposed in the chapter is also aimed at the very poor of the world. In this case, the target population is the 'dollar poor.'[2] It is estimated that some 1.2 bn people presently live at this level of poverty, of whom some three-quarters are in rural areas. The chapter further estimates that about 800 m 'dollar-poor' people depend on access to water for their livelihood. Most grow crops or tend livestock, while others may engage in fishing, agro-forestry or aquaculture. The opportunity arises from the observation that relatively low-cost measures are available that could improve access to water, or make that access more secure, thus increasing the output of the productive activities.

The proposal is for a range of interventions not greatly different from the first opportunity: low-cost technology transfer, social marketing of technology, provision for micro-credit, and various kinds of institutional support. It is hoped that farmers would be motivated to adopt such technologies as low-cost drip irrigation systems (which both reduce water use and improve yield, compared to traditional irrigation practices) and treadle pumps (which may make irrigation a feasible alternative to rain-fed agriculture). Other low-cost technologies are also available.

---

[1] The goals are based on the paragraph 19 of the United Nations Millennium Declaration (2000) as expanded by the recommendations of the World Summit on Sustainable Development (2002).

[2] 'Dollar poor' is defined as those with household incomes of less than US$1.00 per capita per day, measured in 1985 Purchasing Power Parity (PPP).

It is assumed that 100 m farm families would adopt the small-scale technology, and that the result would be a stream of benefits in the form of increased crop value. The present value of the anticipated direct benefits is estimated in the range of US$150 m to US$300 m, for discount rates of 10 per cent and 5 per cent, respectively. Costs are on the order of US$50 m to US$100 m, giving a BCR of 3. It is further noted that increases in farm output and agricultural activity can be expected to produce increased economic activity in the region, possibly multiplying benefits by a factor between 2 and 4. Choosing the median of this range gives a BCR of 9, as reported in the chapter. However, no details are provided on the nature of the expected indirect benefits, or to what extent the calculation has excluded transfers.

Water and Sanitation as Commodities[3]

In the early 1990s, an international conference formulated four principles for the development of water resources in the twenty-first century (Dublin Statement 1992). The fourth and most controversial of the Dublin Principles is: 'Water has an economic value in all its competing uses and should be recognised as an economic good.' This was widely and probably correctly interpreted as meaning that water should be treated like any other market good,[4] a view that runs counter to considerable opinion, then and now.

The notion that 'water is different' is embedded deeply in the psyche of most water engineers, planners and managers. After all, the argument goes, water is essential to life. While the same can be said for food, shelter and clothing, there are few advocates for a 'food is different' or 'clothing is different' position. Throughout history these essential

services have been almost universally commodified and traded in markets. But not water. Over the six millennia separating the first irrigation systems in ancient Babylon from the vast water supply systems of today's megacities, water supply and wastewater management has been the work of government much more often than not. This historical fact seems congruent with our cherished beliefs. Water is, after all, the 'enabler and sustainer of civilisation' (NRC 1991). It is said to be the very 'source of life' and an 'inalienable individual and collective right' it has even been argued that 'society must collectively assume all of the costs' of water supply.[5]

One might conclude, therefore, that water is truly 'different', and not a market good like food or shelter. One might also conclude that various modern innovations such as full cost recovery and privatisation are inappropriate or harmful. But these conclusions are not correct. They arise from a basic misunderstanding about the subject of the debate. Water supply, especially in the developing world, is a distinctly different thing from the stylised, even mythical, notion of water embodied in the 'water is different' arguments.

There are at least three pieces to the argument. First, it is asserted that 'water is different': it is not an economic good like ordinary market goods. The second piece of the argument is that water is, in effect, a public good which should be available to all and, at least for basic uses, unpriced. Finally, the argument says that it is the responsibility of government to determine how much water should be provided, when and where, and to assume the costs of this service. Parallel arguments can be asserted for many sanitation services.

In economics, we make a distinction between public goods and market goods. Market goods are said to be rival and excludable. It is these characteristics that make it sensible and possible for a market to allocate market goods. When one or both of these characteristics are missing, the good is said to be some form of public good. This attribute is associated with market failure, where markets either cannot allocate the good at all, or do so inefficiently.

But what kind of good is water? If we are speaking of water in the environment, then it cannot be a market good except in very special circumstances. Normally, water is ubiquitous. It is everywhere around us. It would be impractical or impossible to

---

[3] The arguments in this section are paraphrased and abbreviated versions of material that previously appeared in Boland (2001, 2003).

[4] Little noticed in the ensuing controversy was the sentence that immediately followed the Fourth Principle: 'Within this principle, it is vital to recognise first the basic right of all human beings to have access to clean water and sanitation at an affordable price' (Dublin Statement, 1992).

[5] These statements first appeared on the internet (Committee for the World Water Contract 1998). The Contract was later elaborated and published in book form by Ricardo Petrella (2001).

levy a charge for water in the environment, and then exclude non-payers. So this is clearly a public good.

But water in the environment is not what the writers of the Water Manifesto had in mind. They were concerned about water that is collected, stored, transported and then made available for human uses at the time and place of need. To accomplish this requires a set of services that we know as 'water supply'. And water supply is clearly rival (water supplied to one person is not available to another) and excludable (if a charge is levied, nonpayers can be excluded). Water supply is, therefore, a market good, while water in the environment is not.

But this is not the whole story. Water does more than wash faces, flush toilets and irrigate driveways. Universal access to a supply of safe water, coupled with safe means for disposing of human wastes, brings important health benefits – taken for granted in industrial countries, but yearned-for in many developing countries. And the benefits are not just to the users of water individually, but to communities collectively, e.g. as communicable disease incidence drops. Also, water supply systems free household members, usually women, from the time-consuming and laborious tasks of carrying water and managing its use. This expands the labour force, increases income and improves the quality of life. The point is that these water-related services are not market goods – they are collectively consumed public goods.

The Water Manifesto takes a rather simple line: water is a public good and not a market good. Reality is more complex. Water in the environment is generally a public good, while water supply is a market good, but one with important public good aspects. Similarly, the safe disposal of human wastes into the environment is a public good, while the safe removal of such wastes from human contact is a (mostly) market good, again with important public good aspects.

This intertwining of public and market goods is not unique to water and sanitation. Similar arguments can be made for many other services of urban infrastructure: electric energy, public transportation, communications, etc. By comparison, water and sanitation services are distinguished by the relative prominence of the public good aspects, and by a history of public sector provision which has tended to obscure the market good aspects.

Once it is accepted that water and sanitation are commodities, it becomes clear that efficient provision and use can be achieved through appropriate pricing and related commercial practices. But if it is also accepted that these commodities have important public good aspects, it is also clear that their provision must be subject to government (or at least public) control, so as to protect the public goods. Where the provider is not the government, it may have no incentive to provide universal access, to meet safety and environmental standards, to insure that the poor receive adequate services, etc. Interventions which help the provider become financially sustainable and which promote efficient pricing do not ensure that public goods are provided in the proper amounts. Similarly, interventions which focus on the public goods may not lead to efficient provision of the market good. Proposed interventions must recognise this complexity, and must be clear about their specific objectives.

Limited Scope for Economic Intervention

Both opportunities described in the chapter can be characterised as 'bottom-up' strategies. That is, they seek to improve the ability of individuals, households and communities to take actions that will result in improved water and sanitation services. In this sense, these opportunities are consistent with the lessons of decades of disappointing initiatives. Time and again, attempts to impose 'top-down' solutions (institutional strengthening, institutional reform, reorganisation, regulations and standards, etc.) have produced little or, at best, temporary improvement. On the other hand, there are distinct limitations to what can be accomplished through 'bottom-up' approaches.

The chapter describes the proposed opportunities in very general terms, with few details. In the case of the first opportunity, it can be assumed that social marketing, training and community mobilisation activities will be used to help develop an organisation competent to deliver improved water supply and sanitation services. The community organisation would then be acquainted with a range of appropriate low-cost technologies. A variety of financing and self-help measures would be needed to construct the facilities. Finally, users will be expected to pay fees and/or contribute labour in return for the improved services. Most practitioners agree that this is a sound approach.[6]

According to a conventional rational analysis of this problem, because the benefits to the community may far outweigh the cost, the community is expected to welcome any assistance in achieving these benefits. But whether all of this is feasible in any given location depends on many factors beyond the control of the intervenor. There may be reasons why the community is unable or unwilling to organise (internal divisions, prior negative experience with similar efforts, etc.). The proposed technologies may be unsuitable for historical or cultural reasons. It may be difficult to achieve financial sustainability because of problems with levying charges or collecting sufficient revenues.

These issues are real, but they do not preclude success. The problem is to understand exactly what barriers may be encountered and to craft a place-specific intervention that avoids them. Different forms of organisation may be appropriate in different places; not every community can achieve a locally managed activity. Even private sector firms can be considered, provided that regulation and oversight can be provided.

The relative social acceptance of alternative technologies is a complicated topic, especially in the case of sanitation. Issues of habit, privacy, cleanliness, etc. may result in rejection of certain types of facilities (e.g. latrines) in certain places. It is important to understand what will be acceptable before proceeding.

Financial sustainability requires a tariff which is socially acceptable and which can produce the needed revenues.[7] Even in very poor countries, this is almost always achievable in the case of water supply. All households demonstrate significant willingness to pay for improved water services. Some urban households may already pay a substantial fraction of disposable income for water obtained from vendors.[8] Of course, the tariff must also provide for those households which cannot or should not be required to pay the full cost of improved water service. There are a number of ways to accomplish this, generally by providing a basic level of service at a low cost or at no cost. Proper tariff design allows this to be done without distorting the price signals received by other households (Whittington, Boland and Foster 2002).

Sanitation services present a different problem. Because of the large public good component of sanitation services, household-level willingness to pay may be low to non-existent. Industrial countries solved this problem by bundling wastewater services with water supply, thus exploiting the higher willingness to pay (WTP) for water as a revenue source for wastewater management. But the pattern in developing countries has been to provide water supply first, then attempt to implement sanitation improvements later. This requires increasing the water tariff to pay for sanitation, a highly unpopular approach. A better strategy is to bundle the services from the outset where possible, and to make maximum use of contributed labour to reduce the cost of sanitation improvements.

The argument for 'bottom-up', user-driven approaches is that they respond to the actual needs and constraints of the affected community, and thus have a much higher likelihood of success. A corollary to this argument is that each local intervention must be prepared to adapt to those needs and constraints; it must identify each possible barrier to success and attempt to provide a solution. While economic tools are important, much barrier identification and adaptation relies on the skills of other social scientists (sociologists, anthropologists, etc.). There is no 'one size fits all'.

Critique and Conclusions

Chapter 9 focuses on two areas of great need: (1) the several billions of people who presently lack access to safe water and/or safe means for disposal of human wastes and (2) the nearly 1 billion very poor people whose livelihood depends on an adequate supply of water for irrigation, stock watering, etc. The first opportunity is described as a set of

[6] Early reports of apparent success of interventions of this kind are steadily accumulating; most recently in Kazakhstan (Michael Curley, personal communication).

[7] This assumes that the tariff is correctly set, that users are billed accurately and that most bills are paid. Each of these conditions represents a major challenge in most developing countries, although early indications are that community managed systems may have fewer collection problems.

[8] Whittington and Choe (1992) found water vendor costs ranging up to 40 per cent of disposable household income.

'bottom-up' interventions designed to facilitate the formation of community managed, self-sustaining organisations which can deliver improved water and sanitation services. The second opportunity involves the introduction and social marketing of a number of low-cost technologies which promise to increase the net income of those who use water for productive purposes. In both bases, the interventions are expected to provide large net benefits, with BCRs of 2.7 and higher.

One major question, applicable to both opportunities, is how to predict the degree of successful implementation. In the case of the first opportunity, each individual intervention must be tailored to the culture, history and situation of the affected community. Some of these adaptations will be successful in leading the community to develop improved water supply and sanitation services; others will not. The chapter avoids this issue by merely stating that the MDGs will be met: that is, half of the unserved population will be served by 2015. Whether this is achievable in the stated time frame, or at all, is unknown. While experience with approaches of the kind proposed has been encouraging, it can also be assumed that the easiest problems have been addressed first (the 'low-hanging fruit'). No one can say how effective this approach will be if implemented on the massive scale and in the compressed time frame contemplated by the chapter.

The second opportunity raises a similar question. In this case, it is assumed that there exist low-cost, cost-effective technologies that can increase the income of some 100 m very poor families. If this is true, one must ask why there is not already a large demand for and widespread adoption of these technologies. The answers implied by the chapter are that the technologies are not widely known and that there are financial barriers to their adoption (the potential beneficiaries have insufficient cash and no credit). The nature of the opportunity is that providing information and financing (micro-credit arrangements) will lead to widespread adoption. In fact, the chapter assumes 60 per cent adoption.

Despite these criticisms, it is probably true that both interventions are highly beneficial. Even if the first opportunity was limited to several hundred million people, instead of several billion, the benefits would likely exceed the costs by a large margin. Similarly, a more limited application of

the second opportunity would still produce large benefits. Since each of them consists of numerous individual, mostly independent projects, there are few economies of scale in implementation. If the sites are first screened for expected benefits, it would possible to pick the best applications first, producing BCRs even higher than those estimated in the chapter.

In presenting evaluations of the two opportunities, the chapter notes the prevalence of cost effectiveness analyses in the literature, many of them measuring outcomes in terms of infrastructure built, or institutions created, rather than as services delivered. In other words, benefits are measured in terms of inputs, not outputs.[9] The chapter recognises this problem and attempts to avoid it by providing, in each case, an economic measure of the value of services provided. On the other hand, the number of persons served is predetermined for both opportunities, so there is an element of rigidity in this analysis, as noted above.

Another issue for the first opportunity arises out of the need to develop financially sustainable community managed service delivery organisations. This is perhaps the most difficult achievement, especially in countries where water utilities have traditionally depended on subsidy, where there is no tradition of cost recovery, where many water bills go unpaid without consequences, where utility managers feel no accountability to their customers, etc. There is little or no experience with devising public institutions that will reverse this set of expectations. Some cases of privatisation appear to have achieved this, but it is not clear that a community managed organisation will succeed immediately.

Finally, there is the issue of public goods. Where water and sanitation services have been provided by government, it has been presumed that government would promote and protect the public goods. In fact, government-owned agencies in some developing countries have been severely dysfunctional, failing to provide adequate quantities of the market goods as well as the public goods. Where private sector firms are the providers of service, the responsibility for ensuring that public goods are

---

[9] One (unnamed) industrial country has recently been heard to count as beneficiaries of improved water supply the entire population of a river basin, where the only action taken was the organisation of a new water management agency.

adequately provided falls squarely on government, and government may or may not fulfil this charge. It is not yet clear what advantages a community managed organisation may have. One argument is that it will attend to the public goods at least as well as a government agency would and that it will also be a more effective provider of the market goods. A contradictory argument is that the community managed organisation will have little incentive to protect health, environment, etc., relying on the government to attend to these matters.

In summary, the chapter presents two provocative and meritorious opportunities. Their justifications would be more persuasive if they either used more realistic adoption goals, or if they were presented in terms of phased, incremental adoption. Also, the chapter is silent on the considerable difficulty and complexity of adapting each intervention to local beliefs, customs and situations. However, this omission does not detract from the potential benefits to be gained, it merely casts further doubt on the assumed level of adoption.

The proposed opportunities are well worth further elaboration and development. In the case of the first opportunity, particular attention should be given to the two issues for which there is little satisfactory experience: (1) the means of adapting interventions to local conditions and (2) the strategies for achieving financially sustainable delivery of services. In the case of the second opportunity, efforts to promote the adoption of low-cost technologies must begin with a clear and detailed understanding of why those technologies will not be adopted in the absence of intervention.

References

Boland, J.J., 2001: Should water be considered a commodity: Yes. in *History in dispute; 7, water and the environment: global perspectives*, St James Press London, 281–284
  2003: Thinking about the demand for water services: why is it so difficult to understand?, The 2003 Abel Wolman Distinguished Lecture, National Research Council of the National Academies, Washington DC

Committee for the World Water Contract, 1998: The water manifesto
Dublin Statement, 1992: International conference on water and the environment: development issues for the 21st century, 16–31 January Dublin, Ireland, World Meteorological Organisation, Geneva
Esrey, S.A., J.B. Potasch, L. Roberts and C. Shiff, 1991: Effects of improved water and sanitation on ascariasis, diarrhoea, dracunculiasis, hookworm infection, schistosomiasis and trachoma, *Bulletin of the World Health Organisation*, **69**(5), 609–21
Evans, B.G., L. Hutton, and L. Haller, 2004: Closing the sanitation gap – the case for better funding of sanitation and hygiene, Paper prepared for Roundtable on Sustainable Development, 9–10 March 2004, OECD, Paris
NRC.1991: *Opportunities in the hydrologic sciences*, National Academy Press, Washington, DC
  1996: Water and sanitation services for megacities in the developing world, in *Meeting the challenges of megacities in the developing world: a collection of working papers*, Washington, DC
Petrella, R., 2001: *The water manifesto: arguments for a world water contract*, Palgrave Macmillan, New York.
Rijsberman, F., 2004: Sanitation and access to clean water, chapter 9 in this volume.
UN Department of Economic and Social Affairs. 2004: Plan of implementation of the World Summit on Sustainable Development, Division for Sustainable Development
UN General Assembly, 2000: Millennium declaration (55/2)
UNWWDR (UN World Water Development Report), 2003: *Water for people, water for life*, UNESCO, Paris
Whittington, D., J.J. Boland, and V. Foster, 2002: Understanding the basics, in *Water tariffs and subsidies in South Asia*, Water and Sanitation Programme-South Asia, New Delhi, India, at http://www.wsp.org/pdfs/Water%20Tariff%201_press_27th%20Feb.pdf, 1–16.
Whittington, D., and K. Choe, 1992: Economic benefits available from the provision of improved water supplies, WASH Technical Report 77, US Agency for International Development, Environmental Health Project, Washington, DC

Perspective Paper 9.2

HENRY VAUX, JR

There can be little question but that 'water and sanitation' represent one of the great challenges facing the world. Although I have a major concern about Rijsberman's characterisation of the importance of water scarcity in providing water and santitation services, I am in substantial agreement with much of the substance of his paper. I begin this chapter 9 Perspective paper with a series of short comments on the principal points found in the chapter. These are matters where I differ only by degree, if at all, with the substance of the chapter. Following that I present a more extensive treatment on the general question of water scarcity and argue, contrary to Rijsberman, that the pervasive scarcity of water world-wide and the absence of institutions which allocate it effectively among competing demands is central to the problem of providing adequate water and sanitation services to the unserved.

Short Points of Commentary

There are a number of important points in chapter 9 that invite further elaboration. They are treated briefly below.

The Millennium Development Goal (MDG): The author is correct in identifying the provision of water and sanitation services to the 'unserved' as a critical challenge. He is also correct is noting that net benefits will likely be maximised by investing jointly in the facilities needed to supply water and wastewater treatment. While it is convenient to use the MDG of halving the number of unserved by 2015 as a framework for the quantitative analysis, the goal itself seems unreasonable and unlikely to be obtained no matter how much is invested. If the MDG is to be achieved

it will be necessary to bring sanitation services to 825,000 unserved people *each day* (between now and 2015). The companion figure for water supply is 581,000 unserved/each day. This goal does not seem physically, institutionally or economically attainable.

Benefit-Cost Analyses: The benefit-cost analysis (CBA) is incomplete but necessarily so for the reasons that the author advances. The chapter contains a good survey of the available cost and benefit data but the data are far from sufficient and the resulting BCR must be interpreted as simply an indicator that the net benefits of the proposed investments would be significant.

Multiple, Combined Interventions: Rijsberman notes both explicitly and implicitly that the strategic focus of efforts to address this challenge should be on a combination of interventions including technology and institutions. This point is critically important for, as is noted, here and there throughout the chapter, the purely technical solutions of the past have not always solved the water problems to which they were directed and, in some instances, have led to worse problems. In many instances, the neglect of institutional problems has undermined efforts to solve significant water problems.

Water and Economic Growth: The evidence cited in the chapter confirms the widely ignored notion that water is a necessary but not sufficient condition for economic growth. All too frequently, politicians and others assume that the provision of water and sanitation services *by themselves* will guarantee economic growth. The evidence suggests that water and sanitation must be available if significant growth is to occur, but their presence does not assure such growth.

The Role of Desalinisation: Desalinisation has been widely heralded at one time or another as the solution to many of the world's water problems. It is true, as Rijsberman states, that the costs of desalinisation have been coming down, but that is not the full story. Desalinisation costs are very sensitive to the salinity of the feed water. Desalinisation of brackish waters and waters that are mildly saline can be economically justified for some high-valued uses. Sea water desalination remains enormously expensive when all costs are fairly accounted for. There is a tendency to promote seawater conversion projects that are joint with power plants. The resulting costs are almost always understated because the power is subsidised and all of the joint costs are allocated to power production. Seawater conversion is unlikely to be the solution to water problems except in a few instances where there are no alternative sources of supply and there is considerable wealth to defray the costs of seawater desalinisation.

The Problem Of Water Scarcity

The principal shortcoming of chapter 9 centres on Rijsberman's assertion in his introductory section that the problems of water supply and sanitation have little to do with water scarcity which, he avers, 'is not the issue for all but the largest cities in dry areas'. Here it is argued that water scarcity is indeed the issue (floods and flood control excepted) and that the pervasiveness of such scarcity the world over will likely constrain, even severely, the extent to which we are able to provide adequate water and sanitation services to most if not all of the world's population. Rijsberman notes that 'because water for domestic purposes is of such high value and clear priority that it takes precedence over other uses'. This argument would be more compelling if reasonably well-functioning markets or other allocative institutions which respond to relative values to ensure that water is allocated to its most valuable uses (more or less) exist and are reasonably widespread. Unfortunately, such institutions are the

exception rather than the rule. Additionally, scarcity is further exacerbated by declarations that all have certain fundamental rights to water. The fact is that water is not freely available nor freely allocable as between domestic, agricultural, environmental and other uses. It is for this reason that communities in both dry and humid areas struggle to obtain the water supplies needed to support existing and anticipated population and economic growth. In the USA, for example, the Atlanta, Georgia urban area in the humid southeast struggles to obtain additional water in the same way that Las Vegas, Nevada in the arid southwest does. Spain is embroiled in a paralysing political conflict over how to provide water for the rapidly urbanising Mediterranean Coast even though those demands could be met by relatively modest reallocations from the agricultural sector. And, in the continuing absence of effective reallocative institutions, significant numbers of Mexico's urban residents may be hard pressed to find domestic water supplies in the future (NRC 1995). Other examples abound.

Beyond the absence of market institutions, there are circumstances which promise to intensify water scarcity in the future. Rijsberman alludes to these circumstances but does not elaborate sufficiently to show how they will lead inevitably to heightened water scarcity. The compelling and urgent nature of these problems likely means that in the absence of effective allocative institutions, the solutions to these problems may stretch or even crowd out the financial resources needed to provide adequate water and sanitation services to most, if not all, of the world's population. Stated differently, the need to resolve these water problems which affect both rich and poor, will generate formidable competitors for the expertise and resources needed to develop the water and sanitation services for the world's unserved. These problems, which include the maintenance of sustainable ground water resources, the maintenance and enhancement of water quality and the need to feed a more populous world, will in the future compete to some extent for the resources that might otherwise be devoted to the water problems of the poor. The remainder of this chapter is devoted to a discussion of these three problems and how they may come to dominate our thinking and action about water resources.

The Importance of Sustainable Ground Water

Ground water accounts for approximately a third of the world's usable water supply. Ground water is a particularly attractive component of the water supply because its availability is not linked directly to precipitation and runoff. This means that ground water is specially important in times of drought when surface water supplies may be significantly reduced. Ground water overdraft, in which the quantities of water pumped exceed the quantities recharged threatens the sustainability of many of the world's ground water resources. Overdrafting may be justified and economically appropriate in the short term as, for example, when it contributes a supplementary source of supply during drought periods. In non-drought periods overdrafting stops and aquifers have the opportunity to recover. By contrast, long-term overdraft is not sustainable. Long-term overdraft is always self-terminating and the mechanism of termination is the economic exhaustion of the aquifer which occurs when water tables fall to the point where pumpers can no longer afford to extract.

Rijsberman notes in his introduction that: 'The fall in groundwater (*sic*) levels, particularly in India and China, threatens the livelihoods of the farmers in these areas as well as the food supply for a significant share of the world population.' Ground water depletion in China appears to be occurring on an enormous scale. Evans, Foster and Garduno (2003) report that there have been 'massive declines' in ground water levels in the Hai, Huai and Huang river basins which cover an area where 430 m people live. Falling water tables are not confined to China and India but are found virtually everywhere around the globe. Thus, for example, it has been well documented that the Mexico City Aquifer, which is relied upon by a significant proportion of Mexico City's 14 m residents, has been continuously overdrafted for nearly a century (NRC 1995). Postel (1999) reports that ground water depletion is now widespread in central and northern China, parts of India and Pakistan, the western United States, North Africa, the Middle East and the Arabian Peninsula. The sustainability of ground water resources around the world is threatened and unless ways are found to address and attenuate persistent overdraft, accustomed supplies of water will be lost and the costs of extracting ground water that remains will rise.

Perhaps the most common way in which ground water overdraft has been addressed in the past is by constructing additional surface water storage and conveyance facilities which then permit new increments of surface water to be substituted for the depleted ground water. In the absence of effective controls over ground water extractions, this strategy is just a short-term palliative. For example, it has been documented that in the southern Central Valley of California there have been three recurring cycles of ground water depletion, followed by surface water importation, which is then followed by depletion again as the economy and population of the region grows (Vaux 1986). Moreover, this strategy of alleviating ground water overdraft by importing additional surface supplies is becoming less viable as surface water supplies become fully appropriated.

Continuation of persistent ground water overdraft threatens to reduce supplies at a time when demands for water world-wide are growing. The continuation of the widespread failure to address problems of persistent overdraft serves only to intensify further the generalised global scarcity of water and to make scarcity even more acute in areas where long-term ground water overdraft occurs. The need to maintain and sustain local and regional economies that are dependent upon ground water overdraft will create especially vexing problems in areas where alternative supplies are not available. The need to rescue such communities will create additional competition for both water supplies and appropriate infrastructure and render the problems of providing water and sanitation services to the unserved even more difficult to solve.

Water Quality

The availability of water is inextricably a function of water quality. Any discussion of the adequacy of existing or potential water supplies carries – explicitly or implicitly – assumptions about the suitability or lack thereof of the quality of water to serve intended uses. Some uses, such as domestic use, require waters of very high quality. Others, such as landscape irrigation, require waters of lesser quality. Rijsberman notes that the cleanup of surface waters in western Europe and North American that began with the provision of sewage collection and disposal a century ago and was followed by significant investment in wastewater treatment facilities over the last several decades has been a real success story. While the trends in surface water quality in Europe and North America have generally been positive in recent decades, water quality trends in the rest of the world have not and there are reasons for suspecting that a continuing decline in water quality world-wide is to be expected (Ongley 1999).

New chemicals, whose biological properties are not understood, appear every day. At least some of those chemicals and their byproducts and residues will find their way into the environment along with existing chemicals that will continue to be discharged to the environment. Given the pace and sophistication modern industrial research and application, it appears likely that both ground and surface waters will be subject to continuing contamination from both natural and synthetic chemicals. In addition, past land use practices have left toxic residues in the soil, many of which are migrating inexorably toward some nearby aquifer. With time more aquifers will become contaminated with chemicals that have migrated through the soil profile over very long periods (NRC 1993). Inappropriate land use practices, which occur because land use is largely unregulated in most parts of the world, will result in new chemical legacies that will lead to further ground water contamination.

Even granting that the provision of sanitation services to the unserved will lead to improvements in the quality of local receiving waters, there is an irony in the fact that the poorest countries are least able to manage, enhance and maintain water quality. This will almost always mean that declining water quality will lead to declines in the availability of water – increasing scarcity – in the poorest countries. In fact, the general relationship between GDP and water quality suggests that the poorer a country, the less able it is to manage water quality so that inevitably water availability itself is a function of the

country's relative wealth (Ongley 1999). The likely declines in water quality will contribute further to water scarcity. This will be especially pronounced in areas where the demand for high-quality water is growing and may interfere directly with efforts to make domestic water supplies available to the unserved.

Feeding a More Populous World

The criticisms of irrigated agriculture often mask its importance in feeding the world. Rijsberman notes this fact and cites studies which document that irrigated agriculture contributes significantly to the reduction of rural poverty. However, the importance of irrigation and the availability of water for irrigation may be far more critical than is suggested by the contribution of irrigated agriculture to poverty reduction. Agriculture water users are frequently thought of as the supplier of last resort when additional water supplies are needed for critical domestic and environmental purposes. This is because agriculture accounts for such an overwhelming proportion of consumptive water use and because many agricultural water uses of are relatively low value. Nevertheless, in a report from the World Watch Institute, Postel and Vickers (2004) note that water shortages will soon manifest themselves as food shortages. If such shortages are to be averted, irrigated agriculture will probably have to be expanded. Yang *et al.* (2003) show that as an empirical matter when water availability in a country falls below 1500 m^3/*capita*/year, the country begins to import foodstuffs which are predominantly cereal grains. These food imports compensate for the local water deficits since the water needed to produce the imported food does not have to be taken from the local water budget.

As population grows, the demand for food increases. So long as foodstuffs can be traded relatively freely in world markets, increasing demand for food drives increases in the world-wide derived demand for water. Again, so long as trade can be accomplished relatively freely, countries whose water supplies are insufficient to allow them to grow the food needed to feed their populations can import 'virtual water' in the form of imported food (Yang and Zehnder 2002). In this way, the demand for water in water poor countries is transmitted as demand for food to water rich countries. The significance here is that although agriculture, which is now regarded as the suppliers of last resort, will find itself the focus of intensifying demand. Yang *et al.* (2003) examined water availability worldwide and identified twenty-one African and Asian nations whose indigenous water supplies were less than 1,500 m^3/*capita*/year in 2000. Using a range of population projections these authors identified an additional fourteen countries in Asia and Africa that will fall below the threshold by 2030. (*Note*: The status of China is uncertain. To avoid a deficit below the 1500 m^3 annual *per capita* threshold the Chinese will need to develop virtually all of their surface supplies (Zehnder 2003).) They estimate that the water deficit of both groups of countries in 2030 would be 1,150 km^3/year, roughly thirteen times the annual discharge of the Nile River.

There are two immediate implications of these circumstances. First, for water-deficient countries that have insufficient wealth to purchase needed foodstuffs in international markets, the need to feed additional numbers of people who might otherwise starve will compete for resources that might have been used to provide water supply and sanitation serves. The need to provide such services as well as the food that cannot be grown because of water scarcity will require investments considerably in excess of those presented by Rijsberman. Second, to the extent that water-deficit countries are able to translate their water deficiencies into effective demand for food in world markets, the derived demand for water for agriculture in the water-surplus countries of North America, western Europe and – possibly–Australia. This means that increasing world population will intensify the scarcity of water, not just in rapidly growing, water-deficient countries, but in the water surplus-countries as well.

Conclusions

The provision of water and sanitation services to the unserved as well as the provision of water and the implements of water management to the poor is surely one of the great challenges facing the world. This challenge is embedded in the more general challenge posed by world-wide water scarcity. The daunting tasks of providing water and sanitation services and improving the lot of the rural poor in developing countries will be difficult enough where water is plentiful or susceptible of being reallocated. In a world confronted with sharply intensifying water scarcity, the task will be even more difficult.

The persistence of long-term ground water overdraft world-wide threatens to diminish absolutely the availability of ground water in terms of both quantity and price. If overdraft cannot be attenuated, regions and economies that are dependent on ground water overdraft will require additional supplies from elsewhere if they are to survive. Widespread institutional solutions to the problems of overdraft seem unlikely and the result will be intensifying water scarcity, particularly in regions where alternative sources of supply are either non-existent or very costly. Some of these regions will have significant numbers of people who do not have access to water and sanitation services. Intensifying water scarcity will increase the difficulty of bringing such services to these people.

Similarly, general trends of water quality decline world-wide are unlikely to be reversed in the near future. Water quality decline is a particular problem in the developing world where the financial and institutional resources needed to manage water quality are generally unavailable. It is true that the provision of sanitation services to the unserved will have substantial positive impacts on the quality of local receiving waters. Nevertheless, growing water contamination from industrial and agricultural sources as well as 'legacy pollution' of ground water suggests that water quality will continue to decline in many parts of the world and reduce the quantities of water available for high-valued uses, including domestic uses. The resultant increase in the scarcity of water for domestic uses will further complicate the problem of providing water and sanitation services for the unserved.

Finally, as has been observed, water scarcity may in the future manifest itself in food shortages. It is instructive to note that four of the nine countries which Rijsberman lists as high-priority countries for water supply service are also countries whose annual *per capita* water availability will fall below 1,500 m³ by 2030. These countries will come to be water deficient in the same time frame that efforts will need to be made to provide water services to significant numbers of unserved. In addition, the observed tendency of countries to import cereals once they have become water deficient means that increasing population will result in further intensification of water scarcity world-wide.

While Rijsberman makes a useful distinction between the problems of managing water scarcity and the problems of providing water access and sanitation services to those who don't have them, it is simply not true that water scarcity and the need to manage that scarcity will have no impact on the ability of world to address the water and sanitation challenge. In the absence of reallocative institutions which can facilitate the movement of water from relatively low-valued uses to higher-valued uses, the problem of providing the water itself as well as the problem of providing access to water for the un-served and the poor promises to be more formidable than chapter 9 suggests.

References

Evans, R., S. Foster and H. Garduno, 2003: *Achieving groundwater use efficiency in Northern China*, Proceedings of the 3rd Rosenberg International Forum. Canberra, Australia

National Research Council, 1993: *Groundwater vulnerability assessment: contamination potential under conditions of uncertainty*, National Academy Press, Washington, DC

National Research Council (NRC), 1995: *Mexico City's water supply: improving the outlook for sustainability*, National Academy Press, Washington, DC

Ongley, E., 1999: Water quality: an emerging global crisis in S.T. Trudgill, D. E. Walling and B. W. Webb (eds.), *Water quality: processes and policy*, John Wiley & Sons, Inc., New York

Postel, S. 1999: *Pillar of sand*, W.W. Norton, New York

Postel, S. and A. Vickers, 2004: Boosting water productivity, in L. Brown (ed.), *State of the world 2004*, Worldwatch Institute, Washington, DC

Vaux, H., 1986: Water scarcity and gains from trade in Kern County, California. In K. Frederick, *Scarce water and institutional change,* Resources for the Future. Washington, DC

Yang, H. and A. Zehnder 2002: Water scarcity and food import: A case study for Southern Mediterranean countries, *World Development*, **30**(8), 1413–30

Yang, H., P. Reichert, K. Abbaspour and A. Zehnder, 2003: A water resources threshold and its implications for food security, *Environmental Science and Technology*, **37**(14), 3048–54

Zehnder, A., 2003: Personal communication, 7 October, 2003

Subsidies and Trade Barriers

CHAPTER 10

KYM ANDERSON

The Copenhagen Consensus project is looking for an answer to the question: if there was a desire to spend US$50 bn over the next five years to improve the world, what opportunity offers the highest pay-off? This chapter argues that putting effort into phasing out wasteful subsidies and trade barriers should be ranked highly among the opportunities being addressed in this project, for three reasons:

- It would require only a small fraction of that $50 bn to make a significant impact in this area, via greater advocacy, and cuts to subsidies could reduce government outlays by hundreds of millions of dollars leaving plenty to spend on the next-best opportunity too
- Trade reform would allow citizens to spend more also on other pressing problems (because under freer trade the world's resources would be allocated more efficiently), thereby *indirectly* contributing to opportunities to alleviate other challenges
- Trade reform would also *directly* alleviate poverty and thereby reduce environmental degradation and address some of the other challenges identified in this project, namely climate change, communicable diseases, conflicts and arms proliferation, education underinvestment, financial instability, poor governance and corruption, population and migration issues, water issues, and undernutrition and hunger.

The Challenge

Despite the net economic and social benefits of reducing most government subsidies[1] and opening economies to trade, almost every national government intervenes in markets for goods and services in ways that distort international commerce. Those

distortionary policies harm most the economies imposing them, but the worst of them (in agriculture and clothing) are particularly harmful to the world's poorest people. The challenge addressed in this chapter is to rid the world of such wasteful and anti-poor policies. The geographic scope is thus global, although some of the opportunities for alleviating the problem involve action by just sub-sets of the world's national governments.

To keep the task manageable, the policy instruments considered will be limited to those trade-related ones over which a government's international trade negotiators have some influence, at both home and abroad. That thereby excludes measures such as generic taxes on income, consumption and value added, government spending on mainstream public services, infrastructure and generic social safety nets in strong demand by the community, and subsidies (taxes) and related measures set optimally from the national viewpoint to overcome positive (negative) environmental or other externalities. Also excluded from consideration here are foreign exchange policies, as they are being considered in chapter 5 in this volume (Eichengreen 2004).

This challenge in its modern form has been with us for about seventy-five years. The latter part of the nineteenth century saw a strong movement towards laissez faire, but that development was reversed

Thanks are due to Denmark's Environmental Assessment Institute and *The Economist* for sponsoring the Copenhagen Consensus project, to numerous colleagues for their ideas and suggestions and to Lona Fowdur for research assistance with the spreadsheet underlying figure 10.1. Remaining shortcomings are the author's responsibility.

[1] Not all subsidies are welfare-reducing, and in some cases a subsidy-cum-tax will be optimal to overcome a gap between private and social costs that cannot be bridged *à la* Coase (1960). Throughout this chapter all references to 'cutting subsidies' refer to bringing them back to their optimal level (which will be zero in all but those exceptional cases).

following the First World War in ways that led to the Great Depression of the early 1930s and the conflict that followed (Kindleberger 1989). It was during the Second World War, in 1944, that a conference at Bretton Woods proposed an International Trade Organisation (ITO). An ITO charter was drawn up by 1948, along with a General Agreement on Tariffs and Trade (GATT), but the ITO idea died when the United States failed to progress it through Congress (Diebold 1952). Despite that, the GATT during its forty-seven-year history (before it was absorbed into the World Trade Organisation, WTO, on 1 January 1995) oversaw the gradual lowering of many tariffs on imports of manufactured goods by governments of developed countries. Manufacturing tariffs remained high in developing countries, however, and distortionary subsidies and trade policies affecting agricultural and services markets of both rich and poor countries continued to hamper efficient resource allocation, economic growth and poverty alleviation.

The Uruguay Round of multilateral trade negotiations led to agreements signed in 1994 that saw some trade liberalisation over the subsequent ten years. But even when those agreements are fully implemented by end-2004, and despite additional unilateral trade liberalisations since the 1980s by a number of countries (particularly developing and transition economies), many subsidies and trade distortions will remain. They include not just trade taxes-cum-subsidies but also contingent protection measures such as anti-dumping, regulatory standards that can be technical barriers to trade and domestic production subsidies (allegedly decoupled in the case of some farm support programmes, but in fact only partially so). Insufficient or excessive taxation or quantitative regulations (QRs) in the presence of externalities such as pollution also lead to inefficiencies and can be trade-distorting. Furthermore, the on-going proliferation of preferential trading and bilateral or regional integration arrangements – for which there would be little or no need in the absence of trade barriers – is adding complexity to international economic relations. In some cases, those arrangements are leading to trade and investment diversion rather than creation.

The reluctance to reduce trade distortions is almost never because such policy reform involves government treasury outlays. On the contrary, except in the case of a handful of low-income countries still heavily dependent on trade taxes for government revenue, such reform may well benefit the treasury (by raising income and/or consumption tax revenues more than trade tax revenues fall, not to mention any payments forgone because of cuts to subsidy programmes). Rather, distortions remain largely because further trade liberalisation and subsidy cuts redistribute jobs, income and wealth in ways that those in government fear will reduce their chances of remaining in power (and possibly their own wealth in countries where corruption is rife). The challenge involves finding politically attractive ways to phase out remaining distortions to world markets for goods, services, capital and potentially even labour.

This chapter focuses primarily on distortions at national borders (trade taxes and subsidies, QRs on international trade and technical barriers to trade) plus a few significantly trade-distorting production subsidies. While global in coverage, the chapter distinguishes between policies of developed countries and those of developing (including former socialist and least-developed) countries. Among other things, it emphasises the consequences, in the absence of other policy changes, for the UN's key Millennium Development Goals (MDGs) as encapsulated in the other nine challenges being addressed by the Copenhagen Consensus project – since trade reform, perhaps more than any of the other opportunities under consideration, has the potential to impact positively on most of those challenges.

The chapter is structured as follows. The next section summarises the arguments for removing trade distortions, along with critiques by sceptics. This includes examining not only the economic benefits and costs but also the social and environmental consequences of such reform, to make the case that opening markets is a worthy cause. Four opportunities to reduce these distortions over the next five years are then laid out in the third section. They are, in decreasing order of potential contribution to global openness and economic growth: full trade liberalisation globally (to provide more a benchmark than a politically likely scenario), non-preferential legally binding trade liberalisation following the WTO's current Doha round of multilateral trade negotiations, a reciprocal preferential agreement in the form of a Free Trade Area of the Americas (FTAA) and a non-reciprocal preferential agreement by OECD countries to provide least-developed countries (LDCs) with duty-free market access for their exports of 'everything but arms' (EBA).[2] The core of the chapter is the fourth section, where estimates of the economic benefits and costs of these opportunities are presented, along with a methodological critique of the various empirical studies surveyed, an assessment of the likely social and environmental consequences of reducing subsidies and trade barriers,[3] and finally an overall net present value (NPV) assessment.

The Arguments for (and Against) Removing Subsidies and Trade Barriers

Even before examining the empirical estimates of the costs and benefits from grasping various trade-liberalising opportunities, the case can be made that such reform in principle is beneficial economically. It then remains to examine whether particular reforms are also at least benign in terms of social and environmental outcomes. The latter is particularly important because there are many non-economists who believe or assume the social and/or environmental consequences are adverse and seek to persuade others through such means as mass (and sometimes violent) street protests.

Static Economic Gains from Own-Country Reform

The standard comparative static analysis of national gains from international trade emphasises the economic benefits from production specialisation and exchange so as to exploit comparative advantage in situations where a nation's costs of production and/or preferences differ from those in the rest of the world. This is part of the more general theory of the welfare effects of distortions in a trading economy, as summarised by Bhagwati (1971). Domestic industries become more productive as those with a comparative advantage expand by drawing resources from those previously protected or

subsidised industries that grow slower or contract following reform.

The static gains from trade tend to be greater as a share of national output the smaller the economy, particularly where economies of scale in production have not been fully exploited and where consumers (including firms importing intermediate inputs) value variety so that intra-industry as well as inter-industry trade can flourish.[4] In such cases the more efficient firms within expanding industries tend to take over the less efficient ones. Indeed theory and empirical studies suggest the shifting of resources *within* an industry may be more welfare-improving than shifts between industries.[5] They are also greater the more trade barriers have allowed imperfect competition to prevail in the domestic marketplace, which again is more common in smaller economies where industries have commensurately smaller numbers of firms.

Dynamic Economic Gains from Own-Country Reform

To the standard comparative static analysis needs to be added links between trade and economic growth. The mechanisms by which openness contributes

---

[2] A non-preferential but non-binding trade liberalisation opportunity by the Pacific rim members of APEC is also mentioned, but it is not considered in detail because its timeframe is to 2020 and in any case it is a sub-set of the opportunity to move to global free trade.

[3] Throughout the chapter, governmental 'triple-bottom-line' terminology is used to distinguish economic effects from social and environmental effects, rather than the economist's standard terminology of private effects for the former and social effects for the latter.

[4] Some may question the value of intra-industry trade, given that transaction costs such as freight can be non-trivial, but consumers are willing to pay for a greater variety of products. Those consumers include producers using those products as intermediate inputs. Feenstra, Markusen and Zeile (1992) suggest the welfare cost of tariff protection can be underestimated by as much as a factor of ten when this consideration is not included. In a study of US import data from 1972 to 2001, Broda and Weinstein (2004) find that the upward bias in the conventional import price index, because of not accounting for the growth in varieties of products, is approximately 1.2 per cent per year, and suggest that the welfare gain from variety growth in US imports alone is 2.8 per cent of GDP.

[5] See Melitz (1999) on the theory of this point and Trefler (2001) for an empirical illustration.

to growth are gradually getting to be better understood by economists, thanks to the pioneering work of such theorists as Grossman and Helpman (1991), Rivera-Batiz and Romer (1991) and the literature those studies spawned. In a helpful survey of the subsequent literature, Taylor (1999) identifies several channels through which openness to trade can affect an economy's growth rate. They include the scale of the market when knowledge is embodied in the products traded, the degree of redundant knowledge creation that is avoided through openness (Romer 1994) and the effect of knowledge spillovers.[6] More importantly from a policy maker's viewpoint, the available empirical evidence strongly supports the view that open economies grow faster (see the survey by USITC 1997).

Important econometric studies of the linkage between trade reform and the rate of economic growth include those by Sachs and Warner (1995) and Frankel and Romer (1999). More recent studies also provide some indirect supportive econometric evidence. For example, freeing up the importation of intermediate and capital goods promotes investments that increase growth (Wacziarg 2001). Indeed, the higher the ratio of imported to domestically produced capital goods for a developing country, the faster it grows (Lee 1995; Mazumdar 2001). Rodrigeuz and Rodrik (2001) examine a number of such studies and claim that the results they surveyed are not robust. However, in a more recent study that revisits the Sachs and Warner data and then provides new time-series evidence, Wacziarg and Welch (2003) show that dates of trade liberalisation do characterise breaks in investment and GDP growth rates. Specifically, for the 1950–98 period, countries that have liberalised their trade (raising their trade–GDP ratio by an average of 5 percentage points) have enjoyed on average 1.5 percentage points higher GDP growth compared with their pre-reform rate. There have also been myriad case studies of liberalisation episodes. In a survey

of thirty-six of them, Greenaway (1993) reminds us that many things in addition to trade policies were changing during the studied cases, so ascribing causality is not easy. That, together with some econometric studies that fail to find that positive link, has led Freeman (2003) to suggest that the promise of raising the rate of economic growth through trade reform has been overstated. The same could be (and has been) said about the contributions to growth of such things as investments in education, health, agricultural research and so on (Easterly 2001). A more general and more robust conclusion that Easterly draws from empirical evidence, though, is that people respond to *incentives*. Hence getting incentives right in factor and product markets is crucial – and removing unwarranted subsidies and trade barriers is an important part of that process. Additional evidence from thirteen new case studies reported in Wacziarg and Welch (2003) adds further empirical support to that view, as does the fact that there are no examples of autarkic economies that have enjoyed sustained economic growth, in contrast to the many examples since the 1960s of reformed economies that boomed after opening up.

Specifically, economies that commit to less market intervention tend to attract more investment funds, *ceteris paribus*, which raise their stocks of capital (through greater aggregate global savings or at the expense of other economies' capital stocks). More open economies also tend to be more *innovative*, because of greater trade in intellectual capital (information, ideas and technologies, sometimes but not only in the form of purchasable intellectual property (IP)). Trade liberalisation can thereby lead not just to a larger capital stock and a one-off increase in productivity but also to higher *rates* of capital accumulation and productivity growth in the reforming economy because of the way reform energises entrepreneurs. For those higher growth rates to be sustained, though, there is widespread agreement that governments also need to (a) have in place effective institutions to efficiently allocate and protect property rights, (b) allow domestic factor and product markets to function freely and (c) maintain macroeconomic and political stability (Rodrik 2003; Wacziarg and Welch 2003; Baldwin 2004). Or to paraphrase Panagariya

---

[6] Openness allows society's knowledge capital to grow faster. If an x per cent increase in that stock generates a more than x per cent increase in individual firms' outputs, as assumed by Romer (1986) and Lucas (2002), then that economy's GDP growth rate will rise. A study of North–South trade (Schiff and Wang 2004) provides empirical support for this assumption.

(2004), trade openness is necessary, but may not be a sufficient condition, for sustained economic growth.

Why, Then, are Countries Protectionist?

Despite the evident economic gains from removing trade distortions, most countries retain protection from foreign competition for at least some of their industries. Numerous reasons have been suggested as to why a country imposes trade barriers in the first place (infant-industry assistance, unemployment prevention, balance of payments maintenance, tax revenue raising, protection of environmental or labour standards, etc.). All of them are found wanting in almost all circumstances in that a lower-cost domestic policy instrument is available to meet each of those objectives (Corden 1997; Bhagwati 1988), but nonetheless there are well-meaning people who still believe that trade measures are needed for one or other of those reasons or to avoid the social costs associated with removing them. So part of the present challenge is to convince such people that the gains from reform would far exceed the costs and that there are more direct means of addressing their concerns.

The more difficult part of reforming trade policies relates to the fact that the most compelling explanation for their persistence is a *political economy* one. The changes in product prices that result from trade liberalisation or subsidy cuts necessarily change the prices for the services of productive factors such as land, labour and capital. Hence even though the aggregate income and wealth of a nation may be expected to grow when trade distortions are reduced, not everyone need gain, and social safety nets, where they exist, typically provide only partial compensation for such losses. This is the source of resistance to policy reforms: the expected losses in jobs, income and wealth are concentrated in the hands of a few who are prepared to support politicians who resist protection cuts, while the gains are sufficiently small per consumer and export firm and are distributed sufficiently widely as to make it not worthwhile for those potential gainers (not to mention foreign producers/exporters) to get together to lobby for reform, particularly given their greater free-rider problem in acting collectively (Hillman 1989; Grossman and Helpman 1994). Thus the observed pattern of protection in a country at a point in time may well be an equilibrium outcome in a national political market for policy intervention. In that case, reform requires a shock to that equilibrium.

What Can Induce Reductions in Subsidies and Trade Barriers?

That political market equilibrium may indeed be altered from time to time. Changes are induced by such things as better information dissemination, technological changes, reforms abroad and new opportunities to join international trade agreements.

Better Information Dissemination

One way that political markets for policy intervention can change is better dissemination (e.g. by national or international bureaucrats, think tanks, local export industries, foreign import suppliers) of more convincing information on the benefits to consumers, exporters and the overall economy from reducing subsidies and trade distortions, and on alternative means of achieving society's other objectives more efficiently, so as to balance the views of single-issue non-government organisations (NGOs), labour unions and the like who tend to focus only on the (often overstated) costs of reform to their constituents. Since the 1980s the spreading of more balanced benefit-cost information has contributed to unilateral economic reforms and a consequent opening to trade in numerous developing countries as well as richer countries such as Australia and New Zealand. More recently, several major NGOs, together with the OECD Secretariat, have begun to focus on providing better information about the wastefulness of environmentally harmful subsidies that has already started to have an impact (e.g. in reducing coal mining subsidies in Europe).

Technological Change

Another way the political equilibrium is altered is technological innovation. The information and telecommunications revolution since the 1980s, for example, has dramatically lowered the costs of doing business across national borders, just as happened with the arrival of steamships and the telegraph during the latter part of the nineteenth century. That increased trading opportunity has made (actual or potential) exporters more eager to get together to counter the anti-trade lobbying of import-protected groups and NGOs.

Unilateral Opening of Markets Abroad

A country's political equilibrium could also be upset by trade opening by one or more other countries, in so far as those reforms alter international prices and volumes of trade and foreign investment and provide greater market access opportunities for exporters. Such opening abroad also adds to the evidence of the net gains and (particularly in the case of phased reforms) the relatively low adjustment costs associated with trade reform, making it easier for exporters to counter the alarmist lobbying of protectionists.

A coincidence of this and the previous two types of shocks has given rise to the latest wave of globalisation. This is raising not only the rewards to economies practising good economic governance but also the cost of retaining poor economic governance. Just as financial capital can now flow into a well-managed economy more easily and quickly than ever before, so it can equally quickly be withdrawn if confidence in that economy's governance is shaken – as the East Asian Financial Crisis of the late 1990s demonstrated all too clearly. A crucial element of good economic governance is a commitment to a permanently open international trade and payments regime (along with sound domestic policies such as an absence of subsidies, secure property rights and prudent monetary and fiscal policies).

Opportunities to Join International Trade Agreements

In seeking to find politically expedient ways to open their economies, governments are increasingly looking for opportunities to do so bilaterally, regionally or multilaterally. The reason is that the political market equilibrium in two or more countries can be altered in favour of liberalism through

an exchange of product market access. If country A allows more imports, it may well harm its import-competing producers if there are insufficient compensation mechanisms; but if this liberalisation is done in return for country A's trading partners lowering their barriers to A's exports, the producers of those exports will be better off. The latter extra benefit may be sufficiently greater than the loss to A's import-competing producers that A's liberalising politicians too become net gainers in terms of electoral, financial or other support in return for negotiating a trade agreement. When politicians in the countries trading with A also see the possibility for gaining from such an exchange of market access, for equal and opposite reasons, prospects for trade negotiations are ripe.[7]

Such gains from trade negotiations involving exchange of market access are potentially greater nationally and globally the larger the number of countries involved and the broader the product and issues coverage of the negotiations. That is the logic behind negotiating multilaterally with nearly 150 WTO member countries over a wide range of sectors and issues. That WTO process is becoming increasingly cumbersome, however, which has led countries to negotiate also bilaterally or regionally in the hope that faster and deeper integration will result. Preferential free trade areas (FTAs) involving just a sub-set of countries need not be welfare-enhancing for all participant nations, however, because of trade diversion away from the lowest-cost supplier; and non-participants in the rest of the world may be made worse off, too (Pomfret 1997; Schiff and Winters 2003). Hence the need for empirical analysis of the likely gains from different types of prospective trade agreements.

What About the Social and Environmental Consequences of Trade Reform?

Trade liberalisation in recent years has attracted a considerable amount of attention from NGOs, as witnessed by their presence on the streets of cities where trade ministers meet (e.g. during the WTO Ministerial in Seattle in late 1999). The groups attracted see trade reform as contributing to the spread of capitalism and in particular of multinational firms, and believe those aspects of globalisation add to innumerable social and

---

[7] Elaborations of this economists' perspective can be found in Grossman and Helpman (1995), Hillman and Moser (1995), Maggi and Rodriguez-Clare (1998) and Hoekman and Kostecki (2001). Political scientists take a similar view. See, for example, Goldstein (1998).

environmental ills in both rich and poor countries. But just as the traditional economic arguments for protection have been found wanting, so too have the social and environmental ones, both conceptually and empirically. For example, there has not been a systematic 'race to the bottom' in environmental or labour standards of rich countries as a result of trade and foreign direct investment (FDI) growth, and in poor countries foreign corporations often have among the highest environmental and labour standards (Bhagwati and Hudec 1996). Nor has trade growth been a major contributor to the stagnation of wages of unskilled workers in OECD countries (Greenaway and Nelson 2002).

The number of such claims by anti-globalisation groups – almost invariably not supported by credible empirical evidence – makes it a huge task to address them all systematically. However, some attention is given on pp. 548ff. to the social and environmental benefits and costs associated with cutting subsidies and trade barriers, with the focus on their potential impacts on the other nine challenges being addressed in this project (chapters 1–9 in this volume).

The Opportunities for Reducing Subsidies and Trade Barriers

The gains from reducing government interventions in markets have been well known since the writing of Adam Smith's *Wealth of Nations* more than two centuries ago, and popular magazines such as *The Economist* and more and more daily newspapers continue to remind the public of the virtues of market opening.[8] Even so, greater dissemination of empirical information on the net economic benefits of reducing trade distortions, to balance the often-exaggerated claims by potential losers and their supporters of the adjustment costs of reform, can no doubt assist the liberalisation process. Empirical studies can also shed better light and take some of the heat out of debates about whether, in the presence of domestic distortions such as under-taxed pollution, subsidy and trade reform is welfare-reducing. Such studies can also point to the domestic policy reforms that should accompany trade reform so as to guarantee not only national welfare improvement in aggregate but also that there

is no significant left-behind group, no unexpected new damage to the environment, etc. Clearly there is an opportunity for well-meaning interest groups, think tanks and national and international economic agencies to spend more money and resources on such empirical studies, and in particular on the effective dissemination of their findings. In an idealistic world in which such studies were able to persuade all governments to fully liberalise their trade unilaterally, the benefit derived from that opportunity would be measured by the gain from moving the world to one free of subsidies and trade barriers (Opportunity 1). Unlikely though such an outcome may seem in the foreseeable future, it provides a benchmark against which all other opportunities partially to meet this challenge can be measured.

Among the more feasible opportunities available today for encouraging trade negotiations to stimulate significant market opening, the most obvious is a non-preferential legally binding partial trade liberalisation following the WTO's current round of multilateral trade negotiations (Opportunity 2). That round was launched in Doha, the capital of Qatar, in 2001 with the intention of completing negotiations at the end of 2004, when implementation of the last of the Uruguay Round commitments under WTO are scheduled to be completed. It now seems uncertain as to how long the current round will take, what issues will be kept on its agenda and indeed even whether it will come to a successful conclusion. That uncertainty is all the more reason for assessing the potential of this opportunity, given that it involves almost 150 WTO member countries, plus another twenty-five in the midst of accession, and hence all but a tiny fraction of global trade.

There are at least three other types of trade negotiating opportunities that, while they involve only a sub-set of the world's economies, have the potential to generate deeper integration in the medium term and so are worth comparing to the WTO Doha Round. One is *non-preferential but non-binding trade liberalisation*, as currently being pursued by

---

[8] On the intellectual history of the virtues of free trade, see Bhagwati (1988, chapter 2) and Irwin (1996). Bhagwati notes that the virtues of division of labour and exchange were cited twenty-four centuries ago in Plato's *Republic* (see the back cover of the October 1985 issue of the *Journal of Political Economy*).

the Pacific rim members of the Asia-Pacific Economic Cooperation (APEC) forum. APEC member countries agreed in 1994, and have since reiterated that commitment several times, to move to free trade in the Asia Pacific region by 2010 in the case of developed countries and 2020 in the case of developing countries. Even though there is no legal binding on members to achieve that goal and retain that status beyond the deadline, the distinguishing feature of this long-term commitment is that, as with WTO commitments, the market opening is to be provided to all trading partners of each APEC country (a most-favoured-nation or MFN reform), and not just to other APEC members as in an FTA. That makes its effects simply a sub-set of those derived from moving to global free trade, so the APEC initiative can be considered as part of Opportunity 1.

A second type of trade negotiating opportunity involving a sub-set of the world's economies is a *reciprocal preferential agreement*. This could take the form of an FTA, a customs union, or a broader economic union. Typically such an agreement would be legally binding and, even though it would be notified to the WTO, it would provide greater market access only to signatories to that agreement and hence would not be MFN. An example is the agreed enlargement of the EU from fifteen to twenty-five members, to be implemented from May 2004. Even though implementation will be spread over the next few years, for present purposes enlarging the EU to twenty-five is considered an opportunity already seized rather than in prospect (and further eastern enlargement is unlikely before the 2010s). Efforts are also being made to negotiate an FTAA, which potentially would bring together all the economies of North, Central and South America. This is by far the largest and most ambitious preferential agreement currently in prospect: it dwarfs the bilateral FTA negotiations that the USA and EU are having with a range of other countries, and it is also more advanced than other proposed FTAs such as in South Asia and between China and Southeast Asia. Hence the FTAA provides an upper limit on the gains that might be expected from this type of trade agreement (Opportunity 3).

There is also the opportunity to enter into non-reciprocal preferential trade agreements, as the EU has with its former colonies (the so-called ACP countries of Africa, the Caribbean and the Pacific) and as most OECD countries have with developing countries in the form of a Generalised System of tariff Preferences (GSP). The EU's initiative to extend preferences for UN-designated 'least developed countries' (LDCs) provides duty- and quota-free access to the EU for exports of 'everything but arms' (EBA). It received in-principle, best-endeavours endorsement by other OECD countries at the WTO Ministerial in Doha in November 2001, but without any specific timetable. While this opportunity (Opportunity 4) clearly involves only a small volume of global trade, it has a relatively high probability of being implemented unilaterally by numerous countries and is perceived to be of direct benefit to the world's poorest people – even though that view may be misplaced.

Benefits and Costs of Reducing Subsidies and Trade Barriers

To estimate the benefits and costs associated with the opportunities just outlined, this section first looks at economic benefits, particularly for halving subsidies and trade barriers by 2010. That is a rather optimistic scenario for the Doha Round (Opportunity 2), but one that is not politically infeasible if enough resources were to be expended globally to alter the balance of power between narrow pro-protection private interest groups and broader community interests in free trade. The economic costs associated with that strategy are then examined, followed by an assessment of its social and environmental benefits and costs, before concluding as to the overall net present value (NPV) and benefit-cost ratio (BCR) for society from reducing subsidies and trade barriers.

Economic Benefits from Opportunities to Reduce Subsidies and Trade Barriers

The Computable General Equilibrium Approach to Measuring Economic Benefits

All the estimates considered below of the potential global economic welfare gains from these opportunities are generated using computable general equilibrium (CGE) models of the global economy, the most common of which (GTAP) is described in the appendix. The CGE welfare gains refer to the equivalent variation in income (EV) as a result of each of the shocks described.[9] While not without their shortcomings (see Francois 2000, Whalley 2000, Anderson 2003 and the list of caveats below), CGE models are far superior for current purposes to partial equilibrium models, which fail to capture the economy-wide nature of the adjustments to reform whereby some sectors expand when others contract and release capital and labour; and they are also superior to macroeconometric models which typically lack sufficient sectoral detail (Francois and Reinert 1997). They were first used in multilateral trade reform analysis in *ex post* assessments of the Tokyo Round of GATT negotiations in the late 1970s and early 1980s (Cline *et al.* 1978; Deardorff and Stern 1979, 1986; Whalley 1985). Since then, they have been used increasingly during and following the Uruguay Round, as shown in the various studies summarised in Martin and Winters (1996).

Empirical comparative static studies of the economic welfare gains from trade liberalisation typically generate positive gains for the world and for most participating countries. (Exceptions are when a country's welfare is reduced more by a terms of trade change or reduced rents from preferential market access quotas than it is boosted by improvements due to reallocating its resources away from protected industries.) When economies of scale and monopolistic competition (IRS/MC) are assumed instead of constant returns to scale and perfect competition (CRS/PC), and when trade not only in goods but also in services is liberalised, the estimates of potential gains can be increased severalfold. A few economists have also examined the effects of lowering barriers to international capital flows or labour movements, and some have included estimates of a lowering of trade costs as a result of trade facilitation measures such as streamlining customs-clearance procedures. Even so, in most studies the sum of these comparative static CGE model estimates tends to amount to only a tiny fraction of GDP.

Those low estimated gains seem to fly in the face of casual empiricism. Irwin (2002), for example,

notes that three different countries on three continents chose to liberalise in three different decades, and *per capita* GDP growth in each of those countries accelerated markedly thereafter (Korea from 1965, Chile from 1974 and India from 1991, see Irwin 2002, figures 2.3–2.5). Admittedly those historical liberalisation experiences involved also complementary reforms to other domestic policies and institutions that would have contributed significantly to the observed boosts in economic growth. Even so, both theoretical economists and econometricians have sought to demonstrate that trade can promote not only static efficiency gains but also dynamic gains. Some CGE modellers have tried to proxy that effect by adding an additional one-off total factor productivity (TFP) shock to their trade reform scenarios. But reform may also raise the *rate* of factor productivity growth and/or of capital accumulation. Such endogenous growth has yet to be satisfactorily introduced into CGE models,[10] and in any case it is unclear how to interpret a model's estimated welfare effects if households are reducing current consumption in order to boost their or their descendants' future consumption by investing more.

It should be kept in mind that all the experiments in the comparative static CGE studies surveyed below reduce only trade barriers plus agricultural production and export subsidies. The reasons for including subsidies only in agriculture are that they were the key subsidies explicitly being negotiated at the WTO (where non-agricultural export subsidies are illegal),[11] they represented an estimated 38 per cent of all government expenditure on subsidies

---

[9] EV is defined as the income that consumers would be willing to forgo and still have the same level of well-being after as before the reform. For a discussion of the merits of EV versus other measures of change in economic, welfare, see for example, Just, Hueth and Schmitz (1982), Ng (1983) and Martin (1997).

[10] For an early attempt to develop a dynamic version of the GTAP model, see Ianchovichina and McDougall (2000).

[11] Production subsidies in non-agricultural sectors, however, have come under close scrutiny through the WTO's dispute settlement procedures (DSPs) since the Uruguay Round's Agreement on Subsidies and Countervailing Measures came into force with the WTO's formation in 1995 (Bagwell and Staiger 2004). Fisheries are also explicitly under consideration by negotiators in the WTO's Doha Round.

Table 10.1. Comparative Static Estimates of Economic Welfare Gains from Full Global Liberalisation of Goods and Services Trade

Study	Market assumptions[a]	Sectors liberalised	Baseline year (of EV welfare measure)	Welfare gain, non-OECD (US$ bn)	Welfare gain, global (US$ bn)	Year of currency (US $)
ADFHHM (2002)	CRS/PC	Goods only	2005	108	254	1995
BDS (2003)	IRS/MC	Goods, services and FDI	2005	431	2,080	1995
FMT (2003)	IRS/MC	Goods and services	1997	113	367	1997
WBGEP (2003a)	CRS/PC	Goods only	2015	184	355	1997
WBGEP (2003b)	CRS/PC plus productivity boost	Goods only	2015	539	832	1997

Note: [a] CRS/PC: constant returns to scale/perfect competition; IRS/MC: increasing returns to scale/monopolistic competition/firm-level differentiated products.
Sources: Anderson *et al*. (2002); Brown, Deardorff and Stern (2003); Francois, van Meijl and van Tongeren (2003); World Bank (2003).

globally during 1994–8[12] and they were fully represented in the GTAP database whereas subsidies for most other sectors were not included so it is not possible to estimate their welfare cost within the same framework. The reason for not also explicitly estimating the welfare impacts of other domestic policies and institutions that, because of their complementarity, affect the pay-off from opening up is that typically they are beyond the sphere of influence of international trade negotiators.

With this as background, we consider first the economic benefits associated with each of the four opportunities in turn.

Removing All Trade Barriers and Agricultural Subsidies Globally

Only a few CGE modelling studies have reported simulations of complete liberalisation of trade. The ones of most relevance are those that incorporate in

their baseline the implementation of all the Uruguay Round agreements, since that process is due for completion at the end of 2004. The results are reported in table 10.1 and each study is discussed in turn.

The ADFHHM study (Anderson *et al*. 2002) provides the simplest scenario: global liberalisation of just merchandise trade using a comparative static version of the GTAP model with CRS and PC in all product and factor markets (first described in Hertel 1997). The GTAP Version 4 database (McDougall, Elberhnri and Truong 1998), which provides data for 1995, is used in that study to generate a new baseline for 2005 by projecting the world economy forward a decade and assuming that all Uruguay Round commitments (including the politically sensitive Agreement on Textiles and Clothing, ATC), and those of China and Taiwan (made on their accession to the WTO) are implemented by then. This baseline for 2005 is then compared with how it would look after full adjustment following the removal of all countries' trade barriers and agricultural subsidies. The economic welfare gain is estimated to be US$254 bn per year in 1995 dollars as of 2005 (and hence slightly more each year thereafter as the global economy expands). Of that, $108 bn p.a. is estimated to accrue to developing countries. These are the lowest of the estimates

---

[12] See van Beers and de Moor (2001, table 3.1), whose estimates suggest that energy subsidies are the next biggest group, at 22 per cent of all subsidies, followed closely by road transport (21 per cent) and then water (6 per cent), forestry and mining (each 3 per cent) and fisheries (2 per cent), with manufacturing subsidies making up the residual 5 per cent. For more details on energy and transport subsidies, see OECD (1997); von Moltke, McKee and Morgan (2004).

Table 10.2. Sectoral and Regional[a] Contributions to Comparative Static Estimates of Economic Welfare Gains from Completely Removing Goods Trade Barriers Globally, Post-Uruguay Round, 2005 (percentage of total global gains)

Liberalising region:	Benefiting region	Agriculture and food	Other primary	Textiles and clothing	Other manufactures	Total
High-income						
	High-income	43.4	0.0	−2.3	−3.2	38.0
	Low-income	4.6	0.1	3.5	8.8	16.9
	Total	**48.0**	**0.0**	**1.3**	**5.6**	**54.9**
Low-income						
	High-income	4.4	0.1	4.1	10.9	19.5
	Low-income	12.3	1.0	1.4	10.9	25.6
	Total	**16.7**	**1.1**	**5.5**	**21.7**	**45.1**
All countries						
	High-income	47.9	0.1	1.9	7.7	57.5
	Low-income	16.9	1.0	4.9	19.6	42.5
	Total	**64.8**	**1.1**	**6.8**	**27.3**	**100.0**

Note: [a]High and low income here are short-hand for developed and developing countries.
Source: Anderson *et al.* (2002).

summarised in table 10.1. Using the decomposition algorithm developed by Harrison, Horridge and Pearson (2000), table 10.2 shows that only two-fifths of this study's estimated gain to developing countries are derived from policy changes in developed countries. Changes in policies in developing countries make a more substantial contribution to other developing countries' economic welfare, and almost half of that gain comes from policy changes in their agricultural sector. This reflects the importance not only of own-country reform but also of expanding South–South trade.

The BDS study (Brown, Deardorff and Stern 2003) uses the same Version 4 GTAP database also projected to 2005, but they embed it in their static Michigan Model of World Production and Trade (www.ssp.umich.edu/rsie/model and Deardorff and Stern 1986) to produce the highest of the surveyed estimates of global welfare gains from complete removal of trade barriers and agricultural subsidies: $2,080 bn p.a., of which $431 bn would accrue to developing countries. These much larger estimates are the result of several features of this study: not having China and Taiwan's implementation of their WTO accession commitments in the baseline; the inclusion of IRS and MC for non-agricultural sectors and therefore product heterogeneity at the level of the firm rather than just the national industry;

liberalisation of services in addition to goods trade (with IRS/MC assumed for the huge services sector); and the inclusion in services liberalisation of the opening to FDI. The latter boosts substantially the gains from services liberalisation, which accounts for 63 per cent or $1,310 bn of this study's estimated total gains.

All other estimates of the gains from complete trade liberalisation are between these two extremes. The FMT study (Francois, van Meijl and van Tongeren 2003), which builds on Francois (2001), uses the more recent Version 5.2 of the GTAP database for 1997 (Dimaranan and McDougall 2002) and a variant of the GTAP model to include IRS/MC (see www.intereconomics.com/francois and Francois 1998). As in the BDS study, the latter feature ensures that the inclusion of the agglomeration effects of reform that are emphasised in the new economic geography literature.[13] Its economic welfare gain is estimated to be US$367 bn per year in 1997 dollars as of 1997, of which $113 bn p.a. is estimated to accrue to developing countries. Just over 40 per cent of that total ($151 bn) is due to trade facilitation measures such as streamlining

[13] See, for example, Fujita, Krugman and Venables (2001), Neary (2001), Fujita and Thisse (2002) and Baldwin *et al.* (2003).

customs clearance,[14] while only 14 per cent ($52 bn) is due to services trade reform. The global gains from removing just merchandise trade barriers is $163 bn in 1997 (compared with ADFHHM's gain of $254 bn for 2005 when the global economy is considerably larger). Part of the reason for these gains being lower than those from the BDS study is that this one includes in its baseline China's WTO accession, the EU's Agenda 2000 and eastern enlargement, which lowers its estimate of the gains from removing residual EU-25 trade barriers. But the main reason has to do with the quite different way in which services trade barriers are measured and their reform modelled.

The final study reported in table 10.1, WBGEP (World Bank 2002), uses the same 1997 GTAP database as FMT but projects the GTAP model to 2015. With the world economy considerably bigger then than in 1997 or 2005 one would expect WBGEP to provide larger dollar estimates, other things equal. Two are provided, both assuming CRS and PC and both with only merchandise trade reformed. The first estimate, which is comparable to the ADFHHM study, provides a global gain of $355 bn p.a. for 2015. That is in line with

ADFHHM's estimate of $254 bn for 2005 as both represent 0.7 per cent of GDP for their respective years, as projected by the World Bank (2003, table A3.1). The slightly larger share of that gain going to developing countries (52 per cent in 2015 compared with ADFHHM's 43 per cent) is also in line with the expected growth in developing countries' share of the world economy over that decade.

The second WBGEP estimate assumes that liberalisation boosts factor productivity in each industry according to the extent of growth in the share of production exported by the industry. While the precise formula used for this adjustment is somewhat arbitrary, it nonetheless gives a feel for how the overall size and composition across economies of the gains from trade can change when allowance is made for an openness-induced productivity boost. The case presented suggests that the gains would rise 2.3 times to $832 bn p.a. with that adjustment,[15] and since trade of developing countries grows more than that of OECD countries under full liberalisation, they receive 65 per cent of those gains ($539 bn) instead of the 52 per cent or $184 bn generated without that productivity adjustment.

In both WBGEP simulations, agriculture contributes 70 per cent of the gains from liberalising all merchandise trade. This is very similar to the estimate of two-thirds by both the ADFHHM and FMT studies.[16] The extent to which these results are dominated by agriculture is remarkable, given that agriculture is responsible for only one-twelfth of global GDP and exports. It simply reflects the fact that agricultural sectors of both rich and poor countries are still highly protected from import competition, and in some rich countries are also subsidized directly, despite the efforts of the Uruguay Round.

By contrast to the similarity in welfare results for goods trade liberalisation, the gain from services trade reform reported in the FMT study ($53 bn in 1997) is only a small fraction of the BDS estimate of $1,280 bn in 2005 ($220 bn of which goes to developing countries). The FMT estimate is in line with an estimate by Verikios and Zhang (2001) of $47 bn globally just for telecoms and financial services, while the BDS estimate of $220 bn for developing countries alone is exceeded by the WBGEP study which also reports an estimate of the

---

[14] The OECD defines 'trade facilitation' as the simplification and standardisation of procedures and associated information flows required to move products internationally from seller to buyer and to pass payment in the other direction. For an in-depth discussion of the nature and importance of reducing trading costs, see World Bank (2003, chapter 6). Francois, van Meijl and van Tongeren (2003) assume that full trade liberalisation would be accompanied by a reduction in trading costs (the difference between fob and cif valuations) of 3 per cent of the value of trade.

[15] This greater gain is consistent with the consensus that developed over the 1990s that incorporating endogenous growth effects in CGE models raises the welfare gains from trade liberalisation by several orders of magnitude. A study by Rutherford and Tarr (2002), using a generic model of a small open economy, reinforces this consensus.

[16] By contrast, BDS estimate a share close to zero. The explanation BDS provide for this result is that the expanding of agriculture in lightly protecting countries draws resources from the non-agricultural sectors which, unlike agriculture, are assumed to have increasing returns to scale and monopolistic competition. Apparently that IRS/MC feature is having a much stronger effect in the BDS model than it is in the FMT one (which also has IRS/MC), since the FMT estimated contribution of agriculture is close to the estimates from the CRS/PC models.

gain from liberalising services trade just for developing countries, of $884 bn in 2015. These vastly different results for services reflect the great deal of uncertainty that still prevails in estimating the extent and effects of services trade barriers (see Findlay and Warren 2001; Whalley 2003). Even though this is widely recognised as a major area of trade policy concern for both developed and developing countries, there is clearly much more research required in this area before we can expect a convergence of empirical estimates for the services sector.

The huge estimate for gains from services reform in the BDS study appears to be a consequence of their model explicitly allowing for foreign investment flows, in contrast to the standard GTAP model where such flows play a very modest role. What this highlights is that trade in products need not – as suggested by the simplest of trade models (Mundell 1957) – be a complete substitute for trade in factors of production such as capital and labour. Indeed, as Markusen (1983) has shown (and see also Ethier 1996), factor trade can be a *complement* to product trade. Nor are we able to say *a priori* which might grow more when trade in all factors and products is opened simultaneously (Michaely 2003).

None of the above empirical studies examines the global welfare gains from allowing greater international movement of labour. Historical analyses of global migration by Hatton and Williamson (1998, 2002) conclude that the effective demand by developing country workers to move to higher-income countries is likely to grow considerably up to 2025, with wage differentials a major driving force. It appears that national governments, however, are becoming more rather than less restrictive of migrant inflows in the wake of that growing demand. How costly are such restrictions? A CGE study in the mid-1980s suggested that complete liberalisation of world labour markets, in the presence of existing barriers to trade in products and capital, could double world income and in so doing raise several-fold the economic welfare of people working at that time in developing countries (Hamilton and Whalley 1984). The more recent resurgence of interest in this subject has encouraged one group of GTAP modellers to examine this issue afresh, but in the context of Mode 4 of the WTO's GATS, the so-called 'temporary movement of natural persons'. Winters *et al.* (2003) simulate the effect of raising worker immigration quotas of developed countries enough to increase labour forces there by 3 per cent (which sums to a temporary migration flow from developing countries of 8.4 m unskilled and 8 m skilled workers or just 0.6 per cent of the labour force in developing countries). A movement even as modest as that is estimated to raise annual world welfare by $156 bn (0.6 per cent of global income), with most of that benefit accruing to those currently in developing countries who migrate.

These welfare results underscore two points: first, migration restrictions are very costly to people in poor countries; and second, if rich countries are to persist with those restrictions in the wake of growing demands for lifting them, even more effort should be made to alleviate poverty through liberalising international capital flows and trade in products exportable from developing countries, most notably agricultural goods.

The above studies do not provide an estimate of the net welfare gains from reducing direct government subsidies to domestic production or consumption of non-farm products. They would be small compared with those from trade reform, bearing in mind that an estimated 38 per cent of all government subsidies go to agriculture (van Beers and de Moor 2001) and hence are captured in the above estimates. They nonetheless represent significant transfers from taxpayers to special interest groups, estimated by van Beers and de Moor (2001, table 3.1) to be $1,065 bn per year globally between 1994 and 1998 (4 per cent of GDP) and by others to be between half and twice that amount. Cutting those subsidies therefore has the potential to provide a great deal of revenue for meeting society's other pressing challenges.

Reducing Trade Barriers and Agricultural Subsidies Following the WTO's Doha Round

The WTO is in the midst of its first round of multilateral trade negotiations following the Uruguay Round, whose implementation programme is scheduled to be completed at the end of 2004. The present round, known as the Doha Development Agenda, is currently at an early stage, and even the

Table 10.3. Comparative Static Estimates of Economic Welfare Gains from a 50 per cent Multilateral Liberalisation of Goods and Services Trade (Optimistic Doha Round) and from the Proposed FTAA

Study	Market assumptions[a]	Sectors liberalised	50% cut to bound or applied tariffs?	Baseline year (of EV welfare measure)	Welfare gain, non-OECD (US$ bn)	Welfare gain, global (US$ bn)	Year of currency ($ US)
Optimistic Doha round							
BDS (2003)	IRS/MC	Goods and services incl. FDI	Applied	2005	216	1,040	1995
FMT (2003)	IRS/MC	Goods and services	Bound	1997	88	196	1997
FMT (2003)	CRS/PC	Goods and services	Bound	1997	51	132	1997
HRTG (2003)	CRS/PC	Goods only	Applied	1997	97	186	1996
FTAA							
BDS (2003)	IRS/MC	Goods and services incl. FDI	Applied	2005	24	83	1995
HHIK (2003)	CRS/PC	Goods only	Applied	1997	na	3	1997
HRTG (2003)	CRS/PC	Goods only	Applied	1997	6	4	1996

Notes: [a] CRS/PC: constant returns to scale/perfect competition; IRS/MC: increasing returns to scale/monopolistic competition/firm-level differentiated products. na = Not available.
Sources: Brown, Deardorff and Stern (2003); Francois, van Meijl and van Tongeren (2003); Hertel *et al.* (2003); Harrison *et al.* (2003).

list of issues to be negotiated is yet to be finalised, even though the Round was originally scheduled to conclude at the end of 2004, presumably with implementation to begin in 2006 following ratification by national governments in 2005. Given the slow progress to date, assessing the *likely* benefits is therefore difficult, even though we know that the *potential* benefits are those associated with full trade liberalisation as discussed above.

Typically *ex ante* analyses by CGE modellers in this situation involve uniform across-the-board tariff cuts. The above-mentioned BDS study, for example, reports a one-third cut in applied rates of protection and, because their model is linear, the results are simply one-third of those reported above. If their tariff cuts were 50 per cent, they would generate a global welfare gain of $1,030 bn p.a., of which $216 bn would accrue to developing countries. This is again hugely greater than what other analysts are reporting (table 10.3).

[17] That represents 15 per cent of the gains from the agricultural portion of the reform. This is consistent with other studies which also find that domestic support measures are a relatively minor part of agricultural assistance measures. See, for example, Rae and Strutt (2003) and Hoekman, Ng and Olarreaga (2004). Those findings vindicate the present chapter focus on border measures.

For example, the FMT study reports a 50 per cent across-the-board cut to tariffs and farm subsidies, plus half the liberalisation in services and half the trade facilitation modelled for their full global liberalisation reported above. The authors estimate a global welfare gain from that 50 per cent reform of just $196 bn p.a., which is slightly over half their estimate for full liberalisation although the component parts differ (e.g. the gain to developing countries would be 44 per cent of that total, compared with only 31 per cent of the gains from full reform). An important reason for this non-linearity is that FMT cut *bound* tariffs on merchandise by 50 per cent, not the (often much lower) applied rates that typically are used by modellers, including BDS. Since it is the rates that are bound in WTO commitments that are negotiated, this feature of FMT's study is more realistic. Of that $196 bn, only 4 per cent is due to the halving of domestic subsidies to agriculture.[17]

The FMT's global welfare gain is very similar to that estimated for a 50 per cent across-the-board cut to tariffs and farm export subsidies by Harrison *et al.* (HRTG) (2003). That is pure coincidence, though, as there are some features of the HRTG study that would lead one to expect larger estimates (they use higher price elasticities than most other trade modellers, and cut applied rather than bound tariffs), and other features that would lower their estimates (they assume CRS, do not liberalise services trade or domestic farm subsidies and there is no trade facilitation included).

On the one hand, all three of these studies are probably excessive in the sense that no previous multilateral trade reform has agreed to anywhere near as much as a 50 per cent across-the-board cut in (especially applied) rates.[18] On the other hand, these studies all underestimate the potential gains, perhaps by a wide margin, because they exclude any endogenous growth effects and effects of liberalisation of trade in labour or capital (with the exception of the BDS study where FDI in services is allowed).

Removing Intra-American Trade Barriers Following the FTAA Negotiations

The negotiations to create an FTAA – the largest such FTA negotiations currently under way or in prospect – have begun but are running into political problems so it is not clear if/when they might conclude. The reason for considering this opportunity here is simply to point out that the potential global gains from such an FTA are only a small fraction of those obtainable from multilateral negotiation (because the major economies of Europe and North America are already well integrated and so any new initiatives involve relatively small economies joining one of those hubs or integrating among themselves). Two studies that examine both Doha and the FTAA are reported in table 10.3, together with one, by Hertel *et al.* (HHIK)(2003), that looks just at the FTAA. The global gain from the FTAA in the BDS study is estimated to be just one-twelfth of that from a 50 per cent multilateral trade liberalisation (hence one-sixth of that from a 25 per cent multilateral reform, etc.); and for the HRTG study the difference is even greater. Furthermore, these studies take no account of the dampening effect of the rules of origin that almost invariably constrain the extent to which firms can take advantage of any FTA's removal of bilateral tariffs (Krueger 1999; Anson, Cadot and de Melo 2003); nor of the fact that such FTAs typically have phase-in periods that stretch more than a decade for some products and exclude altogether the most sensitive products.

FTAs of this type are pursued nonetheless for a wide range of reasons, including preferential access to an important protected market (often at the expense of other countries), insurance against anti-dumping by that partner and deeper and faster integration than has been possible or is in prospect through the multilateral reform route (Schiff and Winters 2003). The gains to just one or a few developing economies from joining with North America or the EU may be non-trivial, but so too would be the gains from a similar degree of multilateral reform. According to the HRTG study, a multilateral reform involving even just a 25 per cent reduction in merchandise tariffs would benefit South America more than the FTAA, for example.

Moreover, even leaving aside the potential systemic cost of FTAs on the WTO rules-based multilateral trading system, such preferential agreements can harm excluded developing and/or developed countries through *trade diversion*. For example, the estimated gains to FTAA members are nearly fully offset by losses to excluded economies, according to the HHIK and HRTG studies. Harmful trade diversion would also result from an FTA between, say, South Asia and either North America or the EU, according to GTAP results reported in Bandara and Yu (2003). Indeed an examination of eighteen existing preferential trading arrangements found that twelve diverted more merchandise trade from non-members than they created among members (Adams *et al.* 2003). That review was able to conclude more positively about the benefits of FTAs in reforming such things as investment, services, competition policy and government procurement, but was unable to say whether those benefits tended to be sufficient to offset any losses from trade diversion. Another review, by Nielsen (2003), came to similar conclusions, and added that the

---

[18] Francois (2001) compares gains from a 50 per cent cut in bound tariffs with a 50 per cent cut in applied tariffs and finds the global gains from the former to be one-sixth less than from the latter. A complete elimination of agricultural export subsidies is conceivable, as could be true too for developed countries' tariffs on manufactures other than for textiles and clothing; but a halving of applied agricultural tariffs in this first WTO round seems unlikely, especially given the considerable extent to which bound tariffs exceed current applied rates.

greatest gains for developing countries from FTAs would come if developed countries were to liberalise trade in their politically sensitive sectors, most notably agriculture but also textiles and clothing. That is likely in preferential agreements only with the smallest of developing countries whose impact on protective developed economies is tiny, examples of which are examined in the next subsection.

Removing Developed Country Barriers to Exports from Least-Developed Countries

The EU's recent initiative to extend preferences for UN-designated LDCs provides duty- and quota-free access to the EU for exports of 'everything but arms' (EBA). That initiative received in-principle, best-endeavours endorsement at the WTO Ministerial in Doha in November 2001, but without any specific timetable. Liberal though that proposal sounds, note that it does not include trade in services (of which the most important for LDCs would be movement of natural persons – that is, freedom for LDC labourers to work on temporary visas in the EU or other high-wage countries, see Winters *et al.* 2003). A number of safeguard provisions are also included in addition to the EU's normal anti-dumping measures. Furthermore, access to three politically sensitive agricultural markets – bananas, rice and sugar – would be phased-in by the EU only gradually over the rest of this decade (and would be subject to stricter safeguards).

Several empirical studies of the proposal have already appeared. A World Bank study by Ianchovichina, Mattoo and Olarreaga (2001) compares the EU proposal, from the viewpoint of SSA, with recent initiatives of the USA and Japan. Its GTAP modelling results suggest that even the most generous interpretation of the US Africa Growth and Opportunity Act (which they model as unrestricted access to the USA for all SSA exports) would benefit SSA very little because the US economy is already very open and, in the products where it is not (e.g. textiles and clothing), SSA countries have little comparative advantage. By contrast, the EU proposal, especially if it were to apply to all QUAD countries (the EU, the USA, Canada and Japan), would have a sizable effect on SSA trade and welfare – provided agriculture is included in the deal. Just from EU access alone, SSA exports would be raised by more than US$0.5 bn and SSA economic welfare would increase by $0.3 bn per year (a 0.2 per cent boost).[19] The results overstate the benefits of the EU proposal, however, as this World Bank study assumes that all SSA countries (excluding relatively wealthy South Africa and Mauritius), not just the LDCs among them, would get duty- and quota-free access.

Another World Bank study, by Hoekman, Ng and Olarreaga (2002), uses a partial equilibrium approach and looks at the benefit of the EU initiative for LDCs not just in SSA but globally. It finds that trade of LDCs would increase by US$2.5 bn p.a. if all QUAD countries provided LDCs with duty- and quota-free access on all merchandise.[20] However, almost half of that increase would come as a result of trade diversion from other developing countries. The authors suggest this is trivial because it represents less than 0.1 per cent of other developing countries' exports (about $1.1 bn).[21] But if the forty-eight LDCs are given such preferences, they will become advocates *for* rather than *against* the continuation of MFN tariff peaks for agriculture and textiles – diminishing considerably the number of WTO members negotiating for their reduction. It may be true that MFN reductions in agricultural and textile tariffs would help LDCs much less than it would help other developing countries, as the study by Hoekman, Ng and Olarreaga (2002) finds; but the gains to consumers in the QUAD would be more than sufficient to allow them to increase their aid to LDCs to compensate many times over for the loss of LDC income from the preference erosion that necessarily accompanies MFN reform.

[19] This is very similar to the estimate by UNCTAD/Commonwealth Secretariat (2001, chapter 3).

[20] This and other estimates of gains from preferential market access provisions need to be discounted to the extent that such things as rules of origin, anti-dumping duties and sanitary, phytosanitary (SPS) and other technical barriers limit the actual trade allowed. For a detailed analysis of these types of restrictions on EU imports from Bangladesh in recent years, see UNCTAD/Commonwealth Secretariat (2001, chapter 5).

[21] The impact outside the LDC group would be far from trivial for Mauritius, however, since the vast bulk of its exports are quota-restricted sales of clothing and sugar to the EU and USA. See the discussion in UNCTAD/Commonwealth Secretariat (2001, chapter 6).

How Best to Reduce Subsidies and Trade Barriers Globally by 2010?

To open markets in the face of the political economy pressures for retaining subsidies and trade barriers requires seizing on not just one of the above-mentioned four opportunities but rather adopting a multi-pronged approach. That approach would seek to achieve unilateral reform at the national level and multilateral reform at the WTO level, supplemented by regional support for both as adopted by APEC members in what its supporters call 'open' (that is, MFN) regionalism. Exploiting this set of opportunities requires developing stronger lobbies for freer MFN trade and investment, to counter the lobbying of entrenched protectionist forces. That in turn requires sponsoring policy think-tanks and other suppliers of international trade policy analysis and advocacy, so that the vast majority of the community who would gain from freer trade are made more aware of the inefficiencies and inequities associated with subsidies and trade restrictions. Just $1 or $2 bn per year over the next five years could go a long way in altering the climate of public opinion on this issue. The aim would be to encourage national governments to engage not only in unilateral reform but also to embrace the opportunity to negotiate an ambitious outcome from the WTO's current Doha Development Round of multilateral trade negotiations. The latter is important because if other countries also agree to liberalise, that makes it easier for any one government to persuade its constituency to liberalise too; and if it is done within the WTO framework, those commitments will be MFN and they will be legally bound so that backsliding in the future becomes much less of an option. With the forces of globalisation encouraging good (and penalizing bad) economic governance more than ever before, an ambitious target is appropriate. For the rest of this chapter, the target is assumed to be a 50 per cent reduction in subsidies and trade barriers as bound in the WTO (hence a smaller reduction in applied tariff rates, particularly for developing countries, given the large degree of 'binding overhang' in current WTO tariff commitments, see Francois and Martin 2003).[22]

Preferential trade agreements would not be an explicit target in this approach, even though they will no doubt continue to be pursued in the years ahead. Non-reciprocal trade preference agreements in particular are of questionable value, for at least five reasons which apply to the EBA initiative discussed above and equally to the agreement the EU has had with its former colonies, known collectively as ACP developing countries. First, many other equally poor butnon-LDC/non-ACP developing countries (e.g. Vietnam) are harmed by such preferences. This was made abundantly clear in the 1990s during the infamous dispute-settlement case that was brought to the WTO concerning the EU's banana import regime. One background study showed that for every $1 of benefit that the banana policy brought to producers in ACP countries, the regime harmed non-ACP developing country producers by almost exactly $1 – and in the process harmed EU consumers by more than $13 (Borrell 1999a). It is difficult to imagine a more inefficient way of transferring welfare to poor countries, since EU citizens could have been, through ODA payments, thirteen times as effective in helping ACP banana producers and not hurting non-ACP banana producers at all.[23] Such wasteful trade diversion is avoided under non-discriminatory, MFN liberalisations that result from multilateral trade negotiations under the WTO.

Second, the additional production that is encouraged in those LDCs or ACP countries getting privileged access to the high-priced EU market is not

[22] This 50 per cent across-the-board cut is in between two other possibilities: an ambitious Swiss formula which would cut higher tariffs by a larger percentage, and a conservative approach which at the extreme would exclude tariff peaks (as was effectively done in earlier GATT rounds in which agricultural and textile protection was not lowered). A study by Fontagné, Guérin and Jean (2004) uses a new and very detailed tariff data set to compare these three possible modalities. They find that the conservative approach (excluding cuts to tariff equivalents in excess of 15 per cent for manufacturing and of 85 per cent for agriculture) generates only half the welfare gains of the across-the-board approach, while the Swiss formula approach gave considerably larger gains, especially for those countries with the highest tariff peaks.

[23] The EU is contemplating moving by 2006 to a tariff-only regime for banana imports from non-ACP countries, and in the process raising its tariff from the current 75 Euros. That could raise the protective effect of the tariff for ACP countries currently enjoying duty-free access, so yet again harming other developing countries (Borrell and Bauer 2004).

internationally competitive at current prices (otherwise it would have been produced prior to getting that preferential treatment). Indeed the industry as a whole might not have existed in the LDC/ACP country had the preference scheme not been introduced.[24] In that case, its profits are likely to be lean despite the scheme, and would disappear if and when the scheme is dismantled or EU MFN tariffs are reduced. Efforts to learn the skills needed, and the sunk capital invested in that industry rather than in ones in which the country has a natural comparative advantage, would then earn no further rewards.

Third, these preference schemes reduce very substantially the capacity for developing countries as a group to press for more access to developed country markets. Perhaps if such preferences had not been offered in the first place, developing countries would have negotiated much more vigorously in previous GATT rounds for lower tariffs on agricultural and other imports to developed countries.

Fourth, because these preferential access schemes are not reciprocal agreements (that is, the developing countries are not required to open their markets to developed countries' exports) they contribute nothing to the removal of the wasteful trade-restrictive policies of the LDC/ACP countries. This contrasts with market access negotiations under WTO, which are characterised by reciprocity.

Points one–three also apply to South–North reciprocal FTAs. Furthermore, the latter agreements are rarely just a simple sentence such as: there shall be free trade between the parties. On the contrary, they can run to thousands of pages involving long lists of exceptions, complex rules of origin and DSPs, differing phase-in periods for different products, safeguard mechanisms, requirements to meet

the trade partner's myriad standards and so on. So complex are such features that it is not uncommon for firms to pay the MFN tariff rather than do all the paperwork necessary to get duty-free access within an FTA. And while they are potentially able to deliver gains to those who join them, FTAs do so to some extent at the expense of excluded countries and so, as was clear from the discussion on p. 00 of the FTAA studies, they contribute only a small fraction of the gains that can come from WTO-based multilateral reform – and yet they can involve a major diversion of trade negotiator attention away from WTO negotiations. In any case, the more MFN tariffs are reduced the less need there is for preferential trade agreements.

Summary of Gross Economic Benefits from Reducing Subsidies and Trade Barriers by 2010

What can be concluded from the range of estimates in table 10.3 of the gross economic benefits that would flow, to developing countries and to the global economy as a whole, from a halving of subsidies and trade barriers if that was agreed in 2004–5 and was phased-in equally over five years from 2006? Some people will claim some of those estimates are too high, for reasons that include the following:

- Modellers should be cutting not applied but bound tariffs (as in the FMT study)
- IRS should already have been exploited by producers, so those modellers assuming IRS are exaggerating the gains from reform
- The gains to developing countries enjoying tariff preferences in developed country markets are exaggerated if (as is the case) those preferential rates are not included in the models' tariff profiles[25]
- Domestic distortionary policies and exchange rate policies, which can inhibit the benefits of opening up, are not all included in the models
- Existing but currently redundant technical barriers might cease to be redundant and become binding constraints to trade as tariffs fall, in which case the rate of protection would fall less than the applied tariff rate
- Re-instrumentation of assistance to industries will reduce the gains and may even turn them into

[24] Alternatively, the ACP scheme may have caused an existing industry to become less competitive. An extreme example of an industry that has ossified as a consequence of regulations introduced to share the expected benefits of EU preferences is sugar in Mauritius (Borrell 1999b).

[25] To the extent that the gains to preference-receiving developing countries are offset by losses to other countries because of trade diversion, the global welfare effects of accounting for preferences (given the smallness of recipient economies) will be very small. The GTAP Version 6.0 database is expected to include preferences when it is released in mid-2004, so future modelling studies should be able to account for this.

losses if sufficiently inferior policy instruments (e.g. new technical barriers to trade) replace the ones being liberalised.

On the other hand, there are numerous reasons for believing some of the estimates in table 10.3 may be too low, including the following:

- Services as well as goods trade reforms need to be factored into the calculation, together with trade facilitation and FDI liberalisation if not also international migration
- The opening up of government procurement to foreign suppliers also needs to be modelled
- Non-agricultural subsidies (which are estimated to be around 60 per cent of all direct government subsidies globally) are not modelled for removal in the reform scenarios
- Some of the productive factors initially absorbed to fuel reform-induced output growth, particularly unskilled labour, may have been previously underemployed
- Monopolistic competition and product variety/heterogeneity between firms needs to be modelled
- Price elasticities in the standard GTAP model arguably err on the low side
- Endogenous growth effects need to be included as a benefit
- Account needs to be taken of wasteful spending of resources on lobbying, as that will fall if assistance to industries (including re-instrumentation of existing protection) is announced to be a thing of the past
- If trade reform encourages domestic policy and foreign exchange policy reforms as well, the benefits from those changes too need to be added; and, perhaps most important of all
- The counterfactual to reform is not the status quo as assumed by modellers but *increased protection*, particularly for agriculture and conceivably also for other sectors without tariff bindings in place or for which technical barriers to trade or anti-dumping duties may then restrain trade.

With these claims and counter-claims it is not possible to be precise about the gross benefits that would result from any particular reform such as a halving of subsidies and trade barriers. A

lower-bound estimate might be that provided in the IRS/MC part of the FMT study, which is the only study to consider cuts to bound (as distinct from applied) tariffs. That estimate amounts to 0.67 per cent of GDP in 1997. It contrasts with the estimate from the BDS study, in which services trade liberalisation includes dramatic growth in FDI. The latter's gain amounts to 3.0 per cent of GDP in 2005. The HRTG study is between those two but refers only to goods trade reform. In the light of these estimates it is assumed in what follows that the comparative static gains after full adjustment is an unweighted average of the BDS and FMT estimates, which is 1.8 per cent of GDP for the world as a whole and 2.5 per cent for developing countries (implying 1.6 per cent for developed countries). And it is assumed that those gains will accrue fully after a five-year phase-in period, prior to which the gains will begin in 2006 at one-fifth the full amount as of 2010 and rise by a further one-fifth each year until 2010.

There are dynamic gains from trade to consider in addition to those comparative static ones (not to mention the net benefits from non-farm subsidy cuts and the potentially massive gains from freeing up migration). The experiences of successful reformers such as Korea, China, India and Chile suggest that trade opening immediately boosts GDP growth rates by several percentage points. To err on the conservative side, it is assumed here that reform boosts GDP growth rates – projected to 2015 by the World Bank (2003, table A3.1) to be 2.7 per cent for developed countries, 4.6 per cent for developing countries – by one-sixth for developed countries and one-third for developing countries, that is, to 3.1 and 6.1 per cent, respectively, and hence from 3.2 to 3.8 per cent globally. Those rates are assumed to continue to 2050.[26]

To move from those gross effects to the net effects of these assumptions, it is necessary to consider the economic costs associated with reform, and also associated social and environmental benefits and costs.

---

[26] It may be that the growth rate rises more than this initially and then fades in later decades, in which case the increase assumed can be considered the appropriately discounted average over the period.

Economic Costs of Reducing Subsidies and Trade Barriers

The above benefits from reform are not costless, of course. Expenditure on negotiating, and on supporting policy think-tanks and the like to develop and disseminate a convincing case for reform, could be expanded manyfold before running into declining returns. But even if it did expand enormously, the increase globally would be trivial compared with the gains from reform (less than $2 bn per year over the next five years). Of much more significance are the *private costs* of adjustment for firms and workers, as reform forces some industries to downsize or close to allow others to expand (Matusz and Tarr 2000; Francois 2003). Those costs are ignored in the full-employment CGE models discussed above.

There are also *social costs* to consider. They include social safety net provisions in so far as such schemes are developed/drawn on by losers from reform (e.g. unemployment payments plus training grants to build up new skills so that displaced workers can earn the same wage as before), and perhaps increased costs of crime in so far as its incidence rises with transitional unemployment.

All three types are one-off costs to weigh against the non-stop flow of economic benefits from reform. The private and social costs of adjustment tend to be smaller the longer the phase-in period or smaller the tariff or subsidy cut per year (Furusawa and Lai 1999). CGE simulation studies also suggest that the annual change in an industry's terms of trade due to phased trade reform is typically very minor relative to changes due to exchange rate fluctuations, technological improvements, preference shifts and other economic shocks and structural developments associated with normal economic growth (Anderson *et al.* 1997; Dixon, Menon and Rimmer 2000).

Estimates of the magnitude of those costs are difficult to generate, but all available estimates suggest they are minor relative to the benefits from reform. An early study by Magee (1972) for the USA estimated the cost of job changes including temporary unemployment to be one-eighth of the benefits from tariff and quota elimination initially. Even assuming that transition took as many as five years, Magee estimated a BCR of 25. A subsequent study which examined a 50 per cent cut in US tariffs (but not quotas) came up with a similar BCR estimate (Baldwin, Mutti and Richardson 1980). In more recent debates about trade and labour, analysts have had difficulty finding a strong link between import expansion and increased unemployment (see Greenaway and Nelson 2002). One example is a study of the four largest EU economies' imports from East Asia (Bendivogli and Pagano 1999). Another European example is a study of the UK footwear industry: liberalising that market would incur unemployment costs only in the first year, because of the high job turnover in that industry, and those estimated costs are less than 1.5 per cent of the benefits from cutting that protection (Winters and Takacs 1991). A similar-sized estimate is provided by de Melo and Tarr (1990) using a CGE model that focuses just on US textile, steel and auto protection cuts and drawing on estimates of the cost of earnings lost by displaced workers (later reported by Jacobson, LaLonde and Sullivan 1993).

For developing countries the evidence also seems to suggest low costs of adjustment, not least because trade reform typically causes a growth spurt (Krueger 1983). In a study of thirteen liberalisation efforts for nine developing countries, (Michaely, Papageorgiu and Choksi 1991) found only one example where employment was not higher within a year. A similar study for Mauritius by Milner and Wright (1998) also found trade opening to be associated with employment growth rather than decline.[27]

A survey of 18 Latin American countries for the period 1970–96, by Marquez and Pages (1998),

---

[27] A further impact of trade policy reform about which concern is often expressed is the loss of tariff revenue for the government. This is of trivial importance to developed and upper middle-income countries where trade taxes account for only 1 and 3 per cent of government revenue, respectively. For lower middle-income countries that share is 9 per cent, and it is more than 20 per cent for more than a dozen low-income countries for which data are available, so how concerned should those poorer countries be? The answer depends on whether/how much that revenue would fall and, if it does fall, on whether/how much more costly would be the next best alternative means of raising government revenue. On the first of those two points, government revenue from import taxes will rise rather than fall with reform if the reform involves replacing, with less-prohibitive tariffs, any import quotas or bans, or tariffs that are prohibitive (or nearly so) or which encourage smuggling or underinvoicing or corruption

found some increases in short-term unemployment, but mainly in countries where the real exchange rate appreciated as a result of capital inflows that had accompanied the reforms. That small short-term negative effect soon reversed as production became more labour-intensive following reform, according to studies by Moreira and Najberg (2000) for Brazil and de Ferranti et al. (2001) for a wide range of Latin American and Caribbean countries over the 1990s.

If the adjustment costs are so small and may lead to more rather than fewer jobs even during the adjustment period, why are governments so reluctant to open their economies? The reason is because the losses in jobs and asset values are very obvious and concentrated whereas the gains in terms of new job and investment opportunities are thinly spread, are less easily attributed to the trade reform, and are often taken up by people other than those losing from the reform.[28] The few losers are prepared to support politicians who resist protection cuts, while the gains are sufficiently small per consumer and unassisted firm as to make it not worthwhile for those many potential gainers to get together to lobby for reform, particularly given their greater free-rider problem in acting collectively (Olsen 1965). Hence the need for publicly funded trade policy think-tanks and the like to play an advocacy role.

A prime example of the role analysis can play has to do with effects on developing countries in reforms to support for agriculture in OECD economies. The primary channel for such effects is through the terms of trade, which in turn depend in part on whether a country is a net exporter or importer of the affected OECD products. Long-term support for agriculture in OECD countries, coupled with often-negative assistance to farmers in many developing countries, has left developing countries as a group dependent on imports of these subsidised products. As a result, an across-the-board cut in all domestic support for OECD agriculture leads to welfare losses for many developing countries and to declines in farm incomes in Europe, Japan and North America. Such a reform package is therefore unlikely to be implemented on its own. An alternative approach is to focus on *broad-based reductions* in market price support, as has begun

occurring in the European Union where domestic support has increasingly replaced border measures. As Dimaranan, Hertel and Keeney (2003) show, a shift from market price support to land-based payments could generate a win–win–win outcome whereby OECD farm incomes are maintained and yet world price distortions are reduced and economic welfare rises for most developing countries and globally. Provided these increased domestic support payments are not linked to output or variable inputs, the trade-distorting and welfare-reducing effects are likely to be small, thereby providing an effective way of offsetting the potential losses that would otherwise be sustained by OECD farmers. This type of policy re-instrumentation increases the probability that such reforms are politically acceptable in the reforming economies while simultaneously increasing the likelihood that they will be beneficial to developing countries. That analysis suggests that developing country governments should focus their efforts on improved access to OECD food markets while permitting wealthy

by customs officials. It is even possible in a tariff-only regime that lower tariffs lead to a sufficiently higher volume and value of trade that the aggregate tariff collection rises. Examples of recent trade policy reforms that led to increased tariff revenue are Chile and Mexico (Bacchetta and Jansen 2003, 15) and Kenya (Glenday 2000). See also Greenaway and Milner (1993) and Nash and Takacs (1998). Since the economy is enlarged by opening up, income and consumption tax collections will automatically rise too. On the second point, about the cost of raising government revenue by other means if tax revenue does fall, Corden (1997, chapter 4) makes it clear that in all but the poorest of countries it will be more rather than less efficient to collect tax revenue in other ways. Even countries as poor as Cambodia have managed to introduce a value-added tax. Hence from a global viewpoint there is no significant cost that needs to be included in response to this concern. To the extent that subsidies are also cut as part of the reform, the chances of government revenue rising are even greater. Income and consumption tax revenue will also rise as the economy expands following reform. In any case, CGE modellers typically alter other taxes when trade tax revenues change, so as to keep the overall government budget unchanged.

[28] In the Australian context of high unemployment in the later 1970s, Max Corden was prompted to write a deliberately non-technical paper called 'Tell us where the new jobs will come from?', because he knew the answer was not obvious to a non-economist (Corden 1979). The paper proved so popular that thousands of offprints were distributed and in 1985 it was reprinted in *The World Economy*.

countries to increase their decoupled domestic payments as import tariffs are lowered.

So as not to exaggerate the net gains from trade reform, it is assumed here that there would be an adjustment period as long as five years following a 50 per cent across-the-board liberalisation, and that in each of those years the adjustment costs would be as much as 30 per cent of the annual comparative static benefits as of 2010 (and zero thereafter). That amounts to $219 bn per year during 2006–10 globally, of which $64 bn is expended in developing countries, when expressed in 2002 US dollars by using the projection to 2010 of global GDP provided by the World Bank (2003, table A3.1).

A 100 per cent (25 per cent) liberalisation would yield roughly twice (half) the gross benefits as a 50 per cent liberalisation but would have a much lower (higher) probability of being politically acceptable. This is because adjustment costs would be proportionately greater (less) with the bigger (smaller) reform. For the purposes of comparison, it is assumed here that a 100 (25) per cent liberalisation would involve adjustment costs equal to 40 (25) per cent of the annual comparative static benefits as of 2010 and zero thereafter, instead of the 30 per cent assumed for a halving of subsidies and trade barriers.

Social and Environmental Benefits and Costs of Reducing Subsidies and Trade Barriers

Because trade reform generates large and on-going economic gains while incurring comparatively minor one-off adjustment costs, it would allow individuals and governments to spend more on other pressing problems, thereby *indirectly* contributing to the alleviation of other challenges facing society. But in addition, trade reform would also *directly* alleviate some of those challenges. This section first focuses on the impact of trade reform on poverty alleviation, since that is the solution to many of the world's problems. It then turns to trade reform's impact on the environment, before briefly commenting on its impact on several of the other specific challenges being addressed in this project – namely climate change (chapter 1), communicable diseases (chapter 2), conflicts and arms proliferation (chap-

ter 3), access to education (chapter 4), financial instability (chapter 5), governance and corruption (chapter 6), population and migration issues (chapter 8) and malnutrition and hunger (chapter 7).

Poverty Alleviation

Evidence presented by Dollar and Kraay (2002) and Sala-i-Martin (2002), among others, suggests that aggregate economic growth differences have been largely responsible for the differences in poverty alleviation across regions. Initiatives that boost economic growth are therefore likely to be helpful in the fight against poverty, and trade liberalisation is such an initiative. But cuts to subsidies and trade barriers also alter relative product prices domestically and in international markets, which in turn affect factor prices. Hence the net effect on poverty depends also on the way those price changes affect poor households' expenditure and their earnings net of remittances. If the consumer and producer price changes (whether due to own-country reforms and/or those of other countries) are pro-poor, then they will tend to reinforce any positive growth effects of trade reform on the poor.

The effects of trade reform on global poverty can be thought of at two levels: on the income gap between developed and developing countries, and on poor households within developing countries. On the first, the CGE estimates surveyed above suggest that current developing countries, which produced just 19 per cent of global GDP in 2002, would enjoy nearly half of the NPV of the global static plus dynamic gains to 2050 from halving trade barriers. Clearly that will reduce substantially the income gap between developed and poorer countries on average.

How poor households *within* developing countries are affected is more difficult to say (McCulloch, Winters and Cirera 2001; Winters 2002). What is clear from table 10.2 is that the agricultural policies of developed countries provide a major source of developing country gains from reform, and lowering barriers to textiles and clothing trade is also important. Both would boost the demand for unskilled labour and for farm products produced in poor countries. Since two-thirds of the world's poor live in rural areas and, in least-developed countries, the proportion is as high as 90 per cent (OECD

2003a, 3), and since most poor rural households are net sellers of farm labour and/or food, one would expect such reforms to reduce the number in absolute poverty (Anderson 2004; Cline 2004a).[29] A preliminary analysis by Hertel *et al.* (2003), in which GTAP results are carefully combined with household income and expenditure survey data for fourteen developing countries, tests this hypothesis and finds strong support for it in most of the fourteen cases considered.

The Environment

The effects of trade reform on the environment have been the focus of much theoretical and empirical analysis since the 1970s and especially since 1990 (Beghin, van der Mensbrugghe and Roland-Holst 2002; Copland and Taylor 2003). Until recently, environmentalists have tended to focus mainly on the *direct* environmental costs they perceive from trade reform, just as they have with other areas of economic change.[30] That approach does not acknowledge areas where the environment might also have been *improved*, albeit indirectly, as a result of trade reform (e.g. from less production by pollutive industries that were previously protected). Nor does it weigh the costs of any net worsening of the environment against the economic benefits of policy reform of the sort described above.

The reality is that while the environmental effects of reform will differ across sectors and regions of the world, some positive and some negative, there are many examples where cuts to subsidies and trade barriers would reduce environmental damage (Anderson 2002; Irwin 2002, 48–54).

For some time the OECD has been encouraging analysis of these opportunities (OECD 1996, 1997, 1998, 2003b). Environmental NGOs are increasingly recognising them, with Greenpeace currently focusing on energy subsidies, WWF on fisheries subsidies (WWF 2001) and IISD and Friends of the Earth on subsidy reforms generally (e.g., Myers and Kent 1998; FOE *et al.* 2003). They and the better-informed development NGOs such as Oxfam seem to be coming to the view that the net social and environmental benefits from reducing subsidies and at least some trade barriers may indeed be positive rather than negative, and that the best hope of reducing environmentally harmful subsidies and trade

barriers is via the WTO's multi-issue, multilateral trade negotiations process.

If there remains a concern that the net effect of trade reform on the environment may be negative nationally or globally, that should be a stimulus to check whether first-best environmental policy measures are in place and set at the optimal level of intervention, rather than a reason for not reducing trade distortions. This is because if they are so set, we would then know that the direct economic gains from opening to trade would exceed society's evaluation of any extra environmental damage, other things equal (Corden 1997, chapter 13).

Much environmental damage in developing countries is a direct consequence of poverty (e.g. the slash-and-burn shifting agriculture of landless unemployed squatters). In so far as trade reform reduces poverty, so it will reduce such damage. More generally, the relationships between *per capita* income and a wide range of environmental indicators have been studied extensively. Because richer people have a greater demand for a clean environment, income rises tend to be associated with better environmental outcomes once incomes rise above certain levels.[31] Even though more pollutive products are being consumed as incomes rise, many abatement practices have been spreading fast enough to more than compensate. And openness to trade accelerates that spread of abatement ideas and technologies, making their implementation in developing countries affordable at ever-earlier stages of development.

Estimating the global cost to society of all environmental damage that might accompany a reduction in subsidies and trade barriers, net of all environmental gains, is extraordinarily difficult both

[29] Das (2001) describes independent India's lack of openness prior to the 1990s as 'a great betrayal' that kept hundreds of millions of people in poverty for two generations longer than necessary.

[30] See the critique by Lomborg (2001).

[31] This is the theme of the book by Hollander (2003). For statistical evidence of the extent to which different environmental indicators first worsen and then improve as incomes rise (sometimes called the 'environmental Kuznets curve'), see the special issue of the journal *Environment and Development Economics*, 2(4) 1997 and the more recent papers by and cited in Harbaugh, Levinson and Wilson (2002) and Cole (2003).

conceptually and empirically.[32] In the absence of any sufficiently comprehensive estimates, it will be assumed that the net effect of reform on the environment would be zero.

Climate Change

When the environmental impact is global rather than local, as with greenhouse gases and their alleged impact on climate change, international environmental agreements may be required (see Cline 2004b). When developing countries are not party to such agreements, however, it is difficult to prevent 'leakage' through a relocation of carbon-intensive activities to those non-signatories. An alternative or supplementary approach that is likely to achieve at least some emission reductions, and at the same time generate national and global economic benefits rather than costs, involves lowering coal subsidies and trade barriers. Past coal policies have encouraged excessive production of coal in a number of industrial countries and excessive coal consumption in numerous developing countries including transition economies. Phasing out those distortionary policies has both improved the economy and lowered greenhouse gas emissions globally – a 'no-regrets' outcome or win–win Pareto improvement for the economy and the environment (Anderson and McKibbin 2000). Additional opportunities for reducing greenhouse gases through cutting energy subsidies are pointed to in the UNEP study by von Moltke, McKee and Morgan (2004).

Communicable Diseases

Communicable diseases are more common among the poor, so again trade reform's contribution to

poverty alleviation will in turn impact on human health in general and the reduced incidence of diseases in particular. Furthermore, the greater openness of economies ensures that medicines and prevention technologies are more widespread and cheaper, particularly following the Doha WTO conference of trade ministers and the subsequent Decision of 30 August 2003 on the TRIPS Agreement and Public Health. That Decision by the WTO General Council ensures that developing country governments can issue compulsory licences to allow other companies to make a patented product or use a patented process under licence without the consent of the patent owner, while developing countries unable to produce pharmaceuticals domestically can now import generic copies of patented drugs made under compulsory licensing by other developing countries.

Conflicts

Openness tends to break down the common prejudices that accompany insularity, and to broaden mutual understanding between people with different cultures and customs. It also expands economic interdependence among countries, which raises the opportunity cost of entering into conflicts with trading partners. In so far as it reduces income inequality across countries, then that too diffuses tension between nations – a point that has even greater significance following the terrorist attacks of 11 September 2001. Indeed there is now statistical support for Immanuel Kant's hypothesis that durable peace is supported by representative democracy, trade and membership of international organisations: Oneal and Russett (2000) find that all three contribute independently to more peaceful relationships with other countries.[33] Casual observation also suggests that more autarchic economies tend to be less democratic.

Where openness involves also greater international migration, there tends to be less intercultural conflict and more social gains from multiculturalism. Conversely, it is in societies that resent immigrants and impose strict migration quotas where cultural clashes seem to be more common. Clashes between ethnic groups are also more common where a minority prospers greatly relative to the majority or other significant minorities (Chua 2003). Such income and wealth inequality within a country

---

[32] A beginning nonetheless is being made, with several governments funding *ex ante* evaluations of the WTO Doha Round's potential impact on the environment. The EU's efforts include a workshop on methodological issues which are laid out in CEPII (2003), and further work has been contracted to the University of Manchester; progress can be traced at http://idpm.man.ac.uk/sia-trade/Consultation.htm. *Ex post* analysis are also being undertaken by NGOs. See, for example, Bermudez (2004) for WWF's sustainability impact assessment of trade policies during 2001–3.

[33] A survey of the evidence did not find a significant direct link between poverty and terrorism, however. Rather, Krueger and Maleckova (2002) concluded that terrorism was more a response to political conditions and long-standing feelings of indignity and frustration.

tends to be less common the more open is the economy, at least after the initial adjustments to reform (Williamson 2002).

Education Underinvestment

Parents and governments are less likely to underinvest in education the higher their incomes, other things equal. So to the extent that trade reform raises incomes, it contributes to better educational outcomes. That is especially so for the very poorest who cannot afford even primary education: even a slight increase in the cash income of poor farm families, for example following a reform-induced increase in international prices of farm products, can make it possible to pay the (often relatively high) school fees that are otherwise unaffordable.

Financial Instability

Trade reform 'thickens' international markets by raising the share of global production that passes through them. That typically reduces the variation across time in prices for traded products. It also expands the demand for international financial services to transfer the required payments and often to provide temporary credit. Together these forces contribute to the long-term stability of financial markets.

Openness also tends to reduce inflation. It can do so by increasing competition in domestic markets, which drives down prices and reduces political pressure on the central bank to inflate, and by providing more options for people to hold savings in foreign currencies, which reduces the ability of governments to inflate savings away (Rogoff 2003).

Poor Governance and Corruption

A tolerance for subsidies and trade barriers breeds rent-seeking by special interests seeking protectionist policies for their industry. If those policies include import licensing, that breeds corruption through encouraging bureaucrats responsible for allocating licences to accept bribes from would-be importers. Together those activities ensure that the welfare costs of trade barriers are higher than is typically measured, since a share of the private rents they generate are wasted in these lobbying activities. Tax-avoiding corruption is also encouraged

in the case of import tariffs, for example through bribing customs officers or through smuggling. For these reasons it is not surprising that statistical analysis has found less open economies to be more corrupt (Ades and Di Tella 1999).

Population and Migration Issues

The challenge in developed countries of a shortage of low-skilled workers has been eased by merchandise trade with and FDI flows to labour-abundant developing countries, most notably China since the 1980s. But that has been far from sufficient to equalize wages across countries. Historical experience in the fifty years before the First World War showed that by far the fastest way to bring about a convergence in living standards is through international migration (Williamson 2002). Notwithstanding the liberalisation of much merchandise trade post-Second World War, and the opportunity through the WTO's Doha Round to reduce those and services trade barriers further, the CGE analyses by Hamilton and Whalley (1984) and Winters *et al.* (2003) suggest that this will still be the case in the foreseeable future. When coupled with an ageing population in developed countries, there is a compelling case for them to expand their quotas on immigrants from developing countries. Indeed Mattoo and Subramanian (2003) argue that this would be essential if the Doha Round is to deliver on its promise of being development-friendly.

Undernutrition and Hunger

Food security is always a great concern in poor countries, especially those dependent on food imports where there are fears that reducing agricultural subsidies and protectionism globally will raise the price of those imports. But food security is defined as always having access to the minimum supply of basic food necessary for survival, so enhancing food security is mainly about alleviating poverty. That suggests this issue needs to be considered from a *household* rather than national perspective.[34] If

---

[34] Even from a national viewpoint, it is not necessarily the case that a country that is currently a net food importer will lose from a rise in the international price of food. If, for example, it is close to self-sufficient in food without price supports, and reform abroad raises the international price of food, it

an international food price rise from trade reform abroad is transmitted domestically, the vast majority of the poor in low-income countries would benefit directly. This is because the poor are found predominantly in farm households and are net sellers of food. Even poor landless farm labourers who are net buyers of food would benefit indirectly from an agricultural price rise via a rise in the demand for their unskilled farm labour if that raises their wage enough to more than offset the rise in food prices in rural areas. The earnings prospects for other landless rural poor will have risen, too, along with the demand for labour in local enterprises that grow as farmers spend their enhanced income on simple manufactures and services produced nearby. Since the typically more affluent people in cities would find it relatively easy to pay a little extra for food, the only other major vulnerable group is the underemployed urban poor. But even that group may not be worse off in so far as trade reform generates a more-than-offsetting increase in the demand for that group's unskilled labour, which is used relatively intensively in (often informal sector) services or, if developed countries were to reduce also their barriers to imports of textiles and clothing, the apparel industry.

may switch to become sufficiently export-oriented that its net national economic welfare rises. A second possibility is that a developing country's own policies are sufficiently biased against food production that the country is a net importer, despite having a comparative advantage in food. In that case, it has been shown that the international price rise can improve national economic welfare, even if the price change is not sufficient to turn that distorted economy into a net food exporter (Anderson and Tyers 1993). That comes about because the higher price of food attracts mobile resources away from more-distorted sectors, thereby improving the efficiency of national resource allocation. Because of these two possibilities, the number of poor countries for whom a rise in international food prices might cause some hardship is much smaller than the number that are currently net importers of food products.

[35] These expectations are supported by the household-focused CGE analysis by Hertel et al. (2003). An interesting exception, though, is Mexico: poverty there has been reduced by Mexico's preferential access into the US market via NAFTA, and the benefit of those preferences would decrease with multilateral reform because Mexico would then have to share some of those earlier gains with other developing countries. This result highlights the beggar-thy-neighbour nature of FTAs, as discussed above.

What about in developing countries where multilateral agricultural trade liberalisation means lower domestic prices for agricultural products because such countries had kept domestic food prices above international levels via import restrictions? It is true that removing those distortions will reduce farm incomes in those countries (but by more for larger than smaller farms), and urban households will benefit from lower food prices. However, food self-sufficiency will fall – and it is the fall in both farm earnings and food self-sufficiency that focuses the attention of those who argue that agricultural trade liberalisation is bad for poor households. Focusing on just the direct effects of agricultural trade policy reform can be misleading, however, not least because it does not take account of the fact that such reform would be undertaken in the context of multilateral, economy-wide liberalisation. Being multilateral means that other countries' farm protection cuts raise international food prices, and so less of a price fall occurs than when a country cuts its agricultural protection unilaterally. And being economy-wide means that the decline in demand for farm labour is more or less offset by a growth in demand for labour in expanding non-farm industries such as apparel.[35]

Hunger and undernutrition can be eased by trade not only in goods but also in agricultural technologies, in particular newly bred varieties of staple crops (Runge et al. 2003). The introduction of high-yielding dwarf wheat and rice varieties during the 'Green Revolution' that began in Asia in the 1960s is a previous case in point, whereby producers and consumers shared the benefits in terms of higher farm profits and lower consumer prices for cereals. A prospective case in point is the possibility of breeding crop varieties that are not only less costly to grow but are 'nutriceuticals' in the sense that they contain vitamin and mineral supplements. The most promising is so-called 'golden rice'. Consumers in many poor countries suffer from chronic vitamin A deficiency that can lead to blindness, weakened immune systems and increased morbidity and mortality for children and pregnant and lactating women. 'Golden rice' has been genetically engineered to contain a higher level of beta-carotene in the endosperm of the grain and thereby

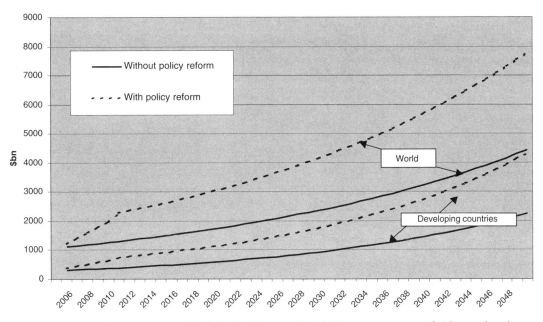

Figure 10.1. *Annual increment to global GDP without and with 50 per cent cut to subsidies and trade barriers, 2006–2050 ($US 2002 bn)*

provide a vitamin A supplement. By being cheaper and/or more nutritionally beneficial, it would improve the health of poor people and thereby also boost their labour productivity. Anderson, Jackson and Nielsen (2004) estimate that the latter economic benefit from this new technology could be as much as ten times greater than just the traditional benefits of lower production costs – not to mention that poor people would live longer and healthier lives. This new technology has yet to be adopted, however, because the EU and some other countries will not import grain from countries that produce food that may contain genetically modified organisms (GMOs) – even though there is no evidence that GM foods are a danger to human health (see, e.g., King 2003). That trade barrier may be challenged at the WTO because it is seen by adopters of GM corn and soybean simply as a disguised form of economic protection for European farmers (an hypothesis that is not inconsistent with empirical research showing that the EU's moratorium on GM food boosts EU farm household incomes even though it denies them the opportunity to adopt the new technology – see Anderson and Jackson 2004).

Global Net Present Value and Benefit-Cost Ratio from Lowering Subsidies and Trade Barriers by 2010

The previous section points to numerous examples of net social benefits from trade liberalisation, but is unable to quantify them, let alone all the other social and environmental benefits and costs of such policy reform. For present purposes of estimating the NPV of this opportunity to reduce subsidies and trade barriers, they will therefore be ignored even though, like the net gains from migration, they are most likely positive and large.

With that in mind, lower-bound estimates of the overall net benefits from halving subsidies and trade barriers are calculated as the differences each year between the economic benefits and costs discussed on pp. 558–62. As shown in figure 10.1, these benefits would roughly double the annual increment to global GDP after the initial adjustment period. Even if the benefits ceased after fifty years, their NPV in 2005 at a discount rate of 5 per cent would be $23,040 bn for the world economy, of which $11,500 bn, or almost half, would accrue to the current developing countries (expressed in 2002

Table 10.4. Summary of Benefits and Costs of Liberalizing Subsidies and Trade Barriers (2002 US$ Billion)

Opportunity[a]	Benefit (NPV in 2005) ($)	Cost (NPV in 2005) ($)	BCR	Key assumptions
Optimistic Doha: 50 per cent liberalisation of trade barriers and agricultural subsidies	23,040	947	24.3	5 per cent discount rate, benefits rise each year even after the five-year phase-in to 2010 (because the economy is growing) and last to 2050, costs are $219 billion per year and last from 2006 to 2010
Full reform: 100 per cent liberalisation of trade barriers and agricultural subsidies	46,080	2,104	21.9	As above, except costs are $583 billion per year
Pessimistic Doha: 25 per cent liberalisation of trade barriers and agricultural subsidies	11,520	395	29.2	As above, except costs are $91 billion per year

Note: [a]Based on the estimates in the BDS study, the FTAA opportunity would yield benefits of (possibly very much) less than one-twelfth of that for the Optimistic Doha opportunity above, and a lower BCR, because of standard FTA complexities such as rules of origin. The EBA opportunity for least-developed countries to get preferential (duty- and quota-free) access to developed country markets would yield global benefits of less than one-hundredth of the above, and those benefits would diminish as and when developed countries lowered their MFN tariffs. While the least-developed countries would be the main beneficiaries in proportional terms from EBA, their benefit would be at the expense of other developing countries (including ones as poor as Vietnam) who lose from the trade-diverting nature of this preferential agreement.

US dollars, when global and developing country GDPs were $32,016 and $6,079 bn, respectively). That implies a BCR of 24.3 globally and 37.9 for developing countries. If the dynamic gains (in addition to prospective migration gains and social and environmental net benefits) are ignored, the global gains are $17,100 bn in terms of NPV, implying a BCR ratio of 18.1 for the world as a whole. Table 10.4 summarises these results as the Optimistic Doha opportunity. For comparison it also shows the BCRs for a 100 per cent liberalisation and for a Pessimistic Doha outcome of a 25 per cent liberalisation, assuming proportionately higher (lower) costs of adjustment when the reform is greater (smaller) as discussed above.

Even if one believes that the probability of a successful Doha Round is low, that it might take some years beyond 2005 to complete and beyond 2010 before its full impact is felt, that it might involve much less than a halving of subsidies and trade barriers, that the comparative static gains are closer to the lowest estimate in table 10.3 and that the dynamic gains would boost GDP growth rates by less than one-sixth for developed countries and

one-third for developing countries, the alternative NPV estimates one would generate are likely still to be enormous – both absolutely and relative to the cost associated with this reform. And that benefit would be even larger if the counterfactual was not the status quo but a rise in protectionism and a decline in the WTO institution and the rules-based global trading system that it supports.

The estimated net benefit to developing countries after adjusting to greater access to developed country markets is large compared with ODA currently provided by OECD countries to developing countries (around $60 bn p.a). It is large also compared with the FDI funds that flow from OECD to developing countries (between $120 and $150 bn per year). Yet it would not be costly for developed countries to provide that greater market access. On the contrary, those countries would gain even more in dollar terms than developing countries from such policy reform (see table 10.2), giving them extra resources to expand their development assistance and FDI and thereby to further reduce global income inequality and poverty, particularly if non-farm subsidies were also cut. All that is required is bold leadership to grasp the opportunities before us for unilateral and multilateral trade reform and associated subsidy cuts, particularly via the WTO's Doha Round of negotiations.

Conclusion

The theory and available evidence surveyed above show that subsidies and trade barriers are not only economically wasteful but many also have harmful social and environmental effects. Even where the latter effects are not harmful, there are almost always cheaper ways of obtaining those social and environmental effects than via trade and subsidy measures. The reasons these inefficient measures persist is partly lack of understanding of the benefits being forgone, but mostly it is because a small number of vested interests lobby for their retention.

The challenge is to find politically feasible opportunities for ridding the world of subsidies and trade barriers. This chapter suggests that the most obvious way is currently before us in the form of the Doha Development Agenda of multilateral trade negotiations under the WTO. Seizing that opportunity for reform could reduce government outlays by hundreds of millions of dollars. It could also allow citizens to spend more on other pressing problems (because under freer trade the world's resources would be allocated more efficiently), thereby *indirectly* contributing to opportunities to alleviate other challenges facing the world; and it could also *directly* alleviate poverty and thereby reduce environmental degradation and address other challenges such as communicable diseases, conflicts and arms proliferation, education underinvestment, corruption, migration issues, water issues and undernutrition and hunger.

Appendix The Global, Economy-Wide GTAP Database and Model

To estimate the potential economy-wide effects of regional and multilateral trade liberalisations, by far the most common methodology since the 1980s has involved a global computable general equilibrium (CGE) model and database.[36] It is a daunting task to compile and periodically update all the necessary data for such a model so, under the direction of Professor Tom Hertel of Purdue University, a Consortium was established for this purpose in the 1990s. Known as GTAP (the Global Trade Analysis Project), it is currently providing Version 5 of its database, with Version 6 to be released in the spring of 2004. That latest database provides reconciled production, consumption and bilateral goods and services trade data plus subsidies and trade distortion estimates[37] (including developing country preferences) as of 2001 for seventy-eight countries or country groups spanning the world, each divided into fifty-seven sectors spanning the entire economy (see www.gtap.org). Earlier versions based on 1997 or 1995 data had less country and product disaggregation and did not include tariff preferences. This database is the foundation of most global CGE trade models in use today. The current version is described in detail in Dimaranan and McDougall (2002).

In addition, the GTAP Center at Purdue University has developed its own family of applied general equilibrium models (Hertel 1997). The core GTAP model is a standard, multi-region CGE model that is currently being used by several hundred researchers in scores of countries on five continents. (The GTAP database builds on contributions from many of these

individuals, as well as the national and international agencies in the GTAP Consortium.) Perfect competition (PC) and constant returns to scale (CRS) are assumed for all sectors of each economy in the core comparative static version.

The GTAP model utilises a sophisticated representation of consumer demands that allows for differences in both the price and income responsiveness of demand in different regions depending upon both the level of development of the region and the particular consumption patterns observed in that region. On the supply side, differences in factor endowments within and between countries interact with different sectoral factor intensities to drive changes in the sectoral composition of output in response to structural or policy shocks. The GTAP production system distinguishes sectors by their intensities in five primary factors of production: agricultural land, other natural resources, unskilled labour time, skilled labour time and physical capital. Thus in a region where physical capital is accumulating rapidly relative to other factors, for example, that region's relatively capital-intensive sectors tend to expand at the expense of other sectors. In addition to differences in intermediate input intensities, import intensities are also permitted to vary across uses. Since much trade is in intermediate inputs, the distinction between sales to final consumers and sales to other firms can be important. Lowering the cost of imported goods to consumers is quite different from lowering the cost of intermediate inputs to domestic firms that may be competing with imports in the final product market. Products are also differentiated by place of production. The linkage between the different prices of a product is typically quite strong, but will depend on the degree of substitutability in consumption. In addition to matching up more effectively with reality, this approach has the advantage of permitting

---

[36] On the need for adopting a general rather than a partial equilibrium methodology, see Anderson (2002).

[37] Estimating the height of trade barriers is a non-trivial task in itself, even for merchandise (Evans 2003) but especially for services (Findlay and Warren 2001) and if technical barriers to trade are involved (Maskus and Wilson 2001).

bilateral trade to be tracked, as opposed to simply reporting total exports net of imports.

References

Adams, R., P. Dee, J. Gali and G. McGuire, 2003: The trade and investment effects of preferential trading arrangements: old and new evidence, Staff Working Paper, Productivity Commission, Canberra, May

Ades, A. and R. di Tella, 1999: Rents, competition, and corruption, *American Economic Review*, **89**(4), 982–93

Anderson, K. 1992: Effects on the environment and welfare of liberalising world trade: the cases of coal and food, chapter 8 in K. Anderson and R. Blackhurst (eds.), *The greening of world trade issues*, Harvester-Wheatsheaf and University of Michigan, London and Ann Arbor

2002: Economy-wide dimensions of trade policy reform, chapter 2 in B. Hoekman, A. Matoo and P. English (eds.), *Development, trade and the (WTO): a handbook*, World Bank, Washington, DC

2003: Measuring effects of trade policy distortions: how far have we come?, *The World Economy*, **26**(4), 413–40

2004: Agricultural trade reform and poverty reduction in developing countries, in S. Jayasuriya and P.J. Lloyd (eds.), *International trade and development: essays in honour of Peter Lloyd*, Edward Elgar, Cheltenham

Anderson, K., B. Dimaranan, J. Francois, T. Hertel, B. Hoekman and W. Martin, 2002: The burden of rich (and poor) country protectionism on developing countries, *Journal of African Economies*, **10**(3), 227–57

Anderson, K., B. Dimaranan, T. Hertel and W. Martin, 1997: Economic growth and policy reforms in the APEC region: trade and welfare implications by 2005, *Asia-Pacific Economic Review*, **3**(1), 1–18

Anderson, K. and L.A. Jackson, 2003: Standards, trade and protection: the case of GMOs, paper presented at a seminar at the World Bank, Washington DC, 2 October

Anderson, K., L.A. Jackson and C.P. Nielsen, 2004: Who would benefit from the adoption of golden rice in Asia?, University of Adelaide, February, mimeo

Anderson, K. and W. McKibbin, 2000: Reducing coal subsidies and trade barriers: their contribution to greenhouse gas abatement, *Environment and Development Economics*, **5**(4), 457–81

Anderson, K. and L.A. Jackson 2004: Standards, trade and protection: the case of GMOs, paper presented at the Annual Conference of the American Agricultural Economics Association, Denver CO, 1–4 August

Anderson, K., L.A. Jackson and C.P. Nielsen 2004: Who would benefit from the adoption of golden rice in Asia?, paper presented at the 7th Annual Global Economic Analysis Conference, Washington, DC, 19 June

Anderson, K. and R. Tyers 1993: More on welfare gains to developing countries from liberalising world food trade, *Journal of Agricultural Economics* **44**(2), 189–204

Anson, J., O. Cadot, J. de Melo, A. Estevadeordal, A. Suwa Eisenmann and B. Tumurchudur 2003: Rules of origin in North–South preferential trading arrangements with an application to NAFTA, CEPR Discussion Paper, **4166**, London

Bacchetta, M. and M. Jansen, 2003: Adjusting to trade liberalisation: the role of policy, institutions and WTO disciplines, Special Studies, 7, World Trade Organization, Geneva, April

Bagwell, K. and R.W. Staiger, 2004: Subsidy agreements, NBER Working Paper, **10292**, Cambridge MA, February

Baldwin, R.E., 2004: Openness and growth: what's the empirical relationship?, in R.E. Baldwin and L.A. Winters (eds.), *Challenges to globalization: analysing the economics*, University of Chicago Press for NBER and CEPR, Chicago

Baldwin, R.E., R. Forslid, P. Martin, G.M. Ottaviano and F. Robert-Nicoud, 2003: *Economic geography and public policy*, Princeton University Press, Princeton

Baldwin, R.E., J. Mutti and J.D. Richardson, 1980: Welfare effects on the United States of a significant multilateral trade reduction, *Journal of International Economics*, **6**, 405–23

Bandara, J. and W. Yu, 2003: How desirable is the South Asian free trade area? A quantitative economic assessment, *The World Economy*, **26**(9), 1293–1324

Beers, C. van and A. de Moor, 2001: *Public subsidies and policy failures: how subsidies distort the natural environment, equity and trade and how to reform them*, Edward Elgar, Cheltenham

Beghin, J., D. van der Mensbrugghe and D. Roland-Holst, 2002: *Trade and the environment in general equilibrium: evidence from developing economies*, Kluwer Academic, Norwell, MA

Bendivogli, C. and P. Pagano, 1999: Trade, job destruction and job creation in european manufacturing, *Open Economies Review*, 10, 156–84

Bermudez, E. 2004: *Sustainability assessments of trade policies and programmes,* WWF International, Gland

Bhagwati, J.N., 1971: The generalized theory of distortions and welfare, in J.N. Bhagwati *et al.* (eds.), *Trade, balance of payments and growth*, North-Holland, Amsterdam

    1988: *Protectionism*, MIT Press, Cambridge, MA

Bhagwati, J.N. and R. Hudec (eds.), 1996: *Fair trade and harmonization*, MIT Press, Cambridge, MA

Borrell, B., 1999a. Bananas: straightening out bent ideas on trade as aid, paper presented at the World Bank/WTO Conference on Agriculture and the New Trade Agenda from a Development Perspective, Geneva, 1–2 October

    1999b: Sugar: the taste test of trade liberalisation, paper presented at the World Bank/WTO Conference on Agriculture and the New Trade Agenda from a Development Perspective, Geneva, 1–2 October

Borrell, B. and M. Bauer 2004: EU banana drama: not over yet, Centre for International Economics, Canberra

Broda, C.M. and D.E. Weinstein, 2004: Globalization and the gains from variety, NBER Working Paper, **10314**, Cambridge MA, February

Brown, D., A.V. Deardorff and R.M. Stern, 2003: Multilateral, regional and bilateral trade-policy options for the United States and Japan, *The World Economy*, **26**(6), 803–28

CEPII 2003: *Methodological tools for SIA: report of the CEPII workshop held on 7–8 November 2002 in Brussels,* Paris: CEPII Working Paper **2003-19**, at http://www.cepii.fr/anglaisgraph/workpap/pdf/2003/wp03-19.pdf

Chua, A., 2003: *World on fire: how exporting free market democracy breeds ethnic hatred and global instability*, Random House, New York

Cline, W.R., 2004a: *Trade policy and global poverty*, Center for Global Development, Washington, DC

    2004b: Climate change, chapter 1 in this volume

Cline, W.R., T.O. Kawanabe, M. Kronsjo and T. Williams, 1978: *Trade negotiations in the Tokyo Round: a quantitative assessment*, Brookings Institution, Washington, DC

Coase, R., 1960: The problem of social cost, *Journal of Law and Economics*, **3**, 1–44

Cole, M.A., 2003: Development, trade, and the environment: how robust is the environmental Kuznets curve?, *Environment and Development Economics*, **8**(4), 557–80

Copland, B. and M.S. Taylor, 2003: *Trade and the environment: theory and evidence*, Princeton University Press, Princeton

Corden, W.M., 1979: Tell us where the new jobs will come from?, *Bank of New South Wales Review*, 30; reprinted in *The World Economy*, **8**(2), 183–88, 1985 and as chapter 7 in W. M. Corden, *The road to reform: essays on Australian economic policy*, Addison-Wesley, Melbourne, 1997

    1997: *Trade policy and economic welfare*, 2nd edn., Clarendon Press, Oxford

Das, G., 2001: *India unbound*, Knopf, New York

Deardorff, A.V. and R.M. Stern, 1979: *An economic analysis of the effects of the Tokyo Round of multilateral trade negotiations on the United States and other major industrial countries*, MTN Studies, 5, US Government Printing Office, Washington, DC

    1986: *The Michigan model of world production and trade: theory and applications*, MIT Press, Cambridge, MA

de Ferranti, D., G.E. Perry, D. Lederman and W. Maloney 2001: *From natural resources to the knowledge economy: trade and job quality,* Latin American and Caribbean Studies, World Bank, Washington, DC

Devarajan, S., D.S. Go and H. Li, 1999: Quantifying the fiscal effects of trade reform, World Bank Working Paper, **2162**, Washington, DC, August

Diebold, W., Jr., 1952: *The end of the ITO*, International Finance Section, Essays in International Finance, 16, Princeton University Press, Princeton

Dimaranan, B., T. Hertel and R. Keeney 2003: OECD domestic support and the developing countries, GTAP Working Paper, **19**, Center for Global Trade Analysis, Purdue University, West Lafayette

Dimaranan, B.V. and R.A. McDougall (eds.), 2002: *Global trade, assistance, and production: the*

GTAP 5 data base, Center for Global Trade Analysis, Purdue University, West Lafayette

Dixon, P., J. Menon and M. Rimmer, 2000: Changes in technology and preferences: a general equilibrium explanation of rapid growth in trade, *Australian Economic Papers*, **39**, 33–55

Dollar, D. and A. Kraay, 2002: Growth is good for the poor, *Journal of Economic Growth*, **7**(3), 195–225

Easterly, W., 2001: *The elusive quest for growth*, MIT Press, Cambridge, MA

Eichengreen, B., 2004: Financial instability, chapter 5 in this volume

Ethier, W.J., 1996: Theories about trade liberalisation and migration: substitutes or complements?, in P.J. Lloyd and L.S. Williams (eds.), *International trade and migration in the APEC region*, Oxford University Press, London and Melbourne

Evans, C., 2003: The economic significance of national border effects, *American Economic Review*, **93**(4), 1291–1312

Feenstra, R.C., J.R. Markusen and W. Zeile, 1992: Accounting for growth with new inputs, *American Economic Review*, **82**(2), 415–21

Findlay, C. and T. Warren, 2001: *Impediments to trade in services: measurement and policy implications*, Routledge, London and New York

FOE *et al.* 2003: *Green scissors 2003: cutting wasteful and environmentally harmful spending*, http://www.foe.org/res/pubs/pdf/gs2003.pdf

Fontagné, L., J.-L. Guérin and S. Jean 2004: Market access liberalisation in the Doha Round: scenarios and assessment, CEPII, Paris, mimeo

Francois, J.F., 1998: Scale economies and imperfect competition in the GTAP model, GTAP Technical Paper, 14, Center for Global Trade Analysis, Purdue University, West Lafayette, September

2000: Assessing the results of general equilibrium studies of multilateral trade negotiations, Policy Issues in International Trade and Commodities Study Series, 3, UNCTAD, Geneva

2001: *The next WTO Round: North–South stakes in new market access negotiations*, Centre for International Economic Studies, Adelaide and Tinbergen Institute, Rotterdam

2003: Assessing the impact of trade policy on labour markets and production', in *Methodological Tools for SIA*, CEPII Working Paper, **2003-19**, CEPII, Paris

Francois, J.F. and W. Martin, 2003: Formula approaches to market access negotiations, *The World Economy*, **26**(1), 1–28

Francois, J.F., H. van Meijl and F. van Tongeren, 2003: Trade liberalisation and developing countries under the Doha Round, CEPR Discussion Paper, 4032, London, August

Francois, J.F. and K.A. Reinert (eds.), 1997: *Applied methods for trade policy analysis: a handbook*, Cambridge University Press, Cambridge and New York

Frankel, J.A. and D. Romer, 1999: Does trade cause growth?, *American Economic Review*, **89**(3), 379–99

Freeman, R.B., 2003: Trade wars: the exaggerated impact of trade in economic debate, Research Paper, 2003/42, Leverhulme Centre for Research on Globalization and Economic Policy, University of Nottingham

Fujita, M., P. Krugman and A.J. Venables, 2001: *The spatial economy: cities, regions and international trade*, MIT Press, Cambridge, MA

Fujita, M. and J. Thisse, 2002: *Economics of agglomeration: cities, industrial location and regional growth*, Cambridge University Press, Cambridge and New York

Furusawa, T. and E.L.C. Lai, 1999: Adjustment costs and gradual trade liberalisation, *Journal of International Economics*, **49**, 333–61

Glenday, G. 2000: Trade liberalization and customs revenue: does trade liberalization lead to lower customs revenue? The case of Kenya, African Economic Policy Discussion Paper, **44**, Kennedy School of Government, Harvard University

Goldstein, J., 1998: International institutions and domestic politics: GATT, WTO and the liberalisation of international trade, chapter 4 in A.O. Krueger (ed.), *The WTO as an international organization*, University of Chicago Press, Chicago and London

Greenaway, D., 1993: Liberalizing foreign trade through rose-tinted glasses, *Economic Journal*, **103**, 208–22

Greenaway, D. and C. Milner 1993: The fiscal implication of trade policy reform: theory and evidence, UNDP/World Bank Trade Expansion Program Occasional Paper, **9**, World Bank, Washington, DC

Greenaway, D. and D.R. Nelson (eds.), 2002: *Globalization and labour markets*, 2 vols., Edward Elgar, London

Grossman, G.M. and E. Helpman, 1991: *Innovation and growth in the global economy*, MIT Press, Cambridge, MA

1994: Protection for sale, *American Economic Review*, **84**(4), 833–50

1995: Trade wars and trade talks, *Journal of Political Economy*, **103**(4), 675–708

Hamilton, B. and J. Whalley, 1984: Efficiency and distributional implications of global restrictions on labor mobility, *Journal of Development Economics*, **14**, 61–75

Harbaugh, W.T., A. Levinson and D.M. Wilson, 2002: Re-examining the empirical evidence for an environmental Kuznets curve, *Review of Economics and Statistics*, **84**(3), 541–51

Harrison, G.W., T.F. Rutherford, D.G. Tarr and A. Gurgel, 2003: Regional, multilateral and unilateral trade policies on MERCOSUR for growth and poverty reduction in Brazil, World Bank, Washington DC, May, mimeo

Harrison, W.J., J.M. Horridge and K. Pearson, 2000: Decomposing simulation results with respect to exogenous shocks, *Computational Economics*, **15**, 227–49

Hatton, T.J. and J.G. Williamson, 1998: *The age of mass migration: causes and economic impact*, Oxford University Press, London and New York

2002: What fundamentals drive world immigration?, CEPR Discussion Paper, 3559, London, September

Hertel, T.W. (ed.), 1997: *Global trade analysis: modelling and applications*, Cambridge University Press, Cambridge and New York

Hertel, T.W., D. Hummels, M. Ivanic and R. Keeney, 2003: How confident can we be in CGE-based assessments of free trade agreements?, GTAP Working Paper, **26**, Center for Global Trade Analysis, Purdue University, West Lafayette, May

Hertel, T.W., M. Ivanic, P.V. Preckel and J.A.L. Cranfield, 2003: Trade liberalisation and the structure of poverty in developing countries, paper prepared for the Conference on Globalization, Agricultural Development and Rural Livelihoods, Cornell University, Ithaca, 11–12 April

Hillman, A.L., 1989: *The political economy of protection*, Harwood Academic, New York

Hillman, A.L. and P. Moser, 1995: Trade liberalisation as politically optimal exchange of market access, in M. Canzoneri, W. Ethier and V. Grilli (eds.), *The new transatlantic economy*, Cambridge University Press, Cambridge and New York

Hoekman, B.M. and M. Kostecki, 2001: *The political economy of the world trading system: the WTO and beyond*, 2nd edn., Oxford University Press, London and New York

Hoekman, B., F. Ng and M. Olarreaga, 2002: Eliminating excess tariffs on exports of least developed countries, *World Bank Economic Review*, **16**, 1–21

2004: Agricultural tariffs versus subsidies: what's more important for developing countries?, *World Bank Economic Review*, **18**

Hollander, J., 2003: *The real environmental crisis: why poverty, not affluence, is the environment's number one enemy*, University of California Press, Berkeley

Ianchovichina, E. and R. McDougall, 2000: Theoretical structure of dynamic GTAP, GTAP Technical Paper, 17, Center for Global Trade Analysis, Purdue University, West Lafayette

Ianchovichina, E., A. Mattoo and M. Olarreaga, 2001: Unrestricted market access for Sub-Saharan Africa: how much is it worth and who pays?, CEPR Discussion Paper, 2820, Centre for Economic Policy Research, London, June

Irwin, D.A., 1996: *Against the tide: an intellectual history of free trade*, MIT Press, Cambridge, MA

2002: *Free trade under fire*, Princeton University Press, Princeton

Jacobson, L.S., R.J. LaLonde and D.G. Sullivan, 1993: Earnings losses of displaced workers, *American Economic Review*, **83**(4), 685–709

Just, R.E., D.L. Hueth and A. Schmitz, 1982: *Applied welfare economics and public policy*, Prentice-Hall, Englewood Cliffs, NJ

Kindleberger, C.P., 1989: Commercial policy between the wars, in P. Mathias and S. Pollard (eds.), *The Cambridge Economic History of Europe*, 8, Cambridge University Press, Cambridge

King, D.K., 2003: *GM science review: first report*, prepared by the GM Science Review Panel under the chairmanship of Sir David King for the UK Government, July

Krueger, A.B. and J. Maleckova, 2002: Education, poverty, political violence and terrorism: is there a causal connection?, NBER Working Paper, 9074, Cambridge MA, July

Krueger, A.O., 1983: *Trade and employment in developing countries*, 3: *Synthesis and conclusions*, University of Chicago Press for NBER, Chicago

1999: Free trade agreements as protectionist devices: rules of origin, in J. Melvin, J. Moore and R. Riezman (eds.), *Trade theory and econometrics: essays in honour of John S. Chipman*, Routledge, London

Lee, J.-W., 1995: Capital goods imports and long-run growth, *Journal of Development Economics*, **48**, 91–110

Lomborg, B., 2001: *The sceptical environmentalist: measuring the real state of the world*, Cambridge University Press, Cambridge and New York

Lucas, R.E. Jr., 2002: *Lectures on economic growth*, Harvard University Press, Cambridge, MA

Magee, S.P., 1972: The welfare effects of restrictions on US trade, *Brookings Papers on Economic Activity*, **3**, 645–701

Maggi, G. and A. Rodrigeuz-Clare, 1998: The value of trade agreements in the presence of political pressures, *Journal of Political Economy*, **106**(3), 574–601

Markusen, J.R., 1983: Factor movements and commodity trade as complements, *Journal of International Economics*, **13**, 341–56

Marques, G. and C. Pages 1998: Trade and employment: evidence from Latin America and the Caribbean, IDB Working Paper, **366**, Inter-American Development Bank, Washington DC

Martin, W., 1997: Measuring welfare changes with distortions, chapter 3 in J. Francois and K. Reinert (eds.), *Applied methods for trade policy analysis: a handbook*, Cambridge University Press, Cambridge and New York

Martin, W. and L.A. Winters (eds.), 1996: *The Uruguay Round and the developing countries*, Cambridge University Press, Cambridge and New York

Maskus, K. and J. Wilson (eds.), 2001: *Quantifying the impact of technical barriers to trade: can it be done?*, University of Michigan Press, Ann Arbor

Mattoo, A. and A. Subramanian, 2003: What would a development-friendly WTO architecture really look like?, IMF Working Paper, **WP/03/153**, Washington DC, August

Matusz, S. and D. Tarr 2000: Adjusting to trade policy reform, in A.O. Krueger (ed.), *Economic Policy Reform: The Second Stage*, University of Chicago Press, Chicago

Mazumdar, J. 2001: Imported machinery and growth in LDCs, *Journal of Development Economics*, **65**, 209–24

McCulloch, N., L.A. Winters and X. Cirera, 2001: *Trade liberalisation and poverty: a handbook*, Centre for Economic Policy Research, London

McDougall, R., A. Elberhnri and T.P. Truong (eds.), 1998: *Global trade, assistance, and protection: the GTAP 4 data base*, Center for Global Trade Analysis, Purdue University, West Lafayette, December

Melitz, M., 1999: The impact of trade on intra-industry reallocations and aggregate industry productivity, Economics Working Paper, Harvard University, Cambridge MA, November

Melo, J. de and D. Tarr, 1990: Welfare costs of US quotas on textiles, steel and autos, *Review of Economics and Statistics*, **72**, 489–97

Michaely, M., 2003: Goods versus factors: when borders open, who moves?, *The world economy*, **26**(4), 533–54

Michaely, M., D. Papageorgiou and A. Choksi (eds.), 1991: *Liberalizing foreign trade*, 7: *Lessons of experience in the developing world*, Basil Blackwell, Oxford

Milner, C. and P. Wright, 1998: Modelling labour market adjustment to trade liberalisation in an industrializing country, *Economic Journal*, **108**, 509–28

Moltke, A. von, C. McKee and T. Morgan, 2004: *Energy subsidies: lessons learned in assessing their impact and designing policy reforms*, Greenleaf Books for UNEP, London

Moreira, M. and S. Najberg 2000: Trade liberalization in Brazil: creating of exporting jobs?, *Journal of Development Studies*, **36**(3), 78–99

Mundell, R.A., 1957: International trade and factor mobility, *American Economic Review*, **47**, 321–35

Myers, N. and J. Kent 1998: *Perverse subsidies: tax dollars undercutting our economies and environments alike*, International Institute for Sustainable Development, Winnipeg

Nash, J. and W. Takacs 1998: Lessons from the trade expansion program, in J. Nash and W. Takacs (eds.), *Trade policy reform: lessons and implications*, World Bank, Washington DC

Neary, J.P., 2001: Of hype and hyperbolas: introducing the new economic geography, *Journal of Economic Literature*, **39**(2), 536–61

Ng, Y.-K., 1983: *Welfare economics*, Macmillan, London

Nielsen, C.P., 2003: Regional and preferential trade agreements: a literature review and identification of further steps, Report 155, Danish Research Institute of Food Economics, Copenhagen, November

OECD 1996: *Subsidies and the environment: exploring the linkages*, OECD, Paris

1997: *Reforming energy and transport subsidies: environmental and economic implications* OECD, Paris

1998: *Improving the environment through reducing subsidies*, OECD, Paris

2003a: *Agricultural trade and poverty: making policy analysis count*, OECD, Paris

2003b: *Environmentally harmful subsidies: policy issues and challenges*, OECD, Paris

Oneal, J. and B. Russett, 2000: *Triangulating peace: democracy, interdependence and international organizations*, Norton, New York

Oxfam 2002: Boxing match in agricultural trade: will WTO negotiations knock out the world's poorest farmers?, Briefing Paper, **32**, Oxfam International, Brussels

Panagariya, A., 2003: Miracles and debacles: do free-trade skeptics have a case?, University of Maryland, mimeo

Pomfret, R., 1997: *The economics of regional trading arrangements*, Oxford University Press, London

Rae, A.N. and A. Strutt, 2003: The current round of agricultural trade negotiations: should we bother about domestic support?, *Estey Centre Journal of International Law and Trade Policy*, **4**(2), 98–122

Rivera-Batiz, L. and P. Romer, 1991: International integration and endogenous growth, *Quarterly Journal of Economics*, **106**, 531–56

Rodrigeuz, F. and D. Rodrik, 2001: Trade policy and economic growth: a skeptic's guide to cross-national evidence, in B.S. Bernanke and K. Rogoff (eds.), *NBER Macroeconomics Annual 2000*, MIT Press, Cambridge, MA

Rodrik, D., 2003: Growth strategies, NBER Working Paper, **10050**, Cambridge, MA, October

Rogoff, K.S., 2003: Disinflation: an unsung benefit of globalization, *Finance and Development*, **40**(4), 54–5

Romer, P., 1986: Increasing returns and long-run growth, *Journal of Political Economy*, **94**(5), 1002–37

1994: New goods, old theory, and the welfare costs of trade restrictions, *Journal of Development Economics*, **43**(1), 5–38

Runge, C.F., B. Senauer, P.G. Pardey and M.W. Rosegrant, 2003: *Ending hunger in our lifetime: food security and globalization*, Johns Hopkins University Press for IFPRI, Baltimore, MD and London

Rutherford, T.F. and D.G. Tarr, 2002: Trade liberalisation, product variety and growth in a small open economy: a quantitative assessment, *Journal of International Economics*, **56**(2), 247–72

Sachs, J.D. and A. Warner, 1995: Economic reform and the process of global integration, *Brookings Papers on Economic Activity*, **1**, 1–95

Sala-i-Martin, X., 2002: The world distribution of income (estimated from individual country distributions), NBER Working Paper, **8933**, Cambridge, MA, May

Schiff, M. and Y. Wang 2004: On the quantity and quality of knowledge: the impact of openness and Foreign R&D on North–North and North–South technology Spillovers, World Bank Policy Research Working Paper, **3190**, Washington DC

Schiff, M. and L.A. Winters, 2003: *Regional integration and development*, Oxford University Press for the World Bank, London

Taylor, M.S., 1999: Trade and trade policy in endogenous growth models, chapter 15 in J. Piggott and A. Woodland (eds.), *International trade policy and the pacific rim*, Macmillan for the IAE, London

Trefler, D., 2001: The long and short of the Canada–US free trade agreement, NBER Working Paper, **8293**, Cambridge, MA, May

UNCTAD/Commonwealth Secretariat, 2001: *Duty and quota free market access for LDCs: an analysis of Quad initiatives*, UNCTAD, Geneva and Commonwealth Secretariat, London

USITC, 1997: The dynamic effects of trade liberalisation: an empirical analysis, Investigation 332–375, Publication 3069, United States International Trade Commission, Washington, DC, October

Verikios, G. and X.-G. Zhang, 2001: Global gains from liberalising trade in telecommunications and financial services, Staff Research Paper, Productivity Commission, Canberra

Wacziarg, R., 2001: Measuring the dynamic gains from trade, *World Bank Economic Review*, **15**(3), 393–429

Wacziarg, R. and K.H. Welch, 2003: Trade liberalisation and growth: new evidence, NBER Working Paper, **10152**, Cambridge, MA, December

Whalley, J., 1985: *Trade liberalisation among major world trading areas*, MIT Press, Cambridge MA

2000: What can the developing countries infer from the Uruguay Round models for future negotiations?, Policy Issues in International Trade and Commodities Study Series, 4, UNCTAD, Geneva

2003: Assessing the benefits to developing countries of liberalisation in services trade, NBER Working Paper, **10181**, Cambridge, MA, December

Williamson, J.G., 2002: Winners and losers over two centuries of globalization, WIDER Annual Lecture, 6, United Nations University, Helsinki

Winters, L.A., 2002: Trade liberalisation and poverty: what are the links?, *The World Economy*, **25**(9), 1339–68

Winters, L.A., N. McCulloch and A. McKay, 2004: Trade liberalisation and poverty: the empirical evidence, *Journal of Economic Literature*, **62**(1), 72–115

Winters, L.A. and W.E. Takacs, 1991: Labour adjustment costs and British footwear protection, *Oxford Economic Papers*, **43**, 479–501

Winters, L.A., T. Walmsley, Z.K. Wang and R. Grynberg, 2003: Liberalizing temporary movement of natural persons: an agenda for the development round, *The World Economy*, **26**(8), 1137–61

World Bank, 2003a: *Global economic prospects and the developing countries 2002: making trade work for the poor*, World Bank, Washington, DC

2003b: *Global economic prospects 2004: realizing the development promise of the Doha agenda*, World Bank, Washington, DC, September

WWF 2001: *Hard facts, hidden problems: a review of current data on fisheries subsidies*, WWF, Washington, DC

Alternative Perspectives

Perspective Paper 10.1

JAN PRONK

In chapter 10 in this volume, Kym Anderson argues that phasing out wasteful subsidies and trade barriers should be given first priority, for three reasons:

1 The direct economic costs are low and the benefits in terms of trade expansion and economic growth are high
2 Trade liberalisation and reform would enable the world to allocate resources more efficiently and would set resources free in order to meet other pressing needs (including the other challenges addressed in the Copenhagen Consensus)
3 In addition, trade liberalisation and reform would also directly address these other challenges, including poverty (and poverty-related-issues in the fields of education, health, water and nutrition), environmental degradation, climate change, governance (conflicts, corruption, financial instability) and migration.

I will argue that the first two reasons are valid, but that their relevance requires further scrutiny of the political options. The third reason, in my view, is true only if specific conditions are met, outside the realm of trade itself. I will call them 'sustainability conditions'. Meeting them requires political action in other fields than trade. Not meeting them is also jeopardizing the political opportunities to make better use of the potential of trade liberalisation and economic reform.

The Challenge

Anderson defines the challenge as a global one: to rid the world of wasteful and anti-poor distortionary trade policies. In order to keep the task manageable he limits the consideration of the policy instruments to those trade-related ones over which a government's international trade negotiators have some influence. Limiting oneself to trade distortions at national borders and trade-distorting production subsidies for reasons of measurement and comparison is fully understandable. Since the 1980s an impressive global database has been developed that includes data on trade tariffs, taxes and subsidies, on quantitative restrictions (QRs) and technical barriers to trade as well as on trade-distorting production subsidies. Building and refining the data base for about eighty counties and country groups, together spanning the world, and about sixty sectors, spanning the entire economy is an important accomplishment. In the early 1980s, in UNCTAD, when I had the responsibility for a smooth functioning of a number of specific multilateral trade negotiations, we were still lacking such a comprehensive database. We had to limit ourselves to simple world models and multi-sectoral national and regional models that were complemented by sectoral and national cost-benefit analyses (CBAs) of alternative trade policies. Using global multi-sectoral computable general equilibrium (CGE) models is a great step forward in the analysis of different scenarios. It provides policy makers with much more insight into the effects of possible alternative policies.

Among these policy makers trade negotiators play an important role. In the practical reality of international trade negotiations they take crucial decisions. However, behind them there are the governments themselves. They give the instructions. They are accountable *vis-à-vis* the population and the business sector for the results or non-results of the negotiations. The governments, not the trade negotiators, are responsible for the overall economic, social, financial and budgetary policy of a country. That includes decisions concerning taxation, public expenditure on infrastructure, social welfare, the environment as well as health and education. Consideration of this category of policy measures has been excluded from the analysis. This is understandable because there is not yet a comprehensive global database that includes the data concerned and because corresponding world models would become unmanageable. However, an analysis of the challenge to redress distortionary policies and opportunities to free resources in order to meet social and economic needs and to alleviate poverty – as intended in the Copenhagen Consensus – should not be limited to a consideration of trade policies. In practice, governments are managing their economies with the help of all the policy instruments at their disposal, and they try to harmonise them. That implies also harmonisation between trade measures and domestic policies. Trade policies do affect the economic and social perspectives of both people and business. Domestic policies will either positively or negatively influence the social, economic and political capacity of a country to commit itself towards more free trade. Examples of such policies, that can boost or retard the ability and willingness of a government to engage itself into a speedy trade liberalisation, are the facilitation of production capacities, investments in research and education, the establishment of social safety nets and measures to avoid environmental pollution and a deterioration of the biodiversity. In a consideration of opportunities to alleviate major challenges confronting the population of the various nations of the world, it is up to (democratic) governments to assess the alternatives. Governments, more than

experts or bureaucrats responsible for specific sectors, have the duty to weigh the various objectives. More than anybody else they can influence, directly as well as indirectly, the allocation of resources and the application of all relevant policy instruments concerned. For this reason a consideration of trade policies should go hand in hand with a consideration of domestic policies.

There is a second reason. The distribution of the fruits of trade among countries as well as within countries will be unequal. Trade is not the culprit, trade takes place in the context of a given degree of inequality between nations and population groups. The allocation of production factors, their remuneration and the distribution of costs and benefits among market partners will reflect that inequality. Whether the resources set free by open and more efficient trade relations will be used to address the challenges concerned will depend on their allocation, and thus on a combination of market forces and public policies.

A third reason why we should not limit our attention to the potential benefits of trade expansion is that trade is not an aim in itself. The ultimate objective of economic policy making is not to expand trade, but to increase income and welfare. Trade is an instrument. Its expansion should be assessed against the objectives. It is always the relationship that matters: trade and growth, trade and welfare, trade and development, trade and the environment. And because the objectives are manifold trade should also be seen in relation to other intermediary instruments and policies: trade and investment, trade and finance, trade and competition, trade and labour, trade and technology.

The Arguments

In his chapter Anderson presents the well-known arguments for free trade: static economic gains resulting from an optimum allocation of resources in a world characterised by competition, plus dynamic gains, because openness contributes to investment, knowledge, innovation, productivity and growth. This is classical theory, more and more refined in the latter half of the twentieth century. It has been substantiated by econometric studies and empirical evidence.

The author mentions two caveats. First, ascribing causality is not easy, because parallel to trade many other factors influence economic growth. Though recent developments in the theory of economic growth have provided us with more insight into the relative importance of factors explaining growth, we will never be certain about the causality and the mutual relations between those factors in specific circumstances. However, as is also argued by Anderson, economic history shows that open economies grow faster and that autarkic economies tend to stagnation. So, policy makers and governments can safely assume that openness is better. However, that does not mean that openness is enough. There is a second caveat, also mentioned by the author: trade openness is a necessary, but not a sufficient, condition for sustained economic growth. In order to make good use of openness a country needs good institutions, functioning markets and macroeconomic and political stability.

These are important conditions. What if the domestic conditions are not fulfilled? Is more openness and more free trade always good under such circumstances? Moreover, do these conditions determine trade or does trade also affect the conditions? In other words: could more and open trade not result in a weakening of institutions, less stability and a deterioration of market relations? That complete openness is not always necessary is shown by the example of the Asian 'tigers'. The newly industrializing countries of East Asia in the 1970s did experience unprecedented trade expansion and high economic growth with the help of much public intervention, aggressive policies, managed trade, gradual opening of markets.

Fast market reforms can also create problems. For a long period China has witnessed two-digit growth figures, among others facilitated by a massive and speedy access to world markets. But within China this unprecedented growth rate gives rise to economic and environmental distortions. Pollution is enormous, jeopardizing people's health. Easy lending has resulted in a huge overhang of bad loans, threatening the banking system, financial stability and people's confidence. Moreover, in the world outside China Chinese competition on the basis

of its comparative cost advantage may lead to an increase in unemployment that cannot easily be matched by increased exports to China. Without a comprehensive international approach, integrating policies concerning trade, investment, finance and money, this could violate the stability of trading partners and of the world economy.

That a gradual and conditional opening of markets can be a wise policy is shown by the EU. Long negotiations had to take place in order reach agreement with the accessory countries. These negotiations dealt with the consequences of European expansion for markets in both the old and the new Europe: agriculture, transport, internal migration, competition, environmental legislation. Nobody dared, for instance, to argue in favour of a prompt establishment of a fully free agricultural market within the enlarged EU. Countries were willing to further liberalise agriculture, because everybody realised that the allocation of resources was highly inefficient and that subsidies could not be sustained. But at the same time there was fear for social consequences, as had also been the case during the negotiations to enlarge the then 'old Europe' with Spain, Greece and Portugal. Were those fears not justified? The position of farmers outside Europe is much worse. That alone would justify a removal of the barriers that those farmers have to overcome when they want to export to Europe. But this does not render the fears inside Europe itself irrational. Rural conditions within Europe are not only a burden on the European economy; they also reflect certain values. For similar reasons, Austria was afraid that a free transportation market would irreversibly violate the environment in the Alps. Not everything can be compensated through a reallocation of resources set free by expanded trade.

Many fears are related to specific interests. They can be addressed with rational economic counterarguments. However, are all such fears irrational? Can all arguments for protectionism be 'found wanting in almost all circumstances in that a lower-cost domestic policy instrument is available to meet each of those objectives' (Anderson 2004)? Anderson argues that the most compelling explanation for their persistence is a political economy one. Indeed, but that does not render them irrational or inferior.

Anderson points out that the source of resistance to policy reforms is that 'the expected losses in jobs, income and wealth are concentrated in the hands of a few who are prepared to support politicians who resist protection cuts, while the gains are sufficiently small per consumer and export firm and are distributed widely as to make it not worthwhile for those potential gainers to lobby for reform.' I agree that this is often the case. However, resistance to reforms often also is based on more general considerations, instead of specific group interests. Anyway, whether the resistance were socially justified or not, it is a political fact, related to questions of distribution. To address such resistance would require a broad analysis of all relevant factors, perhaps with the help of models that include political variables and equations. Anderson seems to admit this himself, when he concludes the paragraph concerned with the statement that 'the observed pattern of protection in a country at a point in time may well be an equilibrium outcome in a national political market for policy intervention' (Anderson 2004).

If so, then the policy measures suggested are not adequate. Better information dissemination concerning the potential benefits from reducing trade distortions will not be sufficient. Many parties – consumers, labourers as well as producers – do not see these feature as trade distortions, but as mechanisms to restore, protect or sustain a socio-economic and political balance in the economy or in the nation. To inform them about the costs involved, for them as well as for others, and thus about the potential benefits of removing the costs, will not suffice. They will envisage the removal of the trade distortions as paving the way for other distortions and as a possible source of uncertainty and instability. They will therefore weigh the costs and potential benefits differently. Is that irrational? Sometimes, but not always, because the initial situation preceding trade reform and before more freedom is introduced on markets, is one of inequality in welfare as well as in political power.

Will technological change and the unilateral opening up of markets abroad contribute to a different understanding and weighing of the benefits and costs? Yes, in so far as trading costs are lowered and economic gains to be reaped come nearby. Anderson rightly points out that this is happening in the present era of globalisation. However, at the same time the perceived uncertainties and threats come closer. Financial and monetary instabilities increase with globalisation, and economic inequality as well. Foreign control of investments, and thus of production, commercial and trade systems and sales, also increases with globalisation. This may retard the willingness to actively contribute to a further opening up. Because of the inequalities mentioned earlier, such reluctance is not irrational. Even when it is clear that further liberalisation will contribute to growth and will help create more resources, it is uncertain who will reap he benefits and whether inequalities may not increase. It is too simple to conceive of this in terms of an 'alarmist lobbying of protectionists' (Anderson 2004) alone. Such lobbies exist and do harm; however, there are also legitimate fears that cannot be taken away by merely more and better information. Such fears can be countered only through a serious and comprehensive approach that goes beyond creating expectations and beyond promises.

International trade agreements, as widely representative for all the interests concerned as possible, would be the most credible way to begin addressing these fears. They form the best opportunity to bargain and exchange access and opportunities. Anderson rightly points out that the chances of success are greater the larger the number of countries involved and the broader the product and issues coverage of the negotiations. But here again, it will not be simple. Like all other modalities of trade policy making multilateral negotiations take place in a context of both international and national inequality. Inequalities at home imply rigidity in the position of the negotiation partners. They may fear instability at home resulting from a different assessments and weighing of the outcome of the negotiation among various groups at home. For this reason, they cannot afford to be very flexible in the negotiations. Their governments can try to prevent or compensate this by means of specific domestic economic and social policies. However, these policies are costly and will have to be financed out of the economic gains resulting from the expanding trade opportunities. Sometimes these opportunities have a different time frame. Often they cannot easily be taxed. All this will mean that the governments will be rather cautious in their instructions to their trade negotiators and that the negotiators themselves will exercise restraint.

This will add to a cautious approach that the same governments will choose because of the other inequality – that between the negotiating countries themselves. It is self-evident that this inequality leads to a lengthy negotiation process. The fact that previous rounds of negotiation have led to quite unequal results for the trading partners – the OECD countries benefited much more than most developing countries – and also the fact that many commitments and promises resulting from these negotiations have not yet been implemented will add to the reluctance to engage themselves in further rounds of talks, not to speak of new negotiations. Even if new rounds more or less objectively could be considered as beneficial to the world economy as a whole, weaker negotiation partners will stay reluctant. This, for instance, is the case for negotiations concerning services and investment. The reluctance of weaker developing countries to engage themselves in the (MAI) negotiations and in talks concerning the so-called 'Singapore issues' is understandable in the light of the above.

It is also understandable that other countries are eager to speed up negotiations and action. They want to expand trade and boost the opportunities for growth and they are less afraid of an unequal distribution of the results. Because in their view multilateral negotiations become more and more cumbersome, they increasingly choose a different path: bilateral and regional negotiations, with free trade areas (FTAs) involving only a sub-set of countries. Anderson rightly warns against such an approach. Trade may be diverted from lower-cost developing countries, worsening the situation for non-participants in these talks. It is therefore meaningful to analyse empirically the likely gains from different types of prospective agreements. This is done in Anderson's chapter, where he presents the results of a variety of empirical studies. The usage of the term 'empirical' is a little misleading, however. It remains a theoretical exercise, with the help of quantifiable data and empirically tested models that by their very nature cannot reflect political realities. The outcome of the scenario exercise remains

an abstract possibility. Whether it can be turned into a reality will depend on many factors outside the limits of trade policy alone.

The Opportunities

Anderson present estimates for four different categories of trade liberalisation: (1) a world free of trade barriers and subsidies, (2) non-preferential legally binding partial trade liberalisation, (3) reciprocal preferential legally binding trade liberalisation, and (4) non-reciprocal preferential trade agreements. The potential benefits of full trade liberalisation are tremendous, though their estimates widely diverge, depending on the assumptions made. The author carefully mentions the assumptions underlying the estimates: the definition of the baseline scenario (full implementation of the commitments made in the Uruguay Round, with or without the completion of the accession of China to the WTO and of the EU eastern enlargement), constant returns to scale versus economies of scale, perfect versus monopolistic competition, with or without trade in services in addition to trade in goods, static versus dynamic efficiency gains. Possible benefits resulting from the lowering of barriers to international capital and labour movements and from the lowering of subsidies outside the sector of agriculture, notably the energy subsidies are generally excluded in most of the scenarios. There are also different assumptions concerning the extent to which the liberalisation of agricultural markets will draw resources from other sectors in the economy. The wide divergence between the outcomes strongly reflects different combinations of the assumptions underlying the various models. However, some general conclusions can be drawn. First, trade liberalisation by developing countries is very important, in particular in the framework of South–South trade. This conclusion reflects the predominance of protection in developing countries themselves. Second, liberalisation of the services sector, including capital services, foreign direct investment (FDI) and labour migration will offer many opportunities for growth, though the precise magnitude of the effects is still uncertain. Third, trade facilitation, an area that is often neglected, deserves more attention. This last conclusion can be interpreted as an indication that non-tariff barriers (NTBs) are an even greater barrier to trade and more difficult to handle than tariffs and subsidies. Examples of such NTBs, other than customs clearance, are health and sanitary regulations (SPs) and safety measures. These trade measures are not so easily quantifiable and comparable as tariffs and subsidies and not easily manageable in negotiations that require a bargain. But they have become quite popular and increasingly replace traditional trade barriers.

There is no reason to dispute the outcome of the computations. They represent the state of the art. The question is not whether the estimates are right, but whether they are relevant. After all, also without the help of global modelling in the period following the Second World War policy makers knew that the macroeconomic benefits of trade liberalisation could be enormous. They knew that also before the war, there was ample economic literature making a convincing case for trade liberalisation. Before the war; and in particular after the Crash of 1929, policy makers had not listened well. After 1945 they had learned their lesson and gradually embarked on a mutual removal of barriers to trade. The result was a series of multilateral negotiations, though not world-wide. Experience with the trade rounds is not bad. Governments were serious. They knew what was at stake (Cairncross *et al.* 1982). In the course of half a century many tariffs were substantially reduced, though there are still rather high tariff peaks and tariff patterns discriminating against processing of raw materials and intermediate products in countries where they have been produced, increasingly countries that had shown a clear preference in favour of protectionism and import substitution became willing to liberalise trade and to implement market reform. At first this was a by-product of adjustment policies that were more or less imposed upon them by financing institutions, but later this tendency became more endogenous. There is, however, a mixed reading of that experience. Some authors claim that developing countries have shown a substantial willingness to unilaterally opt for reform (Whalley 1989). Others, like Bhagwati, were much more sceptical (Bhagwati 1991).

Negotiations were limited to tariffs and to manufacturing sectors. These limitations constrained the capacity to liberalise fully among all countries, but they also made the negotiations manageable. During the Dillon Round, the Kennedy Round and the Tokyo Round the 'low-hanging fruit' was reaped. These negotiations also helped to counter inclinations to return to protectionism. But protectionist tendencies still had their way in the form of NTBs and restrictive business practices. Moreover, commodities and agriculture still were outside the scope of these rounds. These subjects were dealt with in different international gremia. The Uruguay Round negotiators reached the limits of what was possible within the prevailing trading system. No wonder that, after about half a century, it was deemed necessary to broaden the scope. GATT was turned into WTO, which meant that investment, services and agriculture got a prominent place on the agenda, next to trade in goods. It also implied a broadening from tariff barriers to all barriers to trade. And it meant a widening of the partnership in the negotiations: with the Former Soviet Union (FSU) and with China as well as with developing countries. The latter had been followers of what basically were West–West negotiations. The entry into force of WTO as the successor of GATT increased their chances to become equal partners in the talks. Formally that was the case, but it had to be given shape and content in the negotiations that followed.

No wonder that since the early 1990s the broadened negotiation process slowed down. The reason was not that countries had become more protectionist; governments had not become less aware of the potential benefits of trade liberalisation, such as the benefits estimated in macro terms by the economists that built the GTAP database and variations of the CGE model. However, they found it more difficult than before to cope with the institutional intricacies of globalisation and with the uncertainties resulting from globalisation. They had to learn to deal with the complications resulting from the multiple broadening of the negotiations, as reflected in the mandate and the composition of the WTO.

No wonder, also, that many governments resorted to alternatives to real multilateral negotiations on a world scale. The 1990s saw a preference for regional reciprocal or non-reciprocal trade liberalisation areas. Governments chose such options not because they had become less oriented to free trade, but because they wanted to combine more free trade with more speed than would be possible in a fully multilateral framework and with more certainties than would be possible in a fully global context.

One could explain the efforts emerging towards the end of the millennium in two different ways, either as tendency towards more protectionism, or as trade liberalisation in stages. The failure in Cancun to further the implementation of the Doha commitments, the harsh language used by the EU as well as the USA and the newly established group of bigger and more advanced developing countries and the regional approaches chosen by the USA as well as the EU (combining regional free trade areas with trade measures against non-members) can be conceived as a return to protectionism. The estimates of the benefits of various regional approaches towards trade expansion, as summarised by Anderson, indicate that, to a great extent, these benefits are achieved to the detriment of third parties. Harmful trade diversion may arise from the establishment of a Free Trade Area of the Americas (FTAA) as well as from the EU 'everything but arms' (EBA) initiative to provide duty- and quota-free access to exports of all LDCs.

However, are these examples of a conscious choice in favour of protectionism or are such policy steps meant to be a gradual approach towards a further liberalisation of markets? Recent developments in trade policy can also be explained as an effort to follow a 'two-track' approach, parallel or in stages: a slow WTO process in combination with an intensification of bilateral and regional trade negotiations, both with the objective to enlarge trade, but in such a way that the economic and social consequences of that enlargement can be managed. The problem, however, as has been made clear by many authors, is that the second track renders the first track less and less feasible, because it undermines the rule-based character of a global system, eroding the principles which in earlier stages had been agreed by all countries. It is not enough to address such a tendency by highlighting the wonders of trade liberalisation or by investing, as suggested by Anderson, $1 or $2 bn per annum in research and advocacy, in order to counter the lobbying of entrenched protectionist forces and to change public opinion. I agree with Anderson that in present circumstances a policy choice has to be made in favour of what the author calls 'a multi-pronged approach': unilateral reform at the national level and multilateral reform at the WTO level, supplemented by regional support for both, in a form of open MFN regionalism. I consider this politically feasible, because I interpret recent developments not as a tendency towards protectionism but as a preference for a double-track approach. I also agree with Anderson that in such a multi-pronged approach there is no place for an expansion of regional preferential trade arrangements. These would harm third parties, erode an efficient allocation of resources at home and undermine efforts to achieve a better multilateral agreement later. It is my personal experience from trade negotiations that temporary preferential treatment, enjoyed by initially less developed countries and granted to them on the basis of infant-economy considerations in order to overcome time-bound handicaps, turns out to stay. It is difficult to reduce preferences, let alone to remove them, because beneficiaries see them as established rights; it is nearly impossible to replace them by other measures intended to assist the integration of the country into the world economy at equal footing.

However, to choose in favour of a multi-pronged approach is more easily said than done. It certainly cannot be confined to trade measures only. More information dissemination regarding the benefits of free trade is not sufficient. Advocacy is not enough: policy makers are already aware of the potential effects; they are weary about the uncertainties. Vos, for instance, has shown that since 1980 trade liberalisation in Latin America has resulted in import dependence rising more strongly than the capacity to export. As a result, for these countries' capital flows have become more important to sustain a growth path built on a combination of increasing reliance on exports and a structural rise in the trade deficit. Moreover, as Vos found out, capital flows reinforced this pattern by pushing up real exchange rates, cheapening imports and squeezing profits for exporters in the short run (Vos *et al.* 2004).

A multi-pronged approach should therefore be constructed in such a way that the real impediments can be removed: unequal treatment, social instability, transition costs, financial constraints and increasing foreign debt. Impediments to trade should be dealt with in conjunction with other macroeconomic constraints. The answer to the fears lies in elaborating a world trading system that (1) is truly rules-based, (2) guarantees equal treatment of all partners, (3) is comprehensive and in tune with the world financial system and that (4) ensures sustainability. After the end of the Cold War and in response to the international economic stagnation and adjustment of the 1980s the world trading system has been reformed, in order to render it more adequate to address the needs that could not be taken care of by GATT (Pronk 1987). However, the new impetus to globalisation since then demands a further reform of the world economic system, without which claims to further open up economies will not easily be honoured by all participating countries. This will require, among others, a further reform of WTO in relation to a reform of the Bretton Woods system and of international debt management procedures (Carlsson and Ramphal 1995; Sampson 2000).

Benefits and Costs

Provided that such a comprehensive, multi-pronged approach could be followed, then the estimates of the gross economic benefits, by 2010, from a 50 per cent reduction of subsidies and trade barriers ('optimistic Doha Round'), as summarised in table 10.3 of Anderson's chapter, would not only have a strong theoretical basis but could also become politically realistic. In that table a range of estimates is presented, on the basis of different assumptions. The author concludes that the comparative static gains could lie somewhere between the extremes presented in the table. Both estimates refer to liberalisation of trade in both goods and services. The low estimate (Francois, van Meijl and van Tongeren 2003–2) assumes cuts in bound tariffs, constant returns to scale and perfect competition and does not include liberalisation of services. The high extreme (Brown, Deardorff and Stern 2003) assumes cuts in applied tariffs, increasing returns to scale, monopolistic competition and firm-level differentiated products. It is strongly dependent on the inclusion in services liberalisation of the opening to FDI. One

can safely assume that many (not all) sectors are characterised by oligopolistic competition and by economies of scale. Whether or not negotiations will result in cuts of applied or bound tariffs is uncertain and may partly depend on the size of the cuts. This is a political choice, as is the decision to include services and investment. All in all Anderson's conclusion that the static welfare gains could lie somewhere in the middle seems to be reasonable. However, they may take more than five years to accrue fully, because (in particular) the liberalisation of services and trade will call for capacity adjustments.

A 50 per cent reduction in trade barriers is an optimistic scenario. Full liberalisation is not on the cards. Presently modest cuts are more likely – for instance, a pessimistic Doha Round scenario, implying 25 per cent reduction of trade barriers. However, the degree of optimism attached to the scenarios may depend more on the *coverage* than on the size of the cuts. It is likely that agricultural products – though not all – will be included. It is also likely that tariffs and subsidies will be more heavily reduced than other NTBs. Including services and investment is still disputed strongly. In particular, the inclusion of the latter could lead to more dynamism in the world economy than the more likely further reductions of trade barriers in agriculture and industry.

It would not be far-fetched to assume that additional dynamic gains from trade will be higher the greater the coverage of trade liberalisation. Reducing only tariffs will produce less additional endogenous economic growth than reducing tariffs and subsidies and NTBs. The latter will provide more certainties to entrepreneurs and will be a greater incentive to investment. Including services and investment will lead to even much greater dynamic gains, because wholly new investment opportunities will arise and new markets will open up. Anderson's expectation, that in addition to the static welfare gains the dynamic gains from trade will be substantial, is plausible. However, their size will depend on the coverage of the liberalisation. This is in particular true for developing countries. Anderson assumes that trade reforms may boost economic growth in developing countries by one-third and in developed countries by one-sixth. In his view, this is a conservative assumption in the light of the experience of successful reformers such as China, India, Korea and Chile. I agree. So, I have no reason to dispute the summary estimates presented by the author in the chapter: GDP growth in 2015 of 3.1 per cent for developed countries, 6.1 per cent for developing countries and thus 3.8 per cent for the world as a whole. However, I wonder whether it is justified to assume that those rates will continue until 2050. The dynamic gains from trade will gradually diminish, sustaining them may require new initiatives.

These estimates result from calculations on the basis of a combination of both conservative and optimistic assumptions. In the light of economic history, such growth rates is attainable. The assumptions are not overly ambitious. For instance, the growth rate of 6.1 per cent for developing countries is in line with internationally agreed policy targets for GDP growth of developing countries that since 1960 have been laid down in the subsequent Strategies for the United Nations Development Decades. However, such rates will not easily be achieved.

Why not? There are three reasons. First, the benefits are *not distributed equally among trading partners*. The positions taken by various country groups during the first phase of the Doha Round, and in particular at the Cancun mid-term review, show that countries are aware of this and acting correspondingly. To a certain extent this is due to a lack of experience of negotiators in a new setting and this can be overcome. However, there are also substantial differences. Francois, van Meijl and van Tongeren show that agricultural liberalisation offers a mixed set of results, even against expectations: positive for Europe, Asia and Northern Africa, negative for SSA, potentially negative for the Asia-Pacific region and North America, neutral for Latin America. The same authors also show that China will be hurt by a liberalisation of manufacturing. It will meet stiffer competition from other developing countries and experience a decreasing terms of trade (Francois, van Meijl and van Tongeren 2003–4). Vos *et al.*, with the help of CGE models for Latin American countries, found that, unlike the Asian experience, export-led growth in Latin America has proved so far to be anything but a 'development miracle'. They show that for some Latin American

countries free trade under the WTO or the FTAA will have a negative impact on agriculture which is not compensated by sufficient employment and income growth in other sectors (Vos *et al.* 2004). These are examples only. The results of the calculations depend strongly on the assumptions made, and some assumptions are less realistic than others. Will liberalised and expanding agricultural sectors (with constant returns to scale) really draw substantial resources from modern industry that is characterised by increasing returns to scale? But the examples make clear that, for good reasons, different negotiation partners will have different expectations. This cannot easily be solved, either in negotiations of a rather limited scope, nor in the framework of negotiations which are fully representative for all interests concerned.

The second reason is that the *benefits per country are also distributed unequally*. The benefits of international trade policies so far have been utterly unequal. These policies are a combination of free trade and protectionism, *à la carte*, selective and characterised by a fair amount of arbitrariness in the granting of preferences and the mix between reciprocity and non-reciprocity. The benefits were bought at the cost of many poor countries and many poor people, within both more and less advanced economies. Europe, for instance, in combining ACP free trade with the continuation of its Common Agricultural Policy (CAP) has done much harm to farmers both within ACP countries and in other developing countries. Poor farmers world-wide have suffered from the functioning of international commodity markets (sugar, bananas, cotton, rubber, cocoa and others) with decreasing terms of trade, overproduction, subsidies to commodity producing farmers in the USA and the EU, preferential treatments, unilaterally set rules of origin, market speculation and the development of technologically new substitutes. International talks to remove all of these and other barriers will create a new perspective for the victims of these practices. But the winners of today will be the losers of tomorrow and it is not only a matter of rich versus poor. It is much more complicated, and this explains why negotiations in the field of trade will have to be complemented by *internationally harmonised domestic policies* that can result in a fair balance in all countries.

The third reason is that for all negotiation partners there are *costs* involved and these costs are higher than often is assumed. Anderson, referring to studies in particular of manufacturing in the USA and Europe, argues that the costs involved – private costs of adjustment for firms and workers and social costs in the form of social safety nets, unemployment schemes and retraining and reintegration – are minor. They are one-off costs, transitional, and should be weighed against the non-stop flow of economic benefits from reform. Anderson does not want to overstate the net gains from trade and therefore presents an estimate of the costs amounting to 40 per cent of the gross static benefits under full liberalisation and 30 per cent (resp. 25 per cent) in an optimistic or pessimistic Doha Round. Anderson also assumes that these costs will last no longer than five years. In my view, however, the costs are much higher. It is difficult to question overall average percentages. But trade negotiations seem to relate only to whole economies. In fact, they concern specific sectors and industries. In macro terms the costs of trade liberalisation may be far less than the benefits, but per sector or region this is often very different In some cases, for instance when full liberalisation threatens the continuation of an industry, these are higher than the benefits. The benefits will accrue elsewhere and will not easily be used to finance compensation or restructuring benefiting the industry or region concerned. For a number of traditional sectors one cannot speak of one-off costs. The costs involved will have to be borne by a full generation consisting of people that can no longer be retrained and reintegrated in the economy. In such cases one may have to take into account a period of twenty-five rather than five years. Often the next generation – the children of workers laid off in extractive industries or in traditional manufacturing enterprises that are downsized or closed – will also be affected. In agriculture the costs will also be borne by others: people living in rural areas, not only in the less productive agricultural sectors in Europe and the USA, but above all in developing countries. For many of these people small-scale subsistence agriculture is more than an economic activity; it is a means to survive, a living, a culture, a way of life. Some of these people can be hired as farm labourers, others as unskilled labourers in industry. Many would be fully

uprooted, they themselves as well as their families and the next generation. The economic, social, psychological and cultural costs are neither minor, nor one-off or transitional. They are long-term, structural and major.

They will be complemented by costs for the environment because traditional production techniques in harmony with the natural environment and with available scarce natural resources will get lost. There will also be a possible loss in terms of landscape and biodiversity. All this may easily translate into political costs: more poverty, less cohesion, more turmoil. In theory, policies to redress and compensate all this ought to be financed out of the benefits resulting from reform. However, as argued above, these benefits often accrue to population strata that cannot easily be taxed by the government, in particular because the reforms take place in the framework of an economic philosophy that emphasises the market and demands a retreat of the public sector. Moreover, not all such costs are of an economic character, lending themselves to specific forms of compensation. And they last much longer than a transition period of five years. All this explains a reluctance of governments to engage themselves in opening up their economies. The reason is not only, as argued by Anderson, that the losses in jobs and asset values are concentrated, whereas the gains in terms of new jobs and investment opportunities are thinly spread, and are less attributable to trade reform, taken up by people other than those losing from the reform. For many countries and sectors this is a relevant political analysis, not only in the Western industrialised countries, but also in developing countries such as India, where the middle class is benefiting from new opportunities due to the opening of markets such as in information services. However, in many sectors and countries, in particular in agriculture in less advanced Northern economies and in the Third World, it is the other way around: the losses are widely spread and cut deeply into the existence of people while the initial concrete benefits are concentrated in the hands of a new class. Whether there will be also long-term benefits in the form of structural employment opportunities for many people is often uncertain, also because new industries, often financed with foreign capital, disregard the comparative advantage of the countries involved and rather choose capital-intensive production technologies. Especially nowadays, in a more and more globalised economy, the ample availability of labour becomes a relatively less important factor in decisions of enterprises to invest and to choose a particular location. The resulting uncertainty is, for governments, an additional reason to go slow with reforms.

For these reasons, I am less positive than Anderson about the relation between trade reform and poverty alleviation. Trade reform can reduce the income gap between developed and developing countries, provided that it takes place within a comprehensive approach. In doing so, trade reform will enhance the capacity and help increase the resources necessary to implement pro-poor policies within poorer countries. Trade reform will also contribute to higher economic growth within developing countries. Whether the increased capacity will be used for that purpose, however, will depend on the policies pursued and on the economic and social structure of the country. Market reforms can also lead to new distortions and new inequalities, to the detriment of the poor people, and to more rather than less poverty. As has been documented by many studies, since the early 1990s inequalities have widened both within and between countries. That phenomenon took place at the same time that, parallel to increasing trade and a strong emphasis on economic liberalisation and market reform, world economic growth was very high and sustained for an unprecedently long period. The conclusion is warranted that the world has never been so rich as in the period just before the end of the millennium. Foreseeing this, after the end of the Cold War at the World Summit on Environment and Development in 1992, governments promised to use the additional resources which would be set free by reforms and growth for the implementation of policies to reduce poverty. Commitments were made to increase international income transfers to poor countries and to carry out specific anti-poverty programmes in the fields of water, health, education and food and agriculture.

A decade later, we must admit that this promise has not been kept. International assistance went down, anti-poverty programmes stagnated,

inequalities increased and the number of poor people in terms of income poverty as well as human poverty is as high as it used to be. No wonder that poor countries are suspicious with regard to the promise that new trade negotiations after Doha will lead to less poverty. Some market liberalisation in the field of agriculture, for instance, will lead to increased consumer prices in food-importing developing countries. Other reforms will result in upsetting traditional agrarian systems and land use patterns, depriving the poor of the use of essential resources. Market reforms aiming at price liberalisation, a retreat of the public sector and more incentives for private enterprise in essential sectors such as health and education have similar consequences. It not only a matter of good governance along the lines set out in studies such as the ones by Dollar and Kraay (2002) that could countervail this. Criteria of good governance accompanying market reform, as advocated since 1990, and applied in international policies concerning trade, finance, aid and debt have often produced a counterproductive effect. Governments were more or less forced to diminish public efforts to decrease poverty (Pronk, 2001, 2003a, 2003b). Expectations similar to those quoted by Anderson on the basis of recent studies and estimates concerning the number of poor people in rural areas who could find a better living after reforms, because there would be an increased demand for both farm products and their off-farm labour, were also raised in the late 1980s. They have not been fulfilled. China was an exception, but in Africa and in South Asia urban and rural poverty increased, despite a certain degree of liberalisation (UNDP 2003). One could perhaps say that these reforms did not go far enough, but those who realise how much policy change has been implemented since 1980 – first as a necessity due to adjustment policies, later on the basis of the universally applied 'Washington Consensus' – will understand the scepticism regarding the acclaimed future speed and depth of further reforms.

Trade and Environment

A similar line of reasoning would apply to the relation between trade reform, economic growth and the environment, including climate change. I will only briefly touch upon this. The logic of the argument resembles the discussion of the relation between trade reform and poverty alleviation. Rather than assuming that trade does have a direct impact on the environment, be it positive or negative, I prefer to discuss environmental effects as resulting from *economic activities* in the real sphere, such as investment, production and income growth, transportation, consumption and exploitation of natural resources, including energy. All such economic activities in the real sphere are linked through trade. It is trade that facilitates their combination and provides them with more opportunities to create value added. So, environmental consequences result not from trade in isolation, but from trade in combination with one or more of the other economic categories. For instance, more free trade resulting from a decrease of trade-distorting agricultural and energy subsidies will produce a positive environmental effect because of the reallocation of resources and production following this trade liberalisation. Anderson rightly points out that there are many examples of such 'win–win' relations in the field of trade and environment. I agree with Sampson (2000) that, even within the present WTO framework, this offers opportunities which regretfully still seem to be neglected.

Not all expanded trade in combination with increased investment and production results has negative consequences for the environment. Anderson refers to the fact that, contrary to fears expressed at the beginning of the new phase of economic globalisation, when international investment started to pick up again, there was no systematic 'race to the bottom' in environmental standards. He also points out that trade, in so far as this does lead to poverty alleviation, can result in less harmful land use patterns (less slash-and-burn agriculture). It may also result in a substitution of non-renewable sources of energy (wood-cutting, for instance) by other sources. The same is true for a substitution of coal by environmentally less harmful sources of energy that could result from the removal of coal subsidies. In my view, however, trade in combination with activities in the real sphere of the economy has other environmental effects as well: increased energy use, increased use of other scarce natural resources, risk-

ing depletion, loss in animal welfare, spread of animal diseases, loss of biodiversity, climate change, depletion of fish resources, overutilisation of water resources, land degradation due to overgrazing and so on. Trade is not the culprit, production and consumption are. But specific trade policies, including trade liberalisation, have consequences for investment, production and consumption patterns, for land use systems and transportation systems. Trade policy rules, as agreed in the WTO, to a great extent determine the use of the world's resources. Of course, it is also the other way around: trade and the opportunities for trade policy making are influenced by developments and decisions in other areas and by technological change. But this means that the combined effects for the environment cannot be neglected when choices in the field of trade itself are on the agenda. The discussion of environmental consequences of our economic behaviour should also be brought within the scope of world trade talks.

Sustainability

Poverty alleviation and environmental concerns, together with food security and access to medication and some other issues, are sometimes called the 'non-trade concerns' in international trade. At the 2002 Johannesburg Summit on Sustainable Development they were high on the agenda. Calls have been made on trade negotiators to broaden the Doha Agenda in order to incorporate so-called 'sustainability questions' into the talks. Within WTO there is still a reluctance to do so. This is understandable, because the incorporation of concerns other than trade as such would further complicate the process. It is also understandable in so far as negotiators believe that more free trade, next to higher growth, on balance will always result in less poverty, less environmental damage and more sustainability. Empirical evidence and development theory teach us that this is not automatically the case. Specific conditions ensuring an integrated and comprehensive approach will have to be fulfilled. I have mentioned a few of these conditions above. Many are of a political character. Meeting such conditions is not only a non-trade concern; it would also be in the interest of trade itself. When policy makers are uncertain about specific consequences of trade liberalisation, they may refrain from it. When trade liberalisation brings about unintended harm for a society, a backlash may result.

For many governments, the main challenge is to create new jobs for ever-more new young people without unduly destroying jobs for others. Failing to do so will have major social and political consequences, world-wide. When expectations are not met, when aspirations are violated, when unemployed young people are denied a fair perspective, economic instability, social unrest, political strife and violence may result. People without a stake in the labour market, in particular the young among them, may feel themselves excluded not only from the economic system, but from society as a whole. In reaction to this they may turn against society. To bring openness and fairness into a society is a first responsibility of policy makers in the economy, including trade.

Presently the process of globalisation seems to strengthen economic forces that are in favour of trade liberalisation. But there always will be a natural inclination to protect. It is a struggle between entrepreneurship and fear: where fear prevails, protectionism will be on the rise. Stemming a return to protectionism as an unintended result of a combination of policy reactions – out of fear, or in order to guard specific interests against dangers from outside – is perhaps even more important than to enforce further liberalisation. But a defensive approach will not suffice. It is important to keep the economy dynamic and oriented towards innovation. A standstill can easily turn into regression. Rendering trade policy making more comprehensive can be a contribution towards such a dynamic approach.

The stakes are high. As I indicated above, I do not dispute Anderson's estimates. I can agree with his estimates of gross economic benefits from reducing subsidies and trade barriers. Both the static gains and the dynamic gains as presented by him are reasonable, given the assumptions made. Maybe these benefits will take more time to accrue and not last as long as assumed, but this is a minor consideration. However, in my opinion the economic costs will be higher than Anderson assumes. They will

last longer. Still, in macro terms they are much less than the benefits.

I do not share Anderson's optimism with regard to the social benefits and costs. Anderson argues that the net social benefits from trade liberalisation for poverty reduction, the environment, diseases, education, nutrition, governance, stability and conflict management are most likely positive and large. I have argued for two of them – poverty and the environment – that this is only true under specific conditions, which will not easily be met. If not, the effects may on balance be negative rather than positive. The same line of reasoning will in my opinion apply to the other categories. However, because the effects cannot easily be quantified, Anderson ignores them. This is not unreasonable. I am aware that the purpose of the Copenhagen Consensus is to compare and weigh alternative financial and policy efforts in these and other fields. To present plausible estimates would require a different world model, much more comprehensive than those available, highlighting all the linkages concerned.

The most important caveat with regard to Anderson's figures is that their theoretical validity may be politically less relevant. The figures can be turned into reality only through political negotiations. In these negotiations, the conditions underlying these figures will also have to be met. Many of these conditions concern the distribution of the benefits and costs. Who will benefit – which countries, which sectors, which people? Who will have to bear the burden? Can they be compensated? Certainly, because the macro benefits are very high. Will they be compensated? That is uncertain, and this uncertainty adds to the costs. The question is not whether the stakes are high, or how high they are, but how to *share them*. It is the distribution of the costs and benefits, rather than the size, which will determine action.

References

Anderson, K., 2004: Subsidies and trade barriers, chapter 10 in this volume

Bhagwati, J., 1991: Threats to the world trading regime, in A. Koekkoek and L.B.M. Mennes (eds.), *International trade and global*

development: essays in honour of Jagdish
Bhagwati, Routledge, London

Brown, D., A.V. Deardorff and R.M. Stern, 2003:
Multilateral, regional and bilateral trade-policy
options for the United States and Japan, *The
World Economy*, **26**(6), 803–28

Cairncross, A. *et al.*, 1982: *Protectionism: threat to
international order. The impact on developing
countries*, Commonwealth Secretariat, London

Carlsson, I. and S. Ramphal, 1995: *Our global
neighbourhood: the report of the Commission
on Global Governance*, Oxford University
Press, Oxford

Dollar, D. and A. Kraay, 2002: Growth is good for
the poor, *Journal of Economic Growth*, **7**(3),
195–225

Francois, J., H. van Meijl and F. van Tongeren,
2003a: Economic benefits of the Doha Round
for the Netherlands, report to Ministry of
Economic Affairs, The Hague

    2003b: Trade liberalisation and developing
    countries under the Doha Round, CEPR
    Discussion Paper, 4032

    2003c: Economic implications of trade
    liberalisation under the Doha Round, Paper
    prepared for the 6th Annual Conference on
    Global Analyis, The Hague, 12–14
    June 2003.

Pronk, J.P., 1987: Towards a new international trade
organization?, in J. Harrod and N. Schrijver
(eds.), *The UN under attack*, Gower, Aldershot

    2001: Aid as a catalyst, *Development and Change*,
    32(4), 611–29

    2003a: Aid as a catalyst: a rejoinder, *Development
    and Change*, **34**(3), 382–400

    2003b: Collateral damage or calculated default?
    The Millennium Development Goals and the
    politics of globalisation, Inaugural address,
    Institute of Social Studies, The Hague

Sampson, G.P., 2000: *Trade, environment, and the
WTO: the post-Seattle agenda*, Overseas
Development Council, Washington, DC

**United Nations Development Programme
(UNDP)**, 2003: *Human development report
2003. Millennium Development Goals: a
compact among nations to end human poverty*,
Oxford University Press, New York and Oxford

Vos, R., E. Ganuza, S. Morley and S. Robinson
(eds.), 2004: *Who gains from trade
liberalisation? Export-led growth and poverty
in Latin America*, Routledge, London

Whalley, J. (ed.), 1989: *The Uruguay Round and
beyond: the final report from the Ford
Foundation supported project on developing
countries and the global trading system*,
University of Michigan Press, Ann Arbor

Perspective Paper 10.2

ARVIND PANAGARIYA

Introduction

Kym Anderson has done an excellent job in chapter 10 in this volume of articulating the challenge of trade liberalisation facing the world economy today. He correctly points out that this challenge has been with us for seventy-five years. While substantial progress has been made, barriers to trade in goods and trade-distorting agricultural subsidies continue to cost the world economy billions of dollars each year. Luckily, there is ample opportunity to eliminate these remaining barriers.

Anderson identifies four such opportunities that can be exploited:

- *Opportunity 1*: Unilateral, non-discriminatory liberalisation by countries acting solely on their own
- *Opportunity 2*: Reciprocal, non-discriminatory liberalisation on a multilateral basis under the auspices of the WTO Doha Round
- *Opportunity 3*: Region-wide liberalisation either on a non-discriminatory basis as under the auspices of APEC or on a discriminatory basis as under the auspices of customs unions and free trade areas (FTAs) such the EU and Free Trade Area of the Americas (FTAA), respectively

- *Opportunity 4*: One-way trade preferences by the rich to the poor, especially least developed countries.

In the key sub-section entitled 'How best to reduce subsidies and trade barriers globally by 2010?,' (p. 557) Anderson is critical of both FTAs such as NAFTA and FTAA (opportunity 3) and one-way trade preferences (opportunity 4) and urges that we hang the future liberalisation strategy on unilateral and multilateral liberalisation (opportunities 1 and 2, respectively).[1] I wholeheartedly endorse this conclusion. In my own writings, I have been critical of the preferential approach – whether reciprocal or one-way (Bhagwati and Panagariya 1996; Bhagwati, Greenaway and Panagariya 1998; Panagariya 1999a on reciprocal preferences; Panagariya 2002 on one-way preferences) – and have advocated sticking to the non-preferential, non-discriminatory approach implemented at the national, regional, or multilateral level.[2] I am therefore delighted with Anderson's key recommendation.

Unfortunately, my role here is that of an opponent, which means I must criticise the chapter. Being in agreement with the bottom line offered by the author, my criticisms have to be in the form of suggestions and qualifications, which is what I shall offer in what follows. In the next section, I offer some broad criticisms of the paper, in the next suggestions for how we can beef up the case for free trade; in the next section are further reasons why opportunities 1 and 2 are desirable and 3 and 4 are not and in the final section some concluding remarks.

Broad Concerns

The Anderson chapter has three substantive sections. The first section offers a general discussion

---

[1] I must admit, however, that the message does not come out as sharply in the paper as stated here. For example, the language at the end of the first paragraph of p. 9 and at the beginning of the second paragraph leaves the impression that Anderson does not view unilateral liberalisation as a realistic option for meeting the challenge of trade liberalisation. Likewise, the discussion on p. 10 seems to endorse both the FTA route and unilateral trade preferences. It may be best to state the conclusion sharply in the introduction.

[2] Indeed, I was among the first to articulate the case for non-discriminatory liberalisation on a region-wide basis in East Asia (in Panagariya 1994).

of why the elimination of trade barriers is beneficial; the next section identifies the four opportunities; and the next section offers estimates of the benefits from liberalisation by seizing each of the four opportunities followed by a general discussion of the costs of liberalisation and its relationship to the other challenges, including the environment, poverty and climate change.

Let me begin by making four broad points that may be worthy of attention. First, the reader will benefit from being told of the barriers and subsidies that exist in different countries. These can be presented in some aggregate form – as done, for example, in Gillespie and Low (1999) and Panagariya (1999b) in the case of trade barriers. Without a clear sense of how high the barriers are, for which products and in which countries, one cannot fully appreciate the political economy of liberalisation and hence the cost of available opportunities to be exploited. Countries do view liberalisation through the mercantilist lens – lately even more so since the rich countries have begun to fear trading with the poor countries – and therefore informing them of the computable general equilibrium (CGE) estimates of the gains from liberalisation is far from sufficient to persuade them to liberalise. They need to know what market access they can get in return for the access they yield.

Second, in a number of places, the chapter strays from the challenge at hand – border barriers and agricultural subsidies – reporting instead on the gains that can be had from the liberalisation of trade in services, investment and even labour mobility. While such extension is interesting in itself, it is not a part of the challenge undertaken.

Third, in some key areas that I will point out in my discussion of the specific opportunities below, there is a need to disaggregate the global effects into those relating to country aggregates. I am not suggesting a country-by-country analysis, which will be obviously counterproductive, but by broad groups of countries according to the way their welfare is qualitatively differently impacted. Sometimes, the effects on some developing countries may be negative while on others it is positive. In such cases, the aggregation of these two groups into a single category can be quite misleading.

Finally, I think the chapter relies excessively and uncritically on the estimates derived from the CGE models. These models are not based on detailed time-series data in the way econometric models are and do not have the predictive power of the latter. Instead, they assume a certain structure of the economy with functional forms and parameter values, calibrate the initial equilibrium around a base year and then change the trade policy parameters to solve for the change the model implies. Thus, only the data from the base year are used to build the model.[3] Not surprisingly, in a recent *ex post* evaluation of the NAFTA CGE models written in the late 1980s and early 1990s by some of the same researchers cited frequently in the present paper, Kehoe (2003) demonstrates entirely convincingly that these models uniformly failed to predict the changes in the Mexican economy by a long shot. In my own work (Panagariya and Duttagupta 2001), I have systematically demonstrated how the model structure, specific functional forms and parameter values can alter the results in these models even qualitatively.

I am not unsympathetic to the use of the model estimates since these are (almost) all we have by way of numbers relating to the future liberalisation. But I would prefer some warning and qualification regarding the likely errors and also somewhat greater reliance on the qualitative arguments and, especially, country experiences that amply demonstrate the value of outward oriented policies. I elaborate on this theme below.

Making the Case for Liberalisation

In making the case for liberalisation, the chapter relies almost exclusively on the cross-country regression studies for empirical evidence. While these studies are a useful complement, they have come under severe criticism from not just free trade sceptics such as Rodriguez and Rodrik (1999) but also the most prominent pro-free trade

---

[3] In addition, some of the parameters may be estimated though even these are often taken from the existing literature rather than estimated for the specific economy under analysis.

economists Srinivasan and Bhagwati (2001). Conclusions along the lines that a 10 per cent reduction in trade barriers *leads to* an *x* per cent jump in the growth rate, offered by these studies, are quickly countered by the sceptics, who point to the many countries in Africa and Latin America that liberalised trade during the 1980s and 1990s but actually saw their growth rates plummet.[4]

The case for openness has therefore to be more nuanced. The proposition that is entirely defensible and is consistent with the cross-country regression studies without relying on them is that the countries that have grown rapidly on a sustained basis have almost always done so in the presence of either low or declining barriers to trade. Or, more precisely, openness is necessary but not sufficient for sustained rapid growth. Making the case this way anticipates the criticism that openness does not always lead to faster growth right away.

In Panagariya (2004a), I have offered a systematic defence of free trade along these lines. I identify all countries that have grown at 3 per cent or more in *per capita* terms since the 1960s and show that these growth 'miracles' uniformly took place in the presence of low or declining barriers to trade. I also identify the growth débâcles – the countries that did not experience any growth in *per capita* terms on a sustained basis or actually declined – and show that they are rarely the outcome of openness. Thus, while openness is an important part of the miracles, it does not lead to débâcles.

Making the case in this manner also allows one to bring individual country experiences documented in the landmark studies of Little, Scitovsky and Scott (1970), Bhagwati and Krueger (1974) and

Balassa (1982) as evidence supporting the case for outward oriented policies. Country experiences such as those of East Asia starting in the 1960s; China, India and Chile starting in the 1980s; and many Latin American and African countries during the 1960s and the early 1970s offer compelling evidence favouring the hypothesis that an outward oriented trade regime is a necessary ingredient in the high-growth recipe. Indeed, it is difficult to come up with examples of countries that grew rapidly on a sustained basis while maintaining high wall of protection that was not coming down during the growth process.

The Opportunities

Let me now turn to the specific opportunities identified in the chapter and suggest improvements that can be made in the light of the existing studies not covered by Anderson.

Opportunity 1: Unilateral Liberalisation

There is now ample evidence of many developing countries embracing unilateral liberalisation and benefiting from it. A volume edited by Bhagwati (2002), entitled *Going Alone*, systematically documents the experience of Asia and Latin America. I would urge making a stronger pitch for working toward exploiting this opportunity than is done in the chapter. Among other things, it will be useful to document at some length the experience of India and China, which did poorly over the years 1950–80 under autarkic policies but were able to grow at 'miracle-level' growth rates during the 1980s and 1990s while following the path of unilateral liberalisation.[5]

Critics of trade liberalisation have seized on the observation that Latin America aggressively liberalised trade during the 1980s and 1990s but found its growth rates plummet. But such criticisms are misplaced. The key source of Latin America's plight in the 1980s was the macroeconomic instability resulting excessive foreign borrowing with or without capital account convertibility and had little to do with trade liberalisation. The 1970s had been characterised by rising foreign debt in many Latin

---

[4] The common assertion that each country can crawl along the fitted cross-country regression line provided it adopts the policy changes represented by the independent variables in the line is seriously flawed. Even after we ignore the errors in the measurement of variables, which are especially serious in the cross-country regressions, *and* accept all the assumptions relating to the distribution of various error terms and the functional form – usually linear and therefore separable in the policy variables – the estimation gives us a *bend* of estimates (or what is called the *interval* estimate in technical terms) with a specified probability rather than the mean value of these estimates shown by the regression line.

[5] The experience of India is documented in Panagariya (2004b).

American countries with debt service as a proportion of exports rising to 30 per cent or more by the early 1980s in many cases. On top of that came the Volcker-era interest rate increases in the USA, which led capital to flow out of Latin America abruptly and choked all growth potential.

But even the Latin America of the 1980s onward offers an example that supports the hypothesis that trade openness is necessary for growth. Since the 1980s, Chile is perhaps the only major country in Latin American that has registered sustained rapid growth. Its GDP grew annually at rates of 5.3 and 5.9 per cent, respectively, during 1981–91 and 1991–2001. During the same time periods, exports of goods and services grew annually at 8.6 and 9 per cent, respectively, with the imports: GDP ratio rising from 26.8 per cent in 1981 to 32.7 per cent in 2001.

Like many other Latin American countries, Chile opened up its economy to trade by slashing tariffs unilaterally and undertaking reforms such as privatisation. What distinguished it, however, was the management of macroeconomic affairs. For example, on average, Chile had a balanced budget during the 1980s and a fiscal surplus during the 1990s. Through prudent management of monetary policy, Chile also brought inflation down from 21 per cent in 1989 to 3 per cent in 1999. Above all, Chile avoided financial capital flow crises through a credible policy regime in general and judicious taxation of capital inflows that loosely corresponded to the local version of the Tobin tax.

Opportunity 2: Multilateral Liberalisation via the Doha Round

In discussing this opportunity, the chapter considers industrial and agricultural goods simultaneously and focuses on achieving a 50 per cent reduction in all tariff barriers and the same for agricultural subsidies. In my judgement, it is worth de-linking the discussion of the liberalisation in industrial goods from agricultural protection and subsidies.

Multilateral liberalisation in industrial goods has now been under way since the 1950s and the remaining barriers are relatively low. It is therefore realistic to consider complete elimination of the existing barriers in this sector as a part of the Doha Round.

Admittedly, the actual elimination of the barriers by 2010 is unrealistic, as is even the 50 per cent reduction proposed in the chapter. But an *agreement* to eliminate the remaining industrial tariffs by a certain date as a part of the Doha Round agreement is not unrealistic. Indeed, the current proposal on the table by the USA proposes just that. According to this, the WTO members would agree to eliminate all industrial tariffs by 2015. Because there is some concern that developing countries need a longer phase-out period owing to their lack of adjustment assistance programmes and social safety nets, the US proposal may be modified to move the date for developing countries to eliminate the tariffs to 2020. Given the benefits from unilateral liberalisation for the developing countries that have little market power in the global economy and their failed attempts since the 1970s to get developed countries even to lower tariffs on labour-intensive products including apparel and footwear, let alone eliminate them, this is an attractive option to explore.

In agriculture, the scene is more complicated. For one thing, the process of liberalisation in this sector began only in the 1990s and the existing border barriers and subsidies are very high. As such, the achievement of an agreement for zero tariffs and subsidies in this sector in the foreseeable future is unrealistic. The goal of 50 per cent reduction in the barriers as considered in the chapter would seem to be a reasonable benchmark.

It is important, however, to recognise that the majority of the least developed countries (LDCs) will actually be hurt by the removal of agricultural subsidies and perhaps even tariffs in the case of the EU. It has become a cliché to assert that the subsidies in the rich countries are hurting the poorest countries in the world. The reality, however, is that the major beneficiaries of the removal of these subsidies will be the countries that give them, and the Cairns Group of countries that include developed and relatively richer developing countries with comparative advantage in agriculture. Perhaps the largest beneficiary will be the USA, which stands to benefit both from reduced distortions domestically as it lowers its own subsidies and tariffs as well as from increased market share as its highly competitive agricultural sector expands in response to tariff liberalisation and removal of subsidies by the EU.

Table 10.1.1. Net food importers

	LIC	LMIC	UMIC
NFIM	48	35	22
NFEX	15	17	11
Total	63	52	33

Source: Valdes and McCalla (1999).

Table 10.1.2. Net position in agriculture

	LIC	LMIC	UMIC
NAIM	30	32	23
NAEX	33	20	10
Total	63	52	33

Source: Valdes and McCalla (1999).

In so far as the poor countries are concerned, drawing on the work of Valdes and McCalla (1999), I have argued in Panagariya (2003a) that a large majority of them stand to lose from the liberalisation of subsidies in agriculture.[6] Consider tables 10.1.1 and 10.1.2, taken from the Valdes and McCalla study, which show the status of various developing countries in international trade in food and agriculture. There are 148 developing countries in all, which the World Bank divides into sixty-three Low-Income Countries (LIC), fifty-three Lower-Middle-Income Countries (LMIC) and thirty-three Upper-Middle-Income Countries (UMIC). Based on 1995–7 trade data, Valdes and McCalla further divide these countries into Net Food Importing (NFIM) and Net Food Exporting (NFEX) countries, on the one hand, and Net Agricultural Importing (NAIM) and Net Agricultural Exporting (NAEX), on the other. The two-way division is shown in tables 10.1.1 and 10.1.2.

According to table 10.1.1, as many as forty-eight out of sixty-three LICs are net importers of food. Even among the LMICs, thirty-five out of fifty-two are net food importers. In so far as the subsidies apply with potency to food items, their removal will raise the world prices of the latter and hurt the real incomes of the importing countries.

Table 10.1.2 classifies the three groups of countries according to their net position in agriculture as a whole. Here more LICs appear as exporters – thirty-three versus only fifteen when we consider trade in food. But the picture is less pretty if we focus on the LDC only. At the time that Valdes and McCalla wrote, there were forty-eight LDCs. Of these, as many as forty-five were net food importers and thirty-three net agricultural importers.

Some argue that the end to subsidies will nevertheless benefit the poor countries because even those that currently import food and agricultural

goods will become exporters of these products. For one thing, the basis of this assumption is far from clear: true, the rise in the prices will expand output, but how can we be sure that this will be sufficiently large to change the status of a large number of the countries from net importers to net exporters? But more importantly, as I explain in appendix 1, the change of status from net importer to net exporter is far from sufficient to ensure net gains. As the countries turn into exporters, initially the losses from terms of trade deterioration as importers would dominate the gains from the terms of trade improvement as exporters. Only if the exports of the country cross a critical level will the loss be offset by the gains.

A closely related issue concerns the existing trade preferences that the LDCs enjoy in the EU market. As explained in appendix 2, in so far as these preferences also apply to agriculture, the removal of tariffs would hurt even the net exporters of the agricultural products even as the subsidies are removed simultaneously. Domestic and export subsidies lower the world prices but the tariffs keep the EU *internal* prices above the latter. The exporting poor countries with tariff-free access to the EU market benefit from the arrangement since they have access to the high internal EU prices. While subsidy reductions will raise the world price, tariff reductions will lower the EU internal price. In so far as the LDCs sell at the latter price, they will be hurt from the change.

The simulations conducted by Yu and Jensen (2003) offer numerical examples supporting these points. For example, they simulate the combined effect of implementing the 'everything but arms' (EBA) initiative and a 50 per cent reduction in the EU import tariffs on food and agriculture. They find that this leads to a loss in the real incomes of the majority of the LDCs, especially in SSA. In another simulation, they combine EBA with EU

---

[6] See also Panagariya (2003b) in this context.

export subsides on all food and agricultural products, and obtain similar results.

It is important for the policy community to stop repeating, without critical examination, the assertion that subsidies are hurting the poorest countries and that they constitute the most important obstacle to the development of the poorest countries. While there is no doubt that the subsidies constitute a major distortion of agricultural trade and must be removed, such removal is likely to hurt the majority of the LDCs and is surely not about to put many of them on a sustained, higher-growth trajectory. Only after we recognise this fact will begin to design appropriate social safety nets and adjustment assistance for the poor countries that are net importers of agricultural products and will actually lose from the increase in the price of agricultural products following the removal of the subsidies. If we continue to assert that the poorest countries stand to benefit from the end to agricultural subsides, there would be no case for sinking resources into such assistance and safety nets.

Opportunity 3: Preferential Trade Liberalisation

I entirely agree with the chapter that there is no need to proactively promote preferential trade areas (PTAs) such as NAFTA and FTAA. To the arguments made in the chapter, I will add four more.

First, the *growth effects* of PTAs remain unproven. Whereas there is overwhelming country evidence supporting the hypothesis that low or declining trade barriers on a non-discriminatory basis are necessary for growth, similar evidence in favour of PTAs is simply lacking. One is hard-pressed to find examples of countries that have chosen to hang their growth strategy on FTAs and have grown successfully on a sustained basis. Mexico, in particular, consciously chose the path of preferential liberalisation and has also implemented the policy package that is usually associated with reforms but has not been able to achieve high rates of growth. Portugal and Spain may offer some favourable evidence but such evidence has two limitations. (1) These countries went on to become a part of a customs union that was truly striving to be a single market, which is not what the rest of the PTAs today are doing. And

(2), as these countries joined the EC/EU, they also achieved considerable *external* liberalisation since the EC tariffs were well below theirs. As such, their success should be attributed at least partially to unilateral, non-discriminatory liberalisation.

Second, there is already political momentum for more of these arrangements than are desirable. The trading system has come to be fragmented on account of the large number of FTAs negotiated in the 1990s. The competition for FTAs has created so much discrimination in tariff policy in the major markets based on the origin of the product that the Most Favoured Nation (MFN) principle of the General Agreement on Tariffs and Trade (GATT) can scarcely be recognised. In the name of free trade, we now have what Bhagwati has called the 'Spaghetti Bowl' phenomenon whereby the tariff on a product depends on the stage of implementation of the FTA with the trading partner exporting the product and the concomitant rule of origin (Bhagwati and Panagariya 1996). The only way to clean up the system now is not more FTAs but *multilateral liberalisation.*

Third, in so far as agricultural subsidies are concerned, their liberalisation necessarily requires the *multilateral context.* Domestic production subsidies are not aimed at specific trading partners and therefore will not be eliminated in the context of an FTA. Likewise, preferential removal of export subsidies is politically problematic. Preferential removal of tariffs makes within-union suppliers more competitive relative to outsiders and therefore finds political support among producers of the member countries. But preferential removal of export subsidies does just the opposite: it makes outsiders more competitive relative to insiders! Not surprisingly, the negotiations for the FTAA have come to a standstill on account of differences on agricultural subsidies (among other things).[7]

Finally, from the viewpoint of the poorest countries, FTAs involving the USA come with various strings attached. These latter include the link between trade and labour, restrictions on the use of capital controls, a WTO plus intellectual property rights (IPR) regime and commitments in the area of the investment regime whose desirability for the

---

[7] This paragraph is based on Bhagwati and Baldwin (2004).

host country is questionable. Indeed, a close examination of the US FTAs suggests that the driving force behind them is not market access but these *'non-trade' commitments* it is able to obtain from small countries such as Chile, Jordan, Singapore and various Central American countries.[8]

Opportunity 4: One-way Preferences by the Rich to the Poor Countries

Once again, let me add two arguments to those already provided by Anderson to support the view that this opportunity is of dubious value even though the political pressure for its implementation remains intense.

First, like FTAs, these one-way preferences have by and large failed to produce major success stories in terms of growth. They have largely helped shift some rents from the rich to the poor countries but without generating an upward shift in long-term growth.[9] There are a number of reasons for why this happened, some of which are discussed by Anderson while others can be found in Panagariya (2002). An important one, not mentioned by Anderson, is that the existence of the preferences has had a detri-

mental effect on the trade liberalisation in the recipient countries. The export lobby that often drives the liberalisation process has been diluted.

Second, even though the Enabling Clause requires that the preferences be entirely unilateral and thus without *any* strings attached, they have effectively turned reciprocal. In the USA, they have been used to promote tougher IPR protection and higher labour standards in the recipient countries. Likewise, the EU preferences under the Generalised System of Preferences (GSP) have come to be used as a reward for enforcement against drug trafficking.

Conclusions

I wholeheartedly endorse according the highest priority to the removal of trade barriers and subsidies advocated by Anderson as also the strategy of exploiting actively opportunities 1 and 2 for this purpose. The *economic* cost of meeting this challenge being negligible – unlike the fight against the AIDS epidemic, the removal of trade barriers and subsidies does not require the investment of financial resources – the rate of return on the small investment in building pro-liberalisation constituencies is very high. Indeed, meeting the 'trade and subsidy liberalisation' challenge is essential to meeting all other challenges. If we fail in this area, it is unlikely that we will achieve significant success in the others.

---

[8] See Bhagwati and Panagariya (2003) for a more detailed exposition of this argument.

[9] Indeed, it is the existence of these rents in favour of the exporting firms that has created a lobby in favour of the continuation and expansion of the schemes.

Appendix 1 Agricultural Subsidies and Net Importer Developing Countries

In figure 10.2A1.1, *DD* and *SS* denote the demand and supply curves of a net importer of an agricultural product, wheat. The price in the presence of subsidies by the rich countries is given by line $p_s p_s$ and the gains from trade to the country are represented by the triangular area marked '*a*'. The removal of the subsidy raises the price to the free – trade level indicated by $p_f p_f$. The gains from trade are now given by the triangular area *b*, which is smaller than area '*a*'. The country thus loses on a net basis.

To explain the effects further, observe that the equilibrium under autarky would be at point *A* with the consumers' plus producers' surplus given by the area enclosed by the demand and supply curves and the vertical axis. Under the subsidy regime with imports permitted freely, Imports at price p_s permit the consumers' surplus to expand to the area under the demand curve and above $p_s p_s$ while the producers' surplus shrinks to the area above the supply curve and below $p_s p_s$. The net increase in the surplus relative to autarky is thus area '*a*'.

The removal of the subsidy leads to a rise in the price to $p_f p_f$. The area below the demand curve and above $p_f p_f$ plus that above the supply curve and below $p_f p_f$ exceeds the surplus under autarky by '*b*'. As drawn, this area is smaller than area '*a*'.

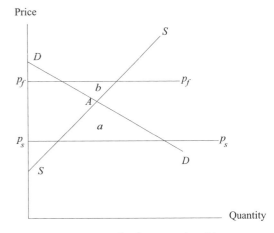

Figure 10.2A1.1. *Subsidy removal and impact on importing countries*

Even though the country turns into an exporter upon removal of the subsidy, it thus ends up losing from the change. Those who argue that the a net importer country also stands to gain from the removal of the subsidy because it will turn into a net exporter miss the point that the price increase initially constitutes a *deterioration* in the terms of trade and only after point *A* is crossed does it turn into an *improvement* in the terms of trade.

Appendix 2 The Impact of Tariff and Subsidy Removal on a Preference-Receiving Exporter Country

Subsidies have kept world prices low while tariffs have held internal prices in the rich countries high by preventing arbitrage between the two prices. Leaving aside a few sensitive items, the EU grants the LDCs duty-free access to its high internal price. The lowering of subsidies will raise the world price while lowering of tariffs will lower the internal EU price. Since the least developed exporters have access to internal EU price, they will actually be hurt by the change.

Figure 10.2A2.1, which relates to the EU, helps explain this point. DD and SS denote the EU demand and supply curves for an agricultural commodity in which it lacks comparative advantage. Under free trade, it would be an importer of the product with the price settling at $p_f p_f$. But an export subsidy combined by a tariff turns it into an exporter of the product. Thus, suppose it gives an export subsidy equal to $p_t p_s$ per unit, complemented by a tariff at the same or higher rate. These measures push the external (world) price to p_s (since the EU is a large exporter in the world market) and the internal price up to p_t. The LDCs with duty-free access to the EU market sell at the internal price, p_t. When the subsidy and tariff are removed, the world price settles at p_f, which is lower than p_t. The least developed exporters are hurt.

It is easy to extend this analysis to the case in which the EU is an exporter of the product under free trade but pushes the exports beyond the free-trade level through an export subsidy supported by a tariff. All we need to do is to shift up all three prices shown in figure 10.2A2.1 by the same fixed amount until p_f lies above point A.

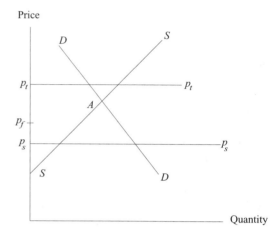

Figure 10.2A2.1. *Impact of the removal of the EU export subsidy and tariff on the EU internal price*

References

Bhagwati, J. (ed.), 2002: *Going alone: the case for relaxed reciprocity in freeing trade*, MIT Press, Cambridge, MA

Bhagwati, J. and R. Baldwin, 2004: Doha is the only option for advancing trade, *Financial Times*, 18 December

Bhagwati, J., D. Greenaway and A. Panagariya, 1998: Trading preferentially: theory and policy, *Economic Journal*, 1128–48

Bhagwati, J. and A. Krueger (eds.), 1974: *Foreign trade regimes and economic development: a special conference series on foreign trade regimes and economic development*, Cambridge University Press, New York

Bhagwati, J. and A. Panagariya, 1996: Preferential trading areas and multilateralism: strangers, friends or foes?, in J. Bhagwati and A. Panagariya (eds.), *The economics of preferential trading*, AEI Press, Washington, DC, 1–78; reproduced as chapter 2 in J. Bhagwati, P. Krishna and A. Panagariya (eds.), *Trading blocs: alternative approaches to analyzing preferential trade agreements*, MIT Press, Cambridge, MA, 1999

   2003: Bilateral trade treaties are a sham, *Financial Times*, 13 July

Gillespie, J. and P. Low, 1999: Free trade at the border by a date certain?, in J. Bhagwati (ed.), *The next negotiating round: examining the agenda for Seattle*, Proceedings of the conference held at Columbia University, 23–24 July 1999, 187–210

Kehoe, T. J., 2003: An evaluation of the performance of applied general equilibrium models of the impact of NAFTA, Research Department Staff Report, 320, Federal Reserve Bank of Minneapolis

Little, I., T. Scitovsky and M. Scott, 1970: *Industry and trade in some developing countries*, Oxford University Press, London

Panagariya, A., 1999a: The regionalism debate: an overview, *World Economy*, June, 477–511

   1999b: Free trade at the border, in J. Bhagwati (ed.), *The next negotiating round: examining the agenda for Seattle*, Proceedings of the conference held at Columbia University, 23–24, July, 2119–225

   2002: EU preferential trade arrangements and developing countries, *World Economy* **25**(10), 1415–32

   2003a: Trade liberalisation and food security: conceptual links, chapter 3 in A. Panagariya, *Trade reforms and food security*, Food and Agricultural Organization of the United Nations, Rome, 25–42.

   2003b: Think again: international trade, *Foreign Policy*, November–December, 20–28

   2004a: Miracles and debacles: in defense of trade openness; available at http://www.bsos.umd.edu/econ/ciepanag.htm.

   2004b: India in the 1980s and 1990s: a triumph of reforms, IMF Working Paper, WP/04/43, forthcoming in W. Tseng and D. Cowen (eds.), *India's and China's recent experience with reform and growth*, Palgrave Macmillan, Basingtoke

Panagariya, A. and R. Duttagupta, 2001: The 'gains' from preferential trade liberalisation in the CGEs: where do they come from?, in S. Lahiri (ed.), *Regionalism and globalization: theory and practice*, Routledge, London, 39–60

Rodriguez, F. and D. Rodrik, 1999: Trade policy and economic growth: a skeptic's guide to cross-national evidence, NBER Working Paper, W7081

Srinivasan, T. N. and J. Bhagwati, 2001: Outward orientation and development: are revisionists right?, in D. Lal and R. Snape (eds.), *Trade, development and political economy*, Palgrave Macmillan, Basingtoke

Yu, W. and T. V. Jensen, 2003: Tariff Preferences, WTO negotiations and the LDCs: the case of the 'Everything but Arms' initiative of the EU, Danish Research Institute of Food Economics, Rolighedsvej, Copenhagen, mimeo

PART II

Ranking the Opportunities

Expert Panel Ranking

JAGDISH N. BHAGWATI, ROBERT W. FOGEL, BRUNO S. FREY,
JUSTIN YIFU LIN, DOUGLASS C. NORTH, THOMAS C.
SCHELLING, VERNON L. SMITH, NANCY L. STOKEY

The Goal of the Project

The goal of the Copenhagen Consensus project was to set priorities among a series of proposals for confronting ten great global challenges. These challenges, selected from a wider set of issues identified by the United Nations, were: climate change; communicable diseases; conflicts and arms proliferation; access to education; financial instability; governance and corruption; malnutrition and hunger; migration; sanitation and access to clean water; and subsidies and trade barriers.

A panel of economic experts, comprising eight of the world's most distinguished economists, was invited to consider these issues. The members were Jagdish N. Bhagwati of Columbia University, Robert S. Fogel of the University of Chicago (Nobel Laureate), Bruno S. Frey of the University of Zurich, Justin Yifu Lin of Peking University, Douglass C. North of Washington University in St Louis (Nobel Laureate), Thomas Schelling of the University of Maryland, Vernon L. Smith of George Mason University (Nobel Laureate) and Nancy Stokey of the University of Chicago.

The panel was asked to address the ten challenge areas and to answer the question: 'What would be the best ways of advancing global welfare, and particularly the welfare of developing countries, supposing that an additional $50 bn of resources were at governments' disposal?' Ten challenge papers (chapters 1–10 in this volume), commissioned from acknowledged authorities in each area of policy, set out more than thirty proposals for the panel's consideration. During the conference, the panel examined these proposals in detail. Each chapter was discussed at length with its principal author and with two other specialists who had been commissioned to write critical appraisals in the form of Perspective papers, and then the experts met in private session. The panel then ranked the proposals, in descending order of desirability (see table on p. 606).

Ranking the Proposals

In ordering the proposals, the panel was guided predominantly by consideration of *economic costs and benefits*. The panel acknowledged the difficulties that cost-benefit analysis (CBA) must overcome, both in principle and as a practical matter, but agreed that CBA was an indispensable organising method. In setting priorities, the panel took account of the strengths and weaknesses of the specific cost-benefit appraisals under review, and gave weight both to the institutional preconditions for success and to the demands of ethical or humanitarian urgency. As a general matter, the panel noted that higher standards of governance and improvements in the institutions required to support development in the world's poor countries were of paramount importance.

Some of the proposals (for instance, the lowering of barriers to trade or migration) face political resistance. Overcoming such resistance can be regarded as a 'cost' of implementation. The panel took the view that such political costs should be excluded from their calculations: they concerned themselves only with those *economic costs of delivery*, including the costs of specific supporting institutional reforms, that would be faced once the political decision to proceed had been taken.

For some of the proposals, the panel found that information was too sparse to permit a judgement to be made. These proposals, some of which may prove after further study to be valuable, were therefore excluded from the ranking.

Final overall ranking

		Challenge	Opportunity
Very Good	1	Communicable diseases	Control of HIV/AIDS
	2	Malnutrition and hunger	Providing micronutrients
	3	Subsidies and trade	Trade liberalisation
	4	Communicable diseases	Control of malaria
Good	5	Malnutrition and hunger	Development of new agricultural technologies
	6	Sanitation and water	Community-managed water supply and sanitation
	7	Sanitation and water	Small-scale water technology for livelihoods
	8	Sanitation and water	Research on water productivity in food production
	9	Governance and corruption	Lowering the cost of starting a new business
Fair	10	Migration	Lowering barriers to migration for skilled workers
	11	Malnutrition and hunger	Improving infant and child nutrition
	12	Communicable diseases	Scaled-up basic health services
	13	Malnutrition and hunger	Reducing the prevalence of LBW
Bad	14	Migration	Guest worker programmes for the unskilled
	15	Climate change	Optimal carbon tax
	16	Climate change	The Kyoto Protocol
	17	Climate change	Value-at-risk carbon tax

Each expert assigned his or her own ranking to the proposals. The individual rankings, together with commentaries prepared by each expert, will be published in due course. (The chapters and other material have already been placed in the public domain.) The panel's ranking was calculated by taking the median of individual rankings. The panel jointly endorses the median ordering shown above as representing their agreed view.

Communicable Diseases

The panel ranked at 1 new measures to prevent the spread of HIV/AIDS. Spending assigned to this purpose would yield extraordinarily high benefits, averting nearly 30m new infections by 2010. Costs are substantial, estimated at $27 bn. Even so, these costs are small in relation to what stands to be gained. Moreover, the scale and urgency of the problem – especially in Africa, where AIDS threatens the collapse of entire societies – are extreme.

New measures for the control and treatment of malaria were jointly ranked at 4. At $13 bn in costs,

the benefit-cost ratio (BCR) was somewhat lower than for the proposals on HIV/AIDS and malnutrition and hunger, but still extremely high by the ordinary standards of project appraisal, especially for the provision of chemically treated bednets (ITNs). Again, the scale and urgency of the problem are very great. Scaled-up basic health services were ranked at 12.

Malnutrition and Hunger

Policies to attack malnutrition and hunger were ranked at 2. Reducing the prevalence of iron-deficiency anaemia by means of food supplements, in particular, has an exceptionally high BCR; of the three proposals considered under this heading, this was ranked highest at $12 bn. The expert panel ranked a second proposal, to increase spending on research into new agricultural technologies appropriate for poor countries, at 5. Further proposals, for additional spending on infant and child nutrition and on reducing the prevalence of LBW, were ranked at 11 and 13, respectively.

Global Trade Reform

The panel considered three main proposals for global trade reform: first, multilateral and unilateral reduction of tariffs and non-tariff barriers (NTBs), together with the elimination of agricultural subsidies; second, extension of regional trade agreements (RTAs); third, adoption of the 'Everything But Arms' (EBA) proposal for non-reciprocal lowering of rich-country tariffs on exports from the least developed countries (LDCs). In the case of trade reform, lives are not directly and immediately at risk. However, the first proposal – free trade – was agreed to yield exceptionally large benefits, in relation to comparatively modest adjustment costs, both for the world as a whole and for the developing countries. Accordingly it was ranked at 3. (Some members of the panel argued that since this proposal need not involve any budgetary outlays, it should be acted upon in any case, regardless of the resources available for additional budget outlays.) The proposal to extend regional free trade areas (FTAs) was not ranked, for lack of information on particular agreements. The proposal for non-reciprocal lowering of barriers to exports of the LDCs was also not ranked, with some members of the panel noting that this proposal would harm many poor countries not participating in the arrangements, while encouraging those that did participate to invest in activities that were not internationally competitive.

Sanitation and Access to Clean Water

The panel agreed with chapter 9 on sanitation and access to clean water that the lack of safe and affordable access to these services is a great burden for more than a billion of the world's poorest people. Almost half of the people living in developing countries suffer at any given time from one or more water-borne diseases. Three proposals, including small-scale water technology for livelihoods, were regarded as likely to be highly cost-effective and were ranked at 6, 7 and 8.

Governance and Corruption

The experts considered five proposals for improving governance in developing countries. While agreeing, as already noted, that better governance is very often a precondition for progress of any kind, the panel thought it inappropriate to include four of these proposals in their ranking. This is because these reforms involve costs of implementation that will differ greatly according to each country's particular institutional circumstances. The experts felt they had too little specific information to make a judgement about what those costs might be. The panel did, however, express its support for the proposal to reduce the state-imposed costs of starting a new business, on the grounds that this policy would not only be enormously beneficial but also relatively straightforward to introduce. This proposal was ranked at 9.

Migration

Policies to liberalise international migration were regarded as a desirable way to promote global welfare and to provide economic opportunities to people in developing countries. A lowering of barriers to the migration of skilled workers was recommended, and ranked at 10. Guest-worker programmes, of the sort common in Europe, were not recommended, owing to their tendency to discourage the assimilation of migrants.

Climate Change

The panel looked at three proposals, including the Kyoto Protocol, for dealing with climate change by reducing emissions of carbon. The expert panel regarded all three proposals as having costs that were likely to exceed the benefits. The panel recognised that global warming must be addressed, but agreed that approaches based on too abrupt a shift toward lower emissions of carbon were needlessly expensive. The experts expressed an interest in an alternative, proposed in Mendelsohn's Perspective paper 1.1, that envisaged a carbon tax much lower in the first years of implementation than the figures called for in chapter 1, rising gradually in later years. Such a proposal, however, was not examined in detail in the presentations put to the panel, and so was not ranked. The panel urged increased funding for research into more affordable carbon-abatement technologies.

Access to Education

The panel considered proposals to improve the provision of education in developing countries. It agreed that in countries where spending on education at present is very low, the potential exists for large benefits in return for modestly increased spending. However, the institutional preconditions for success are demanding and vary from case to case: experience suggests that it is easy to waste large sums on education initiatives. Given this variety of circumstances and constraints, the panel chose not to rank any proposals in this area. However, the experts did endorse the view that externally supervised examinations improved accountability of schools and should be promoted. They also expressed an interest in schemes to reduce, in a targeted way, the fees charged in many developing countries for public education, and to pay grants to families which send their children to school. More research on experience with such schemes is needed.

Conflicts

In considering a series of proposals for reducing the incidence of civil wars, the panel unanimously agreed with chapter 3's assessment that the human and economic costs of such conflicts are enormous – even larger, in fact, than is generally assumed. Measures to reduce the number, duration, or severity of civil wars would stand very high in the ordering, if they could be expected with any confidence to succeed. Members of the panel were not persuaded that the proposals put before them met that test. The panel noted the strong *prima facie* case for additional financial support for regional peace-keeping forces in post-conflict countries which meet certain criteria, but felt that the information before them was insufficient for them to assign a ranking. The experts also noted the evidence that growth in incomes reduced the long-term incidence of civil war; to the extent that their highest-ranked proposals raised incomes, they would have the additional benefit of reducing the incidence of conflict.

Financial Instability

Four proposals before the panel addressed the issue of international financial instability. The panel, noting the complexities and uncertainties in this area, chose not to come to a view about which, if any, of these proposals to recommend. They were therefore not ranked.

Individual Rankings

JAGDISH N. BHAGWATI

Communicable Diseases (Chapter 2)

- *HIV/AIDS* is different from other diseases and health problems. The disease has an impact on the whole society and the economy involving catastrophic consequences. Again the economies hardest hit are some of the weakest, mainly in sub-Saharan Africa (SSA). Control of HIV/AIDS should receive the highest priority.
- *Scaled-up basic health services* will benefit some of the poorest people and this goes for all regions. It will improve the value of life for all ages, from babies to the elderly. The benefits are significant relative to the costs and there is a great need for resources for investments in basic health services.

Malnutrition and Hunger (Chapter 7)

- Generally speaking the opportunities in this challenge represent excellent, high benefit-cost ratio (BCR) investments in global human welfare.
- Reducing micronutrient *deficiencies* in populations in which they are prevalent should be prioritised highly, since it entails modest costs and very high positive effects for a large number of people in developing countries. 2 billion people suffer from iodine deficiencies and 3.5 billion people are malnourished due to Vitamin A and Zinc deficiency alone.

- In the practical implementation of the opportunities, it is crucial to be aware of the different *infrastructure* needs. For reduction of micronutrient deficiency they would appear to be relatively modest.
- Investment in *technology* in developing agriculture is another very good opportunity. It is important to focus attention on these sort of structural opportunities as a fundamental development strategy. This opportunity would help some of the poorest groups.
- Improving *infant and child nutrition* in populations with high prevalence of child malnutrition requires low costs and brings large benefits, much like the opportunity to reduce a micronutrient deficiency. The infrastructure needs do, however, seem to be somewhat larger.
- Reducing *LBW* for pregnancies with high probabilities. LBW has a smaller scope than some of the other opportunities and will probably hit diminishing returns sooneest.

Governance and Corruption (Chapter 6)

- Many developing countries, including China and India, have very *big government sectors and enterprises*. These become conduits for corruption and for inefficiency, often at the cost of the poor.
- There are big payoffs therefore in having *procurement* subjected to rules and transparency.
- By contrast, the WTO Procurement Code exempts developing countries from joining the Organisation. This is counterproductive.
- Democratic politics requires that politicians are able to raise money to fight elections. If procurement becomes transparent and money for politics cannot be raised that way, we also need to advocate and introduce *general political reforms* so that election money can be provided in other ways. Otherwise, procurement reform will not work as intended: it will be evaded.
- We also need to distinguish among different *types of corruption*. All politics is corrupt since it involves patronage. But certain forms of patronage are less costly than others. Where politicians

indulge in rent-creating corruption, by awarding monopolies to their friends and cronies, this is expensive. Where they indulge in profit-sharing corruption, by having their friends and relatives get a share of profit, politicians have an interest in increasing profits and exploiting the pie: this is far less expensive than rent-creating corruption. Developed country politicians also have friends, relatives and cronies whom they favour, but in ways that are less expensive to the economy. We need therefore to rank different forms of corruption analytically. The World Bank studies and TI (Transparency Index) indices lack conceptualisation and should be discounted as helpful contributions to the study of corruption.

Climate Change (Chapter 1)

Regardless of the interest rates used, all opportunities suggested in this area appear to have quite low BCRs compared to other opportunities.

Migration (Chapter 8)

While objections were raised to temporary worker programmes, especially by Mark Rosenzweig (Perspective paper 8.1), who raised the issue that temporary workers will not assimilate well, Martin was enthusiastic about them. I believe that the Panel threw the baby out with the bathwater. Guestworker programmes are perhaps the only political way to accept large numbers of unskilled immigrants and reduce the incidence of illegal immigrants. Most likely, if we ask for large-scale permanent immigration outright, it will be turned down, whereas large numbers of temporary immigrants will be more acceptable even though *de facto* they become permanent!

I was disappointed that the Panel considered temporary immigration (which is really mostly unskilled) to be a below-the-line item while putting skilled immigration above the line. I thought this was ridiculous, since it gives the appearance that developed countries should take the skilled but not the unskilled from the poor nations, an argument that will not stand scrutiny among immigration experts unless they are of conservative persuasion:

- As far as the impact on developing countries is concerned, *lower barriers to unskilled migrants* can be of enormous benefit to both the migrants and those not migrating because of remittances, etc. Such remittances, and the return of migrants with new cash and skills, can transform source villages, as is seen from experience in Kerala, Mexico and Morocco, for example. The payoffs in development of the poor countries are enormous compared to the cost of migration.
- For skilled migrants, as in the IT sector, the developing countries can be considered under two templates: (1) those such as India, the Philippines and China, which see skilled outmigration as an *opportunity* and (2) those such as countries in Africa which see it as a *'brain drain' problem*. For the former, migration reflects a welcome opportunity, for the latter it reflects a perilous phenomenon.
- In each case, policies will have to be devised to maximise benefits and minimise the costs of migration. These include proposals such as the 'Bhagwati' tax proposal for income tax jurisdiction to be extended to *nationals migrating abroad* – recent estimates suggest huge revenue returns from small tax rates-tax revenue-sharing proposals, etc. For unskilled, low-income migrants, proposals to improve returns from remittances and to enhance their development potential can also be considered.

Financial Instability (Chapter 5)

Financial instability can undermine the welfare-improving beneficial effects from opportunities provided by, for instance, trade liberation or by measures to reduce malnutrition, because it *disrupts the whole society and economy*, as in the East Asian Financial Crises in the late 1990s. It is therefore of very high value to reduce financial instability. Unfortunately no credible solution has been found. Chapter 5 presents a sophisticated analysis of the solutions, and some analysis, but no consensus could be reached on how effective the proposed global solution would be.

Sanitation and Access to Clean Water (Chapter 9)

- The first opportunity presented in chapter 9 focuses on *small-scale technologies in community-managed programmes*. This is an opportunity with a high payoff and great value. There is little mention of the connection between the growth in community-managed small-scale technology and innovations in large technology. On could ask if, perhaps, the real innovation is the focus on community-managed activity and not the choice of technology in itself. This is an area of development where participatory collective action and the role of NGOs seems to be quite useful.
- *Any technology that works* should be prepared in this area. For the purpose of irrigation, big dams can be an alternative to small pumps. Let us focus on the non-technological aspects. Maybe small is beautiful, but especially for the purpose of drinking water, there is also an aspect of human health and safety. In larger-scale technologies it is usually less expensive and more reliable to secure a high level of safety.
- In the areas where water is scarce, perhaps one could consider technologies that *optimise the use of water*. Looking at the possibilities of reducing the need for water seems a worthwhile opportunity in these areas. There are no separate suggestions for reducing the need for water in chapter 9. In the 'Green Revolution', the output from crops increased dramatically through spreading of high-yielding dwarf cereal varieties. These were, however, quite water- and fertiliser-intensive. If GMOs are economical with respect to water need, and they can surmount the concern for undesirable effects on nature, and should be considered among the opportunities.
- One important consideration that should be borne in mind is that larger technologies for the supply of water for irrigation have one considerable advantage over decentralized systems: with a central water supply, one has the opportunity to make decisions on *distribution of water*. Decision makers and planners can transfer water from areas with abundance of water to villages in places where water is less abundant.

Subsidies and Trade Barriers (Chapter 10)

Very substantial benefits follow from trade liberalisation, with estimates depending on the assumptions made about what and how to model in computable general equilibrium (CGE) models. There are huge differences among them, some even showing losses to poor countries, such as in Africa. One has thus to be circumspect, while accepting that most models come up with significant payoffs from liberalization. But this does not extend to *bilateral preferential trade agreements* (PTAs) as a way to liberalise trade. Hardly any meaningful numbers can be yet attached to the damage they do, for they create a 'spaghetti bowl' of chaotic preferences across countries, representing system damage to the multilateral trading system, and also lending themselves to exploitation by hegemonic countries is such as the USA, distorting the world trading system by introducing non-trade features into the WTO. Anderson in chapter 10 was very critical of them, as were Pronk and Panagariya in Perspective papers 10.1 and 10.2, respectively. Anyone familar with the issues would have therefore classified them as below the line, worse than Kyoto Protocol, as a plague on the trading system from which we all expect so much. I was astonished that they were simply not ranked, instead of being ranked as disastrous:

- Multilateral trade liberalisation is the best way of reducing trade barriers and removing agricultural subsidies. It will ensure the highest payoff for all countries when trade is liberalized.
- *Unilateral trade liberalisation*, where undertaken, is also a high-benefit approach.
- PTAs are deplorable because their proliferation is destroying the world trading system.

- *Non-reciprocal trade liberalisation* for the poorest countries also creates additional preferences for a sub-set of developing countries and are therefore contributory factors to a deplorable deterioration in the world trading system, even though they are designed to reduce trade barriers and benefit the developing countries. EBA, GSP and such measures are therefore, on balance, not helpful and desirable ways to liberalise trade to benefit developing countries. Instead, *MFN non-preferential trade liberalisation* in products of export interest to all developing countries is a vastly preferable way of helping the developing countries as a group.

Access to Education (Chapter 4)

- *Educational reform* offers big payoffs relative to cost.
- In particular, programs to *eliminate tuition fees* offer huge returns, particularly because they enable the children of poor families to access highly profitable educational opportunities, not otherwise open to them due to lack of funds.
- Equally, high BCRs characterise the introduction of *external examiners*.

Conflicts (Chapter 3)

Conflict prevention evidently has enormous benefits, both economic and in relieving human anguish. But the efficiency and value of specific opportunities to prevent conflicts is not clearly and convincingly established. Policies to assist management of post-conflict situations is, however, better understood, though difficult.

Ranking the Opportunities: Jagdish N. Bhagwati

Challenge	Opportunities	Ranking
Communicable diseases	Control of HIV/AIDS	1
Malnutrition and hunger	Reducing the prevalence of iron deficiency anaemia and iodine, Vitamin A and zinc deficiencies	2
Subsidies and trade barriers	Trade liberalisation	3
Communicable diseases	Scaled-up basic health services	4
Malnutrition and hunger	Improving infant and child nutrition and exclusive breastfeeding promotion	5
Sanitation and access to clean water	Community-managed low-cost water supply and sanitation	6
Sanitation and access to clean water	Small-scale water technology for livelihoods	7
Sanitation and access to clean water	Research in water productivity in food production	8
Migration	Guest worker policies (unskilled)	9
Migration	Active immigration policies (skilled)	10
Governance and corruption	Lowering the costs of starting a new business	11
Communicable diseases	Control of malaria	12
Malnutrition and hunger	Investment in technology in developing country agriculture	13
Malnutrition and hunger	Reducing the prevalence of LBW	14
Climate change	Optimal carbon tax	15
Climate change	Value-at-risk carbon tax	16
Climate change	The Kyoto Protocol	17

ROBERT W. FOGEL

Malnutrition and Hunger (Chapter 7)

Reducing micronutrient deficiencies in populations in which they are prevalent was ranked high because of the low cost and high BCR. This opportunity gives a quick payoff. The opportunity of reducing *LBW* for pregnancies with high probabilities of LBW is also considered important.

Communicable Diseases (Chapter 2)

Control of *HIV/AIDS* is considered the most important challenge for ethical reasons. It is also important to control *malaria*, because malaria is not only a disabling disease with a high mortality rate but also weakens the immune system of individuals, thus raising susceptibility to other diseases.

Governance and Corruption (Chapter 6)

It is difficult to rank the opportunities in this challenge because the BCRs have not been estimated. However *reduction in state-imposed costs* of establishing a new business and in the costs associated with ongoing business/government relations is ranked as the most important of the five opportunities.

Climate Change (Chapter 1)

The three opportunities of climate change are given low ranks because of their low BCRs. However, it is important to produce scientific personnel to keep monitoring climate change. There should therefore be a budget for *continued scientific research* in this area. The environment is considered to be important, but it is not yet time to do anything massive about climate change. But with continued research and development (R&D) it will be possible to address future catastrophes and climate change mitigation and adaptation.

Migration (Chapter 8)

It is not possible to rank the opportunities given. There are too many unsettled issues about *social and political costs* as well as about economic costs to the complementary labour of left behind in sending countries.

Financial Instability (Chapter 5)

The first three opportunities are not proposals. On the need to pursue an international solution to the currency-mismatch problem, I have no basis for judgement, so the opportunity isn't included in the ranking.

Sanitation and Access to Clean Water (Chapter 9)

Community-managed low-cost water supply and sanitation is important in the control of malnutrition

by reducing the loss of essential nutrients. Research in water productivity should focus on the problems of very poor countries. Research in food productivity should be part of the investment in technology for developing the food resources of poor countries. *Small-scale water technology* is an important means of improving agricultural productivity in very poor communities.

Subsidies and Trade Barriers (Chapter 10)

In some countries the political battle over trade liberalisation can be so divisive as to nullify the economic benefits. In the case of small countries with weak infrastructure, *tariffs* may be the only feasible way of financing necessary government activities. Regional trade agreements (RTAs) and non-reciprocal access for low-income countries were not discussed in enough detail to provide a basis for ranking.

Conflicts (Chapter 3)

Religious and ethnic factors have much more to do with civil wars than economic factors. This has been true in the past, and remains true today.

Ranking the Opportunities: Robert W. Fogel

Challenge	Opportunities	Ranking
Communicable diseases	Control of HIV/AIDS	1
Malnutrition and hunger	Reducing the prevalence of iron deficiency anaemia and iodine, Vitamin A and zinc deficiencies	2
Sanitation and access to clean water	Community-managed low-cost water supply and sanitation	2
Malnutrition and hunger	Reducing the prevalence of LBW	3
Communicable diseases	Control of malaria	4
Sanitation and access to clean water	Research in water productivity in food production	5
Malnutrition and hunger	Investment in technology in developing country agriculture	5
Malnutrition and hunger	Improving infant and child nutrition and exclusive breastfeeding promotion	6
Sanitation and access to clean water	Small-scale water technology for livelihoods	6
Governance and corruption	Lowering the costs of starting a new business	7
Communicable diseases	Scaled-up basic health services	8
Subsidies and trade barriers	Trade liberalisation	9
Climate change	The Kyoto Protocol	10
Climate change	Optimal carbon tax	11
Climate change	Value-at-risk carbon tax	12
Migration	Guest worker policies (unskilled)	–
Migration	Active immigration policies (skilled)	–

BRUNO S. FREY

General Comments

Here only the four most important points relating to all the challenges will be discussed:

Inadequate Knowledge and Assumptions

The task to prioritise the ten challenges and the particular opportunities in each challenge is daunting. Reading the background chapters, the perspective papers and listening to the discussions, the dominant thought occurring was: 'How little do we know!' For many, if not most, of the issues the existing theoretical – but, in particular empirical – knowledge is quite inadequate. Moreover, there is often a large gap between the general discussion in the background chapters and

the BCRs the Experts panel is asked to indicate. But knowing little is in my view certainly no excuse for refusing to seriously attempt to establish the priorities envisaged in the Copenhagen Consensus. It is still far better to try to do the relatively best, than to do nothing – the problems addressed in the ten challenges are much too important.

The fact of inadequate knowledge should also remind us to be well aware of the assumptions which must necessarily be made. These often strongly affect the BCRs and, more generally, the prioritisation. It is also important to intensify efforts to improve our knowledge by research applied to these 'grand' issues rather than to the issues analysed in 'normal' research which are often devoted to the neat and tractable issues defined within the academic community itself. Economic education should also pay more importance to these 'grand' problems. In particular, it should be possible to pursue an academic career if a scholar is prepared to tackle such issues, even if they do not lend to easy, well-defined approaches and solutions.

Institutions and Institutional Reform

The discussions of the ten challenges revealed the crucial importance of institutions and of institutional reform. Two aspects can be distinguished:

(a) Several challenges can be met by undertaking *appropriate reforms of institutions*. This is most clearly visible in the case of governance and corruption (chapter 6). Improved public governance requires institutional changes, involving low direct economic costs but likely to yield very high economic and social benefits. They therefore should be undertaken. Such institutional reforms require little, if any, monetary outlays; in some cases the expenditure of money may even worsen the situation (thus, for example, it may increase, rather than lower, corruption). But many institutional changes are not costless in another sense. Effort must be expended to overcome *political opposition* to change. A major concern for dealing with the challenges is to devise strategies to successfully approach this task.

(b) What institutional conditions are being assumed when the BCRs are discussed? In the vast majority of the opportunities the expenditure of money makes sense only when institutional conditions are reasonably well developed. In particular, political governance must be such as to allow funds to reach their targets, rather than being diverted to other tasks, or being stolen. In the latter case, the expenditure of public money leads only to waste and fruitless corruption.

Unequal Nature of Challenges

The challenges are of an unequal nature. Some of them address issues in the *utility function* of individuals such as hunger or diseases. Others refer to *mechanisms* which help to achieve worthy goals. The dampening of financial instability and the lowering of protection are thus of no value in themselves but serve to raise GDP, which in turn raises individuals' well-being.

GDP Effects

Most studies measure the effects of the opportunities discussed in terms of GDP – i.e. consider only the productive side. In contrast, the utility side is neglected. This is most relevant for the challenges referring to hunger and diseases which are accompanied by great human suffering, or climate change and migration which involve many aspects affecting utility, but not productivity.

Individual Utility

The effects on individual utility can be captured by various methods such as contingent valuation surveys or hedonic pricing estimates. But these are confronted by major shortcomings. In particular, contingent valuation surveys tend to prompt the results implicit in the questions, while the hedonic pricing approach works only if the housing and labour markets are in perfect equilibrium – and this is most unlikely to be the case. The development of 'economic happiness research' (see Frey and Stutzer 2002) has offered an alternative way to consistently measure the effects of the opportunities on individual utility. Life satisfaction, subjective reported well-being (for short: happiness) can be measured in a satisfactory way by carefully designed surveys. A happiness function econometrically identifies the determinants, which can be ordered into personal, socio-demographic, economic and institutional–political factors. The effect of a particular factor, such as environmental quality or civil war, on happiness can then be identified. This approach has already been used in a few instances. One study (Luechinger, Stutzer and Frey 2004) has been able to measure the effect of civil war and terrorism on individual utility. The estimates suggest that the effect on life satisfaction is substantial. Thus, for example, the inhabitants of Paris would, on average, be equally well off with 14 per cent lower income if the level of terrorist activity is reduced to the level in the rest of France. The population of Northern Ireland would even be prepared to accept 40 per cent lower income if the civil war activities were as low as in the rest of the UK. These estimates are only preliminary and should be taken only as indicative, but they suggest that in future research on world challenges this method can be used, provided that more data on individual life satisfaction than currently available will be produced.

Specific Comments

Malnutrition and Hunger (Chapter 7)

1 The chapter does not deal with *famine*, though it still is of considerable importance today.
2 Malnutrition and hunger do not only affect productive capacities reflected in GDP, but entail high suffering from *hunger*. The need to exploit the opportunities discussed increases as the benefits are higher than indicated in the estimates shown in the chapter.

Communicable Diseases (Chapter 2)

The discussion focuses on AIDS and malaria which are without doubt of major importance. But it would also be desirable to consider *internationally transferred diseases*. SARS caused only a few victims and was quickly controlled, but it may well be that this is less the case for (yet unknown) future diseases. It may well happen that, due to air travel, they are distributed all over the world within one or two days, with potentially catastrophic consequences. While little is known about this challenge, money should be extended to establish an effective way to control future international communicable diseases.

Governance and Corruption (Chapter 6)

This is a clear case in which *institutional reform* is required. Many attempts to reduce corruption have failed, partly because it is deeply entrenched in many developing countries. To raise transparency is therefore likely to have little effect, because the persons involved see little or no wrongdoing. Transparency may in fact even have counterproductive effects: when people are made aware of the extent of corruption elsewhere, they may well be induced to follow suit. There is an analogy to the compensation

of managers: when it was made transparent in the USA, it resulted in a further explosion of salaries because the lower-paid managers became aware of their situation and demanded equal treatment with the better-paid managers.

In view of the many failed attempts to curb corruption, I venture to advance a new approach. It relies on the idea that the rulers and public bureaucrats in developing countries must be given an incentive to effectively use the aid provided from outside. This can be achieved by officially giving them a certain percentage (say, 25 per cent) of the aid given for their own purposes, provided they effectively use the remaining percentage (say, 75 per cent). If they do not comply, they will in the future not receive any money at all, and will therefore lose their share (the 25 per cent). This scheme has two advantages:

(a) Aid recipients have a strong incentive to use the money effectively
(b) The share given to the disposition of aid recipients is not unethical.

Migration (Chapter 8)

Martin rightly stresses that migration increases GNP as the migrants move from low- to high-productivity occupations. But this beneficial outcome depends on a crucial assumption, namely that the migrants are *productively employed in their new country*. But this is often not the case; in the EU, with an unemployment rate of about 10 per cent, immigrants are often unemployed, but receive full social security benefits. To some extent, migration into EU countries is motivated by the fact that it is possible to receive public transfers without having to work. Under these circumstances, migration does not raise overall GDP but rather puts an additional strain on the social security system. Its financing requires higher taxes on persons in productive employment, or burdens the economy by higher public debts. In any case, the growth of the economy will be negatively affected.

Subsidies and Trade Barriers (Chapter 10)

The reduction of tariffs and subsidies is a major contribution to overall welfare. However, there are costs associated with this beneficial move which should be taken into account. The level of tariffs and subsidies represents a *politico-economic equilibrium*; in particular, it reflects the power of organised interest groups. It would be naive to assume that this power disappears when the extent of protection against foreign competition is reduced. It just takes different forms: one is non-tariff restrictions (which are more difficult to observe and to work against), the other is social legislation (especially in labour markets). Both reduce the static and dynamic efficiency of the economy. The question, then, is whether the distortions by trade restrictions or those in other areas are larger. In my view, the available evidence suggests that the reductions of tariff restrictions is strongly beneficial, even when induced distortions elsewhere are taken into account.

Ranking the Opportunities: Bruno S. Frey

Challenge	Opportunities	Ranking
Communicable diseases	Control of HIV/AIDS	1
Malnutrition and hunger	Reducing the prevalence of iron deficiency anaemia and iodine, Vitamin A and zinc deficiencies	2
Communicable diseases	Control of malaria	3
Subsidies and trade barriers	Trade liberalisation	4
Governance and corruption	Lowering the costs of starting a new business	5
Sanitation and access to clean water	Small-scale water technology for livelihoods	6
Malnutrition and hunger	Investment in technology in developing country agriculture	7
Migration	Active immigration policies (skilled)	8
Sanitation and access to clean water	Re-use of wastewater for peri-urban agriculture	9
Malnutrition and hunger	Improving infant and child nutrition and exclusive breastfeeding promotion	10
Communicable diseases	Scaled-up basic health services	11
Malnutrition and hunger	Reducing the prevalence of LBW	12
Climate change	Optimal carbon tax	13
Climate change	The Kyoto Protocol	14
Sanitation and access to clean water	Research in water productivity in food production	15
Migration	Guest worker policies (unskilled)	16
Climate change	Value-at-risk carbon tax	17

References

Frey, B. S. and A. Stutzer, 2002: *Happiness and economics*, Princeton University Press, Princeton

Frey, B. S., S. Luechinger and A. Stutzer, 2004: Valuing public goods: the life satisfaction approach, Institute for Empirical Research in Economics, Working Paper, 184, University of Zurich

JUSTIN YIFU LIN

Introduction

The world we live in is not a perfect one – we face a wide range of daunting challenges. The Copenhagen Consensus 2004 has been a very useful exercise, not only bringing our attentions to ten of the most important problems confronting the world but also reviewing opportunities for addressing these problems. If all these challenges can be overcome successfully, we are going to have a much better place to live.

In my view, the most important opportunity for improving well-being in developing countries is the *governance reform*. Many governments in the developing countries distort prices, intervene in the functions of markets and deprive people of the opportunities of doing businesses freely. Those distortions and interventions result in corruption, stagnation, poverty and other miserable situations in their economies. From experience in China, Vietnam, India and other developing countries, I find that market-oriented reform, if carried out appropriately, will have the highest payoff. The economy will start to grow dynamically and many other problems, identified in the Copenhagen Consensus will be solved or alleviated. However, if the approach to market-oriented reform is not appropriate, the economy may collapse, as evidenced in the former Soviet Union (FSU) and Eastern Europe, bringing more problems for people in the country. Unfortunately, while the importance of good governance in developing countries is discussed, the approach of governance reform is not addressed in great detail at the Copenhagen Consensus.

It is also important to note that many projects in the developing countries, initiated by donors from the developed countries, failed after support from the donors was terminated. Many reasons are responsible for this failure. Institutional infrastructures in developing countries are poor. Without donors' direct involvement in implementation, local communities lack the ability to carry out projects. However, the donors' support and direct involvement are unlikely to last for ever. Failures may also arise from differences in priorities or discount rates due to the different constraints in developed and developing countries. People in the developing countries are facing various challenges to their very survival. They tend to give high priority to activities that will bring immediate material returns or alleviate direct threats to their survival. Due to the lack of capital and wealth, people in developing countries in general have a higher discount rate for future income and benefits than people in developed countries. Projects favoured by donors may not be worthwhile from the local people's point of view due to the high discount rate. Once support from donors ends, local people may not have the incentives to continue the projects. In evaluating the various opportunities related to developing countries, I will use a discount rate of at least 8 per cent, which is less than one-third of the market interest rate in most developing countries.

The Copenhagen Consensus assumes that we have US$ 50 bn at our disposal to allocate among thirty-eight opportunities for addressing ten problems in the world, especially in developing countries. When prioritising the opportunities, I will adjust the benefits and costs provided by chapters in the volume according to my judgements about whether the required institutions to implement the proposals and the priorities and appropriate discount rate exist for people in developing countries.

Malnutrition and Hunger (Chapter 7)

- Reducing the prevalence of iron deficiency anaemia and iodine, vitamin A and zinc deficiencies (opportunity 3) is a cost-effective way to improve the health of people in low-income countries. Empirical evidence and medical data clearly support this proposal. The proposed intervention is relatively easy to implement in developing countries, and the improvement of health is itself a desirable good. Moreover, health also contributes to people's *productivity in learning and working*. In my view, this option has the highest BCR, and should be listed at the very top of the opportunities.

- Most poor people rely on agriculture for their living. The 'Green Revolution' in Asia and Latin America shows that investments in agricultural technology (opportunity 4) have made important contributions to the increase of farmers' income and improvement of people's nutrition in many developing countries in Asia and Latin America. In the past, the 'Green Revolution' occurred mainly in those areas with good irrigation due to the difficulties of developing drought-resistant high-yield modern varieties through conventional breeding approaches. The maturity of *gene engineering* has made the breeding of new varieties with traits of resisting various insects, cold and other constraints to high yield much easier. Investments in international agricultural research institutions and national agricultural research systems will have a high return for increasing food supply and solving the problem of malnutrition in low-income countries in Africa and other parts of the world.

- The other proposed opportunities are not sufficiently cost-effective to deserve a high ranking compared to the opportunities 3 and 4.

Communicable Diseases (Chapter 2)

- HIV/AIDS is the most urgent challenge confronting the world, and is especially threatening in some parts of Africa. If there are no proper interventions from the global community, catastrophic results are inevitable in many countries. As effective means of *preventing HIV/AIDS* are available at reasonable costs now, it is ethically unacceptable to continue to ignore this problem in many poor countries.

- Opportunity 2 (control of HIV/AIDS) deserves a high ranking, in my judgement next to the provision of *micronutrients*. As a necessary institutional infrastructure is required to implement the package of HIV/AIDS prevention nationwide, the BCR is unlikely to be 52, as indicated by some pilot experiments mentioned in chapter 2. The ratio is more likely to be in the range of 19 or lower, as illustrated in the Thai case. Nevertheless, even taking the need for institutions for implementing the proposed intervention into consideration, the BCR of this proposal is still one of the highest among all opportunities.

• The control of *malaria* also has a high BCR. However, the issue is not as urgent as HIV/ AIDS.

• The investment to *scale up basic health services* (opportunity 3) sounds attractive. This opportunity, however, will have a high BCR only if the government is not corrupted and the required institutions at local level exist, which is doubtful in many poor countries.

Governance and Corruption (Chapter 6)

• Clearly, the preferred opportunity is 4, which proposes to enable people in low-income countries to *exploit profitable market opportunities* by reducing the state-imposed costs of establishing a new business. This option does not depend on setting up any new specific institutions, nor need it require substantial costs to carry out the proposal. As argued in chapter 6, governments in many developing countries obstruct the proper functions of markets and deprive poor people of the chance to pursue profitable market opportunities. From the experiences of East Asia, once governments in poor countries liberalise controls and allow people the freedom to exploit market opportunities for their own benefit, their economies will start to grow dynamically, creating conditions for solving other urgent challenges identified in the Copenhagen Consensus. In my judgement, the BCR of this option is one of the highest.

• Success in *procurement reform* (opportunity 2) will contribute to highly needed transparency in developing countries. It is likely that this reform will reduce the corruption and improve government services for poor people. International agencies such as the World Bank and other regional development banks may condition their aid to developing countries on procurement reform. However, the success of this reform will require a committed political leadership as well as a well-functioning civil society.

• It is important to note that it is only option 4 which can create new *streams of wealth* in developing countries. All other opportunities mentioned in association with this challenge work through allocating *existing* resources more efficiently. In my view, it is more important to create a new stream of wealth than to improve the efficiency of allocating the existing stock of resources.

Climate Change (Chapter 1)

• None of the opportunities for solving the issue of global warming is attractive. If a discount rate of 8 or even 5 per cent is used, all the three opportunities proposed by chapter 1 have net negative benefits.

• If the proposed *optimal tax of US$20* is implemented in China, according to the current level of carbon emission (3,108 million tons in 1998), the total carbon emission tax will reach about 5.5 per cent of China's GDP. The Chinese government's tax revenue is about 18.5 per cent of GDP; the proposed carbon tax will therefore lead to a 30 per cent increase in overall tax. Coal-using intensity is also different across sectors, which means that some coal-intensive sectors' tax rate may increase much more than the average 30 per cent. If the proposed optimal carbon tax were implemented, it could wipe out the coal-intensive sectors and be extremely harmful to economic growth in China. It would be more acceptable to impose the US$2 per ton of carbon emission tax, proposed in Perspective paper 1.1, than the optimal tax of US$20 per ton, proposed by Cline.

• The carbon emission *per capita* in low-income countries is substantially lower than that in high-income countries. The high-income countries should therefore take a larger responsibility for reducing carbon emissions than the low-income ones. Among the various options, Kyoto Protocol (opportunity 2) is more attractive, because it takes into account the existing low emissions in the developing countries and requires the high-income countries to take a leading position in the carbon emissions reduction.

Migration (Chapter 8)

- Migration is beneficial for migrants, skilled and unskilled alike, and will also be beneficial for the *receiving country* as a whole, although workers with similar skills in the receiving country may be potential losers. There will be some costs to the sending countries, such as the loss of returns to public investments in the migrants' education. The negative impact will be larger if the migrants possess scarce talents that are important for the development of the sending countries. If a migrant's children are left in the sending countries, the sending country will also be responsible for providing education and other services to them while receiving no tax revenues from the migrant.
- Opportunity 3, migration for development, is a more favourable choice than the other two if some new international arrangement such as a World Migration Organisation (WMO) can be formed. The receiving countries of migration may make a contribution to the WMO, proportional to the tax revenues collected from the migrants. The WMO in turn transfers the contributions from the migrant receiving countries as grants to the sending country, allowing the latter to use the grants for investing in education, health and other social development projects. As such, migration will be a win–win situation for both receiving and sending countries.

Financial Instability (Chapter 5)

- Financial instability is a very important issue for developing countries and *currency mismatch* is one of many causes of financial crises. However, currency mismatch is most likely to be linked to other fundamental causes of financial crisis, such as excessive corporate leverage, overheating and

fiscal deficits, rather than the cause of crisis itself. The proposal to deal with the currency mismatch problem advanced by chapter 5 does not address other fundamental reasons for financial crises. The opportunity to borrow internationally in local currency may encourage the developing country to borrow more and cause more crises. I support the Expert panel's decision to drop this proposal from the list of considered opportunities.
- Option 2, to reimpose some form of *capital control*, may be desirable for the developing countries. The capital market in developing countries is extremely small, so a large outflow of capital will inevitably trigger a financial crisis, and international capital flows will be intrinsically unstable. If fact, Japan and the four 'small dragons' of East Asia should all maintain some form of capital controls until their *per capita* income reaches the level of the high-income countries. If the reimposition of some form of capital controls in the developing countries is used to shield them from the shock of unstable international capital flows rather than to protect a distorted, inefficient domestic financial sector, the opportunity should have a high BCR.

Sanitation and Access to Clean Water (Chapter 9)

- Opportunity 5, research into *improving water productivity in food production*, is the most desirable. Researches in developing drought-resistant crops have not been successful. However, as discussed in chapter 7 on malnutrition and hunger, with the maturity of gene engineering, research is likely to be successful in the near future and to produce a high BCR in terms of increasing farmers' income and reducing the incidence of malnutrition and hunger.
- Opportunity 2, *small-scale water technology for livelihood*, is available at low cost. If the information is available and farmers in low-income countries have access to financial services (such as micro credit) for obtaining funds to purchase the technology, this opportunity will have a high BCR.

- *Community-managed low-cost water supply and sanitation* can be a very effective opportunity in countries with good community structures such as India, China and other East Asian countries. However, in Africa the required community institutional structures are questionable. The overall BCR will therefore not be as high as for opportunity 2.

Subsidies and Trade Barriers (Chapter 10)

- The removal of all kinds of trade barriers should be listed as a top priority. Chinese experience confirms this wisdom: the annual growth rate of trade has been 16 per cent per annum since the reform and 'open-door policy' began in 1978. According to research I carried out, a 10 per cent increase in trade contributes to a 1 per cent increase in GDP growth. Trade growth has therefore contributed to about 1.6 per cent of GDP growth annually in China since 1978.
- The elimination of *agricultural subsidies* in developed countries will lead to the increase of agricultural prices in the world market. This will be most beneficial to the rural poor in developing countries if they produce and sell part of their agricultural produce to the market. However, the urban poor and farmers that do not produce enough agriculture produce for their own consumption will be hurt by the price increase. Therefore, some compensation for those losers due to the increase of agricultural prices will be desirable.

Access to Education (Chapter 4)

While education has been universally endorsed as a key to improve the well-being of people in underdeveloped countries, empirical studies have often failed to find positive impacts of education on economic growth in developing countries. The main reason may be that the increase of education will enhance people's ability to handle the *disequilibrium situations* arising from structural change, industrial upgrading, introduction of new technology, etc. The effect of education on economic growth will therefore depend not only on how effectively educational programmes are carried out but also on the government's macroeconomic management, two aspects often highly correlated in developing countries. I support the Expert panel's judgement that the increase of resources to education itself may not be enough to contribute to the improvement of people's well-being in developing countries.

Conflicts (Chapter 3)

The economic, social, and human costs of civil wars are enormous, as chapter 3 ably documented. The payoff for avoiding civil wars in developing countries would be extremely high. However, an effective prevention of civil war requires a good understanding of the *causes and circumstances* that lead to each individual conflict. Chapter 3 provides a useful framework for understanding these causes. While post-conflict intervention from the international community, as proposed in chapter 3, seems to be an interesting idea, overall the proposals fail to provide convincing arguments for reducing the civil war in developing countries.

Ranking the Opportunities: Justin Yifu Lin

Challenge	Opportunities	Ranking
Malnutrition and hunger	Reducing the prevalence of iron deficiency anaemia and iodine, Vitamin A and zinc deficiencies	1
Communicable diseases	Control of HIV/AIDS	2
Governance and corruption	Lowering the costs of starting a new business	3
Subsidies and trade barriers	Trade liberalisation	4
Malnutrition and hunger	Investment in technology in developing country agriculture	5
Sanitation and access to clean water	Research in water productivity in food production	6
Sanitation and access to clean water	Small-scale water technology for livelihoods	7
Sanitation and access to clean water	Community-managed low-cost water supply and sanitation	8
Communicable diseases	Control of malaria	9
Migration	Active immigration policies (skilled)	10
Migration	Guest worker policies (unskilled)	11
Malnutrition and hunger	Improving infant and child nutrition and exclusive breastfeeding promotion	12
Malnutrition and hunger	Reducing the prevalence of LBW	13
Communicable diseases	Scaled-up basic health services	14
Climate change	The Kyoto Protocol	15
Climate change	Optimal carbon tax	16
Climate change	Value-at-risk carbon tax	17

DOUGLASS C. NORTH

WITH THE ASSISTANCE OF

SONJA THOMSEN

Introduction

The issues discussed at this conference are of great importance and deserve a lot more attention than the week of intensive scrutiny and debate that we undertook. Nevertheless, both the chapters in this volume and the related Perspective papers were, in general, of excellent quality and the ensuing discussion explored in depth the complex issues involved in evaluating and prioritising the issues. While some of the opportunities advanced in the chapters could be realised by simply redirecting resources, others would entail altering the existing institutional structure.

I wish to elaborate briefly on the significance of the institutional framework, since it is the key to successfully undertaking reforms and was not given sufficient attention by either the chapters or the Perspective papers. *Institutions are the structure that humans impose on human interaction* and therefore constitute the *incentive system* that underlies both the problems to be solved and the opportunities essential to a solution. While overall national institutions are important, the local institutional setting plays an equally significant part. 'Bottom-up' institutional reform entails creating a structure that is appropriate to community needs and preferences and reaches people living in the poorest areas – not an easy task if the institutional infrastructure is not in place. Altering institutions through the political system is problematic because the organisations that have come into existence as a result of the existing institutional framework will be threatened by changes in that framework and accordingly will oppose them. Institutional changes have also to be made taking the history and culture of the specific country into consideration when considering implementation and delivery of opportunities. The chapter authors had a tendency to slight the cost of institutional reform, but the radical difference between the private and social rate of return makes clear that the political market works differently from the economic market and that altering the political market in order to realise the high social returns in many of the opportunities poses fundamental problems.

Malnutrition and Hunger (Chapter 7)

In this challenge, four opportunities were given. My ranking is as follows. Reducing micronutrient deficiencies in populations in which they are prevalent is 2. The BCR is perceived to be high and there should be few institutional obstacles to realising this opportunity. Reducing LBW for pregnancies is 9; improving infant and child nutrition in populations with high prevalence of child malnutrition is 11. Both of these opportunities require an *institutional structure* in place in order for them to be successful and to get the perceived benefits. The costs of securing the institutional setting are likely to be very high in some areas and relatively low in others. The key is the degree to which there is an *existing infrastructure of institutions at the local level* to deliver the essential services.

Communicable Diseases (Chapter 2)

Control of HIV and AIDS ranks as 1. The costs seem underestimated, but so do the benefits; the BCR is surely very high. The HIV epidemic requires both treatment and preventative interventions, and as chapter 2 makes clear 'requires political and social commitment at all levels' (p. 97). Moreover as van der Gaag stressed in Perspective paper 2.2, government interventions have frequently been ineffective and 'too little attention given to what the private sector can do' (p. 128). The challenge of

controlling HIV and AIDS is linked primarily to SSA, where the situation is very severe. AIDS is one of the main threats to the African continent, posing the risk of disabling it both economically and socially. The opportunity is therefore primarily focused on this geographical area. Benefits are assumed to be high because control of AIDS can play a critical role in improving *economic performance* in the entire continent.

Of the other opportunities in this challenge, I rank control of malaria as 10; again there are very high benefits in eliminating a scourge that kills more than 2 million persons (mostly children) a year. A major problem has been developing an infrastructure for delivery of an antidote in Africa where a scattered population and high information costs exist. Scaled-up basic health services ranks as 12, and again it is necessary to develop the essential institutional infrastructure.

Governance and Corruption (Chapter 6)

Susan Rose-Ackerman has provided an excellent survey of the sources of corruption and poor governance in chapter 6, but as the study and illustrations make clear, the problem does not lend itself to overall general reform. The opportunities are difficult to rank because corruption is rooted in the specific society and economic activity in which it takes place and therefore solutions must be tailored to the specific institutional setting so that no generalised solution can be prioritised. However, I rank one of them, lowering the cost of starting a new business, as 8. It has a positive BCR: reducing regulations that *raise the cost* of *starting new businesses* is clearly worthwhile.

Climate Change (Chapter 1)

Compared to the other opportunities, the climate change opportunities presented I rank as 'bad projects.' The reasoning is straightforward. Most of the benefits are far into the future and the substantial costs are upfront and immediate. Given the uncertainties associated with both the projections and the consequences, climate change cannot compete with the other urgent issues we confront, although it is clear that some steps must be taken now to forestall adverse consequences down the road.

Migration (Chapter 8)

The only opportunity I ranked within this challenge was lowering the barriers to migration of skilled workers. I ranked it as 7, due to its good BCR. The *institutional setting* is very important if migration is to have positive effects for both receiving and sending countries. For the receiving countries there must be a structure that will encourage assimilation and integration of the immigrant. For the sending countries there must be compensation for the loss of such skilled labour (although it is doubtful that compensation can make up for the loss of skills associated with emigration). The guestworker programmes opportunity seems to have a negative BCR and therefore I did not rank it.

Financial Instability (Chapter 5)

Opportunities 1–3 (regulating markets, imposing capital controls, a single world currency) are either unfeasible because they have negative BCRs (according to Eichengreen) or for practical reasons and are not considered actual opportunities. But 1, regulating financial markets, had negative BCRs only because of the way Eichengreen framed the issue. All markets are structured by an institutional framework that provides the *incentive structure* of that market. One can structure a financial market at a moment of time to provide the incentives that will encourage expansion while the institutional structure will concurrently discourage destabilising activities (and such a structured market constitutes a positive form of regulation). However, it is also important to be aware that it is a non-ergodic world, and any policy that is likely to work today may be obsolete tomorrow. Indeed it has been the radical change in information costs, technology and political organisation that has made any lasting solution impossible. The only opportunity that had

promise is 4, the currency mismatch; however, this issue lacks substantial information on various externalities.

Sanitation and Access to Clean Water (Chapter 9)

The opportunity of community-managed low-cost water supply and sanitation I rank as 3, the opportunity of small-scale water technology for livelihoods is 5 and the opportunity of research in water productivity in food production is 6. All these opportunities are considered to have a very high BCR and are likely to be feasible. Small-scale technology development and community-managed water supply and sanitation were perceived to be opportunities that would *reach the poor almost immediately* and therefore I rank them higher than the others here, even though they are all considered very important.

The challenge of providing water and sanitation for the population of the world is very important, but also a challenge that is dependent on an appropriate and well-functioning institutional setting. The costs of delivery and implementation do not seem clear in chapter 7 and are most likely much higher than described. This is also evident when considering the necessary infrastructure. However the benefits are equally estimated to be high and the BCR is therefore considered high. *Implementation* is a major problem in SSA, since the infrastructure is mostly non-existent.

Subsidies and Trade Barriers (Chapter 10)

Three opportunities presented in this chapter were gathered into one and named trade liberalisation and removal of agricultural subsidies. This opportunity I ranked as 4. It is important as it has a very high BCR; however, we deliberately ignored the political costs of implementation, and the institutional structure to be put in place in regard to liberalising trade and removing agricultural subsidies has to be very *specific to the context* of the specific country.

Access to Education (Chapter 4)

The opportunities within the challenge of education I cannot rank, as we still lack substantial information. Pritchett acknowledges as much. As in the case of governance and corruption, there are few generalisations that apply across diverse countries and levels of education. As (Perspective paper 6) said to me, an investment of $100 m in well-structured research would yield immense benefits in providing definitive understanding of the *basic sources of educational improvement*. Such research has not been done, even though it appears that this should be a high priority item for research.

Conflicts (Chapter 3)

I consider the elimination or reduction in violence and warfare as the most crucial problem of human survival. More humans were killed in warfare in the twentieth century than in all of previous history, and given the awesome power of modern military technology for mass destruction it should clearly have top priority. But there is little convincing research on effective means of *reduction or elimination*. While eliminating civil wars would be a step in this direction we were not persuaded that the opportunities advanced in chapter 3 would have general applicability.

Ranking the Opportunities: Douglass C. North

Challenge	Opportunities	Ranking
Communicable diseases	Control of HIV/AIDS	1
Malnutrition and hunger	Reducing the prevalence of iron deficiency anaemia and iodine, Vitamin A and zinc deficiencies	2
Sanitation and access to clean water	Community-managed low-cost water supply and sanitation	3
Subsidies and trade barriers	Trade liberalisation	4
Sanitation and access to clean water	Small-scale water technology for livelihoods	5
Sanitation and access to clean water	Research in water productivity in food production	6
Migration	Active immigration policies (skilled)	7
Governance and corruption	Lowering the costs of starting a new business	8
Malnutrition and hunger	Reducing the prevalence of LBW	9
Communicable diseases	Control of malaria	10
Malnutrition and hunger	Improving infant and child nutrition and exclusive breastfeeding promotion	11
Communicable diseases	Scaled-up basic health services	12
Climate change	The Kyoto Protocol	13
Climate change	Optimal carbon tax	14
Climate change	Value-at-risk carbon tax	15

THOMAS C. SCHELLING

General Points

- One cannot value life or cost of death in terms of lost productivity. Life as such has no value, since the dead person is removed from the equation. If a person produces the same amount as she consumes, it makes no difference to GDP if she is dead. The value of life thus depends fully on the person's relations in life: father and breadwinner vs ten-year old vs five-year old, etc. GDP *per capita* is thus not an appropriate measure by which to value life. If death brings loss, whose loss is it (i.e. not the dead person's)? Grief and orphanage is real, GDP is not. Death should be evaluated in terms of what is left behind: only externalities count.
- Valuing the life/cost of death must be detached from GDP in order to avoid a BCR dependent on nationality, because GDP is not a valid measure.
- One must deduct the growth rate from the discount rate, since it is essential to assume overall growth in *per capita* income (global GDP) *if* valuing life from GDP measure.
- One must assume a reasonable level of institutional framework development.
- This suggests a net 3 per cent discount rate.

Malnutrition and Hunger (Chapter 7)

- Providing essential vitamins and nutrients in the form of animal products, although reported to be highly effective, is probably a very expensive way to deal with the problem.
- This identifies a possible fifth opportunity, namely to avoid pregnancy in addressing LBW.

Communicable Diseases (Chapter 2)

- BCRs should include the suffering of a life lived with disease.

- Death is not a 'bad' if one is terminally ill or living in unbearable pain.

Governance and Corruption (Chapter 6)

- One should begin by targeting petty corruption: the 'trickle-up' effect is possible to improve the morale of citizens.
- The opportunities presented do not compete: if given three hours with a corrupt president, I would emphasise only one opportunity. If given more time to engage in dialogue with various organisations, etc., I would advocate several options and approaches.
- The only costs of reform are human resources (enthusiasm and commitment). The costs are strictly country-dependent.
- In the case of corruption, it is safer *not* to evaluate in terms of money.
- We need a social CBA.
- We need $50 bn to attract attention to the issue in targeting citizens' moral incentives, not to spend on reform as such.

Climate Change (Chapter 1)

- The discount rate as presented in the chapters in this volume is not a discount for time, but a discount for the greater wealth of future populations.
- The discount rate loses significance when discounting over 300 years.
- Future generations will be much richer than current ones, and it thus makes no sense to make current generations 'pay' for the problems of future generations.
- A fourth opportunity should be to invest resources in R&D: this will give future generations a choice and a base for comparison which we currently lack.
- None of the relevant chapters mentions geo-engineering (i.e. changing the reflectivity of the earth and its atmosphere), possibly by putting particulates in the stratosphere, as suggested by the US National Academy of Sciences in 1992.

Migration (Chapter 8)

- Discriminatory aid policies will not play well with the public or the international development agencies – i.e. compensating some but not other countries by replenishment of the gap that migrants leave behind. This is, however, a political problem.
- Migration is exceedingly beneficial for the migrants, but problematic for the sending and receiving countries. An important consideration thus becomes: does migration benefit GDP or does it merely benefit the people who migrate from the poor to the rich country?
- In addressing the issue of replenishment, an option could in theory be to establish medical schools in developing/sending countries, paid for by the developed/recipient countries, and by this process export doctors to the USA and Europe. This will benefit both the sending and receiving country – if richer countries finance the education of highly qualified technicians, for example. This benefits the sending country by targeting the people who migrate anyway, and it becomes costless for the country to 'lose the brains', and the receiving country gains the skilled labour of which it is in need.
- However, the receiving countries cannot and will not determine the question of migration on the basis of a BCR. The subject is too political. Populations of rich countries will not care about an increase in global GDP as an incentive to lower barriers to migrants. They will worry about jobs and the strain on the social security system. Thus, the many externalities that cannot be valued in terms of costs or benefits make the ranking of the opportunity in coherence with the other thirty-five opportunities difficult.
- One basic problem concerning unskilled labour migration is: what are the skills learned in the receiving country that can possibly be a benefit to the sending country upon return? It strikes me that making beds in hotel rooms, mowing lawns or loading and unloading trucks are not new skills for which there will be much demand back home.

Sanitation and Access to Clean Water (Chapter 9)

- The ranking of the five opportunities presented by Rijsberman is based on the following grounds:

(1)   *Small-scale water projects*: ranked 6 in the hope that it will catalyse a widespread diffusion. The idea is that once small-scale projects begin to gain terrain, they will spread to neighbouring communities. There is some empirical evidence of this happening in India, and it seems reasonable to imagine the same could happen in Africa, where the problems are apparent.

(2)   *Small-scale irrigation*: ranked 9, ahead of immigration, but behind all the disease and malnutrition projects.

(3)   *Re-use of wastewater*: ranked 19, since it is not yet ready for implementation.

(4)   *Wetlands*: ranked 17, simply because there was no basis for any higher ranking.

(5)   *Research on water productivity in food production*: this should be combined with the agricultural research opportunity of chapter 7 on malnutrition and hunger, and then the opportunity raised from rank 5 to 4, ahead of malaria.

Financial Instability (Chapter 5)

No comment.

Subsidies and Trade Barriers (Chapter 10)

No comment.

Access to Education (Chapter 4)

- In the absence of drastic systemic change, little or nothing can be accomplished by providing the things that money can buy – not books, teacher training, televisions, furnishing.

- Resistance to such systemic change is like a stone wall.
- A breach in the wall of resistance might occur through the initiation of externally administered exams, the results being publicly available. Such a procedure might generate local demands for necessary reforms.
- A major obstacle to school attendance is the cost to families of sending children to school. In many school systems there are fees for attending public schools. Outside funds might make it possible to waive the fees, most cost-effective would be if this policy could be targeted at children who would otherwise not attend. One way to achieve this would be to waive fees in rural areas. (Waiving fees across the board might have the effect of reducing some families' sense of responsibility for schools.)
- Cash grants to poor families conditional on children attending school are promising. Again, it helps to target the children who would not otherwise attend, if that can be done.

Conflicts (Chapter 3)

- If one were to use aid as a prevention of civil war, one would probably do just the things we talked about under communicable diseases, malnutrition and hunger, sanitation and access to clean water, etc. Therefore we have already covered the subject.
- Possibly a proposal for military intervention should be considered. The costs appear remarkably low, and if the troops are to be provided from other poor countries they may indeed need compensation for the military expense.

Comment on Nancy Stokey's Expert Ranking

I find Nancy Stokey's ranking comments (pp. 639ff.) not only persuasive: she covers most of what I would want to say, so my main ranking discussion above is basically an endorsement of what she says.

I do have, however, a comment about climate change. Neither chapter 1 nor Perspective papers 1.1 and 1.2 introduced any kind of programme for utilising part of the $50 bn in the next few years. They might have proposed, for example, billions of dollars of research and development (R&D) that could immediately be undertaken and that would reduce the cost of carbon abatement over the long run; they did not. None of their proposals was pertinent to our task. I think there were two reasons for this: each of them had been working the field for many years and each of them had a well-established position and was intent on making his case. Perhaps the invitation to them did not emphasise sufficiently that we were engaging in a budgetary exercise and the task of the chapter author was to make a case for spending some part of the $50 bn, which he did not do. I think that instead of classifying the three climate proposals as 'bad', we should have classified them as 'inapplicable'. Also, Kyoto was never a proposal. It may have been implicitly an 'option,' but Cline does not offer Kyoto as something worth financing, nor does Mendelsohn (Perspective paper 1.1) or Manne (Perspective paper 1.2). Our group thought that Kyoto was not a good approach, but it should not have been on the agenda because none of the three authors thought it worth considering.

Ranking the Opportunities: Thomas C. Schelling

Challenge	Opportunities	Ranking
Malnutrition and hunger	Reducing the prevalence of iron deficiency anaemia and iodine, Vitamin A and zinc deficiencies	1
Communicable diseases	Control of HIV/AIDS	2
Malnutrition and hunger	Improving infant and child nutrition and exclusive breastfeeding promotion	3
Sanitation and access to clean water	Research in water productivity in food production	4
Malnutrition and hunger	Investment in technology in developing country agriculture	4
Communicable diseases	Control of malaria	5
Sanitation and access to clean water	Community-managed low-cost water supply and sanitation	6
Malnutrition and hunger	Reducing the prevalence of LBW	7
Communicable diseases	Scaled-up basic health services	8
Subsidies and trade barriers	Trade liberalisation	9
Governance and corruption	Lowering the costs of starting a new business	10
Migration	Active immigration policies (skilled)	11
Migration	Guest worker policies (unskilled)	12
Sanitation and access to clean water	Small-scale water technology for livelihoods	13
Climate change	Optimal carbon tax	14
Climate change	The Kyoto Protocol	15
Climate change	Value-at-risk carbon tax	16

VERNON L. SMITH

Introduction

In considering each opportunity I ask two questions: does it increase freedom for somebody, and/or does it help people help themselves to become self sustaining?

Some items are strong complements, and difficult to separate. Alternatively, think of them as *merged opportunities*.

In the highest-rated category – very good – my ratings differ somewhat in order and content from those in the Copenhagen Consensus items: control of HIV/AIDS, providing micronutrients, trade liberalization, and control of malaria. I moved the following up from lower Consensus ratings for further elaboration: development of new farm technolo-gies, small-scale water technologies for livelihood, and lowering barriers to migration that, to me, is integral to free trade.

Communicable Diseases (Chapter 2)

Control of Malaria

Malaria appears to be a disease that may have escaped control because of an overreaction to early environmental concerns about the widespread use of DDT for insecticide spray. Although its primary use was in agriculture, where acceptable substitutes were available, its effectiveness in Malaria control was very negatively impacted by the overreaction that banned it where close effective substitutes were available. I think that it is fair to say that science collided with politics and a bad press, and the failure fully to appreciate the tradeoff between small, tolerable environmental costs and potentially large loss of life produced an unbalanced policy.

But success is in the future not the past, and we should get on with incurring the relatively small costs of interventions that promise a large return in saved lives. The great success in KuaZulu Natel resulting from the use of insecticide spray (40 per cent DDT, 60 per cent delta methrin) and combination drug therapies shows that major reductions in malaria cases can be achieved.

HIV/AIDS

This disease carries the promise of killing or disabling so many people that entire economies are threatened with rapid negative growth and potential collapse in economic continuity and network sustainability.

One would think that the challenge was too overwhelming to admit the biased and arbitrary exclusion of private response initiatives, some of which have already invested in a delivery system, on the ideological grounds that no one should be permitted to profit from AIDS. Yet I am dismayed to learn in this challenge session that:

> International donors are generally reluctant to involve private insurers or private providers. NGOs are usually involved in development efforts, including the prevention and treatment of diseases. But the for-profit private sector is often ignored or excluded, especially when it comes to health care provision. Still, the little bit of success in providing drug treatment for HIV/AIDS patients is largely a private sector story...
>
> The total problem is daunting, but more can be done if donors were willing to lift constraints that currently prevent a much larger role for the private sector. For instance, an HMO in Nigeria covers about 65,000 patients and has contracts with about 200 hospitals. This organisation exists, and the infrastructure exists. Unfortunately, the organisation is under tremendous financial stress, up to the point that it is no longer capable of treating (in-hospital) end-stage AIDS patients. The same organisation could provide drug treatment for about 10,000 patients, if only someone would put up the money for the drugs and for the work involved. But organisations that can be accused of trying to 'make money from AIDS' are not eligible for interna-

tional financial support. Governments are supposed to deal with the problem, but fail to do so. Those who have the organisation and the infrastructure to, at the very least, provide a modest contribution, are not asked (and financed) to do so. (Van der Gaag, Perspective paper 2.2)

Wherever private organisations can make a contribution, funds should not be denied them. Support should not be arbitrarily restricted to governments, especially if there is evidence of their failure, and the private sector can be effective with donor support. Why not provide matching donor funds to private agencies? The rhetoric of 'market failure' should not become a means of protecting government failure, especially as in this case the private sector has shown some progress, even if small compared to the magnitude of the problem.

Donor biases against private initiatives leave me sceptical about the chances of success of major expenditure programmes to alleviate the HIV/AIDS problem. Much of the funding is likely to be wasted in trying to deliver help through governments poorly motivated to provide adequate infrastructure. Spraying programmes to control malaria seem more deliverable without heavy involvement by local governments.

Subsidies and Trade Barriers (Chapter 10)

There is no other world policy – with the exception, perhaps, of free migration – that would be more effective in creating human betterment and reducing poverty through wealth creation than removing all restrictions on trade and all subsidies to private businesses. Goods, services and people must be free to move where they command the highest individual value, which in turn provides the greatest world value.

This is not widely appreciated and understood by the average citizen or her political representatives because wealth creation through increasing specialisation is no part of the intentions of individuals myopically seeking to improve their own lot. The fundamental theorem in economics is still that specialisation is limited by the extent of the development of the market. What has changed since the theorem was stated over 225 years ago has been the increasing empirical support for it.

'Globalisation' is just a new word for pushing the extreme geographical limits of specialisation and wealth creation. The archeological and DNA evidence is that it started over 40,000 years ago when our common Cro-Magnon ancestors walked out of Africa, no doubt in search of betterment.

Malnutrition and Hunger (Chapter 7)

Development of New Farm Technologies

What makes this opportunity so attractive is the enormous success demonstrated by agricultural technology in the 'Green Revolution' from the 1960s to the 1990s in bringing foodgrain self-sufficiency to Mexico, Pakistan, India (even a net exporter for awhile), China, etc. and preventing the deaths of hundreds of millions of people – new seed varieties increased the nutritional yield of wheat, rice and maize; reduced plant production of fibrous waste; improved metabolism of water, fertiliser and trace elements in the soil; improved natural resistance to pests, and to climate variation; shortened maturity times; and reduced dependence on traditional soil erosion tilling methods. This happened in the face of dire predictions (e.g. The Population Bomb) of mass starvation. From 1965 to 1992, world grain output rose 170 per cent, with land cultivation increasing only 1 per cent.

But this revolution barely impacted SSA. Nor has it reached areas of poverty still dependent on subsistence agriculture which are outside the market system and lack transport facilities or access to commercial distribution systems. The 'Green Revolution' needs to expand to a new generation of seed varieties (including GMOS) and technologies that can improve productivity not only in traditional commercial grains but also *for the very poor who are dependent on diverse garden products to supplement their food supply*. That the result may not

yield the dramatic results of the 'Green Revolution' is beside the point, because that is not the alternative for these people. The need is to deliver better technology that the recipients can relate to in their immediate circumstances, gain improvement and help to launch them on a recovery path that can exploit grain technologies after infrastructure has improved, building on local knowledge to produce visible local results. This option also leverages the other opportunities by reducing malnutrition. Particularly important is the fact that delivering the fruits of new farm technologies enables people in regions of food impoverishment to help themselves by increasing their food self-sufficiency. They become a part of the solution rather than only accepting welfare gifts.

Although intervention to reduce malnutrition is as important as reducing hunger through these new farm technologies, the difficulties of *delivery* are far more formidable. Farmers can see the immediate personal benefits of adopting higher-yield seeds that can be planted without ploughing, weeds controlled without hoeing, etc. The benefits of Vitamin A supplements are neither visible nor convincingly demonstrable to them. Their use cannot be related to people's experience as can food growing methods.

Sanitation and Access to Clean Water (Chapter 9)

Small-Scale Sanitation and Water Technologies for Livelihoods

These opportunities clearly complement both the communicable diseases and malnutrition/hunger opportunities. Moreover, unlike most of the challenges, this one lends itself to CBA, in the sense that money might actually be spent for specific purposes – irrigation, sanitation – to get specific garden crop and health benefits.

I particularly like the local small-scale delivery of water and sanitation equipment to community-based systems for managing the commons. This builds on community social structure, uses local information and draws on local resources. It strengthens local communities by increasing their self-sufficiency, while central system water resource development goes in the opposite direction. There are no more important initiatives – opportunities to support – because it involves direct delivery, and the locals who benefit must invest their time and resources to make it a success. Moreover, especially in irrigation communities can see directly the value of the technology and are motivated to learn to use it. In juxtaposition with irrigation, although the recipients may not understand the invisible microbes controlled by sanitation, those delivering the help have a better chance of being credible. This is the type of aid that Elinor Ostrom's research has shown to be efficacious, precisely because it is not dependent on big-time market/rocket science.

Migration (Chapter 8)

There are high benefits from the small direct costs that are achievable by migration, particularly into the USA, in spite of formidable national barriers. The gain is generated by the movement of people from low-productivity regions to high-productivity ones. It is the individual, but also the community, and in particular the support community, that can jump-start the gains. The gains are captured by the migrants and the destination country, but except for migrants that eventually return to their origin country (as with Iceland, China and India), there is a loss to the originating country.

Although one can imagine schemes that compensate the sending countries for their loss, I think this would be bad policy. Sending countries are failing to provide opportunities for their people that cause them to want to stay. As always, the problem of any society is the *utilisation of knowledge*: to institute structures, or allow them to emerge that, as Hayek would say, induce people to do the desirable things without anyone having to tell them what to do. The need is for those countries suffering from a 'brain drain' to change their policies, not hamstring movement. China and India are examples of countries that today provide more self-development opportunities for their people than in the past, and as a result many past migrants are returning. Countries can change: don't reward their natural inclination

to do the wrong thing. The best way to get back experienced and productive migrants is to make sure that their return will be rewarded with ground-floor development opportunities that build on what they have learned in the receiving country.

The high BCRs from migration are indicators of the value created by freer movement of people, but not a measure of the net gains attainable by new international spending programmes, unless you know how to spend the money. I come out as an eager supporter of reduced barriers to migration, but I am not a supporter of programmes that attempt to micromanage migration.

Looking at the opportunities presented in chapter 8, I believe that reducing barriers for migration of skilled workers is the soundest opportunity. Modest barriers to the more unskilled workers may actually serve as a good filter; only the most upwardly mobile surmount them. And without a support community in the receiving country, they are less likely to leave permanently. The leaky US–Mexican border is a case in point; it takes some ingenuity to get in, and the underground system has produced some effective breeches that allow people to travel back and forth between families remaining in the South and filling temporary service jobs in the North. It's called 'gains from trade', and deserves a better press.

Governance and Corruption (Chapter 6)

Rose-Ackerman's chapter 6 notes that: 'All political systems need to mediate the relationship between private wealth and public power. Those that fail risk a dysfunctional government captured by wealthy interests. Corruption is one system of such failure with private willingness-to-accept trumping public goals. Private individuals and business firms pay to get routine services and to get to the head of the bureaucratic queue.'

I do not find this sort of rhetoric – evil private interests derailing lofty social ends – a useful way to introduce and define the problem. What are the decisions and the structures within which corruption occurs in these private – government exchanges? There is time enough to identify the devils, of which there are no doubt more than enough to go around in both the private and the public domain. Why is there a bureaucratic queue? Are there perverse incentives that cause it? The immediate substance of corruption is the transfer of a right by a seller to a buyer for a price. The gain from the transfer necessarily involves willingness-to-accept by the seller as much as willingness-to-pay by the buyer. Are 'wealthy interests' capturing a dysfunctional government, or are government gatekeepers personally profiting by privately taxing the wealth-creating activities in the economy? Or is it a two-sided equilibrium? The meat of chapter 6 actually provides some great examples, after a disheartening rhetorical start:

(1) Corruption in the sense of bribes stems primarily from the government regulation of *rights to act* – 'legitimate' or not – on the part of citizens and their organisations. It is significant that every US proposal to deregulate industry X is opposed by the regulators and the regulated of X.

(2) The primary focus should be on the *rules and rights* to be defined by government regulations, the latter designed so that they best promote, encourage and protect citizen productive activities. You start with that principle then ask if there is a rule structuring the incentives so that they are self-regulating and self-disciplining, with the state simply enforcing the resulting (property) rights to act. Then you ask whether there is need to monitor the enforcer or a need for better incentives for the enforcer, etc.

(3) It is not possible to evaluate the effectiveness and efficiency of government without first recognising (1), and acting on (2).

In some cases it is clear that the rule restricting the exercise of rights should be repealed or substantially liberalised. The Chinese Constitution prohibited individuals from owning and therefore exchanging private property, but community norms and practices permitted ownership and property was in fact bought and sold. This led to bribes being collected to allow such illegal activities. Concern over the resulting widespread corruption led the government early in 2004 to revise the constitutional rule to permit ownership of private property that 'had been legitimately acquired'. The latter Catch-22 was a political compromise that did not

entirely close the door on corruption, but it was believed that the change would substantially reduce corruption recognised by the state to be contrary to the public interest. Maybe it was the profiting bureaucrats that retained the Catch-22, disguising it as a way of providing some protection 'for the people'.

Rules such as those against theft, robbery, kidnapping and murder clearly violate legitimate wealth-creating rights to act, and, should be enforced and defined so that they are practically enforceable. Where police corruption is a problem, as in the USA, it is most commonly evident in the enforcement of laws against the voluntary exchange of illegal commodities such as alcohol under prohibition, drugs and sex. In these cases, if repeal is not politically acceptable you must perforce probably expect a certain amount of corruption as part of the cost of trying to prevent voluntary exchanges judged by other people's opinion to be unjustified.

Rights of access to public resources such as the airwaves, public land, import markets and state owned extractive resources are best simply privatised at auction or by other means, perhaps even free access, thus eliminating the need to have a gatekeeper tempting bribery. Here the crucial issues are auction design (information and incentives to bid value), auction objectives (efficiency or revenue) and the need to define clear alienable rights to the assets being auctioned.

Should a public resource be auctioned for the account of the Treasury as a tax offset, or for the account of the citizens whose incomes are taxed? The advantage of the latter is that the government must acquire rights to spend public funds by having all their tax and spending policies approved through the ballot box. Thus Prudhoe Bay oil royalties were divided between the government and the Alaskan Permanent Fund, shared equally by all Alaska's citizens. The outcome of this controlled natural experiment is that today the government has a budget gap – having repealed its income tax with the run-up of oil prices – while the citizens' fund invested in securities has a market value of some $26 bn.

I see the control of corruption as an *institutional design problem* with appropriate checks, balances and incentives in which legitimate rights of access are transferred *qua* auction, while limitations on private rights are either repealed as unworkable or retained and enforced even if the enforcers – maybe 'grassroots' citizen councils – have to be watched. Such government may also have greater potential for being less corrupt and corrupting.

Climate Change (Chapter 1)

The Science

It is clear from both the science and the economics of intervention that those of us who care about the environment are not well advised to favour initiating a costly attempt to reduce greenhouse gases (ghgs) build-up in the atmosphere in the near future based on the available information. Although the ultimate dangers may turn out to prompt action, the current evidence indicates that it is much too soon to act *relative to the many other important and pressing opportunities that demand immediate attention.* This is an indictment of the *timeliness* of this opportunity, not its potential importance for action in the future.

Chapter 1 and Perspective papers 1.1 and 1.2 all accept the proposition that the science has produced a consensus: global warming and climate change over the last century or so is attributable to anthropogenic releases of ghgs, but there are differences in the assessment of the *economic efficiency* of near-term action. I want to note, however, that there has been substantial trend fluctuation in the estimates of the earth's surface temperature over the past century and a half: temperatures:

(1) Changed little (1860–1910)
(2) Rose rapidly (1910–40)
(3) Declined steadily, but not greatly (1940–80)
(4) Increased (since 1980).

Cline, Mendelsohn and Manne acknowledge that these short-run movements are not clearly related to changes in ghgs, and therefore are thought to be simply random variations due to other factors within an overall upward trend attributed to ghg.

The Economics

I have some scepticism about the above consensus on the science, but there are other far more compelling reasons for delaying action besides our lack of scientific certainty.

(1) As noted by Mendelsohn in Perspective paper 1.1, the logic of the planning problem is one of optimal control and the appropriate decision rule at time t is to equate the marginal cost of abatement to the discounted value of the future marginal damage, *both evaluated at the time t.*

Hence, the damage due to emissions that are expected to occur after 100 years from now has no bearing on abatement today. It is sub-optimal to devote resources to incur abatement costs now for damages attributable to emissions after 100 years. Optimal abatement now applies only to the expected future damage from current emissions. If we ignore this rule of optimality and begin abatement now for damages caused by emissions after 100 years, we leave our descendants with fewer resources – 100 years of return on the abatement costs not incurred – to devote to subsequent damage control. The critical oversight here is in the failure to respect *opportunity cost.* Each generation must be responsible for the future effect of that generation's emission damage. Earlier generations have the responsibility of leaving to subsequent generations a capital stock that *has not been diminished by incurring premature abatement costs.*

(2) Optimal delay in this sense also has the enormous advantage that, given past trends in human knowledge accumulation, 100 years from now people will be smarter than we are by a factor so large that we would hardly recognise them as our descendants. Just imagine the astonishment of a person in 1904 learning of our knowledge utilisation, c. 2004. The formal analysis leaves out of the equation the effects of growth in the future stock of *scientific knowledge.* Our descendants will also be much more productive unless we starve them their legitimate stock of capital.

(3) Moreover, optimal delay has the advantage that the improving state of the science and of the growing database will allow our descendants to make far better *estimates of when the damage will begin.* Thus they may discover that our

estimates today were wrong – damage is expected to begin earlier (fifty), or later (150) years from now – and they can take appropriate action.

Adaptations

An alternative to abatement is to refrain from action in trying to stop the damage from the build-up of ghgs, and instead *use resources to adapt to climate change*. This might be cheaper and preferable in the event that the damage is expected to be much smaller than originally thought, or if it is found that the build-up is due primarily to non-anthropogenic causes and the damage is inevitable, or in the event that reversing ghgs build-up will not reverse the damage as expected. Thus, it was much warmer 130,000 years ago (roughly when our Cro-Magnon ancestors appeared in Africa) than it is today, and the temperature of the earth cooled on its own. In fact, our more pressing concern may in time be one of adapting to cooling. The earth's temperature was also more volatile earlier than anytime in the last 12,000 years. Optimal delay may also enable us to learn more about the efficacy of *adaptation*.

Carbon Tax vs Tradable Quotas

Finally, I want to object strongly to a carbon tax as emphatically not the effective means to provide incentives for abatement, as opposed to tradable direct emission quotas that would be tightened in the aggregate over time as new information becomes available. Unfortunately the hypothetical theorem claiming their equivalence is not based on an analysis of the economic world in which we live (ideal loan markets do not exist). Grandfathering baseline rights to pollute allows those for whom abatement is naturally very costly to buy rights from those who can naturally abate more cheaply *within the desired same overall aggregate emission standard*, which should be the instrumental variable that we all want to limit – if such be the right approach – in a way that is directly observable.

A tax arbitrarily, and therefore unfairly, impacts those with higher abatement costs who need time to adapt, and any given tax may be too high or too low

to incentivise the target reduction in carbon emissions. Knowing how much to reduce emissions does not tell *regulators the tax level needed to target that reduction*. Don't require regulators to estimate the uncertain tax rate that will yield the uncertain abatement level they are supposed to estimate. Good environmental policies should never be a lame excuse for collecting revenue from taxes. Information on abatement cost is dispersed among all emitters and is not given to any one mind, including the regulator. It is far better to set the aggregate target directly, observe the emission price response and adjust it marginally over time as needed based on continuous observation. The tightening schedule of allowable emissions over time will motivate the exchange of permits from those whose permits can fetch a price higher than their abatement cost to those for whom abatement costs are greater than the permit price. The market price that emerges for the emission rights enables emitters to plan ahead for introducing abatement technologies.

Simultaneously, it allows those emitters who face higher clean-up costs to buy time before facing bankruptcy, and perhaps avoid it, in the event that technical innovations induced by the price of the permits lowers the cost of clean-up. Necessity – a high permit price – is the legitimate mother of invention, which must necessarily vary across the disparate sources of CO_2. She should be given a chance. This mechanism of control for SO_X and NO_X emission permits has worked very effectively in many applications.

Access to Education (Chapter 4)

If money were used for educational improvement, it may be that the way to motivate exposure to the educational system in poor countries is to pay families the opportunity cost of keeping their children in school until they finish. This alleviates poverty while tying payments for school attendance to the wage alternatives that pressure families to take their children out of school early. Instead of welfare transfers to help the poor, you invest in their schooling and thereby provide them with the *tools to extricate themselves*, or at least the next generation, from poverty.

Being in school, however, clearly does not guarantee performance. Hence, perhaps, the need to raise family incomes further by paying the students for performance: learning multiplication tables, writing, reading and spelling skills, etc. This is just the routine learning, and no one knows better than academics that this is not the same thing as educational accomplishment in which the most important thing to learn is how to learn, and be in a life that never ceases self-teaching. That is a tough one, and the world is replete with examples like that of Einstein, bored and regimented by the system thought best to serve all.

The problem with systemic reform proposed in chapter 4 is the lack of empirical evidence showing the effectiveness of systemic reform. The more effective schools may be good systemic models, but they no doubt emerged from unobservable factors that are hard to identify, and certainly were not designed by an outside country sending funds to a country committed to top-down management of everything. Good educational systems, like good economic systems, evolve from the bottom up in good incentive environments.

Financial Instability (Chapter 5)

This challenge topic is a technical specialty, a field still in an early process of learning how to structure institutions the hard way: by trial and error modification in the field. Every trial followed by error is enormously costly. As I see it, the primary problem arises from *intergovernment transfers for private development*, with too few of the funds finding their way into sustainable productive activities monitored and controlled by business entities who have risked their own equity funds. Development comes from the bottom up: entrepreneurs risking their own funds and motivated to find ways to make those investments pay off. Nobody knows by what other process development can happen. Government-to-government transfers are pushing on a development string and suffering from the other people's money problem.

Why is the foreign country not attracting private investment funds? Why is the government that wants to see development not facilitating private opportunities, reducing impediments to entry, simplifying business regulations and devising the property rights that will sustain development? Why are there so few equity funds available to help with financial stability? The answers to these microeconomic questions will provide guidelines for what is to be done about structure and incentives. If these are the questions that are not finding answers, then no new schemes for moving the money around between entities with dollar-denominated liabilities and unproductive assets denominated in local currencies is going to bring financial stability. Financial stability derives first from *underlying real investments* that are high-yielding.

It does not advance understanding to say that the problem of financial instability is a problem of asymmetric information and adverse selection in loan markets. Compared with what? Is the comparison standard an ideal non-existent world in which loan markets clear at a uniform equilibrium interest rate? As Adam Smith well knew, the profligate borrower is first in line to offer a high interest rate. Every market has its own characteristic features, and surely the essence of the loan market is default risk. If the question concerns default, the answer is to know your borrower. And that means having local information, being close to the situation, monitoring it and noting that *ceteris paribus* better borrowers have an equity stake in their entrepreneurial activity. If they do not, the lender needs to ask why. I do not think this process will be encouraged by government-to-government loans, trusting the recipient government to know how to spend or lend to produce a return.

Globalisation has brought a new discipline to governments, and they need to listen up: governments are in global competition with each other to follow stable monetary and fiscal policies and to provide the kind of opportunities that incentivise people to invest at home, and to attract private foreign investment.

Conflicts (Chapter 3)

The basic theorem that applies to the challenge of conflicts and arms proliferation was stated well by the great French economic journalist Claude

Fredric Bastiat, described aptly by Schumpeter as 'the most brilliant economic journalist who ever lived': 'If goods don't cross borders, soldiers will.' Chapter 3 is about civil war, on average two per year these days; about soldiers who do *not* cross borders.

But there is a connection with Bastiat: chapter 3 finds that the three most important factors in determining the risk of war are level of income, income growth and primary commodity exports. Higher income and higher growth reduce the risk of war and dependence on extractive resources for income increases the risk of war. Low income levels and low growth mean that the gains from exchange are thin, people's economic fortunes are not interdependently well connected to each other and this encourages soldiering; conflict is greater when value flows more from below ground and less from brow sweat. Chapter 3 also finds that aid is not a cost-efficient way to avoid war, while Intriligator, in Perspective paper 3.1, states flatly that many counterexamples suggest that aid spurs conflict, feeds corruption and provides the military resources for war. Bastiat would have said, I believe (and, if so, I agree), that if you want development you won't get it from external aid. War is thus encouraged by inadequate exchange whether across borders or within borders, and by resources pumped in from country donors rather than created internally by the populace.

The unimportance of borders to Bastiat's theorem is further underlined by the fact that civil war not only decreases the country's income, but also by the empirical finding that it decreases the income of its neighbours. I would also argue that the increased risk of war attributable to a country's dependence on extractive resources is a consequence of government control over these resources, as opposed to their private ownership. The right model for oil development is for the country to:

(1) Auction exploration and development rights on public land to private concerns for whom the rights command the highest value
(2) Place the proceeds of the auction into a permanent fund for the account of all the citizens who share equally in the fund after it is invested in world security markets.

This gives ownership of public assets directly to the people who pay the taxes required by the government to do its business. To give the government direct free drawing rights on oil wealth is to encourage corruption, and bypass control by the people.

The practical problem in achieving this desirable objective is how to get there from the current world in which, unfortunately, public assets have already been claimed directly by most of the peoples' governments.

Ranking the Opportunities: Vernon L. Smith

Challenge	Opportunities	Ranking
Malnutrition and hunger	Development of new agricultural technologies	1
Sanitation and access to clean water	Small-scale water technology for livelihoods	2
Communicable diseases	Control of malaria	3
Communicable diseases	Control of HIV/AIDS	4
Sanitation and access to clean water	Community-managed water supply and sanitation	5
Subsidies and trade barriers	Trade liberalisation	6
Migration	Lowering barriers to migration for skilled workers	7
Migration	Guest worker programmes for the unskilled	8
Malnutrition and hunger	Providing micronutrients	9
Communicable diseases	Scaled-up basic health services	10
Malnutrition and hunger	Reducing the prevalence of LBW	11
Malnutrition and hunger	Improving infant and child nutrition	12
Migration	Migration for development	13
Sanitation and access to clean water	Research in water productivity in food production	14
Sanitation and access to clean water	Sustainable agriculture in wetlands	15
Sanitation and access to clean water	Re-use of wastewater for peri-urban agriculture	16
Climate change	Optimal carbon tax	17
Climate change	The Kyoto Protocol	17
Climate change	Value-at-risk carbon tax	17

NANCY L. STOKEY

Introduction

Two general issues arise in ranking the proposals: *choosing a discount rate* and *valuing lives saved* (premature deaths averted). Most of the Expert panel members, myself included, adopted a 5 per cent discount rate. It is a reasonable figure and has the practical advantage of being the one used in most of the chapters in the volume.

Many of the chapters value Disability-Adjusted Life Years (DALYs) at the average *per capita* income of the relevant country or region, usually around $1,000. The panel quickly agreed that this figure was far too low. An ethical principle suggested by one panel member was adopted instead: *to value a life as the individual herself would value*

it. To arrive at a figure, one estimates how much people are willing to spend, out of their own pockets, to reduce the risk of accidental death. Individuals in developed countries evidently value their lives at around five times their lifetime earnings. For an annual income of $1,000 and a discount rate of 5 per cent, this leads to a figure of $5 \times \$1,000/0.05 = \$100,000$.

For some of the proposals, subsidies or the extension of credit could be used instead of outright provision of goods or services. These strategies would increase the number of projects that could be implemented from a fixed budget.

Communicable Diseases (Chapter 2)

All three of the opportunities presented here are excellent projects. The *HIV/AIDS initiative* seems most important for several reasons: the scale of the problem, the large public good aspect and the urgency of quick intervention. Several countries in SSA have very high infection rates already, and disaster seems imminent in these countries if something is not done soon. The proposal for *malaria control* also offers benefits that are very large relative to the costs, and the proposed interventions have good track records. The benefits from using ITNs are largely private, so subsidising their purchase might be an alternative to outright provision. Switching from SP to ACTs for malaria treatment has a public good aspect because drug-resistant strains develop, but subsidies might be an alternative to outright provision here as well.

Subsidies and Trade Barriers (Chapter 10)

Liberalising international trade and reducing developed country subsidies to agriculture would yield huge economic benefits (the estimate in chapter 10 is about $45 trillion) around the world. The (direct) costs are negligible by comparison: the main obstacles are political. Developing countries would enjoy special benefits, since the *inflow of new technologies and new ideas* that accompany free trade would boost their growth rates.

Establishing free trade areas (FTAs) is much less useful. The FTAA would probably be advantageous to the participating countries, but partly – if not wholly – at the expense of the rest of the world, which would suffer from the loss of diverted trade. The EBA proposal currently before the EU seems to be even worse, viewed from a global perspective. The losses to LDCs that would *not* have preferential access to EU markets would more than offset the gains to the participating countries. These proposals were not ranked.

Malnutrition and Hunger (Chapter 7)

Two of the Opportunities in this area are excellent projects; the other two are worthwhile but have lower priority. Reducing *micronutrient deficiencies* produces very large improvements in health

and productivity, at a modest cost. Investing in developing *better crop varieties* should also be a high priority. In the past this has proven to be a very successful strategy for raising incomes for millions of families, and there is every reason to think that its success can continue. A similar investment project was proposed as part of the water challenge (chapter 9), and my rankings of these two should be viewed as a tie.

Reducing LBW pregnancies and improving child nutrition are also worthwhile, but more expensive. In addition, the programmes need to be carefully organised and targeted to be effective.

Sanitation and Access to Clean Water (Chapter 9)

All three of the opportunities in this area are excellent projects. Projects of each type have been implemented before, with great success. Treadle pumps and other technologies that allow individual farmers to control irrigation of their crops are extremely effective in raising rural incomes. Since both the costs and the benefits of low-tech irrigation methods accrue to the individual farmer, these investments seem to be excellent candidates for financing with *micro-credit lending arrangements*. Financing them in this way makes them especially attractive, and for this reason I ranked this opportunity 1 in the group.

Clean drinking water and better sanitation are extremely effective in reducing water-borne diseases, especially diarrhoea. Thus, providing a domestic water service has many of the same benefits as providing better nutrition and preventing disease. Chapter 9 stresses that water provision (village standpipes) and wastewater management (public latrines) should be linked. Willingness-to-pay is high for the former, since water is a private good, and much lower for the latter, since sanitation is a public good. But both must be financed in a *self-sustaining way* for communities to enjoy the health benefits.

The cost of providing a domestic water and sanitation service is very high. But Rijskerman noted that most of the currently unserved are in Asia. Information about the relevant technologies is available in those countries, and local financing for the required initial investment is likely to be forthcoming, so little outside intervention seems to be needed; by contrast, in SSA little is likely to happen without outside intervention. Even in that region, however, the villages being served can be expected to bear part of the cost.

The proposal for R&D to develop drought-resistant and water-saving crop varieties is similar to the R&D proposal in chapter 7 on hunger and malnutrition.

Migration (Chapter 8)

The costs and benefits of altering policies on migration can be assessed from the viewpoint of individuals or nation-states, or both. I prefer to concentrate on individuals. Substantial benefits clearly accrue to the migrants themselves, and there are few direct costs associated with lowering barriers to mobility. The question, then, is whether there are additional benefits or (indirect) costs to other individuals in the receiving and sending countries.

In receiving countries possible losers are workers with skills similar to those of the immigrants. Their wages may fall and they may have more difficulty finding jobs. Possible gainers are employers and workers with complementary skills, who will see their profits and wages rise. For sending countries the effects are reversed. The magnitude of these effects depends on the *size of the migrant group relative to the total population*. In most cases, these secondary effects should be small. The exception is if a large number of highly skilled people leave a country where such skills are scarce. This may be an issue for some countries in SSA, where an excessive 'brain drain' could be costly for those left behind.

In addition, there may be social costs. For the receiving country these include increased social tension, political conflict and (possibly) crime. The importance of these social costs seem to be very different across countries: higher in western Europe and substantially lower in the USA, Canada, Australia and New Zealand. The 'New World' nations are populated almost entirely by descendants of earlier waves of migrants, and their institutions and social norms are geared to accepting and assimilating new ethnic groups. In Europe, immigrants more often live in ethnic enclaves, and their children remain attached to them. They are perceived, rightly or wrongly, as contributing to crime. These issues are less important for highly skilled immigrants, however.

Lowering barriers for high-skill immigrants seems thus to be a good idea, for the USA and for western Europe. There are no direct (out-of-pocket) costs, the benefits to the migrants are large and the ancillary effects for other individuals in the sending and receiving countries are an order of magnitude smaller.

The other two proposals, guest worker programmes and the (poorly named) migration for development policy seem very flawed. The former maximises the social costs for the receiving country, requires a large bureaucracy and creates adverse incentives (to cheat) for employers. The latter involves a misplaced emphasis on remittances and returns. Both proposals seem to be bad ideas, for both the USA and Europe.

No proposal was offered for simply *lowering barriers to all migration*; it would have been much more difficult to evaluate. The US economy is well equipped to absorb new workers and the social costs would probably be modest. The situation in Europe is quite different. European labour market policies make their economies much less flexible, ethnic groups are not as quickly assimilated and immigration has already produced a strong political backlash. Even in the USA a proposal of this type would probably also have to limit access by recent immigrants to various welfare programmes. The chief benefit from migration comes from raising the productivity of migrants, and it accrues only if the migrant works. Compensation to the sending country for financing the migrants' education might also be reasonable, especially for countries with large numbers of emigrants.

Governance and Corruption (Chapter 6)

Poor governance is a fundamental problem in many developing countries. A poorly functioning or deeply corrupt government makes progress on other fronts much more difficult, if not impossible. Economic development is stifled and outside agencies attempting to improve health, education, etc. face much higher costs.

What aspects of governance are important for economic development? *Stability* is crucial. Civil liberties are desirable, but evidently not critical for growth. Democracy is neither necessary nor sufficient for economic growth. In low- and middle-income countries democracy often produces pressure for redistribution that discourages investment, effort and innovation. Corruption is deplorable, but historical evidence suggests that moderate corruption does not hinder growth. Chicago was called 'the city that works' not because corruption was absent but because it was organised and not excessive. A corrupt but stable and forward-looking government, one that wants a share of the pie, will want to promote economic growth.

The ideas in chapter 6 are good ones, but the best ways to implement them will vary from place to place. In this sense, they are not specific enough to suggest particular action, so the panel chose not to rank most of the proposals in this section. The exception is the proposal to lower state-imposed costs of establishing a new business. Encouraging entrepreneurial activity should be a high priority for any government interested in stimulating economic progress.

Climate Change (Chapter 1)

Chapter 1 presents an alarmist view about the costs of global warming. Three facts are important in assessing its conclusions. First, the author uses an extremely long time horizon, 300 years. Second, he uses very low discount rates, 0 per cent (his preferred figure) to 3 per cent, compared with 5 per cent in other chapters in the volume. Third, he makes no allowance for technical change in the next 300 years that will allow the world to cope more effectively with CO_2 emissions and their climatic effects. All three of the opportunities entail high costs and few benefits over the next hundred years, and (relatively) lower costs and higher benefits over the subsequent two centuries. Using a shorter horizon

(100 years) and a more standard discount rate (5 per cent), all of the proposals produce BCRs well below unity.

Does this mean that the issue is unimportant and should be ignored? No. There is evidence that global warming is real and that eventually it will become an important problem. Perspective paper 1.1 recommends a more moderate measure, a modest tax, for the short run. Modest efforts over the next couple of decades will (a) reduce the stock of emissions in the upper atmosphere in 2024; (b) reduce adverse effects on fragile environments that may already be occurring; (c) help to develop international institutions/treaties to deal with the problem; (d) encourage R&D in abatement technologies. During this time our understanding of the relevant scientific issues will improve, as will the list of available technologies. Future decision makers will be better equipped to decide whether more aggressive action is needed.

Access to Education (Chapter 4)

Chapter 4 argues that in less developed countries, as in rich ones, there are many ways to spend additional funds for education badly. Are there any ways to spend funds well? The only serious proposal presented in chapter 4 is for 'systemic reform'. But little is known about what *specific types of institutional (systemic) reforms* improve school quality, and without such detail the proposal is not very useful.

Three good ideas did emerge. The first is the use of *achievement tests* to measure school performance. Evidence suggests that testing is a cost-effective way to improve accountability at the local school level. The second is using financial incentives to encourage *school attendance*. Evidence shows that reducing school fees (as in Uganda) or providing direct subsidies for school attendance (as in Mexico) raises enrolment and discourages dropping out. The third is an idea that would increase our information about the effectiveness of specific programmes in raising student achievement. The World Bank and other organisations already make large expenditures on education. These organisations should design programmes with an eye to the information, the data, they will produce. The PROGRESA programme in Mexico is an example of how this can be done, and of how useful the information can be.

Financial Instability (Chapter 5)

Chapter 5 identifies two sources of financial instability. The first is *macroeconomic mismanagement*: unsustainable fiscal deficits, a weak financial system and so on. The evidence shows quite clearly that these sources of financial instability are important, with Argentina and Brazil as leading examples. The second consists of *exogenous shocks*, such as business cycles and commodity market fluctuations. The claim is that if the country issues dollar-denominated debt, these shocks can set off a financial crisis, while a crisis will not occur if the debt is denominated in local currency. The author sees this as a flaw in the structure of international financial markets.

Chapter 5 offers four proposals: re-regulating domestic financial markets, re-imposing capital controls, adopting a common currency and pursuing an initiative to create markets for debt denominated in LDC currencies. The first three are straw men: the first two are patently bad ideas and the third is infeasible, at least at present. The fourth is the author's own recent, novel idea. It is a serious proposal, but I have serious reservations as well.

As the author acknowledges, the proposal will do nothing about financial crises that arise from macroeconomic mismanagement. Will it prevent or ameliorate financial crises of the second type? To answer this question, it is useful to ask why markets *do not already exist* for the asset(s) the chapter proposes to create. Financial markets are for the most part very efficient. Their business is to bring together borrowers and lenders, and investment banks are continually looking for (creating) new financial instruments that will appeal to their clients. Interest in emerging markets is strong, so one would expect them to be eager to invest in new securities that would facilitate lending to these countries. Their lack of interest (evidently they have been

approached) makes one suspicious that the costs are higher or the benefits lower than chapter 5 suggests. In addition, it is not clear that debt denominated in a 'basket' of emerging market currencies would allow an individual country to hedge much exchange rate risk.

It is also instructive to remember that Japan, Korea, Taiwan and Hong Kong enjoyed extremely high growth rates with almost no foreign borrowing. Domestic saving rates in those countries were extraordinarily high, and it was domestic saving that financed rapid growth. Since there is no experience or evidence on which to base an evaluation, the panel chose not to rank this proposal.

Conflicts (Chapter 3)

Chapter 3 does a good job quantifying the costs of civil conflicts, and they are enormous – especially when the numbers are revised (upward) to reflect the panel's valuation ($100,000) for a life saved. The proposals to reduce the number of conflicts were less convincing, however. No role was allowed for the bitter ethnic, religious and other rivalries that are often part of such conflicts. To the extent that higher incomes and faster economic growth reduce 'proneness' to conflict, many of the other opportunities should promote peace. One proposal did seem worthwhile: using *peace-keeping troops* from LDCs when hostilities cease, to reduce the probability that conflict resumes.

Conclusions

It is important to remember that the Expert panel ranked *solutions*, not problems. Poor governance, financial instability and civil war are important problems, but at present there are few clear, concrete, convincing suggestions for how to deal with them. SSA stands out as a region facing problems on many fronts: hunger, disease, war and poor government. Does this suggest a different approach for intervention in this region? The final priorities reflect very basic desires: life, health and the ability to be productive.

Ranking the Opportunities: Nancy L. Stokey

Challenge	Opportunities	Ranking
Communicable diseases	Control of HIV/AIDS	1
Subsidies and trade barriers	Trade liberalisation	2
Malnutrition and hunger	Reducing the prevalence of iron deficiency anaemia and iodine, Vitamin A and zinc deficiencies	3
Communicable diseases	Control of malaria	4
Sanitation and access to clean water	Small-scale water technology for livelihoods	5
Sanitation and access to clean water	Community-managed low-cost water supply and sanitation	6
Sanitation and access to clean water	Research in water productivity in food production	7
Malnutrition and hunger	Development of new farm technologies	8
Migration	Lowering barriers to immigration for skilled workers	9
Governance and corruption	Lowering the costs of starting a new business	10
Malnutrition and hunger	Reducing the prevalence of LBW	11
Malnutrition and hunger	Improving infant and child nutrition	12
Communicable diseases	Scaled-up basic health services	13
Migration	Guest worker programmes for the unskilled	14
Migration	Migration for development	15
Climate change	The Kyoto Protocol	16
Climate change	Optimal carbon tax	17
Climate change	Value-at-risk carbon tax	18

Epilogue: Youth Forum Human Benefit Analysis

CHRISTIAN FRIIS BACH

Background: The Copenhagen Consensus Youth Forum

If you thought that young university students belong to a fast-food, zapper culture and think only about the night tonight and the day tomorrow, then the Copenhagen Consensus Youth Forum would have made you think again. Eighty young graduate students from twenty-five countries met in Copenhagen to repeat the same exercise as the eight senior economists: to prioritise the challenges and opportunities of the world.

Over five intensive days in Copenhagen, the young people debated the global challenges in parallel to the deliberations of the experts in the Copenhagen Consensus. Each day, they heard the authors of the chapters and Perspective papers present their views, and they had plenty of time to ask questions and propose their own opportunities to meet the challenges. After listening to and discussing the issues raised, a group of eight participants made a presentation championing each challenge, followed by a second group arguing against a high priority for it. At the end of the day, votes were cast on the challenges and opportunities put forward – including any additional opportunities identified by the Youth Forum. In this way, a rolling list of priorities was established, not completed until the voting on the last challenge had taken place on the final day (see the table on p. 646).

The Youth Forum delegates were chosen by the Environmental Assessment Institute with special attention to providing graduate students with dissimilar academic backgrounds and the widest possible geographical representation of the world's population: 56 (70 per cent) came from developing countries, 4 (5 per cent) from Russia and 20 (25 per cent) from rich countries.

To further ensure diversity, participants were chosen (where possible) to represent both urban and rural areas and their parents' income was considered. Priority was given to applicants with scholarships, to counter the tendency for university students to come from the wealthier part of the population. Equal gender representation was also aimed for and achieved.

Human Benefit

If you take a quick glimpse at their prioritised list of challenges, it may not look that different from the list produced by the experts. But if you delve deeper into which opportunities they selected. it is. In general, the Youth Forum prioritised broad, long-term solutions that tackled structural problems, politics and inequalities – although these solutions often had quite low BCRs. In fact, they almost consistently selected opportunities with some of the lowest BCRs, disregarding a fair bit of the advice they received from the economists. As Joanna Cabello from Peru and Sethuraman Janardhanan from India expressed it at the final press conference: 'We have not prioritised according to cost-benefit analysis. We have used human benefit analysis.'

Surprisingly, the Youth Forum delegates were, despite the huge diversity of the group, fully in agreement on their highest and lowest priorities.

Long-Term Solutions

Ranked 1 by the Youth Forum was malnutrition and hunger. This is not a surprise. It came in at 2

Christian Friis Bach was the moderator at the Youth Forum. These comments reflect his personal interpretation of the arguments made by the Youth Forum delegates during the week of the conference.

on the list from the 'real' Copenhagen Consensus. However, as their best opportunity, they chose to invest in technology in agriculture in the world's poorest countries rather than handing out vitamin pills and micronutrients – although the latter had much higher BCRs and was the preferred economic choice of the experts. The Youth Forum participants recognised that distribution of micronutrients was a short-term and partial solution, while investments in agricultural technology were long-term. Moreover, such a policy could tackle problems of both poverty and hunger *at the same time*. This is far from fast-food politics.

The Youth Forum ranked communicable diseases at 2, which the expert forum ranked at 1. However, while the experts preferred to hand out condoms and provide information campaigns on HIV/AIDS, the Youth Forum participants preferred to invest in scaled-up basic health services. The reasoning behind this was that other interventions would be useless without a basic health care structure and that basic health services could permit countries to tackle a broader range of diseases than HIV/AIDS. The Asian participants were still worried about SARS and for many participants malaria was a key concern. Again, condoms and information campaigns had much higher BCRs and could yield much faster results. Still, the students preferred long-term and long-lasting solutions: clinics instead of condoms. In doing so, they defied the stereotyped image of the young as impatient and short-sighted. But perhaps it is logical: they will, hopefully, live for many years while the older economists will not be around for quite as long. They may thus look for quick progress and care less about long-term impacts. They may have different discount rates.

Voice and Accountability

Perhaps surprisingly, governance and corruption were ranked at 3 by the Youth Forum. To overcome the burden of corruption one needs experience and networks – something young people often lack. Corruption may, therefore, pose higher costs and barriers for young people than for old. Good governance is synonymous with more opportunities if you are young and relatively poor. The Youth Forum again differed from the experts in their choice of op-

portunity. The experts preferred to lower the barriers to starting a new business. The Youth Forum preferred to give voice to the people: grassroots monitoring and service delivery combined with more transparent governance systems.

Similarly, the opportunity they preferred within this challenge (ranked at 6) was community-managed low-cost water supply and sanitation systems. Strengthening the influence of local communities was crucial for the participants.

Power and Politics

Protecting them may be critical as well. While the Youth Forum did recognise that there were significant benefits from trade liberalisation, they stressed that lower trade barriers can create problems such as poverty and inequality in the short run. So despite the enormous BCRs presented in chapter 10 – some approximating to infinity – the Youth Forum ranked subsidies and trade barriers only at 8. It is not as simple an issue as often believed by economists. Their preferred opportunity was a balanced Doha Round in the World Trade Organisation (WTO), with stronger support for institutional development in poor countries and institutional improvements at the global level. Without proper institutions, local communities may not be able to reap the benefits of globalisation. Moreover, they believed that the decision-making structure within global institutions must improve.

This was even more clearly expressed within the challenge of financial instability, which was ranked at seven. Here, the Youth Forum disregarded the range of technical solutions presented in chapter 5 and preferred a political one: the governance structure of the World Bank and the International Monetary Fund (IMF) should be changed to give more power to developing countries. If developing countries had a stronger say they could, themselves, fight for more fair and effective solutions to financial instability. In a CBA, changing the voting system in the global financial institutions would be almost costless. The Youth Forum believed that it would also be effective. Many opportunities have not been taken up despite having high BCRs: political power and influence plays an enormous role, as was clearly recognised by the Youth Forum.

No.	Challenge	Opportunity
1	Malnutrition and hunger	Investment in technology in developing country agriculture
2	Communicable diseases	Scaled-up basic health services
3	Governance and corruption	Grassroots monitoring and service delivery with technical assistance and information provision provided centrally by government or NGOs
4	Access to education	Quality of education, with emphasis on a holistic model, including informed life decisions, health, civic awareness, ethical and cultural issues
5	Conflicts	An international peace fund to support regional solutions to regional conflicts
6	Sanitation and access to clean water	Community-managed low-cost water supply and sanitation
7	Financial instability	Change the governance structure of the World Bank and the IMF to give more power to developing countries
8	Subsidies and trade barriers	A balanced Doha Round with stronger support for institutional development in poor countries and institutional improvements at the global level
9	Climate change	Kyoto Protocol plus awareness raising and development of new technology and allowing tariffs (in the WTO) against countries which do not meet Kyoto targets
10	Migration	Active immigration policies, including lower barriers, promoting cultural understanding, policies to attract professionals and cross-country dialogue

Finally, Climate Change

This was perhaps the most contentious challenge, ranked at 9. Only active migration policies were ranked lower (at 10). However, again the Youth Forum differed from the experts. The experts and economists preferred an 'optimal' carbon tax. The Youth Forum recognised that when it came to global warming, one might wish to buy into other opportunities, but the Kyoto Protocol is the only shop in town. They selected an opportunity which in the jargon was labelled 'Kyoto plus-plus-plus' – the Kyoto Protocol *plus* rising awareness, *plus* faster development of new technology and *plus* countervailing tariffs (in the WTO) against countries which did not meet Kyoto targets. The logic behind the latter proposal was that failure to adhere is an implicit subsidy. If countries do not join, they should be met with countervailing measures. Surprisingly, perhaps, this proposal was brought forward by a Russian participant.

Conclusions

In conclusion, the priorities presented by the Copenhagen Consensus Youth Forum provided an insightful addition to the work of the Copenhagen Consensus experts. It also provided them with constructive criticism. In the words of one of the speakers, Professor Mendelsohn: 'Dealing with the Youth Forum was tougher than talking to the experts.'

The Youth Forum did indeed appreciate the economic insights provided by the chapters and Perspective papers. However, they were also sceptical and critical. Again and again the participants asked about lack of information, unaccounted-for externalities and missing data. They argued that better health would give you better education; easy access to clean water would save lives but also save time, especially for women. Such effects should have been included in the cost-benefit calculations, but were not. They also argued that it would not help to prioritise education if the kids and teachers died of malaria or HIV/AIDS. Clean water had no meaning if you had to flee from war and oppression. The challenges are *interlinked*. They argued that 'instead of fighting over which part of the cake to eat, we should go back into the kitchen and make the cake bigger'. They argued that what matters were not only costs and benefits but the *distribution* of costs and benefits. They asked about happiness, mutual understanding and cultural values – and when it came to education they prioritised an education system with a focus on informed life decisions, civic awareness and ethical and cultural issues. They criticised putting a price on human beings, but also recognised that in fact the economists continuously argued that the price of the life of a poor person in a poor country was – and should be – a lot higher than the price we implicitly put on his or her life today. We already price human beings differently, when we carry out heart surgery in rich countries (which is extremely costly) but fail to save children in Africa who die of malaria (although the cost of doing so is cheap). The evidence presented during the week in Copenhagen showed that it really pays to invest in poor people in poor countries. Thus, the price of a life in Africa, Asia or Latin America went up. This is perhaps the most important outcome of the Copenhagen Consensus conference.

The priorities by the Youth Forum reflect their concerns and their critique. But it also reflects the fact that the task given to the students was different from that given to the professors. The Youth Forum delegates did not only prioritise according to costs and benefits. They could prioritise – not only as economists – but as biologists, anthropologists, sociologists, political scientists, or engineers. They could prioritise according to what they believed in – not only based on what the numbers told them. They could prioritise with their hearts and feelings. They could prioritise according to their dreams and visions. So they did.